16 & Market
5 Penn Center
1:30

STRATEGIC MANAGEMENT
TEXT AND CASES

Wiley Series in Management

STRATEGIC MANAGEMENT
TEXT AND CASES

Glenn Boseman
The American College

Arvind Phatak
Temple University

Robert E. Schellenberger
East Carolina University

JOHN WILEY & SONS

New York   Chichester   Brisbane   Toronto   Singapore

Copyright © 1986 by John Wiley & Sons, Inc.

All rights reserved. Published simultaneously in Canada.

Reproduction or translation of any part of
this work beyond that permitted by Sections
107 and 108 of the 1976 United States Copyright
Act without the permission of the copyright
owner is unlawful. Requests for permission
or further information should be addressed to
the Permissions Department, John Wiley & Sons.

Library of Congress Cataloging in Publication Data:

Schellenberger, Robert Earl.
   Strategic management.

  (Wiley series in management, ISSN 0271–6046)
   Rev. ed. of: Policy formulation and strategy
management. 2nd ed. c1982.
   Includes indexes.
   1. Strategic planning. 2. Strategic planning—
Case studies. 3. Business logistics. 4. Business
logistics—Case studies. I. Boseman, F. Glenn.
II. Phatak, Arvind V. III. Schellenberger,
Robert Earl. Policy formulation and strategy
management. IV. Title. V. Series.
HD30.28.S34 1986   658.4′012   85–9553
ISBN 0-471-88059-0

Printed in the United States of America

10 9 8 7 6 5 4 3 2

PREFACE

Strategic Management: Text and Cases is designed to introduce the reader to the basics of strategic management. The contents of the book are built upon three pedagogical pillars: text, cases, and practical insights from the real world.

The textual material is covered in six concise, easy-to-read chapters that were written with the idea of taking the student quickly to case analysis. The organization of the chapters is guided by a conceptual model of the strategic management process which is presented early in Chapter 1. The model provides a top-management perspective on strategic planning, and strategy implementation and control. It displays the major components of the strategic management process and how the components are theoretically related and sequenced throughout the process. Chapters 2 through 5 discuss in detail one or more major elements of the model. Chapter 6 draws heavily on Chapters 1 through 5. Its purpose is to provide the student with a comprehensive, yet concise approach to how the strategic management concepts and techniques may be used in case analysis. As such, the reader will find substantial repetition of material covered in earlier chapters. Therefore, instructors may prefer to not discuss this chapter in class but just assign it to students as a home-reading assignment.

This book is aimed at the undergraduate capstone course in business policy or strategic management. We realize that the field of strategic management can be dealt with at different levels in a college setting. Indeed, there are graduate and doctoral courses being offered in several universities on various aspects of strategic management. Our purpose is to give the student in a case-oriented undergraduate business policy or strategic management course the necessary framework and background to conduct case analysis.

The text part of the book is followed by 33 up-to-date cases, ranging from simple to complex, drawn from different types of industries. There are three cases on entrepreneurship, two dealing with the nonbusiness sector, 12 in the service sector which is becoming increasingly important in the economies of the United States and Western Europe, 10 in the converting and manufacturing sector, four focusing on the international aspects of business, and two concerning social responsibility issues.

We have also included eight short, single-issue cases that can be discussed in a relatively short period of time. These short cases are useful for illustrating the problem-solving process and basic strategic analysis in a rather simple environment.

We have made an extra effort to illustrate the use of strategic management concepts in actual practice. Interwoven with the text are numerous *practical insights* that illustrate the application of the concepts discussed in the chapters. The reader should find the practical insights both informative and interesting.

An instructor's manual comprising analysis of cases and sample objective questions is available. We have also prepared a sufficient number of overhead projector transparencies for Chapters 1 through 5 that we have class-tested. Instructors may want to use them as teaching aids.

Many instructors use a management game to complement the strategic management course. We have used MANSYM IV and found it to be very worthwhile. MANSYM IV is an extremely flexible management game with 1 to 3 products for 3 to 10 firms involving 10 to 33 decisions. The game forces players to plan over a three-period planning horizon and expects planning over a full year's planning horizon. To this end it includes a *pro-forma* option so firms may see the effect of various strategies on their financial and production statements for any number of quarters before the actual decision is made. The strategic emphasis is further enhanced with the availability of a computerized worksheet used to make short-run production decisions. The market research option provides data on which sales forecasts may be made. The output of this option may be used directly with some mainframe programs and via minimal data input with some inexpensive microcomputer programs to obtain sales forecasts. With the performance evaluation option and the multifaceted decision support system, the game can function effectively with very little instructor assistance. The game promotes and enhances computer literacy via the decision-support system which includes microcomputer programs and permits interaction with standard packages. Four different industries are simulated and with easy-to-make changes in the parameter values, a different game may be used each semester. The game is written in Fortran 77 and is available on a mainframe or microcomputer (IBM PC and PC compatibles). Write John Wiley & Sons, Inc. or ask your Wiley representative for more detailed information about MANSYM IV.

We are indebted to the authors who have contributed their cases. Their interest and cooperation is most appreciated. Without their assistance this book would not have come into being.

The following persons did an outstanding job of reviewing the manuscript and offering many penetrating comments and recommendations for improving it: Dr. Richard F. Barton, Professor of Business Administration, Texas Tech University; Dr. William Brant, Director of Planning, The American College; Dr. Davis W. Gregg, Distinguished Professor of Economics, The American College; Dr. Solomon Montoya, Professor of Management, St. John's University; Dr. Jugoslav Multinovich, Associate Professor of Management, Temple University; Mr. Daniel L. White, Assistant Professor of Management and Organizational Sciences, Drexel University; Dr. Francis Wolek, Research Director, College of Commerce and Finance, Villanova University; Dr. Irvin A. Zaenglein, Associate Professor, Northern Michigan University.

We thank Dr. Edward M. Mazze, Dean, School of Business Administration, Temple University, for his support and encouragement. Dr. Robert M. Crowe, Senior Vice-President of Academic Affairs, The American College, was very helpful and supportive of our writing efforts. We thank him for that. Mr. Paul Myerson and Ms. Virginia Patton, Arvind Phatak's graduate assistants, played a crucial role in organizing the practical insights presented in the chapters. Ms. Kay Powell, Editorial Director, and Ms. Barbara Keyser, Assistant Editorial Director, The American College, have our gratitude for their fine editorial work on the manuscript prior to its submission to the publisher.

Finally, without the dedicated and hard-working Amy McLean, who typed the many drafts of the manuscript in record time, this book never would have been published on schedule. Thanks, Amy!

Glenn Boseman
Arvind Phatak
Robert E. Schellenberger

ABOUT THE AUTHORS

Glenn Boseman is Bingay Professor of Leadership at The American College in Bryn Mawr, Pennsylvania. He has taught Business Policy, Strategic Management, and Organization Behavior at both the graduate and undergraduate levels. A native of North Carolina, he earned his DBA in organization and management from Kent State University. He is an active member of the Academy of Management, the American Institute for Decision Sciences, the Academy of International Business, the Eastern Academy of Management, and Phi Beta Gamma.

Boseman is an active consultant for financial services organizations. One of his primary activities is developing systems for organization development as well as conducting managerial training and development programs. He is the author of four books and numerous scholarly articles and presentations.

Arvind Phatak is Professor of Management and International Business Administration at the School of Business Administration, Temple University. Phatak received his Ph.D in Business Administration from the University of California at Los Angeles. He chaired the Management Department at Temple University and served as the Director of the International Business Program for several years. He is the author of three books and has authored or co-authored several articles in academic journals and proceedings. Phatak has lectured extensively in the U. S. A., Europe, and the Far East on topics ranging from strategic management to international business. In 1984 he received Temple University's School of Business Alumni Association Distinguished Faculty Award. He is a member of Beta Gamma Sigma.

Robert E. Schellenberger is a Professor at East Carolina University, Greenville, North Carolina. He chaired the Department of Management at Temple University and Southern Illinois University. Schellenberger has taught graduate and undergraduate courses in Business Policy, Entrepreneurship, Operations Research, Operations Management, Management Information Systems, and Quantitative Methods.

Schellenberger received his Ph.D from the University of North Carolina. He has been actively involved as an officer and member of the Academy of Management and four of its divisions, as well as the American Institute for Decision Sciences and the Institute of Management Sciences. He is a member of Beta Gamma Sigma and was twice cited in Outstanding Educators.

Schellenberger has numerous articles published in academic journals and proceedings. He is also author of five books and monographs. He consults extensively in both the public and private sectors.

CASE AUTHORS

Sexton Adams
Roger M. Atherton
Jeffrey A. Barach
M. Edgar Barrett
Kenneth Beck
Glenn Boseman
William M. Brant
Julius S. Brown
Mark W. Bushell
Joseph P. Caliquri
William G. Callarman
Mary Pat Cormack
Lincoln W. Deihl
X. Gilbert
Adelaide Griffin
Jacques Horovitz
James R. Lang
Victor J. LaPorte, Jr.
Richard Levin
R. Lorenz
Thomas J. McNichols

Michael Martin
Timothy Mescon
G. Michael
Laura L. Nash
Kenneth W. Olm
Bettye Painter
E. L. Parke
Richard Robinson
Philip Rosson
Robert E. Schellenberger
David C. Shaw
Alan Sheldon
Matthew C. Sonfield
Melvin J. Stanford
Denzil Strickland
Marilyn L. Taylor
Richard S. Tedlow
Joe G. Thomas
Joseph Tomey
William H. Warren
A. K. Wickesberg
Dan R. Willis

Case Coauthors

Andy Abroms, M. Agee, Jeff Bell, Bernie Berger, David Berry, Robert Broadbent, Jim Buchanan, J. Buckeye, Business Policy Classes at the College of William and Mary, Marlene Carle, Robert Carle, Bill Clark, Teresa Dawn, Richard Edwards, Leonard A. Fuchs, III, Monya Giggar, John Greening, Gregg Gunchick, Robert D. Hamilton, III, Monique Hensel, Mark Kever, Curt Leathers, Janet Lorenzen, George Macias, David Miller, Peter Nerby, Serge Oreal, John Sanders, Ken Schoenherr, Dave Thompson, Paula Walters, Deborah Weaver, Terry White, and James J. Wiley.

CONTENTS

PART ONE THE CONCEPTS OF STRATEGIC MANAGEMENT AND CASE ANALYSIS 1

1 UNDERSTANDING STRATEGIC MANAGEMENT 3
Strategic Management Dimensions 5
The Strategic Management Process 6
Characteristics of the Strategic Management Framework 11
The Nature of Strategic Decisions 12
Organizational Levels and Strategic Management 14
The Evolution of Formal Strategic Management in Organizations 16
Summary 18

2 SWOT ANALYSIS 20
Conceptual Framework for SWOT Analysis 21
Identification of Opportunities and Threats 22
Key Success Factors 27
Identification of Key Success Factors 28
Evaluation of Firm's Strengths and Weaknesses 36
Summary 41

3 FORMULATING A DIRECTION FOR THE COMPANY 43
Organizational Mission 45
Organizational Philosophy 49
Organizational Policies 52
Strategic Objectives 53
Generic Corporate Strategy Alternatives 58
Summary 68

4 ORGANIZATIONAL STRATEGY 71
Identifying Current Corporate Strategy 75
Corporate Strategy Analysis 76
Business Strategy Analysis 83
Functional Strategy Analysis 90
Choosing an Organizational Strategy 90
Summary 91

5 IMPLEMENTATION AND CONTROL OF ORGANIZATIONAL STRATEGY 93
Implementation of Organizational Strategy 95
Control of Organizational Strategy 115
Summary 118

xii Contents

6 UNDERSTANDING CASE ANALYSIS — 121
Introducing the Case Method — 122
Preparing for Written and Oral Case Analysis — 123
Major Steps in Case Analysis — 123
A Scheme for Evaluation: The Appraisal Framework — 127
Concluding Comments on the Strategic Management Process — 142
Summary — 143

PART TWO CASES — 145

1 ENTREPRENEURSHIP — 147
The Apartment Store — 147
Crested Butte Athletic Club — 160
Slumbering Valley, Inc. — 173

2 NONBUSINESS — 196
The Theatrical Society — 196
Midland County Hospital — 201

3 SERVICE — 234
Wal-Mart Stores, Inc. — 234
Overnite Transportation Company — 246
The Casual Male: Off-Price Men's Apparel Retailing — 267
The McLean Trucking Company — 287
Electronic Data Systems Corporation — 307
Diamond Valley Savings and Loan Association — 325
The American Express Company — 333
Mary Kay Cosmetics, Inc. — 350
Oshman's Sporting Goods, Inc. — 367
Albertson's, Inc. — 390
Parker Drilling Company (1984) — 417
Holiday Inns, Inc. — 439

4 CONVERTING AND MANUFACTURING — 460
CML Group, Inc.—Twelve Years Old — 460
Kerr-McGee Corporation — 478
Masco Corporation — 497
Allied Chemical Company — 506
Apple Computer, Inc. — 519
ASDIC Limited — 533
Dickenson Mines Limited — 544
Marion Laboratories, Inc. — 559
Mobil Corporation — 576
Ammco Tools, Inc. — 601

5 INTERNATIONAL — 620

Bordados Maty, S. A. — 620
F. W. Woolworth and Co., Limited (Woolworth, U. K.) — 632
Nautica, S. A. — 666
John Currie and Internav Ltd., Sydney, Nova Scotia — 692

6 SOCIAL RESPONSIBILITY — 703

Welgro Chemical Company — 703
The Anaconda Smelter — 721

7 SHORT CASES INVOLVING STRATEGIC ISSUES — 739

Moldex Company — 739
Keystone Instruments, Inc. — 739
Alabama Clothing, Inc. — 741
Gulf Coast Seafood — 750
The Khashoggi Affair — 755
A Community Coalition Plans a Conference on Employee Assistance Programs — 763
The Classic Car Club of America — 766
The Charger Company (A) and (B) — 775

APPENDIX A   Additional Sources of Information — 779
APPENDIX B   Financial and Ratio Analysis — 787
APPENDIX C   Student Case Analysis — 797

Case Index — 803
Name Index — 807
Subject Index — 809

PART 1
THE CONCEPTS OF STRATEGIC MANAGEMENT AND CASE ANALYSIS

CHAPTER 1

UNDERSTANDING STRATEGIC MANAGEMENT

Strategic Management Dimensions

The Strategic Management Process

    Assessment of Organization Strengths, Weaknesses, Opportunities, and Threats
    Formulation of Organization Mission
    Formulation of Organization Philosophy and Policies
    Determination of Strategic Objectives
    Determination of Organization Strategy
    Implementation of Organization Strategy
    Control of Organization Strategy

Characteristics of the Strategic Management Framework

The Nature of Strategic Decisions

    Organization Level
    Temporal Impact
    Future Orientation
    Systems Perspective
    Open-System Orientation
    Framework for Lower-Level Decision Making
    Deployment of Resources

Organization Levels and Strategic Management

The Evolution of Formal Strategic Management in Organizations

Summary

References

4 The Concepts of Strategic Management and Case Analysis

PERFORMANCE OBJECTIVES

When you have finished reading this chapter, you should be able to

1. Explain the concept of strategic management.
2. Describe the strategic management process.
3. Explain the six subprocesses of the strategic management process.
4. Explain the differences between societal, corporate, business, and functional strategies.
5. Understand the nature of strategic decisions.
6. Describe top- and middle-management responsibilities for strategic management.
7. Explain how the strategic management process differs in single-business and multiple-business organizations.
8. Describe how strategic management typically evolves in organizations.

Strategic management is concerned with determining the future direction of an organization and implementing decisions aimed at achieving the organization's long and short-term objectives. Business magazines and periodicals are always reporting on companies that have changed for the better or worse because of key management decisions. When one analyzes why companies such as IBM, Xerox, McDonald's, Coca-Cola, Delta Airlines, and Federal Express have grown and prospered, whereas others such as W. T. Grant, Braniff Airlines, and American Airlines either have gone out of business or have been close to bankruptcy, one finds that successful companies have something in common: they were able, through the strategic management process, to attain and retain in the long run the strategic advantage that helped them to prosper. Companies that either have failed or are not doing well were unable, because of poor strategic management, to retain in the long run their short-term strategic advantages.

The strategic management process is applicable to all businesses, large or small, profit or nonprofit, private or public. The concepts and logic of strategic management are just as useful to a small insurance agency, restaurant, or retail hardware store as to a large company such as Sears or the Chase Manhattan Bank. Similarly, strategic management is necessary for success in organizations such as the U. S. Department of Defense, the Catholic Church, the American Cancer Society, the University of California, and the Carnegie Foundation.

Strategic management involves paying attention to several critical business areas. Marvin Bower, a successful management consultant and former managing director of the management consulting firm McKinsey and Company, listed 14 basic components of the strategic management system that should be performed by managers at some level in all organizations (see Figure 1–1).

FIGURE 1-1
Strategic Management Responsibilities of Managers

1. *Establishing the mission*—deciding on the business or businesses that the company or division should engage in and other fundamentals that will guide and characterize the business, such as continuous growth. A mission is usually enduring and timeless.
2. *Formulating a company philosophy*—establishing the beliefs, values, attitudes, and unwritten guidelines that add up to "the way we do things around here."
3. *Establishing policies*—deciding on plans of action to guide the performance of all major activities in carrying out strategy in accordance with company philosophy.
4. *Setting objectives*—deciding on achievement targets within a defined time range. Objectives are narrower in scope than the mission, and are designed to aid in making operational plans for carrying out strategy.
5. *Developing strategy*—developing concepts, ideas, and plans for achieving objectives successfully and meeting and beating the competition. Strategic planning is part of the total planning process that includes management and operation planning.
6. *Planning the organization structure*—developing the plan of organization and the activities that help people work together to perform activities in accordance with strategy, philosophy, and policies.
7. *Providing personnel*—recruiting, selecting, and developing people to fill the positions in the organization plan.
8. *Establishing procedures*—determining and prescribing how all important and recurrent activities will be carried out.
9. *Providing facilities*—providing the plant, equipment, and other physical facilities required to carry on the business.
10. *Providing capital*—making sure the business has the money and credit needed for working capital and physical facilities.
11. *Setting standards*—establishing measures of performance that will enable the business to best achieve its long-term objectives successfully.
12. *Establishing management programs and operational plans*—developing programs and plans governing activities and the use of resources that, when carried out in accordance with established strategy, policies, procedures, and standards, will enable people to achieve particular objectives. These are phases of the total planning process, which includes strategic planning.
13. *Providing control information*—supplying facts and figures to help people follow the strategy, policies, procedures, and programs; to keep alert to forces at work inside and outside the business; to measure overall company performance against established plans and standards.
14. *Activating people*—commanding and motivating people to act in accordance with philosophy, policies, procedures, and standards in carrying out the plans of the company.

Source: Marvin Bower, *The Will to Manage: Corporate Success through "Programmed Management,"* © 1966, McGraw-Hill, Mc-Graw-Hill Copyrights and Permissions Department.

STRATEGIC MANAGEMENT DIMENSIONS

The entire strategic management process has two major dimensions: (1) strategic planning, and (2) strategy implementation and control. In Figure 1–2, the shaded section represents strategic planning and the unshaded section represents strategy implementation and control.

6 The Concepts of Strategic Management and Case Analysis

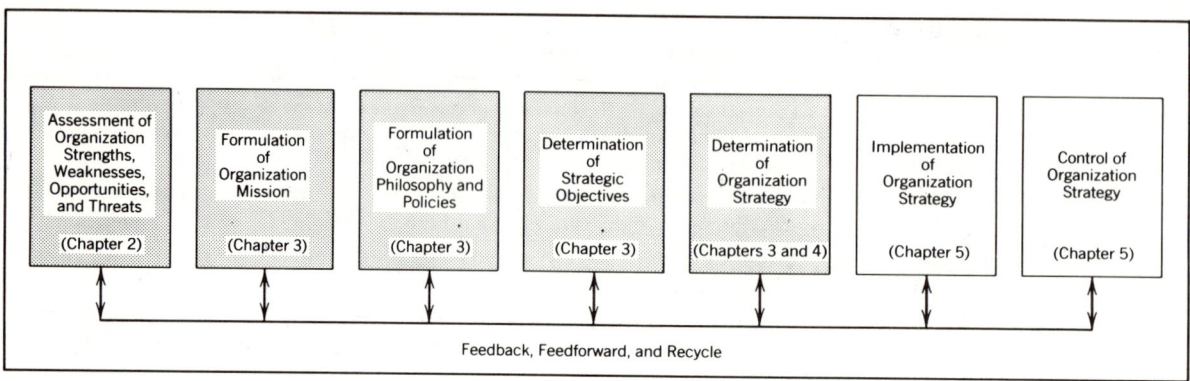

FIGURE 1-2
A Model of the Strategic Management Process

In strategic planning *strategic* decisions are made concerning the total organization's mission, philosophy, policies, and objectives, and methods of achieving organization objectives. Strategic decisions are those that have long-term impact or consequences for the total organization. They are made in response to the anticipated environmental threats and opportunities in the future. (The nature of strategic decisions will be discussed in greater detail later in this chapter.)

Strategy implementation and control is concerned with making a variety of managerial decisions, such as the type of organization structure, leadership styles, management information systems, and monitoring and evaluation systems used to ensure that the organization objectives are achieved effectively.

THE STRATEGIC MANAGEMENT PROCESS

Our model of the strategic management process (Figure 1–2) shows that it consists of seven major interrelated subprocesses:

1. Assessment of organization strengths, weaknesses, opportunities, and threats (SWOT).
2. Formulation of the organization mission.
3. Formulation of the organization philosophy and policies.
4. Determination of the strategic objectives.
5. Determination of organization strategy.
6. Implementation of organization strategy.
7. Control of organization strategy.

Let us examine each of these subprocesses in some detail.

Assessment of Organization Strengths, Weaknesses, Opportunities, and Threats

Strengths are the internal capabilities of an organization that promote organization objectives in a competitive industry. Weaknesses do just the opposite: they restrict the accomplishment of organization objectives. Opportunities are external circumstances, events, or situations that offer an organization the chance to achieve or exceed its objectives. Threats are the opposite of opportunities. Threats are external forces, factors, or situations that might potentially create problems, harm the organization, or endanger its ability to achieve its objectives.

The process of assessing an organization's strengths, weaknesses, opportunities, and threats is generally referred to in the business world as SWOT assessment or analysis. SWOT analysis provides the decision makers in an organization with information that could serve as the basis for decisions and actions that, if implemented effectively, would enable the enterprise to achieve its objectives. SWOT analysis enables an organization to exploit future opportunities while combating threats and problems, and to do so through strategies founded on its distinctive competencies and strengths.

The entire strategic management process conceptually begins with SWOT assessment, because an organization's SWOTs may suggest a change in either the mission, objectives, policies, or strategies of the organization. A firm gains many benefits from a skilled analysis of possible opportunities and threats and relating them to an objective assessment of its own strengths and weaknesses. Not doing so could be disastrous, as both General Electric and RCA learned in the early 1970s, when they attempted to compete with IBM in the mainframe computer market, but did not have the necessary financial resources to achieve even a marginal market share at acceptable cost. Both companies eventually withdrew from the market after suffering millions of dollars in losses.[1]

Formulation of Organization Mission

All organizations have a mission. The mission is the reason for the organization's existence. It answers the basic question, "What business are we in?" "To market agricultural chemicals globally" is an example of a mission. Defining the mission of an organization is very important, because it sets the boundaries for its operations and prevents the organization from overlooking any related fields of endeavor. It is the ultimate guiding force that governs where the firm's critical resources will be deployed. The mission statement may be written in very broad or very narrow terms. How the mission statement is written has a profound effect on the future development of the organization. Many years ago, the railroad industry defined its business as just railroading. Theodore Levitt raised the penetrating question, "Would the railroad industry be better off today if its management had thought of their business as being not just railroads but transportation?"[2] Unquestionably the railroads suffered because of this narrow definition of its mission. It would have been to the railroads' advantage to identify the needs of their customers (transportation) and to provide the service. Limiting their activities only to railroading prevented the railroads from entering new arenas of opportunity.

Formulation of Organization Philosophy and Policies

An organization *philosophy* sets forth the values and beliefs of the organization that guide the behavior of its members in all aspects of business activities. Many companies have a written "code of conduct," reflecting the organization philosophy. The code does not try to prescribe action for every business encounter but attempts to capture the basic general principles to be observed by all employees. The organization philosophy of Caterpillar Tractor Co. with regard to relationships with employees world-wide is shown in Figure 1–3.

Organization *policies* provide the guidelines that define the "ball park" within which objectives are established and strategies are determined, implemented, and controlled. Policies provide managers with a set of broad constraints that all decisions must satisfy. They establish a universe in which action should be taken. Policies allow managers to choose one alternative among the many available, and to identify those that are totally unacceptable. For example, a policy stating that "our products shall be marketed in retail stores that cater to the affluent customer" precludes the use of a discount outlet as a channel of distribution. Organization policies are formulated by top management, thus, reflecting their attitudes and beliefs. It is important that organization policies facilitate the successful accomplishment of organization mission and objectives and the implementation of strategies. A change in the mission and objectives should lead to a review of and possible reformulation of appropriate organizational policies.

Determination of Strategic Objectives

Strategic objectives are the results that the *total* organization wishes to attain during a given period. They translate into specific terms the results an organization must have in order to fulfill its mission. "We will grow at an annual rate of 8 percent for the next five years" is an example of a strategic objective derived from the organizational mission "to market personal-care products for men."

The process that leads to the determination of strategic objectives is influenced by various power configurations both inside and outside the organization, such as the managers at various organization levels, the union, the stockholders, the customers, the suppliers, the government, and various social interest groups such as the Sierra Club and the Friends of the Earth.

Determination of Organization Strategy

A strategy is a means to an end. Organization strategy describes the organization's method for achieving its strategic objectives. This step in the strategic management process includes the identification of the strategic alternatives to achieve organization objectives, the evaluation of the strategic alternatives using certain criteria, and the selection of an alternative or group of alternatives that might become the organization strategy.

There are four different levels in organization strategy: societal, corporate, business, and functional.

Societal strategies are "concerned with the role of an organization in the society of which it is a part, with the process by which that role will be defined, and with the organization's involvement in those processes."[3] Societal strategies focus on the relationship between an organization and its external environment, as well as on the broad issues of corporate citizenship, social responsibility and accountabil-

FIGURE 1-3
Human Relationships

We aspire to a high standard of excellence in human relationships. Specifically, we intend:

1. To select and place employees on the basis of qualifications for the work to be performed without discrimination because of race, religion, national origin, color, sex, age, or handicap unrelated to the task at hand.
2. To place people only on jobs that are truly productive and necessary for the achievement of approved organization objectives.
3. To show each employee the purpose of his or her job and work unit and to insist that work be done efficiently and well. We ask that people give their best efforts, including their ideas and suggestions for improvement.
4. To maintain uniform, reasonable standards of work, and to strive to offer people opportunities to be challenged and to make the best use of their abilities.
5. To encourage self-development and to assist employees in improving and broadening their job skills.
6. To protect people's health and lives. This includes maintaining a clean, safe work environment as free as practicable from health hazards.
7. To provide employees with timely information concerning company operations and results, as well as other work-related matters in which they logically have an interest.
8. To promote from within the corporate organization—in the absence of factors that argue persuasively otherwise.
9. To compensate people fairly, according to their contributions to the company, within the framework of national and local practices.
10. To develop human relationships that inspire respect for, and confidence and trust in, the company whether or not employees are members of a union. Union membership and representation are matters that are decided within the framework of national laws and prevailing practices. Where employees elect in favor of, or are required by law to have some form of, union representation, Caterpillar will endeavor to build a company–union relationship based upon mutual respect and trust.
11. To make employment stabilization a major factor in corporate decisions. We shall give high priority to providing people the most stable, secure employment consistent with the long-term success and growth of Caterpillar.
12. To refrain from hiring persons closely related to members of the board of directors, administrative officers, and department heads. When other employees' relatives are hired, this must be solely the result of their qualifications for jobs to be filled. No employee is to be placed in the direct line of authority of relatives. Nepotism—or the appearance of nepotism— is neither fair to employees, nor in the long-term interests of the business.
13. To place operating decisions at the lowest level in the organization at which they can be competently resolved. This includes giving employees opportunities, commensurate with their capabilities, to make work decisions that will lead to improved performance.
14. To create an environment that develops a feeling of responsibility within every employee for the overall performance and well-being of Caterpillar—especially as we seek improvement in containment of costs, avoidance of waste, adherence to quality standards, greater productivity, and better utilization of assets.
15. To give special effort to working directly with each other in a helpful, friendly way—seeking to avoid bureaucracy and other hazards common to large organizations—and remembering that the Golden Rule is as applicable to human relationships in the workplace as it is in the community and home.

Source: *A Code of Worldwide Business Conduct and Operating Principles*, Caterpillar Tractor Co., 1982.

ity, and business ethics. The main concern of societal strategy is how the organization intends to function as a member of the immediate community, the society, the country, and the global community.

The *corporate strategy* is developed in response to three basic questions: (1) What business or businesses are we in? (2) What business or businesses should we be in? (3) How should the business or group of businesses be managed in order to fully enhance the organization's ability to achieve its strategic objectives? The answer to the first question is identical to the organization's mission. The answer to the second question is the key to the organization's survival because staying in the wrong business may prove to be suicidal in the long run. The answer to the third question is concerned with deciding how much of the company's resources should be invested in its own business; in the case of a firm that has several businesses, deciding how much of the company's resources each of the businesses should receive.

Business strategy is designed to achieve the corporate strategy of the firm. It focuses on deciding how a company can most effectively compete in a particular business or industry once the organization has decided how the business is going to be managed, what results it expects, and the amount of resources it should receive. Its thrust is on integrating the various functional activities (marketing, production, finance, research, and development) to optimize the use of its resources within that business. The purpose of business strategy is to position an organization in an industry in a way that gives it a *competitive advantage* in the marketplace. (Please note that throughout this text we have used the terms business and industry interchangeably.)

Functional strategy is concerned with the formulation of strategies in each of the functional areas of business (production, marketing, finance, and so on), which, when properly implemented, collectively should achieve the business strategy. Functional strategies are the means of carrying out the business strategy. For example, suppose the top management of the organization has decided in its corporate strategy to invest its resources in the soft-drink industry, with the objective of increasing its market share. Suppose that to increase its market share in the soft-drink industry the top management has chosen the introduction of a new product that would appeal to the older segment of the market as its business strategy. After funds have been allocated, each of the functional areas of the organization must develop their respective functional strategies to achieve the business and, in turn, the corporate strategy successfully.

Implementation of Organization Strategy

All tasks and activities that constitute the strategic management process discussed so far would be a waste of valuable management time if the organization strategy (societal, corporate, business, and functional) is not converted into concrete action and results. Implementation of organizational strategy is, therefore, of great importance. According to George A. Steiner, a scholar in strategic management, "the implementation process covers the entire range of managerial activities including such matters as motivation, compensation, management appraisal, and control processes."[4]

According to Schendel and Hofer, implementation is achieved through a variety of administrative tools that can be grouped into three categories: (1) *structure*—including physical structure, methods of specialization, methods of departmentation, methods of coordination, delegation of authority, and informal organization; (2) *processes*—including resource allocation systems, information systems, measurement and evaluation systems, rewards and sanctions, personnel selection, development, and promotion systems; (3) *behavior*—including interpersonal behavior, leadership style, and uses of power.[5] Implementation, then, involves actually executing the strategic game plan of the company.

Control of Organization Strategy

Control is fundamentally concerned with measuring actual performance against planned performance; detecting significant deviations between results and expectations, and identifying the reasons for these deviations; and finally taking corrective action. This process applies equally to the control of the company's organization strategy. Performance indicators that are directly linked to the company strategy (such as market share, return on sales, competitive response, and so forth) may be used to provide early warning signals of its long-run effectiveness. Such early assessments are important not only to effective strategy implementation, but to the review of and possible reformulation of an ineffective strategy. The ultimate effectiveness of a company strategy is decided in the marketplace.

Control of organization strategy is often called "strategic control," because of its focus on actions taken by the organization to achieve strategic objectives. Such actions and the ensuing results are monitored to ensure that the actual strategy implemented is in fact the planned strategy and that it is producing the desired results.

The formulation of contingency plans also is included in the process of strategic control. Contingency plans are plans that can be put into action quickly if environmental circumstances change unexpectedly or the already implemented plans are not achieving the desired results.

We should recognize that the strategic management process involves decision-making by *people* in the organization. People by nature tend to look after their own interests. They form groups and coalitions in order to protect their turf. Strategic management decisions require making choices that may not be equally agreeable to everybody in the organization. Therefore, the relative power and influence of the relevant managers and groups in the organization are manifested in the *political* bargaining that occurs before strategic decisions are made.

CHARACTERISTICS OF THE STRATEGIC MANAGEMENT FRAMEWORK

The strategic management process shown in Figure 1–2 consists of several subprocesses or steps that are theoretically carried out sequentially, beginning with the firm's identification of its strengths, weaknesses, opportunities, and threats, and ending with the control of organization strategy. However, in actual practice, the entire strategic management process is dynamic, and many of the subprocesses are performed simultaneously or iteratively. For example, an organization's mission and policies may evolve simultaneously. Similarly, strategic objectives and organization strategy may be developed simultaneously. Moreover, as the strategic management process is performed in the organization, new feedback information may necessitate changes in the outputs of one or more subprocesses to achieve a certain level of internal consistency in the entire process. To illustrate, suppose an organization is unable to achieve its overall objectives. This may lead to an evaluation of the current strategy showing that the current strategy is ineffective in light of the changed environmental circumstances (changes in the competitive structure in the industry, change in consumer tastes, and so on). Consequently, a new strategy may be formulated to replace the old and now ineffective strategy. However, a check against the organization's strengths and weaknesses may show that the new strategy cannot be implemented because of limited financial resources and human skills. This cyclical process would continue until an acceptable solution is found that is internally consistent in terms of the objectives sought, strategy selected, and the resources available to implement it.

Internal consistency among the subprocesses of the strategic management framework is important. Therefore, executives are required to change the decisions made in the various subprocesses until the results of such decisions are consistent with each other. The framework incorporates several time dimensions. Different companies have different time frames for their strategic management systems. A large multinational company may have objectives that extend five, ten, or twenty years into the future, and long-range implementation plans with time frames of three to five years or more. A small automobile parts dealer may have objectives and plans that do not extend beyond three years. The model of the strategic management process applies to both large and small companies and various planning time frames or horizons.

THE NATURE OF STRATEGIC DECISIONS

Strategic management involves making and implementing strategic decisions that are by nature unique and nonroutine. Often, it is not readily apparent when a strategic decision needs to be made. To comprehend strategic management, it is important to understand the nature of strategic decisions.

Organization Level

The impact of strategic decisions is felt throughout the organization and across all functional areas. Only top management has a broad enough perspective to understand the broad ramifications and implications of strategic decisions. Top management also has the power to allocate resources to implement strategic decisions. Therefore, issues that call for strategic decision-making are best handled by the top-management of the organization. Typical issues that require top-management participation are a firm's decision to go into or get out of a particular business ("Should we divest ourselves of the fertilizer business?"), establishment of objectives for the entire organization that might affect the derivative objectives and plans of various departments and functions in the organization ("Our objective is to double our total sales in five years or less"), and formulation of strategies to achieve company-wide objectives ("We will achieve this sales objective by geographical diversification into national markets where our competitors are not dominantly entrenched").

Temporal Impact

Strategic decisions have long-term consequences for the firm. When a firm decides to engage in a certain line of business and to compete in a well-defined market segment with a distinctive strategy designed to give it a competitive advantage, it has decided on a course of action that it will pursue for many years. This does not mean that under no circumstances will management change the firm's fundamental direction; the firm will change direction if circumstances warrant such a drastic change. However, firms become known for certain products, certain markets, and certain features. For example, when one thinks about the Campbell Soup Company, a certain image comes to mind—a company that makes quality soups. The success of Campbell is intricately tied with its image. Once a firm has committed itself to a certain strategic direction, its competitive image and advantages are tied to it. To move away from the businesses, products, markets, and technologies that have helped a firm build its competitive advantage is not easy. Thus, strategic decisions may be made in a short period of time (the decision to enter a new line of business could conceivably be made in a few weeks or months), even though the decisions have an enduring, long-term impact on the entire organization.

Future Orientation

Strategic decisions are future oriented. Management is required to make a forecast of the future environmental characteristics and an objective assessment of the threats and opportunities embedded in it. Armed with this information, management is in a better position to make strategic decisions such as what the firm should look like in the future (in terms of products, markets, corporate image, size, competitive position, and the like) and what presently should be done to realize their aspirations (spend more money on research and development, invest in the acquisition of modern technology, purchase a dynamic company in a growth industry, and sell divisions in the company whose products are nearing maturity). The future orientation of strategic decisions implies deciding the current course or courses of action that will enable the firm to transform itself from its present state to a desired future state.

Systems Perspective

Strategic decisions are made after a thorough evaluation of their impact and consequences on the whole organization as well as its component parts. In making strategic decisions, management recognizes that the organization is a system of interrelated and interdependent parts; decisions that impact on one part (for example, a production unit) have repercussions on the operations of another part (e.g., marketing) and vice versa.

Open-System Orientation

An organization is said to be "open" to its external environment in the sense that the internal functioning and operations of every firm affects and is in turn affected by the external environment. For instance, a dramatic drop in the birthrate will most certainly adversely affect the sales of a company that markets baby food or diapers. A company that discovers a cure for cancer will have a dramatic impact on the health-care industry. If a firm wants to remain vibrant and successful in the long run, it must make strategic decisions that take into account the impact the external environment, especially such relevant groups as competitors, customers, suppliers, creditors, and government, will have on its operations.

Framework for Lower-Level Decision Making

Strategic decisions provide the umbrella under which managers at lower levels can make decisions that are consistent with the thinking and wishes of top management and contribute towards the total organization's objectives. Every day thousands of major and minor decisions are made throughout the organization; all of these decisions should flow from and be consistent with the organization's strategy. Strategic decisions provide managers who make such decisions with guidelines to ensure that what they decide is consistent with top management's directional plans for the company.

Deployment of Resources

Typically the implementation of strategic decisions involves the allocation of substantial resources. Strategic decisions commit the organization to a stream of actions, extending far into the future, that require substantial resource support.

ORGANIZATION LEVELS AND STRATEGIC MANAGEMENT

Who is responsible for strategic management in an organization? The answer depends on the size of the organization. In a small enterprise, the chief executive officer (who is usually the owner as well) is responsible for the various steps in the strategic management process. As the organization grows, the strategic management responsibilities get spread among managers at different levels. In a large organization, top management is heavily involved in the entire process, with middle management participating in the planning and implementation of programs aimed at the successful fulfillment of organization strategy (societal, corporate, business, and functional).

Some firms are in a single business and others are engaged in more than one business. The former are single strategic-business unit (SBU) firms, the latter are multiple SBUs. An SBU is an operating unit that has a single product, product line, or service(s) that is sold to a clearly defined market segment, and identifiable external competitors. The manager of an SBU has the complete authority to manage it within the broad corporate guidelines and expectations formulated by top management. Examples of single SBU firms are Kentucky Fried Chicken franchises, Pan American Airlines, and Apple Computer Company. Examples of organizations with many businesses are Philip Morris, General Foods, General Electric, and Atlantic Richfield.

In a single SBU firm, the societal, corporate, and business strategies are formulated by the senior managers. Managers in charge of functional departments (marketing, finance, production, and so on) are responsible for the functional strategy formulation, subject to the approval of the senior managers.

In multiple SBU firms, top management at the corporate headquarters is responsible for the entire company's societal and corporate strategy. Each SBU sets its own business and functional strategies under the umbrella of the corporate strategy, which defines the scope of each SBU's operations.

Even though the different types of strategies—societal, corporate, business, and functional—are formulated and implemented by company executives, the Board of Directors of a corporation has the ultimate responsibility for effective strategic management because they are responsible to the stockholders. The chief executive officer therefore must consult with the Board and obtain its approval, especially when it comes to the formulation of corporate and business strategies that he or she wishes to implement in view of the firm's current and future expected situation. Strategic management responsibilities in single SBU and multiple SBU firms are shown in Figure 1–4.

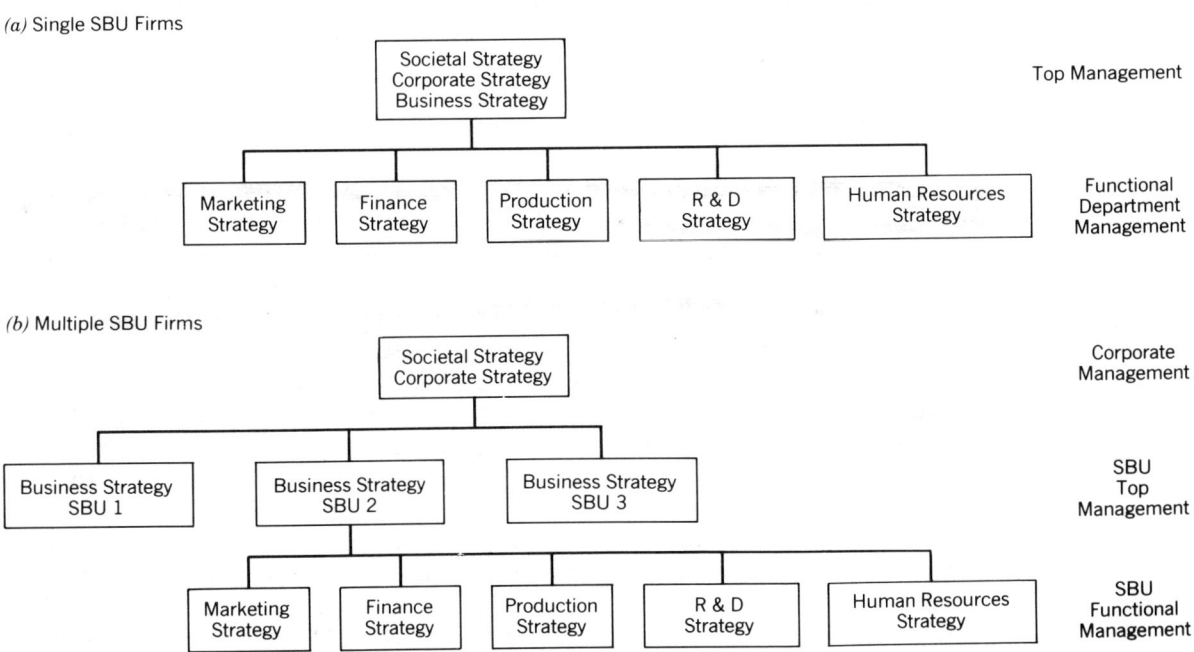

FIGURE 1-4
SBUs and Strategic Management

Although the four types of strategies involve different levels of management making different types of decisions, the strategies should be consistent with one another. If societal, corporate, business, and functional strategies do not fit vertically, the organization will encounter serious difficulties very soon. Each level of strategy must be developed under the umbrella of the strategy of the next higher level: functional strategies should be developed under the umbrella of business strategies, business strategies under that of the corporate strategy, and corporate strategy under that of societal strategy, and so on.

THE EVOLUTION OF FORMAL STRATEGIC MANAGEMENT IN ORGANIZATIONS

In the not-too-distant past, the managerial focus in most businesses was on current decisions for today's operations in today's business. The biggest decision that managers had to make was how to serve the needs of the customers by efficiently producing goods and services at prices that were competitive and consumers were willing to pay. Organizations that performed this task well expected to prosper. Although the basic philosophy of serving the customer's needs by producing goods and services efficiently is still the dominant concern of management in all organizations today's rapid, turbulent, and often unpredictable environmental changes have caused the focus of managers to shift. Managers now try to anticipate the future and prepare for it by formulating and implementing effective strategies. According to George A. Steiner, "A company may overcome inefficient internal resource use if its basic strategy is brilliant, but it is not likely to overcome the wrong strategies even with excellent production and distribution performance. The ideal situation, of course, is for an organization to design brilliant strategies and to implement them efficiently and effectively."[6]

Gluck et al.[7] have suggested that strategic management in most companies evolves along similar lines, albeit by varying rates of progress, from basic financial planning to an overall strategic management framework (see Figure 1–5). In phase *one*, management is most concerned with developing an annual budget; planning is seen as a financial problem. Procedures are designed to develop expense budgets, and information systems are established to compare functional performance against budgetary targets.

In phase *two* of the evolution, the emphasis is on forecast-based planning. The time frame for planning increases as plans are based upon multiyear forecasts. At first, forecasts are made by treasurers struggling to make the most effective financial plans. Initially these forecasts are mere extrapolations of past trends, but often the real world varies significantly from the forecast and the desired results do not occur. Sometimes faulty forecasts bring about disastrous consequences. During the advanced stages of phase two, the planners apply more sophisticated forecasting tools. This causes some improvement, but not soon enough. The predictive models often fail to warn the manager of major environmental shifts that appear obvious after the fact, but the consequence of not providing warning signals is usually a negative impact on profits. Still, phase two does improve the effectiveness of strategic decision making. It forces management to assess the consequences of

Understanding Strategic Management

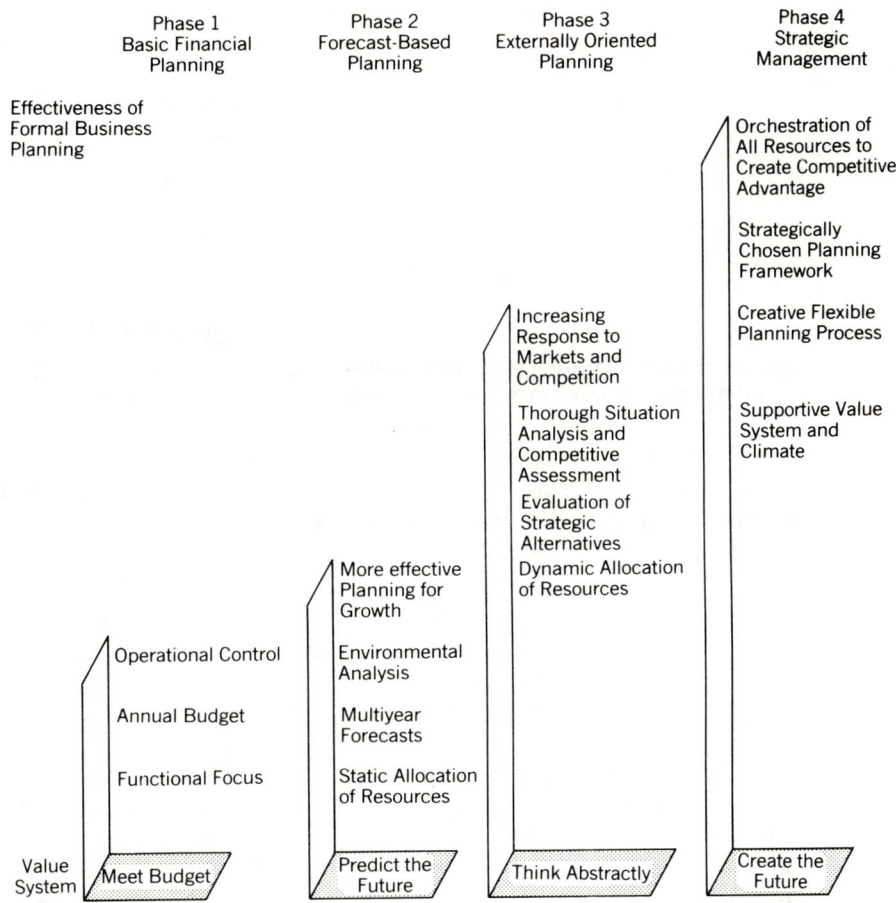

FIGURE 1-5
Four Phases in the Evolution of Formal Strategic Management

Source: Reprinted by permission of the *Harvard Business Review*. An exhibit from "Strategic Management for Competitive Advantage," by Frederick W. Gluck, Stephen Kaufman, and A. Steven Walleck, (July/August 1980). Copyright © 1980 by the President and Fellows of Harvard College; all rights reserved.

current decisions and estimate the potential impact on company operations of discernible trends and events long before they are reflected in current income statements.

In phase *three*—externally oriented planning—managers, having lost faith in forecasting because of repeated failures caused by rapid environmental changes, try to understand the basic marketplace phenomenon bringing about change. They obtain a better understanding of the key factors that determine success in a particular business. In this phase the allocation of resources is dynamic and creative, and managers search for new ways to identify and meet customer needs. They do so by assessing objectively their companies' strengths, weaknesses, and product mix compared to those of their competitors, which may force the company to redefine its markets and develop newer competitive strategies. Planners and lower-level managers are expected to offer top management several alternative ways to allocate resources. Each alternative offers a different risk to a different objective. It is in this phase that top managers recognize that the bottom-up process of identifying alternatives, that is, planners and lower-level managers choosing alternatives for top management consideration, has given planners and lower-level managers the power to significantly influence the future character of their companies without top-level participation. This knowledge disturbs top management and forces it to become heavily involved in the planning process. This marks the beginning of phase four.

In phase *four*—strategic management—companies develop and use sophisticated and effective planning techniques. Techniques are developed as managers face up to the challenge of planning in an organization comprising many different and rapidly evolving businesses, and serving a variety of products/markets in many different countries. However, the feature that distinguishes companies in phase four from those in the three previous phases is the close linking of strategic planning to operation decision-making. To a large measure this linkage is achieved by developing a planning framework that facilitates strategic decision-making as it cuts across organization boundaries, developing a planning process that fosters entrepreneurial thinking, and a corporate value system that reinforces managers' commitment to the company's strategy.

SUMMARY

Strategic management is a process concerned with determining the future direction of an organization and implementing decisions aimed at achieving an organization's long and short-term objectives. The strategic management process consists of seven major interrelated subprocesses: (1) assessment of organization strengths, weaknesses, opportunities, and threats (SWOT); (2) formulation of the organization mission; (3) formulation of the organization philosophy and policies; (4) determination of the strategic objectives; (5) determination of organization strategy; (6) implementation of organization strategy; (7) control of organization strategy. These subprocesses are conceptually carried out in sequence. However, in actual practice, the entire strategic management process is dynamic and iterative by nature.

Strategic management involves the making of strategic decisions. The impact of strategic decisions is felt throughout the organization and have long-term consequences for the organization. In a small organization, the chief executive is responsible for the various strategic management steps. In a large organization, top management is heavily involved in the entire process, with middle management participating in the planning and implementation of programs designed to achieve organizational strategy.

There are four types of organizational strategy: societal, corporate, business, and functional. In a single-business firm (single SBU), societal, corporate, and business strategies are formulated by top management, and functional strategies are the responsibility of the functional department managers. In multiple-business firms (multiple SBUs), corporate headquarters establishes societal and corporate strategies, and each business unit (SBU) sets its own business and functional strategies.

The typical evolution of strategic management in companies consists of four phases: (1) basic financial planning, characterized by operation control, annual budgets, and a functional focus; (2) forecast-based planning characterized by more effective planning for growth, environmental analysis, multiyear forecast, and a static allocation of resources; (3) externally oriented planning characterized by an increasing response to markets and competition, a thorough situation analysis and competitive assessment, evaluation of strategic alternatives, and dynamic allocation of resources; (4) strategic management characterized by orchestration of all resources to create competitive advantage, strategically chosen planning framework, creative and flexible planning processes, and a supportive value system and organization climate.

References

1. William E. Fruhan, Jr., "Pyrrhic Victories in Fights for Market Share," *Harvard Business Review* (September–October 1972), p. 102.
2. Theodore Levitt, "Marketing Myopia," *Harvard Business Review* (July–August 1960), p. 45.
3. Charles W. Hofer, Edwin A. Murry, Jr., Ram Charan, and Robert A. Pitts, *Strategic Management: A Casebook in Business Policy and Planning* (St. Paul, Minn.: West Publishing Company, 1980), p. 11.
4. George A. Steiner, *Strategic Planning: What Every Manager Must Know* (New York: Free Press, 1979), p. 21.
5. Dan E. Schendal and Charles W. Hofer, *Strategic Management: A New View of Business Policy and Planning* (Boston: Little Brown and Company, 1979), p. 222.
6. Steiner, *Strategic Planning*, p. 5.
7. Frederick W. Gluck, Stephen P. Kaufman, and A. Steven Walleck, "Strategic Management for Competitive Advantage," *Harvard Business Review* (July–August 1980), pp. 154–161.

CHAPTER 2
SWOT ANALYSIS

Conceptual Framework for SWOT Analysis
Identification of Opportunities and Threats
    External Environmental Analysis
Key Success Factors
Identification of Key Success Factors
    Industry Characteristics
    Nature and Degree of Competition
    Barriers to Entry
    Competitive Power of Substitute Products
    Buyer Power
    Supplier Power
Evaluation of Firm's Strengths and Weaknesses
Summary
References

SWOT Analysis

PERFORMANCE OBJECTIVES

When you have finished reading this chapter, you should be able to

1. Conduct analysis of industry characteristics.
2. Identify key factors for success in business.
3. Understand how to assess a firm's strengths and weaknesses to successfully exploit the opportunities and avoid the threats in an industry.
4. Understand the relationship between the external environment and assessment of a firm's internal resources and skills.
5. Explain an approach to determine a firm's future opportunities and threats.

CONCEPTUAL FRAMEWORK FOR SWOT ANALYSIS

The concepts and process of strategic management were introduced in the last chapter. A model of the strategic management process was presented, and the steps in the process were enumerated and explained. Figure 2-1 illustrates that conceptually the entire process begins with an assessment of an organization's strengths, weaknesses, opportunities, and threats (commonly referred to as SWOT analysis). SWOT analysis enables an organization to formulate and implement strategies aimed at accomplishing its organizational mission and objectives. Information collected and analyzed in the SWOT analysis may suggest that changes be made in either the mission, objectives, policies, or strategies of the organization.

We will begin by presenting a conceptual framework for conducting SWOT analysis (shaded area in Figure 2-1). A method for assessing the impact of changes in the external environment on the industry and identifying threats and opportunities is then discussed, followed by the presentation of an approach to evaluate the strengths and weaknesses of a firm.

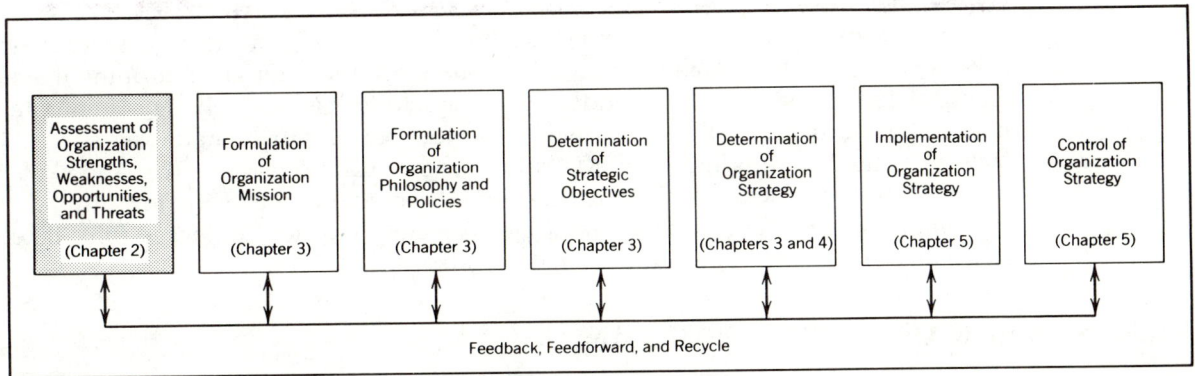

FIGURE 2-1
A Model of the Strategic Management Process

22 The Concepts of Strategic Management and Case Analysis

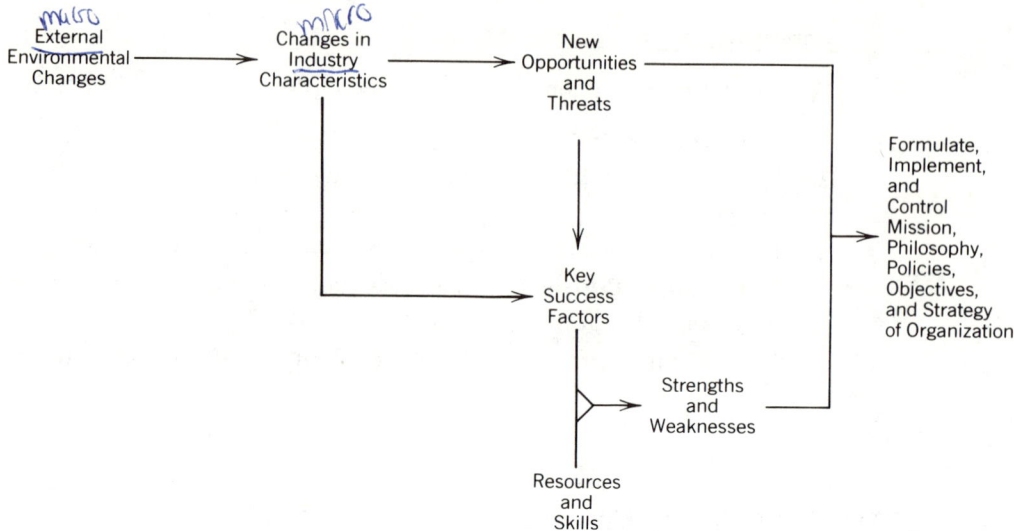

FIGURE 2-2
Framework for Assessing SWOTs of an Organization

The framework for SWOT analysis presented here is for a single-business company. A company engaged in several different businesses must conduct a SWOT analyses for each business in its' portfolio.

A company attempting to analyze its own SWOTs first must start by defining its business. Second, it must identify the opportunities and threats in the business at that time. Third, it must determine the business's *key success factors*—those activities or areas in which the company must be especially proficient to succeed in the business by fully exploiting the opportunities available to it and combating the threats that endanger it. Fourth, it must look inward and evaluate its own capabilities in terms of the skills and competences present in the organization that would enable it to do especially well in those areas identified as the key success factors for the business. *Objectively matching its capabilities against the key success factors will provide the company with a good estimate of its own strengths and weaknesses.*

A conceptual framework for establishing the SWOTs of an organization is presented in Figure 2–2, which shows that changes in the external environment are responsible for changes in the industry's characteristics. Such changes generate new opportunities and threats as well as a new set of concomitant key success factors for the business/industry. Matching the organizational resources and skills to the key success factors of the business provides data that are useful for formulating, implementing, and controlling strategic plans designed to successfully take advantage of opportunities and combat threats.

IDENTIFICATION OF OPPORTUNITIES AND THREATS

Changes in the external environment of the firm are the principal source of the current and future opportunities and threats for the firm. The external environment is composed of those trends, events, and forces that are beyond the direct control of the management of the firm. Changes in the external environment affect different industries or businesses in different ways. For example, a demographic change, such as a drop in the birth rate and a gradual aging of the population, will adversely affect a company in the baby food business. However, this very trend will have a favorable impact on the health-care and retirement-home industry. Thus, the same environmental change could pose a threat to one industry and be an opportunity for success in another industry.

There are four segments of the external environment: economic, sociocultural, political, and technological. Figure 2–3 shows the factors usually found in each segment of the environment, although it is by no means a complete list of all factors in each segment.

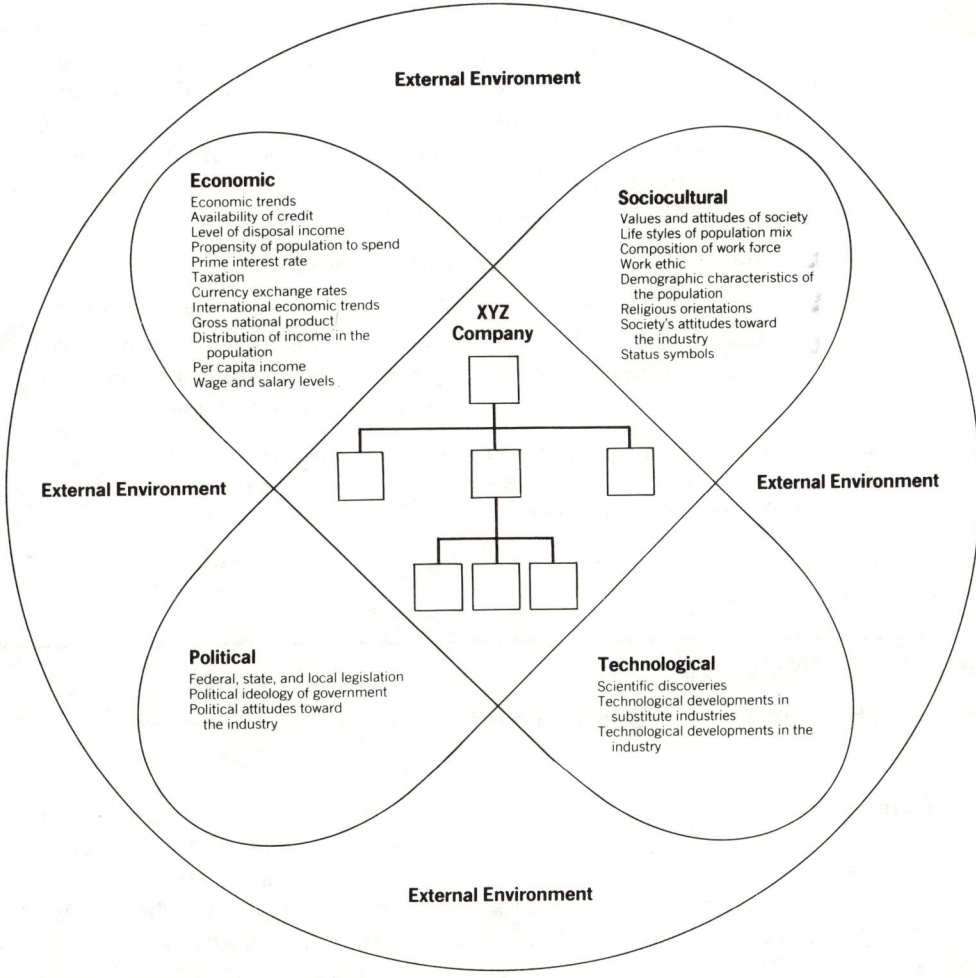

FIGURE 2-3
Factors in the External Environment

External Environmental Analysis

The external environment never remains static. For example, dramatic external environmental changes occurred in the 1970s, and most scientists and futurists agree that even greater and more rapid changes should be expected in the years ahead. The critical responsibility of managers is to identify future opportunities and to position the firm to avail itself of the opportunities for growth and profitability. However, managers face the constant problem of innumerable changes in trends and events and the impossibility of keeping track of all of them. The key to making this task manageable is to focus only on critical environmental factors.

Critical environment factors are the trends, events, and forces that might have a significant favorable or unfavorable impact on the firm's operations. Not all industries or businesses have the same critical environmental factors, as noted earlier. For example, to a firm whose products are petroleum based, the world price of petroleum would be critical, but it is not critical to a firm that makes shoes. For a multinational company, changes in a foreign country's political ideology would be critical because a change from a capitalist to a socialist orientation could result in expropriation or nationalization of the company's assets in that country. This would not be the case for a purely domestic company. The following steps are suggested for forecasting the opportunities and threats that might result from changes in the external environment:

1. Identify the critical environmental factors.
2. Monitor the changes that appear in the critical environmental factors.
3. Forecast the cumulative impacts on the *industry* characteristics of the critical environmental factors. Will the impact on the industry be favorable and present opportunities or be unfavorable and pose threats to the firm?

Practical Insights 1 illustrates the opportunities and threats identified by a personal-computer manufacturer because of environmental changes affecting the microcomputer industry.

PRACTICAL INSIGHTS 1
Opportunities and Threats Facing a Personal-Computer Manufacturer

Opportunities

New segments are emerging in the present markets for microcomputers, giving rise to new opportunities for growth. Trends towards increased portability, smaller size, and battery operation are becoming more pronounced. The company could capitalize on this trend through development of products to fit these new needs. An example of a new product could be a notebook-sized, "dedicated" computer, meaning the computer is dedicated solely to one or two specific preprogrammed functions, such as word processing or portfolio analysis. There are also new opportunities for microcomputers in regulating home environments (temperature, air quality, appliances) and programming robots for routine tasks. Most universities are purchasing microcomputers for their students' specific needs, instead of one large mainframe system.

Opportunities also exist within previously neglected demographic groups to a certain degree. The largest increases in population are projected to be the number of people aged 30–39 years old and children under five years of age. The 30–39-year-old age group is maturing into their peak earning years and is having children. We see growth potential in the projected overall population increases, but it is the younger generation that has the greatest potential for repeat and upgrading purchases, and it is the segment we feel holds the most opportunity for increasing sales. Educational games and programs are the next big opportunity in microcomputer software; the education segment presents a growing opportunity to cement brand image and recognition in consumers' minds at a young age, thus increasing the probability of repeat purchases. The deregulation of the telecommunications industry affords opportunities for extension into satellite communications via microcomputers, electronic mail, and other forms of electronic communication.

The expected shakeout of the microcomputer industry, in which many fledgling companies may go under because of an inability to remain competitive against the more established microcomputer firms, will present an opportunity to acquire additional valuable related assets necessary for microcomputer manufacturing. These assets could include manufacturing facilities, individuals with technical training and expertise, and even inventories—all of which could be purchased at reduced costs to the company. We would be able to increase our assets while minimizing investment.

Threats

The trend towards increased nationalism is a major threat to our company. Many nations have developed an increased orientation towards protection of local companies from foreign competition. Rising tariff and nontariff barriers, specifically local content laws and government subsidies of competitors, could significantly alter our Division's profitability since 70 percent of total revenues are from foreign markets. It was recently announced that the British Broadcasting Company has pooled its resources with numerous British computer firms underwritten by the government to develop an advanced microcomputer system dubbed the Acorn.

A significant threat to our Computer Systems Division is the expected movement of manufacturers towards standardization on a particular operating system. Our systems utilize the CP/M system, while IBM offers a MS–DOS system. MS–DOS offers many advantages over CP/M and if it becomes the standard, software companies will concentrate on writing programs for MS–DOS. This could limit our Division's software offerings until we change over to the accepted standard. Further complicating this situation is the impact of the U. S. Government on the selection of the standard. It is possible the government may request that a totally new system that, because of its influence as a major purchaser, could, become the industry standard.

The Computer Systems Division will be confronted by new market entrants, primarily large American and/or Japanese firms. Many of these firms have considerably greater resources and skills than our company's.

The cost of crude oil and the demand for gasoline and other oil products are two critical environmental factors for the oil-refining industry. Practical Insights 2 illustrates the severely adverse impact on U. S. independent oil refineries of the

PRACTICAL INSIGHTS 2

Independent Oil Refiners are Still in Shock

Through first-hand experience, Andrew E. Hill, Chairman of Hill Petroleum, sees "no more room for the independent refiner." In February 1984, his small Houston refining company filed for reorganization under Chapter 11 of the bankruptcy laws. Before this, Hill Petroleum laid off one-third of its workforce, reduced salaries, and installed a $175 million "cracking" unit to squeeze more valuable fuels out of each barrel of crude oil. Despite these actions and a slight surge in gasoline demand, Hill Petroleum continued to lose money. "It was like being a cancer patient waiting to die," says Hill, who still remains president of the American Independent Refiners Association.

During the last several years, weak demand and fierce competition have created much red ink for most refiners. But the independents, who have no wellhead profits to carry refining losses, have been particularly hard hit.

The problems began for independent refiners with the end of federal price controls on oil in 1981. The cost of crude oil began to rise just when pump prices for gasoline were beginning to sag, which resulted in shrinking margins. During this same period, the federal government phased out its entitlements program, which required crude-rich refiners with cheap domestic reserves to pay crude-poor ones cash subsidies. As a result, a large number of small, old refineries bit the dust.

Now, even the larger independents are feeling the effects of the oil glut. Tosco Corp. lost $378 million last year on sales of $2.5 billion. Tosco is attempting to sell two of its three refineries, in order to pay off some $754 million in debt. Charter Oil Co. has laid off half of its workers at its Houston refinery. Coral Petroleum Inc.'s United Refining Co. and Hudson Oil Co. have filed under Chapter 11.

The struggle is most intense on the West Coast, which is a traditional stronghold of the independents. Major oil companies such as Shell Oil, Atlantic Richfield, and Standard of California have battled for market share. This has driven prices down, "putting the squeeze on all of us," says Richard W. Matson, president of Paramont Petroleum Corp., a California refiner. Gasoline prices have inched up of late, easing the pressure, but unless prices move still higher, industry specialists believe a dozen or more California refiners could fall.

According to James D. Francis, president of Charter Oil's refinery division, "the majors can afford to sit there and wait until the market rationalizes, independents can't." One major reason for this is the independents' lack of financial muscle. Lenders, burned by billions of dollars in bad energy loans made during the 1970s, have gotten tough. As a result, many banks froze the credit lines of borrowers, drying up the independents' liquidity.

This crunch has come as funding needs have mushroomed. For one thing, crude procurement has changed radically. Up to 1980, most small refiners could buy on credit. Working through exchanges, they used that leverage to buy, then swap barrels in one region for barrels near their plants to save on transportation. Now, the majors routinely require letters of credit, so that more refiners are shipping instead of swapping.

During the 1970s, small, less efficient refiners could profit, even though they produced large proportions of so-called residual fuel—a low-grade product used mainly to generate electricity. After 1978, when prices surged, electric utilities switched to other energy sources, lessening the demand for residual fuel. At the same time, world oil production shifted to heavier crudes that yield more residual oil.

The major oil companies have retooled

their refineries, at costs of up to $1 billion per plant. Such sums are beyond most independents' resources. With more profitable refineries, the majors can afford to distribute products to new markets, often shattering the independents' regional niches.

A few independents have attempted to upgrade, often with disastrous results. Powerline Oil Co., a 50-year-old West Coast refiner, spent $160 million upgrading its equipment. The hardware failed to deliver and Powerline, caught in the midst of a price war with less gasoline than expected, maintaining losses and impossible debt payments, was forced to file for bankruptcy under Chapter 11 in March 1984.

Even going out of business has grown costlier. There are so many old refineries on the block that values have plummeted. Says one owner, "after trying for months to find a buyer, I finally called the scrap dealers, but they wanted to charge me $1 million to haul it off."

Compounding these problems, the EPA is expected to propose that lead in gasoline be reduced by 90 percent, to 0.1 grams per gallon. It is estimated that compliance will cost about $500 million, most of which will be incurred by small refiners.

Even the well-heeled independents are not immune to these costly problems. In 1980, Valero Energy Corp. purchased 50 percent of the small Saber Energy Inc. refinery in Texas, planning a state-of-the-art facility that could process residual fuel into gasoline. Today, after spending $572 million, Saber is going through serious start-up problems. The price spread between residual fuel and gasoline has shrunk from $12 to $5, and its debt repayments start coming due within the next six months. Although Valero representatives deny that the project is in trouble, industry consultants warn that "a year from now the banks will be knocking on Valero's door. Then we will see how deep [the company's] pockets are."

Source: Business Week, April 23, 1984, pp. 52–54.

---

end of federal price controls on oil coupled with a drop in the demand for oil products.

To sum up what has been discussed thus far, changes in the external environment bring about changes in the characteristics of the industry in which the firm competes. Changes in industry characteristics in turn create a new set of opportunities and threats and corresponding key success factors. In order to evaluate the strengths and weaknesses of the company and its consequent probability of succeeding in the business, managers must assess the resources and skills of the company in light of the new set of key success factors. Next we will discuss an approach for identifying the key success factors of a business.

KEY SUCCESS FACTORS

The most important element in the framework for analyzing the SWOTs of a business is the accurate determination of its key success factors. Misjudgment of the key success factors could have disastrous consequences for an organization because it might lead to the development of an inappropriate organization strategy. Accurately determining the key success factors of the business must be a high priority for top management, since the organization strategy must be founded on these factors. Top management must ensure that organization strategy is consistent and never at odds with the key success factors.

Not only do key success factors differ from business to business, but they change over time. For example, the key success factors in the automobile industry prior to 1974 and the oil embargo by OPEC were comfort and attractive styling, competitive price, effective channels of distribution (dealerships), and efficient service after sale. After the rapid rise in the price of gasoline in 1974 and the inroads into the U. S. market by foreign imports, particularly from Japan, the rules of the game and key success factors for the automobile industry changed considerably. In addition to those existing prior to 1974, three more key success factors were added to the industry: quality, safety, and fuel economy.

The key success factors are different in other industries. For example, in the soft-drink industry key success factors are distinctive taste, brand identification, and effective advertising to obtain more shelf space in supermarkets and grocery stores than competing brands. In the supermarket business, the key success factors are low price, good advertising of products and prices, fast checkout, sufficient inventory to prevent stockouts of products on shelves, and ample parking. Sometimes the same factors may be responsible for success in two or more industries. In such cases, a closer examination will reveal variations in the relative role, importance, and subtle differences among the key factors in each industry.

In determining the key success factors for a business, managers must be extremely careful not to identify anything and everything as a key to success. An exhaustive list serves no purpose, because it does not focus on the small number of factors that hold the key to success in a business. Managers must study, evaluate, and analyze the facts uncovered during SWOT analysis and boldly put forth the handful of key success factors that will serve as the basis for strategy formulation.

IDENTIFICATION OF KEY SUCCESS FACTORS

We will begin by describing an approach based on the analysis of the opportunities and threats originating from the industry characteristics. We will assume that changes in the industry characteristics resulting from the changes in the external environment already have occurred. We will further assume that at the moment managers of the firm are faced with the task of determining the organization's strengths and weaknesses to exploit the opportunities and reduce the threats in the business. Our focus will be on the existing industry characteristics and their analyses.

Industry Characteristics

In conducting an analysis of industry, we are principally concerned with determining its characteristics, its long-term prospects, and how it functions. We will examine industry characteristics along five dimensions: nature and degree of competition, barriers to entry, the competitive power of substitutes, buyer power, and supplier power. Changes in the characteristics of each of these five dimensions are responsible for generating new opportunities and threats and a new set of key success factors.

Nature and Degree of Competition The opportunities and threats as well as the key success factors in an industry are a function of the intensity of rivalry and the competition's tactics such as price competition, introduction of new products, advertising wars, improved customer service, and better warranties.

Rivalry among competing firms is intense when there are numerous firms in the industry or the major competitors are nearly equal in size.[1] When there are numerous firms, there is a greater chance of some firms falsely believing that they could improve their position without being noticed and thereby incurring a retaliatory action from competitors. However, it rarely happens that such moves go unnoticed by competitors. Competition is also intense when major competitors are fairly equal in strength, size, and resources, whether this be four firms with 25 percent of the market or 100 firms with one percent of the market.[2] Firms try to improve their respective market shares through strategic moves that are immediately countered by competitors. However, when the industry is dominated by one firm, the degree of competition decreases because the market leader establishes the rules of competitive behavior in the industry and other firms do not have the resources to stage a "coup" against the "ruler."[3] Therefore, the number of firms competing in an industry has a dramatic impact on competition.

The intensity of rivalry among firms is high when industry growth is slow.[4] When industry growth is high and demand for the product is increasing rapidly, there is enough business for everybody, hence rivalry among firms is low. When the industry growth rate slows, firms that want to continue increasing their sales volume can do so only at the expense of others. Actions to increase market share among growth-oriented firms precipitate moves and countermoves in the competitive arena that leave weaker firms either permanently crippled or dead. Therefore, industry growth has great impact on competitiveness.

Rivalry among firms is intense when firms are pressured to produce at or very near full capacity. This situation is more prevalent in industries that typically have *high fixed* costs such as copper and aluminum. When demand for the product is high, firms experience high capacity-utilization rates. When demand decreases, rival firms resort to high sales volume maintenance tactics, such as volume discounts, rebates, extended warranties, and secret price concessions. Such high sales volume maintenance tactics also are used by firms when their products have a short shelf-life or seasonal use or either are difficult or costly to keep in inventory.[5]

Competition is weaker when the products or services of competing firms are differentiated enough to provide protection against competitive onslaughts. Obvious differentiation that leads to strong customer loyalty makes it difficult for the customer to switch easily to another product.[6] An example of such product differentiation is the customer loyalty shown to the double-edged razor blades made by Gillette.

Competitive rivalry is intense in industries characterized by scale economies that dictate increases in a firm's capacity be made in large increments.[7] When one or more firms raise their capacity, the total industry's capacity for a period of time may exceed the level justified by total demand for the product, resulting in price cutting and other tactics to raise sales volume. Examples of industries that have so suffered are ammonium fertilizer, vinyl chloride, and chlorine.

The more diverse are industry competitors in their strategies, their personalities, their countries of origin, their goals, and their corporate priorities, the greater will be the degree of competition.[8] Diversity among firms enhances the chances of their adopting different competitive strategies and misreading each other's real strategies. Uncertainty and insecurity result as firms are unable to obtain a correct reading on the "rules of the game" in the industry. A strategy that may be beneficial for one firm may be harmful to another. For instance, a small firm may be quite happy to have a lower rate of return than the industry average and be willing to adopt pricing and promotion strategies that may be quite unacceptable to a large company. A foreign company may have different objectives for competing in the industry, for example, unloading products at cost in order to operate at full capacity at home. Such a strategy can totally disrupt the industry, as happened in the United States steel industry because of the "dumping" of foreign-made steel. In short, diversely oriented companies have different concepts of the market and the best ways to compete; therefore, they continually clash with each other as each strategic move by one firm is attacked by a counter-strategy of another.

Rivalry in the industry is intensified if there are firms that have much to lose from failure or much to gain from success in the market.[9] Companies that have committed many resources and whose future "health" is associated with success in the industry are likely to adopt strategies that may greatly intensify interfirm rivalry. For example, Philip Morris' entry into the beer industry by purchasing the Miller Brewing Company resulted in intensified competition and rivalry among firms in that industry.

Interfirm rivalry is aggravated if exit barriers, which prevent a firm from dropping out of the industry, are high.[10] There are a variety of exit barriers, such as specialized assets that are tied to a certain business or location, assets with low liquidation value, and assets that cannot be converted to another use or moved to another location except at great expense. In many foreign countries, the government may disallow plant closings because of the negative effects on the regional economy. Management personnel may have strong personal attachments to a business that may induce them to hold on to it even if it is declining. When exit barriers are high, as in the case of airlines, excess capacity remains and companies continue to increase competition. As competition becomes keener, the profitability of the healthy firms suffers and the weaker firms are forced out of business.

To sum up, the nature and degree of competiton in an industry, which determines the opportunities and threats and the key success factors, is influenced by several factors: the number of firms in the industry and their relative sizes, the growth rate of the industry, the pressure to operate at near full capacity, the shelf life and seasonality of the product, the difficulty or cost of storing the product in inventory, product or service differentiation, scale economies in the industry, diversity in the orientation of firms in the industry, top management's commitment to stay and succeed in the business, and the height of the exit barriers.

Barriers to Entry. A new firm entering an industry adds to the production capacity of the industry if the new entrant has not bought an existing firm as a means of entry. New entrants come with a plan to obtain market share, and often command substantial resources and skills. Strong firms entering an industry can cause a major shake-up in the market, particularly when the new firm is a large company diversifying through acquisition, for example, Philip Morris and its purchase of Miller Brewing and 7-Up. A competitive onslaught by the new firm can result in lower product prices; the costs to the incumbent firms rise as they respond to the new competitor. For example, the massive radio, T. V., and newspaper promotional campaign by Philip Morris on behalf of Miller beer increased the advertising and other marketing-related expenditures of Anheuser-Busch, the producer of Budweiser and Michelob beers.

The significance of the competitive threat of entry by new firms in the market depends on the barriers to entry, especially the potential entrant's expectations about how the incumbent firms will *react* to it. The threat of entry is low if barriers to entry are high and/or the new entrant expects massive, hostile retaliation from the older firms in the industry.[11]

There are a number of important barriers to entry in a particular industry.[12] The first major barrier is *economies of scale*. If scale economies exist (that is, if there is a decline in unit cost and greater efficiency associated with an increase in absolute volume per period), the new entrant has two choices—either to enter on a large scale and enjoy lower costs or on a small scale and accept a cost disadvantage. Scale economies can occur in every function of a business, including production, marketing, purchasing, finance, research and development, customer service, and distribution. For example, scale economies exist when a chain with 20 stores in one city does not have to spend twice as much for local advertising as a competitor that has only 10 stores, since the cost of advertising is independent of the number of stores. Similarly, larger discounts on inventory purchases may be available with increases in the volume of inventory purchased.

The new entrant must face the problem of entering on a small scale of operations and experiencing the disadvantage of higher costs, or entering on a large scale and facing the risk of aggressive retaliation by the incumbent firms. The older firms may resort to strategies designed to protect their market shares or continue operating at existing capacity levels. Because both entry options—small or large scale—are unattractive, economies of scale lessen the threat of a new entry.

The second major barrier to entry is capital. The larger the total amount of financial resources needed to enter the market and compete successfully, the more limited will be the pool of likely entrants. Capital is needed not only for production equipment and plant, but for financing inventories, working capital, providing credit to customers, advertising, and absorbing start-up losses. Xerox and IBM created significant capital barriers to entry with their strategy of renting or leasing their equipment instead of selling their products outright, which greatly increased the working-capital requirements.

A third major barrier to entry is access to distribution channels. A new entrant must either create its own channels of distribution or use already established ones. Creating new channels of distribution may be uneconomical or prohibitively expensive, and the new firm must face the task of inducing the established distributors to carry its product. The distributor may be reluctant to carry a product that lacks buyer recognition. The distributor also may prefer not to offend firms with competing brands. Quite often, limited warehouse space may mean that the new entrant's product must displace competitors' products. The more limited the wholesale or retail stores and the stronger the relationships that existing competitors have with the wholesalers and retailers, the more difficult will be entry. To overcome this barrier, potential entrants may have to implement a variety of methods to obtain distribution channels, such as price reductions, higher margins, demand creation advertising, and so on.

Brand identification is a fourth barrier to entry. When a firm's product enjoys brand identification, it has generally been successful in differentiating its product and creating customer loyalty. Massive dollar expenditures are involved in creating brand identification and customer loyalty. Therefore, a new entrant must be prepared to spend more than the entrenched competitors on advertising and sales promotion to shift customer loyalties away from the competitors' products. Creating brand identification and customer loyalty also can be very time-consuming unless the new entrant's product is overwhelmingly superior in some aspect, such as quality, performance, or efficiency. Finally, expenditures on projects aimed at establishing brand identification are especially risky. If the project fails, there is no liquidation or salvage value as there is with physical assets such as plant and equipment. Established brand identification and customer loyalty have created high barriers to the entry of new firms, such as in the information-processing industry where IBM is the established leader. Similarly, established brand names have created entry barriers in cosmetics, soft drinks, and the manufacture of airplanes.

Cost advantages independent of size constitute the fifth major entry barrier. Existing firms may possess cost advantages that are unavailable to potential entrants regardless of the size or economies of scale of the new entrant, such as access to cheaper and better quality raw materials, favorable locations, assets purchased at preinflation prices, and capital at lower interest rates. Entrenched firms also may have advantages that are derived from such factors as a patented product or process, a secret formula (for example, the formula of the coke syrup is a closely guarded secret of the Coca-Cola Company), or proprietary technology.

A sixth major entry barrier is the learning or experience curve. In some industries, especially those involving a high labor content performing intricate tasks and/or complex assembly operations, it has been observed that unit costs decline at a predictable and measurable rate when a firm gains cumulative experience in producing a product.[13] The decline in unit costs is the result of greater efficiencies and productivity obtained not only in manufacturing but in other functional areas, such as research and development, marketing, and purchasing. This phenomenon has been observed in aerospace, automobile, electronic, petrochemical, airline transportation, and semiconductor businesses. Entrenched firms that have lower unit costs because of accumulated experience can make life in the industry miserable for a new firm by adopting strategies such as aggressive price cutting, which a new entrant may not be able to afford because of its higher cost structure.

The seventh major barrier to entry is government policy. Entry into certain industries is difficult, limited, or even disallowed by government policy. In the United States, laws for the protection of the environment and safety promotion have indirectly created entry barriers. Licensing requirements limit entry in the radio and television broadcasting industry. The government controls entry in some industries like trucking, railroads, and liquor retailing. In Pennsylvania liquor stores are state-owned and private ownership of liquor sales outlets is prohibited.

The eighth major barrier to entry is the reaction of existing competitors. Even though the new entrant feels that it has the ability to overcome the entry barriers, its expectations about how the existing competitors will react to its entering their industry will influence its decision. If it expects the incumbent firms to forcefully retaliate, making its entry in the industry both risky and unpleasant, it may decide to forgo entry. Circumstances such as the following increase the probability of strong retaliation by incumbent firms and discourage new entrants:

- The incumbents have substantial financial resources, including cash and unused borrowing capacity that they can use to unleash an aggressive promotion campaign and price war to defend their market positions.
- In the past, the incumbents have aggressively resisted "territorial" encroachments by new entrants.
- Incumbents have sufficient influence over distributors and customers to maintain market share.
- Incumbents are likely to cut prices because of overcapacity in the industry or to protect their market share.
- The industry has established firms that are committed to staying in it profitably, and exit barriers for such firms are high.
- There has been a reduction in the growth rate of the industry, thereby limiting its ability to accommodate a new entrant without affecting the sales volume and profitability of the incumbent firms.

Switching costs is the ninth and final major entry barrier. The higher the costs incurred by a buyer for switching from one supplier's product to another, the more benefits a new supplier must offer to induce the buyer to switch from an existing supplier. Switching costs include: training employees to use the new product, product redesign, rearranging work, new physical layout, and so on. High switching costs is one of the significant barriers to entry in the mainframe computer industry.

To sum up, the competitive threat of new firms is mitigated by the entry barriers into the industry. Among the most significant entry barriers are economies of scale, capital requirements, access to distribution channels, brand identification and customer loyalty, cost advantages independent of size, lower costs of entrenched firms because of the experience curve, government policy, retaliation by existing firms in the business, and high switching costs.

Competitve Power of Substitute Products. For most products, it is possible to identify related products that can serve as substitutes. For example, steel competes with aluminum and in some cases plastics, sugar competes with saccharine and aspartame, coffee with tea, and fiberglass insulation with styrofoam and cellulose. Substitutes can limit the potential of an industry by putting upper limits on the prices that an industry can charge for its products.[14] When a customer buys a product, he or she expects value for money spent. This value is determined by the level of satisfaction derived from using the product. The more attractive the price–satisfaction tradeoff of substitute products, the greater is the danger of losing industry sales to the substitute products. Unless the industry can improve the price–satisfaction tradeoff offered on its product by somehow differentiating it via marketing or improving its quality and/or performance, it will be unable to improve its profit potential by raising prices.

An industry should be most concerned about a substitute industry that is experiencing technological developments that may improve its price–satisfaction tradeoff. Also of concern are substitute industries that are highly profitable because of their potential to price their products at levels that improve the substitute's price–performance tradeoff. An industry may unexpectedly encounter stiffer competition from substitutes if firms in the substitute industry begin to encounter increased competition within their own industry, thereby forcing them to drop prices or improve product performance.

Buyer Power. Buyers can influence competition in an industry by demanding lower prices, higher quality, better service, improved warranty terms, and forcing sellers to outdo each other for the buyer's business.[15] How much influence buyers can exert depends on their power. The buyer group is powerful when[16]

- The buyers are few, and their purchases represent a significant percentage of the total sales of the supplying industry.
- The purchased products account for a significant portion of the total purchases or costs of the buyer. Buyers are more likely to shop around for a better price and purchase selectively.
- The supplier industry's products are undifferentiated and standard. As a product approaches the status of a commodity, product differentiation becomes difficult and buyer power increases. Such is the case with products like copper, zinc, and bananas.
- The supplier industry's product is not an important ingredient or component determining the quality of the buyer's product or service. Pressures on the supplier industry to lower prices are smaller when the quality of the buyer's product is critically based on the purchased product.
- The buyer can purchase the product from any number of different sellers without incurring great switching costs. In this case, the buyer can play off one seller firm against another in order to get the best deal.
- When the buyer industry has low profits. This forces buyers to seek cheaper goods and materials.
- When there is a threat of backward integration by the buyers. This can happen when the seller industry is profitable and has good long-term prospects, in which case the buyer may purchase a firm in the selling industry. A buyer may

integrate backwards and not only increase profits but assure a reliable source of supply and stable prices.

Supplier Power. The more powerful are the suppliers, the greater their ability to influence the competitive conditions and profitability of the industry that purchases their products. Powerful suppliers can influence the buying industry's costs, prices, quality, and ultimately its overall prospects for growth and profitability. If suppliers can force the buyers to accept their terms on prices and quality of purchased goods or services, they have power over them. Powerful suppliers can shrink the profit margins of the buying industry unable to raise the prices of its products or services. A supplier group is powerful when[17]

- There are a few large supplier firms and many firms in the buying industry.
- The products of each supplier firm are so differentiated that they make it very costly for the buyer firms to switch suppliers. Buyers cannot play one supplier against another.
- The supplier industry does not have to worry about competition from substitute products. The fact that glass, aluminum, and plastics act as substitutes in the packaging and bottling industry has limited the power of these industries. A similar situation exists in the sweetener industry, in which firms producing alternative sweeteners, albeit large individually *vis-a-vis* the individual buyers, are engaged in intense competition.
- The suppliers sell to a number of industries and the buying firms in the industry do not account for a significant portion of the suppliers' total business. In such instances, the suppliers are not very concerned about offering reasonable prices or improving product quality, because their own financial health and future well-being are not significantly affected by the volume of sales to one particular industry.
- The supplier's product is an important ingredient in the success of the buyer's manufacturing process or product quality.
- One or more firms in the supplier industry present a credible threat of forward integration into the buyer industry. This may happen when the profitability and future prospects of the buyer industry are better than those of the seller industry. Such a threat places constraints on the ability of the buyer industry to strike a favorable bargain on the purchased items.

An objective and thorough analysis of the competitive environment in which the firm is operating, plus diagnoses of the barriers to entry, the competitive power of substitutes, and the relative power of the buyer and supplier industries should provide the firm with a list of key success factors. Practical Insights 3 illustrates key success factors in the personal-computer industry identified by a company that is competitive in that product/market segment.

Fiat's withdrawal from the prestigious American market because of its inability to score high on the key success factors for the automobile industry, such as a strong dealer network, a strong service system, and a reputation for high quality, is described in Practical Insights 4.

PRACTICAL INSIGHTS 3

Key Success Factors Identified by a Firm in the Personal-Computer Industry

- Availability of a large library of high-quality, user-friendly software is critical.
- Technological equivalence with competitors' products in the marketplace is necessary to be competitive. Product lines must offer at least the same level of technology as the market leaders.
- Continuous product development is essential to maintain equivalence in this dynamic, high-technology industry.
- Marketing and distribution effectiveness to reach target markets is critical.
- Strong advertising, promotion, and distribution capabilities are essential.
- High brand recognition and good brand image are key ingredients for success. Products must be well-known and perceived as a good buy.
- Competitive pricing is critical.
- A strong customer service network is necessary to offer product support and service.

PRACTICAL INSIGHTS 4

Fiat's Turnaround Strategy

Fiat's turnaround strategy has worked. It captured 12.7 percent of Europe's 9.8-million car market by the end of 1983, up from 11 percent in 1979, and was running neck-and-neck with Ford's European operations for top spot. In Italy, it reversed a 14-point drop in its market share during the 1970s and ended the year with 55.4 percent of that market, up from 50.3 percent in 1980. To accomplish such a coup, the company spent an average of $1 billion a year to overhaul all versions of Fiat's 14 models from the Lancia to the Panda. Many are entirely new; the rest are completely restyled.

Fiat sold its steelmaking operation to the Italian government and two assembly operations in Argentina and Columbia to local investors. It withdrew from the U. S. market last year, where its weak network of dealers lost heavily on sales of only 12,000 cars in 1982, down from 59,000 in 1979. The Strada, its leading model, competed in price with U. S. and Japanese economy cars, but because of a weak service system could not overcome a reputation for poor quality. Romit, the chief executive officer now feels that: "Prestige does not come from being in a market. It comes from making a profit."

Fiat failed in the U. S. market and lacks the resources to effectively compete with the Japanese, despite its excellent recent performance at home. Consequently, it is stuck in the slow-growing European and trouble-ridden Latin American markets.

Source: *Business Week,* January 23, 1984, pp. 81–83.

EVALUATION OF A FIRM'S STRENGTHS AND WEAKNESSES

Refer to Figure 2–2 again. Having identified the threats and opportunities that exist in the business and the key success factors, the firm now can proceed in the evaluation of its own strengths and weaknesses. The process involved in the evaluation of a firm's strengths and weaknesses to compete successfully in the marketplace includes the following steps:[18]

1. Identify the small number of key success factors for the business.
2. Develop a profile of the firm's resources and skills.
3. Compare the firm's resources and skills profile to the key success factors of the business.
4. Identify the areas of major strengths on which the firm can build a viable strategy to exploit opportunities in the business and the critical weaknesses it must minimize to prevent failure.
5. Compare the firm's strengths and weaknesses with the strengths and weaknesses of its major rivals in the business.
6. Isolate areas in which the firm's resources and skills are significantly stronger or weaker than those of its major competitors.

The resources and skills capability profile of a firm (step 2) can be organized around a series of penetrating questions. The types of questions that may provide answers leading to the development of such a profile are suggested in Figure 2–4.

FIGURE 2-4
Sample Questions for Resources and Skills Capability Profile

Marketing

- What is the firm's current market share in the total market and the major market segments? Is this a strong position? Does the firm enjoy a unique position in the industry?
- Is the market as a whole expanding or contracting? At what rate is the size of the total market changing? How is the firm's market share changing?
- Where in the product life-cycle are the firm's major products? What is the position of prices and margins of the major products? How strong and complete is the product line?
- How good is the reputation of the products among present and potential customers? What are the strengths and weaknesses of the products in terms of prices, patents, quality, design, customer loyalty, etc.?
- How effective and efficient are the channels of distribution?
- Is the market research system capable of providing valid and reliable information to keep the firm's R & D programs tailored to current and potential customer's needs?
- How effective and efficient is the sales force? Does it have good rapport and ties with key customers?
- How effective is the firm's advertising program? Has it helped the firm establish a strong product-brand position against competing brands, a strong market niche, customer loyalty, etc.?
- How effective and efficient is the service after sales program?
- Does the organization have an appropriate mix of products?
- Does the organization properly appraise and identify the potential for present and prospective production?

Research and Development

- How many commercially successful products has R & D created in the past five years? What return have R & D expenditures produced?
- Is the R & D effort guided by needs uncovered by the marketing department? Is it customer oriented?

(Continued)

FIGURE 2-4 (Continued)

- What are the strengths and weaknesses of the total R & D efforts in terms of people involved, facilities, and equipment?

Finance

- How good is the financial health of the firm based on various financial ratios in four major categories: leverage ratios, liquidity ratios, activity ratios, and profitability ratios?
- Based on expense ratios (cost-percentage analysis), how efficient are operations over time?
- Does the firm have adequate financial resources to enable it to maintain its present position or obtain needed resources and skills in the future?
- Can the firm raise capital through the sale of securities, equity financing, or debt financing?
- Does the firm have sufficient working capital?
- Are the financial controls sound and effective?
- How good is the quality of financial management in the company? Does the firm have short and long-term financial plans that are well integrated with the overall company-wide plans of the same duration?
- Are there effective and efficient accounting systems for cost, budget, and profit-planning procedures?

Production

- How efficient are the production facilities and manufacturing processes compared to those used by the major competitors? Are they suitable to meet future product-volume requirements?
- Is the manufacturing plant technologically advanced or obsolete?
- How do the operating costs compare with those of the major competitors?
- Are the facilities fully or partially utilized given the current demand?

Management

- What image does the management have in the business community? Is it considered dynamic or stodgy?
- How successful has management been in the past in meeting its stated objectives for the company? How does this record compare with that of the company? How does this record compare with that of the major competitors?
- What is the age distribution of the key executives? Are there a sufficient number of dynamic executives who can take charge if and when turnover of key executives does occur because of retirement or executive mobility?
- Is the top management of the firm capable of coping with the challenges of the future?
- Does top management understand the relevant forces in the external environment?
- Does top management engage in effective, long-range planning?

Corporate Structure

- Can the organization structure effectively coordinate the firm's product and geographic diversity?
- Does the organization structure expedite making and executing of corporate decisions?
- Is the organization structure appropriate in light of the nature of the technology and people in the firm and its environment?

Human Resources

- Does the organization have the appropriate mechanisms to obtain, retain, and improve human resources?

FIGURE 2-5
Matching Key Success Factors and Company Resources and Skills Relative to Major Competitors

	Key Success Factors				
Resources and Skills	1	2	3	4	5
Strengths	XXX[a]		XX		X
Weaknesses		XXX		X	

[a] XXX = high. XX = medium. X = low.

The importance of objectivity in the entire process should not be overlooked. Without it, the process will be nothing but an exercise in futility.

A matrix similar to that presented in Figure 2–5 may be used to pinpoint the areas in which the company is especially stronger or weaker than major competitors. Note that the company is stronger than its major competitors in key success factors 1, 3, and 5, but weaker in key success factors 2 and 4.

It should be noted that a company's strength or weakness is relative to the particular opportunity or threat that exists at the time, the key success factors that are derived from the business opportunity under consideration, and the competition. What may be a strength in one set of circumstances could be a limitation in another. There are many examples of great armies being defeated by much smaller, poorly armed bands of rebels. For example, the United States had superior arms and air power in Vietnam, but was ineffective because success required the ability to first recognize the enemy, win the loyalty and friendship of the populace, and counter the enemy's overwhelming strength in guerilla warfare. Practical Insights 5 presents a self-assessment of the strengths and weaknesses of a firm in the personal-computer industry.

PRACTICAL INSIGHTS 5

Strengths and Weaknesses of a Personal-Computer Manufacturer

Close information of the Computer Systems Division Resource and Skills Capability Profile in relation to the key industry success factors has led us to the following compilation of our business strengths and weaknesses.

Strengths

1. Our division has developed an extensive marketing and distribution network in the European Common Market, thus assuring our continued dominance in overseas target markets. Having entered the European market early, we have established dominant market share by cultivating an extensive dealer network, particularly in Great Britain and Germany. Additionally, early entry permitted our division to select and lock in the best Europen dealers on our products. We have subsequently main-

tained an excellent working relationship with European dealers, who are characteristically more loyal than their American counterparts, thus further securing our position in the channels and serving to inhibit our competitors.

2. We offer microcomputer systems at very competitive prices. Price is a major consideration in the selection of a brand and we are among the leaders in this category. Our position as a price leader is attributed to the structure of our manufacturing operations. Because our company is vertically integrated backwards, the Computer Systems Division is assured a supply of semiconductors and most major components at much lower costs than our competitors.

Another advantage of our vertically integrated structure is that we can design systems and chips simultaneously, which means we can bring new microcomputers to the market in half the time, since our competitors must wait until the chip is designed before designing their system. We gain both speed and continuity of design at the same time as our cost advantage is maintained.

Furthermore, with manufacturing plants in Canada, Germany, and Hong Kong, we gain additional cost advantages through minimization of duties and tariffs. Moreover, we benefit from comparative tax and labor advantages by partial manufacturing in Hong Kong, thus further reducing costs. Last, our registration as a Bahamian company permits us additional tax savings that may be passed on to the consumer in the form of lower prices.

3. Successful product development and efficient utilization of our marketing, production, and distribution skills has enabled our division to establish and maintain a strong niche in the home market. Offering two full-feature systems at prices unmatched by competitors, our division has 26 percent of the market for systems under $1,000. We are the industry leader in this price segment.

Weaknesses

1. A weakness of our division has been our inability to duplicate our European success in the home market. We have not established a strong dealer network for our entire product line. Our primary dealers are the mass-merchandise department stores that are reluctant to carry the higher-priced systems targeted for the small-business, personal, and education markets. Secondary distributors such as the Computerland franchises cater to better-known competitors. Many of these stores dropped our machines when the competition offered a more advanced system.

2. The sales of our products are inhibited by our company's poor brand recognition and image in the United States. A recent survey of 35,000 households concerning personal computer attitudes and buying plans, confirms our weakness. Apple had the highest recognition, while our company finished sixth. Further compounding our predicament is our brand image, which is perceived as synonymous with merely acceptable quality.

3. We have not generated a sufficient variety of user-friendly software for our systems. In addition to our marginal capacity to produce software internally, the majority of independent software firms are more inclined to write for our competition.

4. Our existing machines priced in the $1,000–$3,000 category have not been upgraded sufficiently to maintain technological equivalence. Competitors' machines have the edge in many areas, including memory capability, ease of operation, and graphics.

5. We have not developed a strong service and support network for our products. Technical support for our products compared to the industry leaders is weak.

Once a firm has evaluated its SWOTs, it can proceed to the next stage in the strategic management process, which theoretically is the formulation of organizational mission (Figure 2–1). However, the company's SWOTs in reality impact on the entire strategic management process, as shown in Figure 2–1.

SUMMARY

We have examined a method of evaluating the strengths, weaknesses, opportunities, and threats (SWOTs) of a company. SWOT analysis is conceptually the first stage in the strategic management process and, therefore, the most important. Failure to objectively evaluate SWOTs could lead to disastrous results for a company, because it would cause managers to make strategic decisions inconsistent with the facts confronting the company.

The conceptual framework for SWOT analysis suggests that changes in the external environment bring about changes in the industry characteristics, which in turn generate new opportunities and threats for firms and a new set of key success factors. These factors are the areas in which one company must excel in order to take advantage of the opportunities and combat the threats in the business. Matching the key success factors against the resources and skills of the company provides managers with a picture of their company's strengths and weaknesses.

Identification of the threats and opportunities requires analysis of the external environment. Making external environmental analysis manageable requires monitoring the so-called critical environmental factors, that is, those trends and events that might have a significant favorable or unfavorable impact on the business.

An approach to determining the key success factors involves an analysis of the characteristics of the industry along five dimensions: nature and degree of competition, the competitive power of substitutes, the barriers to entry into the industry, the power of buyers, and the power of suppliers. Analysis of the industry along these five dimensions gives managers an idea of what it will take to succeed in the business, that is, what constitute the key success factors.

Comparing the key success factors to the firm's resources and skills identifies the major strengths and weaknesses of the company. However, before managers can develop a viable strategic company plan, they must first compare the company's strengths and weaknesses to those of its major competitors. Such a comparison will help isolate areas in which the firm's resources and skills may be significantly stronger or weaker than those of its major competitors.

References

1. Michael E. Porter, "How Competitive Forces Shape Strategy," *Harvard Business Review*, vol. 57, no. 2 (March–April 1979), p. 142; Charles W. Hofer and Dan Schendel, *Strategy Formulation: Analytical Concepts* (St. Paul: West Publishing Company, 1978), p. 126.
2. Hofer and Schendel, *Strategy Formulation*, p. 126.
3. Michael E. Porter, *Competitive Strategy: Techniques for Analyzing Industries and Competitors* (New York: The Free Press, 1980), p. 18; Hofer and Schendel, *Strategy Formulation*, p. 126.

4. Porter, *Competitive Strategy*, p. 18.
5. Porter, *Competitive Strategy*, pp. 18–19.
6. Porter, *Competitive Strategy*, p. 19.
7. Porter, *Competitive Strategy*, p. 19.
8. Porter, *Competitive Strategy*, pp. 19–20.
9. Porter, *Competitive Strategy*, p. 20.
10. Porter, *Competitive Strategy*, p. 20.
11. Porter, *Competitive Strategy*, p. 7.
12. Porter, "How Competitive Forces Shape Strategy," *Harvard Business Review*, pp. 138–40.
13. Derek F. Abell and John S. Hammond, *Strategic Market Planning* (Englewood Cliffs, N. J.: Prentice-Hall, Inc., 1979), pp. 103–33.
14. Porter, "How Competitive Forces Shape Strategy," p. 142.
15. Porter, "How Competitive Forces Shape Strategy," pp. 140–41.
16. Porter, *Competitive Strategy*, pp. 24–26.
17. Porter, *Competitive Strategy*, pp. 27–28.
18. Hofer and Schendel, *Strategy Formulation*, p. 145.

CHAPTER 3
FORMULATING A DIRECTION FOR THE COMPANY

Organizational Mission

Organization Philosophy

Organization Policies

Strategic Objectives

    Factors Impacting on Strategic Objective Formulation
    Characteristics of Effective Objectives

Generic Corporate Strategy Alternatives

    Stability
    Growth
    Retrenchment
    Combination
    Summary of Alternative Strategies

Summary

References

PERFORMANCE OBJECTIVES

When you have finished reading this chapter, you should be able to

1. Understand the concept of organization mission.
2. Distinguish between the purpose and the mission of an organization.
3. Explain an effective way of defining organization mission.
4. Explain the role of organization philosophy and policies in strategic decision making.
5. Identify and explain the factors that must be considered when strategic objectives are formulated.
6. Identify and explain the four major generic corporate strategies.

Strategic management is the process of determining the future direction of an organization and implementing decisions aimed at achieving the organization's long and short-term objectives. In Chapter 1 we described the major interrelated subprocesses of the strategic management process: (1) assessment of an organization's strengths, weaknesses, opportunities, and threats; (2) formulation of the organization mission; (3) formulation of the organization philosophy and policies; (4) determination of the strategic objectives; (5) determination of organization strategy; (6) implementation of organization strategy; (7) control of organization strategy. The conceptual process of strategic management is presented again in Figure 3–1.

In the last chapter we discussed one approach for assessing a company's strengths, weaknesses, opportunities, and threats. In this chapter we will focus on steps 2–4 and some aspects of step 5 (shaded areas in Figure 3–1).

We will begin with a discussion of the organization mission and the issues that should be effectively addressed in the mission formulation process. Next we will consider the concept of organization philosophy, which will be followed by the

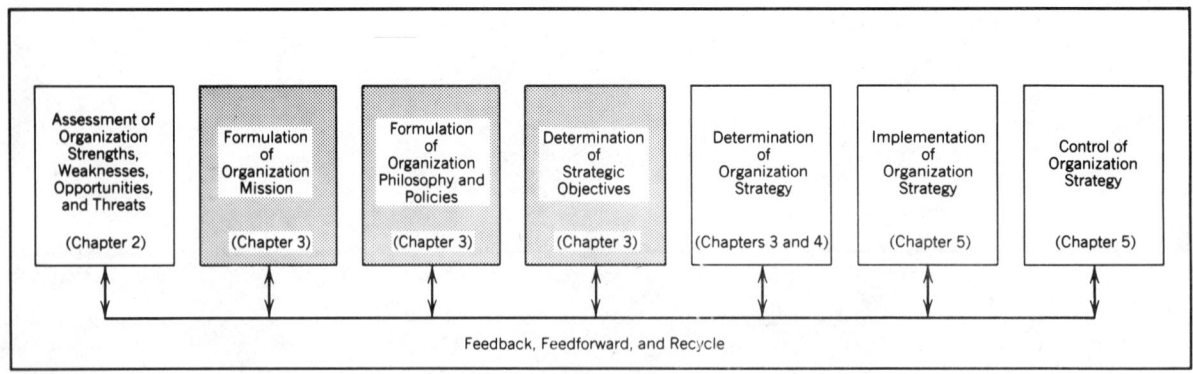

FIGURE 3-1
A Model of the Strategic Management Process

concept of organization policies and the nature of strategic objectives. This chapter will conclude with a presentation of generic corporate strategy alternatives from which corporate strategists can formulate the organization's strategy. As was discussed in Chapter 1, there are four levels of organization strategy: societal, corporate, business, and functional. The next chapter will address the details of the various corporate strategy formulation models and business strategy approaches.

ORGANIZATION MISSION

We will begin our examination of the concept of mission by making a distinction between the terms *mission* and *purpose*, which are often used interchangeably. The *purpose* of an organization is the dominant role that society expects it to play. This role is what is expected of *all* similar organizations in society. The basic purpose of any organization is to use society's resources to produce needed goods and services as efficiently and responsibly as possible. In a capitalist society, the purpose of a business is to offer products and services within the legal, ethical, and moral constraints put upon it by the society and to produce a surplus or profit for itself in the process. The purpose of a hospital is to provide health care. The purpose of a university is to search for new knowledge through research and make it available to students through formal teaching in the classroom and the laboratory. The purpose of a country club is to provide social and recreational opportunities for its members. The purpose of a state highway department is to design, construct, and operate a network of roads and freeways in the state. The purpose of the courts is to interpret and apply laws. In short, the purpose of an organization is the basic function or task assigned to it by its society.

The *mission* of an organization flows from its overall purpose. Purpose defines the broad role the organization plays in meeting society's needs; its mission defines more specifically and precisely the scope of this societal purpose. Mission defines the business of an organization.

For example, a company could state its purpose as follows: "To be continually responsive to the needs of customers and the public, and to design, produce, and market safe and reliable products." On a higher level, the purpose of any enterprise is to strive for those objectives assigned to it by society. At a lower level, the purpose of an enterprise is whatever the manager says it is, for example: "To recognize and appropriately discharge our responsibilities for the welfare of our employees, the community, and society." The mission of an organization, on the other hand, is written in narrower terms. An organization strives to achieve its purpose through its mission and to commit its resources toward its achievement.

An organization can define its mission in terms of its *products* or *services*. Thus, a railroad could say that it is in the transportation business, a pharmaceutical company in the pharmaceuticals business, and a tire company in the tire business. Firms also can define their mission in terms of the *markets* or *customers served*. For instance, a firm could see itself in the business of supplying fertilizer to farmers, while a health clinic could view its mission as providing outpatient care to residents within a 25-mile radius.

A far more effective way of defining an enterprise's mission is in terms of a *product* or *service* aimed at a specific *market segment*, consisting of homogeneous subsets of buyers having some common characteristics, such as age, income, class, geographic location, or religion. For example, the mission statement may read "providing patient care to individuals in the 45–60 age group who earn over $40,000 a year and live in west Los Angeles." The mission statement indicates both the service provided and the market segment. An enterprise must decide which market segment it wishes to serve. A product that is tailored to serve the needs of one market segment may not be appropriate for the needs of another. For example, furniture sold to offices and factories is quite different from that sold to families. Similarly, security safes sold to businesses and banks are different from those sold for private use. The clientele of a neighborhood community college is not quite the same as that of a major urban university.

A firm may define either broadly or narrowly the market segment served. The choice of the breadth of the market segment should be made only after carefully evaluating the alternative market segments. Defining a company mission too broadly may be just as bad for a company's future as defining it too narrowly. For instance, a company's mission statement that "we are in the business of communication" does preclude allocation of resources to the development, production, and marketing of products outside the communications field. However, such a broad definition of its mission may not be operationally useful for the firm because it does not specify whether it is in the business of marketing data-processing equipment, telephones, movie cameras, or television sets, all of which are products used for communication.

Thus, a mission statement that is too broad does not provide managers with guidelines or constraints to help them focus their activities. But a company mission that is too narrow may be too limiting and eventually prevent the company from applying its resources and capabilities to various market opportunities, as happened in the case of the Baldwin Locomotive Works. "Making steam locomotives" was its mission, which prevented the company from exploring other technologies for locomotives. If the company had stated that it was in the business of making locomotives for railroads, it probably still would be in business. The broader mission would have permitted it to develop diesel and electric locomotives, which were ultimately produced by competitors.

The nature of a company's mission determines the opportunities it pursues, its competitors, and ultimately its chances of succeeding in the business given its strengths and weaknesses as opposed to the strengths and weaknesses of its competitors. For example, a company in the "copier and duplicating business," such as Savin Corporation, would face a totally different set of opportunities and key success factors if it broadened its mission to become a "supplier of automated office systems." It is therefore important for management to judge its chances of success in the business on the basis of the definition of the company mission. Although too narrow a mission might prevent a firm from taking advantage of opportunities that a broader mission could offer, it is still crucial before redefining the mission to determine whether the company has the competitive strength to fight the new group of competitors associated with the broader mission.

An example of redefinition of a company mission is that of the Compugraphic

Corporation. The company's original mission could be defined as "marketing photocomposition equipment to newspapers, commercial printers, and corporate print shops." Now it has broadened the scope of its mission to include the technical-publishing market segment. Practical Insights 1 describes the expanded scope of Compugraphic's activities as a result of its broadened mission and its new competitive arena. By entering the newer technical-publishing market, Compugraphic is in a new business segment and therefore will confront a new set of key success factors. Only time will tell whether the company has the necessary skills and resources to succeed!

PRACTICAL INSIGHTS 1

Compugraphic: Trying to Move Typesetting from the Shop to the Office

Compugraphic Corp., the company that makes photocomposition equipment, is embarking on a mission that will move typeset copy from the back shop to the front office, replacing the office typewriter. "It's the idea of using typesetting to replace regular typewriters, as Xerox has replaced carbon paper," explains Susan L. McGarry, senior analyst with the Yankee Group. Compugraphic, which has sold phototypesetters to newspapers, commercial printers, and print shops for years, will find itself in a new market if its strategy works.

This new extension of its product line seems logical for Compugraphic, which already dominates the $1.3 billion world-wide phototypesetting market with a 25 percent market share. Although the firm's 1983 profits soared 79 percent to $13 million and sales rose 11 percent to $306.3 million, Compugraphic's new product will push it into the far more competitive environment of the office-automation market.

Compugraphic hopes to ease into this market by carving out a niche in technical publishing. By 1986, it plans to introduce a system that will include computer work stations, software, typesetters, and scanners to merge text and graphics which would enable a firm to produce the service manuals, product instructions, and training booklets that they now have printed commercially. The system will be targeted at the nation's top 1,000 corporations. Compugraphic's president and chief executive, Carl E. Dantas, says that customers will be able to write, design, and typeset documents themselves at costs ranging from about $50,000 to $200,000. Getting into the technical-publications market could lead to heady growth for Compugraphic in the future, hopefully tieing or beating the market's current 18–20 percent growth rate.

Last October, Compugraphic introduced the Personal Composition System (PCS), a typesetter for photographic paper driven by Apple Computer Inc.'s Lisa computer and Compugraphic software. PCS sales have been encouragingly brisk. By July Compugraphic will begin combining its software with Lisa and a Canon Inc. electronic laser printer—putting Compugraphic typefaces on plain paper and thus taking a firm step into the office.

Since 1981 Compugraphic has concentrated on developing software to bypass much of the complex computer coding that has made many printing jobs a task for professional printers. The company is now allocating 7 percent of sales into research and development—twice its 1982 R & D budget. It is ahead of its main competitors, AM International Inc.'s Varityper Div. and Mergenthaler Linotype Co., in developing and packaging new gear.

Other established firms producing office-automation products, such as Data General Corp. and Wang Laboratories, will be offering strong competition.

One difficulty Compugraphic will face is how to sell to a wider market without competing head-on with these powerhouses. In addition, many companies may decide that they can meet their document reproduction needs less expensively with typewriters and high-quality copiers. The company's current lines for the in-house market run the risk of being cannibalized by its new office products.

Chief executive Carl Dantas insists that developing software to connect Compugraphic's type and typesetters to computers and printers produced by others will enable the company to avoid direct competition with Wang and Data General. Compugraphic's systems should be cost-efficient since they are targeted for the office market, where a company can spread the cost of a single machine over several departments.

Compugraphic hopes that it has turned a corner toward profitability after losing $6.7 million in 1981. Its' software-based Modular Composition System, a group of typesetting machines, now accounts for 75 percent of sales.

When, in February 1982, a Belgian photo products company called Agfa–Gevaert bought 69 percent of Compugraphic's stock, Compugraphic was able to reduce its debt and increase R & D spending. Agfa–Gevaert, which holds nearly 80 percent of the company's stock and will probably acquire the rest eventually, has been able to help to increase sales in Europe. Compugraphic stock has climbed from a low of 14 in 1983 to a present price of 33.

A study by Boston University concluded that typeset business documents can be read 27 percent faster that those typewritten or reproduced on a dot-matrix printer, and that they are more credible. Compugraphic is hoping that this opinion will be adopted by offices around the world.

Source: Business Week, July 2, 1984, p. 89.

To sum up, the mission statement of a firm should not be either too broad and ambiguous, or too narrow and confining for the effective allocation and utilization of its resources and skills. In defining its mission, a company should realize that the more it engages in unfamiliar activities as it broadens its mission, the greater the danger that it will fail. That is, there should be a common thread or synergy in the firm's activities. A firm can obtain synergistic benefits if it adds a product to its existing product line that uses one or more of the items already being used, such as plant and equipment, channels of distribution, technology, customers, or source of raw materials. For example, a firm that makes toothpaste may benefit from the synergistic effect of adding a mouthwash to its product line because it would be using the same channels of distribution and probably the same customers.

Those who support the common-thread concept offer the bad experiences of Litton and Singer to prove that far-flung diversification into unrelated activities can be disastrous—Litton with typewriters and shipbuilding, and Singer with aerospace operations, housing, and business machines. But the jury is still out on this issue, as companies such as ITT, Textron, and Gulf and Western are quite successful in spite of the absence of a common thread in their numerous activities; Textron is into helicopters, snowmobiles, watchbands, iron castings, and insurance; ITT's enterprises include telephone equipment, hotels, lawn-care products, car rental, and other services and products. The truth is that conglomerates such as ITT, Textron, Gulf and Western, and Litton have multiple missions, each corresponding to the product/market segment served by each of their unrelated businesses.

Of course, the mission of a firm is not etched in stone. On the contrary, a firm's mission should be in step with both the external environment and the firm's internal capabilities. As the external environment changes, so should the mission of the firm. The needs of new consumers may make old needs obsolete, new technologies may make old products obsolete, and new markets may emerge where none previously existed. Such environmental changes may necessitate changing a firm's mission. However, in redefining its mission, a firm must take into account the internal resources—financial, physical, and human—which set the limits on what it can accomplish.

ORGANIZATION PHILOSOPHY

An organization philosophy represents the values, beliefs, commitments, and aspirations of the company. The philosophy serves as a guide for the behavior of its employees as well as how the organization conducts its business. It reflects the "culture" of the enterprise. Many companies have publicized statements, which critics call public relations gimmicks, that convey their philosophies to the public. Although it is true that many written philosophies are designed to improve the public image of a company, they can be and often are the cornerstone of a company's direction and method of operation.[1] Jerry McAfee, the former chairman and chief executive officer of Gulf Oil Corporation, has credited the company's philosophy of international corporate citizenship for its business success globally (see Practical Insights 2). The philosophy of the IBM Corporation regarding its corporate responsibility is embodied in its corporate principles, presented in Practical Insights 3. Mitchell D. Kapor is the president and founder of Lotus Development Corporation. His beliefs, shaped in the era of the 1960s, are reflected in Lotus's company philosophy (see Practical Insights 4), which encourages an equitable work environment, teamwork, dignity of the individual, and ethical behavior.

PRACTICAL INSIGHTS 2

Gulf Oil Corporation—Philosophy of International Corporate Citizenship

Gulf's international involvement began in 1912, and today we are represented in 88 countries. Thus, we have had the opportunity to adapt and adjust to the changing needs, expectations, aspirations, and sensitivities of many host countries throughout the globe.

One of the reasons that we have been able to survive—and prosper—in this changing environment is that we base our involvement in each of these foreign countries on a simple, but effective philosophy of international corporate citizenship.

Three Responsibilities of MNCs

We have three important responsibilities in each host country: to do the job, to do it at a profit, and to do it in accordance with the limits established by the host country. Our primary responsibility—in fact, the very reason host countries invite us to participate in their economies—is to do the job and do it well. By effectively fulfilling this basic economic function, the multinational corporation performs its most important role in the host country because of the many beneficial multiplier effects it can have.

In producing its goods or performing its services, the multinational corporation creates jobs, develops human skills, develops and transfers technology, and thereby shares the tools and techniques of societal uplift with the people of the host nation. In short, the multinational creates wealth where it did not exist—and by wealth, I mean not just monetary wealth, but cultural wealth as well.

Our second responsibility is to do the job at a profit. Let there be no misunderstanding about this point. Our very existence depends on our ability to earn a return on our shareholders' investment that is more attractive than competing forms of investment. Indeed, over a period of time, profit determines whether or not a given company has the right, to say nothing of the ability, to survive. If we can't survive, we can't make any contributions to the host country—economic, social, or otherwise.

Our third responsibility is to do the job within the limits established by the host country—the ethical limits, environmental limits, and social limits. Gulf's Code of Business Principles requires that we conduct our activities in accordance with both the letter and the spirit of the laws of the governing country. Where there is no law or where it is vague, the Code requires us to conduct our business in such a manner that we would be proud to have the full facts disclosed. Similarly, in the environmental area, the Code states that "Gulf assigns a high priority to its obligations to assure a clean, safe environment in every locale in which it has operations and to comply with applicable environmental laws and regulations."

In the social area, Gulf does not view its investment in any country solely in terms of sales, profits, and dividends. As a profit-making corporation, Gulf wants to be part of the economic expansion throughout the world. But Gulf does not participate in the economic development of any country purely and simply in the interests of our company's bottom line. As a responsible member of the international corporate community, Gulf firmly believes that it has performed its job well only when its activities both assist in the economic development of the host nation and widen the educational and occupational horizons of Gulf employees from that host country.

Source: Jerry McAfee, "Three Responsibilities for Multinational Corporations," *Corporate Citizenship: Outstanding Examples Worldwide* (Washington, D. C.: International Management and Development Institute, 1979), pp. 20–21.

PRACTICAL INSIGHTS 3

IBM's Philosophy of Corporate Responsibility

The philosophy [of corporate responsibility] is embodied in the corporate principles of IBM. They are central to IBM policies and a yardstick against which company decisons are made. They imply much more than simply making contributions to charities, education, and the arts. Rather, they mean the application of basic philosophy to the day-to-day operation of the business.

The basic beliefs of IBM, as first articulated by Thomas J. Watson, Sr., are:

- Respect for the individual.
- Service to the customer.
- Pursuit of excellence.

In addition to these beliefs, IBM has certain fundamental principles, among which are effective leadership by managers, fulfillment of obligations to the stockholders, fairness with suppliers, and good corporate citizenship.

In concrete terms, these principles are applied by discharging our responsibilities in four ways:

1. Assuring the employment and satisfaction of employees and suppliers.
2. Giving stockholders a reasonable return on their investment.
3. Offering customers good products and services at competitive prices.
4. Understanding the impact that the enterprise may have on society, in order to avoid any negative effects and to enhance the positive ones. In other words, business should have a social conscience.

Source: Jacques G. Maisonrouge, "Safeguarding the Future," *Corporate Citizenship: Outstanding Examples Worldwide* (Washington, D. C.: International Management and Development Institute, 1979), p. 23.

PRACTICAL INSIGHTS 4

A Bit of the 1960s Lives on at Lotus

During the 1960s, Mitchell Kapor revered the Beatles, sported long hair, and protested against the Vietnam War. In the 1970s, he worked as a disc jockey for a rock station, taught transcendental meditation, and earned a master's degree in psychology. In the 1980s, Kapor became a millionaire.

Mitchell Kapor is a rather extreme example of a baby boomer who turned from protests to profits. Kapor is president and founder of the two-year-old Lotus Development Corp., which earned $14.3 million on sales of $53 million in 1983. Lotus's first product was a software package named 1–2–3 that integrates computer graphics, information management, and spreadsheet analysis. It has been on top of the software best-seller list for more than a year. Symphony is the latest addition, which adds word processing and communications.

Kapor still clings to the ideals of the 1960s. Although he describes much of the turmoil of the 1960s as "no more than standard, adolescent growth pains," it left him with a sense of social obligation that he has brought with him into corporate life. Kapor explains the philosophy in the following terms: "It's possible to make money and at the same time to have a company where people are proud to work and can be happy."

Kapor has attempted to create an equitable work environment. Two of the six line vice-presidents are women. Kapor also explains company developments, introduces new workers, and answers questions at weekly meetings that are open to all 520 employees.

Kapor also has worked hard to encourage teamwork. He avoids the prima donna mentality because it demoralizes the workforce, and he likes to give as much control as possible to his management team.

Kapor does believe that there is some need for bureaucracy and hierarchy. He says, "If you've got someone making $22,000 a year, you don't want them responsible for a $3 million decision."

However, Kapor concedes that if Lotus continues to grow at its current rapid rate, the company's carefree management approach will have to change. The weekly employee meetings are already becoming unmanageable, and procedures are being developed to govern everything from hiring practices to planning sessions.

So that management could preserve Lotus's distinctive character, a statement of company philosophy has been drafted. The key features include the dignity of the individual, ethical behavior, and a sense of humor. Kapor is attempting to keep his corporate culture as healthy as its financial performance. Says he: "It's a balancing act between people and profits."

Source: Business Week, July 2, 1984, p. 59.

ORGANIZATION POLICIES

Policies were defined in Chapter 1 as guides to action that define the "ball park" within which objectives are established and strategies are determined, implemented, and controlled. Policies should be consistent with and flow logically from the organization philosophy. Generally policies tend to limit the scope of alternatives that must be considered in implementing of organization strategy. For instance, a company's strategy may call for the dropping of a business or product lines, whereas an implementing policy might spell out the criteria that must be satisfied before a business or product line can be considered a candidate for liquidation or divestiture. Policies provide executives with a framework for decision making; they do not remove managerial discretion in decision making. Consider a policy that states that "in politically stable countries our businesses should provide a minimum of 15 percent return on investment, but in politically unstable countries we expect a minimum of 25 percent return on our investments." Note that the policy statement does not decide which countries are stable or unstable, nor does it indicate in which specific countries the corporate resources should be invested. Such decisions are left to the discretion of the appropriate managers. The policy merely states that investments in politically stable and unstable countries should yield a minimum return of 15 percent and 25 percent, respectively.

In Chapter 1 we referred to the two major parts of the strategic management process, namely, strategic planning and strategy implementation. Organization policies can be segmented into two categories—strategic policies and implementation policies—to correspond with strategic planning and strategy implementation, the two major aspects of strategic management. Strategic policies are designed to guide the strategic planning process in an organization; implementation policies are designed to do the same for the strategy implementation process. Thus, the overall purpose of organization policies is to guide the thinking, decision making, and actions of managers in the strategic management of an enterprise. Organization policies guide the organization's strategists as they determine and implement the strategic objectives and organization strategy of the firm. Figures 3–2 and 3–3

FIGURE 3-2
Issues Involved in Formulating Strategic Policies

Scope of the corporation's business—defining the product(s) of the corporation and the market segment(s) served.

Criteria for entering or existing in a business or industry.

Geographical scope of company activities.

Nature of technology utilized in production process.

Channels of distribution.

Product quality.

Company image.

Fundamental organizational objectives—growth, stability, retrenchment, turnaround, divestment, liquidation.

Dominant method of competition.

Social responsibility of corporation.

Role of corporation in society.

Philosophy regarding management style and organizational climate.

Organization structure.

Corporation orientation—marketing vs. production.

FIGURE 3-3
Issues Involved in Formulating Implementation Policies

Type of organization structure—divisional vs. functional.

Leadership styles—authoritarian, democratic, participative.

Motivation systems—incentive programs, reward system.

Staffing practices—matching executives to job requirements.

Coordination techniques—quality circles, project teams.

Information needs of managers and systems to meet those needs.

Promoting entrepreneurship in managerial behavior.

Employee's career paths and promotion methods.

Performance evaluation systems.

Measures for evaluation of total organization performance.

present the types of issues an organization's strategists have to resolve. These figures in no way represent an exhaustive list; there are many more issues that strategists must deal with in actual practice. Moreover, the organization policies that are the output of the deliberations and discussions of the issues vary from firm to firm.

Organization policies are not etched in concrete. They should be consistent with the environment of the firm, both inside and outside. For example, a strategic policy that requires that "organization growth should come from diversifying into new businesses through internal development rather than the acquisition of already existing firms" may need a revision if the price/earnings ratios of firms in the targeted industries fall significantly because of economic conditions. In such a circumstance it may make economic sense to pursue the acquisition route to diversification instead of the strategy of internal development of new businesses. Similarly, an implementation policy in a paternalistic organization that says "promotion should be based primarily on seniority and secondarily on performance" may have to be changed if a new generation of younger employees rejects the paternalistic attitudes of management and demands upward mobility based on individual performance. Organization policies must remain flexible to serve the best interests of the organization.

STRATEGIC OBJECTIVES

The formulation of a company's mission, philosophy, and policies provides its executives with an important frame of reference and direction for planning. However, the managers must then formulate organization strategies designed to guide their own actions and those of their subordinates toward the fulfillment of certain desired results. The time required to achieve the results may vary from the short range to the long range; that is, some strategies may be implemented and results obtained in a day or a month, while other strategies may take as long as five or more years for their fulfillment. Whatever the time frame of the strategies, all must aim at the fulfillment of well-defined results. Although the mission of a firm defines its business in terms of both its product or service and its market segment, it is not specific enough to facilitate the development of strategies within the firm for which managers need to know what results they are expected to achieve and the time frame within which they must achieve them. Managers need well-defined objectives that specify desired results that can guide the design of strategies for their fulfillment and can serve as standards of performance. Without an objective a manager is like a ship captain whose company may have a well-defined mission to provide a floating resort for the single-set vacationers, but does not let him know where he is supposed to take his ship, how many ports he is supposed to visit, and for what period of time he will be gone.

Strategic objectives are the ends that the total organization hopes to achieve in fulfilling its basic mission. These desired outcomes serve as benchmarks against which an organization can measure its progress as it implements its plans. A strategic objective should be consistent with and derived from the mission, policies, and philosophy of the organization. For instance, the mission of an enterprise may be to "promote hygiene and personal attractiveness through personal-care products for men." The strategic objectives arising from this mission may include sales objectives such as "increasing our total sales by 8 percent a year" or market share objectives like "obtaining at least 25 percent of the market in the next five years."

Objectives are the end points of all functions of management—organizing, leading, staffing, controlling, and planning. An organization has a hierarchy of objectives. Although an enterprise may have strategic objectives for the enterprise as a whole, each division and department within the enterprise also should have its own subobjectives derived from and consistent with the major enterprise objectives. For example, a firm that has as its major strategic objective the attainment of a 25-percent market share in the next five years may have as an objective of its research and development department "the introduction within the next two years of a new product aimed at the middle-class consumer."

One of the major functions of a firm's board of directors is to establish the strategic objectives of the firm. The board of directors relies heavily on the judgment and recommendations of the chief executive officer in setting objectives. However, instead of rubber-stamping the recommended objectives, the board of directors should question and scrutinize the chief executive's recommendations.

Factors Impacting on Strategic Objective Formulation

The chief executive does not set the strategic objectives unilaterally, because there are forces in both the internal and external environments that present threats and opportunities to the firm. The managers of the firm should aspire to exploit oppor-

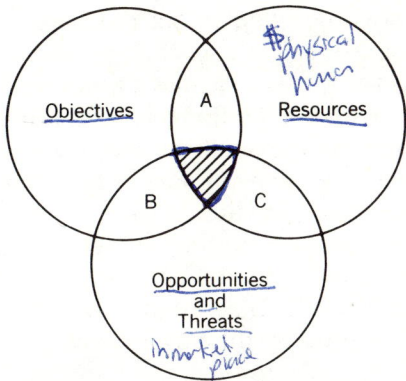

FIGURE 3-4
Formulation of Strategic Objectives

tunities and combat environmental threats. The objectives they set for the firm should reflect these aspirations. When the overall strategic objectives are formulated, the board must examine current objectives, current and obtainable resources, and current and future opportunities and threats in the marketplace. Figure 3-4 depicts how these overall objectives are set. Notice that the only logical area at which to set the objectives is the *intersection* of objectives, resources, and opportunities and threats. To commit resources to objectives that are geared toward opportunities that do not exist in the marketplace will not work (area A). For example, developing and producing a product for a market that refuses to accept the product is unreasonable. To set objectives when there are opportunities but insufficient resources (area B) is not acceptable. An example of such misjudgment is a firm whose objective is a 100 percent increase in sales within the next 12 months, but whose financial resources are insufficient to achieve this objective, even though there is sufficient demand to support the objective. The objectives should fully use the resources of the organization and exploit the opportunities available to it.

Many companies have reformulated their objectives to be consistent with their resources and external environment. For example, large cigarette empires such as R. J. Reynolds and Philip Morris, finding that cigarette sales have reached a plateau because of the controversy over the health hazards of smoking, have diversified into nontobacco businesses. R. J. Reynolds has acquired Sea-Land Service (containerized shipping), Aminol International (oil and gas), and Del Monte (processed food). Philip Morris is not only the second biggest producer of cigarettes behind R. J. Reynolds, but is also the second largest brewer of premium beer. When Philip Morris purchased the Miller Brewing Company, it was the eighth largest brewer in America; Philip Morris has boosted the company to the number-two spot because it had the marketing expertise and financial resources for huge advertising outlays, it introduced new products such as Lite beer, it improved and enlarged its distribution system, and it improved production efficiencies and market segmentation strategies. R. J. Reynolds and Philip Morris saw the threats that the external environment—in the form of the American Cancer Society—posed to the cigarette industry and proceeded to set the objective of establishing beachheads in non-tobacco businesses. They were able to do so mainly because they had the financial and human resources to achieve this objective.

A firm, without the financial and human resources of these companies could not have aspired to diversify the same way as R. J. Reynolds and Philip Morris did. Naturally the objectives of such a firm would be far more modest. For example, firms whose main product markets are leveling off or declining and whose resources cannot withstand the competition from larger and resource-strong firms in the industry often have the objective of merging with another firm. For example, the F & M Schaefer Corporation, which lost $63 million on sales of $173 million in 1978, was acquired by the Stroh Brewery, the eighth largest brewer in the United States.

In setting strategic objectives for the firm, managers must always be aware of political realities. Every organization has individuals, groups, and cliques that are constantly striving to attain their interests. What happens if the interests of two or more individuals or groups are at cross-purposes with each other? In such circumstances, the conflicting objectives of the individuals or groups need to be reconciled through negotiations and bargaining so that the objectives that emerge are acceptable to all parties. For example, if a firm is in financial jeopardy—such as the Chrysler Corporation was in 1979/1980—but the labor union demands higher wages and better fringe benefits and the stockholders want the firm to show higher profits and pay out a higher dividend, the top management of the company will have to negotiate and bargain with the coalitions of interests involved (employees and stockholders) and establish objectives acceptable to both parties.

The personal value systems of managers also have an impact on the choice of strategic objectives. For example, to be the biggest company and the leading innovator company in the industry are objectives that reflect the values held by the chief executive or the top-management of the company. Similarly, objectives in growth, product quality, social responsibility, community relations, and managerial style reflect the values of the managers who participated in their formulation.

The strengths and weaknesses of the firm's internal resources can place constraints on the aspiration levels of the firm's managers and influence what they hope to achieve in terms of the strategic objectives. The objectives should be set at the intersection of the human, financial, and physical resources of the firm as shown in Figure 3–5. Setting objectives at the intersection of human and physical resources (area A) without having the financial resources available is not sound, nor is setting objectives between financial and physical resources (area B) without considering human resources, or setting the objectives between human and financial resources (area C) without regarding the physical. Of course, formulating objectives does not occur in a vacuum; the external environment must be considered.

Characteristics of Effective Objectives

Strategic objectives for the organization as a whole are necessarily broader in context than those for a department, such as the assembly group in the production

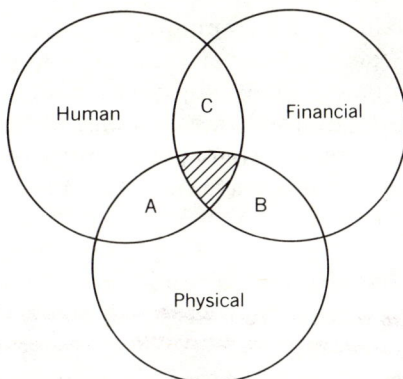

FIGURE 3-5
Internal Resources and Strategic Objective Formulation

department. Regardless of whether we are referring to the overall strategic objectives or the much narrower objectives of the subunits of an organization, all objectives should have certain essential characteristics for them to be effective. Let us review some of these characteristics.

Objectives Must Have Some "Reach" in Them. An objective that is easily attainable is not challenging to the individual and, therefore, not as motivating as one that has some built-in difficulty but is still attainable. An objective should be high enough to make an individual stretch in order to reach it.

Objectives Should Be Attainable. Even though stretch aspects must be built into every objective, an objective that is so far above the reach of an individual does not serve any useful purpose. For example, a person who has been running at an eight-minute-a-mile pace is not about to make any effort to compete in a race in which the best runners run a consistent five-minute-a-mile-pace.

Objectives Should Be Measurable. One of the purposes of having measurable objectives is to use them to determine the degree to which expected results have been attained. As such they can be useful in performance appraisal of the company, department, or individual employee. Objectives can be made measurable by quantifying the attributes sought. For example, an objective that calls for a growth in sales can be quantified by putting a figure on the amount of growth in sales desired, for example, "increase sales by 10 percent every year." Understandably, not all objectives can be easily quantified. However, if an effort is made, surrogate measurable variables can take the place of unquantifiable attributes. For example, if the attribute desired is improved morale, a surrogate variable for measuring morale is the rate of turnover. Another surrogate variable for morale measurement is the rate of absenteeism. Even if the objective reads "We should improve the morale of our clerical personnel," the effectiveness of plans designed to achieve this objective could be evaluated by examining the absenteeism and turnover rates of the clerical employees before and after the plan was put into effect.

Unfortunately many objectives cannot be quantified, nor are there surrogate variables to make them measurable, in which case it is advisable to state them qualitatively. Pushing too far to quantify objectives can backfire if managers, finding that they are unable to quantify certain worthwhile objectives, choose not to state them at all.

Objectives Should Have a Time Frame for Their Fulfillment. Setting a time frame within which the desired results should be achieved allows the budgeting of time and resources required to complete the necessary tasks. Setting a time frame also enables those responsible for the tasks to measure the progress being made toward the achievement of the objective and the likelihood of meeting the established deadlines.

Objectives Should Be Mutually Consistent. If objectives are not consistent with one another, plans to fulfill them will also be inconsistent, which could lead to disastrous results. For example, if the production department has the lowering of per-unit production costs via long production runs and a simplified product line as one of its objectives, this would be inconsistent with the marketing department's objective of increasing the total sales volume by offering a variety of custom-made products to meet the needs of different market segments.

Short-Range Objectives Must Be Derived from and Consistent with Strategic Objectives. Strategic objectives are the desired results in pursuit of the organization mission. Short-range objectives are performance targets, with a time frame of up to one year, that managers shoot for in order to achieve the organization's long-range objectives.

Although objectives vary greatly from one organization to another, Peter Drucker[2] suggests that there are eight areas in which objectives have to be set: market standing, innovation, productivity, physical and financial resources, profitability, manager performance and development, worker performance and attitude, and public responsibility. Figure 3–6 illustrates areas in which most organizations could establish strategic objectives.

GENERIC CORPORATE STRATEGY ALTERNATIVES

After assessing a firm's strengths, weaknesses, opportunities, and threats, and formulating its organization mission, philosophy, policies, and strategic objectives, strategic managers should be in a position to answer the following questions:

1. What business(es) are we in?
2. Are we going to continue functioning in our existing business(es) now and in the future at the same level of effort as in the past (stability)?
3. Are we planning to grow by either adding new businesses to our existing business portfolio or increasing the level of effort in our existing business (growth)?

FIGURE 3-6
Areas for Establishing Strategic Objectives

Profitability	Attain a 20 percent return on investment within the next two years.
	Increase net income by $50 million within the next three years.
Market Standing	Attain a 30 percent share of the market in less than five years from now.
	Increase noncosmetics products sales to 60 percent of total sales.
Research and Development	Develop at least one patented product every year.
	Increase the research and development budget by 5 percent a year for the next five years.
Financial Resources	Decrease long-term debt by $30 million within the next three years.
	Increase working capital to $15 million within the next four years.
Human Resources	In the next four years, put all top-management personnel through an executive development program developed in conjunction with a leading business school in the area.
	Reduce employee turnover by 3 percent within the next three years.
	Reduce absenteeism by 5 percent in the next two years.
Productivity	Produce at the rate of at least 100 units per hour in the next two years.
Physical Resources	Increase production capacity in the mid-Atlantic states by 25 percent within the next five years.
Customer Service	Increase the on-time delivery rate to 95 percent before the end of next year.
	Reduce customer complaints by 30 percent within the next two years.
Social Responsibility	Allocate at least 0.5 percent of earnings before income taxes for philanthropy.
	Donate the time of at least five managers per year for teaching in colleges and universities.

4. Are we now going to reduce the effort or completely get out of our existing business (retrenchment)?
5. Are we planning to implement the above strategies simultaneously or sequentially depending on the business or product concerned (combination)?

The answers to the above questions clarify and define the organization's corporate strategy (discussed in detail in the next chapter). Corporate strategy deals with deciding how much of the company's resources should be invested in the existing business or businesses and the new businesses that the company plans to add to its portfolio. If the answer to question 2 is yes, the company would follow a *stability* strategy, which requires allocation of resources at the same levels as in the past. A yes answer to question 3 would lead to a *growth* strategy for a business that means larger amounts of resources allocated to a business. A *retrenchment* strategy would be indicated if question 4 is answered yes. This means a partial or total cutback in the resources received by a business. An organization that has a portfolio of several products or businesses will have a *combination* strategy when it gives a yes answer to question 5.

Thus, stability, growth, retrenchment, and combination are the four principal generic corporate strategy alternatives that a company could choose for each of its businesses with the ultimate aim of achieving its mission and strategic objectives. The following pages present an explanation of these four generic corporate strategy alternatives.

Stability

The stability strategy suggests that the organization should continue to do what it is currently doing. This strategy assumes that the environment will not change significantly in the near future.

Stability strategy is used frequently. Glueck[3] has suggested that the stability strategy is effective under three conditions: (1) the firm is in a mature industry, (2) the firm is currently successful, and (3) the environment of the firm is changing very slowly.

There are several logical reasons why management may choose a stability strategy. The organization is currently performing at a high level. Although there are a few adjustments that can and should be made in the internal operations, why risk failure by changing strategies when the organization is currently performing at a satisfactory level? Why not learn from the mistakes of other firms before adopting a new strategy? It also may be that the organization has recently undergone major changes and needs time to stabilize and develop a routine.

Although the stability strategy is often used, it also can be very dangerous in the sense that the strategy of continuing the present routine can lull management into complacency. While management is in such a complacent state, the organization's external environment may change without an attendant change in the internal environment. By the time management recognizes the changes, it may be too late for the organization to capitalize on new opportunities. In other cases, the organization may not have recognized threats; by the time it does, a significant share of its market may be lost.

The stability strategy adopts the attitude of "wait and see." This attitude may be an advantage or disadvantage depending on how the organization responds. If the organization possesses an effective system to monitor the changes in the environment, such an attitude may be an advantage. The organization must decide, however, on the most appropriate time to enter the market. If it enters the market too early, it may turn soft; if it enters too late, the opportunity for a decent market share may be lost to other organizations that established early entry. The key to success for the stable strategy, therefore, is a strong system for monitoring the external environment and an experienced management to determine the appropriate time to respond to changes in market conditions.

Growth

During the past three decades, organizations have subscribed to the attitude of "the termination of growth spells the beginning of death" and "bigger is better." With this attitude, growth became the objective of many businesses. Although businesses may have overemphasized the growth objectives, growth is a culturally derived American goal. A public business firm must generate enough growth in real terms to satisfy its owners, the stockholders. The expectations of the owners are derived through culture and current economic conditions.

Growth of a firm most often results from the firm's financial resources, its product or service, its external environmental conditions, and the skills of its management. Management's ability to assess these variables accurately is essential for growth. The organization must be constantly concerned about size. A firm that is too small cannot effectively compete if it lacks productive capacity or market strength; neither can it compete if the firm grows so large that it becomes unmanageable for its current management.

The greatest motivation for growth is the perception of individual managers. Many managers believe that a "growing organization is a healthy organization." As long as the firm is growing, it gives the impression that management is effective. Further, managers want to leave a larger firm than when they arrived—another measure of effective management. The final and perhaps most logical reason for growth is that growth ensures long-term survival. If one product fails, the large company probably will not suffer major losses. For a small firm, product failure may result in financial disaster.

Internal Growth. An organization may grow by internal or external means. One that chooses to grow by internal means continues its current strategy, but increases its efforts to improve those things that the company considers it does best. The company emphasizes its strengths and tries to improve on them by increasing the resources needed for such a task. Bates and Eldridge[4] have suggested that internal growth may occur either by penetration or expansion.

Internal growth by penetration emphasizes growth by increasing market share, sales, or profits with the current product. The advantages of penetration are that management is familiar with the product and the market. The disadvantage is that if the product is in a stable environment and one firm emphasizes penetration, there may be retaliation by a competitor. This strategy, therefore, is most effective for firms with a small market share operating in an expanding market. Penetration may be accomplished by increasing product demand through encouraging new uses of present products for present consumers, attracting new nonuser–consumers, and attracting consumers from competitors.

Internal growth by expansion allows for more variation in the strategy than penetration. Firms can expand by moving into new geographical areas with a currently successful product. The disadvantage of this expansion form is that the firm is moving into a market area in which management may know very little and the firm has no image.

Another form of expansion may occur by modifying the product in some way to provide new product features that may satisfy buyer preferences or offer better customer services. To accomplish this form of expansion, the firm may provide a larger number of models and sizes; make the product lighter, stronger, thinner, restyled, more durable, or introduce or change any other feature the consumer desires; or promote the product differently.

External Growth. An organization that chooses to grow by external means will add functions or operations to the current organization. The firm will expand its operations using one of two different strategies: integration, in which the firm stays essentially with the same products, and diversification, in which the firm moves into products of related or unrelated industries.

Integration. There are basically three substrategies in the integration strategy. The first substrategy is horizontal integration, in which the firm acquires other firms or products that can use existing facilities. Usually the acquired firm is a competitor. The second substrategy is vertical forward integration, in which the firm buys the distributors. Vertical forward integration allows the firm to control the flow of finished goods to consumers and reduces promotion cost by reducing intermediaries. As Bates and Eldridge[5] pointed out, higher profit margins are usually closer to the point of final sale. The acquiring firm therefore increases its profits by reduced promotion costs as well as higher profits at the point of final sale. The third substrategy is vertical backward integration, in which the firm acquires its dominant raw material supplier. Thus, the acquiring firm assures itself of a raw material supply and reduces promotion costs, which is usually passed on to the consumer. Based on the reduced costs of raw materials, the acquiring firm may be in a position to offer the product to the final consumer at a cheaper price that increases demand, or the firm is able to maintain the current price with higher profit margins. From a negative standpoint, it should be recognized that vertical integration often increases the organization's dependency on demand for the final product, therefore rendering the organization more vulnerable to decreases in demand for the final product. The major problem with all forms of integration is the cost of the capital required to acquire other firms.

Diversification. Uyterhoeven[6] has defined diversification as an alternative way of committing one's resources. The organization may envision a decreased demand for the current product or service. Diversification requires the organization to move into similar or new products or services, while at the same time exploiting existing products or services. If the current market is decreasing very rapidly, the organization may choose to completely phase out its current product and phase in the new. There are other reasons why a firm may diversify, such as (1) competitive pressure, product obsolescence, or antitrust and tax legislation; (2) excess cash flow; (3) spreading the risks among more products; (4) new challenges for management.

There are two ways a firm may diversify. It may use *concentric diversification*, where the firm buys a business whose product, service, or technology is similar to or related to the product, service, or technology of the current organization. This form of diversification is attractive because the firm's management already has experience with similar products; it could probably use the same salespersons and distribution channels; it may use similar production processes or already existing plant capacity that is not currently being used; it would probably use the same raw material suppliers. A company that has adopted this route to diversification through acquisitions is Dean Foods. Practical Insights 5 shows how the executives of Dean Foods Company select and acquire companies in the dairy and specialty foods segment of the food industry.

The second form of diversification is the *conglomerate*. The acquiring firm purchases a business whose product, service, or technology is unrelated to its present products, services, or technology. The conglomerate may serve as a useful vehicle by which a firm can get out of a declining industry or reduce its risk by moving into more than a one-product market. To be successful, a conglomerate will usually do

PRACTICAL INSIGHTS 5

Concentric Diversification at Dean Foods Company

Dean Foods Co. isn't likely to bowl anyone over with flashy acquisitions.

Its latest purchase, little Bluhill American Pickle Co., has annual sales of $8 million. Bluhill's only plant squats on a gravel parking lot in a cloud of pickle brine vapor, churning out five-gallon jugs of hamburger dills.

Compared with many other takeover bids these days, Dean's acquisition forays are dull. In its slow-growth, food-industry segment—dairy and specialty foods—Dean must buy other companies to grow rapidly, but its purchases are usually small and mundane.

Nevertheless, Dean's growth record is remarkable, competitors and analysts say. Profit has grown ninefold in 10 years, to $18.4 million in 1982 on sales of $747.2 million. Return on total invested capital has been 25 to 30 percent since 1977, a high rate for the food industry, Standard and Poor's Corp. says. Dean's stock price and dividends have risen steadily; its total return to shareholders during the last decade was about 30 percent, according to a recent Standard and Poor's survey.

Expert at Acquisitions

A top executive at a major Dean competitor says: "They're one of the best-managed companies in the business, and they get among the best returns on investment of any company." That record is largely because of Dean's acquisition strategy. In more than a decade of steady purchases, Dean has become expert at picking candidates, and its discipline has paid off financially. Usually, Dean follows a few simple rules: It sticks to the stodgy businesses it knows best. It pays cash, avoiding dilution of future earnings. It works hard at finding and evaluating candidates, lavishing the time of top management on maintaining industry contacts and examining candidates' facilities and financial data. It shuns bidding wars, which helps it hold down the prices it pays for acquisitions.

Dean, which is based in Franklin Park, Ill., also uses operational yardsticks, as well as financial criteria, to size up acquisition candidates. Bluhill, for example, will add to Dean's sales and profit. But it should also increase Dean's distribution and marketing clout, making the company the nation's No. 2 pickle packer behind Campbell Soup Co.'s Vlasic subsidiary. By folding Bluhill into the company's other pickle operations, Dean can cut costs and fatten its pickle profit margins.

Dean is one of a growing number of corporate suitors that are reluctant to venture into unfamiliar territory when making acquisitions. It has made mistakes in the past. In the 1960s, its ventures into highly processed, packaged frozen meat entrees and specialty baked goods flopped. In both cases, Dean raised the quality of the ingredients, then hurt its sales by raising retail prices. "We weren't as smart as we thought we were," says Kenneth J. Douglas, Dean's chairman since 1969.

More recently, Dean again was taught to avoid unfamiliar turf by its 1978 acquisition of money-losing Vita Food Products, a herring processor. Dean tried to turn around the operation, but herring prices doubled in three months and sales suffered. Dean sold Vita in 1982.

Dean isn't alone in such failures. "I think there's a certain disenchantment with going out and buying something for financial reasons and not integrating it into the operations," says Alfred Rappaport, an expert on acquisitions who teaches at Northwestern University. He cites Mobil Corps.'s acquisition of Montgomery Ward, a retailer, as an example. "My guess is, there's going to be a certain degree of reticence to get involved in completely unrelated businesses."

So far, Dean's usually disciplined approach to acquisitions has paid off in the form of a high success rate—Vita is the only failure in the last decade—and steady profit gains. A look at the Bluhill acquisition, completed in July, shows how Dean operates.

To most observers, Bluhill early this year would have looked like a loser. Kellogg Co., which had acquired Bluhill in 1979, had lost interest in commodity businesses such as pickle packing and decided to stick to highly processed, branded products, a spokesman says. Sales were falling and Bluhill was losing money. In March, Kellogg sold Bluhill back to its former owner, Morris Ginsburg.

Mr. Ginsburg, who says he ran Bluhill profitably for 26 years before selling it to Kellogg, set about cutting costs. As the company's results began to improve, he contacted a Dean executive, Robert Antoine, to ask if Dean was interested in Bluhill.

That was no accident. Dean tries to cultivate a reputation as a good corporate parent. Mr. Douglas sometimes courts prospects for months through golf outings and lunches, and other top executives belong to industry associations to build contacts. Mr. Ginsburg knew Mr. Antoine, a Group Marketing Vice-President in Dean's pickle operations, through Pickle Packers International, an industry group. Mr. Ginsburg liked what he had seen of Dean, which had begun expanding its pickle operations. "They were on the track of what I felt needed to be done in the industry," he says. He cites combining regional pickle packers into a national company to increase clout with big customers like McDonald's Corp.

Even though Bluhill was small, top Dean executives turned their attention to it. William D. Fischer, Vice President of Finance, spends about half his time on acquisitions. "I always tell people, 'Have gun, will travel,'" he says. "I'll get on an airplane and go anyplace" to look at a prospect. (Sometimes, their curiosity gets Dean executives into trouble. Mr. Douglas, a former FBI agent, once posed as a milk-bottle salesman to get a good look at a dairy he was thinking of buying. "It was fine until they started asking me about bottle prices," he says.)

Mr. Fischer flew to Arvada for the first of three visits by Dean executives. Bluhill's plant, warehouse and other facilities were in good shape, and the company had a commanding share of the growing Denver market. But Mr. Douglas wanted to see specific plans to raise Bluhill to the 22 percent rate of return on equity of other Dean pickle operations. That required a lot of scrutiny of Bluhill by Dean executives.

They figured out how to increase Bluhill's volume sharply and cut its costs by buying cucumbers from Dean's Midwestern and Southeastern sources, as well as Bluhill's Colorado and Texas suppliers. Dean's trucking unit and refrigeration facilities could distribute Bluhill products more widely and cheaply. And the executives planned fuller use of the cucumbers Bluhill buys. In the past, Bluhill had to sell the small pickles it couldn't use to make hamburger dills. Now, Dean could use the little pickles in its retail pickle packing plants.

"Dean understands the business," says Mr. Ginsburg. Although he has "high respect for the personal integrity of the people at Kellogg," he says, "they just didn't know our business." When Kellogg bought Bluhill, Mr. Ginsburg says, he looked to Kellogg's sales force to broaden distribution, but "they didn't know the product."

Check Each Other

Dean had no competition in bidding for Bluhill, and it won't say what it paid. But Ronald Strauss, an analyst with William Blair and Co., Chicago, notes that the company has usually paid about four to eight times earnings for its purchases. That contrasts with prices as high as 15 times earnings that are sometimes paid for companies making highly processed, packaged products. Mr. Fischer says he tries hard not to "fall in love with an acquisition" and pay too much, and top executives check each other in making bids. "Ken accuses me of giving away the store," Mr. Fischer says. And Mr. Douglas responds, "I have to hold onto his coat sometimes."

Mr. Ginsburg says Dean has tried hard to maintain morale at Bluhill. After the experience with Kellogg, its 70 employees were afraid of being acquired again, so Dean kept the talks secret, he says. Then, when the deal was closed, Messrs. Douglas, Fischer and Antoine took a dozen Bluhill employees to dinner. As they piled into the car, a salesman offered Mr. Douglas the front seat, Mr. Ginsburg recalls. "He said, 'No, no, you've got long legs. I'll sit in the back.' How many chairmen of Fortune 500 companies would react like that?" Dean also hasn't made any drastic changes in Bluhill's operations, a process that can hurt morale. "They've been very open to what people here have to say," says Bonnie Wright, Bluhill's office manager.

Despite all the work Dean put into it, the Bluhill acquisition drew little notice on Wall Street. Asked about leading pickle packers, an analyst said, "Well, Campbell is in it, and Heinz. And there's a third company—I can't remember the name."

But Mr. Douglas says obscurity doesn't bother him. "I get a little insidious pleasure—a certain amount of pride—that this organization is able to take a mundane, stodgy food business and achieve the results it has," he says. Eventually, Dean may have to diversify outside the food industry, "but I don't see that now," he says. "I don't think we'll change our strategy unless it's not working. If it's not broke, why fix it?"

Source: Reprinted by permission of the *Wall Street Journal*, © Dow Jones and Co., Inc., 1983. All rights reserved.

---

more than increase total sales or profits. The conglomerate should add synergy to the present organization, that is, the total sales and profits of the conglomerate should be greater than the combined sales and profits of the two separate firms. So why would a firm become a conglomerate? The strategies and current operating position of the two individual firms provide the impetus. For example, the operating positions of the two firms may be that (1) one has little cash and much opportunity in the marketplace, while the other has much cash and little opportunity in the market place; (2) one has great opportunities in the marketplace but few skills, while the other has limited opportunities but many skills; (3) one has low debt and the other high debt; (4) they are in products with countercyclical sales.

American Can Company has adopted the strategy of conglomerate diversification. Practical Insights 6 shows the unrelated businesses that the company has acquired. American Can has deliberately moved away from the canning and packaging business and into financial services and retailing.

The various external growth strategies are summarized in Figure 3–7.

Retrenchment

A firm that follows a retrenchment strategy perceives that it is not meeting its basic objectives via its current strategy. The company therefore reduces its scale of operations. Retrenchment is not a popular strategy since businesspersons generally equate success with growth. The degree to which a firm should retrench depends on how serious the problems are with the current strategy. The retrenchment may

PRACTICAL INSIGHTS 6

Conglomerate Diversification at American Can Company

Source: Reprinted with permission of *USA Today.*

range from temporarily reducing personnel and other cost-saving methods to complete liquidation of the company.

Cutback and Turnaround. Glueck[7] has proposed that this strategy can be utilized effectively when the current strategy is threatened by short-term environmental changes, such as reduced sales or the cutting of operational costs if they are out of control. The cutback and turnaround strategy is considered temporary and consists of the firm's reducing the internal cost of operations. The firm may suffer from decreasing sales, which management expects to be only temporary. In an effort to

FIGURE 3-7
Integration and Diversification Matrix

		New Products	
	Products Customers	Related Technology	Unrelated Technology
New Mission	Firm Its Own Customer	Vertical Integration	
	Same Type	Horizontal Integration	
	Similar Type	Marketing and Technology-Related Concentric Diversification	Marketing-Related Concentric Diversification
	New Type	Technology-Related Concentric Diversification	Conglomerate Diversification

Source: I. Ansoff, *Corporate Strategy*, © 1965, McGraw-Hill, McGraw-Hill Copyrights and Permission Department.

reduce costs so that the product or service can be retained, it may be necessary to cut back on internal costs. This may be accomplished through the reduction of costs in three areas: administration, production, or sales. For example, promotion may be reduced or transportation costs of raw materials may be reduced. The most dramatic reduction in cost is personnel. The company must carefully weigh the temporary benefits of saving personnel costs against the cost associated with rehiring and retraining new personnel, not to mention the damage to the company's image.

Divestment. The firm may find that the reduced profits or sales are not temporary, or that there are new technologies associated with the product or service that the company does not possess and whose acquisition would be costly. In such cases the firm probably would decide to reduce its scale of operations by selling off the product line. Divestment is usually a difficult decision to make because management already has the product line and is familiar with it; also, management has been commited to that line and to give it up indicates failure.

Liquidation. The most severe of all types of retrenchment is liquidation or selling the entire organization. There are a number of reasons why a company might liquidate. It may be that top management is approaching retirement with no trained successors, management may feel that the company is at its peak and there is no place to go but down, another firm may be willing to buy the company for more than management thinks it is worth, or the firm has allowed itself to become inefficient in operations.

Liquidation is a difficult decision for management to make. The company may have been in business for a long time; management may feel that it is a mature firm, which they nurtured from infancy. In many cases top management spent their "lives" developing the company. Little wonder they are reluctant to sell.

Combination

The three basic strategies discussed thus far—stability, growth, and retrenchment—may lead one to believe that a firm pursues only a single strategy at a time. With the increasing size of businesses in the past two decades, it should be obvious that a firm may pursue more than one strategy at a time. With a small firm in a one-product line, only one strategy may be used. Most firms that have increased in size to multiproduct lines, however, will find it necessary to carry out multistrategies simultaneously. It may well be that one division of a company is growing, while another division of the same company is retrenching. General Electric is a good example. It might retrench in consumer appliances, yet be in a growth strategy in aerospace at the same time.

Another combination strategy may be sequential. A firm might plan to allow several periods of stability before resuming a growth strategy per se. The period of stability gives the firm the opportunity to catch up with the competition and reorganize before it returns to a growth strategy. The sequential combination strategy allows the organization to adopt any temporary strategy designed to better its position for a return to its long-run strategy.

Summary of Alternative Strategies

The four types of strategies, their substrategies, and their usefulness are provided in Figure 3–8.

SUMMARY

The mission of an organization is distinct from its purpose. The purpose defines the broad role the organization plays in meeting society's needs. The basic purpose of any organization is to use society's resources to produce efficiently and responsibly goods and services needed by that society. The mission of an organization defines its business. An organization's mission should be defined in terms of a product or service aimed at a specific market segment. The mission statement should be neither too broad and ambiguous, nor too narrow and confining for the effective allocation and utilization of its resources and skills.

An organization philosophy represents the values, beliefs, commitments, and aspirations of the company. It reflects the "culture" of the company and, as such,

FIGURE 3-8
Types of Strategies and Their Usefulness

Strategy	Substrategy	When Useful
Stability		In mature industry; environment of firm is changing slowly; firm is currently successful.
Growth	Internal	
	Penetration	Firm has small market share operating in an expanding market.
	Expansion	Firm is early in product life-cycle; firm has resources to move into new geographical areas or modify current product(s) or service(s).
	External	
	Integration	Company needs to control finished products or raw materials. Requires massive capital.
	Diversification	Firm has excess cash flow; product has become obsolete; new tax legislation implemented; competition has increased.
Retrenchment	Cutback and Turnaround	Firm is faced with short-term environmental changes.
	Divestment	Short-term environmental changes become permanent.
	Liquidation	Firm can no longer compete effectively.
Combination		Firm faces economic transition; firm is in transition for new product or service offered.

guides the behavior of its employees. It governs how the organization conducts its business.

Organization policies are guides that define the "ball park," within which objectives and strategies are determined, implemented, and controlled. They provide a framework for decision making in the organization. Generally policies tend to limit the scope of alternatives that may be considered in making decisions.

Strategic objectives are the ends that the total organization hopes to achieve in fulfilling its basic mission. They are the desired outcomes and serve as the benchmarks against which an organization can measure its progress as it implements its plans.

There are four principal generic corporate strategy alternatives: stability, growth, retrenchment, and combination. With a stability strategy, the organization continues what it is currently doing. The growth strategy can be pursued through internal growth via penetration or expansion, or through external growth via integration or diversification. Under a retrenchment strategy the organization deliberately reduces the scale of operations of a business. The retrenchment may range from temporarily cutting back on personnel and other costs to a complete divestment or liquidation of a business. Companies with many products or businesses in their portfolios use a combination strategy, that is, some products may be in a growth phase, some may be in the stability phase, and a few may be undergoing retrenchment.

References

1. George A. Steiner, *Strategic Planning: What Every Manager Must Know* (New York: The Free Press, 1979), p. 151.
2. Peter F. Drucker, *The Practice of Management* (New York: Harper and Row Publishers, 1954), p. 63.
3. William F. Glueck, *Business Policy and Strategic Management*, 3e (New York: McGraw-Hill, 1980).
4. Donald L. Bates and David L. Eldridge, *Strategy and Policy: Analysis, Formulation, and Implementation* (Dubuque, Iowa: William C. Brown, 1980).
5. Bates and Eldridge, *Strategy and Policy*.
6. Hugo, E. R. Uyterhoeven, Robert W. Ackerman, and John W. Rosenblum, *Strategy and Organization: Text and Cases in General Management* (Homewood, Illinois: Richard D. Irwin, 1977).
7. Glueck, *Business Policy*, pp. 223–229.

CHAPTER 4

ORGANIZATION STRATEGY

Identifying Current Corporate Strategy

Corporate Strategy Analysis

    Techniques for the Analysis of Corporate Strategy
    The BCG Growth-Share Matrix
    The GE Business Portfolio Matrix

Business Strategy Analysis

    Generic Business Strategies
    Strategies for Dominant Firms
    Strategies for Low Market-Share Firms
    Strategies for Firms in Stagnant Industries
    Strategy Contingencies: Competitive Strength and
        Product Life-Cycle Stage

Functional Strategy Analysis

Choosing an Organization Strategy

    Internal Considerations
    External Considerations

Summary

References

72 The Concepts of Strategic Management and Case Analysis

PERFORMANCE OBJECTIVES

When you have finished reading this chapter, you should be able to

1. Distinguish between the four levels of organization strategy.
2. Explain the need for corporate strategy analysis in a diversified firm.
3. Show the relationships between corporate, business, and functional strategy.
4. Explain the techniques used for corporate strategy analysis.
5. Describe some situational business strategies.

After establishing the strategic objectives of the organization, the next step in the strategic management process is the determination of the organization strategy (see Figure 4–1). There are four levels in organization strategy: societal, corporate, business, and functional. The formulation of societal, corporate, business, and functional strategies involves identification, evaluation, and selection of strategic alternatives. The sum total of the societal, corporate, business, and functional strategies constitutes the organization strategy of the firm.

The societal strategy of an organization is formulated by the board of directors. The functional strategies are taught in various functionally oriented courses such as marketing, production, finance, and personnel; therefore they will not be covered in this chapter. We will concentrate on corporate and business strategy, because it is the process of formulating corporate and business strategy that integrates the various functional areas when strategic decisions are made.

Let us start by redescribing the four levels of organizational strategy: (1) societal, (2) corporate, (3) business, and (4) functional.

Societal Strategy

Societal strategy is concerned with the relationships between an organization and its external environment, as well as the broad issues of corporate citizenship, social

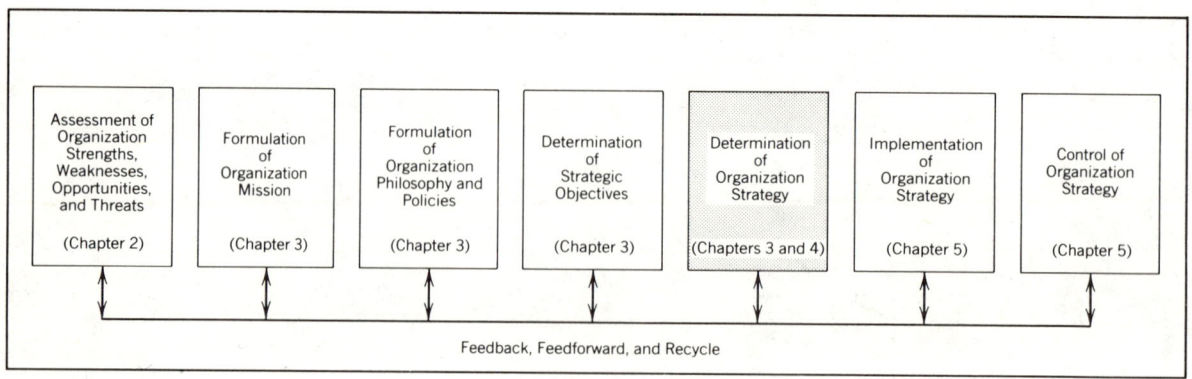

FIGURE 4-1
A Model of the Strategic Management Process

responsibility and accountability, and business ethics. The main concern of societal strategy is how the organization intends to function as a member of the immediate community, the society, the country, and the global community.

Corporate Strategy

Corporate strategy is top management's grand design for managing the whole organization. The aim of corporate strategy is to manage the company's current and future portfolio of businesses to effect the fulfillment of the company's strategic objectives. According to Hofer and Schendel, corporate strategy "is concerned primarily with answering the question: what set of businesses should we be in? Consequently, scope and resource deployments among businesses are the primary components of corporate strategy."[1] Corporate strategy is developed in response to the following questions:

1. What business or businesses are we in?
2. Will our current business or businesses enable us to achieve our long and short-run strategic objectives, particularly growth, profitability, and financial performance?
3. Should we get into new businesses that will enable us to achieve our strategic objectives?
4. Which and how many resources do we have at our disposal now; which and how many resources that could be allocated to our businesses are we capable of garnering in the near future?
5. Which and how many of our resources should we allocate to each of our businesses? Are there any businesses that do not deserve to receive resources in the future at the same level as in the past?

The answer to question one should define the company's basic mission, and in the case of a diversified company, the mission of each business in its portfolio. Question one also may clarify and refine the mission. To illustrate, the executives of a company that manufactures frozen pizza may want to give serious attention to the issue of whether it is in the food business, the frozen-food business, or the frozen pizza business.

In answering question two, strategists would determine whether the company's current business activities are capable of generating the desired level of performance demanded by strategic objectives. This would require examining the competitive position of each business, critical environmental forces and changes that could have significantly favorable or unfavorable impacts on each business, and a SWOT analysis of each business. After making such assessments, if it is found that a substantial gap is likely to develop between the expected and desired levels of performance from the current set of businesses, company strategists might choose to lower their strategic objectives. If the decision is against lowering strategic objectives, the only viable choice is to answer question three with a yes and diversify into other businesses. In answering question four, the company strategists determine the availability of resources now and in the foreseeable future.

Question five implicitly recognizes that there are limits to the resources that any company can muster at a certain point, therefore company strategists must ration resources among the various businesses. Some resources might be used to enter new businesses, some to help a few existing businesses to grow (growth strategy), and still others to maintain some of the businesses at their present levels (stability strategy). Strategists may even decide to slowly starve some businesses or to sell or liquidate others (retrenchment strategy).

Business Strategy

The focus of business strategy is on "how to compete in a particular industry or product/market segment."[2] The time test of a successful business strategy is whether it provides the firm with the competitive approach that enables it to achieve its business objectives, as defined by the firm's corporate strategy, given the industry environment and the firm's position in that environment. For example, what competitive approach should a company's business take if the corporate strategy has designated it a growth business and it has a low market-share in the industry, or how should the business compete if the industry has become stagnant? The purpose of business strategy is to position an organization in the industry so that it has a strategic advantage in the marketplace, thereby enabling it to outperform its competitors. Strategic advantage is the competitive edge that a firm has over its competitors, based on its distinctive competence.[3] Distinctive competence refers to a firm's superiority in a particular aspect of the industry compared to its competitors, for example, quality service, product innovation, or distribution system.

Functional Strategy

Functional strategy is concerned with the development of strategies in each of the functional areas within a business, for example, production, marketing, finance, and R & D. The effectiveness of functional strategies is measured by the extent to which they collectively achieve the objectives of a strategic business unit, that is, the extent the business strategy is successfully implemented. According to Hofer and Schendel, the principal focus of functional strategy is "on the maximization of resource productivity. Synergy and the development of distinctive competences, therefore, become the key strategy components."[4]

The interrelationships between the various levels of organizational strategy are presented in Figure 4–2, which shows that there is a hierarchy of objectives and a corresponding hierarchy of strategies. It also shows that the formulation of objectives and the corresponding strategy at one level must take into consideration and be consistent with the objectives and corresponding strategy at levels *above* and *below* that level. For example, if the corporate strategy for a strategic business unit calls for a growth strategy, the objectives of the business unit must be oriented towards growth and the business strategy must be aimed at achieving the growth objective. However, should the strategic business unit be unable to implement the growth strategy because of reasons such as its inability to implement functional

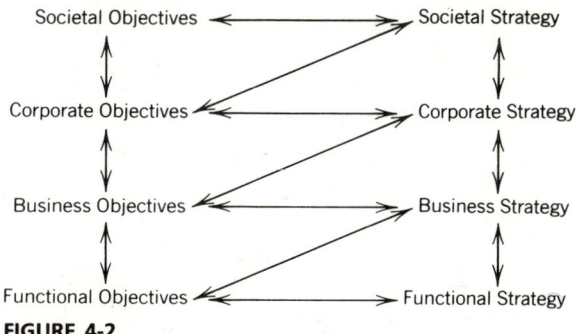

FIGURE 4-2
Hierarchical Strategy Interrelationships

strategies because of a scarcity of functional skills and resources, both business and corporate objectives and strategies must be reformulated.

IDENTIFYING CURRENT CORPORATE STRATEGY

In a multibusiness organization, the analysis of corporate strategy is principally concerned with determining the attractiveness of the total business portfolio and formulating ways of improving its performance through the determination of the appropriate role that each business is expected to play in the company's game plan. The authority for the development and implementation of specific business strategies is generally delegated to general managers in charge of specific business units.

Although the concept of corporate strategy has special relevance to multibusiness organizations, it is equally applicable to single-business enterprises concerned about the future profitability of their core business and thinking about diversifying into other business areas with superior future prospects. Thus, in either single or multibusiness enterprises, corporate strategy formulation involves evaluation of the current business or businesses and making decisions about which business deserves greater or fewer resources in the future; which business should be divested or liquidated; whether new businesses should be added, and if so, which should be added; how each business should be managed in the future.

But before a company can arrive at a determination of its corporate strategy, it must have a thorough understanding of its present strategy. Only then can the strategists evaluate and decide whether the current strategy is the proper one in light of the future realities and whether any changes are mandated. Figure 4–3 identifies the "spokes" of corporate strategy and the dimensions that ought to be examined in order to obtain a proper perspective of the organization's current corporate strategy.

Analysis of the current corporate strategy may show an extremely well-managed firm that has carefully assessed its strengths and weaknesses in each business area, knows what is necessary to succeed in each business area, and has used this knowledge to develop and implement a corporate game plan capable of fully exploiting the opportunities and combating the threats in each business area. At the

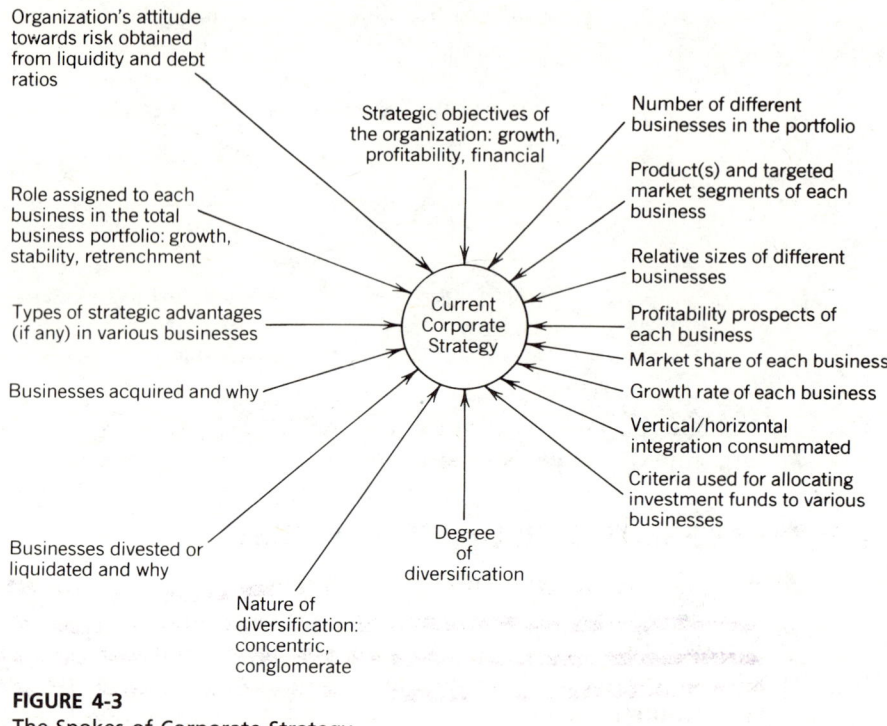

FIGURE 4-3
The Spokes of Corporate Strategy

other extreme, a picture might emerge of a firm that is drifting aimlessly without a sound corporate strategy.

CORPORATE STRATEGY ANALYSIS

An effective corporate strategy gives the firm a balanced portfolio of businesses, that enables it to achieve its strategic objectives, especially those in the areas of profitability, growth, and financial performance. Corporate strategy formulation requires the making of investment decisions by corporate strategists, that is, corporate strategists must decide where to allocate the organization's resources among the existing businesses in its portfolio or to enter new businesses. In any financial investment portfolio, the investor's purpose is to obtain a portfolio of investments that provides the best performance at least cost with an acceptable degree of risk. A similar objective is desired by corporate strategists, who also want the corporate funds invested in a business portfolio that represents an acceptable balance between risk and return. Corporate strategy analysis techniques are meant to help the corporate strategist obtain such a business portfolio. An illustration of the corporate strategy and business portfolio of Union Carbide is presented in Practical Insights 1.

PRACTICAL INSIGHTS 1
The Six-Business Strategy of Union Carbide Corporation

Industry analysts looking at Union Carbide Corp., the country's second largest chemicals producer (as of 1979), see a company that has allowed its chemical lines to grow like cancer, with the same debilitating effects of cancer. Costs have risen so high that Carbide was forced to divest almost all of its European chemicals and plastic operations last year. At the same time, ethylene prices fell to 13¢/lb., causing a cash squeeze. This made bankers skittish, as they forced Carbide to retire the $292 million long-term debt of its Gulf Coast Olefins Co.

According to Warren Anderson, Carbide's president, ". . . only 37 percent of our revenues [$79 billion in 1978] came from chemicals and plastics." In fact, Anderson believes that by 1983, chemicals will make up only 25–30 percent of revenues.

Through the use of strategic planning, Carbide is cutting back some businesses and classifying others as cash cows. "If you look back, we gave too much support to poor businesses and not enough to our good businesses," explains Anderson. The result was that Carbide lost its clear leadership in areas such as phenolic resins and vinyl products.

The company has now decided to focus on "making tradeoffs in a limited resource situation." Six businesses have been identified, which according to Anderson, will comprise 75 percent of Carbide's assets by 1983, up from the current level of 66 percent. These businesses are graphite electrodes, batteries, agricultural seeds and chemicals, polyethylene, industrial gases, and a mixed-bag of other chemicals.

Most analysts, feel that Carbide is moving in the right direction. G. James Williams, Vice President of Finance at Dow Chemical Co. concludes that Carbide is well suited for diversification. "Dow has a monolithic identity with chemicals, Carbide has management people with expertise outside the chemicals business."

Along with the divestiture of their $378 million European petrochemicals business, Carbide has also sold off 11 other businesses in the last two years (1978–1979), accounting for $204 million in revenues. They have also been able to eliminate an additional $20.9 million in operating costs by abandoning 25 sideline businesses that they were developing.

The chopping is far from over. Although Anderson will not state which businesses are on the chopping block, sources close to the company point to ferroalloys, coatings, and possibly food casings as fields Carbide might exit.

Source: Business Week, Sept. 24, 1979, p. 97.

Techniques for the Analysis of Corporate Strategy

Portfolio analysis is the predominant approach of corporate strategy analysis in diversified firms. In the following pages, we will examine two major portfolio analysis techniques: (1) the Boston Consulting Group (BCG) growth–share matrix and (2) the General Electric (GE) business portfolio matrix. Hofer and Schendel[5] recommend that they be used in a two-stage process. In the first stage, the BCG matrix should be used to obtain a tentative plot of the corporate portfolio because it is the simplest and requires the least data. During stage two, the GE portfolio matrix may be used to highlight those businesses that require special attention either because of their importance or they do not perform as expected on the initial BCG plot.

The portfolio techniques are equally applicable in less diversified and single-business firms in which the main concern is not getting a "good" mix of business to improve overall performance, but assessing whether the firm should consider entering new businesses and/or deemphasizing the current business.

The BCG Growth–Share Matrix

One of the most publicized and written about corporate strategy analysis and evaluation techniques is the BCG growth–share matrix.[6] Figure 4–4 represents a hypothetical company's diversified business portfolio that consists of 15 businesses. Each of the businesses represented by a circle is placed in one of the four cells in the matrix, whose dimensions are growth rate and relative market share. The size of the circle represents the size of the business, usually in terms of sales volume. Where a certain business gets placed in the matrix depends on the growth rate of the business (corrected for inflation) and its relative market share. According to the BCG approach, the separation between high and low-market–growth-rate businesses on the horizontal axis is made at 10 percent, and the separation between high and low relative market-share is at 1.0. *Relative market share* is defined

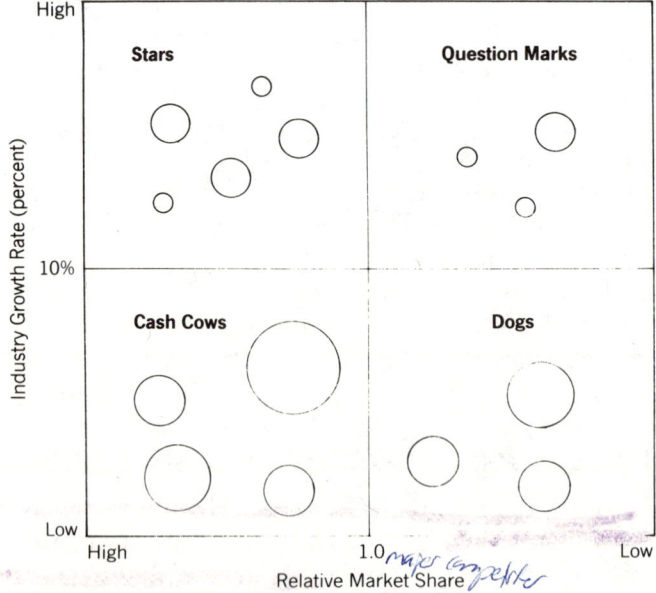

FIGURE 4-4
The BCG Growth-Share Matrix

as the ratio of the business's market share in units sold (not dollars) to the market share of the largest competitor. (Note: there is no rigid rule stipulating that the business growth-rate dividing line should be set at 10 percent. The principle is that businesses above the dividing line should be growing rapidly and those below it ought to be in the low-growth, maturity, or declining stage in the business life-cycle. As for relative market share, the dividing line could be put at points above or below 1.0, the idea being that businesses to the left of the dividing line have strong market positions—not necessarily leadership—and those to the right of it have a relatively weak market share. Thus businesses that are market leaders will be placed to the left of the relative market share dividing line.

How a business should be managed is suggested by the placement of the business in the BCG matrix (see Figure 4-4).

Stars. A "star" is a business that is growing rapidly and has a high market-share. It is in a high-growth business and, hence, may need large amounts of cash to maintain its relative market share position. Being a leader in the business, it might generate large amounts of cash. Therefore, a star business may be generating sufficient cash flow to provide for its cash needs. It represents a superior growth and investment opportunity for a firm and deserves the resources needed to maintain its position in the market. At times this may require a firm's cash-investment in the star business over and above that which the star can generate internally. Eventually, when the growth rate of the business slows, as it does in all businesses, the star drops into the "cash cow" category. However, if no attempt is made to hold the market-share position of a star business, it may slip into the "dog" category.

Cash Cows. A "cash cow" business has a high market-share position, but is in a low-growth business. Such businesses generally generate large amounts of cash, far more than they can profitably invest. Because of their superior market position, their costs are expected to be low and their position in the low-growth market reduces their need for cash investments in plant and equipment. Hence, cash cow businesses generally generate large amounts of cash and are quite profitable. Cash cows are "milked" for the cash to pay dividends and interest on corporate debt, cover corporate overhead, finance research and development, finance new acquisitions, support stars, and provide cash to the "question mark" businesses, whose market share the company wishes to increase in order to make them into future stars.

Question Marks. "Question mark" businesses are high-growth businesses, but with a low-market share. Their low share often means low profits and weak cash flows from operations. At the same time, because they are in rapidly growing markets, they require large amounts of cash to maintain market share and even larger amounts to increase market share. The dilemma that such a company faces is whether to pump in high amounts of cash to make them into future stars or to let them drop into the "dog" category.

Dogs. "Dog" businesses have low growth rates and low market-share. Their poor competitive position puts them in a poor profitability situation. If they are lucky, they are able to generate their own cash needs, but at times they do not generate sufficient cash for investment in the business just to maintain the low competitive position. Dog businesses are unlikely to ever become a significant source of cash; therefore they are often called *cash traps*. Hence, BCG recommends that unless exceptional circumstances demand that they be retained, dog businesses ought to be harvested, divested, or liquidated (these terms are explained later in this chapter) depending on which alternative provides the most attractive cash flow.

The Basic Postulates of the BCG Matrix. The BCG matrix has adopted relative market share and business growth rate as the two dimensions in the matrix for several reasons. The relative market share determines the rate at which a business generates cash; the stronger the business's competitive position, the higher should be its profitability and cash flows as a result of the experience-curve effect. Note: the experience-curve effect refers to the phenomenon where the cost per unit of a product declines by a predictable percentage each time a company's experience at producing and selling it doubles.[7] Relative market share is used as a convenient proxy measure of relative competitive position.

Business growth rate indicates the relative ease and, hence, cost of gaining market share. It is easier to gain market share in high-growth businesses than low-growth businesses. In the former, because the total market for the products that the business has to offer is growing rapidly, any gains in market share by one firm do not come at the expense of a decrease in the sales volume of its competitors. In fact, competitors may not even realize that they are losing market share because their actual sales volume may not be affected. On the other hand, in businesses whose growth rates have slowed or become stagnant, share increases by one firm must come at the expense of a reduction of the sales volume and market share of competitors. In such circumstances competitors are bound to fight back with price-cutting moves and increased marketing and service expenditures to maintain sales volume and market share. Intense competition in the business results in lower profitability and cash flows.

Consequently, BCG recommends that a company's business portfolio should be balanced, that is, there should be enough cash cow businesses to support the stars. Furthermore, there should be an ample number of stars because they will eventually turn into cash cows.

Limitations of the BCG Matrix. The BCG growth–share matrix is open to several major criticisms:[8]

- The high–low classification system does not give enough attention to businesses in an intermediate position; in other words, not all businesses fall neatly within one cell.
- The two-factor comparisons do not give explicit considerations to other impor-

tant strategic factors, such as strategic fit across products, competitive advantage, and the like.

- Growth rate and market-share factors are not always good indicators of cash flow, profitability, and business attractiveness.
- The matrix is not helpful in comparing relative investment opportunities across businesses; for example, is a star always better than a cash cow?
- There is sufficient evidence that not all dog businesses deserve to be so described. In one study of 87 organizations that would have fallen in the dog category, 40 earned a return on investment greater than 20 percent.[9]
- Firms often find it difficult to define the scope of the strategic business units; for example, is the company in the whiskey or scotch whiskey business? How it defines its business in terms of its scope determines its market-share ranking in the matrix.
- It is often difficult to define the scope of the market segment served; for example, is the company in the generic tire market or the replacement market? The business growth-rate positioning of a business in the matrix depends on how much market segmentation is involved.

The Business Portfolio Matrix

Recognizing the shortcomings of the BCG matrix, General Electric (with help from McKinsey and Company) developed a second type of business portfolio matrix. The GE business portfolio matrix consists of nine cells with long-term product/market attractiveness on one axis and business strength/competitive position on the other axis (see Figure 4–5).

The long-term product/market attractiveness is a composite of factors such as the nature of the market or market size; market growth rate (units and real dollars); competitive environment; profitability; technological, social, legal, environmental, and human impacts. The business strength/competitive position is viewed as a function of market size and growth rate, market share, profitability, margins, technological position, skills or weaknesses, image, environmental impact, and quality of management.[10]

Figure 4–5 shows the investment strategies suggested for a business in each of the nine cells in the business portfolio matrix. Each business is represented by a circle whose size corresponds to the sales volume of the business. Let us examine the alternative investment strategies.

Invest and grow. A business that falls within the boundaries of those cells that call for an invest-and-grow strategy is expected to grow and have considerable profit potential. Therefore this business receives substantial investments for technology, production capacity, product improvements, product design, and improved marketing. These investments increase the total sales volume and market

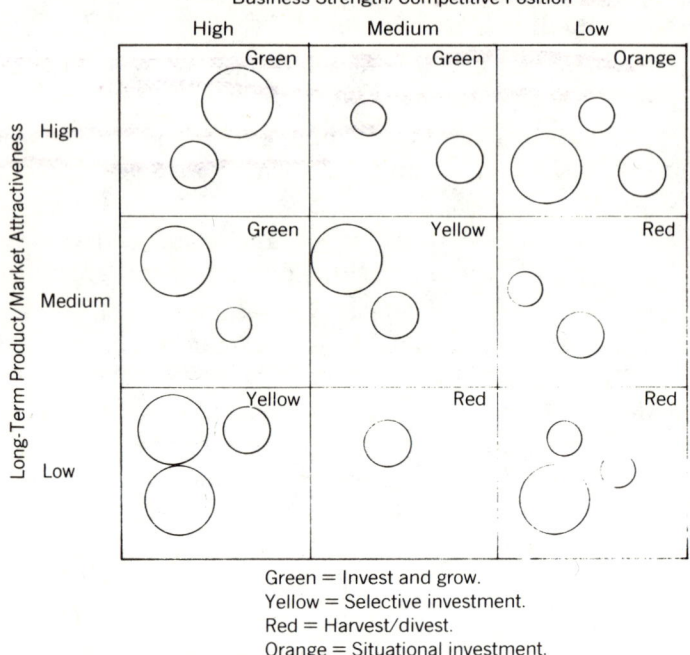

FIGURE 4-5
The GE Business Portfolio Matrix

share of the business. Another purpose may be to maintain the existing competitive position of the business in a rapidly expanding total market.

Selective Investment. A business that qualifies for a selective investment strategy receives investments in order to maximize the returns on its existing assets, resources, and skills. The cash generated in excess of its reinvestment needs is generally reinvested in those businesses that fall into the invest-and-grow category. Any new investments in the business are aimed at maintaining existing investment levels and improving existing competitive advantages.

Harvest/Divest. A business that falls in this group is a loser. It should be harvested by selling idle equipment, tightening up spending, cutting costs, aggressively reducing working capital, pruning products, making only maintenance investments in manufacturing, and investing proceeds in more promising areas.

Businesses that have been thoroughly milked or are likely to drain the long-term profits of the firm should be liquidated or divested. A divestment strategy may require some investment in advertising, pricing, and distribution to make the business attractive to potential buyers. The key is to make just the right amount of investment; too much investment may reduce the return on investment of the business and too little investment may run down the business enough to reduce or eliminate potential buyers.

Situational Investment. The level of investment in a business that falls in this category is based on the judgment and experience of the managers who make this decision. If the managers believe it would be feasible and in the long-term best interests of the company to build the company's strengths to succeed in the business, the invest-and-grow strategy is applied. If not, the harvest/divest strategy is adopted.

The GE business portfolio matrix is considered better than the BCG portfolio matrix because it allows for intermediate rankings between high and low, and strong and weak, and incorporates explicit consideration for a much larger number of relevant factors. However, the portfolio matrix approach still does not suggest the correct strategies for the average and near-average businesses.[11] This is a serious weakness given the direction-setting function of corporate strategy and the fact that every business needs a specific strategy that will lead to the best possible performance, regardless of its attractiveness and competitive position. Hofer and Schendel[12] also have pointed out that the GE approach does not depict well the positions of those businesses about to emerge as winners or losers before the product or market has entered the takeoff (rapid growth) stage. There are more advanced portfolio models designed to correct these shortcomings, but they are beyond the scope of this text.[13]

BUSINESS STRATEGY ANALYSIS

As stated earlier, the focus of business strategy is how the firm should compete in a particular industry or product/market segment to obtain a strategic advantage over the competition. Porter[14] has identified three generic strategic approaches to obtain a competitive advantage designed to outperform competitors.

Generic Business Strategies

Overall Cost Leadership. A low-cost position yields above-average returns in the industry in spite of strong competition. A strategy to obtain cost leadership involves construction of efficient-scale facilities, vigorous efforts to get cost decreases from any learning and experience-curve effects, severe cost and overhead control, dropping of marginally profitable customers, and cost minimization in areas such as R & D, service, sales force, and advertising.

A low-cost position defends a firm against competitors should they choose to compete by lowering prices. In such cases only firms with lower costs than the competition can expect to make money; high-cost producers will quickly go out of business. A low-cost position can serve as a shield against powerful buyers who may drive down the price of their purchases to the level of the next most efficient producer. Having a low-cost position protects a firm against powerful suppliers by providing greater flexibility to handle input cost increases. Being a low-cost producer also helps to put a firm in a better position than competitors to cope with the competitive pressures from substitute products. Finally, factors that lead to a low-cost position could prove to be substantial entry barriers to new entrants in the industry.

Differentiation. This strategy focuses on creating a product or service offering perceived by the customer as unique. The idea is to attract the customer and increase sales volume. Differentiation can take many forms. A firm should ideally differentiate along several different dimensions. Some examples of differentiation are technology (IBM in computers), dealer network (Caterpillar Tractor in construction equipment), service (IBM in computers), brand image (Coca-Cola and Pepsi-Cola in soft drinks), and superior quality (Rolls Royce in automobiles). Effective differentiation strategies protect the firm against competitors because of customers' brand loyalty and the resulting lower sensitivity to price. Brand loyalty allows the firm to price the product or service higher than competitive products, thus generating higher margins.

Focus. This strategy involves focusing the firm's attention on a particular buyer group, segment of the product line, or geographic area. The aim is to serve a particular target market exceptionally well, which is why functional strategies (marketing, finance, and production) are developed. The idea is to serve a narrow strategic market more efficiently and effectively than across-the-board competitors. Consequently, the firm is able to achieve low cost, differentiation, or both from the perspective of its narrow market target, if not from an industry-wide perspective.

Implementing the three types of generic business strategies requires different resources and skills and different organizational, control, and incentive systems. Figure 4–6 illustrates the requirements that a firm must be capable of meeting if it is to successfully implement the overall cost leadership, differentiation, or focus strategies.

The key to getting a strategic advantage in the market is to adapt the generic business strategies to the industry situation and the firm's position. Several authors have recommended specific business strategies for firms in specific situations. In the following pages, we will examine:

1. Strategies for dominant firms.
2. Strategies for low market-share firms.
3. Strategies for firms in stagnant industries.
4. Strategies contingent on competitive strength and product life-cycle stage.

Strategies for Dominant Firms

A firm with a dominant position in the industry (like IBM in computers, General Motors in automobiles, and Campbell's Soup Company in canned soups) is concerned mainly about maintaining or improving its position in the industry. Philip Kotler[15] suggests the following strategies for dominant firms:

Be on the Offensive. Continue efforts to increase market share. Continue to offer new and improved products and innovate in areas such as customer service and distribution channels. Make cost-cutting discoveries, lower product price, and increase value received by the customer from the product. A good example of a firm using this strategy effectively is IBM.

FIGURE 4-6
Requirements of the Generic Business Strategies

Generic Strategy	Commonly Required Skills and Resources	Common Organization Requirements
Overall Cost Leadership	Sustained capital investment and access to capital Process engineering skills Intense supervision of labor Products designed for ease in manufacture Low-cost distribution system	Tight cost control Frequent, detailed control reports Structured organization and responsibilities Incentives based on meeting strict quantitative targets
Differentiation	Strong marketing abilities Product engineering Creative flair Strong capability in basic research Corporate reputation for quality or technological leadership Long tradition in the industry or a unique combination of skills drawn from other businesses Strong cooperation from channels	Strong coordination among R & D, product development, and marketing Subjective measurement and incentives instead of quantitative measures Amenities to attract highly skilled labor, scientists, or creative people
Focus	Combination of the above policies directed at the particular strategic target	Combination of the above policies directed at the particular strategic target

Source: Reprinted with permission of the Free Press, a division of MacMillan, Inc. from *Competitive Strategy: Techniques for Analyzing Industries and Competitors*, by Michael E. Porter, Copyright © 1980 by the Free Press.

Fortify Against the Enemy. Plug holes in the company's product line to keep a competitor from moving in, and introduce a number of additional brands to compete with the company's own and already successful brands in order to tie up scarce shelf space in distribution centers and lock out some of the competition. Procter and Gamble has perfected this strategy with its many brands of toothpaste and soaps, as has Philip Morris with its numerous cigarette brands.

Confrontation. Defend the company's territory by engaging in expensive promotional or price-cutting wars to punish aggressive competitors.

Strategies for Low Market-Share Firms

Companies with low market-share positions are most concerned about improving their competitive position and market standing. Small firms cannot achieve this aim by imitating the market-share leaders; they must do something unique. Hamermesh, Anderson, and Harris[16] propose that low market-share companies adopt one or all of the following strategies:

Segment Markets. Select and compete in market segments in which the firm has expertise. For example, Crown Cork and Seal has chosen to concentrate on two product segments: metal cans for beer and soft drinks and aerosol cans.

Efficient Use of R & D. Smaller companies cannot win any R & D battles because larger firms can afford bigger R & D budgets. Hence, low market-share companies must use R & D funds efficiently by channeling R & D spending into areas that are most likely to produce the greatest benefits for them. The suggested approach is to focus R & D on lowering process costs or to bring new products to the market.

Think Small. Another feature of successful low market-share companies like Crown Cork and Seal and Burroughs is that they are all content to remain small. They emphasize profits rather than sales growth or market share and specialization rather than diversification.

The following strategies for low market-share companies are offered by Philip Kotler:[17]

The Vacant Niche. Find the market segment that the large firms are not competing in and focus on different areas than the major competitors. The Japanese carmakers like Toyota and Honda and the makers of the German Volkswagen successfully filled the vacant niche in the small-car market that the large American carmakers like General Motors and Ford had ignored. An illustration of an effective vacant niche strategy of Armstrong Rubber Company is presented in Practical Insights 2.

PRACTICAL INSIGHTS 2

The Niche Strategy at Armstrong Rubber

Armstrong Rubber Co. would seem to be caught in an industrial crevice. Sixth among U. S. tiremakers, with only about 4 percent of the U. S. tire market, it is squeezed between muscular giants above and more specialized rivals below. "Some learned and scholarly people have proved that we can't exist," says James Aloysius Walsh, the New Haven-based company's chairman and chief executive. "But so far, they've been wrong."

Lately they've been more wrong than ever. After getting through the 1970s with lackluster if steady growth, Armstrong bounced back from a 1980 deficit of $16.4 million to ring up record sales ($560 million) and profits ($17.4 million) in the fiscal year that ended last September. Despite the recession, both sales and profits continued to rise slightly through the first three quarters of fiscal 1982, surprising Wall Street analysts who had been predicting a small decline in net earnings. . . . Armstrong's turnaround stands out in an industry flattened on top by the prolonged slump in new auto sales and plagued by overcapacity. Tire manufacturers have closed 19 plants since the beginning of 1978, idling some 30,000 workers. Profits have fluctuated wildly; so far this year they are down for all of the Big Five and one, General Tire, is in the red. But profits are up for all three of the smaller domestic tiremakers.

. . . Armstrong has been sheltered from the industry's worst woes because it makes tires almost entirely for the replacement market. About 40 percent of its tire sales are to Sears Roebuck, which it has been supplying for 46 years. Moreover, the company has benefited from its well-honed habit of grabbing small opportunities overlooked by rivals.

. . . Frank R. O'Keefe, president of the company, also has revved up Armstrong's five-year strategic planning, through which the company tries to focus resources and investments on segments of the business where growth looks promising. Wherever he goes he carries with him a 100-odd-page loose-leaf notebook crammed with charts and tables spelling out the details; he refers to it frequently with associates, most of whom have copies of their own. "If you've got a plan," he explains, "communicate it. Don't keep it hidden away in a drawer or in the hands of a select few. If everybody in the organization knows the game plan and his or her mission within the plan, you don't have any trouble making judgments and evaluating performance."

At the same time, O'Keefe has been astute enough to recognize and respect Armstrong's fundamental strengths. One of the greatest is that skill for picking and exploiting profitable specialized niches where Armstrong can exert more clout in what O'Keefe calls "a truly segmented business." Niche picking has been a major element of the company's strategy since well before Walsh became chairman.

Today, O'Keefe figures, Armstrong ranks second in industrial tires, "probably second" in the replacement market for all-season radials (which he expects will someday make snow tires obsolete except in the snowiest areas), and second or third in tires for farm equipment and offroad recreational vehicles. "When you really excel in a market segment, you get paid for it," he says. The niches' contributions to profits ought to increase since, O'Keefe contends, "all of these markets are coming out of troughs right now."

Source: Reprinted by permission from *Fortune* Magazine; © 1982, Time Inc. All rights reserved.

"Ours Is Better Than Theirs." Simultaneously implement focus and differentiation strategies keyed to product quality. Target marketing efforts to the performance and quality-conscious buyers. An example of this strategy and its effective use is the Mercedes–Benz automobiles' strength in the luxury car segment of the market.

Distinctive Image. Obtain a strategic advantage via a distinctive image or appeal. Examples of this strategy include 7-Up's "Uncola" campaign and Avis' "We try harder" image.

Channel Innovation. Find innovative ways of distributing the product. Timex experienced rapid sales growth by entering nontraditional outlets like drugstores and discount stores at a time when the watch industry was geared to sales through jewelry stores. Avon avoided shelf space battles in retail outlets by its cosmetics door-to-door selling.

Strategies for Firms in Stagnant Industries

For firms that do business in industries where demand has weakened or reached maturity, milking or harvesting, divestiture, or liquidation may be appropriate strategies. However, abandoning a business just because it has stopped growing and become very competitive may not always be the correct alternative. A stagnant business may still be making a substantial contribution to the total sales, profits, and overhead of the firm. It is most appropriate for a stagnant business to abandon the growth objective in favor of realistic cash flow and return-on-investment criteria.

William K. Hall has found that profitable companies in eight stagnant industries all had accomplished the following:

- "... achieved the lowest delivered cost position relative to competition, coupled with both an acceptable delivered quality and a pricing policy to gain profitable volume and market-share growth."[18]
- "... achieved the highest product/service/quality differentiated position relative to competition, coupled with both an acceptable delivered cost structure and a pricing policy to gain margins sufficient to fund reinvestment in product/service differentiation."[18]

Hamermesh and Silk[19] suggest that successful firms in stagnant industries do the following:

- Identify, create, and exploit the growth segments in the industry. Most industries consist of various segments. Usually at least one of the segments is growing. The trick to success is to analyze and study the industry thoroughly and detect segments that are expanding. In so doing, firms can avoid getting bogged down in a stagnant mode. For instance, in a generally stagnant beer industry, Philip Morris was able to grow in the calorie-conscious beer-consumer segment by pushing its Miller Lite brand.
- Emphasize product quality and product innovation. In a stagnant coffee industry, General Foods was able to earn huge profits by introducing freeze-dried coffee. Consumers perceived freeze-dried coffee as better tasting and more like brewed coffee. Consequently, demand for freeze-dried coffee grew in spite of a drop in general demand for coffee. Innovation could create consumer interest in the firm's product and rejuvenate demand, allowing it to compete on a basis other than price.
- Systematically and constantly improve efficiency of production and distribution systems. The Japanese have been able to capture the U. S. market for automobiles, cameras, and steel by the effective application of this strategy.

The various situational strategies are summarized in Figure 4–7.

Strategy Contingencies: Competitive Strength and Product Life-Cycle Stage

Patel and Younger[20] have developed a contingency model that proposes strategies contingent on the position of the business or product in its life cycle and the competitive position of the firm. This model, presented in Figure 4–8, is self-explanatory.

FIGURE 4-7
Situational Business Strategies

Dominant Position	Low Market-Share Position	Stagnant Industry
Be on the offensive	Segment markets	Lowest delivered cost position
Fortify against the enemy	Efficient use of R & D	Product/service quality differentiation
Confrontation	Think small	Identify and exploit growth segments
	Fill the vacant niche	Emphasize product quality and innovation
	"Ours is better than theirs"	Constantly improve production and distribution efficiency
	Channel innovation	

The situational business strategies presented are by no means exhaustive. There are several other situations and corresponding business strategies that have been suggested by various authors. Moreover, each of the corporate strategic alternatives such as growth, stability, and retrenchment, which were discussed in the last chapter, also have business strategy counterparts. We chose the particular situational business strategies discussed here because most firms have businesses that face these situations.

FIGURE 4-8
Strategy, Product Life Cycle, and Competitive Position

	Embryonic	Growing	Mature	Aging
Dominant	All out push for share	Hold position	Hold position	Hold Position
	Hold position	Hold share	Grow with industry	Hold position or harvest
Strong	Attempt to improve position	Attempt to improve position	Hold position	Hold position
	All out push for share	Push for share	Grow with industry	
Favorable	Selective or all out push for share	Attempt to improve position	Custodial or maintenance	Harvest
	Selectively attempt to improve position	Selective push for share	Find niche and attempt to protect	Phased withdrawal
Tenable	Selectively push for position	Find niche and protect it	Find niche and hang on or phased withdrawal	Phased withdrawal
Weak	Up or out	Turnaround or abandon	Turnaround or phased withdrawal	Abandon

Source: Reprinted with permission from Peter Patel and Michael Younger, "A Frame of Reference for Strategy Development." © 1978, Pergamon Press.

FUNCTIONAL STRATEGY ANALYSIS

Functional strategy includes the strategies developed in each functional area of the business to support the business strategy. Analysis of functional strategy focuses on the evaluation and selection of strategies in areas such as finance, production, R & D, marketing, personnel, industrial and labor relations, government affairs, and public relations. We will not define or describe the characteristics of strategies in each function because they are covered in other courses. What must be remembered is that functional strategies should be internally consistent, both vertically and horizontally. Functional strategies are horizontally consistent when strategies in one functional area are consistent with those in all the other functional areas. They are vertically consistent when they effectively and efficiently contribute as a unified system to the fulfillment of the business strategy.

CHOOSING AN ORGANIZATION STRATEGY

The following list of questions will serve as a guide to selecting an organization (societal, corporate, business, and functional) strategy. A negative response to all or a part of the questions does not mean the strategy should not be selected. Indeed, it is possible that no strategy can be found for which all questions are answered favorably. A negative response should be taken as an incremental measure of risk. The list of questions to be addressed in selecting a strategy could be extremely long and complex. Since the selection of a strategy will result in success or failure, its selection should receive maximum attention. There is no simple or unequivocal way to make the selections. Selection of a strategy is an art that rests on the managers' reasoning and creativity.

The questions are divided into those dealing with the internal environment and those dealing with the external environment of the firm. The reader will recognize that external considerations reflect opportunities and threats, while internal considerations reflect the ability to take advantage of those opportunities or the ability to withstand external threats.

Internal Considerations

- Does the strategy effectively utilize the financial, human, and physical resources of the company?
- Is the strategy consistent with the strategic objectives?
- Is the strategy consistent with the personal values of the managers and employees of the company?
- Is there a direct relationship between the market expectations resulting from the strategy and the internal capabilities of the company?
- Does the strategy provide sufficient flexibility to change or alter it if it proves inappropriate?
- Is the company capable of the planning and development required from the strategy, for example, is the strategy consistent with managerial abilities?

- Does the strategy emphasize the company's strengths and avoid its weaknesses?
- Does or will the company have adequate financial resources for the strategy?
- Has the company adequately planned the processes of implementation for the strategy to ensure a reasonable chance of success, for example, are the strategy and structure consistent?

External Considerations

- Does the strategy lead to a market niche or niches now unfilled by others?
- Does the strategy improve competitive conditions for current market or product lines?
- Is the minimum attainable market sufficient to produce the minimum return on investment?
- Does the strategy utilize or take advantage of existing market and product strengths?
- Does the strategy include products and markets outside the current sphere of products and markets so that the risk of threats is spread?
- Does the strategy fit within the legal and political frameworks so that the success of the strategy will not raise legal or political questions?
- Will the strategy be perceived by society as a responsible and ethical one?

Because there are no set rules for selecting a strategy, the strategist must use judgment and experience. He or she may ask what other companies are doing in general and what the competing companies are doing in particular. In examining these data, however, certain caveats must be heeded. First, strategic choices change over time. Strategies popular at one time may find themselves in disuse at other times. Second, strategic choices vary by industry. Third, company size and the product life-cycle have a dramatic bearing on the strategy that is adopted.

SUMMARY

The focus of this chapter is on corporate and business strategy. Corporate strategy is top management's grand design for the total organization. The aim of corporate strategy is to manage the company's current and future portfolio of businesses to facilitate the fulfillment of the company's strategic objectives.

Business strategy entails decisions on how the company should compete in a particular industry or product/market segment. Business strategy positions an organization in an industry so that it gets a strategic advantage in the marketplace.

The Boston Consulting Group's (BCG) growth–share matrix and GE's business portfolio matrix are the two corporate strategy analysis techniques that were presented. The BCG matrix dimensions are business growth rate and relative market share. The two dimensions of GE's business portfolio matrix are long-term product/market attractiveness and business strength/competitive position.

There are three generic business strategies: overall cost leadership, differentiation, and focus. Implementing the three types of generic business strategies requires different resources and skills, as well as different organizational, control, and incentive systems. The key to getting a strategic advantage in the market is to adapt the generic business strategies to the situations of the industry and the firm's position. Several authors have recommended specific business strategies for firms in specific situations. We discussed strategies for firms in four common situations—strategies for dominant firms, strategies for low market-share firms, strategies for firms in stagnant industries, and strategies contingent on the firm's competitive strength and product life-cycle stage of the business or product.

References

1. Charles W. Hofer and Dan Schendel, *Strategy Formulation: Analytical Concepts* (St. Paul: West Publishing Company, 1978), p. 27.
2. Hofer and Schendel, *Strategy Formulation*, p. 27.
3. Philip Selznick, *Leadership in Administration* (Evanston, Ill: Row, Peterson, and Company, 1957), p. 42.
4. Hofer and Schendel, *Strategy Formulation*, p. 29.
5. Hofer and Schendel, *Strategy Formulation*, p. 33.
6. For an excellent explanation of the BCG growth–share matrix, see Barry Hedley, "Strategy and the Business Portfolio," *Long Range Planning*, vol. 10, February 1977, pp. 9–15.
7. For an excellent explanation of the experience effect, see Derek F. Abell and John S. Hammond, *Strategic Market Planning* (Engelwood Cliffs, N. J.: Prentice-Hall, Inc., 1979), Chapter 3.
8. Abell and Hammond, *Strategic Market Planning*, p. 211–12; George S. Day, "Diagnosing the Product Portfolio," *Journal of Marketing*, April 1977, pp. 35–36.
9. Carolyn Y. Y. Woo and Arnold C. Cooper, "Strategies of Effective Low Market Share Businesses," *Academy of Management Proceedings*, August 1980, pp. 21–25.
10. William K. Hall, "SBUs: Hot, New Topic in the Management of Diversification," *Business Horizons*, vol. 21, no. 1, February 1978, p. 20.
11. D. E. Hussey, "Portfolio Analysis: Practical Experiences with the Directional Policy Matrix," *Long Range Planning*, vol. 11, no. 4, August 1978, pp. 4–5.
12. Hofer and Schendel, *Strategy Formulation*, p. 33.
13. See Product/Market Evolution Portfolio Matrix in Hofer and Schendel, *op. cit.*, pp. 33–34; see also S. J. Q. Robinson, R. E. Hitchens, and D. P. Wade, "The Directional Policy Matrix: A Tool for Strategic Planning," *Long Range Planning*, Vol. 11, No. 3, June 1978, pp. 8–15.
14. Michael E. Porter, *Competitive Strategy: Techniques for Analyzing Industries and Competitors* (New York: The Free Press, 1980), pp. 35–41.
15. Philip Kotler, *Marketing Management: Analysis, Planning, and Control* (Englewood Cliffs, N. J.: Prentice-Hall, 1980), pp. 273–81.
16. R. G. Hamermesh, M. J. Anderson, Jr., and J. E. Harris, "Strategies for Low Market Share Businesses," *Harvard Business Review*, May–June 1978, pp. 95–102.
17. Kotler, *Marketing Management*, pp. 281–84.
18. William K. Hall, "Survival Strategies in a Hostile Environment," *Harvard Business Review*, September–October 1980, pp. 78–79.
19. R. G. Hamermesh and S. B. Silk, "How to Compete in Stagnant Industries," *Harvard Business Review*, September–October 1979, pp. 161–68.
20. Peter Patel and Michael Younger, "A Frame of Reference for Strategy Development," *Long Range Planning*, April 1978, p. 8.

CHAPTER 5
IMPLEMENTATION AND CONTROL OF ORGANIZATION STRATEGY

Implementation of Organization Strategy
    Corporate Culture and Strategy Implementation
    Organization Structure and Strategy Implementation
    Human Resources and Strategy Implementation
    Organization Rewards and Strategy Implementation
    Matching Rewards to Corporate Strategy

Control of Organization Strategy
    Framework for Strategic Control
    Strategic Diagnosis
    Operational Diagnosis

Summary

References

PERFORMANCE OBJECTIVES

When you have finished reading this chapter, you should be able to

1. Explain the concept of corporate culture.
2. Explain the importance of corporate culture in strategy implementation.
3. Discuss the role of organization structure in the successful implementation of strategy.
4. Explain the need for a "fit" between the characteristics of the strategy and individual characteristics of the manager responsible for its implementation.
5. Show how the reward system can be designed to facilitate the successful implementation of strategy.
6. Discuss the essential elements in the strategic control framework.
7. Explain the differences between strategic and operational diagnosis.

Implementation and control of organization strategy are the last two phases in the strategic management process. Strategic planning and strategy implementation and control are two sides of the coin called *strategic management*. One cannot have effective strategy implementation and control without the objectives, standards of organization performance, and strategy established through strategic planning. The opposite is also true: the organization must have a sound strategy implementation and control system that provides the necessary feedback so critical to the development of strategic plans.

We will begin by discussing the essential aspects of organization strategy implementation (Figure 5-1). Control of organization strategy will be discussed later in this chapter.

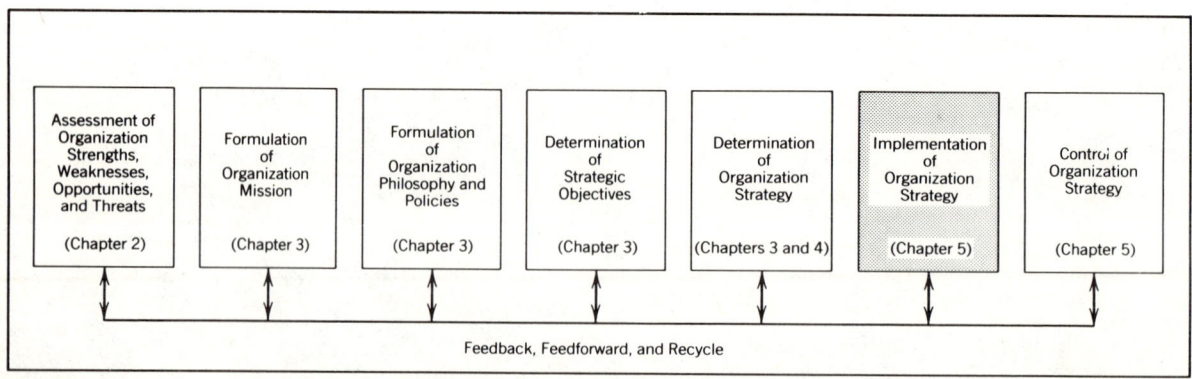

FIGURE 5-1
A Model of the Strategic Management Process

IMPLEMENTATION OF ORGANIZATION STRATEGY

Organization strategy must be converted into concrete action and results; otherwise all tasks and activities constituting the strategic management process will end up a waste of management time and effort. The task of implementing organization strategy is critical to the future success of an organization and may be the key to its very survival; unless the desired results dictated by organization strategy are achieved, the organization will be incapable of exploiting the future opportunities and combating threats effectively. As Steiner has pointed out, "the implementation process covers the entire managerial activities including such matters as motivation, compensation, management appraisal, and control processes."[1] Pierce and Robinson say that "to effectively direct and control the use of the firm's resources, mechanisms such as organizational structure, information systems, leadership styles, assignment of key managers, budgeting, rewards, and control systems are essential strategy implementation ingredients."[2] According to Higgins, "almost all the management functions—planning, controlling, organizing, motivating, leading, directing, integrating, communicating, and innovation—are in some degree applied in the implementation process."[3]

We agree with these authors that the implementation of organization strategy involves the application of the management process to obtain the desired results. Each of the management functions—planning, organizing, staffing, leadership, and controlling—has been the subject of extensive writing and research by scholars and practitioners and has been covered extensively in management books. Since full coverage of each management function is beyond the scope of this book, we will focus on the four factors that are probably most critical to effective implementation of organization strategy and may not be covered at length in other courses. This approach assumes that organization strategy cannot be effectively implemented unless there is consistency between the strategy and the corporate culture, organization structure, human resources, and organization rewards (see Figure 5-2). We will begin by discussing the relationship between corporate culture and strategy implementation.

FIGURE 5-2
Key Factors in Successful Implementation

Corporate Culture and Strategy Implementation

There are as many definitions of culture as there are books on anthropology. Herskovits has defined culture as "that complex whole which includes knowledge, beliefs, art, morals, customs, and any other capabilities and habits acquired by man as a member of society."[4] In other words, culture denotes the distinctive way of life of a group of people and their complete design for living. We can define corporate culture as a system of norms, attitudes, values, beliefs, and customs that governs the behavior of people within an organization. The corporate culture is the sum total of how people in an organization think and act as members of the organization. Once a culture is learned and accepted, it tends to persist.[5] This is also true of organization culture. All cultures, including organization cultures, are gradually and continuously changing, even though human beings tend to resist changes.[6]

All organizations have an enduring culture. For example, the IBM Corporation has a corporate culture that encourages teamwork, innovation, open communications, and customer service. Morgan Guaranty Trust, an investment banking firm, has a culture that is very conservative, secretive, and stoic, and the people who work for the bank have internalized these features in their own behavior.

The corporate culture of a firm can be a major strength if it is consistent with its organization strategy. However, managers will experience difficulty implementing a strategy at odds with the corporate culture. This is illustrated in Practical Insights 1, which describes the problems created by the culture in the Bell System during the government-imposed divestiture and break-up into several independent regional companies.

PRACTICAL INSIGHTS 1

Corporate Strategy and Corporate Culture at the Bell System

The split-up of the Bell System not only represents the biggest break-up in corporate history, but the most enormous task of reorienting managers that any company has ever had to face. AT & T and the seven regional operating companies are redefining manager jobs, teaching them new skills, and perhaps most important, changing their mind sets.

Redeploying Bell's personnel is a monumental task; 13,000 to 15,447 employees at AT & T headquarters are to be dispersed throughout the system. The Bell operating companies (BOC) will contribute 68,000 people to AT & T, which will provide intrastate and interstate long-distance service; 88,000 other BOC personnel (mainly technicians) are to be reassigned to AT & T Information Systems.

Meanwhile, AT & T and the regionals are overhauling their management systems, redistributing decision-making power, and encouraging teamwork. AT & T must also exist in an unstable business environment.

This last restructuring ends a decade-long period of reorganization. The last one, which was aimed at making the company more market-driven, began in 1978. However, as AT & T President William Ellinghaus has said, "The biggest difference now is we have a deadline, and the change with divestiture is more critical. In 1978, we could do it in our own good time."

So far, it appears that the company has met its goal of making the divestiture "transparent" to customers.

There is, however, "a cauldron of activity," as one Bell executive puts it, beneath this smooth surface. There have been two guiding principles for divestiture—that people shortages and surpluses would be shared and people would follow their work. Even so, it appears that those in high demand—including regulatory, procurement, and financial specialists—have been able to pick from the multitude of Bell suitors. In fact, some industry analysts claim that AT & T Information Systems has skimmed off more than its fair share of the marketing talent.

Although most people being moved to new organizations will perform the same jobs at the same location as before, a major problem has been melding disparate management systems. AT & T Communications predecessor, the Long Lines Dept., set hiring and pay rules that managers transferred from BOCs and AT & T headquarters had to abide by, a policy that caused much resentment. Asserts Robert H. Gaynor, AT & T Communications designated vice president for Personnel, "The feeling was, 'We don't want to get involved in your bureaucratic procedures.'"

Political infighting escalated in the new or merged organizations as executives jockeyed for position. One middle manager retired early rather than face this problem in the Central Services Organization, which handles systems engineering and research jobs. "It is going to be much more of a dog-eat-dog environment," the former manager mourns. Rumors abound of battles between the managements of the 22 BOCs that have been merged into seven regionals, although NYNEX Corp.'s designated chief executive, Delbert C. Stanley, denies it.

One of the reasons American Information Technologies Corp. is remaining decentralized, asserts James J. Howard, its president-designate, is to avoid the difficult task of merging five top managements. Another reason is to counter the reorganization that occurred in the late 1970s and early 1980s, that robbed the operating companies of a great deal of autonomy. The potential problems of merging managements led Ameritech to employ a psychologist to attend the first meeting of its five state presidents.

These insights indicate how difficult it has been to alter Bell's culture. NYNEX's Stanley, for one, believes the new regionals will have to be careful that they don't "revert to where they were in marketing," a possibility because "the real thrust came from AT & T."

Although Archie J. McGill, the architect of AT & T's marketing program, left the company last spring, he wonders how deeply marketing is imbedded at AT & T. Says McGill, "their relative success in making that transition from a monopoly to a competitive enterprise, from a telephone company to an information-systems supplier will be determined by their ability to shift the culture. They haven't arrived yet."

Source: Business Week, Sept. 26, 1983, pp. 112–116.

Yet another example of the constraints imposed by corporate culture is the Johnson & Johnson Corporation. This company, which is well-known for its consumer products such as Band-Aids and Baby Shampoo, has now diversified into very different and highly sophisticated medical technology businesses. Practical Insights 2 illustrates the problems that the company's corporate culture poses to the successful implementation of its "new" corporate strategy.

Similar experiences to those of the Bell System and Johnson & Johnson have been repeated in many firms. Corporate culture cannot be ignored by strategists, because it will have a significant impact on the success or failure of organization strategy. Strategists must recognize that a major shift in the firm's organization

PRACTICAL INSIGHTS 2
Corporate Strategy and Corporate Culture at Johnson and Johnson

Although Johnson and Johnson (J & J) is best known to consumers for such brands as Band-Aids and Baby Shampoo, they have embarked on an accelerated move into far more sophisticated medical technologies. There are risks involved, since success will depend on whether J & J can manage businesses very different from those it has dominated. To achieve these goals, Chairman James Burke is making subtle, but important changes in management style and corporate culture that have long been central to the company's success.

In addition to its consumer brands, J & J has powerful and profitable franchises in hospital supplies and prescription drugs, which for years have flourished under a marketing-dominated, decentralized-management structure.

The people that run its 170 "companies" have autonomy unheard of in most corporations. Most divisions have their own boards, and there are only 750 people in corporate staff. Only one layer separates division presidents from the 14 member executive committee to whom they report.

J & J is an example of the virtues of decentralization. Its earnings growth during the last 10 years has averaged 13% annually. Fifty-five percent of 1983's $6 billion in sales came from products that are number-one in their markets. Its resuscitation of Tylenol pain reliever after the 1982 deaths of seven people who had taken cyanide-laced capsules, its repositioning of Baby Shampoo for the adult market, and its come-from-nowhere move to number-2 in infants' toys demonstrate its legendary marketing prowess.

While the core businesses are solidly profitable, their markets are maturing and have limited long-term growth potential. Moreover, scientific and technological advances will revolutionize health care. As a result, Burke states that the company must make a push into the technology field, because "it is absolutely critical to the future and to the present, without it, we would be heading toward being just another company."

Since 1980, J & J has acquired 25 companies, many in promising high-tech markets. J & J is now positioned in products ranging from intraocular lenses and surgical lasers to magnetic resonance scanners for diagnostic imaging.

Now it appears that the long-time dominance of marketing and sales executives and the insularity of J & J's divisions could seriously impede the company's ability to successfully push into new businesses and to react swiftly to changing competitive conditions in health care. Burke concedes that the company's success will require greater cooperation among corporate units...

...Many successful CEO's have found that changing a company's mix of businesses is a lot easier than changing managers' attitudes. William Ylvisaker successfully transformed Gould, Inc. into an electronics company only after replacing dozens of key managers. In Emerson Electric Co., the company's corporate culture that has always put emphasis on cost cutting and bottom line, threatens Charles Knight's ambitions in high-tech. Ruben Mettler has had some problems trying to get TRW, Inc's. divisions to share their expertise so the company can make maximum use of its considerable technological strengths.

Source: Business Week, May 14, 1984, pp. 130–138.

strategy (societal, corporate, business, or functional) will require a supportive corporate culture that may be radically different from the old corporate culture, and that steps must be taken to close the gaps between the current and the needed culture. If the cultural gap cannot be closed sufficiently and within a reasonable period of time, then there are two alternatives. One alternative is to modify the strategy to align it with the corporate culture. The other is to abandon the strategy and search for one that is compatible with the corporate culture.

Organization Structure and Strategy Implementation

An organization is a system of people, technology, resources, and information designed to achieve specific objectives. An effective organization facilitates the completion of tasks derived from the strategy chosen by the organization to achieve its objectives. An organization structure conveys how work is divided and assigned to people, and how the activities of people performing their duties are coordinated in the enterprise. Because the nature of the work is determined by the firm's organization strategy, the organization structure that coordinates the people performing the tasks must follow the firm's organization strategy. For example, a firm that has a simple business will use the functional structure; as it grows and gets into new businesses, it will adopt the multidimensional structure. If the firm chooses to diversify by acquisition into unrelated businesses, it will adopt the holding company or conglomerate structure. The more an organization structure is suited to the firm's current strategy, the easier the task of strategy implementation. "The evidence shows that for any strategy, the high performers are those who have achieved a fit between their strategy and their organization."[7] Practical Insights 3 describes the changes in the organization structure that the Hewlett–Packard Company used to implement its strategy of becoming more competitive with IBM and gaining a bigger share of the scientific and engineering markets.

PRACTICAL INSIGHTS 3

Strategy and Structure at Hewlett–Packard

Ninety-five of Hewlett–Packard Co.'s top managers retreated to Monterey, California for a week-long immersion in the gospel of marketing. This action was unprecedented in the 35-year history of the giant manufacturer of electronic instruments and computers, and it paralleled even more dramatic changes going on back at the company's Palo Alto (California) headquarters.

In July 1984, HP announced a structural reorganization designed to accelerate its transition from a company run by engineers for engineers to one with the marketing clout needed to reach a wider audience and compete with an increasingly aggressive IBM Corp. This action taken by HP will unify the marketing efforts of its two biggest businesses—computers and instruments. The new structure regroups HP's dozens of product divisions under sectors that are focused on markets rather than product lines. Two of these sectors will now sell computers—one concentrating on business customers, the other concentrating on marketing computers and instruments to scientific and manufacturing customers. HP is merging its two biggest businesses because industrial customers are increasingly buying computers linked with instruments for testing and process control.

Since 1973, HP's revenues have grown at a 21.5 percent compound annual rate. But the fast-growing computer markets require an all out effort by HP to grow even faster to keep up with industry leaders and maintain its market share.

John Young, president and CEO, feels that restructuring is a logical follow-up to a 1983 corporate reshuffling. However, industry experts feel that this is necessary because of the disappointments and glitches HP has experienced in the computer markets it has targeted for growth. A change was needed to develop a stronger profile among the company's nontechnical computer customers and to tighten its grip on scientific and engineering markets.

According to E. David Crockett, president of market researcher Dataquest, Inc. and a former HP executive, the transformation may be "the only chance HP has of continuing to grow and be successful in a market more dominated by IBM each day."

Even more important, this overhaul will result in the merging of the computer and instrument lines. Until now, each had its own sales force. But, increasingly, they were pursuing the same customers.

Industry analysts feel that these changes were overdue. They point to the disappointing performance of HP's 9000 series of computer work stations, which was intended to spearhead the company's drive into the fast-growing computer-aided engineering market. However, the 9000, "did not come out with the software it needs to do computer-aided design and engineering," says Galen Wampler, president of Prime Data, a California market researcher.

It is now quite possible that the organizational changes will make it easier for HP to sell the "integrated solutions" that customers demand, such as electronic networks that enable computers to swap information. These solutions take the form of complex combinations of computers and electronic instruments. As Wampler says, "Increasingly, computers used in computer-aided engineering are tied to test instruments, and HP is uniquely situated to bring these together."

Source: Business Week, July 30, 1984, pp. 111–112.

NCR was facing difficulties in developing new products. Realizing that the organization structure of the company was inhibiting its ability to innovate and adapt, management changed the organization structure from functional to divisional. Details of the reorganization at NCR are presented in Practical Insights 4.

PRACTICAL INSIGHTS 4

A New Organization to Match Strategy at NCR

NCR (formerly National Cash Register Co.) is a multinational electronics and computer-manufacturing corporation with 1983 revenues of $3.7 billion. During the 1920s, this 100-year-old company was *the* dominant concern in office equipment and cash registers. Thomas Watson, Sr., founder of IBM, was NCR's star salesman early in his career.

More recently, in 1979, NCR was a troubled company. Management had begun to wonder whether its very structure was inhibiting its ability to innovate and adapt. William

Buster, an NCR executive vice-president, recalls: "The first step was to realize that the product development process was not yielding products that hit the market as squarely as desired or as timely as the market required."

NCR commissioned the McKinsey and Co. consulting group to study the attributes of several highly successful companies. They looked at corporations such as Sperry, IBM, and Hewlett–Packard to see if what they had done might be applied to NCR. NCR used this study as a basis for the development of a plan to restructure itself. The path of a product from idea to implementation was analyzed and some obvious impediments were discovered. At NCR, the development, production, and marketing of a new product involved three separate divisions. This system "created opportunities for false starts and misinterpreting what the market really was . . . ," says Buster. "It took a long time to get a product through this entire process, and sometimes products get lost in translation." NCR then proceeded to break up its product-management organization and move the parts to units that would develop, manufacture, and market products. In other words, NCR had gone from a "functional" to a "divisional" organization.

NCR retained a functional organization in some divisions, while pushing the entrepreneurial aspects considerably further in others. This transformed NCR from a highly centralized operation into a series of stand-alone units. The different divisions now are able to make their own decisions about how they want to structure themselves with regard to such activities as marketing.

The change was difficult for many managers. They did not all adapt well to their new freedoms and responsibilities. During the 18-month transition period, many managers could not believe it was for real, continually double-checking decisions with senior management, while at the same time, many others thrived in the new environment. One of those who thrived was Donald Coleman, vice-president in charge of Data Entry Systems.

Coleman's division of 3,000 people is responsible for, among other things, NCR'S entry into the highly competitive personal-computer market. Within his division, he has repeated the business-unit concept, breaking the institution into the smallest feasible units. He set up five independent units ranging from 500 to a little over 1,000 people. Each unit has its own general manager, finance department, personnel department, research and development budget, and manufacturing division. Each unit is a fully operational, stand-alone business. In 1982, Coleman went a step further, breaking down these five units into relatively autonomous subunits, so that his division now consists of 13 elements, each of which has its own plan and balance sheet. The annual sales of the units range in size from $10 million to $100 million per year. To a certain extent, the individual units are allowed to set up their own internal incentives, financial and otherwise, to reward initiative.

Coleman has forced planning decisions down the line to the level closest to user needs. This has freed enormous innovative energy in his employees. "I've got a whole array of self-service terminals that we introduced [because of this system] for gas stations, hotels, ski lifts, and airlines," says Coleman.

Coleman mentions the self-service terminals for gas stations as a good example of this innovative energy. They devised a charge-card slot for gas stations, so that customers would be able to easily charge their purchases. An employee in one of the business units came up with the idea, which the unit developed into an installed product within five months (something that would have been impossible under the old system). The concept has since been extended to other markets with similar success. One result of all of this, and a good measure of success, is that 50 percent of the division's revenues in 1983 came from products it did not sell the year before.

Source: Eugene Linden, "Let a Thousand Flowers Bloom," *INC*, April 1984, pp. 66–70.

Human Resources and Strategy Implementation

Just as the culture and organization structure of a firm must be suitable for the implementation of its strategy, there also must be a proper "fit" between the nature of the strategy and the individual with the responsibility for its implementation. For instance, a manager who has been highly successful in managing a high-growth "star" business may not be the right person to manage it when it becomes a "cash cow." As stated by Lorange and Murphy,

> ... mature "cash cow" businesses and newly emerging businesses pose very different managerial challenges. In the former case, competitive success depends heavily upon highly efficient, cost-conscious management. A streamlined internal organization might significantly lower such a business's cost function and thereby provide it with critical competitive advantages. In the latter case, success in the competitive battle would probably hinge much more on the ability to "adapt" effectively to a rapidly changing environment by means of new or revised product and/or market alignments. Certain managers will excel at cost-conscious, efficient management in a relatively stable environment, while others will find their true metier in an entrepreneurial setting where the external parameters are constantly shifting. From a human resources point of view, therefore, the critical problem is the attainment of an optimal match between competitive strategic needs and the skills and strengths of individual managers.[8]

A useful framework for linking the strategic situation with the specific characteristics of ideal candidates, developed by Gerstein and Reisman,[9] is shown in Figures 5-3 and 5-4.

As we can see in Figure 5-3, Gerstein and Reisman first identified a set of seven "pure" strategic situations on the basis of discussions with operating executives, case examples, and the strategy literature. Second, the authors developed a set of characteristics associated with each strategic situation. Next, the major job thrusts

FIGURE 5-3
Characteristics of Various Strategic Situations

I.	Start-up	High Financial Risk
		Limited Management Team Cohesiveness
		No Organization, Systems, or Procedures in Place
		Endless Workload: Multiple Priorities
		Generally Insufficient Resources to Satisfy All Demands
		Limited Relationship with Suppliers, Customers, and Environment
II.	Turnaround	Time Pressure for "Results": Need for Rapid Situational Assessment and Decision Making
		Poor Results, but Business Is Worth Saving
		Weak Competitive Position
		Eroded Morale: Low-esteem/Cohesion
		Inadequate Systems: Possible Weak or Bureaucratic Organizational Infrastructure
		Strained and Eroded Relationships with Suppliers, Customers, and Environment
		Lack of Appropriate Leadership: Period of Neglect
		Limited Resources: Skills Shortages: Some Incompetent Personnel

Figure 5-3 (Continued)

III.	Extract Profit/Rationalize Existing Business	"Controlled" Financial Risk Unattractive Industry in Long Term: Possible Need to Invest Selectively, but Major New Investments Not Likely to Be Worthwhile Internal Organizational Stability Moderate-to-High Managerial/Technical Competence Adequate Systems and Administrative Infrastructure Acceptable to Excellent Relationships with Suppliers, Customers, and Environment
IV.	Dynamic Growth in Existing Business	Moderate-to-High Financial Risk New Markets, Products, Technology Multiple Demands and Conflicting Priorities Rapidly Expanding Organization in Certain Sectors Inadequate Managerial/Technical/Financial Resources to Meet All Demands Unequal Growth across Sectors of Organization Likely Shifting Power Bases as Growth Occurs Constant Dilemma between Doing Current Work and Building Support Systems for the Future
V.	Redeployment of Efforts in Existing Business	Low-Moderate, Short-Term Risk/High Long-Term Risk Resistance to Change: Likely Bureaucracy in Some Sections High Mismatch between Some Organization Skill Sets, Technology, People vs. Needs Created by Redefined Strategy Likelihood of Lack of Strategic Planning for Some Historical Period—Highly Operational Orientation to Executive Team
VI.	Liquidation/Divestiture of Poorly Performing Business	Weak Competitive Position, Unattractive Industry, or Both Likely Continuance of Poor Returns Possible Morale Problems and Skills Shortages Little Opportunity for Turnaround or Redeployment because of Unsatisfactory "Payback" Need to Cut Losses and Make Tough Decisions
VII.	New Acquisitions	Acquisitions may be classified into one of the above situations. In addition, the following conditions characterize a recent acquisition situation: Pressure on New Management to "Prove Themselves" Existing Management Ambivalent Defensive about Change Fundamental Need to Integrate Acquired Company with Parent at Some Levels

Source: Reprinted from "Strategic Selection: Matching Executives to Business Conditions," Marc Gerstein and Heather Reisman, *Sloan Management Review*, Vol. 24, No. 2, Winter 1983, p. 36, by permission of the publisher. Copyright © 1983 by the Sloan Management Review Association. All rights reserved.

and specific characteristics of ideal candidates corresponding to each of the seven strategic situations were formulated (Figure 5-4). Figures 5-3 and 5-4 show that because of the differences in the characteristics of each strategic situation, the major job thrusts of each situation are different as well. Consequently, the specific characteristics of ideal candidates also differ from one strategic situation to another. A

FIGURE 5-4
General Management Requirements of Various Strategic Situations

Situation	Major Job Thrusts	Specific Characteristics of Ideal Candidates
I. Start-up	Creating Vision of Business Establishing Core Technical and Marketing Expertise Building Management Team	Vision of Finished Business Hands-on Orientation: A "doer" In-depth Knowledge in Critical Technical Areas Organizing Ability Staffing Skills Team-Building Capabilities High-Energy Level and Stamina Personal Magnetism: Charisma Broad Knowledge of All Key Functions
II. Turnaround	Rapid, Accurate Problem Diagnosis Fixing Short-Term and ultimately Long-Term Problems	"Take Charge" Orientation: Strong Leader Strong Analytical and Diagnostic Skills, especially Financial Excellent Business Strategist High-Energy Level Risk Taker Handles Pressure Well Good Crisis Management Skills Good Negotiator
III. Extract Profit/Rationalize Existing Business	Efficiency Stability Succession Sensing Signs of Change	Technically Knowledgeable: "Knows the Business" Sensitive to Changes: "Ear-to-the-Ground" Anticipates Problems: "Problem Finder" Strong Administrative Skills Oriented to "Systems" Strong "Relationship Orientation" Recognizes Need for Management Succession and Development Oriented to Getting Out the Most: Efficiency; Not Growth
IV. Dynamic Growth in Existing Business	Increasing Market Share in Key Sectors Managing Rapid Change Building Long-Term Health toward Clear Vision of the Future	Excellent Strategic and Financial Planning Skills Clear Vision of the Future Ability to Balance Priorities, e.g., Stability vs. Growth Organizational and Team-Building Skills Good Crisis Management Skills Moderate–High Risk Taker High-Energy Level Excellent Staffing Skills

Figure 5-4 (*Continued*)

V.	Redeployment of Efforts in Existing Business	Establishing Effectiveness in Limited Business Sphere Managing Change Supporting the "Dispossessed"	Good Politician/Manager of Change Highly Persuasive: High "Interpersonal Influence" Moderate Risk Taker Excellent "Systems Thinker": Understands How Complex Systems Work Good Organizing and Executive Staffing Skills
VI.	Liquidation/Divestiture of Poorly Performing Business	Cutting Losses Making Tough Decisions Making Best Deal	"Callousness": Tough-Minded, Determined—Willing to Be the Bad Guy Highly Analytical re: Costs/Benefits—Does Not Easily Accept Current Ways of Doing Things Risk Taker Low-Glory Seeking: Willing to Do Dirty Jobs—Does Not Want Glamour Wants to Be Respected, Not Necessarily Liked
VII.	New Acquisitions	Integration Establishing Sources Information and Control	Analytical Ability Relationship Building Skills Interpersonal Influence Good Communication Skills Personal Magnetism—Some Basis to Establish "Instant Credibility"

Source: Reprinted from "Strategic Selection: Matching Executives to Business Conditions," Marc Gerstein and Heather Reisman, *Sloan Management Review*, Vol. 24, No. 2, Winter 1983, p. 37, by permission of the publisher. Copyright © 1983 by the Sloan Management Review Association. All rights reserved.

manager who may have the characteristics that make him or her the ideal candidate to manage a business at the start-up phase may be unsuited to manage a business in the turnaround phase, which requires a different set of individual characteristics. Similarly, a manager who has experience in one type of business may have developed and internalized the "culture" of that business, making that person unsuitable for management of another type of business with a substantially different "culture." For example, managers who have been successful in a marketing-oriented business may not be comfortable and equally adept at running a high-technology-oriented business, a point illustrated by the case of Johnson & Johnson:

> Learning to manage new businesses is also a major task, as evidenced by the management problems that have plagued the push into medical equipment, where losses have been heavy . . . Johnson and Johnson is discovering that developing and marketing high-tech equipment requires markedly different management skills than selling the

products that generated its rapid growth . . . Because its strength is in making and marketing consumer products, some competitors and Johnson and Johnson alumni doubt that the company can become a leader in medical equipment. What pill people have done well in hardware, and what hardware people have done well in pills?"

asks GE's chairman, John F. Welsh, Jr.[10]

The hiring of James F. McDonald as president of Gould Inc. in 1984 illustrates a change in a company's strategic direction and the resulting necessity of putting a person who can manage the company effectively under the new circumstances in the president's chair. Within three years, William T. Ylvisaker, the chairman of Gould, turned what was an old-line manufacturing company that made bearings, pistons, electrical equipment, and batteries into a bona-fide force in high technology. In 1983, electronics accounted for 75 percent of Gould's $1.7 billion in sales and all of its $79.2 million in earnings, up from 25 percent of sales and 33 percent of earnings in 1979. The company bought nine high-tech companies ranging from a manufacturer of integrated circuits to a minicomputer maker. Realizing that the skills needed to coordinate and manage an electronics enterprise may be quite different from those required to run an auto-parts operation—skills that the top-management executives at the company did not have—at the risk of losing some of his top-management personnel, Chairman Ylvisaker hired James F. McDonald away from IBM as the president of the company. McDonald held key positions in vital businesses ranging from office automation to robotics during his 21 years at IBM, but more important to Ylvisaker, during the previous four years, McDonald had been the chief of IBM's new manufacturing-systems products group—which is an IBM independent business unit that operates free of conventional corporate controls until its products are established in the market. Ylvisaker hopes that McDonald can generate in Gould an entrepreneurial drive similar to IBM's manufacturing-systems products group, and he believes that McDonald has the right background to run the "new" Gould Inc.[11]

According to Richard J. Herman–Taylor, Vice President of Boston Consulting Group, the link between human resources planning and organization strategy is not explicitly recognized by most companies when they consider significant changes in strategy.[12] This may be because it is difficult to appraise an individual's characteristics, managerial orientation, and style, and then determine whether that person matches the type needed for a specific job. Moreover, if someone from the outside is hired as a manager, it may be demoralizing to current managers. Small companies with few divisions and products might find it impossible to find suitable and challenging positions elsewhere in the organization for otherwise competent managers who were unlucky enough to be in a business or division whose strategy has changed because of a corporate-level decision. However, "several companies are trying hard to formalize programs that will at least keep them heading in the direction of making perfect managerial meshes."[13] Practical Insights 5 presents the efforts of companies such as Chase Manhattan Bank, Heublein, Corning Glass, Texas Instruments, and General Electric to bring about a fit between the managerial orientation and style and the major thrusts of their strategies.

PRACTICAL INSIGHTS 5

WANTED: A Manager to Fit each Strategy

Chase Manhattan Bank.

When the trust manager retired, corporate management decided to focus on an aggressive growth strategy for the department, as opposed to its previously stable condition. Chase hired a man who had been with IBM previously, and had a ". . . strong IBM customer marketing orientation." In a similar vein, when Chase changed its retail banking operation from a low-margin operation to a more expansionary enterprise offering broader consumer financial services, they hired an executive with strong entrepreneurial skills. The former head of retail banking, who was viewed as a strong cost-cutter, is now successfully whipping some of Chase's European operations into better financial shape.

Heublein's United Vintners, Inc.

United Vintners split its wine operations in two in 1977, forming a premium wine division that stresses quality over volume and a standard division that emphasizes aggressive pricing and efficient volume production. A wine professional, Robert Furek, was chosen to run the premium wine business. A former personal products manager for Gillette Co. was chosen as general manager of the Standard Wine Division. The sales staff was reorganized, so that according to a company representative, "People in our premium wine company tend to have more wine background, while those in our standard wine company come out of consumer products and food companies."

Corning Glass Co.

Fast growth was projected for Corning's optical fibers business over the next decade, so the head of the company's television tube business was shifted to direct the new venture. The manager had shown entrepreneural flair and seemed to fit perfectly into the optical fiber business, which ". . . is clearly an entrepreneural thing," according to Richard Shafer, Corning's director of management and professional personnel.

Later that year, ironically, Corning concluded that the electronics market was starting to expand again and that a growth-oriented manager was needed. In this case, a manufacturing specialist who had "shown a great deal of flair in working with customers" was hired to run the division. According to Shafer, "it looks like he's turning it around."

The TI Story.

"As a product moves through different phases of its life-cycle, different kinds of management skills become dominant," says Charles H. Phipps, manager of strategic planning at Texas Instruments. Although TI takes great pains to assess its managers in terms of personal orientation, it failed to capitalize on its early lead in integrated circuits largely because it misjudged the style needed to manage the product line. One of TI's foremost researchers and a pioneer in integrated circuit technology, Jack Kilby, was labeled a brilliant scientist, but a weak manager. In 1959, TI began its IC development program and placed an administrator in charge, with Kilby subordinate to him. TI ignored Kilby's "strong desire to lead his brain child into the marketplace."

In 1961, TI let Kilby manage the IC department. Not surprisingly, Kilby stressed innovation and research at the expense of financial controls. He was eventually eased out and replaced by managers who provided tighter cost controls.

The new management provided tighter controls, but did not provide the technical push needed to get the IC operation, which was still in the development phase, off to a fast commercial start. In 1967, J. Fred Bucy became head of TI's semi conductor operations and replaced most of the IC management with technically oriented people. As a result, TI went on to pioneer brilliantly in bipolar integrated circuits and became a competent follower in the newer metal-oxide semiconductor technology.

General Electric.
At GE, strategic objectives for the company's wide-ranging products are defined as "grow," "defend," and "harvest," depending on the product life-cycle. Currently, its general managers are being classified by personal style or orientation as "growers," "caretakers," and tongue-in-cheek as "undertakers," to match managerial type with the product's status. Says one industry analyst: "I hear they have a shortage of growers, but they are making great efforts to remove the undertaker types who are heading up growth businesses."

Looking at the situation at GE's Lighting Business Group in Cleveland tends to support that observation. According to Harry Rein, manager for strategic planning, "the lighting business is mainly mature, but we just designated international operations as a growth area in our five-year forecast." Therefore, they have decided to move in a manager from GE's motor division who had an industrial rather than lighting background, but who seemed to show an entrepreneurial flair.

Corning's Match-Ups.
Corning Glass may have the most formal integration of personal managerial styles and strategic objectives. Each of the company's top 100 managers are assessed for qualities such as entrepreneurial flair by a personnel director. Eleven other personnel development managers gather skills data for about 300 lower echelon managers. All this is done, ". . . because we want to know what goes into success," says Richard Shafer.

It is easier for small companies to assess the types of managers employed by larger competitors and emulate their approach to staffing. In 1974, Kenneth Fisher left Honeywell, Inc. to become president of Prime Computer Inc., a small minicomputer maker with sales of $6.5 million, operating in the red. Fisher immediately began hiring new managers from companies like his former employer.

Fisher explains: "We wanted people from big companies that had already been through what we were going through; we assumed that we were going to succeed extraordinarily, and we needed men who had been through all the plateaus before." Since then, Fisher has increased the managerial staff from 15 to 260 people, and sales are up to $153 million, net income up to $17 million.

Fisher feels that the recruitment of executives with the sophistication gained at giant companies has enabled Prime to automate its process for laying out printed circuit boards much earlier than competitors of the same size. The computerization of factory scheduling, material control, and other functions have let the company operate with a much smaller administrative staff than otherwise would have been required. Fisher claims that Prime has revenues of about $70,000 per employee compared with an average in the industry of about $35,000.

In spite of such successful results from strategic manpower planning, many companies remain uninterested in the concept. For instance, Tenneco, Inc. still prefers versatile, jack-of-all-trades managers. Many behavioral scientists shudder at such views, but they hope that 10 years from now fewer executives will feel this way.

Source: Business Week, February 25, 1980, pp. 166–173.

Organization Rewards and Strategy Implementation

Financial and nonfinancial rewards over and above an executive's salary package are used in organizations to elicit desired behavior from members of the organization. Most large companies rely on financial rewards—principally in the form of bonuses and stock options—to encourage managers to achieve organization objectives. As top management attempts to influence the behavior of managers through incentives, the important question becomes how to make the financial incentives consistent with the organization strategy and how to motivate managers to implement the desired strategy aimed at predetermined objectives.

We will be mainly concerned with offering a few guidelines for designing an incentive compensation system for top-management executives, a group that includes corporate executives and heads of divisions in a multidivisional company, or senior managers and heads of functional departments—marketing, production, finance, R & D, and so on—in a functionally organized single-business firm. These are the executives directly responsible for implementing the organization strategy.

Before an effective compensation system can be designed—one that motivates managers to implement the required strategies—top management must come to grips with four main generic organization strategy issues:[14] (1) short run vs. long run, (2) risk aversion vs. risk taking, (3) interdivisional relationships, and (4) company–division relationships. We will examine each strategic issue briefly.

Generic Organization Strategy Issues

Short run vs. long run. Is corporate management interested in maximizing profits and obtaining the desired results in a short period of time, or is it willing to wait a long period for the results?

Risk aversion vs. risk taking. Does corporate management want executives to take prudent risks, or is it interested in minimizing risks? Does corporate management encourage entrepreneurial behavior by executives or does it want them to be "caretakers" of business?

Interdivisional relationships. Which is more important to corporate management—substantial joint effort and cooperation between divisions or decentralization and autonomy for the divisions with independent operations of each other?

Company–division relationships. Does corporate management play the principal role of resource allocator to the divisions? Does it consider each business at the divisional level to be a portfolio investment and, therefore, of primary interest only because of its financial return? Or does corporate management play a more active role in the management of each business or division?

The answer given by top-management executives to these four generic organization strategy issues will determine the characteristics of the incentive compensation program. Once these potential or existing strategic issues have been resolved in the context of the company's objectives and strategy, the principal parameters will have been established for answering the difficult questions pertaining to six aspects of incentive compensation: financial instruments, performance measures, degree of discretion to corporate management in allocating rewards, size and frequency of incentive payments, degree of uniformity in performance measures and rewards among levels of corporate management and divisions, and the method of funding the incentive-bonus pool.[15]

We will now examine the six key aspects of incentive compensation. In looking at the salient features of each, we will assume that there exists an equitable and competitive salary structure in the organization.

Key Aspects of Incentive Compensation Program

Financial Instruments. A variety of financial instruments are available such as cash, deferred cash, company stock, and deferred company stock. Current awards like annual bonuses encourage short-term performance, whereas deferred awards deemphasize annual results.

Performance Measures. This is one of the most difficult aspects of planning an executive compensation program. There are a wide variety of methods by which executive performance can be measured: qualitative as well as quantitative measures. Product quality, image, customer service quality, employee morale, and quality of personnel are examples of qualitative measures. Examples of quantitative measures are profits, market share, cash flow, return on equity, and return on assets. Also at issue is the question of how some measures such as profits are applied, that is, should total corporate profits, divisional profits, or some combination of the two be used? The same question could be asked in regard to return on assets. Qualitative measures generally emphasize long-run considerations and send the message that the total performance will be evaluated for purposes of bonus awards. Also, bonuses based upon total corporate profits encourage interdivisional cooperation and minimize any exaggerated divisional self-interest.

Corporate Management Discretion. At issue is whether the chief executive officer, the compensation committee, and the board of directors should play a significant role in making awards or whether awards should be made on the basis of some fixed formula. If corporate management wishes to promote interdivisional cooperation and encourages a balance between the short-run and long-run points of view, then a fixed-formula-based bonus plan is not suitable. Instead, corporate management might use several measures in combination with their own evaluation of performance to make incentive awards.

Size and Frequency of Awards. The size of the awards should be commensurate with the degree of risks assumed by the executives. The higher the risk that corporate management wants executives to take given the company's situation, the higher should be the rewards. As for frequency of awards, the more frequently bonuses are given, the greater is the likelihood that executives will focus on short-term performance.

Degree of Uniformity. Whether there should be uniformity in performance measures and rewards among levels of top management and divisions depends on what corporate management wants to achieve. If corporate management is deeply involved in supervising and advising divisions, then the incentive program of each level should be structured similarly. However, if corporate management treats divisions as merely portfolios of businesses and has adopted a hands-off approach to managing the divisions (except for supervising resource generation and allocation among them), then the basis for corporate management's rewards should be different than the divisions. When divisions generate outstanding results, division heads should receive bigger bonuses than those of corporate-level executives because they shoulder much greater operating risks and responsibilities.

Funding of Bonus Pools. The question that management faces with the funding of the bonus pool is this: Should the bonus pool be funded from total company profits or should each division have its own bonus pool based on the division's profit? The choice between these two alternatives is governed by the measures of performance used to allocate bonuses. Funding the bonus pool from total company profits is logical when company-wide measures are the basis for allocating rewards; when divisional performance is the criterion for allocating rewards, divisional profits ought to be the source of divisional pools. Another consideration in the issue of company vs. divisional bonus pools has to do with corporate headquarters control over divisions, which is greater when bonus pools are funded exclusively from corporate profits.

The relationship between the four main generic organization strategy issues and the six key aspects of an incentive compensation program are presented in Figure 5-5, developed by Malcolm S. Salter.

Matching Rewards to Corporate Strategy

The material presented above should give us a better understanding of the issues, problems, and factors that must be considered in designing an executive incentive compensation program. Let us see how a company could use rewards for motivating executives to implement the desired strategy.

The desired strategy is one that, if implemented effectively, should enable the organization to achieve its objectives. Every business is in a specific situation at a given point in time. Some businesses may be in a growth phase, whereas others may be in the stability or declining phase. The fundamental emphasis or thrust of a business is determined by its corporate strategy; therefore the objectives of a business with growth strategy would be necessarily different from those businesses with stability or retrenchment as strategies. It follows logically that the business strategies of various businesses at different stages also should be different because of the differences in their respective objectives.

Figure 5-6 illustrates the relationship among the business situation, major business thrusts, and business objectives. We can see in Figure 5-6 that the business objectives are quite different, depending on the situation and major thrust of each business.

The corporate strategy of a company has a greater chance of fulfillment when each division's rewards are based on the degree to which divisional objectives are achieved. Under such a scheme, a division whose business has been designated as a "cash cow" (stability) by the corporate strategy and, therefore does not have increasing market share as an objective, will not strive to implement a business strategy that increases its market share because increasing market share is an objective of a "star" division. Hence, the chances of implementing the "correct" business strategies of divisions should be enhanced, because division heads know the basis for the incentive rewards, and are aware that the objectives that their respective divisions are being asked to achieve are consistent with the stages that

FIGURE 5-5
Key Aspects of Incentive Compensation

Policy Issues	Financial Instruments	Performance Measures	Degree of Discretion in Allocating Bonus Awards	Size and Frequency of Awards	Degree of Uniformity	Funding
Short run vs. long run	Mix of current bonus awards and stock options should reflect the relevant time horizon for policy level executives Deferred instruments are weak reinforcers of short-term performance	Mix of quantitative measures of performance and more qualitative measures should reflect the relevant time horizon for executives Qualitative measures usually reflect long-term considerations more effectively than quantitative measures	Nondiscretionary, formula-based bonuses tend to encourage a short-run point of view	Frequent bonus awards encourage concentration on short-term performance		
Risk aversion vs. risk taking	Current bonus awards, in cash or stock, can reinforce risk-taking behavior	Qualitative measures of performance can reinforce initiative by assuring executives that total performance will be evaluated for purposes of bonus awards	Completely discretionary, highly personalized bonuses do not clarify the "rules of the game" and as a result can discourage risk taking behavior	The size of both salary and incentive awards should be commensurate with the business and personal risks involved		
Interdivisional relationships		Bonus pools can be based on divisional performance, total corporate performance, or some mix of the two. Each arrangement sends different signals in terms of interdivisional cooperation	Nondiscretionary formula-based bonuses for division managers are most practical in companies where little cooperation among divisions is required Discretionary bonuses are practical when top management wants to encourage cooperation among divisions		Uniformity among divisions in the design of measurement and reward systems facilitates interdivisional cooperation	The choice between divisional and corporate bonus pools should reflect the reasoning used in selecting appropriate performance measures
Company–division relationships	Stock options can effectively link the interests of division personnel to the interests of the corporation	Use of objective measures of performance for division managers is more meaningful where the primary role of headquarters is to allocate capital than it is in instances where the head office plays an important role in "managing the business" of the divisions	Nondiscretionary formula-based bonuses are most practical in companies where headquarters does not interfere in management of the profit centers Discretionary bonuses are most useful when top management wants to exert a direct influence on decisions in the divisions		Uniformity among divisions in the design of measurement and reward systems facilitates the resource allocation process at the corporate level With respect to uniformity among levels of management, the more decentralized the organization, the more reason there is to differentiate the reward systems of each group	Bonus pools funded solely from divisional profits tend to limit the ability of corporate headquarters to use financial incentives as an instrument of control Bonus pools funded solely from corporate profits tend to increase the influence of headquarters over the divisions and other profit centers

Source: Reprinted by permission of the *Harvard Business Review.* An exhibit from "Tailor Incentive Compensation to Strategy," by Malcolm S. Salter, *Harvard Business Review,* March–April, 1973, pp. 100–101. Copyright © 1973 by the President and Fellows of Harvard College. All rights reserved.

FIGURE 5-6
Relationships Between Business Situations, Major Business Thrusts, and Business Objectives

Business	Major Business Thrust	Business Objectives
Growth (Star)	Increase market share	Increase market share from 20 to 35 percent in next three years
	Return on assets	Increase on assets to 15 percent within the next two years
Stability (Cash Cow)	Cash flow	Provide funds for reinvestment in growth businesses
		Increase cash flow by 20 percent in next three years
	Debt capacity	Increase debt capacity by 15 percent in next two years
	Return on assets	Maximize return on existing assets
		Earn a minimum of 10 percent on existing assets
	Market share	Maintain existing market share, allow no slippage
Retrenchment (Dogs)	Expenses	Reduce marketing expenditures by 20 percent
		Reduce plant and equipment expenditures by 40 percent
		Stop R & D expenditures
	Find a "niche"	Prune the number of products in product line
		Reposition product line in a "niche" that is defensible against competitive inroads

their businesses are in. It is therefore the responsibility of top management to specify the objectives of each business and reward divisions for fulfillment of divisional objectives. Such conditions are an essential prerequisite for the effective implementation of organization strategy.

Many companies now are tying rewards to the objectives and strategies they want their executives to pursue. In the Union Carbide Corporation, managers in areas such as basic chemicals are rewarded for providing cash rather than growth, although managers of operations targeted for expansion are judged on sales and profit growth.[16] Practical Insights 6 describes the efforts made by companies such as Emhart Corporation, Sears, Roebuck, and Company, Combustion Engineering Inc., and the Lummus Group Inc., to link rewards to strategic objectives.

PRACTICAL INSIGHTS 6

Tying Rewards to Strategic Objectives

Taking a long-term view of its business recently enabled Emhart Corp. to more objectively evaluate short-term opportunities. The decision was whether or not to expand and modernize an already profitable industrial hardware plant. In the past, Emhart's executives might have turned down the proposal, because their bonuses were based mainly on the company's profit growth. Expansion would sacrifice short-term earnings and, therefore, reduce their bonuses. But Emhart had recently changed its executive compensation plan, tying bonuses to long-term stock price. As a result, Emhart executives approved the expansion, which they saw as adding value to their interests in the long run.

Similar positive results can be seen at Sears, Roebuck, and Co., where a "shareholder-value" plan motivated top executives to make such difficult moves as the recent divestiture of retail operations in Venezuela and other countries. The Sears board's belief that chairman Edward A. Brennan could quickly turn around the company's ailing merchandise group prompted them to add incentives to his compensation package that rewarded a rapid increase in his business' real return on equity. The merchandise group's health has improved considerably, thanks to the foreign divestitures and other moves, confirming Sears' belief that business plans are best made with an eye on a return on equity target.

Mounting evidence that earnings per share have very little long-term impact on a company's stock prices has caused companies to search for measures of performance that do. A growing number of companies, including Sears Roebuck, Emhart, Borden, and Combustion Engineering, have been daring enough to experiment with compensation plans that link executive pay to performance measures that experts believe increase shareholder value by increasing stock prices and dividends. Although the experts agree that shareholder value cannot be measured by changes in earnings per share, they are still arguing over which measure is best—ranging from discounted cash flows to deflated return on equity.

Experience has shown that linking managers' pay to strategic goals and financial measures more meaningful than earnings per share has motivated them to change the way they operate their businesses. CEOs who have implemented pay-for-performance plans are discovering that they can be a powerful management tool.

Combustion Engineering, Inc. has instituted shareholder-value plans for nearly 600 top managers. Top executives at this engineering, construction, and oil-field equipment manufacturer earn an annual bonus, in addition to a long-term stock option plan if the company earns an amount ranging between its cost of capital and return on equity. Bonuses for many operations managers are tied to the deflated return on equity invested in their individual units rather than on sales growth.

"The system," says a Combustion Engineering executive, "has spurred a healthy examination of each and every business. Top management has to sit down and analyze what each unit's contribution is to real return on equity and then think about ways that it can be maintained or improved. And that's resulted in changes in how division heads are running their business."

These positive results have shown up in the oil-field equipment division, for example. A division manager's proposal to merge the distribution systems of four product lines will reduce the division's asset base while sacrificing little in sales or profits. Such a decision would probably not have been made if the managers involved were being compensated solely on sales growth.

Several obstacles had to be overcome before CE could implement its shareholder-value plan. President Charles E. Hugel realized that division general managers had been ignoring the company's strategic plans and were operating merely to meet budget targets instead. Strategic planning and budgeting departments, which had been operating at cross purposes, had to learn to work together.

Top management, group heads, strategic planners, and the budget department now cooperate to evaluate the prospects for each of CE's four main operating divisions and set individual targets for real rates of return on capital invested by each unit. With these targets in mind top management attempts to tailor each division manager's compensation to his unit's financial and strategic goals.

The additional incentive this method provides can be seen comparing targets set for Lummus Group, Inc. and CE's oil-field equipment business. Lummus, CE's engineering and construction arm, has a small capital base and shows unusually large positive spreads. Financial objectives for it were a high rate of return and increased cash flow. A lower rate of return-on-equity was set for the less profitable oil-field equipment business with a stated goal of improving slightly on a marginal real rate of return. This realistic goal gives this division's managers a chance for an annual bonus by meeting the financial goal and the strategic objective of an increased penetration of a few key foreign markets. Under the old system, division managers in this slow-growth segment would not receive an annual bonus because of an inability to generate sufficient sales or stimulate earnings growth. "People who were driven strictly by profit-and-loss statements are now driven by real returns and strategic goals," boasts an executive.

Major changes in the way people are measured and paid cannot be made overnight, despite the apparent success of pay-for-performance plans at companies such as CE, Sears, and Emhart. Many chief executives who have been raised on the importance of earnings per share and other short-term measures are reluctant to adopt something new, and fear that if new compensation systems are enacted too quickly they could backfire.

"A key to any plan is that it can be communicated effectively through the ranks, and that can take time," says Peter T. Chingos, a compensation expert at Peat, Marwick, Mitchell, and Co. At Libby–Owens–Ford Co., the corporate office is beginning to include the contribution to shareholder value that each division makes in its monthly management reports. The goal, says vice president Howard Selland, "is to get people comfortable with the concept." But Libby–Owens–Ford won't actually determine manager's pay on this contribution for several years. People need to understand change and the reasons for it, before they can be asked to accept it.

Source: Business Week, April 2, 1984, pp. 99–100.

CONTROL OF ORGANIZATION STRATEGY

In the rest of this chapter, we will focus our attention on the last phase of the strategic management process—the control of organization strategy, henceforth referred to as strategic control (see Figure 5-7).

The control process is concerned with determining what the actual performance is and ensuring that it is consistent with expected performance. There are five basic steps in the control process:

1. Establish the standards of performance.
2. Measure and evaluate actual performance against established performance standards.
3. Diagnose the reasons for deviations (if any) between the actual performance and performance standards.
4. Take corrective action to match performance standards and actual performance.
5. Continue to get feedback from internal and external environment and monitor actual performance.

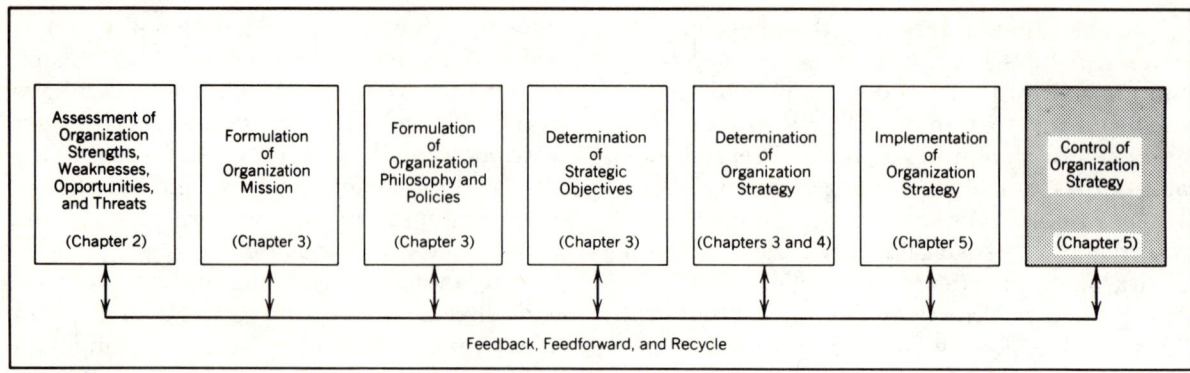

FIGURE 5-7
A Model of the Strategic Management Process

Framework for Strategic Control

A framework for strategic control that incorporates the basic control steps is presented in Figure 5-8.

Let us look at the essential features of the various elements of the strategic control framework. Conceptually, strategic control begins when managers obtain information about the results of the current strategy as it is being implemented. The results are compared with the strategic objectives of the firm.

At the very least, the business should compare favorably with other competing firms in the industry. The following factors can be used to make this evaluation:

- Net profit
- Market share
- Return on equity
- Return on sales

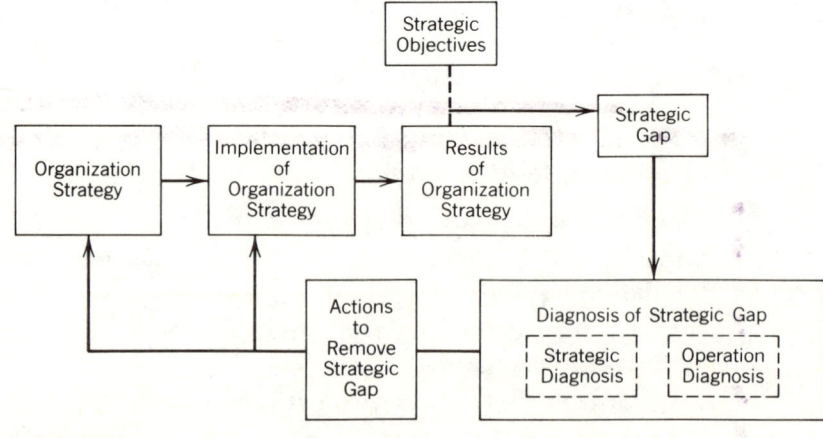

FIGURE 5-8
Framework for Strategic Control

- Stock price
- Sales growth
- Asset growth

A significant "strategic gap" between the performance of the total firm and the results expected by top management indicates that serious problems exist; if they are not removed, they will cause a deterioration of the firm's financial health and long-term survival prospects. Diagnosis of the causes of the strategic gap is conducted at two levels: strategic and operational. *Strategic diagnosis* is concerned with evaluation of the current organization strategy and determination of whether a change in the firm's strategy is required. *Operational diagnosis* focuses on the evaluation of how effectively the current strategy is being implemented and on changes in implementation methods and processes that must be made to improve the current operations of the firm. Diagnosis of the causes of the strategic gap leads to executive action to close the strategic gap, which may include formulating a new strategy (corporate, business, or functional) and/or changing the systems and methods used to implement the organization strategy.

Strategic Diagnosis

Strategic diagnosis involves going back to the first phase in the strategic management process—assessment of organization strengths, weaknesses, opportunities, and threats (SWOT) (Figure 5-7)—and reexamining the premises and assumptions that were originally used in formulating the organization strategy. In a single-business company, this process occurs at the corporate level with the involvement of the board of directors, the chief executive officer, and senior functional managers. In a diversified company with related businesses, the SWOT analysis takes place with the participation of corporate executives and heads of relevant divisional strategic business units (SBUs). In a conglomerate, the process occurs at the divisional SBU level. Often in a conglomerate the corporate-level executives bring in major outside consulting firms to evaluate the strategic problems of some of the businesses in the conglomerate family, because corporate management cannot effectively evaluate the performance of every business in the company's diverse business portfolio.

Questions such as the following may be asked in the strategic diagnosis of each business:

- Have changes occurred in the external environment that have negatively affected the success of the current strategy, for example, demographic factors, values and attitudes of society, technological developments in industry, technological developments in substitute industries, availability of credit, interest rates, currency exchange rates, or governmental controls (or decontrols)?
- Have changes occurred in the strategies of major competitors, buyers, or suppliers?
- Have changes occurred in the nature of the industry: exit barriers, entry barriers, capacity, product differentiation, substitute products, buyer characteristics, or power of key suppliers?

- Have new opportunities and/or threats emerged as a result of changes in the external environment, competitor strategies, or industry?
- Have the key success factors for the industry changed?
- Is the current strategy consistent with the changes that have occurred in the external environment, competitor strategies, or industry?

This is by no means an exhaustive list of all the questions that can be asked to determine the causes of the strategic gap facing the company. Answers to diagnostic questions may result in a change in the company's strategy and the adoption of a strategy more consistent with the situation. However, more dramatic changes in the company's total posture may result as well. Corporate strategists may come to the conclusion that the existing business is not unattractive anymore and not worth the investment of resources in it—in which case the company's mission would change and corporate management would guide the investment of the company's resources into another business. Naturally this would cause the strategic objectives and organizational strategy to change as well.

Operational Diagnosis

Operational diagnosis is concerned with evaluating the results of the implementation of current strategy. It focuses on assessing the current performance of the firm and determining the reasons for the strategic gap. The first step in operational diagnosis is to determine in which areas operating performance is below acceptable levels and need improvement. The most commonly used measures of firm performance are analyses of the income and balance-sheet statements using ratio analysis and cash-flow analysis. Analysis of financial statements points out areas in which changes must be implemented and what the nature of such changes should be in order to restore the financial health of the company. (Analysis of financial statements will be covered at length in the Appendix.)

The firm's strategic gap may be due to problems in functional areas like production, marketing, research and development, personnel, and so on. It also may be due to faulty management practices in planning, organizing, leadership, motivational systems, communications and information systems, and control systems.

Operational diagnosis can result in changes in the methods adopted to implement the current business strategy—changes in the functional strategies (production, marketing, finance) and/or changes in the management practices and techniques implemented to achieve the current business strategy.

The strategic control framework (Figure 5-8) is dynamic by nature. It is equally applicable to small and large firms and firms in different industries.

SUMMARY

Implementation of organization strategy and control of organization strategy are the last two steps in the strategic management process. Implementation of the organization strategy involves the application of the entire management process and all the management functions: planning, organizing, staffing, leadership, and control. Four factors are considered critical to effective implementation of organization strategy. Effective implementation of organization strategy will not take place unless there is consistency between the strategy and each of these factors: corporate culture, organization structure, human resources, and organization rewards.

Corporate culture is the system of norms, attitudes, values, beliefs, and customs that governs the behavior of people in an organization. It is the sum total of how people in an organization think and act as members of the organization. The corporate culture can be a major strength if it is consistent with the organization strategy. Difficulties with the implementation of organization strategy will be experienced when the strategy is at odds with the corporate culture.

An organization structure shows how work has been divided and assigned to people and how the activities of people performing their duties are coordinated in the enterprise. The firm's organization strategy determines the nature of the work, and therefore the organization structure that coordinates the people performing the tasks must follow the firm's organization strategy. The greater the consistency is between the current organization strategy and the organization structure in place, the easier will be the task of strategy implementation.

There also must exist a proper fit between the nature of the strategy to be implemented and the characteristics of the manager responsible for its implementation. It is suggested that a manager who may have the ideal individual characteristics to manage a business in the "star" category may not be the right person to run a "cash cow" or a "dog" business. The specific business situation dictates the particular characteristics of managers most suitable to manage the business.

The nature of the rewards system can have a significant impact on the effective implementation of strategy. Rewards should be tied to the achievement of business objectives. The objectives of a "star" business will be different from those of a "dog" business, and therefore the results expected of a "star" should be different from those of a "dog" business. Rewards should be given for accomplishing the desired results dictated by the corporate strategy.

Conceptually, the control of organization strategy or strategic control begins when the results from the implementation of organization strategy and the strategic objectives of the organization are compared. A strategic gap exists when there is a significant discrepancy between the results of organization strategy and the strategic objectives. When a strategic gap occurs, the diagnosis of its causes is conducted at two levels: strategic and operational. Strategic diagnosis is the evaluation of the current organization strategy and determination of whether a new organization strategy is warranted. Operational diagnosis is the evaluation of the organization strategy's implementation and what changes in implementation must be made to improve the current operations of the firm.

Executive actions to close the strategic gap following the strategic and operation diagnosis may lead to a reformulation of the organization strategy and/or to changes in the methods and processes used to implement the organization strategy.

References

1. George A. Steiner, *Strategic Planning: What Every Manager Must Know* (New York: Free Press, 1979), p. 21.
2. John A. Pierce II and Richard B. Robinson, Jr., *Strategic Management, Strategy Formulation and Implementation* (Homewood, Ill.: Richard D. Irwin, Inc. 1982), p. 287.
3. James M. Higgins, *Organizational Policy and Strategic Management, Text and Cases,* 2ed. (Chicago: Dryden Press, 1983), p. 196.
4. Melville J. Herskovits, *Man and His Works* (New York: Alfred A. Knopf, 1952), p. 17.
5. David Dressler and Donald Carns, *Sociology, the Study of Human Interaction* (New York: Alfred A. Knopf, 1969), pp. 56–59.
6. *Ibid.*
7. Jay R. Galbraith, "Strategy and Organization Planning," *Human Resource Management,* 22, no. 1/2 (Spring/Summer 1983):63.
8. Peter Lorange and Declan C. Murphy, "Strategy and Human Resources: Concepts and Practice," *ibid.,* p. 113.
9. Marc Gerstein and Heather Reisman, "Strategic Selection: Matching Executives to Business Conditions," *Sloan Management Review,* Winter 1983, pp. 33–49.
10. "Changing a Corporate Culture: Can Johnson and Johnson Go From Band-Aids to High Tech," *Business Week,* May 14, 1984, pp. 131–32.
11. "A New President to Fit Gould's New Shape," *Business Week,* July 30, 1984, p. 78.
12. "Wanted: A Manager to Fit Each Strategy," *Business Week,* February 25, 1980, p. 166.
13. *Ibid.,* p. 168.
14. Malcolm S. Salter, "Tailor Incentive Compensation to Strategy," *Harvard Business Review,* March–April 1973, p. 95.
15. *Ibid.,* pp. 95–101.
16. "Union Carbide: Its Six-Business Strategy Is Light on Chemicals," *Business Week,* September 24, 1979, p. 100.

CHAPTER 6

UNDERSTANDING CASE ANALYSIS

Introducing the Case Method
Preparing for the Written and Oral Case Analysis
Major Steps in Case Analysis
    Understanding the Environment
    Appraising and Evaluating the Environment
A Scheme for Evaluation: The Appraisal Framework
    Assessing Organization Strengths, Weaknesses,
        Opportunities, and Threats
    Formulating the Organization Mission
    Formulating the Organization Philosophy
    Formulating Organization Policies
    Formulating Strategic Objectives
    Formulating Organization Strategy
    Implementing Organization Strategy
    Formulating Strategic Control
Concluding Comments on the Strategic Management Process
Summary
References

PERFORMANCE OBJECTIVES

When you have finished reading this chapter, you should be able to

1. Understand the nature of case analysis.
2. Write or present an oral case analysis in strategic management.
3. Describe the steps in case analysis.
4. Use the appraisal framework in analyzing and evaluating the environment of a company.

Case analysis is the vehicle that this text, coupled with the contributions of your instructor and colleagues will use to fulfill the objectives of a strategic management course. This chapter introduces the student-analyst to the case method and provides a framework for analyzing cases so that an appropriate strategy or course of action can be recommended. This framework does not assume that the correct or optimal strategy or course of action is recommended, only that the appropriate factors have been considered—thus, producing better recommendations. It should be remembered that the goal of case analysis is to make suggestions for managerial actions.

INTRODUCING THE CASE METHOD

A case is defined by Glueck and Jauch as a written description of an enterprise.[1] A case details the events and circumstances surrounding a particular organizational or managerial situation. A case usually contains information about numerous aspects of the organization, including its history, external environment, and internal environment.[2] Therefore, the case and its analyses are expected to be comprehensive.

The cases used in this book are not intended to be examples of right or wrong or good or bad management. They were selected because each was interesting and provided a relevant analytical situation. They are about real organizations; in most examples the real names of the organizations are used. Where the cases are disguised, the companies wish to remain anonymous; however, this does not change the usefulness of the case.

Most of the cases in this book are comprehensive. Even so, the student frequently asks for additional information before making a decision. Many instructors have their students make decisions based on the information given in the case, reasoning that a manager never has all the information necessary to make a decision. Since case analysis is a representation of reality, the analyst should be required to make decisions based on less-than-complete information. Some instructors have students do supplemental library research; Appendix A provides a list of helpful reference materials.

Most instructors require the student to present both written and oral presentations throughout the semester. Therefore, a short introduction on how to prepare both a written and an oral case are included.

PREPARING FOR THE WRITTEN AND ORAL CASE ANALYSIS

There are many different approaches for preparing written and oral case analysis.[3] Essentially, the analyst's preparation for the written or oral analysis is the same. Usually a comprehensive written analysis is between 8 and 12 double-spaced typewritten pages long. When the case is to be presented orally, the student may be given anywhere from 30 minutes to an hour and a half to present the case, depending on the comprehensiveness of the case. Many times the instructor will divide students into groups of four or five people. The formation of the groups is based on the diversity of student backgrounds. In preparing for the oral or written presentation, students learn from each other. For example, one student's background may be weak in finance, but a finance major in the same group may be able to provide the expertise to help that student.

When presenting an oral case before the class, the analyst should not just read the report. The analyst should know the material well enough to be able to discuss the material from a topical outline. In oral case analysis the analyst must be very precise and in many cases more convincing than in written case analysis. The audience may not have time to digest all of the presenter's facts. Useful tools include an overhead projector or handouts, so that the audience can better follow what the analyst is trying to convey. The oral presenter also must be well-organized and prepared to accept criticism. Frequently, someone in the audience will question the analysis or interpret the case data differently. An analyst must accept criticism when it is due. It is not necessary to defend every point, especially if the analyst has not discussed it. In case analysis there are no right and no wrong answers. What is important is that the recommended actions be based on the analysis.

Students find written case analysis difficult, because an effective analysis on paper must be concise. Most students taking a strategic management or business policy course have spent a great deal of time writing term papers. Somehow they have gained the idea that a term paper should be a certain length to obtain a high grade. But the length of the paper and its quality are not correlated. In written case analysis the grammar must be clear, and the paper must be concise and precise. The use of vague words should be avoided. For example, what does "good" or "bad" performance mean?

Because the purpose of case analysis is to present, discuss, justify, and defend recommended courses of action, the analyst may want to prepare certain financial documents and place them in the appendix of the paper to justify major arguments and recommendations in the text body. Over time the analyst will acquire a certain style of presentation. Until an analyst has developed his or her own style of presenting the case, however, we suggest the following approach. Also the novice case analyst no doubt will find the appraisal framework a useful approach to both written and oral case analysis.

MAJOR STEPS IN CASE ANALYSIS

Although there are many different approaches to understanding strategic management through the use of case analysis, the steps that the analyst must proceed through are more or less the same. This textbook will divide the case analysis process into two parts: understanding the environment, and appraising and evaluating the environment.[4]

Understanding the Environment

Although there is no substitute for at least two thorough readings of a case, there are a number of concepts and aids that are very useful in helping the analyst to understand a case. We will look first at the distinction between the nature of the internal environment, over which the firm has a high degree of control, and the external environment, over which the firm exerts little control. Next we will look at three useful techniques for understanding the environment: (1) the time line, (2) the customer scenario, and (3) the extended organization chart.

External vs. Internal Environment. The environment of an organization is usually divided into external and internal categories. The organization's external environment includes the behavior of each task agent, such as consumers, distributors, suppliers, community, creditors, governments, and competitors. The internal environment of an organization includes (1) its human resources, (2) its financial resources, and (3) its physical facilities.

One major aspect of knowing the environment is a thorough understanding of the personal goals and values of the people making major decisions, because these goals and values greatly affect the decision-making process. In the United States, successful business managers are usually characterized as pragmatic, dynamic, and achievement-oriented. What makes these managers successful is they have values that emphasize making decisions in a rapidly changing environment. This is not to suggest that all successful managers work in dynamic environments, are pragmatic, and are achievement-oriented. But the analyst must understand the goals of the major decision-makers before recommending actions that may affect the organization's objectives. The goals of the major decision-makers may be both professional and personal in nature.

The internal–external classification scheme is valuable in case analysis primarily for convenience. As mentioned, the organization can maintain a great degree of control over the internal environment, but relatively little control over the external environment. In the external environment, the organization must take into account customer behavior and act accordingly or attempt to influence the behavior. In the internal environment, the organization can, for example, place its machines in a particular fashion, but this placement is limited by the available space, capabilities of machines, and purpose. Thus, no behavior is entirely discretionary, but some behaviors are more discretionary than others. Each decision further delineates the realm of future discretionary actions.

Aids in Understanding the Environment. Knowing the environment is primarily a matter of assimilating the information in the case. The appropriateness of any aid to the understanding of the environment depends on the aspects of the case that are difficult to grasp or need to be singled out for attention. In the following pages,

FIGURE 6-1
Sample Time Line

Personnel events:	Hire manager A		Union problems		
Market events:	Add product A		Delete product B		
	Yr 0	Yr 1	Yr 2	Yr 3	Yr 4
Financial events:		Sell stock		Lose money	
Facility events:			New plant		

three aids will be examined: (1) the time line, (2) the customer scenario, and (3) the organization chart. All or none may be useful for any particular case.

The Time Line. Sometimes the events affecting the organization can be put into better perspective by listing them in chronological order. Only the major events that helped shape the current organization are recorded. Events similar in character may be listed on the same level, with time being reflected on the horizontal scale. Usually the type of events categorized are market, financial, and facilities. A sample time line is shown in Figure 6–1, which indicates the major events in the organization for four years. The time line not only allows the analyst to digest complex information, but helps identify patterns of managerial actions and outcomes.

The Customer Scenario. It is very important to develop an understanding of what motivates a customer to purchase from the company. This involves having an understanding of who the customer is, how he or she buys, and why. Some of this information is directly available, but some must be inferred. The customer scenario begins with a cross-match between customer types and product classes or services. The identification of product class or service depends so much on the individual case that further elaboration is not possible here. Customer classifications may be few or many. The basic criterion in deciding how extensive a classification should be is to seek common reasons why customers buy the product. The extent to which this can be done depends on the information or inferences that can be made regarding the motivation to buy. In some instances, the breakdown may be a simple dichotomy, such as civilian/military or institutional/individual, and so on.

The Organization Chart. The case analyst should understand (1) the identity of the principals in the case; (2) the background of the principals, at least in terms of education, experience, and age; (3) the goals and values of the principals; (4) the formal authority and responsibility of each principal; (5) the informal relationships and communications among principals. When such relationships are complex or numerous, an extended version of an organization chart as illustrated in Figure 6–2 is helpful. The analyst who has a complete understanding of the relevant external and internal environments is then prepared to move on to the second step in case analysis: appraising and evaluating the environment.

FIGURE 6-2
Extended Organization Chart

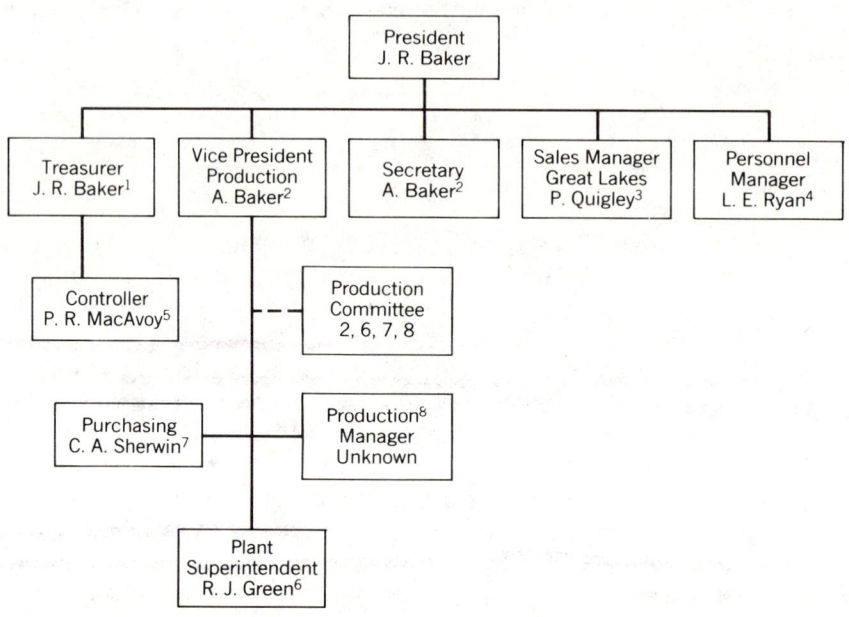

Personnel Information:
[1] About 55-years-old, college graduate, 34 years with company in all phases of business (1950).
[2] About 45-years-old, all phases, especially production (1966).
[3] At least in 40s, 15 years in newspaper advertising, 5 years advertising and sales promotions manager (1980).
[4] No information.
[5] Age unknown, controller, U. S. Mineral Wool Corp. public accountant, experience as accountant with Allis Chalmers (1969).
[6] Age unknown, mechanical engineering degree, experience with automatic parts manufacturing (1969).
[7] No information, hired 1974.
[8] No information.

Appraising and Evaluating the Environment

In this step of case analysis, the analyst gathers and evaluates information on the external and internal environments of the organization. To accomplish this the analyst will assess each step in the strategic management process as illustrated in Figure 6–3.

In Figure 6–3 (the model flows from left to right), it should be clear that assessing organization strengths, weaknesses, opportunities, and threats (SWOT) relates the internal environment (strengths and weaknesses) to the external environment (opportunities and threats). The mission is developed from the SWOT analysis. The organization's philosophy and policies flow from the mission. Objectives consistent with the mission, philosophy, and policies are established. The

Understanding Case Analysis

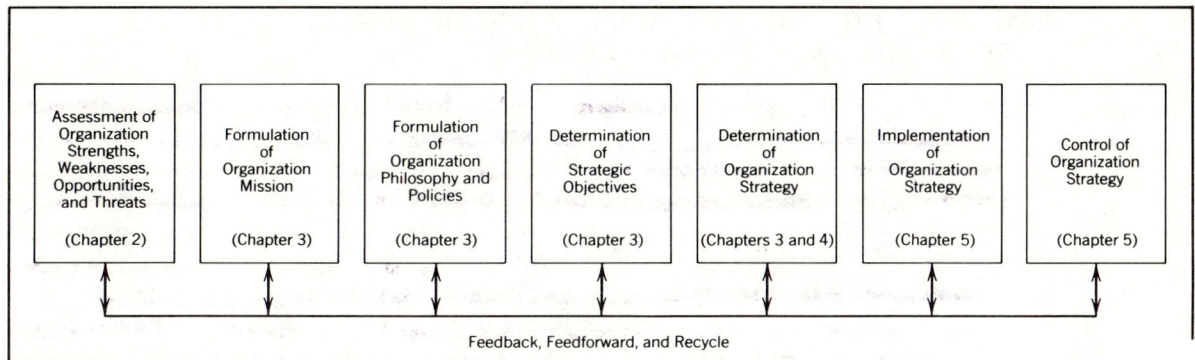

FIGURE 6-3
A Model of the Strategic Management Process

strategy then is developed based on the SWOT analysis, mission, philosophy, policies, and objectives. Finally, the strategy is implemented and a control system is established.

In summary, there are many approaches to case preparation. Many students use the following steps:

1. *Understand the environment.* Read and reread the case. Prepare time lines, a customer scenario, and an organization chart. Thoroughly understand both the internal and external environments of the firm.

2. *Appraise and evaluate the environments.* Gather and evaluate information on the external and internal environments of the firm, then conduct a SWOT analysis. State and evaluate the organization's mission, philosophy, policies, and objectives. Examine the current strategy and recommend that the old strategy be retained or changed; when a change is recommended, develop an implementation plan and a system of evaluation and control.

The following evaluation scheme should help the novice starting out on the strategic management case-analysis journey.

A SCHEME FOR EVAUATION: THE APPRAISAL FRAMEWORK

The appraisal framework is designed to facilitate analysis of the external and internal environments of the company. The hoped-for outcome of the appraisal is an *evaluation of current organization strategy* and *recommendations for future courses of action*. The recommended future courses of action may be as major as a generic strategic change or as minor as the correction of existing problems within the organization. The analyst will note that the figures in this chapter are reproduced from figures in earlier chapters. This was done for convenience. The appraisal framework will follow the strategic management process shown in Figure 6–3, which has been a central focus throughout this textbook.

Assessing Organization Strengths, Weaknesses, Opportunities, and Threats (SWOT)

This assessment requires several steps. First, the analyst must define the business that the organization is competing in and in which it wants to fully exploit the opportunities and combat the threats. Second, an analysis of the opportunities and threats in the external environment must be conducted. Third, key success factors (activities or areas in which the company must be especially proficient in order to succeed in the business) must be determined. Fourth, the analyst must look internally and evaluate the strengths and weaknesses in terms of skills, resources, and competences of the persons within the company who would enable it to do especially well in those areas identified by the key success factors. Finally, matching the capabilities with the key success factors objectively will provide the analyst with a good estimate of the organization's ability to successfully exploit the opportunities and fight off the threats in the external environment. Let us take a closer look at each of the steps in the SWOT analysis.

Defining the Business. At both levels of strategy—corporate and business—defining the business is intended to force the organization to constantly examine its mission. In Figure 6–3 one can see that defining the mission is the second step in the strategic management process. Note that the strategic management process is an iterative model, and as such, it constantly reexamines each step in the model. Mission defines the business of an organization. Defining the overall corporate mission involves defining the mission of each business in its portfolio. Business missions are normally written in terms of products or services aimed at a particular market segment.

The analyst should remember that in conducting SWOT analysis one should work with the already stated corporate or business mission if there is one. However, this does not preclude the analyst's investigating the feasibility of either expanding or contracting an organization's mission to include or exclude a business. Indeed, the analyst may recommend such an action based on the analysis. Having defined the business, the analyst should examine the opportunities and threats in the external environment that will help identify the key success factors.

Assessing Opportunities and Threats. The external environment is composed of trends, events and forces that are beyond the direct control of a firm's management. Changes in external environment affect different industries in different ways. The external environment may be divided into four segments: economic, sociocultural, political, and technological. Figure 6–4 shows the factors typically found in each segment of the environment, although it is by no means inclusive.

A critical responsibility of managers is to identify future opportunities and to position the organization to avail itself of the opportunities presented by the changes. However, managers face innumerable changes in the trends and events that occur continuously, and it is impossible to keep track of all of them. The key to making this task manageable is to monitor and forecast factors in the external environment critical to the firm's operations. These critical environmental factors

Understanding Case Analysis   129

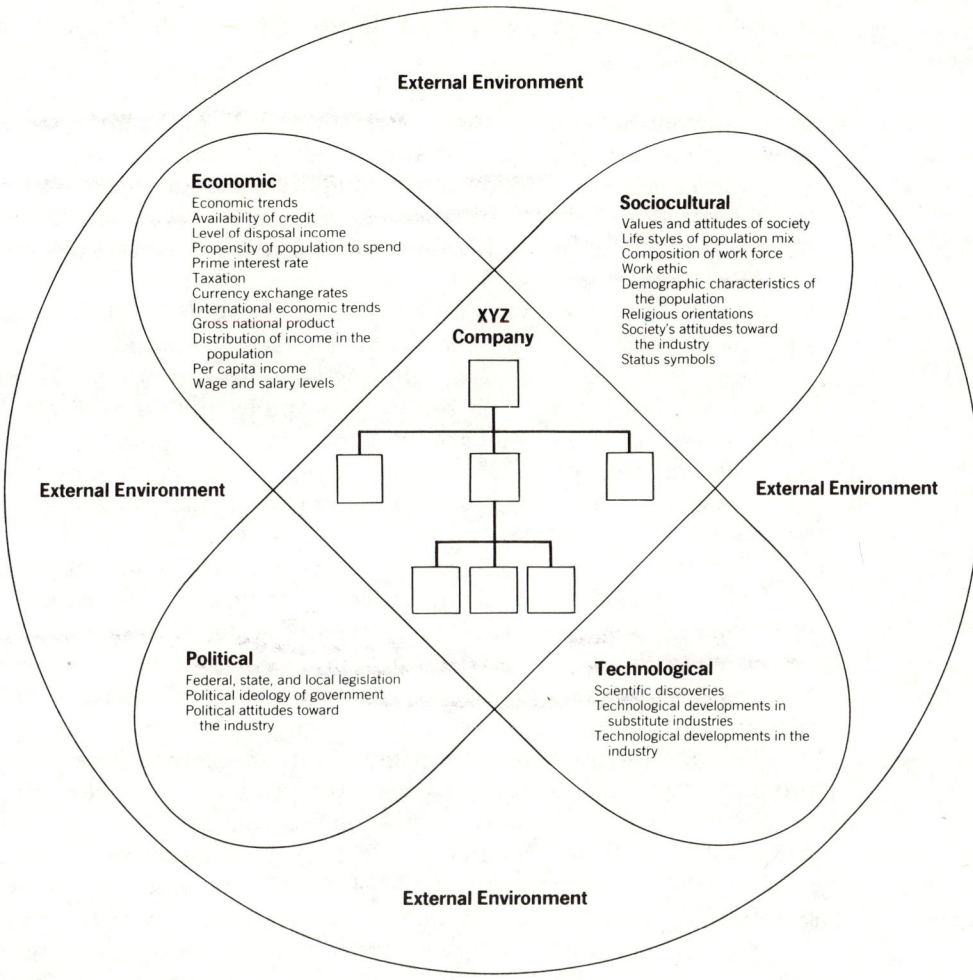

FIGURE 6-4
Factors in the External Environment

are the trends, events, and forces that might have a significant favorable or unfavorable impact on the firm's operations. The following steps are suggested for forecasting the opportunities and threats from the changes occurring in the external environment of a firm:

1. Identify the critical environmental factors.
2. Monitor changes as they appear in the critical environmental factors.
3. Forecast the cumulative impact on the industry characteristics and the firm of the critical environmental factors. Will the changes be favorable and present opportunities or unfavorable and pose threats?

The analyst should recognize that the critical environmental factors change over time and, hence, require close monitoring. The analysis of opportunities and threats is invaluable to the analyst. It provides the foundation for determining the key success factors.

Defining Key Success Factors. Key success factors change from industry to industry. They also change over time within the same industry. To determine key success factors, the analyst must thoroughly understand the industry. The analyst should carefully investigate the following industry characteristics: nature and degree of competition, barriers to entry, competitive power of substitutes, buyer power, and supplier power.

In examining the nature and degree of competition, the analyst should investigate the intensity of rivalry and the tactics used by competitors in market positioning, such as price competition, introduction of new products, advertising, customer service, and product or service warranties. Other indicators of competitor intensity include the number of firms already in the industry, the industry growth rate, the idle capacity of competitor firms, the differentiation of products among the firms, and the strategies, history, mission, and personalitites of competitor firms.

There are a number of barriers to entering an industry that the analyst should be aware of inasmuch as a firm enters an industry in hopes of obtaining market share. These barriers include economics of scale, capital requirements, access to distribution channels, establishing brand identification, cost advantages enjoyed by existing competitor firms, government policy, and the reaction of existing competitors to the entry of a newcomer.

The analyst must be concerned about the competitive power of substitute products. There are substitutes for most products. A customer expects satisfaction from a purchased product, and one measure of the satisfaction is the price–performance tradeoff. Further, the analyst must be aware of the development of substitute products, because a technological breakthrough may reduce cost, thereby upsetting the price–performance satisfaction of the customer.

How much power is possessed by the buyers of a product or service may greatly influence competition in an industry: they can demand lower prices, higher quality, better service, better warranty terms, or force sellers to be more competitive for the business.

The case analyst must understand supplier power because the more powerful the supplier, the greater its ability to influence competition. Powerful suppliers can influence the buying industry's costs, prices, quality, and ultimately its growth and profits.

Assessing an Organization's Strengths and Weaknesses. Having identified the key success factors for the business, the analyst can now turn attention to an evaluation of the organization's own capabilities—its strengths and weaknesses—to exploit opportunities and fend off threats from competitors in the industry. The evaluation of a firm's strengths and weaknesses includes:

1. Identifying the key success factors for the business.
2. Developing a profile of the firm's resources and skills.

3. Comparing the firm's resources and skills profile to the key success factors of the business.
4. Identifying the major strengths on which the firm can build a viable strategy to exploit opportunities in the business, and the critical weaknesses it must eliminate to prevent failure.
5. Comparing the firm's strengths and weaknesses with those of its major rivals in the business.
6. Isolating areas in which the firm's resources and skills are significantly stronger or weaker than its major competitors.

Step 1, identifying the key success factors for the business, has already been completed in the previous analysis. Step 2, the resources and skills capability profile, can be organized around a series of penetrating questions. Figure 6–5 provides sample questions for each of the important factors in the resources and

FIGURE 6-5
Examples of Questions Used in a Resources and Skills Capability Profile

Marketing

- What is the firm's current market share in the total market and the major market segments? Is this a strong position? Does the firm enjoy a unique position in the industry?
- Is the market as a whole expanding or contracting? At what rate is the size of the total market changing? How is the firm's market share changing?
- Where in the product life-cycle are the firm's major products? What is the position of prices and margins of the major products? How strong and complete is the product line?
- How good is the reputation of the products among present and potential customers? What are the strengths and weaknesses of the products in terms of prices, patents, quality, design, customer loyalty, etc.?
- How effective and efficient are the channels of distribution?
- Is the market research system capable of providing valid and reliable information to keep the firm's R & D programs tailored to current and potential customers' needs?
- How effective and efficient is the sales force? Does it have good rapport with key customers?
- How effective is the firm's advertising program? Has it helped the firm establish a strong product-brand position against competing brands, a strong market niche, customer loyalty, etc.?
- How effective and efficient is the service-after-sales program?
- Does the organization have an appropriate mix of products?
- Does the organization properly appraise and identify the potential for present and prospective production?

Research and Development

- How many commercially successful products has R & D created in the past? What return have R & D expenditures produced?
- Is the R & D effort guided by needs uncovered by the marketing department, that is, is it customer-oriented?
- What are the strengths and weaknesses of the total R & D effort in terms of people, facilities, and equipment?

(Continued)

FIGURE 6-5 (Continued)

Finance

- How good is the financial health of the firm based on various financial ratios in four major categories: (1) leverage ratios, (2) liquidity ratios, (3) activity ratios, and (4) profitability ratios?
- Based on expense ratios (cost-percentage analysis), how efficient are operations over time?
- Does the firm have adequate financial resources to enable it to maintain its present position or obtain needed resources and skills in the future?
- Can the firm raise capital through the sale of securities, equity financing, or debt financing?
- Does the firm have sufficient working capital?
- Are the financial controls sound and effective?
- How good is the quality of financial management in the company? Does the firm have short and long-term financial plans that are well integrated with the overall company-wide plans of the same duration?
- Are there effective and efficient accounting systems for cost, budget, and profit-planning procedures?

Production

- How efficient are the production facilities and manufacturing processes compared with those used by the major competitors? Will they meet future product volume requirements?
- Is the manufacturing plant technologically advanced or obsolete?
- How do the operating costs compare with those of the major competitors?
- Are the facilities currently fully or partially utilized?

Management

- What image does the management have in the business community: dynamic or stodgy?
- How successful has management been in meeting its stated company goals? How does this record compare with that of the company? How does this record compare with that of the major competitors?
- What is the age distribution of the key executives? Are there a sufficient number of dynamic executives who can take charge if and when there is a turnover of key executives because of retirement or executive mobility?
- Is the top management of the firm capable of coping with the challenges of the future?
- Does top management understand the relevant forces in the external environment?
- Does top management engage in effective, long-range planning?

Corporate Structure

- Can the organization structure effectively coordinate the firm's product and geographic diversity?
- Does the organization structure expedite making and executing corporate decisions?
- Is the organization structure appropriate in light of the nature of the technology and people in the firm and its environment?

Human Resources

- Does the organization have the appropriate mechanisms to obtain, retain, and improve human resources?

skills capability profile. These questions are examples of the kinds of questions that may provide answers leading to the development of the resources and skills capability profile.

To answer each of the questions in Figure 6–5 requires a basic understanding of all the functions of business. By examining the questions in Figure 6–5, the student should be able to see the interrelationships among the business functions. Since many students have a problem understanding the financial function of business, Appendix B includes ratio analysis, cost-percentage analysis, and sources and uses of fund statements for individuals who need a refresher.

Having assessed the firm's resources and skills, the analyst can compare that profile with the key success factors of the business (step 3). This evaluation will help the analyst carry out step 4 in the strengths and weaknesses process—identifying the major strengths on which the firm can build to exploit opportunites in the business and the critical weaknesses it must eliminate to prevent failure.

Step 5 in the strengths and weaknesses evaluation process requires the analyst to compare the firm's strengths and weaknesses with those of major competitors. Of course, this requires the analyst to acquire as much material about competitors as possible. Finally, in step 6, the analyst will isolate areas in which the firm's resources and skills are significantly stronger or weaker than its major competitors, which will lead to an understanding of what really are the firm's strengths and weaknesses. For example, an analyst may find that the firm's resources and skills profile indicates that it could effectively achieve the industry key success factors, but the firm has major weaknesses relative to its competitors and few strengths relative to its competitors. This may require the analyst to consider reformulating the organization mission.

Formulating the Organization Mission

Mission defines the business of an organization. In the discussion on SWOT analysis, we assumed that the business was adequately defined, but that may not be the case. The external environment may have changed to such an extent that a new or redefined mission is needed. Usually the mission is written in terms of products or services aimed at particular markets or customers. A more effective way of defining the mission is in terms of a product or service aimed at a specific market segment or homogeneous subsets of buyers.

The mission provides guidelines as to where managers should focus their activities. The analyst must recognize that the nature of a company's mission determines which opportunities will be pursued, who its competitors will be, and ultimately what will be its growth and profitability.

In conducting case analysis the analyst first does the SWOT analysis as though it is a strategic review. A strategic review ensures that the strengths and weaknesses of the firm are exploiting the opportunities and fending off threats in the external environment. The strategic review assumes that the organization's mission has not changed. However, after the strategic review is complete the analyst may conclude that a redefined or new mission is in order if the organization is to exploit opportunities for growth and profits.

Formulating the Organization Philosophy

Having conducted the SWOT analysis, formulated the organization mission, philosophy, policies, and strategic objectives, the analyst is in a position to determine the organization strategy. The organization strategy of a company is the method that the company uses to achieve its strategic objectives. Determination of organization strategy includes the identification of strategic alternatives to achieve organization objectives, the evaluation of strategic alternatives, and the selection of alternatives that will become the organization strategy. Of the four levels of organization strategy—societal, corporate, business, and functional—we will emphasize corporate and businesss.

Formulating Organization Policies

Policies are guides to action that define the boundaries within which objectives are established and strategies are determined, implemented, and controlled. Policies flow from the organization's philosophy and should be consistent with it. The purpose of the policies is to limit the scope of alternatives that must be considered in making and implementing strategic decisions. Policies may be divided into strategic and implementation. Strategic policies guide the planning process, and implementation policies guide the strategy implementation process. Figure 6–6 presents the issues that the strategists must face in developing policies.

In conducting a strategic review, the analyst will want to ensure that the policies are consistent with the mission and philosophy. If there is a recommended strategic change because of the strategic review, the analyst should specify how the change will require changes in both strategic and implementation policies.

Formulating Strategic Objectives

Managers need well-defined objectives. The objectives should specify the desired results, which will guide the design of strategies to fulfill them and serve as standards of performance. Strategic objectives are the ends that the organization hopes to achieve in fulfilling its basic mission. A strategic objective should be consistent with and derived from the mission, philosophy, and policies of the organization. The mission provides the umbrella under which the strategic objectives are formulated. The objectives are established by the board of directors of the firm, who rely heavily on the judgment and recommendations of the senior management.

In recommending strategic objectives, senior management takes into account the forces in the internal and external environments that present threats and opportunities to the firm. The managers should aspire to exploit opportunities and combat environmental threats; the objectives they set for the firm should reflect these aspirations. When establishing strategic objectives, senior management and the board of directors must examine current objectives, current and obtainable resources, and current and future opportunities and threats in the marketplace. The analyst will want to ensure that the firm has set its strategic objectives at the

Understanding Case Analysis

FIGURE 6-6
Issues Involved In Formulating Strategic Policies

- Scope of the corporation's business—defining the product(s) of the corporation and the market segment(s) served.
- Criteria for entering or existing in a business or industry.
- Geographical scope of company activities.
- Nature of technology utilized in production process.
- Channels of distribution.
- Product quality.
- Company image.
- Fundamental organizational objectives—growth, stability, retrenchment, turnaround, divestment, liquidation.
- Dominant method of competition.
- Social responsibility of corporation.
- Role of corporation in society.
- Philosophy regarding management style and organization climate.
- Organization structure.
- Corporation orientation—marketing vs. production.

Issues Involved in Formulating Implementation Policies

- Type or organization structure—divisional vs. functional.
- Leadership styles—authoritarian, democratic, participative.
- Motivation systems—incentive programs, reward system.
- Staffing practices—matching executives to job requirements.
- Coordination techniques—quality circles, project teams.
- Information needs of managers and systems to meet those needs.
- Promoting entrepreneurship in managerial behavior.
- Employee's career paths and promotion methods.
- Performance evaluation systems.
- Measures of evaluation of total organization performance.

intersection of resources, objectives, and opportunities and threats. To commit resources to objectives geared to nonexistent opportunities in the marketplace will ensure failure. To set objectives when there are opportunities but insufficient resources is unacceptable. This discussion has emphasized the objective criteria used in formulating strategic objectives. However, of equal importance, are the subjective or behavioral criteria that affect strategic objectives formulation.

In setting the strategic objectives for the firm, managers must always be aware of political realities. Every organization has individuals, groups, and cliques that are continuously striving to protect and enhance their interests. Another behavioral consideration is the personal value system of the managers. Different managers strive toward different goals; this must be considered in formulating objectives. Finally, the strengths and weaknesses of the firm's internal resources can place restraints on the aspiration levels of the firm's managers and thereby influence what they hope to achieve in terms of the strategic objectives. For example, if management wants to introduce a new product within its line, but no financial sources are available or potentially available, management will be required to lower its aspiration level and wait until the resources are available before it introduces the new product.

The case analyst should determine what the firm's objectives are during the strategic review. If changes are recommended after the SWOT analysis, the analyst should be careful to spell out the recommended new objectives clearly. Areas where one would normally find strategic objectives are:

1. *Profitability.* Expressed in terms of profits, return on investment, earnings per share, or profit-to-sales ratios.
2. *Markets.* Expressed in terms of share of the market or dollars or unit volume of sales.
3. *Productivity.* Expressed in terms of a ratio of input to output or cost per unit of production.
4. *Product.* Expressed in terms of sales and profitability by product line or product or target dates for development of new products.
5. *Financial resources.* Expressed in terms of the capital structure, new issues of common stock, cash flow, working capital, dividend payments, and collection periods.
6. *Physical facilities.* Expressed in terms of square feet, fixed costs, or units of production.
7. *Research and innovation.* Expressed in terms of the amount of money to be spent or projects to be completed.
8. *Organization structure and activities.* Expressed in terms of changes to be made or projects to be undertaken.
9. *Human resources.* Expressed in terms of rates of absenteeism, tardiness, turnover, or number of grievances. It also can be expressed in terms of the number of people to be trained or number of training programs that are to be conducted.
10. *Customer service.* Expressed in terms of delivery times or customer complaints.
11. *Social responsibility.* Expressed in terms of types of activities, number of days of service, or financial contributions.

Formulating Organization Strategy

Having conducted the SWOT analysis, formulated the organization mission, philosophy, policies, and strategic objectives, the analyst is in a position to determine the organization strategy. The organization strategy of a company is the method that the company uses to achieve its strategic objectives. Determination of organization strategy includes the identification of strategic alternatives to achieve organization objectives, the evaluation of strategic alternatives, and the selection of alternatives that will become the organization strategy. Of the four levels of organization strategy—societal, corporate, business, and functional—we will emphasize corporate and businesss.

Corporate Strategy. Corporate strategy is the grand design for managing the whole organization. The analysis of corporate strategy principally concerns determining the attractiveness of the total business portfolio and formulating ways to improve its performance by elucidating the appropriate role for each business in the company's total game plan, and/or adding a new business to the business portfolio. Although the concept of corporate strategy has special relevance to multibusiness organizations, it is equally applicable to single-business enterprises concerned about the future profitability of their core businesses and thinking about diversifying into other business areas with superior prospects. Thus, in both single-business and multiple-business enterprises, corporate strategy formulation involves the evaluation of the current businesses and decisions as to which businesses deserve greater or lesser resources in the future, which businesses should be divested or liquidated, whether new businesses should be added, and how each business should be managed in the future.

Before a company can determine its corporate strategy, it must have a thorough understanding of its present strategy. Only then can the analyst conclude whether the current strategy is the proper one in light of its future realities and whether any changes are mandated. Figure 6–7 provides the "spokes" of corporate strategy and the dimensions that should be examined to obtain a proper fix on the organization's current corporate strategy.

The analyst must decide if the current strategy is effective, that is, if it gives the firm a balanced portfolio of businesses that will enable it to achieve its strategic objectives. Obviously, to determine if the current corporate strategy is effective, it is necessary to analyze each of the business units in the portfolio. At the corporate strategy level, the analyst is really determining whether each of the businesses within the portfolio contributes to the success of the strategic objectives, as defined in the corporate strategy. In the financial investment portfolio, the investor wants to obtain a portfolio that provides the best performance at the least cost and an acceptable degree of risk. Similarly, corporate strategists want the corporate funds invested in a business portfolio that represents an acceptable balance between risk and return.

Having identified the current corporate strategy, the strategist or analyst is now in a position to make a recommendation for future strategies. The recommen-

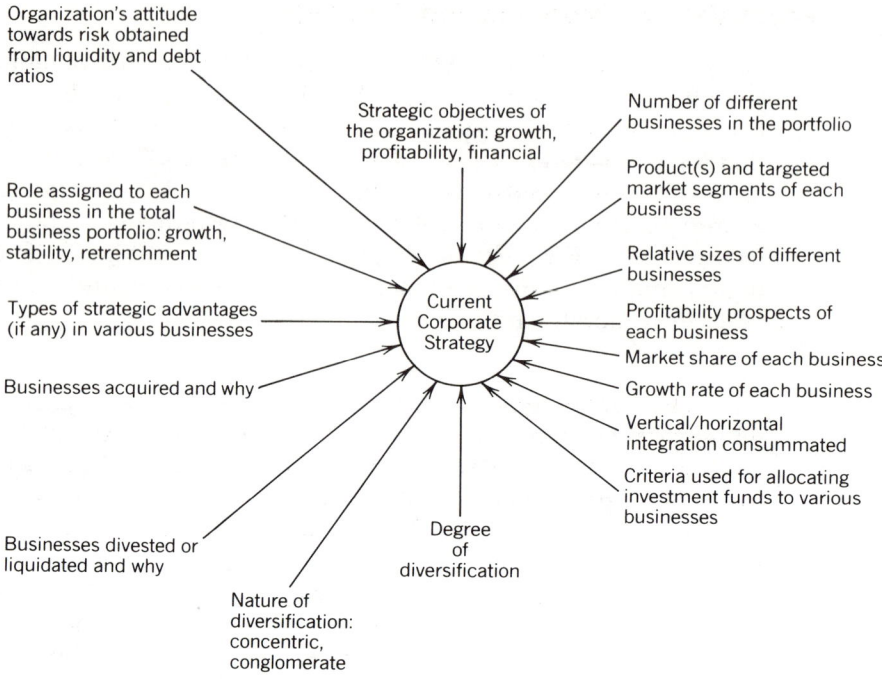

FIGURE 6-7
The Spokes of Corporate Strategy

dation may be a minor one—adjustments to the current strategy—or it may be a major strategic change. For example, a business in a stability strategy may change to a retrenchment strategy.

Business Strategy. As discussed under corporate strategy, the strategist or analyst must analyze the strategy of each business within its portfolio. Therefore, understanding the business strategy is of major importance to both the business and corporate strategist. The focus of business strategy is on how the firm should compete in a particular industry or products/market segment in order to obtain a strategic advantage over the competition. Three generic business strategies already have been discussed: cost leadership, differentiation, and focus.

The cost-leadership strategy provides a product or service to the marketplace that is priced less than that of competitors. A differentiation strategy focuses on creating a product or service perceived as unique in the marketplace. The focus strategy involves focusing the firm's attention on a particular buyer group, segment of the product line, or geographical area. The aim is to serve a particular target market more efficiently and effectively than competitors.

The key to gaining strategic advantage in the marketplace is to adapt a generic business strategy to the specific industry situation and the firm's position. Although there are many business strategies that could be adopted for firms in specific situations, we have recommended corresponding strategies for four situations most commonly experienced by firms (see Figure 6–8).

FIGURE 6-8
Firm Situations and Recommended Strategies

Situations	Strategies
Dominant firms	Be on the offensive Fortify against the enemy Confront enemy by promotion
Low Market-Share Firms	Segment market Use R & D efficiently Think small Build image Channel innovation
Firms in stagnant industries	Identify, create, and exploit growth segments in the industry Emphasize quality and innovation Improve efficiency of production and distribution
Stages of product life-cycle and competitive strength of firm	Contingent upon where product is in life cycle and firm's competitive position

Evaluating the Recommendation. When analyzing a case, the analyst is constantly faced with the problem of separating the important issues from the trivial ones. Recommendations should be presented in terms of their long-term impact on the firm. The recommendation must be sufficiently supported to warrant its acceptance. The only wrong recommendation in case analysis is a logically inconsistent one. The degree to which the recommendation is correct is judged by the long-term effect of the recommendation on the future success of the company. Schellenberger and Boseman[5] have proposed that the following criteria be used in examining any recommended strategies: it should be appropriate, feasible, realistic, specific, conclusive, and flexible, and it should be a logical outgrowth of the analysis.

Selecting an Organization Strategy. By now the analyst has developed a number of alternative strategies for the corporate or business level. One of these strategies is recommended for implementation. Since the strategy will result in a success or failure for the organization, its selection should receive maximum attention. There is no simple way to make the selection; it is an art that rests on the manager's reasoning and creativity. There are a number of questions that can guide the analyst in selecting the strategy; we have divided them into those that deal with the internal environment of the firm and those that deal with the external environment. The following list of questions is certainly not inclusive, but is only meant to be a guide to the internal and external considerations for the analyst.

Internal Considerations

1. Does the strategy effectively utilize the company's financial, human, and physical resources?
2. Is the strategy consistent with the strategic objectives?
3. Is the strategy consistent with the personal values of the company's managers and employees?
4. Is there a direct relationship between the market expectations resulting from the company's strategy and its internal capabilities?
5. Is the strategy sufficiently flexible to be changed or altered if it proves inappropriate?
6. Is the company capable of the planning and development required by the strategy, for example, is the strategy consistent with managerial abilities?
7. Does the strategy emphasize the company's strengths and avoid its weaknesses?
8. Does the company have adequate financial resources for the strategy or will it have them?
9. Has the company adequately planned the implementation of the strategy so as to give it a reasonable chance for success, for example, is the strategy and structure consistent?

External Considerations

1. Does the strategy lead to a market niche or niches not now filled by others?
2. Does the strategy improve competitive conditions for current market or product lines?
3. Is the minimum attainable market sufficient to produce the minimum return on investment?
4. Does the strategy utilize or take advantage of existing market and product strengths?
5. Does the strategy include products and markets outside the current sphere of products and markets so that the risks are spread?
6. Does the strategy fit, within the legal and political frameworks so that the success of the strategy will not raise legal or political questions?
7. Will the strategy be perceived by society as a responsible and ethical one?

Implementing Organization Strategy

Having developed the organization strategy, the analyst is now prepared to write an implementation plan, which converts the strategy into concrete action and results. Implementation of the strategy involves application of the total management process to obtain the desired results. The management functions of planning, organizing, staffing, leadership, and controlling are essential in implementing a strategy. Most students spend a considerable time studying these functions, so a full coverage is omitted here. But there are four areas critical to effective strategy implementation: corporate culture, organization structure, human resources, and organization rewards. In developing or reviewing the implementation plans, the analyst should be sure that there is consistency among these four factors and the newly developed strategy.

Organization culture is a system of norms, attitudes, values, beliefs, and customs that govern the behavior of people within an organization, the sum total of how individuals in an organization think and act as employees. Once the culture is established, it tends to persist and can be a major strength if it is consistent with the firm's organization strategy. For example, an organization that has a very radical strategy would tend to employ people who display aggressive behavior.

The organization structure should be consistent with the strategy. The organization structure conveys how work has been divided and assigned to people and how the activities of people performing their duties are coordinated. The nature of the work is determined by the firm's strategy. The organization structure that coordinates the people performing the tasks should follow the firm's strategy. If there is a major strategy change, there most likely will be a change in organization structure to realign the tasks carried out by people in the organization. If the organization tries to continue with the same organization structure after a strategy change, the implementation process will be hampered if not destroyed.

There should be a proper "fit" between the human resources and the strategy of the organization. Each organization strategy requires different major job tasks. As these job tasks change, they require different types of personal characteristics among those who carry out the task. For example, a turnaround strategy requires a rapid, accurate problem diagnosis. An executive who can accomplish that task is usually a "take-charge" person or a strong leader. Therefore, the analyst must be very careful to consider human resources when writing the strategy implementation plan. Finally, organization rewards should be consistent with the new strategy. Senior management may influence the behavior of managers through financial incentives. Senior management must come to grips with the type of performance they want to reward. Does senior management want to reward short-run or long-run performance? the risk averter or the risk taker? joint effort between division managers or decentralization and autonomy for managers? However, management decides to settle these issues, all managers must understand the reward system. The reward system should match the organization strategy.

Formulating Strategic Control

The final step in the strategic management process is developing a control system for the on-going or newly implemented strategy. Strategic control begins when managers obtain information about the results of the current strategy as it is implemented. The results of current performance are compared with the strategic objectives of the firm. If a significant gap exists between the performance of the firm and the results expected by top management, a serious problem may exist. Such a problem could cause a deterioration of the firm's health and prospects for long-term survival. Diagnosis of the cause of the gap may be handled at two levels—strategic or operational. The strategic diagnosis involves evaluating the current organization strategy and determining whether a change in the firm's strategies is required. An operational diagnosis focuses on the how effectively the current strategy is being implemented and on implementation changes that must be made to improve the current operations of the firm.

In conducting a strategic diagnosis, the analyst goes back to the first phase of the strategic management process—SWOT analysis—and reexamines the premises and assumptions originally used in formulating the organizational strategy. Then the analyst examines each step in the strategic management process. The following are some of the questions that may be asked to determine the causes of the strategic gap facing the company:

- Have changes occurred in the external environment that have negatively affected the success of current strategy, for example, demographic, values and attitudes of society, technological developments in industry, technological developments in substitute industries, availability of credit, interest rates, currency exchange rates, or governmental controls (or decontrols)?
- Have changes occurred in the strategies of major competitors, buyers, or suppliers?
- Have new opportunities and/or threats emerged as a result of changes in external environment, competitor strategies, or industry?
- Is the current strategy consistent with the changes that have occurred in the external environment, competitor strategies, or industry?
- Have the key success factors for the industry changed?

Answers to such diagnostic questions may result in a change in the company strategy and the adoption of a strategy more consistent with the situation facing it. The analyst may conclude that the existing business is not attractive anymore and, hence, not worth investment of resources. If so, a change in the company mission would lead corporate management to invest resources in other businesses. Naturally this would cause the strategic objectives and organization strategy to change.

An operational diagnosis concerns evaluating the results derived from the implementation of the current strategy. Its major focus is on assessing the current performance of the firm. The operational diagnosis determines the areas of the business in which operating performance is below acceptable levels and, hence, needs improvement. Usually the performance measures of the firm are financial. The operation diagnosis may result in changes in the methods used in implementing the current business strategy.

CONCLUDING COMMENTS ON THE STRATEGIC MANAGEMENT PROCESS

The strategic management process shown in Figure 6–3, is meant to serve as a guide for the analyst in conducting a strategic review. The strategic management process involves seven steps that the analyst needs to go through. However, it an iterative process: as one step is concluded, it moves back to the previous step. For example, a formulation of organization mission requires the analyst to examine the SWOT analysis again. Athough the strategic management process indicates that the firm should start the process with a SWOT analysis, in reality the analyst or strategist may start the process at any step in the strategic management process.

There are other strategic management models, but we have found this model to be extremely useful in teaching strategic management in the classroom, as well as representing the reality of how the strategic management process is carried out in the real world.

SUMMARY

This chapter introduces the analyst to cases and the case method. It explains the nature of cases and how they can be used to understand the operations of a company in the real world.

Some attention has been devoted to how to prepare for both the written and oral presentation of a case in a section containing helpful hints formulated over many years of teaching business policy and strategic management.

The major steps in case analysis are understanding the environment and appraising and evaluating it. For this analysis, the environment is divided into two parts—external and internal. The external environment includes the behavior of each task agent within the environment of the organization: consumers, suppliers, etc. The internal environment includes human resources, financial resources, and physical facilities. Three aids help in understanding the internal environment: a time line, a customer scenario, and an organization chart.

In appraising and evaluating the environment, we followed the steps in the model of the strategic management process that has been the central focus of this book. An appraisal framework for appraising and evaluating each step in the model is presented. The outcome of this step in case analysis is an evaluation of current strategy with recommendations for future courses of action.

References

1. William F. Glueck and Lawrence R. Jauch, *Business Policy and Strategic Management*, 4th ed. (New York: McGraw-Hill Publishing Company, 1984), p. 422.
2. Arthur A. Thompson, Jr. and A. J. Strickland III, *Strategic Management: Concepts and Cases*, 3d ed. (Plano, Tex., Business Publications, Inc., 1984) p. 276.
3. For an excellent review of how a case should be analyzed, see Robert Ronstadt, *The Art of Case Analysis* (Dover, Mass., Lord Publishing, 1980), Chapter 3.
4. This approach was adapted from Robert Schellenberger and Glenn Boseman, *Policy Formulation and Strategy Management*, 2d ed. (New York, John Wiley and Sons, 1982), Chapter 3.
5. *Ibid.*, pp. 68–70.

PART 2
CASES

1 ENTREPRENEURSHIP

THE APARTMENT STORE

"Our next big step is to arrange the bank financing we will need to start our new venture," Paula Cox said to her two partners on January 5, 1984. "When that matter is settled, we can actually make some physical arrangements and open the business in a matter of weeks." Because Katherine Wallace and Alice Bennett agreed with her, all three founders sat down to go over all the material they had collected.

While working on their MBA degrees at a nearby university, the three women had become interested in opening their own business. Since they wished to utilize their special talents, they decided to begin a venture called, "The Apartment Store." The Apartment Store would be a retail business oriented toward serving the furniture and accessory needs of a rapidly growing market: young people with moderate incomes generally living in rental housing. To serve these needs at a reasonable cost and to retain design flexibility, The Apartment Store was planned as an integrated operation from manufacture to retail.

Organization

The founders felt that the success of the venture would largely be a function of the blend of the special talents of the management team. Paula Cox, as president, would have overall coordination responsibility, as well as responsibility for handling the financial/accounting duties. Because she had experience as an interior designer, Cox was familiar with the industry. All marketing matters, including the sales effort, would be the direct concern of Katherine Wallace as Vice President—Marketing.

Finally, Alice Bennett, as Vice President—Operations, would have direct responsibility for production and distribution.

Despite their well-defined primary responsibilties, all three would act as a team in strategy decisions. Any questions of product design, store locations, and long-range planning would require input from and a decision by the entire group. In this manner, they felt that the strengths of the members could be best utilized to achieve success.

Initially, virtually all work will be done by the three-person management team, including selling, bookkeeping, production supervision, and so on. When growth of the organization occurrs, additional personnel then will be added, primarily in production and sales. The organization chart in Exhibit 1 presents the organization's approach to growth.

Marketing

Market to be Served

The Apartment Store, as the name implies, is designed to serve the needs of apartment dwellers and other renters. These needs are furniture and accessories that are moderately priced, easily transportable, designed for flexibility, and value-oriented. The market is characterized by single people and young families (head of household under 34-years-old). In general, the customer has a minimum income of $15,000 annually, although this may not be true of students and others with parental support. The market is both price and value-conscious, in addition to demanding innovative styling.

Competition

Competition comes from other retailers and furniture-rental agents. The rental agents tend to have close ties with specific apartment complexes. Considerable business is generated as a

---

Source: Prepared by Richard Levin and Bettye Painter of the University of North Carolina at Chapel Hill. Support to write the case was provided by the North Carolina Business Foundation. Permission to use granted by the authors.

EXHIBIT 1
Organization

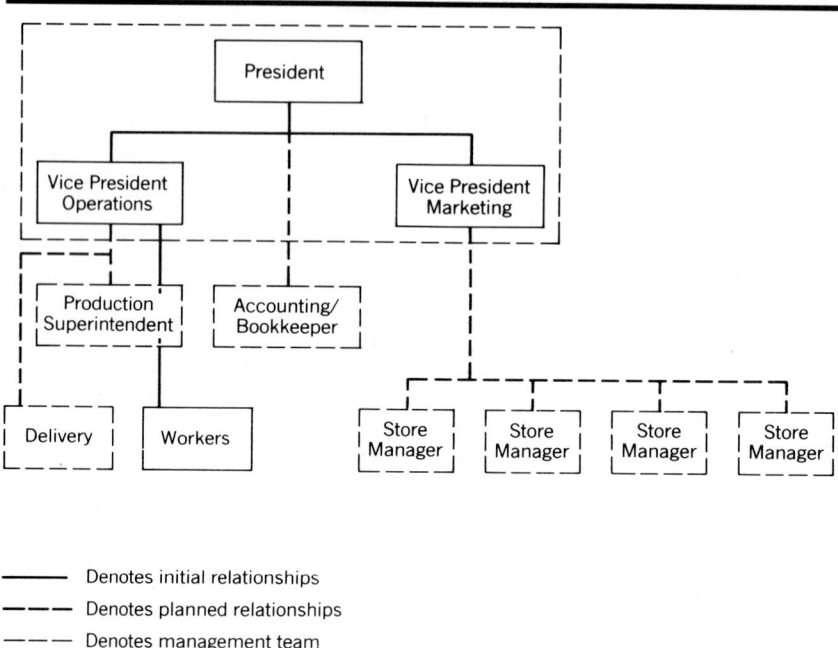

result of referrals. Rental's major appeal is threefold: (1) minimal investment by apartment dweller, (2) no moving/storage problems, and (3) ability to change furniture as styles change. Major problems that rental agents face include high rental cost, desire for ownership, and the fact that young people wish to avoid the "plastic" atmosphere implicit in rental furniture.

Furniture retailers typically offer a broad range of furniture, most of which has been designed for single-family homes, not apartments. Although the retail trade has developed along price lines to some extent, other types of segmentation are developing. Recent years have seen the development of waterbed stores, unfinished furniture stores, and other specialty approaches. Where such stores have been successful, they have served a sufficiently large market that desires their product. The founders of The Apartment Store hope to use a similar concept.

Product Concept

The Apartment Store would retail two basic product lines: in-house manufactured items and purchased accessories. The latter would be purchased from distributors and include lamps, wall decorations, and bed frames. The purpose of this line is to meet customer needs that cannot be better served by in-house manufacture. The products manufactured by The Apartment Store are fully described in the writings and drawings in Exhibits 2 and 3. In brief, the product line includes furniture for the living room, dining room, and bedroom. It is characterized by compactness and flexibility. The apartment dweller places a high premium on both because of frequent moves, limited space, and a limited furniture budget. The products will be made of solid wood and available in several finishes or unfinished. The products have been designed to blend well in furniture groups.

EXHIBIT 2
Product Descriptions

TRUNDLE BED

This delightful, moderately priced trundle bed is a modern, comfortable couch by day that converts into a comfortable 60″ wide bed by night. The overall dimensions of the couch are $76\frac{1}{2}″ \times 31\frac{1}{2}″$. By sliding out the top drawer, a $76\frac{1}{2}″ \times 61\frac{1}{2}″$ queen-size bed is formed. Two super-firm, 6″ polyfoam mattresses covered in decorator fabrics (or available uncovered for your own fabric) are supplied.

CHAIR BED

By day this is a $30″ \times 36″ \times 12″$-high chair that converts into a full-size bed by night. The chair is made of two $30″ \times 36″ \times 6″$ thick polyfoam mattresses with a detachable $36″ \times 6″ \times 15″$ high bolster. When laid end-to-end, the chair converts into a full-size single bed. Two or more chairs can be used in modular form, placed side-by-side, to create a sofa.

DINING ROOM TABLE

With the two tops stacked, this table measures $34″ \times 44″$, providing dining space for four. By telescoping out the third pair of legs and turning over the upper top, a $34″ \times 88″$ table is formed providing dining for eight. For storing or moving, the top lifts off the legs (attached by pins) and the three pairs of legs collapse to form a compact unit making storage easy.

COFFEE/DINING ROOM TABLE

Wherever space is at a premium, this table is perfect. With its legs on end, it is a $52″ \times 29″ \times 20″$ high coffee table. By turning the legs onto its side and placing the top across the two upper legs, the table converts into a $52″ \times 29″ \times 29″$ high dining table.

MODULAR SYSTEM

This storage and shelving system is based on a $25″ \times 16″ \times 16″$ box with almost infinite flexibility. Boxes can be stacked to produce any size book case or storage shelf. Steel pins inserted into mating holes on the top and bottom of the boxes being stacked lock the boxes securely. Drawers can be added to produce drawer cabinets or, by stacking, to produce four, six, and eight-drawer chests. Each drawer comes with two-drawer guide bars that fit into position holes in the box sides. These bars then form the guide bars on which the drawers slide.

Drawers come in three sizes: $24″ \times 7\frac{1}{2}″$ high, $24″ \times 5″$ high, and $15″ \times 4″$ high. All drawers are 16″ deep. The first two are used with the mod box horizontal. By stacking boxes and using the $7\frac{1}{2}″$ drawer, bedroom chests of different sizes can be created. The 5″ drawers can be used to create different sized general-storage cabinets.

The $15″ \times 4″$ drawer is used with the mod box vertically to produce general-storage cabinets or with the available desk top to form a four, six, or ten (with two mod boxes) drawer desk. The desk top measures $47\frac{1}{2}″ \times 24″$ wide and contains two $24″ \times 5″ \times 16″$-deep open-storage bins that can take two $24″ \times 5″$ drawers. The desk top can be used with the mod boxes fitted with drawers or with shelves or four 25″ legs.

Product Pricing

The market for furniture of this general type is value-conscious. If The Apartment Store was strictly a retail operation, it would be difficult to exceed the value offered by established competition. Because the founders plan to control both manufacturing and retailing, The Apartment Store will be able to offer furniture with a competitive style, quality, and price combination. This combination represents value to the consumer. Exhibit 4 indicates prices by product; in all cases, the price is 10 to 40 percent below that of competitive merchandise. Prices for purchased items are comparable to competitive levels (see Exhibit 5).

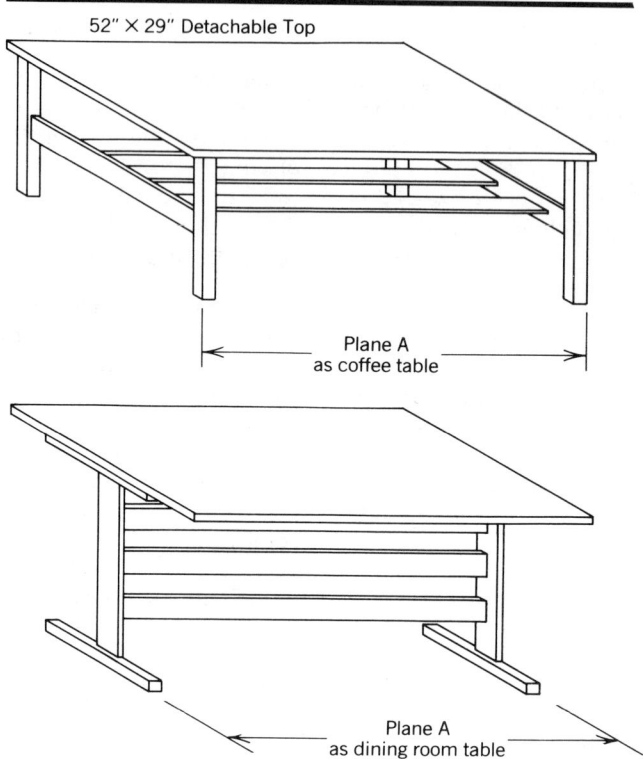

EXHIBIT 3
Coffee/Dining Room Table

Market Location

Because of the market it will serve, Cox, Wallace, and Bennett wished to locate The Apartment Store in a reasonably young, affluent metropolitan area. They limited their search to several nearby states because of manufacturing considerations, the management team's familiarity with the customs and needs of the area, and family considerations. Analysis of the alternatives centered on several quantitative factors: (1) absolute size of rental living population, (2) level of affluence, (3) mobility, and (4) age of renters. In addition, strength of competition, area growth, local customs, and other qualitative factors were considered.

The three-person management team used data from the 1980 U.S. Census to make the quantitative evaluation. The largest market area was excluded because of the heavy saturation of its retail and apartment rental markets. Manufacturing and marketing costs would also have been much higher. The city of Alexandria was selected because it was more compact geographically, had a slightly larger mobile population, and was more centrally located to the long-run market area than the other choices. Since 17,800 (73 percent) of the 24,400 rental units (with monthly rental in excess of $200) were occupied within two years of the census, Alexandria has a large market of mobile rental dwellers. In addition, 7,700 or 32 percent of the total units had a 1980 income greater than $15,000.

EXHIBIT 4
Manufactured Products

Product	Labor Cost ($)	Material Cost ($)	Total Cost ($)	Sales Price ($)	Sales Mix[a]
Table, dining	23.50	25.10	48.60	100	0.12
Table, coffee	43.50	12.30	55.80	110	0.05
Chair, low	3.70	30.10	33.80	100	0.10
Chair, high	3.70	40.10	43.80	120	0.05
Desk, basic	30.60	10.80	41.40	80	0.07
Desk, drawer optional	14.40	10.00	24.40	40	0.05
Sofa, trundle	71.50	44.70	116.20	200	0.03
Sofa, drawer optional	9.00	11.30	20.30	40	0.01
Headboard (single)	10.60	3.30	13.90	30	0.05
Headboard (double)	11.50	4.50	16.00	40	0.10
Module	12.10	5.30	17.40	30	0.15
Drawer (one)	4.70	3.30	8.00	15	0.05
Shelf	1.20	1.60	2.80	5	0.10
Magazine rack	4.50	.60	5.10	15	0.07

Source: Costs—engineering estimates. Prices—desired mark-up and competitive pressures. Sales Mix—management estimate.

Note: In all income and cash flow statements, manufactured products are assumed to constitute 80 percent of total dollar sales volume. For computation purposes, the weighted average figures above are used.

[a]Sales Mix is an estimate of relative unit sales within this group of manufactured products. Based on it, the following figures were derived:
  Weighted average cost = $29.65.
  Weighted average selling price = $59.80.

Retail Strategy

The founders of this venture realized that their ultimate success rested on retail success. Although considerable effort was devoted to choosing a market area, the second-level decision was the actual location of the initial store. The management team planned to locate the store adjacent to the plant in Alexandria. They decided against locating The Apartment Store in a shopping mall to avoid the expense of casual shoppers and the high overhead of such a location. The site for the free-standing location is advantageous, because it is convenient to major apartment locations and high traffic thoroughfares, has a reasonable rental fee, and is zoned to allow a combination retail/manufacturing facility. Since Cox's experience indicated that most furniture is sold to the serious shopper rather than the casual looker, she felt that the free-standing approach was sound.

Wallace plans to use two techniques for attracting customers. First, a substantial advertising budget would be used mostly to run newspaper ads periodically. The remainder of the budget would be used for yellow pages, apartment guides, and specialty newspapers (e.g., college papers). In all instances, ad copy would stress the value of the furniture: modest costs, flexibility, compactness, and durability. The second promotion technique would be simply displaying the merchandise. This would, of course, be accomplished primarily at the retail store. Displays would emphasize innovative room settings. Wallace also plans to make supplemental display techniques, used effectively by rental agents, such as providing furnishings for model apartments, part of The

EXHIBIT 5
Purchased Products

Product	Cost ($)	Sales Price	Sales Mix[a]
Mattress and box spring (double)	$120	$200	0.06
Mattress and box spring (twin)	90	150	0.03
Mattress, air, double	30	60	0.03
Mattress, air, twin	20	40	0.01
Bed frame	8	16	0.12
Bean bag chair	20	25	0.15
Dining chair	12	24	0.10
Bed lamp	6	12	0.10
Table lamp	10	20	0.10
Floor lamp	20	40	0.10
Pole lamp	12	25	0.05
Pictures, framed	10	25	0.15

Source: Costs—quotations. Prices—estimates based on competitive pricing. Sales Mix—management team estimate.

Note: In all income and cash flow statements, purchased goods are assumed to constitute 20 percent of total dollar sales volume. For computation purposes, the weighted average figures above are used.

[a]Sales mix is an estimate of relative unit sales within this group of purchased products. Based on it, the following figures were derived:
  Weighted average cost = $20.90.
  Weighted average selling price = $38.95.

Apartment Store display approach. Finally, the owners plan to make shopping convenient for the apartment dweller by accepting cash, checks, and bank credit cards as payment. They also hope to assist in arranging bank credit through their bank. Store hours would be 10:00 A.M. to 8:00 P.M., Monday through Saturday, for the convenience of the working customer, and free delivery would be provided within the metropolitan area.

Long-Range Marketing Strategy

Within five years of the initial opening, the management team plans to expand The Apartment Store to five metropolitan areas in a two-state region. Details on this expansion are given in the financial exhibits. This expansion would follow the same approach as was used in the original location in Alexandria. Retail and advertising skills, tested in Alexandria, would become more effective with experience. In general, the limits on growth would be primarily financial and organizational. The latter is crucial, since store managers must be hired and developed as the network of retail outlets expand. Since a poor manager could destroy an excellent marketing effort, future growth is purposely limited to five stores in five years to prevent undertrained management.

Production

Physical Requirements

Furniture production requires a substantial investment in equipment, tools, and inventory. These requirements are detailed in a layout (Exhibit 6) and equipment list (Exhibit 7). Since the production requirements are for short runs of differentiated products, a job-shop approach is planned for manufacturing. The system calls for three basic operations: machining, assembly, and finishing. The proposed facility would be adequate for production levels anticipated in the first three years. The purchase of additional equipment (less than $10,000 in cost) would allow the five-year production targets to be met. The proposed facility is designed to meet all applicable OSHA (Operational Safety and Health Act) and pollution controls regulations.

Staffing

Initially, the operation would be under the direct supervision of Bennett, Vice President—Operations. For most of the first year, her duties would include production guidelines and quality control. During that year, the direct labor force would not exceed three people. In the second year, it would grow to a maximum of five people. With the exception of a lead person, these employees would be semi-skilled.

Costing

Bennett has developed product costs based on material and labor estimates made by graduate

EXHIBIT 6
Floor Layout of Initial Factory/Sales Showroom

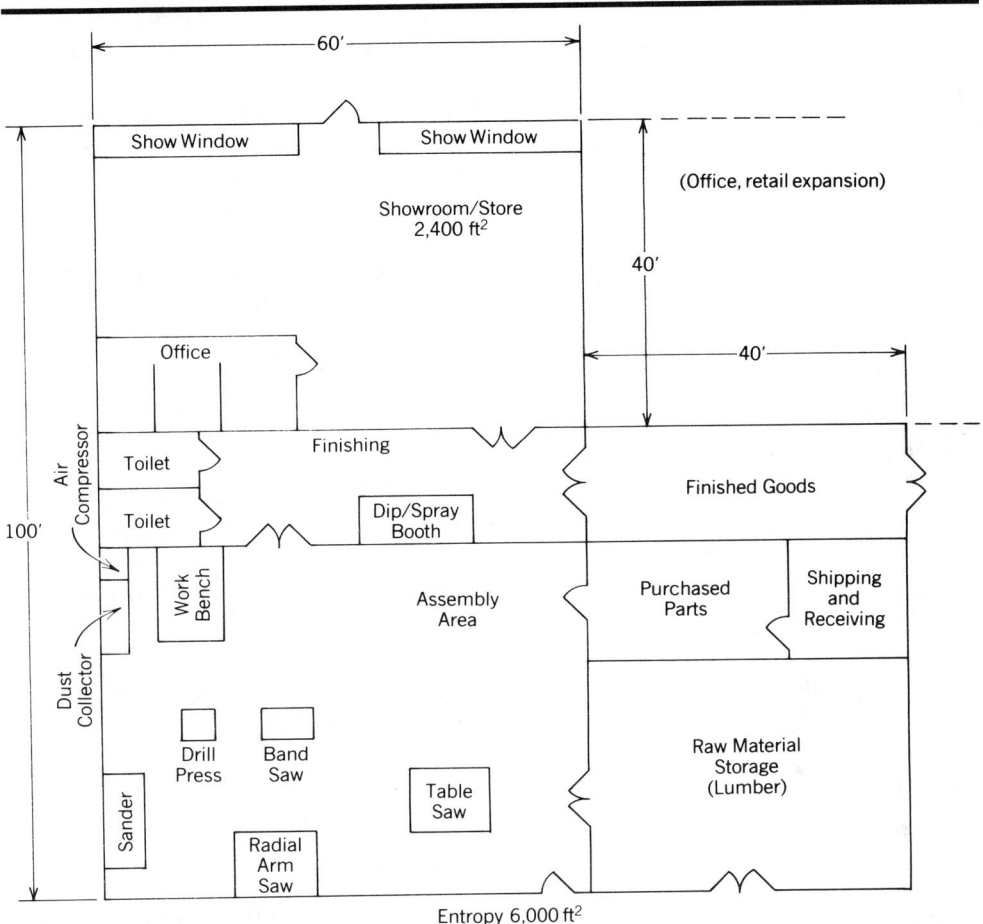

engineers. In all cases, reasonable allowances were made for additional costs because of inefficiency, scrap, and purchasing variances. All estimates assume sales volume as estimated in the exhibits and the resultant product lot sizes.

Long-Range Production Considerations

All production has been planned to be accomplished in the initial building with the addition of some equipment in year three. As volume grows, a production superintendent will be added. Growth in volume will result in reduced cost, principally because of labor and purchasing efficiencies. This improvement is reflected in all *pro-forma* statements (see Exhibits 8–11).

Finance

Sales Forecast

A five-year forecast is presented in Exhibit 8. The estimates were based on three considerations: (1) selling prices, (2) sales levels of competitors and similar businesses, and (3) market size (Census data). Sales growth will come partially from individual store growth; it is planned,

EXHIBIT 7
Plant and Equipment

Item	Price ($)
Dust collector	4,500
Air compressor with tank	1,000
Contour sander	2,000
Band saw	600
Radial arm saw	600
Router	500
Drill	400
Table saw	400
Total	10,000

Plant Improvements	Cost ($)
Equipment wiring	7,500
Dust collection pipes	3,000
Compressed air pipes	500
Total	11,000

Miscellaneous	Cost ($)
Material handling carts	1,000
Tools (hammers, buffers, etc.)	1,200
Office equipment	800
Total	3,000
Total cost, plant and equipment	$24,000

Source: Estimates by a woodworking manufacturer. Prices are for top condition used equipment when available.
Annual straight-line depreciation, based on a seven-year life: $3,400.

however, to achieve it primarily by expansion. The forecast includes the slow growth that is characteristic of new furniture retailers at any given location.

Financial Structure

The initial financing is planned to consist of $32,000 in common stock, $12,000 in unsecured convertible debentures, and a $20,000 secured bank loan. Each member of the management team is participating financially by contributing capital and accepting a reduced salary ($8,000 annually) to start.

The common stock will be issued with a par value of $100. Of the authorized 1,000 shares, the management team plans to purchase 40 each and sell 200 shares to outside investors. There will be only one class of common stock, with all having equal voting rights per share.

The convertible debentures are $1,000 face value with an interest rate of 10 percent, payable in the year 2000. The three founders plan to purchase four debentures each. The conversion ratio will be one debenture for 10 shares of common stock, with conversion taking place at the request of the holder. The debentures will be unsecured.

The $20,000 bank loan will be secured by equipment and inventories. The founders anticipate an annual interest rate of 10 percent and that the note will be payable on demand. The pledged security would amount to approximately 175 percent of the loan amount. With such a structure, the debt-equity ratio would be 0.625 not including convertibles, 0.50 if they are included.

The Apartment Store will be incorporated in the state where the founders live and will be organized under the provisions of Subchapter S. The Apartment Store meets all Internal Revenue Service requirements for Subchapter S election.

Potential Return

The founders plan to defer debenture interest payments in the first year. This would give The Apartment Store a positive cash balance of $8,540 (Exhibit 9) and a net loss of $27,200 (Exhibit 10). Under Subchapter S, this loss would be passed on directly to the investors. The management team hopes this will be a major selling point for acquiring outside investment. Each investor, if in the 60 percent tax bracket, would realize a tax saving of $5,100 during the first year. In the second year, the return is anticipated to be small. Beginning in the third year, Subchapter S would be revoked, and the operation would begin as a normal corporation. With positive earnings in year three, the investor would receive stock appreciation plus

EXHIBIT 8
Five-Year Sales Forecast

Year	Month/Quarter	City 1	City 2	City 3	City 4	City 5	City 6	Total
1	1							$ —
	2	$4,000						4,000
	3	5,000						5,000
	4	5,000						5,000
	5	6,000						6,000
1984	6	6,000						6,000
	7	7,000						7,000
	8	7,000	$3,000					10,000
	9	7,000	4,000					11,000
	10	8,000	4,000					12,000
	11	8,000	5,000					13,000
	12	8,000	5,000					13,000
Annual Total		71,000	21,000					92,000
2	1	9,000	6,000					15,000
	2	9,000	6,000					15,000
	3	9,000	6,000					15,000
	4	9,000	6,000	$3,000				18,000
	5	9,000	6,000	3,000				18,000
1985	6	9,000	6,000	4,000				19,000
	7	10,000	7,000	4,000				21,000
	8	10,000	7,000	4,000				21,000
	9	10,000	7,000	4,000				21,000
	10	10,000	8,000	4,000				22,000
	11	10,000	8,000	5,000	$3,000			26,000
	12	10,000	8,000	5,000	3,000			26,000
Annual Total		114,000	78,000	36,000	6,000			234,000
3	1	30,000	24,000	15,000	12,000			81,000
	2	30,000	24,000	15,000	12,000			81,000
1986	3	30,000	25,000	18,000	15,000			88,000
	4	30,000	25,000	18,000	15,000	$9,000		97,000
Annual Total		120,000	98,000	66,000	54,000	9,000		347,000
4	1	30,000	25,000	21,000	18,000	12,000		116,000
	2	30,000	25,000	21,000	18,000	12,000		116,000
1987	3	30,000	25,000	24,000	21,000	15,000		125,000
	4	30,000	25,000	24,000	21,000	15,000	$9,000	134,000
Annual Total		120,000	100,000	90,000	78,000	54,000	9,000	491,000
5	1	30,000	25,000	25,000	24,000	18,000	12,000	144,000
	2	30,000	25,000	25,000	24,000	18,000	12,000	144,000
1988	3	30,000	25,000	25,000	25,000	21,000	15,000	151,000
	4	30,000	25,000	25,000	25,000	21,000	15,000	151,000
Annual Total		120,000	100,000	100,000	98,000	78,000	54,000	590,000

EXHIBIT 9
Pro-forma Cash Flow Statement

Year One 1984 Month	1	2	3	4	5
Sales collections	—	3,880	4,850	4,850	5,820
Misc. inflows	44,000			20,000	
Purchased goods	2,000	200	250	250	1,900
Labor	740	980	1,110	1,110	1,110
Materials	3,500	1,370	680	2,700	680
Overhead					
Manufacturing	2,020	2,020	2,020	2,020	2,020
Selling	1,800	2,500	2,000	2,000	2,000
Administrative	1,160	760	760	760	760
Interest	—	—	—	200	200
Miscellaneous		10,000	10,000	4,000	
Total outflow	11,220	17,830	16,820	13,040	9,670
Inflow less outflow	32,780	(13,950)	(11,970)	11,810	(3,850)
Cash, end of month	32,780	18,830	6,860	18,670	14,820
Inventory, end of month					
Raw/purchased parts	2,590	2,740	2,050	3,380	2,710
In-process	900	1,200	1,350	1,350	1,350
Finished	900	1,360	1,900	2,580	2,880
Purchased goods	2,000	1,800	1,550	1,300	2,600

Year Two 1985 Month	1	2	3	4	5
Sales collection	13,580	14,550	15,520	16,490	17,460
Misc. inflows					
Purchased goods	2,900	750	800	3,500	900
Labor	2,450	3,170	3,170	3,460	3,600
Materials	6,700	1,670	1,670	7,460	1,270
Overhead					
Manufacturing	2,050	2,050	2,050	2,050	2,050
Selling	3,800	3,800	3,800	5,100	5,100
Administrative	1,200	1,200	1,200	1,300	1,300
Interest	500	200	200	500	200
Miscellaneous					
Total outflow	19,600	12,840	12,890	23,370	14,420
Inflow less outflow	(6,020)	1,710	2,630	(6,880)	3,040
Cash, end of month	2,730	4,440	7,070	190	3,230
Inventory, end of month					
Raw/purchased parts	7,100	5,400	3,700	7,500	5,000
In-process	2,200	2,800	2,800	3,100	3,200
Finished	2,000	2,600	2,700	3,200	3,400
Purchased goods	3,600	2,800	2,000	3,800	2,900

Notes: 97 percent of gross sales are collected in the month of the sale; the remainder is lost to service charges. All proceeds of bank loan. Year 1, Months 2–4—Miscellaneous outflow is related to purchase of equipment and plant

6	7	8	9	10	11	12	Total
5,820	6,790	9,700	10,670	11,640	12,610	12,610	89,240
300	350	500	3,600	600	650	650	
1,110	1,110	2,010	2,300	2,450	2,450	2,450	
680	4,570	1,220	1,290	5,180	1,290	1,290	
2,020	2,020	2,020	2,020	2,020	2,020	2,020	
2,000	2,200	3,500	2,400	2,500	2,400	2,400	
760	760	1,320	1,120	1,120	1,120	1,620	
200	200	200	200	200	200	200	
7,070	11,210	10,770	12,930	14,070	10,130	10,630	
(1,250)	(4,420)	(1,070)	(2,260)	(2,240)	2,480	1,880	
13,570	9,150	8,080	6,820	4,390	6,870	8,750	
2,040	5,240	4,130	2,980	5,570	4,270	2,900	
1,350	1,350	2,100	2,400	2,550	2,550	2,200	
3,180	3,050	2,490	2,580	2,700	2,580	2,400	
2,300	1,950	1,450	3,950	3,350	2,700	2,050	

6	7	8	9	10	11	12	Total
18,430	19,400	20,370	21,340	22,310	23,280	24,250	226,980
950	4,700	1,050	1,100	4,000	1,200	1,600	
3,750	3,750	3,750	3,750	4,470	4,470	4,760	
1,320	7,920	1,330	1,320	9,440	2,360	4,000	
2,050	2,050	2,050	2,050	2,050	2,050	2,050	
5,100	5,100	5,100	5,100	6,400	6,400	6,400	
1,300	1,300	1,300	1,300	1,400	1,400	1,400	
200	500	200	200	500	200	200	
						8,000	
14,520	5,320	14,770	14,820	28,260	18,080	28,410	
3,860	(5,920)	5,600	6,520	(5,950)	5,200	(4,160)	
7,090	1,170	6,770	13,290	7,340	12,540	8,380	
2,400	6,300	3,700	1,000	5,800	3,400	2,400	
3,400	3,400	3,400	3,400	4,000	4,000	4,300	
3,600	3,400	2,900	1,800	1,800	1,500	1,500	
2,000	4,700	3,600	2,500	4,200	3,000	2,100	

inventories are at cost. Year 1, Month 1—Inflow is from stock and debenture issues. Year 1, Month 4—Inflow from improvements. The delay reflects expected purchase terms.

EXHIBIT 10
Pro-Forma Income Statements

		Year One 1984		Year Two 1985
Gross sales		$92,000		$234,000
Less: Discounts and Losses		2,800		7,000
Net sales		89,200		227,000
Cost of goods sold		46,000		117,000
Gross margin		43,200		110,000
Overhead				
Manufacturing				
Salaries	$8,000		$8,000	
Rent	15,000		15,000	
Utilities	1,200		1,500	
Depreciation	3,400		3,400	
Total Manufacturing Overhead	27,600		27,900	
Selling				
Salaries	10,000		25,000	
Advertising	7,000		15,000	
Delivery	4,000		9,000	
Rent	6,000		12,000	
Utilities	800		1,800	
Total Selling Overhead	27,800		62,800	
Administrative				
Salaries	8,000		8,000	
Transportation	1,800		3,600	
Telephone	600		1,000	
Office	600		1,000	
Professional services	500		800	
Miscellaneous	500		800	
Total Administrative Overhead	12,000		15,200	
Total overhead		67,400		105,900
Earnings before interest and taxes		(24,200)		4,100
Interest		3,000		3,000
Earnings		$(27,200)		$1,100

Note: Three percent discount allows for losses and service charges for credit sales. Income taxes begin in year three

dividends. The tax savings plus appreciation should be sufficient to attract investors. In addition, the downside risk would be minimal. If the entire venture fails in the second year, the outside investors would lose a maximum of $3,500. This includes the $5,100 tax savings, plus balancing a capital loss against a capital gain.

The purpose of the convertible debentures is to increase the tax loss the outside investor can take by reducing the equity position of the management team. In addition, it offers the management team the benefit of capital appreciation. As can be seen in Exhibit 10, the owners of The Apartment Store anticipate dividends of $4,000 in year three, $20,000 in year four, and $40,000 in year five. This, combined with a repurchase of the total outside stock for

	Year Three 1986	Year Four 1987	Year Five 1988
Gross sales	$347,000	$491,000	$590,000
Less: Discounts and Losses	10,400	14,700	17,700
Net sales	336,600	476,300	572,300
Cost of goods sold	173,500	245,500	295,000
Gross margin	163,100	230,800	277,300
Overhead			
Manufacturing	36,200	36,500	37,400
Selling	93,400	111,000	138,600
Administrative	22,500	25,400	28,300
Total overhead	152,100	172,900	204,300
Earnings before interest and taxes	11,000	57,900	73,000
Interest expense	2,000	2,000	2,000
Earnings before taxes	9,000	55,900	71,500
Taxes	2,000	20,500	27,500
Net income	$ 7,000	$ 35,400	$ 44,000
Dividends	$ 4,000	20,000	40,000

because of discontinuance of subchapter S election.

$50,000 in year five, would give the outside investors an annual return over five years of over 30 percent after taxes. Without stock repurchase, the annual after-tax return exceeds 10 percent.

Conclusion

As their meeting came to a close, Katherine Wallace turned to her two partners and said, "I think we have completed our plans. When we meet with our bankers this afternoon, we will have to convince them that we have made logical plans, have a marketable idea, and can attract those outside investors." After chatting a little longer, the three founders of The Apartment Store idea gathered their notes and exhibits and prepared to leave for the meeting at the bank.

EXHIBIT 11
Pro-forma Balance Sheets

	Year One 1984	Year Two 1985	Year Three 1986	Year Four 1987	Year Five 1988
Assets					
Cash	$ 8,800	$ 8,400	$10,800	$11,000	$13,000
Inventory					
Raw materials/purchased parts	2,900	2,400	3,500	5,000	6,000
In-process	2,200	4,300	5,500	5,000	6,000
Finished	2,400	1,500	2,500	3,500	4,000
Purchased goods	2,100	2,100	3,000	3,100	3,900
Total inventory	9,600	10,300	14,500	19,100	21,900
Plant and equipment	24,000	24,000	24,000	24,000	24,000
Less: depreciation	3,400	6,800	10,200	13,600	17,600
Net plant and equipment	20,600	17,200	13,800	10,400	10,600
Total assets	$39,000	$35,900	$39,100	40,500	45,500
Liabilities and equity					
Accounts payable	$ 1,000	$ 800	$ 2,000	$ 3,000	$ 4,000
Interest payable	1,200	1,200	1,200	1,200	1,200
Notes payable	20,000	16,000	16,000	—	—
Total liabilities	22,200	18,000	18,200	4,200	5,200
Convertible debentures	12,000	12,000	12,000	12,000	12,000
Capital stock ($100 par)	32,000	32,000	32,000	32,000	32,000
Paid-in capital			(26,100)	(26,100)	(26,100)
Retained earnings	(27,200)	(26,100)	3,000	18,400	22,400
Total equities			20,900	36,300	40,300
Total liabilities and equity	$39,000	$35,900	$39,100	$40,500	$45,500

Note: Since all sales are cash or credit card with prompt collection, accounts receivable are assumed to be zero.
Note: Convertible debentures are considered equity in anticipation of their conversion. The negative paid-in capital reflects the dropping of Subchapter S and resultant reorganization.

CRESTED BUTTE ATHLETIC CLUB

It is three o'clock in the afternoon. Seventeen women bend and stretch in sweaty silence on the blue-pile carpet in Monica's Health Spa. Tiffany Montrose stands at the front of the room. With her back to the group, she leads them through an exercise routine, choreographed to the rhythm of a pop-music hit. She studies the women's reflections in the mirrored wall before her. They seem to be doing okay—better than she is at the moment. This is the fourth time Tiffany has gone through the routine today. She wants a break.

When the music stops, she switches tapes and tells the women they're on their own for awhile. After checking the front desk to be sure that someone is on duty, she slips to the back of the room. She buys herself a fruit juice

Source: This case was prepared by M. Agee and J. Buckeye under the supervision of Professor A. K. Wickesberg, University of Minnesota. Permission to use granted by A. K. Wickesberg.

and perches on a wooden bench. From this spot, she can see her group exercising, keep an eye on the front desk, and still have a moment to herself.

"How much longer will I be doing this?" she wonders. "Will I ever have my own spa? Do I even want it?" These questions have troubled Tiffany for months—ever since her best friend, Mary Turner, suggested they open their own business in the Colorado ski resort where Tiffany's boyfriend works. At first, the idea had seemed so right that the two friends rushed ahead with plans to move. But as the time drew near to make a final decision, Tiffany became less confident. They had worked hard on the plan for their business. Tiffany really believed the idea would work. But today she is pensive again. Does she want to leave her home in Minneapolis? Is she ready to start her own business? Is their plan as solid as she thinks?

The Business Plan

The Principals

At age 23, Tiffany had just graduated from the University of Minnesota with a B.S. in business. She had earned mostly "A's," in spite of a busy schedule of sorority activities, a part-time job, a steady boyfriend, and a daily commute to campus from her parents' lakeside home in the far western suburbs of Minneapolis.

Tiffany considered her work experience quite "extensive in the area of spa management." She had managed a branch facility for the Spa Petite chain and had been a program coordinator for a European Health Spa. In addition, she had been a YMCA member and visited many health clubs. Her business studies had included a concentration in management, which she also considered good preparation for operating her own business.

Throughout college, Tiffany had planned to seek a job with some local corporation when she graduated. She wanted to stay in Minnesota. She also wanted to start a career in a large company, where she could benefit from training programs and a variety of work experiences. But when she graduated in fall 1981, jobs like that were scarce. So she decided to take a winter job in Crested Butte, the Colorado ski resort where her boyfriend managed a small condominium. When Tiffany returned to Minnesota the following spring, she found a "temporary" job as an instructor at Monica's Spa. She hoped this would keep her going until she found the corporate job she really wanted.

Six months later, she was still looking for that job. Then her friend, Mary, suggested that the two of them move to Colorado to start their own business. Tiffany took the suggestion seriously because she liked and trusted Mary. The two women had been friends since childhood, their fathers had shared a medical practice, and their mothers had worked together on numerous volunteer projects. Besides, the job hunt was not going well and Tiffany's boyfriend was urging her to move to Crested Butte.

Mary had earned a B.S. in Physical Education and had coordinated corporate physical fitness programs for two different companies. She also was an aerobic dance instructor and had spa management experience. She was a year younger than Tiffany and had just graduated from the University. Tiffany thought Mary would make an ideal partner.

When the two women discussed the idea of starting a business in Crested Butte, they decided that any business they got into would have to meet several shared personal objectives. First, it would be ["extremely important" that the business be in some industry in which both had some general knowledge.] "This will allow us to start out with a feel for what needs to be done in order to succeed," they said. [Second, they were interested in a business "that would better the community and improve the quality of life."] It should be service-oriented, so that customers and staff could know each other personally. This, they thought, would allow them to "control the image we want to portray."

With those objectives in mind, they decided to open an athletic club. As Tiffany explained it:

> The health area is a growing industry, one in which my partner and I have experience and it fills a vital role in society. Athletic clubs allow people to work out their aggressions along with providing relaxation after a hard day. With heart attacks and obesity on the rise, athletic clubs will play a valuable role in making the American way of life a healthier one.

Both women were willing to spend the time and energy needed to make the athletic club a success. They expected personal rewards to come from seeing their "energies and hard work result in a successful and fulfilling business."

Tiffany and Mary decided they would incorporate the business to avoid any personal liability; they would seek appropriate legal counsel to accomplish this. In addition, the two partners would have a legal contract between them in order to protect either or both parties in case of a split. They would call their business the "Crested Butte Athletic Club."

The Industry

With the personal objectives that Tiffany and her partner had in mind, Tiffany began to seriously investigate the athletic club industry. Adding to experience and her belief that health clubs would play an increasingly valuable role in making the American way of life a healthier one, she began to read what the "experts" were writing.

Actually, athletic clubs were known by a variety of names: gyms, workout studios, health salons, health clubs, body boutiques, and others. Their growth was following the American obsession with fitness and health.

According to the President's Council on Physical Fitness and Sports, fewer than one in four American adults exercised regularly 20 years ago. At that time, President Kennedy began programs to encourage children and adults to become more physically fit. Today, about one out of three adults (around 72 million) claim to exercise on a regular basis.

Tiffany discovered that this new emphasis on exercise and health has generated an estimated $30 billion annually in sales of sports and health equipment, memberships, books, records, company fitness programs, health foods, and diet aids. Tapes, records, and books by famous people such as Jane Fonda and Richard Simmons, made it possible for people to exercise at home, but from all the programs available in the Twin Cities, she was sure that people preferred to exercise in group settings. For example, Jackie Sorenson aerobic dance classes were offered in nearly 100 locations in the metro area.

The statistics supplied by the President's Council on Physical Fitness and Sports indicated that Americans spend $1 billion a year on sports shoes, $5 billion for health foods and vitamins, $5 billion for health clubs and corporate fitness memberships, $240 million for diet and exercise, and $2 billion a year on sports medicine.

Tiffany remembered that Wheelock Whitney had mentioned the rising corporate interest in "wellness" in his senior management course two years earlier. He indicated that companies such as Control Data Corp., 3M, Northwest Mutual Life Insurance Co., and Wilson Learning Co. believed that they were reducing employee absenteeism by adding fitness programs with names such as "SHAPE" and "StayWell." Corporate membership rates also were available at a number of athletic clubs in the area.

Nautilus Sports/Medical Industries, the world's largest manufacturer of exercise equipment, showed an increase of 100 percent in the sales of equipment in the past two years. Tiffany believed that this was consistent with the development and marketing of weight-training equipment and machines from other companies such as Universal and Olympic. Other industries that seemed to be involved were the fashion industry's exercise/dancewear market and the book industry. Just the other day she had been amazed when she visited her local B. Dalton bookstore and noticed all the fitness books, including *Thirty Days to Thinner Thighs.*

There seemed to be many social and physical benefits to exercise, including improved cardiovascular performance, reduced hypertension, stress reduction, appetite modulation, greater physical strength and flexibility, increased self-confidence, improved sleep, and better sexual stamina. The fitness professionals that Tiffany talked to seemed to think that the focus on health is a permanent one.

One exercise instructor said:

> It's not a trend that will peak and then drop off because exercise is literally addictive—that rush that runners get is the same thing you can get from an exercise routine. People are looking at exercise as a way of incorporating preventive medicine into their lives in daily activities, not just running out to a gym and doing an isolated workout. They are reading more about health and fitness, watching their diets, trying to lower their stress levels. It's a new way of life.

The Market

Location

Several objectives were included in choosing a suitable location:

1. An area in which the partners want to live.
2. A growing community.
3. Little or no competition exists in the area.

With those objectives in mind, the location selected for the athletic club was an expanding ski resort in Colorado. Crested Butte Mountain Resort (CBMR) is located 230 miles southwest of Denver (see Exhibit A). There is only one road to the town of Gunnison, 31 miles away. A vast majority of the mountain workers live in Gunnison and public transportation is highly used between towns. The women had concluded that the distance between Crested Butte and Gunnison would not be a factor affecting club membership, because of the way of life and the normal amount of traveling done. Therefore, the club's market will be the Crested Butte and Gunnison areas.

The town of Crested Butte was started in the 1880s during the gold and silver boom and served as the railhead and supply station for many mining camps. The spirit of those days still lives on in Crested Butte, and the warmth and intimacy of the town has never been lost.

The ski resort and community are growing at an unbelievable rate. This is where the main source of growth to the Club will come. By getting in at the start of the growth and peaking with the growth of the community/resort, the Club will establish a niche and benefit from a prosperous economy.

In the last year, sleeping capacity on the mountain increased by over 500 pillows and four new condominiums were built in a two-year period. Snow-making equipment was purchased last year that will allow the ski season to be extended and guarantees a consistent early opening. This is insurance against bad snow years and guests will be able to book reservations with confidence that snow conditions will be good. A new mountain adjacent to the present butte will also be opening, with skiing capacity increasing from 4,300 skiers a day to 6,400 skiers a day. The project is estimated to be completed in five-to-seven years.

Crested Butte is at the beginning stages of growth and will be growing at a fast pace for the next 10 years. Many have said that Crested Butte is the next Aspen and the opportunities for business are limitless. The area successfully

EXHIBIT A

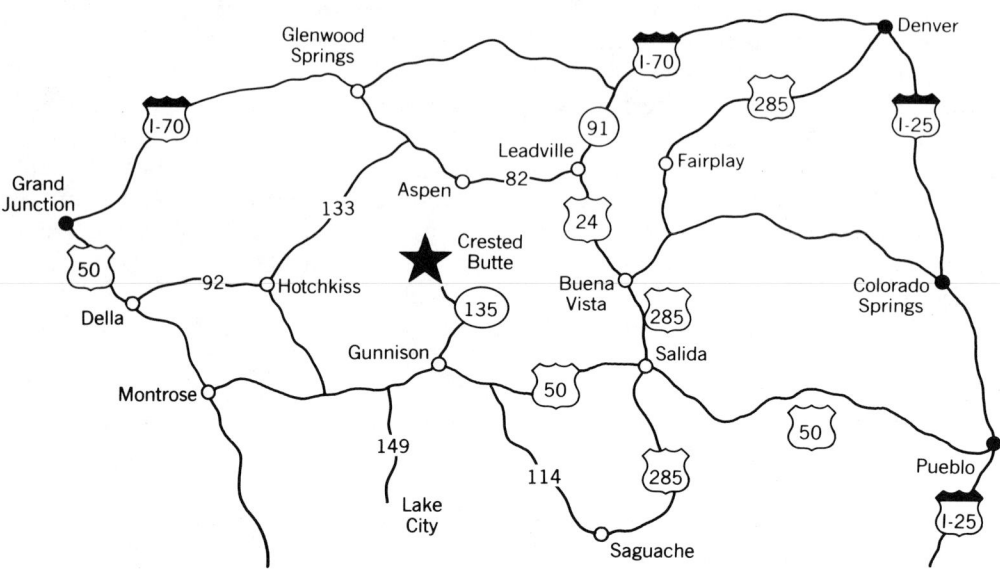

Average Distance from Crested Butte to:

Albuquerque—115 miles	Denver—230 miles	Oklahoma City—715 miles
Chicago—1,250 miles	Kansas City—790 miles	Phoenix—660 miles
Dallas—870 miles	Los Angeles—975 miles	Minneapolis—1,060 miles

meets the first two criteria in the location objectives.

The third and last criterion concerning location was an area with little or no competition. No athletic clubs exist in Crested Butte or Gunnison now. There is no competition whatsoever. Of the 33 condominiums in operation, only six have pools, saunas, and jacuzzis. Nine have saunas and jacuzzis. Five have just saunas and one has a jacuzzi only. None of the condos has gym equipment. The partners anticipate no competition from the condos and will attempt to reach a cooperative arrangement with them.

Crested Butte meets all the partners' location requirements and the site selected will utilize the free 15-minute interval shuttle bus service from downtown Crested Butte to the condos. The Club site is also within walking distance to many of the condos (see Exhibit B).

Target Market

The markets for the athletic club have been divided into three categories and are listed in order of importance:

1. *Vacationers/Guests.* With the increase in mountain capacity and snow-making equipment lengthening the ski season, this market will grow larger each year. All facilities at the Club will be geared toward this market along with the majority of the advertising budget.

   In order to market to this group, the condominium owners and mountain management will be approached because guests have first and continuous contact with these people. The selling point and emphasis used to elicit advertising will be a mutual improvement approach. An athletic club will increase the marketability of the condos

EXHIBIT B

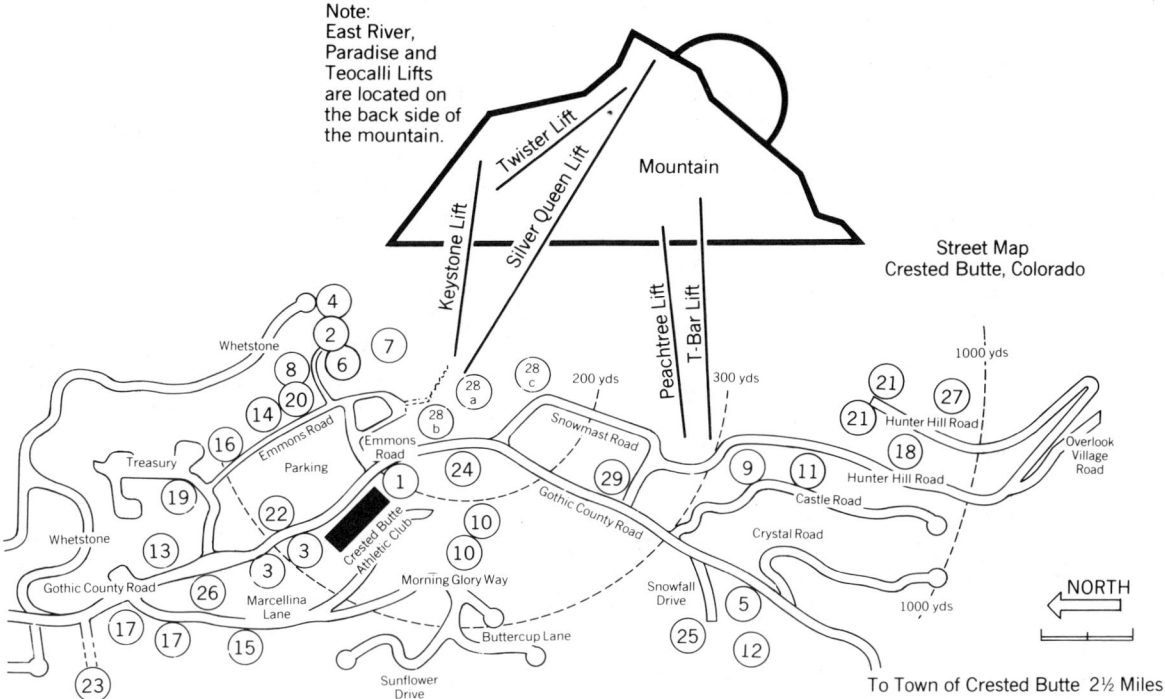

1. Alpine Condominiums
2. The Buttes Condominiums
3. Chateaux Condominiums
4. Columbine Condominiums
5. Crest House Condominiums
6. Crested Butte Lodge
7. Crested Mountain Condominiums
8. Crested Mountain North Condominiums
9. Crystal View Condominiums
10. Eagle's Nest Condominiums
11. Elk Ridge I Condominiums
12. Elk Ridge II Condominiums
13. Elk Ridge III Condominiums
14. Evergreen Condominiums
15. Moutain Sunrise Condominiums
16. Nordic Inn
17. Outrun Condominiums
18. Paradise Condominiums
19. Ponderosa Condominiums
20. Redstone Condominiums
21. San Moritz Condominiums
22. Ski Crest Lodge
23. Ski Jump Condominiums
24. Snowcrest Condominiums
25. Snowfall Point Condominiums
26. Three Seasons Condominiums
27. Timberline Condominiums
28. Village Center Condominiums
    28 a. Axtel Building
    28 b. Emmons Building
    28 c. Whetstone Building
29. Woodcreek Condominiums

Shuttle buses stop at all condominiums and run every 15 minutes between 8:30 and midnight.

---

and draw more guests to the mountain. It will add prestige and help the resort. Listing the club with the mountain's literature and the information service will be effective advertisements. The condo owners who do persuaded to buy full condo memberships not have pools, saunas, and jacuzzis will be that would allow anyone who stays in the condo to use the club facilities.

Posters and table stands will be put in the condos (assuming the owners agree) that will almost guarantee that every guest is made aware of the club. Location also helps to accomplish visibility, since the club is on the one and only road leading to the resort.

The cost involved in these approaches is negligible, but it is time-consuming. Both partners have lived and worked in Crested Butte and have contacts with the mountain management and some of the condo owners. Although this does not guarantee their success, they believe it will help.

2. *Locals.* Locals are people who live in Crested Butte or Gunnison year-round and will be the second market for the Athletic Club. Many people live in Gunnison and work in Crested Butte, but travel between the two cities is not considered a problem. Advertisements will be placed in local newspapers with special discounts on memberships offered when the club opens. Flyers and posters will be put in supermarkets, the post office, and other heavily traveled areas. Also, word of mouth will be a major source of recognition. Special programs lasting several weeks (e.g., racquetball lessons, swimming lessons, aerobic dance classes) will be offered to draw people to the Club.

The partners will approach bigger businesses to begin a total corporate fitness program using corporate memberships at the Club. Depending on the club's success, contests between stores for most weight loss could be encouraged.

3. *One-timers.* No advertising money will be spent directly on this group. The club will offer free, one-day passes to increase awareness of the club and to get people to try out the facility with the hope that they will join. This group will be charged a daily membership fee.

Physical Facilities

The club building is already standing, plumbing has been installed, and it is properly zoned. The Crested Butte Athletic Club will feature a complete exercise room, steam bath, sauna, whirlpool, pool, hot tub, and masseuse room (see Exhibits C and D). Since most club members will use the bus, the small parking lot, with space for 12 cars, should be adequate.

Providing that the Athletic Club is successful, expansion will include a pro shop in year three and an indoor tennis court in year six. Crested Butte and Gunnison have only two outdoor tennis courts and no indoor courts. This should be a big selling point for the club, and the local market should increase with this addition.

The two partners will supply typewriters, stereo, and other general office supplies at no cost to the club, so that money can be spent on other things.

Financial Plan

Tiffany and Mary will each put up $50,000 to cover set-up costs for the Crested Butte Athletic Club. Tiffany will get her money from personal assets, family, and bank loans. The $100,000 should cover equipment purchases, set-up of facilities, remodeling, and initial inventory, and still leave the club with more than $3,000 in cash (see Exhibit E).

The club will be housed in a building that sits on land that Mary owns. The building requires extensive remodeling and a $400 monthly payment is due on it through 1995.

Crested Butte's population is expected to increase an average of 30 percent per year for the next 10 years. More guests, capacity use of condominiums, and more locals mean more business for the Athletic Club. The peak season for the club should be December 1–April 15, the usual Colorado ski season. Although guests patronize the resort year-round, summer occupancy is now about 35 percent. But this figure also is expected to increase.

Tiffany and Mary used these population figures to forecast sales for years one through five (see Exhibits F and G). They believe their sales revenue projection for year one ($49,066) is modest. They have projected a 10 percent increase in revenue for year two, a 15 percent

EXHIBIT C
2 Racquetball Courts

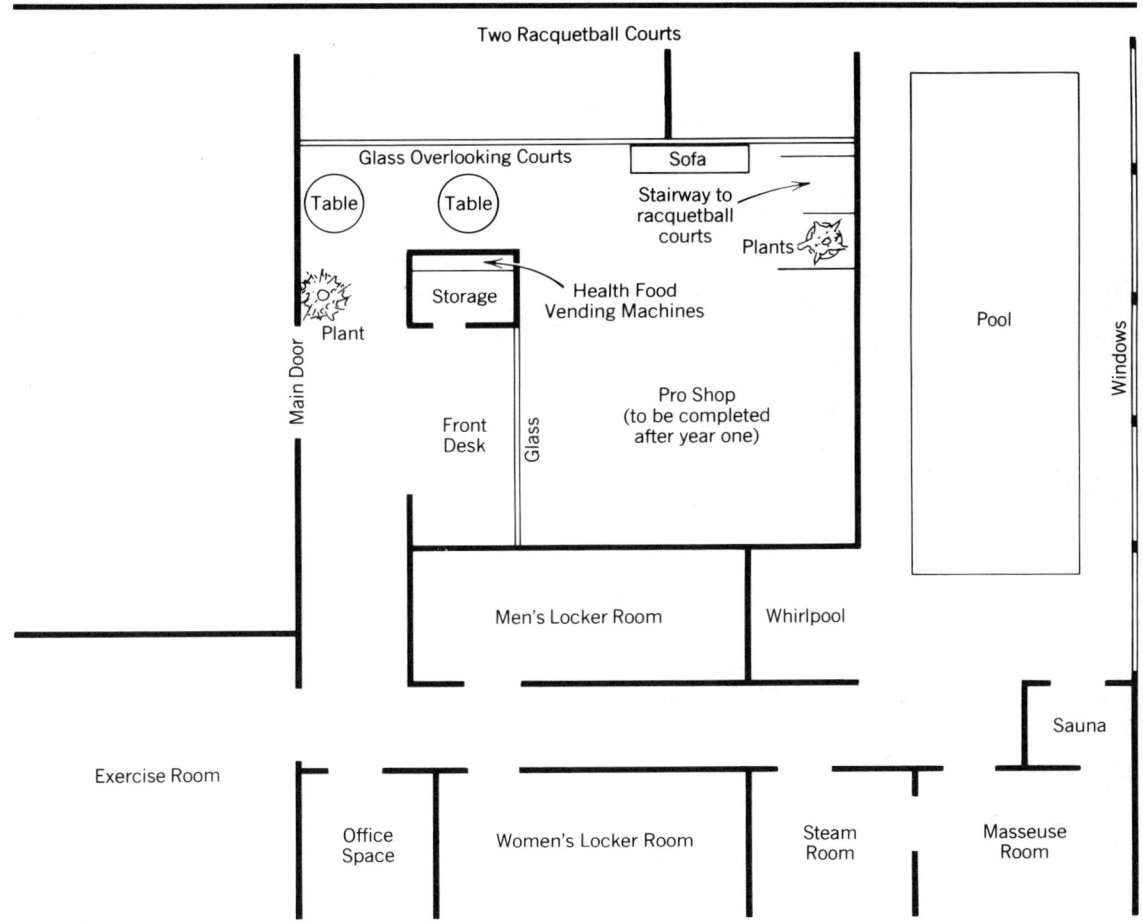

increase for year three, and a 20 percent increase each in years four and five.

By year three, the partners expect to be doing well enough to open a pro shop stocked with racquets, bags, warm-up suits, and other equipment. This addition to the club should cost about $20,000, which they expect to finance with a loan through the local bank.

Athletic Club expenses are expected to increase each year. For example, the cost of goods sold, estimated at $3,000 for year one, should increase 15 percent each year, because of inflation. "Cost of goods sold" includes electricity and water (the basic ingredients for the pools, saunas, etc.), laundry, and other miscellaneous items (e.g., shampoo, lotion, powder) (see Exhibit H).

The club's major operating expense will be salaries, totaling $28,550 in the first year. This figure includes pay for one full-time employee at $4 per hour during the peak season and one part-time year-round employee at $3.75 per hour. Worker turnover after the ski season should make this employment pattern possible. The partners believe these wages will be higher than what the other resorts offer. In

EXHIBIT D
Exercise Room Layout

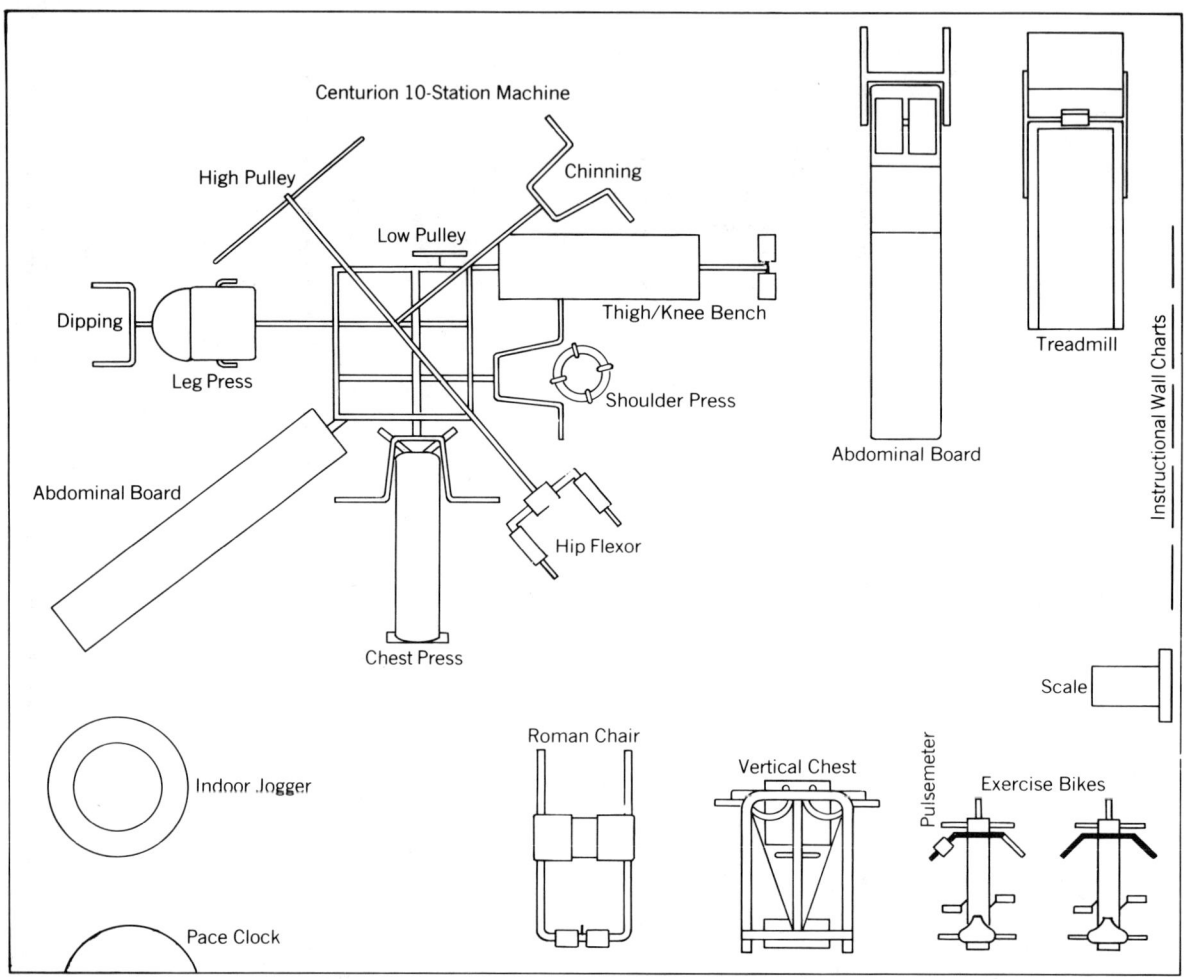

Item	Cost
Centurion 10-Station Machine	$5,935
Abdominal Board	95
Treadmill	1,225
Indoor jogger	176
Roman Chair	525
Pace Clock	305
Vertical Chest	591
Exercise Bikes (2)	500
Scale	300
Total	$9952.00

EXHIBIT E
CB Athletic Club Inventory and Equipment

Item:	Initial Cost:	Yearly Maintenance (Year 2–5):[a]
Equipment		
Exercise room	$ 9,950	$ 500
Table (2)/desk/chairs	1,200	0
Sofa	400	0
Pool	12,000	1,000
Whirlpool	6,000	100
Steam room	9,000	50
Sauna	8,000	80
Hot tub	5,000	50
Racquetball courts (2)	20,000	200
Locker room (showers, lockers, miscellaneous)	5,000	50
TOTAL	$76,550	$2,300
Inventories		
Four racquetball Racquets	$80	
Eight cans of balls	32	
Typewriters (supplied by owners)	0	
Miscellaneous Office Supplies and Towels	150	
TOTAL	$262	

[a]For the first five years, most items will not have high maintenance fees because of warranties and the newness of the items.

year three, when the pro shop opens, additional staff will be needed. By that time, the partners expect to employ two full-time workers during the peak season (at $4.10 per hour) and two part-time year-round workers at $3.80 per hour. Employees' wages will increase to $4.30 per hour (full-time) and $3.95 per hour (part-time) in year five.

In addition to their other employees, the partners plan to contract with a masseuse, to be on call for appointments only. Half the fee for a massage will go to the masseuse, half to the club.

The partners plan to take $10,000 each in salary for the first two years. In year three, they'll raise that to $12,000 each and $14,000 in years four and five.

Other operating expenses include advertising (for posters, newspapers, flyers, and magazines), depreciation (figured at straight line over 10 years on the exercise equipment), telephone, and insurance. The partners also have projected extraordinary legal fees for the first two years to cover incorporation expenses.

According to the revenue and expense projections for the next five years, the Crested Butte Athletic Club should earn a profit for the owners in years two, four, five, and beyond. Tiffany and Mary believe their five-year revenue forecast is modest, considering the market potential for the area. Although both women concede that "a projected ROI of 0.08 in year five is not the best," they are not bothered. In Tiffany's words:

> We are doing this business venture because we enjoy the industry, community, and our freedom. Over the long-run we expect to have the building and facilities paid for, and we expect to have a list of condo and business memberships. During these years, our only costs besides regular bills will be maintenance bills. We see the club as being profitable over the long-run and are willing to stick it out till the end.

Objectives

Tiffany and Mary believe that by pooling their financial and personal resources they can develop a successful business in Crested Butte. As they see it now, Mary will be in charge of personnel and maintenance, and Tiffany will handle bookkeeping and administrative duties. Both will be responsible for marketing and conducting lessons. They also would like to maintain a fully trained staff, employees who are familiar with all club facilities. Staff cooperation and familiarity with equipment and club facilities will be necessary in order to carry out the club's mission:

> ... to provide first-class accommodations giving guests red-carpet treatment. The atmosphere will be a fun and warm one, allowing

EXHIBIT F
CB Athletic Club Sales for Year 1 and First Year of Pro Shop

Type	Cost	Estimated Number of People	Yearly Revenue
Membership			
Total condominium	$2,000	Six condos a year	$12,000
Yearly	150	200	30,000
Weekly	18	16 people/week	4,608
Daily	8	100/year	800
TOTAL			$47,408
Lessons			
Racquetball	$8/hour	4 people/4 lessons each	$ 128
Swimming	$15/six weeks	30/year	450
Aerobic dance	$15/session	10 people/4 sessions/year	600
TOTAL			$1,178
Masseuse[a]			
Contracted out when needed. Club will receive $10 and masseuse will receive $10, plus tips.		48/year[a]	$480
TOTAL			$480
Pro Shop (not opening until after year 2)			
Based on Revenue of Sports Shop in CB			$3,000 (year 3)

Total Revenue from above items

$49,066 (without Pro Shop)
  3,000 (Pro Shop)

Expected Revenue Increases (does not include 10 percent increase in Pro Shop/year)

Year 2: 10 percent
Year 3: 15 percent
Year 4: 20 percent
Year 5: 20 percent

[a]Taking 16 weeks for the peak ski season, with only three people using the service during this time.

guests to relax and enjoy the facilities. The staff will be trained in the proper use of the exercise equipment and other areas of the club. Top-level, friendly service is what the club will be known for.

It is 3:25 P.M. Tiffany is suddenly aware that the music has stopped and the 17 women in her exercise class have headed for the showers. One young woman approaches her. "Do you have extra towels in the storeroom, Tif?" she asks.

"Just a minute. I'll check," Tiffany replies. She heads for the storeroom in search of towels. But her mind is on Crested Butte and the athletic club. "What am I going to tell Mary when I see her tomorrow?" she asks herself. "Is this business a good idea or should I just head for the placement office and try to set up some more interviews?"

EXHIBIT G
CB Athletic Club *Pro-Forma* Income Statement

	Year				
	1	2	3	4	5
Sales					
Membership	$47,408	$51,315	$58,111	$72,025	$78,923
Lessons	1,178	1,878	2,778	3,778	5,278
Masseuse	480	780	1,180	1,680	1,100
Pro Shop	0	0	3,000	3,300	6,600
Total Sales	$49,066	$53,973	$65,069	$80,783	$91,901
Cost of goods sold					
Raw materials	3,000	3,450	3,968	4,563	5,248
Gross Profits	$46,066	$50,523	$61,101	$76,220	$86,653
Operating Expenses					
Salaries	28,550	28,550	41,440	45,440	50,220
Depreciation	7,655	7,655	7,655	7,655	7,655
Legal	1,000	1,000	0	0	0
Payroll taxes	3,426	3,426	4,970	5,450	6,000
Telephone	240	240	240	250	250
Insurance	4,000	4,000	4,000	4,000	4,000
Advertising	1,200	1,200	1,300	1,400	1,500
Miscellaneous (includes mortgage)	600	600	600	600	600
Total operating expenses	46,671	46,671	60,215	64,795	70,225
Net Income	$ (605)	$ 3,852	$ 886	$11,425	$16,428

Notes:
In Year 2, sales will increase by 10 percent; Year 3, 15 percent; Year 4, 20 percent. In five years we will double the initial sales. This is because of the increased capacity and the growing community. Also the Pro Shop is growing at 10 percent a year.
Cost of goods sold will increase 15 percent each year because of inflation.
Salaries will increase because of an increased number of employees.

EXHIBIT H
CB Athletic Club Cost of Goods Sold and Operating Expenses

Raw Materials	Cost Per Year
Electricity	$1,200
Water	960
Laundry (towels)	480
Miscellaneous (hair dryers, shampoo, lotion, powder)	360
Total	$3,000 (this will increase 10 percent each year)

(*Continued*)

EXHIBIT H (Continued)

Salaries	Description	Cost Per Year
Full-time	40 hours/week @ $4 (30 weeks)	$ 4,800
Part-time	20 hours/week @ $4.75 (50 weeks)	3,750
Tiffany	Owner	10,000
Mary	Owner	10,000
Total		$28,550

EXHIBIT I
CB Athletic Club Balance Sheet (Year End)

	Year 1	Year 2	Year 3	Year 4	Year 5
Assets					
Cash	$ 3,188	$ 10,238	$ 3,000	$ 12,000	$ 15,000
Accounts Receivable	4,906	5,397	6,506	8,078	9,190
Inventory	262	412	562	712	862
Total Current Assets	8,356	16,047	10,032	20,790	25,052
Building/Land	100,000	100,000	100,000	100,000	100,000
Equipment	76,550	76,550	76,550	76,550	76,550
Depreciation	(7,655)	(7,655)	(7,655)	(7,655)	(7,655)
TOTAL ASSETS	$177,251	$184,942	$178,963	$189,685	$193,947
Liabilities					
Accounts Payable					
Notes Payable	$ 40,500	$ 45,500	$ 50,500	$ 53,000	$ 55,000
(Loan)	100,000	92,000	92,000	84,000	76,000
Payroll Tax	3,426	3,426	4,970	5,450	6,000
Miscellaneous	13,325	14,016	1,493	7,235	6,947
Retained Earnings	20,000	30,000	30,000	40,000	50,000
TOTAL LIABILITIES	$177,251	$184,942	$178,963	$189,685	$193,947

Notes:
Accounts Receivable is figured at 10 percent.
Depreciation is figured straight line for ten years.
Cash Flow = Net Income + Depreciation

	Year	1	2	3	4	5
Net Income		$ (605)	$ 3,852	$ 886	$11,425	$16,428
Depreciation		7,655	7,655	7,655	7,655	7,655
Cash Flow		$7,005	$11,507	$8,651	$19,080	$24,083

SLUMBERING VALLEY, INC.

Paul Fleetwood, owner of a large tract of land and manager of a firewood operation, joined Barry Goldberg to develop the multiple-use potential of his land which is located in a state known for its tourist attractions. Ambitious plans conceived by the entrepreneurial pair during the summer of 1979 exceed their initial ability to obtain financing. Tough environmental regulations, designed to protect the natural beauty and tourism related enterprises, prove to be major barriers. The weather, always capricious in mountainous terrain also hinders the seasonal venture.

The Entrepreneurs

Paul Fleetwood, a multitalented, dynamic 45-year-old takes pride not only in his strong belief in God and his business accomplishments achieved despite adversity, but in his wife, their five teenage children, and his American Indian heritage. The son of a lumberjack, Paul grew up in the mountains of a rural state, developing a love of nature and a desire to own enough land to provide privacy as he matured. By 1979 he had acquired 700 acres of land approximately 20 miles from Sawersville, the largest metropolitan area in the state. A year of civil engineering and physics before transferring to nursing at Sawersville University provided Paul with an understanding of mechanical devices and engineering approaches to roads, bridges, and water control, and a framework of analysis for solving problems and making decisions.

At 43 years of age, Barry Goldberg recently sold his CPA practice, leaving public accounting to concentrate on his faculty duties in the business program at Sawersville University. Over the past dozen years, Barry had advised Paul on tax and regulatory matters, while Paul had assisted in making improvements to Barry's home. Both had many local business contacts and their friendship flourished.

Paul's Business History

As registered nurses, Paul and his wife, Mary, had started an eight-bed nursing home in 1963 with an initial investment of 32¢. By personally constructing an addition to the original building, they eventually expanded the nursing home to 18 beds. However, even with a 98 percent occupancy rate, an 18-bed nursing home proved to be economically untenable when state and federal safety regulations imposed increased financial burdens. In 1975, with their profit margin severely squeezed, Paul and his wife sold their nursing home.

The experience as a nursing home administrator led Paul to develop a concept of a community convalescent center that would provide intermediate patient care (between the levels provided by a hospital and a nursing home) at greatly reduced costs. Convinced that Paul's concept was viable, the National Hotel Corporation (NHC) built their first convalescent-care center in Sawersville, hiring Paul as their developer and administrator. This position provided national exposure for Paul, who wrote articles, served on national panels, and was elected president of the State Nursing Home Association. After three years as a very active, successful administrator of the 160-bed facility and 175 employees, Paul was ousted in a power struggle with the center's medical director. Two years after making the physician an administrator, NHC experienced operating losses and closed the center.

Paul retired to his land and started working on his spacious, but unfinished house. During the 1973 Arab oil embargo, realizing that his 700 acres of trees constituted a renewable asset, Paul entered the firewood business, because people in the state began converting

---

Source: This case was prepared by G. Michael, E. L. Parke, and R. Lorenz of the University of Vermont School of Business Administration to serve as a basis for class discussion rather than to illustrate either effective or ineffective handling of an administrative situation.

their home heating from expensive oil to firewood. The initial operation was strictly a family affair as the cutting, splitting, and any delivery of the wood was done by his five children in their two-cord dump truck. Reluctant to use a skidder to bring fallen trees to a landing, Paul used a bulldozer to cut logging roads wide enough for the dump truck, reducing both operating costs and damage to the land. Because firewood sales looked promising in the near future, Paul purchased an adjacent parcel of timberland (250 acres) when it came on the market at a distressed price, and incorporated his operations as the Slumbering Valley Wood Products, Inc. In 1978, he harvested 540 cords of firewood.

Barry's Involvement

Within a week of returning from his 1979 sabbatical leave in Israel, Barry went to see Paul and the progress on Paul's 4,700 square foot, two-story house. In the course of conversation, Barry inquired about the firewood business. To Barry, the firewood enterprise appeared to be a very strenuous, low-paying venture, because a cord of firewood was being sold and delivered for only $75 to $80.

Each cord weighs 2.5 tons and is moved three times before being delivered to a customer's driveway. True to his training, Barry roughed out a cost calculation of a cord of wood at $63, which did not include Paul's effort and taxes on payroll and real estate. Barry's calculations appear in Exhibit 1.

Paul disagreed with Barry's calculations, and explained the error of Barry's approach. Pointing to a cord of wood stacked near the house, Paul said, "a cord of wood on the stump becomes 1.1 cords of firewood when we use a five-star splitter. After all, we sell air in stacked wood." Continuing, Paul demonstrated, "Barry, you are thinking like an auditor again. Accrual accounting is wrong in this case. The only salary I pay is for felling and cutting, and there are no payroll taxes because I get independent contractors. The kids

EXHIBIT 1
Slumbering Valley Wood Products, Inc.

Costs of Producing One Cord of Firewood

Felling trees/cutting to 16" lengths[a]	$24
Moving wood to splitter[a]	4
Splitting[a] (two cords/hour)	2
Delivery[a]	5
Fuel for splitter, saws, and truck	6
Interest and principal payments on bulldozer, truck, and splitter	10
Maintenance of equipment	4
Insurance—Liability	3
Office and telephone	2
Newspaper advertising	2
Miscellaneous	1
Total	$63

[a]Salary items.

do everything else for family unity. Besides, I'm behind on most of my fixed payments."

Paul and Barry walked around the land adjacent to Paul's home brainstorming ways of improving Paul's cash flow. After many poor ideas including bankrobbing, their discussion took a positive turn.

Barry: Gee, Paul. You really put a lot of work into these logging roads. The water bars look good.

Paul: Sure. My truck needs room to operate. I don't have a skidder because they are expensive and do considerably more damage to the forest.

Barry: You don't cut wood in the winter! Have you ever considered converting these logging roads into cross-country ski trails?

Paul: No.

Barry: I bet there are many nordic skiers in Sawersville who would pay to ski on your land.

Barry had long harbored a goal of acquiring an apartment in Israel where he could enjoy the good life when not teaching accounting at the university. In order to reach this goal,

Barry needed some additional capital, and getting in on the ground floor of a potentially profitable small business fit his plans.

Inspired by the possibilities, Paul and Barry began to explore the steps necessary to enter the ski-touring business. Drafting business plans separately, the two men met weekly to exchange ideas.

Barry: How many kilometers of logging road do you have?

Paul: About 20 miles, but I haven't cut any roadways through the new 250 acres. Are the logging roads adequate for ski-touring trails?

Barry: Adequate! Our families and my senior class could race from a mass start and not trip one another. Those 15-foot-wide logging roads can accommodate side-by-side skiing in one direction. And the slope for your truck is great for ski inclines. We should construct a trailboard at the trailhead and intersections to post information about the trail network, and print some trail maps. The local newspaper is quietly in the printing business at rates designed to yield a contribution margin, but not cover full costs.

Paul: I know a part-time signmaker five miles from here.

Barry: There is a short section of trail just north of your house—we could run some power to illuminate that loop for night skiing.

Paul: That's not short. It's over two miles. Wire alone would cost $10,000 plus the fixtures. I couldn't run that much wire in time for the November snows. But I could clear the logs from the landing site and we could park cars close to the house.

Barry: Okay. But the driveway from the state road to your parking lot is only one lane wide and half a mile long. With any amount of traffic in winter, we'll need to widen that driveway to two lanes. And, we will need a shed to sell tickets and permit skiers to wax and warm up.

Paul: To cut costs, we could convert the living room with the fireplace for ticket sales and warming area. Part of the basement could be used for a waxing room.

Barry: If we could use the whole first floor (2,400 square feet) of your house, we could put in a snack bar, an office, and a shop to rent skis. Since neither of us have ever sold skis, someone had better look into any trade secrets.

Paul: I'll talk this over with my family. I wouldn't object to earning off-season income, but would you have the time to develop some business plans?

Barry: Of course.

Business Planning

The business planning agenda included topics such as (1) estimating the market, (2) estimating revenue and expenses, (3) financing the start-up period, (4) obtaining the necessary legal permits from governmental agencies to operate the business, (5) securing contractors to perform both inside and outside work, (6) developing an advertising campaign, and (7) insuring the business.

Market Data

To develop detailed estimates of expected revenues and expenses of a ski-touring operation, Barry collected and analyzed data from various sources. From a survey of local recreation shops in the adjacent metropolitan area, Barry learned that 35,000 pairs of nordic skis had been purchased by local residents, 75 percent of whom were considered to be "backyard skiers." Several colleges with a total enrollment of nearly 10,000 students were located within a 30-mile radius.

An interstate highway could be used to travel 12 of the 20 miles from Sawersville, with its year-round population of 100,000 plus seasonal college students, to Slumbering Valley. Located 40 miles to the northeast and 35 miles southeast of Slumbering Valley were two nationally known alpine ski resorts. These re-

EXHIBIT 2

Activity	Popularity Score	Participated
Hunting	13.2	20.7%
Ski touring	13.2	20.1
Alpine skiing	10.4	14.6
Snowmobiling	10.4	13.6

sorts attracted many out-of-state alpine skiers, but there has been a growing resistance among the skiing public to steep increases in the prices of downhill lift tickets. One nordic ski industry source predicted a constant growth of nordic skiers because of economic and health concerns, with the majority of skiers selecting the nordic variety of skiing as early as 1990.

The State's Agency of Environmental Conservation released the results of a study of recreational demand citing the comparative popularity of leisure time recreational activities among natives of the state. Barry was interested in the selected items shown in Exhibit 2.

A major manufacturer of alpine and nordic skis had recently located a manufacturing facility in Sawersville. From directories of ski-touring centers, Barry counted seven local ski-touring areas that he considered competitors in this market. Six of these ski areas were small operations, apparently operated for fun or as minor sidelines. One ski operation located 45 miles from Sawersville was well established with better vistas than those from Paul's land, but whose trails were steeper, narrower, and of generally lower quality than Paul's logging roads. Barry made a note to himself to check with other state agencies, for example, Development and Community Affairs, Forests and Parks, and Tourism, for more potential market data.

The Decision

After a month of weekly brainstorming sessions, Paul and Barry convinced themselves that the costs of converting the areas discussed as well as a skidoo for trail grooming and a warming hut on the far end of the trail network were reasonable and worthwhile investments. Barry estimated initial cash requirements at $40,000. Details appear in Exhibit 3.

Barry: I have $5,000 in a passbook account at $5\frac{1}{4}$ percent interest, and if we borrow an additional $35,000 at 14 percent, we can surely repay the $35,000 loan in four seasons.

Paul: I will contribute the land, floorspace in my house, equipment, tools, and a bulldozer to cut new ski trails.

Thus, a month after their initial discussions, Paul and Barry agreed to venture into the ski-

EXHIBIT 3
Slumbering Valley Recreation Corporation
Initial Cash Requirement

Alternate Sewer Design		$ 350
Tucker Sno-Cat—used		4,500
Drags and Sled		1,000
Lodge		
Carpet—245 yds. @ $15/yd.	$3,675	
Bathrooms	5,000	
Stair treatment	800	
Wire	400	
Woodwork	1,000	
Fixtures	500	
Drywall	500	
Taping	500	
Painting	1,000	
Other	2,025	15,400
Driveway—double width—$\frac{1}{2}$ mile dirt and 150-car parking area—dirt		5,000
Signs		350
Hut		3,500
Promotion		5,000
Maps		500
Snack bar		
Tables and chairs	2,000	
Food inventory	1,000	
Paper supply	500	3,500
Miscellaneous		900
Total		$40,000
Less Goldberg loan		5,000
Need		$35,000

touring business, and named it Slumbering Valley Recreation Corporation after a nearby valley. Their short term goal was to offer ski touring facilities during the 1979–1980 ski season.

Terms of the Agreement

Income from trail fees, snack bar sales, and ski rentals would be distributed as follows: 40 percent to landowner and partner Paul who needed current income to support his family and satisfy old debts; the balance to operating expenses (maintenance, repairs, insurance, advertising, salaries, utilities), and any profit to be equally divided between partners Paul and Barry. With the brief time left before the first snowfall, the partners wanted to find a tenant who would operate the ski shop, provide ski equipment, fit skiers with proper boots, skis, and poles, and pay rent based on sales. Such a tenant, separately insured, would limit the liability on the partnership. Paul would continue to operate his firewood business, and Barry's teaching schedule would permit him to serve as an active accountant for the firm. The business was incorporated in September 1979.

Search for a Tenant

Knowing little about ski equipment rentals and wishing to limit the liability of the partnership, Barry approached the owner of a popular cross-country ski shop in Sawersville about the possibility of establishing a branch ski shop in the Slumbering Valley lodge.

John: For years I've wanted to be associated with a recognized ski-touring center. Will Slumbering Valley be one of the top 10 centers in the United States?

Barry: I like cross-country skiing but I don't know if our trails will be that good. What makes a good ski-touring area?

John: I'll send two of my employees to look over your trails and let you know.

Peter, a forester, and Rick, a former U. S. Ski Team member, made three visits to Slumbering Valley. Paul's habit of showing visitors the trail system in stages, with the more scenic trails last, made an impact. While walking the trails, Paul elaborated on some potential development ideas as Rick and Peter took in the views and suggested trail-marking systems, locations for trail maps, and extending a few trails to make turns safer. The glowing reports to John resulted in his agreeing to open a branch at the lodge. Independently, Peter and Rick offered to operate a ski school on a fee-sharing basis with Paul and Barry.

Thoughts of being part owner of a top 10 ski-touring center exhilarated Barry. Paul, meanwhile, contemplated further development of tourist facilities for other seasons, possibly year-round use, to smooth income flows—a restaurant, tennis courts, a pool, a golf course, condominiums, and a hot tub for the ski center. Land improvements would increase his land values at least fivefold, permit him to ease out of the strenuous firewood business, and return to administration.

Because time was short, Paul moved rapidly to secure bids from contractors to widen the driveway and gravel the parking lot, remodel the first floor of Paul's house as a lodge, construct a warming hut, and install a larger sewage system. Despite the lack of funds, contracts were awarded to those contractors who promised completion of work before the first snowfall and would accept installment payments after the work was completed. Paul supervised this activity.

Organization

Barry, Paul, Peter, and Rick formed an *ad hoc* board of directors for the overall venture, covering trailmaking, ski shop and ski school operations, wood operations and marketing. Paul emerged as the leader because of his insight, experience, and major financial risk bearing. This group met every Monday to establish a list of projects and goals, and to implement them in the time remaining before the first snowfall.

Advertising/Promotion

Everyone recognized that advertising would play an important part in the success of the project. Much time was spent discussing advertising methods. Financial constraints precluded a total media program. However, without good advertising, money would be lost. The group decided to hire the advertising agency that John's Ski Shop used. The advertising agency agreed to develop a logo and a brochure, the latter to be distributed by mail to known X–C skiers and groups in the area and displayed in ski shops. In addition, they agreed to accept payment in January 1980. Trail maps and the brochure were printed by the local newspaper.

After much debate, the group decided to name their ski-touring center Slumbering Valley, thus, helping people in Sawersville to recognize its location. Where better to look for the Slumbering Valley Ski-Touring Center than on Slumbering Valley Road.

Ads used on a scatter basis would be placed in the Thursday and weekend editions of the *Metro Free Press*, the major newspaper of the state. Color ads would consistently feature the name, logo, map of the ski center's location, and a description of the activity that was on hand. Half of the advertising budget ($5,000) was allocated to the print media; the remainder would be spent on radio spots, posters, and flyers.

The promotion campaign to draw skiers to Slumbering Valley included a schedule of events: a gala grand opening featuring a female personality (more women than men cross-country ski) and prizes provided by 10 of Barry's former accounting clients; demonstrations of cross-country ski equipment by various manufacturers; a citizen's race that pits skiers against other skiers in a similar age bracket; a spring skiing/suntan lotion day to get an early tan; free trail passes for high-school nordic teams to spread the news by word of mouth. The partners were convinced that the wheel of fortune would be set in motion by getting the skiing public to make that first visit—once on the Slumbering Valley trails, they would return repeatedly for the sheer beauty of safe, scenic trails.

Insurance

Over the past decade, most of the state's alpine ski slopes had been sued by patrons who fell or tripped while speeding down the slopes. Court-awarded settlements to plaintiffs of $500,000 were not uncommon in such cases. To protect their assets, Paul and Barry sought insurance from the unexpected. Local insurance firms made little distinction between alpine and nordic ski operations and were reluctant to insure either. The partners turned to the National Ski-Touring Operators Association (NSTOA). For a modest 2 percent of sales revenue, Lloyd's of London insured NSTOA members for liabilities up to $500,000 per accident. Paul and Barry elected to take an additional $1 million umbrella policy above and beyond the basic Lloyd's minimum policy.

Industry associations such as NSTOA provide business people with an opportunity to discuss common problems, to organize lobbying efforts for the benefit of the entire industry, and a chance to meet competitors, When NSTOA scheduled an autumn meeting at a ski area in the southern regions of the state, Paul and Barry attended. Dressed in suits, they found everyone else dressed casually. Their initial unease turned to confidence as they heard their fellow operators talking about trails six-feet wide. "By comparison," said Barry, "our trails are skiways." Any fall on a six-foot-wide trail could lead to a collision with bordering trees and result in possible head injuries. Pleased with their double-tracked, one-way, 15-foot-wide trails, Barry's hope that Slumbering Valley would achieve recognition as one of the top 10 ski-touring centers changed to absolute confidence. Euphoric, the partners bought

EXHIBIT 4
Sawersville Meteorological Data Averages (1906–1967)

Month	Temperature (°F)	Rainfall (Inches)	Snowfall (Inches)	Percent Sun	Cloudy Days[a]	Thunderstorms	Wind Velocity
Jan	18	1.8	18	39	20	0	10
Feb	19	1.7	18	46	17	0	10
Mar	30	2.1	11	52	18	1	9
Apr	43	2.4	2	48	18	1	10
May	55	3.0	0	55	16	3	9
Jun	65	3.5	0	60	14	5	8
Jul	70	3.6	0	63	12	8	8
Aug	67	3.4	0	61	13	5	8
Sep	60	3.3	0	55	13	3	8
Oct	49	2.9	1	49	15	1	9
Nov	37	2.7	10	30	22	0	10
Dec	23	2.0	15	33	21	0	10
ANNUAL	45	32.3	71	51	199	30	9

[a]Cloudy means no sunshine showing during 50 percent or more of the daylight hours.

some space announcing the opening of Slumbering Valley in the NSTOA publication.

Ski-Touring Expenses and Revenues

Paul informed Barry that the 900 to 1200 foot elevation of the Slumbering Valley trail network promised skiable amounts of snow for a 13-week ski season. Barry checked with the Agricultural Extension Service at Sawersville University which provided the average snowfall each month found in Exhibit 4. Since Slumbering Valley was 600 feet higher in elevation than Sawersville where the measurements were made, these averages could be considered minimums. Barry also noted that the average maximum temperature in Sawersville for the period of December 25 to January 2 was 29°F and the average minimum was 11°F from 1885 to 1967. Paul claimed the winter temperature at his lodge was always 10 to 12 degrees lower than the temperature reported at Sawersville.

Barry reasoned that a $5,000 advertising campaign would draw 2,000 skiers per week to the ski center. Multiplying this estimate by a 13-week season, Barry came up with a base of 26,000 "skier days." Going one step further, he recognized a concept of steady patrons and placed this as an average of four visits per season, or 6,500 ski patrons. Assuming 10 percent of the ski patrons would buy a season pass, the

EXHIBIT 5
Projected Revenue from Ski-Touring Activities

1. Average 2,000 skier/week × 13 weeks = 26,000 skier days.
2. 26,000/average of 4 visits per season = average number of ski patrons (6,500).
3. 6,500 ski patrons minus 650 season-pass holders = 23,400 skier days.
4. Revenue from daily trail fees @ $3 ... $70,200
5. Revenue from season passes: 650 @ $40 ... 26,000
   Estimated total trail revenue ... $96,200
6. Equipment rental—20% of skier days @ $7.50 ... $39,000
7. Ski school—2% of skier days @ $9.00 ... 4,680
   Estimated gross revenue ... $139,880

remainder would purchase one-day trail passes. At $40 and $3, respectively, a trail revenue of $96,200 was estimated. Ski lessons and equipment rental revenues were estimated at almost $44,000, with gross ski revenue reaching nearly $140,000. An itemized projection of the ski revenue is included in Exhibit 5. Projected ski expenses are found in Exhibit 6.

Financing

In September, Barry approached friends, who in August had encouraged his venture, but

EXHIBIT 6
Projected Expenses of Ski-Touring Operation

Trail grooming	$ 3,250
Salary: Tickets and grooming	2,000
Supplies: Misc., payroll tax	3,000
Utilities	3,500
Rental equipment	2,500
Ski instructors	1,872
Advertising, P. R.	10,000
Sales tax (3%)	4,074
Insurance (2%)	2,798
Total estimated expense	$32,994

EXHIBIT 7
Slumbering Valley Recreation Corporation Estimated Cash Flow (1979–1980)

Revenue	Estimated Paying		
Week (1 to 18 Weeks)	Adults	Children	
1 Opening week free	0	0	
2	200	100	
3	300	150	
4	400	200	
5	450	225	
6	500	250	
7	500	250	
8	550	275	
9	600	300	
10	700	350	
11	750	375	
12	750	375	
13	750	375	
14	750	375	
15	500	250	
16	500	250	
17	500	250	
18	500	250	
Total	9,200	4,600	
Rate	$3	$1	
	$27,600	$4,600	
Total Trail Fees			$32,200
Food Net Income			
½ people yield 50¢	2,300	1,150	3,450
Wine–Beer / ¼ adults 50¢	1,150		1,150
Rentals—10% commission / 10% of people @ $8 (13,800 × $8 × 0.10)			1,104
Sales—10% commission estimate sales 15,000			1,500
School—25% commission / 10% of people one $10 lesson (13,800 × 0.10 × $10 × 0.25)			3,450
Total Estimated Revenue			$42,854

found his appeal for loans being turned down in preference for the 14 percent no-risk return from treasury bills. Pursuing the necessary financing, Barry approached Larry, a neighbor who was a loan officer at the Last National Bank.

Barry: Can your bank lend my skiing operation $50,000 for four years at the going interest rate (16 percent at this time)?

At this point, the costs of converting the house into a lodge were running over budget and adequate trail grooming required something larger than a snowmobile. A used Tucker Sno-Cat was found for $4,500.

Larry: What do you need the money for?

Barry: My partner and I have formed Slumbering Valley Recreational Corporation and are building a ski-touring center that we expect will be one of the top 10 centers in North America.

Larry: We are already financing a cross-country ski area that got off to a late start last year. The bank doesn't want to finance a second ski area. One's enough.

Barry: Would you look at my projections to see if the estimates are reasonable, and slipped schedules of initial cash requirements and estimated cash-flow schedules (Exhibits 3, 7, and 8) in front of Larry.

Larry: After a quick scan, these are right on the money. Probing the matter further, Barry quizzed Larry about income and cost relationships, and expenses possibly overlooked in this initial projection. A change of mind occurred.

Larry: Perhaps I was too quick. Let me present your request to the bank's loan committee. I'll get back to you in a week.

A week later, Larry called and said, "It's good. You will be successful, but the Loan Committee prefers treasury bills at 17 percent to ventures."

EXHIBIT 8
Slumbering Valley Recreation Corporation
Estimated Cash Flow (1979–1980)

Expense		
Insurance—2% of trail fee and food and wine sales + 2% tax	$ 751	
Membership in NSTOA	150	
Principle and Interest $40,000, 4 year, 14%	13,118	
Salary—Paul $300 × 18	5,400	
Other salary—Net of food sales	0	
Equipment rental	900	
Tucker—Repair	1,000	
Gas, oil, insurance—Tucker	1,000	
Office	300	
Professional Service	1,000	
Trial fees 50%	16,100	
Total Estimated Expense	$39,719	
Revenue		$42,854
Expense		39,719
Cash Increase		$ 3,135

Pressing on to another bank and another acquaintance from his days as a CPA, Barry broached the idea of a loan.

Barry: I am involved in a cross-country ski area. Here are the financial projections. I want to borrow $50,000 from your bank.

Stan: These are interesting projections. We don't mind financing, but because of current interest rates, we don't want to touch risk areas. But if you have a strong personal balance sheet, we will finance you.

Barry: You mean if I personally guarantee everything?

Stan: Yes, of course.

From his briefcase, Barry reluctantly retrieved his personal balance sheet showing assets, debts, and $20,000 of equity, and the joint assets, liabilities, and $115,000 of equity held in common with his wife.

Stan: We won't loan to you, but we will loan to you *and* your wife.

Barry: I'll check.

A discussion followed between Barry and his wife, who had the final word.

Barry's wife: I'm just finishing my B.A. in history which I started 24 years ago. I'm doing well and really enjoying it. I didn't mind when you took out $5,000 and put it into the ski area; I don't mind if you take a little bit more, but NO WAY, NO WAY AM I GOING TO SIGN AND RISK MY HOUSE. ABSOLUTELY NOT!"

When Barry explained his wife's attitude to Stan, Stan said, "Barry, you're lucky. You've got a smart wife. No loan."

In October 1979, Paul and Barry concluded that debt financing was not a practical alternative to their capital needs. Paul recognized that the land was the only asset upon which people would base an investment. Market values of the land parcels had increased substantially since Paul and his wife, Mary, had acquired them.

Paul: What are the tax implications if we form a parent corporation to own the land, the wood company, and the recreation corporation?

Barry: Paul. If you and Mary transfer the land into a new corporation for common stock, you qualify for a Section 351 tax-free exchange. But you need to own at least 80 percent of the initial stock.

Paul: Fine. Mary and I will own 80 percent, and you will receive the remaining 20 percent. Then, we'll sell stock publicly to raise working capital.

Barry: Why should you give me 20 percent of the land?

Paul: Had you not lent me $13,000 for a down payment, I would have lost the 250-acre parcel of prime land for skiing and development. The 1,300 foot easterly road frontage and large meadows makes it ideal for condominiums. In time, real profits will come from that land. Incidentally, I put a $1,000 deposit on Mrs. Smith's land. You know, her land is on both sides of the road. The piece on our side is the last piece to the puzzle. We now have over a mile of road frontage to the west. On the other side, we could build luxury housing. She thinks there are 200 acres in both parcels, but she's wrong—there are 350 acres. Land deeds in this area used only rough estimates. The price is $100,000 and we don't need the balance of the price until May 1980.

Barry: Thank you. I accept your stock offer. As part of the original stock for land transfer, I too, will come under Section 351. Granted my basis is only $13,000, but I'll worry about capital gains in five years. We can transfer in the two operating companies as wholly owned subsidiaries, and sell equity . . . PAUL! WHERE DID THE $1,000 COME FROM?

Paul: I'll get our lawyer right on the land transfers and the establishment of Slumbering Valley, Inc. as a land-holding company . . . oh, I called an old friend and borrowed the $1,000 from her Master Charge. I told her we would pay $1,015 in 30 days.

Sixteen hundred shares were issued to Paul, Mary, and Barry in exchange for $380,000 net equity in the market value of the land, subsidiary companies, and a modest $32,956 excess cost over book value of the subsidiaries. Each owner's share was worth roughly $238 per share.

Slumbering Valley, Inc. (SVI), the parent holding corporation, was formed on November 1, 1979. Immediately Paul found some people, both resident and nonresident, who invested $2,500 each in SVI stock at $250 per share. Barry had been advised by his business school colleagues that the interstate sale of less than $100,000 was exempt from SEC regulation. A printer of stock certificates was found and an ample supply of certificates ordered. Barry developed a budget of $99,999 and results of funding through December 19, 1979 which is displayed in Exhibit 9.

Part of the new money was used to pay off the $4,500 Tucker Sno-Cat. Immediately, Paul refinanced the asset at the Sawersville Bank for

EXHIBIT 9
Slumbering Valley Cash Flow and Obligations (Nov. 1, 1979–Dec. 19, 1979)

	Budget	Receipts		Probable Debt Conversion	Uncommitted Balance
Financing					
Stock	100,000	22,500		9,000	68,500
Short-Term Debt	0	32,500		(9,000)	23,500
	100,000	55,000		0	45,000

	Budget	Expended	Accounts Payable	Expenditure	Uncommitted Balance
Expenditures					
Act 250 Requirements	1,500	2,245	700	300	(1,745)
Tucker Sno-Cat	4,500	4,500			0
Drags and Sled	3,500	500	3,000	100	(100)
Leasehold Improvements—Lodge	20,000	10,800	6,500	5,000	(2,300)
Driveway and Parking Lot	5,000	9,950	1,700		(6,650)
Signs	750	375	100	200	75
Warming Hut	4,000			3,400	600
Promotional Advertising	5,000	375		3,829	796
Maps	500			350	150
Snack Bar Equipment	4,000		375	600	3,025
Lighting-Phase I	20,000	10,000	10,000		0
Equipment Barn	8,000			4,000	4,000
Tools—Parts	2,000			1,500	500
Wood—Moving Equipment	13,500				13,500
Working Capital	7,749	7,600			149
Lodging Roads	0	8,500		1,000	(9,500)
Waxing Room	0		1,250	1,250	(2,500)
	99,999	54,845	23,625	21,529	0

Note: Expended amounts subject to reclassification after treasurer examines each bill for proper classification.
No lighting work performed. Contractor to take 10,000 stock. Must wait for Act 250 approval. Approval expected 12/21/79.

EXHIBIT 10
Projected Revenue, Expenses, and Contribution Margin for Six Activities in Year 1

Venture	Estimated Revenue	Estimated Expenses	Contribution Margin
A. Ski-touring	$139,880	$32,994	$106,886
B. Snack Bar	43,030	26,387	16,643
C. Ski shop	8,400	5,010	3,390
D. Firewood	100,000	60,000	40,000
E. Three-Season Activities	68,888	11,644	57,244
F. Hot tub	10,000	5,750	4,250
Total Revenues			288,413
General and administrative expenses			177,700
Balance			50,713

$5,000 on a 90-day, 18½ percent note. Additional funds were borrowed from friends and from Peter and Rick.

To promote the sale of SVI stock, the partners decided to host a party for potential investors. Kelly Services was hired to type and duplicate the SVI business plan. Figures for year 1 and projected revenue, expenses, and contribution margin are found in Exhibits 10 and 11.

One of the pigs that Paul raised for his family's food was slaughtered for the main course. The party in the unfinished lodge attracted many friends and acquaintances of the partners, but monies generated from the promotion failed to meet current needs. Pledges of future money made the party a partial success.

In the weeks following the party, the promised stock monies did not arrive at the same rate as the bills. To cover these expenses, the partners turned to relatives and acquaintances for short-term personal loans. Soon this money was spent, and only in mid-December did the first big stock sale ($15,000) occur. Their checking accounts overdrawn and in the position of owing the builder, the carpenter, the bulldozer payment, the attorney, and others, the partners consoled themselves with news of how ski sales in the county were rising and looked to the skies, hopeful for signs of the first snowfall.

The Trails

Paul's land, located at a high elevation, held snow from early winter through late spring. The 40-kilometer trail network brought skiers

EXHIBIT 11
Slumbering Valley, Inc. Projected Summary Schedule

	1979–1980	1980–1981	1981–1982	1982–1983	1983–1984
Contribution Margin					
Skiing—Schedule A	106,886	166,412	216,283	340,367	440,551
Restaurant–Lounge—Schedule B	16,643	26,859	36,150	46,687	60,005
Ski Shop—Schedule C	3,390	3,820	4,280	4,710	5,130
Firewood–Timber—Schedule D	40,000	50,000	45,000	50,000	60,000
Three-Season—Schedule E	57,244	91,481	107,228	137,344	150,180
Hot Tub—Schedule F	4,250	9,688	14,725	19,613	23,125
Total Revenues	228,413	347,260	468,666	598,721	738,991
General and Administrative Expense					
Salary—Administrative	87,000	115,000	125,000	125,000	130,000
Payroll Tax and Fringe	8,700	11,500	12,500	15,000	17,000
Interest	34,000	32,000	24,000	16,000	14,000
Utilities: Heat, Light, Phone	8,000	10,000	10,000	12,000	12,000
Insurance	5,000	5,000	6,000	6,000	7,000
Professional Service	15,000	15,000	20,000	20,000	20,000
Other Salary (and Tax)	10,000	12,000	12,000	12,000	12,000
Real Estate Tax	6,000	8,000	8,000	8,000	9,000
Miscellaneous	4,000	5,000	5,000	6,000	7,000
Total Costs	177,700	212,500	222,500	222,000	228,000
Balance	50,713	134,760	246,166	378,121	510,991
Land Appreciation		1,400,000	1,800,000	2,500,000	2,900,000
Total Annual Growth	50,713	1,534,760	2,046,166	1,878,721	3,410,991

to scenic viewpoints of the entire range of Iron Mountains to the west, a view of the third highest of the Blue Mountain range to the east, and Lake Wallenpaupack which divides the two. At the end of one trail was a ledge overlooking a 600-foot drop to the floor of the valley. Butternut Lodge, a warming hut, was under construction at this lookout. On its spacious porch, skiers could rest on benches and enjoy the view.

A 3.5-kilometer loop, called the Ridge Trail, was selected as the night ski trail. The entire trail was illuminated by 69 lighting fixtures, each containing three bulbs. The night trail concept was designed to attract people who work regular hours and would enjoy an after-dinner workout. Barry had determined the electric bill for the 6 to 10 P.M. period to be $30, and a break-even point would be 10 paying skiers per night session.

Government Regulation

The state, rural and naturally blessed with mountains, clean rivers, dairy farms, and tall church steeples, became a magnet to tourists in seasons—vacationers in the summer, hunters and foliage buffs in autumn, and alpine skiers in the winter. Spring was called the mud season, and no one had quite figured how to draw tourists from out-of-state during this season to enjoy the ample supply of mud. When the interstate highway system made the commute from two multimillion population out-of-state metropolies feasible, many vacation homes were constructed in the southern and northern part of the state. Hastily constructed developments on mountain slopes and river floodplains did not take into account the rock's inability to absorb sewage generated by a growing tide of humans. Pressure to preserve the state's pristine attractions, a principal slice of the tourist economy, led state legislators to the enactment of land-use legislation called Act 250. Designed principally to protect floodplains and elevations above 1,000 feet, Act 250 gave the state authority to regulate changes in land use through a system of approvals and permits. Construction in prohibited areas without an Act 250 permit risked $500/day fines for the offending firm and possible imprisonment for the principals.

Barry had budgeted $1,500 for the required plans and attorney fees. Shareholders were informed that the state's environmental criteria must be satisfied before Slumbering Valley, Inc. could open their ski-touring center. A builder named Jack was hired to shepherd the Slumbering Valley, Inc. application through the Act 250 proceedings. Exhibits three inches thick were submitted to the district's Act 250 Environmental Board of Commissioners. Act 250 environmental criteria pertinent to Slumbering Valley, Inc.'s application are listed in Exhibit 12. Neither Paul, nor Barry had realized how slow, tedious, and difficult Act 250 proceedings would become. The Slumbering Valley application was heard by the Commissioners on December 23rd. The exhibits argued that the sewage system was adequate, the well overflowing, soil erosion negligible, the effect on the schools nonexistent, and the trail network would not disturb wildlife.

Meetings of the Environmental Board tend to be lengthy, because the democratic tradition in its purest form permits everyone to speak his mind without a time limit. Six residents residing on the unpaved state road leading to Slumbering Valley attended the hearing, objecting to the potential for increased traffic by their homes. After seven hours of hearing, the Board adjourned without approving the permit application. Objections to the sewage system and traffic remained unsolved. Some of the construction at Slumbering Valley was being performed as improvements to the lumbering operation and house that needed no Act 250 permit. But, items directly related to the skiing operations, for example, installation of the illumination system on the Ridge Trail could not be started without a permit. Fines of $500 per day for violating the law did not both-

EXHIBIT 12
Pertinent Act 250 Environmental Criteria.
Guidelines for Proposed Changes in Land Use in Vermont

1. Will not result in undue water or air pollution.
2. Has sufficient water available for the needs of the subdivision or development.
3. Would not unreasonably burden any existing water supplies.
4. Would not cause unreasonable soil erosion or effect the capacity of the land to hold water.
5. Will not cause unreasonably dangerous or congested conditions with respect to highways or other means of transportation.
6. Will not create an unreasonable burden on the educational facilities of a municipality.
7. Will not create an unreasonable burden on the municipality providing government services.
8. Will not adversely effect the esthetics, scenic beauty, historic sites, or natural areas, and necessary wildlife habitat and endangered species in the immediate area.
9. Is in conformity with local or regional plans.

er Barry, but two years in prison did. The lighting system was placed last on the partners' list of things to do and work proceeded on any projects related to the wood business. Snow had fallen four times and melted by this date. But, since none of the competitors had opened, Paul and Barry were philosophical about the snail's pace of obtaining the essential permit.

The Act 250 hearing resumed on December 27th, with Harry, the Regional Planning Commissioner objecting to the commercial use of land above the 1,000 foot elevation. Parts of the Slumbering Valley network rose to 1,200 feet in elevation, a great advantage in attracting and holding heavy snow accumulations. The argument developed more or less as follows:

Chairman of Environmental Board: Would recreational purposes be acceptable to your overall plan?

Harry: Yes. However, this firm is not recreational, it is commercial. They charge for the use of their trails.

CEB: If the State owned the land, operated a cross-country ski area above 1,000 feet, and charged a modest maintenance fee, would that be acceptable?

Harry: Absolutely. We think the State would do an admirable public service in providing a cross-country ski area above 1,000 feet.

CEB: What difference exists between the State and private enterprise operation of a cross-country ski area?

Harry: Private enterprise is commercial, it is bad.

CEB: Objection overruled.

Compliance to other objections took the form of installing low-water toilets and posting signs warning of children along the state road to be used by skiers. The Environmental Board granted approval, but not the permit; without a permit, no work could be performed on the lighting of the trails. On January 3rd, the permit was issued, ending a three-month process that consumed 300 man-hours and cost $6,488.

Another source of governmental regulation was a safety inspection of the premises by the village fire department. Unanticipated was their interest in barriers to the physically handicapped. Arguing that wheelchair-bound customers should not be excluded from the ski shop, snack bar, or toilet facilities while waiting inside for skiing friends, the fire department cited Slumbering Valley for violating the law by not providing elevator and toilet facilities for the handicapped. The cost of these modifications was estimated to be $50,000. Paul and Barry sought and received an exemption from the regulation as the lodge was an existing building rather than a new one, used primarily as a private home. By mid-January, 1980, temporary permits were in hand, but neither a snack bar nor a bar could be operated because of an incomplete sewage system. The partners resorted to paper plate service in the snack bar.

The 1979–1980 Ski Season

In November, skies darken, temperatures turn brisk, and skiers think snow. Ski sales pick up and conversations turn to the selection of equipment. In the fall of 1979, the media hype about the Winter Olympic Games scheduled in Lake Placid raised expectations higher than usual. What better timing for the grand opening of the Slumbering Valley cross-country ski center?

By mid-January 1980, all trails were marked. Signs at the entrance were erected. The ski shop and snack bar were well stocked. The lodge was beautiful in its new decor. Spot ads in the local newspaper and on radio stations had informed cross-country skiers about Slumbering Valley's existence and location. Only one element was missing—SNOW.

Meteorological records show a consistent history of at least two six-inch snowfalls at Sawersville's low elevation during the month of December, and more at higher elevations. Less snow fell during December, January, and early February 1979–1980 than in the past 68 years. The meteorologists were kind, explaining that this situation could not have been expected. Paul and Barry had opened a ski-touring center in a year of snow drought. By February, the Lake Placid Olympic Games were being run on snow trucked from distant locations.

Slumbering Valley had enough snow for only eight days of skiing in the 1979–1980 season. Revenue from trail fees amounted to $1417. Many skiers had used the free trail passes distributed to promote the center. As an additional promotion, members of ski teams from local schools were invited to ski at no expense. With the Recreation Corp.'s operating expenses for the season amounting to $58,237, the first season's operations ended with a loss.

Paul and Barry owed the builders $25,000. The corporate checkbooks were chronically overdrawn. Common stock sales slowed to a halt at $43,000. The partners consoled each other with the idea that the concept was right, and after all, the next season was only nine months away.

Transition

How to survive until the next season generated a lively discussion. Since this was only mid-February, the weather might turn cold and bring record amounts of snowfall to extend the season and restore income to adequate levels. Neither partner was particularly hopeful that this event would take place. Like the Olympics, Paul and Barry could truck snow from higher elevations, enough, perhaps, to cover the 3.5-kilometer Ridge Trail. A snowmaking system could be purchased and installed for $100,000, plus the cost of developing a pond to hold the water used in snowmaking. Variable costs of covering a kilometer of trail nine-feet-wide with 12 inches of snow were estimated to be $5,000. This option would mean going deeper into debt.

Parcels of land along the road could be sold to raise money, or houses could be built close to the trail network to provide an atmosphere of exclusivity. The time might also be appropriate to develop condominium units in the meadowlands. On the other hand, rather than sell assets, the partners could renew their effort to raise capital by attracting new shareholders to carry SVI over the 1980–1981 season. After all, can lightning strike twice?

Another development eliminated the need to make a decision. NSTOA petitioned Governor Richards to declare the state a disaster area because of the lack of snow, thereby permitting troubled businesses to qualify for federal loans from the Small Business Administration. However, since most downhill ski areas make their own snow and were less hurt by the snow drought, they lobbied against such a gubernatorial declaration, fearing the label "disaster area" would harm downhill ski areas. Ten years earlier, a record snowfall overwhelmed the local town snowplow fleets. To get the economy moving, the then-governor declared the state a disaster area as a step necessary to permit National Guard trucks and plows to be thrown into the snow removal battle. When the national media carried the news, many would-be out-of-state skiers, thinking the state to be immobilized, cancelled their skiing trips and depressed the alpine ski industry.

In a moment of political savy, Governor Richards declared an "economic dislocation" rather than a disaster. Economic dislocation was the buzz word for disaster that kept peace with the alpine lobby, yet permitted loans to affected businesses from the SBA. In one day, Barry completed the necessary SBA forms, requesting the maximum $100,000 to relieve Slumbering Valley, Inc. of all short-term debts and carry the current mortgage payments until the second season.

The SBA Loan

In June 1980, the SBA approved an $84,700 dislocation loan for SVI, but with SBA funds being drawn down by earlier disasters in Louisiana and Alaska, no checks were issued. However, approval of the loan provided hope to the partners and helped to fend off the anxieties of their creditors. In September 1980, a 20-year loan in the amount of $84,700 at $8\frac{1}{4}$ percent was granted to SVI to alleviate the financial stress because of the 1979–1980 snow drought, but the check issued by the SBA was in the amount of $64,700, the balance to be released in the future. Monthly repayments of $729 were scheduled to start in six months.

Some conditions were attached to the SBA loan. The SBA required life insurance be taken out on Paul and Barry. Loan guarantees were required from Paul, Mary, and Barry. In addition, the SBA took first or second mortgages on all land owned by SVI, except the lodge and its surrounding 80 acres since Paul's home had been leased, not transferred to the corporation.

The Smith Land

Even with the expected SBA funds, the partners could not raise enough money to cover all their creditors. The May 1980 payment to Mrs. Smith had been postponed 60 days. Her land was believed to be a vital element in Paul's total development scheme (condominiums, a village of stores, and a 60-bed inn) of reaping huge profits.

Paul was soliciting funds from a wealthy, prior business associate. Ted Rockford was interested in investing, but his money was tied up in his own businesses. Paul made the following offer: Ted would buy the Smith parcel from Mrs. Smith for $100,000 plus closing costs and return the $1,000 deposit to SVI. By contract, Ted would give SVI the use of the Smith land and require corporate consultation prior to reselling any portion of the land. Ten percent of all sales proceeds would come to SVI until Ted recovered his initial investment plus real-estate taxes. Thereafter, 20 percent of sales would belong to SVI. Land values were expected to grow as a result of the ski center's development, thus a conservative estimate of this offer's value was $85,000 to SVI. Therefore, SVI would offer 200 shares of stock valued at $425 per share to Ted in exchange for use of the Smith land. Ted accepted the offer.

Reassessment

Paul's drive to acquire additional acreage was part of his long-term thinking about developing a four-season resort area adjacent to the lodge. Golf, tennis, swimming, skiing, and restaurant facilities, as well as housing accommodations were the major elements in his thinking. In June 1980, Paul had time to examine the situation. Most creditors were appeased with the promise of SBA funds. Only one had quit before the work was completed and taken his case to court, but with the court backlog, that case would not be heard for two years. John had decided to withdraw his branch ski shop operation, but by now Paul and Barry had more time and experience and operating their own ski shop was an opportunity to increase profits from the sales and rental area.

Although SVI had advertised 40 kilometers of trail, 10 were too rough for general use. The summertime would be used to smooth the 10 kilometers and improve the 30 kilometers balance. Water bars were to be replaced by culverts to control water crossing the trail system. Skiers, few as there were, were delighted with the 30 kilometers of trails open during the first season. Acclaim came from out-of-state skiers, Olympic skiers, and European National "A" Team skiers. The eight days SVI was open during the first season proved that the lodge was too small. An expansion was needed for a larger ski shop, with the former ski shop space becoming dining space.

The state wanted a raised mound septic system as a minimum sewage disposal system for the lodge at a price Paul estimated at $15,000. But for an additional $35,000 sewage from the lodge, the planned 60-bed inn, village of shops, and condominium development could be pumped to a gravel pit two miles distant.

Paul: I told you, Barry, that with hard work and belief in the Lord, all good things will come. We are survivors. Do you know any other business that could open during the worst weather in 68 years and still function? It's time to raise our stock price and sell more. Let's expand and show investors that we are alive and strong. You get our lawyers working on stock registration and I'll find a builder to put up a three-story, 500 square foot addition to the lodge on credit. The basement will be showers, the main floor, the ski shop, and the second floor, offices. In the meantime, my family will live on the second floor of the original building.

Barry: Showers?

Paul: For the seven-foot diameter, outdoor, wood-heated hot tub. I'll write a new business plan; investors will want to see one. Oh! Be sure to give me five-year projections of all activities, including revenue and expenses from the three-season elements (restaurant, lounge, pool, and tennis).

First Annual Report

Barry selected October 31st as the end of SVI's fiscal year. The annual report, found in Exhibits 13, 14, and 15, reports data for the consolidated entity, then breaks out the parent land-holding entity (SVI) and the two subsidiaries, SV Wood Products and SV Recreation. Barry used the equity method of accounting. The straight line method of depreciation was used for roads, bridges, and trails (10 years), the trail lighting system (7 years), signs (3 years), organization costs (5 years), the State Act 250 permit (5 years), and leasehold improvements (20 years). Equipment was depreciated by the double-declining balance or straight line methods for periods varying from 3 to 10 years. The wood inventory was recorded at cutting cost plus stumpage fees ($8 per cord when paid to adjacent land owners), where applicable. The market value of 225 cords of firewood on hand was $16,875. Approximately 40 cords were allocated to heat buildings and the hot tub during the winter 1980–1981. Both SVI subsidiaries experienced net losses during their first operating year, amounting to $60,471.

Restructuring the Common Stock

Unhappy with investor response to SVI shares, the partners hired an attorney specializing in public stock issuances. After reviewing the history of SVI stock sales, the lawyer expressed concern over the past practices of talking to too many potential investors (talking "stock" constitutes making an offer and businesses like SVI are limited to a maximum of 35 shareholders) and selling stock to out-of-state investors (California's Blue Sky Law is not subject to the SEC $100,000 exemption), both possibly minor infractions of equity trans-

EXHIBIT 13
Slumbering Valley Consolidated Balance Sheet (October 31, 1980)

	Consolidated	Slumbering Valley Inc.	Wood Products Inc.	Recreation Corp.
Assets				
Current Assets				
Inventory	$ 13,446	$	$ 5,678	$ 7,768
Intercompany receivable		46,926		
Total Current Assets	13,446	46,926	5,678	7,768
Property and Equipment				
Land and Timber	505,650	505,650		
Buildings under construction	13,339	13,339		
Leasehold improvements	34,901	34,901		
Roads and Bridges	56,895	23,939		
Trails	64,977			64,997
Trail Lighting System	20,070			20,070
Equipment	106,389	57,163	49,226	
Waste Disposal System	3,484	3,484		
Signs	1,156			1,156
Subtotal	806,861	638,476	49,226	86,203
Accumulated Depreciation	(29,335)	(3,089)	(22,950)	
Net Property and Equipment	777,526	635,387	26,276	86,203
Other Assets				
Investments in Subsidiaries		50,000		
Deposits	190	190		
Organizational cost	4,370	3,370		1,000
State Act 250 Permit	6,488			6,488
Subtotal	11,048	53,560		7,488
Amortization	(1,523)	(674)		(849)
Net Other Assets	9,525	52,886		6,639
Total Assets	$800,497	$735,199	$31,954	$100,610
Liabilities and Stockholders Equity				
Current Liabilities				
Accounts Payable	$ 49,350	$ 40,840	$ 742	$ 7,768
Room and Meals Tax Payable	39			39
Accrued Salary Payable	708			708
Accrued Interest Payable	9,051	8,127	383	541
Accrued Real-Estate Tax Payable	5,396	5,396		
Withholding and Payroll Taxes Payable	7,522		3,402	4,120
Intercompany Payable			1,576	45,350
Notes and Mortgages Payable	68,963	62,375	6,094	494
Total Current Liabilities	141,029	116,738	12,197	59,020
Long-Term Liabilities				
Notes and Mortgages Payable	203,743	135,469	4,068	64,206

EXHIBIT 13 (Continued)

	Consolidated	Slumbering Valley Inc.	Wood Products Inc.	Recreation Corp.
Other Liabilities				
Oak Pass Unearned Revenue	300			300
Shareholder Loans	34,196	1,292		32,904
Convertible Debentures	25,000	25,000		
Total Other Liabilities	59,496	26,292		33,204
Total Liabilities	404,268	278,499	16,265	156,430
Stockholders Equity				
Common Stock 5,000 shares authorized, no par value, 1,858 shares issued and outstanding	446,700	446,700		
Common Stock of Wholly Owned Subsidiary Companies			16,000	1,000
Retained Earnings	(60,471)		(311)	(56,820)
Total Stockholders Equity	396,299	456,700	16,689	(55,820)
Total Liabilities and Stockholders Equity	$800,497	$735,199	$31,954	$100,610

EXHIBIT 14
Slumbering Valley Consolidated Income Statement and Retained Earnings Statement for the Year Ended October 31, 1980

	Consolidated	Slumbering Valley Inc.	Wood Products Inc.	Recreation Corp.
Revenues				
Lease Income	$	$37,703		$
Ski Income	1,417	$		1,417
Wood Sales	12,017		12,017	
Wood Cost of Goods Sold	(4,489)		(4,489)	
Wood Delivery Income	1,470		1,470	
Total Revenues	10,415	37,703	8,998	1,417
Expenses (Note 1)				
Lodge and Land Lease				
Interest	5,703	20,794		43,406
Depreciation and Amortization	22,867	3,612	1,532	541
Advertising and Promotion	12,295	500	4,538	849
Insurance	6,909	400	386	6,023
Real-Estate Tax	2,964	6,196	800	1,764
Salary	6,196			
Payroll Taxes	2,612			2,612

(Continued)

EXHIBIT 14 (Continued)

		Slumbering Valley		
	Consolidated	Inc.	Wood Products Inc.	Recreation Corp.
NSTOA Membership and Conference	338			338
Equipment Operating Cost	643			643
Telephone	1,302	1,226	1,302	
Electricity	1,826	120	240	360
Legal	1,100	3,789	120	860
Travel	3,789	652		
Office	772	298		120
Licenses and Fees	794	80	199	197
Wood Delivery	221		50	91
Food Service	150		150	
Miscellaneous	41			41
Total Expense	364	36	36	292
Net Loss	70,886	37,703	9,353	58,237
Beginning Retained Earnings	(60,471)	0	(355)	(56,820)
Retained Earnings, October 31, 1980	0	0	45	0
	$(60,471)	$ 0	$ (310)	$(56,820)

EXHIBIT 15
Slumbering Valley Consolidated Statement of Changes in Financial Position for the Year Ended October 30, 1980

Funds Provided By

Common Stock		$446,700	
Common Stock Subscribed		10,000	
Shareholder Loans		34,196	
Convertible Debentures		25,000	
Deferred Revenue		300	
Long-term Notes and Mortgages		203,743	
Total Funds Provided			$719,939

Funds Applied To

Acquisition of Land, Buildings, Roads, Trails, Lighting System, Waste-Disposal Systems, and Other Assets		799,346	
Net Loss	$60,471		
Add Back Expenses not Requiring use of Working Capital	12,295	48,176	
Total Funds Applied			847,522
Decrease in Working Capital			$127,583

Computation of Decrease in Working Capital

Current Assets	$ 13,446
Current Liabilities	141,029
Working Capital, October 31, 1980	(127,583)
Less Beginning Capital	0
Decrease in Working Capital	$127,583

actions. Original SVI shares would be classified as "Class A" shares (23 current shareholders) and a second class, "Class B," was created. Sale of shares would be restricted to state residents. Five shares of the nonvoting Class B stock could be converted into one share of Class A stock after one year, as reflected in Exhibit 16. Upon application, the State authorized an increase to 15,000 of the Class A (original common) stock and 30,000 shares of Class B. To raise $272,000, SVI authorized the sale of 3,200 shares of Class B stock at $85 per share, a price based on the market value of the land and Act 250 permit.

The 1980–1981 Ski Season

Prices of both firewood and trail passes were raised. Revenue from the presale of 90 cords of wood remained less than that of a year earlier. A variety of weather extremes hampered recreation activities. Adequate snowfall was melted by warm spells and rain. The ski season at

EXHIBIT 16
Slumbering Valley Balance Sheet (March 31, 1981)

	Slumbering Valley Inc.	Wood Products Inc.	Recreation Corp.
Assets			
Current Assets			
Cash	$ 1,341		
Prepaid Insurance	0		$ 1,400
Accounts Receivable	540		
Contracts Receivable	85,000		
Intercompany Receivable	114,446	$ 2,191	
Inventory		5,003	17,638
Total Current Assets	201,327	7,194	19,038
Property and Equipment			
Land and Timber	504,650		
Buildings	25,785		
Leasehold Improvements	89,999		
Roads and Bridges	23,939		
Trails			75,495
Equipment			23,917
Waste-Disposal System	46,911		
Signs			1,288
Subtotal	751,144	49,226	110,601
Accumulated Depreciations	8,425	26,570	5,615
Net Property and Equipment	742,719	22,656	104,986
Other Assets			
Investments in Subsidiary	50,000		
Deposits	190		
Organizational Costs	3,370		1,000
State Act 250 Permit			6,488
Subtotal	53,560		7,488
Amortization	954		1,474
Net Other Assets	52,606		6,014
Total Assets	$996,652	$29,850	$130,038

(Continued)

EXHIBIT 16 (*Continued*)

	Slumbering Valley Inc.	Wood Products Inc.	Recreation Corp.
Liabilities and Stockholders Equity			
Current Liabilities			
Accounts Payable	$114,972	$ 774	$ 58,457
Sales and Meals Tax Payable			483
Accrued Salary Payable			508
Accrued Interest Payable	17,215	1,021	2,036
Accrued Real-Estate Tax Payable	8,850		
Withholding and Payroll Taxes Payable		3,402	6,911
Intercompany Payable			116,637
Notes and Mortgages Payable	66,220	6,094	494
Total Current Liabilities	207,257	11,291	185,526
Long-term Liabilities			
Notes and Mortgages Payable	152,111	4,069	64,206
Other Liabilities			
Deferred Revenue		240	240
Shareholding Loans	60,054		
Convertible Debentures	14,900		
Total Other Liabilities	74,954	15,600	249,972
Stockholders Equity			
Common Stock of Wholly Owned Subsidiaries		16,000	1,000
Common Stock Class A $1 Par Value 15,000 Shares Authorized, 1899 Shares Issued and Outstanding	1,899		
Contributions in Excess of Par Value	457,101		
Common Stock Class B $1 Par Value, 30,000 Shares Authorized, 98 Shares Issued and Outstanding	98		
Contributions in Excess of Par Value	8,232		
Common Stock subscribed	95,000		
Retained Earnings	0	(1,750)	(120,934)
Total Stockholders Equity	562,330	14,250	(119,934)
Total Liabilities and Stockholders Equity	$996,652	$29,850	$130,038

Slumbering Valley lasted seven weeks. However, during three of those weeks, subzero temperatures led to sparse attendance. Barry recorded approximately 3,500 ski visits that yielded trail and food revenues of less than $20,000, as shown in Exhibit 17. When the sewer contractor quit and left the system unfinished, the partners were forced to continue paper-plate service in the snack bar.

September 1981

Slumbering Valley's second ski season's revenues had exceeded those of year 1, but lagged behind expenses. The $20,000 balance of the SBA loan had been impounded by the new President, who both Paul and Barry had helped to elect. The partners owed $600,000 to their creditors, $240,000 of which was over-

EXHIBIT 17
Slumbering Valley Income Statement and Retained Earnings Statement for the Five Months Ended March 31, 1981

	Slumbering Valley		
	Inc.	Wood Products Inc.	Recreation Corp.
Revenues			
Lease Revenue	$32,519		
Gain on Sale of Truck	221		
Trail Fees			$ 9,521
Equipment Rental			1,326
Lessons			69
Sales—Merchandise			3,355
Less Cost of Goods Sold			(1,864)
Sales—Food			1,561
Less Cost of Food Sold			(781)
Sales—Wood		$2,250	
Less Cost of Wood Sold		(675)	
Total Revenue	32,740	1,575	13,187
Expenses			
Land and Asset Lease Expense			41,211
Office			378
Equipment Operating Cost			1,318
Truck Lease			1,100
Salary—Office			3,465
Salary—Kitchen			2,600
Payroll Tax			525
Staff Expense			3,402
Travel			182
Advertising and Public Relations	664		5,307
Memberships and Conferences			185
Racing Supply			283
Telephone			1,165
Electricity			1,612
Lodge Heat			2,350
Real-Estate Tax	3,454		
Insurance			3,054
Professional Service	6,298		
Permits	870		
Miscellaneous	50		
Interest	15,195	638	3,967

EXHIBIT 17 (Continued)

	Slumbering Valley		
	Inc.	Wood Products Inc.	Recreation Corp.
Depreciation and Amortization	6,209	2,376	4,992
Total Expense	32,740	3,014	77,301
Net Loss	0	(1,439)	(64,114)
Retained Earnings November 1, 1980	0	(311)	(56,820)
Retained Earnings March 31, 1981	$ 0	$(1,750)	$(120,934)

due. However, some of the creditors were understanding. Paul and Barry figured that $50,000 to $75,000 in new money would hold things together until January 1, 1982. The 1981–1982 ski season was too distant to put off all their creditors for 90 days. The sale of firewood was not generating enough of a cash flow to keep the venture afloat. One Wednesday, Paul called Barry with some news.

Paul: Barry! Great news! The state agency of environmental conservation has just approved our permit for the total project sewage system. This means we will be able to open the season with the large hot tub, restaurant, bar, and showers. Ted will lend me $60,000 at 21 per cent. I'll reloan to CVI at 21 percent. I put a down payment on the hot tub and hired workers to finish the shop in time for the Second Annual Charity Footrace. I have asked Ted to send $18,000 of the loan to me on Friday and the balance as I call for it. That way we save some interest.

Barry: I guess you were right, Paul. God works in His own time.

Paul: I told you.

On Friday of the same week, Paul called Barry again.

Paul: I was just informed that Ted died of a heart attack at 10:30 this morning.

2 NONBUSINESS

THE THEATRICAL SOCIETY

The Theatrical Society was founded in 1981 in Boston, Massachusetts by Turk Heart. During its first year of existence it sold over 17,000 seasonal ticket subscriptions and realized revenues of approximately $500,000. The Theatrical Society was a not-for-profit corporation that produced classical, stock plays featuring star actors.

Turk Heart, founder of the Theatrical Society and Chairman of its Board of Directors, was a lawyer by profession. His initial exposure to the theater occurred while he was a law student at Stanford University. A friend took him to a small community theater for a performance. He enjoyed it so much that he joined the group. While he was with the group he did everything from collecting tickets to producing his own play.

After graduating from law school Mr. Heart returned to his home town of Boston. About three years later he decided to become involved with theater. Drawing on his community theater experience, he and a few friends formed the Commonwealth Playhouse. At first they used the community hall of an area church and built their own sets. Heart's wife and a few of her friends sewed all the costumes. In short, the members of the group did everything that was necessary to present the plays.

During the first few years of the Commonwealth Playhouse's existence, there were very few productions. Most of its audience consisted of friends and relatives of members. The ticket prices generally were $1, and on many occasions the members had to dip into their own pockets to pay for production expenses not covered by box office receipts. Heart realized at this time that the survival of his theater and its ability to produce classical plays depended upon his ability to develop a broader audience. He realized he did not stand a good chance of cultivating an adult audience, so he looked to the secondary-school market. Through a business associate, Heart arranged a meeting with the city's school superintendent. The superintendent thought the idea had great possibilities and arranged to have students bused to the theatre.

To help with expenses (the school board was only paying 25¢ per student), Heart began to look for outside funding. Based on the Playhouse's student program he was able to get a grant of $3500 from I. B. M. At the beginning of the second full year of the student program the school board awarded the Playhouse a grant of $10,000. For the most part, the members of the group still did everything themselves. A portion of the grant money was spent on more elaborate costumes and sets. The remainder was used to rent a small theater hall on the fringe of Cambridge. Heart's wife, Ellen, kept the books. Her only source of records was the cancelled checks from the Playhouse's account.

In 1978, because of the large amount of grant monies involved, Heart assumed responsibility for the books. Since he no longer acted and only occasionally wrote plays, he felt he could adequately handle the financial records. He developed an expense and revenue ledger that invariably was rescued from confusion by the Playhouse's monthly check statement. In 1979, the school board did not renew its grant. By this time, the Commonwealth

---

Source: Prepared by Robert Broadbent, Leonard A. Fuchs, III, and James J. Wiley of Temple University under the supervision of Glenn Boseman. Permission to use granted by Glenn Boseman.

Playhouse had developed a reputation as an excellent amateur group. On weekend evenings it was playing to near capacity crowds who were paying $2 for admission. In fact, its theater reputation in the community was so good that the State Street Foundation gave it $15,000 to continue its student program.

Halfway through the 1979 season (October–March) Heart found himself embroiled in a dispute with several other members of the group. They were opposed to his hiring professional actors (Heart felt that by doing so he would improve production quality); moreover, they wanted to produce Harold Pinter's *The Homecoming* next season. Heart still felt strongly about producing only classical plays so he opposed the Pinter production. Although the Commonwealth Playhouse could afford to hire a few inexpensive professional actors, some members felt doing so would dilute their amateur status. Again, Heart felt that the Playhouse was moving forward and that its survival and ability to produce better classical productions depended on its ability to adapt to its new role. Heart eventually won the dispute but at the expense of the group's solidarity.

During the summer of 1979, Heart met John Dearborn, a successful actor who was performing at the famous Woods Hole's Summer Playhouse. During one of their conversations Heart mentioned he would like to produce professional classical plays. Dearborn replied that he had a friend who packaged plays for summer theater and that this individual perhaps would be interested in working with Heart. Dearborn arranged the meeting between his friend, Bradford Telli, and Heart.

Telli, after hearing Heart's plan, endorsed it enthusiastically. Telli only worked during the summer; he liked the concept of taking the summer theater package of a three-week rehearsal and a three-week run and adapting it to a winter season. The three-week rehearsal would be done in New York City and to a small extent would be controlled by Telli. For the most part, either the director or star would have the final say about production decisions.

The only obstacle in Heart's way was securing a theatre. His first consideration was the Beacon Street Theatre. It had just been renovated and was owned by the State Street Foundation. Heart knew many of the Foundation members professionally; consequently, he was able to secure a three-year lease beginning in November 1981. The lease gave the Theatrical Society use of the theater for three weeks per month, November through February. All operational costs for the theater were included in the cost of the rental. Costs for the first year were $5000 per month.

Some of the Board members openly expressed doubt regarding the wisdom of leasing to Heart because they felt his chances of success were small. Furthermore, they felt the terms of the lease were too generous. Heart's corporation, the Theatrical Society, was to pay its rent from actual box-office sales.

By the time Heart completed the leasing agreement for the Beacon Street Theatre, the Commonwealth Playhouse was beginning its 1980 season. Heart realized he could not continue with the Playhouse, create his Theatrical Society, and practice law, so he withdrew from the Playhouse.

Heart chose four plays for his first season, and Telli went about signing big-name actors and directors for each play. The Society's first play was *Born Yesterday*, featuring Dotty Sands and John Randell. On the strength of the stars, Heart initiated a media campaign in April 1981 offering season subscription plans for the Society's first season (1981–1982). He placed advertisements in Boston's largest papers and used a few spot commercials on two of Boston's FM radio stations.

By July 1981, season subscription sales reached 16,000. By the end of October, they climbed to 17,000. Revenue from subscription tickets amounted to about $350,000. Based on a theater capacity rate of 93 percent, box-office sales were expected to add another $100,000 of revenue. Heart also had arranged to receive grants from the Commonwealth of Massachusetts Council on the Arts and the State Street Trust Foundation. These grants provided for money in the amount of 10 percent of ticket sales up to a maximum of $50,000. A further stipulation of the foundation grant was that the Society have no consecutive yearly operational deficit. Total revenue, including grant money, for the Society's first season was expected to easily exceed $500,000.

In their early discussions, Heart and Telli agreed that each production would cost approximately $110,000. This figure did not include the Beacon Street Theater rent. Because Heart had prepared no formal budget, he was quite pleased to see that revenues would adequately cover all production expenses.

When requests for subscription tickets first started coming in, Heart, along with his wife and a few friends, attempted to handle the disbursement of tickets. After a few days, they found themselves inundated with subscriptions and were compelled to hire outside help. Heart's wife suggested that in the future more thorough planning would have to be done. Heart replied that they had always managed in the past and, besides, an occasional crisis was enjoyable.

The Theatrical Society's first play opened in November 1981. It was a tremendous success. Its total production cost was $109,000. Telli told Heart he might have been able to bring the production in at an even $100,000 but unexpected expenses pushed the final cost higher. Heart informed Telli that it was no problem because the money was available. He did not, however, tell Telli that he was upset with the director's interpretation of the play. Heart realized that the artistic style and direction of the Theatrical Society would escape his control for a period of time, but that eventually he would gain complete control. At this time, however, he did not want to change anything for fear it might adversely affect the Society's success.

Production expenses included everything from the actors' salaries to the advertising and publicity costs. All rehearsals were done in New York. The show then moved to Boston for its run at the Beacon Street Theatre. This arrangement caused no problems as long as sufficient funds were available and the show's expenses stayed within Telli's initial estimation.

The Society's second and third productions were also successful, but a small decline in box-office sales was noted by the box-office treasurer, the Society's only full-time employee.

A week before the final play was to go on, word arrived from New York that Tammy Grimes, the production's star, was withdrawing. Heart immediately called Telli who informed Heart that Ms. Grimes could legally do so because of an out clause. When Heart asked Telli why he had allowed such a clause, Telli informed Heart that he was not a theatrical lawyer.

When word hit the Boston press that Tammy Grimes had withdrawn from the Theatrical Society's *The Imaginary Invalid*, box-office sales plummeted. What should have been a $25,000 box office amounted to only $3500. The show did go on with an understudy and, fortunately, the critics enjoyed her performance. The show, however, did require the use of the company's excess revenues.

All things considered, the first season for the Theatrical Society was a success in that expenses and revenues were about even. Heart was concerned about the artistic and management functions being in New York City, but felt that a change at this time was not in the interest of the Society. In March 1982, he presented a report to the Theatrical Society's Board, of which he was Chairman. In his report he discussed a brief expense and revenue statement and suggestions for next year's program. The Board consisted of a few business friends of Heart's and several members of his family. When a Board member asked for a specific breakdown of expenses for the Society's first production, Heart informed him that the information had not as yet arrived from New York.

Approximately a week after the March Board meeting, Heart and Telli signed contracts (all with no out clauses) with the next year's star performers. Tom Morebary, one of the stars, insisted that he be allowed to choose not only his own artistic director, but the play. Heart was reluctant to agree and did so only when he was assured Morebary's selection would be a classic. Heart and Telli agreed (without any formal budget) that production costs would be $120,000 per play.

In early April seasonal subscriptions were offered. Newspapers and FM radio were again used to announce the coming season. By the end of July subscription sales numbered only 12,000. By the end of October they had reached only 14,000. Even with the increase in the price of subscriptions, revenues amounted to only $322,000. Since no records had been kept on the first year's subscription holders, there was no way to determine how many of them were included in the 14,000 figure. Heart had planned on subscription sales increasing slightly. Their decline alarmed him. He felt, however, that the big names he had signed for the coming season would come through at the box office. To be on the safe side he told Telli to keep New York expenses to a minimum. Telli assured Heart he would do his best.

The Society's first play for the 1982–1983 season, *Rose Tattoo*, was a smashing success. The theater was sold out for the last two weeks of its run. Heart was pleased because box-office sales amounted to $29,000 (ticket prices were raised slightly). More important, Telli was able to keep the New York rehearsal costs to $100,000. If box-office sales continued to be good and Telli was able to hold New York costs down, Heart felt the Society would be able to break even.

The rest of the season, however, was a disaster. When the last play closed, Heart found that he had a $49,000 deficit. A major

EXHIBIT 1
Theatrical Society

Expense and Revenue Statement: 1982–1983 Season

Revenue		
Subscription sales	$322,000	
Box office sales	78,000	
Grant money	65,000	
Total		$465,000
Expenses		
Play 1	$116,000	
Play 2	126,000	
Play 3	131,000	
Play 4	141,000	
Total		$514,000
Profit or Loss		($ 49,000)

snowstorm crippled the city for two of the three weeks that *Hedda Gabler* ran. The effect was devastating on ticket sales. The next two plays, *The Last Mile* and *Key Largo*, received bad reviews; consequently, there were virtually no box-office ticket sales. Total revenue and expense figures appear in Exhibit 1.

Heart realized in early January that the season might be a financial disaster, so he asked an accountant friend what he could do to offset any deficits. Heart was told to close his books the day of the last performance and to begin immediately to sell subscriptions for next year's season. Revenue from these sales could be used to pay any outstanding debt. To play it safe, Heart had Telli negotiate all the contracts for the next year's actors in early February. When the final curtain fell on *Key Largo*, Heart was ready to announce again through Boston's three newspapers next season's stars and shows. To move subscription sales he gave a 5 percent discount to those who paid for their tickets before March 25th. *Key Largo* closed on February 28th.

By March 25th the Theatrical Society had received money for 6,000 season subscription tickets ($150,000). Heart immediately paid all obligations from the society's second season. He realized he needed to become more organized. He also realized he needed better financial controls. With his accountant friend he developed a revenue and expense (R & E) budget for the Theatrical Society's coming year (Exhibit 2). He also expanded his advertising campaign by using direct mail (100,000 pieces).

By early August subscriptions sales reached only 10,000. Two weeks before the Society's third season was to open they were still only 12,000. The figure never changed and was considerably below that projected by Heart and his budget.

The Society's first play received indifferent reviews and box-office sales responded accordingly. The next play, Shaw's *Arms and the Man*, also got mediocre reviews. One critic stated, "Like most recent Society productions, *Arms and the Man* lacked artistic togetherness." During the *Arms and the Man* run, Heart was informed that the State Street Foundation was not going to continue its grant next year. When he asked why, he was formally told because of insufficient assets and more important priorities. A close friend privately told Heart it was because the Theatrical Society's Board did not have enough clout in the community.

Prior to the Society's fourth and final play, Heart was given the organization's cash position (see Exhibit 3). Needless to say, he was worried. The Society used prominent stars and outstanding directors, and still the audiences continued to turn away. On the last Saturday night of *Arms and the Man*, Heart noticed at intermission that the majority of the audience appeared to be in the 35 and up category. He wondered why there were not more young people in attendance.

The following morning Heart called a friend who was an instructor at Boston University's School of Business. In their conversation the professor gave Heart many suggestions, one of which was the hiring of a managing

EXHIBIT 2
Theatrical Society

Revenue and Expense Budget: 1983–1984 Season

Revenue	
Subscription—regular	$390,000
Subscription—patrons[a]	10,000
Subscription—schools	12,000
Box-office sales	100,000
Interest income	1,500
Earned income	$513,500
Grant income	78,000
Total income	$591,500
Expenses	
Actors' and Directors' salaries	$134,000
Stage cost	38,000
Casting cost	5,000
Costume cost	22,000
Set cost	46,000
Lighting	2,500
Rent for theater (Beacon Street)	68,000
Rent for theater (New York Rehearsals)	70,000
Royalties	24,000
Union expenses	10,500
Program and tickets	3,500
Advertising and publicity expenses	56,000
Box-office cost	12,000
Administrative	25,000
Miscellaneous	75,000
Total expenses	$591,500

[a]Tax deductible amounts added to patron subscription.

EXHIBIT 3
Theatrical Society

Cash Position: January 1984

Play 1—November		
Cash on hand	$251,000	
Box-office income	17,000	
Less production expenses		$147,000
Play 2—December		
Cash on hand	121,000	
Box-office income	14,000	
Less production expenses		143,000
Play 3—January		
Cash on hand	(8,000)	
Box-office income	12,000	
Less production expenses		129,000
Play 4—February		
Cash on hand	(125,000)	

director, particularly one with strong credentials. Heart realized he could no longer operate the Theatrical Society from his law office. Perhaps with some professional management, the Theatrical Society could rebuild its once substantial audience.

MIDLAND COUNTY HOSPITAL

As Ken Mason considered the future of Midland County Hospital, he reviewed the mission statement, last year's statistics, and the HSA guidelines. (See Appendices 1–4.) He felt strongly that although Midland County could remain a small-community general hospital providing a fairly broad range of acute care for some time to come, its days in this capacity were numbered, and that it was his responsibility to guide the institution toward a more viable future.

Looking back on his tenure at the hospital, he felt that he had accomplished much in the two and one-half years that he had been there, but still experienced frustration at not having been able to make more progress in delineating a viable long-range strategy. Now the opportunity had opened up, although perhaps earlier than he might have desired, to explore some form of collaboration with Johnston Memorial Hospital. Not only had trustees of the Johnston Memorial board and his own expressed an interest in such a move, but those trustees, key members in each case, would only remain on their respective boards for another year or two. The long-time chief executive officer of Johnston Memorial Hospital had resigned a little earlier than expected and had been replaced by a younger man who had a history of bringing off collaborative endeavors. The time seemed right, yet Ken was not at all sure whether to proceed, how to proceed, or for what he should aim. Should they be aiming at a full merger, a consolidation, some kinds of joint ventures, or simply starting a process of exploring possibilities. He did not know, for example, whether to involve the doctors in any process of exploration. If he involved more people early, would they become threatened and undercut the process? If he left them out, would they be resentful and undermine it later?

Background

The city of Johnston has 350,000 people and is below the four per thousand bed limit so there are no excess beds. Johnston Memorial in the north has 588 beds and used to be run by Mike Stone who, after 19 years was retiring early. It is the oldest hospital—100-years-old. Midland, with 201 beds, is in the southwest area of the town. St. Stephens is in the southeast, has 384 beds, and is run by a lay administration for the Daughters of Charity. The building is three-years-old. The HSA has recommended that at least one pediatrics and obstetrics unit close and that only one of the two hospitals presently doing elective cardiac surgery continue.

Midland County started when a Jewish surgeon at Johnston Memorial felt he was not compatible. Some of the community still think that Midland is Jewish and Johnston Memorial is antisemitic. The Johnston Memorial board is somewhat WASPish, but this really is not a problem any longer.

Historically there had been bad feelings between Johnston Memorial and Midland for several years. There was a fund-raising drive on the part of Midland who said that in order to make it easy for the fund raisers and the community, that people should leave their lights on if they wished to give. Johnston Memorial

Source: This case was prepared by Alan Sheldon, Harvard University. Permission to use it was granted by Alan Sheldon. Copyright © 1980 by the President and Fellows of Harvard College. Reprinted with permission of the Harvard School of Public Health.

heard about this and went out an hour ahead of the Midland fund raisers and cleaned up.

Mike Stone was proud of his institution and knew nothing and cared less about multi-institutional relationships. His application for emergency room expansion was turned down three times by the cost commission and he blamed this on the Midland trustees. In his last year he got into trouble with the union. He was dominated by his doctors, and his management had been having such problems that a consulting firm had to be brought in. The cardiac surgery group decided to leave Johnston Memorial for St. Stephens for mixed reasons. Johnston Memorial raises the most money, but has suffered a big loss in prestige. They are now trying to recruit a replacement for the cardiac surgeons. The head of the cardiac surgery group was the head of long-range planning at Johnston Memorial, and its board was really upset when they left.

St. Stephens is not a candidate for merger because their chief executive officer is dead set against it and their governing structure and board is nonexistent. There has never been and will not be any discussion with that organization. However, Ed Thomas of Midland, who has the best medical group there, is exploring cooperation with St. Stephens. Midland County M. D.s have the greater loyalty to St. Stephens because 70 percent of them have affiliations there. Johnston Memorial insists on its M.D.s not having privileges at other hospitals.

Events of the Last Few Weeks
Unexpectedly the possibility of merger was aired at a recent meeting of the chief executive officers by the Johnston Memorial Hospital people. There was also a rumor of St. Stephens being interested in buying Midland County. As a result, the board presidents of Johnston Memorial and Midland County and a small number of key trustees started talking.

Johnston Memorial has convinced Ken they want to move rapidly, although his own trustees do not want to go so fast. The president of their board wants a merger. He is responsible for much good in the town, for example, his bank underwrote a regional health-planning study. This is not the first time collaboration has been suggested. An elderly trustee at Midland, a leader of much social change, some seven years ago suggested merger at a board meeting. Half of the Midland board then visited Johnston Memorial. At that time, the Midland administration did not want it.

Midland may have some leverage in discussions because both hospitals have applied for CAT Scanners. Why should the Johnston Memorial chief executive officer bother? In addition to their need to regain psychological prestige, they want open-heart surgery back, and they want Midland to help them develop outreach; then they would be more competitive with St. Stephens. Also they see the association, especially with the good management of Midland, as helping them with three major problems: their labor problems, their poor management, and their very unhappy medical staff. The goal would be to consolidate rather than merge and to keep the institutions separate initially.

In Ken's eyes the reasons for merger include:

1. They want psychiatric beds, will not get them, and we have them.
2. We could close our in-patient pediatrics and put it there.
3. We do not have any educational programs and need residents to come here.
4. We would become more attractive and could more easily get doctors if we have more specialties.
5. Ambulatory care development is easier from a bigger base.
6. We could not get a CAT Scanner without being involved with them.
7. The OB/GYN report. (See Appendix 5.)

Ken considered the somewhat surprising results of informal discussions that he had with members of the medical staff. He found them to be more realistic about the future of Midland County Hospital than he had expected and more open to considering the possibility of some future, however unattractive to them, that they recognized as probably being necessary. Even the long-range planning committee, which met for the first time in two years, commented favorably when Ken brought up the fact that merger had been raised as a possibility. One doctor said, "Merger does not sound ridiculous anymore and ten years ago I would have left the room if it had been raised." A trustee said, "There has been a change from a backstabbing environment to a backscratching environment as far as the hospitals relating to each other are concerned." But whom they should woo and how was not clear.

The chairman and president of Ken's board are both in favor of proceeding with negotiations, and think they might carry the necessary twenty-four (24) of thirty-six (36) trustees with them—if the M.D.s do not get to them first should they become alarmed. They feel an urgency as their terms of office end in two years.

In the last month a consulting company has been retained by the two hospitals, who share expenses equally. They have put on a presentation to both boards on the merger process.

Conclusions

Ken reviewed the events of the last few weeks in his mind as he struggled with these issues and tried to formulate an overall strategy. What part in it should collaboration play?

Ken Mason felt that the paramount issue facing him was how to create the widest set of options for the future, and keep control over them rather than being forced into some corner. Would merger or consolidation secure this? Since a consolidation might mean Midland retaining psychiatry, pediatrics and obstetrics, and emergency medical services, would such a possible future role be acceptable to the medical staff?

When he first came people questioned whether there was a need for three hospitals. He convinced himself then that there was a need for the continued existence of Midland in acute care. But with the increase in government control it is hard to survive as an acute-care hospital. Since they offer much the same care as the other two hospitals, although ideally he would like that, practically he had doubts. He felt that their role might be determined by others. He does not believe that Midland County could specialize because the others would not allow it. Unless, of course, that specialization did not conflict with the others. But why would they want a partner? He was very skeptical about the success of any alternative, including collaboration, other than perhaps becoming a welfare institution. Historically, at best, there had been coolly cordial relationships between the other two behemoths. Even such things as dual staff memberships had taken six months of discussion to get anywhere. It was only just possible that if the boards got together something might happen and that there might be a consortium.

Probably both Johnston Memorial and St. Stephens would ultimately refuse merger because they each have large shelled-in space and would do better to build on-site. He recognized that a pressing need to do anything is five to ten years away, but then it might be too late to keep control of their fate. He also wondered how to manage the M.D.s who already had concerns about the role of Midland County and preferences for possible partners. Would they simply leave for St. Stephens as soon as wind of what was even being considered got out? What could he negotiate that might head off such a move?

Ken's conclusions were that there were no imperative and pressing reasons for Midland County Hospital to entertain collaboration now. But since it would eventually have to do so if it were not to deteriorate as an institution, and since there were some happy conjunctions of circumstances now that made the possibility of collaboration hopeful, he felt he should probably proceed. But he was uncertain as to with whom he should talk and in what direction he should move.

APPENDIX 1
Statistical Comparison of Services Rendered
(As of September 30, 1978)

Category of Services	1977/1978	1976/1977
Total Admissions	10,093	9,908
Infant Deliveries	986	905
Pediatrics Admissions	678	739
Short Stay Admissions	1,072	851
Home Care Admissions	517	508
Emergency Room Visits	33,081	31,400
Days of Patient Care	64,199	64,537
Operations	4,622	4,748
EKG's	9,439	9,261
Respiratory Therapy	10,962	10,151
Physical Therapy	10,209	8,052
Prescriptions Filled	52,294	50,940
Meals Served	283,978	275,394
Personnel Man-hours	1,240,632	1,203,489
Pounds of Laundry Processed	939,595	924,510
Pediatrics Center Patient Visits	8,915	9,354
Prenatal Clinic Patient Visits	1,147	893
Dental Clinic Visits	2,042	2,772
Medical–Surgical Average Length of Stay (Days)	7.1	7.1
Maternity Average Length of Stay (Days)	3.7	3.7
Newborn Average Length of Stay (Days)	4.0	4.1

APPENDIX 2
Mission Statement

Midland County Hospital's mission is stated below. Of necessity, the statement is couched in terms of broad generalizations rather than specifics. Although it is not intended to last permanently without change, the statement articulates the fundamental purposes of the institution for the next several years. It provides a basic set of criteria that will guide the institution, against which Midland County's Board of Trustees, Medical Staff, and administrative leadership, as well as the community at large, can measure the Hospital's performance.

Midland County Hospital is an acute-care community hospital that dedicates itself to provide high-quality diagnostic, therapeutic, and rehabilitative services, including appropriate professional, nursing, technical, and support services, to meet the basic health-care needs of its constituency. This constituency includes its neighbors who have historically depended upon it as a key health resource; other residents of Johnston and adjacent communities whose clinical needs can be met by particular professional competencies among the medical and dental staff of the Hospital; and all persons living or working nearby who, because of their own or their physicians' perferences, wish to receive care at Midland County Hospital.

Midland County Hospital must be viewed within the context of its community; it is one element in a complex network of health-care providers, including a variety of institutions and professional practitioners. In order to avoid unnecessary duplication of services and excessive costs and to assure rational development of community resources, Midland County commits itself to meaningful cooperation with the members of this health-care network, as well as with recognized planning and regulatory agencies.

Midland County perceives its role as multidimensional, involving the provision of in-patient, out-patient, and emergency services in all major specialties. Its out-patient activities must respond effectively to the needs of an inner city population that depends heavily on Midland County for access to health-care services.

Midland County's emergency services are of considerable importance because of its location at the intersection of the Idaho Turnpike (I-95) and the Colonel Connector (Route 3-26). This key relationship to major traffic arteries requires that Midland County Hospital fulfill a particularly important role in trauma care.

Notwithstanding its sensitivity to a significant inner city responsibility, Midland County will maintain and strengthen its effectiveness as a key resource for its medical staff members whose patients require a hospital setting geared to their needs.

In its provision of medical care, its appointments to the Medical Staff and its employment practices Midland County Hospital will not discriminate against any person or group of persons on the basis of race, color, religious creed, national origin, age, sex, marital status, or physical handicap. Midland County will respond with compassion and skill to patients from all age groups and all socio-economic backgrounds.

Midland County Hospital will maintain high standards in making appointments to its medical and dental staff and in hiring all professional and nonprofessional personnel. It will seek to provide educational opportunities to physicians, nurses, and other professional, technical, and support personnel.

Midland County Hospital will maintain a physical facility that is modern, clean, comfortable, and conducive to high-quality patient care from the point of view of patients, physicians, and all Hospital personnel.

Midland County Hospital will seek to develop and maintain activities that increase the public's awareness of its own health needs. It will utilize health-education techniques that stress health promotion, preventive services, and the constructive use of the community's medical, dental, hospital, and other health resources.

Midland County Hospital must be flexible; its mission must be under continuing review, so that it will remain responsive to a changing environment and changing needs. Midland County must continue to improve the quality of the care and services it renders to its community. Moreover, the Hospital must continue to pursue more linkages and integration of services with the various components of the regional health-care network.

Midland County is particularly sensitive to the potential impact that a hospital can have on the community in which it is located. Every hospital is an important employer in its community and operates a facility that inevitably sets a tone for its own neighborhood. Midland County is keenly aware of its relationship to its community and commits itself to do those things—in terms of physical facilities and operating policies—that will strengthen its neighbors and its neighborhood.

There is obviously more on this "menu" than Midland County Hospital can reasonably digest. Although there is something to be said in favor of a program in any one of the areas discussed, it would be imprudent for Midland County to attempt to respond to every one of these challenges. It will be necessary to select from among these the ones that are most responsive to community need, that are least likely to involve duplication of services or provoke destructive competition with the other hospitals in Johnston, and the ones that offer the best prospects for implementation.

Such a process of selection from among a wide range of options will require the most serious attention on the part of the Hospital's Long-Range Planning Committee. The agenda of items for potential action, will be more than sufficient as a starting point for future Committee deliberations. A few concluding observations about these various program areas may be useful.

Ambulatory surgery is an idea whose time has come. Conservative opinion will point to clinical hazards for patients and economic hazards for hospitals but it is believed that if proper limits are placed upon ambulatory surgery programs, the disadvantages are minimal and are far outweighed by the advantages.

Emergency Medical Service is the example *par excellence* of a program requiring the greatest degree of cooperation among the three hospitals in Johnston. Midland County's demonstrated capability in this field suggests that its role in any cooperative venture should be a prominent one.

Geriatrics is clearly an area in which the needs of the public will experience considerable growth in the years ahead. Whether a specific Department of Geriatrics would be the best way to respond to these needs, or whether it would be preferable to develop a geriatric capability that would infuse all of the clinical departments of the Hospital is a complex question with many philosophic, political, and administrative ramifications. There can be little doubt, however, that some type of activity in this field would enable Midland County to respond more effectively to the needs of the community.

Industrial medicine appears to be an activity that could be developed imaginatively, with considerable benefit to the health of employed individuals and to industry in the area. It is believed that the strong resistance to any industrial health program expressed by members of the medical staff is based on a misconception that such a program would represent a form of financial competition. Quite the contrary, a properly designed industrial health program can be a source of referrals rather than of competition. Both physicians and hospital can benefit economically from a program that is responding to a significant community need.

In light of the recent appointment of a full-time Director of Psychiatry, activity in the field of mental health will almost certainly receive major consideration. As noted above, we recognize the concern that the general public might react unfavorably to expansion of psychiatric services at Midland County, but we do not regard this as a certainty. We are inclined to give the public credit for a more forward looking and open-minded view of the place of psychiatry in modern health care. Accordingly, we believe that carefully designed programs in this field would be well received and that such programs would complement significantly the existing range of services provided by Midland County.

Obstetrics is one of the thorniest issues confronting Midland County. The obstetrical service is one of which the Hospital is understandably proud. Nevertheless, regulatory pressure to correct the existing surplus of facilities places this service in jeopardy. Justifiable pride in the existing program should not blind the Hospital to its vulnerability on this issue. Given the circumstances, the most reasonable solution might be for Midland County to relinquish obstetrics as part of a program trade-off agreed to by the hospitals in Johnston, the HSA, and the Commission on Hospitals and Health Care, restructuring various programs in a way that would best meet the needs of the community. Midland County should not allow its institutional pride—however justifiable—to interfere with rational planning. This is not to suggest that the proper cause of action is for the Hospital to relinquish its obstetrical department. The decision should be made in the context of calm and thoughtful discussions among the three hospitals, the Health Systems Agency, and the Commission on Hospitals and Health Care. Such discussions are most likely to produce a result that is in the community interest, if every institution and agency involved approaches the matter open-mindedly, without rigid adherence to positions that may have been taken at an earlier time.

Rehabilitation medicine has some appeal, in terms of broadening the range of services provided by the Hospital. However, there is a strong possibility that such a program would duplicate services already available in the community. If so, it would be more appropriate for Midland County to continue (and, if necessary, to strengthen) its referral patterns with the Rehabilitation Center.

Each of the several clinical areas discussed above is dependent, to greater or lesser degree, upon effective nursing care. Indeed, in virtually every medical program that Midland County currently maintains or might develop in the future, nursing care is an essential component. Although nursing care was not discussed in detail by the Long-Range Planning Committee or the subject of specific analysis, the Nursing Department's reputation for sensitive, caring service is widely recognized throughout Midland County. It is important that the special character of nursing service at the Hospital be preserved, regardless of what programmatic directions are eventually decided on.

The potential for educational programs is extremely varied. Within the area of graduate medical education, the most reasonable program for Midland County to pursue, if any, would appear to be development of a residency in the field of primary care. Whether such a program could be developed and sustained will depend upon the range and quality of clinical services provided by Midland County. In this connection, it is important to recognize that several of the program areas discussed above would be rooted in—or very closely related to—a major institutional thrust towards ambulatory care. This overall issue deserves more extended comment.

At this time, Midland County Hospital's out-patient activity is modest, at best, particularly for an institution that provides services to an inner city population. Its Emergency Room provides a rather substantial 30,000 visits annually, but its out-patient clinics provide a relatively small volume—about 10,000 visits annually in pediatrics, somewhat more than 2,000 in dentistry, and barely 1,000 in the pre- and postnatal clinics.

An optimum level of commitment to ambulatory programs is not easy to define. Certainly much can be said for increasing the emphasis on ambulatory care; it would be responsive to needs of the inner city area served by the Hospital and it would serve as a significant source of in-patient referrals. On the other hand, overemphasis on ambulatory programs would produce considerable anxiety on the part of the medical staff (some of whom have shown themselves to be sensitive on issues of personal economics) and it would tend to bring about gradual changes in the overall socio-economic mix of patients at the Hospital that might discourage middle class users.

The middle course, which would appear to be most reasonable, would require a sensitive perception of clinical, social, economic, and political issues. However, it should not be difficult to find a solution that would result in a balanced program providing services to patients of varying socio-economic levels—Medicaid, medically indigent, and self-pay patients. Imaginatively conceived, this goal could be attained by establishing an attractive group practice arrangement that would enable members of the medical staff to see their own practice patients (and bill them directly), to carry out ambulatory surgery in a specially designed facility, and to see Medicaid patients as well on some type of group practice basis. Even an industrial hygiene program could be coordinated with such an effort.

Designing and implementing such a program would require considerable leadership skills (which they believe to be available at Midland County) and a considerable degree of flexibility, imagination, and foresight on the part of the medical staff. We believe the long-range gains—to the community, to the institution, and the members of the medical staff—would be well worth the effort.

The issues outlined above are ones that Midland County Hospital should address as promptly as possible. They cover an extremely broad range, encompassing psychiatry, geriatrics, emergency services, industrial medicine, rehabilitation medicine, obstetrics, graduate medical education, ambulatory surgery, and the broader area of ambulatory care in general.

APPENDIX 3
Monthly Statistics (January 1980)

Page	
1	Admissions and Discharges
2	Patient Days and Personnel Report
3	Out-Patient Area and Special Services
4	Maternity Statistics
5	Analysis of Admissions by Medical Service
6	Admissions by Race and Nationality
7	Radiology Statistics
8	EKG and Phonocardiogram Statistics
9	EEG Statistics
10	Respiratory Therapy Statistics
11	Physical Therapy Statistics
12	Professional Fees
13	Man-Hour Report

Monthly Statistics (January 1980)

	Jan '80	Dec '79	Jan '79	YTD 1979–1980	YTD 1978–1979
Pt. by Admission (Fin)					
State Aid—Title XIX	192	161	205	714	666
Compensation	11	10	20	49	56
Blue Cross	299	228	305	1,122	1,140
Medicare	152	128	143	545	537
Under 65	27	14	13	63	65
Commercial Insurance	164	151	189	667	682
Self-Pay	25	27	37	95	115
Other	32	42	26	166	136
#21 Employee	5	7	2	22	24
Total	907	768	940	3,443	3,421
Pts. by Admission (Dist)					
Medicare—Med/Surg	175	136	150	590	583
Adults Non-Maternity	450	404	504	1,814	1,769
Psychiatric	36	32	41	126	133
Pediatrics	88	65	64	271	220
Total Non-Maternity	749	637	759	2,801	2,705
Maternity	81	68	92	336	368
Sub-Total	830	705	851	3,137	3,073
Newborn	77	63	89	306	348
Total	907	768	940	3,443	3,421
Pts. by Discharge (Fin)					
State Aid—Title XIX	179	161	196	711	648
Compensation	8	13	12	48	50

Monthly Statistics (January 1980) (*Continued*)

	Jan '80	Dec '79	Jan '79	YTD 1979–1980	YTD 1978–1979
Blue Cross	290	238	297	1,123	1,151
Medicare	141	135	134	537	534
Under 65	22	13	13	58	64
Commercial Insurance	156	150	166	664	662
Self-Pay	31	23	36	100	116
Other	33	42	26	168	136
#21 Employee	3	9	1	24	23
Total	863	784	881	3,433	3,384
Pts. by Discharge (Dist)					
Medicare—Med/Surg	156	144	143	577	580
Adults Non-Maternity	427	429	452	1,800	1,733
Psychiatric	29	35	45	126	136
Pediatrics	90	59	68	268	219
Total Non-Maternity	702	667	708	2,771	2,668
Maternity	83	62	88	348	367
Sub-Total	785	729	796	3,119	3,035
Newborn	78	55	85	314	349
Total	863	784	881	3,433	3,384
Patient Days (Fin)					
State Aid—Title XIX	1,021	833	1,072	3,972	3,788
Compensation	62	73	108	314	282
Blue Cross	1,592	1,296	1,536	5,801	5,791
Medicare	1,508	1,478	1,438	5,651	5,730
Under 65	200	165	123	565	620
Commercial Insurance	954	753	953	3,485	3,599
Self-Pay	112	108	162	406	514
Other	216	275	163	1,043	863
#21 Employee	24	42	11	204	125
Total	5,689	5,023	5,566	21,441	21,312
Patient Days (Dist)					
Medicare—Med/Surg	1,615	1,558	1,528	5,959	6,147
Adult Non-Maternity	2,581	2,270	2,574	9,946	9,473
Psychiatric	503	500	553	2,080	2,216
Pediatrics	275	192	181	802	653
Total Non-Maternity	4,974	4,520	4,836	18,787	18,489
Maternity	315	246	340	1,275	1,385
Sub-Total	5,289	4,766	5,176	20,062	19,874
Newborn	400	257	390	1,379	1,438
Total	5,689	5,023	5,566	21,441	21,312
Average Length of Stays (Days)					
Medicare—Med/Surg	10.3	10.8	10.7	10.3	10.6
Adult Non-Maternity	6.0	5.8	5.7	5.5	5.5
Psychiatric	17.3	14.3	12.3	16.5	16.3
Pediatrics	3.1	3.2	2.7	3.0	3.0
Total Non-Maternity	7.1	6.8	6.8	6.8	6.9

(*Continued*)

Monthly Statistics (January 1980) (Continued)

	Jan '80	Dec '79	Jan '79	YTD 1979–1980	YTD 1978–1979
Maternity	3.8	4.0	3.9	3.7	3.8
Sub-Total	6.7	6.5	6.5	6.4	6.5
Newborn	5.1	4.7	4.6	4.4	4.1
Total	6.6	6.4	6.3	6.2	6.3
Occupancy Rate (%)					
Medical/Surgical	85.4	77.3	83.3	81.4	80.1
Psychiatric	81.1	80.6	89.2	84.5	90.1
Pediatrics	126.7	88.5	83.4	93.1	75.8
Total Non-Maternity	86.5	78.1	84.0	82.2	81.0
Maternity	65.2	55.0	69.8	66.5	70.0
Sub-Total	84.8	76.4	82.9	81.0	80.2
Newborn	56.1	36.0	54.7	48.7	50.8
Total	56.1	72.3	80.0	77.7	77.2
Personnel Report					
Total Man-hours paid	111,925	108,860	108,195	435,903	424,306
Avg Daily Man-hours paid	3,610	3,512	3,386	3,544	3,405
Full-time Employees	512	509	491	509	490
Part-time Employees	188	184	181	183	180
Full-time Equivalents	631.8	614.5	610.8	620.2	603.7
Employee–Patient Ratio	3.4	3.8	3.4	3.6	3.5
Out-Patient Area					
Emergency Room Visits	2,608	2,343	2,354	9,860	9,482
E.R. Adm.—Adults	269	240	265	991	1,024
—Pediatrics	37	22	33	126	117
Pedi Office Hours	1,168	784	960	3,891	3,537
Prenatal Visits	110	59	79	320	347
Home-Care Admissions	31	32	47	141	173
Ophthalmology	3	10	12	22	25
Dental Clinic	278	181	192	879	811
Total	4,504	3,671	3,942	16,230	15,516
Special Services					
Anesthesia	379	308	395	1,448	1,397
Operations	381	306	399	1,456	1,412
Deliveries	77	62	90	308	353
EEG	39	38	70	147	207
EKG	779	756	803	3,052	3,036
Phonocardiograms	6	7	8	31	51
(P) Respiratory Therapy	852	896	846	3,717	3,463
(T) Physical Therapy	755	653	896	2,912	3,440
(R) Radiology—Diagnostic	11,375	9,749	12,905	43,218	48,280
Nuclear Med.	2,547	2,049	1,929	9,245	9,278
Rad. Ther.	933	665	2,268	3,954	6,444
Ultrasound	1,664	1,331	1,156	6,115	5,014
Total	16,519	13,794	18,258	62,532	69,016

Monthly Statistics (January 1980) (Continued)

	Jan '80	Dec '79	Jan '79	YTD 1979–1980	YTD 1978–1979
(R) Laboratory—In-patient	755,145	677,500	725,742	2,817,701	2,892,846
—Out-patient	156,379	115,768	145,224	533,379	525,654
Total	911,524	793,268	870,966	3,351,080	3,418,500
Pharmacy Prescriptions	4,858	4,543	4,711	18,590	18,387
Short Stay Patients	85	94	94	415	372
Intravenous (M/S)	3,184	2,958	3,022	13,091	12,201
(Mat)	154	111	197	554	691
Laundry (pounds)	64,934	60,054	69,451	252,027	284,316
Meals Served	25,300	23,190	23,240	98,349	93,057
Autopsy Rate	6.7%	6.7%	26.3%	14.8%	20.0%
Mortality Rate	1.6	1.9	2.0	1.6	2.0

(P) Patient Days.
(T) Treatments.
(R) Relative Value Units.

Maternity Statistics (January 1980)

	Jan '80	Dec '79	Jan '79	YTD 1979–1980	YTD 1978–1979
Pts. by Admission (Dist)					
O.B. Patients	78	65	80	305	333
Prenatal Clinic	3	3	12	31	35
Newborn—male	45	29	45	170	178
—female	32	33	44	135	171
Total Admissions	158	130	181	641	717
Deliveries	77	62	90	308	352
O.B. Patients by Disch (Fin)					
Blue Cross	41	27	29	142	156
Commercial Insurance	14	16	19	82	77
State Welfare	20	14	30	89	99
Self-Pay	6	2	7	15	19
Other	2	3	3	20	16
Total	83	62	88	348	367
Newborn by Disch (Fin)					
Blue Cross	41	23	27	131	153
Commercial Insurance	13	14	20	75	72
State Welfare	18	12	29	78	91
Self-Pay	4	3	7	13	17
Other	2	3	2	17	16
Total	78	55	85	314	349

(Continued)

Cases

Maternity Statistics (January 1980) (Continued)

	Jan '80	Dec '79	Jan '79	YTD 1979–1980	YTD 1978–1979
O.B. Patient Days (Fin)					
Blue Cross	170	109	124	558	616
Commercial Insurance	40	62	78	271	274
State Welfare	78	56	105	330	352
Self-Pay	21	6	26	49	89
Other	6	13	7	67	54
Total	315	246	340	1,275	1,385
Newborn Patient Days (Fin)					
Blue Cross	228	110	132	607	618
Commercial Insurance	55	68	80	290	274
State Welfare	98	59	142	375	409
Self-Pay	13	7	31	46	67
Other	6	13	5	51	70
Total	400	257	390	1,379	1,438
	715	503	730	2,654	2,823
Pediatrician's Office					
Patient's visits	1,168	784	960	3,891	3,537
Prenatal Clinic	110	66	79	327	347

Analysis of Admissions by Medical Service for Period Ending January 31, 1979

	Current Month		Percentage of Change	Year-to-Date		Percentage of Change
	This Year	Last Year		This Year	Last Year	
Medical	298	299	(.3)	1,150	1,105	4.1
Surgical	81	103	(21.4)	332	340	(2.3)
Obstetrics	81	92	(12.0)	336	368	(8.7)
Gynecology	95	95	—	380	363	4.7
Ophthalmology	25	30	(16.7)	88	82	7.3
Otorhinolaryngology	22	37	(40.5)	87	109	(20.2)
Urology	19	24	(20.8)	79	82	(3.7)
Orthopedic	49	38	28.9	187	168	11.3
Dermatology	—	1	—	—	1	—
Pediatrics	88	63	39.7	271	219	23.7
Psychiatry	37	41	(9.8)	130	134	(3.0)
Proctology	19	14	35.7	53	52	1.9
Newborn	77	89	(13.5)	306	348	(12.1)
Dental	7	6	16.7	22	22	—
Maxillo & Recon.	9	8	12.5	22	28	(21.4)
	907	940	(3.5)	3,443	3,421	.6
One Day Stays	(99)	(102)	2.9	(445)	(392)	13.5
	808	838	(3.6)	2,998	3,029	(1.0)

Admissions by Race and Nationality (January 1980)

	Jan '80	Dec '79	Jan '79	YTD 1979–1980	YTD 1978–1979
Caucasian	530	422	550	2,011	2,064
Black	182	190	224	776	775
Puerto Rican	179	142	135	591	501
Cuban	1	1	0	5	1
Portuguese	10	9	20	43	54
Oriental	2	3	7	8	10
Other	3	1	4	9	16
Total	907	768	940	3,443	3,421

X-Ray Monthly Statistics (January 1980)

	January 1980		YTD 1979–1980		YTD 1978–1979	
	Exams	Units	Exams	Units	Exams	Units
Diagnostic						
In-Patients	1,498	6,728	5,605	24,868	6,324	27,611
Out-Patients	1,237	4,647	4,857	18,356	5,345	19,959
Total	2,735	11,375	10,462	43,224	11,669	47,570
Shift Breakdown	Pts.	Exams	Pts.	Exams	Pts.	Exams
12–8 A.M.	168	232	596	928	667	1,009
8–4 P.M.	1,403	1,762	5,377	6,806	6,012	7,835
4–12 P.M.	582	759	2,187	2,962	2,291	3,123
Total	2,153	2,753	8,160	10,597	8,970	11,967
Ultra-Sound	Pts.	Exams	Pts.	Exams	Pts.	Exams
In-Patients	112	115	368	386	339	353
Out-Patients	47	51	231	240	193	196
Total	159	166	599	626	532	549
Nuclear Scan	Pts.	Exams	Pts.	Exams	Pts.	Exams
In-Patients	110	149	433	569	394	538
Out-Patients	40	57	99	142	63	83
Total	150	206	532	711	457	621
Radiotherapy	Pts.	Exams	Pts.	Exams	Pts.	Exams
Patients Treated	23		97		100	
Treated as In-Patient		101		399		440
Treated as Out-Patient		377		1,334		1,168
Total		478		1,733		1,608

(Continued)

X-Ray Monthly Statistics (January 1980) (*Continued*)

	January 1980		YTD 1979–1980		YTD 1978–1979	
	Exams	Units	Exams	Units	Exams	Units
Film Count:						
14 × 14 – 35 × 35	100		1,625		1,000	
9 × 9 – 24 × 24	1,450		7,425		3,625	
14 × 17 – 35 × 43	3,675		13,525		16,625	
11 × 14 – 30 × 35	500		2,825		3,000	
10 × 12 – 24 × 30	2,525		10,500		11,750	
8 × 10	200		2,750		6,125	
Total	8,450		38,650		42,125	

Films Discarded	395			
Films on Hand	9,050	*Films Received*	8,000	
Films on Hand for	FEBRUARY 1980 :		8,600	

EGK Statistics (January, 1980)

	Jan '80	Dec '79	Jan '79	YTD 1979–1980	YTD 1978–1979
In-Patient					
Private	409	373	443	1,587	1,736
Medicare	293	285	267	1,120	968
Employee	3	2	9	20	30
Total	705	660	719	2,727	2,734
Out-Patient					
Private	63	83	67	267	237
Medicare	10	13	13	50	43
Employee	1	0	4	8	22
Total	74	96	84	325	302
	779	756	803	3,052	3,036
Phonocardiograms					
In-Patient	1	1	6	7	24
Out-Patient	5	6	2	24	27
Total	6	7	8	31	51
Treadmill Stress Tests					
In-Patient	9	2	2	17	12
Out-Patient	6	4	6	16	15
Total	15	6	8	33	27
Dynamic Cardiogram					
In-Patient	33	25	19	113	72
Out-Patient	29	26	12	107	38
Total	62	51	31	220	110

EKG Statistics (January, 1980) (Continued)

	Jan '80	Dec '79	Jan '79	YTD 1979–1980	YTD 1978–1979
Impedance Phlebography					
In-Patient	6	2	2	16	23
Out-Patient	4	2	2	6	2
Total	10	4	4	22	25
In-Patient					
Private	17	19	34	76	101
Medicare	15	9	11	41	51
Employee	0	0	0	0	0
Total	32	28	45	117	152
Out-Patient					
Private	7	10	25	30	53
Medicare	0	0	0	0	1
Employee	0	0	0	0	1
Total	7	10	25	30	55
	39	38	70	147	207

Department of Respiratory Therapy Monthly Statistical Reports

	Jan '80	Dec '79	1980 Oct–Jan	1979 Oct–Jan
	Monthly		Year-to-Date	
	Current	Previous	Current	Last
Pt. Days	852	896	3,717	3,463
Avg. No. Pts./Day	27.4	28.9		
Avg. No. R_x Days/Pt.	4.7	4.0		
Total Hours O_2	4,952	6,173	23,417	21,575
Nasal	339	473	1,634	1,566
Cold/Warm/Steam	35	60	293	157
IPPB R_x	432	350	2,010	4,006
IPPB (Pt. Days)	148	123	660	1,433
Croupette	98	56	243	728
Respiratory Exerciser	257	173	921	734
Air Compressor	108	54	309	175
Aerosol Nebulizer	342	416	1,778	185
Induced Sputum	7	8	23	39
Continuous Ventilation	12	6	276	415
Postural Drainage	350	328	1,516	890
Walking Exercise		1	22	13
Extended Therapy	114	75	521	197

(Continued)

Department of Respiratory Therapy Monthly Statistical Reports (*Continued*)

	Jan '80	Dec '79	1980 Oct–Jan	1979 Oct–Jan
	Monthly		Year-to-Date	
	Current	Previous	Current	Last
Ultra-Sonic Nebulizer	5	40	184	1,106
Pulmonary Function Test				
Lung Volumes	14	9	58	53
Lung Volumes (2 studies)	8	4	39	
Diffusion Test	17	10	72	
Functional Residual Vol.	16	7	65	
Pulmonary Screening Test	8	0	23	29
Other				

Monthly Statistics (January 1980)

	Jan '80	Dec '79	Jan '79	YTD 1979–1980	YTD 1978–1979
In-Patients—Total	101	84	93	254	367
Treatments	674	607	818	2,036	3,020
Out-Patients—Total	18	12	18	31	84
Treatments	81	46	78	121	420
Modalities:					
Hydrocollator	206	119	319	580	1,029
Ultrasound	89	62	264	338	916
Massage	41	29	260	231	880
Ther. Exercises	266	205	607	1,099	2,476
Gait Training	362	253	489	1,518	1,807
Diathermy	—	—	—	—	—
Whirlpool	33	65	35	239	119
Elec. Stimulation	—	1	—	3	15
Infra-Red	—	—	—	—	—
Traction	9	4	48	13	109
A.D.L.	74	119	53	445	281
Cold Packs	1	—	—	1	2
Ultra Violet	—	—	—	—	—
Paraffin	—	—	1	—	2
Medco-Sonol	30	26	32	90	116
Others	12	11	3	30	28
Stump Conditioning	—	—	—	9	5
Evaluation	106	80	87	334	300
General Tonic Exerc.	192	207	—	829	—
Debridement	13	25	—	49	—
Total	1,434	1,206	2,198	5,808	8,085

Professional Fees (January 1980)

Department	Income Tests or Units Current Month	Rate	Due Physician Current Month	January 1979	YTD 1979–1980	YTD 1978–1979
Laboratory	902,162 (u)	$.0234 per unit	$20,867.83	$16,826.54	$ 74,736.12	$ 64,065.06
Radiology	16,519 (u)	$1.6875 per unit	$31,686.37	$33,463.13	$123,997.63	$128,535.37
Respiratory Therapy	$ 18,889.00	$1.700 + 3%	$ 2,266.67	$ 2,328.99	$ 9,575.28	$ 9,800.45
EKG	775 (t)	$7.00	$ 5,425.00	$ 4,740.00	$ 19,673.00	$ 18,720.00
EKG	39 (t)	$15.00	$ 585.00	$ 1,050.00	$ 2,205.00	$ 3,090.00
Phonocardiograms	6 (t)	$50.00	$ 300.00	$ 350.00	$ 1,550.00	$ 2,500.00
Ophthalmology—Angio	3	$60.00	$ 180.00	$ 600.00	$ 1,140.00	$ 960.00
—Fundus	—	$5.00	$ —	$ 10.00	$ 15.00	$ —
—Retina*	—	$35.00	—	—	—	—
—Retina	—	$27.00	—	—	—	—

(u) Relative value units.
(t) Tests.
* With visual fields.

Man-Hour Report

	January 1980	January 1979	Percentage of Change	Year-to-Date 1979–1980	Year-to-Date 1978–1979	Percentage of Change
Straight Time Worked	83,710.8	80,607.6	3.7	355,365.2	344,806.4	3.0
Sick Hours	3,256.4	3,337.3	(2.5)	12,939.2	15,108.3	(16.7)
Overtime Premium	3,882.8	3,672.1	5.4	14,004.6	12,521.2	10.6
Vacation	5,056.8	4,979.8	1.5	21,678.5	21,564.9	0.5
Holidays	4,886.3	4,064.1	5.8	15,149.0	14,417.0	4.8
Other	300.0	523.5	(74.5)	2,591.0	2,089.5	1.9
Total Man-Hours	101,093.1	97,724.4	3.3	421,727.5	410,507.3	2.7
Total Man-Hours Worked	87,593.6	84,279.7	3.8	369,369.8	357,327.6	3.3
Average Daily Man-Hours Pd	3,610	3,386	6.2	3,544	3,450	2.7
Full-Time Equivalents Pd	631.8	610.8	3.3	620.2	603.7	2.7
Full-Time Equivalents Worked	547.6	526.7	3.8	543.2	525.5	3.3
Full-Time Personnel	512	491	4.1	509	491	3.5
Part-Time Personnel	188	181	1.6	183	180	1.6

APPENDIX 4
Excerpts from HSA Report

INTRODUCTION

Acute in-patient care consists of diagnostic, therapeutic, rehabilitative, and support services provided in a short-stay or general hospital to patients requiring, at minimum, an overnight stay, but at least 50 percent of whom do not require hospitalization beyond a 30-day period. In our discussion, we consider seven (7) general hospitals operating under voluntary control. In addition, a private psychiatric hospital, a state psychiatric hospital outside of HSA I, and a non-profit community mental health center are considered in formulating bed need estimates and projections. In-patient mental-health services are addressed in-depth in Chapter VIII on Mental Health and Substance Abuse Services.

Acute-care hospitals are hardly homogeneous in size, services, or in the ways in which medicine is practiced within their labyrinthine structures. They vary greatly in bed capacity. They may provide basic services (medical/surgical, pediatric, and obstetrical), specialized services (e.g., psychiatric or alcohol detoxification), and/or highly specialized services (e.g., a burn center or neonatology unit). They may provide outpatient clinic services either in hospital-based and/or in satellite facilities. Their emergency departments may serve as *de-facto* primary care resources to the poor and near poor who lack such services in their communities. In any event, hospitals are operating in a transitional era; an era in which their traditional in-patient focus is widening to include new roles and models for meeting the health needs of the community.

The concern of policy makers has turned to the presence of "excess" hospital capacity. Questions have been raised as to how much excess capacity actually exists and the extent to which it contributes to spiraling medical costs without substantial benefit to the health of the population. Since it makes sense economically to use costly medical facilities only when necessary, a logical first step in hospital cost containment is to identify and eliminate hospital beds that may be in excess of population need. The following principles provide a framework within which to plan for future in-patient care services.

PRINCIPLES FOR ACUTE IN-PATIENT CARE PLANNING AND RESOURCE DEVELOPMENT

1. The acute in-patient care system should be a cohesive, regional, stratified system of care that links hospitals of more limited capabilities with those hospitals in and outside of the region capable of providing services of increasing complexity. Such cooperative arrangements should provide services of optimal quality with minimal duplication of highly trained personnel and expensive facilities in order to maximize cost-effectiveness.

2. It is not necessary for any given hospital to provide comprehensive specialized services for all disease categories, nor is it necessary for the region to be self-contained for all tertiary services. On the contrary, hospitals should be encouraged to plan the delivery of specialized services jointly to avoid unnecessary and costly duplication. Each hospital should have a well-defined role in this stratified system.

3. Hospital services should be responsive to the needs of the community served. That responsiveness should include consideration of the social, economic, mental, and physical needs of the population within the context of resource availability and the need to develop cost-effective services. Other considerations such as the geographic isolation of the community, the availability of the hospital, and the size of the hospital should be considered in the planning and provision of hospital services.

4. Hospitals should, whenever physically and economically feasible, and without compromising quality, make every effort to share manpower and other resources.

5. Hospital planning should be consistent with the goals of the total health-care system. The appropriate role and function of the hospital in education, prevention, and the provision of diagnostic and therapeutic acute-care services should be defined in a way which takes into

account other elements of the health-care system.
6. Opportunities for consultation and referral should be readily available to physicians. Channels should exist for referring a patient transferred to distant hospitals with more highly specialized services back to their primary physicians with a recommended program for continuing care and follow-up.
7. In order to facilitate continuity of care, hospitals should have both formal and informal linkages with other service providers in the health-care system.
8. All hospitals should be part of a coordinated system for providing opportunities for the continuing education of physicians, nurses, and allied health personnel.
9. Although a hospital plan should reflect recognition of legal, fiscal, and other existing constraints, the plan should, above all, identify and address the health-care needs of the population within its service area. While system development may imply expansion, it does so only to the extent that expansion may be appropriate in order to provide more effective and efficient health care to an area where need for services has been substantiated. In this context, each hospital should provide a range of services appropriate to its size, utilization, and resources.
10. Since the hospital's core function is the delivery of patient services, teaching and research functions should be appropriately related but subordinate to patient care.

AREAS OF PRIORITY CONCERN

As noted, HSA has seven nonfederal, general short-stay hospitals all of which are centrally located within each of the three metropolitan areas that comprise our region. They range in size from 201 licensed beds to 634, and total 2,612 beds. In addition, there are an estimated 117 short-stay mental-health beds used by residents in two psychiatric facilities in the region and in a state institution out of the region.

Based on patient-origin data from the Idaho Hospital Association, the service areas of our general hospitals are generally congruent with metropolitan area boundaries. Notable exceptions are Grandview Hospital whose patients are virtually all Grandview residents and St. Margaret's Hospital which serves predominantly Marin residents. Relatively few patients from out of the region seek care in Southwest Idaho hospitals.

Access to area hospitals is facilitated by two major highways that transverse the entire length of the region, the Morton Parkway and the Idaho Turnpike. Furthermore, the region is well served by 35 ambulance services employing some 930 emergency medical technicians for emergency care. At least 95 percent of Southwest Idaho residents are within 30 minutes travel time by automobile to a hospital.

As stated above, a major concern of the HSA is rising health-care costs and the extent to which excess hospital resources contribute to this inflationary trend. Consequently, the supply of hospital facilities in Southwest Idaho relative to the need is of prime importance.

1. *Hospital Bed Supply and Utilization.* There were an estimated 4.1 beds for each 1,000 Southwest Idaho residents in 1978. This is higher than that recommended by DHEW—less than 4 beds per 1,000 population—in its National Guidelines for Health Planning, and more than adequate to meet our needs.

This is substantiated by a regionwide acute-care bed occupancy rate of 72 percent; rates for individual hospitals range from a low of 55 percent to a high of 83 percent. It is clear that not all hospitals in the region are operating at optimum efficiency. Of course, this variance might be explained somewhat by demographic and diagnostic differences in individual hospital's patient mix. Even though the age–sex distribution of the three metropolitan areas is similar, the Johnston Area hospitals, which serve about half the region's population and many more of the region's poor and elderly, average shorter lengths of stay and higher occupancy rates, and thus appear to be more efficient than the hospitals in the Marin/Grandview area. By comparison to the national standard of at least an 80 percent overall occupancy, we are significantly deficient.

It is unlikely that occupancy rates will improve given recent trends in number of patients, patient days, and existing hospital bed capacity and organization. In order to improve occupancy rates either the number of patients must be increased or the number of patient days must be increased, or the number of beds and/or units reduced. Given inpatient trends of the recent past and the projected slow growth in the population, the latter alternative must be considered. The number of patients in our region's hospitals has decreased steadily albeit slightly since 1971—3 percent patient days have likewise decreased—2 percent. Below, the performance of specific hospital service units are analyzed and projections of local need made.

2. *Obstetrical Units.* Perhaps the area of greatest inefficiency is obstetrical services. All seven hospitals have obstetrical patients only, the 1978 from 17 to 49 beds. Based on obstetrical patients only, the 1978 regionwide occupancy rate was 43 percent compared to the national standard of 75 percent and the state standard of 65 percent.

All hospitals appear to have "Level II" obstetrical units in terms of equipment and staffing. That is, they provide a full range of maternity and neonatal services for uncomplicated deliveries, the majority of complicated obstetrical deliveries, and certain types of neonatal illnesses. They also provide 24-hour in-house anesthesia, 24-hour blood bank, continuous maternal/fetal monitoring as well as other services. Only Johnston Hospital, however, meets the national standard for minimum number of births—1,500.

No regional plan for obstetrical services exists as recommended in the National Guidelines. For the most part, each hospital has established informal agreements and protocols concerning transfer and tertiary care for high-risk neonates. Johnston Memorial Hospital has the only neonatal intensive-care unit and resusitation team in the region. The neonatal resusitation team is available to assist other hospitals in neonatal emergency situations. Presently, only St. Stephens Hospital and Midland County Hospital utilize these resources. The other four hospitals in the region have informal transfer arrangements with Lincoln and Twin Falls hospitals. As with obstetrical services, no neonatal regional plan exists.

Given the current low level of use of obstetrical units by *obstetrical patients,* it appears that greater efficiencies could be achieved through regionalization of obstetrical services; that is, the consolidation of units and all appear to be relatively equivalent with respect to quality and level of care. As it is, however, expensive obstetrical resources such as delivery rooms, specially trained personnel, and equipment are underutilized.

We estimate that there are at least 53 excess licensed obstetrical beds in our region's hospitals and that by 1985 an additional bed should be eliminated. These estimates and projections are based on a number of findings and assumptions: (1) the decline over the past eight years (1971–1978) in the number of obstetrical patients; (2) a modest increase in births due to an increase in the number of women of childbearing age (1970–1977); (3) a stabilization in the proportion of births by ceasarean sections; (4) stabilization in average length of stay.

3. *Pediatric Units.* All seven general hospitals in Southwest Idaho maintain pediatric units that accommodate a total of 186 beds. Bed capacities range from 7 at Midland County Hospital to 42 at Johnston Memorial Hospital. Only Midland County's unit does not meet the national minimum bed capacity of 20.

None of the units in the region's hospitals meet the 65 percent minimum annual occupancy rate standards recommended in state and federal guidelines—based on pediatric patients only. Pediatric occupancy rates varied from a low of 27 percent in Marin Hospital to 96 percent in Midland County Hospital.

Pediatric patient trends over the past eight years indicate that optimum utilization of existing pediatric units is likely given current bed complements. Data show that the number of pediatric patients declined by over 25 percent since 1971. Accordingly, patient days also declined—15 percent. These trends will probably continue into the next decade since the number of children in the region is expected to drop by 11 percent by 1985.

In order to improve the occupancy rates of pediatric units, either the number of patient days must be increased or the number of beds and/or units reduced. Given the trends of the recent past and the projected decrease in the pediatric population, the latter alternative must be considered. We estimate that there were at least 44 excess pediatric beds in the region in 1978, most of them in the Greater Marin Area. By 1985, 18 more beds should be eliminated, or a total reduction of 62 beds.

4. *Medical/Surgical Units.* There are 2,118 beds in medical/surgical units in the region. Unit size

vary from 149 beds at Midland County Hospital to 512 at Johnston Memorial Hospital. The overall occupancy rate for Johnston area hospitals was 84 percent. In contrast, the overall occupancy rate for Marin area hospitals was 70 percent—nearly a 15 percent difference.

Data on medical/surgical patient discharges show a generally level trend since 1971; a steady increase in medical patients was more than offset by a steady decrease in surgical patients. Similarly, patient days, overall, have been declining.

Our calculations of the current (1978) medical/surgical bed need for the region show that we had an excess of 232 beds, 50 percent of which were in Marin area hospitals. However, by 1985, most of these excess beds will be pressed into service. Based on a 6 percent increase in the population aged 19 to 64 and, even more important, a 20 percent increase in the over-65 population, all but 15 of the existing supply of medical/surgical beds will be needed.

5. *Hospital Costs in Southwest Idaho.* Over the period 1974 through 1977, hospital charges, as measured in the Consumer Price Index, rose 42.6 percent nationally; regionally the rise was 44.8 percent. Because the price stabilization program for hospitals was not lifted till after April 1974 and hospitals used that year as a "catch up" period, a more useful measure of the increase in process is the period from 1975 through 1977. For this period the rate of increase for the United States as a whole was 24.0 percent; for Southwest Idaho the rise in prices charged was 24.6 percent, for an average annual compound rate of 7.64 percent.

Some of the more significant findings in our region are:

- Between 1974 and 1977, hospital net in-patient revenues rose 42 percent; from $97.7 to $139.0 million.

- Between 1974 and 1977, hospital (net) expenses incurred for providing in-patient care increased by 44 percent.

- Patients paid $129.70 for each day of care in 1974; by 1977 patients were paying $183.63 for the average day, an increase of 42 percent.

- Patient payments for the average hospital stay rose from $996 in 1974 to $1,428 in 1977, an increase of 43 percent.

- Hospital costs for out-patient services rose 44.8 percent.

- Net revenues for providing out-patient services rose 70.0 percent.

Our analysis of hospital bed supply and utilization indicates a decrease in in-patient hospital days. Over the five-year period, 1974 through 1978, there was a decline of 2.5 percent in in-patient days or close to 17,979 days.

A decrease in in-patient days has a significant economic impact on hospitals because of their large investment in plant and equipment. Given a fixed investment in plant and equipment, a decrease in days of hospitalization leads to (1) a rise in charges, (2) a rise in operating deficits, or (3) some combination of these alternatives.

Hospitals have raised charges and have suffered losses in several of their departments. For example, in 1977 the combined operating losses of maternity and newborn services were $1.9 million, up from slightly less than $1.5 million in 1974. Out-patient expenses exceeded revenues by $2.8 million in 1977. Using the final audited financial statements of the hospitals in our region, reported net operating income was $666,844. (This figure takes account of the maternity, newborn, and out-patient losses and is calculated *before* any endowment income or bequests are added.) 1977 was not an aberration, it merely continued a trend.

Thus, other departments and other services had revenues of over $5.4 million *more* than their costs to compensate for the losses in maternity, new-born, and out-patient services. Put another way, there were $5.4 million of cross-subsidization.

Goal AC-1: TO CONTAIN TO THE EXTENT POSSIBLE ACUTE IN-PATIENT CARE COSTS BY MAXIMIZING APPROPRIATE AND EFFICIENT USE OF ACUTE IN-PATIENT CARE FACILITIES IN SOUTHWEST IDAHO

Objectives

1. To achieve a 3.7 licensed bed per 1000 population ratio by October 1983 by elimination of 131 licensed beds in accordance with the following subregional distribution (Table A):

TABLE A

	Johnston Area	Walkland Area	Marin Area	Region
Medical/Surgical	+9	−22	−63	−76
Obstetrical[a]	−28	+2	−28	−54
Pediatric[b]	−22	−7	−33	−62
Psychiatric	+32	+9	+20	+61
Total Reduction	−9	−18	−104	−131
(HMO Reduction)[c]	(−29)	(−12)	(−20)	(−61)

[a]By 1983 each obstetrical unit should have at least 1500 births.
[b]By 1983, each pediatric unit should have a minimum of 20 beds.
[c]Based on estimates of reduced hospital bed utilization by projected HMO members; will be adjusted as experience dictates.

2. By October 1983, a regionwide annual occupancy rate of at least 80 percent should be achieved. Occupany rates in specific units in each hospital should be no less than the following:

Medical/Surgical	85%
Obstetrical	75%
Pediatric	65%
Psychiatric	85%

Recommended Actions

1. With the aim to achieve objectives 1 and 2, area hospitals should immediately initiate joint planning activities on a metropolitan area basis to: (1) systematically reduce obstetrical beds; (2) consolidate obstetrical units; (3) develop regional plans for the delivery of obstetrical services. Linkages between obstetrical and neonatal units delivering less than 1500 births annually. Any party seeking an exemption or discretionary adjustment should present written justification in an application to the HSA prior to August 31, 1980 as per HSA Board policy.

2. Area hospitals should immediately initiate joint planning activities on a metropolitan area basis for the systematic reduction of beds and consolidation of pediatric units to achieve objectives 1 and 2. No pediatric unit should contain less than 20 beds. Any party seeking an exemption or discretionary adjustment should present written justification in an application to the HSA prior to August 31, 1980.

3. The HSA Board through its Health Systems Plan Committee should evaluate and approve or disapprove written requests from parties seeking exemption from the above objectives and attendant actions.

4. The HSA through its review function should evaluate hospital proposals for alterations in and/or expansions of in-patient services in accordance with objectives 1 and 2, and the principles of acute in-patient care planning and resource development.

5. All hospitals should expand their ambulatory surgery programs to 15–20 percent of all hospital surgery. The HSA should favorably review financially sound proposals for the expansion of ambulatory surgery programs in accord with its principles for acute inpatient care planning and resource development.

6. The PSRO of Landfair County and the region's hospitals should develop appropriate guidelines and protocols for identifying procedures (including surgical) and tests that can be reasonably performed on an out-patient basis, and implement strategies for reducing unnecessary hospital admissions.

6. *Speciality Services.* As previously stated, acute in-patient care has become increasingly intensive and sophisticated. Technological advances make available services and equipment that contribute significantly to the cost spiral because of the expense of the equipment and the requirement for

highly skilled manpower. Unless patient volume is sufficient, specialty services are not cost-effective investments of scarce health dollars. Thus, the distribution of these services should be thoughtfully planned to ensure optimal utilization and equitable access.

The specialty services of particular concern in this Health Systems Plan are: neonatal special care units, open heart surgery, cardiac catheterization, radiation therapy, computerized tomographic scanners, and end-stage renal dialysis. As with the general hospitals services addressed above, planning and standards guidelines have been developed by the U.S. Department of Health Education and Welfare regarding the supply, distribution, and organization of these services.

Neonatal Special-Care Units provide highly specialized services required by only a very small percentage of infants. Standards contained in the National Guidelines, to promote regionalization of services, indicate that a single Level II or III neonatal special-care unit should contain no less than 15 intermediate or intensive-care beds. This standard is based on the recommendation of the American Academy of Pediatrics.

Level III units are staffed and equipped for the intensive care of newborns as well as intermediate and recovery care. Level II units provide intermediate and recovery care as well as some specialized services.

Currently, two hospitals in HSA I have neonatal special care units—Walkland and Johnston. Walkland Hospital is a Level II unit. Johnston Memorial, which has both intermediate and intensive-care beds, approximates a Level III unit. Their units contain 10 and 16 beds, respectively, for a ratio of 3.4 beds per 1000 live births. This is within the national standard of maximum of 4.0. (Only Johnston Memorial meets the minimum bed capacity standard.) A determination must be made regarding where future beds should be placed and whether two units in the region are necessary.

This determination should be made within the context of a regional plan for neonatal and obstetrical services. Such a plan does not currently exist as suggested in the National Guidelines. Only the Johnston hospitals have formal agreements regarding the transfer of high-risk infants to neonatal intensive-care units within and outside of the region, although informal understandings and protocols are operational in other hospitals.

Open Heart Surgery for congenital and acquired heart and coronary artery disease is very costly requiring highly specialized manpower and hospital resources such as a heart–lung bypass machine to perform circulatory functions during surgery. It is currently performed at two hospitals in the region: Johnston Memorial and St. Stephens Hospital share a surgical team and major equipment. These two hospitals have recently agreed to consolidate this service at St. Stephens Hospital.

The National Guidelines suggest a standard of a minimum of 200 open heart procedures annually in order to maintain and strengthen skills. The total number performed in 1978 at the 2 hospitals was 101; a 19% decrease from 1977.

Megavoltage Radiation Therapy equipment is expensive to purchase and to operate. Most radiation therapy treatments are performed on an out-patient basis and therefore, it may not be necessary for each hospital to have this service available for its in-patients. However, six of the region's hospitals have radiation therapy units. (St. Margaret's Hospital shares the Marin Hospital service.)

Until the last few years cobalt 60 units were the most common type of megavoltage equipment. Now, hospitals are changing to the more sophisticated and costly linear accelerator when a unit must be replaced.

Currently, four hospitals meet the National Guideline of more than 300 cancer cases annually and two are below this standard. Only Walkland's Unit is performing an optimal number of treatments per year.

Computerized Tomographic Scanners, more commonly known as CT or CAT Scanners, are sophisticated diagnostic devices that combine x-ray and computer technologies to provide advanced diagnostic capabilities. CT scanners are costly to purchase ($600,000–$750,000) and are costly to operate. Specialists in this field must be available at the hospital to operate this equipment.

At present, there are scanners in five of the seven hospitals in the region. Only two have been in operation for more than one year—Johnston Memorial's "head" scanner and Grandview Hospital's more comprehensive "full body" scanner.

Currently, there is an over-abundance of scanner capability in the area. In accordance with the National Guidelines, no additional or replacement scanners are needed until each existing scanner is performing at least 2,500 medically necessary scans per year.

The *End-Stage Renal Dialysis* Program was created pursuant to Section 2991 of the Social Security Amendments of 1972 (Publ. L. 92-603), which extends Medical Benefits to any individual who has end-stage renal disease requiring dialysis or transplantation, provided that such individual: (1) is fully or currently insured or entitled to monthly benefits under Title II of the Social Security Act; or (2) is the spouse or dependent child of an individual so insured or entitled to such monthly benefits in order for an End-Stage Renal Dialysis facility to qualify for reimbursement under the program, the facility must meet the conditions for coverage of suppliers of end-stage renal disease services as established by regulation. These conditions incorporate standards that relate to supply, distribution, and organization of End-Stage Renal Dialysis facilities. National standards were developed by the Department of Health, Education, and Welfare based on extensive consultation with professionals and other persons knowledgeable in the areas of nephrology and transplant surgery, and published as regulations. The regulations do not try to encourage any particular type of dialysis setting. It is widely recognized, however, that self-care dialysis can significantly contain costs without impairing the quality of care of the suitably chosen patient. The organization of resources to support self-care dialysis is therefore encouraged to the maximum extent practicable.

There are currently three End-Stage Renal Dialysis facilities in the region—in Walkland Hospital and in two free-standing proprietary facilities in Johnston. Walkland Hospital recently received approval for an additional five stations and seven new stations have been approved for Johnston. With these additions, no additional stations will be needed by 1985.

Goal AC-II: TO REGIONALIZE SPECIALTY CARE SERVICES IN SOUTHWEST IDAHO IN ORDER TO FOSTER OPTIMAL UTILIZATION OF EQUIPMENT AND PERSONNEL WHILE ENSURING REASONABLE ACCESS TO MEDICALLY NECESSARY CARE.

Objectives

1. By October 1983, a regional plan should be developed which details the distribution and location of neonatal intermediate care beds (level II) and which contains treatment guidelines and protocols for the transfer of high-risk infants. Johnston Memorial's neonatal intensive care unit should continue as the region's only level III resource. Services should be organized and utilized in accordance with standards contained in the National Guidelines.

2. By October 1983, existing open-heart surgical units that do not meet the National Guidelines of a minimum of 200 procedures should be discontinued.

3. By October 1983, Grandview, Marin, and St. Margaret's Hospitals should consolidate their cardiac catheterization services in order to be consistent with recommended national standards. Additionally, the performance of pediatric cardiac catheterizations in the region should be discontinued.

4. By October 1983, megavoltage radiation therapy units should be treating a minimum of 300 patients annually and no new units should be permitted unless existing units are performing at least 6,000 treatments annually.

5. By October 1983, all CT scanner(s) in the region should be performing at least 2,500 medically necessary patient procedures per year.

6. Until 1985, no new ESRD stations should be established unless there is a demonstrated need for such an expansion.

Recommended Actions

1. Area hospitals should immediately begin joint planning on a regionwide basis to determine the distribution and location of neonatal intermediate care beds. Walkland Hospital should submit in writing an application which includes justification of continuation of its neonatal intermediate care unit (level II) in accordance with HSA Board policy.

2. Open heart surgical units in the Johnston area that do not meet the standards should be discon-

tinued and formal referral arrangements made with appropriate hospitals. Justifications or exemptions from this action should be submitted in writing in an application to the HSA by August 31, 1980 as per HSA Board policy.
3. Grandview, Marin, and St. Margaret's Hospitals should immediately develop plans for consolidating cardiac catheterization in one unit in order to meet minimum standards contained in the National Guidelines. Any of these hospitals seeking an exemption from this action should submit written justification in an application to the HSA by August 31, 1980.
4. The HSA should monitor the utilization of megavoltage therapy treatments in Marin–Grandview area hospitals. New or replacement units should be permitted only if existing units are fully utilized in accordance with National Guidelines.
5. No new CT scanners should be established in the region. Replacements should be approved only if existing scanners within the same metropolitan area are fully utilized in accordance with National Guidelines.
6. The HSA should encourage ESRD facilities to increase their efficiency by increasing the number of shifts and thereby meet additional demand. Facilities should also promote and maximize opportunities for home dialysis and self-dialysis.

Comparison of National State and HSA Acute Care Resource Standards

Category	National Standard	State Standard	HSA Standard
Acute care short-stay hospital bed supply	Less than four nonfederal short-stay hospital beds per 1,000 population.		3.7 beds per 1,000 population needed in region in 1985.
Acute care short-stay hospital occupancy rate	Average annual rate of at least 80% for all nonfederal short-stay beds.	Overall minimum occupancy level of 80% for each health service area.	Regionwide annual occupancy rate of at least 80% to be achieved by October.
Medical surgical service occupancy rate		Not less than 80% (and sufficiently above).	Not less than 85% in each hospital.
Obstetrical service bed supply, volume and occupancy rate	Hospitals providing care for complicated obstetrical problems (Levels II & III) should have at least 1,500 births annually. Average annual occupancy rate of at least 75% in each unit with more than 1,500 births annually.	Minimum occupancy level: 20 bed unit: 65% 20–29 bed unit: 70% 30+ bed unit: 75% Bed supply: 0.8 beds per 1,000 females 15–44 years old.	Each OB unit to have at least 1,500 births annually. Occupancy rate of not less than 75% in each hospital. Regionwide bed need for 1985 is equivalent to 0.87 beds per 1,000 females 15–44 years old.
Neonatal special care units size and bed supply	No more than 4 neonatal intensive and intermediate care units per 1,000 annual live births in service area; minimum unit size of 15 beds.		Need to study whether current (1978, ratio of 3.4 beds per 1,000 live births is sufficient; in light of national standard of 4.0; also to study whether 2 existing units of 10 and 15 beds respectively are necessary in light of national standard of minimum unit size of 15 beds.

(Continued)

Comparison of National State and HSA Acute Care Resource Standards (*Continued*)

Category	National Standard	State Standard	HSA Standard
Pediatric service bed supply, unit size and occupancy rate	Minimum unit size of 20 beds in an urbanized area Minimum occupancy rate for a facility with: 29–39 beds: 65% 40–79 beds: 70% 80 or more beds: 75%	Minimum occupancy level: 40 bed unit: 65% 40–79 bed unit: 70% 80+ bed unit: 75% Bed supply: No more than 1.0 beds per 1,000 population 0–14 years old (includes neonatal ICU).	Each pediatric unit to have a minimum of 20 beds by 1983. Minimum occupancy rate of 65% in each hospital. Regionwide bed need for 1985 is equivalent to 0.9 beds per 1,000 population 0–18 years old (includes neonatal ICU).
Psychiatric short-stay in-patient bed supply occupancy rate			Regionwide bed need for 1985 is Service equivalent to 0.3 and beds per 1,000 total population. Minimum occupancy rate of 86% in each hospital.
Heart surgery	Within 3 years of initiation, a minimum of 200 open heart procedures annually in an institution operating on adults; a minimum of 100 pediatric heart operations per year, 75 of which should be open heart procedures. No new units initiated unless each existing unit is operating and is expected to continue to operate at a minimum of 350 adult cases and 130 pediatric cases.		National standard adopted
Cardiac catheterization	A minimum of 300 cardiac catheterizations of which at least 200 should be intracardiac or coronary artery catheterizations, performed per year in an adult unit within 3 years of initiation. A minimum of 50 pediatric cardiac catheterizations performed per year within 3 years of initiation.		National standard adopted

Comparison of National State and HSA Acute Care Resource Standards (*Continued*)

Category	National Standard	State Standard	HSA Standard
	No new units in facilities not performing open heart surgery. No new additional units unless existing adult units perform 500 procedures per year, and pediatric units perform 250 procedures.		
Radiation therapy	A megavoltage radiation therapy unit should serve a population of at least 150,000 persons and treat at least 300 cases per year, within 3 years of initiation. No new units unless existing unit is performing at least 6,000 treatments per year.		National standard adopted
Computerized tomographic scanners	2,500 medically necessary patient procedures per year during the second year of operation and thereafter. No additional scanners unless existing scanners operate at more than 2,500 procedures per year. No additional scanners unless the operation of the proposed equipment will set in place data collection and utilization review systems.		National standard adopted
End-stage renal disease	HSPs should be consistent with standards and procedures contained in the DHEW regulations governing conditions for coverage of suppliers of end-stage renal disease services (20 CFE, Part 405, Subpart U)		National standard adopted

General Policy of the Southwest Idaho Health Systems Agency
Re: *Determination of Adjustment and Full Implementation of National Guidelines*

- In view of the research and the public review and comment process that preceded final issuance of the National Guidelines, it is reasonable for HSA I to adopt them for the purpose of setting voluntary planning goals for this region, subject to discretionary adjustments which may be made.
- The burden of proof for such adjustments should be left with the party or parties seeking adjustment or exception to the guidelines.
- The plan (HSP) should affirm the National Guidelines, and should indicate on *October 1, 1983* target date for full implementation.
- The plan (HSP) should indicate that area hospitals should immediately initiate joint planning activities to achieve consistency with the National Guidelines by the target date.
- In order to gain exception or discretionary adjustment of the guidelines, any party should present justification to the HSA, (through its HSP Committee and Board) prior to August 31, 1980.[a]
- The Board's decision on a "request for adjustment" would be subject to public hearing, preceded by a thirty (30)-day review period consistent with the normal revision process of the HSP.
- In the interim, the Review Committee should be guided by the National Guidelines as adopted by the Board.

---

[a]Discretionary adjustments may be justified when the application of the National Guidelines would result in:

1. Denial of access to necessary health services to area residents.
2. Significantly increased costs of care for a substantial number of patients in the area.
3. Denial of care to persons in need resulting from moral and ethical values.

OB/GYN Study

In 1977, the three hospitals together, through the Johnston Health-Coordinating Committee, undertook a study of the feasibility of consolidating their obstetrical services. The study was initiated at the request of the State Commissioner of Health, who was acting on behalf of the State Public Health Council (SPHC). The Johnston Health-Coordinating Committee report concluded that consolidation or elimination of any of the obstetrical services in Johnston was economically unfeasible not only because of the loss of revenue to a hospital from its maternity cases, but because the hospital would not be able to depreciate assets specific to the lost service, and, because of the related loss of 50 percent of pediatric and gynecologic cases. The report indicated that major increases in other patient charges could be expected if any of the hospitals eliminated its obstetrical unit.

It should be noted that the report of the Johnston Health-Coordinating Committee failed to acknowledge that unused assets might be depreciated at a faster rate given Commission authorization to do so, that some of the assets (especially hospital units) might be used for alternate purposes, or that some of the unused assets might be sold to other providers of obstetrical care. Similarly, the reasons for the Council's working assumptions that 50 percent of pediatric and gynecologic patients might be lost by a hospital relinquishing its obstetrical unit were not clearly documented; in particular, the relationship of a closed obstetrical unit to the use of an on-going pediatric unit was not thoroughly explained.

The Southwest Idaho Health Systems Agency has repeatedly questioned the need for as many obstetrical beds in the county as are currently available. The HSA's concern with obstetrical beds is part of its larger concern about excess hospital capacity. The current *Health Systems Plan. . . . , (for 1980–1985)* proposes the elimination of 28 obstetrical beds (out of 94 obstetrical and OB/GYN beds) specifically in the Johnston area by October 1983. The number of beds that the HSA proposes to have eliminated is based upon calculations that take into account the following findings and assumptions:

1. The decline over the . . . years (1971–1978) in the number of obstetrical patients.
2. A modest increase in births due to an increase in the number of women of childbearing age (1970–1977).
3. A stabilization in the number of births by ceasarean section.
4. Stabilization in average length of stay.

This bed reduction is also proposed, in part, to achieve a minimum occupancy rate of at least 75 percent in each obstetrical unit and a minimum of 1,500 births per year in each obstetrical unit (in accordance with Federal guidelines). The National and State guidelines/standards for obstetrical and pediatric units are presented herein.

The source of concern about the need for the number of existing obstetrical beds in Johnston is shown in the following table. Table 1 indicates for each of the hospitals in the City of Johnston: the average number of obstetrical (only) beds in operation throughout a fiscal year, the number of patient days generated in the obstetrical unit by maternity cases, the average obstetrical daily census, the average occupancy level of the obstetrical unit by maternity cases, and the amount of excess inpatient obstetrical capacity.

The data presented in Table 1 show some degree of year to year variation in the occupancy levels of each of the hospitals' obstetrical (only) units. However, the data make it apparent that at the present level of staffed obstetrical beds, only about two-thirds of the available beds are usually being used for maternity cases. The most recent data on actual utilization (for FY 1979) indicate that 16,110 patient days were generated by maternity cases in all three Johnston hospitals, that is, approximately 44.1 beds of 65.2 available obstetrical beds were occupied. Looking at the hospitals individually, moreover, it is apparent that Midland County and St. Stephens each have been maintaining an obstetrical service to serve fewer than 12 maternity cases on an average day.

Further, the data show that between fiscal year 1975 and fiscal year 1979, between 38.3 and 44.1 beds were utilized on average by Johnston maternity patients, an increase in use of about 1.45 beds on average per day. If we assume that this trend will continue, 45.6 obstetrical beds in Johnston will be used on average by maternity patients in fiscal year 1980 (i.e., the average daily census would be 45.6 patients), 48.5 in 1982, and 52.8 in 1985, etc.

The table that follows (Table 2) indicates the number of beds needed to accommodate a continuation of the recent rate of increase in demand at an average 75 percent occupancy level. Table 2 also indicates the number of beds needed at the 65 percent and 70 percent minimum occupancy standards set by the State for smaller units (were the beds to be available in smaller units) and compares the numbers needed to the total number of beds (94) currently available for obstetrical (only) and obstetrical/gynecological cases.

The table indicates that even if the average daily use of obstetrical beds by maternity patients continues to increase at the rate it has over the period from 1975 through 1979, and if the most conservative (65 percent) occupancy level were implemented, there would be an excess of 12.8 to 26.2 obstetrical-only and obstetrical/gynecological beds. If the more efficient 75 percent occupancy level were applied, an excess of between 23.6 and 35.2 obstetrical and OB/GYN swing beds would remain.

Data developed by the hospitals in Schedule O of their operating budget submissions for FY 1981 indicate that *the Johnston hospitals expect their obstetrical patient days to remain stable* at 16,739 patient days (9241 at Johnston Memorial, 3998 at Midland County, and 3500 at St. Stephens) for the next three to four years. This number of patient days is equivalent to an average obstetrical daily census throughout the City of Johnston of 45.8. Somewhere between 61.1 and 70.5 beds would be needed for maternity patients relative to the occupancy level guidelines listed above: that is, there will be an excess of 23.5 to 32.9 beds. There is sufficient excess capacity in Johnston to justify consideration of the elimination of 28 beds as suggested by the HSA and the consolidation of obstetrical units.

Obstetrical service consolidation could be cost-effective (through elimination of an entire unit rather than reduction of a number of beds at each obstetrical unit in Johnston) if a vacated unit could be used for another needed service, and thus eliminated as a regular expense (cost center) for a particular hospital. It would also be reasonable to expect

TABLE 1
Obstetric Service Utilization in City of Johnston—FY 1975 to FY 1980

	Actual FY 1975	Actual FY 1976 (366 Days)	Actual FY 1977	Actual FY 1978	Actual FY 1979	Projected FY 1980 (366 Days)
Johnston Memorial Hospital						
No. of Ob.-only Beds	30	30	30	30	30	30
No. of Patient Days	8,124	8,081	7,961	8,165	8,671	9,241
Average Daily Census	22.3	22.1	21.8	22.4	23.8	24.6
Average Occupancy (%)	74.2%	73.6%	72.7%	74.6%	79.2%	84.2%
Excess Oper. Capacity	7.7 beds	7.9 beds	8.2 beds	7.6 beds	6.2 beds	5.4 beds
Midland County Hospital						
No. of Ob.-only Beds	17	17	15.1	15.4	16.2	15.8
No. of Patient Days	3,393	3,305	3,458	3,803	3,966	3,998
Average Daily Census	9.3	9.0	9.5	10.4	10.9	10.9
Average Occupancy (%)	54.7%	53.3%	62.6%	67.7%	67.0%	69.1%
Excess Oper. Capacity	7.7 beds	8.0 beds	5.6 beds	5.0 beds	5.3 beds	4.9 beds
St. Stephens Hospital						
No. of Ob.-only Beds	17	16.1	20	19	19	19
No. of Patient Days	2,458	2,755	3,249	3,170	3,473	3,500
Average Daily Census	6.7	7.5	8.9	8.7	9.5	9.6
Average Occupancy (%)	39.6%	46.8%	44.5%	45.7%	50.1%	50.5%
Excess Oper. Capacity	10.3 beds	8.6 beds	11.1 beds	10.3 beds	9.5 beds	9.4 beds
City of Johnston						
No. of Ob.-only Beds	64	63.1	65.1	64.4	65.2	64.8
No. of Patient Days	13,975	14,141	14,668	15,138	16,110	16,739
Average Daily Census	38.3	38.6	40.2	41.5	44.1	45.9
Average Occupancy (%)	59.8%	61.2%	61.8%	64.4%	67.6%	70.9%
Excess Oper. Capacity	25.7 beds	24.5 beds	24.9 beds	22.9 beds	21.1 beds	18.9 beds

Most figures, except as otherwise noted, taken from hospital submissions of Schedule O (includes data relative to Section 19-73k, Idaho General Statutes criteria). The number of beds listed is each hospital's reported "average number of beds used for *obstretrics only*."

TABLE 2

	FY 1979 (Actual)	FY 1980	FY 1981	FY 1982	FY 1983	FY 1984	F 1985
Aver. Daily Census	44.1	45.6	47.0	48.5	49.9	51.4	52.8
Need at 65% Occ. Level	67.8	70.2	72.3	74.6	76.8	79.1	81.2
Need at 70% Occ. Level	63	65.1	67.1	69.3	71.3	73.4	75.4
Need at 75% Occ. Level	58.8	60.8	62.7	64.7	66.5	68.5	70.4
No. of Beds Avail. (inc. Obstetrical and OB/GYN) Swing Beds	94	94	94	94	94	94	94
Excess (Deficit)	26.2–35.2	23.8–33.2	21.7–31.3	19.4–29.3	17.2–27.5	14.9–25.5	12.8–23.6

that the consolidation service(s) remaining would realize certain cost-efficiencies, if not improved quality of care through more regular use, as a result of increased case load.

If elimination and/or consolidation of Johnston's obstetrical services were attempted, they would still be accessible to local consumers. Additionally, there is no firm basis to expect, as the Johnston Health-Coordinating Committee has suggested, that if a hospital's obstetrical unit were eliminated, its gynecology cases could not be accommodated in existing medical/surgical beds and would necessarily be lost, or that 50 percent of the pediatric cases currently being served would be lost. Further, surplus equipment and staff might be absorbed by another unit or hospital, and remaining assets could be depreciated on an accelerated schedule. The financial savings attributable to eliminating the obstetrical unit of any of Johnston's hospitals is detailed herein.

PEDIATRIC SERVICES IN JOHNSTON

As reported earlier, the SPHC expressed its concern about excess pediatric bed capacity and duplicative pediatric services in its review of the Fiscal Year 1980 budget submission of each of the three hospitals in Johnston. The hospitals were instructed to study the feasibility of consolidating pediatric services; their efforts toward developing a plan to curtail underutilization of pediatric services was to be evaluated by the Commission in future budget reviews.

The Southwest Idaho Health Systems Agency (HSA) also proposed reduction of (22) pediatric beds in Johnston by 1984 in its *Health Systems Plan. . . . , 1980–1985* (p. AC-10). The bed reduction figure proposed by the HSA took into account an expected decrease of 11 percent (by 1985) in the number of children in the area. The HSA also proposed that by 1984, each pediatric unit have a minimum occupancy level of 65 percent, and no less than 20 beds in conformance with Federal and State guidelines.

The basic reason for concern about the number of pediatric beds in Johnston is that the number of pediatric admissions/discharges, as well as the number of pediatric patient days, has been declining fairly steadily in Johnston for more than a decade.

The source of concern about the need for the number of existing pediatric beds in Johnston is shown in the following table (Table 3). Table 3 indicates for each of the hospitals in the City of Johnston: the average number of pediatric beds in operation throughout a fiscal year, the number of patient days generated in the pediatric unit, the average pediatric daily census, the average occupancy level of the pediatric unit, and the amount of excess inpatient pediatric capacity.

The table shows that there has been a decrease in the average daily census of each hospital's pediatric unit since 1975. Johnston Memorial has just decreased the number of staffed beds in its pediatric unit (and in the entire hospital) by eight; however, it will still have about 13 empty beds on average in the unit in FY 1980 through 1984 based on its patient day projections.

The three Johnston hospitals have indicated in their FY budget submissions (Schedule O) that they expect their pediatric patient days (13,861) to remain stable through 1984 at FY 1981 levels. City-wide, this will mean that the three hospitals together will have approximately 30 empty beds per day in pediatrics through 1984 according to their combined pediatric patient day projections.

Using the hospitals' combined average pediatric daily census of 37.9 patients through 1984 (based on their patient day projections), the commission's staff has calculated the number of beds needed to accommodate an average of 37.9 patients in unit(s) with a 65 percent, 70 percent, and 75 percent occupancy level. These bed need projections are presented below.

	FY 1980–1984
Average Daily Census	37.9
Need at 65% Occupancy Level	58.3
Need at 70% Occupancy Level	54.1
Need at 75% Occupancy Level	50.5
No. of Beds Available	68
Excess (Deficit)	9.7–17.5

The figures indicate that even with Johnston Memorial's recent pediatric bed reduction (42–34 beds), there will still be an excess of 9.7–17.5 pediatric beds. (The range of excess prior to Johnston Memorial's recent eight-bed reduction was 17.7–25.5, in line with the HSA's suggested elimination of 22 beds).

TABLE 3
Pediatric Service Utilization in City of Johnston—FY 1975 to FY 1980

	Actual FY 1975	Actual FY 1976 (366 Days)	Actual FY 1977	Actual FY 1978	Actual FY 1979	Projected[a] FY 1980 (366 Days)
Johnston Memorial Hospital						
No. of Beds	42	42	42	42	42	34
No. of Patient Days	8,667	9,273	8,888	7,447	7,924	7,659
Average Daily Census	23.7	25.3	24.4	20.4	21.7	20.9
Average Occupancy (%)	56.5%	60.3%	58.0%	48.6%	51.7%	61.5%
Excess Oper. Capacity	18.3 beds	16.7 beds	17.6 beds	21.6 beds	20.3 beds	13.1 beds
Midland County Hospital						
No. of Beds	7	7	7	7	7	7
No. of Patient Days	2,774	2,710	2,291	2,114	2,005	2,098
Average Daily Census	7.6	7.4	6.3	5.8	5.5	5.7
Average Occupancy (%)	108.6%	105.8%	89.7%	82.7%	.5%	81.9%
Excess Oper. Capacity	(0.6 beds)	(0.4 beds)	0.7 beds	1.2 beds	.5 beds	1.3 beds
St. Stephens Hospital						
No. of Beds	24	25.4	27	27	2	27
No. of Patient Days	3,608	3,165	3,653	3,766	4,153	4,104
Average Daily Census	9.9	8.6	10.0	10.3	11.4	11.2
Average Occupancy (%)	41.2%	34.0%	37.1%	38.2%	42.1%	41.6%
Excess Oper. Capacity	14.1 beds	16.8 beds	17 beds	16.7 beds	15.6 beds	15.8 beds
City of Johnston						
No. of Beds	73	74.4	76	76	76	68
No. of Patient Days	15,049	15,148	14,832	13,327	14,082	13,861
Average Daily Census	41.2	41.4	40.6	36.5	38.6	37.9
Average Occupancy (%)	56.5%	55.6%	53.5%	48.0%	50.8%	55.7%
Excess Oper. Capacity	31.8 beds	33.0 beds	35.4 beds	39.5 beds	37.4 beds	30.1 beds

Source: Patient day figures and bed figures taken from Schedule O, FY 1981 budget submissions.
[a] The hospitals project their FY 1980 level of pediatric patient days and staffed beds to continue through 1984.

Additionally, it should be noted that Federal guidelines indicate that there should be a minimum of 20 beds (as shown in Table 4) in a pediatric unit in an urban area; Midland County Hospital does not provide even this minimum level of service. Also, the other two pediatric units in Johnston do not maintain the minimum occupancy level for units of their size according to both Federal and State guidelines/standards. Johnston hospital's 34-bed unit is projected to have only a 61.5 percent occupancy level in fiscal years 1980 through 1984. St. Stephens' 27-bed unit is projected to have only a 41.6 percent occupancy level in fiscal years 1980 through 1984. These levels compare unfavorably with Federal and State guidelines/standards of at least 65 percent for units with 20–39 beds.

It seems reasonable to suggest that somewhere between 9.7 and 17.5 more pediatric beds could be eliminated throughout the city without presenting undue problems of in-patient pediatric service (lack of) availability and accessibility to the local population.

The financial impact of the elimination of the pediatric service by any of the Johnston Hospitals is detailed herein.

DISCUSSION AND CONCLUSIONS

The existing level of obstetrical and pediatric services in Johnston has been considered with respect to the criteria set forth under Section 19-73 of the Idaho General Statutes. Commission staff has con-

TABLE 4
Federal and State Guidelines for Hospital Services

National	State	
Guideline III: Obstetrical Services	*Maternity Services*	
1. Obstetrical services should be planned on a regional basis.	Female 15–44 Age (sex) Group	
2. There should be at least 1,500 births annually in hospitals providing specialty obstetrical care.	0.8 Maximum Beds/1000 20 bed unit: 65% 20–29 bed unit: 70% 30+ bed unit: 75%	Minimum Occupancy Levels
3. There should be an average annual occupancy rate of at least 75% in each obstetrical unit where there are more than 1,500 births per year.		
Guideline V: Pediatric In-patient Services— Number of Beds	*Pediatric Services*	
There should be a minimum of 20 beds in a pediatric unit in an urban area. An adjustment downward may be justified when travel time to an alternate unit exceeds 30 minutes for 10 percent of the population or more.	0–14 Age Group 1.0 Maximum Beds/1000 20–39 bed unit: 65% 40–79 bed unit: 70% 80+ bed unit: 75%	Minimum Occupancy Levels
Guideline VI: Pediatric In-patient Services— Occupancy Rate		
Minimum average annual occupancy rates (excluding neonatal special care units) should be 65 percent for a facility with 20–39 pediatric beds, 70 percent for a facility with 40–79 pediatric beds, and 75 percent for a facility with 80 or more pediatric beds.		

sidered the utilization records of these services in Johnston with regard to Section k, and has formulated several conclusions as set forth below.

Staff notes that there has been a continuing decline in the patient load of pediatric services in Johnston and that the patient load in obstetrics has been growing over the past few years. With regard to both types of service, however, utilization levels are generally too low to be considered efficient and would not reach recommended National and State occupancy levels. In the case of Midland County Hospital, moreover, the number of beds in both the obstetric and pediatric units is below accepted standards.

Staff notes that the availability of each of these services at all three Johnston hospitals appears to be unnecessarily duplicative and as such, constitutes an unnecessary expense for the hospitals in Johnston and, ultimately, for the consumers of health care.

Staff believes that the elimination of excess capacity would not have an adverse affect on the quality of available health care or on the hospitals' ability to meet community or regional need for obstetric and pediatric services.

FINANCIAL IMPACT

Elimination of beds was estimated to result in the following savings:

Johnston Memorial Hospital	Maternity	$1,656,470
Midland County Hospital	Maternity	$ 534,067
St. Stephen's Hospital	Maternity	$ 576,868
Johnston Memorial Hospital	Pediatrics	$ 513,593
Midland County Hospital	Pediatrics	$ 173,696
St. Stephen's Hospital	Pediatrics	$ 260,617

3 SERVICE

WAL-MART STORES, INC.

In January 1982, amid a distressed economy, Wal-Mart continues to pace the discount-chain industry, leaving K-Mart, Target, and Woolco behind. The chain emerged in 1962 with one store serving a small community in Arkansas and has grown to 491 stores serving 13 different states at the close of 1981. Jack Shewmaker, President of Wal-Mart, says the chain will continue to grow into markets where we can get the right profitability and return on investment.

History and Background

Wal-Mart Stores, Inc., headquartered in Bentonville, Arkansas, had its origin in the variety-store business. Sam Walton opened his first variety store, under the Ben Franklin franchise, in Newport, Arkansas, in 1945. One year later, he was joined by his brother, J. L. "Bud" Walton, now Senior Vice-President, who opened a similar store in Versailles, Missouri. The two brothers went on to assemble a group of 15 Ben Franklin stores, and subsequently developed the concept of larger discount department stores in communities of small size. This concept emerged in 1962 when the first Wal-Mart Discount City store in Rogers, Arkansas opened. Wal-Mart Stores, Inc., became a publicly held corporation in October 1970. After the company was listed on the over-the-counter market, stock began trading on the New York Stock Exchange in mid-1972. The founder, Sam Walton, continues to serve as chairman of the board and chief executive officer.

Source: This case was prepared by Monya Giggar, Gregg Gunchick, and David Miller, under the supervision of Professor Sexton Adams. Permission to use granted by Sexton Adams. This case is based on library research.

In 1982, Wal-Mart has 491 discount department stores servicing the general merchandise needs of its customers. The discount stores range in size from 30,000 to 90,000 square feet, with the average store size being about 52,000 square feet. Wal-Mart stores are usually organized with 36 departments and carry merchandise such as wearing apparel for the entire family, household furnishings, appliances, and other hard-line merchandise. These stores are located in 13 states across the south and the southeast.

Unlike many other major discount chains, Wal-Mart has devoted itself almost exclusively to serving small towns and medium-sized cities. In their respective communities, Wal-Mart Discount Cities are the largest nonfood retailers. The largest cities in which the company operates, at this time, are: Little Rock, Arkansas; Shreveport, Louisiana; Springfield, Missouri; Huntsville, Alabama; Nashville, Tennessee.

Management

Wal-Mart has exercised a highly entrepreneurial, participatory, and goal-oriented style of management. Responsibility for Wal-Mart's style has been attributed to Sam Walton, chief executive officer and chairman of the board. Serving below him are some of the most respected top-level management personnel in the discount-store industry. Heading these top-level executives is Jack Shewmaker, President (see Exhibit 1).

One of the chain's historical strengths, though, has been that it has a single-minded philosophy that has kept it on the straight and narrow path established by Sam Walton 36 years ago. Sam's personal attitude has been reflected in the manner which he has estab-

EXHIBIT 1
Organization Chart

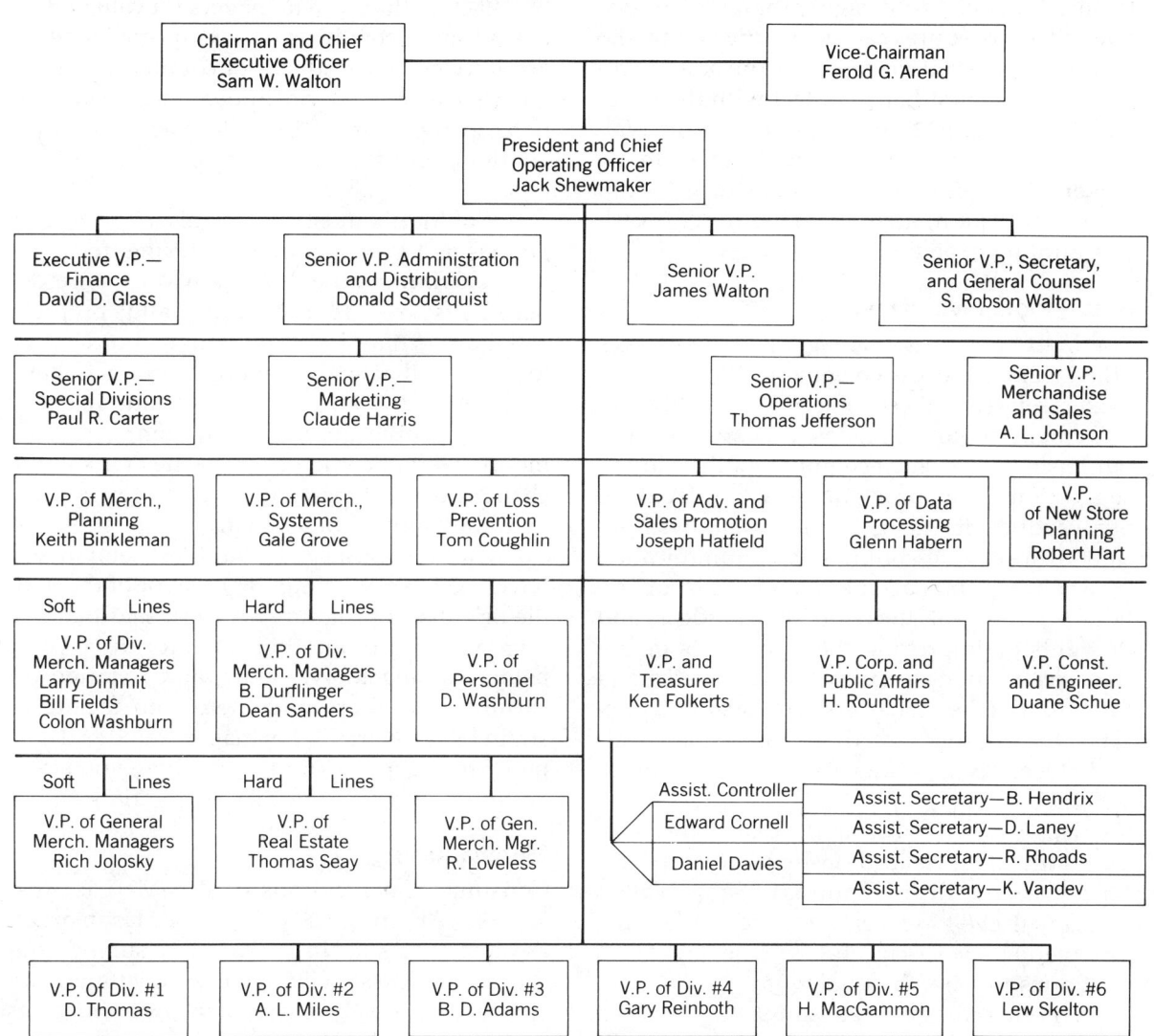

lished special relationships with many of the employees, whom he calls "associates." In the early years at Wal-Mart, Sam visited all the stores twice a year, exchanging open communication on ideas and problems. Theo Ashcraft, Vice-President of the Lease Department, said that Sam has always listened to people . . . learning (from them) everyday.

In 1982, the geographical expansion of Wal-Mart makes it impossible for Sam Walton to visit and communicate at a personal level with the employees of all 491 stores. Therefore, Jack Shewmaker has inherited many responsibilities, handed-down by the aging Sam Walton. Shewmaker, of the Sam Walton mold, is a strong believer in participatory management. He says, "Wal-Mart's system is people supportive. This is a major factor in our operational strategy. We design programs so systems and procedures can be overridden by the manager, assistant manager, or the store manager who has first-hand contact with the problem." In addition to his support of Sam Walton's participatory management style, Shewmaker also maintains a personal relationship with Sam Walton, accompanying him on various hunting expeditions.

Grass-Roots Involvement

Wal-Mart practices management objectives called "grass-roots involvement." Jack Shewmaker refers to these objectives as "the involvement of our associates in every aspect of our business and the recognition of their ideas, suggestions, and problems is a key factor to our productivity gains." This policy was designed to provide continuous communication between top management and field operations. Starting at the store level, ideas and thoughts on improving the company's operations are written down by the associates and forwarded to headquarters. The overall corporate plan consolidates these individual goals and objectives to produce Wal-Mart's plan for action.

However, the corporate plans are composed in a centralized fashion at corporate headquarters. Every Saturday Sam Walton meets with the top-level executives and corporate planners to discuss future strategies. Sam continues to have the final word.

Another facet of Wal-Mart's strategy is an extension of the participatory management style to get employees involved. "We believe in sharing vital information on sales, expenses, and profits with every associate throughout the company," says Shewmaker. Among other vital information available, ". . . each month we prepare departmental reports showing percentage to total and comparative performance on sales, markdowns, inventory turnover, and gross margin. Each person is made to feel that he/she can affect the results."

Each of the store managers is evaluated on overall sales from his store, with consideration given to location and size of community. They are also evaluated on appearance, contributions in the form of ideas to corporate headquarters, and their ability to compete in their region.

Wal-Mart's most successful incentive program is its VPI or Volume Producing Item contest. This program allows individual store departments free rein to price and promote certain merchandise of their own choice. Walton claims that many faltering products have been revived as a result. "This is another way to keep people involved and thinking. Each month everyone knows where they rank in the chain and what percentage of a store's business they have," he explains.

The responses of Wal-Mart employees have been overwhelmingly in favor of the people-orientated programs. A clerk said that she "had worked for another chain for three years before coming to Wal-Mart, and I started off earning more here and there's no feeling of strain or pressure." A manager stated, "It's so much more open. You know where you stand all the time. You're not left in the dark."

Merchandising

Consumers' perceptions of Wal-Mart in Russellville, Arkansas, a typical Wal-Mart market, are just fantastic. In a Wal-Mart survey conducted in Russellville, many consumers responded positively to the chain with comments such as they have better quality merchandise, their prices are lower than K-Mart's, and they have a big selection. Wal-Mart's merchandising program has found the right combination of brand names, low prices, promotions and presentations, item merchandising, and fashion sense to attract and keep its customers.

Wal-Mart combines a strong brand-name merchandising philosophy with its domination of categories and subcategories. An example of its brand-name appeal is the Wrangler program. The complete size assortment of Wrangler jeans are displayed in special dark-stained wooden cubicles. Inside the display or adjacent to it in both the men's and women's departments, are accessories (hats, belts, boots, and shirts) positioned to encourage tie-in sales. Brand programs are also extended to the hard lines. The Wal-Mart strategy is that it carries all the usual hard-line brands, but adds fringe items to bolster the price/value perception of its shoppers. In health and beauty aids, a line of old-favorite fragrances like Wind Song, Jontue, and Emeraud is joined by a selection of limited semirestricted lines, like Charlie, Cie, Sophia, and Scoundrel. These limited additions are stocked heavily in multiple facings on open shelves, unlike many other chains that keep limited lines under lock-and-key. The philosophy for having the lines accessible was that one cannot sell the lines where the shoppers cannot get to them.

Another area where perception plays a key role is in Wal-Mart's pricing policies. As one consumer states, Wal-Mart's prices are lower than K-Mart's. The selection is better, too. Wal-Mart, T.G. & Y., and K-Mart are often locked into intense competition in the markets they all share (small-towns and rural areas). In setting pricing policies, each chain must devise an assortment strategy. Of the two competitors, T.G. & Y. tends to be overassorted—similar to the variety stores of the past. K-Mart, on the other hand, tends to narrow its assortments and fill-in the gaps with private label brands, such as K-Mart toilet tissue and facial tissue. Wal-Mart's strategy calls for splitting the difference. First, it out-assorts K-Mart, then it beats the prices offered by T.G. & Y. Additionally, much of Wal-Mart's perceived lower prices is revealed in a comparison of shelf-prices of the three discount retailers that was conducted in Bartlesville, Oklahoma (1981). The results of the shelf-price study are shown in Exhibit 2. There were four random categories chosen and several subcategories within these categories. The total price differential for a 36-item market basket amounted to less than $7\frac{1}{2}$ percent between competitors. These results are indicative of the closeness of the competition.

Much of Wal-Mart's success in developing consumer perceptions is accredited to its promotional programs. The program emphasis provides the impact of name brands and good values that make key departments dominant in the marketplace. "Power alley," a Wal-Mart promotional characteristic, is the high-powered promotional race track in all the stores. The alley promotions are lined down each aisle in the store's race track. In most stores, the power alley will have 100 or more promotional tables or platforms. These tables/platforms contain merchandise with average tickets that are sometimes 100 percent lower than at most chains. This promotional effort is the key to the volume production that has enabled Wal-Mart to maintain its growth. Included among the 100 or more tables and platforms that make up the total program are assorted 2×2 ft. cubes, 3×3 ft. tables, and 5 ft. square tables and platforms, occasionally joined together. The 2×2 cubes are used in health and beauty aids, with 18 to 24 items set in a double row down the center of an interior aisle. Requiring lower inventory investments, the small cubes are also used to pull shoppers into the automotive department located at the right (or left) rear corner of the race track aisle.

Wal-Mart's strategy also entails the use of item merchandising. It is a concept by which an unusual "item" is positioned near or adjacent to a department to build category dominance. To create a bigger share of the bed-sheet market and to build brand image, Cannon sheets at attractive prices are promoted on a table adjacent to the domestics department. The item sets the scene for the particular department and serves as a way to draw

EXHIBIT 2
Self-Price Comparison
Bartlesville, Oklahoma, Shelf Prices

Item	Wal-Mart	T.G. & Y.	K-Mart
H & BA			
Bayer 100's	$ 1.57	$ 1.60	$ 1.57
Excedrin X-Strength 100's	2.58	3.37	2.06*
Bufferin 100's	2.13	2.13	2.13
Bufferin A.S.	1.67[a]	2.09	2.43
Tylenol X-Strength 100's	3.54	3.27	3.29
Tylenol X-Strength 50's	2.33	2.53	2.33
Anacin 200's	3.68	3.97	3.68
Anacin 100's	1.42[a]	1.99	1.97
Flex 16oz. Shampoo	1.68	1.68	1.74
Suave Baby Shampoo 28oz.	1.06	1.14	1.48
Faberge Organic X-tra Body	1.18	1.18	1.18
No More Tears 16oz. Shampoo	2.62	3.12	1.97[a]
Wella Balsam 8oz. Shampoo	1.78	1.77	1.67
Head & Shoulders 15oz. tube	2.97	2.99	1.58[a]
Head & Shoulders 11oz. bottle	2.46	2.67	2.46
Prell tube 5oz.	1.92	1.72	1.92
Pert 15oz.	1.83[a]	2.44	2.13
Silkience 15oz.	2.56	2.78	2.16
Small Electrics			
Mr. Coffee 10 cup	22.88	22.99	24.97
GE automatic percolator	28.42	28.96	28.87
Regal Poly-Perk hot pot	9.96	9.99	10.62
Automotive			
Rain Dance 16oz.	5.54	5.99	5.07
Turtle Zip Wax 18oz.	1.84	2.17	2.07
Phillips TropArctic oil	0.97	0.95	0.97
Quaker State oil	0.97	0.95	0.97
Penzoil 10W-40	0.97	0.95	0.97
PL nondetergent	0.68	0.77	0.74
Hardware			
Powerlok II 20 ft.	11.57	12.99	12.48
Stanley 16oz.	8.44	5.67[a]	9.97
Steelmaster 16oz.	12.76	14.30	11.88
Black & Decker			
7104 Drill	16.88	17.87	15.77
7004 Drill	12.97	12.99	11.97
7504 Jig saw	12.97	11.77	13.48
7580 VSR drill	42.46	34.57	33.88
7308 Circular saw	29.96	35.97	27.88
7300 Circular saw 5½ in.	24.97	27.77	27.97
TOTAL	$284.19	$290.06	$268.31

Source: Discount Store News Research, December 14, 1981, p. 43.
[a]Sale item.

shoppers into the department. All Wal-Mart chains practice this concept with their "million-dollar" items. These are basic everyday needs (sheets, socks, mattress covers) that help build a category or major brand-name goods that help build the brand-name image.

The profitable lure of apparel is also becoming increasingly evident in Wal-Mart stores. Over the next five years, Wal-Mart intends to build its stake in soft lines to 35 percent, according to the chain's executives. This is evident in the newer stores opened. In recent stores, the format is upgraded and total space-to-apparel and major soft-lines is as high as 43 percent. Wal-Mart has placed large, prominently placed departmental signs that tend to resemble J. C. Penney's signs. Brand emphasis is concentrated more and more on the apparel side of the store as is obvious with the Wrangler brand emphasis in boy's, men's, and women's wear. Most store units also stock Garan knit sport shirts and display them on an eye-catching "brand displayer." Also, Wal-Mart is now trying to build identity in men's socks by displaying signs that read, "Alder from Burlington." Overall, Wal-Mart steers clear of no-names, especially in categories where image counts.

Advertising

The advertising policy, displayed in all Wal-Mart stores, is to take sale advertisements from any other store and match the price. Under this policy, historically, it has held advertising expenditures to 1.5 percent of sales or less. Recent expansion, however, will raise this level to about 1.7 percent of sales or nearly $2.4 billion a year. According to company sources, one third of that total will be spent on newspaper advertising, and television spots will be increased from $6 million to the $7 or $8-million dollar level. Expansion into urban areas has entered Wal-Mart into markets where television time, newspaper space, and radio time are substantially more costly.

In addition to its added level of expansion, Wal-Mart has begun running more expensive, up-scale advertising. In the small town of Fayetteville, Arkansas, where it was opening an 85,000 square foot store, Wal-Mart ran a 36-page, four-color, all-photo, magazine-size, "catalog" circular. This new style resembled a J. C. Penney's catalog. All 36 pages, 11 or so pages of apparel and the remainder of consumables, seasonal merchandise, and hardlines, were full four-color and the circular used models and/or product photography. In contrast to the bigger-store advertisements, smaller units' circulars are usually 10-page broadsheets with false four-color on the front and back and black and white inside.

Wal-Mart is devising two separate merchandising and advertising strategies: the typical hard-line-oriented 40,000 to 50,000 square foot store and the 85,000 to 90,000 square foot stores that give greater emphasis to the fashion apparel side. This strategy is important to Wal-Mart's future in the ever-changing marketplace.

Distribution Centers

A basic practice of Wal-Mart has been to limit its store operations to about a 450-500-mile radius of distribution to centers, to achieve speed of restocking and savings in delivery costs. As Wal-Mart continues pushing its geographical limits, distribution that is cost-effective becomes more critical.

Located near headquarters in Bentonville, a 525,000 square foot distribution complex handled, in the past, 80 percent of all the goods sold by Wal-Mart. The expansion of the chain has resulted in additional distribution centers being constructed. In Searcy, Arkansas, an equal capacity center was opened to aid in Wal-Mart's expansion into southern Arkansas. Long-range plans called for the construction of a 512,000 square foot center in Palestine, Texas. This center fully came on-line, at the close of 1981. In 1982, a 900,000 square foot distribution center will be built in Cullman, Alabama.

The Palestine distribution center helped Wal-Mart penetrate the Texas border and Gulf Coast markets. Sam Walton is convinced that he can "double, even triple" the size of his company, just with locations in Texas and Louisiana. Shreveport, Louisiana, Houston, Corpus Christi, and Dallas–Fort Worth, Texas have been sited for the expansion of Wal-Mart. Management has already sited the Rio Grande valley and eight more sites in the area for prime expansion moves.

The new Alabama distribution center may be even more critical to the chain's expansion than the Palestine center. Coming on-stream in 1983, the center will provide overnight delivery into the states where the Big K acquisition brought the chain. It will extend into the Carolinas, Georgia, and Florida. These areas could be potential sites for Wal-Mart Country expansion.

Wal-Mart distribution centers (existing, as well as those to be built) are mechanized, utilizing conveyor systems to expedite the flow of merchandise and each serve an approximate proportion of the chain's stores. There are two additional distribution centers in Bentonville that are used for the inspecting and processing of fashion clothing; warehousing for jewelry and sporting goods; operations and accumulation of sale merchandise for shipment to stores as close to the sale as possible. The centers' radius span is to allow Wal-Mart's own trucking fleet to make deliveries in one day.

Wal-Mart trucks are expected to travel about 20-million miles in 1982 at a cost of about $18 million. The distribution centers' total expenses run approximately 2.5 percent of the goods shipped through them (now about 85 percent of the chain's total merchandise assortment). Wal-Mart's move toward establishing distribution centers and trucking fleets in Texas and Alabama is part of its long-range plan to expand its markets outward.

The Acquisition of Big K

Wal-Mart acquired the Kuhn's Big K chain, headquartered in Nashville, Tennessee, in August 1981. The total cost for 92 Big K stores, a large distribution center, headquarters, all of Big K's liabilities, and inventories within each store was about $100 million. Each store is estimated at costing $125,000 each to convert to the Wal-Mart label.

The conversion process (at the close of 1981) was first applied to the five least profitable Big K stores. This served as an acid test of the validity of the acquisition. According to Sam Walton, the average sales gains in these renovated stores have been in excess of 150 percent. In the first quarter as part of the Wal-Mart chain, the renovated stores contributed $70 million in sales volume.

The purchase helped Wal-Mart's future plans become more attainable. With the Big K stores, Wal-Mart gained penetration of Tennessee, Kentucky, and large "clusters" in Alabama and Mississippi. It also brought Wal-Mart into the new areas of Georgia and South Carolina. Thus, by purchasing a bargain expansion and getting good locations that are profitable to the chain, Wal-Mart stands ready to face the future.

Financing

The company has financed its capital expenditures for expansion primarily through internally generated funds. Funds from operations, $74 million in fiscal 1981, are the primary source of liquidity for the company. For additional externally generated funds, Wal-Mart offered one-million shares in 1981 that generated almost $33 million for the company. At fiscal year end, 1981, Wal-Mart had access to $176 million of unused short-term credit.

As far as controlling expenses, Wal-Mart has done so using several strategies: (1) negotiating harder with landlords for store sites (its current occupancy cost is 1.75 percent of sales), (2) store payrolls are tight—currently 7.5 percent (store managers work on smaller base salaries but with richer profit-sharing plans), (3) discouraging employee theft by sharing half the savings with employees, (4) tough bargaining stances on key line items

EXHIBIT 3
Consolidated Balance Sheet

	January 31	
	1981	1980
	(Dollar Amounts in Thousands)	
Assets		
Current assets:		
Cash	$ 6,927	$ 5,090
Short-term money market investments	11,528	—
Receivables	12,666	7,806
Recoverable costs from sale/leaseback	31,325	15,557
Inventories	280,021	235,315
Prepaid expenses	2,737	2,849
Total Current Assets	345,204	266,617
Property, plant, and equipment, at cost:		
Land	5,903	15,002
Buildings and improvements	51,200	42,287
Fixtures and equipment	80,411	56,072
Transportation equipment	12,969	9,012
	150,483	122,373
Less accumulated depreciation	33,702	23,613
Net property, plant and equipment	116,781	98,760
Property under capital leases	152,882	109,608
Less accumulated amortization	23,721	17,806
Net property under capital leases	129,161	91,802
Other assets and deferred charges	1,199	700
Total Assets	$592,345	$457,879
Liabilities and Stockholders' Equity		
Current liabilities:		
Notes payable	$ 15,000	$ 25,080
Accounts payable	97,445	100,102
Accrued liabilities:		
Salaries	11,229	12,889
Taxes, other than income	9,627	6,619
Other	25,748	15,148
Accrued federal and state income taxes	11,907	5,365
Long-term debt due within one year	3,375	2,314
Obligations under capital leases due within one year	3,270	2,704
Total Current Liabilities	177,601	170,221
Long-term debt	30,184	24,862
Long-term obligations under capital leases	134,896	97,212
Deferred income taxes	1,355	740
Stockholders' equity:		
Preferred stock	—	—
Common stock	3,234	1,512
Capital in excess of par value	67,481	35,064
Retained earnings	177,594	128,268
Total Stockholders' Equity	248,309	164,844
Total Liabilities and Stockholders' Equity	$592,345	$457,879

Source: 1981 Annual Report.

from suppliers, and (5) advertising cost are kept at less than 1.2 percent of sales.

Wal-Mart's operating, selling, general, and administrative expenses (1981) rose 138 percent since 1977, and the cost of goods sold at the chain increased even more by 139.7 percent. Sales of the company rose 142.2 percent during that same period. Earnings for Wal-Mart also increased 193.8 percent since 1977.

The financial statements that follow detail Wal-Mart's impressive financial record. Exhibit 3 is the consolidated balance sheet, and Exhibit 4 is the consolidated statement of income. Exhibit 5 highlights the two-year comparison and the five-year financial review of Wal-Mart's performance. Exhibit 6 provides a review of 10 years of growth for Wal-Mart.

Wal-Mart vs. "The Other Guys"

Wal-Mart's five-year financial record through 1981 has paced the discount-store industry. Exhibit 7 shows five-year averages for Wal-Mart and two of its competitors. While running above the industry median, Wal-Mart has stiff competition to face. As Wal-Mart moves into larger metropolitan areas, its competition expands from Magic Mart, Gibson's, T.G. & Y., and K-Mart to include Dayton Hudson's Target, Woolworth, Murphy, and the Caldwell chain.

EXHIBIT 4
Consolidated Statement of Income

	Years Ended January 31		
	1981	1980	1979
	(Dollar Amount in 000)		
Number of stores in operation at the end of the year	330	276	229
Revenues:			
Net sales	$1,643,199	$1,248,176	$900,298
Rentals from licensed departments	5,331	4,804	6,344
Other income—net	6,732	5,288	3,271
	1,655,262	1,258,268	909,913
Costs and expenses:			
Cost of sales	1,207,802	919,305	661,062
Operating, selling and general and administrative expenses	331,524	251,616	182,365
Interest costs:	5,808	4,438	3,119
Debt	10,849	8,621	6,595
Capital leases	1,555,983	1,183,980	853,141
Income before income taxes	99,279	74,288	56,772
Provision for federal and state income taxes:			
Current	42,982	31,649	28,047
Deferred	615	1,488	(722)
	43,597	33,137	27,325
Net income	$ 55,682	$ 41,151	$ 29,447
Net income per share:			
Primary and fully diluted	$1.73	$1.34[a]	$.97[a]

Source: 1981 Annual Report.
[a] Adjusted to reflect the 100 percent stock dividend paid on December 16, 1980. See accompanying notes.

EXHIBIT 5
Wal-Mart's Financial Highlights

Two-Year Comparison
(Dollar amount in thousands)

	1981	1980
Current assets	$345,204	$266,617
Current liabilities	177,601	170,221
Working capital	167,603	96,396
Current ratio	1.94	1.57
Stockholders' equity	$248,309	$164,844
Number of shares outstanding	32,342,445	30,242,522*

Five-Year Financial Review
(Dollar amounts in thousands except per share data)

	1981	1980	1979	1978	1977
Net sales	$1,643,199	$1,248,176	$900,298	$678,456	$478,807
Income before income taxes	99,279	74,288	56,772	40,847	30,857
Net income	55,682	41,151	29,447	21,191	16,039
Net income per share:					
Primary	$ 1.73	$ 1.34[a]	$ .97[a]	$ .74[a]	$ .58[a]
Fully diluted	1.73	1.34[a]	.97[a]	.71[a]	.54[a]
Number of stores in operation at the end of the period	330	276	229	195	153

Source: 1981 Annual Report.
[a]Adjusted to reflect the 100 percent stock dividend paid December 16, 1980 to holders of Wal-Mart common stock.

Although K-Mart is Wal-Mart's closest competitor, Target stores have been making moves to expand into Arkansas, Wal-Mart's home state. At the close of 1981, Target and Wal-Mart vie only in Nashville, Tennessee. However, the Dayton Hudson discount chain purchased three shuttered Woolco stores in Little Rock, an 80,000 square foot unit and two 10,000 square footers. The stores are to be remodeled in early 1982. Over the next two years, industry observers say that Texas appears a likely mark for expansion as Target currently covers the state with roughly half the number of stores as Wal-Mart.

The past performance of Wal-Mart in its smaller towns has been aided by its assimilation of technological advances. Exhibit 8 provides the data to support Wal-Mart's operational power among its competition. Thus, the expansive strength of Wal-Mart will be tested by all its competitors in the years to come.

Industry Trends

Within the discount-store industry, there is a definite trend toward upscaled merchandise presentation. K-Mart is adopting a new merchandising program that, for example, is dropping all synthetic fibers in favor of natural blends. In addition, in view of Wal-Mart's success in rural markets, K-Mart is targeting expansion outside of metropolitan areas. Increasing emphasis on promotionally priced goods has caused reductions in many chains' profit margins. According to Kenneth Mache, president of Dayton Hudson (Target), this additional promotional activity will depress the bottom lines for the major chains by cutting into already reduced margins. To combat these problems, many discounters are turning to more updated apparel lines and cosmetics while at the same time reducing the number of items carried.

244 Service

EXHIBIT 6
The Years of Growth for Wal-Mart

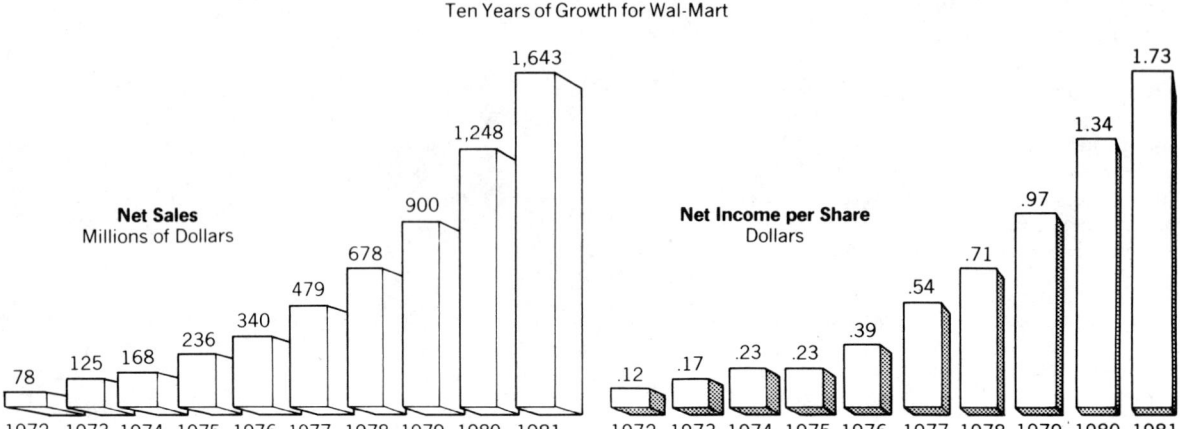
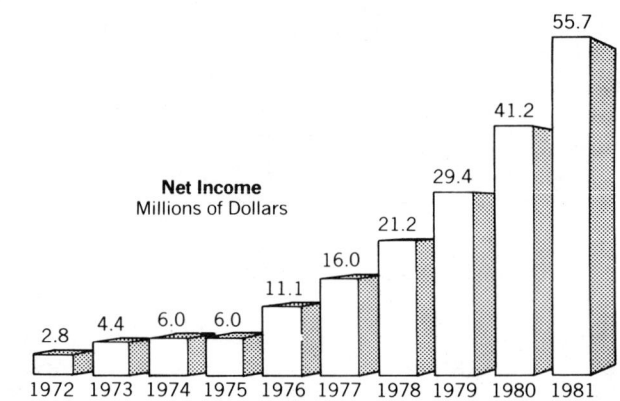
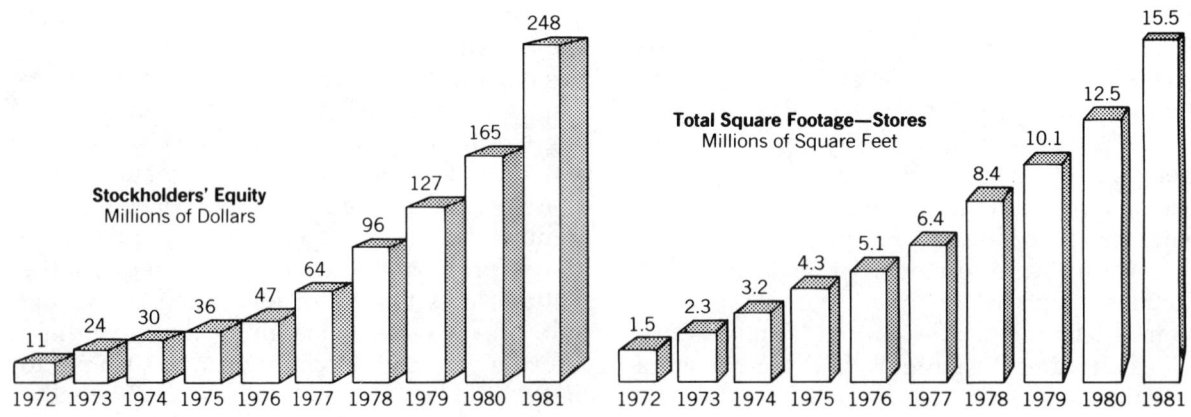

EXHIBIT 7
Five-Year Averages

Stores	Return on Equity	Sales Growth	Profit Margin
Wal-Mart	30.6%	37.4%	3.3%
K-Mart	16.0	17.1	1.5
Woolworth	11.8	9.6	1.6
Industry Median	12.1	9.7	2.2

Source: "Sam's Song," as published in *Forbes,* January 1982.

Macroeconomic factors have a direct impact on industry strategies. In the recessionary environment of early 1982, for example, discounters are caught in a squeeze between declining real income of consumers because of inflation as well as a very high unemployment rate. As a result, consumers are shopping less frequently, and seeking out sale-priced items when they do shop. Of this, a Merrill Lynch analyst, Jeffrey Feiner, remarks, this pattern may reverse itself following the scheduled 10 percent tax cut in July 1982. But retailers believe that consumers are settling into the habit of sale shopping and will not change quickly.

Industry merchandisers are becoming more selective on the merchandise carried in their stores. Today's successful merchant carefully scrutinizes inventories, making sure that goods do not sit on shelves by stepping up promotions. The test for discounters in the future is to combine a low-cost structure with the most innovative merchandising techniques to move the goods.

There is also a trend toward greater similarity between major competitors in the discount-store industry. Many of the more successful innovations of one chain are quickly adopted by its competitors. Examples of this include race-track configurations in store layouts, heavy use of promotional tables in merchandising, and upgraded apparel quality and presentation, to name a few.

Company Outlook

The important things have changed very little for Wal-Mart over the years. The company still makes strong presentations of basic merchandise, still benefits from Sam Walton's entrepreneurial spirit, and still concentrates on the small towns and surrounding rural areas where the store can be the primary source for shoppers. It also still uses the best merchandise techniques and develops or attracts the best merchandise talent, always experiment-

EXHIBIT 8
How Wal-Mart Outruns the Competition (Sales in billions/Earnings in millions)

	T.G. & Y.		K-Mart		Wal-Mart		Target		
1981	—		+14%	16.5	+28%	2.44	+26%	2.07	Sales
	—		−20%	210.0	+30%	79.5	—		Earnings
1980	+22%	1.4	+14%	14.2	+29%	1.7	+27%	1.5	Sales
	—		−27%	260.5	+26%	55.7	—		Earnings
1979	+19%	1.3	+13%	12.7	+38%	1.2	+20%	1.1	Sales
	—		+4%	358.0	+28%	41.1	—		Earnings
1978	+18%	1.2	+18%	11.7	+28%	0.9	—		Sales
	—		+18%	343.7	+17%	29.4	—		Earnings
1977	+14%	1.0	+18%	9.9	+42%	0.5	—		Sales
	—		+12%	302.9	+31%	21.4	—		Earnings

Source: *Discount Store News Research,* December 14, 1981, p. 13–14.

ing with new goods and new ways to present these goods.

Wal-Mart has evolved an intense, high-profile management style that brings together field supervisors and store managers into a chainwide merchandising emphasis, providing new ideas for the company. The best ideas are put into the corporate framework and encouraged to be fulfilled. This is but one of several practices that have helped Wal-Mart gain its current status. Others include the perception of everyday low prices by the consumers, and commitment to innovative, cost-control systems with the savings passed on to the consumer. The company utilizes technological advances in its operations for maximum efficiency and productivity. One example, is that the main computer in Bentonville talks directly to vendor computers, resulting in lower out-of-stocks.

Wal-Mart's 1981 annual report reflects its view of the future:

> The retailing environment is constantly changing. Competition will continue to improve and become more intense. Life styles will change, and today's solutions will soon be obsolete. But, with a flow of new programs, with the continuing contribution of our dedicated associates and with our commitment to avoid any short-term strategy that does not enhance our long-range goals, we are convinced that improved productivity will be achieved. Our people have truly made the difference, and as they respond to the ever-changing environment, we will serve our customers with the "best value in town."

OVERNITE TRANSPORTATION COMPANY

"Do you have any lady truck drivers?" Ken Gentil, President of Overnite Transportation Company, was asked by student casewriters in a business policy class at the College of William and Mary.

> Yes, we have a husband and wife team who've been on the road now for about nine or ten months. There seems to be a trend toward lady drivers, and we've interviewed quite a few ladies. But if we are to make any real go of it, I think it's got to be as a husband and wife team on a sleeper tractor. I don't think it would work out too well as far as singles are concerned.

Mr. Gentil was reminded that EEOC (Equal Employment Opportunity Commission) does not recognize that standard, and that a persistent single woman might challenge it. His response was noncommittal.

___

Source: This case was prepared by business policy classes at the College of William and Mary under the supervision of Professor William H. Warren. Permission to use granted by William H. Warren.

You may be right. But I can say this, in our general office we've done a pretty super job in opening up opportunities to the ladies. But when we get into terminal operations, the work is almost all physical, so I'd say the number of jobs with a lot of responsibility in such operations would be negligible.

Not satisfied, the questioner went on, "We've got several young ladies here. If one were to apply as a single you couldn't accept her, but if she and her husband both applied. . ." Mr. Gentil interrupted the questioner. "Our road drivers would be all for it, 100 percent—I think they'd probably look upon it as a fringe benefit. But I don't know about the management."

The questioner finally gave up, concluding the interchange by acknowledging that "Overnite's always been a Southern company with a traditionally conservative management, so I guess I can understand that." Inherent in the line of questioning by the student casewriters was not specifically the employment / sex-equality issue implied by the opening question, but how Overnite had adapted to the rapidly changing economic, social, and political changes of the latter 1970s and what additional changes the company contemplated for the 1980s.

Overnite, as directed by Chairman Harwood Cochrane and President Gentil, faced a three-pronged economic onslaught, if business forecasters' predictions are accurate: (1) a declining economy, (2) increasing fuel costs, and (3) deregulation of the industry.

A Brief History of Overnite Transportation Co.

In 1933, in Hanover County, Virginia, a 21-year-old high-school dropout, Harwood Cochrane, went into the trucking business with his brother, Calvin. Times were difficult, and Mr. Cochrane and Calvin failed in their first venture after accidents wrecked their two uninsured trucks. The brothers found themselves unemployed and broke. But Calvin was able to give Harwood a used Chevrolet truck to pay off a debt, and with that one truck began the story of Overnite Transportation Company.

Before the Interstate Commerce Act was passed by Congress in 1935, the trucking industry was a cutthroat, depression-ravaged business. Mr. Cochrane, now Chairman of Overnite, told *Nation's Business* in July 1978, how it was in the early 1930s.

> We used to sleep in our trucks, often using an oil lantern and an old quilt to keep from freezing to death... Had I not been young and headstrong, I never could have survived the many ordeals we faced...

The ICC brought order and stability to the motor carrier industry and, although the depression lingered, Overnite held its own for the remainder of the 1930s. By 1940, Overnite, headquartered in Richmond, had established itself sufficiently for Mr. Cochrane to make his first acquistition of a competitor, a landmark decision because acquiring competitors was to become a significant method of expansion for Overnite.

Overnite went public in 1957, and in 1962 its stock was listed on the New York Stock Exchange. The 1960s and 1970s were generally prosperous years for the company, 1966 and 1975 being the only slack years. In 1970, Kenneth Gentil, a 20-year veteran with Freuhauf, most recently heading their international marketing operations, was hired as president, with Mr. Cochrane remaining as chairman.

Mr. Cochrane maintained his belief in growth. In 1979, more than 50 acquisitions later, and with revenues of $300 million, Overnight continued to expand. In November of that year, the company began moving into terminals along the Gulf of Mexico from Jacksonville to Houston, after a four-year ICC review of their request for operating authority to service this area. This addition doubled the scope of Overnite's operation (see Exhibit 1). Although Overnite had yet to penetrate a significant portion of the area acquired in their newest territory, services had been established in most of its major cities.

The Trucking Industry's Hauling and Pricing Procedures

In 1979, there were approximately 48 major carriers nationwide whose average length of haul exceeded 500 miles. Of these, 21 had an average haul length of over 750 miles (Overnite's average haul length was 361 miles).

For a given truck load (TL) shipment there were three sets of operating costs: (1) freight pick-up, (2) line haul, and (3) delivery. Pick-up and delivery remain constant whether the length of the haul is 20 or 2000 miles. Because of this, TL rates tend to be high for short hauls (under 150 miles), for example, and relatively lower for longer hauls.

For any Less-Than-Truckload (LTL) shipment there were the same set of costs. However, rates were roughly determined by the cost for transporting one shipment from point A to point B. If a company were shipping to 10 different customers, the pick-up cost would be distributed among 10 shipments, but the corre-

EXHIBIT 1
Geographic Location of Operations in 1979

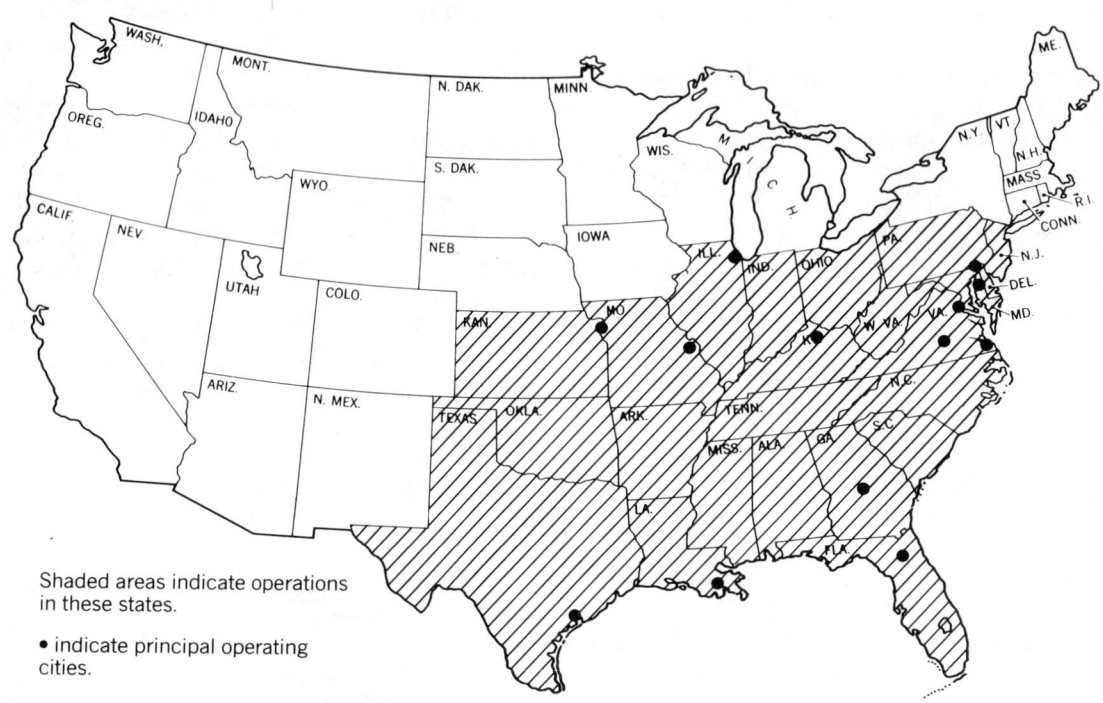

Shaded areas indicate operations in these states.

• indicate principal operating cities.

sponding revenue was calculated for each individual shipment. The same was true for both line haul and delivery. In LTL movements, there were additional expenses incurred. However, when these expenditures could be distributed over a long trip of 1000 miles, for example, LTL freight was clearly more profitable than TL.

A Description of Overnite's LTL System

The terminal in Richmond dispatched trucks to pick-up miscellaneous freight. The freight was unloaded at the Richmond dock and segregated by destination. If an entire load could be composed of freight destined for Baltimore, for example, it was loaded and dispatched. If only a partial load could be made, freight for an intermittent point, perhaps Washington, D.C., would be tail-loaded. In Washington, this merchandise would be "stripped off" and any additional freight for Baltimore would be loaded. The truck then would proceed to Baltimore where the freight was unloaded and reloaded in city trucks for delivery to its final destination.

Once delivery was completed, the city trucks began picking up freight and the process began again. Profits rose as the distance of a haul increased in addition to the multiple shipments and greater tonnage that could be line hauled. Efficient firms (and Overnite considered itself as such) preferred LTL business because they were able to generate enough traffic going to the same destinations to expand profits. This preference for LTL by Overnite was illustrated by their 1979 freight type, volume, and revenue statistics as shown in Table A.

TABLE A

Freight Type	Percent of Total Shipments	Percent of Total Revenue	Percent of Total Tonnage
TL	3	33	50
LTL	97	67	50
	100	100	100

In 1979 Overnite owned approximately 7500 vehicles, employed over 6000 people, and operated almost 70 terminals.

Overnite's Growth During the Early 1970s: A Recap

The casewriters attempted to document from the perceptions of Mr. Gentil the key factors behind the success of Overnite's transition from a regional to a national company and what were its plans for the future. He was asked to explain briefly the dramatic increase in Overnite's net earnings (100 percent +) in the four years after he took office (1970–1974).

> A good part of it was due to our growth by acquisition. But also during that period we centralized our company, which had become somewhat fragmented. We brought more people to Richmond. We put in management controls on things such as purchasing. The industry had some rate increases, and we were able to improve our pricing. Also, early in the 1970s we had assembled a variety of initially independent truck lines, and when you first put something like that together, it is costly. But then they began to come on stream and make a very, very big contribution to our profitability.

Mr. Gentil explained why Overnite's expansion had primarily been by acquisition.

> You can only expand in two different ways. If it's not through acquisition, it must be through what they call "PC & N," for 'Public Convenience and Necessity,' when you have to prove your line can serve an area where service is needed and serve it better than anyone else. PC & N takes a lot of time, and the ICC hasn't been acting very favorably on these, and competing lines are always challenging you before the ICC. So, practically speaking, we must grow by purchasing existing authorities. During the early 1970s many of the truck lines we picked up were operated by individuals 60 to 65 years of age. They had been starter-uppers, and now, as old-timers, they want out, so they can realize their capital gains and take it easy. It has worked very nicely for us.

For many years the trucking industry's hauling tonnage had been increasing at a much faster rate than the growth rate of the transportation industry as a whole. These gains were made primarily at the expense of the rail industry. The relative share by shipment size between truck and rail is presented in Exhibit 2.

Overnite's Financial Posture

The casewriters noted that Overnite had one of the lowest debt-to-equity ratios in the industry and queried Mr. Gentil on his company's conservative financial policy (see Appendix A for details).

> I guess you've got to go back to when we went in business. The company was founded in the early 1930s, when the standard was to keep your debt down. Also, we've found by experience it puts us in a favorable borrowing posture. We've got a revolving credit agreement with the banks that gives us a favorable interest rate, a quarter over prime. This puts us in a position to take advantage of making a quick deal when another truck line becomes available. When an opportunity arises, we like to be in a position to go ahead and take advantage of it. And we don't want to be hamstrung by having overextended ourselves.

Overnite purchased its fleet vehicles, while many other trucking firms believed it more advantageous to lease. The casewriters asked Mr. Gentil for an explanation.

> We think we can borrow money as cheaply as anyone else. We think—we know—we can buy equipment as favorably as anyone else. Our purchasing power is just as good. We

EXHIBIT 2
Distribution of Shipment Size and Distance for all Products (1972)

	Under 1,000 pounds	1,000–9,999 pounds	10,000–29,999 pounds	30,000–59,999 pounds	60,000–89,999 pounds	90,000 pounds or more
Less than 100 miles	Truck	Truck	Truck	Truck	Truck	Competitive
100–199 miles	Truck	Truck	Truck	Truck	Truck	Rail
200–299 miles	Truck	Truck	Truck	Truck	Competitive	Rail
300–499 miles	Truck	Truck	Truck	Competitive	Competitive	Rail
500–999 miles	Truck	Truck	Competitive	Competitive	Rail	Rail
1,000–1,499 miles	Truck	Truck	Competitive	Competitive	Rail	Rail
1,500 miles or more	Truck	Truck	Competitive	Competitive	Rail	Rail

Legend: Truck dominant; Competitive; Rail dominant

Source: American Trucking Trends 1977–1978, published by the American Trucking Association, p. 69.

know a little more. You know, I came here from Freuhauf—tractors, trailers, rigs, and other equipment—we know the business, so we like to take the depreciation ourselves. The key to the equipment part of the business is the trade-in value or the capital gains at the expiration of the depreciation schedule, when we get rid of the rig. If we can borrow for the same amount of money as anyone else can, as far as leasing power is concerned, why give someone else the profit?

For the firms that are not quite as well-off financially as we are, leasing does help them quite a bit. But it is very expensive because of the interest rates that leasing companies have to carry, and the lease is predicated on a vehicle costing probably more than ours. I cannot answer for the industry, but I guess it depends on how strong you are financially. We're interested in rentals only when freight gets very heavy and we don't have the necessary equipment. We might have a peak on one weekend, for example, and are short on trailers. We can get in touch with a leasing company and get trailers on short notice for about 10 or 11 dollars a day. We do not like to rent the tractor, though, because they cost up to about 100 dollars a day. Too expensive.

The Energy Crunch and Other Factors Affecting Overnite's Costs During the 1970s

Overnite has had its problems dealing with the scarcity of fuel and its rising costs, but relatively seemed to be doing quite well. Mr. Gentil explained,

It's been pretty frustrating, but primarily it's costly. We've been blessed by generally warm weather that has really pulled us through. During the decade's middle years our allocation was only about 85 percent of our needs, but we were able to supplement this by buying our #2 fuel from independent home-heating oil companies. We also had increased our storage capacity, and we had purchased four 8,000-gallon road transporters that gave us a back-up contingency from terminal to terminal. So anytime we would have a shortage in any particular area, we would remove from storage. We were also able to contract for some storage with some of the independents. But all of this boosted costs tremendously.

The casewriters, reflecting upon an industry statistic that the transportation industry traditionally had the highest maintenance costs of any industry, asked Mr. Gentil about Overnite's maintenance costs.

> Historically, as a percentage of revenues, maintenance has been running about 12 percent for many companies. Ours in the early 1970s was 12 percent, and now we've got it down to 9. Maintenance is a sticky situation because it's tied to your trade option, meaning how long you keep your vehicles. Everything we repair, we repair in-house. We don't have any work done on the outside. We also do all of our own recapping. So we'd like to shoot for a percent of revenue of between $8\frac{1}{2}$ and 9 percent, which we feel is very good. So we take the difference between 9 percent and the 12 percent industry standard to improve our profits.

Throughout the 1970s, the trucking industry in the United States found itself in a troublesome situation that seemed to be getting progressively worse. The problem was not only how to deal with rapidly rising fuel costs, but also how to cope with spot shortages and the Department of Energy's fuel allocation system.

An offshoot of this situation was that truckers were getting increased competition from the railroads, ironically because they were required to pass less of the increase in fuel costs to customers than trucks, resulting in a relatively more favorable railroad rate structure.[1]

Although railroads used diesel fuel, they could pass on a smaller surcharge than truckers (3.6 percent for railroads vs. 9.5 percent for trucking companies), according to Mr. Gentil. The railroads claimed to have the capability to move one ton of freight approximately 280 miles per gallon of diesel fuel, while the comparative figure for trucks was 77 miles. Many companies consequently began to reevaluate their shipping policies. Safeway Stores, Inc., America's largest grocery chain, Mr. Gentil related, shipped produce on a test basis by rail during June and July 1979. Pleased with the results, Safeway in the fall of 1979 was considering whether it should switch from trucks, which then carried almost all of its freight, to railroads. Some transportation experts predicted that railroads would report an increased share of tonnage in 1979 and 1980, due primarily to rising fuel costs. If the predictions materialized, the trucking industry would suffer accordingly.

Mr. Gentil was quick to point out that the need for trucks would never be completely filled by the railroads, as trucks would still be utilized to transport intracity freight where there are no rail facilities. In addition, there did not seem to be a large threat from air-freight carriers because the cost was prohibitively high. There may be, however, a trend towards shipping perishable and other goods of a similar nature by air.

As of mid-1979, the DOE was predicting that there would be enough fuel and home-heating oil for the winter season, despite the fact that for the first half of the year, stocks of these two petroleum products, which except for minor refining differences are identical, were at or below the "minimum acceptable level" set by the DOE. Viewed realistically, the U.S. supply of diesel fuel was in somewhat of a precarious position in 1979. The instability of the world oil market, due primarily to the cut-off of Iranian oil and the periodic OPEC price increases, made the outlook for adequate supplies uncertain at best.

Overnite had a fuel storage capacity of approximately 860,000 gallons and was con-

---

[1] DOE fuel allocations were established as a percentage of past consumption for the prior year.

structing 420,000 gallons of additional storage. Overnite fueled its own trucks; drivers could not purchase diesel fuel when on the road, except in emergencies. Management tried to keep the tanks full, with a projected supply of 1,280,000 gallons, assuring that Overnite's fleet could be fueled for up to 20 days. The company also had its own 8000-gallon tankers strategically positioned to fill the gap in case of spot shortages. Mr. Gentil expressed concern over prospects for supply as 1980 approached, but for the remainder of 1979 and early into the next year at least, he foresaw no major problems in acquiring fuel.

In 1977, the average fuel cost for Class 1 intercity general freight carrier was 0.086 per vehicle mile. This amount was nearly three times that of 1970. Overnite's fuel expense for intercity hauling was roughly estimated to have increased to $0.10 per mile in 1978, approximately 40 percent above 1974. (See Exhibit 3.)

Steep increases in fuel costs were expected to follow past trends. A government survey reported the price paid by a purchaser of Overnite's size (i.e., one that buys diesel fuel in large quantities and stores it at its own terminals) as $0.69 per gallon in September 1979, and $0.565 in June 1979. The price was $0.39 in September 1978. The survey also reported that the average retail price for diesel fuel at truck stops was $0.994 per gallon in September 1979, while the corresponding January 1, 1979 price was $0.635.

To combat the fuel crisis, Overnite had been investing in fuel-efficient equipment, such as fan clutches, radial tires, low rpm engines, and air deflectors. They were also using "bullnose" units to close the gap between tractor and trailer, thereby improving air flow. The line-haul fleet was primarily composed of "Macks" with 300 Maxidyne engines. In recent years, however, Overnite had acquired tractors from White Motors powered with Cummins Formula 290 engines. These new types of engines raised fleet mpg from an overall average of 3.65 to 5.8 with the Maxidynes, and 5.6 with the Cummins. Such purchases of more fuel-efficient equipment was an expensive proposition (among acquisitions in 1978 were 452 power units costing $14,935,000). According to Mr. Gentil,

> The average price paid for line-haul equipment has increased from $21,000 in 1973 to $43,000 today (1979). City tractors have increased in price from $14,000 to $31,000, and straight trucks from $8800 to $22,000 over the same period. So the trucking industry must face not only rising fuel costs, but also rising costs for new equipment to conserve fuel.

Overnite's Union Posture

Overnite consistently has been one of the most financially successful companies in the trucking industry (see Exhibit 4 and Appendix A). Observers have suggested that it has been the human relations/people management function that earned them this envious position. The casewriters, noting that Overnite was the largest nonunion trucking firm in the United States, asked Mr. Gentil to explain the advantages to Overnite in maintaining a nonunion status.

> Let's put it this way, it's not that Overnite is nonunion. Really, it's our employees who are nonunion. If they wanted it we'd have it because there would be no way we could keep it out. I think our people like our open-door policy to management. They have the prerogative to come visit me at any time, or the chairman of the board, or anyone. We treat everybody as individuals. They are not numbers, and our terminal people know their families.
>
> We're still a little old-fashioned. We have the company picnics and periodic get-togethers, and we have a very competitive retirement plan, one, I think is better than most anybody else can offer. We have a tremendous hospitalization plan. Another thing we have been able to do is to provide a stock-option purchase plan. Over half of our employees by personal choice participate in company stock offerings.

EXHIBIT 3
Fuel Costs per Intercity Vehicle Mile in Cents for Class I
Intercity Common Carriers of General Freight[a]

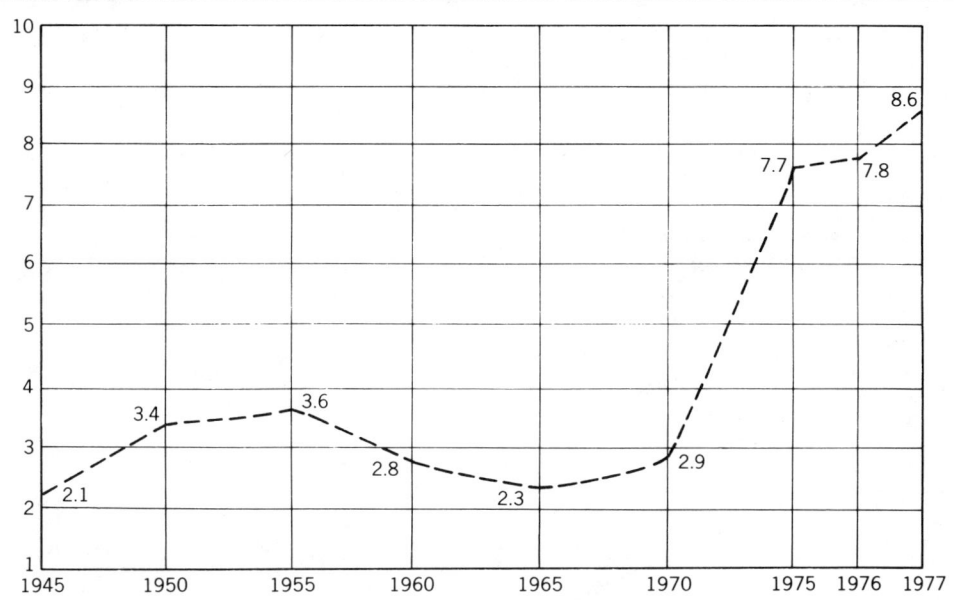

Overnite's Fuel Expense

Year	Intercity Haul Miles[d] (000s)	Average Fuel Cost per Intercity Vehicle Mile[a,c]	Fuel Expense (millions of dollars)	Fuel Expense as Percent of Operating Expenses
1974	79,492	7.0¢	5.6	7.2%
1975	73,411	7.7¢	5.7	7.6
1976	89,470	7.8¢	7.0	7.4
1977	115,561	8.6¢	9.9	8.1
1978	136,534	9.9¢[b]	13.5	8.6

Source: *American Trucking Trends 1977–1978*, published by the American Trucking Association, p. 16.
[a]Excludes State and Federal fuel taxes.
[b]Projected from 1977 (8.6¢ and 14.7% compound growth rate).
[c]Derived by applying the average cost per intercity mile to Overnite's actual miles driven.
[d]Trinc's Red Book of the Trucking Industry.

A main reason is that Overnite's growth has been mainly in the South, rather than the Northern markets, which are perceived as more lucrative by the large trucking teams. According to Ken Gentil, this

has been due to favorable climates. One, of course, is the weather. We're not subject to as much down time as most of the carriers who go North. That's because of snow or ice—mostly ice. We do get ice in Atlanta and Nashville occasionally, but in Northern markets they have to contend with it all the time, four or five months out of the year. Now, second, is the labor climate. There's an element or attitude that's different in the South. The companies

EXHIBIT 4[a]
Selected Operating Ratios (1977, 1978)

	Trucking Industry		Overnite		Arkansas Best		Carolina Freight		Consolidated Freightways		Cooper–Jarrett	
Profitability												
Rate of Return of Total Capital	15.7%	14.7%	17.0%	16.1%	15.3%	8.8%	8.4%	9.3%	19.2%	19.0%	4.0%	NMF
Percent Retained in Co. Equity	14.8	14.2	14.1	13.6	13.9	14.7	11.7	13.6	17.6	16.3	3.1	NMF
ROR on Net Worth	18.8	18.3	18.9	18.2	18.6	19.2	13.2	15.3	22.1	21.2	4.1	NMF
Operating Profit Margin	13.6	13.1	21.7	20.0	13.5	12.0	7.2	8.3	16.1	15.4	5.2	3.4
Net Profit Margin	4.6	4.3	12.1	13.6	4.4	4.4	2.7	3.6	4.8	4.5	.3	1.7
EPS	$3.81	$4.26	$1.96	$2.34	$1.26	$1.65	$1.26	$1.65	$4.24	$4.82	$0.46	$2.28
Liquidity												
Current Ratio	1.34%	1.23%	1.13%	1.24%	1.62%	1.27%	1.22%	1.19%	1.25%	1.14%	1.31%	1.04%
Quick Ratio	1.15	1.07	1.00	1.08	.96	.88	1.14	1.11	.78	.69	1.25	.99
Inventory to Net Working Capital	.71	1.13	1.00	.66	1.06	3.28	.37	.43	2.21	3.20	.19	1.25
Leverage												
Total Debt-to-Asset Ratio	.67	.76	.32	.33	.64	1.01	.96	.95	.84	.86	1.00	1.17
Total Debt-to-Equity	1.10	1.46	.37	.39	.88	2.50	2.02	2.09	.99	.99	2.66	3.70
Long-Term Debt-to-Equity	.53	.75	.15	.17	.38	1.47	1.10	1.19	.19	.14	1.65	2.16
Times Interest Earned				25.1		7.0		3.5		14.0		1.3
Other												
% Debt 6/30/79				15.0		60.0		54.0		29.0		67.0
Number of Employees				5777		26662		4380		24400		1699
Labor Costs %		54.7		53.0		42.0		61.0		45.0		51.0

	Yellow Freight		McLean Trucking		Roadway Express		Smith's Transfer		Transcon Lines	
Profitability										
Rate of Return of Total Capital	18.6%	17.0%	13.5%	11.1%	19.0%	19.6%	11.1%	9.8%	6.8%	8.9
Percent Retained in Co. Equity	16.8	14.4	13.8	11.6	15.0	15.5	14.5	12.7	4.0	7.9
ROR on Net Worth	21.2	18.8	16.6	14.8	19.0	19.6	17.7	15.9	7.8	11.6
Operating Profit Margin	16.3	15.0	9.9	9.0	13.8	13.5	13.4	13.4	8.2	8.8
Net Profit Margin	5.8	5.0	3.5	3.1	5.8	5.8	4.7	3.7	1.7	2.3
EPS	$2.63	$2.73	$2.73	$2.74	$2.28	$2.78	$3.59	$3.69	$1.06	$1.70
Liquidity										
Current Ratio	.86%	.83%	1.23%	1.36%	2.22%	1.68%	1.21%	1.24%	1.36%	1.33%
Quick Ratio	.80	.77	1.09	1.18	2.17	1.65	1.11	1.15	1.21	1.19
Inventory to Net Working Capital	—	—	.59	.51	.04	.04	.47	.38	.45	.44
Leverage										
Total Debt-to-Asset Ratio	.64	.58	.64	.68	.36	.43	.66	.81	.65	.76
Total Debt-to-Equity	.75	.67	.85	1.02	.36	.43	1.19	1.57	.96	1.21
Long-Term Debt-to-Equity	.17	.15	.34	.50	No LT Debt		.79	1.11	.48	.60
Times Interest Earned		22.4		6.2				3.9		3.5
Other										
% Debt 6/30/79		14.0		34.0		0.0		53.0		38.0
Number of Employees		15550		11400		23000		5263		4927
Labor Costs %		55.0		60.0		63.0		55.0		62.0

Source: Valueline, 1979.

[a]This is a composite list of selected large class I, general commodity carriers, whose operating positions are similar to Overnite's; it includes Overnite, Arkansas Best, Carolina Freight, Consolidated Freightways, Cooper–Jarrett, McLean, Roadway, Yellow Freight, and Smith's Transfer.

we're hauling for are primarily nonunion and work very closely with us, and those who do have unions have no constraints or pressures to put on a nonunion hauler, and they're very cooperative. In addition to these two favorable climates, our marketing people believe U.S. business growth is to the South, both east and west, so we are tending to go that direction.

Overnite's operating ratio was approximately 87 percent, which is very good for the trucking industry. "We are able to attain this favorable ratio," according to Mr. Gentil,

> first of all because of our flexibility of not having to conform to any particular work rules. This gets back to our nonunion status. We are able to utilize our people without too many restrictions. If we want to make some personnel changes, we can get rid of the unsatisfactory workers and keep the good ones. And the flexibility we have, due to not having restrictive work rules, makes a big difference. Also, the environment we are working in, the area we serve, the South, Southeast, and Southwest, makes a big difference. And finally, we don't have any absentee management. The people who run this place are always here, and the chairman of the board will compete with you for getting here early in the morning. We're here as a team.

Mr. Gentil said that the unions would like the general public to believe that Overnite works to keep unions out so that it can "chisel" on wages. He readily acknowledged that there are savings in wage costs by not having a union, but not at the expense of the individual drivers.

> As far as the individual is concerned, he does as well or better than his union counterpart. For example, a driver can come in after a road job, and we might ask him to go out in the city and pick-up. He does not say, as a union driver would, "well, I'm just a road driver, not a city driver, to hell with you." We can ask him to work on the dock or anyplace else we need him. In other words, we are able to utilize our people to the utmost.

> The good people like it because they know there is always going to be work for them. If things did get slow, we could take a road driver and put him back in the city. We could take a city driver and put him in the warehouse. And the warehouseman slides back a notch to displace the only people we really get rid of, our casual help. They are students and off-duty policemen who are paid an hourly rate. The system gives our people, especially our good people, a sense of security.

This arrangement enabled Overnite to keep fewer people on the payroll than companies who had contracts with the Teamsters. Mr. Gentil revealed to the casewriters another significant labor saving because of maintaining a nonunion status.

> One of our biggest advantages is that our drivers can and will drive as many as 60 hours a week. This is still within ICC requirements, but the majority of union drivers will pull only 40 hours. The unions are interested in putting people on the union rolls and getting their per capita dues, so the fewer hours their people can work, the more members they will have. Our people pull 60 hours vs. 40 for the union driver, and, of course, at the end of the year, our man's W2 Form is going to reflect more money. We can also pick-up on weekends and after dark. We pride ourselves on really trying to serve the public.

The casewriters asked if Overnite had any problem with union companies being pressured by their plant unions not to permit Overnite's trucks to unload.

> Not really. We've had a little bit of a flare-up on that once in a while when we've gone into a new area. For example, take a place like Louisville which is highly unionized. We've had problems at one or two plants. But when we finally get in and perform the service that we normally do and get to know the people, this barrier is of no real consequence. We have no real problems system-wide.

Teamsters Fail to Organize Overnite

In August 1978 the teamsters attempted to organize Overnite and failed by a vote of 2451 to 1565. Mr. Gentil explained how the Teamsters conducted that campaign.

They spent a fabulous amount of money on a real big drive. It was the most penetrating campaign they've run in a long time. They spend a lot of money, and they get everybody they can to go to work for their cause, and they pay people to distribute handbills and mail and different things like that. But frankly, I guess if I were a union organizer, I would definitely look at Overnite, because we have 6100 employees here, of which there is a potential bargaining unit of up to 4500.

First they go after authorization cards. To get someone to sign they say "your insurance plan is not as good as ours, your pension plan is not as good, you don't have all the fringe benefits we can give you." They're trying to make a case, and, frankly, they can usually get enough authorization cards to at least have an election. They did get the necessary cards in 1978, but when the National Labor Relations Board and we held the election, the company had something like 2500 votes and they had about 1500. So the Teamsters were beaten by roughly 1000 votes. It's still going on, but now they've sort of changed their course to newer ports. They sort of bounce around, but they'll continue spending an awful lot of money trying to organize us.

"When do you think it will be over?", the casewriters asked. Mr. Gentil with resignation said,

Oh, it will never be over. It will be something we live with on a continuing basis. Yet, I'd say our labor climate within this company at the present is better than any time since I've been here. It's good sometimes to have an election like that. It indicated to a lot of our people that the majority of the bargaining unit eligible people wanted to stay nonunion. Since they weren't successful then, it will be very difficult for them to go out and try to do the same thing all over again the following year. You know NLRB won't call another election for at least a year after one has been held.

"Don't they try to get into the new areas where you're expanding?" asked the casewriters.

Well, that's one of the reasons we move our key people. A company's success in resisting a union is a matter of who you surround yourself with. You can be the best guy in the world, but if you surround yourself with a bunch of weak supervisors and workers you're in deep trouble in a hurry. One of our philosophies is to maintain our beliefs and preferences with our own people. Recently we moved one of our most competent and loyal supervisors to Houston. We expect him to carry on our philosophy and hire the proper people. Also, each year I visit all the terminals; that takes about a full week. We ask people to talk to us. I don't think our people are frightened at all to talk to us. Sometimes things they say are kind of hard to take, but they call it like it is. And you do want to hear it, but it will shock you sometimes. I would rather go out there and visit with them and get it first-hand. Also, many of our employees are hesitant to call me on the phone.

Overnite Faces the Decade of the Eighties and a Declining Economy

In 1979, Mr. Gentil discussed with the casewriters the effects of a brief Teamster's Union strike and a longer strike by independent operators (truck drivers who owned their trucks and leased them to shippers, consignees, or trucking companies). This resulted in some violence and a slowdown in traffic for fear of repercussions, but, said Mr. Gentil, "Since Overnite is nonunion, the strikes did not adversely affect us." The independents' strike was triggered not by union wage demands, but by spiraling fuel costs, according to Mr. Gentil. Because of the fuel situation, overall costs escalated faster than inflation, while corresponding rate increases lagged behind the rise in expenses (see Exhibit 5).

A slowdown in the economy, predicted by experts to shift to a recession by the fourth quarter of 1979, significantly reduced the traffic of the trucking industry. *The Wall Street Journal* (November 14, 1979) reported that truck tonnage declined for most carriers by seven to ten percent. Mr. Gentil affirmed that Over-

EXHIBIT 5
Transportation Charges

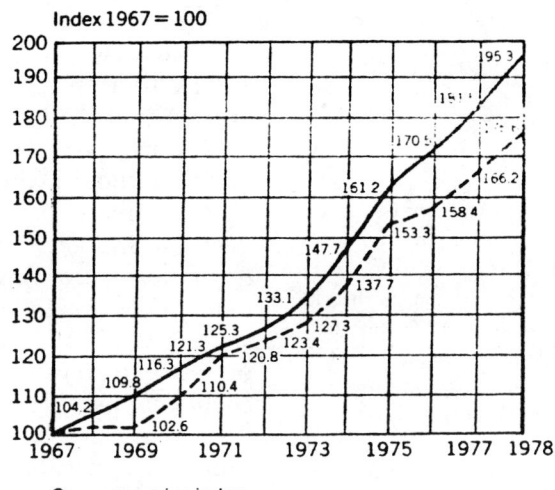

Consumer price index
Regulated general freight carriers

Source: American Trucking Trends 1977–1978, published by the American Trucking Association, p. 50.

In comparison with the consumer price index, the percentage increase in trucking charges for regulated Class I and II general Frieht carriers has been 24.4 percent less. From 1967 through 1978 the CPI has risen from 100 to 195.3, while during the same period the price of regulated motor-carrier service has gone from 100 to 176.6.

nite's receipts were off by about 10 percent, but

> Trucking companies lead in and out of economic slowdowns or recessions. In other words, traffic begins to slack off two quarters prior to when the actual crunch appears in the government figures. On the other side, there is the resulting pickup in business almost two quarters before the economy begins its recovery. The present decline in tonnage reflects a trend that will probably continue through at least the second or third quarter of 1980. Business will probably pick up significantly during the latter half of 1980, but until then companies must be ready for the worst.

Mr. Gentil emphasized that in 1974–1975, Overnite had been unwilling to accept the scope of the economic downturn, but, "we have learned from our mistakes, and will be better prepared to handle what the future might bring."

In 1979 Overnite was doing quite well, considering the somewhat gloomy industry outlook. Mr. Gentil summarized,

> We used to have the ups and downs. By golly, you'd do super in one year, and you were way up there, and then, golly day, that next year you were down like a lead balloon. For the last 10 years we've been fortunate. We've put in a lot of controls, and I think we've done a pretty decent job. Most importantly, except for 1975, our earnings have been accelerating.

Second quarter profits actually were boosted by the ICC rate increases, and by the Teamsters' strike, which worked to the advantage of nonunion firms. Once the strike was over, Overnite scaled back its casual workforce—the part-time help employed during peak periods.

The Threat of Deregulation

In 1979, deregulation of the trucking industry, just as the airlines had been deregulated in 1977, was a major issue. Mr. Gentil gave the casewriters his perspective on this issue.

> Deregulation to the trucking industry is sort of an abrasive word, and the thought of it can drum up a lot of hostility when you talk about it. The two real issues as far as deregulation is concerned, I guess, are what you would call free-entry and the rate-making process. This focus on deregulation you've got going on right now is due to a little bit of a tussle between the ICC and Congress as to who can get in the business and what kind of rates they can charge. Congress is saying, "we think the ICC is overstepping their bounds," while ICC, as in the past, has been taking it upon itself to administer the law as they interpret it. The result will probably be a pretty fragmented deregulation program.

Regulation of trucking, as it existed in 1979, was virtually the same as when it was first enacted in 1935. Basically, the Motor Carrier Act regulated service, entry, and rates. Under this act, Overnite was classified as a common carrier, which was "a firm that holds itself out to carry all persons or the goods of all persons indifferently." In order to obtain a route, a carrier had to obtain a certificate of convenience and necessity that stated the services to be rendered, the specific route, and all stopping points. The ICC then determined if the applicant were fit, willing, and able to perform this service, and that it satisfied a public convenience or necessity. The certificate for each route specified the commodities that each carrier may handle. This limited the firm's ability to fill backhauls. The act required rates to be reasonable and not unjustly discriminatory; the ICC had the authority to suspend a rate if not acceptable, and to prescribe a minimum, maximum, or actual rate. An amendment to the Act allowed carriers to be exempt from the antitrust laws governing rate agreements between carriers. Rates must be published and 30 days notice must be given of any changes.[2]

Advocates for deregulation included President Carter and Senator Kennedy, Chairman of the Senate Subcommittee on Antitrust and Monopoly, who both advocated legislation. The ICC under Daniel O'Neill had also begun a gradual loosening of the reigns it maintained over the industry. The major thrusts of deregulation, according to Mr. Gentil, were: (1) removal or freeing of route restrictions, (2) shifting the burden of proof from applicant to protestor in an ICC hearing (which has already been adopted), (3) allowing shippers to use their own trucks to haul for other companies, primarily as backhaul since shippers otherwise have to return their trucks empty (to some extent this has been permitted), (4) prohibiting carriers from engaging in collective rate-making, and (5) allowing rates to be changed without ICC approval. Although the glamor of airline deregulation was beginning to wear off as airlines cut service and boosted prices, the likelihood of some form of trucking deregulation remained strong.

Overnite's stated policy was against deregulation, but with some reservations. Harwood Cochrane stated to *Transport Topics* (November 5, 1979),

> Deregulate this industry and watch those small economic units, lacking proper and safe equipment and undercapitalized, move into the truckload business. A price war would almost assuredly result, with rates falling as low as the out-of-pocket costs for labor and fuel. Service would certainly deteriorate, and highway safety would be sacrificed.

Mr. Cochrane noted further that trucking companies like Overnite "would vie for the most profitable routes and disregard small and out of the way communities which they are presently obligated to serve."

---

[2]T. G. Moore, *Freight Transportation*, 1972.

"But there are certain things that we like about deregulation," Mr. Gentil told the casewriters. For example, "It took us four and a half to five years to get our route from Jacksonville to Houston approved. If we weren't a strong company, we could have been broke by now." It took that long to get the Jacksonville–Houston route approved, according to Mr. Gentil, because of the regulatory process and the procedures of the administrative law judges that the ICC used.

> You have a hearing, then it's shelved, then they review it, and then they render a decision. Then the protesters, they're the ones who don't want us to get it, ask the Commission to take another look at it. This, of course, is their prerogative, but it's primarily a delaying tactic. This added about a year. Our case was substantial, and finally, in about another year after we had a tentative ruling, the protesters came in again, and finally we had a final ruling. We'd love to see the process speeded up.

But overall, Mr. Gentil believed that deregulation could be frustrating for both Overnite and the industry.

> If the rates fluctuate on a daily basis, how do you know what the rate is for moving flour from Richmond to Pittsburgh? Today it might be $1.18. Well, tomorrow, it might be $1.20. Somebody's got to be in a position to answer that question if Standard Foods or General Mills calls. But if they didn't have a rate, or if it's going to change as often as they're talking about, no rate basis at all, then what is the rate? We think it's going to be very cumbersome.

Mr. Gentil acknowledged that deregulation would increase competition.

> I think that you'll probably see a lot of people experimenting, maybe somebody who hasn't been in the trucking business before. For example, they could rent or lease a tractor from Avis, and 15 or 20 trailers from Freuhauf.

> The real secret to the trucking business, however, is a matter of balance. If a manufacturing company has a two-way haul—products out, raw materials in—then it's going to be profitable. Take a business making widgets that needs laminated wood as a raw material. Overnite's running from Richmond to New York, carrying the laminated wood up to New York and bringing the manufactured product back. We're in a perfect position. But if a hauler doesn't have the two-way haul, I think you're going to find that the cost is prohibitive. And our coverage has an advantage over a small new company leasing its equipment. It'll be easier for us to get two-way hauls.

> Also, a lease has maintenance costs built in, and you've got to remember this, we do our maintenance in-house, which makes it less costly. Contract maintenance is running $30–35 per hour. So with lower volume and higher maintenance costs, how can they beat us?

Overnite's president did not seem overly concerned about losing any of Overnite's share of the truckload market.

> If we lose our TL market, it's going to be on a gradual basis, and, frankly, I think if we continue to move like we're moving into new areas, whatever we lose I think we can generate additional LTL traffic. Overnite is not as vulnerable as many carriers that are, say, 75–80 percent truckload haulers. Much of your truckload traffic is compensatory. In other words, you lose money on some TL hauls to maintain the goodwill of the customer. The difference in rate between TL and LTL is $1.00 vs. $4.00 a hundred.

> Another thing: where are these new companies going to get their drivers? The environment has been such that the drivers they can hire will have been Teamsters, and there are not an awful lot of truck drivers floating around. As a part of maintaining our nonunion status, we train our own drivers. Small operators with Teamster drivers can't compete with us.

> Air freight will certainly enter the picture one of these days, but their costs are exorbitant. Even then, that's got to be a two-ended deal. You've got to have a truck on one end and a

truck on the other. And I think from a competitive standpoint that we'll always be able to pin their ears back if it gets to that.

And something else: if deregulation is going to be so bad, why are big companies trying to buy up major haulers? You've just seen three buys by major conglomerates, the most recent being Smith's Transfer in Staunton, which is Teamster organized, being merged by ARA.[3] That tells you something. They want a ready made business, and they are not concerned with deregulation. This leads you to conclude that these large conglomerates that control an awful lot of money firmly believe that the trucking business is going to be a sound business regardless of the frustrations we're going through with Washington.

Expansion and the Future

Overnite had been following a strategy of expansion, initially by acquisition, but more and more by securing new territories such as the Jacksonville–Houston market. Growth through expansion was an expensive proposition; Overnite spent over $500,000 for legal fees and travel expenses presenting its case before the ICC. Establishing facilities in Houston would cost approximately $3,500,000 for the purchases of the land and building of a terminal. In New Orleans, the management planned to utilize an existing terminal costing $750,000 for both the land and the building. Overnite also would have to purchase or lease facilities at points along the route all the way east to Jacksonville. An increased number of terminals meant that better service could be offered, but an optimum blend of service vs. expense had to be found. There were additional costs, such as the purchase of new trucks and trailers to equip the terminal as well as stocking parts, fuel, and supplies. These were substantial and had to be incurred at each new location.

Overnite's management used two major criteria as inputs to expansion in a given area, according to Mr. Gentil: (1) increased interlined freight[4] to a certain area, and (2) contacts with shippers to determine where their markets were growing and improving. If Overnite's management noticed a lot of freight destined for an area where Overnite had to transfer to a competing carrier, they investigated that area for possible expansion. This philosophy was rooted in the belief that a company could make more money handling both ends of a shipment than it could if it had to interline.

A close relationship with shippers provided a forum for communication, according to Mr. Gentil.

> The shipping public that you're working with at the present time is a good indicator. They will level with you and tell you where they need the service. It's traffic managers of large companies you're working with, and it's their job to move that freight as economically and as quickly as they can. And they're looking for help.

Overnite's sales and marketing staff are always alert for hints and suggestions from customers, Mr. Gentil noted.

> After the decision to expand was made, implementation followed. This process included personnel reassignment, with key positions at new facilities being filled with people who had worked at Overnight for a number of years. This allowed management to have a greater influence on how an operation was run at its inception, which usually determined how it would be run in the future. Absorbing former employees (when the expansion was by acquisition of another company), staffing important positions, and hiring help (not interested in joining the Teamsters' Union) were some of the personnel problems that Overnite had to face when it moved into a new area. When the expansion was broad as was the present Jacksonville–Houston acquisition, it was very diffi-

---

[3] A diversified company with 1979 sales of $2.5 billion, with major operations in vending machines, food distribution, and cafeteria sources for large institutions.

[4] A transaction where one carrier picks up the freight and transfers it to a second carrier who completes the final delivery.

EXHIBIT 6
Organizational Chart

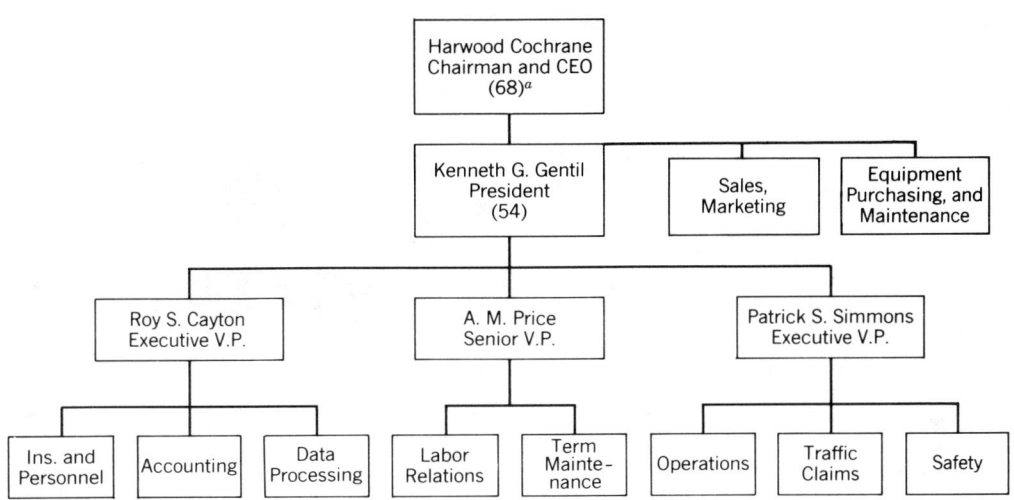

Source: Standard and Poor's Register, vol. 1.

[a] Numbers in parentheses indicate age in 1979.

cult to fill all of the key positions at each new terminal with experienced Overnite employees.

Other important considerations were: making contacts with shippers and consignees, advertising in the new area, dealing with highly unionized companies, and deciding how active to become in a new market. In order to determine the performance of a terminal, a computer printout was run for each facility detailing efficiency, costs, and profits. When expansion occurred, it was often difficult to determine the degree of importance a new operation represented to Overnite as a whole, because of interdependencies with customers and other Overnite facilities. Under ICC regulation, however, a common carrier was obligated to service the region it had been granted authority to serve. As a result, because of price acquisitions of authority, Overnite was required to serve out of the way points in West Virginia and Kentucky. This was typical of the risks encountered when a company decided to expand.

"Although Overnite will remain highly growth-oriented in the future," Mr. Gentil affirmed, "we'll probably slow further expansion for several years, or at least until we're certain we have the Jacksonville–Houston operation fully integrated into the Overnite system. But," he added with the confidence of one who knows where he is and where he is going, "if an appropriate opportunity arose that would let us effectively extend our operating services even further, we would not hesitate to take advantage of it."

When asked to summarize Overnite's situation beyond 1979, with the spectre of deregulation on the horizon, Ken Gentil was cautiously optimistic:

Regardless of what happens with deregulation, again, the work force—the people we've got—will allow us to do a lot of things that other companies cannot do. If it got so bad that everybody sooner or later will be going down the tube, the last survivor will be us, because fortunately we've got the money to hold out the longest. And combined with the financial resources and the good people, the area we're serving is a very good area.

APPENDIX A
Consolidated Balance Sheet (millions of dollars)

	1970	1971	1972	1973	1974	1975	1976	1977	1978
Assets									
Current Assets									
Cash and Equivalent	1.05	1.67	1.08	1.74	1.31	1.08	8.67	2.15	1.02
Net Receivables	3.64	4.22	4.84	6.80	5.21	5.84	7.92	11.16	14.69
Inventories	0.64	0.86	0.86	1.13	1.67	1.37	1.25	1.85	2.49
Other Current Assets	0.50	0.53	0.76	0.84	1.09	1.22	0.78	0.73	1.68
Total Current Assets	5.83	7.28	7.55	10.51	9.29	9.50	18.54	15.89	19.88
Property, Plant, and Equipment (Gross)	42.82	48.81	56.56	66.62	80.74	89.72	98.35	121.93	143.40
Less: Accumulated Depreciation[a]	18.58	20.04	21.88	25.37[1]	28.79	33.67	40.46	48.52	56.71
Property, Plant, and Equipment (Net)	24.24	28.78	34.68	41.25	51.95	55.05	57.90	73.42	86.70
Intangible Assets	0.73	0.78	0.92	1.05	2.10	2.82	2.95	3.45	3.49
Other Assets	0.75	1.00	1.32	1.56	1.47	1.83	2.58	3.61	4.72
Total Assets	31.55	37.85	44.67	54.37	64.81	70.22	82.07	96.37	114.79
Liabilities and Owners Equity									
Current Liabilities (includes Accounts Payable, Debts due in one year, Income Taxes Payable)	5.93	7.31	5.32	7.14	6.80	8.15	15.00	14.07	16.12
Long-Term Debt	5.94	3.57	4.70	6.85	10.53	8.39	4.99	9.36	12.97
Deferred Taxes and Investment Credit	2.14	2.81	3.90	4.93	6.06	7.03	7.40	9.01	11.19
Total Liabilities	14.01	13.70	13.92	18.92	23.39	23.56	27.39	32.44	40.27
Owners Equity									
Common Stock	1.50	3.02	3.02	2.99	2.99	3.13	3.17	3.19	3.21
Other Paid-In Capital	0.32	1.05	1.05	0.41	0.41	1.78	3.22	3.46	3.86
Retained Earnings	15.73	20.08	26.48	32.05	38.02	41.74	48.29	57.29	67.45
Total Owners Equity	17.54	24.15	30.54	35.45	41.42	46.64	54.68	63.94	74.52
Total Liabilities and Owners Equity	31.55	38.01	44.63	54.54	64.84	70.22	82.08	96.37	114.79
Net Sales	54.28	67.73	79.17	91.72	102.14	95.03	120.86	156.28	195.33
Less: Cost of Goods Sold	40.71	46.79	55.45	67.49	78.03	74.77	94.01	122.18	156.23
Gross Margin on Sales	13.57	20.93	23.72	24.23	24.10	20.26	26.85	34.10	39.11
Selling, General, and Administrative, and Other Operating Expenses	4.94	5.64	6.93	8.36	6.63	7.35	7.32	9.48	11.59
Income from Operations	8.63	15.29	16.79	15.87	17.47	12.91	19.02	24.62	27.52
Nonoperating Items:									
Interest Expense	0.61	0.37	0.31	0.46	0.85	1.00	0.54	0.72	1.19
Other Nonoperating Income/Expense	0.13	0.32	0.31	0.03	−0.12	0.04	−0.16	−0.13	−0.01
Income Before Taxes	8.15	15.24	16.79	15.44	16.50	11.94	18.22	23.78	26.32
Income Taxes	3.94	7.37	7.76	6.76	7.07	4.82	8.55	10.07	10.54
Deferred Taxes	0.35	0.44	0.76	1.03	1.13	0.97	0.37	1.61	2.18
Total Income Taxes	4.29	7.81	8.52	7.79	8.20	5.79	8.93	11.68	12.73
Net Income	3.86	7.43	8.27	7.65	8.30	6.15	9.29	12.10	13.59

Source: Compustat Industrial File.
[a]Beginning in 1973, plant, property, and equipment are depreciated using the straight-line method; long-term debt includes current portion; deferred taxes and investment credit are amortized.

APPENDIX A (*Continued*)
Additional Operating Information

	Earnings Per Share[a] (Based on average shares of outstanding stock)				
	1st Quarter	2nd Quarter	3rd Quarter	4th Quarter	Full Year
1970					2.58
1971					2.46
1972					2.74
1973					2.54
1974					2.78
1975					2.03
1976	0.59	0.83	0.84	0.71	2.97
1977	0.58	1.05	1.11	1.07	3.81
1978	0.73	1.18	1.19	1.16	4.26
1979	0.92	1.12	1.48		

	Additional Information[b] (All figures except operating ratio in 000s)				
	1974	1975	1976	1977	1978
Freight Revenue	101,799	94,708	126,537	155,902	194,791
Net Income before Taxes	17,364	12,802	18,681	24,337	27,313
Operating Ratio	82.9	86.5	84.5	84.4	86.0
Intercity Miles	79,492	73,411	89,470	115,561	136,534
Intercity Ton	2,586	2,188	2,669	3,247	3,705

[a] *Source: Valueline, 1979.*
[b] *Source: Trinc's Red Book of the Trucking Industry.*

APPENDIX B
Comparisons of Smith's Transfer

INDUSTRY: 4210	TRUCKING—LOCAL & LONG DISTANCE	TICKER SYMBOL: ABZ
COMPANY: 40789	ARKANSAS BEST CORP.	LISTED: NYSE-NOT S&P 500
RECORD NUMBER: 1472	COMPUSTAT RAW DATA AND RATIOS	

#	DATA ITEM NAME	1970	1971	1972	1973	1974	1975	1976	1977	1978
4	CURRENT ASSETS	15.76	21.41	23.61	28.64	26.43	21.18	27.09	32.61	60.78
5	CURRENT LIAB	9.56	11.78	10.27	12.39	13.50	11.34	14.54	20.08	47.93
9	LONG TERM DEBT	16.31	23.82	21.26	25.77	29.60	23.38	16.07	14.98	68.71
11	COM EQ—TANGIBLE	19.95 RA	20.92 RA	32.28 RA	31.20 BJ	24.64 BJ	20.13 BJ	25.06 OJ	30.08 OJ	29.27 OJ
12	NET SALES	63.92	78.39 AA	100.89	118.62	128.67	113.25	143.08	169.25	205.48 AA
13	OP INC BEF DEPR	9.16	12.99	14.61	17.05	15.39	11.96	20.13	22.80	26.07
15	INTEREST EXPENSE	1.40	1.27	1.67	2.19	3.17	2.78	2.17	2.19	2.63
21	COMMON DIVIDENDS	0.76	0.78	0.92	1.14	1.24	0.71	1.63	1.89	2.11
29	EMPLOYEES	2.73	3.92	4.00	5.62	3.72	3.66	3.83	4.13	7.03
30	CAP EXPENDITURES	6.01	9.36	7.93	6.48	15.85	7.07	11.83	14.69	66.35
42	LABOR EXPENSE	7777.77	7777.77	7777.77	7777.77	7777.77	7777.77	7777.77	7777.77	7777.77

(*Continued*)

264 Service

APPENDIX B (*Continued*)

INDUSTRY: 4210	TRUCKING—LOCAL & LONG DISTANCE	TICKER SYMBOL: CAD
COMPANY: 143897	CAROLINA FREIGHT CARRIERS	LISTED: NYSE-NOT S&P 500
RECORD NUMBER: 1476		

COMPUSTAT RAW DATA AND RATIOS

#	DATA ITEM NAME	1970	1971	1972	1973	1974	1975	1976	1977	1978
4	CURRENT ASSETS	9.05	10.11	11.30	13.30	18.89	17.91	19.14	22.92	24.95
5	CURRENT LIAB	6.26	8.62	7.25	8.63	12.00	12.96	15.11	18.82	20.97
9	LONG TERM DEBT	10.95	6.31	9.38	14.42	23.88	22.71	20.97	22.59	27.96
11	COM EQ—TANGIBLE	6.71	11.21	13.63	15.16 BJ	13.38	11.57	11.96	14.01 RA	16.68 RA
12	NET SALES	60.43	71.97	78.57	88.86	114.36 AA	101.00	123.02 AA	156.52	190.57
13	OP INC BEF DEPR	6.72	8.94	9.02	8.32	10.34	4.84	8.98	12.86	16.32
15	INTEREST EXPENSE	0.93	0.59	0.55	1.12	2.09	2.27	1.88	2.02	2.63
21	COMMON DIVIDENDS	0.51	0.61	0.72	0.78	0.82	0.52	0.41	0.46	0.73
29	EMPLOYEES	3.16	3.40	3.60	3.60	3.70	3.61	3.70	4.00	4.38
30	CAP EXPENDITURES	2.82	4.43	7.26	9.47	14.58	4.87	5.22	9.97	16.70
42	LABOR EXPENSE	7777.77	7777.77	7777.77	7777.77	7777.77	7777.77	7777.77	7777.77	7777.77

INDUSTRY: 4210	TRUCKING—LOCAL & LONG DISTANCE	TICKER SYMBOL: MLN
COMPANY: 582103	McLEAN TRUCKING CO.	LISTED: NYSE-S&P 20 TRAN
RECORD NUMBER: 1484		

COMPUSTAT RAW DATA AND RATIOS

#	DATA ITEM NAME	1970	1971	1972	1973	1974	1975	1976	1977	1978
4	CURRENT ASSETS	26.42	27.29	33.91	35.58	51.21	50.15	58.77	57.88	74.14
5	CURRENT LIAB	21.64	22.98	25.83	24.58	40.34	36.35	50.57	47.08	54.35
9	LONG TERM DEBT	29.82	29.18	29.17	31.55	37.31	41.58	32.43	31.74	52.44
11	COM EQ—TANGIBLE	22.15	26.80	33.62	42.33	50.47	58.69	71.64	84.89	94.62
12	NET SALES	146.71 AA	170.04	195.09	234.06	310.92 AA	320.37 AA	371.70	437.19	493.70
13	OP INC BEF DEPR	16.73	20.70	25.38	28.42	34.39	31.89	42.04	43.61	44.44
15	INTEREST EXPENSE	2.60	2.46	2.20	2.29	3.73	4.18	2.93	2.85	4.22
21	COMMON DIVIDENDS	1.39	1.39	1.67	1.67	1.92	2.01	2.32	2.57	3.26
29	EMPLOYEES	6.59	8.34	8.63	9.66	10.13	9.29	10.17	10.52	11.43
30	CAP EXPENDITURES	7.10	11.77	11.32	16.69	25.03	24.81	23.24	26.49	40.74
42	LABOR EXPENSE	87.88	102.70	119.59	114.42	162.30	175.24	211.13	251.38	294.24

INDUSTRY: 4210	TRUCKING—LOCAL & LONG DISTANCE	TICKER SYMBOL: OVT
COMPANY: 690326	OVERNITE TRANSPORTATION	LISTED: NYSE-NOT S&P 500
RECORD NUMBER: 1487		

COMPUSTAT RAW DATA AND RATIOS

#	DATA ITEM NAME	1970	1971	1972	1973	1974	1975	1976	1977	1978
4	CURRENT ASSETS	5.83	7.28	7.55	10.51	9.29	9.50	18.64	15.89	19.88
5	CURRENT LIAB	5.93	7.31	5.32	7.14	6.80	8.15	15.00	14.07	16.12
9	LONG TERM DEBT	5.94	3.57	4.70	6.85	10.53	8.39	4.99	9.35	12.97
11	COM EQ—TANGIBLE	16.81	23.37	29.62	34.40	39.32	43.82	51.73	60.49	71.03
12	NET SALES	64.28	67.73	79.17	91.72	102.14	95.03	120.86	156.28	195.33
13	OP INC BEF DEPR	11.85	19.00	21.40	21.47	24.10	20.26	26.85	34.10	39.11

APPENDIX B (Continued)

INDUSTRY: 4210	TRUCKING—LOCAL & LONG DISTANCE	TICKER SYMBOL: OVT
COMPANY: 690326	OVERNITE TRANSPORTATION	LISTED: NYSE-NOT S&P 500
RECORD NUMBER: 1487	COMPUSTAT RAW DATA AND RATIOS	

#	DATA ITEM NAME	1970	1971	1972	1973	1974	1975	1976	1977	1978
15	INTEREST EXPENSE	0.61	0.37	0.31	0.46	0.85	1.00	0.64	0.72	1.19
21	COMMON DIVIDENDS	1.05	1.58	1.87	2.08	2.33	2.43	2.74	3.10	3.43
29	EMPLOYEES	3.46	3.73	4.13	4.42	4.49	3.89	4.25	5.35	6.03
30	CAP EXPENDITURES	5.84	8.68	12.51	13.12	18.75	12.26	9.91	25.41	26.07
42	LABOR EXPENSE	27.86	31.93	38.55	46.09	54.60	52.63	66.37	82.68	106.34

INDUSTRY: 4210	TRUCKING—LOCAL & LONG DISTANCE	TICKER SYMBOL: ROAD
COMPANY: 769739	ROADWAY EXPRESS, INC.	LISTED: OTC-S&P 20 TRAN
RECORD NUMBER: 1490	COMPUSTAT RAW DATA AND RATIOS	

#	DATA ITEM NAME	1970	1971	1972	1973	1974	1975	1976	1977	1978
4	CURRENT ASSETS	37.99	72.09	88.88	83.23	109.36	148.22	198.64	210.13	270.76
5	CURRENT LIAB	33.21	47.23	57.19	65.55	79.19	79.56	89.43	125.02	167.77
9	LONG TERM DEBT	0.19	0.11	0.0	0.0	0.0	0.0	0.0	0.0	0.0
11	COM EQ—TANGIBLE	56.68	72.47	91.73	113.93	139.88	158.13	201.87	221.24	266.53
12	NET SALES	232.82	304.71 AA	373.54	447.63	514.48	503.57	613.70	802.01 AA	985.17
13	OP INC BEF DEPR	27.36	44.80	55.69	61.71	76.67	82.11	92.70	107.24	129.91
15	INTEREST EXPENSE	7777.77	7777.77	0.0	0.0	0.0	0.0	0.0	0.0	0.0
21	COMMON DIVIDENDS	1.96	2.21	3.31	3.93	5.16	6.39	8.53	9.70	11.74
29	EMPLOYEES	11.00	12.44	7777.77	16.11	7777.77	15.50	17.20	21.30	23.00
30	CAP EXPENDITURES	17.92	10.90	27.64	45.32	45.26	19.54	21.23	82.83	77.37
42	LABOR EXPENSE	7777.77	7777.77	7777.77	7777.77	7777.77	306.59	382.03	503.77	628.22

INDUSTRY: 4210	TRUCKING—LOCAL & LONG DISTANCE	TICKER SYMBOL: SST
COMPANY: 832407	SMITH'S TRANSFER	LISTED: NYSE-NOT S&P 500
RECORD NUMBER: 1492	COMPUSTAT RAW DATA AND RATIOS	

#	DATA ITEM NAME	1970	1971	1972	1973	1974	1975	1976	1977	1978
4	CURRENT ASSETS	11.36	11.91	13.65	14.69	18.91	16.37	20.33	24.35	33.21
5	CURRENT LIAB	11.74	11.69	14.57	15.46	20.47	18.04	19.57	20.14	26.69
9	LONG TERM DEBT	26.96	29.65	24.34	35.89	38.27	29.28	27.60	40.47	65.03
11	COM EQ—TANGIBLE	10.08	13.91	17.83	21.58	19.50	25.61	34.12	40.37	42.38
12	NET SALES	63.10 AA	87.81	99.61	125.41 AA	137.77	135.15 AA	165.71	193.20 AA	252.00 AA
13	OP INC BEF DEPR	7.77	14.64	16.88	19.06	21.22	20.32	24.80	25.91	33.94
15	INTEREST EXPENSE	1.30	2.25	2.00	3.17	4.49	3.59	2.55	2.65	5.91
21	COMMON DIVIDENDS	0.58	0.82	0.87	0.95	1.01	1.11	1.32	1.64	1.89
29	EMPLOYEES	3.95	3.95	4.10	4.81	4.81	4.47	4.88	5.26	6.46
30	CAP EXPENDITURES	25.91	15.43	7.31	17.09	18.12	5.12	16.44	29.65	42.89
42	LABOR EXPENSE	7777.77	7777.77	7777.77	7777.77	7777.77	86.31	105.55	126.86	162.60

(Continued)

APPENDIX B (Continued)
Comparison of Labor Utilization and Financial Performance—Overnite and Smith's Transfer
(All figures in millions of dollars, except where noted)

	1975		1976		1977		1978	
	Overnite	Smith	Overnite	Smith	Overnite	Smith	Overnite	Smith
Net Sales	95.03	135.15	120.86	165.71	156.28	193.20	195.33	252.00
Labor Expense	52.63	86.31	66.37	105.55	82.68	126.86	106.34	162.60
Labor/Net Sales (%)	.55	.64	.55	.64	.53	.66	.54	.65
Oper. Inc.	20.26	20.32	26.85	24.80	34.10	25.91	39.11	33.94
Op. Inc./Sales (%)	.21	.15	.22	.15	.22	.14	.20	.14
Net Inc.	6.15	4.79	9.29	8.34	12.10	9.02	13.59	9.30
Net Inc./Sales (%)	.07	.04	.08	.05	.08	.05	.07	.04
Employees (#)	3,890	4,470	4,250	4,880	5,350	5,260	6,030	6,460
Sales/Employee ($M)	24,429	30,235	28,437	33,957	29,211	36,730	32,393	39,009
Common Dividends/shr. ($)	2.43	1.11	2.74	1.32	3.10	1.64	3.43	1.89
Retained Earnings	41.74	22.04	48.29	29.06	57.29	36.45	67.45	43.86
Common Equity	43.82	25.61	51.73	34.12	60.49	40.37	71.03	42.38
Ret. on Equity (%)	.14	.19	.18	.24	.20	.22	.19	.22
LT Debt/Equity (%)	.19	1.14	.10	.81	.15	1.00	.18	1.53

Source: Compustat Industrial File.

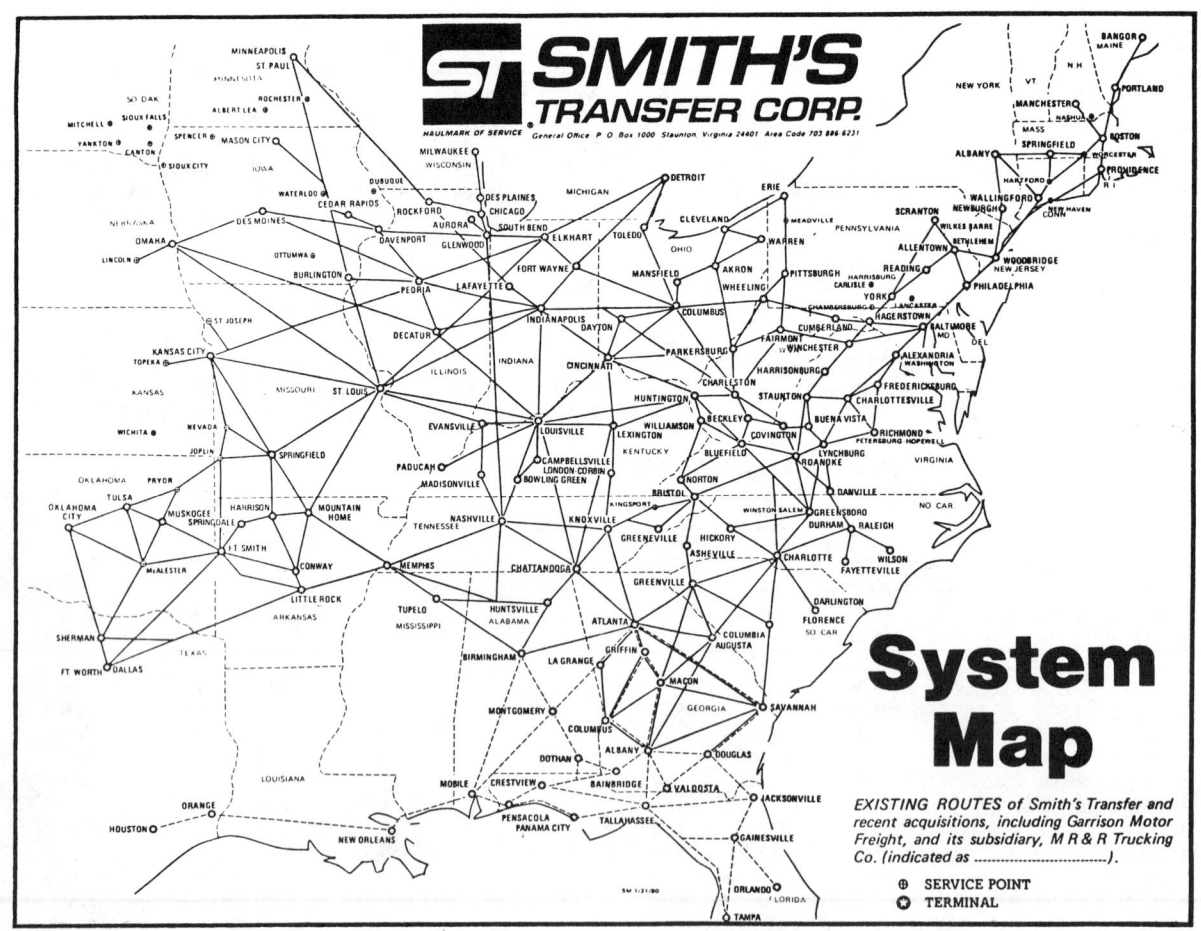

THE CASUAL MALE: OFF-PRICE MEN'S APPAREL RETAILING

In the summer of 1982, Edward Tucker, owner of a chain of off-price menswear retail outlets called The Casual Male, was considering what actions to take to manage his company back to profitability. Sales had increased sharply in recent years and so had the number of stores run by the company. But, because of rising expenses and because of a costly attempt at diversification into women's apparel that failed, profits had not followed suit. (For basic financial data, see Exhibits 1 and 2.) Mr. Tucker, a very energetic man of boundless optimism, felt his company would weather its present difficulties. Most, though not all, of his executives shared this view.

Mr. Tucker decided to launch a thorough examination of The Casual Male in order to determine what strategy would best suit his goal. This review encompassed the industry (with special attention paid to what he viewed as his most direct competition), the consumer, and The Casual Male's strengths and weaknesses.

Apparel Retailing

Apparel moves from the manufacturer to the public through four principal retail outlets: specialty stores, department stores, general-merchandise chains, and discount stores. It is also sold through variety stores, grocery and drug stores (in the case, for example, of hosiery), miscellaneous other outlets, and direct by mail. In 1981, it was estimated that these retail outlets together sold about $85 billion worth of merchandise.

In the latter half of the 1970s, a new philosophy of discounting was developed. This was aimed at the fashion-conscious shopper. These stores, known as manufacturer's outlets or "off-price" retailers, strived, just as traditional discount stores did, to make money through high turnover and low margin, but they focused on a new market segment. Their target was described by one consultant as people who were style-conscious, even "trendy," and enjoyed wearing clothes that expressed that self-image. "These are the people who want to put the coat over the chair so you can read the label." But they were also affected by inflation and were willing to go out of their way to save money purchasing what they wanted. It was to this segment, which one estimate placed at 25 percent of the population, that "off-price" merchandising appealed.

Off-price merchandisers tended to position themselves against department stores. In order to finance their expensive locations and luxurious ambiance, department stores marked up their goods 50 to 60 percent. This mark-up was often taken on as "loaded" cost (i.e., with allowances for advertising, mark-downs, and promotions) that coule be 20 percent above the raw cost. It was this heavily padded price for a heavily advertised, branded garment that served as the off-price merchants' opportunity. They "operated under the umbrella of credibility offered by traditional department stores."

Off-price merchants faced a number of choices concerning how best to bring their merchandise to the public:

1. *Buying.* The basic issue was whether to buy for less and take a larger mark-up vs. whether to buy at full price and take a smaller mark-up. This issue went to the heart of an off-price store's self-definition. Buying for less with a higher mark-up meant the ability to spend more on advertising, fixturing, sales help, and location. It

---

Source: Copyright © 1982 by the President and Fellows of Harvard College. This case was prepared by Richard S. Tedlow as the basis for class discussion rather than for illustrating either effective or ineffective handling of an administrative situation. Reprinted by permission of the Harvard Business School.

EXHIBIT 1
Comparative Unaudited Consolidated Balance Sheet, January 31

	1978	1979	1980	1981	1982
Assets					
Current Assets:					
Cash and Marketable Securities	$ 815	$1,003	$1,187	$ 761	$ 635
Accounts Receivable	127	54	42	357	603
Notes Receivable—Current	0	0	0	0	14
Merchandise Inventory	1,212	2,315	3,142	3,159	3,038
Prepaid Items	36	47	61	45	47
Total Current Assets	2,190	3,419	4,432	4,322	4,337
Property and Equipment	534	733	1,033	1,698	1,961
Less Accumulated Depreciation	179	300	413	564	825
Net Book Value	355	433	620	1,134	1,136
Other Assets	2	5	111	398	296
TOTAL	$2,547	$3,857	$5,163	$5,854	$5,769
Liabilities and Stockholders' Equity					
Current Liabilities					
Loans Payable—Stockholder	$ 0	$ 0	$ 14	$ 17	$ 8
Accounts Payable	510	698	882	2,209	1,707
Due to Customers	74	101	146	231	126
Accrued Expenses:					
Corporate Income Taxes	3	160	345	0	0
Retirement Fund	191	96	51	62	39
Current Maturities of LTD	0	0	0	0	231
Other	146	213	187	43	50
Total Current Liabilities	824	1,268	1,625	2,562	2,161
Other Liabilities	0	0	0	0	282
Total Liabilities	824	1,268	1,625	2,562	2,443
Stockholders' Equity					
Common Stock	5	5	5	5	5
Retained Earnings	1,717	2,584	3,533	3,287	3,321
Total Stockholders' Equity	1,723	2,589	3,538	3,292	3,326
TOTAL	$2,547	$3,857	$5,163	$5,854	$5,769

Source: Company records.

demanded, however, an extraordinarily well-conducted buying operation. The store had to acquire goods in season that the vendor feared being unable to sell. The store had to judge whether these goods would be salable to its clientele at a reduced price if they had not sold well in general. Buying at full price, on the other hand, meant a greater opportunity to acquire merchandise in general demand but with a sacrifice in some of the areas mentioned previously to keep expenses low.

2. *Specialization.* How broad should the offering of the off-price merchant be? Should he carry both men's and women's clothing? If restricted to men's, should he confine himself to low-priced items such as furnishings? These needed little persuasion at the point of sale and thus reduced selling cost.

EXHIBIT 2
Comparative Unaudited Consolidated Statement of Operations and Expenses for the Fiscal Years Ended January 31

	1978		1979		1980		1981		1982	
	$(000)	%	$(000)	%	$(000)	%	$(000)	%	$(000)	%
Sales	13,866	100.0	18,011	100.0	20,233	100.0	24,765	100.0	28,257	100.0
Cost of Sales	8,499	61.3	16,482	58.2	11,411	56.4	14,636	59.1	16,982	60.1
Operating Expenses	3,772	27.2	5,367	29.8	6,070	30.0	8,767	35.4	10,738	38.0
Depreciation and Amortization	69	0.5	108	0.6	162	0.8	223	0.9	424	1.5
Interest Expense	0	0	0	0	0	0	50	0.2	85	0.3
Other Expenses[a]	541	3.9	738	4.1	728	3.6	495	2.0	339	1.2
Total Expenses	12,881	92.9	16,695	92.7	18,371	90.8	24,171	97.6	28,568	101.1
Income (Loss) Before Corporate Income Taxes	985	7.1	1,316	7.3	1,862	9.2	594	2.4	(311)	(1.1)
Provision for Corporate Taxes	389	2.8	558	3.1	850	4.2	272	1.1	(141)	(0.5)
Net Income Loss	$ 596	4.3	$ 756	4.2	$ 1,012	5.0	$ 322	1.3	$ (170)	(0.6)

Source: Company records.
[a] Includes officers' salaries and contribution to employee retirement plan.

But would the consumer go out of his or her way to a less attractive location to save a small amount of money on a small unit purchase? Or, should the merchant seek to offer large dollar savings on big ticket items such as suits or men's outerwear?

3. *Continuity.* Should the off-price merchant seek to assure the consumer that various merchandise would always be in stock, even if the price of that assurance was spending more to buy goods that might be in short supply during a particular season?

4. *Merchandise strategy.* What was the best mix of first-quality clothing vs. irregulars? Did the off-price merchant have the option of selling little-known labels along with those nationally known?

5. *Pricing.* One industry expert believed that off-price merchandise should consistently sell at 20 percent under the department store price. Did this mean that off-price markdowns should be taken at the same time and at the same percentage as department store mark-downs? Was it viable to sell some goods at deeper discounts and heavily advertise them while selling others at full price? How important was it to be price competitive with competing off-price outlets?

6. *Store size.* Off-price outlets ranged from a high of 50,000 square feet to a low of 2,000. What was the optimum?

7. *Store location.* Off-price merchants usually tried to economize on rent expense. What would be the advantage of choosing high traffic locations with a healthy walk-in trade which would not be situated near to competing off-price outlets?

8. *Market penetration.* Off-price retailing seemed to be in the growth phase of its life cycle. Some chains were opening outlets at a very rapid rate to establish themselves prior to an expected shakeout. J. Brannam, for example, was established in October 1979 and had opened 39 stores by 1982. It was planning to open 90 to 100 more stores in the next four years.[1]

---

[1] The above discussion draws heavily on the proceedings of a conference sponsored by Smith Barney, Harris, Upham and Co. on October 21, 1981.

These questions had to be considered within the context of changes in the retailing industry. Perhaps the most important of these questions was the increasing inability of department stores to maintain a price that others could sell "off" of. In part because of the current recession and in part because of the fact that the nation was overstored, some department stores were becoming more price competitive. Trade journals reported that promotions were of lengthening duration, that they were being taken on a broader range of merchandise, and that the discounts offered were deeper than in previous years.

The Company

The Casual Male was founded in 1971 by Edward Tucker. Mr. Tucker was born and raised in Brookline, Massachusetts, and attended college at Ohio State. His first job out of school was at J. M. Fields, a discount chain. In 1966 he moved on to the BVD Corporation, where he sold men's underwear in New England. While still a salesman, he and a partner decided to open up a discount apparel store in the small Boston suburb of Sudbury. "The time seemed right," reflected Mr. Tucker. "People are always looking for bargains in clothing, and there was no low-priced competition nearby." In 1972, Mr. Tucker left BVD and soon thereafter he bought out his partner. Mr. Tucker developed interests in real estate and in a small apparel manufacturer, but the bulk of his business effort was directed at making The Casual Male a success. Mr. Tucker's early efforts paid off well. In fiscal 1980 (ending 1/31/80), sales had reached $20.2 million and profits $1.9 million. (See Exhibit 2.) The Casual Male's strategy had been to locate in suburban or ex-urban areas and to sell branded, first-quality, and irregular merchandise for between 20 and 50 percent less than such merchandise retailed for in department stores during the season. By mid-1980, The Casual Male had 49 outlets.

In the early years, operations were informal and the payroll was very lean. Mr. Tucker did much of the buying himself and even helped with the physical distribution of goods. David Clifford, a buyer, recalled how operations worked prior to the move into the 55,000 square foot warehouse and distribution center in Shrewsbury, Massachusetts, which the company presently occupies:

> At that time, we were operating 40 stores out of a tiny 7,200 square foot warehouse back in Sudbury. If we got freight in on Monday, it had to be worked and split and ticketed and down to be shipped out Monday or you couldn't receive Tuesday. There was so little space. Some nights we worked out in the parking lot until midnight just moving merchandise around and getting it ready to ship out.
>
> Back then, with that system, we were more efficient than we are today. With Eddie [Tucker] I remember being in the market in December 1978, a week before Christmas, in fact, buying holiday goods . . . buying goods to sell for Christmas a week before Christmas. . . . We were in with the manufacturer . . . boom, boom . . . decide what we want . . . boom, boom . . . negotiate a price . . . convince him the season's over. We'd have the merchandise shipped that day—it would be on the back of the overnight trailer to Branch trucking. Branch would get it in at 4:00 in the morning and bring it over to us at 7:00 in the morning because we were very close to their terminal. They'd bring the freight right over to us. We were always first on their run. So we would get that freight and have it split.
>
> The way we split merchandise back then was an abomination, but it seemed to work out. The merchandise would be in some stores that day. We always had a problem, it seemed, with merchandise arriving at our warehouse when we didn't have a purchase order because we were still in New York.
>
> The warehouse people used to lay out 40 cartons. They'd open up the manufacturer's carton and peel off goods just like they were dealing a deck of cards . . . one unit in each box.

All the tickets were put in the box and the shirts—or whatever the item might be—were ticketed at the store. There's a lot of down time at our stores in the morning. From 9:30 to 10:30 they have a lot of time for housekeeping, and they used to use that for stock work. Some stores would get a shipment two or three times a week. There would be 15 to 20 cartons of stock that they would work that day or the next day. They got their stock work done very quickly and got all their merchandise out onto the floor.

To be sure, this system imposed a lot of work on district managers who always had to adjust merchandise when one store started flying and another slowing down. We were forever moving merchandise from store to store to store then. But again, we were running two trucks, and we were running them so often that you could do transfers quite easily. When we did our transfers, we would have our truck schedule right in front of us. We knew which way the driver was going, so if a store was heavy we would look at the stores beyond that were in the truck's delivery line who needed merchandise. The driver would pick up goods at one store at 2:00 in the afternoon, and he would drop it off elsewhere at 3:30 or so. That meant there was very little time the merchandise was not on the selling floor.

We were so quick that we used to be in the market and buy the same merchandise Marshalls [a major competitor] would buy and be sold out of it before they received theirs in their stores. We had a good edge in speed.

As The Casual Male grew, adding 23 stores from 1978 to 1980, this informal method of operation proved impossible to continue. In May 1979, the company moved to a new location in Shrewsbury, Massachusetts, just east of Worcester. There it operated out of a modern 55,000 square foot warehouse adjacent to its offices. The warehouse employed 20 to 40 people, depending upon the season, and was far more systematic in the physical distribution of merchandise to the stores. It was also somewhat slower than the informal system it replaced. It now took at least 10 days from the time apparel was delivered to the warehouse until the time it reached the stores.

Soon after the move into its new headquarters, the company decided to expand into women's apparel. Mr. Tucker felt that since probably about 75 percent of the company's customers were women buying for men, these shoppers would be attracted to merchandise displayed in an adjoining department that they could buy for themselves. Thus, in late 1979, the company began opening a number of stores called The Casual Female. The Casual Female was actually located in the same store as The Casual Male but the outlets leased were about twice the size (averaging 6,000 square feet) of the stores dedicated to men's apparel. Merchandise was displayed in its own area with its own fitting rooms, but it was purchased at the same cash register. These dual stores had four salespeople in the stores at any one time as opposed to two at the men's stores, but they needed no more store managers or district managers. A new partner was taken on and was put in charge of purchasing women's goods.

During the course of 1980, 13 Casual Females were opened. For reasons that no one really understood, however, the experiment proved unsuccessful. Buying posed unanticipated problems difficult to cope with. A cogent advertising strategy was not worked out.

In late 1980, Mr. Tucker and his partner realized that his company should exit the women's business and by late 1981 The Casual Female ceased to exist. The financial consequences of this experiment were serious. The company had signed leases for stores far larger than were economical. Some of these leases were for five years and were difficult to get out of. It took a loss of $755,000 on The Casual Female operations by the time all operations were closed down in late 1981.

Worst of all, perhaps, was the fact that just as The Casual Female experiment was fail-

EXHIBIT 3
Selected Data for All Stores Located in Massachusetts

Store Number	Date Opened	$ Sales 6/82 (000)	$ Sales 6/80 (000)	% Gross Margin 6/82	% Gross Margin 6/80	Square Feet 1982	$ Sales Per Square Foot 1982[a]	Competition
1	2/71	$ 31.9	$35.2	43.2%	45.0%	4,600	$ 83	No major stores nearby
3	11/71	39.4	36.0	44.3	44.3	2,830	167	No major stores nearby
5	11/72	34.5	33.8	42.7	41.3	4,000	103	T. J. Maxx, Marshall's
8	8/73	41.1	33.7	46.7	44.4	2,400	205	No major stores nearby
11	8/74	27.2	31.5	42.8	45.2	2,240	145	Marshall's
17	11/75	27.2	31.5	42.8	45.2	3,500	142	No major stores nearby
20	5/76	36.8	39.8	45.7	45.3	2,400	184	Bradlee's
21	3/76	29.9	33.9	46.9	45.9	3,000	120	No major stores nearby
22	7/76	33.3	33.2	45.6	45.0	3,000	133	Marshall's
31	3/77	41.1	45.0	44.7	43.4	4,000	124	Marshall's
35	8/77[b]	7.4	28.6	34.5	44.8	2,500	N.A.	T. J. Maxx
38	10/77	27.3	25.7	44.5	45.5	2,000	163	No major stores nearby
42	5/78[c]	46.5	72.9	43.6	45.4	N.A.	N.A.	T. J. Maxx
45	11/78	52.5	60.1	46.3	45.3	2,540	247	No major stores nearby
51	8/79	26.7	29.6	43.8	43.1	6,340	50	No major stores nearby
65	11/80	23.2	—	42.0	—	2,340	119	No major stores nearby
66	4/81	101.8	—	47.6	—	11,940	102	T. J. Maxx
67	5/81	43.5	—	47.2	—	4,200	125	No major stores nearby

Source: Company records.
[a] Annualized.
[b] Closed 6/82.
[c] Closed 8/82.

ing, the menswear business was declining in profitability. Competition was sharply increasing in intensity. Total sales of men's clothing were up but expenses were rising more quickly. Sales per square foot in the stores were disappointing. (For store data, see Exhibit 3.) These circumstances resulted in a severe cash squeeze, which sent the company to the bank to borrow funds for the first time. Strict measures, including a freeze on salaries, were taken to bring expenses under control. The company felt it was necessary to show an operating profit by the end of fiscal 1983 (fiscal years ended on January 31). Otherwise, it was feared that the factors through which many apparel vendors sold their merchandise would prohibit sales to the company as a bad credit risk. This development would force a suspension of operations.

The company's difficulties led to considerable discontent among managers and employees. The company, many believed, seemed to have lost its way. It did not have a clear idea of what it stood for and to whom it should cater. Said one, "We have a new logo with a new slogan every two weeks." Some placed the responsibility for the problems at Mr. Tucker's doorstep. They felt he was inconsistent and at times arbitrary. Most important, they felt that he did not let the people he hired do their jobs. He tried to make too many operating decisions, especially those involved with buying, himself. Making decisions on the basis of incomplete data, he was too often mistaken.

Personnel turnover in the company's top positions had been high. In the year preceding August 31, 1982, the chief financial officer, the vice president for distribution, the real-estate director, three buyers, the advertising director, and a couple of district managers had departed. Thus, the company was under a lot of pressure to fill very complex jobs requiring both technical knowledge and people skills.

In the summer of 1982, Mr. Tucker was tackling the store's problems head-on. He was meeting with his key people to solicit advice on how the situation could be improved. The company had gotten by in the good years with a minimum of system but that was a luxury it could no longer afford.

Buying and Merchandising

With competition intensifying, Casual Male executives felt that a greater effort was needed to achieve differentiation. They felt they should try to offer predominantly nationally advertised, branded merchandise which was also sold by major, full-line department stores. They wanted to restrict their sale of irregulars (garments with a minor flaw such as a small stain) and nonnationally advertised merchandise to "hot" fashion items that were impossible to purchase from manufacturers in season. They planned to exclude imperfects (garments with a major flaw such as a tear or broken zipper) altogether.

The Casual Male sold only casual clothing categories. These included dress and casual shirts and slacks, jeans, activewear, outerwear, and accessories. The stores occasionally stocked sports jackets. Within each category, both fashion and basic items were carried.

The company wanted to price its products at 20 to 25 percent below regular-price department stores. Executives believed price was the primary motivator for customers.

Ed Tucker's Views

Ed Tucker loved to buy merchandise, and everyone in the company acknowledged his superior market sense although some criticized his reluctance to delegate buying responsibilities. Mr. Tucker shared the following observations about buying:

The apparel retailer depends on smart buying more than anything else. At this company we have three buying positions, one of which has just been vacated.

Our buying used to be almost totally haphazard. Now, however, we have a plan which I, as merchandise manager, drew up with the aid of an assistant and in consultation with the buyer in question. We have two plans a year—one for each season (fall and spring). These plans are drawn up 90 to 120 days prior to the start of the season. Sometimes I think these plans should be developed six months in advance.

Fall runs from August to February and spring the remainder of the year. This year, for the first time, we stopped shipping spring goods in early June. In previous years we had shipped them into July. We would take last-minute orders, and too often we had to mark them down, thus diminishing our gross profit.

We've had a lot of trouble making up the plan, which is new to us, and a lot more sticking to it. Too often, we take what the vendor has rather than what we think we really need. Too often, we'll buy the first thing that fills our need rather than shopping for the best deal. I know this because I check each order either as it is placed or when it arrives.

The buyer has to know how to strike a bargain. He must understand what I call the pulse of the industry: What's a good deal? How do you negotiate? When do you push? When do you back off? All this comes with time.

He also must understand that sometimes you move no matter what your stock position. A guy will lay a deal on the table, and even though you haven't shopped the market, you know it's dynamite. You grab it. A few weeks ago we were offered Chaps by Ralph Lauren. We had been trying to get that line forever, but they were afraid of us. Probably because of Filene's and Bloomingdales. But this was our chance and we took it.

We have no set mark-up or mark-down percent. We only know that we have to be competitive with our best-known competition: Marshall's and T. J. Maxx.

I determine the salaries of the buyers. A new hire gets in the low $20,000s, while one senior buyer receives about $35,000. A bonus plan has just been introduced that is based upon gross profit and sales improvement.

Dave Clifford

Dave Clifford was with The Casual Male for almost six years. Prior to coming to the company he had bought men's apparel for a Boston specialty store (R. H. Stearn) and department store (Gilchrist), both of which had closed their doors. He graduated from the University of Massachusetts in 1967 and was 36 years old.

Mr. Clifford started buying men's apparel together with Ed Tucker. They worked very closely until he was given his own merchandise classifications to manage. Soon Dave became merchandise manager, with general responsibilities for all buying. After a year and a half in that position he accepted the added responsibility of being a vice president of the company. After another 18 months in both positions, he gave up the vice presidency and focused solely on buying. Mr. Tucker took over general merchandising responsibilities.

Mr. Clifford bought active wear (this classification included items such as tennis shorts and shirts, gym shorts, sweatshirts, and running gear), sweaters, dress shirts, knit shirts, and sport shirts. He placed $8 to $10 million in orders a year. Mr. Clifford made the following comments about buying:

> When I first came to the company, buying was very simple. We bought strictly by price. We had a page for $6.99 sport shirts, $8.99 sport shirts, and $10.99 sport shirts. Three pages. Every time we bought sport shirts we'd add the on-hand to the page and post sales to the page. We virtually bought by fixture. When the $6.99 sport shirt fixtures got thin—which we saw by simply visiting the stores—we'd go into the market and buy more. The fixtures would be stocked again next week. Our only two rules were that the shirt had to be a brand and that we had to be able to sell it for $6.99. Color, pattern, length of collar—all these things didn't matter. All our stores were located in New England at this time, and that was an advantage because styles run behind New York up here. Styles that have died in New York and other trendy areas—and which therefore vendors are stuck with—still sell up here. Now we have numerous locations and this kind of generalization doesn't hold.
>
> Today there are a variety of factors that go into a buy. The first thing we do is look at the sales performance of every SKU we have. This tells us what is and isn't selling. So the first thing we do is project out our needs for what's selling and go into the market to get more. I am in the market in New York City two days a week with my list of preferred vendors, making calls and making purchases.
>
> The second factor is what the store people tell us. Our sales records will say what we are selling but they don't tell us what we didn't sell because we didn't buy in the first place. It's very difficult to evaluate this information and properly act on it, however. Recently the stores were complaining that they were losing business in basic sweatshirts. So we went out and bought sweatshirts that failed to sell because the weather got warm early this year.
>
> A third factor is what the competition, especially Marshall's, is buying. It's easy to find out what they're buying because we go to the same vendors and word gets around. I also know the price they sell at because I know they take a 40–45 percent mark-up. If we feel we can meet their price, we may buy the same goods. But if we do, we can't afford to sell them for one penny more, because if a consumer ever sees the same merchandise at our stores and theirs and ours is more expensive, we've lost that customer for good.
>
> Marshall's buying strategy is determined both by the power they have in the market because of the size of their orders and by the fact that they need enormous quantities of goods. They have money . . . financing. Marshall's just bought in June 50,000 pairs of Levi casual slacks from the Levi sportswear division at $8.75 a pair, and they're paying for them Au-

gust 10. These are summer goods they're going to release to their stores next January. So they're tying up $450,000 for a half year. I can't afford to do that. These are goods I won't be able to get my hands on. I certainly won't be offered a better deal on a smaller purchase than Marshall's.

Marshall's does other things as well. They have a lock on certain vendors like Jantzen and Head sportswear. Whatever the guy has for closeout, Marshall's takes it irrespective of price. One big package deal, they take it all . . . men's, women's, boys'. This is a big advantage to a company because they know that if they overcut, they have an outlet for it. So they can take a little more risk. This means that they can keep three suppliers exclusive. It also means that they can feed this tremendous animal. They have a half-billion dollars of volume. That's a lot of off-price merchandise they've got to acquire.

Marshall's also has their own brand. Melville, which owns Marshall's, bought the rights to Metro Spotwood, which was a $30-million slack company that went out of business a year or two ago. So Marshall's now has slacks manufactured overseas and sells them with the Spotswood, Metro, and Tivoli of Copenhagen labels. They also own the Town 'n Country brand for sweaters. Nobody else carries this brand. But Marshall's has to have 50,000 dozen shetland sweaters every year, and nobody closes out 50,000 dozen shetland sweaters because it's a basic item. So they go direct to a mill, have these goods made up, and sell with their label. To a certain, much smaller extent, we do the same thing with our Himalaya label. We bought this brand and have goods made up under it. To a certain extent every off-price retailer has to do something like this because if you didn't you'd always be out of stock in some classifications. You'd have no continuity.

Our company has some basic decisions to make about merchandise selection and price. When it comes to merchandise, we have to decide whether we want to appeal to the younger fashion-conscious market or to the older market for basic goods. Basic goods are easier to merchandise and your business is more pre-dictable. Furthermore, there has been a definite move among consumers toward traditional looks, called "investment dressing." On the other hand, competition in this segment is tough. Sometimes you can pick up fashion goods at a bargain because the big off-price people don't want to take a chance with them. Recently Marshall's bought 10,000 dozen basic shirts and left 2,000 dozen fashion shirts behind. I told the vendor always to tell me about any split like that because I'll make the buy. Our turnaround from the time of purchase to the time the goods are in our stores is still faster than our bigger competitors: 10 days for us vs. three or four weeks for Marshall's. We can still be in the market the week after Thanksgiving while Marshall's is already buying spring goods. That means that we can buy closer to market, and fashion thus may be a bit less of a risk for us.

There's always a customer at a price. You could buy a lot of short-sleeve plaid sport shirts right now and name your price. You could buy these shirts for $2.00, retail them for $3.99, and probably sell a lot. But I would rather not try to convince a customer to buy something for $3.99 that he really doesn't want. I want to sell him precisely the item he does want.

Like all companies, we're working for more bottom-line dollars. But in that drive, our initial mark-up may be too high. As a result, our mark-downs may be too soon and too steep.

One last thought. I wonder whether we should modify our procedures in buying. The way it works now, we get our open-to-buy, buy merchandise, and plan promotions. Instead, maybe we should plan our promotions first. The planning and scheduling of promotions should be more carefully thought through.

Dave Norton

Dave Norton joined The Casual Male in March. Prior to that, he bought men's apparel at Milton's, a full-price specialty store with three outlets in the Boston area. He had been there for 19 years and decided to leave when passed over for a promotion. He went into some of his own ventures that were not successful. He decided to return to retailing and he wanted to go to the company where there was a chance for growth and where he could make a difference. He observed:

> It's very exciting here. There's no area where improvements can't be made. I enjoy it here, it's great. The fun part is to think not of 50 stores in our chain but to concentrate on one and do it 50 times. I am responsible for outerwear, sport coats, and accessories such as underwear, socks, ties, etc.
>
> When I compare buying at Milton's to here, Milton's seems more scientific. I would do a whole study of what I did the last year or the season in question including price points, percentages, vendors, colors, sizes . . . everything. Before I went to the market, I'd have a whole allocation to the vendors I do business with. I made this plan and submitted it. I adjusted this plan after the merchandise people and the owner looked at it. But before you go to buy, you know what your sales are going to be in what categories. When you actually go to the marketplace, you make changes in accord with what looks good on the spot. But here, you go into vendor X and if you have some money and the deal is right, you buy it. Whoever happens to have the deal that week gets the business. I'm not sure that's best. At Milton's we were never out of stock. But that was because we bought basics . . . white shirts. Here we buy fashion, and that's a different story. From what I can gather, we really don't buy much later than our competition. It seems to me our rule is that we stop buying when money runs out.
>
> I have two basic ideas for making things better here. One is, we ought to consider selling more classifications of merchandise. Suits, for example. We brought in 1,900 suits on a consignment basis this past spring. These suits were made by an established manufacturer. They were irregulars, but they didn't look all that bad. You'd have to examine them pretty closely to see the problems. Anyway, these were traditional, dumb suits. And—without any sales help or alteration assistance—we sold 1,100. If we can get more suits on consignment, so we don't have to worry about turnover, mark-downs, or getting stuck, that would be terrific. Say you can sell a couple of suits at $99.99 and a couple more at $69.99. How many would you have to sell to make a difference? Another category to think about is leather outerwear. This you wouldn't get on consignment because they get beat up, so if you have to return them the guy can't sell them. But it has possibilities.
>
> My second idea is related to the first. We've got to get more men into the stores. In order to do that, we've got to create some excitement with our goods. We could have a designer denim story—that would bring men in because it's a recognized item. Another possibility is something that would be a little higher priced than what we have . . . something that the man will recognize. A man won't travel to buy a $3.99 shirt, even if it's a great shirt, because remember, our stores are out of the way. But he might take a drive to buy a $20 shirt that is regularly $30.
>
> I'm glad to be here. There's no question that if we can get our act together things will go well. There's a feeling of negativism in the company except Ed. That negative feeling is one I don't share.

Selling

The Casual Male operated 54 stores at the end of August 1982. Stores were located primarily in strip shopping centers, downtown shopping districts, and other high-traffic areas. However, executives were willing to experiment with other types of locations (for example, shopping malls) which were more expensive but might help them attract the fashion-conscious young man. The stores tended to be decorated in a low-budget and low-key style. They had wall paneling, neutral carpeting, and soft music. The front windows, however, were plastered with price notices. This atmosphere was originally intended to avoid "turning off" any of the wide variety of customers who might frequent the store. The firm was also considering a new decor with more updated styling and masculine colors.

Stores were arranged in self-contained departments (e.g., slacks, activewear, etc.); however, around the front and central aisle of the store there were also a number of coordinated looks and outfits displayed. The merchandise was placed on "four-ways" (a small rack with a central column and four perpendicular arms that deparment stores use to hang outfits) and small circular racks rather than the straight racks and tables found in most off-price stores. The stores were small (about 2,500 to 3,000 square feet), and two or three sales people were stationed at a central cash register and available to assist customers.

The vice president in charge of stores was Ed Raskin. Mr. Raskin was born and raised in Boston. He graduated from Northeastern University in 1948. His first job was as a stockroom trainee with the J. M. Fields discount chain, and he eventually became a corporate vice-president responsible for half the company's revenues, amounting to $250 million annually. He spent 29 years with Fields and resigned soon after the company was acquired by Food Fair. His next job was at Lechmere, a Boston-based discounter. He managed the branch in Dedham, a Boston suburb, which did about $45 million in volume. Mr. Raskin spent four years at Lechmere which he characterized as mutually satisfactory from the company's standpoint and his.

Nevertheless, late in 1980 he decided to jump to The Casual Male. Ed Tucker, Mr. Raskin explained, had managed a store for him back at J. M. Fields. Mr. Tucker often asked his advice about taking on new executives. When Mr. Tucker told him he was looking for a new director of stores, Mr. Raskin simply said, "Why look any further?"

> We have 54 store managers, one for each store. Above these managers I am presently setting up area managers. I have two area managers scheduled; one has been hired so far. These two area managers run both their own shows as store managers and two or three other stores. These people help absorb some of the work of the district managers in the larger districts, while also getting good training to move up as district managers themselves. Directly reporting to me are six district managers, one new-store-opening manager, a director of operations who handles purchasing, floor planning, and fixturing of new stores, and, of course, my executive assistant.
>
> Ed Tucker is a man of enormous drive and energy and great common sense. I like him, and I think that is reciprocated. But he is not a systems man. He didn't realize that he had to plan for the future. He didn't understand systems. For example, if he had a position to fill at the district or my job itself, he promoted almost on the basis of whim. He looked at store sales but didn't really understand how stores were managed. People got promoted who didn't know anything. Raises were given without the guidance of a budget. Store managers got raises without reason. There was no standard operating procedure, no system.
>
> Ed opened a lot of stores in good times. Sales were there, and so were profits. But as times got tough, all the weaknesses showed: bad leases, bad sites, bad people. It was even worse in merchandising. No planning. People just went into the market and bought whatever they could. The excuse always was that since we only buy off-price merchandise, we have to buy what's available. That's absolute horse ____. A good buy is only good if you can sell it. That's changing now. We're starting to buy by sizes and colors, and, at least in basic merchandising, we're buying to a plan.
>
> My input into merchandising concerning what and how to buy is zero because I don't know the market. But I do have input in terms of distribution into the stores. Too often we send goods to stores where they'll never sell.
>
> All of this has resulted in a great deal of frustration from the field.
>
> I've been involved in a major education effort for the district managers. I've taught them what a P & L really means. I've tried to give them an idea of what gross margin is. What causes shrink. Why is it important. I believe in giving out as much information as possible.

And I've set up a bonus program. I've frozen all wages because of our economic situation. But there is a bonus. Quarterly, store managers will get 3 percent of the sales increase over last year. If it's a new store, 3 percent over plan. The only qualification is that payroll percent—not dollars—has to be the same as last year.

The store managers have no involvement in profit—the district managers get 7 percent of the profit improvement. In the first quarter 25 percent of the managers did get bonus.

There has been a lot of frustration in the field. And there's been a lot of turnover. Some of this has to happen when you have new policies and procedures.

Our problem in this company is not from gross margin down, it's from gross margin up. That means merchandising. The first thing Eddie [Mr. Tucker] has to do is get himself a merchandise manager—a real pro who knows how to handle marketing, distribution, and advertising. He's outgrown it but he doesn't know it.

One of the things that has caused us terrible problems is getting merchandise deliveries right through the second week in December. My God, we paid for that in February, March, and April. That was the lack of planning. People said, "It's a hell of a buy. I've got to grab it." But, if you can't use it, it's not a good buy.

Reviewing last year's P & L figures, I determined that if each store did $400 better sales volume per week, we would have had a great year. Four hundred lousy bucks! We could get these sales in two ways. First, we need better distribution systems. Our stores are classified by sales volume. Goods go out to the stores on that basis. But too many times designer goods will go to a store where they won't sell. The district manager may transfer goods from one store to another within his district, but he doesn't know what's going on in other districts. If he sends these goods back here to our warehouse, more often than not they're shipped back to him the next week. Second, we lose sales because of bad buying decisions. Just recently, somebody made a decision that jeans and sport jackets were not going to be good anymore. These categories did soften nation-wide, but we lost a lot of business here because we were not properly in stock.

Company Finances

Rapid growth and high earnings in 1979 and 1980 led The Casual Male to diversify into the women's off-price clothing market. This venture was terminated by 1982 and resulted in write-offs of $355,000 in fiscal 1981 and $400,000 in fiscal 1982. After the women's operations had been shut down, the company retained lease commitments. Many of these were for space adjacent to men's stores. Through subleases and lease expirations the company managed to get out from under most of these commitments by the middle of 1982. However, in the interim the burden of these costs had to be carried by the men's stores. It was estimated that these additional occupancy costs amounted to $300,000 in fiscal 1982 and would cost another $100,000 in the first half of fiscal 1983. These costs were reflected in low earnings and operating losses up through the second quarter of 1982. The company stated that the second quarter statement would be the last one affected by these expenditures. The persistence of The Casual Female expenses caused some confusion in attempts to isolate The Casual Male's operating performance.

Operating expenses consisted primarily of payroll, occupancy costs, advertising, taxes, insurance, supplies, contract services, and depreciation. Among these selling payroll, occupancy costs, and advertising were considered the major controllable items. Payroll costs had been frozen. Occupancy costs were being pared where possible as the company extricated itself from its women's business. Advertising had been planned at 3 percent of budget, though it was running slightly ahead of that pace as a result of sales being below plan.

With sales lagging, working capital was being tied up in inventory. One consequence was a reduction in the available open-to-buy for the winter season. The firm drew a $1 million loan to ease the effects of this capital shortage. Six-hundred thousand dollars were used in fiscal 1982, and the remainder would be used in fiscal 1983.

Since the company's vendors factored their receivables, all purchases made by the firm's buyers were conditional upon the vendor's factor approving the sale. In approving sales the factors looked closely at financial statements, projections and cash flows, as well as any extraordinary items on the balance sheet or income statement. If a firm began to look as if it would lose its liquidity or was moving toward insolvency, the factors would begin to reduce the limit on receivables that they would factor. In The Casual Male's case, this reduction could mean a purchase ceiling of $50,000 on a single buy, as opposed to current levels of $100,000 to $150,000. This would drastically cut the firm's buying flexibility and efficiency.

Another aspect of the buying and merchandising process had a major impact on the company's financial position. If goods were overbought or out-of-season, mark-downs would have to be taken in order to move the goods out of the stores. New goods usually received about a 52 percent mark-up. With a target gross profit of 42 percent, there was a 10 percent cushion for mark-downs and shrinkage. The cost of shrinkage was about 2 percent of sales. Thus the firm could take mark-downs on goods equivalent to 8 percent of cost or 16 percent of total retail sales at original mark-up. Taking mark-downs meant walking a delicate line between moving goods, thus keeping the inventory turn up, and lowering gross profits. At times when sales were below plan, it was even more delicate because the projected 10 percent cushion for shrinkage and mark-downs diminished in size. The result was a catch-22. Keep the goods near original mark-up, tie-up working capital, and loose liquidity and available open-to-buy, or, take the necessary mark-downs and incur an operating loss.

The firm's chief financial officer was Kevin Steele. A graduate of Nichols College in 1973, Mr. Steele had worked for an apparel financial-service company as an accountant. He had worked as the assistant to the company's chief financial officer for two and a half years and had just assumed his responsibilities.

In Mr. Steele's opinion, the current fiscal year was critical. The firm needed to demonstrate complete recovery from its venture into women's wear, as well as to show an operating profit. The factors wanted to see mid-year financials. These had never been prepared in the past; thus such statements would not be comparable to any others. It was projected that they would show an operating loss. However, it was also felt that projections of year-end statements would show a conservatively estimated profit of $150,000 by the end of the year. How would the firm manage its buying and merchandising so as to conserve cash, maintain volume, and reach the targeted gross profit figure? Any reluctance on the part of the factors could result in insufficient merchandise and failure to attain projected sales volumes. Any overbuying or unseasonal merchandise would have to be moved by mark-downs that would affect the gross profit. Mark-downs taken when sales were below plan would have a much stronger impact on the bottom line.

Reaching the Consumer

Executives at The Casual Male often complained about the advertising, an example of which is reproduced in Exhibit 4. One problem with it, they felt, was caused by the store's lack of success at defining its target customer. The best description of the typical customer these executives could give was that their stores catered to "the fashion and price-conscious younger man." While this statement was recognizable ambiguous, they were uncertain as to how it should be narrowed. For example, what was fashionable? Most specialty stores catered to a very narrow fashion image (e.g., the Gap, the Lodge, Proving Ground, and

EXHIBIT 4
Off-Price Men's Apparel Retailing

Discover the Look of Spring and Save at your nearest CASUAL MALE

Levi's Knit Shirts — $7.99
Short-sleeve, stripes. Sizes S-XL
Regularly $15-$18

BRITTANIA® Western Denim Jeans — $9.99
13¼ oz. stone washed or stretch denim jeans. Sizes 30-40
Regularly $30-$38

FAMOUS BRANDS Belted Poplin Casual Slacks — $12.99
Poly cotton. Sizes 29-38
Regularly $22-$28

Our Version of the Baracuta® Golf Jacket — $18.99
Assorted fashion colors. Sizes S-XL.
Regularly $40

FAMOUS LABEL Western Shirts — $5.99
Long sleeve, assorted plaids. With pearl snap. Sizes S-XL.
Regularly $16

Marco Polo® By Burlington Tube Socks — 4 pr./$6.99
Long length sport socks. Sizes 9-15.
Regularly $11 for 4 pair

The Casual Male
Styling, Service, <u>Real</u> Savings

EXHIBIT 4 (*Continued*)

Brand Name Fashion Discounts for Fathers of All Ages

(3) Lacoste Belts $8
Levi Shirt $9
Shorts $10-13

Interwoven
Plush Terry Crew or Basic Dress Hose
Assorted colors.
3 pair **$5**
Regularly $2.50-$3.25 each

Better Short Sleeve Crew Neck Polo Shirts
Some with vented bottoms. Poly/cotton or silk blends.
$5
Regularly $8-15

Volleyball, Track, Soccer or Boxer Style Swimwear
Poly/cotton.
$6
Regularly $8-13

Chemise
Plush Terry Shirts
Collar model. Stripes or solids.
$8
Regularly $22

3 Lacoste Belts
Gift boxed.
$8
Regularly $22

Short Sleeve Woven Sport Shirts
Poly/cotton. Solids or plaids. One or two pockets.
$8
Regularly $14-20

Levi's Striped Knit Shirts
Short sleeve. Cotton/polyester.
$9
Regularly $16-18

Mountain or Belted Walk Shorts
Multi pockets. Snaps and Zippers. Solids or plaids.
$10-13
Regularly $16-18

Summer Casual Slacks
Comfortable poly/cotton. Assorted colors. Some belted.
$13
Regularly $24-28

The Casual Male
Brand Name Fashion Discounts

items that were typical of each of these outlets but felt that it couldn't have too narrow an identity; it needed to appeal to the masses. In addition, although most of its clothes were styled for men in the 18 to 30 range, the stores did a lot of business with men who were 30 to 45 years old and wished to maintain a youthful image. Moreover, although the store carried only menswear, they saw an increasing percentage of sales made to women who were purchasing gifts. Finally, although the executives were convinced their customers were price-conscious, they felt these customers might be willing to pay a little more for high-fashion merchandise.

In addition, the customer base seemed to vary widely from store to store. One executive remarked that the Boston store catered to business-people, the black community, high-fashion consumers, and gays; the store in East Hartford to low-income and in West Hartford, to high-income customers; the store in South Hadley, Massachusetts, to college students and farmers.

Even with these data, the executives still had a number of unanswered questions about their customers. One issue was whether or not the store had a loyal customer base. Executives were not sure if most customers did all their shopping at off-price stores or if they divided their purchases among various store types. If customers came to off-price dealers only for certain purchases, it was important to know the frequency with which this occurred and what distinguished the items they were looking for from those of other shopping trips.

Executives were not sure how best to attract customers into the store in the first place. They felt that most customers either just "stumbled" onto it or chanced to see an ad. Once they were in the store, they came back because the prices were low, and they liked the quality of the merchandise. The firm had always shied away from advertising that focused on general facts about the store. Instead, the ads featured great prices on certain items in an effort to attract customers.

The Competition

Executives at The Casual Male had differing opinions about which stores posed the greatest competitive threat to their business. This difference of opinion was due, in large part, to the fact that they were not sure of the extent to which The Casual Male had a loyal customer base. The most likely potential competitors could be grouped into four classes: other large, off-price retailers; bargain basements; men's specialty stores; and department stores. Exhibit 5 provides operating data on various types of stores selling apparel, and Exhibits 6 and 7 give data on the consumer. Exhibits 8 and 9 compare prices and breadth of merchandise in selected categories for each outlet. In addition, the classes of stores differed in terms of quality of merchandise and ambience.

Large, Off-Price Retailers

Casual Male executives believed that their most direct competition came from several large, off-price retailers, including Marshall's and T. J. Maxx. These stores were very similar in merchandising strategy and atmosphere. Both stocked a full line of off-price clothing for women and children, as well as menswear.

T. J. Maxx and Marshall's outlets were located primarily in strip shopping centers close to large shopping malls or other high-traffic suburban areas. The stores resembled supermarkets in size and layout, with about 4,000 square feet devoted to menswear. This supermarket atmosphere was retained in the interior decoration: the floors were standard kitchen tile, the walls were neutral, departments were designated by large brightly colored letters near the ceiling, and customers used "buggies" to transport the items they selected. Salespeople were located only in the dressing rooms, where they carefully policed the number of items entering and leaving, and in the numerous checkout lanes by the doors.

The men's department at Marshall's and T. J. Maxx included suits, sports jackets, dress and casual slacks and shirts, activewear, outerwear, and accessories. Each category was

EXHIBIT 5
Comparative Percentage Income Statements for Outlets Selling Apparel, 1980

	Department Stores		Specialty Stores		Discount-Chain Store Sales >$1M	General-Merchandise Chain Sales $10–$20M	Off-Price Store Sales Greater Than $1M
	Sales $10–$20M	Sales $20–$50M	Sales Less Than $1M	Sales Greater Than $5M			
Sales	100.0%	100.0%	100.00%	100.00%	100.00%	100.00%	100.00%
Cost of Sales	62.25	60.24	58.53	59.14	72.20	68.30	60.00
Gross Margin	37.75	39.76	41.47	40.86	27.80	31.70	40.00
Payroll	16.94	18.56	17.56	18.68	12.09	10.95	15.00
Advertising	3.37	3.15	3.09	2.50	2.58	2.55	1.00
Rent	3.28	2.77	4.35	4.21	2.66	2.98	4.00
Other	12.06	13.08	12.90	13.40	6.76	7.82	15.00
Total Expenses	35.65	37.56	37.90	38.79	24.09	24.30	35.00
Profit Before Taxes	2.10	2.20	3.57	2.07	3.71	7.40	5.00

Sources: Financial and Operating Results of Department and Special Stores; *Chain Store Age*; National Mass Retailing Institute; Annual Reports.

physically separated, and the items in the category were displayed on long, straight racks or tables. No outfits or coordinated looks were displayed to suggest how the customer might mix items from various categories. These stores maintained stock levels in a category by size basis only; that is, each store was supposed to display a certain number of medium knit shirts, but there was no control for the mix of colors, brands, styles, or patterns available within a size and category. These stores restricted their off-price buying to "brand names," but T. J. Maxx and Marshall's stocked a much higher percentage of private labels and used private labels to fill out basic categories rather than "hot" fashion items.

There were a number of large, off-price retailers in their trading area that the executives at The Casual Male did not consider to be a direct threat to their business. These included Syms' and Mervyn's, two very profitable chains that built a name based on their wide selection and low prices for designer and brand-name suits. Although these stores car-

EXHIBIT 6A
Clothing Store Awareness (%)

	Total	Sex		Income		Shop Discount Stores	
		Male	Female	Under 25K	25K+	Light	Heavy
Marshall's	68	69	67	63	79	73	62
Filene's Basement	18	24	14	14	23	22	14
T. J. Maxx	16	4	27	15	20	11	23
Casual Male	8	16	2	7	13	6	11
Others	73	67	78	78	62	69	78
Base	(394)	(178)	(215)	(203)	(131)	(208)	(185)

Source: Company records.

EXHIBIT 6B
Importance and Store Ratings on Various Characteristics

	Importance	Casual Male	Marshall's
Good value for money	90%	52%	64%
Having low prices	79	34	70
Return policy	78	56	66
Courteous salespeople	77	55	41
Adequately stocked	77	50	57
Easy to find what you want	74	60	60
Convenient hours	74	61	81
Good sales	71	35	53
Fashionable merchandise	71	65	51
Store cleanliness	70	61	50
Catering to people like myself	69	53	48
Conveniently located	69	54	55
Good parking facilities	67	61	72
Advertised merchandise available	64	42	54
Merchandise on racks	55	61	58
Family-oriented	47	21	73
Modern style store	45	58	50
Merchandise on tables	20	31	48
Having irregulars	19	21	44
Having cut out labels	13	34	42

Source: Company records.

EXHIBIT 7
Consumer Buying Habits: "What is the most important factor in your decision whether to buy men's apparel?"

	Fit/Comfort	Price	Quality	Color/Style	Brand/Store Name
Total, all respondents	36%	24%	16%	12%	12%
Income:					
Under $10,000	29	38	12	10	9
$10,000–$14,999	42	21	13	11	12
$15,000–$19,999	37	24	17	10	12
$20,000 and over	39	16	18	14	13
Age:					
18–24	36	20	14	19	11
25–39	3	20	17	15	9
40–59	32	27	19	8	12
60 and over	37	30	12	5	15
Occupation:					
White collar	38	17	19	12	12
Blue collar	36	22	16	14	12

Source: Daily News Record.

EXHIBIT 8
Comparative Prices for Two Items at Major Competitors

	Casual Knit Shirts			
	Brand Name			
Outlet	Ralph Lauren Polo	Ralph Lauren Chaps	Puritan	Private Label
The Casual Male	$19.00	$16.00	$13.00	—
T. J. Maxx	16.99 (Imper.)	12.99	10.99	10.99
Marshall's	17.99 (Irreg.)	13.99	10.99	11.99
D. H. Roberts	—	—	10.99	12.99
Filene's	31.00	30.00	16.00	13.00
Lord and Taylor	32.00	31.00	—	15.99
Chess King	—	—	—	—
Proving Ground	—	—	—	—

	Calvin Klein Jeans		
Outlet	Quality	Price	Sizes
The Casual Male	First Quality	$29.99	27–38
	Irregular	24.99	assorted
T. J. Maxx	Irregular	19.99	26–44
Marshall's	First Quality	24.99	A few pairs
	Irregular	19.99	A few pairs
D. H. Roberts	First Quality	24.99	A few pairs
Filene's	First Quality	37.00	26–44
Chess King	First Quality	36.00	26–44
Proving Ground	First Quality	36.00	26–44

ried a full complement of off-price menswear, Casual Male executives felt this merchandise appealed primarily to an older and more conservative customer. Syms, especially, had received much publicity lately. Sy Syms owned 10 large stores in 1982, including one in the Boston area. His sales were estimated at $115 million for the previous year with after-tax profits of $10 million. Syms specialized in menswear and was particularly well-known for his suits. His policy was to offer brand-name, nationally advertised merchandise at bargain prices. Low prices were made possible by low overhead (communal dressing rooms, sparse staff, no free alterations, etc.) and cash payment to suppliers. The store ran no sales but did declare periodic "dividends" on selected items that were announced over the store loudspeaker. Although most famous for his suits, Syms actually discounted a wide range of merchandise. In 1981, he sold 1.1 million pairs of branded panty hose for $1.25 per unit. (His purchase price had been $1.00 per unit.) Syms spent 1.5 percent of his gross on advertising, including radio and television. The messages were strictly institutional and quite conservative. The slogan was: "At Syms, an educated consumer is our best customer."[2]

Bargain Basements

A separate class of discount clothing retailers were "bargain-basement" type stores such as Filene's basement and D. H. Roberts. These stores might be connected with a full-price clothing retailer (e.g., Filene's) or run independently.

The distinguishing characteristic of the bargain basements was their lack of atmosphere. The stores were usually located in basements (urban locations) or large abandoned barns or warehouses (suburban or exurban locations). No effort was made at interior decoration. There was no discernible layout between departments, and the merchandise was piled on long tables or crowded on long hanging racks. The stores seemed dirty, crowded, and hot. Dressing rooms and credit arrangements were not provided. A minimal number of salesclerks were stationed at cash registers near the exits. Dave Norton described this ambience as "specifically designed to make the customer feel he or she had suffered so much inconvenience that he or she must be saving a lot of money."

The merchandise mix in these stores was less consistent than that of the off-price re-

---

[2]The above paragraph is based on: Walter McQuade, "The Man Who Makes Millions on Mistakes," *Fortune*, September 6, 1982, pp. 106–116.

EXHIBIT 9
Comparison of Selection in Casual Knit Shirts at Major Competitors

	Department Store	Marshall's and T. J. Maxx	The Casual Male
Sizes:	5	4	4
Colors:	10	No control over colors and patterns	15
Brands:	4 manufacturer brands 1 private label	Numerous brands, but high percentage private label	4 manufacturer brands No private label
Average No. of Units in Stock:	Approximately 1,000	Approximately 1,000	Approximately 300

tailers. Those bargain basements connected with full-price retailers sometimes sold only excess goods from their own stores, without ever buying off-price. It was believed that the independent chains were not yet large enough to have good relations with the preferred vendors. Therefore, these stores carried a mix of brand-name items marked down substantially and "no-name" items for very low prices. They did not make any effort to round out the mix of sizes, styles, and categories, or to keep fashionable items available.

Specialty Stores

Many fashion-conscious young men shopped in specialty stores that conveyed a certain fashion image that closely matches their own. Two of these stores that had merchandise similar to the "fashionable" items found at The Casual Male were Proving Ground and Chess King.

These stores had a very different ambience from the off-price retailers. First, they were usually very small (about 1,250 square feet) and were located in large shopping malls. Second, they defined their image very narrowly and carried this image through to the interior design of the store. Proving Ground and Chess King were decorated in dark contrast colors, chrome, and mirrors. Rock music was played, the lights were soft, and the walls were decorated with art design inspired by rock music or video games. These stores seemed to have a "crowded" feeling from being so full of merchandise.

The merchandise mix at Proving Ground and Chess King consisted primarily of dress and casual slacks and shirts, accessories, and specialty items (such as leather jackets). The items stocked in each category included only fashionable items with no basic looks. All the merchandise was displayed as coordinated outfits, and there were no departments in the store. Two or three young salespeople were stationed at a central cash register and were encouraged to assist customers and make suggestions. These stores carried only first-quality merchandise with infrequent mark-downs at the end of the season.

Department Stores

Executives at The Casual Male were uncertain how their stores competed with typical department stores. The majority of men's clothing shopping was done in department stores. These stores carried the widest variety of clothing categories, stocking virtually all men's items. In addition, their merchandise was presented both in departments (e.g., suits, dress shirts, etc.) and in a number of "boutiques" that conveyed an integrated fashion image similar to that found in various specialty stores. The merchandise was displayed tastefully in coordinated looks, as well as racks and shelf units.

Department stores were seen as a potential threat because of their movement into private label sales, at a price point comparable to that of off-price merchants, and because of the trend towards more frequent sales on branded goods, with substantial storewide markdowns.

Decisions for The Casual Male

Mr. Tucker felt that his company was facing a number of choices. These included:

1. *Merchandise Classification.* What were the arguments in favor and against the suggestion that suits and/or leather outerwear should be carried?
2. *Merchandise Assortment.* Should The Casual Male become more fashion oriented or oriented more to basics? It was presently estimated that 60 percent of dollar sales were derived from fashion goods and 40 percent from basics.
3. *Pricing and Margin Structure.* Should the company take a different mark-up than it was taking at present? Should it sell at a wider variety of price points? Can the store sell regular price fashion merchandise at the beginning of the season?
4. *Advertising.* What was the best strategy? Should expenditures be increased?
5. *Stores.* Was further retrenchment called for? Should the company be willing to pay higher rents for better locations?

Mr. Tucker wondered what combination of the above strategies would prove best? He also wondered whether there were other possibilities he had not thought of.

Mr. Tucker observed:

> This company did $28 million in business last year. The average shopper probably spends about $35 when he visits our stores. That means that three quarters of a million times last year, people went to our stores to buy. We should be able to build on that. There is no reason why we can't be as successful in the future as we have been in the past.

THE McLEAN TRUCKING COMPANY

Amory Mellen, President and Chief Executive Officer of the McLean Trucking Company, is concerned about several significant developments that have impacted the company's operations over the past few months. It has become apparent to him that current planning must be reviewed and updated so McLean will have a firm footing from which to anticipate future changes.

McLean Trucking is the fourth largest Class I motor-freight common-carrier of general commodities in the United States. The company employs more than 13,000 persons and serves 42 states, the District of Columbia, and the Canadian province of British Columbia. McLean operates 206 terminals to service its fleet of 14,000 tractors, trailers, and local delivery trucks. The company is primarily engaged in the transportation of Less-Than-Truckload (LTL) (shipments weighing less than 10,000 pounds) and Truckload (TL) freight. Over 70 percent of the company's operating revenue comes from LTL shipments.

McLean operates a division for specialized freight called Pacesetter Transportation. This division utilizes owner-operated flatbed, reefer, van, and container equipment to transport volume commodities nation-wide. McLean is

---

Source: This case was prepared by Bernie Berger, Jim Buchanan, Teresa Dawn, and Dave Thompson under the supervision of Professor Sexton Adams and Professor Adelaide Griffin. Permission to use granted by Sexton Adams.

EXHIBIT 1
Ten-Year Summary

	1980	1979	1978
Summary of Operations (In thousands except for per share items)			
Operating revenues			
Carrier	$598,352	$483,751	$431,812
Refinery	$121,945	$ 71,712	$ 58,431
Other	$ 4,592	$ 3,897	$ 3,453
Total	$724,889	$559,360	$493,696
Operating expenses	$725,826	$541,372	$465,742
Interest expense	$ 8,158	$ 5,959	$ 4,220
Income (loss) before income taxes			
Carrier	($ 8,368)	$ 9,010	$ 22,290
Refinery	($ 575)	$ 2,959	$ 1,696
Other	$ 1,098	$ 781	$ 570
Total	($ 7,845)	$ 12,750	$ 24,556
Income tax expense (benefit)	($ 5,414)	$ 4,630	$ 9,140
Net income loss	($ 2,432)	$ 8,120	$ 15,416
Net income (loss) per common share[a]	($ .43)	$ 1.44	$ 2.74
Cash dividends per common share[a]	$ .64	$ .64	$ .58
Selected Financial Data (In thousands except for per share items)			
Earnings (loss) retained in the business for the year	($ 6,034)	$ 4,518	$ 12,152
Current assets	$122,686	$ 99,570	$ 74,145
Tangible property cost	$271,509	$261,042	$212,658
Current liabilities	$ 81,251	$ 72,730	$ 54,354
Long-term debt	$111,468	$ 93,956	$ 54,129
Working capital	$ 41,434	$ 26,840	$ 19,791
Shareholders' equity	$102,950	$108,984	$104,458
Book value per common share[a]	$ 18.29	$ 19.36	$ 18.56
Selected Operating Data (Exclusive of noncarrier revenue and expenses)			
Revenue per mile	$ 2.32	$ 1.99	$ 1.85
Revenue per 100 pounds	$ 6.72	$ 4.62	$ 4.20
Pounds billed (in millions)	8,903	10,468	10,280
Number of shipments (in thousands)	6,514	5,601	5,583
Average weight per shipment (lbs.)	1,367	1,869	1,841
Average load (lbs.)	27,663	29,404	29,269
Ton miles of intercity freight carried (in millions)	3,570	3,576	3,413
Intercity miles traveled (in thousands)	258,116	243,252	233,217
Average haul (miles)	802	683	664
Number of employees at end of year	13,767	13,636	11,428
Average carrier revenue per employee	$ 43,463	$ 40,648[c]	$ 37,785
Average ton miles per carrier employee	259,323	300,507[c]	298,652

[a] All "per common share" data have been adjusted to reflect two-for-one stock splits effective January 14, 1972 and July 1, 1976.
[b] Acquired Winston Refining Co. (formerly Fort Worth Refining Company) October 1, 1973.
[c] Based on average number of carrier employees.

	1977	1976	1975	1974[b]	1973	1972	1971
	$375,096	$319,708	$266,132	$277,515	$232,952	$194,226	$169,363
	$ 58,975	$ 49,959	$ 52,594	$ 31,657			
	$ 3,120	$ 2,034	$ 1,643	$ 1,750	$ 1,110	$ 867	$ 672
	$437,191	$371,701	$320,369	$310,922	$234,062	$195,093	$170,035
	$407,738	$341,922	$299,894	$286,200	$213,358	$176,728	$155,782
	$ 2,849	$ 2,927	$ 4,181	$ 3,729	$ 2,291	$ 2,199	$ 2,463
	$ 24,646	$ 24,767	$ 15,325	$ 20,878	$ 18,722	$ 16,176	$ 11,791
	$ 2,280	$ 2,198	$ 1,748	$ 704			
	$ 500	$ 368	$ 351	$ 314	$ 184	$ 146	$ 124
	$ 27,426	$ 27,333	$ 17,424	$ 21,896	$ 18,906	$ 16,323	$ 11,915
	$ 12,125	$ 12,367	$ 7,433	$ 10,338	$ 8,673	$ 7,711	$ 5,886
	$ 15,301	$ 14,967	$ 9,991	$ 11,558	$ 10,233	$ 8,612	$ 6,029
	$ 2.73	$ 2.68	$ 1.79	$ 2.07	$ 1.84	$ 1.55	$ 1.09
	$ .46	$ .415	$ .36	$ .345	$ .30	$ .30	$ .25
	$ 12,727	$ 12,651	$ 7,983	$ 9,634	$ 8,561	$ 6,940	$ 4,638
	$ 57,877	$ 58,773	$ 50,150	$ 51,208	$ 35,579	$ 33,909	$ 27,287
	$179,344	$160,202	$139,703	$124,508	$107,512	$ 95,372	$ 91,102
	$ 47,076	$ 50,568	$ 36,354	$ 40,345	$ 24,580	$ 25,833	$ 18,382
	$ 33,319	$ 34,741	$ 43,910	$ 39,618	$ 33,117	$ 30,561	$ 34,967
	$ 10,801	$ 8,205	$ 13,796	$ 10,862	$ 11,000	$ 8,076	$ 8,905
	$ 92,207	$ 78,860	$ 66,135	$ 58,151	$ 48,490	$ 39,930	$ 32,972
	$ 16.40	$ 14.13	$ 11.86	$ 10.43	$ 8.70	$ 7.16	$ 5.92
	$ 1.73	$ 1.56	$ 1.47	$ 1.33	$ 1.19	$ 1.11	$ 1.02
	$ 3.98	$ 3.70	$ 3.43	$ 3.01	$ 2.83	$ 2.78	$ 2.57
	9,415	8,635	7,700	9,220	8,243	6,979	6,591
	5,752	5,196	4,753	5,284	5,142	4,720	4,755
	1,637	1,662	1,635	1,745	1,603	1,479	1,386
	28,526	27,012	26,940	27,339	25,264	23,963	24,136
	3,087	2,766	2,434	2,843	2,480	2,089	2,006
	216,438	204,776	180,670	207,970	196,330	174,320	166,270
	656	641	626	617	602	599	609
	10,519	10,167	9,295	10,127	9,600	8,635	8,343
	$ 35,700	$ 31,400	$ 28,600	$ 27,800	$ 24,200	$ 22,600	$ 20,400
	293,500	272,000	261,800	285,000	256,700	241,900	240,500

[a] All "per common share" data have been adjusted to reflect two-for-one stock splits effective January 14, 1972 and July 1, 1976.
[b] Acquired Winston Refining Co. (formerly Fort Worth Refining Company) October 1, 1973.
[c] Based on average number of carrier employees.

also the parent currently to four wholly owned subsidiaries: Houston Trailer & Truck Body, Inc., Modern Automotive Services, Inc., Salem Contract Carrier, Inc., and Malja Corporation. These will be discussed in further detail in the next section.

On July 1, 1981, President Jimmy Carter signed into law the Motor Carrier Act of 1980 (1980 MCA). The 1980 MCA completed the federal government's moves toward deregulation of the trucking industry. Bennett Whitlock, Jr., the president of the American Trucking Associations (ATA), an industry trade group representing the larger trucking firms, commented that what the consumer needed was "Reregulation," not deregulation. The ATA is opposed to the 1980 MCA.

Fuel prices increased 85 percent in 1979 and another 30 percent in 1980. This increase is forcing McLean to rethink its route structure and equipment design to improve fuel economy. Recent litigation in both state and federal courts is having an impact on which states will allow length and weight restrictions on vehicles to be relaxed. A work stoppage by the Teamsters union, which represents organized labor in the trucking industry, occurred in April 1979. Significant wage concessions were made to get the freight rolling again. An influx of private carriers have gained a good portion of market share. As Mr. Mellen reflects over these events, it is obvious there has never been a greater need for effective management. A 10-year summary of operations for McLean is presented in Exhibit 1.

Corporate History

McLean trucking began operations in North Carolina in 1934. It has grown since that time through mergers with other trucking firms, purchase of the operating rights held by other firms, and by obtaining new route authorization from the Interstate Commerce Commission (ICC). A summary of the important events in McLean's history is found in Exhibit 2.

The first of the wholly owned subsidiaries is Houston Trailer & Truck Body, Inc. This unit repairs and rebuilds aluminum and stainless-steel tankers and trailers. Many of these units are used in the McLean fleet. The upper photo in Exhibit 3 shows shop operations in the main plant. Houston Trailer is one of the largest suppliers of heavy-duty trailer parts in the Southwest.

The second subsidiary is Modern Automotive Services, Inc., of Winston–Salem. Modern is the maintenance arm of McLean, doing preventive maintenance, major overhauls, repairs, and rebuilds on power units. The firm also operates a tire recapping plant for tires used in the McLean fleet. Purchasing and procurement duties are handled by Modern for the entire McLean company. A picture showing trucks in the shop is also shown in Exhibit 3.

The third subsidiary is Salem Contract Carrier, Inc., which operates as a contract carrier serving the K-Mart Corporation. It is based in Charlotte, North Carolina, where K-Mart

EXHIBIT 2
Important Events in McLean's History

1934	Founded March 10 in North Carolina.
1943	Established general offices in Winston–Salem, North Carolina, June 7.
1945	Purchased operating authority of American Trucking Company, November 1.
1947	Purchased operating authority of Pee Dee Express, Inc., October 31.
1948	Purchased operating authority of Simpson Motor Lines, Inc., April 2.
1951	Purchased operating authority of Fleetway Motor Freight, Inc., November 9.
1952	Acquired Modern Automotive Services, Inc. as a wholly owned subsidiary (maintenance).
1953	Organized Malja Corporation as a wholly owned subsidiary (real estate).

EXHIBIT 2 (*Continued*)

1957	Merged Carolina Motor Express Lines, Inc. (CMX) July 1, following operation under temporary authority since February 18, 1952.
1958	Trading in McLean Trucking Company common stock on the New York Stock Exchange began January 6, first in the industry on the "Big Board."
	Merged Service, Incorporated May 16, following operation under temporary authority since June 26, 1956.
1963	Merged Hayes Freight Lines, Inc. December 31, following operation under temporary authority since July 16, 1958.
1966	Merged Chicago Express, Inc. (CXI) December 31, following operation under temporary authority since December 13, 1962.
1968	Purchased and merged Daily Transport, Inc., June 1.
	Purchased operating authority of Almar's Express Inc., June 24.
1969	Purchased Young–Hall–West Equipment Corp., Houston, Texas, September 30, and merged its principal operating subsidiary, Herrin Transportation Company, October 1.
1970	Purchased operating authority of Harrison Motor Express January 30, following operation under temporary authority since October 1, 1968.
1970	Purchased operating authority of Murray's Fast Express, Inc., April 27, following operation under temporary authority since November 24, 1969.
1971	Purchased operating authority of Boston and Maine Transportation Company, Inc. October 31, following operation under leased rights since May 14.
1973	Organized Winston Refining Co. as a wholly owned subsidiary, and merged Fort Worth Refining Company, Fort Worth, Texas, into Winston Refining Co. November 1. Fort Worth Refining Company was purchased October 1.
1974	Purchased partial operating authority of Valley Express, Inc., Schofield, Wisconsin, May 23, extending service to Milwaukee, Wisconsin.
1977	Purchased operating authority of South Texas Motor Lines, Inc. March 15, following operation under temporary authority since June 18, 1976.
	Merged Topeka Motor Freight, Inc. July 31. Commenced operating under temporary authority October 1, 1972.
	Purchased Wolverine Express, Inc. of Muskegon, Michigan, October 1, extending service to a major portion of Michigan.
1978	Merged Crescent Motor Lines of Spartanburg, South Carolina, August 15. Crescent had been operated as a wholly owned subsidiary since May 1.
	Occupied new corporate headquarters building in Winston–Salem beginning November 6. It had been under construction since May 1976.
1979	Purchased certain operating rights of ET & WNC Transportation Company February 20, following operation under temporary authority since November 15, 1977.
	Received temporary authority from the Interstate Commerce Commission May 1 to lease the operating authority of O. N. C. Freight Systems, the general-commodity motor-freight business of ROCOR International of Palo Alto, California.
	Following ICC temporary approval, organized Salem Contract Carrier, Inc. August 16, 1979 as a wholly owned subsidiary to provide specialized contract carrier service.
	Sold operating authority and equipment of Herrin Petroleum Transport Equipment Corp., September 26, 1979 to the Sunbelt Transport, Inc., of Dallas, Texas.
	Merged Wolverine Express, Inc. December 31, 1979 after operating it as a wholly owned subsidiary since October 1, 1977.
1980	Received initial ICC decision May 16, 1980 pertaining to the grant of permanent authority to acquire the assets of O. N. C. Freight Systems.
	Reorganized Special Commodities Division as Pacesetter Transportation and moved its headquarters June 16, 1980 from Hammond, Indiana to Winston–Salem, North Carolina.
	Sold Winston Refining Co. on October 31, 1980.
1981	Received authority from the ICC to serve all points in Alabama and Mississippi.

EXHIBIT 3
Shop Operations

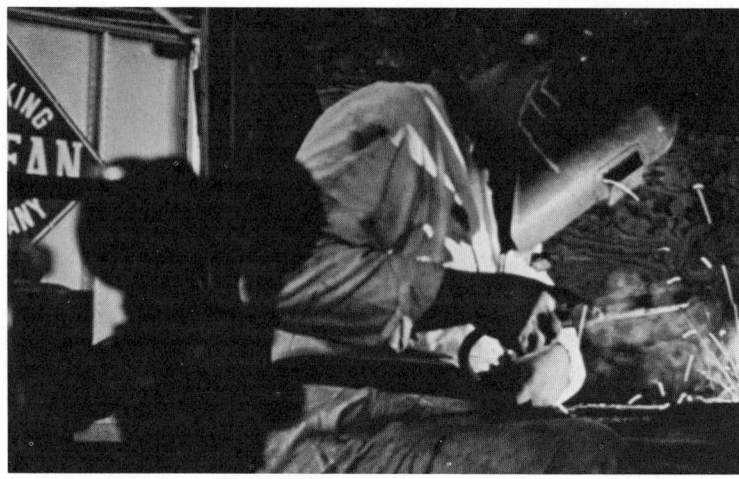

WELDING A PART NEEDED IN THE BODY DEPARTMENT OF THE MAIN SHOPS OF HOUSTON TRAILER & TRUCK BODY, INC.

PREVENTIVE MAINTENANCE ON POWER UNITS IS PERFORMED BY MODERN AUTOMOTIVE SERVICES, INC

has a major distribution facility, and handles K-Mart movements to points in 24 states. This unit was formed in an effort to take advantage of industry deregulation. Contract business provides a guaranteed amount of freight at a prearranged price. According to Lynn Perucca, the sales manager for McLean in Carollton, Texas, Salem has proved itself to be a profitable unit. McLean can be expected to expand its contract operations.

The fourth subsidiary is the Malja Corporation, which is a real-estate holding company for terminals and other properties throughout the McLean system. Malja is responsible for locating and acquiring terminal space, including the construction of new facilities. In fast growing markets, some of these facilities are acquired through lease agreements, and Malja Modern Automotive Services is held for them by Malja.

Management

The top management and directors of McLean are listed in Exhibit 4. The Board of Directors meets monthly to discuss operating results and corporate policy and direction. Exhibit 5 shows the Board during a meeting.

It has been the policy of McLean to stress achievement in its management team, and to use a college recruitment program to obtain persons who can quickly develop into qualified managers. Trainees hired under this program begin their career loading freight in a terminal. After a few weeks, they drive over-the-road trucks for a few months, in order to develop an understanding of the McLean system, where it is, and how it works. Other typical assignments in the first year of employment include Dispatcher, Bookkeeper, and Loading Supervisor. This training and variety of job assignments lets upper management appraise the trainees' potential accurately. Personnel hired under this program are expected to advance beyond first-level supervisory positions.

Management takes pride in the fact that almost all of McLean's executives are college degreed, and believes that this is unique in the trucking industry, but consistent with the innovativeness and complexity of McLean.

EXHIBIT 4
Executive Officers and Directors (Year Elected)

*Paul P. Davis (1948)
    Chairman of the Board.
    Chairman of the Executive Committee.
    Joined the Company in 1943.
    Elected President in 1955.
    Elected to present office in 1970.
*Amory Mellen, Jr. (1968)
    President and Chief Executive Officer.
    Member of the Executive Committee.
    Joined the Company in 1951.
    Elected President in 1970.
    Elected Chief Executive Officer in 1976.
*Fred C. Bauer (1971)
    Executive Vice-President/Marketing.
    Member of the Executive Committee.
    Joined the Company in 1951.
    Elected to present office in 1974.

*Claude M. Hamrick (1975)
    Vice President/General Counsel.
    Secretary.
    Joined the Company in 1977.
    Elected to present office in 1977.
C. R. Jones
    Vice President/Labor Relations.
    Joined the Company in 1975.
    Elected to present office in 1976.
Floyd L. Morris
    Vice President/Maintenance.
    Joined the Company in 1961.
    Elected to present office in 1978.
John R. Morris
    Vice President/Midwestern Division.
    Joined the Company in 1963.
    Elected to present office in 1979.

EXHIBIT 4 (Continued)

*Joe B. Eldridge (1974)
  Executive Vice-President/
    Administration.
  Treasurer.
  Member of the Executive Committee.
  Joined the Company in 1952.
  Elected to present office in 1974.
*David J. Wanchick (1979)
  Executive Vice-President/Field
    Operations.
  Joined the Company in 1979.
  Elected to present office in 1979.
Alvin M. Bodford
  Vice President/Comptroller.
  Joined the Company in 1973.
  Elected to present office in 1978.
Edwin R. Brenegar, Jr.
  Vice President/Personnel.
  Joined the Company in 1949.
  Elected to present office in 1974.
Wilton W. Broadwell
  Vice President/Western Division.
  Joined the Company in 1953.
  Elected to present office in 1979.
Alton Z. Canady
  Vice President/Transportation.
  Joined the Company in 1950.
  Elected to present office in 1977.
S. Vernon Cartner
  Vice President/Traffic.
  Joined the Company in 1949.
  Elected to present office in 1979.
P. Michael Davis
  Vice President/Eastern Division.
  Joined the Company in 1962.
  Elected to present office in 1979.
T. Michael Guthrie
  Vice President/Claims Prevention.
  Joined the Company in 1974.
  Elected to present office in 1980.

James C. Ratcliff
  Vice President/Sales.
  Joined the Company in 1948.
  Elected to present office in 1974.
Myron W. Sexton
  Vice President/Southern Division.
  Joined the Company in 1953.
  Elected to present office in 1976.
Gordon M. Sisk, Jr.
  Vice President/Pacesetter
    Transportation.
  (Special Commodities Division)
  Joined the Company in 1956.
  Elected to present office in 1980.
Charles W. Staley
  Vice President/Real Estate.
  Joined the Company in 1952.
  Elected to present office in 1961.
Robert H. Sykes
  Vice President/Southwestern Division.
  Joined the Company in 1963.
  Elected to present office in 1976.
*James K. Glenn (1971)
  General Partner, Quality Oil Company,
    Winston–Salem, North Carolina
  Member of the Executive Committee.
  Member of the Audit Committee.
*J. Berkley Ingram, Jr. (1977)
  Vice Chairman of the Board, Massa-
    chusetts Mutual Life Insurance Com-
    pany, Springfield Massachusetts.
  Chairman of the Audit Committee.
*Dalton L. McMichael (1979)
  Chairman of the Board
  Chief Executive Officer and Treasurer,
    MacField Texturing, Inc., Madison,
    North Carolina.
*Claude H. Wells, Jr. (1955)
  Retired Vice-President/Operations.
  McLean Trucking Company.
  Member of the Audit Committee.

*Member of the Board of Directors.

EXHIBIT 5
Board of Directors

Seated left to right: Claude M. Hamrick, Henry D. Ward, Joe G. Eldridge, T. W. Andrews, Amory Mellen, Jr., Paul P. Davis, Claude H. Wells, Jr., James K. Glenn, L. T. Bretherton, Fred C. Bauer.

Operations

The organization chart in Exhibit 6 shows that McLean has adopted a geographically divisionalized structure for its trucking operations. Five geographic divisions are headed by a vice president. The sixth division is Pacesetter Transportation, and it is also headed by a vice president.

Each of the division vice-presidents have numerous district managers reporting to them. The district managers are in control of local operations. An integrated computer system, utilizing an IBM 370 mainframe and central processor, speeds the communication and control process. All of the 206 freight terminals are linked to the main computer in Winston–Salem with an input/output printer. Full-period, WATS, and regular telephone lines tie the system together.

The district managers are provided daily operations summaries through the computer. This data organizes such items as fuel and maintenance expense, payroll costs, sales, cash flow, and return on investment. Variances from budget are calculated and highlighted for comparison.

Reporting to the district managers are the safety managers, sales managers, and terminal managers. The local sales representatives report to the sales managers. The terminal managers, who are responsible for the movement of freight into, out of, and within a terminal, supervise drivers, dockmen, dispatchers, and local supervisory personnel. Safety managers are responsible for administering safety procedures within the district.

As the organization chart also shows, the other functional areas are individually headed by vice presidents, who report to executive vice-presidents. McLean is in the business of hauling freight, and these other functions provide support to the trucking operations. National accounts, for example, are handled by sales personnel from the corporate office in addition to local sales representatives.

The McLean Fleet

McLean purchases equipment through special order. The fleet is large enough that the com-

EXHIBIT 6
Organization Chart

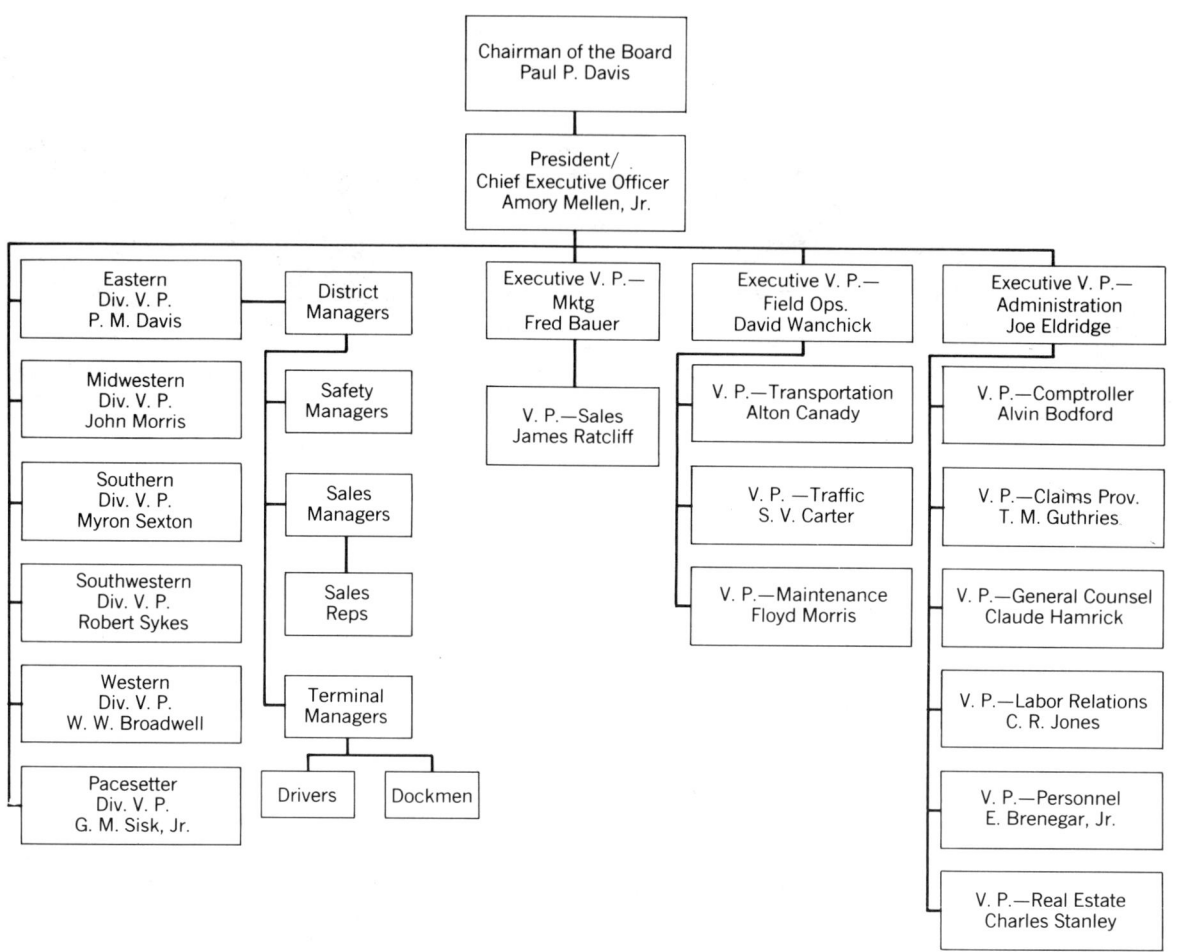

pany feels this can be done economically. The budgeting system, assisted by the computer, helps in the equipment planning process. When the decision is made to purchase units, the bid routine begins. McLean will specify how many units are needed and the exact equipment needed. The trucks will be custom-made for McLean, with the particular engines, transmissions, axles, and other features desired. Specification sheets are sent to all truck manufacturers with requests for bids.

McLean has purchased many makes of trucks over the years. Currently, General Motors Corporation has received the majority of McLean's business. GMC is also one of McLean's largest shippers. Mr. Niendorhf, District Manager for Texas and Louisiana, noted in an interview that Caterpillar Diesel engines are being used almost exclusively now because of their excellent fuel economy and longevity. Company statistics show that a $1.0-million annual savings in fuel expense is achieved for every one-tenth of a gallon improvement in fleet fuel mileage ratings.

The trailer fleet consists mainly of 40 and 45 foot trailers. McLean does have some 27 foot "pup" units that can be operated as doubles, but because the route structure has been based historically in the South and East, it was never deemed feasible to build a large fleet of these. Mr. Perucca, the Carrollton Sales Manager, explained that it can become an operations nightmare to manage a fleet with short and long units intermixed. Clearly, it is not economical to haul pup units individually over long distances as opposed to 40 foot units, so they must always be scheduled as doubles. Although it is possible to track each unit and keep up with each trailer by length so the correct balance of units at each terminal can be maintained, it is a burdensome task even now. With the relaxing of length laws in some states, it may become feasible to begin using more pup trailers.

Trailers typically have a depreciable life of 10 years. Power units will normally last for five to seven years.

The Computer System

McLean uses its computer as a sophisticated tool in moving freight. It keeps up with each bill of lading (the document that in effect is an order for McLean's services) currently in the system, and can be inquired on a real-time basis to locate shipments. If a customer calls wanting to know when his delivery will arrive, it can be located within seconds and advice given. This system also knows at any given time what driver is driving the truck the shipment is in, if it is not on a dock somewhere. Department of Transportation regulations require a driver to work no more than 10 consecutive hours without an eight-hour rest period. The computer keeps up with each driver in this regard; other personnel data are also maintained for administrative functions. A mileage and maintenance history is kept on all units in the fleet. A report is printed daily showing which units are due for an oil change, preventive maintenance, or a major overhaul.

Management believes that the integrated computer system, which it calls its Management Information System, has helped McLean grow to its present size by smoothing operations. McLean delivers over 100,000 shipments weekly; it is felt that the activity needed to coordinate and control this would be ineffective without the computer. It is also used for accounting and record-keeping in many other phases of the business, such as payroll, planning, and tracking operating results. Each district manager is provided a daily report on the profit margin earned by revenue breakdown in his territory.

The Terminal Network

Moving the thousands of pieces of freight that enter the system daily is the most complex task of trucking companies. The management of McLean believes that most Class I and II carriers are basically homogenous in the eyes of the shipper, except for one factor: service. McLean has built its operation strategy around providing more service to each customer. Frequently, this translates into being first and fastest in getting a shipment from its origin to its destination.

McLean has an extensive terminal network. Amory Mellen stated, "Firmly believing in the long-team future of the large, service, and LTL-oriented common carrier, McLean is continuing to expand its operations and the areas it serves." Ten new terminals were opened during 1980.

McLean's present terminal network is concentrated in the Midwest and Southeast and is reflective of the industrial strength in the former and the strength of the furniture, tobacco, and textile industries in the latter. McLean began its operations serving the textile industry. New openings of terminals in 1980 were slightly favored to the South: six vs. four in the Northern states. McLean's strategy has been to open terminals in target geographic regions rather than where certain target customers or industries are. Every shipper is thought to be a potential McLean customer. The terminal network is considered by sources in the industry to be a key factor in the future, especially in the LTL business.

Local Terminals

McLean uses a network concept in routing freight, in which local terminals are clustered around 16 larger terminals that are known as break-bulk terminals. In essence, the local terminals feed freight into their break-bulk, which consolidates freight for shipment to other break-bulk facilities where the process reverses.

The individual local terminals have local trucks operating out of them that make pick-ups and deliveries in their assigned community. A dispatcher is in touch via two-way radio with each driver to tell him/her to make a pick-up at a particular shipper if the truck is not otherwise stopping there. The local trucks, which may be either a tractor-trailer combination or a one-piece "Bobtail" unit, return every evening to their local terminal, with freight moving to any point in the world.

The freight is taken off the trucks, and each individual shipment is weighed. The number of pieces on the bill of lading turned in by the driver is checked and the weight is posted on it. Tariffs provide different rates for many classes of goods, so an accurate description of the particular goods in the shipment is placed on the bill of lading, along with the appropriate charges based upon length of haul and special handling required. This information is fed into the computer system, which prints a final bill of lading for the shipment and sends an invoice for payment to the correct party. Not all shipments are paid for by the shipper.

The next step in processing the freight is to get it loaded onto the appropriate truck for shipment out. McLean uses a cross-dock operation in most of its terminals. A group of local trucks, which have assigned routes, park each evening at their assigned door. A dockman is assigned to handle a group of three to five doors, depending upon the normal volume of freight coming across. The dockman for door set "A," for example, will take freight off the trucks parked at his doors, weigh it, and place it on a cart labeled by destination. He is also responsible for loading the trucks at his door set.

If the "A" dockman is idle but the dockman at door set "B" is busy, "A" will come over and help "B." This helps to utilize each dockman fully. McLean has used constant motion conveyor systems in the past, that require a dockman to be present at his assigned doors at all times. It was felt by management that some dock workers were only utilized productively for four to six hours out of an eight-hour day.

The cross-dock method provides that as the freight is moved off a truck and weighed, it moves to the appropriate truck bound for the break-bulk terminal. This truck will be parked directly across from the local truck, normally. As freight comes in from the break-bulk for local delivery, the same procedure is followed, except there is no need to weigh the goods.

Break-Bulk Terminals

As many trucks as are necessary will move each night from the local terminals to their assigned break-bulk terminals. All freight, unless it will be delivered out of the same terminal that made the pick-up, moves in this fashion. A cluster of local terminals feed their freight into their break-bulk and receive their freight to deliver from their break-bulk.

The freight moves through each break-bulk facility in much the same way it moves through a local terminal. It is off-loaded from a truck and loaded onto another, which is bound for the break-bulk terminal serving the final destination. The over-the-road units will be "Cubed out" (loaded fully), and move their destination break-bulk. A break-bulk terminal is illustrated in Exhibit 7. In the event the dis-

EXHIBIT 7
Interior of the Winston-Salem Break-Bulk Terminal[a]

[a]Freight moving across this dock alone averages over two million pounds a day.

tance from one break-bulk to another is longer than a 10-hour trip, a relief driver will meet the originating driver at a predetermined checkpoint. Two-man driver teams were used formerly, but in those cases one man was inactive at any given time.

Management believes there are two advantages to the break-bulk method of operation combined with the relief driver system. First, with average highway operation costs of $1 per mile, it is very important to move as much freight on each unit as possible. Second, this arrangement keeps equipment and freight moving. Each break-bulk operates a maintenance base to service trucks as they move in and out for routine and preventive items.

Marketing

McLean considers itself to be an aggressive marketer of its services. Sales representatives call on established accounts and seek new ones on a regular basis. During a sales call, the sales person establishes which person at the shipper actually decides which freight line will be used. In some cases, a traffic manager is responsible for the decision, but often it is a shipping clerk who makes the choice. The sales effort keys on the appropriate person. Items such as calendars, note pads, coffee mugs, and terminal directories are used as sales tools.

A nation-wide advertising campaign supplements these personal contact efforts. Ads are placed in a variety of business and industry periodicals. Direct mail is also used to promote special programs. Discount rates are offered to some cities in an effort to balance the flow of shipments from and to any break-bulk pair. McLean has closely controlled this program.

Another promotional effort is the "Diamond Back" service now offered between certain break-bulk pairs. Those pairs having a very high volume of traffic are advertised through direct mail for their quick delivery time. This commitment can be made because of the high volume.

Substantial changes happened to the character of the business in 1980. The average weight of each shipment decreased to 1,369 pounds, the lowest in 10 years. The record high had been set in 1979 at 1,869 pounds. The number of shipments, however, was up to 6.5 million in 1980, a new high that helped offset the lower average shipment weight. The average distance of each haul had been steadily increasing the last nine years, going up 10 to 20 miles per year. A large jump was recognized in 1980, from 683 miles in 1979 to 802. The longer, lighter hauls are more characteristic of McLean today.

McLean was the first of the Class I common carriers to set up a separate contract division (Salem Transportation, Inc.), although Yellow Freight and Carolina Freight are two other Class I common carriers that have followed suit. McLean's plans are to continue expanding the contract operation. The Value Line Investment Survey in January 1981 stated that one of the major reasons TL business has been depressed for common carriers is because of the aggressiveness of some independent, specialized contract carriers. As one manager noted, McLean is going after this business.

Financial Review

Operating revenue in 1980 was up 29.6 percent over that for 1979, but McLean suffered a loss of $2.4 million, as shown in Exhibit 8. This loss equates to a loss of $0.43 per share, the first loss in the company's modern history. Exhibits 8 through 12 show financial data for the fiscal years 1979 and 1980.

On October 31, 1980, McLean sold one of its wholly owned subsidiaries, The Winston Refining Company. This unit is not included as one of the four current subsidiaries. McLean had owned Winston since 1973. The decision to sell the refinery was made primarily for two reasons: to get out of the petroleum industry and to get rid of a significant drain of financial resources. Winston operated at a loss of $575,000 in 1980. The sale of Winston enabled McLean to reduce short-term debt by $3.0 million and long-term debt by $15.0 million.

Current financial reports for operations that will be included in the fiscal 1981 year are presented in Exhibits 13 and 14.

McLean has revolving credit through a group of commercial banks, where a $50.0 million line of credit is available at the prime rate in effect when a borrowing is made. An agreement exists with the banks for this credit; McLean has agreed in this covenant to refrain from retiring capital stock, to restrict dividends, and to incur no more than $50.0 million in long-term debt. McLean has increased its debt under this agreement from $23.0 million in 1979 to 41.0 million in 1980, and thus has a $9.0 million leeway left.

Overall, McLean follows a fairly conservative line of accounting policies. Revenue is recognized on the date the shipment is picked up from the shipper. Inventory is accounted for on the average cost method, and depreciation of tangible property is accounted for on the straight-line basis. Costs of truck maintenance and repairs are expensed as they are incurred, unless the repairs are actually improvements over the original condition of the

EXHIBIT 8
Highlights for the Fiscal Years Ended June 30

	1980	1979
Operating revenues	$724,888,627	$559,360,342
Income (loss) before income taxes	($ 7,845,432)	$ 12,749,781
Net income (loss)	($ 2,431,832)	$ 8,119,781
Net income (loss) per common share	($ 0.43)	$ 1.44
Shares of common stock outstanding	5,628,492	5,628,492
Cash dividends on common shares	$ 3,602,235	$ 3,602,235
Dividends per common share	$ 0.64	$ 0.64
Operating ratio (carrier only)	100.33%	97.20%

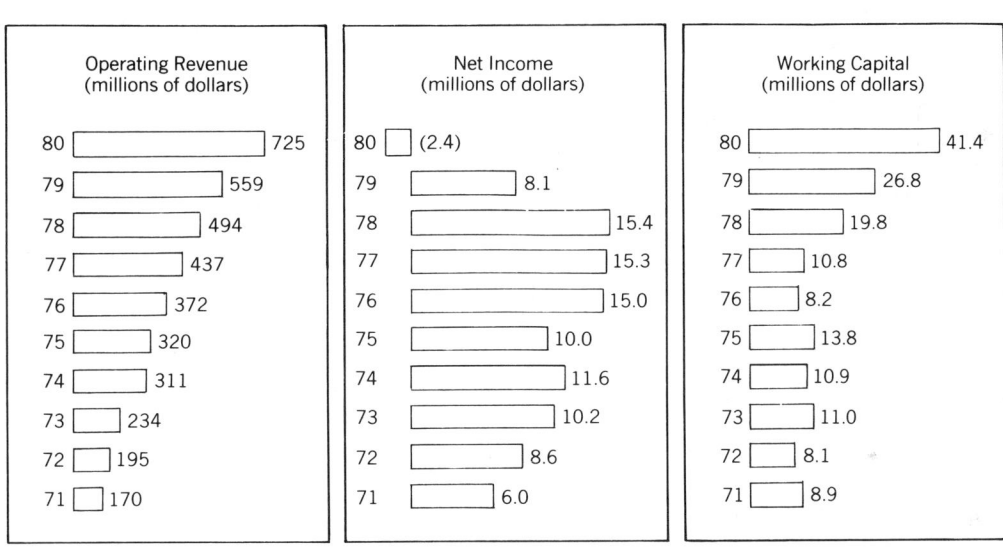

EXHIBIT 9
Distribution of the 1980 Revenue Dollar

Wages, salaries, and employee benefits		
Drivers	$0.290	
Terminal employees	0.206	
Sales and traffic force	0.018	
Maintenance employees	0.042	
General office force	0.015	
Refinery employees	0.003	
Officers	0.002	$0.576
Operation and maintenance		0.371
Operating taxes and licenses		0.023
Depreciation		0.031
Interest and other deductions		0.010
Income taxes		(0.008)
Shareholders' equity { Cash dividends	0.005	
Decrease in retained earnings	(0.008)	(0.003)
Total		$1.00

equipment, in which case the costs are capitalized and subsequently depreciated.

The operating rights granted McLean by the ICC were amortized over a 40-year period, as with most intangibles. Because of deregulation, the value of these rights was written off during the second quarter of fiscal 1981, which ended December 31, 1980. The rights were deemed worthless by the company because of the 1980 MCA. This write-off resulted in a net loss of $10.8 million or $1.92 per share.

A review of McLean's current balance sheet shows increases in cash and short-term investments, an increase in inventories, and a decrease in long-term debt for 1980. McLean had to layoff 3,000 employees in the third

EXHIBIT 10
Comparative Consolidated Income Statements (thousands of dollars)

	June 30			Percentage Increase (Decrease) from Previous Year		Common Size Information		
	1980	1979	1978	1980	1979	1980	1979	1978
Total Operating Revenue	724,889	559,360	493,696	29.6	13.3	100%	100%	100%
Wages, Salaries, and Benefits	409,341	328,763	287,054	24.5	14.5	56%	59%	58%
Operations and Maintenance	110,334	75,957	63,262	43.5	20	15%	14%	13%
Operating Taxes and Licenses	16,796	14,576	13,862	15.2	5.2	2%	3%	3%
Insurance	16,016	13,882	11,003	15.4	26.2	2%	2%	2%
Communications and Utilities	8,261	6,376	5,950	29.6	7.2	1%	1%	1%
Depreciation	21,330	17,571	14,913	21.4	17.8	3%	3%	3%
Rent and Purchased Transportation	18,265	13,074	10,470	39.7	24.9	3%	2%	2%
Total Operating Expenses	600,342	470,199	406,514	30	15.7	83%	84%	82%
Cost of Sales	125,484	71,172	59,228	76.3	20.2	17%	13%	12%
Net Operating Income	(938)	17,988	27,954	(105)	(35.7)	—	3%	6%
Other Income	1,493	961	994	55.4	(3.3)	—	—	—
Interest Expense	8,158	5,969	4,220	36.7	36.7	1%	1%	1%
Other Deductions	242	241	172	0	40	—	—	—
Income Taxes	(5,414)	4,630	9,140	(216.9)	(49.3)	—	1%	2%
Net Income	(2,432)	8,120	15,416	(130)	(47.32)	—	1.5%	3%
Retained Earnings, Beginning of Year	104,474	99,957	87,805					
Dividends	3,602	3,602	3,264					
Retained Earnings, End of Year	98,440	104,475	99,957					

quarter of 1980 because high labor costs and small shipment net volume made the previous force level unnecessary.

McLean reduced some of its operating loss in 1980 by taking advantage of the Investment Tax Credit and by capitalizing interest costs on construction. This produced a net benefit of $7.4 million.

The Outlook

The trucking industry closely tracks economic activity. Consequently, truck traffic dropped in early 1981 and seems unlikely to score a significant rebound until perhaps the second half of 1981, by which time the economy will again be supporting rising freight tonnage. Earnings of trucking companies may be bottoming, as cost reductions come in line with reduced business and weak pricing in the wake of deregulation.

Economic indicators continue to show a slow rise from the recession of early 1980. However, the strong areas of the economy have been services, electronics, and communications, not automotive, steel, and manufactured products. The future of the common carrier is tied to the economy in general, but ecertainly to the manufacturing industries. As Mr. Mellen noted in the 1980 annual report, "Frankly, we do not expect a return to our historical profit margins until there is an improvement in the economy." McLean has set a goal to return to profitability in fiscal 1981.

Drake Sheahan and Stewart Dougall, Inc.,

EXHIBIT 11
Comparative Consolidated Balance Sheets (thousands of dollars)

Assets	June 30			Percentage Increase (Decrease) from Previous Year		Common Size Information		
	1980	1979	1978	1980	1979	1980	1979	1978
Current Assets								
Cash	16,592	9,490	13,042	74.8	(27)	5%	3%	6%
Accounts Receivable	59,305	56,603	36,387	4.8	55.5	20%	20%	16%
Prepayments	15,203	16,156	13,989	(5.8)	15.5	5%	6%	6%
Inventory	24,985	12,628	10,106	97.9	25	8%	4%	5%
Other Current Assets	6,599	4,692	621	40.6	656	2%	2%	0.3%
Total Current Assets	122,686	99,569	74,145	23.2	34.3	40%	35%	33%
Operating Property	271,509	261,042	212,658	4	22.8	90%	92%	96%
Less Depreciation	106,171	90,849	77,304	16.9	17.5	(35%)	(32%)	(35%)
Net Property	165,338	170,193	135,354	(2.9)	25.7	55%	60%	61%
Intangible Property (Net)	12,220	12,002	9,838	1.8	22	4%	4%	4%
Other Assets	2,951	1,628	2,206	81.3	(26.2)	1%	1%	1%
Total Assets	303,195	283,392	221,543	7	27.9	100%	100%	100%

Liabilities and Shareholders' Equity	June 30			Percentage Increase (Decrease) from Previous Year		Common Size Information		
	1980	1979	1978	1980	1979	1980	1979	1978
Liabilities								
Notes Payable	2,000	0	0	—	—	1%	—	—
Accounts Payable	24,222	21,682	15,130	11.7	43.3	8%	8%	7%
Accrued Payroll, Taxes, Etc.	15,284	15,372	14,053	(0.6)	9.4	5%	5%	6%
Bonuses and Other Accruals	18,383	16,633	12,283	10.5	35.4	6%	6%	6%
Federal and State Taxes	0	0	1,295	—	—	—	—	0.6%
Dividends Payable	901	901	816	—	—	0.2%	0.3%	0.4%
Long-Term Debt due in One Year	5,606	5,392	1,693	4	218.5	2%	2%	1%
Other Liabilities	14,857	12,750	9,084	—	—	5%	4%	4%
Total Current Liabilities	81,251	72,730	54,354	11.7	33.8	27%	26%	25%
Long-Term Debt	105,862	88,564	52,437	19.5	68.9	35%	31%	24%
Deferred Federal and State Income Tax	10,306	10,759	8,332	(4.2)	29.1	3%	4%	4%
Other Reserves	2,825	2,355	1,962	20	20	1%	1%	1%
Common Stock	2,814	2,814	2,814	—	—	1%	1%	1%
Premium on Stock	1,696	1,696	1,687	—	—	0.5%	0.6%	0.8%
Retained Earnings	98,440	104,474	99,957	(5.8)	4.5	32%	37%	45%
Total Stockholders Equity	102,950	108,981	104,458	(5.5)	4.3	34%	38%	47%
Total Liabilities	303,195	283,392	221,543	7	27.9	100%	100%	100%

EXHIBIT 12
Statement of Changes in Consolidated Financial Position for the Years Ended June 30

	1980	1979	Percentage Increase (Decrease) from 79 to 80
Additions			
Net Income (loss) for the year	($2,431,832)	$8,119,781	(70%)
Charges to Operations not requiring outlay of working capital:			
Depreciation	22,391,629	18,872,858	19%
Provision for Deferred Income Taxes	(453,343)	2,426,819	(81%)
Amortization and other	604,684	620,044	(2%)
Total from Operations	20,111,138	30,039,502	(33%)
Execution of Long-term debt	30,893,000	36,437,000	(15%)
Proceeds from disposition of tangible property—less gains of $446,831 in 1980 and $742,606 in 1979	6,070,898	2,185,194	178%
Total additions	57,075,036	68,661,696	(17%)
Deductions			
Purchase of tangible property	20,725,099	22,896,045	(9%)
Net assets of business in 1979 exclusive of working capital deficit	3,087,000	18,990,000	(84%)
Reduction of long-term debt	13,594,665	16,542,939	(18%)
Cash dividends on common shares	3,602,235	3,602,235	0
Other deductions (additions)—net	1,471,208	(418,141)	450%
Total deductions	42,480,207	61,613,078	(31%)
Increase in Working Capital	14,594,829	7,048,618	107%
Consolidated Working Capital—at beginning of year	26,839,661	19,791,043	36%
Consolidated Working Capital—at end of year	41,434,490	26,839,661	36%
Changes in Components of Working Capital			
Increase (decrease) in current assets:			
Cash and short-term investments	7,102,469	(3,551,938)	(300%)
Accounts receivable	2,701,656	20,216,702	(87%)
Recoverable federal and state income taxes	2,021,269	3,768,161	(46%)
Prepayments	(952,178)	2,165,971	(56%)
Inventories and other current assets	12,243,022	2,825,642	333%
	23,116,238	25,424,538	(9%)
Increase (decrease) in current liabilities:			
Note payable	2,000,000	0	0
Trade accounts payable	2,540,307	6,551,188	(61%)
Accrued payrolls, payroll taxes, and others	(87,469)	1,318,741	(93%)
Accrued vacation pay	1,749,958	4,349,652	(60%)
Accrued federal and state income taxes	0	(1,295,283)	0
Current maturities of long-term debt	213,425	3,699,642	(94%)
Other current liabilities	2,105,188	3,751,980	(44%)
	8,521,409	18,375,920	(54%)
Increase in Working Capital	14,594,829	7,048,618	107%

EXHIBIT 13
Statements of Consolidated Operations (unaudited)

	Three Months Ended December 31		Six Months Ended December 31	
	1980	1979	1980	1979
Continuing Operations				
Operating revenues	$148,638,398	$150,725,165	$298,872,242	$303,428,092
Operating expenses	149,966,905	155,084,650	296,217,487	304,486,458
Operating income (loss)	(1,328,507)	(4,359,485)	2,654,755	(1,058,366)
Other income and deductions—net	2,146,599	1,785,226	3,958,647	3,115,067
Income (loss) before income taxes	(3,475,106)	(6,144,711)	(1,303,892)	(4,173,433)
Provision for income taxes	(1,433,600)	(1,866,100)	(482,400)	(1,203,600)
Income (loss) from continuing operations	(2,041,506)	(4,278,611)	(821,492)	(2,969,833)
Discontinued Operations				
Loss of Winston Refining Co., less income taxes	(1,293,107)	(389,740)	(2,060,106)	(632,131)
Gain on sale of Winston Refining Co., less income taxes	4,214,283	—	4,214,283	—
Income (loss) from discontinued operations	2,921,176	(389,740)	2,154,177	632,131
Income (Loss) Before Extraordinary Charge	879,670	(4,668,351)	1,332,685	(3,601,964)
Extraordinary Charge				
Write-off of interstate operating rights	(11,703,199)	—	(11,703,199)	—
Net Income (Loss)	$ 10,823,529)	($ 4,668,351)	($ 10,370,514)	($ 3,601,964)
Income (loss) per share				
Continuing operations	($ .36)	($ .76)	($ .14)	($ .53)
Discontinued operations	.52	(.07)	.38	(.11)
Extraordinary charge	(2.08)	—	(2.08)	—
Net income (loss)	($1.92)	($ .83)	($1.84)	($ .64)

a consulting firm that specializes in the transportation industry, issued a forecast in early 1981 regarding rates and costs. This forecast is presented in Exhibit 15.

The highway system is a factor in future plans, also. The Interstate Highway System is virtually complete, and fewer roads are planned. This means no relief from congested roads is expected on federally funded and managed roads. Relief in the form of new roads, expansions, and alternate routes will have to come from the states.

The highway funds that maintain the road system are encountering squeezes today that may get worse. Less driving overall, caused by higher gasoline costs, are resulting in lower gasoline tax revenues. Truckers, however, do not reduce driving because of fuel costs and are thought by many to cause much of the deterioration of the highway system. Higher taxes are an alternative to such deterioration, with perhaps more of the burden on the trucking industry.

Deregulation of the trucking industry is

EXHIBIT 14
Condensed Consolidated Balance Sheets (unaudited)

	December 31, 1980[a]	December 31, 1979[a]
Assets		
Current assets	$ 80,024,142	$105,432,311
Tangible property—net	142,135,554	166,680,720
Operating rights and other assets	7,820,996	14,608,588
Total	$229,980,692	$286,721,619
Liabilities and Shareholders' Equity		
Current liabilities	$ 52,463,760	$ 80,784,339
Long-term debt	72,794,306	91,066,840
Other noncurrent liabilities	13,043,449	11,289,205
Shareholders' equity	91,679,177	103,581,235
Total	$229,980,692	$286,721,619

[a]Winston Refining Co., a wholly owned subsidiary, was sold effective October 31, 1980. At December 31, 1979, the assets and liabilities of the refinery are included in their normal account classifications.

EXHIBIT 15
Trucking Cost and Rate Forecast

Item	Percentage Increase					
	1980	1981	1982	1983	1984	1985
Labor Cost	11	13	12	13	13	8
Fuel Cost	35	13	10	10	12	12
Materials and Supplies	11	11	10	10	12	12
Depreciation	8	5	5	5	5	5
Miscellaneous	9	10	8	9	9	9

Percentage of Costs by Functional Area

	TL		LTL	
	1978	1985	1978	1985
Labor	44.9	44.7	76.3	77.7
Fuel	11.8	18.0	2.9	4.5
Materials and Supplies	16.7	16.9	5.0	5.3
Depreciation	11.2	7.3	5.7	3.7
Miscellaneous	15.4	13.1	10.1	8.8
	100.0	100.0	100.0	100.0

Rate Increase Forecast (Percentage)

	TL	LTL
1980	14	12
Annual Average Through 1985	11	11
Cumulative Increase Through 1985	92	89

Source: Handling and Shipping Management, January 1981.

expected by many industry experts to contribute to an industry "shakeout." Mergers, new entries, and rerouting are expected in large amounts because industry analysts predict "As many as 20 percent of the trucking firms in the country will be out of business by 1981 year end." While some companies are dreading the new rules, obviously the new entrants are anticipating the future as more favorable. Industry analysts expect profitability to permanently suffer, with rate increases to follow after the rate cutting of the shakeout period. McLean's management is uncertain whether their profits will be any more affected than their competitors.

Two trends have shown up that may have a serious effect on common carriers who wish to expand their contract business or, for some, to begin it. D. H. Karel of Cleo Wrap, a contract carrier, feels that contract carriage will be "The name of the game in the near future. . . . More contract rates between common carrier and the shipper." Another aspect of the contract business is the private carrier. Now it is possible for these carriers to carry common freight on backhauls. This right to carry common freight has been limited to regulated common carriers prior to the 1980 MCA. Extension of this right to private carriers is being fought by the Regular Common Carrier Conference of the American Trucking Associations and the Teamsters Union in court. Appeals are pending.

In short, the near future appears to be turbulent as opposed to the last decade. Financial resources and opportunistic management may be the key ingredients for success in the next few years.

ELECTRONIC DATA SYSTEMS CORPORATION

Throughout its 21 years of operation, Electronic Data Systems (EDS) has relied upon a solid teamwork approach guided by strong upper-level management to attain its current strong competitive status. H. Ross Perot, founder and Chairman of the Board of EDS has epitomized the "American Dream" with much flare and, concurrently, much controversy. While building the EDS empire his name has been brought before the public for his noncorporation exploits, such as his leadership of the War on Drugs and his rescue in 1979 of two EDS employees who were captive in an Iranian jail. Nonetheless, Perot's success with EDS has been formidable.

History

Perot founded EDS in 1962 with a mere $1000 investment. He realized that his then-current employer, IBM, was selling hardware to customers, but did not show customers how to utilize it properly. What these customers needed . . . was someone to design, install, and operate their data-processing systems for a fee, thought Perot. This was the basis on which Perot acted when he set out to build EDS, and his desire to fill a gap that IBM neglected has rewarded him handsomely.

EDS began by purchasing unused computer time on the computers of other companies, usually operating from different locations each night. Yet beginning in 1964, EDS's revenues doubled each year until 1968, at which time the first public offering of stock was made (see Exhibit 1).

Unique in comparison to other firms in the computer-services industry, EDS has emphasized its reputation, financial strength, professionalism, and quality of service, which are grounded on five basic tenets:

Source: This case was prepared by Deborah Weaver, Monique Hensel, and Jeff Bell under the supervision of Professor Sexton Adams and Professor Adelaide Griffin. Permission to use granted by Sexton Adams.

1. EDS developed basic philosophies to guide its business:
   - Provide outstanding customer service.
   - Build the finest professional staff in the computer-services industry.
   - Deal with each employee as an individual.
   - Recognize and reward excellence.
   - Build a sound record of financial strength.

2. EDS created the concept of facilities management. In 1962, the computer-services industry consisted of software houses. Under the facilities management concept, EDS becomes the data-processing department of a client such as a large insurance company, bank, or government agency. Facilities management enables EDS to provide a total, long-term agreement for services involving computers, people, and systems at predetermined prices with defined, dependable time schedules and producing desired results.

3. EDS created the concept of a long-term contract in an industry that was accustomed to 90-day contracts. When EDS entered the market, it was generally accepted that no company could sell a five-year contract. Long-term contracts provided EDS with the financial stability it needed for continued growth.

4. EDS formally organized a recruiting group within EDS to identify and bring into the corporation top professionals in the computer industry.

5. EDS initiated data-processing skills development programs because of a scarcity of experienced, qualified operations and systems engineering personnel.

Since its inception in 1962, EDS has grown to become one of the largest firms in the computer-services industry, employing over 11,700 people with assets in excess of $330 million. In

EXHIBIT 1
EDS Yearly Reviews

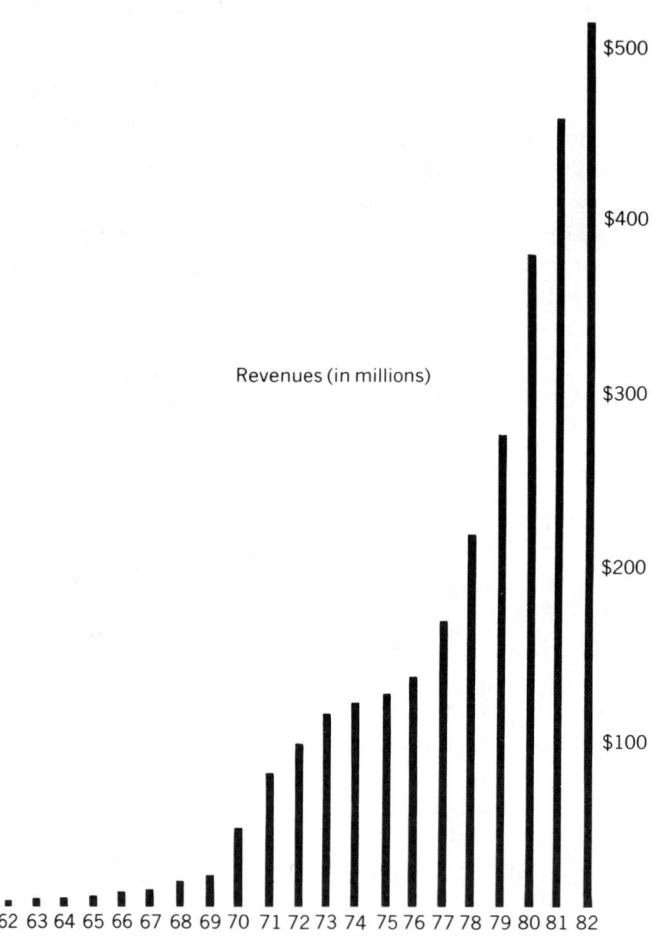

Source: *Electronic Data Systems Corp. Annual Report,* 1982, p. 3.

1975 EDS began offering its services internationally. As of 1983 its international clients include Canada, Kuwait, Belgium, Mexico, Singapore, Spain, Great Britain, Saudi Arabia, Malaysia, and the Netherlands.

Organization

H. Ross Perot appointed Mort Meyerson president of EDS in 1979. Meyerson wasted no time in reorganizing EDS into specialized groups geared towards addressing specific industry and government needs. The Vice Presidents of each group report directly to Meyerson. The five groups are illustrated in Exhibit 2, the EDS organizational chart.

EDS executive officers are usually elected by the Board of Directors at the Board's first meeting subsequent to the Annual Meeting of Stockholders. However, the Board may appoint additional officers as necessary at any time. Exhibit 3 is a list of EDS executive officers as of June 30, 1982.

EXHIBIT 2
EDS Organization Chart

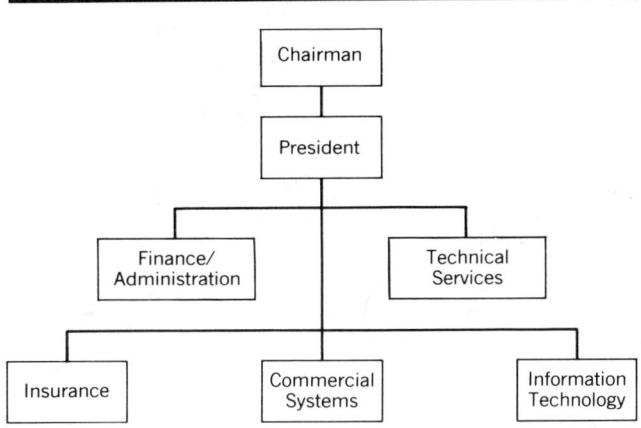

Source: Company Records.

Most of the growth EDS has experienced since beginning operations has been internally generated through acquisitions. Exhibit 4 highlights EDS's subsidiaries as of June 30, 1982.

H. Ross Perot: Chairman of the Board

A leading factor in EDS's success has been its founder and "general," H. Ross Perot. He pre-

EXHIBIT 3
EDS Executive Officers As of June 30, 1982

Name	Office or Position	Served in Position Since	Age
H. Ross Perot	Chairman of the Board	1962	52
Morton H. Meyerson	President	1979	44
Lester M. Alberthal, Jr.	Vice President	1974	38
Thomas D. Behne	Vice President	1971	51
Claude K. Chappelear	Vice President, General Counsel, Secretary	1978	45
R. Michael Farmer	Treasurer	1979	39
Gary J. Fernandes	Vice President	1979	39
R. Frank Furr	Vice President	1971	50
William K. Gayden	Vice President	1970	41
J. Davis Hamlin	Vice President	1969	50
Jeffrey M. Heller	Vice President	1974	42
Gilbert E. Hurley	Vice President, Comptroller	1971 1982	45
Kenneth G. Riedlinger	Vice President	1979	42
Glen D. Self	Vice President	1971	44
J. Thomas Walter, Jr.	Vice President, Chief Financial Officer	1966 1979	48

Source: Company records.

EXHIBIT 4
EDS Subsidiaries as of June 30, 1982

Name	State of Incorporation	Percentage of Voting Securities Controlled by Registrant
National Heritage Insurance Company	Texas	100[a]
EDS Administration Corporation	Nevada	100[b]
EDS Administrative Services, Inc.	New York	100[b,i]
Electronic Data Systems Federal Corporation	Nevada	100[b]
CUNADATA Corporation	Texas	100[b,g]
EDS Federal Corporation	Texas	100[b]
EDS Business Systems Corporation	Nevada	100[b]
Quorum Development Corporation	Nevada	100[b]
EDS International Corporation	Texas	100[b]
EDS Corporation	Texas	100[b]
EDS Management Corporation	Texas	100[b]
EDS Realty Corporation	Nevada	100[b]
ED Systems Corporation	Texas	100[b]
EDS World Corporation	Texas	100[b]
EDS World Corporation (Germany)	Texas	100[b,c]
EDS World Corporation (Kuwait)	Texas	100[b,c]
EDS World Corporation (Netherlands)	Texas	100[b,c]
EDS World Corporation (U. K.)	Texas	100[b,c]
EDS World Corporation (Saudi Arabia)	Texas	100[b,c]
EDS World Corporation (Spain)	Nevada	100[b,c]
EDS World Corporation (Mexico)	Texas	100[b,c]
EDS World Corporation (Far East)	Texas	100[b,c]
EDS Virgin Islands Corporation	Nevada	100[b,g]
Federal Data Systems Corporation	Nevada	100[j]
CUNADATA Corporation (Great Britain)	Texas	100[b,h]
Data Processing of the South, Inc.	North Carolina	100[b]
Electronic Data Systems Leasing Corporation	Texas	100[b]
EDS Engineering Corporation	Nevada	100[b]
Compusource Corporation	Texas	100[b]
Centurion Computer Corporation	Texas	100[b,d]
EDLBV	The Netherlands	100[e,b]
EDSW—Mexico, S. A. de C. V.	Mexico	100[f]
EDS—Bedaux, S. A.	Spain	100[k]
EDS Service Corporation	Texas	100[b]
Electronic Data Systems Corporation (Nevada)	Nevada	100[b]
EDS Airline Systems Corporation	Texas	100[g,b]

Source: FDS Form 10-K, pp. IV-9–IV-11.

[a] Unconsolidated subsidiary accounted for by the equity method.

[b] Included in the consolidated financial statements of the Registrant. See Note 1 to consolidated financial statements of the Registrant's Annual Report to Stockholders for the year ended June 30, 1982, for additional information on principles of consolidation and basis of presentation.

[c] 100 percent owned by EDS World Corporation.

[d] 100 percent owned by EDS Corporation.

[e] 75 percent owned by EDS World Corporation (Netherlands).

[f] 49 percent owned by EDS World Corporation (Mexico).

[g] 100 percent owned by ED Systems Corporation.

[h] 100 percent owned by CUNADATA Corporation.

[i] 100 percent owned by EDS Realty Corporation.

[j] 50 percent owned by Electronic Data Systems Federal Corporation.

[k] 50 percent owned by EDS World Corporation.

The names of other subsidiaries have been omitted. Such subsidiaries, if considered in the aggregate as a single subsidiary, would not constitute a significant subsidiary.

fers to handle matters and tackle challenges by the "one-man, one-job, let's go" approach. In an interview with the *Dallas Times Herald* in September 1982, Perot stated his philosophy on how EDS should be managed:

> The way we get things done around here is everyone takes a small piece of it and does it. Everybody is talking to everybody else, and somebody is always in charge. That's EDS, that's the way EDS is.

Through this managerial style Perot has produced a most formidable product—EDS. The company was originated in 1962, went public in 1968, and has been diversifying from its data-processing base to the production of electronic hardware. A large part of the company's stable growth has resulted from the heavy emphasis Perot has placed on hiring, training, and developing a staff of the highest quality professionals available. EDS is well-known for routinely attracting the best talent and providing formal training that is unsurpassed by its competitors. This philosophy of recruiting is typified by EDS's early recruiting slogan: Eagles don't flock—you have to find them one by one.

In 1979 Perot turned over the presidency of EDS, as well as many of the day-to-day management responsibilities, to Mort Meyerson. But Perot still plays an active part in directing the company he created. He described his emphasis on teamwork as follows:

> If you worked for EDS and you called me and I was really busy, it might take me an hour to get back to you. Normally I just talk to you when you call. Anytime anybody has ever been hurt, anytime an employee has had a serious problem—24 hours a day, 7 days a week—I've known about it and Mort has known about it. We do whatever it takes to deal with it. I think that if there's a secret behind EDS's success, it's that we all just work hard together.

Henry Ross Perot was born June 27, 1930 in Texarkana, Texas, the son of a cattle and horse trader and a cotton broker in east Texas. Perot attended public schools in Texarkana and a two-year pre-law course at a local junior college. He considered his courses neither difficult, nor interesting. Watching his father transact business with nearby farmers may have been more stimulating to him than his educational experience. Perot recalls an episode between his father and a nearby farmer who was interested in selling a horse to Perot's father. His father, no matter how interested in buying the horse, would remain indifferent to any offer. A few days later the deal was settled and the price Perot's father paid was below the original price.

As a boy, Perot enjoyed selling—Christmas cards, saddles, the *Saturday Evening Post*, and the *Texarkana Gazette*. He established a paper route that demanded he travel 20 miles a day on horseback to deliver the paper. Since this route was established because of Perot's efforts, he received 70 percent of the price instead of the customary 30 percent. Later, when the route began to grow and thrive, the newspaper tried to renege on the ratio, but Perot argued against any change.

Perot is considered an achiever and an attention-getter. People in industry may feel his actions are publicity stunts to promote EDS services. However, Perot insists his intentions are concerned with the crisis at hand. An interview with him in December 1980 revealed this statement in *Esquire:* "Ross Perot thinks about the individual and society—about values, the meaning of loyalty, the secrets of success."

Perot's personality and managerial skills have pulled EDS out of several major crises in past years. In building EDS he envisioned the company as a health-insurance industry conglomerate. This dream was realized in the early part of 1979 when an EDS subsidiary bid for a five-year contract to run part of the Illinois Medicare plan. This contract was estimated at 41.8 million for the life of the contract by EDS. The bid established by EDS was $40 million below that of two large insurance companies—Prudential and Metropolitan. The contract began in April 1979, and two major problems soon surfaced that hindered EDS's execution of the contract. First, six months after initiating the job, unprocessed paperwork began to accumulate. The number of unprocessed claims continued to increase, and those claims that were processed often contained mistakes. Second, although comprehensive site location studies were conducted to arrive at the location most suitable for a central office, planners failed to look at actual employment statistics in suburban Des Plaines (the site chosen for the Illinois project). In addition, planners did not investigate the fact that the town had almost no unemployment. These two errors produced a quarterly review for the first year of operation revealing that EDS had failed in five major performance standard tests designed to ascertain whether EDS was fulfilling the terms of the contract. Thus, EDS had to pay contractual penalties amounting to $700,000. Aside from the financial loss, EDS created poor customer relations among aging Social Security and disability dependents who floundered to have the errors EDS created corrected. Early in 1980 claims were again backlogged, although by June 1980 EDS delcared that procedures were efficient in processing claims. Perot and his management team were able to convince the administration of the Illinois Medicare plan that EDS had regained control of its data. However, the decision to allow EDS to continue working on the project was due in part to the costly delays of replacing EDS.

Less than a month after the Illinois Medicare project episode, another experience served to disrupt EDS. On July 15, 1980 the Texas Board of Human Resources announced its decision to take the expiring Texas Medicaid contract away from EDS and to award it to Bradford National Corporation of New York. Bradford was a new low bidder and would take over the contract that EDS had been awarded in 1977. The loss of this "crown jewel" in EDS's empire was good reason for alarm. A few days after the contract had been awarded to Bradford, Hilmar Moore, Chairman of the Texas Board, received a call at his ranch near Richard, Texas from Mort Meyerson. Meyerson and Perot proposed a visit with Moore at his ranch to discuss the misperceptions that had led to the expiration of their contract. Moore readily agreed to the visit; by the end of their visit Moore was convinced that EDS should regain the contract. After personal visits to two other Board members, the Texas Board was willing to submit the matter for reevaluation by a new set of analysts and actuaries. The new hearing began and the new outside consultants affirmed the decision to take the contract away from EDS. The Bradford people celebrated the decision relieved at the renewal of their original victory. However, two days after the second hearing Moore and two of the three Board members announced they were convinced that it would be more advantageous for Texas to remain with Perot, and therefore the contract with EDS would be renewed.

Mort Meyer: President

Mort Meyerson joined EDS in 1966 as a trainee and subsequently built EDS's health-care division into the company's largest division. His noteworthy contributions earned him the presidency of EDS as of 1979. Meyerson recognized that EDS had grown in size and scope and that decentralization was necessary to permit more management to make decisions. Thus, EDS was reorganized into essentially three smaller companies with distinct specialties and markets: (1) the Insurance Group, (2) Information Technology, and (3) Commercial Systems. Each of these divisions is run semiautonomously by EDS executives who spent most of their careers with the company.

EDS Services

EDS services the technology world in the computer-services segment. It delivers services on a long-term basis using four elements: communications, hardware, software, and industry experience. Since EDS specializes by industry, it is the largest computer services firm that can provide specialized services in banking, insurance, and health care.

Four contract arrangements are available to EDS customers: facilities management, program management, professional services, and turnkey. *Facilities management* contracts account for almost 50 percent of EDS's business. In this arrangement EDS essentially becomes the data-processing entity for its client institution. This includes such functions as system design, training, programming, implementation, and operation of any systems it installs and develops. The *program management* contract includes the services of the facilities management contract, in addition to clerical and/or administrative work. Thus, in this contract EDS operates the computer systems, runs the communications network, and provides clerical people, underwriters, and adjusters. These services are typically used in health-care services such as Medicaid and Medicare. The *professional services* contract allows the customer to purchase a highly professional skill, such as software, by the hour, week, month, or on some other basis. This service is provided to help EDS customers in a specific area, and it represents only a small part of EDS's business. Because of its specialized nature, the cost for this service is high, usually around $15,000 to $20,000 a month for one person's time. The final type of contract is the *turnkey* arrangement. With this contract EDS designs a system, installs it, then turns it over to the customer. These four contract arrangements allow EDS to fill the needs of a wide variety of customers, tailoring the services it provides to the special industry in which the customer is competing. In other words, it is a "total system approach."

As previously mentioned, EDS is broken into five major groups (refer back to Exhibit 2). The first two areas are known as the Support Groups and consist of *Administrative/Financial Services* and *Technical Services*. EDS's business

EXHIBIT 5
EDS Service Groups

Insurance Group

Private Sector

Blue Cross/Blue Shield
Life Insurance
Property and Casualty Insurance
Hospitals

Government Agencies

Medicare A and B
Medicaid
State and Local Governments

Commercial Systems Group

Financial	*Industrials*
Banks	Manufacturing
Savings and Loans	Retail
Credit Unions	Distribution
Air Transport Associations	Systems
	Software
Small Businesses	Airlines
Business Systems	Energy
Centurion	

Information Technology Group

Government Services

International

Source: Company records.

essentially consists of the three other Groups, each of which is run by its own Vice President as a semiautonomous business. The *Insurance Group* services commercial insurance, health care, and state and local governments. The *Commercial Systems Group* includes credit unions, savings and loans, and banking. The *Information Technology Group* services government and international business. Exhibit 5 provides an overview of EDS's service groups and the segments serviced.

Strategic Planning System

The method of strategic corporate planning used by EDS can best be described as an intuitive–anticipatory approach. This approach to strategic planning is characterized by comparatively short time horizons and reaction times. The planning decisions are based on the experience and intuition of the corporate management of the company.

EDS used a top-down approach to set annual corporate objectives and goals. Perot emphasizes his "teamwork" orientation when the corporate objectives are established by Perot and the CEO. The Group Vice-Presidents then review the corporate objectives by Perot and the CEO and add their input. Next the CEO and the Group Vice-Presidents discuss the probability of successfully accomplishing each objective until a consensus is reached. Thus, the teamwork that Perot affectionately refers to at EDS is geared to carrying out objectives and goals set by top management.

Mort Meyerson cites the following objectives for EDS during the next five years:

1. To increase revenues and profits by 20 percent annually and to boost after-tax profit margins to 10 percent by 1985.
2. To become a one-billion dollar company in revenues and to become a 100-million dollar company in net income by 1978.

In addition, EDS's corporate policy manual states the following strategic goals for EDS in the long run:

1. To become the most respected computer-services firm in the data-processing industry.
2. To attract and retain the most outstanding computer professionals and to provide them with the career opportunities they seek.
3. To make EDS an exciting and rewarding place to work.
4. To make a fair profit for the organization, its stockholders, and the people that built the company.
5. To have EDS grow into a large company, yet remain a great company.

These long-range goals and objectives are communicated to lower-level managers who put them into operation. Management believes that teamwork at the functional levels is created by the efforts of these managers to meet company objectives.

Divisions

Support Groups

EDS's *Finance and Administrative Group* facilitates the three major service groups in carrying out the routine activities on a day-to-day basis. This group is comprised of three functional departments, each of which maintains and monitors its own operations: Accounting/Finance, Legal, and Personnel and Employee Relations. The Accounting/Finance department is responsible for all capital expenditures and revenue receipts, in addition to analyzing and monitoring these activities. The Legal department handles all legal aspects of EDS's ventures, including customer contracts for services, employee training contracts, acquisitions, and any other activities that may require legal advice or representation. The Personnel and Employee Relations department is responsible for handling selection and placement, compensation, health and safety, training and development, employee relations, and labor relations. All three of these departments act as facilitators for EDS's three customer service groups.

The *Technical Services Group* operates out of five regional data centers. Three data centers are located in the Dallas area, and additional data centers are located in San Francisco and Camp Hill, Pennsylvania. These five regional data centers integrate smaller computer centers and terminals located throughout the offices of EDS customers. The data centers can process information faster and at less cost through the use of several large computers. Thus, the centers run computers, print reports, microfilm documents, and transfer data from one location to another. The concentration of large computers offers back-up capability—a feature small data centers do not have. This convenience is realized when one computer fails to work and processing must be switched to other computers. Another plus of the regional data centers is the sheer volume or capacity. EDS realizes the extreme importance of skilled operations people. It offers an Operations Development Program that is a 12 to 18 month intensive classroom and programmed instruction, including on-the-job-training. Advanced equipment and capable personnel make it happen for EDS.

Service Groups

With its *Insurance Group* EDS has created a profitable niche, providing flexible contracts based upon customer needs. Eleven commercial insurance companies signed contracts with EDS during the 1982 fiscal year. The contracts included existing customers and new firms. New firm contracts contributed to approximately one-half of growth in contract agreements. One of EDS's most recent developments is the Insurance Machine—a computer system designed to help issue and administer life, health, and annuity policies. Also created to help meet the economic challenge of the 1980s in the insurance field is the Universal Life Policy (ULP). Because the ULP pays interest on premiums and allows flexible financial planning, it has become popular among EDS customers.

EDS has been instrumental in cutting the cost of administering health-care programs for 16 years. It developed the first system for processing Medicaid claims, utilizing a joint Medicare plan to process hospital claims in addition to processing claims from doctors and other suppliers. During 1982 EDS is trying to carry this same "one system" idea to computerize doctors' offices. Using such a system doctors and hospitals could file claims on computer terminals and, thus, lower costs and increase the processing of paper work. EDS recognizes that faster claim processing is a main advantage of this new system. Based on this concept EDS installed an Electronic Claims System at Massachusetts Blue Shield, a group healthcare system for Blue Cross, Blue Shield of Iowa, and Blue Shield plans in Montana and Puerto Rico.

Nursing homes and hospitals can also trim expenses by using EDS's computer-based systems. For example, a patient-care system can cut information handling costs by as much as $3,000 per day. In 1982 EDS installed systems in eight hospitals and seven nursing homes. These systems allow health-care professionals to direct their attention towards patient care rather than concentrating on paper work.

EDS's involvement in the Blue Cross and Blue Shield programs dates back to 1966. Diversity may be the key to EDS's future, but as of 1983 EDS is still highly dependent on government business in this area. Within the Blue Cross/Blue Shield segment, EDS has set up 10 plans that account for 93 percent of the current available market. Exhibit 6 highlights the Insurance Group's major account activity during 1982.

The *Commerical Systems Group* experienced a record pace of growth in the financial area. In 1982, seven large banks and thrift institutions signed contracts with EDS that ranged from

EXHIBIT 6
Major Account Activities of the Insurance Group During 1982

Medicare
- 70.0 Million Claims Processed.
- $5.8 Billion Total Benefits Paid.

Medicaid
- 79.3 Million Claims Processed in 15 States.

Blue Cross/Blue Shield
- 10 Plans
- 93 Percent of Current Available Market

Source: Company records.

five to eight years. EDS is the largest processor in banking, serving 650 banks with 10 million accounts in 49 states. Banks in New Mexico, Oklahoma, and Texas have become EDS's customers. These banks add another 180 customers to the company.

In 1982 more than 40 banks purchased the Return on Information System, one of EDS's turnkey contract arrangements. Such an increase in services to the community has required EDS to double the customer base for this product. As with its other service areas, EDS offers a complete range of services to financial institutions, based on the institution's varying needs. The Vice President of this Group feels that EDS's flexibility in providing services greatly assisted the growth in this area.

EDS feels very strongly about keeping pace with rapid changes in the industry. An example is EDS–LINK, which is a breakthrough in electronic-funds transfer technology. This new system permits individuals to make deposits and withdrawals across town or across the country at any participating financial institution. The demand for EDS–LINK is projected to be strong, but this remains to be seen.

Banks are not the only segment of financial institutions that are latching onto EDS's expertise in computer services. The strongest growth area of the Commercial System Group can be attributed to new credit union contracts. In 1983 over 3,000 credit unions used EDS computer systems, serving 7 million members. One thousand credit unions became EDS customers through the purchase of credit union systems from Western Bradford Trust, Missouri League Data Services, Data Processing of the South, and Financial Data Services. A computer system is available for every size of credit union. The newest development is the CUNDATA 2000—a distributing data-processing system that links small-business computers in the credit union with large computers at an EDS data center. The CUNDATA 2000 and the credit-union business in general are examples of remote processing through one master system in Dallas. On-site microcomputers accept and print information while tied to the computer system through a large communication network.

Also within the Commercial Systems Group is the small-business sector, which is not considered to be profitable. As of 1983, Meyerson has considered this area to be a research and development effort, although he is open-minded and optimistic that a market will open in this area in the future.

EDS offers a line of minicomputers that are sold through a national network of 40 independent dealers. These minicomputers are designed and manufactured by one of its subsidiaries, Centurion Computer Corporation. In keeping with EDS's flexible services concept, these minicomputers provide tailor-made systems to customers. Thus, a large department-store chain can use a computer to predict fashion trends. The same computer can decide what advertising and promotional inserts go to specific customers.

A software maintenance plan based on productivity brings about a savings of time and money. One incentive-based contract, for example, brought about a large change. Four EDS systems engineers replaced 34 of the customer's systems engineers. This type of change takes highly motivated, experienced systems engineers to make it work, but it is a new concept that EDS is promoting. Another new idea is a package consisting of computer hardware, software, installation, and maintenance. This package concept has been well accepted since businesses receive data-processing results without the problem of dealing with different vendors.

The *Information Technology* Group has also experienced growth—predominantly in the government and international areas. The largest contract ever made in the computer-services industry was offered to EDS by the U.S. Army in April 1982. Project VIABLE is a

10-year, $656 million contract securing EDS's expertise to build and operate five regional data centers to provide data for processing information for 42 army bases. This project is in the start-up phase as of 1983. Forty-two military posts, each with its own distributed data processing center, will be tied into a network. The number of terminals alone is close to 18,000. EDS is modeling this complex network on the computer and communications network that it built to do the processing for its insurance and commercial business, rather than designing a completely new system. Such an approach to building a new system is not new to EDS, and has been implemented successfully in the past.

The experience with Project VIABLE will put EDS in a good position to win contracts for similar systems from other government agencies and large corporations. Perot has expressed his belief that the Army contract was won by beating companies like IBM and Computer Services, a case of a gnat beating a giant.

The Department of Defense has also signed a contract with EDS for a Defense Enrollment/Eligibility Reporting System (DEERS). The system is a health-care eligibility system for all of the dependents of retired U.S. military personnel. This project was created because of continued fraud and abuse present in the current eligibility system. Dependents simply had to display a card when using medical facilities. Under DEERS dependents are issued a machine-readable plastic card with their thumbprint and a photo. DEERS consists of a network of terminals throughout the United States to determine the eligibility for 9 million people. The challenge for EDS in this service area definitely is linked to the contract awarded by the U.S. Army. Management must find and train 300 people by 1983 and a total of 700 persons by 1985 to meet the demands of the Army contract alone.

In the international market EDS offers the same sophisticated systems used in the United States. Belgium, Canada, Great Britain, Kuwait, Malaysia, Mexico, the Netherlands, Saudia Arabia, Singapore, and Spain are countries that are currently using EDS services. EDS is designing and building an audio processing system that is part of the total command and control system for ships of the Royal Saudi Naval Forces. The system will increase communication between land-based command and the fleet at sea. Although this area is rewarding EDS with profits, there is some skepticism as to whether EDS should rely on or even offer their services to forces that could very possibly confront the U.S. in military action.

Another area EDS has penetrated is entry into the market of higher education. A two-year contract has been set up with Pennsylvania State University to design, develop, and install computer systems to process everything from class schedules to payroll. The future potential of this new market is broad and open to much speculation.

Financial Data

EDS's fiscal year is from July 1 to June 30. Recessionary pressures limited its revenue growth rate to 12 percent in 1982 compared to 21 percent in 1981. In 1982 both earnings per share and net income increased 24 percent compared to a 31 percent increase in 1981. The return on equity was 26 percent, and the return on assets was 16 percent. The company's net profit margin was 9 percent, and the revenue per employee was approximately $50,000. Project VIABLE is expected to provide EDS with $50 million in revenues during fiscal year 1983, and has the potential to add another $320 million in revenues over the 10-year contract period. Pre-tax profits from the Army contract are expected to start at about 7 percent and increase to 10 percent within 2 years. EDS has also negotiated a $500-million contract with Texas Medicaid. The company will handle all of the data-processing activities of National Heritage Insurance Company, an EDS subsidiary, that underwrites certain parts of the Texas Medicaid program. Texas Medicaid is one of

EXHIBIT 7
EDS Consolidated Statements of Income for the Years Ended June 30, 1982, 1981, and 1980

(In Thousands Except Earnings per Share)	1982	1981	1980
Revenues			
Systems and other contracts	$503,335	$448,611	$368,627
Interest and other	6,637	6,003	6,034
	509,972	454,614	374,661
Cost and expenses			
Cost of revenues	378,479	345,160	290,696
Selling, general and administrative	61,111	53,277	41,246
Interest expense	—	—	1,079
	439,590	398,437	333,021
	70,382	56,177	41,640
Provision for income taxes	28,154	22,471	16,585
Income before equity in earnings of unconsolidated subsidiary	42,228	33,706	25,055
Equity in earnings of unconsolidated subsidiary	4,739	4,110	3,835
Net income	$ 46,967	$ 37,816	$ 28,890
Earnings per common share	$ 1.72	$ 1.39	$ 1.06

Source: EDS 1982 Annual Report, p. 26.

the nation's largest processors of medical insurance claims.

EDS has reduced its cost of revenues as a percentage of systems revenue since the second quarter of the fiscal year 1980. The cost reduction reflects the significant impact of EDS's current pricing policy and increased use of strict cost contract measures. Increased levels of marketing activities and increased expenditures to support the company's growth have resulted in increases in selling, general, and administrative expenses. However, as a percentage of systems revenue, these expenses have been declining since the fourth quarter of fiscal year 1981.

The increased use of long-term debt to finance capital expenditures has caused interest costs to increase. EDS's capitalization of interest costs beginning in fiscal year 1981 has resulted in the elimination of interest expenses in both 1981 and 1982.

The financial statements that follow highlight EDS's financial performance as of June 30, 1982. Exhibit 7 is a Consolidated Income Statement. Exhibit 8 is the Consolidated Balance Sheet, and Exhibit 9 is the Consolidated Statement of Changes in Financial Position. Also included is a five-year Summary Financial Information Report (Exhibit 10).

Competition

Company sources cite EDS as a leader in the computer-services industry when ranked by net income, second only to Automatic Data Processing (ADP). Although both EDS and ADP are in the computer-services industry, they service different target markets. ADP concentrates on small businesses, and EDS concentrates on large businesses. Even though EDS does not have a major competitor that competes across the board with its operations, in each of its main business areas there is at least one company that competes directly, and most effectively, with EDS. In the hospital industry EDS competes with Shared Medical. In the health-care industry EDS competes with

EXHIBIT 8
EDS Consolidated Balance Sheets June 30, 1982 and 1981

(In Thousands)	1982	1981
Assets		
Current Assets		
Cash and temporary investments	$ 18,646	$ 7,447
Marketable securities, at amortized cost	20,391	22,074
Accounts receivable	87,872	75,085
Inventories	6,666	6,743
Prepayments	7,864	6,468
Total current assets	141,439	117,817
Property and Equipment, at Cost Less Accumulated Depreciation		
Land	3,922	2,983
Buildings and facilities	26,852	18,112
Computer equipment	17,727	9,821
Furniture and other	13,402	13,186
	61,903	44,102
Other Operating Assets		
Investment in unconsolidated subsidiary	25,544	20,805
Cost in excess of net assets of acquired companies, less accumulated amortization of $459 in 1982; $300 in 1981	5,848	6,007
Purchased software, less accumulated amortization of $6,290 in 1982, $2,041 in 1981	18,186	7,807
	49,578	34,619
Investments		
Land held for investment and development	51,755	49,411
Noncurrent notes receivable, primarily from land sales and other investments	4,487	8,730
Bonds and notes, at amortized cost	21,030	—
	77,272	58,141
	$330,192	$254,679
Liabilities and Stockholders' Equity		
Current Liabilities		
Accounts payable	$ 21,482	$ 21,820
Accrued liabilities	18,591	21,726
Deferred revenue	5,070	1,742
Income taxes	31,041	22,972
Current portion of notes payable	1,867	3,967
Total current liabilities	78,051	72,227
Deferred Income Taxes	3,693	3,526
Deferred Revenue	11,621	—
Notes Payable	32,304	17,229
Commitments and Litigation		

(Continued)

EXHIBIT 8 (Continued)

(In Thousands)	1982	1981
Stockholders' Equity:		
Common stock, without par value; authorized 50,000 shares in 1982	60,554	50,664
and 1981; issued 29,797 shares in 1982; 29,332 shares in 1981	(688)	(652)
Net unrealized loss on noncurrent marketable equity securities	156,795	124,113
Retained earnings	(12,138)	(12,428)
Treasury stock, at cost; 950 shares in 1982; 1,322 shares in 1981	204,523	161,697
Total stockholders' equity	$330,192	$254,679

Source: EDS 1982 Annual Report, p. 27.

EXHIBIT 9
EDS Consolidated Statements of Changes in Financial Position for the Years Ended June 30, 1982, 1981 and 1980

(In Thousands)	1982	1981	1980
Financial resources provided by			
Operations			
Net income	$46,967	$37,816	$28,890
Charges (credits) to income not involving working capital in the current period:			
Depreciation and amortization	15,629	10,259	6,460
Equity in earnings of unconsolidated subsidiary	(4,739)	(4,110)	(3,835)
Other	449	130	394
Working capital provided from operations	58,306	44,095	31,909
Increase in notes payable	17,083	4,954	7,371
Noncurrent deferred revenue	11,621	—	—
Proceeds from sale of land held for investment	858	3,359	3,636
Increase in retained earnings due to acquisition	2,672	—	—
Issuance of common stock (including treasury shares)	10,860	4,853	7,588
Decrease in noncurrent notes receivable	934	2,179	589
	102,334	59,440	51,093
Financial resources used for:			
Additions to land held for investment and development	3,202	11,152	13,210
Additions to property and equipment	28,772	16,496	9,075
Additions to cost in excess of net assets of acquired companies	—	—	3,773
Additions to purchased software	14,628	4,317	3,925
Dividends declared	16,957	15,728	10,365
Purchase of treasury stock	680	10,562	515
Decrease in notes payable	2,258	2,265	3,975
Increase (decrease) in noncurrent notes receivable and other investments	(2,991)	318	6,011
Increase in bonds and notes	21,030	—	—
	84,536	60,838	50,849
Increase (decrease) in working capital	$17,798	$(1,398)	$ 244

Source: EDS 1982 Annual Report, p. 28.

EXHIBIT 10
EDS Summary Financial Information for the Years Ended June 30 (All except per share amounts expressed in thousands)

	1982	1981	1980	1979	1978
Operating results					
Revenues	$509,972	$454,614	$374,661	$274,298	$217,837
Cost of revenues	378,479	345,160	290,696	199,142	156,147
Selling, general and administrative	61,111	53,277	41,246	38,854	31,533
Interest expense	—	—	1,079	582	391
Provision for income taxes	28,154	22,471	16,585	14,246	12,801
Equity in earnings of unconsolidated subsidiaries	4,739	4,110	3,835	2,228	2,701
Net income	$ 46,967	$ 37,816	$ 28,890	$ 23,702	$ 19,666
Per share data					
Earnings per share	$ 1.72	$ 1.39	$ 1.06	$ .91	$ .77
Dividends paid per share	$ .60	$ .56	$ .50	$ .42	$ .36
Average shares outstanding	27,350	27,250	27,374	26,058	25,550
Shares issued	29,797	29,332	29,178	27,792	26,658
Financial position					
Working capital	$ 63,388	$ 45,590	$ 46,988	$ 46,744	$ 46,709
Total assets	330,192	254,679	205,528	175,620	130,431
Property and equipment, net	61,903	44,102	36,246	32,913	28,756
Investments and other operating assets	126,850	92,760	80,060	54,954	30,251
Long-term debt	32,304	17,229	14,540	11,144	2,638
Additions to property and equipment	28,772	16,496	9,075	8,417	5,323
Stockholders' equity	204,523	161,697	145,183	120,076	97,628

Source: EDS 1982 Annual Report, p. 36.

Computer Sciences. The major competitor in the government marketplace is Systems Development Corporation, a subsidiary of Burroughs. EDS's main competitor in the banking business is Systematics. Exhibit 11 presents competitors in the computer-services industry as ranked by net income according to company reports. Exhibit 12 provides a more comprehensive overview of computer-industry competition that was complied by the Gartner Group of Merrill Lynch.

EXHIBIT 11
1983 Competitor Ranking

Company	Net Income in (000,000)
ADP	$57,794
EDS	46,967
Shared Medical	18,710
CSC	17,004
National Data	11,224
Tymshare	11,206
Reynolds and Reynolds	8,454
PRC	7,070

Source: Company records.

Effects of Inflation

To reduce the adverse impact of inflation and increase the effective management of operations and capital, EDS emphasizes asset turnover and operating profit margins. It closely monitors return on capital expenditures and cash flow from receivables to effectively manage its assets. Effective control of operating costs and an increase in sales will serve to spread fixed costs while improving profit margins, company sources contend.

EXHIBIT 12
The Top 20 in Computer Services

	Company	Main Service Area	Revenues (millions)	As a Percentage of Total Revenues	Percent Change in Revenues 1979–1980
Providing software and services to computer users has exploded into a $13 billion business. Here are the 20 largest players, ranked by their 1980 revenues as reported by Gartner Group, a leading research firm. Merrill Lynch assisted with the "main service area" information. As defined by Gartner Group, services noted in the table include: processing (1), custom/contract software (2), remote computing services (3), batch services (4) and facilities management (5).	IBM	2	$2,414.5	9.2%	21.9%
	Control Data	3,4	722.7	19.0	18.6
	Computer Sciences Corp	2	560.3	100.0	34.9
	ADP	3,4	505.0	100.0	24.1
	EDS	5	408.5	98.7	31.1
	Honeywell	3	349.7	7.1	21.0
	General Electric (GEISCO)	3	299.3	1.2	19.3
	Tymshare	3	211.0	89.5	19.7
	System Development Corp[a]	2,5	186.8	100.0	14.6
	McDonnell Douglas (McAuto)	3	160.7	2.6	−21.9
	Bradford National Corp	4	142.7	100.0	18.8
	Planning Research Corp	2	127.4	41.5	24.5
	Informatics Inc	1,2	125.9	100.0	12.0
	Boeing Computer Services	3,4	125.0	1.3	30.2
	Burroughs Corp	2	123.9	4.3	26.8
	General Instrument	2	115.3	14.0	15.2
	United Telecommunications	3	115.1	6.0	20.0
	Shared Medical Systems	2	105.6	99.1	28.3
	Wyly Corp	3	99.0	84.0	13.6
	TRW	1,5	94.2	1.9	32.7

Source: Reprinted in Harold Seneker, "The Growth Industry's Growth Industry," *Forbes*, July 6, 1981.
[a]Acquired by Burroughs Corp., Jan. 5, 1981.

Litigation

In February 1979 Electronic Data Systems Corporation of Iran (EDSCI) filed a breach of contract suit against the Social Security Organization of the government of Iran, the Ministry of Health and Welfare, for breaches of a contract for data-processing services. On May 9, 1980 the case went to trial and the EDS subsidiary won an award in the sum of $19 million plus costs and interest. The subsidiary has attached funds in a New York bank to satisfy the award, and although a federal appellate court upheld the injunction forbidding the transfer of the Iranian funds, EDSCI must pursue its claim before the Iran–United States Claims Tribunal in order to collect this award. A claim was filed before the Tribunal in January 1982, but as of April 1983 the Tribunal has not responded to the claim.

Sportster Incorporated, a 10-year-old chain of sporting-good stores based in Tyler, Texas, filed suit on November 29, 1982 against EDS claiming breach of contract and fraud. Sportster Inc. seeks $88,000 in actual damages and $10 million in punitive damages. The suit claims that EDS sold the company a minicomputer system that never worked properly, that EDS was to modify the system as needed for five years but abandoned the project, and that

EDS personnel made fraudulent claims about the system's capabilities.

On February 16, 1983 EDS filed a breach of contract suit to recover $9,000 from each of three former employees. The suits claim that the three former employees breached an agreement to repay EDS for their training as systems engineers. Two employees resigned approximately one year after signing their contracts and one employee was terminated. According to EDS's employment contract, each employee must sign a promissory note when hired for training. If s/he resigns or is terminated for just cause within two years after training, the employee must repay EDS for the training received—amounting to $9,000 per employee. This suit is currently pending in the court. Such breaches of training contracts are not new to EDS, however, since once an employee has completed EDS's rigorous training program, s/he possesses highly marketable skills. Since EDS's compensation package is competitive, management is unsure of why there seems to be such a mass exodus from the EDS ranks, although it is a well-known fact that an employee's every personal move is scrutinized in addition to on-the-job behavior.

Industry Outlook

The rapid growth of the computer-services market can be attributed to the rising number of computer installations, declining hardware prices, growing user sophistication, productivity improvement efforts, and a shortage of qualified customer-employed programmers. INPUT, a leading international consulting firm, predicts that the $15-billion computer-services market will grow at an annual rate of 19 percent to reach $35 billion by 1985. The firm also comments that "at this pace, the value of computer services—excluding contributions by hardware manufacturers—by early 1984 should exceed that of computer hardware shipments." Exhibit 13 illustrates the value of hardware shipments vs. computer services in the United States. EDS management anticipates computer operations will continue to grow in several specific areas. These areas and their estimated growth are illustrated in Exhibit 14.

EXHIBIT 13
Value of U.S. Hardward Shipments vs. Computer Services
(in Billions of Dollars)

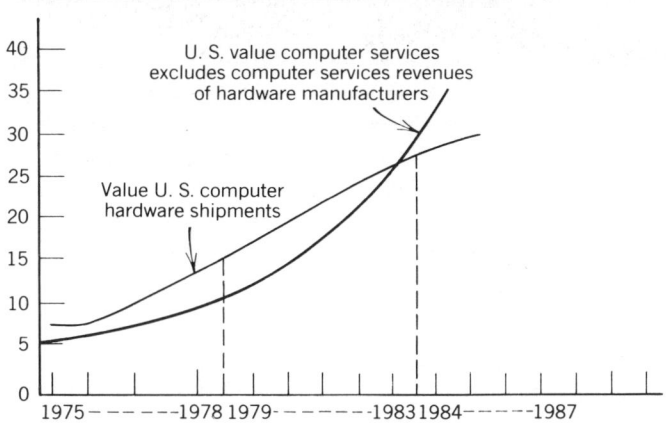

Source: Standard and Poor's Industry Surveys, Office Equipment Systems and Services, July 30, 1981 (Section 2), p. 22.

EXHIBIT 14
Growth in Computer Operations Fiscal Year 1982

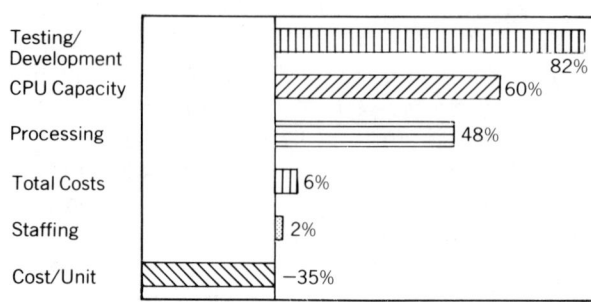

Source: Company Records.

EDS management is deliberating over expectations in the computer industry over the next decade and the challenges they will face. Although they have been successful thus far, several of EDS's top managers are skeptical as to whether such success will continue if EDS does not establish a formalized strategic planning system, especially since EDS has grown so rapidly in recent years. However, these same top managers are aware of Perot's intentions of remaining active in his company, of thus maintaining his militaristic, top-down planning process. The five Group Vice-Presidents have been informally discussing possible avenues for developing a strategic planning system which will meet Perot's approval and yet will also incorporate ideas from lower-level managers who have to live with the day-to-day mechanics of the plans handed down to them.

Another concern of management is centered upon an article appearing in the *Dallas Morning News* "Dallas Life" section on April 17, 1983. The following quote is the opening statement of Jane Sumner's documentary "How Much Do You Make?":

Two things will get you fired at multimillionaire H. Ross Perot's Electronic Data Systems company in North Dallas. One is marital infidelity. The other is talking about how much you make.

Statements such as this are not uncommon when discussing the reputation EDS has built regarding employee practices on and off the job. Although there are no longer strict requirements on clothes, length of hair, and beards, such topics as proper social behavior and pay secrecy are areas that many EDS employees seem to believe are none of EDS's concern if it does not affect their work performance. Perot feels that EDS's staunch image is a positive factor, but some upper-level managers disagree in view of EDS's inability to retain many talented computer professionals once they are trained at EDS. Thus, these managers are also discussing the personality of EDS and what, if any, changes should be made to improve EDS's organizational climate. They plan to bring their comments to Perot's attention for consideration, although they are unsure about Perot's reception of such ideas.

DIAMOND VALLEY SAVINGS AND LOAN ASSOCIATION

Introduction

In spring 1971, it was anticipated that Data Bank Company, the computer-operating subsidiary partnership of Diamond Valley Savings and Loan Association and Helix Savings and Loan Association, would achieve the status of a profitable enterprise. This was a source of great satisfaction to James Sedgwick, President of Diamond Valley, because he had been the driving force in bring his Association to a full on-line computer system and the formation of Data Bank. There had been times in the past when only his faith had sustained the computerization program.

History

Diamond Valley was one of the oldest stockholder-owned savings and loan associations in California. Founded in the 1890s, it enjoyed a slow but steady growth for decades until the 1950s. Then, an enormous number of new people began coming to Southern California and the Association's area changed from rural to suburban. At the same time, federal government policy enabled savings and loan associations to make much longer term loans than they previously had made. The result approximated an exponential rate of growth for Diamond Valley. (See Appendices A and B.)

Mr. James Sedgwick came to Diamond Valley in 1955 as Assistant Comptroller. Thirty years of age, he had had several years experience in banking. The year that he joined the Association it had savings totalling approximately $38,000,000. All bookkeeping was done manually, but this presented no particular problem because computations were routine and only one savings plan—the passbook

Source: This case was prepared by Julius S. Brown, PhD. Permission to use granted by Julius S. Brown.

APPENDIX A
Total Savings (Selected Years 1950–1980) (000 omitted)

Year	Savings
1950	$ 11,944
1955	38,622
1960	72,969
1965	133,532
1970	188,762
1975	202,881
1977	216,322
1980	214,292

APPENDIX B
Net Operating Income Before Income Taxes (Selected Years, 1950–1980) (000 omitted)

Year	Income
1950	$ 507
1955	1,684
1960	3,522
1965	7,486
1970	10,859
1975	12,439
1980	(−)3,289

account—was offered. The rate of interest paid on savings was 4 percent paid semiannually, and interest was paid only on residual balance, that is, interest was paid only on the sum of money in an account on the date of payment and the full six months previously. By 1969, Mr. Sedgwick had been promoted to Vice President and Comptroller (Exhibit 1).

By 1960, savings in the Association had grown to $72,000,000, four branch offices had been opened, and other changes had taken place. Interest was paid quarterly and within a short period of time would change to payment by daily compounding. Interest was now being paid from date of deposit to date of withdrawal and "odd" rates of interest were being

EXHIBIT 1
Senior Officers of Diamond Valley Savings and Loan as Listed on the Annual Statement of December 1969

Thomas Still, Chairman
Patrick Gilbert, President
Donald Osgood, Executive Vice-President
Peter J. Knotz, Senior Vice-President
James J. Bohn, Senior Vice-President
Joseph L. Parent, Senior Vice-President
James Sedgwick, Vice-President—Comptroller
Philip E. Shaw, Vice-President
Jane M. McCollum, Vice President and Treasurer

paid, such as 4.75 percent or 4.85 percent. These factors enormously increased the work of the Association and sometimes caused customer servicing to be very poor. For example, a teller might leave a customer standing at his window for as long as 10 minutes while the teller searched the "tubs" for his ledger card, made calculations and entries, and returned the customer's account book. Another change that added to the Association's book work was the new federal rule requiring that each saver's interest earning be reported on form 1099 annually to both the saver and the Internal Revenue Service.

To meet these changing conditions, the Association did what Mr. Sedgwick considered "make do with patchwork." But from 1957 on he was searching for alternatives; he felt that there simply had to be a better way. One factor that made his search easier was the fact that IBM was located a few doors from the main office of the Association. Mr. Sedgwick did a great deal of what he later described as "going over to watch those crazy people." In fact, he was greatly interested in computer technology and was learning a great deal about it; unlike many executives, Mr. Sedgwick felt no awe at the "mystery" of computers, but enjoyed a sense of familiarity that was to serve him and Diamond Valley well in subsequent years. An example of Mr. Sedgwick's valuable knowledge occurred in 190 when the Association had leased from IBM the standard punch-card system then available. Mr. Sedgwick felt that IBM's prescribed system, which wired teller positions to punch-card machines, was getting "dirty" raw data into the computer, so he improvised a system of wiring the proof machine to the punch-card machine and cut down appreciably on expensive errors.

Mr. Sedgwick was still not satisfied with his computer system, however, and was still searching for alternatives when, in 1962, the on-line[1] real-time computer system came over the horizon. His favorable response was immediate, because he saw a way to get a computer system that he felt would really fill the Association's needs.

The On-Line Computer System: IBM 1440

Investigation of On-Line Systems

In June 1962 the Board of Directors of Diamond Valley appointed a committee to study the feasibility of on-line computer systems. Mr. Sedgwick was named chairman; the other members were Mr. Donald Osgood, Executive Vice-President of the Association, and Mr. Philip Head, a member of the Board of Directors who was a professor of mathematics at a nearby college.

Mr. Sedgwick began an intensive study of on-line systems and soon came to four conclusions: (1) the system could do what otherwise soon would be impossible, such as furnishing instant information on daily compounding; (2) the system would give accurate information, eliminating both errors and the man-hours re-

---

[1] An on-line computer system is one that is based on random access devices, allowing immediate ("real time") output to a terminal's input. For example, a saver's deposit can be recorded by a teller on his terminal, and the teller receives instant information on the depositor's balance including interest compounded to date and the new deposit. An off-line system, by comparison, typically processes the saver's deposit a few hours later and a printout may not be available until the following day.

quired under the current methods to minimize the errors; (3) on-line systems remove people between the account and the computer, and the consequent reduction of errors would be substantial; (4) improvement of the teller line's services and keeping pace with projected growth required an on-line system—there was no alternative.

As to costs, Mr. Sedgwick believed that it was extremely difficult and of dubious value to try to project in detail. He felt that the costs were reasonable, but he also knew that the Association would not fully utilize available computer hours. The potential advantages were so great, however, that he reasoned that the Association could justifiably underwrite the costs for three to five years.

Mr. Osgood favored leasing on-line capability from a time-sharing computer company, which Mr. Sedgwick opposed. Sedgwick felt that Diamond Valley should be independent rather than having to deal with some huge Los Angeles corporation where the Association might get lost in bureaucracy. Mr. Sedgwick's view prevailed.

Mr. Sedgwick made these decisions despite opposition from Osgood; the latter thought Sedgwick's cost-analysis weak and perfunctory. Mr. Head, the outsider, invariably sided with Sedgwick. Head knew that Mr. Sedgwick had a scientifically oriented education (B.S. in chemistry) and that his interest in the knowledge of computers was quite deep. By this time, he had learned programming language and was a competent programmer.

The Computer Studies Committee completed its inquiries and made a presentation of its recommendations to the Board of Directors in fall 1963. Mr. Sedgwick made the presentation in the form of flip charts. Osgood and Head remained silent during this meeting. Following the presentation, the Board voted to accept the Committee's recommendations, and Mr. Sedgwick was instructed to order the hardware from IBM. He was also assigned the responsibility for the installation and operation of the system.

Personnel Policies

Immediately after Mr. Sedgwick ordered the computer hardware from IBM, the Association announced this fact to all employees through its house organ. With the backing of Mr. Gilbert, Sedgwick, who wrote and signed the article, also announced that it would be Association policy that no employee would lose his or her job because of the computer. He told employees that there would be some retraining necessary in some jobs, and that employees might well be asked to shift to a different job, but he reiterated that no one would be discharged. Inasmuch as the computer would, among other things, eliminate the bookkeeping department completely, Mr. Sedgwick knew that a good deal of job shifting would take place. He was confident, however, that attrition would take care of any problem of surplus people.

Mr. Sedgwick was most sincere in his desire to retain employees. One significant measure that he took was to announce to all employees that on a given Saturday morning IBM would give a computer aptitude test to any Association employees who wished to take it, and from this test he expected to find the people who would be the association's programmers. He assured employees that whether they did or did not take the test would have no affect on their personnel record. Second, if they did poorly on the test, the matter was confidential and would not be part of their record. The test was given and led to the identification and development of four programmers. (The highest grade was received by a young woman who was in a rather routine clerical job and had a high-school education. True to his word, Mr. Sedgwick made her a programmer—by 1970 she had become the senior programmer at Data Bank Company at a salary twice her previous pay.) Above all, Mr. Sedgwick felt that it was important to be open and frank with employees. An open house was held in the computer room when the hardward arrived and all employees were invited in to see first-hand what the new equipment looked like. Mr. Osgood took a dim view of this activity, telling Sedgwick at one point that it was a waste of time and money, and that replacement of any disgruntled employee would be quite easy, since their skill levels generally were fairly low.

General Personnel Policies

The general personnel policies of the Association were described by Mr. Sedgwick as "being professional." Once per month an outside professional salary administration consultant came in to join the Association's salary committee meeting. The Association provided fringe benefits that cost 43 percent of wage costs; these included fully paid group health insurance, a retirement plan, a free lunch, and coffee break victuals (doughnuts, rolls, coffee, etc.) in a spacious and attractive cafeteria located in the basement; these same extras were provided at the branches. The style of the cafeteria was very informal. It would be quite common for an officer, particularly Mr. Sedgwick, to be joined at lunch by one or more of the young clerks. The officers encouraged these opportunities for one-to-one conversation with the younger people. Particularly before the arrival of the IBM 1440 hardware, most of the officers found these informal contacts helpful in allaying any fears that employees might feel about the new computer. One thing that they did not discuss with employees at this time, however—not for reasons of secrecy but because they felt that it would pose no additional transition problems—was the fact that before the IBM 1440 arrived they were already investigating the next generation computer, IBM 360. In late summer 1964 the 360/30 was ordered for 1967 delivery.

IBM 360/30: Third Generation Computer

Mr. Sedgwick was aware of the capacity limitations on the IBM 1440, and the decision to go to the 360/30 seemed a logical transition consonant with the Association's policy of planning ahead for expected growth. Although the total cost of the 360/30 was higher than the 1440, its capacity was so much greater that the unit cost of computing was about the same although no detailed cost studies were made. As Mr. Sedgwick later described the situation, "We knew that we were buying more capacity than we needed. We were, however, willing to underwrite it for a time."

Data Bank Company

As the matter evolved, Diamond Valley did not have to go it alone on the IBM 360/30. Mr. Sedgwick happened to be chatting after church one Sunday morning in mid-1965 with a casual acquaintance, Mr. Harold Forbes, whom he knew to be a partner in the Los Angeles management consulting firm of Forbes and Handley. Mr. Sedgwick mentioned that the Diamond Valley Association had an IBM 360/30 on order, and Mr. Forbes told him that his consulting firm had a client, a nearby savings and loan association, that also had a 360/30 on order. He inquired whether Mr. Sedgwick would be interested in discussing the possibility of the two organizations joining in computer orders. Mr. Sedgwick readily assented, and within a few days had, along with Helix Savings and Loan (Mr. Forbes' client), authorized Forbes and Handley to make a full-scale study of a joint computer venture. A few months later the consultants submitted their report, recommending the formation of a computer cooperative, outlining its functions and operations, and estimating a cost savings to Diamond Valley of $38,915 per year and Helix Federal of $49,425 per year. The Boards of both Associations accepted the reports, and meetings were held between the affected officers of the two Associations through spring 1966. By

June, details had been worked out and Mr. Gilbert announced the formation of Data Bank Company in a letter to all Association employees (Appendix C).

Mr. Sedgwick had anticipated that subsidizing Data Bank would be expensive for Diamond Valley in its initial years and it was. He felt, however, that the investment was necessary. He also felt that it was necessary, as the consultants had recommended, that the firm be staffed with people who were not only competent but highly compatible. Their work was so exacting, their work load and hours so irregular, and their mutual interdependence so great that he felt that they must operate almost as a separate unit from the Association itself.

In Retrospect:
The Success of On-Line Computing

In fall 1970 the Board of Directors of Diamond Valley named Mr. Gilbert as Chairman of the Board and Chief Executive Officer and Mr. Sedgwick President of the Association.

Concurrent with these personnel changes in the Association, the hardware, people, and accoutrements of Data Bank Company were moved out of their location adjacent to the Association's head office and into new, specially prepared subsurface offices in a branch of the Association located about five miles from the head office. The main reason for the move was that Data Bank had outgrown its quarters. In the years 1967–1970 Data Bank had been approached by quite a large number of savings and loan associations regarding the possibility of coming into their computer system, the negotiating stage had been reached with many, and some had signed contracts and had been brought on-line. Mr. Sedgwick carried the major responsibility for these negotiations, aided by Mr. Steven Cunningham, Manager of Data Bank. Mr. Sedgwick had discovered in 1967 that his original idea of bringing in other associations on a cooperative, cost-sharing basis was not attractive to other associations, who shied away from what they considered the risks of excessive potential costs. Other associations were interested in buying services, however, on a contractual basis and Mr. Sedgwick accommodated them. As Mr. Sedgwick later explained it, they seemed to "have built a better mousetrap." Data Bank had never actively solicited business among other savings and loans, yet its services were in very high demand. Viewing this high demand, Mr. Sedgwick decided in 1968 that the Company should (1) go to a new IBM 360/40 system to increase capacity, and (2) should purchase the hardware instead of leasing it. The latter decision was based on Mr. Sedgwick's informal estimate that the 360/40 would be the ultimate in computing for the next eight to ten years, and in view of that fact would cost less to own than to lease. As it turned out, he reversed both decisions two years later as Data Bank went to a still higher capacity 360/50 and Mr. Sedgwick decided to sell the 360/40 and lease the new equipment, reverting to the original premise that technology moved too fast to get locked in by purchasing. By the beginning of 1971, Data Bank Company was servicing 22 savings and loan associations with a total of 250 terminals on line. Mr. Sedgwick and Mr. Cunningham had decided that this was about the limit of their present capacity—in the heavy reinvestment period of the first 10 days of January 1971, there had been delays at the terminals as long as 15 seconds—and that no new associa-

EXHIBIT 2
Senior Officers of Diamond Valley Savings and Loan as Listed on the Annual Statement of December 1970

Patrick Gilbert, Chairman and Chief Executive Officer
James Sedgwick, President
Donald Osgood, Executive Vice-President
Peter J. Knotz, First Vice-President
James J. Bohn, First Vice-President
Joseph L. Parent, Senior Vice-President
Philip E. Shaw, Senior Vice-President
Arthur A. Penny, Senior Vice-President
Jane M. McCollum, Vice-President and Treasurer

APPENDIX C
Letter to Association Employees Announcing Formation of Data Bank Company

Diamond Valley Savings and Loan Association Inter-Office Correspondence

TO: ALL EMPLOYEES   DATE: June 8, 1966
FROM: PATRICK GILBERT, PRESIDENT
SUBJECT: COMPUTER COOPERATIVE

The purpose of this memo is to further clarify the relationship between Diamond Valley and the data-processing company that will install the 360 Computer. Data Bank Company has been selected as the name of the organization.

1. Data Bank Company is a new company jointly owned by Diamond Valley and Helix.

2. This new company was formed for the sole purpose of installing and maintaining an *on-line* 360 Computer to service the offices of Diamond Valley and Helix Savings and Loan Association.

3. The Data Bank Company is a partnership form of organization. An Operating Board has overall responsibility for the Company.

   Operating Board

Jim Sedgwick	Diamond Valley
George Stillman	Helix
Bill Sullivan	Helix
Al Goss	Diamond Valley

4. Steve Cunningham is the Managing Officer of Data Bank Company. Steve was formerly the Manager of the Helix Data-Processing Department. Helix has been on-line with the 1440 for over a year.

5. Data Bank Company will rent office space and floor space for the computer from Diamond Valley. The company will be quartered at Main Office of Diamond Valley.

6. Technical staffing of Data Bank Company will be accomplished by transferring Programmers from both Diamond Valley and Helix to the new company. This procedure will take place gradually during the next few weeks.

   By August there will be five employees on the Data Bank Company payroll:

Steve Cunningham	(from Helix)
Bob Herring	(from Diamond Valley)
Charlie Bills	(from Diamond Valley)
Maxine Rand	(from Diamond Valley)
John Brown	(from Diamond Valley)

7. Data Bank Company has the responsibility for designing the new 360 Computer System and writing the programs to implement that design.

8. The 360 Computer will be installed and servicing Diamond Valley and Helix by April 1, 1967.

9. This new approach to Cooperative Data Processing will result in more sophisticated computer systems at reduced cost for both Diamond Valley and Helix. It is anticipated that the operation will be expanded in the future to include other savings and loan associations. Such expansion would further reduce the costs to all member associations.

10. Formation of Data Bank Company does not imply a merger of Diamond Valley and Helix. The cooperative venture is restricted to data-processing only.

11. A temporary office for the new company has been set up on the second floor at Diamond Valley Main Office (Ext. 290).

tions would be accepted for the next two years. Helix and Diamond Valley would both now begin to pay the established rate for Data Bank's services, which would make a profitable year for the company virtually certain.

It was of considerable interest to Mr. Gilbert and Mr. Sedgwick that almost exactly concurrent with Diamond Valley's development of its on-line computer system, another association located in a community approximately 50 miles from Diamond Valley had tried to follow the same path and experienced a costly failure. The other association had, in fact, by 1970 cancelled its hardware leases at a great loss, dissolved its computer operation, and had appealed to and been brought on-line with Data Bank Company.

Mr. Gilbert, in trying to appraise the different results in the two endeavors, felt that the difference was Mr. Sedgwick. He felt that Mr. Sedgwick was quite different in approach to both the computer and the people who worked with it than most executives. Mr. Sedgwick learned to be a programmer; he learned the formal machine language of the computer. But even more important, he learned the esoteric argot of the people who worked with the computer; he became one of them, working side by side with them, gaining an acceptance and a rapport with them. He knew their problems and could discuss the problems in their language. The proof of the importance of Mr. Sedgwick's approach, Mr. Gilbert felt, lay in the fact that the employee turnover in the computer group through the entire period 1964 to 1970 was almost zero. The only loss was one woman who asked to be transferred to another job in the Association. This was noteworthy because of the fact that through this period everyone had a very heavy workload. Working days of 12 or even up to 18 hours were common; working round-the-clock over a weekend to bring a customer on-line was not at all unusual.

In contrast to this, Mr. Gilbert had observed that in the operation of the unsuccessful association's computer venture no officer had become so informed on either computers or people as Mr. Sedgwick. He had also observed that their key programmers, operators, and managers had a way of quitting for another job at critical times.

Last, Mr. Gilbert observed that Mr. Sedgwick had from the first an enormous faith in an on-line computer system as the solution to the mounting paperwork, errors, and personal exasperation and frustration of the people doing the daily work of the savings and loan industry.

Mr. Sedgwick appraised the difference in the two association's success with on-line systems somewhat differently. He did agree with Mr. Gilbert that he had taken great personal interest in both the hardware and the people associated with the computer. Now that Data Bank Company was becoming not only successful but profitable, he did, as he stated it, "bask in the sunshine of their success." (He did not and never had received a dollar of personal compensation from Data Bank.) However, Mr. Sedgwick felt that there were additional factors accounting for the success of Diamond Valley's on-line system. For one thing, he had had a great deal of freedom in decision making; the Computer Study Committee, Mr. Gilbert, and the Board had exhibited a high degree of faith in him. In discussion, Mr. Sedgwick did not mention Mr. Osgood, always referring simply to "the Committee."

Mr. Sedgwick also credited the consultants with making him aware of the most important usage of the computer system—its resource as the core of a management information system. The on-line system had been brought in to improve the services of and help the people on the teller line, which it had done very successfully. By 1973, however, Mr. Sedgwick was becoming increasingly impressed with the computer's aid to him in management decisions. He was, for example, getting reports by 9:30 A.M. every morning telling him (1) savings inflow, loans made, and change in cash position for the previous day, and (2) expected change in cash position for the current day. Based on this information, two things had been possible. Mr. Sedgwick could in a few minutes complete investment decisions for the day, and he could often take advantage of his information to increase the Association's earnings. For example, on a Friday he could often make short-term investments over the weekend instead of leaving a savings inflow idle for the period.

On the whole, the 1970s had been a period of stable, steady growth in both Diamond Valley and Data Bank Company. Interest rates had risen slowly, but Diamond Valley was able to maintain a satisfactory margin between the rate paid savers and the rate charged for mortgages. Data Bank had steadily increased its business and profitability. Mr. Sedgwick had, in 1976, moved up to Chairman of Data Bank and the Board had elevated Cunningham to President. (Data Bank had incorporated earlier and Diamond Valley had bought out Helix for cash.)

By 1980, however, the situation at Diamond Valley had changed dramatically. Interest rates had soared. Deregulation of financial insititutions had brought new, formidable competitors (particularly money market funds) into prominence. To maintain competitiveness, Diamond Valley was offering half a dozen different types and rates of savings and checking accounts were offered in direct competition with banks. A particularly ill omen was the large portfolio of old mortgages at a fixed interest rate below that which now had to be paid to savers.

Mr. Sedgwick, now in his mid-fifties, was deeply immersed in all of the many problems of Diamond Valley. Data Bank Company was still expanding its services to match the new complexities of its customers and was very profitable, but Diamond Valley had begun to suffer losses.

Some members of the Board were advocating the acceptance by Diamond Valley of a takeover offer from one of California's largest financial institutions; their position was, essentially, "bail out of the savings and loan business and get totally in the profitable computer time-sharing business of Data Bank." Mr. Sedgwick differed with these Board members. He explained that his thinking was fourfold. First, Diamond Valley was slowly beginning to lower its losses as more old mortgages went off the books to be replaced with profitable business. Second, the profitability of Data Bank kept Diamond Valley from serious cash flow problems. Third, the beginning of the era of microprocessors foretold a radical decrease in computer costs. (Mr. Cunningham told Sedgwick that Data Bank was fully prepared for any technological changes and could become even more profitable. Sedgwick was not so sure.) Fourth, he had faith in the people of Diamond Valley. He knew that over the years they had adapted well to change and were, he felt, much more loyal than employees of the average thrift institution.

The opposing Board members thought differently. They were uncomfortable, unhappy, and worried about the enormity of changes taking place. They pointed out that the takeover offer, half in cash and half in stock of the huge, blue-chip institution, would net a new, comfortable profit to the stockholders of Diamond Valley, and the cash could be used to further expand Data Bank, perhaps into fields not now tapped.

Sedgwick tended to worry more about what he saw as the tremendous risks of the revolutionary changes in data processing. "Let's stick with the risks we know," he put it, an attitude that amused Osgood, who recalled Sedgwick's "seat of the pants" approach to the risks Diamond Valley had taken over the previous 20 years.

THE AMERICAN EXPRESS COMPANY

By the middle of 1981, the finance-related and insurance industries were in a period of rapid change and turmoil. Each industry was facing problems resulting from general economic conditions and intensified competition. The basis for competition was changing as companies departed from traditional and historic roles, new and powerful entrants threatened, and technological innovation was obvious everywhere. As an active participant in these industries, American Express was also experiencing a year of transition and challenge. James D. Robinson, III, CEO, offered his view of the future:

> By 1990, you'll have a stockbroker in California, a banker in New York, an insurance agency in Maryland, and a realtor jetting between Chicago and Boston. All your purchases will be on the American Express Card, of course. And within the decade you'll have the option of banking by mail or by cable television.[1]

The challenge for American Express was to chart a course for this vision.

The Credit-Card Industry

The first credit cards in the United States were issued in the 1920s by oil companies as a means of promoting brand loyalty and providing a billing convenience for traveling customers. Use of cards was expanded slightly during the 1930s when department stores issued cards to their charge-account customers and major oil companies developed reciprocal billing arrangements. This relatively limited use of cards was abruptly changed in the early 1950s when the credit-card industry was born with the formation of Diners Club. Diners Club began in February 1950 with 22 restaurants and 200 cardholders. After a first-year loss of $158,730, Diners Club earned a $61,222 profit its second year and then continually expanded the scope of its operations during the 1950s. American Express entered the industry in 1958 and took over industry leadership in 1959 by acquiring two smaller competitors. Carte Blanche became competitive in the industry in 1959 when Hilton Hotels added establishments outside of the Hilton chain to its credit-card system.

Banks entered the industry in the late 1950s when the first bank credit card was issued by Franklin National Bank. Through the 1960s the bank cards grew by offering cards to a wider segment of the population and by allowing use for goods and services beyond travel and entertainment.

By 1980 there were over 600 million credit cards in circulation in the United States and it was estimated that there would be 1 billion cards worldwide by 1985. Americans are by far the greatest users of credit cards, holding about 82 percent of all cards. As of 1978 American consumers held an average of 5.2 cards and business persons an average of 11.3 cards each. Of the 1979 total installment borrowing of $300 billion in the United States, about $100 billion was through credit cards.

In spite of their early entry in the industry, travel and entertainment (T & E) cards have not maintained a significant share in terms of number of cards in circulation. In 1980 T & E accounted for one-half of the cards in existance. Sears Roebuck was the single largest issuer; in 1978 Sears alone had 47 million cards in circulation. The proportion of retailers' cards has been on the decline, however, as smaller retailers are being absorbed by conglomerates that tend to favor the use of bank credit cards. In 1979 there were about 115 mil-

---

Source: Dennis W. Callaghan and Robert A. Comerford, *Strategic Management: Text, Tools, and Cases for Business Policy* (Boston: Kent Publishing Company, 1985). © 1985 by Wadsworth, Inc. Reprinted by permission of Kent Publishing Company, a division of Wadsworth, Inc.
[1]Thomas O'Donnell, "The Tube, The Card, The Ticker, and Jim Robinson," *Forbes,* May 25, 1981.

lion bank cards in circulation and that number is expected to increase to 255 million by 1985. Oil companies maintained about 22 percent of the cards outstanding in 1980 and all other types (airlines, etc.) had about 3 percent.

Bank Cards

In 1980 banks held about 22 percent of the number of cards outstanding, but were by far the most aggressive segment of the industry. Traditionally, the bank cards have been differentiated by the fact that they extend a line of credit to the cardholder, whereas the T & E cards demand payment on request each month. Young families, families with children, and families headed by those without a college degree are most likely to use the credit feature of cards, while others use the cards primarily to facilitate transactions. In the mid to late 1970s the use of the credit feature grew rapidly. In 1978, for instance, there was $23 billion of credit outstanding on bank cards, which was a 33 percent increase over the previous year. By the late 1970s interest charges provided 70 percent of the bank's credit-card earnings, which was far greater than the percentages received from merchant discounts (about 2 percent of the amount purchased) and fees. Recently, however, the costs of financing receivables have increased markedly and many banks have begun to charge annual fees of 10 to 15 dollars or transactions fees to offset these costs. Transaction fees are typically 12 cents per transaction. In 1980 about one-half of all bank cardholders paid either annual or transaction fees. In 1979 there were practically none. In other moves to combat higher financing costs, some banks have been moving their operations to states that allow higher than the standard 18 percent interest rate.

In spite of these changes to improve position, most banks lost money on their credit-card operations in late 1979 and 1980. More and more customers were paying off their accounts within the interest-free grace period. In 1980 the banks seemed to suffer no significant drop-off of business because of the institution of fees, but the proportion of billings incurring no interest approached 50 percent. This pay-off phenomenon has led many banks to conclude that they are not selling credit so much as convenience or "transfer of value." This conclusion has led the banks to consider offering other transfer of value instruments such as debit cards[2] and travelers' checks as potential services. For instance, bank cards have teamed up with Western Union's emergency money-order service to allow callers to wire up to $300 to any of 8,100 offices in the United States and to have the amount charged to their credit cards. It is generally felt that if consumers continue to decrease their amount of credit-card debt, the competition will intensify and bank cards will move more aggressively into travelers' checks and other segments of the travel and entertainment segment. In fact, surveys already show that more consumers are using bank cards than are using T & E cards for restaurant checks and hotel bills. As of 1978, Visa and MasterCard claimed 2.5 million outlets accepting cards; Diners Club 400,000; American Express 350,000; and Carte Blanche 250,000.

The two strongest competitors among bank cards are Visa and MasterCard. While Visa has recently overtaken MasterCard as the leader in worldwide volume and number of holders, MasterCard still retains an edge in the United States. Both provide debit cards and are venturing into the travelers' check business.

Visa changed its name from Bank Americard in 1977 in order to shed its national identity with its political connotations and to project more of a worldwide image. The number of Visa cardholders increased dramatically during the late 1970s with over 70 million by 1979. The volume of Visa transactions also has

---

[2]Debit cards operate similarly to credit cards except that when the bank is notified of a sale, it immediately deducts the amount from an account balance that the consumer maintains with the bank, much in the same manner as with a checking account.

increased rapidly (91 percent in 1977–1979 period), primarily from retail stores and restaurants.

Visa presents increasingly formidable competition in the credit-card industry displaying corporate agility that fostered innovations such as the debit card (800,000 accounts in 1980), the single trendy name, and strong initiatives in foreign markets. Although Visa's management sees travelers' checks as a regression into paper processing (which runs counter to their electronic processing strength), they have aggressively entered the travelers' check market. Depending upon cooperation with Barclay's (presently fourth largest issuer of travelers' checks), Visa's business has been growing at a 15 percent annual rate. In 1980 Visa has 8 percent of the U. S. market and is expecting a 40 percent share by 1985. As of 1980 about 90 percent of the checks processed were, in fact, Barclay's. The largest bank to build Visa travelers' checks sales from scratch is First National Bank of Chicago. As of 1980 that bank had sold $50 million in checks. Visa's plan for the travelers' check business is to allow participating banks to place their own names on the checks. Visa hopes this approach will lure banks who have been selling American Express checks.

MasterCard, with its 65 million worldwide cardholders in 1979, has been fighting the Visa challenge with larger advertising outlays (40 percent increase in 1979), a name change from Master Charge to MasterCard, debit cards, and a delayed venture into travelers' checks. The travelers' check delay was caused by a legal roadblock set up by Citibank, a member of the MasterCard system, who already held 12 percent of the world travelers' check market. Along with Visa, the MasterCard system is large enough and integrated enough to provide economy of-scale advantages in authorization and interchange procedures.

Travel and Entertainment Cards

In 1978 it was estimated that $385 billion was spent on domestic and international travel and that by 1988 the amount spent will be $755 billion. American Express is by far the largest T & E card company with 11.9 million cardholders in 1980. The American Express card is held by more than half of the country's families who earn more than $25,000 annually. American Express engages in heavy advertising campaigns and frequently co-sponsors ads with hotels and restaurants that accept their card.

Diners Club intensified their marketing efforts in the late 1970s with large increases in marketing budgets. In 1979 Diners Club claimed 2.5 million cardholders, with about 60 percent of the holders residing outside of the United States. Carte Blanche, with 800,000 holders in 1979, serves the affluent, has snob appeal, and turned down 75 percent of its 40,000 monthly applicants in 1978. Acquired from AVCO by Citicorp in 1979, Carte Blanche was generally thought to be in need of new marketing emphasis in order to survive.

In contrast to bank cards, which credit merchants' accounts on the same day an invoice is received, T & E cards generally cause the merchants to wait several days for payments. T & E cards also charge a higher discount to the merchants, typically 3.5 to 4 percent of the price of purchase. American Express, for instance, offers retailers the option of being paid in from 1 to 30 days after receipt, with the discount rate correspondingly lower as the period is extended.

Travelers' Checks

Closely related to the T & E credit-card segment is the travelers' check industry. Started in 1891 by American Express, which maintains 60 percent of the market, the major competitors are Bank of America, Citibank, Barclays, and Thomas Cook. In 1978, 735 million travelers' checks were sold at a value of $25 billion. The five major U. S. and British issuers earned an estimated total of $239 million. In the five-year period 1974–1979, the industry sales grew 120 percent and by 1979 worldwide sales had reached $30 billion.

Most income on travelers' checks is made not on the nominal fee charged (usually one percent of face value), but on the "float." That is, on checks that are purchased and paid for, but not yet cashed. The average float period for travelers' checks is about two months. The companies can then invest this cash for two months until the checks are cashed. American Express, for instance, had about $2.3 billion in travelers' check float in 1979. Thus, industry experts indicate that it is unlikely that a company can be profitable in travelers' checks with an annual volume of less than $2 billion.

Property–Casualty Insurance Industry

In contrast to the concentration of the credit-card industry, the property–casualty (p–c) insurance industry has a large number of competitors with 200 companies that have written over $40 million in premiums in 1980. Many, but not all, of the leading p–c companies are also leaders in life insurance (See Exhibit 1). Even within the p–c segment, not all companies offer full lines of p–c insurance services. The importance of the various insurance lines in the p–c segment is shown in Exhibit 2.

EXHIBIT 1
Leading Property/Casualty Companies and Groups (1980 Net Premiums Written in Thousands)

	Rank	Total p–c Companies Premiums	Life Insurance Premiums	Total Premium Volume	Rank	Percent Increase 1 Yr	5 Yr Compound
State Farm	1	8,011,787	551,365	8,563,152	3	10.83	19.10
Allstate	2	5,270,426	240,300	5,515,454	6	9.89	12.27
Aetna Life and Casualty	3	4,558,426	3,939,761	10,294,080	1	3.72	16.05
Travelers	4	2,888,253	2,526,244	7,128,640	4	9.05	5.64
Liberty Mutual	5	2,867,423	39,677	2,911,727	10	4.29	18.47
Continental Insurance	6	2,822,595	44,886	2,883,049	11	6.25	7.61
Hartford Fire	7	2,661,964	301,050	3,217,105	9	4.73	9.83
Farmers Insurance	8	2,552,756	133,413	2,719,557	13	7.32	20.69
INA	9	2,550,211	458,050	3,349,209	8	6.08	9.20
Fireman's Fund	10	2,350,283	75,354	2,525,217	17	2.43	12.94
U. S. Fidelity & Guaranty	11	2,043,653	48,008	2,093,985	20	2.63	16.40
Nationwide	12	1,951,339	574,703	2,590,320	15	10.95	18.21
Kemper	13	1,689,683	363,964	2,053,740	21	5.48	12.55
Home Insurance	14	1,689,386	45,964	1,814,049	22	4.04	14.26
Crum and Forster	15	1,620,970	—	1,620,970	25	2.38	13.07
St. Paul	16	1,520,073	96,832	1,682,636	23	9.00	14.18
CNA	17	1,418,916	413,262	2,469,170	18	8.61	16.20
American International	18	1,374,564	203,950	1,632,035	24	10.34	24.82
Chubb	19	1,142,373	88,380	1,281,117	27	6.21	9.31
Commercial Union	20	1,115,897	20,939	1,137,437	28	15.19	8.58
Prudential of America	21	1,023,892	5,847,490	9,681,087	2	11.82	28.79
Connecticut General	22	1,011,796	629,059	2,872,063	12	−1.76	10.88
Royal Insurance	23	957,059	8,890	956,949	35	3.27	7.55
American Financial	24	898,823	177,897	1,079,999	29	9.64	4.82
Reliance	25	875,799	107,299	1,036,609	30	−3.67	10.48

Source: Adapted from *Best's Review: Property/Casualty Insurance Edition*, June 1981.

EXHIBIT 2
Property/Casualty Insurance Industry

	Premium Distribution by Line			Loss Ratio[b]			
	Total Premiums[a]	Percent of Total	Gain in Premiums[a]	1980	1979	1978	1977
Fire	2,887,770	3.0	−19,425	56.1	51.6	47.5	51.0
Allied Lines	1,673,619	1.7	44,043	69.1	67.9	57.1	46.6
Farmowners Multi-Peril	594,335	0.6	60,316	76.5	61.4	60.3	61.0
Homeowners Multi-Peril	10,012,854	10.4	982,901	67.1	61.5	53.5	53.1
Commercial Multi-Peril	7,663,589	7.9	320,269	55.4	52.9	44.4	42.9
Earthquake	53,558	0.1	11,934	5.0	1.8	1.9	.9
Ocean Marine	1,015,670	1.1	74,631	87.9	82.5	66.1	60.8
Inland Marine	2,744,061	2.8	383,791	68.9	58.1	51.6	49.1
Group A & H	1,853,362	1.9	143,767	80.8	76.4	77.5	78.2
All Other A & H	655,389	0.7	1,704	64.2	62.5	62.4	60.2
Workers' Compensation	15,743,510	16.3	1,411,445	70.4	75.3	77.9	74.1
Total Miscellaneous Liability	9,408,956	9.7	−148,140	60.9	55.4	50.6	40.4
Medical Malpractice	1,491,403	1.5	85,412	82.6	75.3	60.6	41.8
Other Liability	7,917,553	8.2	−233,552	57.1	51.6	48.7	40.1
Private Pass. Auto Liability	18,564,090	19.2	1,188,824	67.6	66.4	64.7	63.4
No-Fault	2,170,962	2.2	116,823	78.3	74.0	76.7	78.3
Other Liability	16,393,128	17.0	1,072,001	66.2	65.4	63.1	61.5
Commercial Auto Liability	4,936,684	5.1	136,871	69.0	66.4	61.7	57.9
No-Fault	154,251	0.2	−9,769	71.1	62.7	60.3	64.9
Other Liability	4,782,433	4.9	146,640	68.9	66.5	61.7	57.7
Priv. Pass. Auto Phys. Dam.	13,188,141	13.6	1,161,405	64.9	68.7	65.2	61.6
Comm. Auto Phys. Dam.	2,726,160	2.8	112,358	59.4	59.6	55.4	53.2
Aircraft	389,376	0.4	71,892	82.3	78.6	101.0	63.3
Fidelity	399,686	0.4	18,517	48.1	44.8	55.2	56.0
Surety	1,000,732	1.0	98,180	46.1	33.2	43.5	36.3
Glass	31,666	0.0	−972	54.1	50.6	47.8	46.6
Burglary and Theft	125,653	0.1	−1,831	37.3	36.6	25.8	26.4
Boiler and Machinery	377,519	0.4	8,908	49.4	40.4	31.9	31.7
Credit	79,229	0.1	8,840	56.7	35.1	37.9	38.7
Miscellaneous	584,253	0.6	−54,299	54.3	85.2	46.7	46.2
TOTALS	96,709,863	100.0	6,015,930	65.5	64.3	60.8	57.7

Source: Adapted from *Best's Review: Property/Casualty Insurance Edition*, July 1981.
[a] In dollars, 000 omitted.
[b] Loss Ratio = $\frac{\text{Losses Incurred}}{\text{Premiums Earned−Dividends}}$.

A historical characteristic of the insurance business is the "underwriting cycle." The cycle affects profitability of insurance companies through the relationship between premium pricing and claims costs. At the peak of the cycle, competition is intense and prices are forced to a low level. When claims begin to come in at a level higher than provided for in the reserves, losses occur. At this point there is a shakeout of sorts, with some companies dropping from the competition in their less profitable segments and the remaining companies raising their premiums.

The overall industry growth rate has slowed from 10.7 percent in 1980. This slowing of premium growth rate is indicative of another trough in the underwriting cycle and stiff price competition. In 1980 the top 100 com-

EXHIBIT 3
Summary of Five-Year Industry Results

Year	Premiums Written ($ billion)	Rate of Increase (percent)	Pre-tax Underwriting Profits[a] ($ billion)	Capital Gains ($ billion)	Surplus ($ billion)
1976	60.4	21.9	−2.2	2.0	24.6
1977	72.4	19.8	1.1	−0.8	29.3
1978	81.6	12.8	1.3	0.5	35.2
1979	90.1	10.3	−1.3	2.3	42.8
1980	96.3	6.9	−3.4	4.8	52.3
Five Years	400.8	14.3	−4.5		

Source: *Best's Review: Property/Casualty Edition,* September 1981.
[a]After dividends.

panies averaged an underwriting loss of 3.53 percent of earned premiums (after dividends to policy holders). This loss totaled $2.8 billion for the industry. The forecasts for 1981 indicate that it could be even more competitive with worse results than 1980. Most insurance companies have been able to offset underwriting losses with investment income. *Best's* reported, however, that five of the top 100 firms were not, in fact, able to offset underwriting losses in 1980. Some industry experts predicted that this pressure, following the 1973–1975 trough by only five years, may force weaker firms into insolvency.

The use of investment income to offset underwriting losses has kept the industry profitable, exhibiting a strong capital surplus (see Exhibit 3) in spite of the downturn in the cycle. The increasing dependence of companies on investment income is shown dramatically in Exhibit 4 and may have permanently changed the nature of the insurance business. Some analysts feel that the ability to depend on investment income will delay the normal shakeout of unprofitable lines and companies and will prolong the present trough much longer than usual.

Given the prospect of extended competitive pricing, attention to cost reduction may be one of the keys to survival. The current trends in the industry are summarized in *Best's* as follows:

1. As product and service distinctiveness becomes more difficult to maintain, insurance is taking on the aspects of a commodity game where low-cost producers are winners.
2. Competitive pricing is assuming growing importance.
   - Competition from major new entrants is forcing insurers to offer a competitive price.
   - Independent agencies are undergoing structural changes that are increasing price competition.
   - Customers are becoming more price-conscious as insurance costs rise.
3. As competition increases among all types of insurers, companies are seeking new revenue avenues such as fee-based administration, loss control, and claim services.
4. Since price increases and premium growth are not keeping up with inflation, primarily because of competition, companies with uncompetitive expense ratios[3] may pay a substantial penalty for their inefficiency.[4]

---

[3]Expense ratio = $\dfrac{\text{operating costs}}{\text{premiums earned}}$.

[4]William F. Kinder, "A Look at the Leaders: Has the Game Changed?" *Best's Review: Property/Casualty Insurance Edition* **82** (September, 1981): 132.

EXHIBIT 4
Underwriting and Investment Income Growth Trends

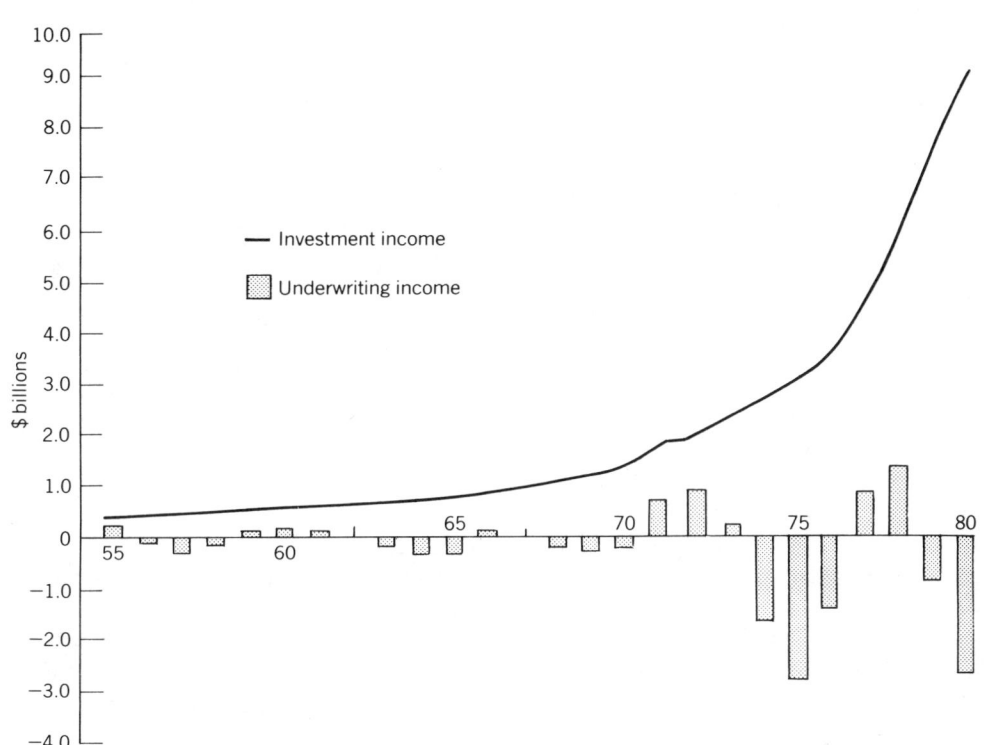

Among the suggestions provided for increasing expense ratios are the following:

1. Programs to increase productivity.
2. Investment in automated systems.
3. Delegation of expense management responsibilities to branches.
4. Building expense accountability into the reward system.

American Express Company

American Express was founded in 1850 and boasts of 114 years of uninterrupted profitability. The Chairman of the Board and Chief Executive Officer is James D. Robinson, III, who succeeded Harold L. Clark in 1977. In the 17 years of Clark's tenure, American Express revenues grew from $77 million to $3.4 billion in 1977. Clark ran the company with a very personal style of management that minimized bureaucratic controls and allowed a great deal of latitude to the division heads. He also recognized the importance of good relationships with banks to the success of American Express's business and used these contacts to build the business. When he left the company, four of the six largest banks were represented on the American Express Board of Directors.

Robinson, who has been at American Express since 1970, has indicated that, "Our prime objective is to provide, directly with banks, the widest variety of consumer financial services available from any single source." The transition from Clark to Robinson was orderly and gradual with Clark maintaining active company involvement for some time after the official transfer of duties in 1977. Although Clark and Robinson are both conservative in financial matters, differences in their management styles have become apparent. American Express has evolved into a more highly structured organization. Along with Roger Morely (who succeeded him as president), Robinson implemented a rigorous system of planning and control, which included not only annual plans, but divisional-level monthly forecasts. Morley was replaced as president in 1979 by Alva Way, formerly the chief financial officer at General Electric. Among the qualities in Way that were found attractive by Robinson were his abilities in strategic planning, data processing, and communications. Observers feel that all of this organizational emphasis has paid off in the form of significant improvements in the coordination among the divisions within the last few years.

A major part of American Express's growth has been through acquisition. In 1968 American Express acquired Fireman's Fund Insurance, the nation's ninth largest property–liability insurer. In 1972 the company bought a 25 percent interest in Donaldson, Lufkin and Jenrette, but sold the interest in 1975 at a $23 million loss. Within Robinson's first three years, American Express attempted to make four acquisitions: Walt Disney Productions, Book-of-the-Month Club, Philadelphia Life Insurance, and McGraw–Hill. The company's recent acquisitions are listed in Exhibit 5, the most significant and most recent being the merger with Shearson Loeb Rhoades.

As of early 1981, American Express was organized into four major business areas: Travel Services Group, Warner Amex Cable Services, International Banking Services, and Insurance Services. The company had assets of $19.7 billion, 44,000 employees, 1,000 travel offices, and 77 international banking and investment offices. Total revenues for 1980 were $5.5 billion with a net income of $376 million. In 1980, dividends were increased from $0.45 to $0.50 per share, the sixth increase in five years. The consolidated financial statements are shown in Exhibit 6 and contributions of the various segments are summarized in Exhibit 7. The scope of the company's international operations is shown in Exhibit 8.

EXHIBIT 5
Recent Acquisitions by American Express Company

Acquisition	Date
American Express Direct Response	April 1979
Warner Amex Cable Communications (Joint venture)	December 1979
First Data Resources	January 1980
Southern Guaranty Insurance Company	September 1980
Food and Wine Magazine	September 1980
Mitchell Beazley Ltd.	November 1980
WATS Marketing of America	December 1980
Interstate Group of Insurance Companies	December 1980
New England Bank Card Association	March 1981
Shearson Loeb Rhoades	Awaiting approval

Source: Moody's Bank and Finance Manual, Vol. 2.

Travel Services Group

The Travel Services Group includes the Card Division, Travelers' Check Division, Travel Division, Communications Division, and the Financial Institutions Services Division. Revenues for the group increased 34 percent from 1979 to $1.7 billion in 1980 and net income rose 17 percent to $177 million, which is 47 percent of the company's total earnings.

The Card Division provides corporate and personal credit-card services to 11.9 million cardholders. The familiar "green card" is marketed not as a credit card implying a line of credit, but as a convenience device. As such, payment in full is required on demand, with the exception of certain tour plans and airplane tickets that can be financed over an extended period. There are approximately 6.5 million personal green cardholders who pay an annual

EXHIBIT 6
Consolidated Income Statement (in millions)

	1980	1979	1978	1977	1976
Revenues					
Commissions and Fees	1,522	1,130	912	738	643
Interest and Dividends	1,264	1,007	759	580	496
Property–Liability and Life-Insurance Premiums	2,589	2,450	2,341	2,080	1,771
Other	129	80	64	48	48
Total	5,504	4,667	4,076	3,446	2,948
Expenses					
Provisions for Losses:					
Insurance	1,545	1,482	1,393	1,255	1,142
Banking, Credit, Financial Paper, Other	214	161	127	108	100
Salaries and Employee Benefits	833	685	578	472	421
Interest	870	572	368	249	208
Commissions and Brokerage	403	371	355	311	275
Occupancy and Equipment	247	187	141	125	105
Advertising and Promotion	187	140	127	84	66
Taxes Other Than Income Taxes	145	133	120	101	85
Telephone, Telegraph, Postage	117	93	83	74	63
Financial Paper, Forms, and Other Printed Matter	82	65	51	45	35
Claims Adjustment Service	78	102	116	130	90
Other	362	285	234	188	162
Total	5,083	4,276	3,693	3,142	2,752
Pre-tax Income	421	391	383	304	196
Income Tax Provision	45	46	69	52	17
Net Operating Income	376	345	314	252	179
Gains on Sale of Investment Securities	—	—	—	10	15
Net Income	376	345	314	262	194
Net Income per Share	$5.27	$4.83	$4.39	$3.65	$2.70
Assets					
Cash	1,069	1,051	844	674	542
Time Deposits	1,084	976	891	858	821
Investment Securities (cost)					
U. S. Government	750	519	435	453	429
State and Municipal	4,070	4,104	3,808	3,167	2,458
Other Bonds and Obligations	1,200	1,044	735	720	710
Preferred Stocks	57	52	48	48	43
Total[a]	6,077	5,719	5,026	4,388	3,640
Investment Securities (Lower of Cost or Market)					
Preferred Stocks	67	83	99	111	95
Common Stocks	99	83	72	66	56
Total[b]	166	166	171	177	151

(*Continued*)

EXHIBIT 6 (*Continued*)

	1980	1979	1978	1977	1976
Investment Securities (Market)					
Preferred Stocks	63	57	50	49	45
Common Stocks	783	652	563	507	506
Total[c]	846	709	613	556	551
Accounts Receivable and Accrued Interest, Less Reserves: 1980, $287; 1979, $213; 1978, $171; 1977, $146; 1976, $125	4,887	3,597	2,705	2,164	1,754
Loans and Discounts, Less Reserves: 1980, $89; 1979, $82; 1978, $75; 1977, $60; 1976, $52	3,690	3,369	3,320	2,571	2,073
Land, Buildings and Equipment (cost); less Depreciation	448	347	285	263	239
Prepaid Policy Acquisition Expenses	271	244	206	153	130
Other Assets	1,171	930	637	542	467
	19,709	17,108	14,698	12,346	10,368
Liabilities					
Customer Deposits and Credits held by Subsidiaries	5,087	4,749	4,192	3,755	3,024
Travelers Checks Outstanding	2,542	2,343	2,105	1,859	1,716
Money Orders and Drafts Outstanding	212	289	324	175	140
Accounts Payable	1,020	889	785	593	471
Reserves For:					
Property–Liability Losses and Expenses	2,589	2,364	2,057	1,723	1,363
Unearned Premiums	1,008	974	875	792	673
Life and Disability Policies	259	227	184	147	130
Short-Term Debt	2,302	1,595	1,117	776	555
Long-Term Debt	1,099	689	479	330	304
Deferred Income Taxes	161	135	108	117	117
Other	1,244	996	852	711	621
Total Liabilities	17,523	15,250	13,078	10,978	9,114
Preferred Stock	24	25	27	28	30
Common Stock (100,000,000 Shares Authorized, $0.60 par value; 71,274,306 Outstanding in 1980)	43	43	43	43	43
Capital Surplus	208	204	202	200	201
Net Unrealized Security Gains	208	115	87	78	116
Retained Earnings	1,703	1,471	1,261	1,019	864
Total Common Shareholders' Equity	2,162	1,833	1,593	1,340	1,224
	19,709	17,108	14,698	12,346	10,368

Source: Annual Reports.
[a]Market: 1980, $4,612; 1979, $5,070; 1978, $4,686; 1977, $4,396; 1976, $3,612.
[b]Cost: 1980, $191; 1979, $192; 1978, $188; 1977, $188; 1976, $167.
[c]Cost: 1980, $531; 1979, $523; 1978, $471; 1977, $433; 1976, $370.

EXHIBIT 7
Industry Segments 1980 (in millions)

	Travel-Related Services	International Banking Services	Insurance Services	Other and Corporate	Adjustments and Eliminations	Consolidated
Revenues	$1,661	$ 930	$2,914	$ 35	$ (36)	$5,504
Pre-tax Income before General Corporate Expenses	236	67	215	16	—	534
General Corporate Expenses	—	—	—	(113)	—	(113)
Pre-tax Income	236	67	215	(97)	—	421
Net Income	177	41	210	(52)	—	376
Assets	$6,877	$6,926	$5,846	$469	$(409)	$19,709

Insurance Services Comprised of:

	Commercial Lines	Personal Lines	Investment Income	Total	Other	Total Insurance Services
Revenues	$1,788	$626	$282	$2,696	$218	$2,914
Pre-tax Income	$ (37)	$(39)	$277	$ 201	$ 14	$ 215

Source: Annual Report.

fee of $35. About 1.5 million customers hold the "gold cards" at an annual fee of $50. In addition to the charge features, the gold card allows members to finance purchases and to obtain cash through a line of credit that American Express has established with 1800 participating banks.

The American Express cards are issued in 23 currencies and are honored by 438,000 establishments worldwide. The company has been attempting to build the number of establishments and about 50,000 new establishments were added during 1980. Expanding beyond the traditional emphasis on food,

EXHIBIT 8
Geographic Operations 1980 (in millions)

	United States	Europe	Asia/Pacific	All Other	Adjustments and Eliminations	Consolidated
Revenues	$ 3,953	$ 700	$ 281	$ 604	$ (34)	$ 5,504
Pre-tax before General Corporate Expenses	435	21	15	63	—	534
General Corporate Expenses	(113)	—	—	—	—	(113)
Pre-tax Income	322	21	15	63	—	421
Assets	11,718	3,704	1,774	2,603	(528)	19,271
Corporate Assets						438
Total Assets						$19,709

Source: Annual Report.

lodging, and travel, is a new emphasis on recruiting prestigious retail and department stores that are likely to provide a high average purchase value.

A major cost of the card business is the financing of card receivables. American Express sells its receivables to Credco, a wholly owned subsidiary. Credco then finances them through commercial paper, equity capital, lines of credit, and long-term debt. In 1980 Credco purchased $19.2 billion of receivables, up from $14.6 billion in 1979. The weighted average interest cost of all Credco financing rose from 8.48 percent in 1978 to 15.7 percent during the first two months of 1980. These increased financing costs have led American Express to tighten its collection policies by reducing the grace period and increasing the finance charge.

American Express cards have achieved a high degree of market penetration in the United States. It is estimated that about 50 percent of the families with incomes greater than $25,000 have the card, as do 64 percent of those with incomes greater than $50,000, and 71 percent with incomes over $75,000. Growth rates in membership have averaged 11 percent over the last three years. A major contribution to the growth rate has come from countries outside of the United States, where the growth rates have been on the order of 25 percent. The number of cardholders outside of the United States was 2.7 million in 1980.

The charge-card volume has increased at annual rates of 26 percent (1978), 29 percent (1979), and 32 percent (1980). This positive trend in the face of government controls on credit spending during the period has reinforced management's view that the card is used by consumers as a convenience rather than a credit device. Customers also seem to be attracted to the country club style of itemizing the bills (a feature not provided by bank cards), the absence of charge limits, check-cashing privileges, and the snob appeal of the card.

American Express travelers' checks are sold through 105,000 outlets worldwide, including banks, travel agents, credit unions, etc. Although check buyers are charged a fee of one percent of the check's face value, the issuing banks retain about two-thirds of that fee. The primary source of travelers' check revenues for American Express is from the "float," or cash the company controls from checks that have not yet been cashed. This float is invested by American Express in tax-free securities and provided a significant amount of the company's total revenues in 1980. The average period that the checks are outstanding is two months. An advertising campaign begun in 1979, featuring actor Karl Malden, appealed to consumers to hold unused checks for emergencies—an attempt to extend the float period. The dollar value of the travelers' checks outstanding at year end has increased from $1.72 billion in 1976 to $2.5 billion in 1980.

Increasing competitive pressure is being felt in the travelers' check industry and the growth rate of American Express checks has been slowing over the last three years. Many banks, which sell the majority of the checks, are now selling their own checks under Visa or MasterCard trademarks. American Express plans to combat this competitive pressure through increased service and new international initiatives. In 1981 the company began construction of a $35 million operations center near Salt Lake City, Utah. It is anticipated that the center will enhance the company's ability to provide cost-effective servicing of travelers' checks. American Express also now owns 34 percent of *Sociéte Francais du Chēque de Voyage*, which began issuing French franc travelers' checks in 1980. American Express has converted all of its French franc business to the new checks.

The Travel Division offers retail and wholesale (tours) travel services worldwide through 1,000 offices in 126 countries. Services include trip planning, reservations, ticketing, and other incidental services. Revenues for the division are earned through commissions from carriers, hotels, etc. and fees from customers for incidental services.

American Express reported major changes in the Travel Division in 1980 including a restructuring of the organization to decentralize along geographic lines. It is anticipated that this move will provide greater flexibility to respond to localized customer needs and opportunities. The company also has been redesigning its tour packages to achieve greater consumer affordability and eliminate low-revenue programs. A major automation step was taken in 1980 with the implementation of a computerized Travel Information Processing System (TRIPS). TRIPS eventually will become an integrated worldwide information and reservation system.

The financial performance of the Travel Division has varied over the years, with weak years during the period 1973–1976. A stronger revenues showing was reported for 1977, although it is not clear whether the division was profitable. In 1979 and 1980 the division reported losses, this in spite of increased revenues during 1980. The company explained that part of the problem in 1980 was due to slackened demand for tours, lower margins on discount ticket purchasing, and the costs of restructuring the division.

The Communications Division was formed in January 1980, and has responsibility for American Express Publishing Corporation, Merchandise Sales, American Express Direct Response (ADR), and Mitchell Beazley Limited, a London-based International publishing house.

The division has recently taken over publishing of *Food and Wine* magazine and has published *Travel and Leisure* magazine (circulation 925,000) since 1970. A growing emphasis in the division is on direct-mail marketing through Merchandise Sales (revenues increased by 70 percent in 1980), supported by the computer services of ADR. ADR also supplies direct-mail marketing services to outside businesses and other American Express divisions.

The Financial Institutions Services Division was formed in 1980 to consolidate operations relating to the financial community. Within the division is First Data Resources, Inc., a recently acquired provider of data and telephone marketing services to financial institutions and merchandisers. Also included are the Money Order Division and Payment Systems, Inc., which provides information and research in payment systems and electronic-funds transfer.

Warner Amex Cable Services

In 1979 American Express paid $175 million for one-half interest in Warner Cable Company, which was owned by Warner Communications. The joint venture includes the subsidiaries, Warner Amex Cable Communications, Inc. and Warner Amex Satellite Entertainment Company. American Express sees the cable systems as the technical hardware link for the financial supermarket of the future that they expect to build around the television screen.

Warner Cable Company owns and operates 141 cable television systems with 736,000 subscribers in 27 states. Among the most recent awards are major franchises in Pittsburgh, Dallas, Cincinnati and in areas surrounding St. Louis, Boston, Chicago, and Akron. These awards provide the potential for entering 1.1 million households.

Most Warner Amex systems have 12 to 30 channels; however, new systems will provide many more channels. The company has a head start on its competition in two-way cable systems with a system called Qube. Warner Amex spent $20 million to develop the Qube system and it is presently operating in Columbus and Cincinnati. Although the talkback feature of Qube is not used primarily for entertainment purposes such as voting on boxing matches, answering viewer polls, and calling plays for football games, the two-way link is critical for potential home selling, burglar alarm, and financial transaction uses. The Qube system is now offering a retrieval service for business analysis and money-management information. A 24-hour security system has recently been added to the Columbus system and is now servicing 2,500 households and businesses.

Warner Amex Satellite Entertainment Company (WASEC) operates five satellite transponders which receive television signals and transmit them over the entire country. The entertainment company offers two major services: "The Movie Channel" and "Nickelodeon." "The Movie Channel" offers 24-hour feature films, while "Nickelodeon" provides varied programming for children and young adults. The company is planning a joint venture with ABC Video Enterprises, Inc., called the Alpha Repertory Television Service, which will provide programming devoted to the performing and visual arts. Firm plans also have been made to offer "The Music Channel," which will provide continuous popular music with complementary visual material.

Although a significant amount of risk exists in the cable video industry in that franchises must be awarded by local governments, Warner Amex has proven to be an effective competitor. In 1980 Warner Amex won 1.1 million of the 1.6 million households up for bids in the United States. The company anticipates a need for significant financing to support future expansion efforts. In 1980 they received a $250 million line of credit from a group of banks, but additional capital will be needed in 1981 from external sources and the parent companies, where appropriate.

Insurance Services

Fireman's Fund Insurance was founded in 1863 and was acquired by American Express in 1968. Fireman's Fund provides a broad range of insurance services including commercial and personal property–liability insurance and life insurance and annuities. Policies are sold in the United States through 11,000 independent agents and brokers. The company also operates overseas through AFIA World Wide insurance, a consortium of U. S. insurance companies. The Fireman's Fund commercial insurance lines include property, general liability, multiple peril, and worker's compensation, and the personal lines include homeowners' and automobile insurance. Life insurance is offered through Fireman's Fund American Life Insurance Company (FFAL), which sells a full portfolio of life insurance products including ordinary and term-life insurance, annuities, group term-life insurance, and group accident and health insurance. FFAL also underwrites the supplemental life insurance offered to American Express cardholders.

Fireman's Fund was caught in the insurance underwriting cycle in 1974 when earnings dropped by 17 percent. Even at this amount, the drop was softened since the company called upon $9 million from a "catastrophe reserve" built up during more profitable years. This practice of banking earnings has since been ordered abolished for the entire industry by the Financial Accounting Standards Board, since it was considered to be misleading to investors.

Following the 1974 experience, American Express decided to institute policies to avoid the cycle. They vowed to price more aggressively when premium rates are rising and not to write unprofitable policies by cutting prices when competition stiffens.

Feeling the competitive pressures of the most recent trough in the underwriting cycle, the growth rate in premiums written has been declining as the company has attempted to concentrate on more profitable business in underwriting and investment. In 1980 $2.4 billion in premuims were written, which is a 2.5 percent increase. The increase in 1979 was 4.5 percent and in 1978 the increase was 9.1 percent.

Fireman's Fund gross revenues for 1980 were $2.9 billion, which is a 7.2 percent increase over 1979. A significant contribution tc the increase in revenues has been from specialized products in rural markets, commercial group packages, and reinsurance. The company has suffered underwriting losses for the past three years because of higher claims costs that were not offset by premiums revenues. The underwriting losses were $76 million in 1980, $53 million (1979), and $13 million (1978). According to *Best's*, Fireman's Fund ranked 53rd in the industry in underwriting performance with a loss ratio of 58.1. These losses were offset by investment income, which increased by 21 percent in 1980. Fireman's Fund is attempting to remedy the losses through rate increases, increased deductibles, and obtaining shorter terms so that premiums can be adjusted more frequently.

The underwriting expense ratio has been increasing over the last three years, from 30.8 percent in 1978 to 33.3 percent in 1980. This increase has been attributed to slower premium growth and long-term development spending. The company has been increasing the number of branch offices, automating its network of offices, and developing a program of standardization of field-office procedures.

International Banking Services

American Express International Banking Company (AEIBC) accounts for 17 percent of American Express's total revenues, 35 percent of the company's total assets, and 11 percent of the net income. AEIBC operates 83 offices in 34 countries, providing commercial banking services, investment banking, wholesale banking, equipment finance, and financial advisory services. It also offers consumer banking service in certain locations, including contracted services on overseas U. S. military bases. The bank does not provide services in the United States except incidentally to its foreign operations. AEIBC is also an active dealer in foreign exchange markets; these activities contributed $35 million in revenues in 1980.

Income from interest increased 21 percent to $197 million in 1980, while commissions fees revenues increased 14 percent to $100 million in 1980. The latter increase reflects an emphasis on the expansion of nonasset related sources of revenues. In 1980 operating costs rose 19 percent, primarily as a result of inflation and automation of the banking network.

The Shearson Merger

In April 1981, American Express and Shearson Loeb Rhoades, Inc., announced that they had reached agreement on a merger. The terms were 1.3 American Express shares for each Shearson share. At the time of the merger Shearson brought into American Express 11,000 employees and $8 billion in assets, mostly in money market funds. The company reported $653 million in revenues in 1980 and had an estimated 500,000 customers.

The level of revenues in 1980 put Shearson in the number-two position in the brokerage industry and is largely the product of eight acquisitions in the 10 years since Shearson went public. Shearson's acquisitions were usually "old-line" brokerage houses that were having financial difficulties. To make the acquisitions work, Shearson cut out levels of management, consolidated and automated the "back office" operations into a strong network, and added new services. The consolidated financial statements for the company are shown in Exhibit 9.

Under the terms of the merger, Sanford (Sandy) I. Weill will remain in charge of Shearson and head American Express's executive committee, and Robinson will become Chairman of the merged entity. After the transaction Weill will personally own an estimated 0.6 percent of American Express's stock. Weill has built a reputation of competence along with his building of Shearson and has demonstrated a willingness and an ability for making fast decisions.

The merger is seen by many as giving strong impetus to a trend in the financial industry where many of the leading brokerage companies are looking for capital inputs to re-

EXHIBIT 9
Shearson Loeb Rhoades, Inc. Consolidated Income Statement (in thousands)

	1980[a]	1979[a]	1978[a]
Revenues			
Commissions	327,497	188,744	136,732
Principal Transactions	82,038	17,427	16,299
Interest	128,961	56,293	36,674
Investment Banking	57,203	23,900	23,339
Mortgage Banking	28,455	6,008	—
Other	28,312	11,658	8,181
Total	652,466	304,030	221,225
Expenses			
Employee Compensation	310,065	152,802	113,078
Floor-Broker Commissions	26,703	16,785	12,658
Interest	57,407	21,178	18,037
Other Operating Expenses	142,653	73,180	57,591
Total	536,828	263,945	201,364
Income Before Distribution	115,638	40,085	19,861
Distribution to Profits Participation	10,669	—	—
Pre-tax Income	104,969	40,085	19,861
Income Taxes	49,162	20,010	9,857
Net Income	55,805	20,075	10,004
Net Income Per Share	$6.99	$3.78	$2.11
Dividends Per Share	$.40	$.34	$.27
Assets			
Cash	52,768	15,372	7,110
Segregated Cash and Treasury Bills	316,739	167,085	123,226
Securities on Deposit	52,514	9,853	13,963
Receivables From Customers	966,759	547,677	485,588
Receivables From Brokers	461,126	135,360	88,676
Mortgages and Construction Loans	69,481	92,146	—
Other Receivables	17,651	7,164	7,176
Spot Commodities Owned	—	—	254
Securities Owned (Market)	248,769	127,586	122,960
Secured Demand Notes	716	7,394	7,394
Exchange Membership	5,175	2,883	2,874
Investments in Affiliates	3,203	—	—
Securities Purchased	1,849	9,630	184,927
Purchased Mortgage Contracts	6,778	7,197	—
Deferred Income Taxes	5,610	—	—
Office Equipment, Etc.	22,011	12,197	8,286
Excess Acquisition Cost	14,559	4,647	4,245
Differed Expenses and Other Assets	21,983	8,359	3,433
Total	2,267,691	1,154,549	1,060,114

EXHIBIT 9 (Continued)

	1980[a]	1979[a]	1978[a]
Liabilities			
Bank Loans	212,668	154,377	149,393
Payables to Brokers	557,752	154,743	109,556
Payables to Customers	607,497	292,992	196,189
Accrued Liabilities, Etc.	341,465	255,874	168,355
Securities Sold[b]	166,260	127,683	115,583
Repurchased Securities Sold	43,517	1,966	211,565
Deferred Income Tax	—	662	749
Term Notes	26,503	17,826	7,513
Subordinate Debt	137,671	61,233	32,994
Secured Demand Obligation	—	7,394	7,394
Contributions of Profit Participation Agreement	30,113	—	—
Preferred Stock	175	1,482	2,026
Common Stock	661	527	487
Paid in Capital	50,665	29,639	26,259
Retained Earnings	96,295	51,713	33,546
Reacquired Stock	(3,561)	(3,562)	(1,496)
Total	2,267,691	1,154,549	1,060,114

Source: Annual Reports, *Moody's Bank and Finance Manual.*
[a]Year ended June 30th.
[b]Securities sold, but not yet purchased.

main competitive on a national scale. The competitive surge appears to be aimed at providing consolidated "one-stop" financial services. Several securities dealers who have survived a tight decade and are showing profitable years now appear attractive to the larger insurance and other financial firms.

The trend in these acquisitions may have been triggered by Merrill, Lynch, Pierce, Fenner, and Smith, which is the industry's number-one brokerage house and has considerable capital ($1 billion) strength of its own. In 1977 Merrill Lynch broke with tradition and created a cash-management account that allows customers to access cash in the account and money funds as well as providing a line of credit. All of this can be accomplished through special VISA cards or Merrill Lynch checks. This move proved attractive to customers and was difficult for the smaller companies to match.

In March 1981 Prudential Insurance merged with Bache Group Inc. Through the merger it is expected that Prudential can provide not only the financial stability to remain competitive and to ride out the fiscal variability that is a problem in the brokerage business, but also to provide marketing and promotional support as well as new services to the Bache customers.

The American Express–Shearson merger announcement caused considerable concern for banks, who see a new kind of financial institution that can offer a broad range of services that banks are not allowed to sell. Banks are presently prohibited from selling securities by the Glass–Steagall Act of 1933. Their reaction has been in several directions. Larger banks have been lobbying to have the government restrictions on themselves lifted so that they can enter the competitive field, but others have been attempting to block formation of such strong competition. The Independent Bankers Association has written to the Justice

Department asking that the American Express–Shearson merger be delayed pending investigation of the deal's "potential anticompetitive effects." The strength of the overall opposition to the merger is difficult to assess without the support of the larger banks. But given the present political trends toward less government involvement, it is unlikely that the merger will be disapproved.

Primary Sources: American Express Company Case

1. American Express Company, *Annual Reports,* 1977 through 1980.
2. *Best's Review,* "Mounting a Concerted Attack on the Underwriting Cycle," October 1981.
3. *Business Week,* "The Everything Financial Service," May 18, 1981.
4. *Dun's Review,* "The Credit Card: Discovering a New Form of 'Money'," June 1978.
5. *Dun's Review.* "Clash of the Credit Cards," June 1978.
6. *Forbes,* "Cached Checks," October 16, 1978.
7. *Forbes,* "Visa Takes Aim at American Express," April 16, 1979, pp. 43–44.
8. *Forbes,* "The Tube, The Ticker, and Jim Robinson," May 25, 1981.
9. *Fortune,* "Quite a Card," April 1977.
10. *Fortune,* "Hazard Down the Track for American Express," November 6, 1978.
11. *Fortune,* "Shifting Shares in Traveler's Checks," November 6, 1978.
12. *Fortune,* "Explosion in the Bank-Card Cafeteria," September 8, 1980.
13. *Moody's Bank and Finance Manual,* Vol. 2, 1982, 1981.
14. Securities and Exchange Commission Form 10K; American Express Company, 1977 through 1980.

MARY KAY COSMETICS, INC.

Mary Kay Cosmetics, Inc. (MKY) is a relatively small manufacturer of cosmetics and skin-care products, marketing its products through an international network of independent sales representatives. Located in Dallas, Texas, the company has five regional distribution centers in the United States, one distribution center in Australia, one in Canada, and one in Argentina. Another distribution center is scheduled to open in Santo Domingo on December 1, 1982. Founded in 1963 by Mary Kay Ash, the company has grown from nine sales representatives to over 150,000. Starting with an initial investment of $5,500, it has grown to net sales of $235 million in 1981. With a relatively small product line that the independent sales representatives, called Beauty Consultants, carry with them, Mary Kay Cosmetics, Inc. has a target market of women ages 25 to 44 who are in the middle and above income brackets.

Mary Kay: The Woman

The story of Mary Kay Ash's life is, to a large extent, the story of MKY. Mary Kay was born Mary Kathlyn Wagner in Hot Wells, a small town in South Texas. At age seven she was helping to support her family and her invalid father while her mother ran the family restaurant in a Houston suburb.

Graduation from high school meant the end of formal education, even though she had graduated from Reagen High School in Houston with honors and hoped to attend college. Mary Kay was soon married to Ben Rogers, a marriage that lasted 11 years and

---

Source: This case was prepared by Mark Kever, George Macias, John Sanders, and Ken Schoenherr, under the supervision of Professor Sexton Adams. Permission to use granted by Sexton Adams. This case is based on a personal interview between Paula Walters and Mary Kay Ash and library research.

resulted in the birth of three children; Marylin in 1935, Ben, Jr. in 1936, and Richard in 1943. World War II meant separation for months at a time from her husband who was drafted and unable to send home more than a few dollars each month. For a while during the time Ben was in the service, Mary Kay attended classes at the University of Houston, but her college career was cut short by the responsibility of three small children.

Selling for Others

To make ends meet Mary Kay went to work part-time for Stanley Home Products in Houston selling household specialties at parties in homes. She had a natural aptitude for selling and quickly became one of the company's leading sales representatives. Mary Kay learned that people liked to talk to her and that her positive attitude enabled her to overcome most of the obstacles she encountered in sales.

Retirement

In 1953 Mary Kay left Stanley after 13 years and went to work for World Gifts Company in Dallas selling decorative accessories. She moved up in this organization to the position of national training director. After 10 years with World Gifts Mary Kay was working 60-hour weeks and making $25,000 a year. A disagreement over proposed policy changes at World Gifts prompted Mary Kay to "retire" in 1963. She had spent almost 25 years in direct selling and intended to spend her time writing.

Mary Kay carefully avoids discussing her age. She comments, "A woman who'd tell that would tell anything." For this reason there are few times when Mary Kay's age is mentioned by writers and reporters who have interviewed her.

Retirement was very unpleasant for Mary Kay. She was unhappy with nothing to do, and within a few days after leaving World Gifts, she began writing down all the direct-selling techniques she had learned in her 25 years in sales. After spending two weeks on this task, she spent another two weeks compiling a list of problems she had encountered in selling, ways of solving these problems, and how she would do things differently in the future if she had the opportunity. Her initial intent was to put this material in a book that would help women sell.

Discovery of the Product

In reviewing and editing the notes she had written, Mary Kay realized that she had prepared everything needed to operate a sales organization. The only thing missing was a product.

Several years earlier, while working for Stanley Home Products, Mary Kay conducted a demonstration of her company's products one evening to a group of approximately 20 women in a home in one of the suburbs of Dallas. The hostess for the party kept the guests after Mary Kay's demonstration to give them little jars of skin treatment, several creams she had prepared using formulas she had been given by her grandfather who had at one time operated a local tannery. The women attending the party were being used to test the formulas. Mary Kay had noticed the beautiful complexions of the women she had met that evening and was anxious to try the skin treatment herself. She took several of the jars, which were various sizes and shapes and were handed to her in an old shoe box. The creams smelled terrible, but they worked. Mary Kay maintains to this day that her own beautiful complexion is the result of using these creams which were eventually to become the first of the MKY product line.

The Beginning of a Company

Soon after the completion of her writing, Mary Kay and her second husband, George Hallenbeck, whom she had married earlier in 1963, decided to use Mary Kay's sales and problem-solving techniques and go into business. George's background included sales and administration. The idea of starting a new business appealed to both of them. The formulas for the skin creams Mary Kay had been given several years earlier were purchased for $500. The woman who owned the formulas had been attempting to produce and market them by herself but had not been successful.

The busy process of organizing their new company was underway. Mary Kay's husband was to be the administrator. He was in the process of planning the physical facilities and caring for other matters regarding the operation of the business, while Mary Kay was preparing the final draft of the sales manual, designing and ordering containers, and recruiting sales people. One month before the business was to open, George died of a heart attack.

Mary Kay discussed her situation with her children, and Richard who was then a 20-year-old insurance salesman in Houston moved to Dallas and helped his mother start the company in September 1963, with $5,000 capitalization. Richard who had attended North Texas State University for a year and a half as a marketing major, was in charge of administration and finance. His mother's duties included training, merchandising, and selling. Six months later, Ben, Mary Kay's older son, joined to take care of warehousing and shipping. Ben later became the vice-president for merchandising but left the company in 1978.

The new company, Beauty by Mary Kay, opened with two full-time employees, Mary Kay and Richard, who drew a salary of $250 a month to start, and nine women who sold the initial skin-care products that were being made with the formulas purchased for $500. One of MKY's strategies from the beginning was that each sales representative buys her own products at approximately 50 percent of retail, pays for all supplies in advance, and carries a sufficient amount of cosmetics with her to fill all orders on the spot. Thus, the company had no accounts payable and no accounts receivable.

Immediate Success

The small staff of beauty consultants was successful both in selling and in recruiting new beauty consultants. The number of people added became so large that a system was established whereby some of the beauty consultants became training directors. An incentive compensation plan was devised that enabled beauty consultants who became training directors to draw an override on the commissions earned by the beauty consultants they recruited and trained. The number of beauty consultants grew from the original nine to 318 in 1964, just one year after the company began operation. Sales for the first year amounted to $198,514. The second year sales exceeded $800,000. The growth continued at an astonishingly rapid pace both in the number of consultants and sales. MKY went public in 1967.

In 1969 it was necessary to add 102,000 square feet to the manufacturing facility in Dallas. Additional space has been added several times. A new distribution center was added in Dallas, and in the late 1960s plans for expansion of sales and distribution centers outside the five-state Texas Southwest were begun. Planning for growth has been necessary from the beginning. The company recently purchased a 177-acre site available for future growth.

Expansion

Rapid growth in the 1960s brought MKY to the $6-million sales level and a point where expansion beyond Texas and into the four contiguous states was a logical next step. In the 1970s expansion was first made into the California market with the opening of a branch in Los Angeles designed to serve the western states. The move westward was tremendously successful, and MKY soon had more beauty consultants in California than in Texas. An Atlanta branch was opened in 1972, and a third branch was opened in Chicago in 1975. In 1978 the first office outside the United States was opened in Toronto.

The small regional company of 1970 that had sales of $6 million grew in the decades of the 1970s to an international company with sales in 1979 of $91 million. In 1980 sales were $167 million, and in 1981 they reached $235 million. The sales force now includes over 150,000 consultants and training directors.

Annual Seminar

One factor that has contributed to the rapid growth of MKY is the ability of the company to instill the spirit of winning and the desire for success in the minds of the beauty consultants, the training directors, and the company employees. A major attraction to many of these people is the annual sales meeting, called by MKY the SEMINAR, which is held in Dallas for three days each August. This is a spectacle that is a combination consisting of beauty pageant, Academy Awards night, party, the sharing of ideas, classes, goal-setting, leadership training, and even bookkeeping. Each person attends the meeting at her own expense, and they come from all states, Puerto Rico, Canada, Australia, and Argentina. The awards include mink coats, diamond rings, diamond bumblebee pins, watches, luggage, typewriters, pocket calculators, exotic vacations, and the year-long use of pink Cadillacs and Buick Regals. Some 16,000 MKY beauty consultants and training directors have attended the seminar for each of the past two years.

International Operations

Attempts to broaden international operations beyond Canada have led to the opening of a subsidiary in Australia, and more recently, another wholly owned subsidiary in Argentina in 1980. These two companies contributed 3 percent of the overall MKY sales in 1981. The Australian company appears to have reasonably good prospects for growth; however, the political and inflationary problems in Argentina and the language barrier are forcing MKY to examine this operation carefully before making a decision on whether or not to attempt to expand its efforts in this market. Recruiting is difficult in Argentina, and keeping sales directors in this country is a problem for MKY. As of December 1, 1982, MKY will begin operations in Santo Domingo.

> In the two countries where we have a different language, we have a language barrier, that we from the home office standpoint find very difficult to hurdle. . . We have tried to find someone who not only knows the cosmetic business well, but who is willing to come over here and spend a year to a year and a half learning *our* way of doing business. I don't think we will open any other market until we have someone who can speak the languages and is trained here and go there to help us.

Not only is language a problem, but brochures must be rewritten in Spanish or the language of that country.

Governmental Regulations and Legal Concerns

The rapid expansion of the business has seen the need for an increase in the number of employees. From the beginning of 1963, from the original two, Mary Kay and Richard Rogers, the Company has grown to over 1400 employees.

The beauty consultants and training directors are technically considered to be independent contractors of MKY, not employees of the Company. However, this status of independent contractors has been under investigation by the Internal Revenue Service since 1978. The Revenue Act of 1978 contained provisions for determining independent contractor status. With this Act, eligible taxpayers, including MKY, were relieved of all liability for . . . federal income tax, withholding, FICA and

FUTA taxes with respect to their sales persons for any period ending before January 1, 1979. Congress extended the interim relief period until July 1, 1982. Any legislation enacted after the period of interim relief could present a financially adverse effect on the Company's future operations. This issue has been magnified as a result of other direct sales companies whose representatives have tried to alter tax deductions.

In 1982 a bill with three provisions was introduced before Congress addressing the status of independent contractors, and was endorsed by MKY and the Direct Selling Association. In a presentation made before the New York Society of Security Analysts on July 22, 1982, Rogers said the bill would require reporting to the IRS commissions paid to sales people when those commissions exceed $600 per year. Another provision would require reporting to the IRS sales of product to individuals when their sales exceed $5,000 per person per year. The third provision that is very important to us is called a "safe harbor provision" that includes several tests which if met would automatically classify a sales person as an independent contractor rather than an employee. Mary Kay suggested that it would be difficult for her independent contractors to avoid the IRS and not report actual commissions because her Company provides the needed information regarding each contractor to the IRS, with this information being maintained on a computer system.

In the third quarter of 1982, the issue was resolved, at least for the time being. The IRS ruled in favor of the independent contractor status. Says Mary Kay, "We won." Rogers indicated that an adverse effect could have impacted the company in several ways.

The Company presently faces a class action suit with regard to the tender offer and purchase of MKY stock from 1979. "Nothing yet has happened," says Mary Kay. "We think, of course, that it's ridiculous. In 1978 and 1979 we as a Company had suddenly realized that our directors weren't meeting the test of a salary requirement except on a secretarial basis. They (women) will take the stable salary rather than a 'maybe' commission. From this, management developed the new compensation plan which has contributed to the success of the growth of the company. In late 1979, we found '60 Minutes' on our doorstep; and after nine days of filming, we came out smelling like a rose. Since that program, our sales have quadrupled and our numbers have tripled. For most companies a loss of the suit could negatively affect financial operations and future plans. It's just for $17 million, and we did $458 million last year in 1981. Anyway, we won't lose it."

Growth

Approximately 40 percent of the 1,400 MKY employees are housed in a modern, eight-story office building in North Dallas. This $7 million structure contains approximately 109,000 square feet of office and meeting space and was completed in 1978. The building is now completely free of encumbrance and is a showplace for employees and others; it is a rounded structure of bronzed-gold glass and beige brick, filled with plants, flowers, and trees, and a colorful display of woods, rugs, and paintings.

According to management, the continued and rapid growth of MKY has necessitated the expansion of the physical plant and plans have begun to build a new facility that will be a campus. Land encompassing 177 acres has been purchased over the past year and in November 1982 ground was broken for the new building. "Almost every department will have its own building, particularly production, distribution, and administrative facilities. We already have our own print shop and legal counsel. In addition, there will be a child-care center and possibly in the future plans to build a hotel." Estimated cost is $100 million for this five-year project; according to Mary Kay it will be paid for from funds generated internally.

Product Line

The intitial product line at MKY consisted of skin-care products for women. Since the introduction of this line in 1963, the line has remained relatively stable. Since 1976, there has been a gradual move toward diversification of products and additions to the Mary Kay line. In 1980, the Skin-Care Line was diversified to meet the needs of the different consumers whose skin types were not alike. Colors have been updated to reflect the colors in fashion. The sunscreen has been reformulated and in 1981, MKY introduced the Body-Care System. The line has also been expanded to include toiletry items, accessories, and hair-care products. The skin-care products for women still account for 50 percent of the sales revenue and will remain the major income producers in all likelihood. Today the products at MKY are still primarily oriented toward skin-care rather than the high fashion market.

Still the line consists of only 45 products. Says Dr. Myra Barker, Vice President for Research and Development, "Our plan is to maintain the present number in our line so that our Beauty Consultants can carry the inventory with them. The best way to service our Consultants is to keep the color line basic when offering the Fashion Forecast for fall and spring." According to Dr. Barker, this strategy allows the Consultants to sell large numbers of basic colors that sell well to customers. This allows MKY to discontinue those colors that do not sell well and provides the necessary flexibility to update our line. Mary Kay quality is instilled in all employees and products.

An 11-year veteran of the pharmeceutical industry, Dr. Bruce Rudy, former Director, Quality Assurance for the Burroughs Wellcome Company, had primary responsibility for governmental, technical, and regulatory compliance in the quality control area. He joined the MKY organization in January 1981 as Director of Quality Assurance, but is now serving as Vice President of Quality Assurance.

"We have one of the strongest quality control programs in existence. Each batch of raw materials is tested in our labs. They must meet our chemical, physical, and microbiological specifications. Bulk products and finished packaged products are audited on the line, with final testing in the lab. Last week, we were inspected by the FDA which is the primary governmental agency responsible for the cosmetics industry."

Says Myra Barker, "We have one of the most sophisticated computer control systems in the industry. Even the FDA was impressed. Our goal is to be the best."

During the past several years, MKY has experimented in the market of skin-care products and toiletry items for men. These are marketed under the product name of "Mr. K.," and to date have accounted for 3 percent of the total company's sales in each of the past three years. "Ten years ago, a man would not have gone into a beauty shop to have his hair done. As time goes on, men will find out that skin is skin. With all the emphasis on youth and keeping trim and fit in this country, skin follows right behind it. For men, skin care is a behind the door thing with cosmetics. I don't have a crystal ball," says Mary Kay, "but it's just one more step to creating the total image, even for men."

"We are faced with the problem of growing too fast. We are constantly reviewing our systems and products for control measures. Typically we are understaffed and have to work a lot of overtime. Give me these problems anyday! They are nice problems to have," reflects Dr. Rudy.

> With the building of our new MKY campus, we are phasing in buildings for the new facility. For example, the Glamour Products manufacturing facility is working closely with the engineering groups to ensure that we meet the criteria for a drug company and can be approved by the FDA. We are looking at meeting not only present, but future requirements for the industry and our company.

Manufacturing, Research, and Development

The manufacturing and research and development facilities for MKY are located in Dallas. Products needed in other geographical areas are shipped to the various distribution centers. Raw materials, fuel, and electrical energy are available in the Dallas area at reasonable costs, and there are no plans to relocate any of the manufacturing or research and development facilities at this time, although the company is studying energy-related costs. Company officials point out that a continuous research and development program is underway and is geared mainly toward the goal of improving present products; however, only a very small percentage of total income is budgeted for the research and development department.

Management and Philosophy

The primary reason for the success of MKY was the motivating reason for starting the company. "This company was really begun to give women an opportunity to advance, which I was denied, when I worked for others." This opportunity to become successful and rewards provided for hard work is evident in the slogan, "I can, I will, I must," which Mary Kay instills in all her employees, particularly during the training seminars. "I train the sales force by example and by relationships."

Although the sales force is independent, it maintains a strong and intimate relationship with the mother company. The organization of the sales force is the brain child of Mary Kay herself. One of the more subtle activities that takes place at the home beauty show is the recruitment of new beauty consultants. A portion of each show is reserved for explaining the MKY sales organization, compensation, and incentive plan.

Recognizing a lag in the sales force and a loss of competitive edge in 1978, MKY changed its compensation program. In addition to the mark-up they receive on the products they sell, sales managers are also eligible for a series of commissions based on their monthly unit sales. To become a sales manager, the beauty consultant must recruit 24 women into the organization to become consultants. The sales manager is then eligible to participate in a training program and later become a sales director. Sales directors spend time on independent sales, but they also manage, train, and recruit other sales consultants. "We expect sales directors to sell a minimum level of $3,000 wholesale products per month, which is $6,000 retail." Mary Kay says that if a sales director falls short of that goal for two consecutive months, then the company contacts that woman to see how they can help. The Chairman of the Board does not just want them to "be" minimum. She wants to help them excel. The average sales director will earn $30,000 in 1982. New sales managers will come to Dallas for one week of training and return from time to time during the year for special training programs. The highlight of the year being the SEMINAR. It consists of workshops conducted by outstanding beauty consultants and directors. Used not only during SEMINAR, but also at other times during the year are training materials such as guides, manuals, tape cassettes, flip charts, films, and other materials developed by MKY staff.

The incentive plan is no small contribution to the motivation strategy employed by MKY. This plan allows sales consultants and managers to set goals for themselves whereby they can earn expensive and extravagant prizes for outstanding sales. The prizes may include opera-length mink coats, diamond rings, diamond bumblebee pins, watches, luggage, typewriters, pocket calculators, exotic vacations, and year-long use of pink Cadillacs, and Buick Regals. Not only is the prize itself a motivator, but its method of presentation serves to provide the recipient with extended measures of recognition from her peers. Promotion from sales director to national sales director is also recognized on awards night during SEMINAR.

Being promoted to National Sales Director is no small task. Each woman must have already proven what she can do. Each person has at least 10 offspring Directors that they have brought into the company and nurtured up the ladder. These 10 offspring Directors must have women who they are working with and motivating, who are called second-line directors. For example, Shirly Hutton earns $32,000 per month and has 26 offspring Directors. Rena Tarbet, who is "living with cancer for seven years now" is working on her third million-dollar year sales.

> Richard and I are the parents of the company. We are really mother and father figures, which I am given the credit for the success, and really Richard deserves as much or at least half of everything that has been done and then some. When I started the company, I didn't know that Richard had an IBM head. I take care of the motivating of the sales force and the public relations work. I don't know the financial condition of the company because I don't have to. Richard knows all of that. I ask for a sales report and the number of recruits that we had for each month. That's all I need. I take it from there.

Communication is considered a high priority motivational strategy at MKY. Monthly publications with circulations of 150,000 weekly bulletins, personalized letters, and 15,000 telephone calls per month keep sales directors and consultants in touch with the home office. MKY also has a computerized tracking system of keeping up with its complex organization of sales consultants, sales directors, and their respective sales and recruiting data.

Sales Staff

Today there are over 150,000 independent Beauty Consultants selling MKY products. The company places a great deal of emphasis upon the rapport with others inside the organization; however, company policy is very clear on the requirements that must be fulfilled in order to be a Beauty Consultant. These requirements are:

- Submit a signed agreement with cashier's check or money order in advance in order to receive the Beauty Showcase that is the basic sales kit.
- Attend three beauty shows or sales demonstrations.
- Schedule five beauty shows for the first week's activity.
- Attend training classes conducted by a sales director in the area.

The beauty shows are the company's marketplace and are held in homes with no more than six customers in attendance.

Future of MKY

It would seem that MKY would merge or be acquired by another company. Mary Kay's reply,

> All the time, but no thanks. These companies believe they can bring in their male executives and take over this 2×4 company and show them how to run it. You can't run a direct sales company like that. We must operate in a different way. Right now we are in the top 10 in the cosmetics industry. Richard's and my goal is to be the largest and best skin-care company in the world. I'm sure we are the best. Now we have to concentrate on becoming the largest.

The future of MKY lies in the hands of the National Sales Directors. These NSD's are carbon copies of Mary Kay herself. She constantly feeds into their computers that they are Mary Kay. Wherever you go, whatever you do, be careful what you do, because you are Mary Kay. You are the future of the company. When I'm not here anymore, you will be taking over. Each of you are in training to be Mary Kay.

Mary Kay's goal is for every single day that passes, she tries to touch as many of these women's lives that she can. "If I see one more woman today become greater than she ever thought she could be by my persuasion that she is great, then it's a good day."

Richard Rogers, 38-year-old son of Mary

EXHIBIT 1
Organization Chart
President's Staff

Board of Directors, Chairman		Mary Kay Ash
President and Chief Executive Officer		Richard Rogers
	Executive Secretary	Cindy Puckett
	President of Mary Kay Cosmeticos S. A. (Argentina)	Dr. Gerardo Segura
	President of Mary Kay Cosmetics, Ltd. (Canada)	Richard J. Bennetts
	Managing Dir. of Mary Kay Cosmetics Pty. Ltd. (Australia)	John Watt
	Vice-President, Administration	Gerald Allen
	Vice-President, Finance and Treasurer	Gene Stubbs
	Vice-President, Controller	Jack Dingler
	Vice-President, Manufacturing Group	John Beasley
	Vice-President, Research and Development	Dr. Myra Barker
	Vice President, Manufacturing Operations	Pat Howard
	Vice President, Quality Assurance	Bruce Rudy
	Vice-President, Marketing	Richard Barlett
	Vice-President, Operations	Phil Bostley
	Director of Personnel	Betty Bessler
	Director of Purchasing	Ron Pearce
	Vice-President, Secretary and General Counsel	Monty Barber
	Director of Internal Audit	Wayne Furman
	Director of Protective Services	Dave Leopard

Kay Ash, is positioned at the helm of Mary Kay, serving as President and CEO of the Company since 1968. He is responsible for setting the tone and direction for the company. In the plans are the building of a new MKY campus (Exhibit 1).

The Industry

Mary Kay Cosmetics, Inc. is a participant and competitor in two basic industries: the cosmetics and personal-care industry and the direct sales industry, the latter composed of approximately 2200 direct sales companies. Among MKY's competitors in the cosmetics industry are Avon, Revlon, Estee Lauder, Gillette's Jafra, Richardson–Vick, Faberge, Cheeseborough–Ponds, Inc., and Noxell Corp. With well over two billion in sales in 1981, Avon, Revlon, and Gillette are the industry leaders. Cheeseborough–Pond's 1981 sales were 1.5 billion. Ranked within the top 10 of the cosmetics industry sales for MKY were 235 (net) million with Faberge and Noxell in the same sales category as MKY. Skin care, which is MKY's niche, is the focus of the competition.

With its appeal to older women in middle to high-income brackets who are entering the work force in record numbers, skin care and quality are the targets for a growing number of women according to industry analysts. They have more purchasing power but less time to spend their money. They want health, fitness, and value. Appealing to these women with major marketing thrusts are: Gillette with Aapri, a facial scrub containing ground apricot pits, and Silkience, which is a self-adjusting moisture lotion; Richardson–Vick with Oil of Olay moisturizer; Noxell with Raintree Hand and Body Lotion and Noxema; Cheeseborough–Pond's Vaseline Intensive Care; Estee Lauder's Clinique as well as a number of products from both Revlon and Avon. Noxell and Cheeseborough–Pond's sell the low-cost products. Avon and Revlon products are in the mid-price range with Estee Lauder products in the high-price range. MKY's products are in the mid to high-priced range. With the exception of Avon and MKY, all of these companies sell their products over the counter in department stores, drug stores, discount stores, and super markets.

The cosmetics industry as a whole is seeing a gradual downturn for the first time in its history, according to *Forbes'* Richard Stern. What has been classified as a recession-proof industry is now seeing growth that is mainly attributed to inflation. Volume sales are declining and the assumption that growth is eternal is gone. The skin-care treatment portion of the industry is the only one with any expectation for growth with perhaps 2 percent for 1982. Even though the recession is motivating a shift to more reasonably priced products, Avon and

Revlon are hurting the most. The industry has survived other recessions because of the increasing numbers of women entering the work force. But the rate of increase has been declining in recent years. To further complicate the volume of sales, virtually every cosmetic company has sales promotions on the concept of a free gift with purchase. MKY is different. Says the Chairman of the Board Ash, "They would love to get out of that business. We don't have to do that. We don't need to."

Both Stern and Mintz of *Sales and Marketing Management* note that Avon's problems stem from a less captive home market and an inadequate compensation program for sales representatives. Retail outlets such as drug stores, mass merchandisers, and food stores are capturing some of Avon's low-to-middle income market. Avon's reward program of gifts and vacations to outstanding sales representatives has failed to improve productivity which has been declining since 1979.

Other industry analysts speculate that the leveling of sales in the cosmetics industry can be attributed to consumers cutting back on purchases traditionally categorized as luxury items because of inflation and recession; women entering careers is leveling off; and the bulge in the teenage market that was seen in the 1960s and early 1970s is beginning to decline. The portion of the cosmetics industry that has had some immunity to this decline is the skin-care portion of the industry.

Some analysts believe the biggest threat to the industry, however, is the threat of regulation by the FDA.

> If a cosmetic item is regarded as a drug, the industry could be confronted with expensive regulations. These include detailed manufacturing controls, more frequent government inspections, product registrations, labeling requirement changes, and other reviews. The Toxic Substances Strategy Committee, a special White House panel studying cancer, has asked Congress to review cosmetics legislation and bring the industry under tighter federal control.

Increased regulation would mean higher production costs and higher prices to the consumer. Research and development divisions would require expansion into more scientifically oriented segments. Industry experts suggest that this would especially be burdensome to the smaller cosmetics companies and would in fact make it very hard for them to exist.

The other industry in which MKY competes is the direct sales industry. Competition is not only for customers willing to provide their home as the market place but also for recruits for sales representatives upon which the industry is totally dependent. Competitors include Amway which sells home products, Shaklee which has organic, non-pollutant household products, Home Interiors and Gifts, and Princess House which sells a fine line of crystal and other table accessories. All of these companies apparently understand the importance of acquiring and motivating large numbers of recruits. Use of exciting contests with flashy rewards such as big cars, furs, expensive jewelry, and extravagant vacations is a motivational factor overlooked by none of these companies. Family harmony and devotion to God are emphasized not only by MKY but by others such as Amway and Home Interiors and Gifts, the latter of which parallels many of MKY's motivational practices and was in fact founded by Mary Kay Ash's former sister-in-law, Mary Crowley.

Another characteristic shared by the direct sales companies is investigation by the Internal Revenue Service regarding the status of their direct sales personnel. MKY, as do many of the others, claim that their "beauty consultants" are independent distributors and not employees of MKY. Consequently, MKY pays no federal withholding or employment taxes for any of their 150,000 direct sales representatives. MKY and other direct sales companies are currently protected from liability under an interim relief act passed by the Congress.

Other pressure being exerted by the Internal Revenue Service on direct sales organizations such as Amway targets individual sales representatives' use of business expenses as tax shelters. In a copyrighted article appearing in the *Fort Worth Star Telegram*, reporters Bowles, McKinsey, and Magmusson claim that Amway recruiters use the advantage of tax shelters as an enticement to become an Amway distributor. The pitch is to use the Amway distributorship as an excuse to write off new clothes, Christmas gifts, appliances, long-distance calls, new cars, vacation houses, and expensive vacations. In IRS audits of the tax returns of 300 Amway distributors in Baltimore last year, all but two resulted in back taxes and penalties being assessed. The average payment was $1,350 not including interest and penalties. Currently 1,000 more Amway distributors in Baltimore are undergoing IRS audits. According to Roscoe Edgar, Jr., the IRS Commissioner,

> It appears that the tax benefit aspects of many of these activities may be the primary reason large numbers of people become involved. Promotional schemes, recruitment methods, and other information we have on these activities frequently highlight the anticipated tax benefits above all else. This indicates to us that the individuals involved know full well what they are doing.

External Environment

Economic Forces

There are several factors of the economy that impact on the cosmetics industry in general and MKY in particular. Among these factors are consumer demand, competition, and the general state of the national economy. For one reason or another the once-held assumption of eternal growth for the cosmetics industry seems to have vanished. The supposedly recession-proof cosmetics industry has for the first time in its history experienced a downturn in business. According to Jack Salyman of Wall Street's Smith Barney and industry consultant Allan Mottus, unit sales have been flat for years with nearly all of the growth (43 percent) since 1978 attributable to a 39 percent increase in the cost of living. The shakeout appears to be focused on the middle market. This leaves the effect on MKY uncertain.

As in any other retail industry consumer demand is the key factor that influences a company's business decisions. Competition to meet the consumers' needs has stiffened considerably in the cosmetics industry as evidenced by the fact that many companies formerly in totally unrelated businesses now have lines of cosmetics. Clothes designers are a good example. One economic factor that is affecting consumers and industry alike is the present higher cost of borrowing money, that is, the prime lending rate. This makes it more expensive for MKY to produce and sell its products and results in higher cost to the customer.

Technological Forces

If a company is not on the "leading edge" of industry technology, it will be at a competitive disadvantage. The cosmetics industry is not a high-technology industry in the sense of the product produced. But, a company needs the latest technology to be able to produce its product cost effectively which is instrumental in gaining a competitive advantage. In the cosmetics industry technology revolves around research into how the skin relates to the rest of the body and how it relates to its environment. Of major concern is the safety and efficacy of the product.

Social Forces

Two keys to the success of the cosmetics industry, factors that greatly influence MKY's business strategy, are population demographics and sociological changes. As noted by Richard Stern of *Forbes*, "The key is the underlying demographics. The industry rode out previous recessions by riding the skirts of ever more working women. More working women meant increased women's spending and more cosmetics to wear to the office. But the rate of increase in the number of working women has declined in recent years." Stern also sees sociological changes afoot as well. Working women now seem to prefer convenience to ambience, prompting a shift in distribution channels toward more merchandizers, discount drug stores, and even supermarkets and away from department stores.

These changes would appear to enhance the appeal of direct marketing because from a convenience standpoint it is much easier to have a product brought to you than it is to have to go get it. Also, the recession seems to have caused a shift in buying habits that may impact the middle market cosmetics significantly. As in other retail industries, consumers of cosmetics have gone to lower priced goods in an effort to economize or have switched to higher priced goods for quality. Population distribution is very important to the cosmetics industry in helping determine target markets. There has been a definite change in the distribution of the population. Between 1970 and 1980 the number of people over the age of 30 increased 40 percent while the total population grew only 11.4 percent. America is growing older.

Political and Legal Forces

The factors that affect MKY in this area fall into two categories. First, there are laws that affect the cosmetics industry as a whole. Then there are factors that are concerned just with regulating firms that sell through direct-sales marketing techniques as does MKY. MKY, as is the rest of the industry, is subject to regulation by the FDA and the Alcohol and Tax Unit of the Treasury department. The FTC regulates the company's advertising and sales practices. Plus, the company's marketing, packaging, package labeling, and product content are regulated by many other federal, state, local, and foreign laws.

Of more immediate concern to MKY and all other companies that use direct sales to market their products is a battle with the IRS over whether the sales person should be considered an employee or an independent contractor. To quote Richard Rogers, "We (MKY) are sure you can appreciate the administrative overhead and expense that we would incur if we were required to maintain employee-type records, withhold taxes, pay social security taxes, etc. for the over 150,000 persons in our sales force." A bill that has been before Congress recently decided the independent contractor issue. To quote Mary Kay Ash, when asked about the status of the independent contractors' bill, she replied, "We won." What she meant is that during the third quarter of 1982 Congress enacted The Tax Equity and Fiscal Responsibility Act of 1982. This act contains provisions that classify people in the sales force of direct-sales marketing firms as "statuatory non-employees." Thus ends a 10-year battle with the IRS.

Internal Environment

Human Resources

Today MKY employs approximately 1,400 persons. These employees are nonunionized. Of the 1,400 around 40 percent are employed in the management and administrative end of the business. The other 60 percent are employed in areas such as research and development, manufacturing, etc. Even more important to the organization are the more than 150,000 "beauty consultants" that operate as independent contractors in selling the MKY products.

When considering human resources, the value of a company's employees must also be considered. In a direct sales organization such as MKY, motivation is the grease that keeps the wheels turning. In that respect Mary Kay Ash is the head "cheerleader." She is the one ultimately responsible for the motivation of the over 150,000 beauty consultants. Without the proper motivation sales would suffer. The company's motivation and communication have already been covered in detail but the philosophy behind it all is summed up in the following quote by Mary Kay. "Somebody said, if you act enthusiastic, you will become enthusiastic. We try to generate enthusiasm by example."

Physical and Production Resources

MKY is headquartered in Dallas, Texas and has facilities in Atlanta, Chicago, Los Angeles, Piscataway, New Jersey, Victoria, Australia, Toronto, Canada and Buenos Aires, Argentina.

The executive offices are housed in an eight-story, 109,000 square food building in Dallas. The company's lone manufacturing facility is housed in a building of some 300,000 square feet, also located in Dallas. This facility is partitioned such that there are approximately 110,300 square feet for manufacturing, 51,300 square feet for office space, and 116,000 square feet for use as a warehouse. This building and the eight-story office tower are owned by the company free of encumbrance. The company leases a third building in Dallas that has approximately 450,600 square feet. This building houses operations for distribution, printing, data processing, and more warehouse space. MKY's office and warehouse facilities in Atlanta, Chicago, Los Angeles, and Australia total approximately 200,000 square feet and are owned free of encumbrance. The office and warehouse facilities in New Jersey, Argentina, and Canada total about 100,000 square feet. These facilities are leased with an option to purchase the Canadian facility. The manufacturing facilities and equipment are at least modern and in many cases state-of-the-art and well maintained. Every machine that comes in contact with an MKY product is disassembled, cleaned, and sanitized at regular intervals.

In the interest of future growth MKY has purchased 177 acres in Dallas at the cost of approximately $6.5 million. The project to develop this land will cost an estimated $100 million, according to Mary Kay. At the present time, believes Richard Rogers, "we have in place facilities to support an annual sales volume of approximately $400 million."

Market Resources

Market resources are the elements necessary to transfer possession of MKY's products to the consumer. MKY's two most important market resources are channel of distribution and advertising (although it has taken MKY time to understand and properly utilize this resource). MKY's channel of distribution is comprised solely of one element, a sales force of 150,000 beauty consultants who operate as independent contractors. The products are distributed via one wholesale sale and one retail sale channel. The products are transferred from the company to the consultant at wholesale, then from consultant to the consumer at retail. The beauty consultants' profit is directly derived from the sale of the product to the ultimate consumer. Her profit is the difference between the wholesale price paid MKY for the product and the price the customer paid for the product. Every consultant can sell products wherever she wishes because MKY does not set territories or sell franchises.

Until recently advertising was used infrequently in MKY's marketing plan. Historically, most advertising was done by word of mouth relying upon direct sales personnel to spread the word. In the past, when there was an advertising budget it was set at or below 1 percent of sales. When national advertising was used, ads usually appeared in magazines such as *McCalls, Redbook, Better Homes and Gardens,* and *Ladies' Home Journal.* Since the appearance of Mary Kay

Ash on "60 Minutes" in late 1979, the company's view of advertising has been changing. Gerald Allen, MKY's Administrative Vice-President, said the company learned a lesson in the past two and one-half years thanks to "60 Minutes." He considers the show partially responsible for the tremendous growth of MKY's sales force. Mr. Allen also believes the show to have been worth the equivalent of $40 million worth of national network advertising and says, "That made believers out of us." In the third quarter of 1982 MKY launched its first nationwide television advertising campaign. The advertising budget for the third and fourth quarters of 1982 will total $3 million and raise the total advertising budget for the year to $4 million (more than double the budget for any previous year).

Research and Development Resources

According to John Beasley, Vice-President of Manufacturing for MKY, research and development is the leading edge in obtaining the corporate goal of being the finest teaching-oriented skin-care company in the world with sales of $500 million by 1990. Since 1975, the company's research and development staff has grown from two to 47. Mr. Beasley also said that, "We go after the top 10 percent of the people in the country who have the skills that we're looking for and personal integrity." MKY funds research all over the world in an effort to develop new technology. Again, to quote Mr. Beasley, "We (MKY) are having to stretch current technology in establishing some new standards in the industry in the area of cosmedogenicity, the interaction of the product, the environment, and skin causing comadnes (acne). Of great importance to the company is that research maintain a fast-response attitude because of the rate at which tastes and fashions change. During a recent interview, Mary Kay Ash indicated that the research and development budget would continue to be approximately one percent of sales as has been the case in recent years.

Results of Operations

In 1981 net sales increased at a rate of 41 percent compared to 83 percent for 1980 and 70 percent in 1979. At the same time the number of beauty consultants increased 42 percent, 64 percent, and 33 percent in 1981, 1980, and 1979, respectively. During the same period, individual productivity of the beauty consultants declined. In 1979 average annual productivity for a consultant increased 27 percent compared with an increase of 12 percent for 1980 and a decrease of one percent for 1981. At the same time, selling and general and administrative expenses held fairly constant at approximately 51 percent of sales. It should also be noted that MKY instituted price increases of 15 percent in 1981 and 5 percent in 1980. As a result of all the above-mentioned factors net income increased from $4.8 million in 1978 to $24.2 million in 1981. Refer to Exhibit 2.

Financial Condition

In 1981 *Business Week* ranked MKY as the 12th fastest growing company in the country. When asked in a recent interview her opinion concerning the current financial condition of the company, Mary Kay Ash responded, "I think we're doing great!" However, she also admitted that she let her son Richard Rogers, the president and CEO, handle the financial matters of the company.

With the phenomenal growth in the last three years MKY's total assets have grown from $36 million in 1978 to $101 million in 1981. Working capital for the same period was $5.7 million in 1978, $2.3 million in 1979, $4.0 million in 1980, and $7.8 million in 1981. At the same time, capital expenditures were increasing faster than both working capital and total assets. In 1981 capital expenditures were $25.3 million compared to $12.5 million in 1980, $4.7 million in 1979, and $2.1 million in 1978. There were approximately 14.3 million shares of common stock outstanding in 1981. This represents a 25 percent decrease compared to the 19.6 million

EXHIBIT 2
Growth

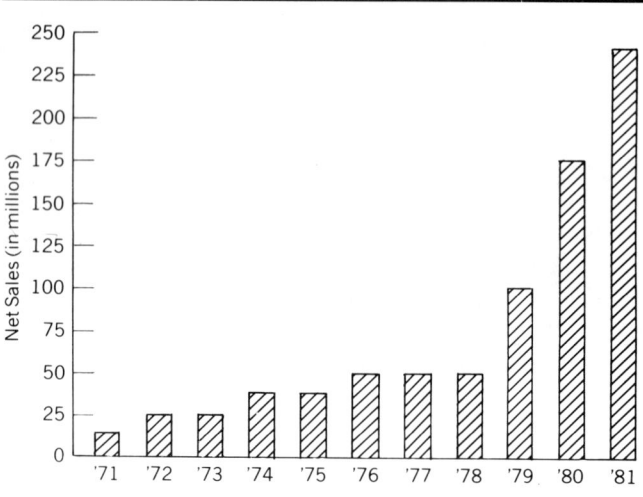

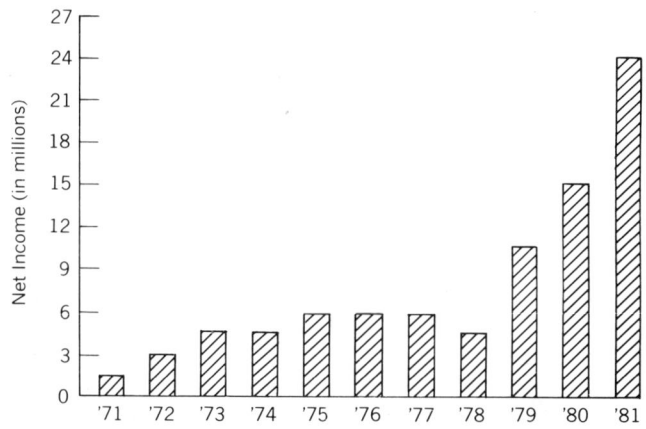

shares outstanding at the end of 1976. The decrease resulted from MKY tender offers in 1977 and 1979. Other information on the company is detailed in Exhibits 3 through 5.

Present Strategic Posture

Strategic posture is determined by the answers to questions such as What is our product mix? and What is our customer mix? The most important factor in MKY's strategic posture is its niche in the skin-care products area of the cosmetics market where larger competitors such as Avon are a minor factor. Also, Mary Kay Ash believes that a limited product line maximizes the sales force's efficiency. Thus, the company's product line is limited to approximately 45 items. Also important is the company's target market. The company perceives its prime market to be women ages 25 to 44 who are in or a little above the middle-income bracket, have some college education, and live in suburbia or exurbia.

Environmental Research

Environmental research is used to determine if an organization can keep pace with external change. As MKY continues to grow it must be able to recognize and react to changes in competition, consumer demand, and economic conditions. The company believes that to do this it must be capable of supporting rapid sales volume growth with consistently high-quality products and reliable service.

EXHIBIT 3
Consolidated Balance Sheets
December 31, 1981 and 1980

	1981	1980
Assets		
Current assets		
Cash and cash equivalents	$ 7,953,000	$11,085,000
Accounts and notes receivable	2,715,000	1,109,000
Inventories		
Raw materials	8,888,000	6,380,000
Finished goods	18,193,000	15,218,000
	27,081,000	21,598,000
Deferred income tax benefits	2,948,000	2,036,000
Prepaid expenses	1,213,000	666,000
Total current assets	41,910,000	36,494,000
Property, plant and equipment, at cost:		
Land	12,298,000	3,793,000
Buildings and improvements	23,869,000	21,348,000
Furniture, fixtures, and equipment	28,299,000	14,963,000
Construction in progress	4,829,000	3,877,000
	69,295,000	43,981,000
Less accumulated depreciation	10,519,000	7,653,000
	58,776,000	36,328,000
Notes receivable	—	1,087,000
Other assets	290,000	522,000
	$100,976,000	$74,431,000
Liabilities and Stockholders' Equity		
Current liabilities		
Note payable to bank	$ 1,260,000	$ —
Accounts payable	8,061,000	8,900,000
Accrued liabilities	16,659,000	13,063,000
Income tax	5,712,000	4,214,000
Deferred sales	1,321,000	4,363,000
Current portion of long-term debt	1,058,000	1,000,000
Total current liabilities	34,071,000	31,540,000
Long-term debt	2,366,000	3,000,000
Deferred income taxes	2,587,000	1,258,000
Stockholders' equity	61,952,000	38,633,000
	$100,976,000	$74,431,000

EXHIBIT 4
Consolidated Statements of Income
Years Ended December 31, 1981, 1980, and 1979

	1981	1980	1979
Net sales	$235,296,000	$166,039,000	$91,400,000
Interest and other income, net	1,485,000	712,000	493,000
	236,781,000	167,650,000	91,893,000
Costs and expenses			
Cost of sales	71,100,000	52,484,000	27,574,000
Selling, general, and administrative expenses	120,880,000	86,998,000	45,522,000
Interest expense	1,014,000	635,000	958,000
	192,994,000	140,117,000	74,054,000
Income before income taxes	43,787,000	27,533,000	17,839,000
Provision for income taxes	19,632,000	12,398,000	8,207,000
Net income	$ 24,155,000	$ 15,135,000	$ 9,632,000
Net income per common and common equivalent share	$1.65	$1.05	$.65
Average shares	14,662,000	14,442,000	14,720,000

EXHIBIT 5
Consolidated Statements of Changes in Financial Position
Years Ended December 31, 1981, 1980, and 1979

	1981	1980	1979
Source of funds			
Operations			
Net income	$24,155,000	$15,135,000	$ 9,632,000
Depreciation	2,866,000	1,987,000	1,569,000
Increased in deferred income taxes	1,329,000	351,000	177,000
Gains on sales of real estate not used in business	—	—	(116,000)
Funds provided from operations	28,350,000	17,473,000	11,262,000
Proceeds from exercises of stock options	1,922,000	1,338,000	164,000
Decrease in notes receivable	1,087,000	120,000	—
Increase in long-term debt	366,000	—	5,442,000
Proceeds from sales of real estate not used in business	—	—	1,182,000
Other	325,000	—	276,000
	32,050,000	18,931,000	18,326,000
Application of funds			
Additions to property, plant, and equipment, net	25,314,000	12,457,000	4,510,000
Dividends declared	2,851,000	2,458,000	1,764,000
Reduction of long-term debt	1,000,000	1,000,000	5,000,000
Purchase of treasury shares	—	—	9,422,000
Increase in notes receivable	—	—	1,047,000
Other	—	369,000	—
	29,165,000	16,284,000	21,743,000
Increase (decrease) in working capital	$ 2,885,000	$ 2,647,000	$(3,417,000)

OSHMAN'S SPORTING GOODS, INC.

History

Oshman's got its start in 1919 as a general store in a small town 30 miles outside of Houston, Texas. A short time after the opening, the sole proprietor, Jake S. Oshman, had a chance to purchase the hunting and fishing inventory from a store in liquidation. When Jake was able to turn this inventory at considerable profit in a short time, he decided to enter the sporting-goods business on an expanded basis. By 1931, Oshman was well-established in the Houston market and was organized as a proprietorship. The stores continued to expand and prosper as Houston grew. In 1946, the company was incorporated under Texas law as Oshman's Outdoor Store, finally changing the name to Oshman's Incorporated in 1958. The corporation continued to grow and for the first time expanded outside the greater Houston area to other Texas Gulf Coast cities.

In the early 1960s, Jake Oshman contracted a terminal illness and the company turned to his son-in-law, Al Lubetkin, then a successful lawyer, for leadership. After joining the company in 1964 and assuming total responsibility for planning following Jake Oshman's death in 1965, Lubetkin was appointed Chief Executive Officer, and he led the corporation to a period of unprecedented expansion and profitability. By the end of the decade, Oshman's held a considerable segment in the sporting-goods market along the Texas Gulf Coast and had placed retail outlets in the four largest Texas cities. While part of this expansion could be financed with existing internal cash flows, the total sum needed was available only through outside financing. On January 22, 1970, Oshman's, Inc. entered into a plan of reorganization to merge, effective January 31, 1970, into a recently formed wholly owned subsidiary (Oshman's Sporting Goods, Inc., a Delaware corporation), with the Delaware corporation being the surviving entity. The new corporation authorized 4,000,000 shares of $1 per value common stock and 500,000 shares of $1 per value preferred stock. In connection with the merger, 1,207,650 shares of the new corporation's common stock were exchanged for all of the Class A and B common and preferred stock outstanding.

Operations as of 1970

The company entered the 1970s with 11 retail stores located in the four largest cities in Texas, eight of these stores in Houston. Sales from February 1, 1969 to January 31, 1970 were $19.3 million, of which $13.3 million were retail sales and $6 million represented institutional and wholesale sales. Net earnings during this period were $789,000. These stores represented a departure from the traditional "Mom & Pop" sporting-goods shop. The typical Oshman outlet averaged in excess of 10,000 square feet of floor space, close to three times the size of a normal sporting-goods store. A stock inventory of over 20,000 items provided the customer with an extraordinary selection of quality merchandise. The stores were much more lavish than the traditional sporting goods store. Resembling a small department store, a typical Oshman's outlet was spacious and attractive, decorated by professional designers, and located in a major regional or suburban shopping center. Oshman's retail target market was the upper to middle-income family with sufficient disposable income and leisure time to be attracted to high-quality, brand-name sporting goods and sportswear.

The company purchased merchandise directly from the manufacturer or manufacturer's representatives in large quantities, taking advantage of any discount offered. The com-

---

Source: Prepared by Robert E. Schellenberger of East Carolina University and Kenneth W. Olm of the University of Texas at Austin. Permission to use granted by the authors.

pany then maintained a substantial inventory in large warehouses until retail inventories had dipped to a pre-established reorder level. Sometimes the company would commit itself to a quantity of stock sufficient to last an entire year or sport's season in a single transaction. Similarly, sportswear orders might be contracted for on a wholesale seasonal basis, however, the company had no long-term contracts with any supplier and no single supplier accounted for as much as 10 percent of the total purchases. Institutional sales (professionals, university and college teams, school districts, industrial leagues, etc.) formed a small but highly profitable market. These sales were large volume, usually for a full season, and many times were based on price alone, even to the point of sealed bids for exceptionally large contracts. The institutional goods were almost exclusively those of brand-name manufacturers, and often were items whose specification was originally set by the leagues themselves. The major competitors in this market were large sporting-goods wholesalers or manufacturer's representatives from producers themselves. In 1969, roughly 4 million dollars of sales came from institutional sales. Institutional sales were made in the Texas and western Louisiana area. However, the wholesaling division was discontinued in January 1, 1974, because of poor performance relative to other parts of the business. In addition to the reduced purchase cost of supplies, Oshman's executives felt that this distribution system provided improved customer service in the form of rapid restocking of shelves and reduced order time for customer's special purchases.

Oshman's hopes and desires for the 1970s can be gleaned from a summary of a presentation made by President Alvin N. Lubetkin in 1971 for the Houston Society of Financial Analysts. As President Lubetkin pointed out, activity and exercise were becoming an important part of American culture. People were consciously setting aside time for their particular activity. Recreational desires were becoming recreational needs. These factors have created what he defined as a "super sports market." He went on to say:

> The more affluent and sophisticated sports enthusiasts will demand larger selections, greater depth, more service, in surroundings that he can comfortably identify with. This is where our opportunity lies. Our stores are three to four times the size of the average sporting-goods store. We offer in-depth selection of the widest range of sporting goods for the beginner; for the would-be pro, there is the right item at Oshman's. You can choose from over 40 different tennis rackets, representing seven different manufacturers, priced from $3.95 to $70.00; six different brands of tennis balls; over 20 models of golf clubs in all price ranges; 15 footballs ranging from a kid's football at $3.95 to the NFL ball at $24.95; 60 different models of baseball gloves from $4.95 to $49.95. Even in large items like pool tables, we offer 15 models priced from $59.95 to $1,500. Obviously the point is you do not need to look elsewhere. We are capable of satisfying the increased requirements of the new sports buff. We have been doing just that for many years in Houston.

He went on to say that the expansion that had taken place in recent years for Oshman's was a result of a 1966 decision to become something other than a regional firm. The recent and expected expansion came about from a thorough analysis of operations and development of capacities and capabilities to effectively and profitably expand into new markets. This required development of people, expansion of facilities, and development of strong systems and controls. Expansion areas were carefully selected after much study. Mr. Lubetkin had the following to say about the future:

> Up to this point, all our expansion has been from the opening of new Oshman's stores where the nature of the average sporting-goods store gives us a competitive advantage, it at the same time precludes an aggressive acquisition policy. There are, however, some sit-

uations that appear to make good sense in terms of management talent in potential markets, and we are pursuing these. As I indicated in my opening remarks, we are in an industry that has great potential, and we are prepared to take advantage of this opportunity. We will continue to expand in our existing market areas and will reach out to new ones. We are studying new ways to develop the full potential of market areas.

We are planning a store for the latter part of next year that will be a departure from our present approach and if successful will open up many new markets with substantial and additional potential. In areas where opening multistores may not be justified, we are thinking in terms of one huge world of sporting goods approach—a free-standing freeway location with good access and strong advertising capable of bringing customers from all parts of the city. These units would be approximately 20,000 square feet, and offer even larger selections of camping and outdoor equipment than our existing units. I want to emphasize that this is an experiment—our first one should be open in San Antonio in late 1972. If it works out we will move ahead with this approach in certain areas while still developing our shopping center locations where they make the most sense.

I have been asked many times, how many stores are you going to open next year? I can answer this only one way, we are young, experienced, and aggressive. We will take advantage of every good opportunity that is presented or can be developed, however, we will not open stores just to have more units. Each one of our stores has the potential of doing well over one million dollars and contributes as much as 15 percent or more to profits and corporate overhead. We are very selective in choosing these sites. In short, we are taking a proven concept and applying it to the sporting-goods industry.

There are many successful national chains in the food, apparel, drug, jewelry, and discount areas. At present there is not one national chain in the sporting-goods industry. We think Oshman's sporting goods will be the first.

Current Conditions

From 1970 until January 1983 sales grew more than 13 fold from $18.3 million to $247 million and the number of stores from 11 to 177. The following descriptions are taken from the annual report for January 29, 1983.

Description of Business

Oshman's Sporting Goods, Inc. is widely recognized as an industry leader operating a chain of 177 full-line retail sporting-goods specialty stores. Oshman's offers in-depth selections of high-quality name brands as well as private label sporting-goods equipment and sportswear for all sporting activities. At year end the Company was operating 166 Oshman's stores throughout the Sun Belt area and Hawaii. Oshman's acquired the world-renowned Abercrombie and Fitch name in 1978. Since then, Abercrombie and Fitch has opened 11 stores in major cities throughout the country and under its banner has also entered the mail-order business. The Company also operates a team division selling athletic equipment and uniforms to schools and amateur and professional teams.

Financial Condition

The Company ended 1982 in excellent financial condition. Working capital increased to $43,469,000 at January 29, 1983, from $40,773,000 at January 30, 1982 and $40,034,000 at January 31, 1981. Cash and equivalents equaled $14,540,000 compared to $6,241,000 and $11,015,000 for the two previous years. The reduction in cash and equivalents and the increase in merchandise inventories, fixed assets, and accounts payable in 1981 were interrelated and primarily due to merchandise inventories and capital expenditures for the 33 sporting-goods stores acquired and other new stores opened during 1981. The increase in 1982 in cash and equivalents is related to the increase in accounts payable and the relatively modest increase in merchandise inventories of $2,760,000 which translates to a reduction in average per store inventories of 11 percent. This was the result of a successful inventory management program implemented in 1982. The increase in fixed assets in 1982 is primarily due to the 35 stores acquired and opening during the year.

Plans for 1983 are to open from 8 to 12 stores. Because of its financial condition, the Company expects to handle future planned expansion without reliance upon additional outside financing. Planned capital expenditures for 1983 are about $4,800,000. The Company presently has available a $12,000,000 line of credit that it expects to use to meet its normal seasonal requirements.

Results of Operations

Sales for 1982 increased 14.2 percent compared to 49.4 percent in the previous year. Approximately 82 percent of the increase in 1982 is due to new stores opened and acquired during the year. The balance of the increase is due to increased sales in units existing prior to 1982. Same-store sales increases for the last five years have been: 2.7 percent in 1982, 8.8 percent in 1981, 1.3 percent in 1980, 8.3 percent in 1979, and 12.0 percent in 1978.

Cost of goods for 1982, 1981, and 1980 were 60.8, 60.0, and 60.9 percent respectively. The increase in cost of goods sold in 1982 was caused by earlier end-of-season ski markdowns in 1982 compared to the prior ski season. The decrease in cost of goods sold from 1980 to 1981 resulted from a lower LIFO charge in 1981. The effect of the LIFO adjustment was to increase cost of sales as a percentage of sales 0.4, 0.4, and 1.1 percent, respectively, for 1982, 1981, and 1980.

For 1982, the after-tax LIFO charge was $541,000 or $0.08 per share compared to $493,000 or $0.07 per share the prior year. The fourth quarter LIFO adjustments resulted in an after-tax credit of $6,000 compared to a credit in the prior year of $128,000 or $0.02 per share.

Selling and administrative expenses as a percentage of sales were 33.9, 33.2, and 32.8 percent, respectively, for the last three years.

The increases in both 1982 and 1981 are primarily due to the fact that expenses of acquired and new stores opened in each year (35 in 1982 and 18 in 1981, plus the 33 stores acquired in January 1981) were proportionately higher than their contribution to sales. The unusually large number of new stores acquired and opened during the last two years has magnified this normal relationship.

Historically, sales increases on a same-store basis have been sufficient to overcome the inflationary effects on salaries and other costs of doing business. 1982 and 1980 have been exceptions. The low same-store sales gains in 1980 were primarily due to a depressed economy and an extremely poor ski season in the Western United States. 1982 same-store gains are also lower than normal and primarily due to the overall slow economic condition and the negative effect of the "oil glut" on a large part of the Company's marketing area and, to a lesser extent, the devaluation of the Mexican peso. The Company anticipates being able to overcome the effects of future inflation through same-store sales increases, especially when economic environments improve.

Demand for Sporting Goods[1]

The Recreation Market

During the 1970s one of the fastest growing segments of consumer spending was for recreational-related products and services. Between 1970 and 1980, recreational expenditures increased from $41 billion to $106.4 billion, an increase of 260 percent. This compares with the 213 percent increase in recreational expenditures experienced in the 1960s. These increases are consistent with the overall growth in consumers' leisure-time spending. According to a study in *U. S. News and World Report* consumer outlays for sports, recreation, and

---

[1]Oshman's 1981 Annual Report.

EXHIBIT 1
Recreational Expenditures as a Percent of Total Personal Consumption Expenditures

1960	1965	1970	1975	1980
5.63%	6.07%	6.32%	6.79%	6.40%

entertainment in 1981 were $244 billion, an increase of 321 percent over 1965.

Recreational expenditures, as a percent of total personal consumption expenditures, also increased steadily over the period 1960–1975, reaching a high of 6.8 percent (Exhibit 1). Since 1974 this relationship has fluctuated between 6.4 and 6.8 percent. This leveling is most likely a result of the rapid inflation experienced in the late 1970s in the basic consumer necessities of food, shelter, and transportation. In the 1980s, as income increases, recreational expenditures should get an even larger share of the consumer's dollar.

Another way to view the increasing importance that Americans place on outdoor recreation is to examine recreational expenditures in relation to disposable personal income and consumer discretionary spending. Recreational expenditures are, over time, positively related to changes in disposable personal income. This relationship suggests that if consumers experience an increase in disposable personal income they normally increase recreational expenditures. Of course, a decrease in disposable personal income should result in a corresponding decrease in recreational expenditures. In practice, this downside sensitivity to lower income levels has not proven necessarily true. Many consumers seem to become accustomed to a particular level of recreation activity and are reluctant to reduce their activity, even when experiencing an income decline or increasing living costs.

Americans now place an ever-increasing value on recreation for its own sake rather than as a reward for hard work. Exhibit 2 shows that recreational expenditures continue to in-

EXHIBIT 2

Year	Discretionary Spending ($ billions)	Percent Change Previous Year	Recreation Expenditures ($ billions)	Percent Change Previous Year	Recreation Expenditures as a Percent of Discretionary Income
1981	$705.1 (E)	6.14%	$122.4 (E)	15.0%	17.36%
1980	664.3	2.94	106.4	7.4	16.02
1979	545.6	23.34	99.1	8.7	15.35
1978	523.3	18.21	91.2	12.3	17.43
1977	442.7	8.71	81.2	11.2	18.34
1976	407.2	20.44	73.0	9.8	17.93
1975	338.1	5.39	66.5	9.1	19.67
1974	320.8	1.90	60.9	10.3	18.98
1973	314.8	12.22	55.2	12.4	17.53
1972	280.5	11.57	49.1	12.4	17.50
1971	251.4	8.22	43.7	12.3	17.38
1970	232.3	−.01	41.0	7.5	17.65
1966	190.4	8.55	28.9	9.9	15.18
1961	129.9	−.05	19.5	6.6	15.01

Source: A Guide to Consumer Markets, 1980/1981, Conference Board Report and July issues of the *Survey of Current Business.*
(E) = estimate.

crease when discretionary spending growth is near zero, as was the case in 1961, 1970, and 1974. Even in 1980 and 1981, which were years of modest growth in discretionary spending, recreational expenditures continued to grow at a healthy rate. The fact that a significant percentage of discretionary spending continues to be allocated to recreational expenditures indicates the importance consumers attach to this activity. Recreation, especially active, outdoor recreation, is part of the American way of life. The majority of active, outdoor recreation involves the use of various types of sporting goods. Thus, sporting-goods sales are an important part of recreational expenditures.

Sporting-Goods Sales

Between 1973 and 1976 total sporting-goods and recreational equipment sales increased 26.0 percent and experienced an average annual growth rate of 8.0 percent. Over this four-year period sporting-goods sales alone represented approximately 45 percent of the total and grew at a rate faster than other types of recreational equipment including bicycles, boats, snowmobiles, and recreational vehicles. During the period 1973–1976, sporting-goods sales increased 77.3 percent, growing at an annual rate of 11.6 percent. This growth pattern has continued through 1981 but at a somewhat slower rate. Between 1977 and 1981 total sporting-goods sales increased 29.3 percent, growing at an annual rate of 6.6 percent as shown in Exhibit 3. This represents a slowing of the growth rate compared to the 1970s. However, when one considers the economic conditions prevalent during this period and the lackluster retail environment, the growth rate is still quite good.

Sporting-goods sales in 1982 are expected to increase only 5 percent to about $12 billion. This projected small increase for 1982 considers the negative impact of the current recession. The longer term demand for sporting goods remains much more favorable as the trends discussed here continue to accelerate in the mid and late 1980s.

EXHIBIT 3
Sporting-Goods and Recreational Equipment Sales

	Total (billions)	Sporting Goods (billions)	Recreational Equipment (billions)
1982	$20.25 (E)	$12.20	$8.05 (E)
1981	18.69	11.68	7.01
1980	16.70	11.35	5.35
1979	16.83	10.38	6.45
1978	18.37	9.57	8.80
1977	17.43	9.03	8.40

Source: The National Sporting Goods Association.
(E) = estimate.

Demand Determinates

During the 1970s Americans demonstrated both increasing interest and greater participation in outdoor recreation activities. Many factors contributed to this phenomenon including an increased awareness of physical fitness and access to better recreational facilities. In addition, certain socio-economic factors were at work, significantly altering Americans' values toward recreation. Other important factors include basic changes in attitudes toward and availability of leisure time (social values), more affluent families, a better educated population, and shifts in that population's age distribution. The impact of trends experienced in the 1970s will continue throughout the 1980s, having a very positive impact on recreation in general and the sale of sporting goods in particular.

Leisure Time

Spending for recreational activities is very dependent upon time, time when consumers are not working or sleeping. This is time available to consumers to pursue recreational activities. It will continue to be an important factor in determining levels of recreational spending. The amount of time free of work, which represents nearly one-third of the days in the year, has not dramatically increased in over 20 years. What has changed significantly is the way leisure time has been redistributed. This redistribution of free time has resulted in the American consumer having larger blocks of leisure time. For example, the U. S. Congress shifted five mid-week holidays to Monday, creating a series of three-day weekends that were previously unavailable. These new blocks of leisure time presented consumers an opportunity to engage in additional outdoor recreation and sport.

There is still continued interest on the part of unions to seek longer vacations and additional holidays. Moreover, unions continue to maintain an interest in the four-day work week. If the work week is adopted nationally, it will dramatically alter the present leisure-time pattern of the American consumer.

Income

Income is a key factor in determining the levels and growth of recreational and sporting-goods expenditures. To be specific, it is income not used for food, clothing, shelter, fuel, and other basic family needs. It is income that can be spent on leisure-time activities. Thus, disposable personal income is essential in determining economic growth in the leisure industry and actually serves as a barometer of the nation's standard of living.

A study conducted by the Department of Commerce in the 1970s supports the relationship between income and sporting-goods sales. Sporting-goods sales were found to be sensitive to changes in disposable personal income. The measure of the degree of sensitivity is called the income elasticity and for sporting goods a reasonable estimate of its income elasticity is between 1.5 to 2.0; a 1971–1972 study showed an income elasticity of 2.01 for Sporting Goods and Toys. The elasticity reflects the percentage change in sporting-goods sales for each 1 percent rise in disposable personal income. Based on this estimate, projected increases in disposable personal income will have a very positive impact on expenditures for sporting goods.

What happens to disposable personal income growth and how the income is distributed among families is of major significance to sporting-goods sales. Townsend–Greenspan and Company estimated that after-tax family income will experience a real growth of about 19 percent by the year 1990. This 19 percent growth is in addition to any inflationary growth experienced during the decade. Even though this projected real income growth is less than that experienced in the 1960s, the growth will be enough to significantly raise the living standard of millions of families.

According to the Townsend–Greenspan and Company 1990 projections, median family income is expected to rise about $23,800 in 1979 dollars. This median value does not reflect the important income distribution shift that will occur.

Even when there is a general rise in the level of disposable personal income, all families do not allocate the same percentage of their income for recreational activities. The trend is for higher-income families to use a larger percentage of family expenditures for recreational purposes. In a study reported by the Conference Board in 1973, families with income above $20,000 represented only 15.6 percent of all families in the United States. But these same families accounted for 28.3 percent of all personal consumption expenditures and allocated 21.2 percent of these expenditures for recreation.

Exhibit 4 indicates that by 1990, 38 percent of the families in the United States will have an income in excess of $25,000. The number of upper-income families will grow by 10.4 million, while the total number of families is expected to increase by only 9 million. Some of this increase in upper-income families will result from growth in the number of workers in the prime of life, ages 25 to 44.

Exhibit 5 shows the estimated distribution of workers ages 25–44.

EXHIBIT 4
Family Income Distribution

Income Categories[a]	Percentage of Families	
	1980	1990
$50,000–over	2.1	5.8
$25,000–49,999	22.8	32.2
$15,000–24,999	32.1	27.7
$ 7,500–14,999	26.4	21.1
$ 0– 7,499	16.6	13.2

[a] 1977 constant dollars.

EXHIBIT 5
Workers in the Prime of Life

Year	Total Workforce (in millions)	Total Ages 25–44 (in millions)	Percent of Workforce Ages 25–44
1975	91.8	39.0	42.5
1980	105.5	48.8	46.3
1985	113.3	58.6	51.8
1990	120.1	66.4	55.3

This huge number of workers will be experienced, productive, and receive higher salaries. This has significant long-run implications for sporting-goods sales. It is these upper-income families that spend a higher proportion of their income for recreational and leisure activities. More at the top and fewer at the bottom will provide the sporting-goods market with a larger share of consumer expenditures.

Population

Population and, more particularly, its distribution among age groups are also significant factors that impact sporting-goods sales. Population of the United States will continue to grow during the 1980s. The expected growth will be slower than population growth during boom years but the nation can expect to add another 20 to 25 million people. The expected trend is that our population will become better educated, more mature, and more productive. By 1990, people between the ages of 25 and 44 will represent the largest segment of our society.

Aggregate household income from 1980 to 1990 is projected to grow significantly more for families earning $25,000 and above than for families earning less than $25,000. Total income (1977 dollars) to families with incomes of less than $25,000 is projected to grow from $673 billion to $838 billion (an increase of less than 25 percent). Total income (1977 dollars) to families with incomes of $25,000 or more is projected to grow from $616 billion to $1,158 billion (an increase of 88 percent). Moreover, the increase for families in the prime of life is even more dramatic. Families age 35–44 with an income below $25,000 are projected to increase from $120 billion to $154 billion (an increase of 28 percent). Families ages 35–44 with an income above $25,000 are projected to grow from $167 billion to $367 billion dollars (an increase of 220 percent). These income and population trends show a large market segment having the financial ability and desire to purchase sporting goods for leisure-time activities.

The Sun Belt Market

Growth in population and income will not be distributed evenly throughout the United States. In the 1980s the fastest growing part of the United States, in terms of population, will be the Sun Belt.

During the 15 years ending in the 1990s, population is expected to increase by 23.3 percent in the Southeast, 18.3 percent in the Southwest, and in the Far West by 16.1 percent (Exhibit 6). Other regions of the country will grow but at a rate slower than Sun Belt regions.

The Sun Belt is Oshman's market. Major Sun Belt cities where Oshman's is represented are listed in Exhibit 7. These markets will also have strong economic growth in the 1980s, placing many of them among the nation's leaders in buying power and retail sales. Economic trends projected for the Sun Belt markets should continue to provide a stimulating business environment and a focus on outdoor lei-

EXHIBIT 6
Estimated Population Growth 1975–1990 in Percent

Area	Percent Growth	
All 50 States	15.4	
New England	10.4	Maine, Vermont, New Hampshire, Massachusetts, Connecticut, Rhode Island
Mideast	11.0	New York, Pennsylvania, Delaware, New Jersey, Maryland
Great Lakes	12.6	Wisconsin, Illinois, Michigan, Ohio, Indiana
Plains	11.3	Minnesota, Iowa, Missouri, North and South Dakota, Nebraska, Kansas
Rocky Mountains	13.8	Montana, Idaho, Wyoming, Utah, Colorado
Far West	16.1	Washington, Oregon, Nevada, California
Southwest	18.3	Arizona, New Mexico, Oklahoma, Texas
Southeast	23.2	Arkansas, Louisiana, Mississippi, Alabama, Georgia, Florida, Tennessee, Kentucky, Virginia, West Virginia, North and South Carolina

sure-time activities. Oshman's, being the leading force in the Sun Belt leisure market, will certainly participate in this growth.

Competition in the Sporting-Goods Marketplace

The sporting-goods industry is extremely fragmented, made up of a large number of small retailers. Sporting-goods departments are also found in discount and department stores of very large retailers.

Oshman's stores, however, are substantially larger and offer a much wider selection than the typical sporting-goods dealer. Oshman's is extremely well positioned to provide for the expanded needs of the growing number of affluent sports buffs.

It is estimated that the large sporting-goods chains (those with 15 or more stores) have only achieved an 8 percent market share. This compares to estimates of 60–70 percent market share of large chains in the jewelry and drug fields.

Store Expansion and Acquisition Program

From 1970 through 1982, Oshman's opened over 70 new stores and acquired 82 new stores. The first acquisition effective June 29, 1972 resulted in the purchase of five stores doing business as "Stan's Sports." All five stores were located in San Francisco, California, and the purchase price was 40,000 shares of the company's preferred stock that was assigned a value of $713,000. The Company's investment exceeded the net assets of "Stan's" by $379,000, of which $105,000 was allocated to property and equipment and $274,000 was allocated to excess of cost over net assets of business acquired. The 40,000 shares were convertable in whole or in part until August 24, 1977 into 60,000 shares of the company's common stock. The preferred stock had a liquidation value of $25 per share, and any shares that had not been converted had to be redeemed by the company by August 28, 1977 at $25 per share. All 40,000 shares were redeemed on August 28, 1977 at $25 per share. Prior to Oshman's acquisition, the five stores accounted for annual sales of less than 3 million dollars and were producing for Stan's stores a return on sales of approximately 2 percent.

Effective November 28, 1972, the company acquired two stores (one in Fresno, and one in Bakersfield, California) from Mid-Valley Sport's Center. In addition, Mid-Valley operated an institutional sales business in California. Annual sales of Mid-Valley prior to acquisition were less than 2 million dollars. Return on sales was approximately 0.5 percent. These stores were purchased for 14,000 shares of the company's common stock. In the year of acquisition, the approximate market price of the company's common stock ranged from $17.50 to $27.50.

Effective October 12, 1977, the company

EXHIBIT 7
Sun Belt Buying Power Leaders—1985 Projections

	DPI		Retail Sales		Population	
	Total	Percent Change	Household	Percent Change	Total	Percent Change
San Francisco Oakland San Jose	$52,473	90.4	$21,612	71.8	5,498.3	5.1
Los Angeles Long Beach Anaheim	46,859	88.8	21,221	70.6	12,320.5	6.0
Houston	41,825	55.3	24,068	51.1	3,701.8	16.6
San Diego	41,484	83.8	19,544	67.5	2,161.0	13.4
Dallas Fort Worth	37,768	46.9	20,731	45.4	3,340.5	10.5
Atlanta	32,402	38.5	18,609	43.2	2,295.6	11.2
San Antonio	32,121	45.9	19,063	46.8	1,183.7	8.9
Birmingham	29,003	42.1	17,518	42.7	898.0	5.3
Miami Fort Lauderdale	27,487	26.2	18,204	35.9	3,115.4	12.8
Phoenix	27,375	27.5	15,395	34.5	1,835.9	17.8
Tampa St. Petersburg	21,753	24.4	15,096	33.6	1,835.9	14.4
TOTAL U. S.	34,184	54.3	17,879	60.1	241,180.6	5.6

Source: Sales and Marketing Management Survey of Buying Power, Part II, 1981. Base year for percentage is 1980.

acquired 24 retail stores and a warehouse/office in California from United Sporting Goods, Inc., a wholly owned subsidiary of Edison Brothers Stores. Oshman's paid $5,444,000, one-half in cash, and one-half by the execution and delivery of the company's promissory notes payable in four annual installments, and bearing interest at the rate of 5.5 percent per annum. Sales for United Sporting Goods prior to acquisition were somewhat more than $15,000,000. United Sporting Goods had been operating at a slight deficit.

On January 14, 1981 the company purchased the leasehold interests in 33 stores and two warehouse/offices from Cullum and Boren Downtown, Inc., a wholly owned subsidiary of Zale Corporation. Additionally, the company acquired merchandise inventories, trade fixtures, leasehold improvement, and the names "Cullum and Boren," "Houseport," and "H. Cook" for an adjusted purchase price of approximately $5,469,000. Of the total adjusted price, $2,418,000 represents capitalized lease obligations and $1,917,000 represents notes payable to Zale Corporation.

1982 represented a continuation of the acquisition and expansion program with 18 stores acquired from Lucky Stores, Inc., plus new store openings. However, the company also closed seven underperforming stores. On September 20, 1982, the Company purchased leasehold interests and the related leasehold improvement, fixtures, and merchandise inventory in 18 L & G Sporting Goods stores from Lucky Stores, Inc. Total consideration was $2,777,000, including a $2,477,000 note payable to Lucky Stores, Inc.

On June 29, 1978, the company entered into a licensing agreement with Abercrombie and Fitch Company, First National Bank of Chicago, and the First Chicago Banking Corporation for the use of the name "Abercrombie and Fitch," trademarks, patents, and catalogues. The agreement provides for 15 annual payments escalating from $25,000 to $150,000 totalling $1,495,000 or 1 percent of annual sales associated with the trademark name and trademarks, whichever is greater. If payments totaled $3,000,000 for the 15-year period, ownership of the name, trademark, and patents revert to Oshman's. If the payments during the 15-year period are less than $3,000,000, the company has the option of extending the agreement for an additional five years at which time ownership of the name, trademarks, and patents would be transferred to Oshman's for financial statement purposes. The minimum payments were capitalized at their discounted present value using a 10 percent imputed interest rate.

The opening of the first Abercrombie and Fitch store in Beverly Hills, California along with the distribution of a small Abercrombie and Fitch mail-order catalogue brought a flood of national media attention. The Beverly Hills location and use by genuine stars of the Abercrombie and Fitch store made it one of the glamour events of 1979 and 1980. To quote a June 23, 1980 article from *Barrons*, "The first unit appears on target, the sales at the Beverly Hills location running around $200 a square foot, annually. Now Oshman's is branching out. Another Abercrombie and Fitch outlet, this one somewhat larger, is slated to open in Dallas late next month. Two smaller versions called 'Best of Abercrombie and Fitch' are planned for southern California's Newport Beach area, and Las Vegas next Spring." Later in the article it says, "There are no present plans for more Abercrombie and Fitch stores."

In 1982 (fiscal 1983) the company added seven more Abercrombie and Fitch stores. Further, the company plans to add four more in 1983 including one in Seattle, Washington.

In addition to the 82 acquired stores, the Company added over 90 new Oshman's stores. Exhibit 8 shows the growth in stores and location of stores for the organization since 1970.

Institutional and Wholesale Sales

The wholesale division was discontinued effective January 1, 1974. The company's annual report commented as follows:

> The decision to discontinue operation of the wholesale company was made in light of employing our major financial, physical, and human resources in our more profitable retail division. The wholesale division had shown very little sales growth during the past five years and earnings had deteriorated. The company worked under a severe handicap of providing merchandise to competitors, who, everything else being equal, would prefer to purchase their merchandise from a wholesaler who did not have their own retail stores. There was no gain or loss at the close of this operation. Accounts receivable were sold and inventory was absorbed into our retail division.

On January 31, 1977, the company discontinued the institutional operations on the West Coast commenting in the annual report, "Our institutional business showed some improvement over last year and we have decided to confine our efforts in routine business to the Texas area where we are able to effectively service our customers from our distribution facilities in Houston. We had attained a sales volume of $936,000 (in California) but we were not yet making a profit." Shown as Exhibit 9 is a 10-year summary of sales and earnings for retail, institutional, and wholesale businesses from 1971–1980. Since 1980 institutional sales data have not been reported in the annual report. The 1981 report stated "Our team (institutional) business continued to make further progress. Efforts to improve margin and operating efficiency resulted in substantial improvement in profits. However, performance is still below company standards for return on investment."

EXHIBIT 8
Oshman's Retail Store Locations

State	1972	1973	1974	1975	1976	1977	1978	1979	1980	1981	1982
Alabama	0	0	2	2	2	2	2	2	2	2	2
Arizona											
New Mexico											
Nevada	1	1	1	1	1	1	1	1	7	7	8
California	8	12	15	16	19	45	46	47	51	55	71
Florida	0	0	0	2	2	2	2	3	5	6	7
Louisiana											
Oklahoma	0	0	0	0	1	1	1	1	6	7	8
Arkansas											
Georgia											
Tennessee	3	4	4	5	5	7	7	7	8	9	9
Texas	17	20	20	21	22	26	28	29	46	54	55
Hawaii	0	0	0	0	0	0	0	0	5	5	6
TOTAL	29	37	44	47	53	84	87	90	132	149	166

Abercrombie and Fitch Retail Store Locations

State	1980	1981	1982
California	1	2	3
Connecticut	0	1	1
Georgia	0	0	1
New Jersey	0	0	1
Nevada	0	1	1
Pennsylvania	0	0	1
Texas	1	0	2
Washington, D.C.	0	0	1
TOTAL	2	4	11

EXHIBIT 9
Sales and Before Tax Earnings by Business

	1980	1979	1978	1977	1976	1975	1974	1973	1972	1971
Sales										
Retail	128,398	111,814	79,508	62,972	54,259	43,420	33,737	25,435	18,727	15,681
Institutional	6,608	6,378	5,957	6,810	6,631	6,145	5,381	5,077	4,655	4,266
Wholesale	—	—	—	—	—	—	1,873	2,248	1,983	1,863
Before-Tax Earnings										
Retail	11,566	10,392	7,730	6,212	5,524	3,437	3,316	2,827	2,041	1,672
Institutional	153	203	198	252	223	290	284	207	265	204
Wholesale	—	—	—	—	—	—	84	41	49	67

Fiscal year ending in year shown in $1,000s.

EXHIBIT 10
Store Size and Sales Per Square Foot

Year	1983	1982	1981	1980	1979	1978	1977	1976	1975	1974	1973	1972	1971
Number of Stores	177	149	132	90	87	81	52	47	44	34	30	19	15
Total Square Footage[a]	1850	1671	1440	1024	977	919	591	532	486	376	340	235	196
Retail Sales Per Square Foot[b]	134	135	129	128	122	117	112	107	105	95	87	85	84

[a] In 1000's.
[b] For stores in operation a full year or more.

Retail Store Operations

Roughly two-thirds of the sales volume from a typical Oshman's store comes from sports equipment and the balance from apparel, mostly sports-related and much of it bearing private labels. Giftwares, electronic games, and items unrelated to sports or athletics constitute less than 2 percent of sales. The typical Oshman's store has about 11,000 square feet of floor space and an inventory of over 20,000 items. It is spacious, well-furnished, attractive, and decorated by professional designers. It is located in a major regional or suburban shopping center. It has a broad and deep line of items and appeals primarily to the upper and upper-middle income family with sufficient disposable income and leisure time to be attracted by high-quality, brand-name sporting-goods and sporting wear. All retail store locations are leased. The company generally seeks long-term leases. The company is, of course, responsible for all store furnishings. The pattern of sales growth from the time a store is opened is explained by the following quotation from a June 23, 1980 *Barron's* article:

> New Oshman's stores tend to recoup start-up costs and achieve profitability within the first three months, if they are opened in developed areas. It can take from one to three years to turn the corner for units built in wholly new markets. The stores in developed areas usually average sales of from $80 to $110 a square foot on the first full year and 15 to 20 percent more each year for the next two or three years. Thereafter, gains tend to level off at around 10 percent annually. Those in developed areas average $100 to $150 a square foot the first year. The increases are smaller thereafter.

Exhibit 10 shows the number of stores and total square footage for all stores for 1971–1983.

With the exception of the San Antonio store, which has 20,000 square feet, most other Oshman's stores conform to the general pattern. However, the Abercrombie and Fitch store and the plans for the additional stores do not conform to the same pattern. The Abercrombie and Fitch store concept and plans are best illustrated by the following quote, from the 1979 annual report:

> In September 1979, we opened the first all-new Abercrombie and Fitch stores in Beverly Hills, California. We are exceptionally encouraged by the initial results and are pleased to report that we now estimate first year sales to be in excess of $200 per square foot.

> This 16,000 square foot store is the start of an exciting project that we believe will contribute materially in the years ahead. Our second Abercrombie and Fitch store is scheduled to open in Dallas, Texas in July 1980. This store will be 26,000 square feet—a size that we feel should be optimal for most cities.

> Abercrombie and Fitch also mailed its first major catalogue to over 300,000 customers in all parts of the country. Results have convinced us that the investment required to build a mail-order business is warranted. We will, however, proceed at a modest pace with only one catalogue planned this year.

We are also finalizing our concept for a new type of Abercrombie and Fitch store which will make its debut in 1981. This smaller version of Abercrombie and Fitch will appear in the best shopping malls in the country, and will probably be named the 'Best of Abercrombie and Fitch.' We plan on opening two or three in 1981 as a test. Each will also contain a mail-order desk.

Management Information, Distribution, and Merchandise Control Systems

The company's California offices and distribution centers are located in a 115,000 square foot facility in Santa Ana, California. The stores in Texas and in the southeastern United States are serviced by the company's 180,000 square foot distribution facility located in Houston. These facilities also house the institutional sales division. In 1980 the company added two new warehouses adjacent to the Houston facility. In 1980 the company replaced its 10,000 square foot facility with a 30,000 square foot facility. The company also leases a 100,000 square foot facility in Dallas. All stores have point-of-sales registers that are on-line with the central computer. The company has used a computerized merchandise and operating information system for many years. The 1972 annual report said, "Our computerized merchandising and operating information system provides us with current data on sale's margins, inventories, and expenses. This information is constantly reviewed by our store managers, buyers, area supervisors, and merchandisers." The 1974 annual report said, "During the past year we installed a new electronic retail system in our Houston stores. This system has increased our capabilities in gathering information necessary for more effective inventory control—all management information systems are under review. We are developing a long-range plan for full utilization of the updated equipment of managing and controlling our business." The 1978 annual report indicated that the systems department had reorganized with the addition of a full-time systems analyst. It further reported that all stores now have point-of-sales registers.

In 1981 Allan Lisse was named Vice-President, Management Information Systems. Mr. Lisse had been Vice-President, Management Information Systems with Drug Fair. He is expected to work closely with Edward Carlin who was named Vice President and Chief Financial Officer in 1981. Mr. Carlin had been Chief Financial Officer of Ups 'n Downs. An inventory management program instituted in 1982 resulted in a reduction in average per store inventory of 11 percent.

New Venture

On September 22, 1978, the company entered into a partnership with an individual inventor to develop and market an inflatable foot-support device in athletic support shoes. The company believes that the invention has other potential applications, including use in football protective padding. In 1979 the company reported that the American Pneumatics, its 51-percent owned affiliate, had developed prototypes of new athletic protective equipment in association with the National Football League. This equipment included shoulder pads, rib protectors, forearms, and thigh guards that are currently being refined and tested so that the company may ascertain commercial potential of the venture.

Finance

The enclosed statement of income 1972–1983 (Exhibit 11), balance sheets 1975–1983 (Exhibit 12), summary of share of preferred and common stock (Exhibit 13), statement of changes in financial position 1975–1983 (Exhibit 14), along with the accompanying notes represent a detailed picture of Oshman's financial position.

Notes to Consolidated Financial Statements

Note A—Significant Accounting Policies
1. *Fiscal Year.* The Company's fiscal year ends on the Saturday closest to the end of January. Fiscal

EXHIBIT 11
Income Statement[a]

	1983	1982	1981	1980	1979	1978	1977	1976	1975	1974	1973	1972
Net Sales	247,264	216,427	144,889	135,006	118,192	85,465	69,782	60,890	49,565	40,991	32,760	25,365
Cost of goods sold (note A4)	163,405	129,787	88,281	80,795	69,693	51,196	41,977	37,154	30,570	25,911	20,947	16,422
Gross profit	96,932	86,640	56,608	54,211	48,499	34,269	27,805	23,726	18,995	15,280	11,813	8,943
Selling and administrative expenses	83,839	71,902	47,538	42,337	37,354	26,164	21,352	17,904	15,348	11,680	8,810	6,698
Advertising		7,888	5,199	4,514	3,506	2,705	2,146	1,757	1,444	1,107	771	564
Taxes other than income		3,751	2,627	2,341	2,201	1,554	1,205	989	820	629	439	312
Rent		8,563	5,377	4,782	4,207	2,688	2,174	1,903	1,671	1,168	931	714
Depreciation	N.A.	3,029	1,833	1,547	1,176	830	692	555	402	277	211	157
Repairs and maintenance		2,466	1,443	1,232	948	635	530	428	262	152	84	67
Other selling and administrative expenses (Notes A and H)		46,205	31,099	27,921	25,316	17,752	14,605	12,272	10,749	8,347	6,374	4,884
Operating profit	13,073	14,738	9,025	11,874	11,145	8,105	6,453	5,832	3,647	3,600	3,003	2,245
Other income (expense)												
Interest	(2,587)	(2,396)	(897)	(760)	(779)	(503)	(203)	(201)	(229)	(74)	(34)	(35)
Other income and misc.	1,800	1,390	937	605	229	332	214	116	309	158	106	145
Earnings before income taxes	12,286	13,732	9,065	11,719	10,595	7,934	6,464	5,747	3,727	3,684	3,075	2,355
Income taxes (Notes A7 and G)	5,195	6,180	4,066	5,379	4,800	3,720	3,031	2,766	1,678	1,684	1,398	1,048
Net earnings	7,091	7,552	4,999	6,340	5,795	4,214	3,433	2,981	2,049	2,000	1,677	1,307

[a]In $1,000s for fiscal year ending in indicated year.

years 1982, 1981, and 1980 all contained 52 weeks and ended on January 29, 1983, January 30, 1982, and January 31, 1981.

2. *Principles of Consolidation.* The consolidated financial statements include the accounts of Oshman's Sporting Goods, Inc. and its subsidiaries, all wholly owned. In consolidation, all significant intercompany transactions have been eliminated.

3. *Cash and Equivalents.* Equivalents ($13,551,000 at the end of 1982 and $8,780,000 at the end of 1981) consist of short-term, interest-bearing securities stated at cost, which approximates market.

4. *Merchandise Inventories.* Merchandise inventories are valued principally by the retail method and are stated on a last-in, first-out (LIFO) basis, which is lower than cost. Using the LIFO method, as opposed to first-in, first-out (FIFO), had the effect of increasing cost of goods sold for 1982, 1981, and 1980 by $938,000, $897,000, and $1,539,000 and decreasing net earnings for those years by $541,000, $493,000, and $848,000 ($0.08, $0.07, and $0.13 per share). If the FIFO method had been used, merchandise inventories at the end of 1982, 1981, and 1980 would have been $3,994,000, $3,056,000, and $2,159,000 higher than reported under the LIFO method.

5. *Property, Plant, and Equipment.* Depreciation and amortization is provided principally by the straight line method based upon estimated useful lives of 3 to 10 years for furniture, fixtures, and equipment, 3 to 30 years for leasehold improvements, and 40 years for buildings. Estimated useful lives of leasehold improvements represent the remaining term of the lease in effect at the time the improvements are made.

6. *Amortization of Other Assets.* Amortization is computed using the straight line method. Excess of cost over net assets of a business acquired is being amortized over 40 years. The cost of a trade name (Note D) is being amortized over 15 years.

7. *Income Taxes.* Provision has been made for deferred Federal income taxes applicable to the timing differences between earnings for financial reporting purposes and taxable income. For income-tax purposes, the Company uses accelerated depreciation methods and generally recognizes the gain on charge sales on the installment method. For financial reporting purposes, the Company uses the straight line depreciation method and recognizes the gain on contract and charge sales in the period the sales are made. Investment tax credits are accounted for by the flow-through method, which recognizes the

EXHIBIT 12
Consolidated Balance Sheet—Year Ending January 31 (in $1,000s)

	1983	1982	1981	1980	1979	1978	1977	1976	1975
Assets									
Current assets									
Cash and equivalents (note A3)	14,540	6,241	11,015	6,684	9,450	9,193	3,006	2,245	509
Accounts Receivable less allowances	7,235	6,203	8,418	5,893	5,174	4,249	4,249	4,125	4,267
Merchandise inventories (note A4)	58,006	55,246	36,644	31,630	29,404	23,532	17,001	15,598	14,960
Prepaid expenses and other current assets	2,112	1,121	833	565	174	1,091	478	272	324
Total current assets	81,893	68,811	56,910	44,772	45,202	38,022	24,734	22,240	20,060
Property, Plant and Equipment (Note A5)									
Furniture, fixtures and equipment (note C)	21,599	17,035	12,168	10,051	8,551	6,428	5,023	4,032	3,319
Leasehold improvements	18,135	16,429	13,140	8,106	6,336	4,582	2,763	2,673	2,448
Buildings	2,440	1,823	1,806	1,774	1,732	1,719	1,704	915	900
Land	983	719	719	719	528	700	700	856	783
	43,157	36,006	27,833	20,650	17,147	13,429	10,190	8,476	6,559
Less Accumulated Depreciation and Amortization	13,996	10,677	7,907	6,128	4,671	3,760	2,990	2,327	1,834
	29,161	25,329	19,926	14,522	12,476	9,669	7,200	6,149	4,725
Other Assets	638	687	736	788	837	236	243	249	256
Total Assets	111,692	94,827	77,572	60,082	58,515	47,927	32,177	28,638	25,041
Liabilities									
Current liabilities									
Current maturities of long-term obligations (note F)	1,760	720	1,365	1,096	695	679	12	3	750
Trade accounts payable	23,674	14,837	7,580	7,989	11,729	6,791	4,014	4,829	3,414
Accrued liabilities (note E)	7,807	7,090	5,254	4,582	4,328	4,023	2,057	1,809	1,245
Income taxes (notes A7 and G)	5,183	4,572	2,677	2,893	2,815	1,234	754	1,107	117
Total current liabilities	38,424	28,038	16,876	16,560	19,567	12,727	6,837	7,748	5,526
Deferred income taxes (notes A7 and G)	1,365	905	721	672	533	393	316	260	174
Long-term obligations (note F)	19,716	19,860	20,592	7,622	8,718	8,738	1,755	521	2,250
Commitments and contingency (note H)	—	—	—	—	—	—	—	—	—
Stockholders Equity (note I)									
Preferred stock par value $1	—	—	—	—	—	—	40	40	40
Reserve for preferred stock conversion	—	—	—	—	—	—	960	960	—
Common stock par value $1	6,755	6,737	4,482	4,476	4,466	3,179	3,179	3,177	3,109
Treasury stock	—	—	—	—	—	(87)	(87)	(87)	(87)
Additional capital (mostly proceeds in excess of par)	1,153	1,018	908	863	787	638	638	623	1,212
Retained earnings	44,279	38,269	33,993	29,889	24,444	22,339	18,539	15,396	12,702
Total stockholders equity	52,187	46,024	39,383	35,228	29,697	26,069	23,269	20,109	17,091
	111,692	94,827	77,572	60,082	58,515	47,927	32,177	28,638	25,041

EXHIBIT 13
Summary of Status of Preferred and Common Stock

Common Stock Price Range	1983	1982	1981	1980	1979	1978	1977	1976	1975	1974	1973	1972
High bid[a]	22	$15\frac{3}{4}$	$13\frac{1}{4}$	10	$12\frac{1}{4}$	$4\frac{3}{8}$	$6\frac{3}{8}$	$6\frac{3}{8}$	$5\frac{1}{4}$	$11\frac{3}{8}$	13	$6\frac{3}{8}$
Low bid[a]	$14\frac{3}{4}$	11	$5\frac{1}{2}$	7	$4\frac{1}{4}$	$3\frac{1}{4}$	4	$3\frac{1}{4}$	$1\frac{3}{8}$	$4\frac{1}{2}$	$6\frac{3}{8}$	$1\frac{7}{8}$
Dividends per share[a]												
50 percent stock dividend[b]	.16	.15	.13	.13	.09	.06	.04	—	—	—	—	—
Shares of preferred stock outstanding $1 par value[b]	500	500	500	500	500	500	500	500	500	500	500	500
Shares of preferred stock outstanding $1 par value[b]	0	0	0	0	0	0	0	0	0	0	0	0
Shares of common stock authorized $1 par value[b]	10,000	10,000	10,000	10,000	6,000	6,000	6,000	6,000	6,000	6,000	5,000	4,000
Shares of preferred stock outstanding $ par value[b]	6,755	6,737	6,723	6,714	6,699	4,768	4,765	4,754	4,735	4,735	4,708	3,125
Total stock options outstanding at end of year[b]	109	109	107	107	118	99	99		75	59	73	55
Stock options granted during the year[b]	0	0	0	65	54	46	68		55	7	34	0

[a]Adjusted for stock dividends.
[b]In 1,000s.

credits as reductions of income-tax expense in the year utilized.

8. *Expenses of New Stores.* Expenses associated with the opening of new stores are charged to expense as incurred.

Note B—Acquisition of Assets

On January 14, 1981, the Company purchased the leasehold interests in 33 stores and two warehouse/offices from Cullum and Boren Downtown, Inc., a wholly owned subsidiary of Zale Corporation. Additionally, the Company acquired other assets related to the operation of the stores, including merchandise inventory, trade fixtures, leasehold improvements, and the names "Cullum and Boren", "Honsport," and "H. Cook." Total consideration amounted to approximately $5,469,000. As the transaction is accounted for by the purchase method, the results of operations for the acquired stores have been included in these financial statements for the period from the data of acquisition.

Of the total purchase price, $2,418,000 represented capitalized lease obligations and $1,917,000 represented notes payable to Zale Corporation (see Note F).

Unaudited *pro forma* consolidated results of operations for 1980, assuming the purchase of the stores had been consumated at the beginning of the year, are as follows:

Net Sales (in thousands)	$183,717
Net Earnings (in thousands)	3,923
Earnings per common and dilutive common equivalent share	$0.58

On September 20, 1982, the Company purchased leasehold interests and the related leasehold improvements, fixtures, and merchandise inventory in 18 L & G Sporting Goods stores from Lucky Stores, Inc. Total consideration was $2,777,000, including a $2,477,000 note payable to Lucky Stores, Inc. (see Note F). Pro forma data are not presented because they are not considered material to the consolidated financial statements.

Note C—Property, Plant and Equipment

$2,418,000 of these leasehold improvements are in facilities leased under noncancellable operating leases (see Note H).

Note D—Trade Name

On June 29, 1978, the Company entered into a licensing agreement with Abercrombie and Fitch Company, the First National Bank of Chicago, and First Chicago International Banking Corporation for use of the name "Abercrombie and Fitch," trademarks, patents, and catalogues. The agreement provides for 15 annual payments escalating from $25,000 to $175,000 (totaling $1,785,000) or 1 percent of annual sales associated with the trade name and trademarks, whichever is greater. If payments total $3,000,000 for the 15-year period, ownership of the name, trademarks, and patents transfers to the Company. If payments during the 15-year period

EXHIBIT 14
Oshman's Sporting Goods, Inc. and Subsidiaries Consolidated Statements of Changes in Financial Position[a]

	1983	1982	1981	1980	1979	1978	1977	1976	1975
Source of Funds									
Net earnings	7,091	7,552	4,999	6,340	5,795	4,214	3,433	2,981	2,049
Items not requiring the use of funds									
Depreciation and leasehold amortization (note A5)	3,560	3,029	1,833	1,547	1,176	830	692	548	395
Amortization of other assets (note A6)	49	49	52	49	28	7	6	7	7
Deferred income taxes (notes A7 and G)	460	184	49	139	140	77	56	86	72
Funds provided from operations	11,160	10,814	6,933	8,075	7,139	5,128	4,187	3,622	2,523
Additions to long-term obligations	2,857	—	14,066	—	689	7,662	1,248	525	3,000
Exercise of stock options	153	121	51	86	219	—	17	47	67
	14,170	10,935	21,050	8,161	8,047	12,790	5,452	4,194	5,590
Application of Funds									
Additions to property, plant, and equipment	7,392	8,432	7,237	3,593	3,983	3,299	1,743	1,972	2,383
Reductions of long-term obligations	3,001	732	1,096	1,096	3,138	1,679	14	2,264	824
Cash dividends	1,081	1,032	895	895	586	414	290	—	—
Increase in working capital	2,696	739	11,822	2,577	340	7,398	3,405	(42)	2,383
	14,170	10,935	21,050	8,161	8,047	12,790	5,452	4,194	5,590
Increase in Components of Working Capital									
Cash and equivalents	8,299	(4,774)	4,331	(2,766)	257	6,187	761	1,736	(564)
Accounts receivable—net	1,032	(2,215)	2,525	719	968	(43)	124	(142)	74
Merchandise inventories	2,760	18,602	5,014	2,226	5,872	6,531	1,403	638	4,446
Prepaid expenses and other assets	991	288	268	(609)	83	613	206	(52)	(19)
Increase in current assets	13,082	11,901	12,138	(430)	7,180	13,288	2,494	2,180	3,937
Current maturities of long-term obligations	1,040	(645)	269	(401)	16	667	9	(747)	750
Trade accounts payable	8,837	7,257	(409)	3,740	4,938	2,777	(815)	1,415	1,080
Accrued liabilities	(102)	2,655	672	(254)	305	1,966	248	564	142
Income taxes	611	1,895	(216)	(78)	1,581	480	(353)	990	(418)
Increase in current liabilities	10,386	11,162	316	3,007	6,840	5,890	(911)	2,222	1,554
Increase in working capital	2,696	739	11,822	2,577	340	7,398	3,405	(42)	2,383

[a] In 1,000s.

are less than $3,000,000, the Company has the option to extend the agreement for an additional five years, at which time ownership of the name, trademarks, and patents would be transferred to the Company. For financial statement presentation, the minimum payments were capitalized at their discounted present value, using a 10 percent imputed interest rate (Note F), and included in other assets.

Note E—Short-Term Obligations
The following significant amounts are included in accrued liabilities at the end of the year:

	1982	1981
	(in thousands)	
Compensation	$1,419	$1,191
State sales taxes	875	1,459

The Company has a $12,000,000 unsecured bank line of credit for short-term loans and letters of credit. At the end of 1982 and 1981, outstanding letters of credit were $1,295,000 and $1,209,000. There are no commitment fees associated with the line.

Note F—Long-Term Obligations
Long-term obligations as of January 29, 1982 were $19,716,000 at an average interest of approximately 10.55 percent.

Note G—Income Taxes
Deferred federal income taxes of $544,000 and $452,000 applicable principally to charge sales are included in current liabilities at the end of 1982 and 1981. The provision for deferred income taxes for 1982, 1981, and 1980 was $552,000 (including $449,000 related to depreciation differences), $265,000, and $49,000. A reconciliation of income tax computed at the 46 percent statutory federal income-tax rate and income taxes reported in the consolidated statement of earnings is as follows:

	1982	1981	1980
		(in thousands)	
Tax at statutory rate	$5,652	$6,317	$4,170
Increases (reductions)			
State income taxes (net of federal tax benefit)	239	245	206
Investment tax credits	(467)	(452)	(297)
Other items, net	(229)	70	(13)
	(457)	(137)	(104)
Income taxes			
Amount	$5,195	$6,180	$4,066
Effective rate	42.3%	45.0%	44.9%

Note H—Commitments

Operating Leases
The Company conducts certain of its operations in owned facilities with its remaining operations being conducted in facilities leased under noncancellable operating leases. Rentals of the retail locations are based on minimum required rentals and, in certain instances, contingent rentals based on a percentage of sales. Some leases contain renewal options of various terms with provisions for increased rental during the renewal term.

Future minimum annual rental commitments under operating leases at the end of 1982, are as follows:

	(In thousands)
1983	$ 8,400
1984	8,100
1985	7,873
1986	7,660
1987	7,553
Thereafter	69,937
	$109,523

Total rental expense entering into the determination of net earnings is as follows:

	1982	1981	1980
		(In thousands)	
Leased facilities			
Minimum rentals	$ 7,659	$6,447	$3,925
Contingent rentals (based on a percentage of sales)	1,752	1,573	1,082
	9,411	8,020	5,007
Other rentals	780	543	370
	$10,191	$8,563	$5,377

Certain leases that provide for total minimum annual rentals of $290,000 are between the Company and two trusts that are for the benefit of two shareholders.

Capital Leases
In January 1981, the Company incurred capitalized lease obligations in connection with the acquisition of certain assets (see note B). Future minimum lease payments for the assets under these capital leases at the end of 1982 are as follows:

	(in thousands)
1983	$ 452
1984	373
1985	311
1986	268
1987	244
Thereafter	923
Total minimum lease payments	2,571
Less interest at 8 percent on lease obligations	733
Present value of net minimum obligations	$1,838

Profit-Sharing Plan

The Company and its subsidiaries contribute to an employee profit-sharing plan based on consolidated net earnings (before income taxes and profit-sharing contributions) in excess of 10 percent of average consolidated stockholders' equity. The provision for profit-sharing expense was $855,000, $1,087,000, and $621,000 for 1982, 1981, and 1980.

Note I—Stockholders' Equity

Capital Stock

Authorized capital stock consists of 500,000 shares of $1 par value preferred stock and 10,000,000 shares of $1 par value common stock. No preferred stock has been issued. Common stock issued and outstanding was 6,755,000 shares at the end of 1982 and 6,737,000 shares at the end of 1981.

Common Stock Split

On June 26, 1981, the Board of Directors authorized a three-for-two stock split effected in the form of a 50 percent stock dividend that was issued on July 31, 1981. The par value of the shares issued was transferred to the common stock account from retained earnings. Cash was paid in lieu of fractional shares.

Common Stock Reserved

At the end of 1982, the Company had under option 35,751 shares of its common stock for issuance under two stock-option plans, at prices ranging from $4.40 to $19.50 per share, of which 12,700 were exercisable. An additional 188,000 shares are reserved for future option grants; options for 58,250 of such shares were granted in March 1983.

The plans provide for the issuance of options to key employees of the Company at an option price of not less than 100 percent of the market value of the shares at the time the options are granted. All options expire within five years from date of grant. Upon the exercise of options, the proceeds are credited to the common stock account to the extent of the par value of the shares issued, and the proceeds in excess of the par value are credited to additional capital. No amounts are reflected in the statement of earnings with respect to exercise of stock options. During 1982, 1981, and 1980, options were exercised for 18,426 shares, 11,070 shares, and 5,575 shares at prices ranging from $3.56 to $14.50.

Note J—Earnings Per Share

Earnings per common and dilutive common equivalent share are based upon the weighted average number of common shares outstanding during each year after giving retroactive effect to the shares issued in connection with the three-for-two stock split (effected in the form of a 50 percent stock dividend) on July 31, 1981. Outstanding options are included in periods where they have a dilutive effect. Earnings per share assuming full dilution are not significantly different (less than 3 percent) from earnings per common and dilutive common equivalent share.

Interview with Alvin Lubetkin on March 20, 1981

The following is a summary of an interview by one of the casewriters with Alvin Lubetkin on March 20, 1981. During that interview three topics were discussed: (1) the current status of Oshman's, (2) the future of Oshman's various business interests, and (3) a clarification of one aspect of the case. Each of these will be presented below.

Mr. Lubetkin reported that for the first time in 17 years, Oshman's net income declined (in fiscal year ending January 31, 1981). He attributed the decline to the shortage of snow in the Southwest, the slow economy, and operating costs that rose at a faster rate than inflation. Mr. Lubetkin also reported the acquisition of 33 stores in January 1981. Most of these stores are in the Sun Belt, but five are located in Hawaii. Although these stores had not been profitable prior to acquisition, he expected the 28 stores in the Sun Belt would be turning a profit within six months.

Mr. Lubetkin indicated that the team sales area was not producing the desired level of profit. He plans to take whatever actions are necessary to improve profitability. One such action might be to eliminate low volume accounts. He indicated that team sales would be confined to the area in and around Houston.

He saw virtually no future for American Pneumatics, indicating that he probably erred in assessing its potential. In response to a question about pursuing other ventures of this type, he indicated that he would assess other opportunities based on their individual merit.

Mr. Lubetkin pointed out that the future of the "World of Sporting Goods" concept was basically a large Oshman's store that could handle more volume than the other stores. While Oshman's had not formally followed through on the concept he indicated that Oshman's stores would be made larger when volume warranted.

Mr. Lubetkin indicated that the current sales volume for Abercrombie and Fitch was about 10 million dollars and that he expected it to reach 100 million dollars in 10 years. He pointed out that the basic difference between the smaller stores called "The Best of Abercrombie and Fitch" and a typical Oshman's store was the "soft goods." Basically the sporting equipment carried in an Oshman's is the best available. However, Abercrombie and Fitch carries more expensive and better sport clothing and accessories. He also indicated that Oshman's was considering opening "The Best of Abercrombie and Fitch" stores in the Northeastern United States in such cities as Philadelphia and Washington, D.C.

Mr. Lubetkin plans to continue to develop the Abercrombie and Fitch catalogue. Response to the first two catalogues, which were distributed prior to Christmas 1979 and 1980, has been satisfactory. Oshman's is trying to improve the quality of the mailing list. The original list of 190,000 names obtained from Abercrombie and Fitch was old and included no information about the names on the list. no information about the names on the list.

Mr. Lubetkin expects that the third major distribution warehouse would have to be established for the southeastern section of the country. Mr. Lubetkin indicated that he would continue to seek acquisitions in the Sun Belt as long as volume and profit potential were adequate to justify the acquisition. He further indicated that the heaviest expansion of new stores would be in the southeast, with Florida being the most likely center of such expansion.

Mr. Lubetkin indicated that Oshman's purchased a full year's supply of goods only rarely. The purchase pattern depended upon the nature of the good (e.g., a good with a very short season may be purchased for the entire season), the purchase price (including quantity discounts), and other relevant factors. This pattern does not change the company's commitment to ready product availability since assurance of availability is one of the factors considered by the company.

Mr. Lubetkin supplied the following organization chart:

1984 Update

The fiscal year ending January 28, 1984 resulted in record sales and earnings. Sales in 1983–1984 increased 14.5 percent over 1982–1983, whereas earnings in 1983–1984 increased 45 percent over 1982–1983. The 1983 and 1984 Income Statement and Balance Sheet follow:

Consolidated Statements of Earnings
Years Ended January 28, 1984, January 29, 1983, and January 30, 1982
(In thousands except per share amounts)

	1983	1982	1981
Net Sales	$283,238	$247,264	$216,427
Costs of goods sold	170,095	150,332	129,787
Gross profit	113,143	96,932	86,640
Selling and administrative expenses	94,175	85,859	71,902
Operating profit	18,968	13,073	14,738
Other income (expense)			
Interest expense	(2,357)	(2,587)	(2,396)
Miscellaneous income	1,992	1,800	1,390
	(365)	(787)	(1,006)
Earnings before income taxes	18,603	12,286	13,732
Income taxes	8,300	5,195	6,180
Net earnings	10,303	7,091	7,552
Earnings per common and common equivalent share	$1.52	$1.05	$1.12

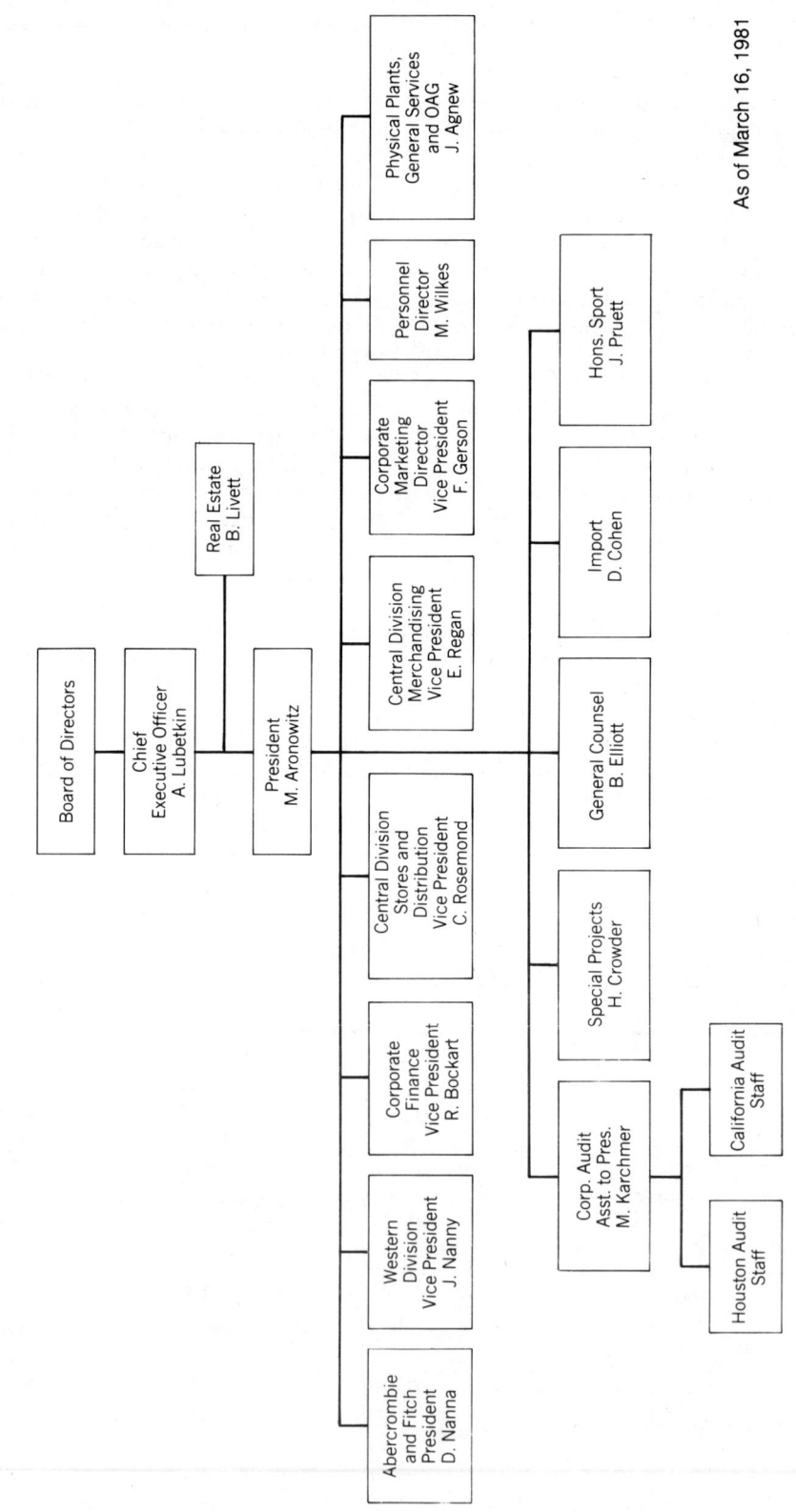

Consolidated Balance Sheets
January 28, 1984 and January 29, 1983 (In thousands)

	1983	1982
Assets		
Current Assets		
Cash and equivalents	$ 23,004	$ 14,540
Accounts receivable, less allowance of $340 in 1983 and $311 in 1982	7,653	7,235
Merchandise inventories	58,688	58,006
Prepaid expenses and other assets	2,333	2,112
Total current assets	91,678	81,893
Property, Plant, and Equipment— at cost	47,294	43,157
Less accumulated depreciation and amortization	17,160	13,996
	30,134	29,161
Other assets	721	638
	$122,533	$111,692
Liabilities and Stockholders' Equity		
Current liabilities		
Current maturities of long-term obligations	$ 2,780	$ 1,760
Trade accounts payable	23,541	23,674
Accrued liabilities	10,318	7,807
Income taxes	5,955	5,183
Total current liabilities	42,594	38,424
Deferred Federal Income Taxes	2,170	1,365
Long-Term Obligations	16,318	19,716
Stockholders' Equity		
Common stock	6,767	6,755
Additional capital	1,252	1,153
Retained earnings	53,432	44,279
	61,451	52,187
	$122,533	$111,692

A number of events and plans will now be reported based on the 1983–1984 annual report. The company made two moves to position itself in the International Market. Woodward Stores Ltd. of Vancouver, British Columbia, Canada, has been granted a license to operate 16 Abercrombie and Fitch stores in Canada. Woodward's is a leading Canadian retail merchandiser with sales of about 2 billion dollars. The first Canadian Abercrombie and Fitch is scheduled to open in September 1984.

The company also reached an agreement with Ito-Yokado Co., Ltd. of Japan whereby they will open and operate Oshman's Sporting Goods stores in Japan. Ito-Yokado is a leading and highly regarded chain store with sales in excess of 5 billion dollars. The coordination of international operations will be the responsibility of Walter Lindenthal.

Abercrombie and Fitch earned its first profit since its inception in 1979. Joe Nanny and Charles Rosemond were elevated from Operations Vice-Presidents to Senior Vice-Presidents and Michael Karchmer was elected to Vice-President, Director of Internal Audits.

Oshman's is enhancing its Management Information System by increasing the detail and accuracy of information with which to plan and control inventories. Also, financial reporting and controls have been upgraded to provide improved planning and allow for continued expansion.

The record results were attained despite the fact that stores in the Houston, Texas area had a decline of 2.3 percent from the previous year in same-store sales. This decline contrasted with an overall increase in same-stores sales of 7.5 percent.

During the 1983–1984 year, Oshman's opened a total of 13 stores and closed a total of four low performing stores. Abercrombie and Fitch expanded from 11 to 16 stores and sales increased 63 percent to 25.3 million dollars.

In 1984–1985 the company plans on opening 15–19 Oshman's Stores and 2–5 Abercrombie and Fitch stores. The Houston economy continues to be depressed. However, the Olympics is expected to increase sales. Oshman's is anticipating and preparing for a surge in sporting activities not only in Southern California where it has 51 stores but throughout the United States.

The difficulties of 1982–1983 appear resolved since cost of goods sold dropped from 60.8 percent in 1982–1983 to 60.1 percent in 1983–1984 which compares with the 60.0 percent in 1981–1982. Likewise, selling and administrative expenses dropped from 33.9 percent in 1982–1983 to 33.2 percent in 1983–1984 which compares with 33.2 percent in 1981–1982.

Telephone Communication with Mr. Lubetkin in April 1984

The following is a summary of an interview by the casewriter with Mr. Lubetkin in April 1984. During the interview three topics were discussed: (1) operation of the various divisions, (2) changing characteristics of store operations, and (3) the future of the company. The discussion with Mr. Lubetkin will be summarized below.

Mr. Lubetkin indicated that each of the divisions was essentially autonomous. While some co-ordination exists within the Oshman's regional division, Abercrombie and Fitch is completely autonomous. Mr. Lubetkin indicated that an eastern division was likely in the not-too-distant future because future growth of Oshman's stores would be concentrated in the southeast. He also indicated that the Atlanta regional warehouse has expanded and will continue to expand as growth dictates. In many respects, future site selection will be more difficult than in the past because many of the obvious sites already have been selected. In addition to the growth of Oshman's stores in the southeast, Mr. Lubetkin also saw substantial growth in Abercrombie and Fitch within the next five years. He felt total sales for Abercrombie and Fitch could increase as much as 10-fold.

Mr. Lubetkin indicated that the merchandise mix varied with the region of the country. He also indicated that the overall merchandise mix is changing. Overall, hunting and fishing merchandise was declining while tennis, golf, and exercise merchandise was on the increase. Ski merchandise was more significant in the California area. He indicated that stores still maintained some nonsport gifts and electronic merchandise, but that it was a relatively small percent of sales. He indicated that most stores were divided into 12 or 13 separate departments and that the recent changes in Management Information Systems involve reporting information on specific merchandise to Houston on-line by phone. Currently, each store receives direct shipments from vendors but replenishment approval must come from division level.

In response to a question regarding the team division, Mr. Lubetkin indicated that it represented less than 2 percent of the company's volume and needed attention. In response to a question regarding the Abercrombie and Fitch catalogue, Mr. Lubetkin indicated that catalogue sales were down, but that he felt comfortable with one catalogue per year.

ALBERTSON'S, INC.

Joseph A. Albertson opened the first Albertson's store in Boise, Idaho in 1939. The store was a supermarket, one of the largest and most modern in the West. Formerly a district manager with Safeway Stores, Mr. Albertson was considered one of the original pioneers of the complete one-stop, self-service concept of supermarketing. Forty-two years after the opening of that first store, the company was operating 327 Albertson's supermarkets in 11 western states in addition to 69 Albertson's combined food–drug stores in four southern states (see map, Exhibit 1).

Consolidated sales in fiscal 1980 reached $3.04 billion, with net profit after taxes of $41.6 million (see five-year summary, Exhibit 2). Total assets as of January 31, 1981 were more than $627 million with stockholders' equity of nearly $209 million (see balance sheets, Exhibit 3). *Fortune* ranked Albertson's in July 1981 as the 19th largest retailer in the United States (in terms of sales), but with the third highest 10-year average return on equity of all U. S. retailers. *Forbes* ranked Albertson's on January 5, 1981, as number 137 in American industry in terms of five-year average return on equity. In that same issue of *Forbes*, Albertson's was number-five out of 30 regional chain stores in five-year average return on equity, number-nine in five-year average return on total capital and number-nine in five-year average earnings per share growth. In the summer of 1981, Albertson's management was looking forward to further growth and profitability for the company.

Source: This case was prepared by Professor Melvin J. Stanford, Mankato State University and Dan R. Willis, Brigham Young University. Permission to use granted by Melvin J. Stanford.

EXHIBIT 1
Areas of Operation

396 Conventional Units and Combination Units at end of Fiscal Year 1980
 30 Stores planned for 1981 (circled)
   Conventional units: 22
   Combination units: 8

Source: Corporate Profile, January 29, 1981.

EXHIBIT 2
Five-Year Summary

	52 Weeks, January 29, 1981[c]	52 Weeks, January 31, 1980[c]	53 Weeks, February 1, 1979	52 Weeks, January 29, 1978	52 Weeks, January 29, 1977
	(Dollars are in thousands except for per share figures)				
Operating Results					
Sales	$3,039,129	$2,673,848	$2,268,970	$1,816,495	$1,490,839
Gross margin	662,566	584,619	516,963	401,109	313,312
Interest expense					
Debt	8,279	8,425	5,924	3,909	3,776
Capital leases	12,856	12,906	11,752	10,862	9,024
Earnings before taxes	77,014	71,635	71,203	48,343	32,425
Taxes on income	35,393	33,312	34,782	23,511	15,352
Net earnings	41,621	38,323	36,421	24,832	17,073
Net earnings as a percent of sales	1.37%	1.43%	1.61%	1.37%	1.15%
Common Stock Data					
Earnings per share[a,b]	$ 2.70	$ 2.49	$ 2.38	$ 1.63	$ 1.13
Dividends per share[a]	.80	.60	.48	.40	.36
Book value per share[b]	14.08	12.07	10.08	8.10	6.81
Financial Position					
Total assets	$ 627,219	$ 572,789	$ 552,215	$ 408,310	$ 335,860
Working capital	111,806	99,343	79,272	46,007	38,727
Long-term debt	82,765	85,748	85,078	43,291	34,205
Obligations under capital leases	122,176	125,882	121,723	113,938	96,902
Stockholders' equity	208,996	178,488	148,872	118,864	99,386
Other Statistics					
Number of stores at end of year	396	384	365	305	292
Number of employees	28,000	25,300	24,440	20,400	17,775

Source: 1981 Annual Report.
[a] Based on average number of shares and equivalents outstanding.
[b] Adjusted for two-for-one stock split paid March 26, 1980.
[c] Reflects the adoption of the LIFO method of valuing certain inventories.

Corporate Philosophy

Albertson's operating philosophy placed a strong emphasis on responsiveness to the consumer, a centralized management information system with decentralized merchandising responsibility, and a fully integrated property development operation. In the low-margin supermarket industry, Albertson's executives believed that careful management of inventory turnover and debt leveraging of real estate and store equipment were the keys to a good return on stockholders' equity. They sought to protect margins by concentrating on store productivity, diversification, implementation of selected private label lines, tight management control through a highly sophisticated management information system, and "most

EXHIBIT 3
Consolidated Balance Sheets

	January 29, 1981	January 31, 1980	February 1, 1979
		(in thousands)	
Assets			
Current Assets			
Cash and short-term securities	$ 74,625	$ 57,754	$ 68,744
Accounts and notes receivable	19,610	13,919	14,113
Inventories	184,427	170,395	155,674
Prepaid expenses	4,932	4,281	4,232
Property held for resale	12,624	12,343	14,793
Deferred income tax benefits	10,155	7,970	6,822
Refundable income taxes		1,336	
Total Current Assets	306,373	267,998	264,378
Other Assets			
Notes receivable	2,285	1,096	1,716
Securities, licenses and other investments, at cost which approximates market	11,904	10,999	9,110
Receivables for capital subleases	3,242	3,276	2,759
	17,431	15,371	13,585
Land, Buildings, and Equipment			
Land	14,152	13,679	13,125
Buildings	47,005	42,097	37,218
Fixtures and equipment	210,487	180,200	156,005
Leasehold improvements	48,214	40,621	36,298
Assets under capital leases	140,082	142,080	136,728
	459,940	418,677	379,374
Less accumulated depreciation and amortization	156,922	129,415	106,116
	303,018	289,262	273,258
Deferred Income Tax Benefits	397		
Deferred Costs, less amortization		158	994
	$627,219	$572,789	$552,215
Liabilities and Stockholders' Equity			
Current Liabilities			
Accounts payable	$151,142	$135,337	$133,735
Salaries and related liabilities	14,166	13,935	13,948
Taxes other than income taxes	11,072	9,043	10,142
Interest payable	3,475	3,337	3,314
Taxes on income	4,722		14,505
Dividends payable	2,968	2,218	1,772
Current maturities of long-term debt	3,506	1,423	5,347
Current obligations under capital leases	3,516	3,362	2,343
Total Current Liabilities	194,567	168,655	185,106

(*Continued*)

EXHIBIT 3 (*Continued*)

	January 29, 1981	January 31, 1980	February 1, 1979
		(in thousands)	
Long-Term Debt	82,765	85,748	85,078
Obligations under Capital Leases	122,176	125,882	121,723
Deferred Credits and Other Long-Term Liabilities			
Deferred investment plan	12,187	9,564	7,828
Deferred compensation	5,021	4,054	2,930
Deferred income taxes		398	678
Deferred rents payable	1,507		
	18,715	14,016	11,436
Stockholders' Equity			
Common stock	14,841	14,791	7,384
Capital in excess of par value	27,375	26,686	33,926
Retained earnings	166,780	137,011	107,562
	208,996	178,488	148,872
	$627,219	$572,789	$552,215

Source: 1981 Annual Report.

important . . . the training of its key assets . . . people."

Responsiveness to the consumer was the basis of a strategy of integrating consumerism programs. Albertson's executives believed that, "It is the heart of our business to initiate consumer services." The company sought to emphasize to its customers that it was the "buying agent" for the customer and not the "selling agent" for the manufacturer. It stated its operating philosophy as follows:

> Albertson's is engaged in the business of operating retail food and drug stores with integrated distribution and manufacturing facilities to support the retail effort for the purpose of satisfying consumer needs. To fulfill this service, we must provide the customer:
>
> 1. Distinctive quality and personalized service in all perimeter departments.
> 2. Helpful, friendly service throughout the store.
> 3. Fast, clean, one-stop convenience.
> 4. Attractive competitive prices.
> 5. Conveniently laid out, well-stocked grocery departments with a good selection of regular and seasonal merchandise.
>
> Albertson's is, in effect, a big store with a specialty store approach. We must be 'big' in terms of low prices, convenience, and wider selection of brands. We must be a 'specialty' store in terms of quality, personal service, and specialized selection.
>
> All programs, plans, and actions initiated and implemented by all personnel should have the objective of satisfying the above criteria.

The company sought to maintain a traditionally conservative financial structure. For some years, it had been using its capital primarily to build stores rather than to develop a distribution system. New store buildings were financed to a large extent by sale and lease-back, with Albertson's internal capital being applied to equipment, inventory, and remodeling. In the long run, management felt that once enough stores were established in a sector of its geographically diversified trading area, investments could then be made in warehouses and distribution facilities with a greater profitability than if such "backstage" support was developed concurrently with the stores. New stores were supplied primarily by wholesalers in their area of operation. Locations for new stores were generally selected in growth areas where price competition would not be intense from existing firms.

Geographically, Albertson's believed that well-run conventional supermarkets still had an important place in the western market. However, the Company's management also saw a trend toward large, one-stop "superstores" with greater emphasis on nonfood, household, recreational, and automotive needs. Accordingly, considerable priority was given to expansion, both in size and product offering, of the combination food–drug units.

A theme of "Grow With the West" had been expressed by Albertson's a decade earlier, but by 1976, management thought that there were many opportunities for new stores in other states where the company was not operating as well as throughout its current operating area. Albertson's referred to itself as the "walking" regional chain. Management believed that the decentralized operation first learned in Idaho would permit the company to go to any attractive store location in its chosen operating area, no matter how remote, rather than slowly expand outward from a central base to neighboring areas. The company expansion that took place in the 1970s, however, led to Albertson's being called by some observers a multiregional and even a national company. There were Albertson's stores within 20 miles of the Canadian border and just short of the Mexican border, as well as units on the Pacific coast of California and the Atlantic coast of Florida.

Albertson's was planning to add some of the states in the Central Plains to its operating area. Expansion into Nebraska and South Dakota was scheduled to begin in 1981 with the introduction of the large combination units there. Opening dates for these stores were planned for early 1982.

Economic Trends and Conditions

The American economic setting of the early 1980s could be characterized as one of extremes:

1. Double-digit inflation. The CPI (cost–price index) for all items rose 13.5 percent in 1980 and 11.3 percent in 1979.
2. Sharp rises in credit demand and interest rates because of fluctuating policies regarding the money supply. During 1980, the prime rate rose above 20 percent and was never under 11 percent.
3. An expanded federal government deficit. In mid-1981, the national debt exceeded $1 trillion.
4. Strains on state and local government budgets.
5. Sagging productivity and rising unemployment, particularly in the automobile and housing industries.

In 1980, the Gross National Product was $2.6 trillion in current dollars, reflecting a one-year increase of over 8.7 percent. In real figures, however, the GNP was $1.5 trillion, a slight decrease from 1979. These yearly averages, however, hid the unprecedented swings of the GNP that had occurred from quarter to quarter. For example, in 1980, the GNP plunged at a 10 percent annual rate during the second quarter. This drop, sparked by President Carter's credit control restrictions, was felt throughout the economy. Surprisingly, though, this plunge did not continue throughout the year; the economy managed to right itself somewhat, primarily because of the accumulated effect of the high interest rates of the late 1970s. Tight money had kept inventories

EXHIBIT 4

	1972	1973	1974	1975	1976	1977	1978	1979	1980
GNP: In actual $ (billions)	1171.1	1306.6	1412.9	1528.8	1702.2	1899.5	2127.6	2368.8	2626.1
Consumer Price Index (CPI)									
All items[a]	125.3	133.1	147.7	161.2	170.5	181.5	195.4	217.4	246.8
Food[a]	123.5	141.4	161.7	175.4	180.8	192.2	211.4	234.5	254.6
Food at Home[a]	121.6	141.4	162.4	175.8	179.5	190.2	210.2	232.9	251.5
Food Away from Home[a]	131.1	141.4	159.4	174.3	186.1	200.3	218.4	242.9	267.0
Wholesale Price Index (WPI)									
All Commodities[a]	119.1	134.7	160.1	174.9	183.0	194.2	209.3	235.6	268.8
Farm Products[a]	125.0	176.3	187.7	186.7	191.0	192.5	212.5	241.4	249.4
Processed Foods and Feed[a]	120.8	148.1	170.9	182.6	178.0	186.1	202.6	222.5	241.1
Disposable Personal Income (actual $ billions)	802.5	903.1	983.6	1076.7	1184.4	1303.0	1458.4	1641.7	1821.7
Personal Consumption Expendit.[b]	729.0	805.2	876.7	963.8	1090.2	1206.5	1350.8	1510.9	1672.8
Durables[b]	118.4	130.3	127.5	128.1	156.6	178.4	200.0	212.3	211.9
Nondurables (incl. food)[b]	299.7	338.0	380.2	409.8	442.6	479.0	531.0	602.2	675.7
Food (At Home and Away)[b]	120.3	136.7	152.3	166.4	180.9	189.3	212.4	238.8	NA
Food Away from Home[b]	36.3	39.7	44.5	51.6	56.3	60.7	66.0	72.5	NA

Sources: Statistical Abstract of the U. S. 1980. Survey of Current Business, April 1981, August 1978.
[a] 1967 = 100.0.
[b] Actual $ (billions).

lean through 1979 and 1980, making it almost impossible to have the massive inventory liquidations that had accelerated previous recessions. This could be seen operating very plainly in the food-marketing industry. Interest costs had become so high that they were a critical part of nearly every inventory decision.

The mid-1980 slump did little to slow inflation. The CPI for all items closed the year at 246.8, up from 217.4 at the end of 1979. The CPI for food at home rose by 8 percent in 1980, lower than the 10.8 percent rise in 1979, while the prices for food away from home rose by 9.9 percent, also significantly less than its 1979 rate of 11.2 percent (see Exhibit 4).

In 1980, consumers spent 16.6 percent of their disposable income on food, 12.2 percent being used for food at home expenditures. While percentages remained stable from 1979, compared to 1975, the proportion of disposable income spent on all food and food at home declined while that for food away from home increased. Overall, disposable income increased in current dollars by 11 percent from 1979, but its real purchasing power actually declined slightly because of the effect of rapid inflation.

Not only was there a drop in real disposable income during the early 1980s, but there also was a rapid rise in unemployment. The 1980 unemployment rate of 7.1 percent was up considerably from the 1979 rate of 5.8 percent. This increase in the unemployment rate and continuing high inflation continued to threaten the nation with another round of recession.

In addition to being affected by these adverse economic conditions, the food-retailing industry also had been subject to consumer boycotts and other negative consumer reactions during the 1970s. These occurred particularly during times of shortages and high prices of specific items, such as beef and sugar. Food processors and retailers had been accused of raising prices more than the increase in their costs, and farmers especially complained that they were being hurt by inflation and that middlemen were taking the profits. This kind of activity had largely subsided by 1976, but the general mood of the food shopper in the early 1980s still seemed to be cautious, thrifty, and worried about prices.

The Supermarket Industry

Total food store sales in the United States were reported by industry and government sources as 235.2 billion in 1980, up from $212.8 billion in 1979 and $190.5 billion in 1978. The total number of stores, however, had declined from 169,500 in 1978 to 168,900 in 1979 and 167,100 in 1980. This pattern was a continuation of the general trend in the United States between 1963 and 1977, during which time the average sales per grocery store increased faster than that of retail trade stores, according to government statistics (see Exhibit 5).

Total sales by U. S. supermarkets were nearly $171 billion in 1980, up 10.8 percent over 1979. The largest increase in sales between those two years were for large supermarkets with annual sales levels of more than $4 million. The sales increase for large chain supermarkets (a "chain" was a company with more than 10 stores) was 15.9 percent; the sales increase for large, independent supermarkets (less than 10 stores per company) was 16.0 percent.

In 1980, there were 12,170 large (over $4 million annual sales) chain supermarkets, a 9 percent increase over the 11,150 stores in 1979 and a 51 percent increase over the 8,050 stores in 1978. The sales of these large chains accounted for 39.5 percent of all U. S. grocery sales in 1980, 37.7 percent in 1979, and 29.9 percent in 1978. All chain supermarkets (including small chain supermarkets, with sales between $1–$4 million) totaled 46.6 percent of all 1980 U. S. grocery sales.

EXHIBIT 5
Retail, Grocery, and Drug Store Data

	Totals, United States			
	1963	1967	1972	1977
Retail Trade, Total				
All Establishments. Number (000)	1,707.9	1,763.3	1,934.5	1,855.1
Sales ($ millions)	244,202	310,214	470,806	723,134
Establishments with Payroll Number (000)	1,206.1	1,191.5	1,286.5	1,303.6
Sales ($ millions)	233,085	295,170	451,987	699,635
Paid Employees (000)	NA	9,381	11,360	13,040
Payroll ($ millions)	NA	36,175	56,385	85,854
Grocery Stores				
All Establishments. Number (000)	244.8	218.1	194.3	178.8
Sales ($ millions)	52,566	65,073	93,328	147,759
Establishments with Payroll Number (000)	132.1	128.7	128.1	126.6
Sales ($ millions)	49,187	61,771	90,048	143,938
Paid Employees (000)	NA	1,242	1,472	1,692
Payroll ($ millions)	NA	4,897	7,846	13,342

Source: *Statistical Abstract of the U. S.*
NA = not available. These government totals are between 3 and 4 percent lower than industry figures because the latter includes some specialty stores that the former did not.

Independent supermarkets (10 or fewer stores in the company) increased from 15,375 stores in 1979 to 16,500 stores in 1980, while their aggregate sales rose from 61.2 billion to 67.9 billion in the same one-year period. Independent supermarkets with annual volumes between $1 million and $4 million increased 5.6 percent in number of stores and 5.9 percent in aggregate sales volume between 1979 and 1980, while independent stores above $4 million volume grew 13.4 percent in number in 1980 while achieving the 16.0 percent sales volume increase mentioned earlier.

Convenience stores, such as 7–11, that tend to stay open longer hours and offer a limited variety of food and related items at higher prices than grocery stores, are not included in the foregoing data on chains and independents (but are included in the industry totals). The number of convenience stores increased from 34,125 in 1979 to 35,800 in 1980, and their aggregate sales volume rose from $10.5 billion to $12.4 billion in that time. A summary of the market shares in number of stores and sales volume for all three categories of stores (in 1978, 1979, and 1980) is as follows:

	1978	1979	1980
Number of Stores			
Independents	69.4%	68.7%	67.4%
Chains	11.4%	11.1%	11.2%
Convenience	19.2%	20.2%	21.4%
	100.0%	100.0%	100.0%
Dollar Sales Volume			
Independents	48.2%	48.2%	47.7%
Chains	46.9%	46.8%	46.7%
Convenience	4.9%	5.0%	5.6%
	100.0%	100.0%	100.0%

A supermarket is defined in the food-store industry as any store, chain, or independent doing $1 million or more in sales per year. Gross profits of supermarkets (without profits of warehouses by those stores that had them) since 1975 had remained near a median of 19 percent of sales for independents and 21.5 percent for chains, with net profits before taxes ranging between 2.1–2.4 percent of sales for independents and 0.84–1.70 percent of sales for chains during that same period (see Exhibit 6). Geographically, the number of grocery stores was decreasing faster between 1967 and 1977 in the Northeast than in other parts of the United States, according to the *Census of Retail Trade* (see Exhibit 7). During that same period, total grocery store sales increased proportionally more in the South and the West than in other regions.

Food retailing in the United States was generally regarded by investment analysts as a mature industry with little overall growth potential. Traditionally a highly competitive, low-margin business, food retailing also faced risks of labor contract negotiation (for larger chains) and pressures from consumer groups and federal agencies, some of which advocated government control of food production and distribution. Despite these conditions, investment observers suggested a consolidation trend in the industry, with the expected result that better-managed food retailing companies would achieve relative growth by increasing their market shares and improving their profitability. Factors for industry growth more important than market share were thought by analysts to be the prospects for a more favorable industry pricing structure and bigger stores capable of carrying a much larger mix of higher-margined merchandise, such as convenience foods (including wines, party cheeses, bakery goods, delicatessen items, frozen foods, and private label items) and general merchandise. Because tight cost control and high sales volume were required in order to make a satisfactory return on investment in the low-margin business, food retailers had traditionally sought special merchandising concepts to stimulate sales and had developed various promotional techniques to improve productivity and reduce costs.

Self-service in grocery stores was an inno-

EXHIBIT 6
Supermarket Industry Data[a] (Medians of stores with annual sales over $1 million)

	1975	1976	1977	1978	1979	1980
Independents						
Gross Profit	18.8%	19.0%	19.5%	19.3%	19.5%	19.6%
Net Profit Before Taxes	2.4%	2.3%	2.3%	2.2%	2.1%	2.3%
Chains						
Gross Profit	21.15%	21.22%	21.35%	21.74%	21.50%	21.71%
Net Profit Before Taxes	1.25%	1.17%	1.12%	0.84%	1.70%	1.39%
All Stores						
Sales/Labor Hour	$54.06	$57.40	$59.62	$71.00	$76.77	$87.27
Weekly Sales/Square Foot	$5.33	$5.50	$5.80	$6.17	$6.49	$6.94
Sales/Customer Transaction	$8.75	$9.39	$9.85	$10.28	$11.60	$12.10
Average Number of Items Carried	8,000	9,000	9,000	11,767	12,745	14,145
Store Labor Expense	8.1%	8.3%	8.4%	8.5%	8.3%	8.4%
Fringe Benefit Expense	1.4%	1.5%	1.7%	2.0%	1.8%	1.9%
Grocery Department Shrink	0.8%	0.6%	0.5%	0.5%	0.5%	0.5%

Sources: "The Supermarket Industry Speaks: 1981." "Grocery Industry Report for 1980," *Progressive Grocer*, April 1981.
[a] Percentages are of sales.

vation in the 1930s, and the constantly increasing store size of supermarkets over the years was the result of efforts to generate higher volume and to increase employee productivity. Other food-retailing techniques included intensive advertising, loss leaders, private brands, central meat processing, and captive food-processing plants (dairies, bakeries, and other high-volume staple items).

During the 1950s, food retailing was in a strong expansion phase. Substantial conversion of the industry to large supermarkets was taking place. That period was characterized by growth and high profits. However, it came to an end when industry capacity became excessive and competition grew more intense. The use of stamps and games became widespread and then subsided. In the 1960s there was a gradual adoption by more food retailers of the discount concept, reaching a climax in 1972 with A & P's WEO (Where Economy Originates) program; in 1972, the industry's average profits (after tax) dropped to 0.49 percent of sales compared to 1 percent in the 1960s.

Discount merchandising was essentially the selling of food in high-volume stores, with all games, gimmicks, stamps, and special services eliminated to achieve lowest prices. With lower overhead and higher volume, earnings could be achieved in spite of lower gross margins.

Greater emphasis on general merchandise appeared to be a major trend for the food industry in the 1970s. Previously, some food retailers had gone into nonfoods blindly on the theory that there was no need to start with expertise in the field. Such firms learned to their regret that general merchandise was a specialty and that a good grocery buyer was not necessarily a good houseware or apparel

EXHIBIT 7
Grocery Store Data by State

Region and State	Establishments (number)			Sales ($ millions)		
	1967	1972	1977	1967	1972	1977
United States	218,130	194,346	178,835	65,074	93,328	147,759
Regions						
Northeastern States	47,739	39,776	35,929	16,254	22,366	32,298
North Central States	49,584	42,011	36,011	18,357	24,641	37,422
South	95,580	88,139	82,583	18,715	29,074	49,215
West	25,227	24,420	24,312	11,747	17,242	28,826
New England	10,743	9,444	9,134	4,080	5,696	8,593
Maine	1,779	1,537	1,474	363	520	836
New Hampshire	959	879	884	290	466	782
Vermont	663	639	653	162	249	375
Massachusetts	4,174	3,528	3,405	1,891	2,593	3,808
Rhode Island	739	659	644	282	378	566
Connecticut	2,429	2,202	2,074	1,092	1,491	2,226
Middle Atlantic	36,996	30,332	26,795	12,175	16,670	23,705
New York	17,603	14,777	12,802	6,009	8,147	10,948
New Jersey	5,890	4,883	4,933	2,481	3,491	5,233
Pennsylvania	13,503	10,672	9,060	3,685	5,032	7,524
East North Central	33,879	28,833	24,477	13,435	18,034	26,956
Ohio	9,418	8,233	7,042	3,512	4,686	7,355
Indiana	4,138	3,513	2,993	1,710	2,265	3,493
Illinois	8,764	7,142	5,631	3,757	4,836	7,111
Michigan	7,516	6,634	5,993	3,127	4,394	6,111
Wisconsin	4,043	3,311	2,818	1,329	1,853	2,886
West North Central	15,705	13,178	11,534	4,922	6,606	10,466
Minnesota	3,223	2,816	2,502	1,043	1,449	2,297
Iowa	2,608	2,156	1,818	890	1,170	1,889
Missouri	5,024	4,014	3,555	1,510	2,013	3,145
North Dakota	684	617	525	162	215	351
South Dakota	688	627	567	175	248	390
Nebraska	1,400	1,105	999	451	581	925
Kansas	2,078	1,843	1,568	693	931	1,469
South Atlantic	42,711	39,353	37,497	9,219	14,509	24,224
Delaware	426	439	431	179	295	434
Maryland	3,212	2,760	2,557	1,247	1,890	2,964
District of Columbia	618	433	396	235	277	326
Virginia	5,821	5,187	5,060	1,413	2,131	3,547
West Virginia	3,207	2,670	2,320	526	771	1,337
North Carolina	9,547	8,411	8,123	1,417	2,240	3,738
South Carolina	5,362	4,956	4,474	720	1,166	1,980
Georgia	7,655	7,117	6,433	1,300	1,998	3,343
Florida	6,863	7,380	7,703	2,182	3,741	6,555
East South Central	24,233	22,350	20,575	3,591	5,524	9,254
Kentucky	6,293	5,237	4,918	904	1,382	2,405

EXHIBIT 7 (*Continued*)

Region and State	Establishments (number)			Sales ($ millions)		
	1967	1972	1977	1967	1972	1977
Tennessee	6,772	6,326	6,038	1,145	1,777	2,934
Alabama	6,197	6,040	5,331	960	1,434	2,392
Mississippi	4,971	4,747	4,288	582	930	1,523
West South Central	28,636	26,436	24,511	5,905	9,041	15,737
Arkansas	4,179	3,557	3,056	548	855	1,417
Louisiana	6,002	5,439	4,830	1,130	1,735	2,961
Oklahoma	3,351	2,963	2,859	780	1,162	2,037
Texas	15,104	14,477	13,766	3,448	5,289	9,322
Mountain	6,493	6,846	6,643	2,561	4,119	7,426
Montana	715	758	681	240	340	579
Idaho	717	734	704	227	335	637
Wyoming	341	282	232	112	151	307
Colorado	1,481	1,380	1,381	662	1,093	1,992
New Mexico	925	1,000	944	279	451	805
Arizona	1,364	1,666	1,675	556	994	1,831
Utah	683	693	629	289	442	774
Nevada	267	333	397	195	314	571
Pacific	18,734	17,574	17,669	9,186	13,127	21,400
Washington	2,682	2,601	2,439	1,172	1,655	2,755
Oregon	1,963	2,000	1,974	702	1,150	1,730
California	13,362	12,238	12,493	6,991	9,773	15,913
Alaska	176	236	273	90	169	410
Hawaii	551	499	490	231	380	592

Source: Census of Retail Trade.

buyer. More recently, companies achieving better results in such diversification reasoned that with proper training on the store level and the hiring of experienced buying and merchandising personnel, supermarkets could compete with general merchandise stores.

Some companies, such as Lucky (automotive, department stores, fabrics, and drugs) and Supermarkets General (drugs, department stores, home improvement centers, and catalogue showrooms), believed that the supermarket industry needed to diversity into a variety of retailing fields in order to improve profitability. Other food retailers, such as Winn–Dixie and Colonial stores, were sticking close to more traditional supermarket operations, on the theory that the supermarket industry was courting trouble if it got beyond its known sphere of operations and competed with professionals in other fields. Investment analysts generally believed that the strength of an operation, not its form (supermarket, discount center, drug store, etc.), determined profitability.

Supermarkets were considered to be in a strong position to capitalize on the one-stop shopping concept, because their stores were generally more conveniently located for the average customer than other retail stores. Moreover, the average customer visited a supermarket about four times per month compared to only about twice a month for general merchandise stores.

In the early 1980s, however, with the rate

of population growth and construction declining, construction of new supermarkets was expected to slow considerably. Consumer buying habits were becoming more diversified, and supermarkets were being challenged to satisfy the needs of an increasingly fragmented society.

The retailing unit of the 1980s was generally agreed in the industry to be 30,000 to 50,000 square foot "superstores" that stocked everything from food to flowers to automotive parts and tried to appeal at the same time to a host of demographic groups. Another trend of the new decade was the revival of low-margin, no-frills markets that stocked large volumes of a limited number of items. This response to the budget-conscious consumer gained acceptance as the impact of inflation was felt more strongly across the nation.

Competition

In the food-retailing industry, competition was perhaps most visible among the large supermarket chains, but the independent operator was also a formidable competitor for several reasons. The independent proprietor was a part of the community in which he or she lived and operated. He or she knew the people and their needs, responded quickly to market changes and trends, worked closely with employees, and had a positive local image. Albertson's management saw this as the challenge to its own growth: to try to maintain these characteristics of local operation in its present and new market areas.

Safeway Stores, Inc., was the largest U. S. food-retailing firm in sales, number of stores, and total earnings (see Exhibit 8). In return on equity capital, Safeway was strong but behind several other firms in the industry. Although it did not rank especially high in balance sheet analysis compared to seven other firms in a recent investment study (see Exhibit 9), Safeway had a reputation of being the best-managed firm in the industry. Albertson's executives regarded Safeway as an "excellent operation, well-managed, good competitors, and predictable" (predictable in the sense that Safeway's size, maturity, and stability of operation would enable others to anticipate what its activities, sales, and profits would likely be in the future).

Safeway was a highly integrated company with its own distribution system. It neither bought nor sold, to any extent, from or to other wholesalers or retailers in the industry. Safeway operated a cost center type of organization that was believed to be typical among large food chains. In 1972 it had overtaken A & P as the number-one food retailer in the United States. Both Safeway and A & P owned large food-processing facilities for their own respective private label merchandise; A & P was one of the largest food-product manufacturers in the United States.

Government Controls

Government regulation had not directly impinged upon the retail food industry since retail price controls, which had been temporarily established in 1972, had expired. The high cost of living, with food prices as a key element of that total cost, was a target of public criticism and government scrutiny during the mid-1970s, especially during the presidential election year of 1976. In response to the public outcry, the joint Economic Committee of Congress had, in 1975, subpoenaed the records and documents of the 17 largest U. S. food chains, including Albertson's. The results of their subsequent study, concluded in May 1977, showed that growing chains did not realize excessive profits, although the amount of overcharge varied among cities and competitive market structures. The average profit rate of grocery chains, in fact, was shown to be less than that of many industries. Two reasons offered for this depressed performance were the government price-control program and A & P's WEO campaign. The study noted, however, a trend toward bigger stores, increased

Albertson's Inc.   403

EXHIBIT 8
Sales and Earnings of 25 Publicly Held Food Chains

	Sales (000$)			Earnings (000$)			No. of Stores
	1980	1979	1978	1980	1979	1978	
Safeway	15,102,700	13,717,861	12,550,569	119,300	143,323	146,118	2,439
Kroger	10,316,741	9,029,315	7,828,071	94,386	85,721	84,596	1,245
A&P	6,811,178 (e)	6,684,179	7,469,659	NA	(3,807)	(52,186)	1,322
Lucky	6,468,682	5,815,927	4,658,409	90,458	98,094	80,400	212
American Stores	6,260,000*(e)	3,786,332	4,183,222	NA	44,434	38,091	760
Winn–Dixie	5,388,978	4,930,538	4,444,255	91,950	94,462	84,014	1,151
Jewel	4,155,750 (e)	3,764,266	3,516,352	NA	50,686	41,142	771
Grand Union (Cavenham)	3,526,700 (e)	3,137,612	2,398,944	NA	30,669	21,863	840
Albertson's	3,045,510 (e)	2,673,848	2,268,970	NA	38,323	36,421	384
Supermarkets General	2,629,200	2,372,574	2,061,873	NA	23,460	17,874	111
Dillon	2,077,265	1,792,217	1,465,277	27,397	33,586	27,757	547
Stop & Shop	2,032,930 (e)	1,878,864	1,762,144	NA	14,948	16,021	151
Giant Food	1,460,078 (e)	1,242,620	1,080,842	NA	17,859	16,957	117
Petrolane (Stater Bros.)	1,425,416	1,143,938	940,827	74,008	60,217	48,414	89
Fisher Foods	1,412,962	1,336,293	1,451,676	6,703	(6,989)	9,829	143
First National	1,259,700 (e)	1,364,797	1,111,691	NA	5,253	3,934	274
Waldbaum	1,233,650 (e)	1,103,443	941,479	NA	7,827	7,016	136
National Tea	1,232,000 (e)	1,045,696	918,635	NA	13,133	12,102	242
Fred Meyer	1,202,270 (e)	1,060,203	927,110	NA	22,380	20,881	61
Food Fair Stores	1,124,067	1,487,270	2,785,899	2,136	37	(52,518)	200
Borman's	984,145 (e)	905,376	783,939	NA	467	5,804	82
Pneumo (P&C)	983,777	771,946	613,356	13,532	10,035	6,599	99
Cullum	864,974	782,520	639,080	11,290	9,406	6,614	114
Weis Markets	684,814	606,346	518,003	33,091	28,880	24,582	99
Foodtown (N.C.)	543,883	415,974	299,267	15,287	13,171	9,481	101

Source: Progressive Grocer, April 1981.

industry concentration, and improved profit margins.

Universal Product Code

A possible target for legislative restriction was the Universal Product Code (UPC) system. The code itself was essentially a 10-digit number. The first five digits identified the manufacturer or the company that controlled the label. The last five digits identified the item of merchandise. The code had been talked about in American industry for more than 40 years, but in order for it to be widely useful, a standard symbol had to be selected that could be read by optical scanners. The coding scheme was adopted in May 1971; two years later a bar code symbol was chosen.

There were three levels of electronic systems that could utilize UPC. The first was a "Stand Alone" electronic cash register (ECR) that would perform all of the functions of mechanical cash registers plus other functions. Some ECRs were upgraded to terminals for a scanning system.

A processor-driven terminal system was the second level, with a minicomputer located in the store and connected to terminals with cables. The processor would contain the mem-

EXHIBIT 9
Comparative Balance Sheet Data for Selected Grocery Chains ($ Millions)

	Albertson's, Inc.		American Stores Co.		Dillon Companies, Inc.	
As Of:	1/81		1/81		6/80	
Net Assets						
Cash and Short-Term Investments	$ 74.6		$ 29.8		$ 24.0	
Other Current Assets	231.7		604.5		148.3	
Total Current Assets	$306.4		$ 634.3		$172.3	
Short-Term Debt	7.0		13.1		12.4	
Other Current Liabilities	187.5		487.8		139.6	
Net Working Capital	$111.8		$ 133.4		$ 20.3	
Net Plant	303.0		630.3		243.3	
Capitalized Property Under Operating Leases(a)	149.0		308.0		102.4	
Other Tangible Assets	17.7		28.4		8.5	
Net Tangible Assets	581.6		1,100.1		374.5	
Intangibles	0.0		0.0		10.8	
Net Assets	$581.6		$1,100.1		$385.3	
Capitalization						
Long-Term Debt						
Senior	$204.9	35.2%	$ 392.2	35.7%	$100.3	26.0%
Capitalized Operating Lease[a]	149.0	25.6	308.0	28.0	102.4	26.6
Convertible	0.0	0.0	0.0	0.0	0.0	0.0
Total Long-Term Debt	$353.9	60.8%	$ 700.2	63.7%	$202.7	52.6%
Other Liab., Def. Items & Min. Interests	18.7	3.2	37.9	3.4	19.8	5.1
Preferred Stock at Liquidating Value	0.0	0.0	118.1	10.7	0.0	0.0
Common Equity	209.0	36.0	243.9	22.2	162.8	42.3
Total Capitalization	$581.6	100.0%	$1,100.1	100.0%	$385.3	100.0%
Capitalized Lease Obligations	$122.2		$180.7		$59.1	
Common Shares Outstanding (000)	14,841.0		9,764.0		16,941.7	
Book Value Per Share[b]	$14.08		$9.83		$9.61	
Tangible Book Value Per Share[b]	$14.08		$9.83		$8.97	
Selected Financial Ratios						
Net Sales/Net Assets[c]	522.5%		583.6%		541.1%	
Pre-Tax Return on Invested Capital[c,d]	20.8		19.0		17.3	
After-Tax Return on Equity	19.9		21.2		16.8	
Interest Coverage	4.6x		3.1x		6.3x	
Fixed Charges Coverage	2.8x		1.8x		2.9	

Source: Lehman Brothers Kuhn Loeb, Inc. Study, July, 1981.
[a] Capitalized at 8x 1981 rental expense.
[b] Excluding capitalized operating leases.
[c] Including capitalized operating leases.
[d] Pre-tax return before interest expense, and capital and operating lease payments.

Albertson's Inc. **405**

	Jewel Companies, Inc.		The Kroger Co.		Lucky Stores, Inc.		Safeway Stores, Inc.		Supermarkets General Corp.	
	1/81		12/80		1/81		12/80		1/81	
	$ 38.0		$ 92.9		$ 64.3		$ 115.8		$ 15.6	
	487.9		952.9		678.8		1,152.5		231.4	
	525.9		$1,045.8		$ 743.1		$1,268.2		$247.0	
	14.6		24.5		14.8		167.4		9.8	
	342.2		794.4		454.9		988.1		207.1	
	$ 169.1		$ 226.9		$ 273.3		$ 112.7		39.9	
	652.3		884.6		622.5		2,033.7		321.5	
	296.8		984.6		422.4		638.4		68.0	
	93.7		49.0		21.7		33.9		4.4	
	1,211.9		2,145.1		1,339.9		2,818.7		433.8	
	17.1		18.2		13.4		3.1		0.0	
	$1,229.0		$2,163.3		$1,353.3		$2,821.8		$433.8	
	$ 349.2	28.4%	$ 386.0	32.7%	$ 409.4	30.3%	$1,051.2	37.3%	$181.0	42.7%
	296.8	24.1	984.6	0.0	422.4	31.2	638.4	22.6	68.0	16.0
	0.0	0.0	0.0	0.0	5.4	60.4	0.0	0.0	4.0	1.0
	$ 646.0	52.5	$1,370.6	32.7	837.2	61.9	$1,689.6	60.0	$253.0	59.7
	72.0	5.9	121.3	10.3	64.5	4.8	68.1	2.4	29.2	6.9
	97.2	7.9	0.0	0.0	17.5	1.3	0.0	0.0	0.0	0.0
	413.8	33.7	671.4	57.0	434.1	32.0	1,064.1	37.6	141.7	33.4
	$1,229.0	100.0%	$2,163.3	100.0%	1,353.3	100.0%	$2,821.8	100.0%	$423.9	100.0%
	$171.0		$121.6		$179.4		$844.0		$126.0	
	11,184.0		27,772.0		50,056.0		26,116.0		8,320.0	
	$36.27		$24.17		$8.67		$40.75		$17.03	
	$36.27		$23.52		$8.40		$40.63		$17.03	
	347.3%		476.9%		478.0%		535.2%		606.0%	
	12.9		15.2		16.2		14.6		15.9	
	13.5		15.3		20.9		11.2		18.4	
	3.9x		5.6x		5.2x		3.0x		4.0x	
	1.7x		2.0x		2.5x		1.9x		2.8x	

ory and logic to drive the terminals. Its computer power would enable it to perform many additional functions, such as:

Look-up prices using item codes.
Accumulate sales for individual items.
Perform check authorization.
Accumulate information for store scheduling.
Consolidate sales from all checkstands.
Control the accumulation of excess cash in the store.

It appeared that the processor-driven system could be expanded to handle numerous other store functions, such as monitoring refrigerated cases, direct delivery, accounting, and payroll timekeeping.

The highest level of electronic system was the full-scan system, which consisted of attaching optical scanners to the processor-driven system. At its full capability, the prices of all items would be stored in the computer. As the symbol was scanned at the checkout stand, the price would be retrieved from the computer memory, displayed, and printed on the customer's receipt.

The full-scan system opened up numerous other possibilities. Manual price marking of each item and checkout errors could be virtually eliminated. Perpetual inventory information could be maintained in the system to reduce both ordering time and stockouts. Such a system could also greatly minimize shrink by pinpointing items that are not rung up at the checkstand. Valuable marketing information on customers and their shopping patterns could also be compiled by a full-scan system. Industry experts estimated that the potential savings from a full-scan system could be as much as 1 to 1½ percent of sales (as much or more than the industry net profit percent margins). According to a survey conducted by the Food Marketing Institute, there were 3,493 scanning installations as of March 1981, and almost 13 percent of the surveyed companies said they expected to be fully scanning by the end of that year.

Another aspect of the survey concerned company personnel staffing for scanning. Of those companies with scanning, 75 percent said they employed at least one person specifically for analyzing the scanning data. For those without such an individual, 16 percent expected to assign someone for this purpose in 1981 and 20 percent expected to do so in 1982. Most companies used their point-of-sale scanning data for monitoring checker performance, work scheduling and coupon allocation, and tracking specials. Other uses include checking on the price elasticity of items, new product evaluation, meat department analysis, and shelf allocation.

Albertson's Operations

Every Albertson's store was a full-line supermarket, with a meat department, produce, groceries, and nonfood items. Many stores had hot bakeries, and some offered a delicatessen and prepared hot foods for takeout. All stores carried a broad range of national brands and offered private labels in most merchandising categories. About 20 percent of Albertson's merchandise was private label, up from 5 percent in 1971. On most items, private labels had wider margins.

"It's good to shop in a well-run store" was Albertson's advertising theme during 1980. This emphasis on being responsible as well as efficient was directed at more knowledgeable and sophisticated consumers burdened with the pressures of spiraling inflation, higher cost of transportation, greater awareness of health and nutrition, and less shopping time.

Each store manager or "Store Director," as they were called, wore a gold-colored blazer jacket so that customers could easily identify and visit with him. He was identified in consumer advertising as the "Man in Gold," with the role of the consumer advisor as a part of his store-management duties. Management believed that customers were responding positively to this approach to personal service. A customer who complained was personally visited by the store manager and sometimes a division officer as soon as possible.

Consumer programs of the Company included:

"Tru-valu' unit pricing. Albertson's had been one of the industry leaders in showing on each shelf label the cost per ounce or other unit of measure for each packaged product.

Uniform beef labeling, using meat industry terminology.

Freshness code dating.

Buyer's choice ground beef program (which showed fat content in percentage).

"See-thru" meat trays.

Fresh bakery products without preservatives.

Longer hours for customer convenience (a number of Albertson's stores were open 24 hours a day, seven days a week).

The "Idea Tree"—a specially designed rack prominently displayed with over 27 different consumer-oriented pamphlets containing budgeting ideas, recipes, and food product information.

Albertson's management information system included both detailed cost controls and budgets and a sophisticated inventory control system. Store managers prepared operating budgets for a year ahead, these were reviewed by district and regional management, and, then were consolidated into a corporate budget. Corporate headquarters prepared weekly operating statements for each store, showing both budgeted and actual figures, and these statements were distributed to regional, district, and store managers, as well as to corporate staff divisions, along with labor analysis, product movement, gross margin by product, and other data.

The inventory control system was operated by computer. Normally, computerized inventory control was not considered feasible unless a supermarket company had its own distribution system. Since Albertson's supplied its stores primarily from outside wholesalers, it had arranged for its major suppliers to provide magnetic tape data on purchases for its inventory control system.

Electronic cash registers that were upgradable to scanning units had been installed in all new and remodeled Albertson's stores from 1974 onward. The Five-Mile Road store in Boise, opened in May 1976, was Albertson's first store to have fixed optical scanners (not wands) installed and operating full scan at the checkstands; however, price labels were still being placed on each packaged item on the shelves in order for customers to see the unit prices in the usual manner. The system had worked well, and Albertson's had proceeded with its plan to have the full-scan system in the majority of its stores by 1986.

At the end of 1980, Albertson's had 31 stores equipped with scanners and planned to add 35 more during 1981. The experiment in Boise had shown that customers could become used to the idea of having merchandise marked only on shelf labels and not on individual packages.

Skaggs—Albertson's

In order to diversify its retail operations and effectively penetrate new marketing areas, Albertson's entered into a partnership with Skaggs Companies, Inc., of Salt Lake City, Utah in 1970. This partnership, one of the first of its kind in retailing, developed large combination food–drug units to serve customers from a common set of checkout stands. During the seven-year life of this partnership, 58 new units were opened and sales increased from $31 million in 1970 to over $626 million in 1976. In January 1977, both companies decided that their partnership had grown large enough and that each could operate the food–drug stores with their own management teams. The partnership was terminated, and Albertson's took over the operation of 31 units in Alabama,

Florida, Louisiana, and Texas, and organized them into the company's Southco Division. Albertson's continued to build upon their experience in drug retailing; the November 1980 *Progressive Grocer* listed Albertson's as having the second largest number of in-store pharmacies in the national supermarket industry.

Growth and Market Share

There were three major thrusts in the expansion of Albertson's operations:

1. Building new stores.
2. Updating new stores through remodeling and renovation.
3. Increasing "backstage" distribution facilities.

Older stores that were declining in profitability were sold if they were not considered feasible to remodel or replace. Although in the past some new market areas such as Denver and Los Angeles had been entered by acquiring existing independent local food-chain stores, all of the new stores and remodels were currently being constructed by the Company's fully integrated property development function, which consisted of real-estate negotiations, lawyers, economic analysts, architects, and construction supervisors. Within the preceding 10-year period, 90 percent of the Albertson's stores had either been newly built or completely remodeled. About one-fourth of floor space was allocated to nonfood items in new stores. A five-year summary of the recent expansion program for Albertson's conventional supermarkets and combination units is shown in Table A.

Albertson's had three full-line distribution centers in the West: a 103,000 square foot center in Boise, Idaho; a 200,000 square foot center in Brea, California; a 340,000 square foot center in Salt Lake City, Utah. During 1981, Albertson's planned to begin construction of a new 338,000 square foot full-line distribution center in Denver to further serve the Rocky Mountain area. The total cost of this facility, scheduled to open in 1982, was expected to be

TABLE A
Albertson's Expansion

	Conventional Supermarkets				
Fiscal	Beginning	Added	Closed	Ending	Square Footage[a]
1976	252	16	7	261	6,135,000
1977	261	19	13	267	6,515,000
1978	267	64	14	317	8,179,000
1979	317	19	11	325	8,568,000
1980	325	14	12	327	8,780,000
	Combination Units				
Fiscal	Beginning	Added	Closed	Ending	Square Footage[a]
1976	26	6	1	31	1,685,000
1977	31	7		38	1,971,000
1978	38	11	1	48	2,536,000
1979	48	11		59	3,128,000
1980	59	10		69	3,666,000

[a] About 70 percent of total square footage is considered to be selling space.

approximately $16 million. Albertson's produce warehouses were operated in Seattle, San Jose, Portland, San Antonio, and Orlando; an additional 135,000 square foot meat and deli distribution center was located in Brea. During 1980, approximately 37 percent of the merchandise purchased for resale in Company supermarkets was received from Company distribution centers. However, management intended to continue to rely on its traditional method of using outside wholesale warehouses and seeking maximum investment return in retailing. At the same time, each operating area was continually being evaluated for other worthwhile distribution investments in the future.

Because of its broad geographical spread, Albertson's traditionally has not had dominant market share in any market except the Boise Valley. It should be noted that market share is difficult to evaluate for a supermarket company, because the stores serve a rather restricted defined market area reasonably close to a store. Geographical characteristics and the amount of competition can make a big difference. Within major defined marketing areas, a single store conceivably could have dominant market share of the area defined as its market, even though another company could have considerably more share of the overall market such as a city or area. Albertson's ability to utilize outside warehouse companies for its merchandise supply has given the company the flexibility to obtain the economies of scale without having market-share domination (see Exhibit 10).

The Company's smaller market share in most markets provides a special opportunity for future growth. Sites obtained in established areas can immediately take advantage of image and cost reduction. Albertson's was focusing its expansion program on established operating areas, along with what could be considered gradual expansion into other states or areas.

Probably Albertson's single greatest advantage from a market environment standpoint

EXHIBIT 10
Analysis of Albertson's Market Share by Major Markets

Boise Valley	33%
Spokane, Washington	19%
Seattle/Everett/Tacoma, Washington	7%
Richland/Kennewick/Pasco, Washington	11%
Montana	7%
Provo/Orem, Utah	20%
Salt Lake/Ogden, Utah	14%
Eugene, Oregon	11%
Portland, Oregon	10%
Southern California	5%
Las Vegas, Nevada	13%
Reno, Nevada	15%
San Jose, California	5%
Denver, Colorado	7%
Colorado Springs, Colorado	13%
Wyoming	9%
Albuquerque, New Mexico	8%
Orlando, Florida	10%
Tampa/St. Petersburg, Florida	13%
San Antonio, Texas	9%
Jacksonville, Florida	8%

Source: Investment Firm Study.

was the location of its market in fast-growing areas. The U. S. Bureau of the Census recently identified the 25 fastest-growing standard metropolitan statistical areas. Exhibit 11 shows that Albertson's has operations in 16 of these areas.

Organization and Management

Albertson's conventional supermarket operation was organized into nine geographical divisions (see Exhibit 12), in addition to the Southco Division of combination food–drug units. Each division included several districts, and each district in turn supervised 7–18 stores. Merchandising policy was a large part of each division's responsibility, recognizing the different nature of the various market areas. A profit center accountability was followed at all levels down to the store. A division staff as well as district managers were supervised by the vice president in charge of a division, and all vice presidents reported to the

EXHIBIT 11
25 Fastest Growing Standard Metropolitan Statistical Areas

Rank	SMSA	Population 1970 Census	Population 1980p Census	Percent Change 1970–1980
1.	Ft. Myers–Cape Coral, Fla.[a]	105,216	204,314	94.2%
2.	Las Vegas, Nev.[a]	273,288	462,218	69.1
3.	Sarasota, Fla.	120,413	201,731	67.5
4.	Ft. Collins, Colo.[a]	89,900	149,278	66.0
5.	Ft. Lauderdale–Hollywood, Fla.[a]	620,100	1,005,507	62.2
6.	Bryan–College Station, Tex.	57,978	93,487	61.2
7.	Reno, Nev.[a]	121,068	193,870	60.1
8.	W. Palm Beach–Boca Raton, Fla.[a]	348,993	551,961	58.2
9.	Provo–Orem, Utah[a]	137,776	217,281	57.7
10.	Phoenix, Ariz.	971,228	1,511,552	55.6
11.	McAllen–Pharr–Edinburg, Tex.	181,535	279,857	54.2
12.	Boise, Ida.[a]	112,230	172,843	54.0
13.	Richland–Kennewick–Pasco, Wash.[a]	93,356	143,287	53.5
14.	Orlando, Fla.[a]	453,270	694,645	53.3
15.	Tucson, Ariz.	351,667	531,896	51.2
16.	Santa Cruz, Calif.[a]	123,790	186,873	51.0
17.	Bradenton, Fla.[a]	97,115	146,048	50.4
18.	Brownsville–Harlingen–San Benito, Tex.	140,368	208,222	48.3
19.	Daytona Beach, Fla.	169,487	250,924	48.0
20.	Austin, Tex.	360,463	532,811	47.8
21.	Houston, Tex.	1,999,316	2,891,146	44.6
22.	Tallahassee, Fla.[a]	109,355	157,076	43.6
23.	Santa Rosa, Calif.[a]	204,885	292,275	42.7
24.	Tampa–St. Petersburg, Fla.[a]	1,088,549	1,550,035	42.4
25.	Lakeland–Winter Haven, Fla.[a]	228,515	321,919	40.9
	25 SMSA's Total	8,559,961	12,951,056	51.3%
	U. S. Total	203,302,031	226,504,825	11.4%

Source: U. S. Bureau of the Census; compilation by NAHB Economics Division.
[a] Areas Albertson's stores are located.

executive vice-president for operations. The latter, together with the corporate headquarters staff, reported to the President.

The organizational philosophy of Albertson's placed considerable emphasis on the role of the store manager. The organization chart that was displayed in the 1970 Annual Report (see Exhibit 13) was still representative of management's viewpoint on organization in 1981. Training received considerable emphasis in the company, and each division had its own training function in addition to the corporate training staff. Store management personnel were well paid and received a percentage of the store earnings each quarter.

Employees of Albertson's were largely unionized; more than 60 percent of the employees were covered by a total of over 350 separate union contracts. Management believed that one of the advantages of its labor relations program was its widespread geographical operation in that a problem with any one contract would not materially affect the entire company. Albertson's negotiated union contracts through employers associations in most areas.

EXHIBIT 12
Division Breakdown as of January 29, 1981

	Number of Stores
1. *Idaho Division*	26
Headquarters: Boise, Idaho	
Southern Idaho (21); Eastern Oregon (4); Elko, Nevada (1)	
2. *Inland Empire Division*	26
Headquarters: Spokane, Washington	
Eastern Washington (17); Northern Idaho (2); Montana (7)	
3. *Utah Division*	29
Headquarters: Salt Lake City, Utah	
Utah (28); Rock Springs, Wyoming (1)	
4. *Western Washington Division*	37
Headquarters: Seattle, Washington	
5. *Oregon Division*	38
Headquarters: Portland, Oregon	
Western Oregon (35), Washington (3)	
6. *Southern California Division*	80
Headquarters: Los Angeles, California	
Southern California (71); Southern Nevada (8); Yuma, Arizona (1)	
7. *Northern California Division*	47
Headquarters: San Francisco, California	
Northern California (42); Northern Nevada (5)	
8. *Rocky Mountain Division*	44
Headquarters: Denver, Colorado	
Colorado (28); Wyoming (4); New Mexico (12)	
9. *Southern Division*	69
Headquarters: Orlando, Florida	
Alabama (4); Florida (40); Louisiana (4); Texas (21)	
	396

Source: Corporate Profile, January 29, 1981.

Management policy was largely established by five executives: Warren E. McCain, Chairman of the Board, President, and Chief Executive Officer; Robert D. Bolinder, Vice-Chairman of the Board and Chief Financial and Administrative Officer; John Carley, Executive Vice-President, Retail Operations; Gary Michael, Executive Vice-President Corporate Development; Robert Huff, Executive Vice-President Distribution and Manufacturing.

Financial Matters

Albertson's common stock was first sold to the public in 1959 and was traded over-the-counter. In 1970, the company was first listed on the New York Stock Exchange, which at that time traded the stock of 1,300 of America's 1.4 million business firms. In 1981 there were over 14.8 million shares of Albertson's common stock outstanding, reflecting the two-for-one stock split that became effective March 14, 1980.

Albertson's leased most of its real estate. The typical lease period was 25 to 30 years, and most leases contained renewal options. Exercise of such options was dependent on the level of business conducted at the location. "Off-balance sheet financing" was the description given by investment analysts to Albertson's past use of sale and leaseback of new buildings, because the lease obligations had not shown directly in balance sheet accounts. Footnotes to the 1976 balance sheets revealed that net minimal rental (lease) payment commitments outstanding were about $303 million, which had a present value of about $135 million when discounted at an average interest rate of 7.8 percent. The Company's exceptional performance in long-term return on equity was attributed, in part, to the financing leverage of such noncapitalized leases. The Company gave up this accounting practice, however, and initiated an "Obligation Under Capital Leases" account on their January 28, 1978 balance sheets.

Total net lease payments in 1980 were $22.8 million, up from $20.4 million in 1979. For 1980, net payments on leases existing at the beginning of the fiscal year were projected at $18.6 million.

Interest payments in 1980 were $8.3 million and in 1979 $8.4 million. Short-term financing was obtained primarily through borrowings on unsecured lines of credit from

EXHIBIT 13
Organization Chart

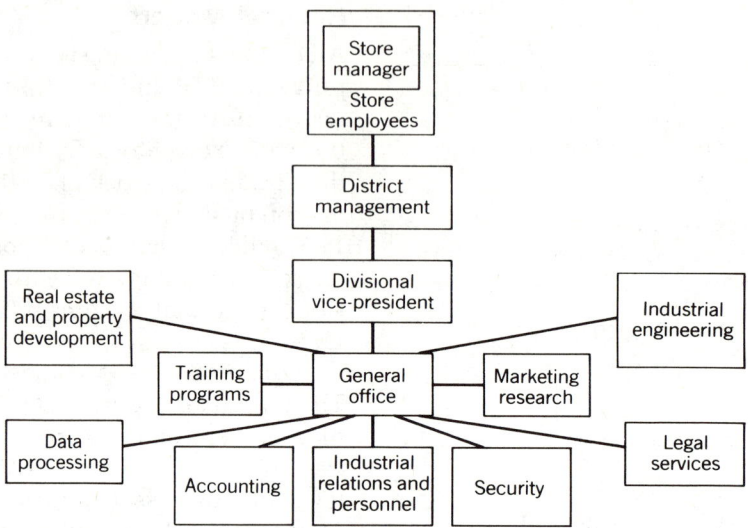

"Are We A Backward Company?"

Well, in one respect. Our organization chart starts in reverse when compared with other corporations. At the very top is the store manager and his people who serve our customers . . .

A typical Albertson's supermarket with its grocery, meat, produce, variety and complex in-store production bakery is a complex business unit . . . and its manager must be a man of many talents . . .

Would you believe he is chief buyer, price setter, goal setter, advertising manager, personnel director, community relations expert, teacher, money manager, accountant, building supervisor, safety engineer, security agent, and merchandise promoter. Enough? No wonder Albertson's puts him at the top of the organization chart . . .

The Company is not interested in building empires for headquarters executives . . . our primary concern is developing the store manager and his people. In the end this is the only place it really counts. Motivated by one of the most forward looking bonus systems, our Albertson's manager is taught to run his store as though he owns it . . .

Source: Annual Report, Fiscal Year Ended March 28, 1970.

---

banks. In 1981, Albertson's had short-term lines of credit at the prime interest rate of 23.5 million, and it was required to maintain compensating balances of 7½ to 10 percent of the total lines of credit plus 7½ to 10 percent of the credit utilized. The company, as of 1981, had not used short-term financing for three years. A five-year summary of Albertson's financial ratios is shown in Exhibit 14.

Future Plans

The outlook of the food-retailing industry was described by industry publications as generally difficult and unpromising for the early 1980s. Among the major problems besetting food retailers were:

1. The sluggish economy, with the austere Reagen Administration economic plan fore-

EXHIBIT 14
Five-Year Financial Ratios

	1980	1979	1978	1977	1976
Working Capital Ratios					
Working capital (in thousands)	$111,806	$ 99,343	$ 79,272	$ 46,007	$ 38,727
Working capital ratio	1.57 to 1	1.59 to 1	1.43 to 1	1.38 to 1	1.40 to 1
Profitability Ratios					
Return on equity	21.7%	23.6%	27.4%	22.9%	18.3%
Return on debt and equity	15.0%	15.4%	19.0%	17.2%	13.4%
Return on debt, equity and obligations under capital leases	10.4%	10.3%	11.7%	9.9%	8.1%
Return on total assets	6.9%	6.8%	7.6%	6.8%	5.5%
Return on sales	1.4%	1.4%	1.6%	1.4%	1.1%
Leverage Ratios					
Long-term debt including obligations under capital leases to equity	98.1%	118.6%	138.9%	132.3%	131.9%
Long-term debt including obligations under capital leases to total assets	32.7%	36.9%	37.4%	38.5%	39.0%
Long-term debt to debt and equity	28.4%	32.5%	36.4%	26.7%	25.6%
Long-term debt including obligations under capital leases to debt, equity, and obligations under capital leases	49.5%	54.2%	58.1%	56.9%	56.9%
Equity to debt and equity	71.6%	67.5%	63.6%	73.3%	74.4%
Pre-tax fixed charge coverage ratio	2.56x	2.53x	2.78x	2.58x	2.29x
Activity Ratios					
Inventory turnover	13.1x	12.8x	12.8x	13.5x	13.8x
Sales to working capital	29.6 to 1	30.6 to 1	38.4 to 1	42.6 to 1	35.0 to 1
Sales to total assets	5.1 to 1	4.8 to 1	4.7 to 1	5.0 to 1	4.8 to 1

shadowing a recessionary decline in late 1981.
2. Changing consumption patterns of shoppers as they cope with inflation.
3. High energy costs.
4. Labor cost increases that outstrip productivity gains.
5. Record costs of financing that slow shopping center development and limit opportunities to open new units, even in fast-growing population centers.
6. Regional price wars as competition grows for market share in older areas oversaturated with stores.

Despite this unfavorable industry-wide scenario, 1981 earnings prospects for grocery chain operators were classified as mixed. Well-positioned, efficiently managed firms were expected to be able to prosper, even while their competitors suffered in the tough operating environment. Factors differentiating individual operators included geographic concentration (especially in the Sun Belt), expansion capability, competitive vulnerability, degree of diversification, relations with labor, modernity of facilities, management's ability to innovate or adjust to innovations, and merchandising strategy. Relative strength or weakness in these diverse areas was expected to determine the performance of industry participants.

Gross National Product was forecast by *Predicasts* to increase 10.8 percent in current dollars and 3.0 percent in real dollars annually through 1990. A quoted forecast for aggregate U.S. grocery stores sales growth to 1988 was 5.4 percent annually, as measured in current dollars.

Robert Bolinder recognized several changes in the business environment that could affect Albertson's way of doing business:

1. Concern over food prices and food expenditures as a percent of disposable income would put pressure on improving productivity, store design, and merchandising concepts.

2. The need to reduce time and distance necessary to shop would require more "one-stop" stores with a wider assortment of merchandise, including nonfood items.

3. "Eating out" would have an effect on grocery sales.

EXHIBIT 15
Capital Required for New Stores

	1/31/82	1/31/83	1/31/84	1/31/85	1/31/86
Equipment					
New stores:					
Albertson's					
Square footage	$ 638,737	$ 760,000	$ 760,000	$ 760,000	$ 760,000
Per square foot (10% inflation)	$ 17.95	$ 19.74	$ 21.71	$ 23.88	$ 26.27
Amount	$11,465,000	$15,000,000	$16,500,000	$ 18,100,000	$ 20,000,000
Southco					
Square footage	452,460	520,000	520,000	520,000	520,000
Per square foot (10% inflation)	$ 17.20	$ 18.92	$ 20.81	$ 22.89	$ 25.17
Amount	$ 7,765,000	$ 9,800,000	$10,800,000	$ 11,900,000	$ 13,100,000
Westco					
Square footage	60,898	300,000	300,000	300,000	360,000
Per square foot (10% inflation)	$ 17.50	$ 19.25	$ 21.17	$ 23.29	$ 25.62
Amount	$ 1,070,000	$ 5,800,000	$ 6,400,000	$ 7,000,000	$ 9,200,000
Grand Total Equipment—					
New Stores	$20,300,00	$30,600,000	$33,700,000	$37,000,000	$ 42,300,000
Capital needed for remodels					
Equipment—remodels	7,300,000	8,000,000	8,800,000	9,700,000	10,700,000
Equipment—replacement	2,500,000	3,000,000	3,300,000	3,600,000	4,000,000
Total store equipment	$30,100,000	$41,600,000	$45,800,000	$ 50,300,000	$ 57,000,000
Real Estate					
New stores:					
Average per square foot	$ 41.60	$ 45.76	$ 50.33	$ 55.36	$ 60.90
Total square footage	1,151,095	1,580,000	1,580,000	1,580,000	1,640,000
Amount—new stores	47,900,000	72,300,000	79,500,000	87,500,000	99,900,000
Amount—remodels	8,900,000	11,000,000	12,700,000	14,700,000	16,900,000
Total store real estate	$56,800,000	$83,300,000	$92,200,000	$102,200,000	$116,800,000

EXHIBIT 16
Five-Year Balance Sheet—Projections (000 omitted)

	1/31/82	1/31/83	1/31/84	1/31/85	1/31/86
Assets					
Current assets	$332,700	$348,600	$374,600	$401,500	$ 437,900
Fixed and other assets	367,700	432,100	493,100	572,600	652,400
	$700,400	$780,700	$871,700	$974,100	$1,090,300
Liabilities and Capital					
Current liabilities	$203,800	$217,700	$233,000	$249,800	$ 269,000
Deferred items	22,200	26,000	30,200	34,800	39,900
Capital:					
Long-term debt	79,400	76,000	72,600	67,500	62,400
Obligations under capital leases	153,000	180,500	209,500	241,500	274,500
Stockholders' equity	242,000	280,500	326,400	380,500	444,500
Total Capital	$474,400	$537,000	$608,500	$689,500	$ 781,400
	$700,400	$780,700	$871,700	$974,100	$1,090,300
Stockholders equity as a percent					
to total capital	51.0%	52.2%	53.6%	55.2%	56.9%
to total assets	34.6%	35.9%	37.4%	39.1%	40.8%
Ratio of long-term debt and obligations under capital leases to stockholders' equity	0.96–1	0.91–1	0.86–1	0.81–1	0.76–1
50 percent of real estate—sale-leaseback uncapitalized off balance sheet	$ 28,400	$ 36,500	$ 40,000	$ 44,000	$ 50,000

4. More convenience foods.
5. Larger quantity sales, such as case lots.

"We have led out in such areas as consumer programs," Bolinder commented. "We are definitely large enough in the industry to lead out when we have the foresight and courage." He added that Albertson's was still committed to the strategies of "aggressively meeting or challenging all price competition" and an "aggressive expansion program." Capital expenditure projections for the five years ending January 31, 1986 are shown in Exhibit 15.

Plans for the expansion of Albertson's stores included emphasis in the Company's current area of operations and expansion into the states of Nebraska and South Dakota (the Westco Division). Funds for expansion over the next five years were projected to be obtained primarily from earnings and sale and leaseback of stores, with a gradual reduction in long-term debt. Albertson's was projecting a 130 percent increase over 1980 sales by 1986 and anticipated no need to add outside funds to working capital during that time period (see Exhibits 16 and 17).

EXHIBIT 17
Five-Year Working Capital Projection Five Years Ending 1/31/86

	1/31/82	1/31/83	1/31/84	1/31/85	1/31/86
Estimated sales	$3,472,000	$4,042,000	$4,813,000	$5,699,000	$6,719,000
Annual increase in sales	14%	16%	19%	18%	18%
Earnings as a percent of sales	1.32%	1.30%	1.30%	1.30%	1.30%
Working capital provided from:					
Earnings	46,000	52,500	62,600	74,100	87,400
Per share, (15,450)	$3.00	$3.40	$4.05	$4.80	$5.66
Depreciation and amortization	35,000	40,000	46,000	53,000	61,000
Deferred taxes and investment credit	3,500	3,800	4,200	4,600	5,100
Capital leases and real estate financing—stores	56,800	73,000	80,000	88,000	100,000
—manufacturing and distribution	12,400	3,000	3,000	5,000	3,000
	$ 153,700	$ 172,300	$ 195,800	$ 224,700	$ 256,500
Working capital applied to:					
Payment of long-term debt	3,400	3,400	3,400	5,100	5,100
Reduction in obligations—long-term leases	10,000	12,000	14,000	17,000	20,000
Dividends	13,000	14,000	16,700	20,000	23,400
Additions to fixed assets:					
Stores:					
Real estate and leasehold	56,800	83,300	92,200	102,200	116,800
Equipment	30,100	41,600	45,800	50,300	57,000
Scanning	5,000	6,000	7,000	8,000	5,000
Manufacturing and distribution:					
Real estate	12,500	2,000	2,000	5,000	5,000
Equipment	4,800	3,000	3,000	5,000	5,000
Office	1,000	5,000	1,000	2,000	2,000
Total fixed assets	$ 110,200	$ 140,900	$ 151,000	$ 172,500	$ 190,800
Total working capital applied	$ 136,600	$ 170,300	$ 185,100	$ 214,600	$ 239,300
Increase in working capital	17,100	2,000	10,700	10,100	17,200
Working capital at beginning of period	111,800	128,900	130,900	141,600	151,700
Working capital at end of period	$ 128,900	$ 130,900	$ 141,600	$ 151,700	$ 168,900

Parker Drilling Company (1984)

History

Parker Drilling Company was started in 1934 by Gifford C. Parker who had spent 20 years drilling oil and water wells. Parker had been involved in a number of ventures prior to the 1934 start of Parker Drilling Company. Although the Depression made success difficult for Parker, the economic recovery of the late 1930s and the war spurred growth and prosperity for the Parker Drilling Company. At the close of the war in 1945, the company dispatched four rigs to Venezuela to drill for the Atlantic–Richfield Company and one rig to Pincher Creek, Alberta, Canada. By the late 1940s Parker had five rigs drilling in Venezuela and 12 rigs operating in Canada, but by the early 1950s, G. C. Parker sold the Venezuelan and Canadian operations. G. C. Parker commented that he had sold his international operations because they were too far from home.

At the age of 31, G. C. Parker's son, Robert L. Parker, Sr., bought the company from his father in 1954 by meeting the highest of five price bids for the firm. The company immediately entered a five-year industry-wide slump in drilling activity. The company struggled, but survived although many of its competitors folded. During these lean years, R. L. Parker realized that he would have to develop a new thrust or continuously fight for survival as part of the pack. Bob Parker's analysis was basic and straightforward. He saw three alternatives for his company. First, he could "get wet," that is, expand Parker's expertise into offshore drilling. Second, he could go deep; this was an unexplored area. Deep drilling was something that had only been hinted at as a new frontier for exploration. Third, he could increase his company's international emphasis. Bob Parker recalled,

> This was before deep gas was discovered, and it was a large gamble to try to go deep, but when I sat down and analyzed it, building a rig to go deep made more sense than hocking the company to go offshore. The difference between going deep and going offshore was astounding. Going deep would cost, per rig, about one-twentieth the cost of going offshore; in addition, there was no competition in the deep field. Of course, there was still some doubt about deep drilling. There was interest in it, but you had to ask yourself how long that interest would last, especially if you found nothng. There were no rigs to 17,000 feet. I went to Gulf and asked what rate they would pay for a rig that could drill to that depth. The rates they quoted were exciting.

The result was a commitment by Bob Parker in the mid-1960s for a total of eight deep-drilling rigs. It was a commitment for more money than Bob Parker had originally paid for Parker Drilling, but first it had to work. The first major deep effort was in Pecos County, Texas for Gulf Oil. Much to Parker's relief, the wells paid off. Very quickly, the demand grew for deeper holes to tap the earth's resources. In addition, Bob Parker decided to go international by expanding a small-scale operation for Gulf Oil in Libya.

The style of the two Parkers was in sharp contrast. G. C. Parker was a gruff and tough task manager. R. L. Parker defines his style as "we're in this together, so let's find a solution together."

In the late 1960s Parker's decision to go deep and to enter foreign operations was going well. Indeed, a third key decision was made by Bob Parker during this period. This decision was to respond to the needs of the marketplace. Bob Parker recalled,

---

Source: Prepared by Robert E. Schellenberger, East Carolina University. Permission for use granted by the author.

Drilling in South America was tough. Transportation was difficult, and many of the locations were so remote, that the only way you could reach them was by helicopter. The obvious answer to the problem of drilling under such conditions was a helicopter-transportable rig. However, no one had ever successfully built a rig that could be both transported by helicopter and tough enough to reach desired depths under adverse conditions. Attempts to lighten the rig had reduced its reliability and durability. Substituting aluminum, for example, was an effective way to cut out weight but gave you a weaker rig. We decided that we would build one that would work.

The assignment to build such a rig was given to Ted Houck who had joined the company in 1937 as a 77¢ per day rig hand. Houck had become a student of drilling and rig design. He was a self-taught expert about drilling rigs, whose expertise had been gained through practical rig-floor experience and study. He was teamed with Ed Phillips, who had an engineering degree and could help translate Houck's practical ideas into reality. In March 1967, a new rig named the HELI-HOIST 1250 made its debut. It worked, primarily because they had discovered new ways to break down a conventional rig into component parts resulting in 109 loads of less than 3900 pounds each.

An additional factor that seemed to indicate a rosy future for the company was a major government contract to drill large diameter holes up to 120-inches-diameter and 6500-feet-deep for the Atomic Energy Commission's tests on Amchitka Island.

Then the roof caved in. Six months after Parker went public, the government of Bolivia nationalized the holdings of Gulf Oil Company. It was October 1969. In addition to the Bolivian shutdown, Parker's four rigs in Colombia were idle for five months because of delays in the drilling programs of Parker Drilling's customers. Also, during 1969, the company constructed, assembled, and winterized five drilling rigs that were delivered to the north slope of Alaska. Because of environmental and production delays, those rigs remained idle for a lengthy period of time. Then, because of cuts in the federal budget, the Atomic Energy Commission halted tests on Amchitka Island. Further, the slowdown in the economy and the availability of "cheap foreign oil" reduced domestic drilling activity.

However, recovery from this adversity began unabated in 1971, and the company again saw an extended period of growth and expansion. During the 12-year span from fiscal 1971 to fiscal 1982, the company sales increased steadily from $27,000,320 to $615,861,000. Likewise, net income increased from $1,000,439 to $76,335,000. Income in 1982 was down from the high of $79,007,000 in 1981. Commenting on the decline in income, the 1982 annual report stated:

> The company's fourth quarter results begin to reflect the negative market conditions which could continue to affect us during much of the upcoming year. Few people saw this change coming one year ago. Our customers did not, nor did we. Several significant changes occurred in our country's economy and in U. S. markets for oil and gas which triggered almost overnight cancellations of many drilling programs. This immediately created an oversupply of U. S. rigs and a very weak domestic market. A recovery from this industry imbalance probably will be slow to occur. We may even see conditions worsen before they improve. Fortunately, our international operations are doing well and providing important financial support to the company. Thus, tightening our belts, reducing our overhead, and disciplining our financial controls are our top priorities.

The Drilling Business

Parker Drilling Company defines itself as a publicly held drilling contractor providing drilling services to major oil companies, independent oil and gas producers, governments, and industrial users that develop their energy sources. Parker specializes in deep drilling (below 15,000 feet) and operates in remote and inaccessible areas from Papua New Guinea to the Arctic zones from South American jungles to environmentally protected areas of the United States. Parker Drilling Company has two wholly-owned subsidiaries, Perry Gas Companies, Inc. based in Odessa, Texas, which specializes in transporting, treating, and processing natural gas, and O.I.M.E. Inc., also based in Odessa, which along with its subsidiary Power Masts and Substructures, Inc., located in Del City, Oklahoma, designs, manufactures, and assembles drilling rigs and major rig components. Over 5200 persons are employed by Parker Drilling Company throughout the world.

The company's 1982 income statement shows $525,945,000 revenue from drilling contracts, $45,627,000 from manufacturing and construction, $38,518,000 from gas transportation and treating, and $5,771,000 from other operating income. In 1982 Parker consolidated its two manufacturing companies into one. The parent is O.I.M.E., a rig-building subsidiary located in Odessa, Texas. Its subsidiary, Power Masts and Substructures, is located in Del City, Oklahoma. O.I.M.E. has been the location of a majority of the R & D activities that have led Parker to its position as one of the top drilling companies in the world. The Odessa location is used for development, end assembly, and testing of rigs as a wholly owned subsidiary of Parker. In 1975, the subsidiary increased its commitment to custom-building deep-drilling rigs. In the late 1970s, the production of rigs for sale to other drillers began to exceed the number built for Parker's use. Indeed, the 1980 annual report said, "Their (O.I.M.E.) ability to build and deliver rigs within 60 days provides Parker with a significant edge over competition in new rig delivery." In 1980, O.I.M.E. built five rigs for Parker plus 18 rigs and other components for outside customers. In 1981, total revenue for O.I.M.E. and Power Masts and Substructures was $154,307,000 of which $69,219,000 was from Parker and $85,088,000 was from outside customers. In 1982 total revenue was $122,350,000, of which $45,627,000 was from outside customers.

In 1980 Parker acquired Perry Gas Company, Inc., as a diversification move outside of the drilling industry. The company saw this move as consistent because Perry was in a field in which the company had knowledge and experience. Perry provides energy services for treating, processing, transporting, and selling natural gas. Perry, based in Odessa, Texas, had major facilities throughout Texas and its Gas Transmission Group stretches across Texas with approximately 750 miles of pipeline. Major lines owned by Perry are the Giddings System, Palo Duro System Line, the Imperial and Pecos River Systems, and the MonDak System in Montana. Perry's gas and oil production group is headquartered in Midland, Texas. This group has the capability to operate its own wells and owns acreage in Texas, Kansas, and New Mexico. Perry has expanded both acreage and pipeline miles since its acquisition by Parker.

Market Considerations

Worldwide demand for energy and international domestic political factors are critical in the operations of a company as widely distributed as Parker. In 1982 the company had 138 rigs, of which 71 were in the continental United States, 10 in Alaska, 12 in Canada, 25 in various countries of South America (including Jamaica), 12 in Indonesia (including Papua, New Guinea), 4 in various countries of Africa, and 4 in both the Middle East and India. As the experiences of 1969 and 1970 clearly show, the company is affected by legal, social, and political factors. Many of these factors are hard to assess and anticipate; however, worldwide energy demands keep increasing. The presence of the Organization of Petroleum Exporting Countries (OPEC) and energy shortages have made many countries want either energy independence or to develop energy resources for sale to other countries. Further, most of the energy resources, particularly oil and natural gas, that were easily accessible, (i.e., accessible at drilling levels above 15,000 feet) have already been drilled. Indeed, it is reported that most of the natural gas reserves available for energy have not been found, have not been drilled, and exist at deep-drilling levels. The advantage Parker has in the face of this demand can be clearly recognized. During 1978 about 330 new land rigs were added to the U.S. market, however, only 50 of these rigs were rated at 20,000 feet or deeper. Of those new U.S. rigs, Parker accounted for approximately 30 percent.

Indeed, the continued research and development has tended to aid Parker's position in the marketplace; in addition to its emphasis on deep drilling and the HELI-HOIST rig it has expanded the concept to TBA (transportable by anything). The concept is the same as the HELI-HOIST rig, where the rig is divided into multiple components for later assembly on-site. It has further continued its development of drilling activity in inaccessible and difficult-to-work-in site locations. It has received widespread attention for its pioneering work in drilling activities that do not disturb the surrounding environment. Although the company has not been engaged in offshore drilling *per se*, it has rented drilling rigs to organizations with offshore drilling platforms. It has used gravel platforms offshore in relatively shallow waters. It is capable of placing its rigs on such platforms in areas as diverse as Alaska and the Great Salt Lake in Utah.

In the United States, Canada, and Alaska the desire for energy independence and the concern for the environment have produced uncertainties, slowdowns, and booms in drilling activity. Further, the regulation of oil and natural gas prices have produced similar results. The 1979 act deregulating natural gas found at levels below 15,000 feet increased demand. While deregulation of oil and natural gas will in the long run considerably enhance drilling activity in the United States, uncertainties regarding natural gas prices, a gas supply excess, the general economic slowdown, and a shrinking of investment dollars makes the short-run domestic market weak.

One consideration that bodes well for Parker is the entry of foreign governments and foreign companies into natural gas exploration because of the ability to liquify and ship such gas to industrial markets.

Drilling Activities

The 1977 annual report suggested that Parker was comfortable with the fact that 43 or one-half of its 86 rigs were operating in the United States and Canada. Nevertheless, the movement in rig count from 1974 through 1982 shows the United States with a higher percentage in rigs than 1974; going from 33 of 69 rigs in 1974 to 94 of 138 in 1982. In addition to the company's desire to maintain a reasonably comfortable mix in foreign and domestic rig assignments, the company also has sought to maintain a reasonable customer mix of major oil companies, independents, governments, and industrial users. The company reports that the company's 20 largest customers accounted for approximately 60 percent of revenue during fiscal 1982 and no single customer accounted for more than 10 percent of the company's contract drilling revenue; approximately 82 percent of the company's current customers previously have used its services during the past five years.

Exhibit 1 shows the number of rigs being utilized by geographic area.

In 1979, the company began a comprehensive rig restoration program. The drilling capacities of each of the rigs can be understood by viewing the distribution of rigs by drilling capacities: twelve with a capacity of 10,000 feet or less, 13 with a capacity of 15,000 feet, 15 with a capacity of 17,000 feet, 55 with a capacity of 20,000 feet, 25 with a capacity of 25,000

EXHIBIT 1
Summary of Rig Assignments by Fiscal Year End

Country	1982	1981	1980	1979	1978	1977	1976	1975
United States								
1. Texas, Oklahoma, New Mexico	53	48	36	33	32	24	24	23
2. Rocky Mountains	14	15	14	14	14	9	6	7
3. Louisiana	4	4	6	6	5	0	0	0
4. Alaska	10	11	9	8	8	10	10	8
Canada	12	11	12	13	6	6	6	6
South America, Jamaica	25	21	17	15	18	18	22	22
Indonesia, Papua	12	11	9	9	8	7	7	8
Africa	4	10	13	13	11	11	5	2
Middle East, India	4	3	1	1	0	1	0	0
Europe	0	1	0	0	0	0	0	0
Total	138	135	117	112	102	86	80	76

feet, and 18 with a capacity of 30,000 feet or over.

Personnel

Since 1948 Parker has had a policy of "no drinking" for all of its employees, management, and operatives. This policy, which is well known throughout the petroleum industry, was not instituted to reflect the personal morality of the company's top management. It is very practical. As Bob Parker, Sr. noted, when discussing the subject in *Forbes*, "When there is a blow-out on a well, it's not the time to go looking for the drilling superintendent at a party." The result according to the analysis by *Forbes* is, "Parker's crews have a reputation for dependability, a reputation that is money in the bank in this business where time is very much money." The article goes on to point out that Parker's reputation is built on innovative technology, well-maintained rigs, and dependability.

It is clear in discussions with Parker employees close to Bob Parker, Sr. that he deeply cares for and is deeply respected by his employees. Some time ago, one long-time employee stated that many employees in the company thought that Bobby "hung on the moon." He also said Bobby was constantly doing something for people in and out of the company. For example, there were no neighborhood stores in Bolivia or Colombia where parents could buy American Christmas trees for their kids. Shortly before Christmas, he sent members of his Tulsa staff scurrying to toy departments to pick out a raft of goodies that, in turn, were flown into the arms of his employees' children. At one point, Mr. Parker stated that "people were hired for what they were and not for what they had done education-wise." The company pays well above scale and has little trouble attracting top-flight workers. Exceptionally good housekeeping on all drilling rigs is insisted upon. Robert Parker, Sr. is not ashamed of his Christian beliefs. He sometimes sends ministers to visit far-flung rigs. The dangers of drilling activities and the need for safety were recognized as early as 1950 when the company appointed a safety director. Further evidence of the character of Robert Parker, Sr. can be seen when prior to public offering of the company stock in 1969, Parker made arrangements to transfer shares of stock to several long-time employees.

Bob Parker, Jr. was elected President and Chief Operating Officer at Parker Drilling

Company in 1977 after a number of years with the company. Bob Parker, Jr. is considered the perfect synthesis of the tough–gruff G. C. Parker and the kind, friendly, participative Bob Parker, Sr. Bob Jr. is an MBA graduate of the University of Texas in 1972. The corporate officers and directors are each described in the following pages.

Robert L. Parker, Sr. (59) is Chairman and Chief Executive Officer of Parker Drilling Company. A petroleum engineering graduate of the University of Texas, Mr. Parker has headed the company since 1954. He is chairman of the board of Saint Francis Hospital and serves as a board member of the Bank of Oklahoma, N.A., Enterra Corporation, Chicago Bridge and Iron Company, Facet Enterprises, Inc., Newpark Resources, Inc., and Philadelphia Suburban Corporation. Mr. Parker also is a board member of the American Petroleum Institute, the International Association of Drilling Contractors, the Independent Petroleum Association of America, and serves on the development board of the University of Texas. Mr. Parker served as chairman of the U. S. Department of Energy Task Force, which wrote the National Energy Plan III.

Robert L. Parker, Jr. (54) was elected President and Chief Operating Officer of Parker Drilling Company in 1977. A graduate of the University of Texas with an MBA in finance, Mr. Parker has served on the board of directors of Parker Drilling since 1973. He has served the company as a contract representative, vice president, and executive vice-president. Mr. Parker is a member of the board of Alaska Airlines, Baker Drilling Company, the International Association of Drilling Contractors, and the University of Tulsa. He also is an advisory director for the Bank of Oklahoma, N.A.

J. Roger Collins (41), Senior Vice-President, is responsible for the company's administrative functions. He is a graduate of Princeton University and received his MBA from the University of Chicago Graduate School of Business. Mr. Collins was executive vice-president and director of a wholly owned subsidiary of Skelly Oil Company prior to joining Parker in May 1976 as vice president. He also serves as a trustee of Hillcrest Medical Center.

William R. Jackson (52), Senior Vice-President, joined Parker Drilling in July 1951. Mr. Jackson's responsibilities include the company's manufacturing operations as well as those of Perry Gas Company. Mr. Jackson has served the company in a variety of capacities, including accounting, price auditing, purchasing, international operations, contract administrator, corporate treasurer, and assistant secretary. Jackson was promoted to assistant vice-president in 1969 and was elected vice president in 1973.

Doris E. Miles (59), Senior Vice-President and Corporate Secretary, joined Parker Drilling in 1946. Her background with Parker includes extensive experience in accounting, purchasing, and expediting material for the company's international operations. Elected a vice president in 1975, she is primarily responsible for company-wide logistics.

R. Michael Still (37), Senior Vice-President and Chief Financial Officer, joined the Parker Drilling Company in 1973. He was named vice-president of finance and treasurer in 1976. A graduate of Oklahoma State University with a BS degree in physics, Mr. Still received his MBA from the University of Rochester.

James W. Linn (36), Senior Vice-President, responsible for North American operations, joined Parker Drilling in 1973. He is a graduate of the University of Oklahoma with a *juris doctor*. Mr. Linn has served in Parker Drilling's international division and was northern U. S. district manager prior to being elected a vice president in 1979. He was promoted to his current position in September 1981.

Robert M. Wadlow (41), Senior Vice-President, is responsible for corporate development and acquisitions. He is a graduate of the University of Oklahoma with a degree in engineering and he received his MBA from Southern Methodist University. He joined Parker Drilling Company in January 1975 and became assistant vice-president in October 1976. He was named vice-president of finance in 1979 and senior vice-president September 1981.

Ronnie R. McKenzie (45), Vice President, western hemisphere/international operations, joined Parker Drilling in 1963 after graduating from the University of Tulsa. He has held management responsibilities throughout the company's South American operations and directed its Singapore division. He was western hemisphere division manager before being named vice president in 1979.

John R. Robertson, Vice President, eastern hemisphere/international operations, joined Parker Drilling Company in 1974 as international division counsel. He is a graduate of the University of Tulsa with a *juris doctor* degree. Prior to his present position, Mr. Roberson served two years as division manager in Lima, Peru.

I. E. Hendrix Jr. (39), Treasurer, joined Parker Drilling in 1976 as manager of the company's treasury department. Mr. Hendrix holds a degree in business from Oklahoma Christian College and an MBA in finance from the University of Oklahoma. Prior to joining Parker, Hendrix was a management consultant with a major accounting firm.

John Savolainen (39) was named Controller of Parker Drilling Company in June 1980. He joined the company in 1978 as finance manager and was named manager of the company's manufacturing and corporate development operations in 1979. Mr. Savolainen is a graduate of Oklahoma State University with a BS degree and he received his MBA in finance from the University of Texas. Prior to joining Parker, he worked for Agrico Chemical Company.

Finance

Eight years of consolidated Income Statements and Balance Sheets are shown in Exhibits 2 and 3. Also shown is a three-year statement of Revenue, Operating Income, and Assets by business and geographic area.

Notes to Financial Statements

Note 1—Summary of Significant Accounting Policies

Consolidation The consolidated financial statements include the accounts of Parker Drilling Company and all of its majority owned subsidiaries (the "company").

Drilling contracts The company recognizes revenue and expenses from each of its drilling contracts as the drilling progresses (daywork contracts) because the company does not bear the risk of completion of the well, as would be the case under other types of contracts.

Gas Transportation and Treating Gas transportation and treating revenue is reported net of the related cost of purchased gas.

Capitalized Interest The company capitalizes interest applicable to the construction of drilling and other equipment. Interest capitalized during the three years ended August 31, 1982, 1981, and 1980 was $1,553,000, $1,987,000, and $526,000.

Property, Plant, and Equipment The company provides for depreciation of property, plant, and equipment primarily on the straight line method over the estimated useful lives of the assets after provision for salvage value. Gain or loss on sales of property, plant, and equipment is treated as an adjustment to accumulated depreciation.

Income Taxes Income taxes for financial statement purposes are calculated on income before income taxes as reported in the consolidated statement of income. Certain items of income and expense are included in the financial statements in different years than they are included in the tax return. The resulting difference between the financial statement income-tax provision and income tax currently payable as shown in the tax return is reported in the financial statements as deferred income tax. The company provides for deferred taxes on undistributed earnings of its foreign subsidiaries and its Domestic International Sales Corporation.

The company reflects investment tax credits as

EXHIBIT 2
Consolidated Income Statement Year Ending August 31 (in $1000s)

	1982	1981	1980	1979	1978	1977	1976	1975
Revenue								
Drilling income	$525,945	$457,336	$339,899	$274,938	$218,350	$141,791	$114,354	$107,733
Gas transportation and treating	38,518	37,340	0	0	0	0	0	0
Other[a]	51,398	87,634	43,181	29,866	22,724	14,284	13,809	4,255
Total Revenue	615,861	582,310	383,080	304,804	241,074	156,075	128,163	111,988
Costs and expenses								
Drilling expense	260,704	250,612	193,579	159,124	126,535	82,631	65,080	67,767
Other operating expenses[a]	45,844	62,701	31,452	20,478	17,112	11,953	10,531	1,802
Depreciation (Note 1 and 4)	75,407	55,008	38,917	31,467	22,277	16,798	14,844	11,380
General and administrative	53,190	44,361	30,209	21,896	18,370	12,283	9,655	6,356
Gas transportation and treating	13,152	9,869	0	0	0	0	0	0
Total costs and expenses	448,297	422,551	294,157	232,965	184,295	123,665	100,110	87,305
Operating income	167,554	159,759	88,923	71,839	56,779	32,410	28,053	24,683
Other income (and expense)								
Interest	(49,628)	(34,286)	(23,105)	(17,557)	(10,623)	(6,665)	(5,294)	(4,679)
Minority interest	(3,991)	(1,373)	(387)	0	0	0	0	0
Other—net	5,358	888	(378)	1,791	2,215	1,444	518	(258)
Total other income and expense	(48,261)	(34,771)	(23,870)	(15,766)	(8,408)	(5,521)	(4,776)	(4,937)
Income before taxes	119,293	124,988	65,053	56,073	48,371	26,890	23,277	19,746
Income taxes (Notes 1 and 4)								
Current	24,649	24,970	12,596	12,046	14,804	8,813	4,221	3,475
Deferred	18,309	21,011	12,664	8,060	2,380	2,661	4,697	4,196
Total taxes	42,958	45,981	25,260	20,106	17,184	11,474	8,918	7,671
Net income	$ 76,335	$ 79,007	$ 39,793	$ 35,967	$ 31,187	$ 15,415	$ 14,359	$ 12,075

[a] Primarily from manufacturing and construction.

a reduction of federal income taxes in the year in which the credit arises ("flow-through" method).

Earnings Per Share Earnings per common share and common equivalent share were computed by dividing net income, after adjusting for dividends on preferred stock, by the weighted average number of common shares and common stock equivalents (common shares issued or issuable under stock options) outstanding during each year.

Earnings per share assuming full dilution are based on the shares outstanding above plus the number of common shares that would have been issued assuming the $8\frac{1}{2}$ percent notes, fully converted in January 1981, had been converted into common stock at the beginning of the year. Interest expense net of income taxes on the convertible notes is eliminated.

Note 2—Accounts Receivable

Because of the general slowdown in the energy industry during the latter half of fiscal 1982, some of the company's domestic customers are experiencing cash flow problems, resulting in substantial in-

EXHIBIT 3
Consolidated Balance Sheet Year Ending August 31 (in $1000s)

	1982	1981	1980	1979	1978	1977	1976	1975
Assets								
Current Assets								
Cash and short term investments (Note 3)	$ 78,335	$ 14,070	$ 6,950	$ 12,572	$ 28,301	$ 20,762	$ 14,778	$ 4,161
Accounts receivable (Note 3)	169,947	148,466	97,168	74,580	64,210	36,603	23,285	23,084
Materials (lower of cost or market)	78,229	58,606	44,699	29,204	19,227	15,319	13,804	13,363
Other current assets	2,010	1,709	919	1,410	1,234	1,379	13,49	2,212
Total current assets	328,521	222,851	149,736	117,766	112,973	74,064	53,216	42,819
Plant and equipment (at cost) (Notes 1 and 3)								
Drilling equipment	654,805	510,544	385,015	306,841	247,692	173,947	140,380	118,270
Construction in progress	28,486	95,613	37,989	43,249	39,449	15,808	17,645	16,093
Gas transport and treating	76,176	57,776	0	0	0	0	0	0
Buildings and improvements	18,979	10,426	8,766	6,978	5,971	4,912	4,236	2,944
Other	88,902	46,066	34,519	22,446	17,460	15,398	9,711	8,195
Less accumulated depreciation	282,958	213,092	156,782	119,881	88,443	68,136	55,017	42,975
Net plant and equipment	584,390	507,333	309,507	259,633	222,129	141,928	116,955	102,526
Deferred charges and other assets	15,383	13,653	5,858	9,814	10,865	11,256	5,566	6,342
Total assets	$928,294	$743,837	$465,101	$387,213	$345,967	$227,249	$174,592	$150,341
Liabilities and shareholders' equity								
Current liabilities								
Notes payable	$ 20,072	$ 21,229	$ 0	$ 500	$ 0	$ 0	$ 2,090	$ 0
Current portion of long-term debt (Note 3)	19,210	26,059	21,921	19,084	9,890	19,319	3,531	5,536
Accounts payable	36,530	56,874	33,806	12,245	20,817	12,770	11,541	9,029
Customers deposits	5,611	6,753	3,342	0	1,372	521	0	1,151
Accrued liabilities	22,612	19,088	7,868	7,760	7,699	6,136	3,095	2,642
Accrued income taxes (Note 1)	10,176	11,606	2,705	5,748	7,934	3,880	2,271	2,173
Deferred income taxes (Note 1)	12,139	10,541	5,955	2,824	3,992	1,984	2,798	1,479
Total current liabilities	126,350	152,150	75,597	48,161	51,704	44,611	25,327	22,010
Long-term debt (Note 3)	332,770	215,625	128,393	128,630	126,890	74,940	60,884	56,662
Deferred income tax (Note 1)	74,502	57,405	39,497	27,085	17,857	17,485	14,010	10,632
Minority interest	10,012	5,944	935	0	0	0	0	0
Preferred stock (Notes 5 and 6)	1,607	1,607	1,462	1,412	129	340	400	400

(*Continued*)

EXHIBIT 3 (Continued)

	1982	1981	1980	1979	1978	1977	1976	1975
Common stock (Notes 5 and 6)	4,814	4,810	4,309	4,298	4,276	3,508	3,413	3,397
Other shareholders equity								
Capital in excess of par	60,480	60,020	52,175	51,546	52,306	23,655	22,056	21,776
Retained earnings	320,624	249,029	163,440	126,851	93,730	63,788	49,353	35,464
Other	(2,865)	(2,753)	(707)	(779)	(926)	(1,068)	(849)	0
Total liabilities and stockholders equity	$928,294	$743,837	$465,101	$387,213	$345,967	$227,249	$174,592	$150,340

creases in the company's accounts receivable. To minimize possible losses, the company has reduced the number of rigs operating for certain customers; obtained, and is continuing to obtain, priority collateral positions on certain customers' oil and gas properties; and recorded a provision for doubtful accounts receivable of $4,000,000. Based on management's evaluation of the financial condition of these customers, it believes that substantially all of the remaining accounts receivable will be collected.

Note 3—Long-Term Debt

Total long-term debt was $332,770,000, of which approximately 31 percent is payable at an average annual rate of about $\frac{6}{10}$ percent above prime and approximately 69 percent is payable at an average annual rate of approximately 14.2 percent. Of the total long-term debt, approximately 21.6 percent is in the name of Perry Gas Companies, Inc. and approximately 2.35 percent is in the name of Adeco Drilling and Engineering Co., Ltd. The remainder are in the name of Parker Drilling Company, Parker Drilling Company U. S. A., Ltd., and Parker Drilling Company International, Ltd.

The company has informal agreements with its principal banks to maintain compensating cash balances of 10 percent of the average loan balance. On August 31, 1982, compensating balances included in the consolidated balance sheet were $665,000.

Parker Drilling U. S. A., Ltd. ("U. S. A.") and Parker Drilling Company International, Ltd. ("Intl.") are wholly owned subsidiaries. Borrowings of these subsidiaries are nonrecourse loans as to the parent. However, Parker Drilling Company has pledged the stock of Intl. as collateral on the loans of Intl. In addition, these companies have pledged their drilling equipment with a net book value of approximately $209,800,000 and accounts receivable of approximately $10,182,000. Adeco Drilling and Engineering Co., Ltd., and Perry Gas Companies, Inc. have pledged substantially all of their assets as collateral on their respective loans.

The notes, among other things, require maintenance of minimum working capital, restrict creation of indebtedness, and limit payment of dividends on common stock. Under the most restriction loan agreements, retained earnings of $88,754,000 were available for the payment of dividends on August 31, 1982.

The aggregate maturities of long-term debt for the five years ending August 31, 1982 are as follows:

1983, $19,210,000; **1984,** $99,560,000; **1985,** $43,199,000; **1986,** $36,233,000; **1987,** $36,305,000.

As of August 31, 1982, the Company had $426,789,000 available in long-term and short-term bank lines of credit, of which $141,818,000 was unused. Commitment fees on unused portions are applicable to certain lines and are generally $\frac{1}{2}$ of 1 percent of the unused commitment.

Note 4—Income Taxes

Parker Drilling Company and its domestic subsidiaries file a consolidated federal income tax return. Federal income taxes are allocated to each member of the consolidated group based on the percentage of pre-tax income.

Deferred income tax expense results from timing differences in the recognition of revenue and expense for tax and financial statement purposes. The sources of these differences and the tax effect of each (in thousands) are shown in Table A.

TABLE A
Deferred Income Tax Expense

	Year Ended August 31		
	1982	1981	1980
Excess of tax over financial depreciation.	$19,514	$18,969	$ 8,894
Daywork drilling and construction contracts recognized on percentage-of-completion method in financial statements and completed contract method in tax return.	1,598	4,586	3,131
Undistributed foreign income included in consolidated financial statements on an accrual basis and included in tax return when dividends are received.	(4,535)	(9,789)	3,748
Foreign tax credits available for financial purposes to reduce U. S. federal income tax under (over) such credits available for tax purposes.	10,603	4,400	(2,339)
Investment tax credits used for financial statements under (over) such credits used in tax return.	(8,564)	1,315	(2,639)
Other	(307)	1,530	1,909
Total deferred income tax expense.	$18,309	$21,011	$12,704

Total income tax expense for the three years ended August 31, 1982 is less than the amount computed by multiplying income before income taxes by the U. S. federal income tax statutory rate. The reasons for this difference (dollars in thousands) are as follows:

On August 31, 1982, the company had an estimated investment tax credit carryforward of $13,800,000 for tax purposes, all of which has been used to reduce the deferred income tax liability for financial reporting purposes. These credits expire within the next 15 years.

Note 5—Redeemable Preferred Stock
Each share of the $0.75 cumulative convertible, Series C preferred stock has one vote and is entitled to $10.00 in 1992, plus unpaid dividends. The company may, under certain conditions, redeem the outstanding Series C preferred stock at decreasing prices of $10.58 to $10.00 per share, plus unpaid

	Year Ended August 31,					
	1982		1981		1980	
	Amount	Percent of Pre-tax Income	Amount	Percent of Pre-tax Income	Amount	Percent of Pre-tax Income
Computed expected tax	$54,875	46%	$57,494	46%	$32,224	46%
Investment tax credit	(13,260)	(11)	(11,752)	(9)	(7,181)	(10)
Other	1,343	1	239	—	217	—
Actual tax expense	$42,958	36%	$45,981	37%	$25,260	36%

dividends. Beginning January 15, 1984, the company must annually redeem one-tenth of the Series C shares then outstanding until all outstanding shares are redeemed.

Note 6—Common Stock and Stock Options
The company has two stock-option plans. The 1969 plan provides for the granting of options to key employees to purchase common stock at not less than $1.00 per share. During the last three years, no options were granted and 2,000 shares were exercised in 1980. At August 31, 1982, no options were outstanding and 223,000 shares were available for granting.

The 1977 plan authorizes the granting of options to key employees and directors to purchase common stock at not less than fair market value at date of grant. On August 31, 1982, no options were outstanding and 1,500,000 shares were available for granting.

The company's 1980 Incentive Career Stock Plan provides for the issuance of 600,000 shares of common stock for no cash consideration to key employees. For the years ended August 31, 1982 and 1981, 28,400 shares and 100,000 shares were granted, respectively, 3,300 shares were cancelled in 1982, and 474,900 shares were available for granting.

Note 7—Employee Benefit Plans
In 1981 the company established a profit-sharing plan for all eligible employees and, accordingly, made a contribution of approximately $1,500,000 and $3,000,000 in 1982 and 1981, respectively. The company also has an Employee Stock Ownership Plan (TRASOP). Contributions to the plan, which are currently based upon property additions eligible for investment tax credit, can be used to reduce federal income taxes. Contributions to the plan for each of the three years ending August 31, 1982, 1981, and 1980 were $1,973,000, $1,749,000, and $759,000.

Note 8—Business Segments
Information regarding the Company's operations by industry segment and geographic areas for the four years ended August 31, 1982, is as shown in Table B.

Total revenue by industry segment includes revenue from both unaffiliated customers and intersegment sales. The profit on intersegment sales has been eliminated. Operating income is total revenue less operating expenses, and includes an allocation of general corporate expenses based on rig-operating days. Operating income excludes interest expense, interest capitalized, equity in earnings of unconsolidated affiliates, nonoperating income or expense, and income taxes.

Identifiable assets are those assets used in each industry segment and geographic area. Corporate assets are principally investments and other assets not identifiable with a particular industry segment.

Note 9—Related Party Transactions
The company has agreed, upon the death of Mr. R. L. Parker, Sr., chairman and a principal shareholder, to purchase the number of shares of the company's stock policies owned by Mr. Parker's estate that can be purchased with the proceeds of any insurance policies owned by the company on the life of Mr. Parker on the date of his death. The purchase price for each share will be quoted market price, less 15 percent on the date of Mr. Parker's death. The value of shares to be purchased cannot exceed the amount qualifying as a stock redemption for federal income tax purposes. At August 31, 1982, the company owned insurance policies on the life of Mr. Parker having a total face value of $7,100,000. If the agreement had been required on August 31, 1982, the company's outstanding common stock would have been reduced by approximately three percent. Except for the above, the Company had no other significant related party transactions with its officers or directors.

Note 10—Supplemental Financial Information Regarding Changing Prices (Unaudited)
In accordance with requirements of the Financial Accounting Standards Board (FASB), the accompanying supplementary information reflects in restated *constant dollars* and *current costs* certain amounts that appear in the traditional, historical cost financial statements. The basic concepts of FASB's requirements are discussed below:

Constant dollar restatement takes into account the effects of general inflation by translating the historical cost of property, equipment, and inventory and the related cost of depreciation and cost of goods sold into dollars having the equivalent of 1982 purchasing power. *Current cost* restatement reflects the changes in specific prices of property,

TABLE B
Company Operations by Industry Segment and Geographical Area

	1982	1981	1980[a]	1979[a]
		(dollars in thousands)		
Operations by Industry Segment				
Revenue, including intersegment revenue				
Drilling	$527,634	$458,443	$350,447	$280,172
Manufacturing	122,350	154,307	51,827	47,274
Gas transportation and treating	41,645	38,889	18,002	10,864
Intersegment	(75,758)	(69,329)	(8,178)	(14,738)
Net income	$615,861	$582,310	$412,098	$323,592
Operating income				
Drilling	$154,224	$113,086	$ 84,834	$ 66,752
Manufacturing	(2,036)	28,000	6,304	5,800
Gas transportation and treating	15,336	18,673	5,678	3,476
Total operating income	167,554	159,759	96,816	76,028
Interest expense	(49,628)	(34,286)	(26,345)	(19,469)
Other income (expense)—net	1,367	(485)	(417)	1,973
Income before income taxes	$119,293	$124,988	$ 70,054	$ 58,532
Identifiable assets				
Drilling	$701,829	$602,800	$413,564	$353,526
Manufacturing	69,503	40,001	46,873	28,379
Gas transportation and treating	127,419	84,404	56,557	28,626
Total identifiable assets	898,751	727,205	516,994	410,531
Corporate assets	29,543	16,632	15,564	14,527
Total assets	$928,294	$743,837	$532,558	$425,058
Capital expenditures				
Drilling	$125,904	$192,699	$ 77,674	$ 70,521
Manufacturing	13,095	2,635	2,693	1,848
Gas transportation and treating	18,742	21,203	27,477	7,344
Total capital expenditures	$157,741	$216,537	$107,844	$ 79,713
Depreciation				
Drilling	$ 66,464	$ 49,170	$ 38,752	$ 31,163
Manufacturing	1,391	878	770	730
Gas transportation and treating	7,552	4,960	2,289	1,326
Total depreciation	75,407	$ 55,008	$ 41,811	$ 33,219
Operations by Geographic Area				
Revenue				
United States	$366,385	$352,931	$228,716	$183,476
Other Western Hemisphere	134,627	92,447	67,869	44,503
Eastern Hemisphere	114,849	136,932	115,513	95,613
Total Revenue	$615,861	$582,310	$412,098	$323,592

(*Continued*)

TABLE B (Continued)

	1982	1981	1980[a]	1979[a]
		(dollars in thousands)		
Operating income				
United States	$ 87,238	$ 99,971	$ 48,061	$ 38,799
Other Western Hemisphere	47,493	30,309	19,229	11,580
Eastern Hemisphere	32,823	29,479	29,526	25,649
Total operating income	$167,554	$159,759	$ 96,815	$ 76,028
Identifiable assets				
United States	$634,321	$519,676	$352,096	$288,821
Other Western Hemisphere	153,655	110,191	73,099	40,211
Eastern Hemisphere	140,318	113,970	107,363	96,026
Total identifiable assets	$928,294	$743,837	$532,558	$425,058

[a] Adjusted to include Perry Gas.

equipment, and inventory from the date of acquisition to the present, thereby differing from *constant dollar* amounts to the extent that specific prices have increased more or less rapidly than prices in general. The Consumer Price Index for all urban consumers was used for restating historical dollars into *constant dollars* while *current cost* estimates were derived from specific indices published by the U. S. Department of Labor.

Gain from decline in purchasing power represents the effect of holding "fixed dollar" (monetary) assets and liabilities during the year (e.g., cash, receivables, debt). Since the company held net monetary liabilities during a period in which purchasing power declined, it experienced a gain to the extent that the net amounts that are presently owed are to be paid with dollars having less purchasing power.

The latest available indices as of August 31, 1982 were used for 1982 *current cost* calculations. It should be noted that because of the continued depressed market conditions, the following *current cost* data does not necessarily present an accurate current value of the Company's inventory and property, plant, and equipment. Management urges that the following restated information be used as a general indicator of the effects of inflation rather than as an exact measuring device.

The following four-year comparison (shown in Table C) shows the effect of adjusting selected historical amounts to average 1982 dollars. The statement of operations for the years ended August 31, 1982 and 1981 and certain other information adjusted for changing prices are in Table D (in thousands).

TABLE C
Restatement of Historical Financial Accounts

	1982	1981	1980	1979
Stated in historical dollars:				
Sales and other revenues (in thousands)	$615,861	$582,310	$412,098	$323,592
Cash dividends declared per common share	$ 0.16	$ 0.15	$ 0.12	$ 0.10¼
Market price per common share at year end	$ 10	$ 23⅞	$ 26¼	$ 16¾
Stated in average 1982 dollars:				
Sales and other revenues (in thousands)	$615,861	$625,042	$487,574	$437,081
Cash dividends declared per common share	$ 0.16	$ 0.16	$ 0.14	$ 0.14
Market price per common share at year end	$ 9¾	$ 24⅝	$ 29	$ 21½
Average Consumer Price Index	282.3	263.0	238.6	209.0

TABLE D
Adjusted Statement of Operations

	Adjusted for General Inflation (Constant Dollar)		Adjusted for Change in Specific Prices (Current Cost)	
	1982	1981	1982	1981
Income from continuing operations as reported in the income statement	$ 76,335	$ 79,007	$ 76,335	$ 79,007
Adjustment to restate cost of goods sold, depreciation, depletion, and amortization expense for the effects of inflation	(27,759)	(24,701)	(53,333)	(32,716)
Income from continuing operations as adjusted[a]	$ 48,576	$ 54,306	$ 23,002	$ 46,291
Per Share	$ 1.69	$ 1.88	$ .80	$ 1.61
Gain from decline in purchasing power	$ 11,071	$ 16,485		
Increase in specific prices of property, buildings, and equipment held during the year[b]			$ 81,861	$ 79,797
Less effect of increase in general prices			33,163	48,414
Net increase in specific prices			$ 48,698	$ 31,083
Net assets at year end	$467,696	$451,429	$581,926	$468,254

[a] While income adjusted for changing prices is reduced from historical amounts, the provisions for income taxes is unchanged, which underscores the "hidden" tax resulting from inflation. The effective tax rates under the various accounting methods are as follows:

	1982	1981
Historical Dollars	36%	37%
Adjusted for general inflation	47%	46%
Current Cost information	65%	50%

[b] At August 31, 1982, the estimated *current cost* of inventory and net property, plant and equipment was $872 million.

Organization, Planning, and Strategy

The company strives to operate on the team management concept. The company does not have a formal organizational chart. Robert Parker, Jr. says, "People know their jobs and their responsibilities and most employees could draw up a rough organizational chart."

The rationale for the Perry Gas acquisition was explained by Robert Parker, Jr.:

In acquiring Perry Gas we hope to do several things. Most of all was to establish another leg to stand on in an area that has high growth potential. We are attracted to this area because it is much like ours. It is a true service area, the customers are the same people, and we do not own the production and compete with our customers. Also this side of the business occurs on a different timing than the drilling business does. In other words, when a new field is discovered it is first drilled, then the pipelines and gas plants are put in, and that service lasts long after the drilling is gone. As you know, we try to relay the message to our customers that we are becoming a total service company and obviously being able to handle their products for them as a service company after the drilling adds credit to that role. We do not plan further acquisitions or I should say we are not out looking for them. However, if a good looking acquisition came along we would certainly take a hard look. Our basic criteria are that: (1) it be a money maker and a very good return on investment, (2) that it be in a rapid growing industry, and (3) that it does not interfere or compete with the type business or customers we have developed in the drilling business.

The company sometimes faces risky political, social, and/or economic situations. The company carries expropriation insurance on most of its foreign rigs and it asks the customer in risky areas to be responsible for getting into the country, operating, and then getting out. Robert Parker, Jr. points out, ". . . it is very difficult many times to compare or rate the risk in various foreign countries. We have been in and out of some of the riskiest countries in the world such as Algeria and Syria, and yet have suffered our worse revenue loss due to governmental actions on the North Slope in our own country. Still we try to stay away from worldwide hot spots."

In response to a question on which contracts are sought and which are accepted Robert Parker, Jr. said:

> The number-one criteria in looking at foreign work is the customer or the operator. A judgement is made as to whether or not they are reputable and a judgement is made to the type of operation that customer usually has. Second we look at the true need to customer may have for our services. If there is no real need for specialized drilling, then we let them know; however, if we see a true need for ultra-deep, remote, or helicopter rig services, we will give that job our priority. Also included in the criterion are the natural considerations of the economics of running a rig in a certain area and the length of term of the project. If it is a six month or less term project, we are not very excited, however, many of them are two years or more and that makes a big difference.

As of 1981 the company did not have a formal planning unit, however, the financial group prepares a one-year forecast of contracts and revenues. Periodically it prepares forecasts for up to five years in advance using general trends to see their effect on long-term capital structure, cash flow, and balance sheet. Parker Drilling also, on occasion, looks at drilling and market trends in the future and strategies the company may follow to take advantage of different trends. Robert Parker, Jr. indicated his feelings about such forecasts as follows, ". . . any forecast past one year is going to be highly inaccurate due to the rapid changes of customer needs in our business."

Marketing

The company does not have a marketing manager. However, in 1981, each division (e.g., West Texas, Oklahoma, Rocky Mountains, South America, etc.) had a division manager in charge of contracts and a division manager in charge of operations. Each area's contracts person and division manager are charged with responsibility of marketing the rigs.

Information to customers about Parker's services are conveyed by word of mouth and by contrast people calling on prospective customers. The company does not advertise, but does distribute literature explaining Parker's services and equipment. The company attempts to keep abreast of which companies do the drilling in each country and each state so that contract personnel can make calls on them.

In 1981, Bob Parker, Jr. said:

> The market was so tight than when a rig was available for work there was no usual problem putting the rig to work for going market rates. Usually a customer we know will call us and will ask us to come see him about his drilling program. He will ask us what work, if any, we could get to with what rigs and then we will tell them what it will cost. In 1981 a few operators insisted on formal bids. On the international front the steps are similar except the customers ask for a proposal on how Parker would mobilize a rig, bring in people, and demobilize the rig. Still, in 1981, the market is tight

enough where the rates are basically negotiated and not bid.

Competition

Parker is the largest contractor in the land rig field. While there are in the neighborhood of 400 drilling contractors, only six are significant participants. They include Hoffland Brothers (a privately owned subsidiary of Ken David Industries, the business interest of Texas millionare T. Cullen Davis), Helmerick and Payne, Noble affiliates, W. R. Grace, and Resource Drilling, Inc. (a subsidiary of Superior Oil), in addition to Parker.

Considering the revenue from contract drilling relative to the total revenue for the consolidated companies, Parker derives the largest percent from contract drilling. In other words, it is the least diversified.

An article in the October 30, 1979 issue of *Forbes* illustrates Parker's commitment to contract drilling by comparing the strategy of Helmerick and Payne. Walter Helmerick, III, head of Helmerick and Payne, expressed concern about the boom and bust character of contract drilling by pointing out that an oversupply of rigs leads to falling rental rates and a wringing out of the business. From over 3000 rigs in the 1950s, the U. S. rig count dropped to 975 in 1971. It is back up to 2323 today, but Helmerick has remained unimpressed. It is Walter Helmerick's ambition to make his company a conglomerate.

Parker, on the other hand, has borrowed heavily for new drilling equipment. Robert Parker says, "You build a service company by reacting to customers."

1983 Update

Fiscal 1983 and 1984 were the worst years in the history of the company. Total revenue in 1983 dropped nearly 44 percent from 618.6 million in 1982 to 348.9 million in 1983. The following consolidated income statement and balance sheet (Exhibit 4) show the 1982–1983 comparison.

The following introduction signed by Robert L. Parker, Sr., and Robert L. Parker, Jr., from the 1983 annual report indicates the problems faced by the Company.

EXHIBIT 4
Consolidated Statement of Income (in 1000's)

	1983	1982	1981
Revenue			
Drilling Contracts	294,426	525,945	457,336
Manufacturing and Construction	5,218	45,627	85,088
Gas Transporting and Treating	45,894	41,303	44,245
Other	3,364	5,771	2,546
	348,902	618,646	589,215
Operating Expenses[a]	345,094	448,203	422,807
Operating Income	3,808	170,443	166,408
Other Income (and Expense)[b]	(46,583)	(51,150)	(41,420)
Income (Loss) Before Taxes	(42,775)	119,293	124,988
Income Taxes (Benefit)	(17,266)	42,958	45,981
Net Income (Loss)	(25,509)	76,335	79,007
Fully Diluted Earnings (Loss) Per Share	(.89)	2.65	2.74

[a]1983 includes 15,536 written-off accounts and 21,578 in written-off assets.
[b]Primarily interest expense.

Consolidated Balance Sheet (in 1000's)

	August 31 1983	August 31 1982
Current Assets		
Cash	$ 15,724	$ 10,969
Short-term investments at cost, which approximates market	112,626	67,366
Accounts receivable, net of allowance for bad debts	67,546	165,367
Notes receivable	16,014	4,580
Inventories, at lower of average cost or market		
Materials and supplies	54,905	62,565
Manufacturing work in process	10,062	15,664
Other current assets	2,244	2,010
Total current assets	279,121	328,521
Property, plant, and equipment, at cost		
Drilling equipment	653,490	654,805
Manufacturing and construction	11,430	14,694
Gas-processing plants and transportation systems	75,082	76,176
Oil and gas properties (full-cost method)	18,028	26,093
Buildings and improvements	19,761	18,979
Other	44,078	48,115
Construction in progress	8,445	28,486
	830,314	867,348
Less accumulated depreciation, depletion, and amortization	349,256	282,958
Net property, plant, and equipment	481,058	584,390
Deferred charges and other assets		
Long-term accounts receivable	15,192	1,323
Notes receivable	6,850	200
Other	23,024	13,860
Total deferred charges and other assets	45,066	15,383
Total Assets	$805,245	$928,294
Liabilities and Shareholders' Equity		
Current Liabilities		
Notes payable to banks	$ 135	$ 20,072
Current portion of long-term debt	16,682	19,210
Accounts payable	26,369	36,530

Consolidated Balance Sheet (in 1000's) (Continued)

	August 31 1983	August 31 1982
Customers' deposits on contracts	767	5,611
Accrued liabilities	17,791	22,612
Accrued income taxes	8,408	10,176
Deferred income tax	—	12,139
Total current liabilities	70,152	126,350
Long-term debt	305,832	332,770
Deferred income tax	59,077	74,502
Minority interest	11,827	10,012
Redeemable preferred stock	$ 1,607	$ 1,607
Shareholders' equity		
Common stock	4,905	4,814
Capital in excess of par value	66,851	60,480
Retained earnings	290,350	320,624
Other	(5,356)	(2,865)
Total shareholders' equity	356,750	383,053
Total liabilities and shareholders' equity	$805,245	$928,294

Note 1—Acquisition

In August 1983, the company acquired all of the outstanding common stock of Separex Corporation ("Separex") in exchange for 331,116 ($4,427,000) shares of common stock. Separex is a high-technology company involved in the development of membrane elements for use primarily in certain gas and organic liquid separation systems. The excess of the purchase price over the fair value of the acquired net assets was $3,948,000, which was recorded as goodwill and will be amortized over 40 years. Additionally, former Separex shareholders will be entitled to receive up to $6.00 per share of Separex stock held prior to acquisition, payable to Parker common stock. This contingent stock payment is based on future gross profits and licensing fees of Separex. Such stock payments will increase the goodwill of Separex. The acquisition was accounted for under the purchase method; therefore, the accounts of Separex have been included in the consolidated balance sheet as of August 31, 1983. Had the purchase been consummated on September 1, 1980, the effect on consolidated results of operations for the three years ended August 31, 1983 would have been insignificant.

Note 2—Contingencies
In January 1983, the company filed claims, through the International Chamber of Commerce Court of Arbitration, against a non-U. S. customer totaling in excess of $33 million. The customer has filed counterclaims against the company of approximately $12 million, plus unspecified amounts in excess of that amount. The claims and counterclaims are in the preliminary stage of proceedings. While management is unable to predict the outcome, they are of the opinion that resolution of these claims will not adversely affect results of operations or financial condition.

To Our Shareholders:

Parker Drilling Company's fiscal 1983 was one year we are thankful to have survived. It was our first loss year ever. Because of many factors, oil and gas operators virtually shut down their search for energy in the United States. Never in the history of the drilling business has the market for our services dried up so quickly. This loss of market followed immediately upon the heels of record activity in 1982. Also, unfortunately, a lot of the slowdown is spreading to international markets. Our subsidiaries, Perry Gas Companies, Inc. and O.I.M.E., were hurt since natural gas transportation markets were in disarray most of the year, and the market for new drilling rigs and equipment virtually disappeared.

It is tough for any company to make adjustments from a strong year to a virtual shut down in most of its areas. We cut operating and overhead expenses to the bone. We worked very hard to keep the markets which we had that were still active. We reemphasized our search for overseas work and we tried not to make any mistakes. Our game plan through the year was to conserve and build cash and hold onto what drilling existed.

Our customers had many problems this year, especially in the domestic market. Nearly all of them have had to cut back their drilling programs. Many of them lacked capital to carry on their search. Several of them have gone bankrupt. Some are broke and don't know it yet. A very few have managed to carry on their normal oil and gas exploration and development programs. When our customers are hurt, we are hurt. Their success or failure greatly determines ours. Much of our time has been spent in solving their problems which, in turn, have become ours. Many of our customers have been unable to pay their bills. Regarding these accounts, we have taken what we consider to be a conservative approach by recording several write-offs. We are working with those accounts in every possible way to help them survive in their business and to help us recover payment for our services. We have done this in the past when our friends were in trouble. We believe this will help us in the future. Some of our best accounts are those that we were able to help in the past in their time of need.

The impact of the recession in this country on its energy consumption has been very dramatic. As a result of this reduced consumption, less oil and gas has been needed, thus fewer holes in the ground. This dramatic cutback in the development of more U. S. oil and gas supplies, while we consume those we had drilled previously, is leading us down a dead-end street. We are once again becoming highly dependent upon outside sources for our energy. Imports already are climbing. It wasn't easy three years ago to stop the decline of U. S. production and to increase exploration efforts so that we could reduce our import dependency. It will be even more difficult the next time around. We are confident there will be a strong need for rebuilding our country's energy supplies.

We now see the light at the end of the tunnel, but do not know how long that tunnel is. Although we can see an improving picture for the first time, we cannot yet determine when that picture will develop or how many other pitfalls lie ahead; so it is with caution that we enter 1984 and look forward to 1985.

Interview with R. L. Parker

The following interview was conducted with Mr. Parker in April 1984.

Q: Please tell us how the company has fared during the first six months of the current fiscal year?

A: The last six months have been bad. They are, in effect, the first six months of fiscal 1984, and we are running about 30¢ a quarter loss and we are projecting that will get larger. We are expecting fiscal 1984 to be somewhere between $1.50 and $2.00 loss.

Q: Is the cause primarily a reduction in domestic drilling?

A: No. It's a uniform reduction in rig utilization. A year ago, the domestic market crashed and hit us hard. In 1984, the international market weakened considerably and we are reversing roles. International rates and activity have slipped. Domestic is picking up in activity but not in rates. The only bright light that we have is that we have been able to reduce our debt substantially and will continue to do so and have accumulated close to $140 million in cash. So, financially, we are stronger than we were a year ago; earnings-wise, we are worse than we were a year ago.

Q: What do you see as the future for the industry in the next year and in the next five years?

A: The next five years are super. We (the world) are just flat running out (of oil and gas) and they (oil companies) are not replacing reserves anywhere. Not overseas and not here. The markets are already firming and the perception (perception is what causes drilling) is we will probably import natural gas into this country within two years to supplement the short-fall. Consequently, the oil search here will greatly increase, primarily offshore. International oil is coming back already—we are talking about five years now. Because each country has its own problems handling its imports, we're not the only country that has that problem. Their pressures are larger than ours due to the value of the U. S. dollar. The two-year picture or even one year should improve significantly starting the last quarter of this year. That perception is from feedback from our customers and two different consulting firms we've employed to give us an outlook on deep on-land drilling which is the only one that affects us in the U. S. The consultants are forecasting a pick-up in demand in drilling activity in the last part of 1984 and really coming on strong in 1985 and 1986. The net activity will not improve day rates enough to help our company. In fact, it will have a negative influence on our company for the first five or six months because it will consume some of that cash we have accumulated for start-up operations and margins will be low until rig activity becomes high. The rule of thumb is two quarters of about 70 percent rig activity before margins resume. That means the middle of 1985 before it has a favorable impact on the company.

Q: What methodology was used by the forecasting organizations?

A: It was strictly economic. They called on 28 customers, I believe. We used two different firms, both of which are very knowledgeable and very well respected in the industry. We don't know if they are right, but they have called the shots pretty well in the last few years. We gave them a specific target market, deep on-land rigs, because most surveys are for the general picture.

Q: Have the events of the last few years at all modified your stance with respect to the absence of an organizational chart, the absence of a formal marketing structure, and the absence of a formal planning unit, particularly as it relates to long-range planning?

A: No, not at all. Let me run through them in order. With respect to organization charts, we operate on a wagon-wheel chart. We depend so much on high-performing, high-productivity field personnel that don't like to be categorized and don't like to be ranked. Organization charts have their way of creating a ladder effect and we want each of them to be his own boss in the area he's in. I see them as the spokes of the wheel and I'm in the middle. Participative management is another word for it. Our chart, as we would draw it now, would simply show the various divisions of the company, finance, research, etc.

In respect to the absence of marketing or sales management *per se*, you must remember that the people that run the oil companies do not award the drilling contracts, and, therefore, the people who award us drilling contracts are men in the field, and they never see Bob Parker or an ad in the newspaper or a letter. What he sees is a fellow in the company car in that area coming up to him and saying, we want to drill your well with this particular rig and I will promise you the same personnel we used on the last well. We have tried a more sophisticated approach and struck out. And we are back with the field personnel on domestic work who do most of our selling and, incidentally, our market share has greatly increased in this down market. Overseas, we have people in each country doing our marketing.

With respect to long-range planning, it is difficult for us. At the moment our long-range plan is not to purchase more drilling rigs but instead to pump up the potential of Perry Gas. We think natural gas is going to offer more opportunities quicker than more drilling rigs will. We had all of our people in during the last two months getting their ideas. Should we dump rigs? Should we burn them? Should we change them? Should we buy more or what? How else could we run the company? Oil? Gas? Cows? Automobiles? After going through the process, it was rather reassuring to come back to staying with what you are doing best and waiting for the marketplace to return. This interchange of ideas occurred way down in the level of the company.

A lot of our friends are having a hard time with diversifications that they entered into. We had pressure from our board to diversify and all the biggest losses that we took in the last two years were from the diversifications we made at their request.

Q: I gather that you have no diversification plans at this point?

A: We would probably put $100 million into a move into the natural gas business right now if we saw the right opportunity to strengthen Perry Gas. Probably in pipelines and transmission. The problem is that there's such a fast-changing set of rules, and we don't know the new rules. It's kind of a conjunction of phased deregulation and congressional opposition. The opportunities are there, but they are both dangerous. One of the dangers is that we must rely upon the judgement of the people that manage Perry instead of our own judgment, because we know nothing about natural gas.

Q: Does O.I.M.E. sell the full line of rigs that you use yourself and what is the current condition of O.I.M.E.?

A: No. They sell a limited line. We do not compete with our own TBA rigs. There are no rigs being manufactured at all right now. O.I.M.E. is still very much there and is a big loss on the company at the moment. It is, of course, greatly reduced in size but it is necessary to maintain the TBA's we own. The major purpose of O.I.M.E. was never making drilling rigs for profit but providing us with drilling rigs that no one else could provide. We are building two rigs right now but they are not for the market. We are building these for a major oil company to use off-shore and we will operate them. They are not TBA's, they're specialized offshore rigs for Alaska.

Q: Does that signal any movement in your direction toward offshore drilling?

A: No. We're not opposed to offshore drilling, but that market is weak, too. It's an opportunity. The building we are doing is on ice platforms. We do most of the ice-platform drilling in the world right now, and, usually, we've been doing it with TBA rigs, so it's a generation of more specialized ice rigs that are not TBA that we're building. These rigs sit on platforms of solid ice used in the winter time, then you must remove the rig quickly before the ice melts.

Q: Is it likely you will continue the lease/purchase arrangement that you had with Mobil Oil or is that a one-time affair?

A: That was in Indonesia. They have finished and we have sold the rigs to them. That was a one-time affair.

Q: What is the status of the suit to recover the $33 million from the government of Algeria? Does the suit signal an end to your relationship with the government of Algeria?

A: The status is that we should have a decision on that in July. We have presented our case and they have presented theirs. The trial judge has indicated that it was not a question of whether they owed us money, but how much they owe us. This does not signal an end of our relationship with the Algerian government. They've already changed governments again. The suit was against the bunch that was in power three years ago.

Q: You've got a large amount of long-term debt falling due this year, do you anticipate any difficulty in meeting it?

A: None at all.

Q: Do you expect any new breakthrough in rig design?

A: No. We've increased our research budget. The newest design was the ice-rig concept. Our research team is looking for a new style rig, but it looks as though the market will be strongest for an improved version of the TBA.

Q: In view of the addition of a large number of MBA's at the executive level, does that signal a change in personnel policy, in the sense that your policy has always been to hire people for what they can do, not for what their education is?

A: It signals our recognition that the world is becoming more sophisticated. We are dealing with a new world, education-wise and computer-wise, and it's a language that we think we're going to have to have and we think we're going to have to have people that can cope with it. We've been pleasantly surprised by the MBA's. I think what we do is take an MBA and try to convert them into being human—and a human MBA is hard to beat.

Let me convey some information and thoughts that might be of interest to your readers. Last year we wrote off $38 million in bad receivables, and we pretty well have that put to bed. Also, we will soon have Algeria clean. We're trying to position ourselves to go fast and obtain good earnings without any burdens when business returns. The last year has given us a good chance to totally reduce the size of our company. It's much leaner and meaner. We can operate on a lower profit margin now.

We are well aware of the current rash of mergers of big oil companies and realize it will have some effect on us, but we don't know what. Further, a large number of drilling companies have been taken over by the banks and have not been written off. We don't know how they're going to shape up as competition. As the oil companies merge with each other, some of those companies have drilling rigs. A few of them in large numbers. Those companies that are merging don't want drilling rigs, so we are being swamped with requests to take over the drilling operations. We are looking at the possible acquisition of a large number of drilling rigs right now at about a dime on a dollar through equity offerings.

HOLIDAY INNS, INC.

The lodging industry is a vast enterprise in the United States and Canada and overseas. In the world, for example, the 10 leading lodging firms can offer more than 900,000 rooms on any given day. Today, almost 50 percent of all lodging properties are affiliated with a chain. Some independents have developed sophisticated reservations networks in an attempt to compete with the tremendous marketing clout inherent in a chain. The largest confederation of independents united through a common reservation system is Best Western International, which represents a total of 150,000 rooms available worldwide.

Motels have come a long way from the days when they were a few small cabins next to the farmhouse. The AAA made an early breakthrough with a listing and rating of motels and hotels for the traveler, but it did not market its service as aggressively as some other operators.

If you travel and stay overnight at a hotel or motel, the chances are that you are most familiar with motels operated and/or owned by the 10 major chains in the lodging industry. The leading chains and the number of rooms each offered in 1978 are given in Exhibit 1. It is readily apparent that Holiday Inns far exceed their competition in number of rooms operated. Indeed, nightly, you can make reservations at any one of 300,000 rooms, in 1,750 Holiday Inns in 60 countries, worldwide! Quite an achievement for a company incorporated on April 30, 1954.

In August 1952, Kemmons Wilson opened his first hotel on the outskirts of Memphis. Wilson entered the business because he was disgruntled by the prices he was forced to pay for cramped lodging on the way to Washington, D. C., while traveling with his wife and five children.

From the original, "Holiday Inn Hotel Courts," the determined Wilson was able to build what ultimately became the largest hotel/motel chain in the world. Growth was pursued in two primary directions: through company owned and franchised operations. Exhibit 2 gives the distribution of the inns and rooms for the two categories.

Holiday Inns, Inc., growth set the pace for the lodging industry. From 1962 to 1978, Howard Johnson more than quintupled its rooms to approximately 60,000, and Ramada Inns went from 6,700 to 95,000 rooms. Since the energy crisis, Holiday Inns has continuously expanded its hotel system. Many of the company operated hotels are operating near capacity. These trends and a favorable economic outlook have led the company to plan to add at least 72,000 rooms by 1983 in United States markets and abroad.

In the past, growth in the industry came (to an extent) at the expense of older hotels and nonchain motels. Hotels offer fewer rooms today than were available 10 years ago. For example, the annual rate of growth in hotel/motel rooms in the late 1960s was about 3 percent. In the latter part of the 1970s this 3 percent growth rate decreased to nearly 1 percent. The number of chain-affiliated properties has drastically increased—to the point where almost 50 percent of rooms available are controlled by the chain operations.

Operations at Holiday Inns, Inc.

When we think "Holiday Inn," we generally are only considering hotels and motels. However, Holiday Inns, Inc., is a $1.2 billion per year diversified multinational corporation. In fact, only 54 percent of total corporate reve-

Source: Prepared by Professor Timothy Mescon. Arizona State University, and Professor Richard Robinson, University of South Carolina. Permission to publish granted by authors.

EXHIBIT 1
Fifteen Leading Lodging Firms *Source:* 1978 Service World International "100" Edition.

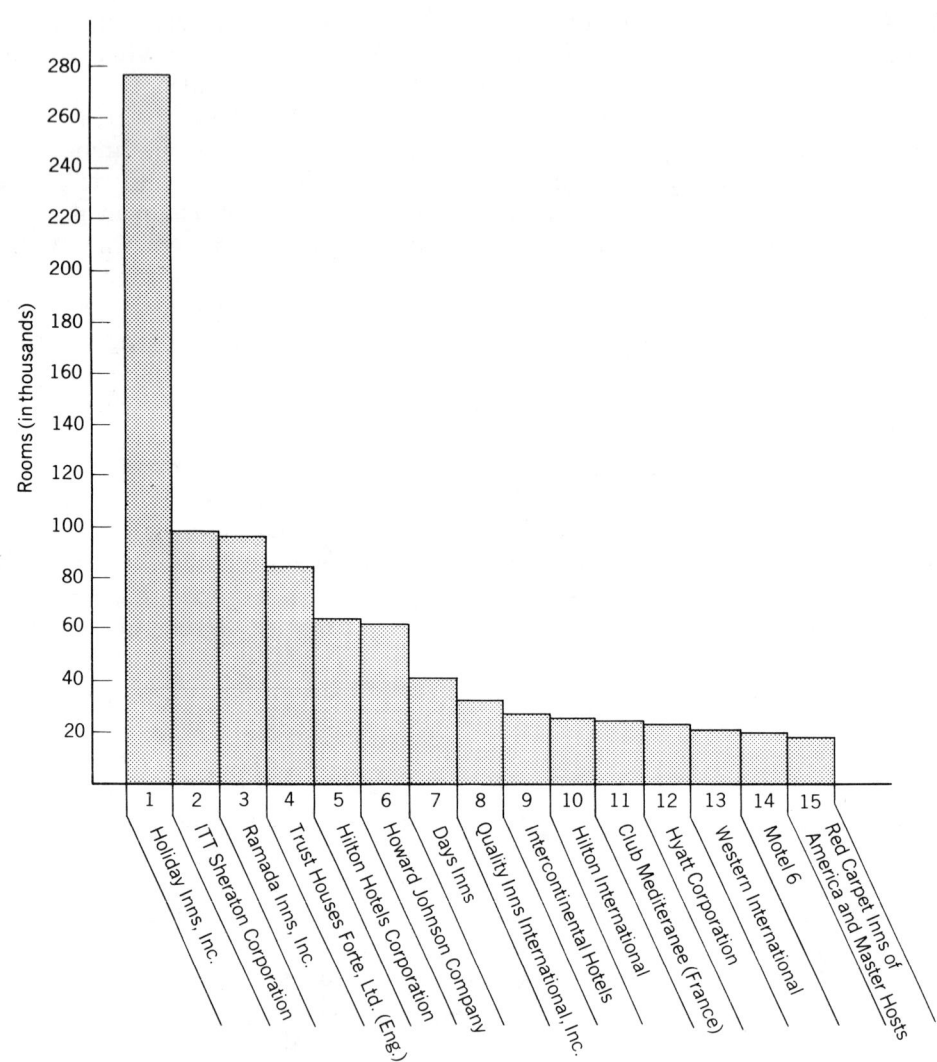

nues results from hotel operations. Today, the company structures itself into four divisions:

1. Hotel group
   a. Parent company
   b. Licensees
   c. International
   d. Products division
2. Transportation group
   a. Trailways, Inc.
   b. Delta Steamship Lines
3. Restaurant group
   a. Good Company
   b. Perkins Cake and Steak
   c. Pipers

EXHIBIT 2
The Holiday Inns System

The Holiday Inns system, comprising both company and licensee-operated inns, is the largest hotel business in the world. On December 31, 1977, there were 1,700 Holiday Inns facilities with a total of 278,957 rooms operated as follows:

	Inns	Rooms
Company-operated		
Owned or leased	247	48,749
Under management contracts	24	8,035
Fifty percent owned	5	1,752
	276	58,536
Licensee-operated	1,424	220,421
	1,700	278,957

4. Gaming
   a. Atlantic City
   b. Las Vegas

The restructuring of the company's operations was initiated in January 1979. The most recent financial data available does not, however, reflect this change. Exhibits 3 and 4 provide some insight into the new look at Holiday Inns, Inc., from a management perspective as well as a reflective look at corporate financial performance through 1978.

The Hotal Group

Since 1976, revenues from rooms in the hotel group have increased 26 percent from $290.0 million to $364.8 million, while revenues from food and beverage operations have increased 16 percent ($148.2 million to $172.0 million) during the same period.

In 1978, the Holiday Inn system worldwide increased its capacity by 7,572 rooms. Since 1975, the system has disposed of 104 hotels with 15,807 rooms. The proceeds generated from these sales were channeled into new hotels or room additions in growing markets which better reflected customer needs. In that same time period, 108 new Holiday Inn hotels with 19,080 rooms have opened, and another 8,287 rooms were added at existing locations where demand warranted them. Today, the company is concentrating its construction efforts on high-demand, inner-city locations.

Hotels that are part of Holiday Inns, Inc., are segregated into two groups. The hotels in the first group are company owned, and those in the second group are licensee owned and operated. Hotel analysis continues to reflect the company's original emphasis on franchising. Today 80 percent of the system is operated by franchisees—independent businesspeople or companies—while Holiday Inns, Inc., operates the remaining 20 percent. By 1978, occupancy at company owned hotels was at a five-year high, approaching 75 percent.

International Operations

Foreseeing the possible obstacles to intensive expansion in the United States, Holiday Inns, Inc., has been rapidly expanding hotel operations abroad. The company's international development strategy is to build strong national chains within the countries where it now operates, as well as to gradually expand into new markets. Holiday Inns, Inc., argues that this strategy differs from that of its competitors who have but one location in each major city overseas.

By the end of 1978, international locations (55 countries) accounted for 195 existing hotels (of which 161 were licensed) and 20 under construction (of which 11 will be licensed) with well over 40,000 rooms. The company reported operating gains in its international operations in 1977 and 1978 compared with losses in previous years. Gains were attributed to higher levels of occupancy, higher average room rates, and increased operating efficiencies. Political difficulties in Lebanon in 1975 forced the closing of a company leased hotel in September of that year.

Holidex Reservation System

Holiday Inns operates the Holidex reservation system, which links over 17,000 terminals

EXHIBIT 3
Business

The following table reflects, for the five most recent fiscal years, operating data with respect to each of the company's industry segments, together with other income, corporate expense, interest, and foreign currency translation (loss) gain.

	Amounts (in Millions of Dollars)					Percentages				
	1978	1977	1976	1975	1974	1978	1977	1976	1975	1974
Revenues										
Hotel	$ 649	$ 589	$540	$526	$502	54.0%	56.9%	55.9%	57.3%	55.5%
Products	148	144	137	116	140	12.3	13.9	14.2	12.7	15.4
Transportation										
Bus	268	244	235	211	203	22.3	23.6	24.3	23.0	22.4
Steamship	155	80	81	83	78	12.9	7.7	8.4	9.0	8.6
Other	14	6	5	4	4	1.2	.6	.5	.5	.5
Elimination of products intersegment revenues	(32)	(28)	(32)	(23)	(22)	(2.7)	(2.7)	(3.3)	(2.5)	(2.4)
Total	$1,202	$1,035	$966	$917	$905	100.0%	100.0%	100.0%	100.0%	100.0%
Income from operations before income taxes										
Hotel	$ 117	$ 90	$ 69	$ 61	$ 52	74.3%	69.1%	66.1%	60.1%	51.4%
Products	6	7	2	1	9	4.0	5.0	1.6	.9	8.9
Transportation										
Bus	20	16	15	20	26	12.6	12.6	14.7	19.7	25.3
Steamship	8	17	17	18	12	5.0	13.3	16.8	17.9	12.4
Other	8	1	2	2	3	5.1	.7	1.9	2.3	3.0
Elimination of products intersegment income	(2)	(1)	(1)	(1)	(1)	(1.0)	(.7)	(1.1)	(.9)	(1.0)
	$ 157	$ 130	$104	$101	$101	100.0%	100.0%	100.0%	100.0%	100.0%
Corporate expense	(15)	(12)	(9)	(10)	(14)					
Interest, net of interest capitalized	(30)	(26)	(28)	(30)	(32)					
Foreign currency translation (loss) gain	(1)	(1)	(3)	6	(9)					
Total	$ 111	$ 91	$ 64	$ 67	$ 46					

The following table reflects, for the three most recent fiscal years, identifiable assets applicable to each operating segment.

	Amounts (in Millions of Dollars)			Percentages		
	1978	1977	1976	1978	1977	1976
Identifiable assets						
Hotel	$579.5	$572.4	$536.6	48.5%	55.0%	55.9%
Products	35.3	52.7	54.8	3.0	5.1	5.7
Transportation						
Bus	177.0	171.3	165.5	14.8	16.5	17.2
Steamship	215.9	163.3	148.6	18.0	15.7	15.5
Other	188.3	79.9	55.0	15.7	7.7	5.7
Total	$1,196.0	$1,039.6	$960.5	100.0%	100.0%	100.0%

EXHIBIT 4
Hotel

The Holiday Inns system, comprising both company and licensee-operated hotels, is the largest hotel business in the world. On December 31, 1978, there were 1,718 Holiday Inns hotels with a total of 286,529 rooms operated as follows:

	Hotels	Rooms
Company-operated		
Owned or leased	235	46,802
Under management contracts	30	9,941
Fifty percent owned	5	1,752
	270	58,495
Licensee-operated	1,448	228,034
	1,718	286,529

The following table sets forth certain historical information concerning hotels operated by the company.

Fiscal Year	Number of Hotels at Year End	Number of Rooms at Year End	Occupancy Rate (%)[a]	Average Daily Revenue per Occupied Room[a]
1978	270	58,495	74.3	$27.81
1977	276	58,536	71.2	$24.56
1976	289	58,332	68.4	$22.17
1975	305	59,384	65.4	$20.86
1974	309	59,898	68.3	$18.38

[a] Excludes hotels operated by the company under management contracts.

The following table sets forth certain information concerning Holiday Inns hotels currently operated by licensees.

As of December 31	Number of Hotels	Number of Rooms
1978	1,448	228,034
1977	1,424	220,421
1976	1,424	219,732
1975	1,409	215,585
1974	1,379	207,134

throughout the world, thus representing the largest reservation system in the hotel industry. The company is devoting considerable resources to creating the second generation of this system. Holidex II will not only be an information system, providing accounting and room inventory services, but will also provide a marketing data base as well as informational services at the unit location by 1980.

Licensees

The 1,448 inns not operated by the company are owned by independent businesspeople called licensees. During the period 1973 to 1978, the number of inns operated by licensees increased from 1,286 to 1,448, and the number of rooms jumped from 188,973 to 228,034. For the years 1976, 1977, and 1978, respectively, licensing operations contributed $34,507,000 (4 percent), $37,933,000 (4 percent), and $47,206,000 (4 percent) in revenues for the company. The company screens all applicants for licenses carefully and places a great deal of emphasis on the character, ability, and financial responsibility of the applicant, in addition to the appropriateness of the proposed location. License agreements establish standards for service and the quality of accommodations The company trains licensee management personnel at Holiday Inn University near Memphis, Tennessee; makes inspections three times a year of licensee operations; and provides detailed operational manuals, training films, and instructional aids for licensee personnel. During the initial period of 20 years, most licenses may be terminated in certain circumstances by the licensee. In the event of a licensee's violation of the agreement, the company may terminate the license. The company's policy in determining whether or not to renew a particular license agreement is in part to evaluate the overall desirability of retaining the licensee's inn within the system. During 1977, the initial 20-year term expired on five licenses, of which two were renewed.

The fees required by newly issued or renewed franchise agreements have been increased from time to time. New or renewed domestic license agreements in 1978 consisted of

1. An initial payment of $5000.
2. A fee of $150 per room (minimum $20,000).
3. A royalty of 4 percent of gross room sales.
4. Conversion of 2.0 percent of gross room sales for marketing and reservation services.

The Legal Status of the Licensee Agreement

The Holiday Inns licensee agreement has been challenged in recent court actions by an increasing number of licensees (franchisees). The agreement is being challenged on two basic points:

1. Violations of antitrust laws.
2. Fiduciary duties to present licensees regarding future locations of Holiday Inns properties.

Litigation is still pending that involves a class action suit by 412 licensees that challenges Holiday Inns right to enter into license agreements with third parties without giving a first option to established licensees for the operation of a Holiday Inn facility in the same local area where a licensee's Holiday Inn facility exists. This same litigation asks for damages against Holiday Inns, Inc., by virtue of its license agreement on prohibiting Holiday Inn licensees from owning interests in inns, hotels, and motels other than Holiday Inn facilities. This latter issue is challenged as a violation of several sections of the Sherman Antitrust Act, including restraint of trade and unlawful interstate commerce.

One franchisee, American Motor Inns, Inc., was awarded $4 million in damages from Holiday Inns on the antitrust issue involving a licensee's right to have non-Holiday Inn facilities. This verdict is still under appeal by Holiday Inns. In 1978, a licensee of three Holiday Inn facilities in Mobile, Alabama was awarded a verdict in excess of $1 million by a jury only to have the verdict set aside by the court. The right to own non-Holiday Inn facilities was at issue, and the decision is being appealed. Another case, initiated in late 1976, is asking $25 million in damages based on Holiday Inns's granting a Holiday Inn franchise in Elizabeth, New Jersey. It is claimed that this franchise hurts an existing operation at the Newark Airport in New Jersey.

Additionally, in 1978, the Domed Stadium Hotel, Inc., a licensee of the company (located in New Orleans), filed suit against Holiday Inns, Inc., hoping to enjoin the parent company from acquiring a competing hotel, The Chateau Lemayne in New Orleans. In January 1979 an affiliate of the Domed Stadium Hotel, Inc., filed suit in Mississippi alleging that the company (Holiday Inns, Inc.) made misrepresentations and fraudulently induced the plaintiff to invest in a motel in Pearl River County, Mississippi. The plaintiff is seeking $550,000 in actual damages and $1 million for punitive damages.

Products Division

The products division distributes institutional furnishings, equipment, expendable supplies, and printed products to the lodging, housing, health-care, and food-service markets. The principal functional groups within the division are:

1. *Inn Keepers Supply (IKS).* IKS accounted for 60 percent of the division's competitive sales in 1978. Distributing furnishings and equipment to the food, lodging, and health-care industries is IKS's principal business. IKS sells its products through 77 salespeople nationwide and four product display centers located across the country. The division has recently expanded operations in Great Britain, agreeing to sell furnishings and equipment to the Grand Metropolitan Hotels.

2. *Dohrmann.* This unit accounted for almost

EXHIBIT 5
Products Division

Financial Performance Data
(in millions)

	1978	1977	1976
IKS	$ 89.0	$ 75.3	$ 70.1
Innkare	21.8	19.4	16.8
Dohrmann	23.6	23.8	22.3
Other	13.7	25.1	28.0
Total revenue	$148.1	$143.6	$137.2
Operating income	$ 6.2	$ 6.6	$ 1.7
Operating margin	4.2%	4.6%	1.2%
Capital expenditures	$ 0.8	$ 0.7	$ 0.6
Assets	$ 35.3	$ 52.7	$ 54.8

16 percent of the division's competitive sales in 1978. Dohrmann, building its reputation for "tabletop" items, now carries over 5,000 products and operates in 10 Western states through 80 sales representatives. Dohrmann is the only in-house distributor owned by the company.

3. *Innkare.* Offering a range of over 4,000 items, including cleaning chemicals, kitchen utensils, and maid supplies, this unit accounted for almost 15 percent of the division's sales in 1978. Operating as a master distributor, the Innkare organization sells to 55 independent distributors nationwide, who sell Innkare products to more than 100,000 motels.

Specific performance data for this division is provided in Exhibit 5.

Transportation Group

The Transportation Division of Holiday Inns, Inc., consists of two major units. Trailways (headquartered in Dallas, Texas), the second-largest intercity bus system, and Delta Steamship Lines. By 1978, the Transportation Division accounted for 35 percent of Holiday Inns, Inc., revenue, with bus operations producing 22 percent and steamship operations producing 13 percent (see Exhibits 6 and 7).

The Trailways route system covers 70,000 miles—5,000 cities and towns in 43 states—and provides package express and charter serfice throughout most of the United States.

J. Kevin Murphy, formerly president of Purolater Services, Inc., was named president of the bus operations in 1977. Placing primary emphasis on new marketing approaches, Mr. Murphy streamlined the company's name, Continental Trailways, to Trailways and adopted a sunburst logo. A new marketing program called the "Anywhere Program" was initiated. It allowed the traveler to go anywhere in the United States—from one origin city to a destination city—with unlimited stopovers for a low, fixed price. Advertising expenditures were increased in 1977 on programs stressing the cost-saving aspects of bus travel as opposed to other transportation forms.

Trailways in 1978 became the first intercity bus company to offer a discount to senior citizens, a group that makes up 25 percent of its market. The idea was initiated as a result of a recommendation from Trailway's Senior Citizen Advisory Council. Also during 1978, Trailways completed a $4 million "terminal of the future" in Houston, Texas. As a result of a movement toward energy efficiency, the company installed speed governors on its buses, which limit the maximum speed to 55 miles per hour.

Two growing segments of bus services are charter operations and package express. Trailways's charter operations serve 26 million passengers a year, representing 9 percent of the total charter market. During the previous five-year period charter sales have grown at a compounded annual rate of almost 13 percent.

Package express, the fastest-growing segment of the Trailways division, accounts for 22 percent of total revenues from bus operations. Package pickup and delivery is offered in more than 110 major United States cities.

Delta Steamship Lines operates a fleet of 24

EXHIBIT 6
Transportation Group: Bus Operations

Bus Operating Statistics

	Fiscal Years				
	1978	1977	1976	1975	1974
Bus operating revenues (000)	$254,495	$240,262	$226,568	$204,421	$195,058
Bus miles (000)	190,770	198,125	207,678	196,682	198,628
Number of intercity buses	2,158	2,203	2,312	2,405	2,271
Passenger miles (000)	2,694,454	2,856,095	2,727,453	2,675,238	2,871,526
Bus occupancy (load factor)	39.5%	40.4%	36.4%	36.6%	39.5%

Bus Operations—Financial Performance
(in millions)

	1978	1977	1976
Passenger	$145.7	$141.9	$136.8
Charter	44.7	41.2	38.9
Express	58.8	51.3	44.9
Other	18.9	10.0	14.1
Total revenue	$268.1	$244.4	$234.7
Operating income	$ 19.7	$ 16.4	$ 15.4
Operating margin	7.4%	6.7%	6.5%
Capital expenditures	$ 21.4	$ 10.0	$ 13.1
Assets	$177.0	$171.3	$165.5

EXHIBIT 7
Transportation Group: Steamship Operations

Steamship Operating Statistics

	1978	1977	1976	1975	1974
Tons of cargo	1,190,552	636,852	727,201	733,583	930,439
Completed voyages	97	45	51	62	60

Steamship Operations—Financial Performance
(in millions)

	1978	1977	1976
Revenue	$155.0	$ 80.1	$ 81.1
Operating income	$ 7.8	$ 17.3	$ 17.6
Operating margin	5.0%	21.6%	21.7%
Capital expenditures	$ 48.8	$ 24.2	$ 0.2
Assets	$215.9	$163.3	$148.6

vessels between Gulf ports, Central America, South America, and Africa. Though revenues were affected by a 59-day work stoppage by longshoremen in 1977, they remained approximately the same as in 1976, but they increased dramatically in 1978. In 1973, Delta introduced LASH (Light Aboard Ship) cargo containers in its operations. The LASH containers (there are four in all) are filled before the arrival of a ship to improve the scheduling of the ship's time in port. For example, the average length of a typical South American voyage has been reduced from 84 to 42 days by using LASH containers.

In June 1978, Delta reached an agreement with Prudential Lines, Inc., to acquire 13 vessels and add five new trade routes (from the East and West Coasts of the United States) over the next two years at a cost in excess of $71.5 million. Approximately half of the Prudential acquisition cost will be financed using Delta's capital construction fund, and the balance will come by Delta assuming low-interest, government-guaranteed mortgages on the vessels.

The Prudential acquisition returned Delta to passenger service, an area in which the line had no involvement since 1968. All four combination passenger/cargo vessels acquired from Prudential have first-class accommodations for 100 passengers.

Restaurant Group

On April 18, 1979, Holiday Inns, Inc., announced that it had signed a formal purchase agreement to acquire Perkins "Cake and Steak, Inc.," a privately held restaurant chain headquartered in Minneapolis. Perkins has approximately 80 company owned and 280 franchised restaurants in some 30 states concentrated in the Midwest. Revenues for the company, for the fiscal year ending March 3, 1979, were $71 million, with system-wide sales of $200 million.

The decision to enter the freestanding restaurant business reflects significant research on consumer trends, as well as a corporate desire to build a broader earnings base. One of the unique characteristics of the food-away-from-home market is its ability to maintain margins and revenues during both recessionary and inflationary periods. Penetrating this market will come through acquiring existing companies, as well as by developing new restaurant concepts. One "grass-roots" development is a new restaurant called "Good Company," featuring a moderately priced menu and entertainment. The company plans to open a second test unit in Dallas in the latter part of 1979.

Gaming Group

In September 1978, the board of directors of Holiday Inns, Inc., announced that it had "expanded" corporate policy to explore potential opportunities for hotel/casino operations in any area where such operations are legal. While the company stressed that this decision implies no firm commitment toward a new development, it does indeed recognize the fact that expansion in this area represents a natural extension of its current hotel operations. Previously, corporate policy restricted the expansion of hotel/casino operations to the state of Nevada and areas external to the United States.

Just two weeks following this announcement, the company approved a proposal to construct and manage a $75 million hotel/casino in Atlantic City, New Jersey. The hotel/casino will be a joint venture between Holiday Inns, Inc., and a Los Angeles-based developer (who happens to own the property on which the hotel is to be built). When it is completed it will include 500 rooms and a 50,000 square foot casino.

In April 1979, Holiday Inns, Inc., announced that it would acquire a 40 percent interest in Riverboat, Inc., a casino operated in conjunction with the Holiday Inn–Center Strip Hotel in Las Vegas, Nevada. For the fiscal year ended June 1978, Riverboat, Inc., had revenues of $36.3 million and a pre-tax income of

$8.8 million. For the six months ended December 31, 1978, Riverboat revenues were $20.1 million and pre-tax income $5.7 million.

The entry of Holiday Inns, Inc., into the casino/hotel business was the culmination of a thoroughly researched and planned effort, which included almost two years of conducting and analyzing detailed feasibility studies and holding discussions with authorities and state officials in both Nevada and New Jersey.

Of the conclusions drawn from this research, the one that most influenced the company's decision to enter the hotel/casino business was threefold: (1) that the overwhelming majority of Holiday Inn guests had no objection to the company's becoming involved in the gaming business, (2) that the hotel/casino industry offers a natural extension of the company's main line of business, and (3) that investment in this industry would produce substantial returns.

This decision, however, triggered the resignation of the company president and chief executive officer, L. M. Clymer. Clymer said that his resignation was incited by personal and religious opposition to this company decision. In a company released statement, Clymer defended his decisions with the following comment:

> This is a personal conviction not involving the financial or business aspect of the industry. The great concern in my heart is that some may erroneously read into this action a silent judgement of those who have reached a different conclusion; this most certainly isn't the case.

Holiday Inns, Inc., Management Team

Many people have made invaluable contributions to Holiday Inns, Inc., through the years. Today the Holiday Inns, Inc., hotel system employs about 150,000 people. Their supportive efforts helped the Holiday Inns, Inc., hotel system exceed $3 billion in revenues in 1978.

Kemmons Wilson, now chairman of the board, recognized in 1951 that the lodging industry was "the greatest untouched industry in the world."

As the business grew, William B. Walton, a young attorney and a graduate of Memphis State, became the company's executive vice-president and chief administrator. Mr. Walton, later president and now vice chairman, was the architect of the company's licensing systems.

In 1957, L. M. Clymer, a Duke graduate and an investment banker with W. H. Morton & Co., was named to the company's board of directors. He contributed to the firm's financial progress and joined Holiday Inns, Inc., as a senior vice-president in 1968. Mr. Clymer was named president in 1973 and in 1976 assumed the additional responsibilities of the chief executive officer. Clymer resigned in 1978.

In 1974, Roy E. Winegardner, a licensee who had one of the company's earliest and largest hotels, joined Holiday Inns, Inc., as first vice-chairman. In 1977, Mr. Winegardner was appointed chief operating officer of Holiday Inns, and in January 1979, he became president and chief executive officer of the company.

Michael D. Rose had worked with Winegardner for many years and in 1976 joined the company as president of the hotel group.

In September 1978, Richard J. Goeglein, formerly a vice president of W. R. Grace & Company, joined Holiday Inns, Inc., as a corporate executive vice-president.

With Clymer's resignation in the latter part of 1978, Winegardner (who had previously shared the recently established office of the president with Clymer) became president and chief executive officer of the company. Joining him in the office of the president are Goeglein (who, while an executive vice-president at W. R. Grace & Company, thwarted every restaurant acquisition attempted by Holiday Inns, Inc.) and Michael D. Rose, who is both a lawyer and an accountant.

In 1976 the company began to restructure

the composition of its board of directors and elected four outside members. At the annual meeting that year, the shareholders voted to reduce board membership from 21 to 15. Today, the board includes six inside members and nine outside members.

The board of directors includes the following persons:

Wallace R. Bunn, 56, president and chief executive officer of South Central Bell Telephone Company, which provides telecommunication service. Prior to 1978, he was president and chief executive officer of Pacific Northwest Bell Telephone Company. He is presently a director of First National Bank of Birmingham.

William N. Clarke, 61, partner in the law firm of Cadwalader, Wickersham, & Taft, New York, New York.

Frederick G. Currey, 46, president of the company's transportation group.

W. M. Elmer, 63, chairman of the board of Texas Gas Transmission Corporation, which is involved in transportation and gas services. Prior to May 1978, he was also chief executive officer of Texas Gas Transmission Corporation.

Nicholas M. Evans, 48, president of the Drackett Co., which manufactures and markets household products and specialty foods. In addition he is vice-president of The Bristol-Myers Co. and director of Ohio National Life Insurance Co.

Richard J. Goeglein, 44, executive vice-president of the company. Prior thereto, he was vice president of W. R. Grace & Company and executive vice-president of its consumer services group.

Richard A. Jay, 60, vice chairman and director of The Goodyear Tire & Rubber Co., which manufactures and distributes tires and other products. He is also a director of Texas Gas Transmission Corporation.

Herbert S. Landsman, 60, executive vice-president and director of Federated Department Stores, Inc., a department store group. He is also a director of Clopay Corporation.

R. A. Lile, 70, president and chief executive officer of Transportation Properties, Inc., Little Rock, Arkansas, a real estate and investment firm. He is also a director of National Old Line Insurance Company.

Archibald McClure, 56, executive vice-president of The Quaker Oats Co., which manufactures and markets consumer products and specialty chemicals. He is also a director of The Wilmette Bank.

Allen B. Morgan, Sr., 70, honorary chairman of the board of First Tennessee Bank, N. A. Memphis, Tennessee, a multibank holding company.

Michael D. Rose, 37, executive vice-president of the company. Prior to his election as executive vice-president, he was president of the company's hotel group and inn development division.

William B. Walton, 59, vice chairman of the board of the company.

Kemmons Wilson, 66, chairman of the board of the company, a control person.

Roy E. Winegardner, 58, president and chief executive officer of the company, a control person.

Financial Performance

Exhibit 8 provides a 10-year summary of the financial performance of Holiday Inns, Inc. Revenues for the year 1978 achieved new record levels. Revenues increased by $167 million—7.2 percent—in 1977. Pre-tax income increased by $20 million—22.4 percent—during 1978 and $27 million—41.4 percent—during 1977. Of particular interest is the increase evident in the transportation division. Since 1974, revenues from this operation have increased by 32.2 percent, and revenues from steamship operations have increased by 99.1 percent. The major force in this increase was the Prudential

EXHIBIT 8
Ten-Year Financial Performance

	1978	1977	1976	1975
Operating results (millions)				
Revenues	$1202.2	$1035.3	$965.6	$917.0
Operating income	$ 156.8	$ 130.3	$104.7	$101.1
Income before income taxes—continuing	$ 111.1	$ 90.8	$ 64.2	$ 67.2
Income taxes—continuing	$ 48.3	$ 38.1	$ 24.9	$ 26.2
Net income—discontinued	—	—	$ (.4)	$ .5
Net income	$ 62.8	$ 52.7	$ 38.8	$ 41.5
Common stock data				
Earnings per share	$ 2.04	$ 1.71	$ 1.27	$ 1.35
Dividends declared per share	$ 0.56	$ 0.465	$ 0.40	$ 0.35
Average number of shares outstanding (thousands)	30,854	30,762	30,657	30,606
Financial position (millions)				
Total assets	$1196.0	$1039.6	$960.5	$957.0
Property and equipment (net)	$ 767.1	$ 705.0	$679.4	$692.4
Long-term debts	$ 322.2	$ 310.2	$299.4	$332.5
Stockholders' equity	$ 552.4	$ 504.8	$465.8	$438.6
Depreciation and amortization	$ 63.1	$ 58.9	$ 56.5	$ 57.1
Capital expenditures	$ 169.1	$ 112.1	$ 70.2	$ 59.5
Performance measurements				
Return on sales	5.2%	5.1%	4.0%	4.5%
Return on invested capital	8.5%	7.8%	6.4%	6.8%
Return on equity	11.9%	10.9%	8.6%	9.8%
Statistical summary				
Number of inns at year end				
Company operated	270	276	289	305
Licensee operated	1448	1424	1424	1409
Total system	1718	1700	1713	1714
Number of rooms at year end				
Company operated	58,495	58,536	58,332	59,384
Licensee operated	228,034	220,421	219,732	215,585
Total System	286,529	278,957	278,064	274,969
Occupancy	74.3%	71.2%	68.4%	65.4%
Average rate per occupied room	$27.81	$24.56	$22.17	$20.86
Passenger miles (millions)	2694.5	2856.1	2727.5	2675.2
Load factor	39.5%	40.4%	36.4%	36.6%
Voyages completed	97	45	51	62
Tonnage carried (thousands)	1190.6	636.9	727.2	733.6

1974	Five-Year Compound Growth Rate (%)	1973	1972	1971	1970	1969	Ten-Year Compound Growth Rate (%)
$905.1	7.4	$808.8	$718.2	$661.8	$557.3	$489.4	10.5
$101.3	11.6	$106.6	$102.5	$ 97.5	$ 88.6	$ 79.4	7.8
$ 46.4	24.4	$ 63.1	$ 74.4	$ 67.7	$ 62.4	$ 57.4	7.6
$ 20.4	24.0	$ 23.9	$ 34.0	$ 31.2	$ 27.1	$ 26.5	6.9
$ .9	—	$ 2.0	$ 1.4	$ 1.5	$ 1.1	$ 0.9	—
$ 26.9	23.6	$41.2	$ 41.8	$ 37.9	$ 36.4	$ 31.8	7.9
$ .87	23.8	$ 1.32	$ 1.37	$ 1.32	$ 1.29	$ 1.18	6.3
$ 0.325	14.6	$ .30	$ 0.275	$ 0.25	$ 0.225	$ 0.20	12.1
30,802	—	31,055	3,532	29,846	28,525	27,950	1.1
$973.5	5.3	$931.9	$892.6	$794.9	$708.7	$607.7	7.8
$720.1	1.2	$706.8	$633.5	$566.6	$500.9	$444.1	6.3
$372.7	(3.6)	$381.9	$381.3	$324.1	$324.0	$257.0	2.5
$408.6	7.8	$395.7	$365.6	$328.6	$251.7	$209.8	11.4
$ 59.5	1.5	$ 48.9	$ 43.1	$ 38.9	$ 34.3	$ 31.3	8.1
$ 86.2	18.4	$127.2	$112.4	$121.7	$ 93.8	$ 89.0	7.4
3.0%	14.7	5.1%	5.8%	5.7%	6.5%	6.5%	(2.5)
5.2%	13.1	6.8%	7.1%	7.5%	8.3%	8.6%	(0.1)
6.7%	15.4	10.8%	15.2%	13.1%	15.8%	16.1%	(3.3)
309	(3.3)	305	297	290	287	265	0.2
1379	1.2	1286	1173	1081	984	899	5.4
1688	0.4	1591	1470	1371	1271	1164	4.4
59,898	(0.6)	57,940	54,643	51,687	49,109	42,559	7.3
207,134	2.4	188,973	166,470	148,777	130,255	116,328	6.6
267,032	1.8	246,913	221,113	200,464	179,364	158,887	6.8
68.3%	2.1	70.6%	70.7%	67.4%	68.5%	72.3%	0.3
$18.38	10.9	$17.63	$16.87	$16.50	$15.55	$14.11	7.8
2871.5	(1.6)	2627.2	2486.5	2899.1	2845.7	2603.1	0.4
39.5%	—	37.1%	36.0%	39.2%	39.8%	38.4%	0.3
60	12.8	45	40	58	48	45	8.9
930.4	6.4	701.9	483.4	661.0	584.3	436.7	11.9

acquisition, and indeed between 1977 and 1978 steamship revenues increased by 93.5 percent. An analysis of the company's 10-year performance shows that the only visible significant drop in income occurred between the years 1973 and 1974, during the peak of the OPEC oil embargo.

In October 1978, Stafford–Lowden, Inc., announced that it had agreed to purchase the assets of the Holiday Press division of Holiday Inns, Inc. The printing operation, accounting for 10 percent of the products division sales in 1977, is a 300,000 square foot facility located in Olive Branch, Mississippi. Its primary activities involve providing business forms and web-press printing. In 1977 this operation had sales of $16.5 million, and for the first seven months of 1978, it showed revenues of $10.4 million. The Stafford–Lowden purchase price was between $12 million and $13 million in cash and notes.

Commenting on this move and after consolidation efforts, R. B. Erskine, corporate senior vice-president for planning and development, stated:

> We took a hard-nosed approach to operations and made demands for excellence. Every operating division and ultimately every individual unit came under scrutiny as to performance and long-term strategic significance. Some hard decisions were made which have been reflected in our improved performance this year and last year.
>
> As a direct result of significant improvements in operating performance, our debt ratio has declined. This, combined with a well thought-out investment posture, also resulted in our current favorable cash position.
>
> As the balance sheet and physical operations came under control, we began to look to the company's future. An in-depth appraisal . . . has culminated in a commitment to develop as a hospitality company. Our emphasis will be heavily consumer oriented, encompassing areas such as lodging, food-away-from-home, leisure-time activities, and related support services.

In keeping with our desire to maintain a strong growth orientation and keep our operations highly profitable, the Products Group has been steadily streamlined since 1974 when it consisted of some 26 operations. The bulk of this activity was completed by 1977, when only six operating units remained . . . all of which were profitable.

With hotel operation still representing over 50 percent of Holiday Inns, Inc., total revenues, continuing growth, and cost efficiency within this division is of paramount importance. When asked to comment on hotel operations now and for the future, Eric Bernard, president of the hotel group, responded:

> We have simplified our management structure from four regions to three. . . . We have sold 10 properties, but replaced them with five new and larger ones in high demand, destination locations. To improve our product, we have committed over $150 million in 1978 for the construction of five new Holidome indoor recreation centers, 1,445 room additions at 15 properties, and three new hotels.
>
> We expect installation of our operational management systems in the balance of our hotels by the first quarter of 1980. By the end of this year, each property will have completed a unit-level business plan. We have tested common menu items and reversed the downward trend in our food and beverage operations and produced increases well in excess of industry averages.
>
> After a systematic study, we came to the conclusion that with the implementation of a common restaurant system with consistent quality and consistent image, we can duplicate with our food operations the success we have had with our rooms.
>
> We are now ready to introduce our new restaurant system, "Pipers," on the national market. It is being implemented in our company hotels in an all-out effort. Sixty installations will be

completed by the end of this year. And 80 more will be completed by the first half of 1979. We have been working diligently behind the scenes to launch a suitable restaurant companion system to our hotel system.

Chains can offer the best value through standardization, which translates into mass purchasing, waste reduction, and labor efficiency. They can effect cost efficiency through multiple-unit advertising. Pipers will be a chain that has all of these attributes and we are confident of its success.

Now, let's turn to our international operations. We have moved forward and grown to 186 hotels open and 24 under construction, a net gain of 29 in one year. . . . We are in the midst of our second profitable year. For the three quarters to date, we have improved our profit by $4.9 million or 72.5% over 1977.

Our international properties can provide business to the U. S. Contributing to our increased referral business was our extension of Holidex this year to Hong Kong, Bahrain, Sydney, Kuala Lumpur, Manila, Sharjah, and Caracas. Further expansion in South America and to Africa is forthcoming.

Today, we are healthy and profitable. We have first-class management, operating on a decentralized basis in five international regions. We will continue to increase the profit from our existing properties and concentrate our energies on development in every part of the world where it is profitable and practical to operate. We will continue our policy of building local chains rather than building only one hotel in capital cities. And we will develop on a wide base to ensure that our profitability is not overdependent on one area of the world.

Additional financial information is included in Exhibits 9, 10, and 11.

Marketing Efforts

In mid-1977, Holiday Inns initiated an aggressive advertising campaign to complement the very successful "The Best Surprise Is No Surprise" theme, which emphasized motel quality and dependability. The new campaign slogan is "Holiday Inn Welcomes You to Some of the Best Hotels in the World." Basically, the campaign is premised on three facts: that the Holiday Inns system has the best location, that the company has the best system of standards, and that a Holiday Inn is the first choice of most travelers over any other hotel. To convey this message, the company has utilized prime-time television spots in addition to advertising in major national publications. The marketing effort emphasizes that preference for the Holiday Inns system is increasing. A recent survey indicates that almost half of the traveling public selects Holiday Inns motels as their first choice in lodging.

In addition to company advertising efforts, Holiday Inns has been working to alleviate a frequent consumer complaint: overbooking. In October 1977, the company initiated the "We Guarantee It" program. This program not only assures the customer of a firm reservation but also improves flexibility in scheduling room demand. The program was the industry's first major attempt to curb the problems of no-shows and diminish the overbooking rate. By the end of 1978, the company estimated that system-wide no-shows declined by more than 40 percent, accounting for a savings in lost revenue of $31 million.

The major theme developed by the company for 1978 described Holiday Inns hotels as "People Pleasin' Places." It stressed locations and standards.

Company research indicates that one-third of the lodging customers purchase 70 percent of the rooms. Holiday Inns continued to recognize the importance of these customers by maintaining the Inner Circle program for its most frequent travelers.

During recent years the company has redirected its sales efforts, changing its emphasis from sales in destination markets to locating its sales offices in cities where trips originate. This

EXHIBIT 9
Holiday Inns, Inc., and Consolidated Subsidiaries—Consolidated Summary of Operations
(In Thousands, Except per Share)

	1978	Percent	1977	Percent
Revenues				
Hotel	$ 649,217	54.0	$ 589,389	56.9
Products	148,102	12.3	143,581	13.9
Transportation				
Bus	268,098	22.3	244,376	23.6
Steamship	155,004	12.9	80,106	7.7
Other	14,177	1.2	6,096	.6
	$1,234,598	102.7	$1,063,548	102.7
Elimination of products inter-segment revenues	(32,389)	(2.7)	(28,274)	(2.7)
	$1,202,209	100.0	$1,035,274	100.0
Operating income				
Hotel	$ 116,548	74.3	$ 90,073	69.1
Products	6,228	4.0	6,561	5.0
Transportation				
Bus	19,717	12.6	16,420	12.6
Steamship	7,776	5.0	17,326	13.3
Other	8,103	5.1	878	.7
	$ 158,372	101.0	$ 131,258	100.7
Elimination of products inter-segment income	(1,570)	(1.0)	(957)	(.7)
	$ 156,802	100.0	$ 130,301	100.0
Corporate expense	(15,317)		(11,769)	
Interest, net of interest capitalized	(29,642)		(26,735)	
Foreign currency translation (loss) gain	(717)		(1,009)	
Income from continuing operations before income taxes	$ 111,126		$ 90,778	
Provisions for income taxes	48,335		38,131	
Income from continuing operations	$ 62,791		$ 52,657	
Discontinued operations, less applicable income taxes	—		—	
Net income	$ 62,791		$ 52,657	
Income per common and common equivalent share				
Continuing operations	$ 2.04		$ 1.71	
Discontinued operations	—		—	
	$ 2.04		$ 1.71	
Cash dividends declared per common share	$ 0.56		$ 0.465	

1976	Percent	1975	Percent	1974	Percent
$539,400	55.9	$525,753	57.3	$502,300	55.5
137,232	14.2	116,185	12.7	139,868	15.4
234,722	24.3	210,723	23.0	202,770	22.4
81,063	8.4	82,816	9.0	77,843	8.6
5,378	.5	4,772	.5	4,482	.5
$997,795	103.3	$940,251	102.5	$927,253	102.4
(32,169)	(3.3)	(23,278)	(2.5)	(22,158)	(2.4)
$965,626	100.0	$916,973	100.0	$905,105	100.0
$ 69,212	66.1	$ 60,878	60.1	$ 51,910	51.4
1,662	1.6	938	.9	9,036	8.9
15,366	14.7	20,011	19.7	25,578	25.3
17,585	16.8	18,100	17.9	12,472	12.4
2,015	1.9	2,360	2.3	3,059	3.0
$105,840	101.1	$102,287	100.9	$102,055	101.0
(1,129)	(1.1)	(953)	(.9)	(996)	(1.0)
$104,711	100.0	$101,334	100.0	$101,059	100.0
(9,200)		(9,745)		(14,161)	
(23,242)		(30,232)		(31,853)	
(3,076)		5,867			
$ 64,193		$ 67,224		$ 46,431	
24,944		26,220		20,442	
$ 39,249		$ 41,004		$ 25,989	
(400)		447		956	
$ 38,849		$ 41,451		$ 26,945	
$ 1.28		$ 1.34		$ 0.84	
(.01)		0.01		0.03	
1.27		$ 1.35		$ 0.87	
$ 0.40		$ 0.35		$ 0.325	

EXHIBIT 10
Consolidated Balance Sheets (In Thousands of Dollars)

	Dec. 29, 1978	Dec. 30, 1977	Dec. 31, 1976 (Restated)
Assets			
Current assets			
Cash	$ 24,216	$ 20,529	$ 18,345
Temporary cash investments, at cost	138,205	70,758	43,257
Receivables, less allowance for doubtful accounts of $7,835,000 and $6,031,000	137,796	87,175	88,448
Inventories, at lower of average cost or market	23,872	27,186	26,996
Other current assets	13,880	11,916	9,020
	$ 337,969	$ 217,564	$ 186,066
Less: Deposits to be made to capital construction fund	3,964	4,258	3,761
Total current assets	$ 334,005	$ 213,306	$ 182,305
Capital construction fund, including above deposits	$ 4,070	$ 26,056	$ 25,010
Investments and long-term receivables			
Nonconsolidated subsidiaries and less-than-majority-owned affiliates	$ 30,934	$ 27,974	$ 20,151
Notes receivable and other investments	37,895	46,025	31,021
	$ 68,829	$ 73,999	$ 51,172
Property and equipment, at cost			
Land, buildings, improvements, and equipment	$1,140,843	$1,068,118	$1,026,586
Less: Accumulated depreciation and amortization	373,707	363,105	347,212
	$ 767,136	$ 705,013	$ 679,374
Deferred charges and other assets	$ 21,966	$ 21,221	$ 22,646
	$1,196,006	$1,039,595	$ 960,487
Liabilities and Stockholders' Equity			
Current liabilities			
Long-term debt due within one year	$ 26,528	$ 28,707	$ 26,948
Notes payable—banks		548	3,771
Accounts payable	60,010	40,145	29,387
Accrued federal and state income taxes	43,779	30,774	16,606
Accrued expenses and other taxes	80,401	49,985	44,630
Other current liabilities	36,337	20,996	18,045
Total current liabilities	$ 247,055	$ 171,155	$ 139,387
Long-term debt due after 1 year	$ 322,177	$ 310,164	$ 299,388
Deferred credits	$ 41,247	$ 10,941	$ 15,404
Deferred income taxes	$ 33,139	$ 42,531	$ 40,557
Stockholders' equity			
Capital stock			
Special stock: authorized 5 million shares; Series A; $1.125 par value; issued 760,296 and 760,358 shares; convertible into common	$ 803	$ 855	$ 855

EXHIBIT 10 (Continued)

	Dec. 29, 1978	Dec. 30, 1977	Dec. 31, 1976 (Restated)
Common: authorized 60 million shares; $1.50 par value; issued 29,999,213 and 29,883,825 shares	45,435	44,999	44,826
Capital surplus	118,648	116,028	114,759
Retained earnings	395,982	350,995	313,301
	$ 560,868	$ 512,877	$ 473,741
Capital stock in treasury, at cost	(7,492)	(6,705)	(6,331)
Unissued deferred compensation shares	(988)	(1,368)	(1,659)
	$ 552,388	$ 504,804	$ 465,751
	$1,196,006	$1,039,595	$ 960,487

new concept, called "outbound sales," evolved from a better understanding of customer travel decisions.

In 1978, in an effort to combat discount fares offered by airlines on selected routes, the Trailways division announced a new series of low fares between major cities in the Northeastern section of the United States. These fares represent a reduction of 30 to 50 percent from regular fares and apply to selected schedules. Additionally, the company announced that it planned to offer a $59 fare on one-way trips averaging 775 miles or more. (Round-trip fares are double the one-way fares.) Trailways noted that the new low fares, which have received ICC approval, apply only to interstate travel.

Touting three major themes—"Price," "Cheaper than Greyhound," and "Senior Citizens"—Trailways, in 1978, advertised 193 times on network television and produced 3,952 radio and television advertising spots in 125 cities nationwide.

Employee Relations

Holiday Inns has outlined five basic principles that form corporate philosophy. These are:

1. Maintain high ethical standards.
2. Provide above-average growth in earnings.
3. Improve our return on invested capital (ROIC).
4. Maintain a strong balance sheet through financial management.
5. People are our greatest asset, deserving careful selection, training, and motivation.

Fulfilling the fifth tenet is no easy task when over 36,000 employees are involved. Labor relations with corporate employees, excluding the 10,000 in the transportation group, have been good.

Management–employee relations in the transportation group (which also includes as many as 2,500 longshoremen employed on an hourly basis) have been satisfactory. There have been several disputes and work stoppages during the past six years, however, including one lengthy strike at a Trailways subsidiary from 1972 to 1976 and an 18-day work stoppage at five Southeastern operating companies during 1976. Since that time, however, there have been no significant problems. In 1979, the company entered into 19 labor contracts covering 2,622 employees. Forty percent of all employees at Holiday Inns, Inc., are unionized.

EXHIBIT 11
Holiday Inns, Inc., and Consolidated Subsidiaries—Statements of Changes in Financial Position
(In Thousands of Dollars)

	Fiscal Years		
	1978	1977	1976
Source of funds			
Net income	$ 62,791	$ 52,657	$ 38,849
Add (deduct) items not affecting working capital:			
Depreciation, amortization, and allowance for property dispositions	67,824	63,034	60,483
Deferred income taxes	(8,068)	7,645	4,844
Other	1,603	1,306	3,906
Working capital provided from operations	$124,150	$124,642	108,082
Proceeds from financing	65,304	51,474	15,501
Decrease (increase) in capital construction fund	21,986	(1,046)	(2,201)
Increase (decrease) in unterminated voyage revenue	9,025	(3,764)	14
Deferred gain on sale of real estate:	21,550	—	—
Depreciated value of property dispositions	40,007	26,470	25,209
Total sources	$282,022	$197,776	$146,605
Application of funds			
Expenditures for property and equipment	$169,116	$112,091	$ 70,247
Payment of mortgages and notes	57,107	43,439	52,393
Dividends declared	16,657	13,787	11,810
Increase (decrease) in investments and long-term receivables	(7,383)	22,721	10,410
Reduction in deferred income taxes	1,324	5,671	1,619
Other	402	834	6,142
Total applications	$237,223	$198,543	$152,621
Increase (decrease) in working capital	$ 44,799	$ (767)	$ (6,016)
Changes in components that increased (decreased) working capital			
Cash and temporary cash investments	$ 71,134	$ 29,685	$ 441
Receivables	50,621	(1,273)	7,517
Inventories	(3,314)	190	(7,210)
Other assets	2,258	2,399	2,426
Long-term debt due within one year	2,179	(1,759)	(361)
Accounts payable and other current liabilities	(65,074)	(15,841)	(6,073)
Accrued federal and state income taxes	(13,005)	(14,168)	(2,756)
Increase (decrease) in working capital	$ 44,799	$ (767)	$ (6,016)

For the Future

Charles Barnette, director of corporate public relations, succinctly summarized the perspective adopted by Holiday Inns, Inc., for the future. He stated, "We want to focus business activities on markets and market segments where we can excel, achieve competitive advantage, and be the cost effective leader."

Some of the specifics that emerge from this statement are: (1) maintain a corporate debt ratio of 35 percent of invested capital; (2) increase corporate ROIC to over 13 percent; (3) grow at a rate of 15 percent or more per year;

(4) achieve a dividend payment representing 35 percent of net income.

During the period 1979–1983, the hotel group wants to increase the number of rooms by 72,000 and sell 75,000 new franchise rooms.

In regard to the transportation group, the company is lobbying vigorously in favor of municipal ownership of bus terminals.

Objectives for the restaurant group include the achievement of an earnings growth of 15.9 percent annually, and an ROIC of 10 percent.

The company invested much money and time in its research on the gaming industry. Company research indicates that casino revenues have grown at a 14 percent compound annual rate since 1948, that the gaming market has been recession-proof, and that gaming has demographics similar to those of Holiday Inn's lodging customers. Increased future emphasis in this area is virtually assured.

Kemmons Wilson, chairman of the board, placed all corporate objectives for the future in a concise framework. He stated:

> Now it's time to embark on a new era of growth and to continue the very favorable trends for our shareholders that we've seen in the past two years. The outlook for tourism in this country and worldwide has never been better. We are truly becoming a unified world where people are traveling farther, more frequently, and for more reasons.
>
> Twenty-seven years ago I had a dream. It has been fulfilled. But even in my wildest dreams I could not see the changes that were ahead. I never dreamed that so many people would travel between countries. Or that people would choose to spend a weekend in their own hometown, or that people would begin to eat more meals away from home than at home, or that forms of acceptable entertainment would change so dramatically.
>
> Today we have a better picture of the future, and at Holiday Inns, Inc. I am proud to say we're anticipating change. In fact, we welcome it. And we're determined to be out in front in whatever markets we are able to serve.

Embarking on a new era of growth will be managed, for the first time in over a quarter of a century, without the presence of Mr. Wilson. On May 16, 1979, Kemmons Wilson announced his retirement, effective June 30. At the annual stockholders meeting, held in Memphis, Wilson made this announcement in conjunction with strong words of praise for his business associates and a strong vote of confidence for the company he founded. Wilson stated:

> I have had an opportunity that no one else has had. I have seen the company take my original vision of a standardized lodging concept and turn it into the largest hotel chain in the world.
>
> As I reflect upon what we have accomplished and I study our plans for the future, I am firmly convinced that we are embarked on a new era of growth. My optimism is based upon our management organization and the favorable trends that we see in tourism throughout this country.
>
> It is also important to recognize that more people are moving into the prime lodging customer age, 25–45 years old. The baby boom has grown up. This trend will favorably impact Holiday Inns, Inc. for many years to come.

4 CONVERTING AND MANUFACTURING

CML GROUP, INC.—TWELVE-YEARS-OLD

In 1969 Charles M. Leighton (age 34) and G. Robert Tod (age 30) decided to strike out on their own. Leaving their positions as group vice-president and group operations manager at Bangor Punta Corporation's leisure time group, they established a new company called CML Group, Inc. The two men planned to locate and buy several small, successful leisure products companies that had outgrown the organizational systems set up by their current owner–founders. Drawing on their business experience and Harvard Business School education, Leighton and Tod would be the ones to provide these companies with the professional management assistance needed to grow further.

With this concept and $40,000 of their own capital, Leighton and Tod purchased 50 percent equity in the new company and in 10 days raised an additional $2 million in outside equity funds. A few months later, CML Group, Inc. had completed its first two acquisitions: Carroll Reed Ski Shops, a $2 million specialty skiwear and rental business in northern New England, and Boston Whaler, Inc., a $5 million manufacturer of high-quality motorboats outside Boston, Massachusetts. Over the next 12 years, CML steadily acquired new companies (see Exhibits 2 and 3) at the rate of about one per year, and in 1981 the combined sales of the 10 CML companies totalled $108.5 million. Tod and Leighton together currently owned about 15 percent of CML's shares; the company's book value was $19.3 million in FY 1981 (see Exhibit 1).

In short, Charles Leighton and Robert Tod had succeeded to grow and manage CML in such a way as to fulfill their personal desires to create their own company and make money in a professionally interesting fashion.[1] In 1982 they were quite optimistic about CML's future growth potential, but they also found themselves seriously questioning whether some of the strategic and organizational assumptions that had sustained the company for over 12 years were the most appropriate way to run CML Group in the 1980s. Whether and how they would sail CML beyond its original charted course was a matter of deep concern to them both.

CML's two founders had originally conceived of a decentralized, diversified company that combined professional management skills with healthy entrepreneurialism; in 1982 much of the company remained true to that vision. The 10 businesses were organized into separate divisions, while the corporate staff was deliberately kept to a minimum: Leighton and Tod plus a chief financial officer to whom two corporate treasurers and a corporate controller reported.

Despite some evolution in their own roles over the past 12 years, Leighton and Tod's involvement with CML's separate businesses was still intense, and even a superficial exposure to the two men revealed just how closely CML reflected their own interests and life style, which might be encapsulated in the

---

Source: Copyright © 1982 by the President and Fellows of Harvard College. This case was prepared by Laura L. Nash as the basis for class discussion rather than to illustrate either effective or ineffective handling of an administrative situation. Reprinted by permission of the Harvard Business School.

---

[1]Original equity breakdown:
  a. C. Leighton and R. Tod: 4,000 shares @ $10/share.
  b. Ford Foundation: 800 convertible preferred shares @ $500/share.
  c. Seventeen outside investors including Dan T. Smith, former HBS Professor of Finance Emeritus, and C. Leighton's father-in-law: 3,200 common shares @ $500/share.

EXHIBIT 1
Consolidated Balance Sheet as of July 31, 1980 and 1981 (000s of dollars)

	1981	1980
Assets		
Current Assets		
Cash	$ 2,149	$ 1,459
Accounts receivable-trade, less allowance for doubtful accounts of $354,000 in 1981 and $270,000 in 1980	9,323	7,467
Inventories		
Raw materials and work in process	4,729	4,822
Finished goods	18,561	14,686
Total inventories	23,290	19,508
Other current assets	2,436	2,547
Total Current Assets	37,198	30,981
Property, Plant, and Equipment, at cost		
Land and buildings	5,721	3,845
Leasehold improvements	2,535	1,773
Machinery and equipment	10,110	7,049
	18,366	12,667
Less accumulated depreciation	5,157	4,363
Restricted certificates of deposit	466	1,628
Goodwill	3,443	3,483
Other assets	2,616	1,115
Total Assets	$56,932	$45,511
Liabilities and Shareholders' Equity		
Current Liabilities		
Notes payable and current portion of long-term debt	$ 908	$ 1,219
Accounts payable	10,896	10,623
Accrued expenses	3,240	2,603
Customer deposits	1,053	1,189
Accrued income taxes	2,317	1,116
Total Current Liabilities	18,414	16,750
Long-term Liabilities		
Long-term debt	15,767	10,689
Subordinated convertible notes	2,700	2,850
	18,467	13,539
Deferred Credits		
Deferred income taxes	228	184
Other deferred items	507	484
Total Liabilities	735	668
Shareholders' Equity		
Preferred stock, par value $0.10 per share		
Authorized—20,000 shares		
Issued and outstanding—1,800 shares in 1981 and 4,642 in 1980—aggregate value in liquidation—$2,250,000	$ 2,191	$ 5,118
Common stock, par value $0.10 per share		
Authorized—30,000 shares		

(Continued)

EXHIBIT 1 (Continued)

	1981	1980
Issued and outstanding—16,008 shares in 1981 and 11,644 in 1980	7,692	2,575
Retained earnings	9,433	6,861
Total Equity	19,316	14,554
Total Liabilities and Equity	$56,932	$45,511

Statement of Changes in Shareholders' Equity

	Preference Stock		Common Stock		Retained Earnings
	Shares	Amount	Shares	Amount	
Balance, July 31, 1979	4,642	$5,118	12,297	$3,110	$4,924
Issuance of 25 shares on exercise of stock option			25	12	
Retirement of common stock			(678)	(547)	
Dividends on preference stock					(113)
Net income					2,050
Balance, July 31, 1980	4,642	$5,118	11,644	2,575	$6,861
Issuance of 1,779 shares			1,779	2,503	
Conversion of preference stock-convertible series 1979	(2,500)	(2,499)	2,500	2,499	
Conversion of $150,000 of subordinated convertible notes			120	150	
Redemption of preference stock-convertible series G	(342)	(428)			
Retirement of common stock			(35)	(35)	
Dividends on preference stock					(113)
Net income					2,685
Balance, July 31, 1981	1,800	$2,191	16,008	$7,692	$9,433

Source: Annual report for FY 1981.

EXHIBIT 2
History of CML Acquisitions and Divestments

		Sales ($ Millions)	FY Prior to Acquisition	1981 Sales
9/30/69	Boston Whaler acquired, stock/earnout	4.9	1969	26.2
10/1/69	Carroll Reed acquired, cash/earnout	1.8	1969	31.0
2/25/70	Hood acquired, stock/earnout			
6/18/70	Mason and Sullivan acquired, cash/earnout	1.3	1970	3.4
5/20/71	Robin Hood acquired, cash			
7/19/71	Ericson Yachts acquired, cash	2.8	1970	7.4
1/26/72	Kelty Pack acquired, common stock			
8/22/72	Sierra Designs acquired, common stock/cash	2.4	1972	9.6

(Continued)

EXHIBIT 1 (Continued)

			1981	1980
3/27/73	HFL acquired, cash			
4/27/78	Sturbridge acquired, cash/common stock	2.6	1973	8.4
10/14/73	Gokeys acquired, cash/common stock	1.9	1973	8.6
7/11/75	(Sold Hood, stock transfer)			
4/77	(HFL disposed, note written off)			
10/78	Hoyt acquired, Pfd stock/cash	1.2	1978	1.6
6/79	(Robin Hood, sold assets)			
7/31/79	(Kelty sold, cash gain $900,000)			
6/30/80	Mother Karens acquired, cash/earnout	2.7	1980	3.9
8/1/80	Supercat acquired, cash			
10/1/80	Outdoorsman acquired, cash plus notes	9.5	1980	10.3[a]

[a] First quarter sales ($2 million) not incorporated into CML's FY 1981 results.

EXHIBIT 3
CML Group Subsidiaries, 1981

CARROLL REED SKI SHOPS, INC., NORTH CONWAY, NH

Founded in 1936, CR marketed a wide range of sportswear, clothing, and equipment for skiing and tennis through direct mail catalogues and company owned retail stores. It also offered a separate collection of gift items. Generally considered to have the ultimate "preppy" image, CR's management emphasized its concern for high-quality, natural fiber clothing and the above-average range of goods offered: many stores, for example, carried 42 different shades or styles of shetland sweaters for men. Carroll Reed's main building was located next to an historic railroad station and tourist train in the White Mountains of New Hampshire. A fully modernized order processing and distribution center was located several miles away. FY 1981 contribution to CML sales: c. $31 million.

MOTHER KAREN'S, SALT LAKE CITY, UT

Founded in 1973, there really was a Mother Karen, who with her husband designed distinctive cross-country and downhill skiwear and other sports outerwear. MK designs used the highest quality sports fabrics, and clothing was marketed through specialty shops and direct mail catalogues. FY 1981 contribution to CML sales: c. $6 million.

ERICSON YACHTS, INC., IRVINE, CA

Founded in 1964, Ericson manufactured award-winning sailboats ranging from 25 feet to 38 feet in length. In 1980 Ericson developed several totally new molds for its boats. The yachts were distributed throughout the United States and abroad. FY 1981 contribution to CML sales: c. $7 million.

BOSTON WHALER, INC., ROCKLAND, MA

Founded in 1958, BW manufactured fiberglass boats ranging from 9 feet to 25 feet in length, which were distributed through dealers throughout the United States and abroad. Whaler's distinctive hull design and innovative technological processes for casting and foam-filled, fiberglass boats made BW a leading U.S. inboard and outboard boatmaker. Customers ranged from private owners to the federal government, and many orders had customized modifications. The company also sold sailboats and inflatables, and had acquired a catamaran manufacturer in Florida in 1980. The latter's former owners were innovative designers who had agreed to join Whaler in a designer/engineering capacity. By 1981 contribution to CML sales: c. $26 million.

GOKEYS, ST. PAUL, MN

Founded in 1950, Gokeys manufactured hunting boots and shoes, the most famous of which was a special boot that was impregnable to the bite of a snake. Gokeys sold sports clothing, camping, hunting, and fishing equipment through direct mail catalogues (which featured golden retrievers on the cover) and retail stores. Its main store in St. Paul was reminiscent of old Abercrombie and Fitch in New York City. FY 1981 contribution to CML sales: c. $9 million.

MASON AND SULLIVAN CO., W. YARMOUTH, MA

Located in its original house on Cape Cod, M & S marketed Early American home and hobby items through direct mail catalogues and company owned retail stores. Its chief products were clock kits, the works of which were imported from Europe and the casings of which were manufactured in another building on the Cape. M & S sponsored assembling workshops, and the weekend sessions drew a variety of hobbyists from all over New England. FY 1981 contribution to CML sales: c. $3 million.

THE OUTDOORSMAN, LAKE TAHOE, CA

Founded in 1961, the Outdoorsman was a specialty retailer whose quality name-brand sporting goods and ready-to-wear clothing were complementary to CR's products. FY 1981 contribution to CML's sales: c. $8 million.

STURBRIDGE YANKEE WORKSHOP, INC, WESTBROOK, ME

Located near Portland, SYW marketed Early American home and hobby items through direct mail catalogues and company owned retail stores. SYW shops carried over 2,000 quality items, and were arranged in mini-room displays with full accessories. Everything from the heavy furniture to the napkins on the table were marketed by SYW. FY 1981 contribution to CML sales: c. $9 million.

HOYT ARCHERY CO, BRIDGETON, MO

Founded in 1931, HA manufactured target and hunting bows that it distributed throughout the United States and abroad. Hoyt target bows had been used by Olympic Gold Medal winners in the 1972, 1976, and 1980 Olympics. FY 1981 contribution to CML sales: c. $2 million.

SIERRA DESIGNS, INC., OAKLAND, CA

Founded in 1965, SD manufactured a variety of high-quality sleeping bags, tents, jackets, and other camping equipment which were sold through company owned retail stores and specialty dealers. Several of SD's tent designs were considered to be unique, and many of its factory workers were experienced campers and hikers. FY 1981 contribution to CML sales: c. $8 million.

TABLE A
Summary of Continuing Operations Ten-Year Review

	Sales (000's)	Income (000's)	EPS
1972	$ 24,563	$ 633	$ 38
1973	31,462	729	43
1974	41,761	973	59
1975	42,276	839	50
1976	52,466	1,011	71
1977	59,198	1,209	84
1978	65,020	1,333	90
1979	73,965	1,709	104
1980	78,447	2,050	118
1981	108,489	2,685	148

phrase, "professional managers and serious athletes." By their own description, CML was first and foremost "a hell of a lot of work and a hell of a lot of fun." The 10 companies were "fun" businesses marketing fun products: sailboats, camping and ski gear, high-quality casual wear, and tasteful colonial furniture. They were for the most part located in suburban areas, housed in converted clapboard houses, or clean small-scale manufacturing and warehouse facilities. The corporate office in attractive suburban Concord, Massachusetts was an old, restored railroad station past which the Boston train rumbled several times a day. In contrast to their leisurely settings, the CML companies had as a group attained a size and professional status that allowed the corporation to compete satisfactorily for outside services, investors, and managers. CML had attracted investments from several prestigious organizations,[2] and by 1982 it had been able to attract an experienced management team.

As Tod and Leighton reflected on CML's history, they felt that in spite of the dramatic changes in the company's size and diversity, and despite the injection of a strong dose of professional management practice into the pristine entrepreneurialism of the acquired businesses, much about CML remained the same. Looking back, Tod asserted, "We're still entrepreneurial in spirit."

Many of the policies that had been instituted over the past 12 years were derived from the two founders' desire to preserve a balance between growth, professional management, and entrepreneurship, but it was nevertheless a balance that new circumstances had continually threatened to unbalance and that was still problematic. What follows is an account of CML's development, how Leighton

---

[2]Total cost of issue (placed privately): $364. The most recent offering was placed in 1981 for $2.5 million at $1,500 per share.

and Tod implemented their original business strategy, and the major issues that concerned them at the time this case was written.

Joining CML—Acquisition Strategy and Assimilation of New Companies

The original financial goals were simple: growth in corporate earnings per share of 20 percent per year, a pre-tax return on CML's investment in acquired companies of at least 20 percent, and a 12.5 percent annual profit growth of acquired companies. In 1981 CML had the same earnings objectives with the revised condition that 15 percent of its growth would arise from existing companies and 5 percent from acquisitions. Annual variations in acquisition activity, however, made this distribution only a rough guideline.

CML's nonfinancial goals had from the start centered on building an organization that was, as the first offering memorandum stated, "devoted to self-expression and individual creativity for profit." Moreover, Leighton and Tod were interested only in "quality companies—quality performance and quality products."

The first acquisition was Boston Whaler in September 1969. As the designer and manufacturer of the first "unsinkable" outboard motorboat, Whaler had an outstanding reputation for technological excellence and distinctive design (as well as processing 700 dealers worldwide), which made it a perfect candidate under CML's criteria.

Whaler's founder, CEO, and principal owner, Dick Fisher, was willing to sell the company because he needed capital for expansion and because he was more interested in the designing side of the business than in instituting badly needed changes in the marketing mix as well as cost control and budgeting policies for the expanding enterprise. Tod and Leighton were already familiar with the company's products. In addition, Charles Leighton had sailed extensively in major sailing competitions, and Robert Tod had once held the U.S. Class B hydroplane speed record. Both had had a long-standing interest in the boat market with their marine company experiences at Bangor Punta. They anticipated that Whaler's long-term sales growth would exceed the industry's 8 percent projected annual average and that CML would achieve fairly quick increases in margin through various cost-saving measures. Fisher would remain head of Whaler after the acquisition, but would be assisted by an experienced manager who could initiate and implement operational policies necessary to meet CML's profit and sales expectations for the company.

Most of CML's subsequent acquisitions followed the Whaler pattern: it sought out healthy, smaller leisure-product companies, privately held, whose original founder(s) had a need to raise capital and/or were personally ready to hand over the managerial reins as the company outgrew its ability to rely on a single person for all administrative decisions.[3] The new parent in turn was expected to provide an infusion of capital and managerial expertise to correct administrative and marketing weaknesses in the business. The original owners would be retained by CML, and were generally assisted by a manager with previous outside experience. All the original companies were distinguished in their markets for technical inventiveness or innovative distribution systems, and they all marketed "elite," high-quality, functional leisure products with which Tod and Leighton had a personal familiarity or interest. As a general principle, this "personal feel" was of greater strategic consideration to them than more formal and financially oriented acquisition criteria. Recalled Leighton:

> One time we made a major mistake by acquiring a particular company because we thought we got a great financial deal, even though we really weren't that excited about the product or its distribution or the people. It looked great

---
[3]For a description of CML's 1982 companies, see Exhibit 3.

for one year, but long-term growth prospects were nil.

The leisure time and discretionary income fields, he explained, were highly ego-intensive and, consequently, a changing market ("Will it be windsurfing or waterskiing?") in which one needed to be personally involved.

> So often if you put down on paper what you actually did, it sounds as though you had deliberately devised an excellent strategy. But a lot of it is gut feel. You go to the national sporting-goods shows, direct mail order shows, the camping and boating shows . . . all of a sudden something hits you.

While "portfolio mix" was never a compelling criterion, Leighton and Tod did begin to factor organizational fit into their acquisition strategy as CML grew in size. By the late 1970s they were looking for larger companies than before and in some instances tried to find businesses that could operate as subsidiaries of existing CML divisions. The Outdoorsman, for example, a $9.5 million company that was acquired in 1981, was chosen partly on the basis of its potential to be a geographic, retail, and seasonal complement to Carroll Reed. Strong in the West, Outdoorsman had the same customer base as Carroll Reed, and in a bad ski season in the East, products could be moved out West, and vice versa. The combined operations also gave Carroll Reed $5 million additional strength in dealing with suppliers.

Neither Leighton, nor Tod underestimated the changes that an acquired company faced in joining CML, and together they tried to smooth the process of assimilation. Charles Leighton concentrated the majority of his attention on the preacquisition process (identifying and negotiating the acquisition as well as maintaining investor relationships), while Robert Tod managed the extensive operational changes which would occur later. Leighton tried to insure that the two parties really got to know each other before agreeing to make a deal.

> Once you find someone—it's like the dating process—you're finding out about each other's idiosyncrasies. Is the chemistry right? That's really what you end up talking about rather than solely the financial aspects.

An essential part of that chemistry was being able to subdue the owner–founder's anxieties over losing control of the company while ensuring his or her continued participation in the business. Leighton would try to explain in detail what life would be like at CML and would ask, "Is it the atmosphere that would be conducive for you to grow in, would you enjoy being a part of it? Would you be excited about it? It's not solely your company anymore, but we have a management system where you have the authority and responsibility for managing it and for its future."

To help achieve a compatible fit between the former owner and, in those cases where a professional manager would be brought into the acquired company, the owner had final authority in selecting the general manager from a pool of candidates recruited and screened by CML, and in firing the general manager should the team prove to be unproductive. This arrangement still held for new acquisitions in 1980 and 1981.

Although most of the original owners stayed with CML until retirement, several eventually chose to leave the company. For Boston Whaler's Dick Fisher, the lure of starting yet another new company of his own was more appealing than trying to run the significantly larger concern that Whaler was becoming. For Ted Hood, who was widely known as one of the outstanding designers and manufacturers of sails for ocean-racing sailboats, CML's refusal to underwrite such ventures as an entry in America's Cup convinced him and CML that Hood Sailmakers was better suited for individual ownership. Hood eventually bought back the company.

Some Consequences of Growth

By 1981, CML had "finished the first phase," to use Robert Tod's phrase, where the professional manager was an adjunct to assist the original owner–founder. With the exception of CML's two most recent acquisitions, where the owners had remained the active presidents, all the companies had professional managers in the top position of division president, primarily because of owner retirement. While clearly intending to steer the CML companies toward a professional administration, Leighton and Tod were insistent on preserving the "entrepreneurial spirit" of the original companies. Mr. Tod stated:

> As an organization we're lean and simple. We place great emphasis on performance: our company presidents know that if they perform they'll be substantially rewarded.

Charles Leighton added:

> We have a corporate culture or philosophy and we've tried to preserve that culture as we've gotten larger. First, from an operations viewpoint, the combination of quality products and quality management should create quality performance for our investors and this process can and should be fun.
>
> Regarding acquisitions, we do not believe in raiding, nor do we believe that once a company has been acquired that we should go in and turn them upside-down. Although some might argue this is effective in the short term, we believe this would greatly reduce our ability to acquire those quality companies that often aren't for sale.

How did the professional managers in charge of divisions regard this entrepreneurship? As one division president put it, "Entrepreneurial? Hell. We're all suicidal! We love to take risks." Charles Leighton quipped to a *Wall Street Journal* reporter, "Street smarts beat the hell out of analytical smarts any time."[4]

CML's entrepreneurial culture, however, did not disguise its general tendency to become increasingly professionalized as the individual companies and overall corporation increased in size. The relative cost of obtaining outside advice became lower; and it also became easier to get attention from the top accounting, legal, and banking institutions. The firm was one of Price Waterhouse's large accounts in Boston, and, for example, if CML needed a tax opinion on a potential acquisition very quickly, PW was right there. The company also had retained what they considered the best corporate lawyer and law firm in Boston. It had had several lead banks since 1974, and was currently using one of the largest banks in the country.

As CML grew, it also became easier to attract more experienced managers. When asked how professional managers made a difference in the company, Robert Tod replied:

> With any small company—3, 4, or 5 million—you have to deal with a lot more intuition; generally you don't have the luxury of an experienced management team.
>
> Now several of our companies have anywhere from 10 to 30 million in sales. They have an organization that is experienced. They've been through problems before with that company and with other companies. They can deal with change. And they have an internal control system and an information system that allows them to make decisions based on facts that are reasonable facts, and not all assumptions.
>
> It's just easier to do things at $100 million in sales than when we were at $40 million; it really is. We're able to solve problems more quickly now.

Charles Leighton summarized the effects of size, business mix, and managerial experience in the current CML group of companies as follows:

> Let's say we're a baseball team: Now we have Boston Whaler and Carroll Reed in the major leagues; Sturbridge Yankee is getting there. And we have a couple of triple A's. We still have a couple of D's, which we've spent more

---

[4]Christopher Grisanti, "One-Time Harvard Teacher Builds Group of Firms by Leaving His Managers Alone," *The Wall Street Journal*, July 12, 1982.

time on than on the major league. But by getting the professional people working with them it's just all coming. And it's because they're doing it, not us. That's the exciting thing.

Organization

Divisions

CML's current organizational structure has not changed radically from Tod and Leighton's original concept of a decentralized divisional grouping. In 1981 the 10 CML companies were self-contained divisions, each with its own president. Although the number and professional experience of division officers varied widely according to the size and activities of each division,[5] there was generally no "second string" subordination at the companies. As Robert Tod put it, "you were either division president or in a functional position, in which case you were classified a vice president. The latter position was not usually viewed as a precursor to being a president."

With the exception of quarterly "Presidents Meetings," where all the division heads would meet to present before the group a quarterly review of their own performance and perhaps participate in a management seminar, the presidents had very little routine contact with each other. The divisions were so decentralized that one company's catalogue did not necessarily stock the items of another CML division. In light of this decentralization, the Presidents Meetings were regarded as a key factor in establishing a sense of belonging to CML and an impressive collection of managers. As one president remarked, "It can get awfully lonely running a company."

Both Tod and the presidents themselves agreed that they all were "entrepreneurial in spirit," but there was less consensus on the "professionalism" of CML's divisional heads.

While some presidents felt it was only a matter of time before all the presidents carried the equivalent of an MBA, others thought CML was beginning to move away from its original pattern of assisting and then replacing the owner–entrepreneurs with professionally educated administrators. As one president asserted, "CML knows the divisions which are doing well today are companies which have shirtsleeve managers with gut-level instincts."

The "professional" backgrounds of the division presidents also seemed to escape generalization, as the following three examples indicate.

Frederick Leighton, president of Carroll Reed, came to CML after 11 years with Fieldcrest, a textile producer, during which time he had filled various management positions ranging from sales manager to marketing manager. John Riddle, head of Sturbridge Yankee Workshop, had worked with a large, quality furniture company before starting up his own gift business, and after it failed for a variety of reasons (including undercapitalization), he was recruited by CML. David Loveless, Boston Whaler's president, had an MBA from Harvard Business School and had been vice president for three years in a large chemical company before being lured to CML in 1969.

Despite their different backgrounds, all three claimed that their initial attraction to CML had been the chance to run their own show. For several of the presidents, the fear or reality of cash restrictions were the only things that had prevented them from starting their own companies or doing so now. They were not, however, a timid bunch. Several complained that CML was, if anything, too risk averse. As one put it, "We love to take risks, do crazy things to meet plan." And another remarked, "If I don't do well, I expect to have to look for a job."

In 1980 five changes were made at the division president level: one president left to join Ronald Reagan's administrative team, two

---

[5]Although CML was generally described as a marketing–distribution company, some of the divisions also had extensive manufacturing operations (see Exhibit 1).

were asked to leave, two existing presidents were transferred to new openings, while the remaining empty position was filled by a person who had received his MBA from Harvard Business School in 1975 and had worked five years at Gillette before CML wooed him away. Although the presidents of Boston Whaler and Carroll Reed had been with CML from its start, Tod estimated that about 70 percent of the overall management team was new to the company within the last five years.

When asked how good CML had been at picking people, Robert Tod replied:

> There has been enough involuntary turnover to indicate that we can do better. I think we look a lot harder at our people now. We are less patient with the professional managers of the company—we give them less time to correct their mistakes than we do the owner–founders. For example, during our recent change of presidents, we saw that profit growth in one company was not very good. We suspected that the president was getting in over his head. We could justify keeping him, but we could also justify removing him—and we made the decision that the time had come to make a move.

Groups

The company recently had established groups under Boston Whaler and Carroll Reed's auspices to link some of the divisions, but in 1981 the structural features of this plan were still evolving. The first group–division relationship had been set up four years earlier when it was decided that Sturbridge Yankee would be put under the jurisdiction of Carroll Reed's president, Frederick Leighton.[6] To help determine the proper reporting system, auditing, and the way that the group would handle cash flow and sales, Leighton hired a new financial officer. A second division was added to this group in 1980 when the Outdoorsman was acquired. Although he did not get involved in the actual negotiations, Frederick Leighton participated in this acquisition to help determine whether or not it seemed to fit well with Carroll Reed's style to see whether the Outdoorsman would offer CR additional market opportunities.

Under the group structure, Fred Leighton wore two hats: president of Carroll Reed and group vice-president for CML Group. Leighton's own compensation and incentive plan were based on CR's performance, but also in part on Outdoorsman and Sturbridge Yankee's results.

In practice, the two divisions had very different relationships with Frederick Leighton, even though they were about the same size (each about one-third of Carroll Reed in sales). Outdoorsman's management (including the president) reported directly to Leighton, and he had the power to hire and fire its staff. He was not, however, an absolute buffer between the corporate office and the new subsidiary. Robert Tod described the corporate–group–division relationship as follows:

> Outdoorsman is a separate company. The president of CR has responsibility for Outdoorsman, but that doesn't mean we just look away and don't pay any attention to it. I was out there last week.

A second type of corporate–group–division relationship was established for Sturbridge Yankee, which was considered in practice more independent from CR than Outdoorsman—"a sort of dotted line relationship between the two, perhaps not as direct as Outdoorsman, but still a strong relationship" (Tod's description). John Riddle, president of Sturbridge Yankee, worked closely with Frederick Leighton partly under the group structuring and partly because SY and CR were setting up retail stores side-by-side in several shopping malls in New England. Frederick Leighton described his relationship with Riddle as follows:

---

[6]Frederick Leighton was Charles M. Leighton's brother, and had joined CML in 1969.

Jack's and my relationship is not quite as defined as the Outdoorsman: it is more of an advisory capacity than a direct reporting. At Sturbridge I feel I could only make a very strong recommendation on certain things concerning what I would or would not wish. I'm aware of the day-to-day operations at SY and where Jack wants to go, but it is his show. I do work on particular things with him—his salary and bonus arrangement, things like that. Between the two of us, we can set up some kind of strategy as to whether or not we want to increase sales for a certain period, or whether we want to decrease cost, or whatever, and we will hash things over to make sure that we all feel that we are going on the same wave length.

Why have a group at all? Frederick Leighton replied:

It wasn't anything that had to happen, it was not in the bylaws. At first we just did things, made things happen after we took on a company. Then we reached a point where it seemed we'd better start systematizing, have a structure that is organized around specializations. For example, we need to be in a position to jump with each new step in automation. For the most part, however, we don't share personnel within the group. I guess the group happened because some of us have made things happen and now need more of a challenge. Also CML's office is small—they can only handle so many people reporting in to Tod.

How did he feel the group system was working?

The structure is somewhat loose now, and the corporate people have to determine how important the group concept should become. Maybe I should be careful of the structure—I don't want it so structured that it does not have any flexibility to it.

Charles Leighton summarized CML's future structural plans as follows:

I hope that each president in our divisions will consider his company as another CML group potential, and so if he develops a good management team with good skills, then he could say 'all right, our expertise is this. Let's find some companies that could use this expertise and which have uniquenesses that we don't have.' And then we will go out and acquire those sort of companies and put them right underneath them, because the presidents have that management skill. And they certainly can manage—if they're the right sort of people—to have three or four of these sort of divisions. So we'll limit the number of companies that come in here to report to Bob (Tod).

But we don't want to do something that becomes very time-consuming for the division presidents so that they lose focus on what they're already doing. Because the little company is more time-consuming than a big company. Now in the case of CR we bought the Outdoorsman, a 10-million dollar company, but it's in a related business in a different location. And so we think there's a good fit there.

Corporate

CML's strong emphasis on decentralization, the presidents' personal responsibility for division performance, and general acceptance of an entrepreneurial independence might suggest that the companies were totally separate from each other and even from the corporate institution that was called CML. Nowhere, for example, would you find CML's name on company catalogues, and when asked what they called the corporate office, most presidents replied with surprise, "Well, I guess we don't call it anything—maybe Concord, or just Bob, Charlie, and Bill!"[7]

Robert Tod and Charles Leighton encouraged the presidents to feel this kind of ownership over their own companies, but they also had organized CML around a belief that they could do more as a diversified group than any one company could do alone. At the same time Tod recognized the difficulty in pinpoint-

---

[7] William Taylor, Chief Financial Officer.

ing what CML had actually contributed to each business.

> One has to look pretty hard at what we're doing to see where the value added is. The value is over time; it's subtle, it's environmentally related, and it's over time performance-related.

Charles Leighton summarized CML's contribution in the following way:

> I think it interfaces in everything we're doing. We're superimposing some good common sense financial discipline over what is, hopefully, a reasonably well thought-out strategy that thinks first of people and motivating those people—choosing, exciting, motivating, and in some cases, demanding performance, or setting high performance goals.

The divisional performance responsibilities of which Leighton spoke were frequently invoked with the statement, "No closets to hide in." A corollary precept for the corporate office might have been, "No status symbols to hide behind."

To the outside visitor, the informality of CML's head office was immediately apparent—there were no special parking spaces; the interior layout of the old railroad station had no corridors; the rooms were divided like an old house, with the same new carpeting and teak decor throughout. Tod and Leighton's personal involvement and style were much apparent in the details of the building: magazines included *Boating* and *The New Yorker* while the conference/board room in the attic was reached via a precariously open circular staircase that was best negotiated in a pair of topsiders. Each floor had one bathroom, which was equipped with a shower and scales for the athletic and weight-conscious members of the office. Visitors were more likely to be offered Tab than a cup of coffee, and corporate officers frequently shared sandwiches with the rest of the staff in a kitchen-dining area in the basement. Tod and Leighton clearly delighted in this kind of attractive informality, and Leighton would frequently meet visitors at the door, mischievously welcoming them—soda in hand—as if he were the receptionist.

Part of this atmosphere coincided with the overall CML philosophy: "lean and simple." But clearly the coroporate structure and setup reflected Leighton and Tod's personal preferences as well. Leighton commented:

> We don't want anyone bowing and scraping around here. This office is made up of nine people—three of them secretaries—who can tell you to go to hell, if they wish. And it's a good indication to potential acquisitions of what life at CML would be like. If you're a manager who needs all sorts of midtown-Manhattan props, you won't fit in here. People come in here to do business and they tend to puff up. We puff them down again, and for the most part they really like that. (Pauses to wait for the Concord train to pass by.) If we can't extract the fun out of doing business, then we might as well sell CML off.

With the exception of visits from the chief financial officer and the corporate controller as well as occasional conversations with Tod, there was no formal staff support at the corporate level for the divisions, and all division presidents reported directly to Tod. At one time CML had taken on a corporate marketing person and a data-processing expert to act as internal consultants for the corporate office and as "free" consulting advisors to the divisions, but neither person had worked out. The corporate office abandoned the idea of expanding its centralized functional staff, and it was currently felt that the division presidents should rely on their own managing teams for day-to-day support.

At the same time, Tod and Leighton felt that they had to stay sufficiently involved in division activities to understand what the presidents were doing and where they were going, and, as Leighton said, "to make sure that we're influencing them as well as they're influencing us." Both men were clearly intrigued on a personal level by the products and style of the CML companies, and their involvement in powerboats, yachts, sporting equipment, and quality clothing was clearly genuine, and clearly maintained on a regular basis.

Despite occasional visits to the divisions, Charles Leighton's day usually centered on corporate-wide financial issues or acquisition activity more than on day-to-day operations. He and the corporate controller spent much of their time screening potential companies and possible new markets for CML; for example, one current area of interest was the health/recreational-type fitness centers that seemed to be gaining in popularity. Leighton also tried to visit at least six outside companies a year to acquaint them with CML and to get a better idea of possible acquisition candidates. The other main aspect of his job was meeting with CML's investors (current and future), and Leighton repeatedly stressed that its prime responsibility was to insure that CML remained financially flexible at all times. Although Robert Tod's daily activities were focused more on operational issues, he also participated in visiting acquisition candidates and in tracking various other corporate matters.

In the early years of CML, Tod felt that the best way to exercise his administrative influence was by knowing the companies' businesses as well as the division presidents did and to involve himself intensively in each company's operations. He would visit divisions at least once every two weeks, and 50 percent of his time was apportioned to on-site contact with division personnel. At that time, Tod's involvement with the divisions included discussions of pricing policy, marketing strategy, production scheduling, personnel problems, and recruiting new managers. In looking back on this period, Tod let out a sigh: "Boy, for the first few years all we did was live and breathe CML! I don't really remember having any outside life at that time. I even knew the phone bills at the divisions." During this period, Tod's involvement with the divisions generated its own symbol, of which every division president knew and related to incoming officers and presidents: it was a small black book containing monthly figures on division budgets, sales, pricing, catalogue deadlines, etc., that Tod carried in his jacket pocket. Whenever he spoke with the presidents by phone or in person, he would frequently have the book in front of him to refer to these figures. In 1981 Tod still kept up his little black book and was ready during any phone conversation to discuss detailed sales figures, catalogue deadlines, and so forth at a moment's notice.

Did he still spend 110 percent of his time on the operating details of the companies? Tod answered:

> No. We still keep track of the major decisions, but this takes less time now. In the past, a lot of my time was spent on just getting up to speed in the companies, their businesses, and their environment. Once you get to know what makes them tick, you can touch base less frequently, because you can judge the decisions being made by management more easily.

In estimating how he divided the time he spent with the divisions, Robert Tod drew the following planning spectrum, which contrasted breadth of outlook with personal time spent on each activity.

As can be seen from this chart, much of his contact with the divisions was financial in substance and the controls were admittedly fairly strict: CML companies daily reported cash, receipts from the previous day, and disbursements for that day to the Concord office. On the first Tuesday of each week every company had to call in sales for the previous week. Robert Tod received those figures by Wednesday. Each president also submitted a monthly report on key indicators for his business (aging of receivables, inventory breakdown, performance by catalogue or store, margins on product lines, etc.), along with a one-page cover letter summarizing problems and challenges. Tod in turn circulated his monthly board report to all presidents.

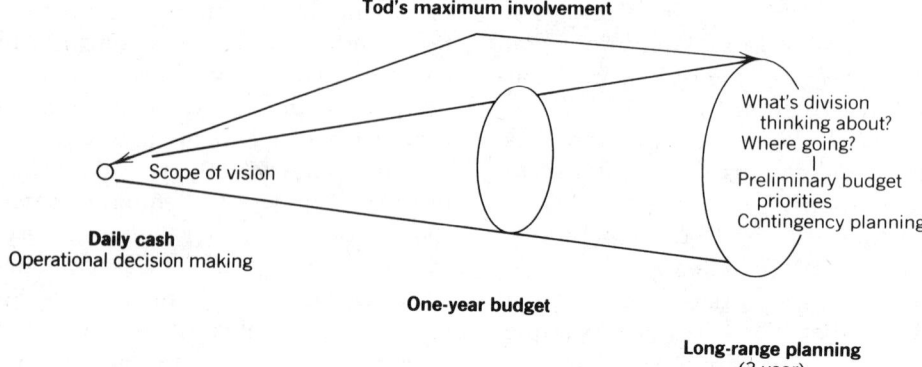

The corporate control system had been significantly tightened in 1976 after one division, named HFL, managed to incur a $1 million loss in a single year. The division, which manufactured clock kits and a limited furniture line, had decided to stimulate sales by launching a major new direct mail campaign, and to simultaneously start up a retail operation selling a new line of finished clocks and kits at several locations. Both efforts failed. A postal strike occurred just after the catalogues were completed, and the retail businesses caused severe production and scheduling problems that quickly hurt the previous high quality of HFL's clock kits. Eventually the company was liquidated. Because of errors in HFL's inventory reporting and a variety of delays in charging committed expenses to the division's budget, CML's corporate officers had been caught by surprise and had not been able, despite repeated efforts, to determine the extent of the problem as it was occurring. Tod's account of this incident was touched with a certain grim humor:

> The HFL incident had a fairly profound change on the company. In retrospect it was the combination of a lot of things: we were starting to move into a bigger company, bigger league, you might say. We were being brought up short in terms of recognizing that problems can develop even in the most attractive situations, because there are so many companies. Company after company you see gets carried away with very rapid growth.
>
> For us, 1975–1976 was a turning point in CML's history. Up to that time, we'd had good growth and were generally pleased with the way the divisions were becoming more professionally run. But an inventory explosion at the start of the 1974 recession had underscored for me just how much we needed to concentrate on some serious long-range planning, and how the corporate office needed to develop more sophisticated control and management information systems. We believed—and still do!—in decentralization and divisional autonomy, but our divisional planning needed to be much stricter than a single minded and hope-ridden concentration on profit growth. Now that's changed. The divisions are required to be more formal about planning and reporting, and I think it's pretty hard to go too much further than we have in terms of reporting at our size and not lose some of the individuality, some of the decentralized responsibility which we expect the divisions to have.

Planning at CML

To help maintain a balance between strict corporate control and decentralized divisional authority, CML placed great emphasis on the budgeting process, which the corporate officers felt was more disciplined and complete than at most of the CML companies' competitors. At the same time, it was felt that it would be inappropriate to ask the divisions to plan in as much detail as some larger conglomerates would demand.

About every year and a half, each divisional manager drew up a detailed strategic plan that included a profile of customers, microeconomic assessment and forecast, industry analysis, capital expenditures, distribution plan, and manufacturing and marketing strategies. The yearly budget process began in February with a rough estimate of current year-end results, performance for the next fiscal year, and a brief shot at the picture two years out.

This estimate was reviewed separately by Leighton, Tod, and the chief financial officer in a review process that was a combination of qualitative analysis and intuition. Robert Tod commented on this review as follows:

> Our chief financial officer consolidates the numbers; we look at them, raise questions about them, play devil's advocate on them. I'm quite concerned about the capital requirements, and then the divisions' objectives, and how they relate to what they say they're doing—does that add up?

To Tod's mind, the most significant information centered around pricing, distribution, and capital expenditure estimates. Any expense over $1,000 had to be included in the capital plan, and all expenses over $5,000, even though approved, were resubmitted as a capital request that required Robert Tod's signature.

For the most part, product strategy relied on knowledge of the customers more than competitive analysis, and in general it was felt that this approach was better suited to a company that had the lead product in a niche market. Consequently, a competitive analysis of the industry was not a primary evaluation tool for the budgets. Nor did the corporate office place a great emphasis on economic forecasts.

> I don't think that companies of our size can afford to do much more than a very gross generalization of what to expect in the financial marketplace—inflation is here with us, therefore we've got to have control over our pricing. Look at our last fiscal year: our bank estimated a prime rate of 11–12 percent and we ended up with a 17 percent average! That cost us an extra $600,000.

After the corporate review of the preliminary budget, Robert Tod and William Taylor met with each president to discuss his plan before a final, formal budget was submitted in May; this budget carried with it a detailed contingency plan for the next fiscal year. Within the first two months of FY 1981, four of the companies were already in a contingency mode, and all had identified problems with their performance vs. budget. Tod stressed the importance of the contingency plan, and much of his attention concerning the divisions was spent on performance vs. plan. The financial goals to which they had committed were considered binding, but the plans for achieving them were regarded as fluid—as conditions changed, so did the updates on the achievement of plan. Summarized Tod:

> Performance is the key. So as long as they have a good strategic plan, and as long as they're performing up to that plan and meeting our expectations, the division presidents are going to get the assets they need. . . .

Financial and Investor Policy

The original CML prospectus in 1969 expressed the founders' intention to take the company public in a few years. As time passed and the company remained private, this intention was not reversed but rather deferred.

In 1981 CML was still privately held. Among the outside investors, Reader's Digest Association, Inc. owned approximately 25 percent and the Ford Foundation, 10 percent. The most recent institutional investor was Save & Prosper, Ltd., one of the oldest mutual funds in Great Britain.

When asked why the investors had remained patient so long about going public,

Leighton attributed part of the reason to their initial expectations, part to company performance, part to the on-going relations that the company had maintained with its investors, and part to the types of investors they had chosen:

> When we first started CML we said, "quality products, quality people, quality performance." We also intended to attract quality investors. Now what does that mean? Well, first of all they had to relate to our company, and the products, and what we are, and what we aren't. Second, we had to be a very small part of their portfolio so that they were less concerned about making a big gain short term on our company; they had to have a long-term viewpoint. As a group their basic goals have been surprisingly similar. They have all tended to be very wealthy people or groups or trusts where we represented a very small part of their assets.
>
> They recognized that they were buying a pie in the sky initially, but they see a private placement at $1,500 a share locked up—which in a public market is probably worth $2,000. So, you know, they begin to sense that they can see four times or five times on their initial investment, which isn't dramatic over 12 years, but it isn't bad.
>
> And then along the way they've had the association, they've been a part of the executive meetings, they've been a part of all activities. I think one of the attractions is the intrinsic value of being associated with some of the products that our company has. It's interesting how much it's meant to them to get a 20 percent discount on Carroll Reed or Gokey's products—they take a tangible result of their investment home to their families, who can relate to our products.
>
> I think their expectations are perhaps a little varied, but they generally expect growth in the range of 15–20 percent a year in terms of the earnings of the company, and it seems their hope is that their investment in CML is doing better than the broad market averages.

Mr. Leighton added:

> Some people say we're too highly leveraged. We don't believe this. Because each of our companies is a strong business entity in its own right, we could, for example, sell a company the size of Carroll Reed tomorrow and pay off our entire bank debt.

The Future

In 1981 Charles Leighton and Robert Tod felt that one of the major questions facing them was how they could best position CML financially to achieve the growth goals that they had defined for the company. As they saw it, CML had the potential to go in three very different directions: stay private, go public, or agree to an upstream merger. At the moment these alternatives were equally possible, and if the alternatives were three points on a triangle, CML was deliberately poised precisely at the center.

How long it would continue to be so, however, was a subject of great concern, and it was clear to both men that any direction they chose would have a strong impact on the way they managed CML Group, Inc. financially, on what sort of acquisitions they would be able to attract and afford, and on the cultural character of the organization they had created. Nor did it escape them that, whatever the final decision was, CML's continued growth could substantially affect the organizational policies now in place.

CML's division presidents had quite varied responses to the possibility of change either through a public offering or an acquisition by a larger company. Several flatly pronounced that they thought it unlikely that the entrepreneurial style of the divisions could remain intact under the control of a large conglomerate, nor did they feel that public shareholders would be as patient about the long-term investments which some divisions had made. "Frankly," said one president, "if a large conglomerate bought us I'd be out the door in a second—and I bet Bob and Charlie would be, too!"

Other presidents saw various advantages as well as disadvantages to being part of a larger company, as the following comments by various division presidents indicate:

> If we were part of a *Fortune* 500 company, we would probably be given a lot more money than we have had, and probably would not have the same responsibility for the bottom line or return on managed assets. Our short-term equity and cash flow would not have been quite the problem they have been and, therefore, we might be quite a bit larger than we are today. As it stands, CML is too risk averse.
>
> . . .
>
> There is a constant battle to have more capital in the company. Most of the companies are small enough that we are in a fast-growth stage. Profit margins are not all that high. We need a lot of cash to finance our growth. I wouldn't mind CML finding a way to enhance that.
>
> . . .
>
> The larger the company, the more political the company is. In a merger you'd find yourself playing the political game.
>
> . . .
>
> Philosophically, I guess the advantage I see is that when the companies are at least the size we are and somewhat larger there are some significant advantages to being run by a close-knit group of entrepreneurs as opposed to getting amalgamated into a corporate structure. It's not good to get homogeneous in thinking, as you do in a corporate environment, and there is an advantage to overall profitability when you don't have huge overhead for meaningless functions.
>
> . . .
>
> My preference would be a large private investor benefactor: to be bought by a privately owned company.
>
> . . .
>
> If I had my way, I would rather see CML go public than merge. That way you have an opportunity to see what the general public thinks of you, and you still have a lot more control over your own destiny.
>
> . . .
>
> I know that although there is a lot of talk about not being a change, there eventually is tremendous change when someone takes over somebody else. The largest companies have a tendency to be quite definite about what they want to do.

Although neither Tod, nor Leighton would discuss a possible date for going public, should that alternative be their final choice, Charles Leighton did explain his reasoning for not committing immediately to a merger with another company:

> Our results overall have been extremely good. And our argument is: If our results are good, if we're going to continue to be able to show 15–20 percent growth in earnings, steady, quality earnings, compounded, we'd be better off not to merge unless we're going to join a company that's growing at 30 or 40 percent. We're in a relatively stable set of businesses, under good control. Probably whatever changes occur in the environment help us rather than hinder us, for the most part.
>
> I'm not saying be all things to all people, but aren't we better off staying independent for a little longer, as opposed to tying our future to another company now? And if we're very comfortable about the next couple of years' performance, one can build a very good case, a logical case, to wait maybe three years to make these decisions—perhaps longer. . . .

KERR–McGEE CORPORATION

It certainly had been a terrific half-century. Rising out of the red dust of Oklahoma in the 1920s as a small oil company, Kerr–McGee Corporation had sprouted into a $3.8 billion energy-resource business by 1981. Kerr–McGee was different from the many other oil industry hopefuls because the company, almost from the beginning, had envisioned itself not just as an oil company but as one whose business was the development of natural resources. Oil was still Kerr–McGee's primary business, but its leadership had the early foresight to push into other resources such as coal, uranium, chemicals, and timber. Dean A. McGee had led the company as either president or CEO for the last four decades. Without a doubt he was one of the most respected businessmen in America in 1981, but McGee would turn 78-years-old in 1982. Trained as a geologist and mining engineer, McGee had skillfully guided the company into one of the strongest mid-sized integrated oil companies in the market.

Experts agreed that the petroleum industry had reached the threshold of a new frontier where stiffened macroeconomic conditions, increased competition, and slackened demand promised to weed out the weaker competitors, either through liquidation or takeovers. Kerr–McGee has been a favorite of takeover speculators because of its financial strength and its expansive and profitable resource base. In 1982, Kerr–McGee was faced with having to give birth to a new management as well as determining a strategic response to this new industry environment. Taken together, these events promised that the next few years would be crucial. Kerr–McGee's basic strategy—to develop natural resources—had been sound in the past because of its ability to generate cash from its petroleum operations to fund ventures into other resource markets. Since this cash would be more difficult to obtain in the future, the strategic issue had become one of deciding where to focus resources so that the next 50 years would be as good as the first.

Petroleum

Petroleum had been Kerr–McGee's bread and butter play since the beginning. In 1981 petroleum exploration, production, refining, and marketing accounted for 77 percent of sales and 72 percent of net income (see Table 1).

The majority of KM's petroleum exploration and production expenditures have been concentrated in the fields in the Gulf of Mexico. This particular area has been the most active in the world in terms of the number of producing wells and was considered mature with limited growth potential. KM had only recently expanded extensive exploration efforts into the less developed areas in the North Sea, Arabian Gulf, and offshore Indonesia. In land-based operations, KM was drilling in Texas, Oklahoma, Louisiana, Wyoming, and North Dakota. KM's working interests in both offshore and land sites ranged from 5 to 100 percent, with the majority falling in the 50–65 percent range. Because of the risk and capital investment required for oil exploration and production, joint ventures were common.

Table 2 indicates KM's oil and gas reserves. Using these reserves and KM's current production of 30,000 barrels a day, assuming

Source: This case was prepared by Mark W. Bushell and by Professor Roger M. Atherton, University of Oklahoma. Permission to use granted by Professor Roger M. Atherton.

TABLE 1
Petroleum Products

	1978	1979	1980	1981
Percent of Total Sales	76%	76%	76%	77%
Percent of Net Income	68%	84%	63%	72%

TABLE 2
Proved Petroleum Reserves

	1978	1979	1980	1981
Crude/Natural Gas Liquids (×1000 Barrels)				
Domestic	59430	57063	63082	66795
Foreign	70038	74770	83350	80053
Totals	129468	131833	146432	146848
Natural Gas (billions of ft^3)				
Domestic	886	826	835	747
Foreign	70	81	125	128
Totals	956	907	960	875

no new oil is found, KM's estimated reserves would be depleted in about 13 years. For natural gas, KM's reserves would last about 10 years. (KM's 1981 oil production rate was 27,800 bbls/day and *Value Line* estimated KM's 1984–86 production would be closer to 42,000 bbls/day.)

KM's capital expenditures in its major line of business had increased dramatically over the last four years, both in real terms and as a percentage of total capital expenditures within the company (see Table 3).

KM's capital expenditures over the same period taken as a percentage of total sales have increased from 13 to 16 percent. These increases in expenditures represented KM's re-cent expansion into foreign exploration, acquisition of more domestic on and offshore leases, as well as the drilling and equipping of new wells. Additionally, part of these increases represented four new rigs that were added to KM's contract drilling subsidiary, Transworld Drilling.

Industry-wide, the approximate norm for capital expenditures as a percent of sales was about 9 percent. Exxon, the industry leader with sales of $108 billion in 1981 had historically committed about 9 percent, but was expected to increase capital outlays by 20 percent to about $130 billion in 1982.

KM also refined and marketed the oil it produced. In 1981, three crude oil refineries were operating in the United States. Finished products flowed through either KM's chain of 1,519 branded service stations or KM's wholly owned subsidiary, Triangle Refineries, Inc. Triangle sold gasoline and other distillates at the wholesale level to buyers through major pipeline and waterway terminals. Profits in this area were off recently because of low plant utilization rates. The current industry average utilization rate hovered around 74 percent. In 1981, KM's rate averaged 63 percent. In the three years prior to this, KM's plant utilization rates were 80, 68, and 62 percent respectively. KM had been processing less oil because selling prices had not been high enough to make operations sufficiently profitable. According to the Company, the lower profit in refining the marketing was due to narrower margins between crude oil prices and refined product prices. While unit costs rise slightly with lower refinery utilization rates, the major reasons for variations in refinery and marketing profits have been margins. This was one line of business where KM performed extensive processing for consumer sales. At one time, Dean McGee had stated that KM's business definition would never take it into consumer markets. He then saw KM strictly as a company dedicated to getting the resource out of the

TABLE 3
Capital Expenditures—Petroleum

	1978	1979	1980	1981
Expenditures (millions)	$142.1	$282.8	$426.4	$513.0
As a percent of Total KM Expenditures	53%	73%	81%	85%

ground and selling it to those whose expertise lay in the consumer distribution field.

The future did not look rosy for the refining industry as a whole. The industry suffered from severe overcapacity that was not expected to be utilized within the next five years. In the interim, success would depend both on increasing operating efficiencies through larger investments in applied technology and expanding production flexibility. In trying to extricate itself from some of the problems related to industry overcapacity, KM had recently tuned up two of its refineries to better meet changed market conditions (greater product flexibility). Additionally, these plants would better meet the upcoming Federal requirements for production of more no-lead and low-lead gasolines as a percentage of total gasoline produced. KM hoped that these modifications, plus the application of more advanced methods of processing petroleum residuum (developed by KM), would improve their deteriorating position in a highly cyclical business and leave the company more competitive in an increasingly price-sensitive market.

In the natural gas segment of the petroleum market, KM operated six processing plants in the United States, with interests in 12 others in the United States and Canada. KM had done reasonably well in this segment of the market and hopes were high that the continuing decontrol of gas wellhead prices would keep profits buoyant. This decontrol mechanism, begun under the Ford Administration and formalized under the 1978 Natural Gas Policy Act (NGPA), mandated that certain gas prices would rise 15–20 percent per year until Jan. 1, 1985, when controls would be lifted altogether. The price of $3 or so per thousand cubic feet some experts predicted would triple by the end of the decade. This legislation explained in part the enthusiastic search that has continued unabated since decontrol began until the early part of 1982 when prices increased and demand dropped.

The demand for natural gas remained 12 percent under the 1973 peak. As the price of crude oil went up, industrial and private gas hook-ups increased substantially. However, with higher prices came conservation in all energy consumption and new and old gas consumers burned their gas frugally and invested in more energy-efficient building designs. The overall result was more customers, but less demand. Even more important, however, nearly every community in the United States had been tapped into gas pipelines leaving very little room for growth through expanded service. In short, the market for natural gas in the United States had become saturated. Additionally, all those incentives discussed earlier with regard to the decontrol of wellhead prices had left utilities (primary users) and gas producers with bulging inventories that demand levels would not burn off for another two years. The business recession was also a major factor in the slowdown in the demand for gas. What precipitated out of this mixed bag of influences was that current short-run conditions would encourage producers to keep their reserves in the ground for the next several years because of excess inventory. Beyond this point, Kerr–McGee expected to see healthy, stable profits as the excess was burned off, crude oil prices rose, and petroleum in general became more valuable.

KM's efforts in petroleum also took the form of contract offshore drilling. One of its strongest suits, KM led the industry in shallow-water contract drilling. KM's Transworld Drilling Company had laid claim to a number of industry "firsts" including being the first company ever to drill a commercial well out of sight of land (1947). The company also developed the first semi-submersible rig (1955) and pioneered floating platforms that could perform double duty as a drilling rig and processing station (1974). In 1981, the company owned 23 rigs with three more under construction for delivery in 1982. Table 4 charts Transworld's progress over the four-year period.

Contract drilling was one of the important

TABLE 4
Transworld

	1978	1979	1980	1981	1982
Number of rigs	18	18	19	23	26
Percent of utilization	99.6%	97.6%	98.7%	96.0%	—

segments of the petroleum industry. As current fields were drained and the price of petroleum increased, there would be intense efforts to find new oil and develop ways to get more oil out of the wells that had already been drilled. In the offshore drilling business this search would be especially profitable for those contract firms that had the expertise to secure long-term contracts with larger oil companies and the reputation for completing contracted wells. KM had demonstrated a real talent for operating on the leading edge of drilling technology. Given this and KM's sound reputation, KM was in an excellent position to maintain its market share in a growing market.

By 1982 the oil industry was feeling the pinch of decreased demand and increased supply. It was argued by many that the industry had indeed reached an inflection point in its growth curve because of the enhanced societal value of energy conservation and the increased usage of alternative fuels. The loss to energy conservation is shown in Table 5 which compares 1978 demand to that in 1981 for various classes of users.

TABLE 5
Petroleum Demand (×1000 bbls)

Segment	1978	1981	% Change
Transportation	9,450	8,510	−9%
Utilities	1,800	1,160	−37%
Residential/Business	2,960	1,810	−38%
Industrial	3,700	3,690	—
Totals	17,910	15,170	−16%

This table shows that homeowners and business people (Residential/Business) were the quickest to adjust their thermostats and the designs of their homes and offices to the rising price of petroleum. If anything, this −38 percent figure understates the true effect because of the higher demand during this period attributed to two unusually harsh winters. The loss in Utilities' demand followed closely behind, dropping 37 percent. This too can be considered relatively permanent as this loss represented conversions to coal-generated energy processes. It was expected that this particular loss would probably grow if petroleum prices went up and new ways were devised to make coal a cleaner source of energy. In the transportation sector, more efficient automobile, truck, and aircraft power plants had significantly reduced demand. As more older, less-efficient engines were replaced in the coming years, this loss could also be expected to grow. *Value Line* believed that, although the coming economic recovery would increase demand somewhat, it was reasonable to assume that most of the losses because of conservation and alternative fuels were permanent.

This is not to imply that oil would no longer be "black gold." Oil was a scarce resource that was rapidly getting more scarce. However, the environment had changed. Oil would become increasingly more valuable, but not by the leaps and bounds projected earlier. Equally important, the current projection that interest rates would remain stubbornly high throughout the rest of the decade (see *Business Week*, April 12, 1982 cover story) meant that the costs and risks inherent to the industry would be higher. Even more important from the perspective of the oil industry, banks and lending institutions would draw harder lines on who would and would not be able to get capital for expansion. As a result, the players that currently made up the industry would decrease in number in favor of those cost-conscious firms that could effectively balance their bread and butter operations with their capital ventures.

Acquisitions would become increasingly popular as the reserves of small companies became more valuable and they were less financially able to get it out of the ground because of increasing production costs and higher risks.

Table 6 shows *Value Line* figures on how KM stacked up against some of its competitors in the petroleum industry in 1981.

Chemicals

As the second largest division in Kerr–McGee's natural resource business, Kerr–McGee Chemical Corporation manufactured industrial chemicals, fertilizer raw materials, and specialty chemical products. Industrial products included magnesium, sodium chlorate (used in the paper industry), boron, soda ash (used in making glass), salt cake, manganese dioxide (for dry cell batteries), ammonium perchlorate, and titanium dioxide (pigment used in paints). Despite the recession at that time, prices for the majority of these products had kept pace with cost increases. Concurrently, KM had kept most of these lines profitable through intensive cost-control programs. In early 1982, the company shut down most of the old Trona plant in Searles Valley, California, citing equipment and process obsolescence, high-energy consumption, and high maintenance costs. This effectively halved Kerr–McGee's total production capacity for soda ash and cost the company an estimated $17 million (one-time charge) against earnings.

Kerr–McGee produced chemically treated railroad ties, utility poles, and hardwood pallets from the company's 265,000 or so acres of timber in the Ohio and Mississippi river valleys. Interestingly enough, Kerr–McGee was the nation's second largest supplier of railroad ties. Sales in this area had been off recently because railroads had postponed maintenance work because of the recession. Sales were expected to reach normal levels as the economy headed toward recovery. Because of the age of the many miles of track in place, Kerr–McGee expected this niche to remain highly profitable through the end of the century.

Exports of industrial products and fertilizers to Europe, South America, Japan, and other Pacific Basin countries represented about one-fifth of division sales. Kerr–McGee considered this a potential growth market. It uses agents and distributors to push KM products

TABLE 6
Value Line Competitive Analysis

Firm	Present Value Proven Res.[a]	Production[b] (Daily)	Sales[a]	Labor Cost Percent Sales	Employees	RONW	Projected RONW 1984–1986
Exxon	$72,035	3,900	$108,108	5.3%	180,000	19.5%	16.0%
Gulf	25,969	615	38,252	6.4%	58,500	12.3%	12.5%
Diamond Shamrock	1,372	NA	3,376	11.0%	13,500	9.0%	21.0%
Kerr–McGee	2,786	28	3,826	6.0%	11,200	14.1%	14.5%
Murphy Oil	3,532	NA	2,447	6.0%	4,800	20.5%	16.0%
Pennzoil	2,790	37	2,682	11.0%	10,100	19.2%	21.5%
Phillips	14,884	409	15,966	8.0%	34,500	16.0%	17.0%
Tesoro Oil	639	25	3,035	3.0%	5,300	18.0%	17.5%

[a] In millions.
[b] Thousands of barrels.

TABLE 7
Exports—Chemical Corporation

	1978	1979	1980	1981
Percent of Sales	35%[a]	18%	20%	15%
Thousands of Tons	1200	860	583	1000

[a]Because of the weakness of the dollar which made US goods particularly attractive overseas.

further into existing markets and to lay the groundwork for expansion into new markets. Table 7 tracks exports over the last four years in terms of percentage of total KM chemical sales and tonnage exported.

Tables 8, 9, and 10 summarize production, sales, and capital expenditures as they apply to the chemical manufacturing division.

For 1982, net profits promised lackluster performance primarily because of the $17 million loss resulting from the Trona plant closure. Because of poor demand in other product lines, KM Chemical was not expected to be able to overcome this loss.

As a major part of the industry, industrial chemicals were taking a real beating as a result of the then-current global recession. Falling demand on almost all fronts and continued high interest rates had dragged industrial chemical profits to all-time lows. As a smaller competitor, KM competed against such giants as DuPont with 1981 sales reaching $21 billion and Dow Chemical with sales of $11 billion. KM's industrial chemicals cover a wide variety of products. Most of these products were tied

TABLE 8
Production History

	1978	1979	1980	1981
Industrial (1000 tons)	1168	1327	1434	1627
Agricultural (1000 tons)	1855	1880	2005	1557
Forest Products (1000 Board ft)	N/A	283	292	325

N/A—Not available.

TABLE 9
Chemical Corporation Sales/Profits

	1978	1979	1980	1981
Sales (Millions)	$375	$420	$501	$543
Net Profit Margin	6.2%	3.4%	4.0%	3.0%
Return on Assets	3.9%	2.3%	3.1%	2.4%
Percent of Total KM Sales	18.1%	14.2%	14.4%	15.6%
Percent of KM Net Income	19.7%	8.9%	10.9%	7.6%

to the manufacturing and construction sectors of the economy. Industrial chemical sales heavily rely on the strength of these particular industrial segments. Like many of the companies in these related manufacturing segments, capital expenditures in this part of the chemical industry had been reduced significantly. The principal reasons lined up behind a common problem found in today's marketplace—severe overcapacity. As a consequence of this and the lower demand levels, plant utilization rates had dropped to an average of 74 percent. Estimates showed that considerable market growth was required to move this figure up to the more reasonable rate of 85–90 percent. Equally distressing, foreign demand had fallen off significantly in the last few years. As domestic prices of oil and gas reached worldwide levels, American companies increasingly lost their competitive edge in terms of lower costs of production. (Pe-

TABLE 10
Chemical Corporation Capital Expenditures

	1978	1979	1980	1981
Capital Expenditures (Millions)	$67	$45.6	$36.3	$43.2
Percent of Total KM Cap. Exp.	25%	12%	7%	7%

troleum normally comprises a significant portion of the raw materials used in producing these chemicals.) Obviously, the global recession had affected a part of this loss, but experts contended the industry would experience some permanent loss in overseas demand.

For fertilizers, the industry news had gone from bad to worse. Fertilizers were marketed by over half of the companies that compete in the industrial chemical segment of the market. Several macroeconomic factors stood out as the biggest anchors holding this segment down. Domestic farm income was lower in real terms than at any time within the last 45 years. While the return on investment of fertilizers in terms of bigger yields remained high, the combination of poor profits and high interest rates had precluded farmers from borrowing the necessary cash. On a global scale, demand for fertilizer had been negatively affected over the last few years as it became increasingly popular to use farm exports as political tools. Recent experience with the Soviet grain embargo pointed to the sensitivity of the food and fertilizer industries to political tinkering. Another aspect of this global demand as it applied to U.S. companies was the long-term effect on demand for U. S. fertilizers as American producers lost their lower cost advantage. (Petroleum also makes up a significant portion of the raw materials used to produce fertilizer.) Like the industrial chemical producers and their products, the leveling of U. S. petroleum prices to worldwide levels took away one production cost advantage U. S. companies have had over other overseas fertilizer producers.

The fertilizer industry had high hopes that these domestic and international problems would dissipate within the next two years as domestic farm income and interest rates improved significantly and worldwide demand increased as a result of the economic recovery. Certainly, food consumption would increase over the next 20 years as the earth's population grew larger. The key for the fertilizer industry is when this demand would turn into operating profits.

As a subsegment of the chemical industry, specialty chemical products historically had been resilient performers even in times of economic downturn. Currently, this could be seen in several companies that specialized in the very profitable segments dealing in oilfield specialty chemicals and specialty adhesives and sealants. The common denominator throughout this segment was the development and production of products (often proprietary) designed for a specific use. The companies competing in this market generally were not capital-intensive. This in part explained the ability of this segment to stand up against falling demand. Large sales organizations also distinguished this particular segment of the chemical industry. In some of the companies, salespeople accounted for more than half the workforce. KM did not market products in either specialty oilfield chemicals or specialty adhesives.

Coal

Consistent with its commitment to develop natural resources, Kerr–McGee began acquiring coal reserves back in 1957. In 1978, profitable coal production began near Gilette, Wyoming with the opening of the Jacob Ranch mine. Since then KM has increased production 700 percent and opened the Clovis Point mine 60 miles from Jacob's. In a move to further increase capacity, KM planned to open its first underground mine near Galatia, Illinois in 1985. (Construction began in July 1981.) As in the case with many new mines, contracts have already been finalized to market the coal from the Galatia mine to coal-burning utility plants near St. Louis. In 1981 KM had coal reserves of 885 million tons in the Wyoming mines and the Illinois mine. Kerr–McGee also holds leases and fee lands in five other states. Widespread drilling has shown the presence of in-place resources of 2.3 billion tons. KM began

TABLE 11
KM Coal Corporation Production and Financial Information

	1978	1979	1980	1981
Coal Shipped (Thousands of tons)	1774	5067	10677	12380
Sales (Millions)	$14.9	$50.5	$101.2	$128.9
Profit Margin	2.7%	26.1%	29.8%	23.4%
Return on Assets	0.5%	12.1%	23.9%	22.2%
Percent of Total KM Sales	1.0%	1.9%	2.9%	3.4%
Percent of Total KM Net Income	0.3%	8.3%	16.5%	14.3%

aggressive efforts to acquire additional reserves of low-sulfur coal. The selection criteria for these acquisitions included prime access to labor markets, transportation facilities, and utility consumers.

KM's Coal Corporation was both the smallest and most profitable operating division in the company. Table 11 provides data on production, sales, profit margins, and sales and net income as a percentage of overall company sales.

Within the coal industry, KM was a small-to-medium-sized competitor. Larger producers such as North American Coal controlled significantly larger reserves (5.5 billion tons for North America vs. 885 million for KM) and annually marketed about double of what KM did in 1981. In the area of critical solvent technology, however, KM was the industry leader. Critical solvent technology involves the process that removes ash, sulfur, and other impurities from coal so that it burns cleanly. The process KM developed was a spinoff of the same type of technology (which KM also pioneered) used in KM's oil refineries to get more product out of crude oil. Under a joint program with the U. S. Department of Energy and the Electric Power Research Institute, the applications of this breakthrough was successfully demonstrated in a pilot plant in Wilsonville, Alabama. Further research was being conducted in a coal liquefaction plant co-located with KM's nuclear facility in Cimarron, Oklahoma. In 1981 the International Coal Refining Company licensed KM's critical solvent process to be used in the SRC-1 refinery, a government coal-liquefaction demonstration plant.

The future for the coal industry looked promising indeed. Increasingly, utility companies here and abroad were turning to coal-based energy generation schemes. In 1981, U.S. utilities used coal to generate 52.4 percent of all electric power compared with 50.8 percent in 1980, 50.5 percent in 1979, and 48 percent in 1978. Several new developments precipitated this trend and promised further gains in coal demand. First, there had been significant progress in developing technologies that processed coal without harming the atmosphere. Untreated coal is notorious in its effects on the atmosphere and indeed the entire environment. Solving these related problems in the past had been cost-prohibitive, but new breakthroughs in technology promised to lower this obstacle in the near future. Technology had also enabled companies to respond to the concerns brought on in the strip-mining process. It had been demonstrated that the land used in strip mining could be "returned" to the environment and, in many documented cases, left better in terms of a more balanced ecosystem.

A second development favoring coal was the rising price of petroleum and the stalled nuclear energy industry. The petroleum pricing development had the most impact of all of the factors discussed. As oil prices increased, coal had become more attractive as an alternative. A subset of rising oil prices was the question of availability. The United States depended upon the Middle East for a significant amount of the petroleum it consumed. Given the volatile politics that governed that area of the world it is very possible that supply could be severed at any time, either by a major war or another embargo by OPEC. Whatever the case, some of the richest deposits of coal in the world rested within U. S. borders. The case to convert to coal seemed most compelling given the precarious situation from which a significant portion of U. S. oil flowed. There was a problem. The coal industry continued to demonstrate significant overcapacity. In numbers this means the industry had the capacity to annually produce 100–150 million tons of coal above the level of demand. Natually, this overcapacity exerted a downward pressure on coal prices. In 1981, this meant that mines were not even considered for opening unless a large, long-term sales contract had been signed for the coal still in the ground. It was simply too risky to commit the huge amounts of capital necessary to obtain the coal without the promise of a buyer. In this environment, the keys to success lay in securing long-term utilities contracts and employing technology and strong management to keep production costs down.

Uranium

Of all the major industries Kerr–McGee competed in, it was the leader in only one. Over the last 30 years KM had been one of the largest producers of uranium concentrates used by nuclear plants to generate power. In 1981, the industry was reeling from the effects of the Three-Mile Island incident, lagging energy demand, massive nuclear plant cost overruns, and increased government intervention. Of all the companies in the industry, KM was probably in the best position to weather the storm. KM had a substantial backlog of contracts for both uranium concentrates and conversion services. To cut costs, four of the 11 KM mines in New Mexico had been put on standby while three mines in Wyoming remained operating at minimum levels. Table 12 below shows KM's uranium production, sales, profit margins, and net income as a percentage of overall company sales and net income.

The longer range projections for nuclear power and the uranium industry revolved around the relative permanency of the financial, environmental, and safety problems. There were 73 plants operating in the United States, with some 80 plants in various stages of construction. Purchase contracts and utility inventories were in place to cover needs until 1985. Additional purchases to replenish inventories and provide uranium for new plants

TABLE 12
Uranium

	1978	1979*	1980	1981
Production (thousands of lbs)	5261	5100	5200	5000
Sales (millions)	115.2	163.4	238.9	201.5
Net Profit Margin	18.3%	—	8.1%	6.3%
Return on Assets	7.8%	—	6.3%	4.2%
Percent of total KM sales	5.6%	6.1%	.9%	5.2%
Percent of total KM Net Income	17.9%	a	10.6%	6.1%

aNet loss $1.1 million.

point to a possible growth market in the late 1980s both in the United States and abroad. Additionally, KM anticipated that 45 percent of any additional power requirements for the 1980s and 1990s would be filled by nuclear power. The current market was forcing several competitors out of this business, thereby strengthening the market for those that could afford to stay. While some experts believed a turnaround in nuclear power and uranium demand was not likely until 1990, Kerr–McGee believed, as it did in 1952, that the use of nuclear power would continue to grow in the United States and abroad. Given KM's strength in the industry, it was hopeful of reaping the fruits of any growth that did occur.

Organization

Kerr–McGee's most valuable asset was not even listed on the balance sheet. Dean A. McGee first came to the company in 1937 as chief geologist for $700 a month. Five years later, McGee took over the reins as CEO, a position he has held ever since. Under his tutelage, KM had successfully expanded from sales of $2 million in 1942 to $3.8 billion in 1981. Even critics praised McGee's uncanny ability to put the company in the right place at the right time. McGee's philosophy of management was best described by the man himself when he told one interviewer he believed in "pitching, not catching." KM followed this strategy closely, creating opportunities by shrewd acquisitions and expansions. For instance, in its role as an energy company in 1954, KM foresaw the potential in uranium. In 1981, KM was poised ready to reap the benefits of a choice made almost three decades past. Under Dean McGee the current business cycle is not where KM planned; it was the long-range prognosis that KM spent its money on. KM's current success reflects McGee's vision of KM as a company in the business of exploiting natural resources—finding them, processing them, and bringing them to the marketplace.

But KM had a problem. Dean McGee would turn 78 in 1982. In 1977, KM's annual report noted that a succession plan had been initiated. Two candidates were chosen by McGee and the board of directors as possible replacements. J. W. McKenny was in 1981 Vice Chairman of the Board (see Figure 1). He was formerly Vice-President of Exploration. F. A. McPherson in 1981 was president of KM and has served as Vice President in charge of both coal and nuclear operations. Both men had been with KM throughout their careers and both were considered well qualified. McGee's selection of the two company men was predictable and expected. Replacing McGee would be no easy task, however. McGee was known throughout the business world as a man of remarkable vision. In 1974, *Dun's Review* rated KM as one of the five best-managed companies in America, noting that KM best demonstrated the ability to move faster than inflation, outpace recession, and weather a crashing stock market. In 1981, the *Wall Street Transcript* selected Dean McGee as the Bronze award winner among chief executives of the domestic integrated oil companies and The American Petroleum Institute gave him a gold medal for distinguished achievement. In early 1982, the *Financial World* selected him for the 1982 CEO of the Year Certificate of Distinction for the petroleum industry.

Like most integrated oil companies that had interests in other resources or businesses, KM was managed divisionally. Unlike the others, however, KM has separated petroleum exploration from the oil and gas divisions; and likewise separated mineral exploration from the coal, nuclear, and chemical divisions. Given KM's success in discovering petroleum and minerals, one could justify this structure on results alone. The ramifications of such a structure, however, raised some interesting questions. Specifically, taking exploration control out of the hands of the operating divisions in some ways hamstrung the division directors as they turned their thinking to intermediate

FIGURE 1
KM Organization Chart

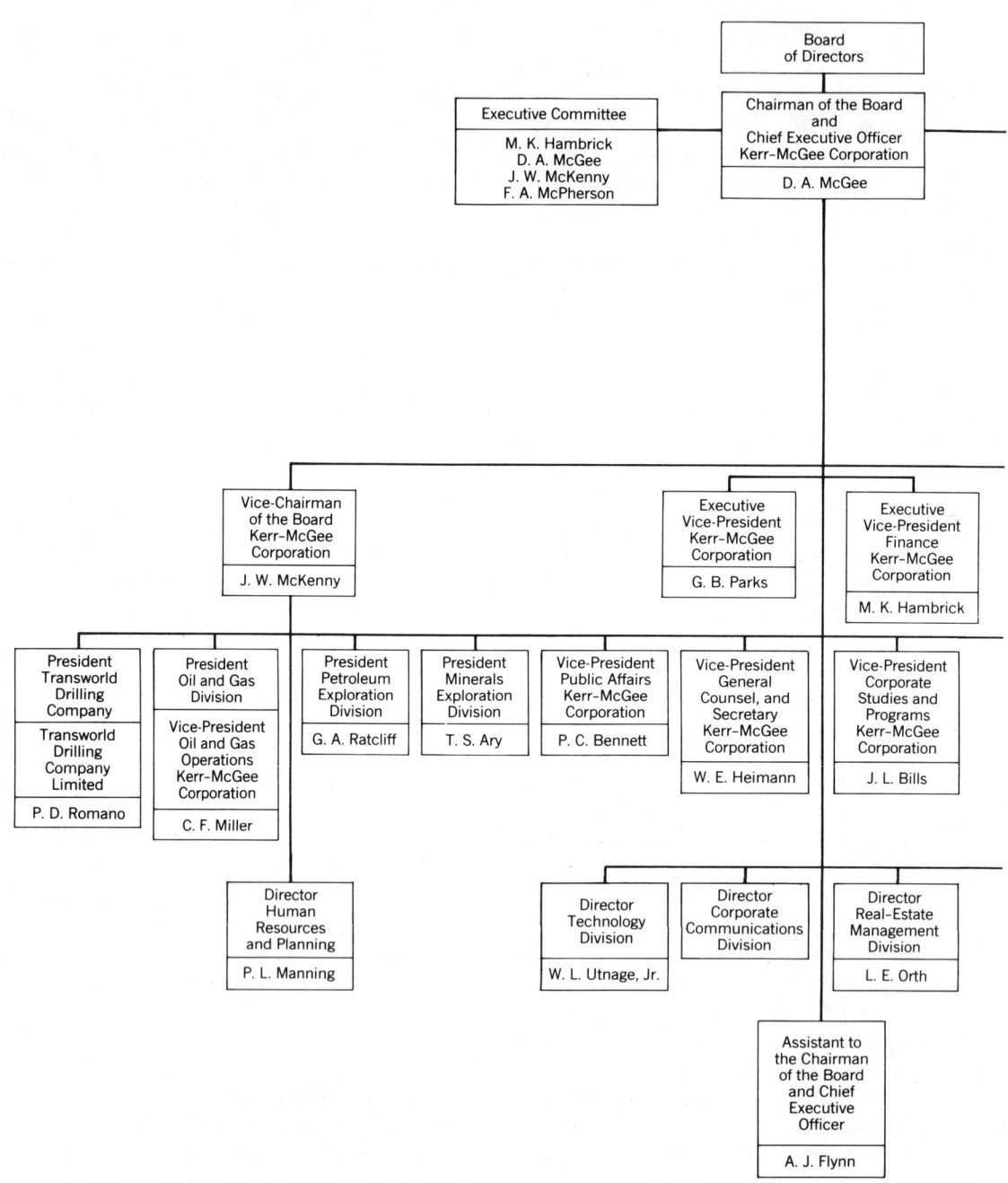

Converting and Manufacturing

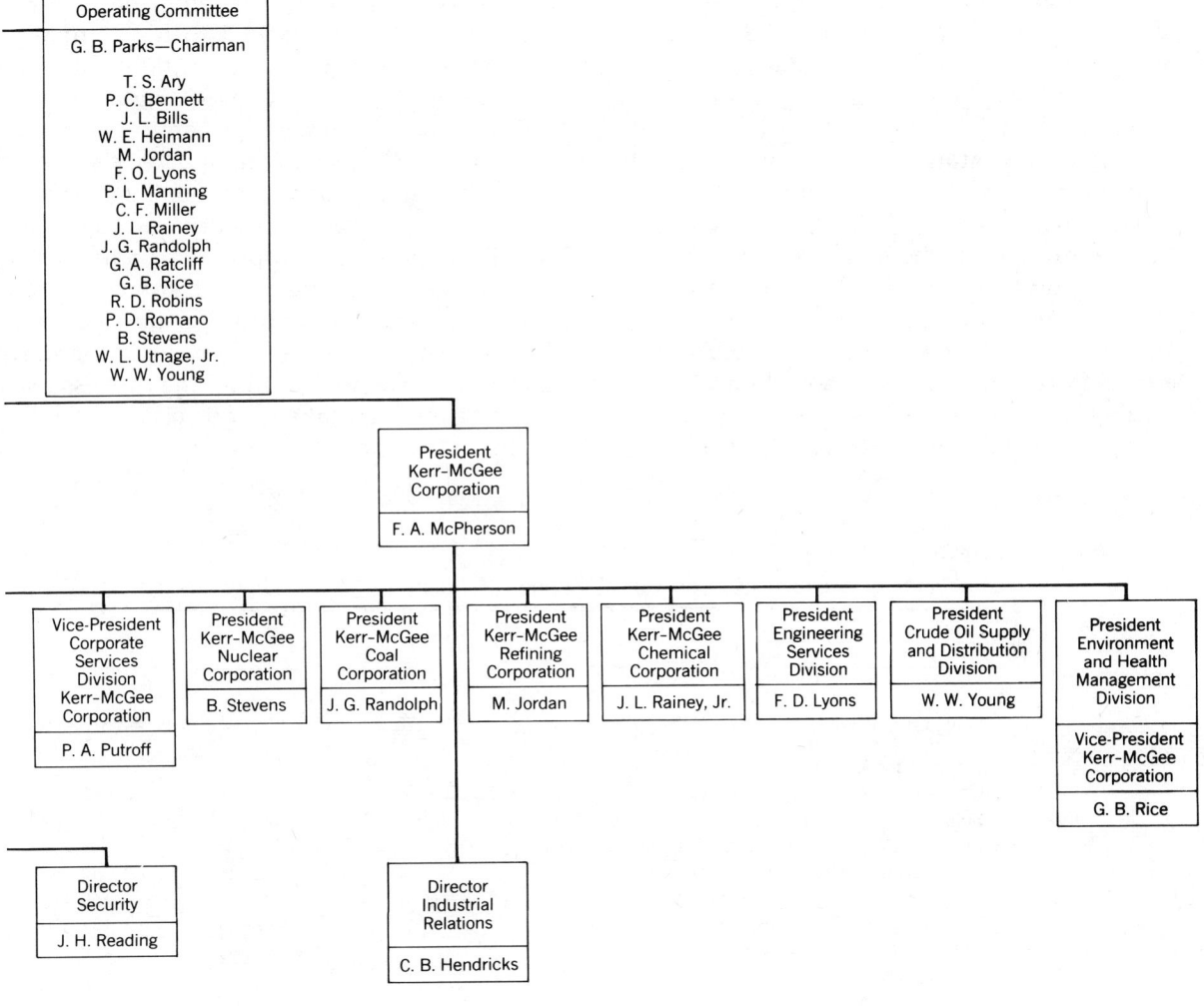

and long-range planning. Basically, they had little control over how big their operation would get and how fast it would get there. Obviously, KM's operating division heads did not live in the dark and were kept reasonably well informed of the current plans of the exploration divisions. Yet it seemed to some that it is antithetical to separate exploration from those that must live with its results. Some have speculated that more than anything else this structure represented McGee's way of maintaining tight control over a diverse number of activities.

Major operating decisions were closely controlled by McGee. Recommendations on expansions, cutbacks, etc., were made to McGee through McPherson and McKenny. All major requests for expenditures are processed through the operating committee. Sometimes an issue would be taken to the operating committee for discussion. Additional inputs concerning market forecasts, government regulations, etc. were solicited from the staff. The final decision was McGee's. This mechanism closely mirrored the budget process and encompassed the strategic planning function with McGee in the driver's seat.

McGee's decision style was described as innovative, deliberate, and to a certain extent, conservative. McGee was particularly noted for his ability to assimilate large amounts of information and identify the important issues and trends as they applied to his company. There is no doubt McGee ran a "tight ship." In the area of strategic planning one could say McGee was something of a genius. His foresight had reaped many benefits. KM's strategic planning process had been institutionalized with all the required staff work on projections and all the necessary upper management discussions. Yet the operational strategic planning process really took place between McGee's ears. So while KM has a recognized vehicle for strategic planning, the process really had never been taken for a serious drive by anyone other than its inventor.

EXHIBIT 1
Consolidated Statement of Income (In thousands of dollars, except per share amounts)

	1981	1980	1979
Income			
Sales and services	$3,826,420	$3,477,881	$2,683,469
Costs and Expenses			
Costs and operating expenses	$2,827,253	$2,705,414	$2,051,897
Selling, general, and administrative expenses	130,932	100,319	96,772
Depreciation, depletion, and amortization	183,999	155,375	116,290
Exploration, including dry holes	83,823	62,726	47,537
Taxes, other than income taxes	156,982	85,824	50,405
Interest and debt expense	91,027	56,005	57,620
Total Costs and Expenses	$3,474,016	$3,165,663	$2,420,521
	$ 352,404	$ 312,218	$ 262,948
Other Income	25,344	20,273	21,137
Net Income before Income Tax Provision	$ 377,748	$ 332,491	$ 284,085
Provision for Income Taxes	166,631	150,268	124,068
Net Income	$ 211,117	$ 182,223	$ 160,017
Net Income per Common Share	$ 4.07	$ 3.51[a]	$ 3.09[a]

[a]Restated to reflect two-for-one stock split on October 21, 1981.

EXHIBIT 2
Consolidated Balance Sheet

	1981	1980
	(In thousands of dollars)	
Assets		
Current Assets		
Cash, including $174,159,000 certificates of deposit in 1981 and $114,688,000 in 1980	$ 204,577	$ 152,689
Marketable securities, at cost	13,371	16,872
Notes and accounts receivable	180,067	203,215
Inventories		
Petroleum and other products	338,583	218,514
Materials and supplies	170,304	118,961
Deposits and prepaid expenses	18,844	16,571
Total Current Assets	$ 925,746	$ 726,822
Investments and Other Assets	$ 75,312	$ 64,976
Property, Plant, and Equipment, at cost		
Petroleum	$2,141,203	$1,648,673
Chemicals	741,164	702,656
Nuclear	334,655	331,605
Coal	179,074	147,049
Other	83,203	82,073
	$3,479,299	$2,912,056
Less reserves for depreciation, depletion, and amortization	1,113,560	949,322
	$2,365,739	$1,962,734
Deferred Charges	$ 48,107	$ 52,027
	$3,414,904	$2,806,559
Liabilities and Stockholders' Equity		
Current Liabilities		
Notes payable	$ 2,300	$ 22,000
Accounts payable	313,009	313,395
Long-term debt due within one year	38,314	9,058
Taxes on income	87,261	91,270
Accrued liabilities	114,733	82,854
Total Current Liabilities	$ 555,617	$ 518,577

(*Continued*)

EXHIBIT 2 (*Continued*)

	1981	1980
	(In thousands of dollars)	
Long-term Debt	$ 841,509	$ 520,599
Advances to be Repaid from Future Production	$ 85,857	$ 95,659
Deferred Credits and Reserves		
Income taxes	$ 324,976	$ 260,269
Other	54,972	34,173
	$ 379,948	$ 294,442
Minority Interests in Subsidiary Companies	$ 50,749	$ 35,310
Stockholders' Equity		
Common stock, par value $1.00—Authorized shares: 150,000,000 in 1981 and 37,500,000 in 1980; Shares issued: 52,088,012 in 1981 and 26,009,646 in 1980	$ 52,088	$ 26,010
Capital in excess of par value	228,213	252,579
Retained earnings	1,222,695	1,064,707
	$1,502,996	$1,343,296
Less common stock in treasury, at cost—224,989 shares in 1981 and 106,840 in 1980	1,772	1,324
Total Stockholders' Equity	$1,501,224	$1,341,972
	$3,414,904	$2,806,559

The successful efforts method of accounting for oil and gas producing activities has been followed in preparing this balance sheet.

In the staff organization, two major areas deserve mention, KM's technology division had been a major contributor to KM's recent growth. This well-funded division had recently gained favorable publicity for the development of the critical solvent process described in the section on Coal. This process, called deashing, represented a real breakthrough in terms of providing cleaner energy from coal. In a related development, the division manufactured another deashing agent that processed petroleum residuum into valuable distillates. Coined ROSE (Residuum Oil Supercritical Extraction), this proprietary proc-

EXHIBIT 3
Industry Segment Data

Selected financial data by industry segment for the last three years are summarized below:

(In Millions of Dollars)	1981	1980	1979
Sales to unaffiliated customers			
Petroleum	$2,951.7	$2,635.7	$2,049.2
Chemicals	542.7	501.2	419.7
Nuclear	201.5	238.9	163.4
Coal	128.9	101.2	50.5
Other	1.6	.9	.7
Total	$3,826.4	$3,477.9	$2,683.5
Operating profit or (loss)			
Petroleum	$ 379.2	$ 284.5	$ 294.6
Chemicals	35.1	36.9	31.8
Nuclear	26.3	30.0	(.2)
Coal	46.6	43.8	17.3
Other	.5	.9	.7
	$ 487.7	$ 396.1	$ 344.2
General corporate expenses	(28.3)	(20.3)	(19.5)
Interest and debt expense	(91.0)	(56.0)	(57.6)
Other income and other expenses—Net	9.3	12.7	17.0
Provision for income taxes	(166.6)	(150.3)	(124.1)
Net Income	$ 211.1	$ 182.2	$ 160.0
Net Income			
Petroleum	$ 152.3	$ 113.9	$ 134.6
Chemicals	16.1	19.8	14.2
Nuclear	12.8	19.4	(1.1)
Coal	30.1	30.2	13.2
Other	(.2)	(1.1)	(.9)
Net Income	$ 211.1	$ 182.2	$ 160.0
Identifiable assets at December 31			
Petroleum	$2,081.9	$1,537.8	$1,197.4
Chemicals	684.7	640.6	624.4
Nuclear	304.5	304.8	288.4
Coal	135.3	126.6	109.2
Other	39.8	26.4	48.2
	$3,246.2	$2,636.2	$2,267.6
Investment in unconsolidated affiliates	41.2	29.6	23.1
Corporate assets	127.5	140.8	48.5
Total	$3,414.9	$2,806.6	$2,339.2
Capital Expenditures			
Petroleum	$ 513.0	$ 426.4	$ 282.8

(Continued)

EXHIBIT 3 (*Continued*)
Industry Segment Data

Selected financial data by industry segment for the last three years are summarized below:

(In Millions of Dollars)	1981	1980	1979
Chemicals	43.2	36.3	45.6
Nuclear	14.2	17.9	28.8
Coal	33.2	39.7	31.2
Other	2.7	6.3	.8
Total Capital Expenditures	$ 606.3	$ 526.6	$ 389.2
Exploration Expenses (excluding abandonment provisions)	63.9	48.5	37.5
Total	$ 670.2	$ 575.1	$ 426.7

ess had already been licensed to five refineries within the United States.

The second area of interest is a smaller division that is unique to KM's divisional management concept. Engineering Services employed personnel whose expertise range from chemical and civil engineering to product scheduling and cost estimation. Used as a project management source, this division provided experts to requesting divisions in the company on a project by project basis. This design provided temporarily expandable services to the different divisions at a fraction of the cost.

A significant amount of KM's stock is reportedly held privately. *Value Line* estimated that 7 percent of the stock is controlled, while insiders placed the figure at a much higher percentage. This is important because KM is one of the most popular Wall Street bets for a merger or acquisition target. The reasons for this are obvious—KM had a good resource base, strong balance sheet, and good management. Given the family-style management KM has had, it is reasonable to expect that most any merger attempt would be viewed with disfavor.

KM's organizational philosophy reflected the experience gained over the last 50 years.

KM had always been a company made up of smaller companies. KM seemed to have a special talent for smoothly absorbing acquired companies into its corporate family. Part of the reason for this was McGee's broad-minded philosophy that when you buy a company you not only buy the resources you can find in the ground, you acquire that company's expertise in the form of its people. This philosophy begets the tactic KM traditionally used to determine the attractiveness of a possible new market. Basically, KM acquired a company already familiar with the ins and outs of the business. From careful observation KM then determined if that particular market fit into KM's corporate expertise. As one might expect from such an organization, the people who made up the KM complex demonstrated a high degree of loyalty. The vast majority of promotions came from within and compensation programs were generous and oriented toward long-term corporate growth. As for the role models in the company, of those men who were division heads most were career KM employees.

Financial Performance

Value Line rated KM A+ in their April 1982 evaluation. (Exxon rated an A++ and Phillips

EXHIBIT 4
Ten-Year Summary of Financial and Operating Data

	1981	1980	1979	1978
Summary of Earnings (Thousands, except per share amounts)				
Sales of products, services, etc.	$3,826,420	$3,477,881	$2,683,469	$2,072,443
Operating costs and expenses	$3,382,989	$3,109,658	$2,362,901	$1,853,217
Interest expense	91,027	56,005	57,620	39,698
Total costs and expenses	$3,474,016	$3,165,663	$2,420,521	$1,892,915
	$ 352,404	$ 312,218	$ 262,948	$ 179,528
Other income	25,344	20,273	21,137	31,363
Net income before income taxes	$ 377,748	$ 332,491	$ 284,085	$ 210,891
Provision for income taxes	166,631	150,268	124,068	92,695
Net income	$ 211,117	$ 182,223	$ 160,017	$ 118,196
Common stock outstanding at year-end	51,863	25,903	25,877	25,857
Net income per common share	$ 4.07	$ 3.51	$ 3.09	$ 2.28
Cash dividends paid on common stock	$ 53,129	$ 46,602	$ 40,099	$ 32,320
Cash dividends paid per common share	$ 1.03	$ 0.90	$ 0.78	$ 0.63
Financial (Thousands)				
Working capital	$ 370,129	$ 208,245	$ 239,799	$ 184,140
Long-term debt and production advances	$ 927,366	$ 616,258	$ 484,876	$ 371,566
Common stockholders' equity	$1,501,224	$1,341,972	$1,204,768	$1,084,084
Total assets	$3,414,904	$2,806,559	$2,339,165	$2,021,742
Capital expenditures	$ 606,257	$ 526,570	$ 389,195	$ 270,185
Operating				
Production (net interest)				
Crude oil/condensate produced (thousands of barrels)	10,522	9,984	10,021	10,199
Natural gas liquids produced (thousands of barrels)	1,885	1,920	2,175	2,458
Natural gas sales (billions of cubic feet)	83	86	89	84
Oil and gas wells completed	65.45	79.71	55.31	44.46
Refining and marketing (thousands of barrels)				
Refinery runs	41,486	41,425	44,976	52,893
Refined product sales (excluding commission				

	1977	1976	1975	1974	1973	1972
	$2,164,754	$1,955,058	$1,798,580	$1,550,349	$727,953	$679,576
	$1,951,008	$1,723,742	$1,570,089	$1,353,609	$632,141	$607,266
	28,623	22,688	14,129	10,736	7,625	8,539
	$1,979,631	$1,746,430	$1,584,218	$1,364,345	$639,766	$615,805
	875,123	$ 208,628	$ 214,362	$ 186,004	$ 88,187	$ 63,771
	13,654	7,165	8,517	10,174	7,412	5,099
	$ 198,777	$ 215,793	$ 222,879	$ 196,178	$ 95,599	$ 68,870
	84,293	81,661	91,799	79,769	32,831	19,955
	$ 114,484	$ 134,132	$ 131,080	$ 116,409	$ 62,768	$ 48,915
	25,854	25,850	25,806	25,020	24,989	24,375
	$ 2.21	$ 2.59	$ 2.57	$ 2.32	$ 1.26	$ 1.03
	$ 32,314	$ 30,660	$ 25,415	$ 21,254	$ 14,741	$ 13,984
	$ 0.63	$ 0.59	$ 0.50	$ 0.43	$ 0.30	$ 0.30
	$ 237,699	$ 273,870	$ 287,414	$ 201,673	$204,128	$198,247
	$ 377,216	$ 336,738	$ 216,409	$ 158,600	$122,819	$124,427
	$ 998,104	$ 915,766	$ 810,556	$ 636,815	$540,738	$463,976
	$1,833,301	$1,625,595	$1,387,882	$1,164,432	$866,671	$806,801
	$ 269,199	$ 332,642	$ 234,734	$ 227,956	$113,041	$ 76,054
	11,195	11,474	10,487	11,193	11,326	12,393
	2,619	2,350	2,245	2,240	2,654	2,775
	81	90	89	104	108	109
	40.90	20.13	34.97	22.50	23.07	19.39
	60,263	60,212	55,842	46,984	14,152	13,612

(*Continued*)

EXHIBIT 4 (Continued)
Ten-Year Summary of Financial and Operating Data

	1981	1980	1979	1978
sales)	52,485	57,666	62,583	75,051
Contract drilling (offshore operations only)				
Number of drilling rigs	23	19	18	18
Number of wells drilled	107	98	93	91
Number of feet drilled (thousands)	1,064	909	921	918
Chemicals				
Industrial sales (thousands of tons)	1,627	1,434	1,327	1,168
Wholesale agricultural sales (thousands of tons)	1,557	2,005	1,880	1,855
Nuclear				
Deliveries of uranium (U_3O_8) (thousands of pounds)	5,354	6,751	5,808	3,959
Deliveries of uranium (UF_6) (uranium content in thousands of kilograms)	6,851	6,897	7,855	5,139
Coal				
Coal shipped (thousands of tons)	12,380	10,678	5,068	1,744
Number of employees	11,202	11,286	10,823	11,148

an A.)[1] This financial strength is in part attributable to KM's ability to finance much of its recent increase in capital expenditures internally. Kerr–McGee's bond rating did permit financing on a favorable basis. However, KM's debt structure had deteriorated somewhat over the last three years as a result of the explosive capital expansions. As if in anticipation of the problems that this weakened position might present in terms of continuing rapid growth, KM authorized a fourfold increase in the number of authorized shares from 37.5 million to 150 million shares in 1981. Exhibits 1 to 4 provide the following financial data: a consolidated statement of income, a consolidated balance sheet, financial data by industry segment, and a 10-year summary of financial and operating data.

---

[1]Sources: *Value Line* (April 16, 1982) and Kerr–McGee *Annual Reports* (1978, 1979, 1980, 1981).

EXHIBIT 4 (Continued)
Ten-Year Summary of Financial and Operating Data

1977	1976	1975	1974	1973	1972
80,255	79,388	83,693	79,201	40,820	47,808
18	18	16	15	14	14
96	99	123	87	85	94
901	935	984	773	860	968
1,129	1,183	1,178	853	784	762
1,514	1,040	1,109	931	1,236	1,348
5,425	4,018	3,638	5,178	5,952	7,553
5,067	3,527	2,162	2,379	3,818	3,157
—	—	—	—	—	5
11,271	11,427	10,305	10,105	8,966	9,217

MASCO CORPORATION

"Nothing we develop is the stuff dreams are made of. They just make lots of money." Richard Manoogian[1]

Masco Corporation is a quiet company. It seems to have no interest in being a star. But when one looks at its earnings growth record, it can be seen that Masco shines very brightly indeed. Masco describes itself as a diversified manufacturing company and diversified it is. Although a major portion of its sales are from the presently depressed housing and automobile industries, it continues to prosper. Masco produces a long list of products from faucets to gear shift levers, from mining drill bits to golf club heads, from Bearcat scanners to water pumps. Production is categorized as follows:

Building products	35 percent of sales
Industrial products	24 percent of sales
Specialty products	41 percent of sales

See Exhibit 1 for a more detailed breakdown by segment.

Over the years, Masco has made many unexciting little acquisitions that have led to

---

Source: This case was prepared by Janet Lorenzen under the supervision of Professor Joe G. Thomas, Middle Tennessee State University. Permission to use granted by Joe G. Thomas.

[1]Steven Flax, "Faucets That Drip Money," *Forbes,* March 16, 1981, p. 132.

EXHIBIT 1
Percentage of Sales by Business Segment
(December 31, 1981)

Business Segment	Sales	
Building Products		
Buildings products	14%	
Home Improvement	21	
Total		35%
Industrial Products		
Automotive Industry	11%	
Trucks, Trailers, Off-Road, Agricultural, and Other Vehicles	9	
Housing-Related (Mobile Homes, Appliances, etc.)	2	
Other	2	
Total		24%
Specialty Products		
Oil-field and Related Products	18%	
Personal Communications	6	
Recreational Accessories	2	
Other	15	
Total		41%
Total		100%

Source: Masco Corporation 1981 Annual Report.

continued growth and spread risk to a degree seldom seen in the corporate world. It seems Masco has built a nearly invincible empire.

History

The First 25 Years: From 1929 to 1954

Alex Manoogian came to the United States from Turkey in 1920 and looked forward to the day he could afford to bring his family to the new world. He worked at several jobs, eventually developing skills as a machinist in the screw machine business. On December 16, 1929, shortly after the Great Depression had begun, Masco Screw Products Company started operations in Detroit. The name "Masco" was an acronym for the first letters of the last names of Manoogian and two other partners who started the business together with "co" for company tacked on the end. The other two partners departed within the first year and left Manoogian to run the business on his own.

Masco's first contract was for $7,000 from the Hudson Motor Car Company. Other contracts came in to produce screws for the production of Chrysler, Ford, Graham Page, and Budd Wheel. Soon Mr. Manoogian was able to bring his family to the United States and eventually two of his brothers joined the growing company.

In those early stages, Masco was completely dependent on the automobile industry, as Exhibit 2 shows, with sales to that industry ranging from 94 percent in 1931 to 100 percent in 1936. Masco first went public in 1936 to finance its growth. In 1948, shares were sold once again to build a new plant in Dearborn, Michigan.

Dependence on the auto industry worked for Masco during World War II when the production of the automakers turned to war goods. Masco's net income jumped from $4,000 in 1941 to $42,000 in 1942, with sales first surpassing the million dollar mark that year. In 1948, Masco once again returned to war production for the Korean conflict. New parts were being demanded that required Masco to gain expertise in areas such as cold extrusion, a metalworking technique that was just being developed. Now Masco is a leader in cold extrusion. While Masco had grown and developed in the years from 1929 to 1954, its

EXHIBIT 2
Percentage of Sales to the Auto Industry in Early Years

Calendar Year	Total Sales	Percentage of Sales to Auto Industry
1930	$ 66,000	98%
1931	26,000	94
1932	29,000	99
1933	48,000	99
1934	77,000	99
1935	162,000	99
1936	234,000	100

Source: Masco 50—The First Fifty Years, 1929–1979.

heavy dependence on the business cycle of the car manufacturers was about to change.

1954 to Present

Alex Manoogian designed a workable, single-handle faucet and built a staff to produce and market it. Four years later, in 1958, sales of the Delta faucet were over the one-million dollar mark. In 1959, a faucet plant was built in Greensburg, Indiana to house the growing segment's production. Richard Manoogian, Alex's son also joined the company in the late fifties and helped to lead the company through continued growth.

In 1961, the first of many acquisitions took place with the purchase of Peerless Industries, Inc., a manufacturer of plumbing valves and fittings. It was at this time that a name change was seen to be in order. Masco Screw Products Company became Masco Corporation. In the period from 1964 to 1978, Masco acquired more than 30 companies, which has made it what it is today, a conglomerate able to withstand great fluctuations in the business cycle and maintain its tremendous growth rate. Exhibit 3 lists the top companies on the New York Stock Exchange (NYSE) that have had at least 25 consecutive years of growth. As can be seen, Masco tops the list with an average annual growth rate of over 36 percent.

In 1968, Richard Manoogian was elected President of Masco, and he continues to hold that position. Presently, Alex Manoogian is Chairman of the Board. He spends most of his time involved with charitable causes and working on faucet design. At the age of 78, Mr. Manoogian is still involved in the company he started 50 years ago. Presently, the Manoogian family holds 15 percent of the common shares of stock outstanding.

Management

In its early stages when Masco was dependent on the auto industry, it was producing by contract to its customers' specifications. Alex Manoogian realized that his hands were tied as far as producing a better product, so he worked to build a reputation of producing high-quality, reliable parts. He also worked hard to make sure that production was efficient. Manoogian continued to manage his company carefully through the 1940s and 1950s essentially by himself. However, with the diversification that came about in the late 1950s and early 1960s came a more fully developed management philosophy. Alex Manoogian knew that when he expanded his operations into two completely unrelated businesses (on one hand, nuts and bolts and other parts for cars and, on the other hand, the new one-handle faucet), he needed two completely separate facilities. This would help him determine individual profitability as well as to become aware of individual problems. It was recognized that effective communication is the key to successful management and it has been a continued effort to keep the number of people down at each plant in order to facilitate communication. See Exhibit 4, an organizational chart.

EXHIBIT 3
Companies on the NYSE with 25 Consecutive Years of Growth

	Annual Earnings Growth
Masco Corporation	36.1%
Xerox Corporation	27.8
Baxter Travenol Laboratories, Inc.	24.6
Perkin–Elmer Corporation	23.0
Petrolane Inc.	22.1
American Hospital Supply Corp.	18.2
Bristol–Myers Co.	17.4
Philip Morris Inc.	17.2
Beatrice Foods Co.	17.1
Central Louisiana Energy Corp.	16.3
Cheesebrough-Pond's Inc.	15.6
PepsiCo Inc.	15.6
Carnation Co.	11.8
American Home Products Corp.	11.7
Kellogg Co.	10.9

Source: Masco 1981 Annual Report, restated from Standard and Poor's Corp.

EXHIBIT 4
Masco's Top Management

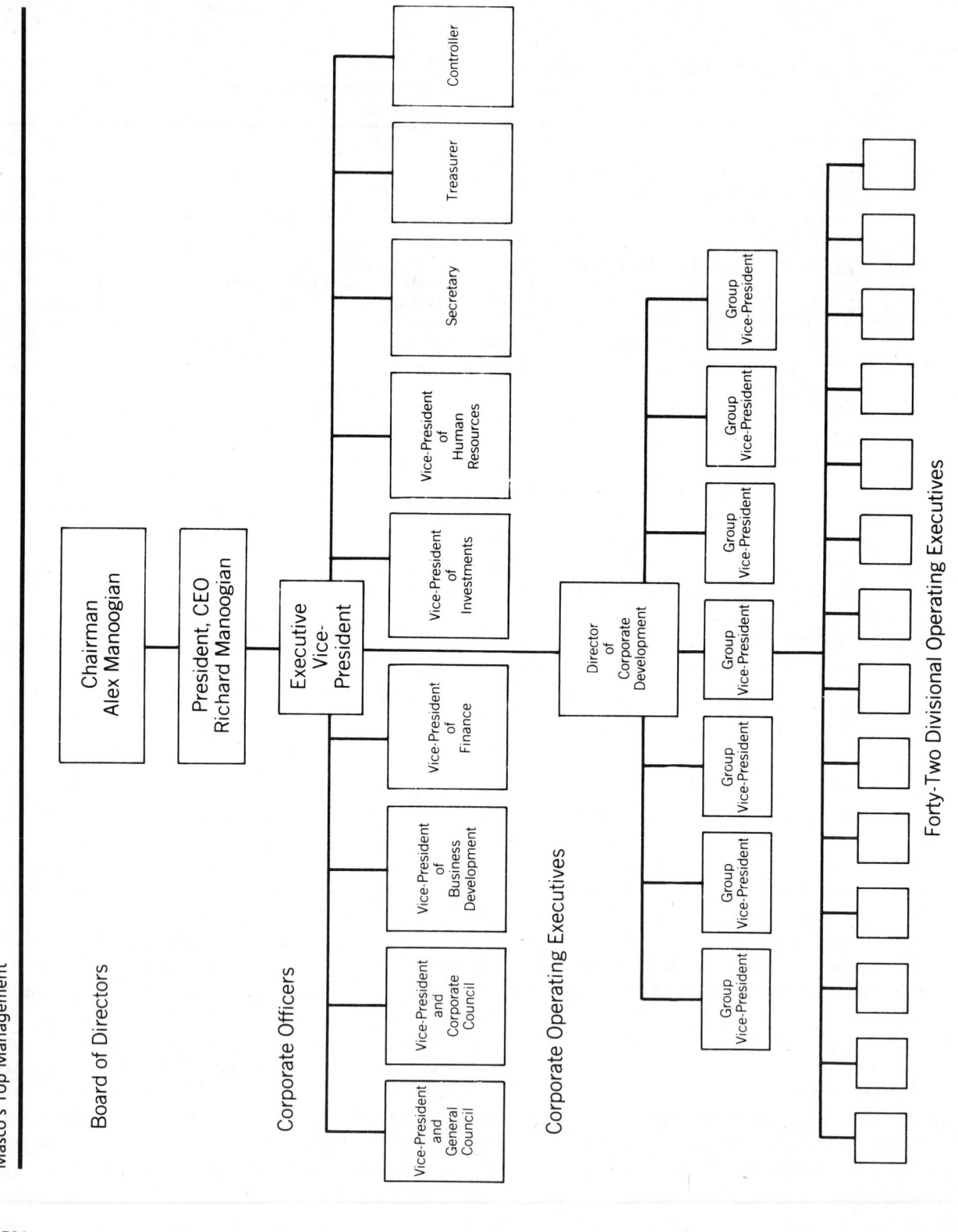

According to the 1981 Annual Report:

> Masco is organized into decentralized, highly autonomous divisional profit centers which are complete, functional business units. As such, we encourage decision making at the cutting edge of product and market opportunity. In our experience, those operations that successfully implement our proven business strategies in pursuit of Masco's objectives and that are entrepreneurially managed will successfully develop their own unique "proprietary" quality.[2]

Masco's policy is to ask the management teams of acquired companies to stay on and continue running the operations they already know. This works well since Masco only acquires solid companies and will not attempt a takeover of an unwilling company. This way, positive relations are developed immediately.

The top management of Masco professes to be very people-oriented. They seek employees that can continue developing the company with the same entrepreneurial spirit upon which it was founded. It is believed that the company could now successfully continue without the Manoogians to guide it. Richard Manoogian explains the success of the company by saying that Masco brings new ideas to dull industries.[3] This means people in the organization need to be bright and innovative to think of ways to keep ahead. Masco operates in what could be stable environments in many of its product lines, but the company is producing new improved products. The people at Masco are preventing many segments from remaining stable, although the products could easily go unchanged and most likely no one would complain.

Some corporate objectives are:

To concentrate on proprietary leadership positions.

To diversify the product base to avoid dependence on any one market.

To utilize existing skills in product development, manufacturing, and marketing.

To manufacture only products of value that ensure an above-average return.

The term "proprietary," as used in the first objective, requires a definition. A "proprietary" product or market position is one that enables the company to earn at least a 20 percent pre-tax profit margin on sales over an extended period of time. See Exhibit 5 for a list of Masco leadership products.

Operations

An operating objective of Masco is to achieve consistent and predictable growth. The company intends to do this as it has done in the past, that is, by diversification into new products and new markets in addition to working to increase its share in existing markets. This is

---

[2]Masco Corporation, 1981 Annual Report, p. 6.
[3]"Dull is Beautiful," *Financial World*, August 1, 1980, p. 36.

EXHIBIT 5
Masco Leadership Products: 1981 Sales

	(In Thousands)	Percent of Total
Faucets	$185,000	21%
Oil-field and Related Products	155,000	18
Specialty Valves and Closures	86,000	10
Cold Extruded Products	81,000	9
Personal Communications Products	57,000	6
Other Plumbing Products	29,000	3
Insulation Products	28,000	3
Ventilating Equipment	27,000	3
Other Specialty Transportation Products	24,000	3
Recreational Accessories	21,000	2
Other	13,000	2
Leadership Product Sales	$706,000	80%
Total Masco Sales	$877,000	100%

Source: Masco Corporation 1981 Annual Report.

EXHIBIT 6
Masco in Periods of Recession

	1981 vs. 1980	1980 vs. 1979	1975 vs. 1974	1970 vs. 1969	1967 vs. 1966	1961 vs. 1960
Sales						
Masco[a]	+14.4%	+5.5%	+21.5%	+16.7%	+19.1%	+6.3%
All Manufacturing[b]	+9.7%	+8.8%	+0.6%	+2.0%	+3.8%	+3.1%
Earnings						
Masco[a]	+14.4%	+5.6%	+25.4%	+15.8%	+3.5%	+61.6%
All Manufacturing[b]	+8.4%	−6.4%	−16.6%	−14.1%	−6.2%	+0.7%

Source: Masco 1981 Annual Report.
[a] As reported in the Annual Report.
[b] Federal Trade Commission Data.

to be accomplished by internal research as well as by carefully selecting acquisitions. There were no material acquisitions in 1981, however.

If Masco's future success can be measured by the past, it should do well. As Exhibit 6 indicates, Masco has been able to weather economic storms far better than the average manufacturer. The company has been able to increase sales and earnings during every recent downswing in the economic cycle. Masco has manufacturing facilities in 16 states and in Puerto Rico, Australia, Canada, Denmark, England, Italy, Mexico, and West Germany.[4]

The company categorizes its products as follows:

Building and Home Improvement Products
    Faucets
    Insulation products
    Venting and ventilating equipment
    Water pumps
    Humidifiers
    Air treatment products
Energy-Related and Other Specialty Products
    Oil-field and related products
    Slide-gate valves
    Industrial closures
    Scanning monitor receivers
    Weight-distributing hitches
    Boat trailer winches
    Air compressors
Cold Extruded and Other Industrial Products
    Cold extruded transmission products
    Hot headed transmission products
    Special fasteners
    Automotive luggage carriers
    Gear shift levers
    Safety reflectors
    Diesel engine exhaust systems

Faucets

In 1981, faucets made up 21 percent of Masco's total sales. Faucets have been important to Masco since the 1950s when Alex Manoogian first diversified into this field to hedge against fluctuations in automobile sales. Masco has also diversified its faucet lines over the years. It started with Delta, the single-handled faucet, which remains strong today with one-third of the total market for such faucets. Delex, double-handled faucets, and Deltique, decorator faucets, give Masco 20 percent of all double-handle faucet sales. But with 1980–1981 new construction down, it seems that

---
[4] Moody's Industrial Manual, Volume I, 1982 ed., Moody's Investors Service, Inc., New York, p. 4029.

Masco should be suffering in this area. That, however, is not the case because the company sells only about 40 percent of its faucets for new construction use. The remaining 60 percent is used in remodeling and replacement and Masco has its whole Peerless line to make plumbing easy for the do-it-yourself market.

Metalworking Technology

Cold extrusion is a metalworking process with which Masco first worked in 1948. At that time, cold extrusion was a new process and Masco, under contract with Chrysler, helped develop it to produce parts for use in the Korean war. At that time, however, Masco was too small and undercapitalized to develop the process further. In 1966, the company was able to start concentrating resources on the development of cold extrusion and today is a leader in the field. The company derives nine percent of its sales from its cold extruded products. These sales go mostly to the automotive market and to some specialty product fields.

The production technique of cold extrusion forces metal into the desired shape without using heat. Instead of heat, great pressure is used to form the metal. A trailer hitch ball is an example of a Masco product made using this process. It is an energy-efficient technique, no waste results, and the structural strength of the product is improved over other methods. Other advantages are that a one-piece cold extruded part can often replace more expensive multipart assemblies, and secondary stages of processing can often be eliminated because the cold extruded part is smooth and complete. With this process, Masco can offer the customer a better product and can successfully compete because of the efficiency of production.

The automobile industry is still a major customer of Masco. Even so, the company has been able to avoid being victimized by the recent automotive slump. Consider the types of parts that Masco produces: wheel bolts, gear shift levers, luggage racks, power transmission gears and shafts, special fasteners, engine manifolds and front-wheel drive components. Several of these parts, such as wheel bolts and gear shift levers, are essential to all cars. Other parts are special in that they require tooling, engineering, and manufacturing skills that few other companies have available. Some parts, such as front-wheel drive components, are fairly new and Masco has gotten an early lead in their production. Masco has been continually increasing the number and dollar value of the parts produced per car. Auto parts sales per domestic car produced have increased at an average annual rate of 14 percent over the last decade.[5]

International Aspect

International production is extensive and the export department is expanding. International sales declined in 1981 for the first time, and this is blamed on the weak European economy. The company has programs going into effect to develop synergy in their world-wide markets including:

> New United States manufacturing techniques and equipment being used in the Danish operation to increase efficiency and manufacturing capabilities.
>
> New product programs to develop products and components that can be manufactured and sold by each of the plumbing operations in the United States and Europe.
>
> New marketing programs to sell products of one division through sales and distribution networks of other divisions.[6]

Another important strategy Masco has implemented world-wide is to capitalize on the high cost of energy. It has accomplished this by using energy-saving production techniques to help it compete successfully, for example, cold extrusion process; by producing products that will save energy for customers, for example, insulation products; by producing parts

---
[5]Masco Corporation, p. 27.
[6]Ibid., p. 31.

EXHIBIT 7
Consolidated Statement of Income for the Years Ended December 31, 1981, 1980, and 1979

Net Sales	$876,530,000	$766,440,000	$726,430,000
Cost of Sales	571,400,000	496,913,000	476,975,000
Gross Profit	305,130,000	269,527,000	249,455,000
Selling, General and Administrative Expenses	139,910,000	116,505,000	107,044,000
Operating Profit	165,220,000	153,022,000	142,411,000
Other Expenses (Income), Net:			
Interest Expense	39,874,000	38,743,000	26,132,000
Other Income, Net	(25,394,000)	(22,611,000)	(16,181,000)
	14,480,000	16,132,000	9,951,000
Income Before Income Taxes	150,740,000	136,890,000	132,460,000
Income Taxes	62,420,000	59,710,000	59,440,000
Net Income	$ 88,320,000	$ 77,180,000	$ 73,060,000
Earnings Per Common and Common Equivalent Share	$3.46	$3.03	$2.80

for those producing energy, for example, oilfield products.

Research and Development

In addition to its method of expansion and development through acquisition, the company also conducts internal research and development. The stated new product objective is to "develop quality value-added products with the potential to realize a 10 percent after-tax profit on sales and 20 percent after-tax profit on investment."[7] The strategies used to obtain the objective are listed below:

> Explore long-range growth potential of appropriate market opportunities.
>
> Evaluate product uniqueness compared to competing products to determine if a premium value will be accorded by the user.
>
> Avoid products where frequent incidence of obsolescence adds inordinately to the risk.
>
> Work closely with customers to insure responsiveness to their needs.[8]

The research team looks to improve materials, production techniques, engineering, facilities planning, and machine and product design. The company estimates that new products, introduced at the beginning of 1980 and later, contributed well over $100 million to 1981 sales. Innovations include faucets for the handicapped, the first synthesized programmable handheld scanner, and various other products that meet such customer needs as energy efficiency in both the housing and industrial markets.

Financial Performance

Masco has experienced growth over the last decade as follows: Net sales, 23 percent average growth per year; Net income, 22 percent; Net income per share, 21 percent; Dividends, 26 percent. Sales revenue increased to $876,530,000 in 1981 from $766,440,000 in 1980. Net income was up $11,140,000 from $77,180,000 in 1980 to $88,320,000 in 1981. Earnings per share, at $3.46 in 1981, increased $0.43 from $3.03 in 1980. Dividends were increased from $0.17 per share, per quarter, to $0.19 in 1981 while in 1980 they had been increased from $0.15 to $0.17. For 1981 the dividend payouts represented about 20 percent of net income. There has been an average 25 percent per year increase in working capital over the last 10 years with current assets over current liabilities of $48,244,000 in 1972 and $381,438,000 in 1981. See Exhibits 7 and 8 for comparative financial statements.

---
[7]*Ibid.*, p. 32.
[8]*Ibid.*, p. 32.

EXHIBIT 8
Consolidated Balance Sheet December 31, 1981 and 1980

Assets				
Current Assets				
Cash and Cash Investments			$ 62,716,000	$ 44,718,000
Marketable Securities			74,829,000	92,778,000
Accounts and Notes Receivable, Net			143,408,000	132,986,000
Inventories, at FIFO			214,529,000	187,624,000
Prepaid Expenses			10,633,000	8,933,000
Total Current Assets			506,115,000	467,039,000
Other Assets				
Investments in Partially Owned Companies			41,531,000	43,611,000
Excess of Cost Over Net Assets of Acquired Companies, Net			51,489,000	53,609,000
Unamortized Purchase Cost of Patents			35,195,000	38,167,000
Accounts and Notes Receivable, Related Party, Net			9,509,000	9,009,000
Other			18,492,000	5,630,000
Property, Plant, and Equipment				
Land and Land Improvements			17,064,000	16,483,000
Buildings			103,644,000	89,694,000
Machinery and Equipment			286,426,000	240,263,000
Less Accumulated Depreciation			(129,452,000)	(245,322,000)
Total Assets			$940,013,000	$862,387,000
Liabilities				
Current Liabilities				
Notes Payable			23,175,000	28,629,000
Accounts Payable			31,761,000	30,656,000
Income Taxes			26,193,000	20,320,000
Accrued and Other Liabilities			43,548,000	38,245,000
Total Current Liabilities			124,677,000	117,850,000
Other Liabilities				
Long-Term Debt, Excluding Current Portion			307,600,000	328,401,000
Deferred Income Taxes, Noncurrent			15,476,000	10,545,000
Total Liabilities			447,753,000	456,796,000
Shareholders' Equity				
Common Stock, $1 Par Value				
Shares (in Millions)	1981	1980		
Shares Authorized	150.000	40.000		
Shares Issued	25.175	25.597	25,175,000	25,597,000
Preferred Stock, $1 Par Value				
Shares (in Millions)	1981	1980		
Shares Authorized	1.000	1.000		
Shares Issued	None	None		
Paid-In Capital			8,157,000	16,007,000
Retained Earnings			458,928,000	388,600,000
Less 981,000 Treasury Shares, at cost				(24,613,000)
Total Shareholders' Equity			492,260,000	405,591,000
Total Liabilities and Shareholders' Equity			$940,013,000	$862,387,000

ALLIED CHEMICAL COMPANY

Allied Chemical is a large, diversified chemical-manufacturing firm headquartered in Morristown, New Jersey, with manufacturing and processing plants located world-wide. Allied Chemical operations are comprised of six segments:

1. *Energy Products and Services.* Production includes liquified petroleum gases (LPG), liquified natural gases (LNG), residue gas, crude oil, and ethylene.
2. *Inorganic Chemicals.* Production includes resins, hydrochloric, hydrofluoric and nitric acids, soda and sodium byproducts, and soda ash.
3. *Organic Chemicals.* Production includes resins used in paints, enamels, and other coatings, and textiles.
4. *Agricultural Chemicals.* Includes ammonia-based products used primarily for the manufacture and application of fertilizers.
5. *Fibers.* Production includes nylon, rayon, and other products.
6. *Other.* Production includes coal and coke operations, automotive safety restraints, paving materials, and packaging films.

1979 was a year of strong contrasts in performance among Allied's business segments. The energy products and services operations, the area of greatest growth in recent years, made a significant gain in sales and earnings. The fibers operations turned in another steady performance. However, these strong performances were offset by lower margins in many of the chemical product lines, substantially higher losses in coal and coke, and a significant loss in agricultural chemicals.

Allied's former Chairman and Chief Executive Officer, John T. Connor, retired under a mandatory retirement program on November 30, 1979. The question of management succession had been under active consideration of the Nominating and Review Committee of the Board of Directors. The committee recommended E. L. Hennessey, Jr. as President and Chief Executive Officer. In a recent discussion, Mr. Hennessey said:

> the economic environment in 1980 will be a challenging one, with much of American industry caught in a profit squeeze between rising costs and competitive and governmental pressures to keep prices down. To deal with the economic uncertainties, Allied has not only moved aggressively to correct loss situations, but has cut costs and trimmed spending plans wherever possible without damaging long-range growth prospects. And Allied continues to believe our growth will pay off in improved earnings for our stockholders over the next few years.

However, Allied, along with other large chemical firms, is having problems maintaining performance, as is shown in Exhibit 1.

While sales continue to increase, net income continues to decline. Allied, along with other large chemical firms, is facing hardships including foreign competition, foreign taxes, governmental regulations, and environmental costs that will only add to the cost–profit squeeze now being felt.

History

Allied Chemical Corporation was incorporated in New York on December 17, 1920 to consolidate the control of The Barrett Co., General Chemical Co., National Aniline and Chemical Co., Semet–Solvay Co., and the Solvay Process Co. It was called Allied Chemical and Dye Corporation, but was changed to Allied Chemical Corporation in 1958. Allied presently operates over 200 plants, research laboratories, mines, quarries, and other facilities throughout the United States, Canada, and Europe.

Source: This case was prepared by Professor Sexton Adams. Permission to use granted by Sexton Adams.

EXHIBIT 1
Profitability (Dollars in millions, except per share amounts)

	1979	1978	1977	1976
Sales and Operating Revenues	$4,332	$3,268	$2,922	$2,630
Net Income	$ 11	$ 120	$ 135	$ 126
Net Income per Share Common	$ 0.20	$ 4.25	$ 4.93	$ 4.52

Source: Allied Chemical Annual Report, 1980, Allied Chemical Corporation, Morristown, New Jersey.

Allied operates these facilities in an effort to reduce shipping costs, because most chemicals are shipped in bulk quantities. It also operates research and development laboratories in close proximity to manufacturing facilities.

The corporation is expanding its oil and gas operations and, as of December 31, 1979, held leases or other interests in oil and gas producing properties in (1) the United States, (2) British sector of the North Sea, (3) Canada, (4) Argentina, and (5) Indonesia. They also have interests in or rights to conduct exploratory activities on undeveloped acreage in (1) the United States, (2) Canada, (3) British and West German sectors of the North Sea, (4) Brazil, (5) Italy, (6) Indonesia, (7) Australia, (8) Tunisia, (9) Bahrain, (10) Jamaica, and (11) on-shore and off-shore Spain.

Organization

With the November 30, 1979 retirement of Chairman and Chief Executive Officer, John T. Connor, and the nomination and election of President and Chief Executive Officer, E. L. Hennessey, Jr., much of the time and energy of the Board of Directors has been diverted from the task of managing the firm. However, with the nomination and election process completed, the Board will be able to direct all attention to managing the company. The company is presently headed by a 15-member Board of Directors that includes 10 external members and five internal members. The Board of Directors, as of December 31, 1979, is as follows:

E. L. Hennessey, Chairman and Chief Executive Officer.

John T. Connor, former Chairman and Chief Exeuctive Officer.

Joseph B. Collinson, Chairman and Chief Executive Officer, Textrom, Inc., a diversified manufacturing company.

John P. Fishwick, President and Chief Executive Officer, Norfolk and Western Railway.

E. Burke Giblin, Chairman of the Executive Committee, Warner–Lambert Company.

Robert T. Mulcahy, former President, Allied Chemical Corporation.

Robert T. Perkins, retired Chairman of the Executive Committee, Metropolitan Life Insurance Company.

Robert R. Shinn, President and Chief Executive Officer, Citibank and Citicorp.

Alexander B. Trowbridge, Vice Chairman, Allied Chemical.

Brian D. Forrow, Vice President and General Counsel, Allied Chemical.

Roger H. Morely, President, American Express Company.

Charles W. Nichols, Private Investor.

John D. Glover, Chairman of the Board, Cambridge Research Institute Inc., business consultants.

Helen S. Meyner, Director, Prudential Insurance Co. of America.

Stanley P. Porter, Retired partner of Arthur Young and Co.

In a recent discussion, President and Chief Executive Officer, E. L. Hennessey, said:

We plan to continue our strategy of redeveloping assets in those businesses we believe have the best future growth potential for Allied Chemical. We will continue to divest ourselves of operations which are marginal in profitability or which for other reasons do not fit into our long-range plans.

Allied Chemical is divided into eight divisions in the six major business segments. Each division is directed by a Division President who is responsible for the day-to-day operations of his or her division as well as communicating with the Board of Directors. The current organizational chart follows:

Marketing

Allied has seen the oil and gas operations grow dramatically in sales and operating income as production continues to grow. The fibers business made significant gains in sales and earnings because 1979 sales were essentially at capacity, and work was started to increase capacity at two major production facilities. However, the earnings of many of Allied's chemical businesses suffered because of industry overcapacity, which kept process below levels needed to cover rising production and overhead costs. Net sales and incomes by product group is shown in Exhibit 3.

Chemical Industry Outlook

Tightening supply conditions sparked by the Iranian oil curtailment early in the year created unusually strong demand for U. S. manufactured petrochemicals, plastics, fibers, and other products through much of 1979. The demand will lead to increased profits that should provide enough momentum to allow chemical firms to report a creditable profit performance for 1980. Sales of chemicals and allied products are forecast to rise to $145 billion in 1979, up from $130 billion in 1978, and with estimated sales of $160 billion in 1980, as can be seen in Exhibit 4.

EXHIBIT 2
Partial Organizational Chart

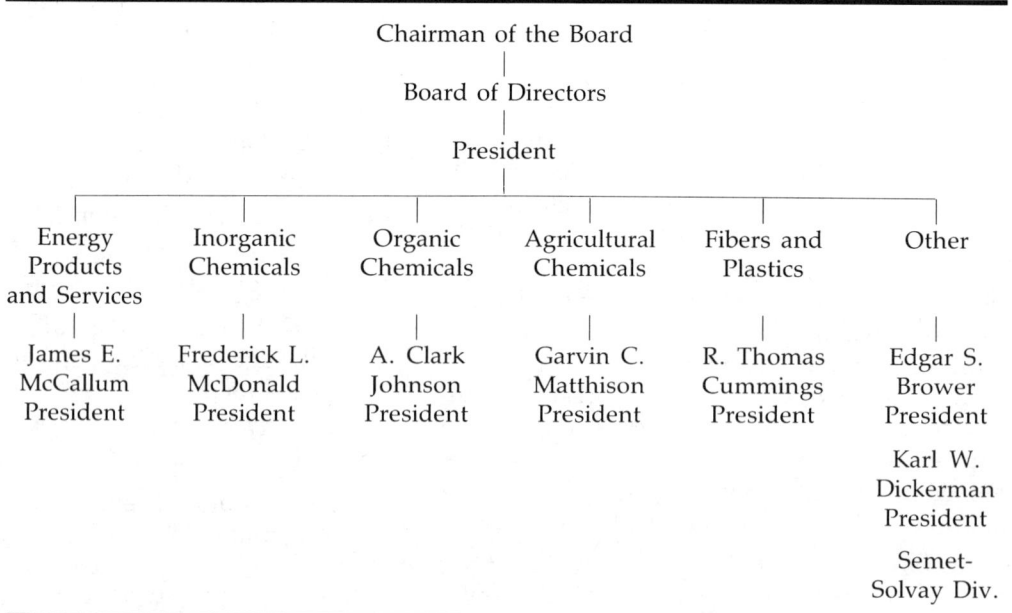

Source: Company records.

EXHIBIT 3
Net Sales and Income by Products Group

In Millions	1979 Total Sales	1979 Operating Income	1978 Total Sales	1978 Operating Income	1977 Total Sales	1977 Operating Income	1976 Total Sales	1976 Operating Income
Energy Products and Services	1,369	392	948	307	676	193	461	31
Inorganic Chemicals	775	22	657	66	623	80	573	91
Organic Chemicals	725	6	537	15	529	31	573	63
Agricultural Chemicals	155	—	162	(31)	180	—	185	38
Fibers and Plastics	940	120	497	85	441	63	380	60
Other	368	24	467	(41)	474	(37)	458	2
Total	4,332	564	3,268	401	2,923	330	2,630	285

Source: Allied Chemical Corporation Annual Report, 1979.

However, major challenges and opportunities face the chemical industry as it anticipates a new decade. Mr. Hennessey, CEO of Allied Chemical Corporation, believes the industry has some major concerns, including:

(1) the tendency for state-controlled nations to subsidize their chemical industries and seek markets for their output at any price, (2) the looming development of a petrochemical industry by OPEC nations in the second half of the decade and the effect this will have on U. S. companies and the world markets, and (3) the on-going takeover of U. S. companies by foreigners through purchases of outstanding stock.

Chemical Industry Profits

"Earnings for most of the large chemical firms should be up about three percent in 1980, and miscellaneous chemicals should have earnings increase about five percent," according to John Baker of Dow Chemical. In a recent conversation, Mr. E. L. Hennessey of Allied Chemical said:

With competition increasing domestically and with more firms trying to capture a larger share of the export market before it shrinks, a moderation or possibly a reversal of recent price increases will be necessary. Prices for all chemicals and related products have risen at a 15 percent annual rate compared to 20 percent for the previous year. On the other hand, manufacturers are faced with an unrelenting climb in raw material costs, energy, and labor costs which should cause profits to decline for the industry. For 1979, the return on sales for the chemical industry was 6.8 percent and should be about 6.3 percent in 1980, and slower price

EXHIBIT 4
Chemical Industry Sales (Billions of dollars)

Year	Industry Sales	Allied Chemical Sales	Allied's Percent of Industry Sales
1969	$ 48.3	$1.316	2.73%
1970	49.3	1.248	2.53
1971	51.9	1.325	2.55
1972	57.4	1.501	2.61
1973	65.0	1.664	2.56
1974	83.7	2.215	2.65
1975	89.7	2.333	2.60
1976	104.0	2.629	2.53
1977	118.1	2.922	2.48
1978	130.0	3.268	2.51
1979	145.0	4.332	2.99
1980 (est.)	160	5.4	3.4

Source; "Chemicals, Current Analysis," Standard's and Poor's Survey, July 3, 1980.

increases should be seen as demand will remain soft through 1980.

Chemical Industry Production

An early projection of 1980 domestic production of chemicals and related products (on a dollar value basis) calls for stable growth of about 12 percent compared to the 1973–1978 average of 15 percent. The area most likely to show gains is industrial chemicals, aided by strong demand from foreign countries arising from lower costs for U. S. manufacturers. Other sectors that should do better than average are cosmetics, pharmaceuticals, and industrial inorganic chemicals. With moderate growth in demand, excess capacities should be gradually absorbed and allow for near-optimum operating rates for producers.

Research and Development

In the 1960s, U. S. industry spent close to three percent of sales for research and development, but spent only 1.87 percent in 1978. A substantial portion of the decline in recent years may be attributable to the 1974 tax code revision, which redefined research and development outlays. Generally, research and development costs are now limited to those expenses that involve the technological aspects of product and process development and that extend knowledge of physical sciences useful in commercial production. Specifically excluded are costs pertaining to routine product improvement, market research, test marketing, seasonal style changes, quality control, and engineering follow-through in production. Also excluded are legal costs related to patents and costs associated with their sale or development outlays as is shown in Exhibit 5.

Financial

According to *Chemical Week* magazine, earnings of the six leading chemical companies are expected to have flat-to-moderate growth in 1980, after an 11 percent increase in 1979 and an 18 percent increase in 1978. The chemical industry enjoyed strong market conditions in 1979, but these conditions are expected to weaken in 1980 as the economy slumps. In recent years, excess capacity hampered the implementation of adequate price relief and squeezed profit margins. The tight supply conditions that prevailed in 1979 created a seller's market and enabled producers to institute long-awaited price increases.

Capital spending is expected to increase 13 percent in 1980, which will only keep up with inflation. Expenditures for investments in new plant and equipment are expected to remain under 10 percent for the third year in succession. A review of industry capital spending as a percent of sales is presented in Exhibit 6.

In mid-1979, the Treasury Department announced that chemical companies would be allowed to reduce to seven-and-one-half years (from nine years) the shortest period over which chemical companies can depreciate their equipment. The new rules should encourage greater spending for new plant expansion.

Industry profitability, measured as a return on stockholders' equity, remained strong at approximately 13 percent. The dividend

EXHIBIT 5
Research and Development Outlays
(As a percentage of total sales)

	1979	1978
Office Equipment	5.70	5.65
Health Care	4.25	4.30
Leisure Time	4.20	4.50
Aerospace	2.75	2.70
Automobile	2.60	2.50
Electronics	2.55	2.45
Chemicals	2.45	2.55
Machinery	1.90	2.05
Rubber Fabricating	1.65	1.70
Home Furnishings	1.60	1.70
Allied Chemical Corp.	1.87	1.77
Composite Average (all industries)	1.83	1.87

Source: "R & D Costs," *Standard's and Poor's Industry Surveys*, September 6, 1980.

EXHIBIT 6
Capital Spending as a Percent of Sales

Year	Percent
1969	10.9
1970	11.6
1971	10.6
1972	8.9
1973	9.9
1974	11.9
1975	12.8
1976	12.7
1977	11.6
1978	9.8
1979	9.8
Projected 1980	13.0

Source: "Chemicals, Current Analysis," *Standard and Poor's Industry Surveys*, September 6, 1980.

pay-out ratio is expected to rise in the next few years, because of an endless quest for growth capital. It appears that industry executives must continue to pay out an increasing percentage of earnings as dividends in order to obtain growth capital.

An additional capital expense for the chemical industry will be in the area of environmental protection. Stricter laws and regulations passed in recent years will continue to drive environmental costs upward at an increasing rate. This is evidenced in environmental spending at Allied Chemical as shown in Exhibit 7.

EXHIBIT 7
Allied Chemical Environmental Costs (In millions)

Year	Expense	Percentage of Sales
1975	27	1.15%
1976	29	1.10
1977	35	1.20
1978	72	2.20
1979	101	3.10

Source: Allied Chemical Corporation Annual Report, 1980.

Environmental Pollution And Other Legal Difficulties

Kepone

Kepone is a chlorinated organic compound similar to DDT. Allied Chemical produced the pesticide from 1966 to 1973 at its Hopewell, Virginia chemical plant. In 1973, Virgil Hundtofte and William Moore, former employees of Allied, formed Life Science Products Company. Life Science Products Company had a total process contract with Allied to produce Kepone solely for Allied until Life Science Products Company was closed on July 24, 1975 by the Virginia Department of Health. Seventy of the plant's 150 employees showed symptoms of Kepone poisoning including tremors, slurring of speech, and chest and joint pains. Disposal of Kepone by Allied followed by Life Science Products Company contaminated a large portion of the James River. According to the U. S. Attorney's Office at Richmond, Allied and Life Science actually dumped Kepone into the river. In December 1975, the river was closed to fishing because the poison was traced to fish caught from the James River.

On October 6, 1976, Federal Judge Robert R. Merhige, Jr. fined Allied Chemical Corporation $13,375,000 for its part in polluting the James River with Kepone. Merhige was quoted as saying, "I hope that the size of the fine will deter employees of other companies from polluting the environment." Besides the employees of Life Science suffering from various nerve disorders, and the fishermen on the James lost their livelihood because authorities banned the sale of fish caught from the James River. Employee and fishermen claims totaled around $200 million in civil suits against Allied. Life Science Products was fined $3.8 million. William Moore and Virgil Hundtofte were fined $25,000 each. After the pronounced sentence, Allied's John T. Connor, who was chairman at the time stated, "We are pleased that the court has found Allied Chemical not guilty of charges of aiding and abetting Life Science

Products Company and conspiring with it to break the law." However, Allied pleaded *nolo contendere* to 940 counts of pumping chemicals into the river. Of the 940 counts, 144 were dismissed against Allied. Connor pointed out that only 312 of the counts involved Kepone and 628 covered two low toxical biodegradeable chemicals, TAIC and THEIC.

Allied is not only being held responsible for pollution of the James River by toxic chemicals, but is being held responsible for dredging about 100 miles of the James River. Approximately 100 miles of the James River was closed to commercial fishing by state health authorities. The estimated cost to Allied of dredging the James River has been around half a billion dollars. Problems exist after dredging the James River such as what to do with the contaminated soil containing Kepone.

Allied ran into problems with solutions to the disposal of the contaminated soil. Allied was planning to dispose of around 100,000 pounds of soil and equipment contaminated with Kepone by burying it in a 16 story deep missile silo in Idaho. However, the state of Idaho rejected the idea of burying the soil in the abandoned silo near Boise. Burning the Kepone stored in barrels turned out to be a nonworkable solution because of the dangerous gases that would be released into the atmosphere. One of the gases released by burning Kepone is a deadly type of gas similar to arsenic gas fumes. The negative results of the burning hampered Allied's plan of using a mobile incinerator for disposing of contaminated materials in Hopewell. Plans for disposing of the Kepone contaminated by Allied include finding locations where the material can be safely buried and disposing of the liquid material by chemical reactions that will leave a safe residue.

Allied set up an original fund of $8 million to help problems caused by its Hopewell, Va. Kepone-making operations. The Virginia Environmental Endowment of $8 million, according to Allied, is to "alleviate the effects of Kepone on the environment and on those whose livelihoods have been impaired by it." The endowment is a separate independent organization whose Board of Directors is appointed by Judge Robert R. Merhige, Jr. The endowment's Board will, according to Allied, "fund scientific research projects to implement remedial efforts and other scientific programs and measures (including financial and economic assistance in the form of loans or such) as the Board of Directors in its sole discretion shall deem appropriate." Allied concedes that the net financial drain to the corporation will probably be around $4 million rather than $8 million because the endowment is considered a charitable contribution. Judge Merhige points out, however, that the endowment does not affect civil suits against Allied by former plant workers claiming injury from unsafe plant conditions at Hopewell or civil suits against Allied by James River watermen for loss of income because of the closing of the river to all commercial fishing. Allied hopes that by creating the endowment, they can express their sincerity on alleviating problems caused by Kepone pollution.

It should be pointed out that in the court proceedings, Allied Chemical experts stated that Environmental Protection Agency levels for action of Kepone pollution could quadruple without changing the safety factor recommended by the Environmental Protection Agency's own experts. Allied Chemical experts also suggested that raising the action level for fish from 0.1 parts per million to at least 0.4 parts per million would be more realistic and consistent with data and would alleviate some of the economic hardship caused by "unnecessarily severe levels." Allied Chemical experts also claimed that the action level for Kepone had been set at a level far more severe than other chemicals that were of far greater potential danger to the environment.

Armco Suit

Allied supplies blast furnace coke and cokeoven gas to Armco's steel production plant at Ashland, Kentucky. Armco filed a suit against Allied for $32 million for Allied's failure to deliver coke and cokeoven gas as specified in a contract to Armco's plant. The suit also asked for $185 million for damages that will occur through 1982. Allied denied breach of contract because of certain contingencies within the contract. These contingencies relieve performance by either party because of equipment failures, labor problems, and failure of supply materials. Allied also claimed that Armco caused operational problems at Allied's Ashland plant by supplying coal of inferior quality. All of Allied's output goes to Armco; likewise, Armco furnishes all of the coal used by Allied. Coke battery damage and excessive deurrage was claimed against Armco by Allied as a result of the inferior coal. After court proceedings lasting most of 1979, Allied was found guilty of charges leveled by Armco. Allied was held responsible to Armco for an initial $34 million, but not long-term damages amounting to $185 million from 1978 through 1980. Allied appealed the verdict; however, the appeal was not successful as other court proceedings arrived at the same verdict. Allied paid the fine and suspended coke business transactions involved with Armco.

Allied Operational Strategies

Plant Modifications

Semet-Solvay is a division of Allied that manages the company's coal and coke operation. In 1977, Allied spent $45 million to rehabilitate a foundry coke plant in Detroit, Michigan. The division's president said, "Rehabilitation of our foundry coke battery in Detroit will serve not only to increase the facility's capacity but also should serve to end concerns among area residents that the plant is a source of environmental contamination." The project brought the screening capacity to 700,000 tons annually. Not only does this action by Allied improve environmental conditions, it includes improvements in coal preheating, coal preparation, and byproduct recovery from operations. Allied is the largest producer of coke in the United States. Operations by Allied's management to revitalize older plants in terms of environmental safety and energy savings is an attempted strategy to meet environmental expectations along with decreasing long-run cost of operations.

Energy Endeavors

Allied's first phase of oil and gas exploration development in the North Sea was Piper Field during 1976. Allied owned a 20 percent interest. This 20 percent cost Allied $250 million. John T. Connor, Allied Chemical's former chairman said, "Allied's commitment to participate heavily in the development of oil and gas in the North Sea was made over five years ago and has had a high priority among its capital spending programs and strategy planning efforts." Allied also owns a 20 percent interest in the Claymore Field located in the North Sea. In late 1980, production of 250,000 barrels per day from the Piper Field and 170,000 barrels of oil from the Claymore Field will reach peak levels for both fields. Mr. Connor stated, "When the two fields reach peak production levels, Allied Chemical will experience substantially increased cash flows. In addition, the flow of crude will provide a raw material back-up for Allied's expanding petrochemicals-based operations." The United Kingdom's energy corporation, British National Oil Corporation, has the option to buy up to 51 percent of the crude oil and natural gas derived from the Piper and Claymore Fields. Connor points out that this arrangement protects the legitimate interest of the United Kingdom. Allied's participation in the North Sea represents the company's largest single endeavor among its oil and gas operations.

Although the North Sea ventures are the largest for Allied in gas and oil, another venture such as the Salou field in the Mediterranean Sea off the coast of Tarragona, Spain, holds significant promise of 15 million barrels. Allied's Union Texas/Espana division is involved not only in the Salou field off Spain but in areas around the Bay of Biscay north of Spain. In Indonesia, Allied Chemical and its partners have natural gas production wells in the Bodak Field in East Kalimantan. Allied's position and strategy involving energy can best be summarized by Mr. Connor's statement, "Clearly, the cash flows derived from the company's participation in these ventures will be most impressive. Moreover, they serve to vindicate a long-term business strategy of our corporation."

Research and Development in Solar Energy

Allied's shift in strategy to all energy fields can be expressed by research and development into solar energy. Allied's research and development division invented a photochemical diode device that simplifies the conversion of sunlight energy into chemical energy. This discovery has been a leading force in solar energy development and utilization. The process uses small simple wafers that create specific chemical reactions when suspended in a chemical liquid and exposed to sunlight. Allied's Materials Research Center actively pursued practical goals for the diode structures. These actions by the Material Research Center developed into high efficiencies for light energy conversion for the solar energy field along with long-term stabilities and low cost to manufacture units for the solar-energy conversion industry. Likewise, Allied benefits from the low cost of manufacture and long-term stability of sales of diodes as many energy experts look to energy from solar conversion for future needs.

Divestments

As was shown previously, Allied Chemical's long-term strategies involve concentrating on improving and expanding its energy aspects of business. For the last five years, Allied's strategy has been to divest themselves of the unprofitable aspects of their business. For example, in 1977, Allied Chemical sold its organic pigments to Harmon Colors Corporation. The sale included all manufacturing facilities, laboratories, and sales offices which were staffed by approximately 325 employees. By this type of divesture, Allied completely disengaged themselves from the organic pigments business. The organic pigments area of their business had turned out to be unprofitable for the past three years. Allied's divestment of unprofitable business segments from 1977 to the present have, along with energy expansion by Allied, reversed a declining shift in earnings per share to an increasing value for earnings per share.

As stated previously, Allied divested itself from unprofitable business aspects from 1977 to present. By divestment and expansion of their participation in oil and gas, Allied's profits from continuing operations more than tripled in 1980 from 1979. Other chemical firms showed a significant drop in earnings as can be seen from Exhibit 8.

The $123.7 million dollar loss of Allied in the third quarter of 1979 was a net loss after nonrecurring, after-tax charges of $163.2 million to cover losses connected with the divestiture of several operations and other one-time costs. All four companies had small sales increases for the third quarter with Allied having the largest of six percent from $1.25 billion to $1.32 billion. Celanese's sales rose one percent from $778 million to $785 million, and Dow's sales increased four percent from $2.43 billion to $2.52 billion. Rohm and Haas's sales were up three percent from $391.9 million to $403.8 million. As is depicted in Exhibit 9, except for Allied, the net income of all three chemical companies for the first nine months of 1980, as compared to 1979, had a negative change.

Rohm and Haas chairman, Vincent L. Gregory, Jr., attributed the company's nine-month drop in earnings to a drop in volume of shipments. G. J. Williams, Dow's financial vice-president, said, "The third quarter was a definite turnaround in the U. S. in virtually all

EXHIBIT 8
Third Quarter Net Income

	1980		1979		Percent Change
	In Millions	Per Share	In Millions	Per Share	
Allied	$ 66.2	$1.80	($123.7)	($4.35)	
Celanese	$ 21	$1.43	$ 37.	$2.47	−43%
Dow	$160.5	$ .88	$198.4	$1.09	−19%
Rohm and Haas	$ 22.6	$1.75	$ 29.2	$2.26	−14%

Source: Wall Street Journal, October 17, 1980.

parts of the economy." However, Williams said that business activity outside the United States, particularly key European markets, had slowed drastically, causing Rohm and Haas and Dow to reduce operations in order to reduce inventory. All companies emphasized a drastic decline in demand for chemicals with an improvement in fibers demand. As an example of industry conditions, Celanese fiber profits were up 36 percent. However, profits from the chemicals business were down 62 percent with profits from plastics and specialties off 70 percent. Edward L. Hennessy, Jr., Allied's current president and Chief Executive Officer, attributed Allied's higher earnings to sales in fibers and the oil and gas industry. Hennessy expressed his opinion that the problems faced in the chemical industry because of poor economic conditions demonstrate the need for large corporations such as Allied to diversify and not depend on one specific industry for survival. Hennessy said that the reason for the chemical and plastic sales decline was poor economic conditions world-wide and especially the auto industry recession from 1979 to the present. Hennessy stated that the most important aspect of the third quarter results for Allied is that 90 percent of Allied's profit from operations came from its oil and gas enterprises. He also pointed out the direct link of profitability to oil and gas operations through Allied's third quarter reports. Allied's oil and gas endeavors accounted for 32 percent of sales while chemicals accounted for 24 percent. However, 90 percent of Allied's third quarter operation profits was from oil and gas.

Future Operations

Allied Chemical has been in a state of transition for the past five years. This transformation

EXHIBIT 9
Nine Months Net Income

	1980		1979		Percent Change
	In Millions	Per Share	In Millions	Per Share	
Allied	$207.5	$5.88	($ 56.6)	($2.00)	
Celanese	$ 82	$5.51	$114	$7.67	−28%
Dow	$562.2	$3.09	$589.6	$3.25	−5%
Rohm and Haas	$ 76.7	$5.95	$ 84.6	$6.56	−9.3%

Source: Wall Street Journal, October 17, 1980.

EXHIBIT 10
Allied's Financial Report

	1979	1978	1977	1976	1975	1974
Net Sales (billions)	4.33	3.27	2.92	2.63	2.33	2.22
Net Income (millions)	11	120	135	117	116	144
Net Income (as a percent of sales)	0.25	3.7	4.6	4.4	5.0	6.5
Cash Dividend per share	2.00	1.85	1.80	1.80	1.80	1.53
Property, Plant and Equipment Additions (in millions)	475	502	465	352	314	306
Rate of Return on Stockholders equity (percent)	0.86	9.7	11.8	11.2	11.6	15.8
Rate of return on total capital	0.64	7.2	8.4	8.0	8.6	10.8

Source: Allied's 1979 Annual Financial Statement.

has involved divestiture of certain operations and a strategy of concentrating in areas of oil and gas. As can be seen readily for the third quarter of 1980, Allied's financial strength is improving on the background of its oil and gas operations. The move five years ago to divest unprofitable businesses and acquire business strength in oil and gas is turning out to be the successful corporate strategy for Allied. Likewise, W. R. Grace is a chemical company that reported a third quarter 1980 net income of $68 million. This was up from $44.5 million during three quarters of 1979. John Spelling, Grace's chief financial officer, explained that Grace's oil and gas operations and its oil-field service business helped push the natural resources segment earnings up 15 percent in the quarter from the same time in 1979. As a result of the drastic decline in production in the auto industry in the United States from 1979 to the present, the demand for chemicals and plastics has been drastically reduced. Likewise, because of a slowdown in the economy of the United States, along with a slowdown of key European markets, the chemical industries demand has become a great deal smaller.

Chemical companies also have faced costly capital expenditures to upgrade plants to meet environmental protection agency requirements. For example, Allied is not only bearing the cost of clean-up and lawsuits steming from Kepone pollution, but negative feelings toward Allied. Chemical companies face difficult times with capital intensive plants producing below capacity because of the falling demand for chemicals. Existence of slowing down economies in the United States and foreign vital markets does not show a promising increase in demand for chemicals. However, the oil and gas industry will continue to be of prime importance with the energy crisis that faces the world.

EXHIBIT 11
Allied's Geographical Operations

	Year	United States	Canada and Europe	Other	Total
Net Sales	1979	3,306	712	314	4,332
	1978	2,606	500	162	3,268
	1977	2,530	351	.42	2,923
Net Income	1979	(100)	75	36	11
	1978	7	76	37	120
	1977	54	59	22	135
Assets	1979	3,062	825	322	4,209
	1978	2,544	629	164	3,228
	1977	2,430	544	96	2,872

Source: Allied's 1979 Annual Financial Statement.
Note: In millions of dollars.

Converting and Manufacturing

EXHIBIT 12
Consolidated Earning Statement (Year Ending December 31)

	Sales and Operating Revenue	Operating Income	Depreciation Amortization and Depletion	Income Taxes	Fixed Charges	Times Interest Earned	Net Income	Earnings per Share	Dividends per Share
1970	1,249	191	120	14	28	2.36	43	1.56	1.00
1971	1,326	207	119	19	29	2.59	52	1.88	1.10
1972	1,500	231	117	31	30	3.06	65	2.38	1.20
1973	1,665	271	109	54	29	4.30	95	22.9	1.29
1974	2,216	363	115	82	28	6.32	144	3.26	1.53
1975	2,333	352	129	73	40	3.88	116	5.17	1.80
1976	2,630	368	136	63	45	3.80	126	4.52	1.80
1977	2,923	446	164	104	55	3.50	135	4.93	1.80
1978	3,268	534	203	148	69	2.75	120	4.25	1.85
1979	4,332	921	225	385	102	2.73	0.11	0.20	2.00

Source: Allied's 1979 Annual Financial Statement.
Note: Millions of $, except times interest earned and earnings per share.

EXHIBIT 13
Financial and Operating Data

	1979	1978	1977	1976	1975	1974	1973	1972
Current assets/current liabilities	1.21	1.43	1.69	1.96	2.14	1.93	2.43	2.81
Percent cash and securities to current assets	7.79	7.22	5.22	7.53	12.24	11.34	19.67	17.33
Percent inventory to current assets	37.28	36.02	39.53	44.83	43.28	44.86	35.52	34.23
Capitalization								
Percent long-term debt	43.67	36.81	33.63	32.26	32.66	26.78	29.09	32.25
Percent common stock and equity	56.33	63.19	66.37	67.74	67.34	73.22	70.91	62.75
Sales/inventory	7.19	9.79	9.03	7.89	7.68	7.70	7.34	7.31
Sales/receivables	5.73	6.56	6.71	7.74	7.86	8.21	6.06	5.32
Percent net income to total assets	0.26	3.72	4.71	4.64	4.97	6.97	4.83	3.62

EXHIBIT 14
Comparative Consolidated Balance Sheet

Balance Sheets	Comparative Consolidated Balance Sheet, as of December 31 (in thousands of dollars)						
	1978	1977	1976	1975	1974	1973	1972
Assets							
Cash	21,260	11,248	22,262	26,858	17,293	20,033	29,856
Short-term securities and time deposits	45,646	31,472	33,701	59,121	35,497	105,604	74,034

(Continued)

EXHIBIT 14 (Continued)

Balance Sheets	Comparative Consolidated Balance Sheet, as of December 31 (in thousands of dollars)						
	1978	1977	1976	1975	1974	1973	1972
Accounts and notes receivable, net	498,209	435,759	339,838	296,991	269,838	274,537	281,990
Inventories	333,701	323,615	333,247	303,941	287,919	226,855	205,194
Other current assets	27,678	16,589	14,321	15,376	11,298	11,654	8,457
Total Current assets	926,494	818,683	743,369	702,287	641,843	638,683	599,531
Marketable securities, cost	3,096	3,396	3,538	3,640	3,728	3,861	3,956
Investments and advances, cost	165,316	134,649	128,612	133,263	113,284	88,881	80,511
Property, plant, and equipment cost	3,739,889	3,450,819	3,129,926	2,901,046	2,703,504	2,500,660	2,381,383
Less: Res. for depreciation, etc.	1,698,480	1,641,446	1,587,589	1,534,056	1,494,220	1,455,727	1,391,037
Net property account	2,041,409	1,809,369	1,542,337	1,366,990	1,209,284	1,044,933	990,346
Goodwill, patents, licenses & def. chgs.	91,634	106,065	109,703	122,026	91,903	85,034	84,053
Total	3,227,949	2,872,162	2,527,559	2,328,206	2,060,044	1,861,392	1,758,397

Liabilities

Accounts payable and accrued liabilities	438,770	388,643	313,214	266,919	254,143	218,589	182,365
Notes and loans payable	47,995	33,176	32,272	25,047	12,411	16,087	8,965
Taxes accrued	144,738	52,963	22,051	24,190	53,148	28,067	22,410
Interest accrued	15,328	10,662	11,309	10,814	7,818	....	....
Long-term debt due in one year	....	....	....	....	4,726	....	....
Total current liabilities	646,831	485,444	378,846	326,970	332,246	262,743	213,740
Long-term debt	741,008	606,612	527,613	503,523	354,071	354,228	383,856
Res. for pensions and contingencies	67,549	70,292	71,109	48,787	61,887	74,086	84,900
Deferred income	46,386	37,369	37,721	26,994	27,894	18,985	19,086
Deferred income tax	247,852	252,197	200,596	170,365	130,544	106,914	91,170
Capital lease obligations	205,999	222,939	203,672	213,366	184,977	180,860	139,178
Common stock (par $9)	375,464	365,932	364,305	364,305	364,305	364,305	364,305
Retained earnings	910,450	846,804	763,508	696,692	631,159	530,117	475,852
Total stockholders' equity	1,285,914	1,212,736	1,127,813	1,060,997	995,464	894,422	840,157
Less: Treasury stock	13,590	15,427	19,813	22,796	27,039	30,846	33,690
Net stockholders' equity	1,272,324	1,197,309	1,108,000	1,038,201	968,425	863,576	806,467
Total	3,227,949	2,872,162	2,527,550	2,328,206	2,060,044	1,861,392	1,758,397
Net Current assets	279,663	333,239	364,523	386,131	309,599	375,940	385,791

Property Account—Analysis

Additions at cost	502,040	464,638	351,613	313,319	302,217	193,812	147,462
Retirements or sales	212,966	143,749	122,733	116,099	101,116	74,535	113,512
Other additions	....	....	....	322	6,641	....	....

Depreciation, Depl., and Res.—Analysis

Additions chgd. to income	202,975	164,307	145,049	136,899	123,276	116,469	123,993
Retire renewals changed to res.	145,941	110,430	91,516	97,013	84,783	51,779	76,411
Other deductions	....	....	....	....	1,685	....	....
Other deductions	....	....	....	....	....	16,666	16,947

APPLE COMPUTER, INC.

A familiar sight at the headquarters of Apple Computer, Inc. in Cupertino, California, is a boyish-looking fellow sporting a stringy mustache and often wearing jeans, boots, and a cowboy shirt. His name is Steven Jobs and at age 28 was chairman of the board of a company that had sales of $583 million in 1982.

Steve Jobs grew up in California in an area referred to as the "Silicon Valley." Tiny semiconductors made with chips of silicon were first manufactured there at the end of the 1960s; hence, the name. Jobs attended high school in Los Altos during the early 1970s where he developed an interest in technology. He also began a friendship with a fellow named Stephen Wozniak. Pooling their talents, the two Steves built and sold so-called blue boxes, which were illegal electronic attachments for telephones that allowed users to make long-distance calls for free.

Jobs entered college in 1972 in Oregon. His college career lasted only two years because of financial hardships. After dropping out, he took a position at Atari designing video games. His close friend, Steve Wozniak, also dropped out of college (Berkeley) to work at Hewlett–Packard as a designer. On his own time, Wozniak began working on the construction of a small computer and, in 1976, he succeeded with a machine about the size of a portable typewriter.

Steve Wozniak did not fully appreciate the commercial potential of his new creation. To him, it was more of a gadget to impress fellow computer hobbyists. Jobs, on the other hand, felt that the invention had real market potential and urged that they form a company. The two raised $1300 to open a makeshift production line by selling Jobs' Volkswagon Microbus and Wozniak's Hewlett–Packard scientific calculator. Jobs wanted the new computer to be something personal with which one could easily become familiar. He rejected any technical-sounding names for the new computer as being inconsistent with this goal. Remembering the pleasant times he had working in the orchards of Oregon, he selected the name "Apple."

Silicon Valley, meanwhile, had developed quite a reputation for having an effective start-up support network for new companies. Says Jobs: "We didn't know what the hell we were doing, but we were very careful observers and learned quickly." Jobs persuaded a public relations specialist to take on Apple as a client. On the recommendation of his former boss at Atari and the public relations firm, Jobs contacted Don Valentine, a venture capitalist, to seek funds for the new company. When Valentine made a visit to inspect the new computer, he found Jobs in cutoff jeans and sandals and wearing shoulder-length hair and a Ho Chi Minh beard. Valentine later referred to his first impression of Jobs as "a renegade from the human race."

Don Valentine did, however, mention the new company to A. C. Markkula, a former marketing manager at Intel (a manufacturer of computer chips) and Fairchild Semiconductor. He was so impressed with the new company's potential that he put up $250,000 of his own money and became an equal partner with Jobs and Wozniak. One of Markkula's first acts was to arrange a credit line with the Bank of America. He also persuaded two venture-capital firms to invest in Apple.

From the very beginning, things went very well for the new company. The original computer was redesigned and called the Apple II. The company also designed instruction manuals to make the computer much easier to use. Sales were $2.7 million in 1977 and, just

---

Source: This case was prepared by Marlene Carle, Robert Carle, Richard Edwards, and Paula Walters, under the supervision of Professor Sexton Adams. Permission to use granted by Sexton Adams. This case is based on library research.

three years later, the young company had sales of $200 million.

The sudden growth, however, had not been without problems. In the words of Markkula, the problem was to keep the race car on the track. According to Markkula, the 1980 introduction of Apple III, a more powerful version of Apple II, was premature because of enormous market pressures. The Apple III had to be reworked before it met its specifications and was temporarily withdrawn from the market. As a result, 40 employees were fired and the project manager of Apple III resigned.

Apple is now at a very critical time. A multitude of aggressive competitors have entered the market. Tandy Corp.'s Radio Shack, with its 8,400 retail outlets has a market share equal to Apple. Xerox has a computer nicknamed "the worm" because they claim it can eat an Apple. More important, however, is the fact that IBM, the computer industry giant, has entered the field.

In addition to competitive threats, Apple must deal with maintaining a superior management team. Although Steve Wozniak is a major shareholder, he is not active in company affairs. Mr. Markkula is retiring and will be succeeded by Mr. John Sculley, former President of Pepsi-Cola Company. Jobs, who took a company that did not exist six years ago and built it to $1 billion entity, must demonstrate that he has the expertise to guide a major corporation.

The Personal-Computer Industry

Since 1977—when Apple Computer, Inc. first introduced the personal computer—the market has grown dramatically. World-wide computer shipments of U. S. based manufacturers, which totaled $29.4 billion in 1981, up 12 percent from a year earlier, are expected to rise 16 percent annually between 1981 and 1986, according to International Data Corp., a Waltham, Massachusetts research firm. The personal computer segment of this industry, which is still in its infancy, is expected to show the most vigorous expansion over the next five years. Personal computers, which currently hold 10 percent of the total computer market, should increase their market share to about 30 percent in 1986, according to IDC. The value of these shipments, which was $3.0 billion in 1981, up nearly 70 percent from $1.8 billion a year earlier, are projected to increase at about 43.5 percent annual compound rate over the next five years.

Growth in the personal computer segment was spurred by improved software, lower hardware costs, and the search by many industries for ways to increase productivity. Which type of software will solve the user's problem is a question constantly asked by potential purchasers of hardware, as buyers have become much more software conscious. *VisiCalc*, a powerful management software package, was the first main breakthrough in personal computer software and, according to Rosen Research, Inc., has proved to be one of the most effective hardware-selling software products ever.

The largest personal-computer market is the business/professional market, which accounted for more than half of the U. S. personal computer units shipped in 1981. Market sources have projected a very healthy growth rate for this segment—some 50 percent through 1986 in dollar value terms. This high rate can be attributed to the very large number of potential buyers—from one-person businesses to large corporations that need to increase productivity—and the increasing applications and capabilities of the machine. Businesses have discovered that white-collar productivity has been declining and that new information/analysis tools are needed to solve this problem. Some advantages of personal computers are their "user-friendly" features, the advantage of not adding to the mainframe load, and the ability to link personal computers to form a load network capable of performing several of the functions of an automated office, such as word processing and electronic mail.

The dollar volume of the home/hobby market is expected to grow at an annual compound rate of about 40 percent through 1986. This rate could be spurred by the continuing decline in hardware costs and increased exposure of people to computers at school and work. Given the 80 million households in the United States, the potential of home/hobby buyers is very large. Sales of lower priced ($100–$1000) home computers have been particularly brisk, benefiting from the popularity of video games.

The scientific/engineering market of the personal computer segment is the third largest in terms of units. This market is expected to grow at a compound annual rate of 15–20 percent in dollar terms through 1986.

The educational market, currently the smallest, is expected to grow at a compound annual rate of 15 percent through 1986. This market is important because exposure to a computer in school may encourage the user—and perhaps the users' parents—to buy a personal computer. This also could lead to increased business sales.

The current trends in the personal-computer industry can be summarized as a shrinking in computer size, a decline in hardware costs, and an increase in the number of personal-computer vendors. A newer trend is a move to 16-bit machines. The 16-bit computer allows more computing power, which is especially useful in the business/professional and scientific markets.

Many large computer manufacturers have been experiencing a stagnant mainframe market and have turned to the personal-computer market for new growth. IBM, for instance, introduced their version of the personal computer in August 1981, and is currently shipping over 20,000 units per month. The increasing number of new vendors is not expected to last and a gradual shakeout is likely to occur over the next few years. John J. McDonald, president of CISIO, Inc. (a Japanese firm), predicts that firms will be unable to maintain profitability with less than 15 percent market share and at least $100 million in revenues. Joel Schwartz, Vice President of DEC, also predicts that the personal-computer market will be dominated by the large companies. David Gold, an industry consultant, predicts that only a handful of the new firms will survive. Firms will either be acquired, go out of business, or end up as small companies with unique applications. The next three to five years should witness an era of price-cutting and intense competition.

Another factor to be considered is the entry of Japanese manufacturers. Initial predictions were that the Japanese would obtain 50 percent of the personal-computer market by 1985. That forecast has since been reduced to a maximum of 25 percent. The primary reason for this reduction is that domestic Japanese demand has increased so rapidly, local manufacturers are hard pressed to satisfy their domestic market. Industry analysts agree, however, that the Japanese will be a major factor in the personal-computer market within the next few years. Exhibit 1 illustrates the trend of the personal computer (sometimes called the desktop computer) segment of the total computer industry.

The Competition

Competition within the personal-computer market is intense as companies scramble for market share and new technological breakthroughs. Currently, there are three major competitive threats confronting Apple Computer, Inc., but instabilities within the market could cause a sudden change in the lineup. Now, however, those firms most competitive with Apple are Tandy, Commodore, and IBM.

Commodore

Commodore International sold $275 million in personal computers in 1982, ranking it number four in the market. Industry analysts see the company's strength in its highly functional, low-priced system. Commodore says that it wants to be known as the American Japanese entry. "Our strategy is to offer more versatility

EXHIBIT 1
The Changing Structure of the Computer Market

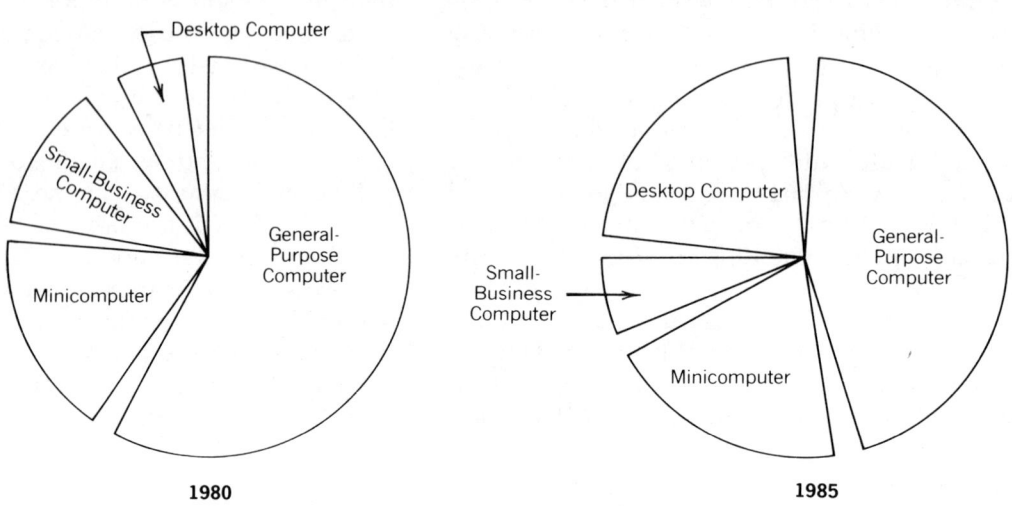

Source: "The Incredible Explosion of Startups," Business Week, (August 2, 1982):63.

in a single desktop computer with peripherals built in at a lower price than anyone else," says Michael Tomczyk, Commodore product marketing manager. "We are more Japanese in our thinking than any Western company because we have been doing business in Japan for a decade."

Commodore recently intensified its efforts in the video-game market by stressing that its products could compute as well as play games. In 1983, Commodore intends to stress price and performance. The message in their ad campaign will emphasize: "Why buy a simple ordinary home computer when you can buy a more powerful one that can be used both at home and at work?"

Commodore spends little on research and development. They have no national sales force and do not plan to create one. Their success in tapping the home market, however, has encouraged other producers to make cost-cutting moves and emphasize new product introductions.

Tandy (Radio Shack)

Tandy's TRS-80 Model I was a pioneer product that quickly gained acceptance and captured a significant market share in the home and small-business market. Tandy is currently targeting Fortune 1000 firms and small businesses. Tandy has an established distribution channel through its Radio Shack stores which has enabled it to become one of the market leaders in the personal-computer market. All of the company's 6,460 stores stock the personal computers. Tandy also distributes its more powerful computers through computer centers and its 480 Super Shacks.

Along with good retail marketing, Tandy offers good service and support. Service has been a problem for most companies, but because of its already existing service centers Tandy has provided excellent service to its customers. According to industry experts, Tandy is fortunate to have such a good service network because some of its products suffer from an image of poor quality. Its TRS-80 line was nicknamed the TRASH-80, and that nickname has persisted in industry circles. Poor quality has probably stemmed from one of Tandy's weaknesses—lack of qualified personnel from the computer divisions management down to the line workers.

IBM

In August 1981, IBM entered the personal-computer market and rapidly captured one-third of the market. IBM sold 200,000 units in 1982 and could double that figure in 1983. Mike Markkula declares that Apple's three biggest rivals are "IBM, IBM, and IBM."

The IBM personal computer offers attractive features and pricing, easy expandability, and most important, the IBM name. IBM is everywhere in corporate America, its image and presence almost intimidating the other manufacturers. Says Charles Johnson of Wang, "IBM sells on their image, we have to sell ourselves first, then the product second."

Software abounds for the IBM personal computer and hundreds of new compatible programs are being created on the assumption that it will eventually be the dominant model. IBM markets only 39 of its own titles, but nearly 1,200 are produced by outside programmers. A marketing rule of thumb in the computer business says that the more programs the computer can use, the more attractive it is for the buyer.

IBM has a network of strategically located dealers and company owned stores. These are located in the largest markets. IBM is also attuned to the potential in the farmer/rancher market and displays a presence in small communities as well. IBM also utilizes 600 retailers to move its product. IBM is industry renowned for the quality of its sales force. Because IBM mainframes are already installed in many companies, the sales force already has a well-established relationship with potential customers for the personal computer. Exhibit 2 presents major product comparisons.

Organization of Apple Computer, Inc.

During Apple's early days, when the company had just a few hundred employees and a single major product on the market, its organizational structure was simple: a few managers backed by small staffs performing whatever needed to be done. With unparalled growth, however, Apple restructured its organization to be certain that activities received the proper attention. Apple's organization is still designed loosely and for maximum freedom and flexibility. The structure is evolving week by week into new areas of specialization and organization form.

Apple's various teams work together and support one another for Apple is, in fact, a team of teams working together to achieve its goals. The company's flexible, decentralized structure tries to ensure enough freedom for individual creativity. According to Steven Jobs, the management philosophy is to give people enough rope to hang themselves. Apple hires specialists to instruct the company what to do. Jobs describes his position as "to help run the company and (plan) the directions we ought to go in."

There are two types of divisions within Apple: (1) product divisions, responsible for developing and manufacturing the various products, and (2) the product support division, which handles marketing, distribution, and post-sale support. There are also a number of administrative departments such as finance, legal, and human resources.

In August 1980, Apple Computer went through a major restructuring phase. Michael M. Scott, was demoted from President to Vice President and lost most of his authority after he fired 40 mid to upper-level managers. He later resigned. Scott's management style was termed decisive, authoritarian, and insensitive. Soon after this shake-out, one Apple executive was quoted as saying: "There seems to be so little control and so much chaos that I can't believe the company isn't flying off into

EXHIBIT 2
Competitor Model Comparison

Computer	Radio Shack TRS-80 Model III	Commodore PET	IBM Personal	Apple III Plus	Apple III
Hardware					
RAM Memory	4 to 48K	16 to 32K	16 to 256K	48 to 64K	128 to 256K
ROM Memory	4 to 14K	18K	40K	12K	4K
B/W Display	yes	yes	yes	yes	yes
Color Display	no	no	yes	yes	yes
Graphics	64 characters + dot graphics	128 full-screen character	line graphic character	15 colors	15 colors
Keyboard	Basic + keypad	basic	83 key, keypad, function keys	basic	basic + keypad
Software					
Languages	Basic, Cobol, Pascal, Author, Pilot, Fortran	Basic	Basic, Cobol, Pascal, Fortran	Basic, Cobol, Pascal	Basic, Pascal
Documentation	20 books, manuals	About 12 manuals	2 manuals	About 100 manuals	About 100 manuals
Consumer Info					
Support	Dealer training	None	Dealer training	None	None
Maintenance	Dealer on-site	Dealer	Dealer	On-site	On-site
Warranty	90 days p + 1	90 days p + 1	90 days	90 days	90 days
Applications					
Personal Investment	yes	yes	yes	yes	yes
Invest, Mgmt.	yes	yes	yes	yes	yes
Personal Finance	yes	yes	yes	yes	yes
Research	yes	yes	yes	yes	yes
Games	yes	yes	yes	yes	yes
Writing/Editing Text	yes	yes	yes	yes	yes
Base List Price	$699 to $2,295	$995 to $1,295	$1,565	$1,530	$3,495

Source: "How to buy a Home Computer," *Forbes*, (August 2, 1982): p. 64.

space in a thousand pieces. On the other hand, it does seem to keep pulling off its plans." A vetern manager of the semiconductor industry describes the company as "Camp Run Amok." Exhibit 3 presents a list of officers and directors of Apple Computer, Inc.

Key Management Personnel

Stephen G. Wozniak cofounded Apple Computer in 1977. He served as Secretary of the company from 1977 to 1980, and as a director from 1977 to 1978. He also has held the position of Vice President of Research and Development. Although Wozniak remains a major shareholder, he is no longer active in company affairs. He has returned to Berkeley where he is pursuing the completion of his college studies. Wozniak received the Grace Murray Hopper Award from the Association for Computing Machinery for his contributions to the computer industry. He has been generous with his recently acquired wealth: he gave

EXHIBIT 3
Officers and Directors

Officers

A. C. Markkula, Jr.	President and Chief Executive Officer
Kenneth R. Zerbe	Executive Vice-President, Finance and Administration
Albert A. Eisenstat	Vice President, Secretary, and General Counsel
Joseph A. Graziano	Vice President and Chief Financial Officer
Gene P. Carter	Vice President, Sales
S. P. Jobs	Chairman and Vice President
C. H. Carlson	Executive Vice-President, Operations

Directors

P.O. Crisp:	A founding and managing partner of Venrock Associates—a limited partnership formed by the Rockefeller family to invest in technology-based firms.
P. S. Schlein:	Chairman of the Board and Chief Executive Officer of Macy's California.
Arthur Rock:	Former general partner of Arthur Rock and Associates, venture capitalists. Currently, a limited partner of a San Francisco based investment banking firm.
H. E. Singleton:	Chairman of the Board and Chief Executive Officer of Teledyne, Inc., a diversified manufacturing company.
A. C. Markkula, Jr.	
S. P. Jobs	

Source: Apple Computer, Inc., 1982 Annual Report.

nearly $3 million in Apple stock to his parents and other family members.

A. C. Markkula (Mike) was promoted to President and CEO in March 1981. He previously held the position of Chairman of the Board and Vice President of Marketing. Markkula was formerly with Intel Corporation where he spent four years as marketing manager. Markkula was also a Product Marketing Manager for Fairchild Semiconductor Corp. as well as a former member of the technical staff of the research and development laboratory at Hughes Aircraft Corp. An electrical engineer, he received his BS and MS degrees from the University of Southern California. Markkula plans to retire shortly from his position, but will remain as a director and consultant, doing long-range research and planning for Apple. He describes his new title as "Markkula-at-large."

Stephen P. Jobs cofounded Apple Computer in 1977 and has served as Vice President and Director since that time. He has also served as Chairman of the Board since March 1981. Previously he held the position of Vice Chairman of the Board. Prior to 1977, he worked as a design engineer for Atari, Inc., a computer games manufacturer. He attended Reed College in Portland, Oregon, but did not receive a degree. Overseeing Apple's growth has kept Jobs too busy to spend his millions. His Tudor-style home in Los Altos Hills is essentially empty because he has not decided how to furnish it. As an executive, Jobs has sometimes been petulant and harsh on subordinates. He says, "I've got to learn to keep my feelings private."

The newest addition to the Apple team is John Sculley, a former President of Pepsi-Cola Company. He will replace Markkula as president and CEO. Sculley is leaving an opportunity at Pepsi to become Chairman of the Board because he says he has to be totally turned on to what he is doing. He sees the computer business as being where the soft-drink business was 10 years ago. Sculley has long had an interest in technology. He applied for a cathode-ray-tube patent at age 14, built projection television sets while at college at Brown University, and designed his home in Greenwich, Connecticut. Sculley has a bachelor's degree in architecture, but later attended business school. He joined Pepsi as a trainee, but worked his way up to President where he built Pepsi into a strong number-two behind Coke. He describes Pepsi as "a Marine boot camp" and believes Apple has a similar work-hard ethic. Apple considered more than 126 executives for the job, but selected Sculley because of his broad domestic and international management and marketing experience. Additionally, his experience in motivating franchised Pepsi bottlers to sell Pepsi-Cola will help him build dealer loyalty at Apple. To induce Sculley to leave a very promising career at Pepsi, Apple will pay him a $1 million bonus when he starts, $1 million in salary and bonuses the first year, and $1 million in severance pay if he leaves. He also gets a package of "wealth creation" benefits, including options on 350,000 shares of Apple stock and financial help in buying a $2 million Tudor-style house with a kidney-shaped pool in Woodside, California.

Product Line

There was nothing really new in the first Apple. It was just a small board fixed up to do simple things for an individual rather than a professional data-processing department. When it became evident that there was real demand for such a product, the prototype was redesigned and christened Apple II. With a capacity of 48K bits of memory storage and a compatibility with virtually every major software system available, the Apple II quickly became one of the top-selling personal computers.

As the computer industry exploded throughout the 1970s, it became evident that the Apple II would be unable to meet growing business demands. As a result, in 1978, the Apple II plus was introduced. This revised model upgraded its memory to 64K, expanded its software capability, allowed itself to be adapted with more peripheral accessories (printers; disk drives, etc.) and more important, maintained cost compatibility with comparable units already in the marketplace.

In 1979 the company unveiled the Apple III and from the start things began to go wrong. Production delays and design foul-ups kept the computer from an earlier release. After it was released, reports started coming in regarding safety hazards. Overheating terminals and electrical current surges were common complaints. The Apple III was withdrawn from the market and later reintroduced after improvements had been made. The Apple III is a more powerful version of the Apple II and as of 1983 its sales were doing very well.

The Apple IIe ("e" standing for enhanced) was introduced in early 1983. Walt Broedner, codesigner, and David Larson, marketing coordinator for the IIe were given the task of redesigning the Apple II plus to include the best features of modern machines, make it less expensive to manufacture, make it compatible with the thousands of Apple II software packages, and to do it quickly. Working alone and with hardware design manager, Peter Quinn, Broedner created two custom computer chips within 22 weeks and Larson was able to demonstrate a fully operational Apple IIe, complete with an expanded keyboard, 128K memory capacity, lower and uppercase typing capability, and a more efficient cooling system.

In 1980 Apple began work on a new machine named LISA (local integrated software architecture) and spent $50 million developing it. Although the LISA was introduced in early 1983, it will not be available to most customers until about June, Apple estimates. This new system is viewed as state-of-the-art in computer technology. Instead of learning complex languages to operate the machine, typing cumbersome commands, and limiting the computer to only a few tasks at a time, LISA enables the user to use the keyboard only for data entry, uses icons (graphic symbols) to replace commands and task descriptions, and employs an electronic pointer called a "mouse." The mouse replaces a cursor and enables the user to select functions and tasks without ever referring to the keyboard. Although LISA is targeted for Fortune 1000 companies, price may be a major issue. At $10,000, LISA is in the high end of the market, according to Egil Juliussen of Future Computing. In addition to price, Juliussen stresses that LISA's novelty will be an issue and it will be about a year before companies start deciding to make volume purchases. Finally, companies want to be assured that Apple will be able to provide the maintenance and program advice that a company like IBM offers.

Work is currently under way on a computer called the "Macintosh" that will utilize elements of LISA technology but will cost less and aim at a different market. The Macintosh will have a video screen, disk drive, and keyboard integrated into one unit that can be transported easily by an individual. The unit will be encased in a soft container and weigh only about 24 pounds. The machine is a 16-bit computer and will have a minimum of 64K random access memory, improved over the old Apple II that had a 8-bit computer. Additionally, Macintosh will have the "mouse" feature as on the LISA. Being able to obtain operational ability in only four to eight hours is the goal of the Macintosh design team. This compares to approximately 20 hours with the Apple II. The computer is expected to sell for $1000 when introduced. It was originally decided that production of the Macintosh would take place in the Carrollton, Texas facility. One building was cleared out specifically to set up work on Macintosh. Project managers were chosen from within the firm and several high-level individuals were hired from Xerox and Texas Instruments to bolster the program. In order to avoid past production problems, an expensive "benchmade" computerized process was to be utilized in production. Just as final production plans were being completed, a memo was received from Steven Jobs instructing the Carrollton facility that the entire production project was being moved to Cupertino, near corporate headquarters.

Marketing, Distribution, and Servicing

Apple does not have the army of direct salespeople that is characteristic of IBM. For this reason it has relied strongly on the ties forged with the 1400 + retail outlets that sells its computers. Among its other marketing tools are sales and product training, toll-free software hot-lines manned by applications specialists, monthly newsletters, and a handsome magazine that focused on a particular application area in each issue.

There is also the Apple Means Business (AMB) program that is designed to help dealers go after targeted markets. ABM provides dealers with a series of objectives and a method of obtaining those objectives. For example, to make dealers more sales-productive, Apple designed sales seminars for 6–20 prospects at a time built around a single application, and created structured presentations the dealers could use, along with a kit of 172 color slides for illustrating the various applications. The dealers are then given tips on seminar organization and post-meeting follow-up.

In 1983, Apple appointed E. Floyd Kvamme as Executive Vice-President of Marketing and Sales with the primary mission of getting Apple into the overseas market and American offices. Assisting Kvamme in his efforts is the National Accounts Program, which was designed to service large customers. This program was also implemented in anticipation of forthcoming products. Sculley, the newly designated president, wants Apple to become a bigger factor in the market for small-office computers, selling whole systems rather than individual units.

Two areas that IBM excels in, a direct selling force and a highly rated dealer network, have presented problems for Apple. Apple has a very small sales force, but it is expanding. Also, Apple was plagued by a rash of sales by its retail outlets to wholesalers, who then sold the machines at discounts. Apple then refused to service computers not sold through an authorized dealer. The problem really became a question of dealer loyalty. Most retail store outlets, however, usually give shelf preference and advertising support to the model that sells, and currently, IBM is selling. "IBM's approach is like the classic Procter and Gamble approach," says the advertising executive that handles Texas Instruments, "If you can sell the consumer, you don't have to sell the grocery store managers in addition."

To meet this challenge, Apple has been making use of TV and magazine advertising. Magazine double gatefolds illustrate the dozens of ways the personal computer can be used from talking to animals to catching a thief, thus using a funny–informational route. Apple also inserted a booklet in *Fortune* and other business publications entitled: What the average business person doesn't know about personal computers could fill a 12-page ad. Paul Wiefels, manager of product advertising, explains Apple's ad philosophy: "People don't fundamentally understand what computers are all about. While other advertisers are talking about 28K versus 48K, we attempt to educate, to show how the personal computer will make meaningful contributions to their lives." Exhibit 4 presents media expenditures by manufacturers.

In the area of service, both Apple and IBM rely on authorized dealers to provide routine repairs. More complicated repairs are provided at regional service centers, of which Apple has six and IBM has 15. Additionally, service contracts providing for on-site coverage of Apple hardware are not offered by every authorized Apple dealer. Service contracts are available at all authorized dealers if you are willing to carry your equipment into Apple-authorized service centers.

Financial Matters

Apple's first four years of operation were financed by private investment and venture capital. The first public offering was in December 1980 when 96.8 million common shares were sold at $22 a share. Apple's steady record of earnings advances has endeared the firm to Wall street and the stock traded at $43 a share on March 30, 1983, then moved to $52 by the end of April. According to *Value Line,* there is little reason to expect the earnings trend to be broken.

Apple makes use of cash management techniques by encouraging dealers to pay in full within two weeks but usually takes six weeks to pay its own suppliers. Exhibits 5 through 8 presents financial data on Apple Computer, Inc.

EXHIBIT 4
Personal-Computer Media Expenditures (January through September 1983)

	Total	Magazines	Newspaper Supplements	TV	Radio
Apple	$3,450.20	$3,110.30		$ 87.10	$232.00
Commodore	650.90	650.90			
Digital	482.80	482.80			
IBM	3,620.40	3,307.00	313.40		
Osborne	1,069.30	954.30		115.00	
Sinclair	1,286.90	1,245.50	19.80	21.60	
Tandy (TRS-80)	2,027.80	652.30		1,375.50	
Texas Instruments	3,183.80			3,183.80	
Timex	2,058.90	756.90		1,302.50	
Wang	918.00	720.70		197.30	
Warner (Atari)	7,786.40	1,306.00		6,480.10	
Xerox	274.00	274.00			

Source: Marketing and Media Decisions, February 1983, p. 144.
Note: Figures are in thousands of dollars.

EXHIBIT 5
Consolidated Statement of Income Three Years Ended September 24, 1982
(in thousands, except per share amounts)

	1982	1981	1980
Net Sales	$583,061	$334,783	$117,126
Cost and expenses			
Cost of sales	288,001	170,124	66,490
Research and development	37,979	20,956	7,282
Marketing and distribution	119,945	55,369	12,619
General and administrative	34,927	22,191	7,150
	$480,852	$268,640	$ 93,541
Operating income	102,209	66,143	23,585
Interest, net	14,563	10,400	567
Income before taxes on income	$116,772	$ 76,543	$ 24,152
Provision for taxes on income	55,466	37,123	12,454
Net Income	$ 61,306	$ 39,420	$ 11,698
Earnings per common and common equivalent share	$ 1.06	$ 0.70	$ 0.24
Common and common equivalent shares used in the calculation of earnings per share	57,798	56,161	48,412

Source: Apple Computer, Inc., Annual Report 1982.

EXHIBIT 6
Consolidated Balance Sheet September 24, 1982 and September 25, 1981 (Dollars in thousands)

	1982	1981
Assets		
Current assets		
Cash and temporary cash investments	$153,056	$ 72,834
Accounts receivable, net of allowance for doubtful accounts of $3,606 ($1,823 in 1981)	71,478	42,330
Inventories	81,229	103,873
Other current assets	11,312	8,067
Total current assets	317,075	227,104
Property, plant, and equipment		
Land and buildings	7,220	4,815
Machinery and equipment	26,136	14,688
Office furniture and equipment	13,423	6,192
Leasehold improvements	10,515	5,129
	57,294	30,824
Accumulated depreciation and amortization	(22,811)	(8,453)
Net property, plant and equipment	34,483	22,371
Other assets	6,229	5,363
	$357,787	$254,838

(*Continued*)

EXHIBIT 6 (Continued)

	1982	1981
Liabilities and Shareholders' Equity		
Current liabilities		
Notes payable to banks	$ 4,185	$ 10,745
Accounts payable	25,125	26,613
Accrued compensation and employee benefits	11,774	7,759
Income taxes payable	15,307	8,621
Accrued advertising	8,815	3,540
Other current liabilities	20,550	13,002
Total current liabilities	85,756	70,280
Noncurrent obligations under capital leases	2,052	1,909
Deferred taxes on income	12,887	5,262
Shareholders' equity:		
Common stock, no par value, 160,000,000 shares authorized	141,070	123,317
Retained earnings	118,332	57,026
	259,402	180,343
Notes receivable from shareholders	(2,310)	(2,956)
Total shareholders' equity	257,092	177,387
	$357,787	$254,838

Source: Apple Computer, Inc., Annual Report 1982.

EXHIBIT 7
Consolidated Statement of Changes in Financial Position Three Years Ended September 24, 1982 (in thousands)

	1982	1981	1980
Working capital was provided by:			
Operations			
Net income	$ 61,306	$ 39,420	$ 11,698
Charges to operations not affecting working capital			
Depreciation & amortization	16,556	8,590	1,377
Deferred taxes on income (noncurrent)	7,625	4,311	747
Total working capital provided by operations	$ 85,487	$ 52,321	$ 13,822
Increases in common stock and related tax benefits, net of changes in notes receivable from shareholders	18,399	112,019	4,569
Increases in noncurrent obligations under capital leases	1,172	1,747	752
Total working capital provided	$105,058	$166,087	$ 19,143
Working capital was applied to:			
Purchase of property, plant, and equipment, net	$ 26,470	$ 24,529	$ 4,878
Reacquisition of distribution rights	—	—	5,401
Other	4,093	1,060	1,298
Total working capital applied	$ 30,563	$ 25,589	$ 11,577
Increase in working capital	$ 74,495	$140,498	$ 7,566

(Continued)

EXHIBIT 7 (Continued)

	1982	1981	1980
Increase (decrease) in working capital by component:			
Cash and temporary cash investments	80,222	72,471	(200)
Accounts receivable	29,148	26,516	6,688
Inventories	(22,644)	69,682	24,089
Other current assets	3,245	4,329	3,685
Notes payable to banks	6,560	(2,895)	(7,850)
Accounts payable	1,488	(12,118)	(9,084)
Accrued compensation & employee benefits	(4,015)	(5,206)	(1,727)
Income taxes payable	(6,686)	(486)	(4,205)
Accrued advertising and other current liabilities	(12,823)	(11,795)	(3,830)
Increase in working capital	$ 74,495	$140,498	$ 7,566

Source: Apple Computer, Inc., Annual Report 1982.

Research and Development

Apple maintains a continuing program of research and development. Apple is developing personal-computer systems to address new markets and applications, including products for use in the office automation and information-processing segments of the business and office market. Several major products resulting from this effort will be announced in 1983 including enhancements to the present line. Investment in research and development was 6.5 percent of sales in fiscal 1982, a total of $38 million or 81 percent more than 1981. Exhibit 9 illustrates Apple's increasing emphasis on research and development.

Plant and Facilities

Apple's dramatic rise in revenues has been matched by its facility expansion. In a little over six years Apple has grown from a two-

EXHIBIT 8
Selected Financial Information Five Years Ended September 24, 1982
(In thousands, except per share amounts)

	1982	1981	1980	1979	1978
Net Sales	$583,061	$334,783	$117,126	$47,867	$ 7,856
Net Income	61,306	39,420	11,698	5,073	793
Earnings per common and common equivalent share	1.06	0.70	0.24	0.12	0.03
Common and common equivalent shares used in the calculation of earnings per share	57,798	56,161	48,412	43,620	31,544
Cash and temporary cash investments	153,056	72,834	363	563	775
Total assets	357,787	254,838	65,350	21,171	4,341
Noncurrent obligations under capital leases	$ 2,052	$ 1,909	$ 671	$ 203	$ —

Source: Apple Computer, Inc., Annual Report 1982.

EXHIBIT 9
Research and Development (In millions)

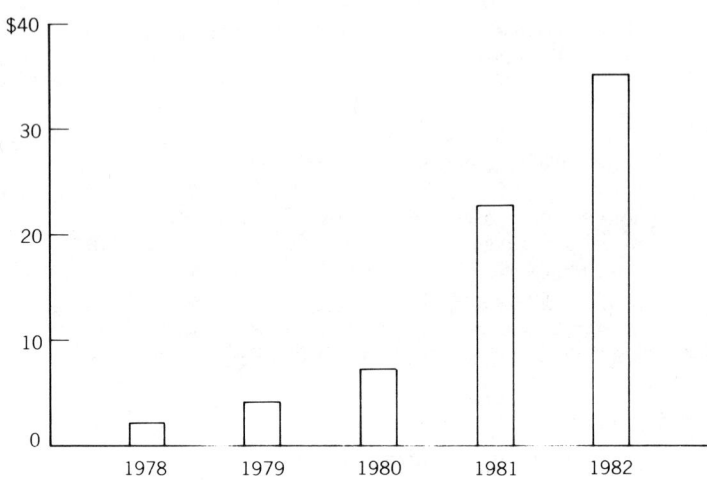

Source: Apple Computer, Inc., Annual Report 1982.

garage to a company that has over 1.5 million square feet of office and manufacturing facilities. Currently, Apple has manufacturing plants in California, Texas, Ireland, and Singapore. Apple's corporate office is located in Cupertino, California. Of the total 1.5 million square feet, over 50 percent is dedicated to manufacturing.

Apple management is very proud of its procedures for new facility implementation. It has a facility crew of five people who oversee the movement into new facilities from the time the request is made until the final person is in place. At one point Apple made five separate facility moves in 10 days with zero production slowdown. This was all accomplished through careful planning, and of course, through use of their computers. Managers are asked to forecast space and personnel requirements for the next few years.

Apple has increased efficiency and reduced inventories, warehousing, storage, and handling costs by what it calls the "just in time" scheduling. This is the procedure of taking delivery of inventory material on a daily basis. Raw materials are delivered on an as-needed basis for the manufacturing of the finished goods.

Management measures its productivity very meticulously, paying attention to small details. With increased emphasis on automation, Apple hopes to increase productivity with its existing facilities. Greater utilization of its plants is one of the goals of management in 1983. Management expects to double capacity in 1983 within its existing plants.

Litigation and Copy Cats

Apple Computer is involved in both defending itself and actively seeking relief from injustices in a number of important lawsuits. In December 1981, six dealers filed suit against Apple seeking to restrain implementation of its prohibition of mail order and telephone sales. The litigation is now in the discovery stage with respect to plaintiff's request for permanent injunctive relief and Apple's counterclaims. On May 12, 1982, Apple brought suit against Franklin Computer Corp. alleging patent, trademark, and copyright infringement. The Franklin Computer Company's Model Ace 1000 is not only a functional copy of the Apple IIe, but it has also been designed to look like the Apple Model. It has almost all the features of the Apple IIe.

Apple Computer is in the process of trying to contain the many "copy cats" such as Franklin that have emerged in foreign markets. Personal computers with names such as "The Orange" and "The Lemon" are having a major impact on Apple's International sales, especially in Japan. In Australia, for example, Apple's market share dropped from 80 percent to 20 percent in two years chiefly because of foreign duplication, according to industry expert John R. Lindel, security analyst at Goldman Sachs.

Until recently Apple has had little luck in prosecuting firms overseas, but some positive signs are surfacing. Taiwan's high court ruled that U. S. companies can initiate criminal cases against Taiwan-based companies, permitting Apple to prosecute companies that copy its computers. In Cupertino, California, Apple's general counsel, Albert A. Eisenstat, hailed the ruling as a spectacular piece of news. "If we can stop these actions out of Taiwan, we will have solved 75 percent of our counterfeit problems. Eisenstat added that Hong Kong was also a major breeding ground for problems. "We feel a little bit like the Dutch boy sticking his finger in the dike." After the Taiwan court decision, Dan Wendin, Head of Apple's Internal Legal Department said, "We will continue to go after the counterfeiters but the fire is under control—maybe even contained."

The Future

Most astute observers agree that the personal computer is going to revolutionize the home and workplace over the next few years. *Time* magazine selected the personal computer as its 1982 person of the year. *Time*'s editorial board had decided that the personal computer had done more to affect mankind than had any single human being. Much has also happened at Apple since it first introduced the personal computer just seven short years ago. Over 1000 competitors have entered the market, including some of the world's most familiar and respected names. In a recent article, Steven Jobs said that within three years no more than five major computer makers will remain, and he vows Apple will be among them. As the industry is not short of challenges, Apple must be careful to relate better than anyone else to the customer's needs and markets.

ASDIC LIMITED

It was a Wednesday in June 1981 and for Mr. Graham James the first item of business that day was a pleasant one. The day before, Mr. James—General Manager of ASDIC Limited—had heard that the company's newly developed satellite transmitter was certified for commercial use. The company had been developing the transmitter for about a year, after having experienced a succession of problems with the "bought-in" transmitters that went into the building of its drifting buoys. Using the new transmitter would mean an end to supply irregularities, better cost control, and more "added value" in the final ASDIC product. All this looked good for ASDIC's drifting

---

Source: This case was prepared by Professor Philip Rosson and Professor Michael Martin, Dalhousie University, Halifax, Nova Scota. The names of the companies, locations, and the personnel involved have been changed to preserve anonymity. The authors gratefully acknowledge the financial support of the Federal Department of Industry, Trade, and Commerce, Technological Strategy Branch in the development of the case. Permission to use granted by Michael Martin.

buoy program, and Mr. James planned to draft a memorandum congratulating those who had worked on the development of the transmitter.

The Company

ASDIC Limited is situated in Shaldon on the Canadian seaboard and occupies a modern plant with a floor area of 125,000 square feet. This plant is equipped for the manufacture of electronic and mechanical components, and equipment from the prototype phase through volume production. More than 300 personnel are normally employed by the company: approximately 25 percent come under the Engineering Department, where engineers, technicians, drafters, and various other people support staff work. The firm is one of the largest private employers in the city of Shaldon. The principal products of the company are:

- Sonobuoys
- Bathythermograph buoys
- Drifting and moored ocean data buoys
- Ice beacons
- Custom buoy systems
- Communications antennas and ionospheric sounders (see Exhibit 1)

EXHIBIT 1
Principal Products

1. Anti-Submarine Warfare
   (a) *Sonobuoy*
       These are air-launched devices designed to detect underwater sounds and relay the information back to listening aircraft by FM VHF radio transmission. The received signals may then be analyzed, leading to identification and location of the underwater sound source. Sonobuoys are used extensively in the search for submarines and ASDIC has the capability of producing 700 units per day.
   (b) *Bathythermograph Buoy*
       This is a device for measuring water temperatures and is deployed prior to acoustic sonobuoys in order to correctly interpret the data recorded and transmitted by the sonobuoy. Again, these are air-

EXHIBIT 1 (Continued)

   launched: minutes after launching their useful life is over and the set is automatically scuttled.

2. Environmental Data Systems
   These are reliable, cost-effective means for gathering data. An important feature is their ability to operate automatically in remote locations, often under harsh conditions. A variety of systems were built, including:
   (a) *Drifting Ocean Data Buoys* (described in the case)
   (b) *Moored Ocean Data Buoys*
       These are large discus buoys used for offshore sensing of:
       - Wind speed and direction
       - Air temperature
       - Air pressure
       - Relative humidity
       - Magnetic north
       - Wave height and period
       - Ocean current and temperature at the surface and depths
   (c) *Ice Beacons*
       These are self-contained units that are used to track the movement of ice flows or icebergs. They are deployed by lowering from a helicopter to the surface, and one-inch spikes prevent "skating" across the ice during windy periods.
   (d) *Custom Buoy Systems*
       New buoy applications can be custom designed and built.
       These systems are all comprised of meteorological and oceanographic sensors, power supplies, data processors, HF, VHF, or UHF communications, and a shore station for data dissemination.

3. Communications Systems
   (a) *Aperiodic Loop Antennas*
       These unique, broadband receiving antennas offer a number of distinct advantages over other products available:
       - Optimum directional characteristics
       - Substantial gain
       - Light in weight and simple, which makes for easy transportation and erection
   (b) *Ionospheric Sounders*
       Long-distance radio communication is dependent on the ability of the ionosphere to reflect the transmitted signal. This system features:
       - Vastly improved capability for long-range HF communications
       - Detection of optimum frequency for HF communications
       - The sounder can be used in a static or mobile role

EXHIBIT 2
Organization Structure

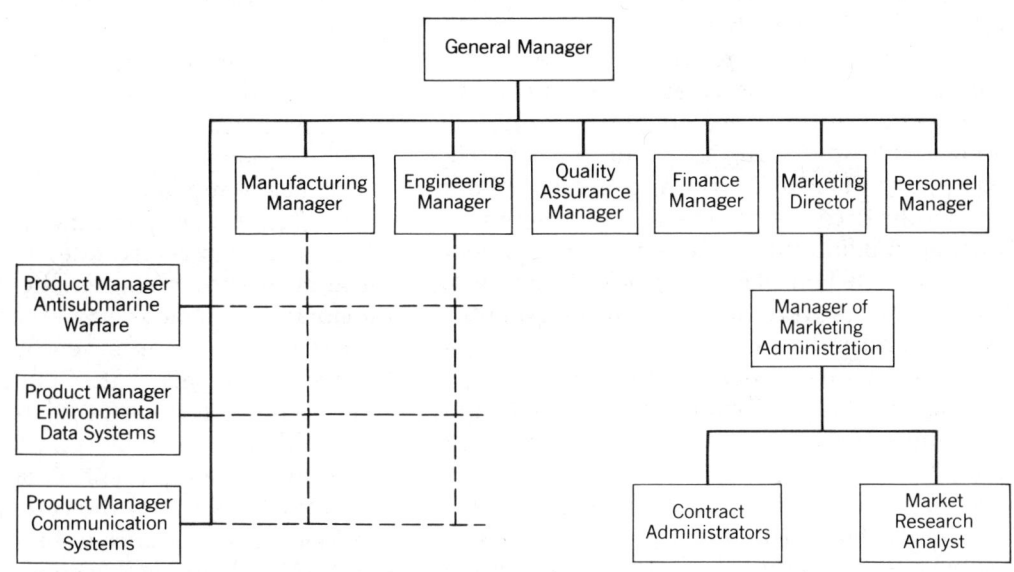

Note: In this matrix organization, each of the three product managers interact with the functional groups as suggested by the dashed lines

The firm is organized in a matrix structure, with functional managers arranged along one edge of the matrix and product managers arranged along the other (see Exhibit 2). The Environmental Data Systems Group, comprising about one-third of the Engineering staff, specializes in the development and production of systems for collecting, analyzing, and disseminating meteorological and oceanographic information. The EDS Group is responsible for the drifting buoys and their development.

Drifting Buoys—CODS and FGGE Contracts

Although ASDIC had prior experience in the area, a Canadian Ocean Data System (CODS) contract in 1975 gave impetus to its buoy programs. This was an "incubator" contract in that the government's objective was to help create a center of excellence in Canada for ocean buoys of all kinds. For two main reasons, this type of contract was particularly valuable to ASDIC. First, the contract award implied that ASDIC was a leading Canadian company in this field. Second, it also provided the opportunity for the company to establish a dominant position in the Canadian drifting buoy market and to penetrate the world-wide market.

Part of the CODS contract required that ASDIC develop a buoy that was to act as a free-drifting platform for the measurement of barometric pressure and sea–surface temperature. Air pressure was to be measured to an accuracy of ± 1.0 millibar (mb) over the range 900 to 1050 mb. Water temperature measurements were to be accurate within ± 0.5°C over the range −5°C to +40°C. The buoys were to transmit data through a special battery-powered transmitter to the Nimbus–RAMS satellite system, which is able to compute the position of the buoy, an important element in the study of weather patterns. Finally, the buoy was to be designed to have a life of between six and twelve months, depending upon the ambient ocean temperature (which affects the life of the battery).

Some 50 buoys were built and tested under the first phase of the contract. Thirty buoys were tested in ocean waters and a further 20 were tested to destruction in the firm's well-equipped test facilities. This process took about 18 months to complete. Then, after design production modifications, a one-year experiment was conducted on 30 more buoys in phase two. Twenty buoys were deployed in the Atlantic, Pacific, and Indian Oceans. Only four buoys failed prematurely because of electrical or mechanical problems. Two buoys collected and transmitted information for more than 18 months. Without independent references, it was difficult to measure data quality from the test buoys, but where this was feasible, performance was to specification. The 10 remaining buoys were tested in controlled situations to gauge the effect of fouling on the buoys and pressure system. As well as meeting the accuracy and working life requirements listed above, launching characteristics were found to be satisfactory. The buoys in question were launched from a variety of ships in motion by untrained crews and without the assistance of a crane.

As a result of its work under the drifting buoy part of the CODS contract, ASDIC was successful in winning the FGGE[1] contract in December 1977. The contract called for the building of 74 drifting buoys that were to be ready for shipment at two dates in March and April 1978. The 74 drifting buoys marked Canada's contribution to FGGE. Other nations also had built buoys for the international program, and the United States made the additional commitment of resources to put the TIROS Satellite in orbit. All of Canada's buoys were built by ASDIC, and because Canada provided more buoys than any other nation, ASDIC effectively became FGGE's largest supplier.

The ASDIC buoys (see Exhibit 3) were shipped to various ports and then deployed in the southern ocean waters where the FGGE experiment was conducted. The buoys measured barometric pressure and sea–surface temperature and then transmitted these data via the TIROS polar orbiting satellites. Despite a higher than expected rate of early failure because of unknown causes, the majority of the Canadian-built buoys gave useful reports for over six months, and seven operated for over two years. The fact that FGGE buoys required a different battery-powered transmitter than that used in the CODS program (because of the different satellite and data collection system) may have led to the early failures.

With its experience in building buoys under the CODS and FGGE contracts, ASDIC began to win orders for drifting buoys from other sources. Some of these were quasi-governmental, in that various oceanographic institutions became interested in the buoys. Other orders came from the private sector; oil companies used the buoys to chart currents in areas like the Beaufort Sea or to assist conducting environmental impact studies in offshore drilling areas. These purchases either came from the oil companies directly or consulting firms working on their behalf. The next spurt of drifting buoy activity, however, came when ASDIC received another government contract in 1979.

The PAPA Buoy Contract

In September 1978, ASDIC submitted a proposal to the Canadian government for the supply of 10-m discus buoys (see Exhibit 4) to be moored in the North Pacific Ocean. The proposal resulted from the company learning that the Canadian government was shortly to announce a decision to terminate the operation of weather ships at Ocean Station PAPA (at 50°N and 145°W in the northeast Pacific Ocean, 1100

---

[1] FGGE is the acronym for "First GARP Global Experiment," where GARP is the acronym for "Global Atmospheric Research Program."

EXHIBIT 3
The ASDIC FGGE Drifting Buoy

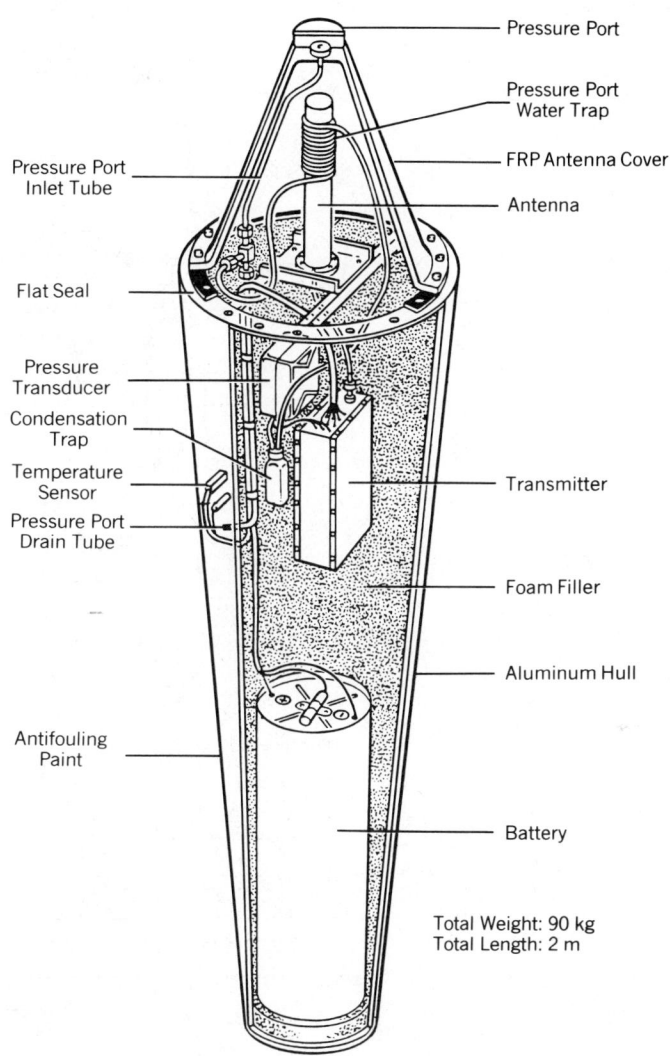

km west of Vancouver Island). Station PAPA was established in 1950 with two refurbished navy frigates. Since 1967, on alternating six-week cruises out of Victoria, B. C., two especially constructed Canadian Coast Guard ships maintained continuous observations at that station. The termination decision was taken because of steadily increasing operating costs, which were estimated at $6 million for 1978. ASDIC believed that their moored ocean data buoy would meet the government's new requirement for an unmanned weather station.

Numerous concerns were expressed about a sudden termination of the ship's observations, and as a result the Atmospheric and En-

538 Cases

EXHIBIT 4
The ASDIC 10 M DISCUS BUOY

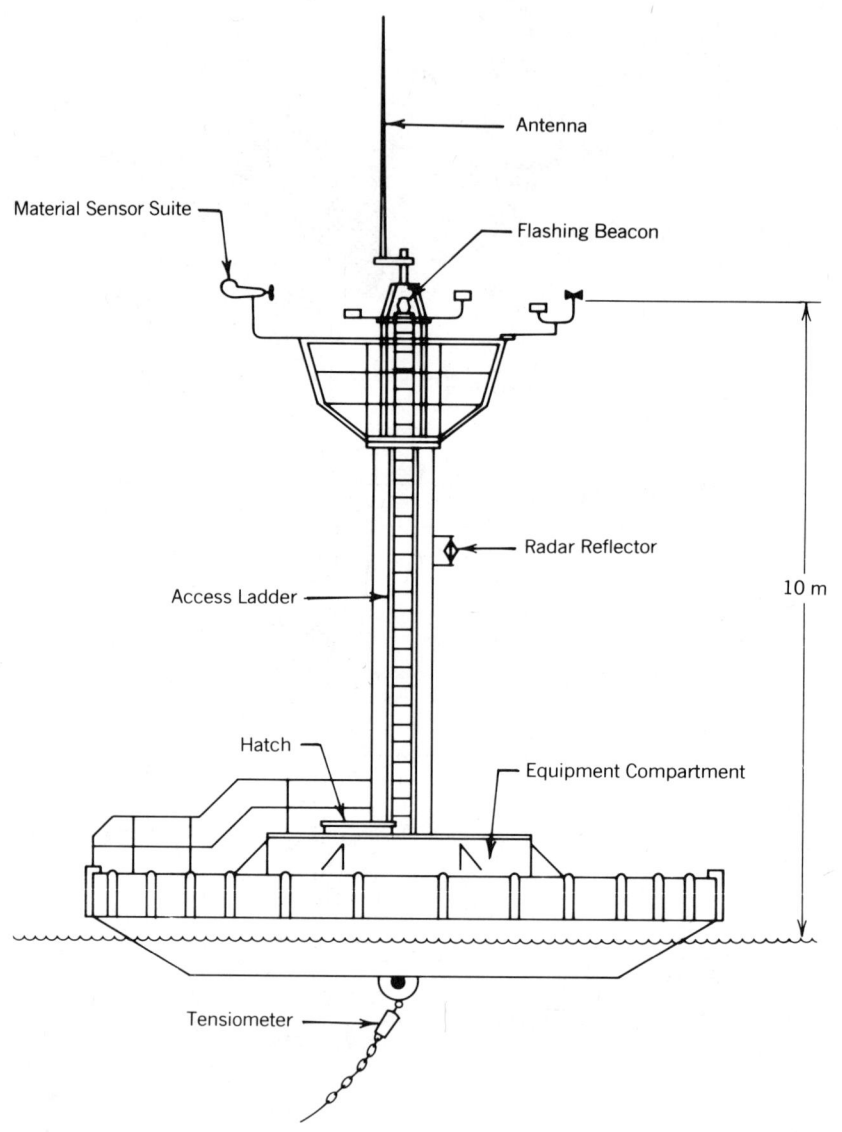

vironmental Service (AES) deferred a number of other programs in order to fund the operation of the ships for two more years. This meant that the first ship would be withdrawn in June 1980 and the second one year later. In November 1978, AES initiated a project to develop and put into operation alternate meteorological observing systems in the northeast Pacific. With a target operating budget of one-quarter that of the ships, no way was seen to duplicate their whole program, which covered upper air, surface, and special observations.

By early 1979, the idea of moored buoys looked less promising. The requirements for two 10-meter discus buoys and their periodic exchange in order to maintain one on station, together with the risk of capsizing or losing a buoy in one of the world's stormiest oceans, made the approach appear too costly. Taking this into account and given the promising results obtained with drifting buoys under FGGE, it was decided to consider a system based on using drifting buoys. In November 1979, ASDIC was awarded a contract, "To undertake research and development on an ocean data buoy system, to develop and test a cost-effective, alternate for the surface level program of the weather ships now serving Ocean Station PAPA in the northeast Pacific Ocean, including a one-year trial of the experimental buoys in the northeast Pacific Ocean." This contract was to take three years to complete.

The AES research program, of which ASDIC's PAPA contract was a part, involved three main steps. In order to develop an economical operational alternative to the high-capability moored buoys, work was necessary to:

1. Establish a real-time data reception facility.
2. Gain initial network experience by using the simple FGGE type buoys with drogues (a drogue is a contrivance used to steady and delay the movement of the buoy).
3. To develop more capable and cost-effective buoys, primarily by improving the drogues and adding anemometers (wind gauges) to the simple buoys.

ASDIC was to produce 28 buoys through the contract, which were to be delivered for testing and development.

Ten drogued buoys were deployed and tested during 1980. Tests by AES showed that when the drifting buoy information was available, better weather maps could be produced. The evaluation procedures showed that the buoy information permitted more accurate location of high and low-pressure centers, better definition of troughs (hence, more accurate placement and better indication of the intensity of fronts), and more accurate determination of pressure gradients. As well as these positive results, certain recommendations for improvements resulted from these tests. One concerned the collection of wind speed and direction data. The work on incorporating an anemometer into the drifting buoy was still underway in June 1981.

By the middle of 1981, the AES program using drifting buoys was looking quite promising, even though some uncertainties remained. The AES real-time TIROS receiving station in Edmonton, Alberta was equipped with a minicomputer system, and computer programs were developed to ingest the buoy reports and decode, sort, verify, and convert data from other data collection platforms. This meant that shortly after completion of the satellite pass (about 5 minutes), weather reports were available for distribution—the whole process from ingestion to distribution being fully automated.

The AES assessment of the drifting buoy program as of July 1981 was that reliable meteorological surface data could be obtained and that a buoy operating life of a year or more was achievable. These were important factors because:

1. The recovery of faulty buoys could not be really entertained when ship costs were of the order of $5,000 a day.
2. Continuous data collection would require 'reseeding' of the northeast Pacific when the buoys deployed drifted out of the area and/or ceased operating.

AES expected to pay at least $10,000 per unit for each of the three types of buoy:

Undrogued drifting buoy—pressure and temperature only.

Drogued drifting buoy—pressure and temperature only.

Drogued drifting buoy—pressure, temperature, and wind.

ASDIC personnel were somewhat unsure of where the PAPA contract would lead them. Some felt that if there was a lack of success with wind measurements, it could signal the end of AES interest in drifting buoys. This was a double concern because ASDIC was not directly responsible for the anemometer development themselves, only for adapting and installing them in the drifting buoys.

Then there was the whole question of cost-effectiveness. One particularly cost-effective method of collecting surface data involved the use of commercial ships; they could make the observations and then transmit it via satellite. Such a program would depend greatly on gaining the cooperation of vessel owners whose ships plied routes that took them through the northeast Pacific. AES had managed to recruit over 100 ships in Canadian Pacific ports in the first six months of 1981 and was interested in this alternative.

Drifting buoys could play an important role in the northeast Pacific and other oceans. A strong case exists for their use in ocean areas that are crossed by few vessels, and generally, the case for their use is stronger as they are made more durable, capable, and economic.

In this connection, the newly certified satellite transmitter was a welcome development. In the past few years, the company purchased transmitters from three sources. Their first supplier, a U.S. based operation was entirely satisfactory for the first year or so, and its product was extremely reliable. Then it began to develop other product lines and decided not to continue regular production of the transmitter ASDIC was buying. Instead, the supplier moved to batch production of the transmitter and ASDIC found that there was a resulting deterioration in product reliability. This problem of poor reliability showed up early in the PAPA program. In fact, the viability of the project was questioned because of this technical problem, but ASDIC instituted a program of reliability shake-down and burn-in testing prior to shipment and was able to turn the program around in time to save it. After this experience, ASDIC looked for alternative sources for the TIROS transmitter. Their next supplier was a French company whose delivery was fine but prices were prohibitive. Finally, ASDIC switched to a Norwegian firm as a stop-gap measure while developing their own transmitter. ASDIC felt that the manufactured cost of its own transmitter would be much less than the price of bought-in units. In view of this difference, it was anticipated that the development costs (shared jointly with government) of the transmitter could be quickly recovered. In addition, scope existed for cost reduction of the final unit, because the transmitter was the most expensive component of the buoy.

ASDIC's accumulated experience with the design and manufacture of drifting buoys was quite considerable by 1981. The 300 buoys it had produced over the last few years were estimated to be at least half of those supplied around the world. ASDIC's main competitors tended to be other firms that had supplied buoys to the Global Weather Experiment in 1978. Yet despite the build up of skills and experience, the drifting buoy business was still small in relation to the company's overall sales. The annual revenue ASDIC derived from drifting buoy work averaged about 4 percent of total sales since 1977. Moreover, for the government contract work described above, the maximum allowable profit margins in effect were 7½ percent (FGGE), and 8½ percent (PAPA), margins that were much lower than those necessary to provide funds for additional R & D.

Company sales exceeded $20 million in 1980, having grown quite steadily from $6 million in 1969. The profitability of the company had, however, been subject to marked fluctuation and this had resulted in changes of ownership and direction.

Company History

ASDIC was founded in 1947. The initial intention was that the company should market a range of instruments, test gear, radar, and radio equipment manufactured in England by the parent organization, a company that had developed an enviable reputation in the fields of radio, radar, and navigational systems. The company moved to Shaldon in 1949 with the promise of assistance from the provincial government if a manufacturing facility was established. The company began manufacturing in modest premises. The first efforts of the new organization resulted in the development of a tactical antisubmarine simulator—an analog computer simulator that was very advanced for its day and remained operational for nearly 20 years. Many defense contracts were filled over the next six years in the fields of antisubmarine warfare, communications, and electronic counter measures. The basis of ASDIC's current engineering expertise in ocean technology was laid during the next 15 years. Variable depth sonars, ionospheric sounders, VHF transmitters, and sonobuoys were developed and produced in the 1950s. The increased volume of work meant that a need existed for increased space and working capital. The problem of space was overcome by building a new plant in Shaldon, while that of financing was resolved by a large U. K. based transnational corporation buying a controlling interest in the company in 1959.

The 1960s saw further development in established areas as well as the initiation of large deep-sea buoys, loop antenna, and automatic direction finders. Employment levels swelled to 550, and two more plant expansions took place during the decade. By 1968, the company was in urgent need of new contracts. The firm's experience in building sonobuoys for the RCN led them to examine the U. S. defense market. One bid for the supply of bathythermograph transmitters to the U. S. Navy was successful. This $2 million contract made the company realize that antisubmarine warfare was an area of great future potential, especially in the United States. As a result, a sonobuoy development program was funded by the firm.

Contract delays and a general slowdown in contract work led to layoffs in 1969 and the possibility of a total closedown of the operation loomed large. This outcome was avoided; in April 1970 the assets and business were purchased by a group headed by a former board member. The group raised money from private investors and gained a Department of Regional Economic Expansion grant, as well as securing a loan from the provincially owned Development Corporation. The new company—ASDIC Limited—won contracts for sonobuoy production and completed jobs that were in progress. Some new contract bids were successful in the 1970s, but problems of maintaining steady business volume continued. One hundred and seventy workers were laid off in 1973, because the company found it difficult to balance its production and research capacity with demand levels.

A $10 million expansion plan was unveiled in 1975, $6 million being provided by the federal and provincial governments. Half of the $10 million was to be used to construct a larger office and production facility. This was necessary in view of the expanded operations of the business, and given the desire to consolidate two production operations, three offices, and two warehouses in one location. The other $5 million was to be spent on capital equipment and inventory. In the summer of the following year, however, the company was in difficulty once again. The bankruptcy of a major supplier caused production interruptions, cost overruns, and a cash flow crisis, and construction of the new facility was incomplete. Gradually the supply and production problems were overcome, and the financial strain placed on the company was offset when control of the company passed over to Titan Industries, a Canadian-owned corporation based in Ontario. Titan was a major supplier of parts and components to the automotive, steel, and aerospace industries, and planned to "balance and diversify" ASDIC's production line, but operate the plant on a decentralized basis.

In March, Titan acquired 54 percent of ASDIC's equity, while previous stockholders remained minority shareholders. In the same month, ASDIC moved to the new plant in the Shaldon Industrial Park.

Company Diversification

One of ASDIC's main problems had been brought into sharp focus during the weeks prior to June 1981. The company learned that a large sonobuoy bid was not successful. As a result, sales and profits would be considerably down in 1981, and a substantial number of assembly workers and other staff had to be laid off. This was not a new situation for the firm, but was nonetheless worrisome. The management of ASDIC recognized that the company was overly dependent upon the military market in general and the sonobuoy business in particular. A number of attempts at diversification had been made over the years, and the establishment of the Environmental Data Systems and Communications Systems product groups reflected these initiatives. However, in 1980 sonobuoy sales were still 90 percent of company sales, with the remainder split between environmental data systems (7 percent) and communications systems (3 percent).

Two previous periods had seen intense attempts at diversification that had come to nothing. In 1968, ASDIC formed a research division that came up with a number of new product ideas, including a heart pacemaker, an electronic stethoscope, and a pipeline crawler that would make x-ray inspections of pipelines. Each of these products would have required quite substantial investments in development and marketing, and these funds were not forthcoming at the time.

Another attempt to diversify had been made in 1973 when ASDIC acquired the assets and products of Sophisticated Sensors Ltd. (SSL) of Ontario. The President of ASDIC at that time, stated that "this step marks a significant turn in direction for ASDIC. While we will continue to generate activity in government-related contract work, it is our intention to move aggressively into the commercial products field." A new department was formed to manage the affairs of SSL, called the Business Products Division, ASDIC Limited.

SSL had entered the nucelar field in 1965 with a device that recorded microinch changes in the size of material specimens and nuclear radiation. The device was developed for use in Canada's nuclear reactor export program. Two other products were manufactured by the company. Ferricare was a product that dealt with the care and handling of magnetic tapes used in the computer and broadcasting industries. Another device was the Floatrex air-cushion support roll. This consisted of a roll air-support bearing much like an elongated cannister. Air was forced into the cannister where it would be allowed to escape through passages cut into the sides. The air flowing out of the cannister was capable of supporting photographic film and other web type materials without solid contact. The product was used in paper, film, and foil processing in North America and Europe. ASDIC management estimated that the new Division would generate $4 million in sales within three years. This was not to be, however, because it transpired that the markets for SSL products were smaller than originally estimated, and/or in some cases, customers developed their own products as solutions to problems identified by SSL.

New Product Planning

The company began to look for new product fields again in 1980. This new search was part of a five-year planning exercise, which was one of the responsibilities of the market research analyst, John Barr. During the year he had been with the firm, Mr. Barr had come to recognize the implications of ASDIC's dependence on the sonobuoy business. In view of the limited sales of the other product groups, he felt it important that the firm come up with other products that would generate substantial revenue. One thing that occurred to him from talking with longer-servicing colleagues was that ASDIC persisted in developing and building *components* rather than product *systems.* He wondered whether this might be due to the way ASDIC tended to operate, that is, as a supplier of technical solutions to problems periodically identified by other organizations (and largely government) rather than applying its technical skills to market needs it identified for itself. Mr. Barr was inclined to think that the company had skills that would allow them to develop a number of markets. He saw these skills as data acquisition and telemetry (or transmission of information from "remote" areas).

New product planning proved to be quite difficult over the months, because ASDIC's marketing group was small and its attention was turned in to the company rather than out towards the market. Because ASDIC was mostly involved in contract work, the marketing group chiefly was involved in administering these contracts. This required attention to the scheduling of work and deliveries, recording costs, and claiming necessary payments. The marketing director spent most of his time on the sonobuoy business, and was away from the office a good portion of the working week. As a result none of the marketing personnel spent much time out in the marketplace attempting to sell the company's existing nonsonobuoy products or investigating new product possibilities. This meant that the Environmental Data System and Communication System group sales really came through ASDIC's reputation for distinctive competence in the field rather than specific marketing efforts. In fact, the company had been completely surprised to receive a recent order for drifting buoys from a European oceanographic institution. Subsequent investigation showed the order to have been planned for 18 months and came the company's way because of contacts between the European institution and members of a federal government laboratory that had been closely involved in the FGGE program. Some promotion of the company's products took place when it exhibited at various trade shows, but again, lack of marketing resources constrained these efforts.

If product innovation was not easy, neither was the process of planning. Mr. Barr felt that the product managers expected him to produce the plan. He, however, saw his role as coordinator rather than creator. The product managers were appointed from the engineering ranks within the company, because the belief was that the highly technical nature of the products demanded managers that could talk to customers in technical terms. This uncertainty concerning the marketing/engineering planning interface needed to be resolved.

DICKENSON MINES LIMITED

In October 1981, Peter Munro, the new President of Dickenson Mines (Dickenson), sat in the Toronto offices of the gold-mining company and wondered what he could do to save Dickenson from bankruptcy. In 1979, Dickenson's former management had undertaken a major expansion of the company's mining and milling operations. Subsequently, interest rates on the debt financing of the project climbed and gold prices dropped. These problems were compounded by cost overruns on the expansion program and higher operating costs at the mine. These factors combined to produce a cash drain on the company and Dickenson was no longer able to service its growing debt. Munro's first priority was to take the necessary steps to ward off bankruptcy and then to restore profitability.

Company History

In 1981, Dickenson Mines conducted gold-mining operations in Ontario and silver-mining operations in British Columbia. Dickenson also held a number of investments in oil and gas ventures throughout Canada and the United States. Most of the company's revenues were generated at the Red Lake Gold Mine in northwestern Ontario.

The Dickenson property was first staked during the Red Lake gold rush of 1926. In 1945, Dickenson Red Lake Mines was incorporated and, by 1947, the first shaft was sunk to a depth of 550 feet. The following year, enough reserves were discovered to justify the construction of a 150 ton per day mill to treat ore. By 1959, the mill was expanded to 450 tons per day, again in response to the discovery of new reserves. In 1961, the first shaft was deepened to 3,300 feet and, in 1968, a second internal shaft was sunk from the 3,300 foot level to 4,400 feet. By 1968, Dickenson was conducting mining operations on 30 different levels off the main shafts.

The period 1945–1971 was difficult for the Canadian gold industry. The selling price of gold was fixed at $35.00 U. S./oz. and production costs were rising. Other metal producers were enjoying increasing prices for their products and therefore were able to lure away skilled miners with the promise of higher wages. These problems led to the introduction of the Emergency Gold Mining Act (EGMA) in 1947 to aid the faltering industry. This act made new gold mines tax-exempt for the first three years of operation and allowed them to accumulate the depletion and depreciation allowances earned during those years for write-offs in the following years. Over this period government subsidies of this sort worked out to roughly $5 an ounce and allowed many companies to stay in operation. In 1971, when gold prices were allowed to float on the open market, profitability returned to the Canadian industry and the EGMA was no longer needed.

After the deregulation of the price of gold, Dickenson's fortunes improved considerably. By 1974, revenues had risen to $11 million and profits were $3 million compared to 1971 when revenues were $3 million and profits were $264,000. The company's major activity was still gold mining, but diversification had begun. Dickenson owned a 36 percent share in Kam Kotia Mines, which had investments in several mining and oil and gas companies and was developing a silver–lead–zinc mine in British Columbia.

In 1975, Dickenson management made the strategic decision to diversify into oil and gas exploration and development. Dickenson entered into a joint venture agreement with Conventures Ltd. of Calgary to develop a gas field

---

Source: This case was prepared by Peter Nerby under the supervision of Professor David C. Shaw, School of Business Administration, University of Western Ontario. Permission to use granted by Carol E. Riley, Coordinator, Case and Text Administration, University of Western Ontario.

in Alberta. Conventures acted as the operating partner and Dickenson supplied a portion of the capital. From June 1975 to December 1978, Dickenson purchased 700,000 Conventures shares for a total of $2.1 million. In 1979, Dickenson invested an additional $1 million and supplied Conventures with some oil and gas leases in Alberta in exchange for 225,000 shares at a share purchase price valued at $8 per share by the two companies. Also in 1979, Dickenson loaned the company money on the basis of a $4.7 million note from Conventures that was convertible into another 681,000 common shares at $6.90 per share until December 31, 1981. If Dickenson decided to exercise the conversion option, they would own roughly 25 percent of the oil and gas company.

By early 1980, the Dickenson group of companies operated the Red Lake Gold Mine in Ontario and the Silvana silver mine in British Columbia. Besides Conventures, Dickenson held non-operating interests in several oil and gas plays throughout Alberta, other parts of Canada, and the United States. In addition, Kam Kotia Mines Ltd. held similar oil and gas interests. Dickenson also held a portfolio of investments in Canadian junior mining companies.

The Mine and Mill Expansion

By 1979, after 31 years of production at the Red Lake Gold Mine, new high-grade ore reserves were no longer being discovered in sufficient quantities to maintain gold production at historical levels. However, Dickenson management believed that large quantities of low-grade ore reserves still existed and that these could best be mined by changing Dickenson from a medium-tonnage, high-grade ore producer to a high-tonnage, low-grade ore producer. The management believed that this shift in mining strategy could best be accomplished by changing the mining method from labor-intensive cut-and-fill mining to mechanized blast-hole mining. Consultants were hired to quantify these low-grade ore reserves and give an opinion on the application of blast-hole mining.

After several months of study, a four-part capital expenditure program was approved. This program would increase mill capacity, deepen the number-two internal shaft of the mine, increase ore hoisting capacity, and utilize newer more mechanized methods of mining. It was estimated that the two-year program would cost between $10 and $11 million and would increase the mine's capacity to 1,000 tons per day.

Deepening the number-two internal shaft from a depth of 4,400 feet to 5,700 feet would open up eight more levels for mining (levels 31–38) and allow access to new ore that was believed to be promising. The cost of the project was estimated to be $2.5 million.

In order to remove 1,000 tons per day from the mine, additional hoisting capacity had to be built. After considerable study, it was decided to modify the #1 shaft to permit utilization of the two hoisting compartments solely for hoisting ore and waste instead of combining this use with the lifting of men and materials. These services then were placed in a third compartment that required the installation of considerable auxiliary equipment. This was expected to cost $4 million.

Finally, milling capacity had to be increased to accommodate the increased ore volumes from the mine. To accomplish this, the consultants proposed that the ore-crushing process be speeded up by reducing the crushing time for a batch of ore and therefore increasing the crusher product size. The size of the crusher product would be doubled, which would increase crusher capacity to 1,400 tons per day. In addition, the fine ore storage bin would be increased in size from 600 to 2,000 tons. The cost of the mill expansion was estimated to be $4 million.

The consultants and Dickenson management believed that these operating changes would allow the company to mine lower ore grades at lower costs per ton. Combined with higher gold prices, these changes would ensure the profitability of the mine in years to come. Dickenson therefore negotiated a $10 million project term loan at a rate of bank prime plus 1 percent and an additional $5 million line of credit to finance the expansion program.

By the end of 1980, approximately $8 million had been spent on the expansion program, yet none of the four components was complete. Dickenson had run the term loan up to $6.6 million and the operating line of credit was up to $3.7 million. Gold production for the year had dropped from 44,000 oz. in 1979 to 29,000 oz. in 1980 primarily because of the mining of lower ore grades. The recovery rate at the mill also fell, as an enhanced recovery process involving the roasting of gold sulfide wastes produced by cyanide leaching had to be suspended because of environmental and employee health reasons. This lowered gold recovery from 93.7 percent to 83.3 percent. Lower ore grades and lower mill recovery rates meant that Dickenson had to treat 4.4 tons of ore in 1980 to produce 1 oz. of gold compared to 2.7 tons in 1979. Fortunately, the average price received per ounce of gold had risen from $356 to $675. The company had revised its estimates of the cost to complete the four-part expansion to an additional $9 million in 1981, because of severe cost overruns during 1980.

Problems in 1981

As the expansion program moved into 1981, several new developments occurred that all started to work against Dickenson. For 1981, anticipating the commencement of the new, mechanized mining operations the company had set out a production budget to mine 210,000 tons of ore at a grade of 0.19 oz. of gold per ton, resulting in the production of 34,700 oz. of gold, assuming a mill recovery rate of about 87 percent. Costs of production were expected to be $63.10 per ton or $381.90 per oz.

As the year progressed, it became clear that Dickenson could not meet this budget. The expansion work in the mine hindered the efficiency of the mining process, and the control of ore-grade quality declined as the new mechanized mining methods were put into use. This resulted in lower tonnages mined at reduced ore grades. The operating and financial statements for the first three quarters clearly indicated the severity of the operating problems at the mine. For the nine months ending September 30, 1981, 133,000 tons of ore had been mined at an average grade of 0.15 oz. of gold per ton, resulting in production of only 16,471 oz. of gold. Once again, the expansion program was experiencing major cost overruns, as total estimated expenditures for 1981 alone were now expected to be roughly $14 million.

Increased financing costs and lower gold prices added to these operating problems. The prime rate hit a high of 22 percent in 1981 and, by October 1981, the price of gold had fallen to $400 U. S./oz. At that point, Dickenson's operating costs were estimated to be $631 Cdn/oz. and interest expense was estimated at $91 Cdn/oz. for a total cost of $722 an ounce. These problems were compounded by the complete lack of capital budgetary controls to the extent that the company relied solely on the external auditors to develop capital cost and cash flow projections. At this time, the company's major banker was exerting considerable pressure to reduce bank debt and infuse new management.

Dickenson's problems were not limited to the gold-mining operations, as the silver division also was operating at a loss. This division was composed of Silvana Mines of British Columbia, and it had been adversely affected by sharply reduced silver prices. For the nine months ending September 30, 1981, Silvana lost almost $1 million as opposed to a profit of $493,000 for the same period in 1980.

Dickenson was also involved in a $21 million lawsuit with Willroy Mines Ltd. concerning the results of an exploration program conducted by New Cinch Uranium Mines of New Mexico, a company in which Dickenson held a 12 percent interest. Willroy was accusing

Dickenson and 15 other firms of misrepresentation regarding the presentation of the New Cinch assay results. The original assays of New Cinch's reserves were found to be inaccurate, but not before Willroy had purchased a large portion of New Cinch shares. When the drilling cores were reassayed and found to be worthless, New Cinch stock dropped dramatically and Willroy Mines incurred a substantial loss. Dickenson contended that it had no knowledge of the inaccuracies in the original assays and indeed that it also suffered a loss on its holdings of New Cinch as a result of the new information.

The Sale of Conventures Ltd.

By September 1981, Dickenson owed $4.5 million in accounts payable and $33.4 million in bank debt, all of which was technically due and payable because the company was in default on servicing this debt. In light of these obligations, Dickenson management decided to sell the company's interest in Conventures Ltd. of Calgary, which now consisted of 1.4 million common shares and the $4.7 million convertible debenture.

On September 29, 1981, Dickenson was able to arrange to sell its interest in Conventures to Oakwood Petroleums of Calgary for $26.5 million. Dickenson received a note from Oakwood for $13.5 million bearing interest equal to the prime rate within a range of 17.5 percent to 23.5 percent. Dickenson also received $13 million in cash which was used to reduce the bank debt. In return, Dickenson gave up 1,453,686 shares of Conventures and the 5 percent–$4.7 million note from Conventures that could be converted into another 680,000 shares by December 31, 1981. On September 24, 1981, Conventure's common stock had closed at $9.00.

The Situation in October 1981

When Peter Munro joined Dickenson from Falconbridge in October 1981, he called in his new Vice President of Finance, John Kachmar also from Falconbridge, to review the situation. The cash proceeds of the Conventure's sales had reduced the floating rate bank debt to roughly $20.4 million. Interest payments amounted to $325,000 a month. Two creditors in particular had become adamant about receiving payment. One bank wanted $1 million by January, and the company's cyanide supplier was threatening to cut off deliveries, which would shut down the mill, if outstanding bills were not settled.

With regard to the expansion program, which had been expected to cost between $9 and $10 million originally, the deepening of the #2 shaft was now complete, and enough equipment had been purchased to begin the mechanized mining processes, but mill capacity had only reached 700 tons per day and the ore haulage system was not finished. The consultants estimated that the cost to complete the program, in addition to the $22 million already spent in 1980 and 1981, was $3.2 million in 1982.

Munro and Kachmar knew that they had to raise cash to pay off their debts or face bankruptcy. They drew up a list of possible options:

1. A public financing issue to institutional investors.
2. A rights offering to existing shareholders and corporate management.
3. Sell assets.
4. Increase gold production with possible use of forward sales to ensure stable gold prices.
5. Reduce costs and cut capital expenditures.

Munro and Kachmar had had some discussions with the company's underwriters regarding the first two financing options. They had come up with a plan to issue a type of "debt unit." This unit would consist of seven $1,000 (U. S.) bonds and 40 gold purchase warrants. Each warrant would allow the holder to purchase one ounce of gold. The warrants would be exercisable in groups of 10 in the years 1986, 1987, 1988, and 1989. Dickenson wanted to sell each unit for $14,000 U. S., the purchase price representing seven $1,000 U. S. bonds and a prepayment of $175 U. S. towards the exercise price of each warrant. The coupon rate on the bonds, the exercise price of the warrants, and the overall size of the issue had yet to be decided.

A rights offering to existing shareholders and management would allow the present shareholders to maintain their proportionate share of ownership and give the new management an opportunity to participate in the ownership of the company at a low cost, given the current price level of Dickenson stock. It was, however, a risky proposition because Dickenson's future was by no means certain.

Selling more company assets was not a pleasant proposition, but had to be considered. First, there was the note from Oakwood Petroleum with a par value of $13,535,000 and interest rates that varied with the prime rate between 17.5 percent to 23.5 percent. Munro and Kachmar also had to consider the possibility of selling a portion of Dickenson's oldest asset, the Red Lake Gold Mine. Munro wondered how much cash he might be able to raise by selling a 50 percent interest in the mine.

Both men clearly recognized the need to cut operating costs and increase gold production. They felt it might be possible to return to more traditional mining methods for a while and work the remaining higher grade stopes and pillars that were still left in the mine. They were also considering the use of the gold futures or options markets in order to gain security against further price drops. Munro was also considering delaying the rest of the capital expenditure program.

Both Munro and Kachmar realized that the initial goal of the mine and mill expansion was a good one in principle. However, it was also clear to them that bankruptcy was imminent if they could not develop a short-run survival plan to raise cash and retire debt. In light of the current problems, the company's five-year plan looked increasingly unrealistic as shown in Exhibit 11.

EXHIBIT 1
Consolidated Balance Sheet (in thousands of dollars)

	September 30, 1981 (Unaudited)	December 31, 1980	December 31, 1979
Assets			
Current			
Bullion and concentrates on hand and in transit, at net realizable value	$ 1,646	$ 1,561	$ 2,943
Accounts receivable	422	580	343
Income taxes recoverable	314	314	—
Marketable securities, at cost (quoted market value 1981–$213; 1980–$383; 1979–$965)	365	347	731
Prepaid expenses	133	110	53
	2,880	2,912	4,070
Long-term investments (note 4)	18,245	22,881	15,826
Fixed, at cost			
Buildings, machinery, and equipment	24,349	16,383	12,041
Less: Accumulated depreciation	9,749	9,293	8,404
	14,600	7,090	3,637

EXHIBIT 1 (*Continued*)

	September 30, 1981 (Unaudited)	December 31, 1980	December 31, 1979
Mining claims	929	1,089	1,179
Townsite lots	287	282	142
	15,816	8,461	4,958
Other, at cost			
Shaft deepening and renovation expenditure unamortized	11,838	6,722	2,922
Interest in and expenditure on outside mining properties	530	1,110	1,129
Interest in and expenditure on oil and gas properties	3,961	3,086	1,905
Stores and supplies	2,712	2,317	1,709
Deferred charges	136	348	186
	19,177	13,583	7,851
	$56,118	$47,837	$32,705
Liabilities			
Current			
Bank indebtedness (note 3)	$ 7,436	$ 4,043	$ 315
Accounts payable	4,378	4,604	2,239
Income and mining taxes payable	142	142	981
Current portion of long-term debt (notes 2 and 3)	6,250	1,043	1,200
	18,206	9,832	4,735
Long-term debt (notes 2 and 3)	6,669	7,746	3,500
Deferred income taxes	5,435	4,916	3,223
	30,310	22,494	11,458
Shareholders' Equity			
Capital stock (note 1)			
Authorized			
30,000,000 Class A common shares without par value			
6,000,000 Class B special shares without par value			
Issued			
Class A shares	4,901	4,879	4,489
Class B shares	4,898	4,879	4,489
Contributed surplus	1,466	1,466	1,466
Retained earnings	17,002	16,688	12,108
	28,267	27,912	22,552
Deduct Company's share of Kam Kotia Mines Limited's holdings of shares of Dickenson Mines Limited	2,459	2,569	1,305
	25,808	25,343	21,247
	$56,118	$47,837	$32,705

Notes to Financial Statements

1. **Amalgamation**

   The consolidated financial statements give effect to the statutory amalgamation (under the Business Corporations Act of Ontario) of Dickenson Mines Limited (Dickenson) and Silvana Mines Inc. (Silvana), both under common control, into the continuing corporation, Dickenson Mines Limited, pursuant to an amalgamation agreement dated October 7, 1980, and the issue of a certificate of amalgamation on October 31, 1980.

   The amalgamation was accounted for on the basis of combining the assets and liabilities of the amalgamating corporations at their carrying value in each corporation's records. The income of the combined corporation includes income of the combining corporations for the year ended December 31, 1980. Income figures for the years 1979, 1978, 1977, and 1976 have been restated on the same basis.

   The amalgamation agreement provided that the authorized capital of the amalgamated corporation shall consist of 30,000,000 Class A common shares without par value and 6,000,000 Class B special shares without par value; each Class A share is entitled to one vote and each Class B share is entitled to ten votes at meetings of shareholders. The Class B shares rank equally with the Class A shares in all other respects.

2. **Long-term debt**

	(In thousands of dollars)		
	September 30, 1981 (Unaudited)	December 31, 1980	December 31, 1979
Term bank loan—$10,000,000 U.S., interest at prime plus 1¼%	$11,919	$ —	$ —
Term bank loan—interest at prime rate plus 1%	—	6,600	4,700
Notes payable—Carl O. Nickle—7% repayable $1,000,000 in September 1981 and $1,000,000 in September 1982	1,000	2,000	—
Finance contract payable—14% repayable $3,036 U.S. monthly up to and including May 1, 1985. Fixed assets have been pledged as security	—	189	—
	12,919	8,789	4,700
Less: Amounts due within one year	6,250	1,043	1,200
	$ 6,669	$7,746	$3,500

3. **Bank loan security**

   The Company has pledged as security for the bank indebtedness and the term bank loan the following:
   (a) A $25,000,000 demand debenture creating a fixed charge over the Red Lake Mine, a fixed charge over the major machinery and equipment of the Company, and a floating charge over all other assets of the Company.
   (b) Security under Section 177 of the Bank Act (Canada) on mineral reserves, inventory, and equipment located at the Red Lake Mine site.
   (c) Security under Section 178 of the Bank Act (Canada) with respect to the Red Lake and Silvana Mines.

(Continued)

Notes to Financial Statements (*Continued*)

(d) An hypothecation of the Company's portfolio of junior stocks, including oil and gas stocks and Kam-Kotia stock.

(e) An assignment of the promissory note from Oakwood Petroleum Limited.

4. Investments in companies accounted for by the equity method:

			(In thousands of dollars)		
			September 30, 1981 (Unaudited)	December 31, 1980	December 31, 1979
Shares and convertible notes					
Kam Kotia Mines Limited	Shares	Quoted Market Value			
at September 30, 1981	2,119,108	$ 4,026,000			
at December 31, 1980	2,119,108	$19,602,000			
at December 31, 1979	2,112,108	$13,465,000	$ 1,041	$ 2,346	$ 2,992
Conventures Limited [Note 1(b)]					
1,453,686 shares and $4,700,000—5% convertible notes (quoted market value at December 31, 1980 $31,128,000)			—	16,826	—
Other (quoted market value)					
at September 30, 1981	$ 2,592,000				
at December 31, 1980	$10,365,000				
at December 31, 1979	$ 7,228,000)		2,855	2,701	2,826
			3,896	21,873	5,818
Loans and advances, at cost			112	72	315
Subtotal			4,008	21,945	6,133
Investment in Conventures Limited (Note 1 (b))					
At December 31, 1979, 1,084,396 shares and $4,700,000—5% convertible notes (quoted market value at December 31, 1979, $23,406,000)			—	—	9,938
Portfolio investments, at cost					
Listed shares					
Shares and warrants of New Cinch Uranium Ltd. (quoted market value)					
at September 30, 1981	$ 274,000				
at December 31, 1980	$12,216,000				
at December 31, 1979	$ 1,388,000)		275	345	198
Other listed shares (quoted market value)					
at September 30, 1981	$117,000				
at December 31, 1980	$385,000				
at December 31, 1979	$365,000)		278	262	320
			553	607	518
Other shares, bonds, advances and participations			1,878	2,188	1,256
Subtotal			2,431	2,795	1,774
Note receivable from Oakwood Petroleums Limited,					

(*Continued*)

Notes to Financial Statements (*Continued*)

(In thousands of dollars)

	September 30, 1981 (Unaudited)	December 31, 1980	December 31, 1979
due September 5, 1983, bearing interest at the prime rate, not to exceed 23.5% and not less than 17.5%	13,535	—	—
Total	19,974	24,740	17,845
Less: Allowance for decline in value	1,729	1,859	2,019
	$18,245	$22,881	$15,826

The quoted market values referred to above do not necessarily represent the realizable value of these holdings that may be more or less than that indicated by market quotations.

The investment in Conventures Limited comprising 1,453,686 shares and $4,700,000 convertible notes was sold to Oakwood Petroleums Limited on September 29, 1981 (with effect from September 4, 1981) for the following consideration:

Cash	$13,000,000
Note receivable, due September 5, 1983	13,535,000
	$26,535,000

The cash portion of the proceeds were applied to reduce the Company's bank indebtedness.

EXHIBIT 2
Consolidated Statement of Income (In thousands of dollars except earnings per share)

	Nine Months Ended September 30,		Year Ended December 31,				
	1981	1980	1980	1979	1978	1977	1976
	(Unaudited)						
Revenue							
Gold bullion production	9,439	16,018	19,857	15,973	13,594	9,650	6,857
Lead and zinc concentrates production	4,584	5,560	7,394	5,207	2,793	1,216	164
Expense							
Mining	8,972	6,548	9,299	6,979	6,256	5,227	4,212
Milling	2,484	2,014	3,073	2,257	1,757	1,343	1,057
Mine management, office and general	2,768	2,326	3,511	2,485	1,930	1,357	1,160
Transportation and treatment costs	1,314	1,251	1,666	1,627	597	498	407
Head office administration, general and short-term interest expense	2,703	629	1,015	796	897	340	28
Marketing	37	62	73	66	65	53	45
	18,278	12,830	18,637	14,210	11,502	8,818	6,909

EXHIBIT 2 (*Continued*)

	Nine Months Ended September 30,		Year Ended December 31,				
	1981	1980 (Unaudited)	1980	1979	1978	1977	1976
Operating Income (Loss) Before Undernoted Items	(4,255)	8,748	8,614	6,970	4,885	2,048	118
Amortization of shaft deepening and renovations	866	960	1,388	393	121	—	—
Depreciation and depletion	671	676	1,206	826	731	583	329
Outside exploration written off	695	516	757	436	9	28	87
Amortization of oil and gas properties	349	257	343	—	—	—	—
	2,581	2,409	3,694	1,655	861	611	416
Income (Loss) from Mining Operations	(6,836)	6,339	4,920	5,315	4,024	1,437	(298)
Investment and Other Income and Expense							
Share of net income (loss) of companies accounted for by the equity method	(106)	104	742	(94)	38	75	(62)
Dividends, interest, and net results of security transactions	736	910	1,093	844	267	258	221
Oil and gas revenue	52	53	70	16	—	—	—
Interest expense, long-term	(985)	(465)	(762)	(674)	—	—	—
Fire loss recovery (net)	32	—	464	—	—	—	—
Amalgamation expense	—	(50)	(332)	—	—	—	—
	(271)	552	1,275	92	305	333	159
Income (Loss) Before Income Taxes and Extraordinary Items	(7,107)	6,891	6,195	5,407	4,329	1,770	(139)
Income and Mining Taxes	—	2,200	1,750	2,691	1,648	541	(346)
Income (Loss) Before Extraordinary Items	(7,107)	4,691	4,445	2,716	2,681	1,229	207
Increase in the carrying value of the Company's interest in Kam Kotia Mines Limited arising from share issues by Kam Kotia	—	503	503	1,200	—	—	—
Provisions for decline in investment in New Cinch Uranium Ltd.	(477)	—	—	—	—	—	—
Share of extraordinary gains (loss) of companies accounted for by the							

(*Continued*)

EXHIBIT 2 (Continued)

	Nine Months Ended September 30,		Year Ended December 31,				
	1981	1980	1980	1979	1978	1977	1976
	(Unaudited)						
equity method	(1,285)	93	93	367	(124)	(75)	(40)
Gain on sale of investment in Conventures Limited (net of deferred tax of $520)	9,183	—	—	—	—	—	—
Net Income for the Period	$ 314	$ 5,287	$ 5,041	$ 4,283	$ 2,557	$1,154	$ 167
Earnings per Share:							
Before extraordinary items							
Class A	(0.76)	0.49	0.48	0.31	0.32	0.16	0.03
Class B	(0.76)	0.49	0.48	0.31	0.32	0.16	0.03
After extraordinary items							
Class A	0.03	0.55	0.55	0.48	0.31	0.15	0.02
Class B	0.03	0.55	0.55	0.48	0.31	0.15	0.02

EXHIBIT 3
Consolidated Statement of Changes in Financial Position (In thousands of dollars)

	Nine Months Ended September 30,		Year Ended December 31,				
	1981	1980	1980	1979	1978	1977	1976
	(Unaudited)						
Source of Funds							
Income (loss) before extraordinary items	$ (7,107)	$ 4,691	$ 4,445	$ 2,716	$2,681	$1,229	$ 207
Charges (credits) not affecting funds							
Amortization of shaft deepening and renovations	866	960	1,388	393	121	—	—
Depreciation and depletion	671	676	1,206	826	731	583	329
Outside exploration written off	695	516	757	436	9	28	87
Amortization of oil and gas properties	349	257	343	—	—	—	—
Share of loss (net income) of companies accounted for by the equity method	106	(104)	(742)	94	(38)	(75)	62
Deferred income taxes	—	2,200	1,692	1,705	710	123	2
Gain on sale of investment in Jameland Mines Ltd.	(118)	—	—	—	—	—	—
Funds provided from (applied to) operations	(4,538)	9,196	9,089	6,170	4,214	1,888	687
Long-term debt, noncurrent portion	1,077	4,100	4,246	3,500	—	—	—

(Continued)

EXHIBIT 3 (Continued)

	Nine Months Ended September 30,		Year Ended December 31,				
	1981	1980	1980	1979	1978	1977	1976
	(Unaudited)						
Issue of capital stock	39	984	986	2,535	852	1,186	264
Decrease in stores and supplies	—	—	—	—	—	93	—
Decrease in deferred charges	219	—	—	14	147	—	—
Proceeds from sale of long-term investments	26,650	—	—	—	—	—	—
Increase in contributed surplus	—	—	—	—	6	—	—
	21,293	14,280	14,321	12,219	5,219	3,167	951
Application of Funds							
Purchase of fixed assets	8,196	3,130	4,482	874	869	1,519	1,686
Shaft deepening and renovation expenditure	5,982	3,332	5,100	2,185	650	35	—
Increase in stores and supplies	395	706	608	275	349	41	141
Investment in and advances to other companies	13,788	7,631	7,501	8,076	1,600	770	342
Exploration expenditure on outside mining, oil, and gas properties	1,338	1,388	2,262	2,238	796	591	115
Increase in deferred charges	—	9	162	—	—	8	173
Dividends paid	—	—	461	190	353	163	259
	29,699	16,196	20,576	13,838	4,617	3,127	2,716
Increase (Decrease) in Funds During the Period	(8,406)	(1,916)	(6,255)	(1,619)	602	40	(1,765)
Funds (Deficiency) at Beginning of Period	(6,920)	(665)	(665)	954	352	311	2,076
Funds (Deficiency) at End of Period	$(15,326)	$ (2,581)	$ (6,920)	$ (665)	$ 954)	$ 351	$ 311

EXHIBIT 4
Forecast of Expenditures to Complete Mine and Mill Expansion (000's)

Expenditure Category	Actual 1980	Actual January 1–September 30, 1981	Estimate 1982
(1) Working Capital and New Machinery for Mechanized Cut-and-Fill Mining	$1,042	$ 2,411	$ 35
(2) Mill Expansion	1,163	5,202	2,882
(3) Deepening of #2 Shaft	3,152	531	0
(4) New Hauling System	2,591	5,776	310
Totals	$7,948	$13,920	$3,227

EXHIBIT 5
Mill Operations

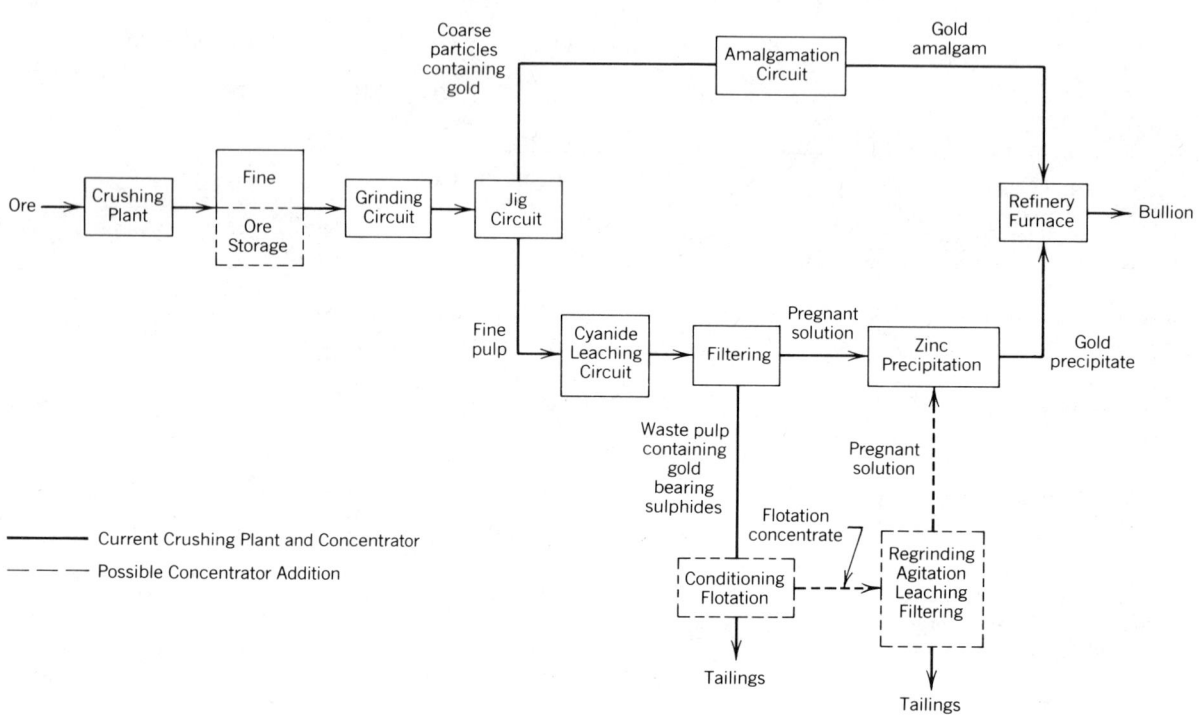

EXHIBIT 6
Operating Results for the Red Lake Mine 1976–October 1981

	1981			Years Ended December 31,				
	Third Quarter	Second Quarter	First Quarter	1980	1979	1978	1977	1976
Ore milled (tons)	49,360	46,467	36,549	128,000	118,000	110,000	129,000	117,000
Average grade of ore milled (ounces of gold per ton)	0.17	0.13	0.15	0.270	0.405	0.576	0.499	0.509
Production of gold (ounces)	7,142	5,047	4,282	29,281	44,367	59,957	60,019	55,488
Operating expenses								
Per ton milled	$ 85.21	$ 83.22	$ 97.21	$ 91.79	$ 86.27	$ 80.94	$ 60.89	$ 58.36
Per troy ounce recovered	$588.33	$765.44	$798.77	$401.25	$229.45	$149.48	$130.89	$123.03
Average price of gold per ounce received during the period	$501.19	$554.04	$687.43	$675.49	$356.33	$226.00	$160.34	$123.30
Revenue received during the period (thousands of dollars)	$ —	$ —	$ —	$19,779	$15,807	$13,560	$ —	$ —

EXHIBIT 7
Proven Ore Reserves

Year	Tons of Ore	Ounce/ Ton	Ounces of Gold
1981[a]	653,700	0.289	189,300
1980	425,000	0.450	191,250
1979	389,000	0.529	205,781
1978	350,909	0.571	200,369
1977	335,622	0.539	180,900
1976	357,382	0.536	191,556
1975	393,057	0.538	211,464

[a]As estimated by consultants.

EXHIBIT 8
Results of Silvana Division

	Nine Months Ended September 30,		Years Ended December 31,		
	1981	1980	1980	1979	1978
Revenue	$3,288,164	$4,214,497	$5,545,193	$3,580,000	$1,896,000
Operating income (Loss)[b]	(352,687)	560,190	413,140	1,255,000	246,000
Income (Loss) before income taxes[c]	(954,898)	493,126	369,488	1,006,000	123,000
Average price received:					
Silver (per ounce)	12.49	23.56	22.56	14.82	6.25
Lead (per pound)	0.44	0.48	0.48	0.63	0.37
Zinc (per pound)	0.50	0.42	0.42	0.41	0.33

[a]In 1976 and 1977 to August 1, Silvana Mines Inc. leased its property to Kam Kotia. Financial information for years prior to 1978 is not comparable to subsequent years.
[b]Before depreciation and depletion, deferred development expenses, oil and gas interests written off, and head office, administration, and general expenses and interest income.
[c]Results were adversely affected in 1981 by a change in the method of accounting for depreciation from the straight line method to the unit of production method.

	Years Ended December 31,			
	1980	1979	1978	1977
Ore milled (tons)	31,110	21,632	17,600	17,499
Average tons per month	2,593	1,803	1,467	1,459
Average grade				
Silver (ounces per ton)	8.63	13.96	14.84	19.34
Lead (%)	3.21	4.87	5.81	7.41
Zinc (%)	3.03	4.51	4.34	6.13
Lead concentrate produced (tons)	1,556	1,654	1,609	2,086

(*Continued*)

EXHIBIT 8 (Continued)

	Years Ended December 31,			
	1980	1979	1978	1977
Metal content				
Silver (ounces)	183,684	185,744	174,799	224,311
Lead (pounds)	1,805,561	2,011,863	1,948,464	2,449,345
Zinc (pounds)	258,200	301,586	299,608	427,384
Zinc concentrate produced (tons)	1,359	1,458	1,071	1,582
Metal content				
Silver (ounces)	71,698	104,301	68,876	101,515
Zinc (pounds)	372,240	491,599	1,108,890	1,578,866
Cadmium (pounds)	9,542	10,937	8,209	12,055

EXHIBIT 9
Common Stock Performance for 1980 and 1981

1981	Dickenson A Shares	Dickenson B Shares	TSE Gold Index	$U.S./oz. Gold Price
September	$ 4.15	$3.60	3423	$431.75
August	5.00	5.00	4101	414.00
July	4.85	4.70	3819	401.50
June	5.37	5.12	3573	428.75
May	7.00	5.87	4449	479.25
April	8.50	7.50	4311	477.25
March	10.50	9.25	4288	539.50
February	8.25	8.00	3796	489.00
January	10.50	9.25	4056	506.50

Note: 1980 Range: $11.25–16.75; $9.75–$17.00.

EXHIBIT 10
Prime Lending Rate of a Major Canadian Bank January 1980–September 1981 (at month end)

		Average Monthly Prime Rate (%)
1980	January	15
	February	15
	March	16.12
	April	17.16
	May	15.18
	June	13.25
	July	12.63
	August	12.25
	September	12.25
	October	12.87
	November	13.83
	December	16.91
1981	January	17
	February	17.11
	March	17.75
	April	18
	May	19.25
	June	20
	July	21
	August	22.50
	September	22.00

EXHIBIT 11
Pro Forma Production Budget

	Year Ending December 31,				
	1982	1983	1984	1985	1986
Ore milled (tons)	240,000	350,000	350,000	350,000	350,000
Average grade of ore milled (ounces of gold per ton)	0.181	0.176	0.176	0.176	0.176
Recovery	83%	85%	85%	85%	85%
Production of gold (ounces)	36,000	52,500	52,500	52,500	52,500
Operating expenses (1982 dollars)					
Per ton milled	$ 56.25	$ 51.65	$ 51.65	$ 51.65	$ 51.65
Per troy ounce recovered	$375.05	$344.38	$344.38	$344.38	$344.38
Capital costs (thousands of 1982 dollars)					
Concentrator	$ 1,443				
Other	$ 1,265	$ 2,853	$ 1,372	$ 1,244	$ 1,244

MARION LABORATORIES, INC.

Michael E. Herman, Senior Vice-President of Finance for Marion Laboratories, had just received word that the Board of Directors was planning to meet in three days to review the Company's portfolio of subsidiary investments. In particular, he and his Senior Financial Analyst, Carl R. Mitchell, were to prepare an in-depth analysis of several of the subsidiaries so that the Board could be better positioned with respect to these subsidiaries compatibility with Marion's overall strategic objectives. The analysis was part of a continuing process of self-assessment to assure future growth for the Company. At the upcoming meeting the Board was interested in a review of Kalo Laboratories, Inc.,[1] a subsidiary that manufactured specialty agricultural chemicals.

Kalo was profitable and in sound financial shape for the fiscal year just ended. (See Exhibit 1: Sales, Profit, and Assets of Major Industry Segments.) But Kalo, in the agricultural chemical industry, was unique for Marion, and Mr. Herman knew that Kalo's long-term status as a Marion subsidiary would depend on more than just profitability.

Marion's future had been the subject of careful study following the first two years of earnings decline in the company's history. In fiscal 1975 net earnings for the company were

---

Source: This case was prepared by Professor Marilyn L. Taylor and Kenneth Beck of the University of Kansas. The development of the case was supported in part by a grant from the University of Kansas Fund for Instructional Improvement. Permission to use granted by Marilyn L. Taylor.

[1] Kalo Laboratories, Inc. was used as the case subject because of the singular nature of the segment information available in Marion Laboratories, Inc., SEC submissions, and does not reflect Marion's intentions as to its investment in Kalo or any of its other subsidiary operations. Materials in this case were generally gathered from publicly available information.

EXHIBIT 1
Sales Profits and Identifiable Assets by Industry Segments

	Year Ended June 30,				
	1978	1977	1976	1975	1974
	(Thousands of Dollars)				
Sales to Unaffiliated Customers					
Pharmaceutical and Hospital Products	$ 84,223	$ 72,299	$59,236	$64,613	$54,165
Specialty Agricultural Chemical Products	9,302	5,227	2,880	4,522	4,044
Other Health-Care Segments	23,853	22,605	18,722	14,961	13,569
Consolidated Net Sales	$117,378	$100,131	$80,838	$84,096	$71,778
Operating Profit					
Pharmaceutical and Hospital Products	$ 27,900	$ 23,439	$18,941	$28,951	$25,089
Specialty Agricultural Chemical Products	905	382	(328)	881	620
Other Health-Care Segments	929	1,251	(593)	686	871
Operating Profit	29,734	25,072	18,020	30,518	26,580
Interest Expense	(1,546)	(1,542)	(898)	(97)	(83)
Corporate Expenses	(5,670)	(4,474)	(3,106)	(2,795)	(2,475)
Earnings Before Income Taxes	$ 22,518	$ 19,056	$14,016	$27,626	$24,022
Identifiable Assets					
Pharmaceutical and Hospital Products	$ 75,209	$ 69,546	$60,376	$43,658	$35,103
Specialty Agricultural Chemical Products	3,923	3,805	1,801	1,942	1,790
Other Health-Care Segments	14,635	14,875	13,902	14,229	12,217
Corporate	5,121	3,424	4,518	3,928	3,770
Discontinued Operations	—	—	—	3,370	6,865
Consolidated Assets	$ 98,888	$ 91,650	$80,597	$67,127	$59,745

Source: 1978 Annual Report.

12 percent lower than in 1974. In fiscal 1976 Marion faced a more serious problem as earnings fell 30 percent below 1974 levels, while sales decreased 4 percent and cost of goods sold rose 12 percent above 1974 levels.

As a result of the interruption in the earnings' growth pattern, Marion sought to reexamine its corporate portfolio of investments. By fiscal year 1977 some results from the reappraisal were seen as earnings rose 28 percent from the previous year. Although sales continued to climb, earnings had not yet recovered to the 1974 level by the end of fiscal year 1978. Marion's long-range planning was an attempt to define what the company was to become in the next 10-year period. Current analysis of subsidiaries and investments were analyzed within this 10-year framework. As part of this long-range planning, a statement of Marion's Corporate Mission was developed.

Statement of Corporate Mission

1. Achieve a position of market leadership through marketing and distribution of consumable and personal products of a perceived differentiation to selected segments of the health-care and related fields.
2. Achieve long-term profitable growth through the management of high risk relative to the external environment.
3. Achieve a professional, performance-oriented working environment that stimulates integrity, entrepreneurial spirit, productivity, and social responsibility.

In addition to these more general goals,

Marion also set a specific sales goal of $250 million. No time frame was established to achieve this goal because the major emphasis was to be placed on the stability and quality of sales. Mr. Herman realized, however, that even though there was no written timetable for earnings growth, it was well understood that to meet stockholder expectations the company must grow fairly rapidly.

On June 8, 1978, in a presentation before the Health Industry's Analyst Group, Fred Lyons, Marion's President and Chief Operating Officer, emphasized Marion's commitment to growth. In his remarks he stated:

> We expect to grow over the next 10 years at a rate greater than the pharmaceutical industry average and at a rate greater than at least twice that of the real gross national product. Our target range is at least 10–15 percent compounded growth—shooting for the higher side of that, of course. Obviously we intend to have a great deal of new business and new products added to our current operations to reach and exceed the $250 million level.
>
> Our licensing activities and R & D expenditures will be intensified. . . . At the same time we'll undertake some selective in-house research business into Marion through the acquisition route. It is our intention to keep our balance sheet strong and maintain an "A" or better credit rating, to achieve a return on investment in the 12–15 percent range, and to produce a net after-tax compared to sales in the 8–12 percent range.

To finance this growth in sales Marion was faced with a constant need for funds. In the past, most of these funds came from the company's operations. To finance a $25 million expansion in its pharmaceutical facilities, the company, in fiscal year 1976, found it necessary to borrow $15 million in the form of unsecured senior notes. The notes were to mature on October 1, 1980, 1981, and 1982 with $5 million due on each of those dates.

In regard to possible future financing, Mr. Herman made the following comments before the Health Industry's Analyst Group. "Most of you realize that industrial companies have debt–equity ratios of 1:1 and, if we so desired to lever ourselves to that level, we could borrow $66 million. However, we would keep as a guideline the factor of always maintaining our "A" or better credit rating, so we would not leverage ourselves that far."

Although Marion was fairly light on debt, the potential for future borrowing was not unlimited. Besides maintaining an "A" credit rating, it was felt that a debt to equity ratio greater than 4:1 would be inconsistent with the pharmaceutical industry.

To analyze Kalo's future as well as the futures of the other nonpharmaceutical subsidiaries, Mr. Herman realized that he and his analysts would have to consider the impact of these financing constraints on Marion's future growth. With unlimited financing in the future, he would have only had to make a "good" investment decision. However, to balance the goals of a strong balance sheet and a high growth rate, Mr. Herman was faced with making the optimal investment decision. It was with these constraints that Mr. Herman would eventually have to make his recommendation to the Board of Directors.

Company History

In 1979, Marion Laboratories, Inc. of Kansas City, Missouri was a leading producer of ethical (prescription) pharmaceuticals for the treatment of cardiovascular and cerebral disorders. (See Exhibit 2: Marion's major ethical products.) Marion also owned subsidiaries that manufactured hospital supplies, proprietary (nonprescription) drugs, eyeglasses, optical accessories, electrical home stairway elevators, and specialty agricultural chemicals.

Marion Laboratories was founded in 1950 by Ewing Marion Kauffman. Prior to establishing his own company, Mr. Kauffman held a job with a field sales force of a Kansas City pharmaceutical company. After four years on the job, Kauffman's sales efforts were so suc-

EXHIBIT 2
Marion's Major Ethical Pharmaceutical Products

Product	Production Application	Estimated Market Size ($000,000)	Marion's Product	Share of Market
Cerebral and Peripheral Vasodilators	Vascular relaxant to relieve constriction of arteries	90–100	PAVABID	22%
Coronary Vasodilators	Controlled release nitroglycerin for treatment of angina pectoris	90–100	NITRO-BID	12%
Ethical and OTC Plain Antacids	Tablets for relief of heartburn	37	GAVISCON	26%
Androgens–estrogens	Product for treatment of calcium deficiencies	12	OS-CAL	46%
Topical burn Antimicrobials	Ointment for prevention of infection in third-degree burns	8	SILVADENE	57%
Urologic antispasmodics	Product for treatment of symptoms of neurogenic bladder	10	DITROPAN	10%

Source: Smith, Barney, Harris, Upham and Co. Research Report (January 19, 1978).

cessful that he was making more money in commissions that the company president's salary. When the company cut his commission and reduced his sales territory, Kauffman quit to establish his own firm.

In its initial year of operation the new company had sales of $36,000 and a net profit of $1,000. Its sole product was a tablet called OS-VIM, which was formulated to combat chronic fatigue. The company's three employees, counting Mr. Kauffman, worked from a 13 × 15 foot storeroom that served as manufacturing plant, sales office, warehouse, and headquarters.

From the Company's inception, the major emphasis for Marion was on sales and marketing. Mr. Kauffman was successful in developing an aggressive, highly motivated sales force. During the mid-1960's the company's sales effort was concentrated on developing Pavabid, introduced in 1962, into the leading product in the cerebral and peripheral vasodilator market.

While other drug companies were spending large amounts on research and development hoping to discover new drugs, Marion concentrated on its sales effort and spent very little on basic research. Nearly all of its research expenditures were directed at improving its current products or further developing products licensed from other drug companies. This particular approach to product development was still being followed in 1979.

Beginning in the late 1960s, Marion decided to reduce its dependence on Pavabid which accounted for more than half of Marion's sales. In the pharmaceutical area, the Company continued to minimize basic research and worked to develop new drug sources. Marion also began diversifying into the hospital and health products sector primarily by acquiring existing firms in those areas. (See Exhibit 3 for a summary of Marion's acquisition and divestiture activities.) Taking advantage of the high market value of its common stock,[2] the Company acquired several subsidiaries engaged in businesses other than pharmaceuticals.

---

[2]Price-earnings ratios for Marion in 1968 and 1969 were 46 and 52, respectively.

EXHIBIT 3
Summary of Subsidiary Acquisitions and Divestitures

Name of Subsidiary	Type of Product(s)	Date Acquired	Date Divested
Marion Health and Safety	First-aid and hospital products	1968	—
American Stair-Glide	Manufacturer of home stairway lifts and products to aid the handicapped	1968	—
Kalo Laboratories	Manufacturer of specialty agricultural chemicals	1968	—
Rose Manufacturing	Industrial fall protection devices	1969	Sold: 1978
Mi-Con Laboratories	Manufacturers of opthalmic solutions	1969	Merged into MH&S: 1973
Pioneer Laboratories	Manufacturer of sterile dressings	50% in 1970	Sold out: 1971
Signet Laboratories	Vitamin and food supplements	1971	Discontinued operations, selling some assets: 1975
Optico Laboratories	Eyeglasses, hard contact lenses, and related products	1973	—
Certified Laboratories	Manufacturer IPC products	1969	Sold: 1978
IPC	Marketed IPC products	1969	Merged into Pharmaceutical Division 1979
Marion International	Distributor of Pharmaceutical products	Incorporated 1971	—
Inco	Industrial creams	1972	Merged into MH&S: 1974
Occusafe	Consulting services; re: OSHA regulation & compliance	Incorporated 1972	Discontinued operations: 1973
Nation Wide	Specialty AG-Chem products	1973	Merged into Kalo
Marion Scientific	Manufacturer and distributor	Acquired by MH&S: 1973	—
Colloidal	Specialty agricultural products	1973	Merged into Kalo 1974
WBC	Holding company for IPC	Incorporated 1976	Sold: 1978
SRC	Specialty AG-Chem products	1977	Merged into Kalo

Organization

In 1979, Marion's operations were divided into two separate groups: the Pharmaceutical Group and the Health Products Group. (See Exhibit 4: Marion Organizational Chart.) The Pharmaceutical Group's operations were a continuation of the original ethical drug line of the Company. The Health Products Group was composed of subsidiaries purchased by Marion in hospital and health-related fields.

Fred W. Lyons, 41, was President, Chief Executive Officer, and a member of the Board of Directors. As President, Lyons was responsible for the total operation and performance of the corporation. This responsibility included the company's pharmaceutical operating group, as well as all subsidiary operations, corporate planning functions, and corporate supportive activities.

Lyons joined Marion in 1970 as Vice President, General Manager, and Director. He came to Marion from a similar position with Corral Pharmaceuticals, Inc., a subsidiary of Alcon Laboratories, Inc. Lyons was a registered pharmacist and had received an MBA from Harvard University in 1959.

Also serving on the Board of Directors was Senior Vice-President and Chief Financial Officer, Michael E. Herman, 37, who joined Marion from an investment banking firm of which

EXHIBIT 4
Organization Chart

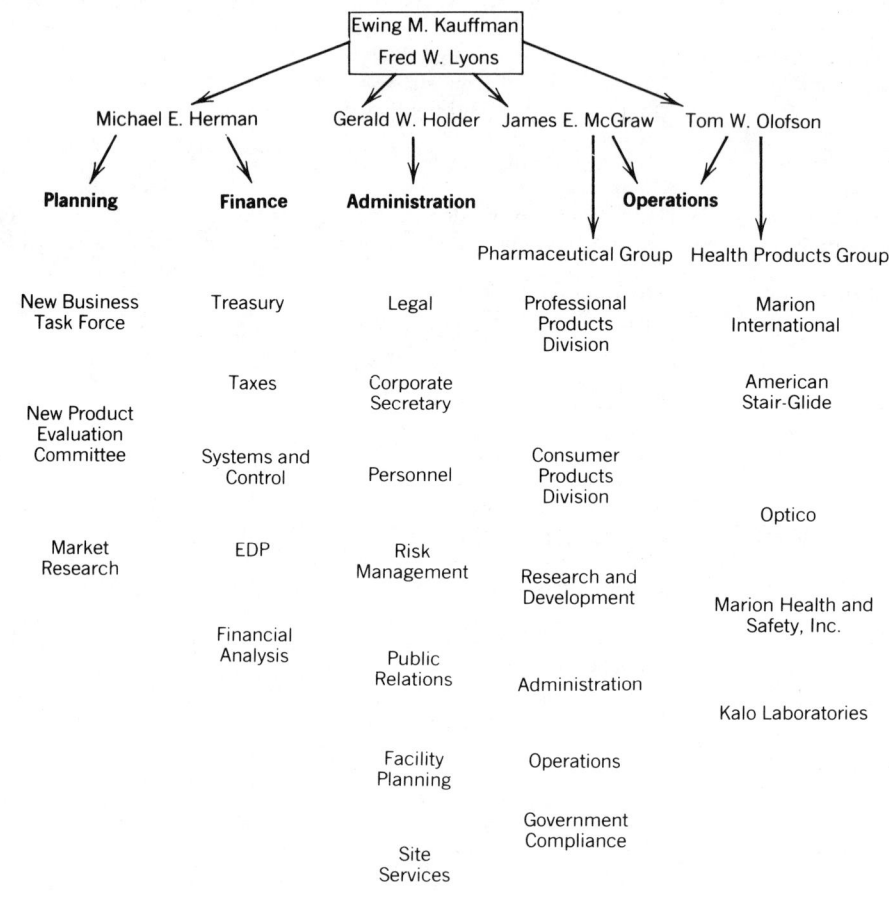

Source: Organization chart as rendered by authors.

he was a founding partner. Herman started with Marion as Vice President of Finance in 1974 and in 1975 was named Director of the Company. His responsibilities were financial planning, financial control of operations, the management information systems, the treasury functions, product development, and strategic long-range planning. Mr. Herman was also Chairman of the company's New Business Task Force Committee, which was responsible for the financial review, planning, evaluation, and negotiation of acquisitions. Herman

earned a BS in metallurgical engineering from Rensselaer Polytechnic Institute and an MBA from the University of Chicago.

Gerald W. Holder, 48, was the Senior Vice-President in charge of administrative functions for Marion. Holder was responsible for all corporate administrative functions, including Marion's legal, personnel, facilities and engineering services, public relations, and risk management staffs. He joined the Company in 1973, rising to the Senior Vice-President level in March 1978.

James E. McGraw, 46, was Senior Vice-President of Marion Laboratories, Inc. and President of the company's Pharmaceutical Group. He was responsible for the manufacturing, marketing, quality control, and accounting functions within the two operating units of the Pharmaceutical Group: the Professional Products Division and the Consumer Products Division. McGraw joined Marion in 1974 from a position as President of the General Diagnostics Division of Warner–Lambert Company.

Tom W. Olofson, 36, was a Senior Vice-President and President of the Health Products Group. His responsibilities included financial and planning aspects for each of the subsidiaries in the Health Products Group.

Within the described organization Marion made some of its operating decisions in small group or task force settings that brought together corporate personnel from several different disciplines. The process of approving certain capital expenditures was an example of the review and analysis process.

Marion had a formal capital expenditure review program for expenditures on depreciable assets in excess of $10,000. At the option of the Group President, the review program could also be applied on expenditures of less than $10,000 with the modification that in these cases only the Group President was involved in the review process.

A form that forced the requesting individual to discount the cash flows of the project had to be completed and submitted, if the net present value of cash flows was positive, to a corporate planning group. This group consisted of corporate accounting and facilities planning personnel who, because the Company was operating with limited funds, decided which projects, based on financial and strategic considerations, should be forwarded to Fred Lyons for final approval or rejection. This process occurred after the planning period and prior to the purchase of the asset. The capital expenditure review program was used for expenditures in both the Pharmaceutical Group and the Health Products Group.

Pharmaceutical Group

Marion's ethical and over-the-counter drug operations were the major components of the Pharmaceutical Group. These operations were split into two divisions: the Professional Products Division and the Consumer Products Division. James E. McGraw headed the Pharmaceutical Group which also was made up of the functions of research and development, administration, operations, and government compliance. Although Marion had been exclusively an ethical drug maker prior to its diversification efforts, the company had recently increased its operations in the proprietary drug area.

In 1978, Marion formed the Consumer Products Division from what had been International Pharmaceutical Corp. (IPC) to market its growing nonprescription product line. This market area, previously untapped by Marion, was expected to be a major ingredient for near-term growth. To aid in the marketing of its nonprescription line, Marion hired a full-scale consumer advertising agency for the first time in the Company's history.

Sales for the Consumer Products Division were boosted when, in fiscal 1978, Marion purchased the product Throat-Discs from Warner–Lamberts' Parke–Davis division. In addition, Marion also purchased two Parke–Davis ethical products: Ambenyl cough–cold products and a tablet for the treatment of thyroid disorders. Because of the timing of the acquisition, most of the sales and earnings were excluded from that year's earnings results. Sales for these three lines were expected to be nearly $8 million in 1979.

Marion's ethical pharmaceutical products were marketed by its Professional Products Division. The Company sold its ethical product with a detail sales force of about 200 that called on physicians, pharmacists, and distributors within their assigned territories. The sales force was very productive by industry standards and was motivated by intensive training and supervision and an incentive compensation system. There was very little direct selling to doctors and pharmacists, the main purpose of the salesman visits being promotion of Marion's products. In addition, Marion had an institutional sales force that sold directly to hospitals, institutions, and other large users.

In fiscal 1978, 80 percent of Marion's pharmaceutical products were distributed through 463 drug wholesalers. All orders for ethical drug products were filled from the Kansas City, Missouri manufacturing plant. Marion's pharmaceutical distribution system is diagrammed below.

During 1978, the company decided to use its improved liquidity position to aid its wholesale drug distributors. Many wholesalers used outside financing to purchase their inventory and were unable to maintain profit margins when interest rates rose. By extending credit on key products, Marion helped its distributors maintain higher inventories and gave the Company a selling edge over competitors.

One of Marion's major goals for each of its products was for the product to hold a market leadership position in the particular area in which it competed. This goal had been accomplished for most of the company's leading products. (See Exhibit 2.)

Capturing a large share of a market had worked particularly well for Marion's leading product, Pavabid, which in 1978 accounted for 18 percent of the entire company's sales. Marion was decreasing its reliance on Pavabid (See Exhibit 5) which, since its introduction in 1962, had been the company's most successful product. Through the 1960s Pavabid had been responsible for almost all of Marion's growth. In recent years, as the product's market matured, sales growth had slowed, forcing the company to become less dependent on Pavabid. The decrease in sales of 3.9 percent in fiscal year 1976 was primarily due to previous overstocking of Pavabid and the subsequent inventory adjustments at the distributor level.

In April 1976 the Food and Drug Administration (FDA) had requested that makers of papaverine hydrochloride (sold by Marion as Pavabid) submit test data to support the safety and efficacy of the drug. Many small manufacturers were not able to submit the data and dropped out of the market. Marion complied with the request and still had not been notified by the FDA of the outcome of the review by early 1979. A negative action by the FDA was not expected since it had taken so long for a decision and papaverine had been used safely for decades. However, if the FDA ruled that compounds such as Pavabid could not be marketed, either because they were not safe or not effective, Marion would lose its leading product.

In August 1977, the FDA requested that

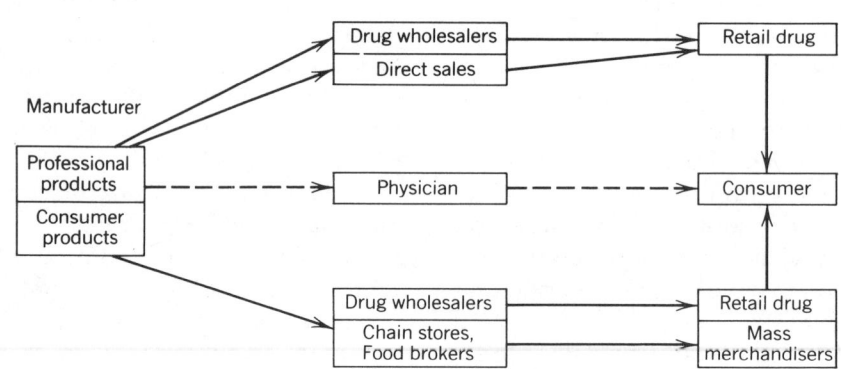

EXHIBIT 5
Changing Product Mix

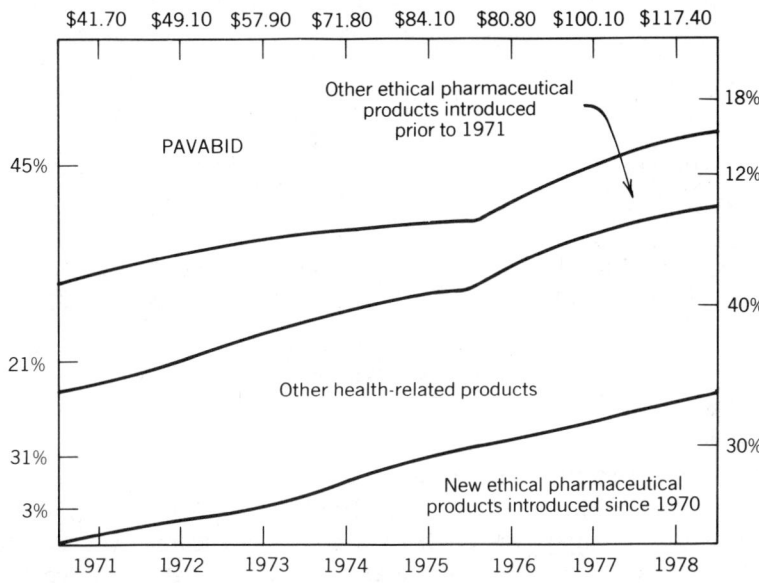

Source: 1978 Annual Report.

manufacturers of coronary vasodilators, including nitroglycerin compounds like Marion's Nitro-Bid, submit test data to prove product safety and efficacy. This review was the same process that Pavabid was subject to and a negative ruling, although not expected, would adversely affect the Company.

Proving its products to be safe and effective was only one area in which the Company dealt with the FDA. Before any ethical drug product could be marketed in the United States, Marion had to have the approval of the FDA. Under the system effective at that time, the company was required to conduct extensive animal tests, file an Investigational New Drug Application, conduct three phases of clinical human tests, file a New Drug Application, and submit all its data to the FDA for final review. With the FDA's approval, the drug firm could begin marketing the drug.

The approval process from lab discovery and patent application to FDA approval took from 7 to 10 years. Often a company had only seven or eight years of patent protection left to market its discovery and recover the average $50 million it had taken to fully develop the drug from the initial discovery stages.

To avoid the R & D expenses necessary to fully develop a new drug entity into a marketable product, Marion's source for new products was a process the company called "search and development." Marion licensed the basic compound from other drug manufacturers large enough to afford the basic research needed to discover new drugs. Generally, the licensors, most notably Servier of France and Chugai of Japan, were companies lacking the resources or expertise necessary to obtain FDA approval and marketing rights in the United States. Marion's R & D effort then concentrated on developing a product with an already identified pharmacological action into a drug marketable in the United States. By developing existing drug entities, Marion was able to

EXHIBIT 6
Selected Ethical Drug Companies, 1977 (In thousands of dollars)

	Net Sales	Cost of Goods Sold	R & D Expenses	Net Income[a]
Pfizer, Inc.	$2,031,900	$978,057	$ 98,282	$174,410
Merck and Co.	1,724,410	662,703	144,898	290,750
Eli Lilly and Co.	1,518,012	571,737	124,608	218,684
Upjohn, Inc.	1,134,325	—	102,256	91,521
SmithKline Corp.	780,337	299,338	61,777	89,271
G. D. Searle and Co.	749,583	345,224	52,645	(28,390)
Syntex Corp.	313,604	132,710	27,648	37,643
A. H. Robbins Co.	306,713	122,374	16,107	26,801
Rorer Group, Inc.	186,020	59,606	5,174	18,143
Marion Laboratories	100,131	37,330	5,907	10,652

Source: Drug and Cosmetic Industry (June, 1978).
[a] After-tax.

shorten the development time required to bring a new drug to market at a lower cost than discovering its own drugs. This enabled Marion to compete in an industry dominated by companies many times its own size. (See Exhibits 6 and 7 for drug industry information.)

In addition to the FDA, the federal government was also affecting the drug industry by promoting the use of generic substitution. In early 1979, 40 states had generic substitution laws that allowed nonbranded drugs to be substituted for branded and often more expensive drugs. The U. S. Department of Health, Education, and Welfare and the Federal Trade Commission had also recently proposed a model state substitution law and a listing of medically equivalent drugs. Under other federal programs, the Maximum Allowable Cost (MAC) guidelines, reimbursement for Medicaid and Medicare prescriptions was made at the lowest price at which a generic version was available.

Generics accounted for 12 percent of new prescriptions being written and were likely to increase in relative importance. To combat the decreasing profit margins that were expected, the industry was looking to its ability to develop new drugs to offset the expected shortfall that was expected in the 1980s caused by a loss of patent protection on many important drug compounds.

The effect that generic substitution laws would have on Marion was unclear. The company had always concentrated on products

EXHIBIT 7
Ethical Drug Industry Composite Statistics

	1978	1977	1976	1975
Sales ($ millions)	12,450	10,859	10,033	9,022
Operating Margin (%)	22.5	22.2	21.9	22.1
Income Tax Rate (%)	36.5	36.4	36.2	36.7
Net Profit Margin (%)	11.8	11.7	11.7	11.6
Earned on Net Worth (%)	18.5	17.9	18.2	18.4

Source: Value Line Investment Survey.

with a unique pharmacological action rather than those that were commodity in nature. Generic substitution required an "equivalent" drug be substituted for the brand-name drug and there were uncertainties about how equivalency would be defined.

Marion's pharmaceutical operations had not produced a major new product for several years. Products that were in various stages of development were diltiazen hydrochloride, an anti-anginal agent; sucralfate, a nonsystematic (does not enter the bloodstream) drug for the treatment of ulcers; and benflourex, a product that reduced cholesterol levels in the blood.

Health Products Group

Subsidiaries selling a wide range of products used in health-care and related fields made up Marion's Health Products Group. The company had bought and sold several subsidiaries since it began to diversify in 1968 (See Exhibit 3). By 1978 the group of subsidiaries was responsible for 39 percent of total company sales and 22 percent of earnings before taxes.

Several times after purchasing a company Marion had decided to sell or discontinue operations of a subsidiary. The divestment decision in the past had been based on considerations such as a weak market position, low growth position, excessive product liability, or a poor "fit" with the rest of Marion.

In his presentation before the Health Industry's Analyst Group, Fred Lyons noted the importance of a subsidiary fitting in with the rest of Marion when explaining the company's decision to sell Rose Manufacturing. "You may have noticed that during this past year we determined through out strategic planning that Rose Manufacturing, in the fall-protection area of industrial safety, did not fit either our marketing base or our technology base. Therefore we made a decision to spin Rose off, and we successfully culminated its sale in November 1977. Rose, like Signet Laboratories three years ago, just did not fit."

In adjusting its corporate profile Marion was always searching for companies that provided good investment potentials and were consistent with the company's goals. To provide a framework within which to evaluate potential acquisitions and to avoid some of the mistakes made in past purchases, Marion developed a set of acquisition criteria to be applied to possible subsidiary investments.

Search Criteria for Acquisitions

Product Area	Health Care
Market	$100 million potential with 8 percent minimum growth rate
Net Sales	$3–30 million
Tangible Net Worth	Not less than $1 million
Return on Investment	Not less than 20 percent pre-tax
Method of Payment	Cash or stock

The Board of Directors made the ultimate decision on the acquisitions and divestment of Marion's subsidiaries. At the corporate level, Mr. Herman was responsible for evaluating changes in the corporate portfolio and based on his analysis making recommendations to the Board. Since Mr. Herman was also on the Board of Directors, his recommendations were heavily weighted in the Board's final decision.

In early 1979 Marion had four subsidiaries in its Health Products Group: Marion Health and Safety, Inc., Optico Industries, American Stair Glide, and Kalo Laboratories. Following is a brief description of each:

Marion Health and Safety, Inc. sold a broad line of hospital and industrial safety products through its Marion Scientific Corp. and Health and Safety Products Division. Recently introduced Marion Scientific products (a consumer-oriented insect bite treatment and a device for transporting anaerobic cultures) both showed good acceptance and growth in their respective markets. Distribution is generally through medical/surgical wholesalers and distributors that in turn resell to hospital, medical laboratories, reference laboratories, etc. Health and Safety Division manufactures and/or packages primarily safety-related products (hearing protection, eyewash, etc.) and first-aid kits and kit products, such as wraps, bandaids, and various OTC products. Sales of these products are made to safety equipment wholesalers/distributors that resell to hospitals, industry, institutions, etc. Sales of Marion Health and Safety, Inc. were estimated to have increased about 17 percent by outside analysts to a level estimated at $19.0 million. Pre-tax margins were about 10 percent in this industry. Marion Health and Safety, Inc., was headquartered in Rockford, Illinois.

Optico Industries, Inc. participated in the wholesale and retail optical industry. Its main products were glass and plastic prescription eyeglass lenses and hard contact lenses. Outside analysts estimated this subsidiary recorded sales gains of about 26 percent for 1978 for sales estimated to be about $8 million. Optico had reduced profitability during 1978 because of expansion of its retail facilities. Pre-tax margins for 1978 were estimated at 6 percent, but this was expected to improve when the expansion program was completed. Optico's headquarters were located in Tempe, Arizona.

American Stair Glide Corp. manufactured and marketed home stairway and porch lifts and other products to aid physically handicapped individuals. These products were principally sold to medical/surgical supply dealers for resale or rental to the consumer. In some instances distribution is through elevator companies. Sales were estimated at about $5 million annually by outside analysts. This subsidiary was expected to grow slowly and steadily and it had a very stable historical earnings pattern. The trend for greater access to buildings for the handicapped was expected to impact favorably on this Grandview, Missouri based subsidiary.

Kalo Laboratories, Inc.

Kalo Laboratories operated in the specialty agricultural chemical market and provided products to meet specialized user needs. In the past, Kalo had been successful in marketing its line of specialty products. (See Exhibit 8: Kalo's Past Earnings Information.) In assessing Kalo's future there were many risks to consider. These risks included competition from large chemical companies, governmental regulatory actions, and uncertain future product potentials.

EXHIBIT 8
Kalo Laboratories Sales, Investment, and Expense Information

	1978	1977	1976	1975	1974	1973
	Dollars in Millions					
Sales	$9 M	$5 M	$2 M	$4 M	$3 M	$2 M
Total Assets	$5.0 M	$4.0 M	$2.0 M	$2.0 M	$2.0 M	$1.0 M
Total Investment[a]	3.0 M	3.0 M	1.0 M	1.0 M	1.0 M	0.5 M
	Expenses as Percent of Sales					
COGS	43%	54%	61%	53%	55%	48%
R & D Expense	8%	7%	7%	5%	5%	3%
Marketing, Selling, and General Administrative Expenses	37%	31%	42%	23%	24%	27%

[a]Includes Marion's equity in Kalo and funds lent on a long-term basis.

EXHIBIT 9
Total and Agriculture-Related Sales Selected Companies, 1979

	Total Sales (millions)	Agriculture Related Sales (millions)	Earnings (pre-tax)
Eli Lilly	$2,520	$920[a]	28.6%
Pfizer	3,030	480[a]	9.8
Upjohn	1,755	280[a]	9.2
Marion (1978)	100	9	9.0

Source: Value Line Investment Survey.
[a]Includes International Sales.

Competition and Industry

The American and Canadian agricultural chemical market was estimated to be $3.2 billion in 1978 and to grow at more than 15 percent a year.[3] The industry was dominated by large chemical manufacturers, such as Dow Chemical, DuPont, Stauffer Chemical, and Gulf Oil. The market was also shared by large ethical drug manufacturers including Eli Lilly, Pfizer, and Upjohn. (See Exhibit 9 for agriculture-related sales.) Economics of scale allowed the larger companies to produce large amounts of what might be perceived as a commodity product (herbicides, insecticides, and fungicides) at a much lower cost per unit than the smaller companies. Diversification of and within agricultural product lines assured the larger manufacturers even performance for their agricultural divisions as a whole.

Since smaller chemical companies like Kalo could not afford to produce large enough amounts of their products to match the efficiency and prices of the large companies, these firms concentrated on specialty markets with unique product needs. By identifying specialty chemical needs in the agricultural segment, Kalo was able to produce its products and develop markets that were very profitable but were not large enough to attract the bigger firms.

Products

Since the larger chemical companies dominated the large product segments, Kalo's products were designed to meet the specialized needs of its agricultural users. Kalo's product line was divided into four major classes: seed treatments, adjuvants, bactericides, and herbicides.

Seed treatments for soybeans accounted for the majority of Kalo's sales. One product in this area was Triple Noctin. Products in the seed treatment class were intended to act on soybean seeds to increase their viability once in the ground. Kalo manufactured seed treatments for soybeans only.

Adjuvants were chemicals that, when added to another agricultural product, increased the efficacy of the product or made it easier to use. For instance, Biofilmo prevented liquid fertilizer from foaming which made it easier to apply, and Hydro-Wet enhanced the soils' receptiveness to certain chemicals, which reduced runoff into surrounding areas.

The newest product for Kalo was the adjuvant EXTEND, a chemical compound added to fertilizer that made it bind chemically with the soil or plant. The binding process helped keep the fertilizer where it was applied, which made each application last longer and more effective. EXTEND was only recently introduced and its success was difficult to assess at such an early stage. Kalo's management was planning to build a family of products around EXTEND. Sales projections showed EXTEND contributing between 60–70 percent of Kalo's future growth through 1987.

Bactericides and herbicides were the final two product classes at Kalo. Bactericides were applied to the soil to either inhibit or encourage the growth of selected bacteria. One product, ISOBAC, was used to control boll rot in cotton. Herbicides, mainly for broadleaf

---

[3]1979 DuPont Annual Report and 1979 Upjohn Annual Report.

plants, were used to control or kill unwanted weeds leaving the desirable crop unharmed.

In the past, Kalo had acquired several of its products by acquiring the company that manufactured the product. When it purchased a going-concern intact, Kalo was able to gain both manufacturing facilities and an existing distribution system. In the future Kalo expected to diversify its product line in a similar fashion. To enlarge its existing product lines, Kalo was planning to use both internal and contract R & D. An example of enlarging the product family was the planned adaptation of its products to different crop applications.

Because Kalo did not have a well-diversified product line, its operations were more cyclical than the overall agricultural sector. Two major factors beyond Kalo's control made its annual performance extremely unpredictable, the weather and spot prices for commodities.

Kalo's operating results were seasonal, because its products were primarily intended to be applied in the spring months. It was not unusual for the subsidiary to show a net loss from operations for the nine months from July until March and then to show a large profit in the three months April, May, and June when the products were being purchased for immediate application. If the spring months were particularly rainy, Kalo's profitability was adversely affected. Heavy farm equipment could not operate on wet fields without getting stuck and application was impossible until the fields dried out. Once the fields were dry, Kalo's agricultural users often did not have time to apply the herbicides or other products, even though it would have been economically advantageous to do so.

The other factor that affected the demand for Kalo's products was the spot pricing of commodities. The price of commodities relative to each other had a large effect on the total amount of each type of crop planted. Because the producer was free to switch crops yearly based on the spot prices, Kalo's demand for the upcoming planting season was uncertain and variable. Kalo was particularly vulnerable to swings in demand caused by the substitutability of crops since many of their products were applicable only to soybeans.

Distribution and Marketing

The end user of Kalo's products was usually the individual farmer. Kalo and the rest of the agricultural chemical industry had a distribution system similar to the one shown below.

Kalo promoted its products with a sales force of about 30 salesmen. The main task of these salesmen was to call on and educate wholesalers/distributors on the advantages, unique qualities, and methods of selling Kalo's products. In addition, some end-user information was distributed to farmers, using "pull" advertising to create demand. A limited amount of promotion was done at agricultural shows and state fairs but because of the expense involved this type of promotion was not used often.

Kalo's Future

Sales forecasts prepared by the staff analysts for Mr. Herman looked very promising because they predicted sales gains of from $4–6

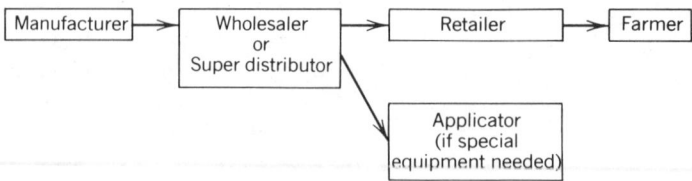

EXHIBIT 10
Kalo Laboratories Forecasted Sales and Asset Turnover

	1979	1980	1981	1982	1983	1984	1985	1986	1987
Net Sales $MM (Current Dollars)	12	16	20	25	30	35	40	45	50
Asset Turnover	1.8x	1.8x	1.9x	1.9x	1.9x	1.9x	1.9x	1.9x	1.85x

Note: After-tax margin expected to increase to 7% by 1984. Authors' estimates.

million for each of the next nine years. (See Exhibit 10.) There were, however, some important assumptions on which the forecasts were based.

As mentioned earlier 60–70 percent of the forecasted growth was to come from a product family based on the new product EXTEND. A great deal of uncertainty surrounded the product, however. Since it was new, the current success of EXTEND was difficult to measure, particularly in determining how current sales translated into future performance. If the market evaluation for EXTEND and related products were correct and if a family of products could be developed around EXTEND, then the sales potential for the proposed product family was very promising provided Kalo was able to exploit the available sales opportunities.

Additional growth projected in the sales forecasts was to come from existing products and undefined future products that were to be developed or acquired. Approximately 20 percent of the growth was to come from the existing products in the next four–five years. Ten to 20 percent of the growth in the later years of the forecast was expected to come from currently unknown products.

For Kalo to realize the forecasted growth, it was necessary for Marion to provide financing. It was going to be impossible for Kalo to generate all the required funds internally. Kalo had been a net user of cash, provided by Marion, since 1976. (See Exhibit 8: Kalo's Sales and Earnings Information, Exhibit 11: Kalo's Balance Sheets at June 30, 1978, Exhibit 12: Balance Sheets and Exhibit 13: Ten-Year Financial Summary for information about Marion's in-

EXHIBIT 11
Kalo Laboratories Balance Sheet June 30, 1978

Current Assets	$2.5MM	Current Liabilities	$1.4MM
PP & E (net)	1.9MM	Long-Term Debt	1.0MM
Other	0.2MM	Capital	2.2MM
Total	$4.6MM	Total	$4.6MM

Authors' estimates.

EXHIBIT 12
Consolidated Balance Sheet 1977 and 1978

	June 30,	
	1978	1977
Assets		
Current assets:		
Cash	$ 381,116	$ 961,588
Short-term investments, at cost which approximates market	2,561,660	10,028,297
Accounts and notes receivable, less allowances for returns and doubtful accounts of $1,845,466 and $2,305,793	28,196,199	20,576,412
Inventories	19,640,945	15,568,170
Prepaid expenses	2,305,403	1,461,367
Deferred income tax benefits	757,585	895,110
Total current assets	53,842,908	49,490,944
Property, plant, and equipment, at cost		

(*Continued*)

EXHIBIT 12 (Continued)

	June 30,	
	1978	1977
Land and land improvements	2,832,588	2,935,671
Buildings	24,458,746	25,224,652
Machinery and equipment	19,671,607	18,110,907
Aircraft and related equipment	1,670,904	1,670,904
Construction in progress	365,311	357,338
	48,999,156	48,299,472
Less accumulated depreciation	10,725,533	8,585,190
Net property, plant, and equipment	38,273,623	39,714,282
Other assets		
Intangible assets	4,774,055	2,042,762
Notes receivable (noncurrent)	890,692	11,589
Marketable equity securities, at market value	688,914	—
Deferred income tax benefits (noncurrent)	318,434	249,647
Miscellaneous	99,597	141,232
Total other assets	6,771,692	2,445,230
Total assets	$98,888,223	$91,650,456

Liabilities and Stockholders' Equity

Current liabilities		
Current maturities of long-term debt	$ 82,102	$ 95,004
Accounts payable, trade	3,979,341	4,224,105
Accrued profit-sharing expense	1,752,515	243,096
Other accrued expenses	3,864,168	3,008,238
Dividends payable	1,260,612	1,198,938
Income taxes payable	4,391,252	5,030,219
Total current liabilities	15,329,990	13,799,600
Long-term debt, excluding current maturities	15,580,072	15,661,399
Deferred income taxes payable	1,107,000	733,000
Deferred compensation	177,975	172,889
Stockholders' equity		
Preferred stock of $1 par value per share Authorized 250,000		

(Continued)

EXHIBIT 12 (Continued)

	June 30,	
	1978	1977
shares; none issued	—	—
Common stock of $1 par value per share Authorized 20,000,000 shares; issued 8,703,346 shares	8,703,346	8,703,346
Paid-in capital	3,474,358	3,475,443
Retained earnings	58,358,925	51,604,550
	70,536,629	63,783,339
Less:		
293,153 shares of common stock in treasury, at cost (189,500 shares in 1977)	3,819,243	2,499,771
Net unrealized loss on noncurrent marketable equity securities	24,200	—
Total stockholders' equity	66,693,186	61,283,568
Commitments and contingent liabilities		
Total liabilities and stockholders' equity	$98,888,223	$91,650,456

Source: 1978 Annual Report.

vestment in Kalo.) Marion's management did not consider the amount of cash provided through the first part of 1979 to be excessive as long as Kalo maintained adequate profitability and steady growth rates. In addition to the long-term funds provided by Marion, Kalo also required short-term financing of inventory during each year because of the seasonality of its sales.

Government Regulation

Another major uncertainty in Kalo's future was an unpredictable regulatory climate. Regulation of agricultural chemicals was under the jurisdiction of the Environmental Protection Agency (EPA). Compliance with the EPA was a similar process to that of the FDA. The process of developing and introducing a new

EXHIBIT 13
Ten-Year Financial Summary (Dollar Amounts in Thousands Except per Share Data)

	Years Ended June 30,									
	1978	1977	1976	1975	1974	1973	1972	1971	1970	1969
Sales										
Net sales	$117,378	$100,131	$80,838	$84,096	$71,778	$57,937	$49,066	$41,692	$35,322	$30,188
Cost of sales	43,177	37,330	29,315	26,078	21,715	18,171	14,932	12,262	10,622	8,985
Gross profit	74,201	62,801	51,523	58,018	50,063	39,766	34,134	29,430	24,700	21,203
Operating expenses	51,718	43,397	37,292	31,699	26,991	21,155	19,164	17,181	13,828	12,453
Operating income	22,483	19,404	14,231	26,319	23,072	18,611	14,970	12,249	10,872	8,750
Other income	1,581	1,194	683	1,404	1,033	722	709	599	630	328
Interest expense	1,546	1,542	898	97	83	109	116	88	198	260
Earnings										
Earnings from continuing operations before income taxes	22,518	19,056	14,016	27,626	24,022	19,224	15,563	12,760	11,304	8,818
Income taxes	10,804	8,404	5,628	13,295	11,791	9,297	7,730	6,364	5,899	4,493
Earnings from continuing operations	11,714	10,652	8,388	14,331	12,231	9,927	7,833	6,396	5,405	4,325
Earnings (loss) from discontinued operations	—	—	—	(3,617)	(120)	76	488	—	—	—
Net earnings	$ 11,714	$ 10,652	$ 8,388	$10,714	$12,111	$10,003	$ 8,321	$ 6,396[a]	$ 5,405	$ 4,325
Common Share Data										
Earnings (loss) per common and common equivalent share										
Continuing operations	$ 1.38	$ 1.23	$ 0.96	$ 1.65	$ 1.40	$ 1.14	$ 0.90	$ 0.76	$ 0.65	$ 0.52
Discontinued operations	—	—	—	(0.42)	(0.01)	0.01	0.06	—	—	—
Net earnings	$ 1.38	$ 1.23	$ 0.96	$ 1.23	$ 1.39	$ 1.15	$ 0.96	$ 0.76[a]	$ 0.65	$ 0.52
Cash dividends per common share	$ 0.59	$ 0.53	$ 0.52	$ 0.48	$ 0.28	$ 0.21	$ 0.20	$ 0.16	$ 0.12	$ 0.12
Stockholders' equity per common and common equivalent share	$ 7.87	$ 7.09	$ 6.63	$ 6.29	$ 5.52	$ 4.16	$ 3.16	$ 2.52	$ 2.01	$ 1.47
Weighted average number of outstanding common and common share equivalents	8,475	8,640	8,707	8,708	8,689	8,715	8,651	8,396	8,377	8,354

Source: 1978 Annual Report.
[a]Before extraordinary charge of $916,000, equal to $0.11 per common share resulting from the disposition of investment in affiliated companies.

chemical product took from eight–ten years, including the two–five years necessary to obtain EPA approval. The costs of developing and bringing a new product to market were generally from $5–10 million.

Once a product was on the market, the EPA had powers of recall similar to the FDA and could require the company to do additional research after the product was introduced. The prospect of having a product removed from the market was an added element of risk for Kalo. No problems were expected for Kalo, although several of the subsidiary's products (particularly its herbicides and bactericides) had a relatively high potential for environmental problems, if not applied correctly.

The Decision

Mr. Herman knew that in making his recommendation he would have to balance the immediate and long-term resource needs and the goals of Marion. Although Kalo looked promising from the forecasts, there were many uncertainties surrounding these subsidiaries' futures that had to be considered.

Since Marion had no new drug products

ready to be introduced soon, the company would have to rely on other areas of the Company to reach its growth goals. Kalo was growing, but it was also requiring a constant input of funds from its parent.

One possibility for growth was to purchase another drug manufacturer and add its products to Marion's, taking advantage of any distribution synergies that might exist. To make such a purchase, the company would need more resources. To sell a subsidiary could provide needed resources, but to do so quickly under less than optimum conditions would surely result in a significantly lower price than could be realized under normal conditions. The income and cash flow impact of this approach would be undesirable.

With the Board meeting so soon, Mr. Herman was faced with analyzing the complex situation quickly. In three days he would have to make his recommendation to the Board of Directors.

MOBIL CORPORATION

Introduction

Having just been given her first formal assignment as a new financial analyst for a well-known New York Bank, Margaret Wells stared pensively at an imposing stack of annual reports, 10-K's, statistical summaries, and previous bank evaluations of Mobil Corporation. She had brought all of this material home in anticipation of a long weekend of preparation for her formal analysis and report on Mobil Corporation to the bank's officer group on Monday morning. Margaret, who was a recent MBA, had just finished the bank's training program, and was eager to do well on her first assignment. She had already reviewed the material several times, but had only the usual collection of figures and statistics to show for her efforts.

She knew, for example, that Mobil Corporation was currently the second largest oil company in the United States, and one of the ten largest industrial corporations in the world. As a fully integrated, multinational corporation, Mobil was actively engaged in both upstream (exploration and production) and downstream activities (refining, marketing, transportation, and chemicals). By 1980, Mobil's assets had grown to $32.7 billion, and both earnings ($3.3 billion) and capital expenditures ($4.8 billion) were at record levels. In fact, capital expenditures had increased by an astounding 225 percent over 1978 levels. For the previous decade (1969–1979), Mobil showed the highest average annual growth in earnings per share (+16.02 percent) among all of the major U. S. oil companies.[1] Moreover, this had been achieved while showing a higher average annual return to investors (15.22 percent for 1969–1979, including capital appreciation) than any of the other majors. Even with the huge capital outlay in 1979, Mobil still showed a 65.9 percent return to investors for that year, second only to Shell Oil at 75.4 percent.[2]

When Margaret considered that Mobil was the smallest of the "seven sisters" (Exxon, Gulf, Standard Oil of California or Socal, Texaco, British Petroleum, and Royal-Dutch Shell) when it was formed back in 1931 and that it always had a competitive disadvantage in natural resources, it was clear that Mobil had been

---

Source: This case was prepared by Bill Clark under the supervision of Professor M. Edgar Barrett, Southern Methodist University. Permission to use granted by Professor M. Edgar Barrett.

---

[1] "The Fortune Directory," *Fortune,* May 5, 1980, pp. 276–277.
[2] *Ibid.*

doing something right, particularly in recent times. There had been dynamic changes in the international petroleum industry during the past decade. Increasing economic and political pressures had placed heavy demands on the management teams, corporate strategies, and operating policies of the major oil companies. Mobil appeared to have handled itself well in the more restrictive and volatile business climate of the 1970s, and Margaret hoped to discover those factors that might distinguish Mobil Corporation from its competitors. She wondered what factors might have shaped Mobil's business strategy and corporate evolution, and how these factors might affect its future development. She therefore decided to start once again from the beginning and outline all of the pertinent material on Mobil's past and present position in the petroleum industry.

Historical Background

Mobil's corporate roots could be traced in one direction back to the formation of Vacuum Oil in 1866, and in another, to John D. Rockefeller's Standard Oil Trust, which later absorbed the smaller company. Vacuum Oil was founded by Hiram Bond Everest and Matthew Ewing, who had invented a new process of distilling crude oil under a vacuum in 1865. At that time, a gallon of kerosene sold for twice as much as a barrel of crude oil, and Ewing believed that his vacuum process could produce more kerosene from a barrel of crude than other known refining methods. Everest, on the other hand, recognized the possibilities of using the oily residue from the distilling process as a petroleum lubricant for machinery and leather. Everest decided to finance the new venture, and Vacuum Oil was founded in 1866.

After some initial consumer resistance, the quality and utility of Everest's lubricants were proven in the marketplace and Vacuum Oil began growing rapidly. The favorable reputation of Vacuum Oil finally attracted the attention of Rockefeller's Standard Oil Company, and in 1879, Rockefeller bought a controlling interest in the smaller company. Under Standard's aegis, Vacuum Oil evolved into a company whose primary functions were refining, domestic and foreign marketing, domestic manufacturing, and distribution of specialty products. By 1912, Vacuum had become an international lubricating oil company, two-thirds of whose business volume was outside the United States.

Standard Oil Company of New York (Socony) was the other of Mobil's immediate ancestors. When the huge Standard Oil Trust was broken up in the historical antitrust action of 1911, Socony was one of 33 fragments of the original company. In 1912, Socony had both an extensive export business and a wide marketing outlet system. However, the company had no crude oil resources, nor was it involved in the lubricating products business. In fact, after leaving the Standard Oil Trust, neither Socony nor Vacuum Oil had any significant strength in exploration or production. Consequently, both companies began trying to integrate operations in the United States and abroad in order to shore up their respective weaknesses. In 1918, Socony acquired 70 percent of the stock of a Texas oil-producing company called Magnolia Petroleum Company that had crude oil production, reserves, refineries, and pipelines in the Southwest. Later, in 1925, Socony, which had assets of $90 million, acquired all of the properties of Magnolia Petroleum Co. Other acquisitions included the General Petroleum Corporation of California (1926), which had production properties, refineries, and marketing facilities on the West Coast, and the White Eagle Oil and Refining Company of Kansas City (1930), which had refineries in Wyoming and Kansas. These acquisitions provided considerable new oil reserves and strengthened the company's marketing network throughout the United States.

Socony and Vacuum Oil merged in 1931, forming Socony–Vacuum, with international capabilities to produce, refine, and market petroleum products. Thus, Socony–Vacuum (later to become Mobil) emerged as the youngest and smallest of the American "sisters." In 1933, Socony–Vacuum pooled its properties and business operations in the Far East with properties owned by Standard Oil Company of New Jersey. Each company owned 50 percent of the stock of the newly formed company called Standard–Vacuum Oil Company, which handled Far Eastern operations.

In 1936, Socony–Vacuum and Texaco, Inc. each acquired a 50 percent interest in South American Gulf Oil Co. and a 49.94 percent interest in Columbian Petroleum Company. Mobil sold its interest in these companies in 1972. In 1955, the company changed its name to Socony Mobil Oil Corporation. By then, Mobil was already heavily dependent on the Middle East, which supplied 50 percent of the company's total crude oil. In 1961, Mobil acquired the oil and gas properties and other assets of Republic Natural Gas Co. In the following year, the company transferred its business and assets in the Far East, representing its 50 percent ownership of Standard Vacuum Oil Co., into a new company called Mobil Petroleum Company, Inc. The new firm's affiliates and branches were later brought under the single management of Mobil International Oil Co. (1965).

Other acquisitions in the 1960s and 1970s included Kordite Corp. (1962); Goliad Corp., a gas processor in Louisiana and Texas (1962); Forum Insurance Company (1963); the worldwide paint and chemical coatings interests of Martin Marietta Corp. (1962); Virginia–Carolina Chemical Corp. (1962); Northern Natural Gas Producing Co. (1962); Industrias Atlas S. A., a manufacturer of industrial and consumer paints in Mexico (1965); Goodling Electric Co., Inc. (1968); Aral Italiana, an Italian subsidiary of Aral AG, West Germany (1971); Pastucol Cos., three Italian firms that manufactured and marketed polyethylene film products (1971); Marcor Corporation, which operated through two subsidiaries, Montgomery Ward and Co., Inc. and Container Corp. of America (1974); and, W. F. Hall Printing Co. (1979).

In terms of the petroleum business proper, Mobil spent the three decades following its formation in 1931 consolidating its diverse holdings and subsidiaries. The company later dropped "Socony" from its name and was known as Mobil Oil Corporation until 1976, after which it was known simply as Mobil Corporation. Throughout its corporate evolution, Mobil continued to be well known as a manufacturer of high-grade industrial lubricants. In 1969, Albert Nickerson, Chief Executive Officer at Mobil, noted:

> In most of the world after World War II, the company had really been just a lubricant marketer. Then we started to expand into one European market after another; we constructed refineries; we improved our crude oil sufficiency.[3]

Even so, Mobil continued to be short of crude oil reserves relative to the other majors, and its reputation in lubricants had followed the company into recent times. An article from the August 1978 issue of *Industrial Marketing* highlighted Mobil's current emphasis on industrial lubricants.

> Mobil Oil Corp. announced a new print ad campaign . . . that will emphasize the company's service and technological expertise in the industrial lubrication market. . . . the new ads are part . . . of an evolutionary communications effort which for the past 10 years has been positioning Mobil as the leader in supplying total lubrication programs to industry.[4]

Thus, Mobil Corporation, now the second largest oil company in the United States, still retained part of its heritage, which could be

---

[3]"How to Rob Peter . . . ," *Forbes*, June 15, 1969, pp. 30–31.
[4]"New Mobil Pro Ad Campaign Stresses Expertise in Industrial Lubricants," *Industrial Marketing*, August 1978, p. 22.

traced to Vacuum Oil, a small producer of petroleum lubricants that had been capitalized in 1866 for $10,000.

Corporate Structure

Mobil's historical and current shortage of crude oil has been an important factor in shaping its corporate structure. Part of the current shortage problem can be traced back to the late 1940s, when Texaco and California Standard, who were then co-owners of Arabian–American Oil Co., offered 40 percent of Aramco to Jersey Standard and Mobil. At that time, the problem was apparently not considered as critical as it became later in the 1970s. As noted in *Forbes*, August 1, 1971:

> Mobil, nervous about the concomitant obligation to absorb its share of crude oil, opted for 10 percent rather than the 20 percent it could have bought. . . . Last year that extra 10 percent would have brought Mobil another 100 million barrels of oil. It could have meant upwards of $25 million in earnings, 25 cents a share.[5]

In the same article, Rawleigh Warner, Jr., Mobil's Chairman, commented:

> That (decision) cost us a tremendous amount of money. . . . the oil companies that year in and year out make the most money because they are balanced. They move their own crude, they refine their own crude, and they sell their own crude.[6]

Although Mobil negotiated a five-year contract in the mid-1970s to acquire another five percent of Aramco, the company still suffered from a shortage of crude oil relative to the other majors. Mobil's dependence on Mideast oil was particularly evident during the Arab–Israeli war in 1956. Mobil's earnings suffered much more than its competitors with the closing of the Suez Canal during that conflict. These events underscored Mobil's corporate vulnerability, and senior management apparently decided that it would have to compensate for its weakness in natural resources through greater efficiency and better organization.

Many of the smaller subsidiaries that had been acquired by Socony and Vacuum were not fully integrated into Mobil's corporate structure upon or even somewhat after their acquisition. These companies often retained their original staffs, operating procedures, and corporate identities. In 1959, Albert L. Nickerson, Chief Executive Officer of Mobil, initiated an extensive company-wide program of reorganization that included the full integration of some of the more independent of Mobil's subsidiaries.

Concerted efforts were made to cut fixed costs in the form of redundant staff services, improve efficiency in exploration and production through better coordination among subsidiaries, and redefine corporate strategy. These efforts were painful. They were, however, thought to be necessary in the shrinking world of international competition and short supply. This new philosophy of lean organizational structure quickly became a continuing corporate policy, and one which Mobil would pride itself on in the future.

In a more recent time, Rawleigh Warner, Jr., Chairman of the corporation since 1969, and William P. Tavoularas, appointed as President the same year, had guided Mobil through the traumatic 1970s. Both men had risen through the ranks of the company on the financial side. This was somewhat unique because the engineering ladder was, for most oil companies, a more normal way. Warner received a liberal arts degree from Princeton. Tavoularas started with Mobil in 1947 in the accounting department, and later received a law degree.[7] Tavoularas was named the first manager of the newly formed planning department in 1959, part of Nickerson's program of

---

[5]"The Lively Tortoise," *Forbes*, August 1, 1971, pp. 18–19.
[6]*Ibid*.

[7]"What Makes Mobil Run," *Business Week*, June 13, 1977, pp. 80–85.

reorganization. Mobil's corporate strategy had become more forward-looking at that time, and formal planning was to play a major role in future development. One oil analyst who worked in planning and finance at Mobil for 10 years said, "Mobil is a lawyer–businessman company rather than an oilman–geologist company. Planning is the real essence of this company."[8]

Both men continued the trend toward leaner staffing and greater consolidation. In 1973, Mobil's U. S. marketing force, which had previously operated through seven divisions, was consolidated into four regional offices, whose greater efficiency was expected to save the company about $10 million a year.[9]

Prior to 1974, Mobil was organized into four operating divisions. The North American Division was Mobil's operating petroleum division for the United States and Canada. The International Division coordinated the petroleum operations of Mobil affiliates outside the United States and Canada. By 1967, it had oil and gas acreage in 18 countries, refining operations in 19 countries, and marketing outlets under the Mobil brand in more than 50 countries. The Mobil Chemical Company was an operating division formed in 1960 that coordinated the chemical operations of Mobil affiliates in the United States and several other countries. This division was involved in the manufacture of agricultural and industrial chemicals, plastics, paints, chemical coatings, and petrochemicals. The fourth division was Transportation, including domestic trucking, pipelines, and deep-sea carriers.

In 1974, the North American Division was reorganized to exclude Canada; the resulting divisions were U. S. Operations and Foreign Operations. Two years later, on July 1, 1976, a holding company was formed called Mobil Corporation, encompassing the Mobil Oil Corporation, which included domestic and foreign energy operations, the Mobil Chemical Company, Montgomery Ward, and Container Corporation. So there were still four operating segments, but they were now distinguished as follows: Energy Operations, including the subdivisions of U.S. Energy Operations and Foreign Energy Operations; Chemical Operations; Retail Merchandising; and Paperboard Packaging.[10]

The latest change (January 1, 1979) in this trend towards greater consolidation was the merger of the marketing and refining segments of Mobil's U. S. and foreign operations within the Energy division.[11]

Exploration and Production

During the 1970s, all of the major oil companies placed more emphasis on exploration and production at the expense of downstream activities—refining and marketing. OPEC played a major role in this upstream movement of the majors. The rate of growth in demand for petroleum products, which had increased steadily since 1940, was finally stunted in the 1970s. This was caused in large part by the fact that OPEC raised prices dramatically (from $2.59 per barrel in 1972 to over $40 per barrel in 1980). In this business climate, the majors were naturally most concerned about ensuring a stable and continuing supply of crude oil.

Like the other majors, Mobil substantially increased its exploration activities during the 1970s. Mobil's commitment to a strong exploration program can be tracked back to the Suez crisis in 1956. Then Mobil's Mideast oil supplies were seriously disrupted and the company paid dearly to acquire crude. Mobil reacted to this situation by reorganizing in 1959. This reorganization served to grant exploration activities a higher priority in the corporation.

---

[8]Ibid.
[9]"Mobil Reshuffle Aims at Cost-Cutting," *National Petroleum News,* September 1973, p. 145.

[10]Mobil Annual Report, 1976.
[11]Mobil Annual Report, 1979.

Exploration operations, previously split between the parent company and two acquired subsidiaries, were pooled. In addition, a planning department was created and the senior planning officer was given a seat on the board in order to counter the board's bias for refining and marketing investments.

During the 1960s, Mobil doubled its land position to nearly 100 million acres. Because some of these drilling rights were acquired between 15 and 20 years ago, they have become incredible bargains. For example, Mobil paid $27,000 for the rights to 13 million acres of Newfoundland in 1965. By contrast, the company paid as much as $36,000 an acre in the Gulf of Mexico 10 years later.[12]

By the late 1970s, Mobil's strategy, which called for an increased emphasis on exploration and production activities, was finally paying off. Mobil held an interest in nine giant oil and gas fields that were discovered during 1979 and the first half of 1980, each of which could net Mobil the equivalent of at least 100 million barrels of new reserves. "We've hit on some kind of formula in exploration," says Tavoulareas. 'We hope we are in a cycle where each year we can find a big field, and if we do, I'm not worried about our future.'"[13]

During 1980, Mobil devoted a record $3 billion in exploration and production capital expenditures and exploration costs that were expensed. This represented an increase of 150 percent over 1978 investments of $1.2 billion. Of the $3 billion, $434 million was spent on lease bonuses (down from $629 million in 1979). Almost $2 billion was spent on exploration and production activities within the United States.

In 1979, the company paid $792 million to acquire the oil and gas operations of General Crude Oil Company. During 1980, Mobil bought Trans Ocean Oil, Inc. for $715 million.

The purchase added over 60 million barrels of proved reserves of oil and natural gas equivalents as well as 2.0 million acres of undeveloped property. This acreage included 500,000 acres along the Overthrust Belt in Wyoming and brought Mobil's total exploration acreage in the United States to 10.1 million acres.

Offshore Activities

More recent improvements may well have made Mobil the leader in offshore geophysics work. The company launched a $14 million geophysical vessel, the T. W. Nelsen, in 1978. It was considered the industry's most sophisticated vessel of its kind. This may explain why Mobil bid so aggressivly in the December 1979 sale of federal drilling leases off Massachusetts. Mobil spent $222 million, more than one-quarter of the money the government took in.[14] Although some people involved in the industry believed that Mobil simply overbid, others suspected that Mobil saw more valuable structures in the area because it had better data.

At the Gulf of Mexico lease sale in September 1980, Mobil spent $301 million for eight tracts off the shore of Louisiana. Mobil spent $1.5 billion from 1970 through 1979 for leases in the Gulf. (Exxon was the only other company to have spent that much in the area.) Mobil has installed 92 platforms in the Gulf since 1970. The company's share of production from all the platforms at year-end 1980 was 261,500 b/d of oil equivalent.

Mobil's exploratory acreage at Mobile Bay, Alabama consisted of 20,000 acres, 100 percent owned. These acres, located in state waters, were acquired in 1969 at low cost. Mobil completed a discovery well in 1979 that flowed 12.2 million cubic feet per day of natural gas. The company recently acquired drilling permits for four additional wells. Mobil has estimated re-

---

[12]"Mobil's Successful Exploration," *Business Week*, October 13, 1980, p. 112.
[13]*Ibid*.

[14]*Ibid*.

serves on the acreage to be between 200 and 600 billion cubic feet. However, industry analysts believed that the potential of the area was much higher—nearly one-trillion cubic feet.[15] A state lease sale in Alabama held in March 1981 had high bonus bids of over $500 million, highlighting Mobil's already strong position in the area.

Foreign Activities

Mobil acquired the rights to drill for oil on 13 million acres offshore Newfoundland in 1965. The company, however, just performed seismic activity in the area. The decision was influenced by results in the vicinity where other companies had previously drilled nearly 50 unsuccessful wildcats. Finally, Mobil got Chevron and Gulf to do the drilling by offering them farm-outs, with shares in its acreage position in exchange.

In 1979, a major oil field was discovered by a Chevron-operated rig drilling 200 miles off the east coast of Newfoundland. This play, known as the Hibernia structure, was estimated to contain 1.5 billion barrels of oil. More important than Hibernia (in which Mobil's share had been reduced to 28 percent) was the surrounding area known as the Jeanne d'Arc Basin. Mobil held a 60 percent interest in this structure that was estimated to contain potential reserves of 10 billion barrels. That would make this the largest oil find since Prudhoe Bay was discovered in 1968.

The Arun Field in Indonesia had reserves of more than 500-million barrels of condensate and 11-trillion cubic feet of recoverable gas. Mobil was developing the field under a production-sharing contract with the Indonesian State Oil Company. Production began in 1977, and Mobil's share from this field averaged 29,000 b/d in 1980. Moreover, the natural gas liquification operations had been quite successful. During 1980, these operations supplied 556-million cubic feet a day to Japan, of which Mobil's share was 451-million cubic feet daily.

Mobil was the holder of the largest pivate interest in the Stratfjord Field. This field had been discovered by Mobil and was located off the coast of Norway in the North Sea. The company's interest in this project was almost 13 percent, the largest of the 12 company partners except Statoil, the Norwegian State Oil Company. Production from the Stratfjord Field, which had reserves of more than 3 billion barrels, began in November 1979 and reached 70,000 b/d by the end of 1980. A second producing platform in this field was under construction and was expected to be operational by 1982. The installation of a third producing platform was planned.

Another of Mobil's major holdings was a 50 percent interest in the Beryl Field in the British North Sea. In 1978, Mobil's net proven reserves in the North Sea were over 500 million barrels of crude oil and 760-billion cubic feet of natural gas. In 1980, production from the entire Beryl Field increased to 110,000 b/d. By the end of 1980, plans had been made to install a second platform to augment production in the field. In addition, several smaller fields in the North Sea in which Mobil owned interests varying from 3 to 20 percent were being developed.

Finally, in 1978 and 1979, Mobil increased its interest in Aramco from 10 to 15 percent. While Mobil had increased its efforts in domestic exploration, it was clear that foreign sources of crude oil were still very important to the company. In 1973, 82 percent of Mobil's oil production came from foreign countries and 70 percent of this total came from the Middle East. Although Mobil's dependence on foreign oil had been relatively stable over the years (85 percent of gross production in 1977), the Middle East had become a much larger supplier to Mobil relative to other foreign sources (81 percent of total foreign production by 1977). By 1979, foreign production was down to 83 per-

---

[15]"Research Brief, Mobil Corporation," Goldman Sachs, April 2, 1981.

cent of the total. Despite this slight drop, it was clear that Mobil would remain particularly vulnerable to the vagaries of foreign politics, especially in the Middle East.

Refining

With the merger of Socony and Vacuum Oil in 1931, the company emerged as one of the strongest refiners in the industry. In terms of refining capacity, Socony–Vacuum was the second largest refiner in the United States. By 1960, however, Mobil had dropped back to third place and its U. S. refining capacity relative to the other major oil companies continued to decline in the following years. By 1978, Mobil was in seventh place behind Exxon, Standard of California, Standard of Indiana, Shell, Texaco, and Gulf. In 1960, Mobil's U. S. refining capacity was 716,700 barrels per day or 7.4 percent of the U. S. total. By 1978, refining capacity was 901,000 barrels per day, representing only 5.2 percent of the U. S. total. (See exhibits for operating data.)

Mobil's actual U. S. refinery runs or product refined had varied over the previous decade from 819,000 barrels per day in 1969 to 907,000 barrels per day in 1973 to 797,000 barrels per day in 1979. In total, the percentage of U. S. runs to capacity decreased from 100 percent in 1969 to 88 percent in 1979.

Mobil's foreign refining capacity was almost twice its domestic capacity, and its foreign refinery runs were about 160 percent of domestic runs in 1979. Although Mobil's foreign refining capacity had increased steadily from 1973 to 1977, the percentage of actual runs to capacity decreased during this period (see Table 1). In recent years, Mobil had been able to reverse this trend slightly, but only by decreasing foreign refining capacity.

As of December 1979, Mobil owned or had interests in 37 refineries in 21 countries. Although there had been some new refinery construction from 1970 to 1980, notably in Joliet, Illinois and Wilhelmshaven, Germany, Mobil spent most of its investment dollars in mod-

TABLE 1
Foreign Refining Statistics

	1973	1977	1979
Runs	1458	1264	1266
Capacity	1688	1832	1770
Run/Cap	86%	69%	72%

Source: Mobil Corporation Financial and Operating Statistics, 1977 and 1979.

ernizing and expanding existing facilities in order to improve production efficiency for gasoline, heating oil, and synthetic lubricants. Mobil had spent over $105 million for environmental protection at its U. S. refineries in the last five years. Moreover, the company had spent over 100 million in the last eight years in energy-saving projects. This resulted in operating efficiencies that lowered the amount of energy needed to refine a barrel of crude oil by 22 percent from 1972 levels. Similar cost reductions had been made in foreign refining operations. Expansion and improvement of foreign refineries in England, Singapore, and Italy were undertaken from 1977 to 1979.

Even so, proportionately fewer and fewer investment dollars had been devoted to refining since 1971. This trend was indicative of the industry-wide concentration on exploration and production at the expense of downstream activities. Mobil's total refining expenditures went from $131 million in 1967 (19 percent of total capital investment for the year) to a high of $244 million in 1971 (24 percent of total capital investment). However, in each year after 1971, there was a decline in the percentage of refining expenditures to total expenditures.

Marketing

Between 1950 and 1970, the major oil companies had been competing fiercely to penetrate as many regional markets as possible. Market share, rather than profitability, was the primary marketing objective. Mobil, on the other hand, followed a different strategy. Albert L. Nickerson, who was then Chairman of Mobil, made the decision to limit domestic marketing expenditures in an effort to develop European markets. In 1969, Nickerson commented on this period of the company's growth.

> From 1948 to 1964 we really starved our marketing people in this country. We just said, 'Look, there are many jobs this company has to do. . . . Give us a chance to strengthen some other elements of the company, and the day will come when we can come back to you. . . .' We had a program that almost required us to lose position.[16]

Mobil's domestic market share dropped from 9.9 percent in 1948 to 6.7 percent in 1967. By 1965, when foreign sales were approaching domestic sales, Mobil finally began to increase its domestic marketing expenditures. By 1969, Mobil's European market share was about 5 percent. Since earnings had improved every year since 1958, Nickerson's strategy was viewed as an overall success.

Since the early 1970s, however, there had been a steady decline in the number of marketing outlets for all companies. Even as late as 1977, Texaco was marketing to every state in the union. At the same time, Mobil was in 48 states, Exxon in 44, Shell in 40, and Socal and Gulf in 39. However, the total number of branded U. S. retail outlets for all companies decreased from 321,640 in 1969 to 232,727 in 1977.

By the late 1970s, Mobil had decided to get out of the Rocky Mountain States because the firm had no refineries in that area. The decision called for pulling out of five states by 1981 and included closing 276 retail outlets that were supplied directly or indirectly by Mobil. From 1969 to 1979, Mobil decreased the number of its retail outlets nation-wide from 25,513 to 17,749.

While the number of Mobil's domestic retail stations decreased by 21 percent from 1974 to 1979, foreign outlets decreased by only 5 percent during the same period. Both at home and abroad, Mobil's strategy was to close down marginal service stations and consolidate areas of marketing strength. Part of Mobil's domestic marketing retrenchment included the introduction of secondary brands, beginning with the "Sello" brand in the Southwest in 1972, and later with "Big-Bi" stations in the Midwest and "Reelo" in North Carolina. Most of these secondary outlets were marginal Mobil stations that were converted to self-serve operations designed to compete with lower-priced private brands. The introduction of these secondary brands caused some confusion among competitors and jobbers, since Mobil was not supplying these outlets with its own product, nor was it closing all of its branded outlets in the areas where secondary brands had been introduced. Amid considerable speculation, Mobil consistently maintained that it did not intend to withdraw the Mobil brand from those areas where secondary outlets had been introduced. The company claimed that it was looking at each of its branded outlets on an individual basis to see if they met various investment criteria.

From 1967 to 1972, Mobil spent an average of 25 percent of its capital expenditures on marketing. This ratio dropped to 14 percent in 1974, and averaged between 7 percent and 8 percent through 1978. In 1979, the ratio fell to 4.9 percent. In 1973, almost twice as much was spent on foreign marketing capital investment as was spent on domestic marketing. By 1979, Mobil was spending almost three times more in foreign marketing investments.

On the consumer front, Mobil was one of the first companies to market super unleaded gasoline (1978). That same year, Mobil introduced engine lubricants, Mobil 1 and Delvac 1 (for commercial vehicles), whose initial sales exceeded company expectations.

Transportation

Although the total number of Mobil's owned or chartered deep-sea carriers decreased from

---

[16]"How to Rob Peter . . . ," *Forbes*, June 15, 1969, pp. 30–31.

118 in 1967 to 96 in 1979, the gross tonnage of the fleet increased from 5.8 million to 12.9 million deadweight tons. From 1967 to 1973, the company increased its investments in marine transportation considerably from 1 percent of total investment to 12 percent. However, by 1975, there was an oversupply of crude carriers world-wide, and Mobil decreased its level of investment to 10 percent of total. This world-wide surplus of Very Large Crude Carriers (VLCCs) continued through 1979, by which time Mobil's capital investments in the marine area were down to 2 percent of the annual total. At the same time, however, the company actually improved its fleet of tankers by purchasing carriers at reduced prices and negotiating charters at low rates. In 1979, Mobil contracted for the conversion of six of its VLCC's from stream turbine to diesel propulsion, which is more cost-efficient. That same year, the company took its first major step in the transportation of liquified petroleum gas (LPG) by arranging a long-term charter of a 75,000 cubic meter LPG carrier to transport large cargoes to Japan.

Total world-wide pipeline increased from 35,071 miles in 1967 (41 percent domestic) to 43,090 miles in 1978 (59 percent domestic). Capital investment in pipeline transportation averaged 2–4 percent of total expenditures each year from 1967 through 1977, with the exception of 1975 and 1976, when investment increased to over 10 percent in support of the Trans-Alaska pipeline project. After completion of the Trans-Alaska pipeline, Mobil's pipeline investment fell to less than 1 percent of total capital investments in 1978 and 1979.

Mobil had a 5 percent interest in the 1.2 million-barrels-per-day Trans-Alaska pipeline and a 2.1 percent interest in the Prudhoe Bay Unit oil field in Alaska. In the late 1970s, Mobil was purchasing extra crude to fill its pipeline share, since its 2.1 percent interest in Prudhoe Bay production was insufficient for that purpose.

In 1977, Mobil was awarded a contract to be project manager for the construction of a 750-mile East–West pipeline for Saudi Arabia's General Petroleum and Mineral Organization (Petromin). The pipeline, which would have a capacity of 1.85 million barrels per day, was due for completion in 1981. It would connect the crude oil fields in eastern Saudi Arabia to the port of Yanbu, on the Red Sea. Mobil also participated in a variety of other joint venture projects with Saudi Arabia, including a refinery in Riyadh and a proposed 450,000 metric ton per year petrochemicals complex.

Chemicals

The Mobil Chemical Company was formed in 1960 to bring the company's world-wide chemical business into one integrated operating division. This division was equipped with its own research and development, manufacturing, and marketing facilities. The primary domestic facilities produced basic petrochemicals such as ethylene, propylene, and butadiene, and aromatics such as benzene and toluene. Early acquisitions included O. & M. Kleemann, Ltd. (Great Britain, 1961) which manufactured plastics; Kordite Corp. (1962), in plastic film products and packaging materials; Virginia-Carolina Chemical Corp. (1963), in fertilizer and phosphorus-based chemical products; the paint and chemical coatings division of Martin Marietta Corp. (1963). The company also opened a new aromatics plant in Naples in 1963.

By the middle 1960s, there was an oversupply of chemicals, resulting in depressed prices and substantial losses for many firms in the business. Mobil also suffered from these conditions, and in 1969, the company terminated its unprofitable fertilizer business, taking a $22 million write-off. Since then, Mobil has not invested as heavily in chemicals. The company's capital investment in chemicals as a percentage of total investment decreased from 13.5 percent in 1966 to 5.5 percent in 1979.

Mobil's strategy in chemicals was one of concentrating on selected areas of business with good growth opportunities, primarily in those fields where the company already had a strong competitive position and could profit from its structural integration and traditional expertise. In addition, Mobil Chemical used much of its output of basic petrochemicals in other manufacturing operations. This large degree of internal utilization made the company somewhat less sensitive to the fluctuations of the petrochemical market.

In the late 1970s, the chemical market had again become oversaturated, and many firms suffered low earnings and losses once more. However, analysts predicted that this would be a shortlived situation and expected a favorable growth market for chemicals in the 1980s. By 1979, Mobil had become the largest manufacturer of plastic packaging in the United States, including such products as HEFTY brand garbage bags, food bags, bread wrapping, and industrial packaging. Another highly successful product of the Plastics division was polystyrene foam, which was used in the manufacture of egg cartons, fast-food containers, and disposable tableware. There had also been considerable growth in sales of a product called Mobilrap, which was a heavy-duty polyethylene stretch film used to wrap pallet loads for industrial distribution.

Mobil also produced "oriented polypropylene" (OPP) under the brand name BI-COR, which was a packaging film replacement for cellophane. This product was receiving rapid acceptance because of its lower cost and higher quality as a cellophane substitute. In 1979, Mobil began an expansion of the company's newest and largest OPP plant (opened in 1978) which would raise total domestic capacity to over 100 million pounds a year by the end of 1980. In addition, a new OPP plant was under construction in Belleville, Ontario that was scheduled for completion in 1981. This plant would make Mobil the first major producer of OPP in Canada. At the same time, a new OPP facility was nearing completion at Virton, Belgium. This plant would inaugurate Mobil's entry into the growing European OPP market.

In 1979, Mobil Chemical was the third largest producer of phosphates in the United States. In December 1979, the company opened a new high-temperature organic phosphates plant in Charleston, South Carolina. This plant manufactured specialty chemicals used in fire-resistant fluids, plasticizers, and uranium extractants, which facilitate the recovery of small amounts of uranium in the rock produced by the phosphate-mining industry.

The company had recently completed facilities in Edison, New Jersey that produced gasoline detergent additives. This plant also manufactured esters, a primary ingredient for Mobil's new synthetic lubricants, Mobil 1 and Delvac 1. The Chemical Coatings Division had greatly increased the production of power coatings in recent years. Power coatings, based on a new technology, were being applied to large diameter pipelines to provide improved performance and environmental advantages over other conventional coatings. Mobil Chemical was using this new powder coating on the 48-inch, 750-mile East–West pipeline being constructed in Saudi Arabia.

Other Energy Sources

Anticipating the future importance of alternative energy sources, Mobil began investing more in research and development for new sources of energy. In 1976, the company formed an Energy Minerals Unit (a subdivision within the Exploration and Producing Division) that had the responsibility for the development of coal, uranium, and other minerals. The objectives of Mobil's energy research efforts were to improve technology for finding and extracting current energy resources and to find viable alternatives to petroleum based energy.

Coal

In 1974, Mobil signed a cost-sharing contract with the Federal Energy Research and Development Administration for the design of a pilot plant, engineered to convert methanol into high-octane gasoline. This process would require the utilization of coal, from which methanol can be made. At that time, Mobil owned 2 billion tons of coal reserves; by the end of 1978, Mobil's coal reserves had been increased to 3.7 billion tons. These reserves were located in Wyoming, Montana, North Dakota, Colorado, and Illinois. The company had already made plans to construct its first coal mine near Gillette, Wyoming. Mobil owned a 50 percent interest in the proposed Gillette mine that was expected to produce 2.5 million tons of coal per year. In addition, Mobil had applied for permits to open a coal mine on another of its properties near Gillette that was expected to have an ultimate capacity of 10 to 15 million tons per year.

Initially, coal was thought to be a very attractive alternative if it could be economically liquified or gasified for transportation through the oil industry's huge pipeline system. The major oil companies had increased their ownership of coal reserves by more than 25 percent since 1970. Exxon was the largest holder with over 8 billion tons. Although there were still some uncertainties over the economics of liquification and gasification, it was estimated in early 1980 that a liquification plant could produce hydrocarbons at a cost of about $40 per barrel of crude oil equivalent. There was certainly the possibility that liquification could become competitive in the volatile seller's market of international petroleum. Although Mobil was a strong advocate of coal as an alternative energy source, coal was not expected to contribute significantly to total earnings in the near term.

Mobil had been conducting oil-shale and tar-sands research since the early 1960s. In 1973, it joined a new group of companies that were testing an improved method of extracting oil from shale through a combination of crushing and heating. Mobil had substantial reserves of oil-shale, but certain environmental problems had to be resolved before large-scale production could begin. In 1975, Mobil joined with nine other companies in developing an underground method for recovering oil from shale. This approach was expected to reduce many of the environmental problems associated with oil-shale extraction. It was estimated that synthetic oil from shale and tar-sands would contribute up to two percent of the country's total energy supply by the year 2000.

Solar

Mobil Tyco Solar Energy Corporation, of which Mobil owned 80 percent, was formed in 1974 for research and development in the field of solar energy. In 1975, the Japan Solar Energy Co., Ltd. was formed under license from Mobil Tyco. Mobil owned a 7.5 percent interest in this company. Mobil committed itself to spending $30 million on research in solar energy through Mobil Tyco. By the end of 1977, the company had invested $10 million in one such project. The program involved the development of a unique silicon ribbon process for the manufacture of solar cells that would convert sunshine directly into electricity. However, without a significant technological breakthrough, this energy source was still expected to be too expensive for any practical application during the next decade. By 2000, it was estimated that solar energy could account for about 3 percent of total energy needs.

Nuclear

The entire oil industry spent over $2.4 billion in uranium exploration, mining, and processing since the 1960s. This form of energy had been one of the most attractive alternate energy sources because its costs were reasonable, and the oil industry could utilize its expertise in geological exploration. Mobil's Rawleigh Warner, Jr. told stockholders at a meeting in 1978:

> . . . in the near term—say, for the balance of this century—we should guard against letting a temporary shortage of deliverable domestic energy force us to make radical and unnecessary changes in our lifestyle, do irreparable

TABLE 2
Total U. S. Uranium Production Capacity
(Estimates based on presently known reserves)

1978	44,000 tons/year
1980	60,000 tons/year
1985	87,000 tons/year

Source: Uranium, A Joint Report by the OECD Nuclear Energy Agency and the International Atomic Energy Agency, 1975, p. 9.

TABLE 3
Total U. S. Uranium Demand Forecasts

1975	18,000 tons/year
1980	50,000 tons/year
1985	100,000 tons/year

Source: Uranium, A Joint Report by the OECD Nuclear Energy Agency and the International Atomic Energy Agency, 1975, p. 9.

damages to our balance of payments, and create confrontations in both domestic and international politics. The U. S. can buy a lot of time—invaluable time—by taking the nuclear route.[17]

Warner said that between the late 1970s and 1990, the United States could depend only on oil, natural gas, coal, and nuclear power for any significant contribution to its energy requirements.

Total production of uranium ore in the United States (including production by the oil industry) was taken from about 3,670 properties, 200 of which accounted for 96 percent of total production. At the beginning of 1976, total cumulative production was about 282,400 tons of uranium processed from 124 million tons of ore. By contrast, 1975 production was only 12,300 tons of uranium. Tables 2 and 3 depict estimated uranium production capacity and demand through 1985.

In 1975, Mobil discovered new uranium deposits in Texas, and the following year began field programs to evaluate production methods. The process of extracting uranium by forcing chemical solutions through the underground ore body was successful, and Mobil anticipated commercial production could begin after receipt of the required licenses and permits. Mobil also had discovered commercial-grade deposits near Gallup, New Mexico in 1977. By the end of 1978, Mobil had uranium holdings of 50 million pounds. However, the future of nuclear power as an acceptable energy source remained problematic because of adverse public opinion and increasingly complex litigation surrounding the building of new nuclear power stations.

Nonenergy Diversification

Real Estate

Mobil made its first significant real-estate investment in 1966 when it moved its Hong Kong terminal, thereby vacating a choice 40-acre site. Mobile decided to build a huge middle-class apartment complex called Mei Foo Sun Chuen rather than selling the land for an estimated $15 million. This complex was completed in 1979, and houses more than 70,000 people. The apartments were initially offered at $16 per square foot, but heavy demand eventually pushed the rates to $80 per square foot. By August 1978, this residential complex had already contributed more than $150 million to Mobil's after-tax earnings, and the company was still earning management fees and renting commercial space. The success of the Mei Foo project led to the decision that real estate should become a major diversification for Mobil. As one Mobil executive said, "Mobil is firmly committed to making real estate a major part of its business."[18]

In 1970, a mangement team was formed to explore further opportunities in real estate. In a period of three years, 55 U. S. metropolitan areas were analyzed, and in 1973, Mobil made

---

[17]"Mobil Urges Boost in Nuclear Program," *The Oil and Gas Journal*, May 15, 1978, pp. 38–39.

[18]"Mobil's Broad Acres," *Forbes*, August 21, 1978, pp. 31–32.

its first U. S. purchase. The area selected was a residential community comprised of 3,300 bayfront acres near San Francisco. Since 1973, Mobil had spent more than $100 million for real estate and paid property taxes of $1.5 million annually. Most of Mobil's land was owned by Mobil Land Development Co., a nonconsolidated subsidiary located in San Francisco. Mobil's holdings were large tracts of land strategically located in high growth areas, and were well suited to large-scale communities of at least 1,000 homes.

Early in 1977, Mobil began bidding for southern California's Irvine Co., which was the owner of America's largest real-estate development. Beginning with an offer of $24 per share (or $202 million), Mobil finally bid more than $336 million for the property before losing out to a private group that included Henry Ford II, John Irvin Smith, Max M. Fisher (Detroit industrialists), and others. In July 1978, Mobil purchased the undeveloped half of Reston, Virginia from Gulf Oil for over $30 million. Gulf previously had sizable interests in real estate, but later divested itself completely of these projects. Gulf maintained that they were not closely enough related to the company's basic business, and that they had not made a meaningful contribution to corporate profits. By 1978, Mobil had acquisition offices in Atlanta, Dallas, Ft. Lauderdale, Washington, Denver, and New York. Table 4 is a partial list of the location and acreage of Mobil's real-estate holdings.

Marcor

In 1968, Mobil made the decision to diversify outside of the energy business, and it formed a diversification study team to analyze various industries and select individual companies as possible candidates for acquisition. Mobil's objective was not to become a large conglomerate, but to acquire one major diversification subsidiary. Mobil's Rawleigh Warner, Jr., commented on Mobil's motivation:

> We had become aware that governments would interfere with our business. We thought they would be oil-producing countries, not consuming nations. But after the oil embargo we realized that the consuming nations would also play a greater role. That impelled us forward with the diversification program.[19]

Senior management established certain criteria for any potential acquisitions. These criteria required that any company being considered have a strong management team, considerable experience in their own field, good earnings growth and rate of return possibilities, different business cycles and business risks from the oil industry, and a strong competitive position within its own markets.

After reviewing over 100 companies in a five-year period, Mobil began looking very closely at Marcor, Inc., a holding company formed in 1968 which consisted of two main subsidiaries, Montgomery Ward and Container Corp. Montgomery Ward was a retailer in the United States, and Container Corp. was the largest U. S. producer of paperboard packaging.

> By 1973, we were looking at individual companies. Marcor had turned around—it seemed to have a management that knew what they

TABLE 4
A Partial List of Mobil's Real-Estate Holdings

Location	Acreage
Redwood City, California	3,300 acres
Dallas, Texas	944
Arlington, Virginia	56
Reston, Virginia	3,700
Buford, Georgia	1,820
Atlanta, Georgia	3,000
Stuart, Florida	4,835

Source: Forbes, August 21, 1978.

---

[19]"Big Oil's Move into Retailing," *Chain Store Executive,* September 1976, pp. 29–32.

were about—yet it was not fully priced in the stock market.[20]

Mobil then bought 4.5 percent of Marcor's stock for an average cost of $23 per share. When the Arab oil embargo hit, the stock market fell sharply and oil prices skyrocketed. By 1974, Mobil had a lot of extra cash on hand, and Marcor's stock looked like more of a bargain than ever. In August 1974, Mobil made a tender offer for shares that would give them a majority interest in the smaller company. The price at that time was still below $25 per share. Marcor's price per share rose sharply that same year. Later in 1974, three Marcor executives were elected to Mobil's Board of Directors, and four officers of Mobil, including Warner and Tavoulareas, were elected Directors of Marcor.

In July 1976, Mobil bought Marcor. The 1976 Annual Report contained the following message to the stockholders:

> By merging with Ward and Container, Mobil effectively realized its major diversification objective. Both firms are extremely well managed and have the growth potential to contribute materially to Mobil's U. S. based earnings. They helped Mobil to increase significantly the percentage of total earnings produced in the United States. Moreover, they operate in business areas with different cycles and risks from oil's and are not subject to the vagaries of oil industry regulation.[21]

During the period of acquisition, Mobil drew considerable criticism from members of Congress and the Federal Energy Administration. John C. Sawhill, chief of the FEA, who had previously defended higher oil profits as necessary for capital investment in domestic exploration and production, said the Mobil offer to acquire controlling interest in Marcor was "like having a wet dishrag thrown in your face." Walter F. Mondale (D-Minn.) said in July 1974 that the proposed acquisition:

> . . . is the best sign yet that the oil industry is engaged in a desperate search for ways in which to get rid of embarrassingly high profits. (It) lends substantial weight to the wisdom of repealing the oil depletion allowance immediately.[22]

Sen. Thomas J. McIntyre (D-N.H.) said that the acquisition plan was "irresponsibility at its worst."[23]

For its part, Mobil maintained a calm resolution throughout the two-year proceedings, citing limited domestic oil–investment opportunities as one factor in their decision to diversify. Rawleigh Warner Jr. commented extensively on the uncertainties facing the oil industry both at home and abroad:

> The oil industry is very different from what we knew five years ago. . . . Governments are interfering. The U. S. Government certainly is. The Federal Energy Administration tells us to whom we must sell our crude and what we can charge. They threaten us with a federal oil company that will have access to the top 20 percent acreage offshore and be a yardstick to see how effective we are. There are 3000 bills before Congress, each one of which would do something to the oil industry.[24]

Warner noted that the Federal Trade Commission was suing Mobil and other oil companies to require substantial divestiture of refining properties and pipeline assets. He also felt that it was only a matter of time before 100 percent of the oil concessions were taken by Mideastern governments, and that long-term rights in the British North Sea and Canada were also subject to uncertainty. Under these circumstances, Mobil's Chairman felt that the Marcor acquisition made good sense.

---

[20]"What Makes Mobil Run?" *Business Week,* June 13, 1977, pp. 80–85.
[21]Mobil Annual Report, 1976.
[22]"Congressional Barbs Hit Mobil–Marcor Deal," *Oil and Gas Journal,* July 1, 1974, p. 32.
[23]*Ibid.*
[24]"Recycling the Oil Profits, Mobil Style," *Forbes,* November 15, 1974, pp. 66–67.

I'm not saying all these things are going to happen, but I don't think we are overreacting, (said Warner referring to the Marcor deal). We think there's enough going on to put an anchor to windward in the interests of our shareholders.[25]

Warner's reply to the criticism that the Marcor acquisition siphoned off cash that should have been used in exploration and production was that Mobil was already exploiting as many E & P opportunities as it could find.

> The limit to our spending isn't dollars, (said Warner). It's the availability of offshore concessions and the limitations of the people we have. We are looking for oil in 24 countries around the world, and that takes competent people. And it's the availability of rigs, platforms, and pipe. It isn't cash or the lack of cash.[26]

While Mobil never revealed the total price for Marcor, it was estimated that they must have paid about $1.8 billion, spending around $800 million for the first 54 percent in 1973 and 1974. Mobil put $200 million of cash directly into Marcor's treasury in exchange for new preferred stock, but maintained that it had no plans to pump additional capital into the retailing chain. Ward was definitely expected to pull its own weight, and Mobil emphasized that its new subsidiary would be granted operational autonomy in the conduct of its business.

However, Ward was encouraged by its new parent to formalize and standardize long-range planning procedures. It was anticipated that Mobil could offer Ward very helpful counsel in the area of corporate planning, a facet of business activity for which the parent company had long been well known. It was also felt that Ward would have less difficulty raising capital when needed in the open market with a parent the size of Mobil behind it.

On the financial side, the Marcor acquisition increased the percentage of Mobil's U. S. earnings but lowered its return on equity. Oil analyst Bruce Lazier commented:

> Without Marcor, Mobil would be earning substantially more overseas than domestically by the end of the decade. Marcor balances foreign and domestic income for Mobil.[27]

Mobil's U. S. based earnings had increased to 58 percent (net operating earnings) in the year of the Marcor acquisition, this was up from only 32 percent in 1973. Marcor contributed 11.8 percent to total operating earnings in 1976. However, by 1979, Mobil's U. S. earnings had fallen back to 34 percent of total operating earnings, with Marcor contributing only 4 percent of total foreign and domestic operating earnings. Mobil attributed the relatively weaker performance of Ward in 1979 to "higher interest rates on Ward's borrowings to finance credit operations, increased markdowns in a highly competitive market, and inflationary pressures on operating expenses."[28]

Container Corporation, on the other hand, showed marked increases in operating income, going from $5 million in 1978 to $35 million in 1979. Mobile cited "improved foreign earnings and a lower provision for litigation settlements" as reasons for Container's improved performance. The 1979 Annual Report noted that "improved U. S. volumes and prices for shipping containers and containerboard were offset by lower margins for folding cartons and boxboard."

Although the Marcor acquisition was seen by some analysts as one of the boldest diversification efforts by a major oil company into a nonenergy field, some oilmen viewed the acquisition as overly conservative. One oil executive said:

> They were far ahead with the idea, but maybe they were too timid. Why not diversify into

---

[25]*Ibid.*
[26]*Ibid.*

[27]"What Makes Mobil Run?" *Forbes,* June 13, 1974, pp. 80–85.
[28]Mobil Annual Report, 1979.

drugs, instruments, office equipment, electronics, or computers—all of which have higher rates of return.[29]

By 1980, Mobil's management was admitting that the scenario surrounding Marcor had not panned out as they had predicted. "'We probably wouldn't buy Marcor this year, right now,' concedes William P. Tavoulereas, Mobil's President."[30] As of 1981, Mobil still had heavy overseas earnings. However, they were more diversified out of the Middle East. The government was far less threatening to the oil industry than it was in 1974. Finally, with the oil price increases that were recorded since the merger, there was little hope that Marcor, even if it had been healthy, could have matched oil industry returns.

Marcor, however, had not been healthy. Montgomery Ward lost $162 million in 1980. To maintain its bond rating Mobil was forced to pump $200 million into the company. In July 1980, Mobil granted Wards a three-year, interest-free loan. Mobil took great care to label the transaction as a loan.

Public Relations

Beginning in the early 1970s, Mobil developed a public relations strategy that was outspoken, controversial, and definitely atypical compared to the other members of the conservative and usually silent oil industry. This strategy did not result from any single decision by senior management.

> ... Mobil's "high profile" operation developed gradually, in response to an increasingly perceived need for the company to become more visible and articulate.[31]

By the late 1970s, Mobil was well known for its efforts to sponsor and promote cultural events on both public and commercial television networks.

> (There was) ... an effort to generate good will by financing a variety of cultural projects—public television shows, outstanding dramatic works on commercial TV, all manner of art books and exhibits. Mobil was a pioneer among corporations in funding public television, making its first grant in 1970 to launch "Masterpiece Theatre," a notable success.[32]

In 1977, Mobil budgeted $1.6 million to finance a full 52 weeks of first-run television shows.

The other facet of Mobil's public relations strategy resulted in a willingness to address "issue oriented" or "advocacy" questions in the media. While much of their "advocacy" advertising was aimed at problems within the oil industry, Mobil also editorialized on other controversial issues that the company thought were of national interest. Mobil was quick to attack any treatment of the oil industry (by the media or the government) that they perceived as "unfair." At the same time, many of their views were somewhat surprising when first aired. For example, the endorsement of an effective mass transit policy for the nation's large metropolitan areas initially surprised many observers. At one time or another, Mobil's readiness to defend its interests led it into extended public conflicts with such powerful media forces as the CBS and ABC televisions networks. Mobil had also not hesitated to break ranks with the other members of the industry on particularly sensitive issues, such as the question of oil price controls.

> Mobil Oil Corp. caught the rest of the oil industry by surprise ... when it proposed that price controls be retained on part of domestic oil production that the Carter Administration wants to free from price constraints.[33]

---

[29]"The New Diversifications Oil Game," *Business Week*, April 24, 1978, pp. 76–88.
[30]"Mobil's Successful Exploration," *Business Week*, October 13, 1980, p. 112.
[31]Ross, Irwin, "Public Relations Isn't Kid-Glove Stuff at Mobil," *Fortune*, September 19, 1976, pp. 106–202.

[32]*Ibid.*
[33]"What Made Mobil A Decontrol Maverick," *Business Week*, May 21, 1979, pp. 32–33.

EXHIBIT 1
Consolidated Statement of Income (In millions except for per share amounts)

Year Ended December 31	1980	1979	1978
Revenues			
Sales and services (including excise and state gasoline taxes: 1980—$3,313; 1979—$2,764; 1978—$1,948)	$62,823	$47,485	$36,684
Interest, dividends, and other revenue	903	807	739
Total Revenues	63,726	48,292	37,423
Costs and Expenses			
Crude oil, products, merchandise, and operating supplies and expenses	41,485	30,477	23,679
Exploration expenses	524	359	253
Selling and general expenses	4,773	4,265	3,632
Depreciation, depletion, and amortization	1,399	1,086	930
Interest and debt discount expense	479	459	420
Taxes other than income taxes	8,390	7,084	5,765
Income taxes	3,863	2,555	1,613
Total Costs and Expenses	60,913	46,285	36,292
Income Before Extraordinary Item	2,813	2,007	1,131
Extraordinary item—Gain on sale of interest in Belridge Oil Company (less applicable income taxes of $189)	459	—	—
Net Income	$ 3,272	$ 2,007	$ 1,131
Income Before Extraordinary Item Per Share	$13.24	$9.46	$5.34
Net Income Per Share	$15.40	$9.46	$5.34

Source: Mobil Corporation Annual Report 1980.

Mobil's proposal suggested that "old" oil (existing reserves) would remain subject to existing price controls, but that 'new' oil (not yet discovered) could be sold at prevailing world levels without being subject to any "windfall profits tax." Industry sources were quick to point out that Mobil, as a relatively crude-short company, stood to benefit most by its proposal. As one Exxon spokesman noted: "Our reaction is that it (the proposal) was self-serving."[34]

For the moment, Mobil seems committed to its rather aggressive public relations policies. While there was some question as to the efficacy of "advocacy" advertising, there was no doubt that more people were now aware of Mobil's stand on various issues. A recent poll indicated that Mobil's advertising had very high visibility, reaching an estimated 90 percent of "Administration, Congressional, and other government leaders."[35]

---

[34]Ibid.

[35]Adkins, Lynn, "How Good Are Advocacy Ads?" *Dun's Review*, June 1979, pp. 76–77.

EXHIBIT 2
Consolidated Balance Sheet (in millions of dollars)

December 31	1980	1979
Assets		
Current Assets		
Cash	$ 698	$ 621
Marketable securities, at cost (approximating market)	1,220	1,257
Accounts and notes receivable	5,718	5,060
Inventories	6,463	4,951
Total Current Assets	14,099	11,889
Investments and Long-Term Receivables		
Investments in unconsolidated subsidiaries	1,091	987
Other investments and long-term receivables	1,122	1,043
Total Investments and Long-Term Receivables	2,213	2,030
Net Properties, Plants, and Equipment	15,840	13,103
Prepaid and Deferred Charges	553	484
Total	$32,705	$27,506
Liabilities and Shareholders' Equity		
Current Liabilities		
Notes and loans payable	$ 949	$ 1,064
Accounts payable and accrued liabilities	7,864	7,092
Income, excise, state, gasoline, and other taxes payable	3,218	2,377
Deferred income taxes	546	467
Long-term debt and capital lease obligations maturing within one year	126	170
Total Current Liabilities	12,703	11,170
Long-Term Debt	3,256	2,962
Capital Lease Obligations	315	342
Deferred Income Taxes	2,087	1,605
Accrued Restoration and Removal Costs	148	114
Deferred Credits and Other Noncurrent Obligations	621	315
Reserves for Employee Benefits	412	398
Minority Interest in Subsidiary Companies	94	87
Shareholders' Equity		
Preferred stock	—	—
Common stock	797	796
Capital surplus	896	880
Earnings retained in the business	11,376	8,837
Total Shareholders' Equity	13,069	10,513
Total	$32,705	$27,506

Source: Mobil Corporation Annual Report 1980.

EXHIBIT 3
Consolidated Statement of Changes in Financial Position (in millions of dollars)

Year Ended December 31	1980	1979	1978
Sources of Funds			
Operations			
Income before extraordinary item	$2,813	$2,007	$1,131
Depreciation, depletion, and amortization	1,399	1,086	930
Deferred income taxes	482	585	234
Dividends in excess of (less than) equity in income of unconsolidated companies	129	(50)	(157)
Funds available from operations	4,823	3,628	2,138
Extraordinary item	459	—	—
Book value of properties, plants, and equipment sold	99	78	79
Other, net	297	104	(18)
Funds Available Before Financing	5,678	3,810	2,199
Application of Funds			
Cash dividends to shareholders	733	541	456

(*Continued*)

EXHIBIT 3 (Continued)

Year Ended December 31	1980	1979	1978
Capital expenditures	3,525	2,641	1,863
Acquisition of the operations of:			
TransOcean Oil, Inc.	715	—	—
General Crude Oil Company	—	792	—
Other applications			
Increase in—			
Investments and long-term receivables	312	136	29
Accounts and notes receivable	658	870	271
Inventories	1,512	823	338
(Increase) decrease in—			
Accounts payable and accrued liabilities	(772)	(1,428)	(691)
Income, excise, state, gasoline, and other taxes payable	(841)	(637)	(291)
Deferred income taxes—current	(79)	43	(71)
Application of Funds Before Financing	5,763	3,781	1,904
(Decrease) Increase in Funds Before Financing	(85)	29	295
Total Financing			
Increases in long-term debt	525	202	190
Decreases in long-term debt	(231)	(287)	(453)
Decrease in capital lease obligations	(27)	(20)	(20)
(Decrease) increase in notes and loans payable	(115)	461	19
Increase (decrease) in long-term debt and capital lease obligations maturing within one year	(44)	1	(18)
Issuance or sale of common stock	17	10	4
Total Financing Increase (Decrease)	125	367	(278)
Increase in Cash and Marketable Securities	$ 40	$ 396	$ 17

Source: Mobil Corporation Annual Report 1980.

EXHIBIT 4
Distribution of Earnings and Assets (In millions of dollars)

Segments	Energy U.S.	Energy Foreign	Chemical	Retail Merchandising	Paperboard Packaging	Other	Adjustments and Eliminations	Total
				Year Ended December 31, 1980				
Revenues								
Nonaffiliated	$13,804	$39,707	$1,891	$5,916	$1,729	$ 169	$ 510	$63,726
Intersegment	786	3,519	136	—	14	37	(4,492)	—
Total Revenues	$14,590	$43,226	$2,027	$5,916	$1,743	$ 206	$(3,982)	$63,726
Pre-tax operating profit	$ 1,729	$ 5,284	$ 175	$ (213)	$ 126	$ 66	$ —	$ 7,167
Finance charges	23	8	5	(106)	(23)	(134)	—	(227)
Income taxes	(818)	(3,286)	(61)	157	(38)	57	—	(3,989)
Segment Earnings	$ 934	$ 2,006	$ 119	$ (162)	$ 65	$ (11)	$ —	$ 2,951
Corporate expenses, net of in-								

(Continued)

EXHIBIT 4 (Continued)

Segments	Energy U.S.	Energy Foreign	Chemical	Retail Merchandising	Paperboard Packaging	Other	Adjustments and Eliminations	Total
come taxes								(138)
Income Before Extraordinary Item								$ 2,813
Capital expenditures	$ 1,263	$ 1,424	$ 248	$ 322	$ 153	$ —	$ —	$ 3,525
Depreciation, depletion, and amortization	$ 760	$ 396	$ 67	$ 88	$ 69	$ —	$ —	$ 1,399
				At December 31, 1980				
Total Segment Assets	$ 9,323	$16,692	$1,547	$3,942	$1,482	$ 226	$ (728)	$32,484
Corporate assets								221
Total Assets								$32,705
				Year Ended December 31, 1979				
Revenues								
Nonaffiliated	$10,213	$28,792	$1,633	$5,652	$1,476	$ 135	$ 391	$48,292
Intersegment	618	3,022	85	—	11	27	(3,763)	—
Total Revenues	$10,831	$31,814	$1,718	$5,652	$1,487	$ 162	$(3,372)	$48,292
Pre-tax operating profit	$ 1,278	$ 3,449	$ 165	$ 149	$ 105	$ 9	$ —	$ 5,155
Finance charges	(12)	(75)	(1)	(80)	(28)	(134)	—	(330)
Income taxes	(586)	(2,033)	(51)	(15)	(42)	60	—	(2,667)
Segment Earnings	$ 680	$ 1,341	$ 113	$ 54	$ 35	$ (65)	$ —	$ 2,158
Corporate expenses, net of income taxes								(151)
Net Income								$ 2,007
Capital expenditures	$ 1,187	$ 825	$ 146	$ 250	$ 117	$ —	$ —	$ 2,642
Depreciation, depletion, and amortization	$ 542	$ 334	$ 58	$ 74	$ 65	$ —	$ —	$ 1,086
				At December 31, 1979				
Total Segment Assets	$ 7,830	$13,681	$1,160	$3,746	$1,382	$ 229	$ (637)	$27,391
Corporate assets								115
Total Assets								$27,506

Geographic	U.S.	Foreign Canada	Foreign Other	Foreign Total	Adjustments and Eliminations	Total
		Year Ended December 31, 1980				
Revenues						
Nonaffiliated	$22,635	$766	$39,815	$40,581	$ 510	$63,726
Intergeographic	683	84	3,374	3,458	(4,141)	—
Total Revenues	$23,318	$850	$43,189	$44,039	$(3,631)	$63,726
Geographic Earnings	$ 826	$ 97	$ 2,028	$ 2,125	$ —	$ 2,951
Corporate expenses, net of income taxes						(138)
Income Before Extraordinary Item						$ 2,813
		At December 31, 1980				
Total Geographic Assets	$15,644	$969	$16,765	$17,734	$ (894)	$32,484
Corporate assets						221
Total Assets						$32,705
		Year Ended December 31, 1979				
Revenues						
Nonaffiliated	$18,400	$685	$28,816	$29,501	$ 391	$48,292

(Continued)

EXHIBIT 4 (Continued)

Segments	Energy U.S.	Energy Foreign	Chemical	Retail Merchandising	Paper Packa...
Intergeographic			508	38	2,990	3,0..
Total Revenues			$18,908	$723	$31,806	$32,529
Geographic Earnings			$ 739	$100	$ 1,319	$ 1,419
Corporate expenses, net of income taxes						
Net Income						
At December 31, 1979						
Total Geographic Assets			$13,696	$788	$13,716	$14,504	$ (809)
Corporate assets						
Total Assets							$27,5..

Source: Mobil Corporation Annual Report 1980.

EXHIBIT 5
Supplementary Oil and Gas Disclosures

Capitalized Costs Related to Oil and Gas-Producing Activities (in millions)	United States	Foreign Canada	Foreign Europe	Foreign Other	Total
At December 31, 1980					
Capitalized costs					
Unproved properties	$1,574	$ 77	$ 14	$ 62	$ 1,727
Proved properties, wells, plants, and other equipment	6,086	713	1,385	960	9,144
Total capitalized costs	$7,660	$790	$1,399	$1,022	$10,871
Accumulated depreciation, depletion, and amortization	$3,044	$283	4 309	$ 267	$ 3,903
Mobil's share of capitalized costs of investees accounted for on the equity method	$ —	$ —	$ 61	$ 135	$ 196
At December 31, 1979					
Capitalized costs					
Unproved properties	$1,018	$ 66	$ 8	$ 51	$ 1,143
Proved properties, wells, plants, and other equipment	5,022	576	965	772	7,335
Total capitalized costs	$6,040	$642	$ 973	$ 823	$ 8,478
Accumulated depreciation, depletion, and amortization	$2,504	$248	$ 218	$ 220	$ 3,190
Mobil's share of capitalized costs of investees accounted for on the equity method	$ —	$ —	$ 53	$ 115	$ 168

Costs (Expenditures) Incurred in Oil and Gas-Producing Activities (in millions)	United States	Foreign Canada	Foreign Europe	Foreign Other	Total
Year Ended December 31, 1980					
Property acquisition costs	$1,119	$ 18	$ 10	$ 22	$ 1,169
Exploration costs	378	123	109	234	844

(Continued)

EXHIBIT 5 (Continued)

Estimated Quantities of Net Proved Crude Oil and Natural Gas Liquids Reserves (Unaudited) (Millions of barrels)	United States	Foreign			Total
		Canada	Europe	Other	
Development costs	417	51	292	113	873
Production (lifting) costs	896	101	201	177	1,375
Total expenditures	$2,810	$293	$ 612	$ 546	$ 4,261
Depreciation, depletion, and amortization	$ 544	$ 37	$ 66	$ 50	$ 697
Mobil's share of certain expenditures incurred by investees accounted for on the equity method	$ —	$ —	$ 35	$ 135	$ 170
Year Ended December 31, 1980					
Net proved reserves					
beginning of year	869	259	524	463	2,115
revisions of previous estimates	49	2	11	28	90
purchases (sales) of minerals in place	18	—	—	—	18
extensions, discoveries, and other additions	61	12	74	80	227
production	(107)	(21)	(25)	(46)	(199)
Net proved reserves					
end of year	890	252	584	525	2,251
Net proved developed reserves					
beginning of year	763	259	182	424	1,628
end of year	759	252	174	449	1,634
Mobil's share of net proved reserves of investees accounted for on the equity method	—	—	7	460	467
Quantities under long-term and special arrangements in which the company acts as producer					
quantities received during the year	—	—	—	37	37
estimated future quantities, excluding quantities anticipated to be received under arrangements being negotiated	—	—	—	9	9
Year Ended December 31, 1979					
Net proved reserves					
beginning of year	854	284	530	473	2,141
revisions of previous estimates	30	(5)	10	14	49
purchases (sales) of minerals in place	68	1	—	(26)[2]	43
extensions, discoveries, and other additions	24	1	5	60	90
production	(107)	(22)	(21)	(58)	(208)
Net proved reserves					
end of year	869	259	524	463	2,115
Net proved developed reserves					
beginning of year	735	284	133	438	1,590
end of year	763	259	182	424	1,628
Mobil's share of net proved reserves of investees accounted for on the equity method	—	—	6	464	470
Quantities under long-term and special arrangements in which the company acts as producer					

(Continued)

EXHIBIT 5 (Continued)

Estimated Quantities of Net Proved Natural Gas Reserves (unaudited) (Billions of cubic feet)	United States	Foreign			Total
		Canada	Europe	Other	
quantities received during the year	—	—	—	46	46
estimated future quantities anticipated to be received under arrangements being negotiated	—	—	—	35	35
Year Ended December 31, 1979					
Net proved reserves					
beginning of year	6,806	2,021	2,207	3,906	14,940
revisions of previous estimates	(63)	(14)	(53)	170	40
purchases of minerals in place	249	58	—	1	308
extensions, discoveries, and other additions	238	16	25	—	279
production	(732)	(77)	(146)	(172)	(1,127)
Net proved reserves					
end of year	6,498	2,004	2,033	3,905	14,440
Net proved developed reserves					
beginning of year	6,356	2,021	1,275	3,906	13,558
end of year	6,104	1,993	1,331	3,905	13,333
Mobil's share of net proved reserves of investees accounted for on the equity method	—	—	73	227	300
Year Ended December 31, 1978					
Net proved reserves					
beginning of year	7,222	1,750	2,157	3,944	15,073
revisions of previous estimates	49	11	11	—	71
extensions, discoveries, and other additions	268	329	198	—	795
production	(733)	(69)	(159)	(38)	(999)
Net proved reserves					
end of year	6,806	2,021	2,207	3,906	14,940
Net proved developed reserves					
beginning of year	6,525	1,750	1,266	2,075	11,616
end of year	6,356	2,021	1,275	3,906	13,558
Mobil's share of net proved reserves of investees accounted for on the equity method	—	—	86	232	318

Summary of Oil and Gas-Producing Activities on the Basis of Reserve Recognition Accounting (unaudited) (In millions)

Year Ended December 31,	1980	1979
(1) Additions and revisions to estimated proved oil and gas reserves		
Additions to estimated proved reserves, gross	$ 4,577	$ 1,533
Revisions to estimates of reserves proved in prior years		
Changes in prices	13,002	14,551
Other	(2,125)	(1,480)
Accretion of discount	3,061	1,748
Subtotal	18,515	16,352
(2) Evaluated acquisition, exploration, development and production costs:		

(Continued)

EXHIBIT 5 (Continued)

Summary of Oil and Gas-Producing Activities on the Basis of Reserve Recognition Accounting (unaudited) (In millions)

Year Ended December 31,	1980	1979
Costs incurred, including impairments	1,243	777
Present value of estimated future development and production costs	2,653	490
Subtotal	3,896	1,267
Additions and revisions to proved reserves over evaluated costs—fully consolidated operations	14,619	15,085
Pre-tax results of oil and gas-producing activities on the basis of reserve recognition accounting of investees accounted for on the equity method	(129)	1,780
Pre-tax results on the basis of reserve recognition accounting	14,490	16,865
(3) Provisions for income taxes	10,366	11,507
(4) Results of oil and gas-producing activities on the basis of reserve recognition accounting	$ 4,124	$ 5,358
(5) Pre-tax results of oil and gas activities as reported in the consolidated financial statements, based on generally accepted accounting principles	$ 4,224	$ 2,899

Changes in Present Value of Estimated Future Net Revenue from Proved Oil and Gas Reserves (unaudited) (In millions)

Year Ended December 31,	1980	1979
Beginning of year	$33,786	$19,140
Increases:		
Additions and revisions	18,515	16,352
Less related estimated future development and production costs	2,653	490
Net additions and revisions	15,862	15,862
Purchase of reserves in place	465	661
Expenditures that reduced estimated future development costs	657	613
Net (decrease) increase in Mobil's share of proved reserves of investees accounted for on the equity method	(507)	1,517
Subtotal	16,477	18,653
Decreases:		
Sales of oil and gas and value of transfers, net of production costs of $1,375 in 1980 and $800 in 1979	5,426	4,007
Net increase	11,051	14,646
End of year	$44,837	$33,786

Source: Mobil Corporation Annual Report 1980.

Note 1: Reserves for the Arun field in Indonesia are based on Mobil's share of hydrocarbons under a production-sharing contract, assuming a continuation of the present liquefied natural gas facility of three liquefaction trains. Negotiations are currently under way which, if successful, will result in the construction of two additional liquefaction trains. This would increase Mobil's share of recoverable natural gas reserves from 3,700 billion cubic feet to approximately 6,300 billion cubic feet.

Note 2: Reflects an increase in the participation interest of a producing country government.

AMMCO TOOLS, INC.

Ammco Tools, Inc., was a North Chicago based, family-owned company specializing in the manufacture and marketing of automotive engine-rebuilding, brake-service, and wheel-alignment tools and equipment. Under the leadership of its president, Fred G. Wacker, Jr., Ammco enjoyed steady growth. Sales grew from $6.2 million in 1967 to $33.8 million in 1980. (Financial statements are shown in Exhibits 1 and 2.)

President and Chief Executive Officer: Business Objectives and Philosophy

Fred Wacker, Jr., entered the company in 1947 and became President and Chairman of the Board of Directors after his father's death in 1948. Sales at that time were $1 million. Wacker moved the company into brake-service tools and further diversified in the 1950s in order to reduce the company's dependence on the automobile industry. He bought the patents for a newly invented positive displacement meter for measuring any liquid, including petroleum, chemicals, and food products. He organized the Liquid Controls Corporation (LCC) in 1954 to manufacture and sell these products.

Fred Wacker (62) graduated from Yale in 1940 with a BA in English. He worked in the machine shop at the AC Spark Plug Division of General Motors while simultaneously studying at General Motors Institute. He was later moved to the time–study department of the AC division. In 1943 he left General Motors for a four-year stint in the U. S. Navy. When he returned from the war, he formed the Fred Wacker Swing Band, which provided him with a comfortable income. In addition to his musical talents, Wacker was an ardent auto racer. He drove on the European Grand Prix Circuit as a member of the French racing team. He also raced with Phil Hill as his teammate in the Le Mans 24-hour race. In 1951 he won the first Sebring Endurance Race. He also sought unsuccessfully to break a motorcycle world speed record at the Bonneville Salt Flats in 1974 and again in 1975.

Fred Wacker possessed a distinct personal and business philosophy which guided Ammco. He considered his chief executive role ideal in a company that was well positioned in the automotive after-market. He noted that the company was technically oriented, and while "you don't have to be a technical genius, you don't have every Tom, Dick, and Harry trying to get into this business." He noted, "what is important to me is to be independent. I don't have to reach for the *Wall Street Journal* every morning to look at the stock quotes. I maintain a no-debt policy and operate a privately held company which assures me of protection from a takeover."

Wacker expressed his views on the common practice of management by committee in these terms: "I'm not much for committees where you tend to sit around and just talk about things." In discussing his philosphy of long-range planning, Wacker vowed that his long-range goal was to "make a profit every month." He was "not much for long-range planning" and was absolutely opposed to making long-range commitments: "You shouldn't make promises you can't keep." Wacker singled out Henry Ford, Eddie Rickenbacker, and William Patterson (founder of United Airlines) as men he admired as entrepreneurs and managers. Wacker believed that the Bible was the best guide for business and personal behavior. He felt that the Ten Commandments were the most important laws to guide a person's life.

> We may not do formal strategic planning, but we have morning meetings of the key personnel to review our operations. We use the

---

Source: Prepared by Serge Oreal and Robert D. Hamilton, III, under the direction of Professor Thomas J. McNichols. Permission to use granted by Robert D. Hamilton, III.

EXHIBIT 1
Income Statements 1972–1980 ($000)

	1972	1973	1974	1975
Automotive				
Gross shipments	$14,965.5	$16,206.9	$17,830.9	$21,150.9
Less returns/allowances	189.3	236.9	229.5	427.2
Net shipments	14,776.2	15,970.0	17,601.4	10,723.7
Cost of sales	6,301.1	7,197.1	8,825.9	9,727.2
Gross Profit	8,475.1	8,772.9	8,775.5	10,996.5
Other costs				
Commissions	1,964.0	2,141.0	2,304.4	2,755.4
Freight out	211.8	256.3	306.1	308.7
Other	(33.9)	(32.5)	(46.8)	(60.5)
Automotive Income	$ 6,333.2	$ 6,408.1	$ 6,211.8	$ 7,992.9
LCC Income	2.9	4.2	4.2	4.9
Total Income	$ 6,336.1	$ 6,412.3	$ 6,216.0	$ 7,997.8
Departmental Expenses				
Engineering expense	$ 215.1	$ 332.3	$ 396.0	$ 540.0
Selling expense	867.3	918.4	1,006.6	1,183.7
Administrative expense	1,813.1	1,956.8	2,065.4	2,420.6
Other expense, net	103.7	27.0	156.4	250.2
Total departmental	2,999.2	3,234.5	3,624.4	4,394.5
Operating Income	3,336.9	3,177.8	2,591.6	3,603.3
Interest expense	56.8	56.8	57.5	31.5
Net Income	3,280.1	3,121.0	2,534.1	3,571.8
Tax provision	1,619.0	1,508.0	1,280.0	1,800.0
Net profit	$ 1,661.1	$ 1,613.0	$ 1,254.1	$ 1,771.8

Arthur Young charts, which give us a good indication of what has been happening in the company in terms of production and cost trends; the charts allow us to track our product lines. We also have used the Strategic Planning Institute, which produces the PIMS data.

But you have to be careful in using certain measures and should not go overboard on any single system. For example, too much adherence to the return on investment concept can lead you to do the wrong things. Our morning meetings may not last very long. We spend time on problems that need solving. We don't know what is going to come up each day. We try to remain flexible and take things as they come up. Our department heads meet once a month. We try to keep them informed and look at the problems they are encountering.

Fred Wacker, Jr., owned 9.6 percent of the outstanding shares of Ammco; the remainder were owned by the Wacker family. The board of directors was made up of Fred Wacker, Jr. as Chairman, Mrs. Wacker, Sr., Fred Wacker's brother, his sister, and Mark Anderson, Chairman of the Board of Aro Corporation of Bryan, Ohio.

Wacker maintained a personal interest in Ammco's employees. He kept 3 × 5 inch cards with pictures of each employee so that he would know them by name. He also tried to keep personal contact through the sponsorship of all-day company outings or parties that included employees and spouses.

Wacker had decided several years ago not to put a cap on the cost-of-living escalator

	1976	1977	1978	1979	1980	1981 Budget
	$23,336.4	$26,732.5	$30,537.1	$34,831.6	$34,713.2	$38,920.0
	421.2	544.1	653.9	797.6	863.3	920.0
	22,915.2	26,188.4	19,883.2	34,034.0	33,849.9	38,000.0
	10,802.8	12,084.9	12,858.3	14,321.0	15,734.4	16,770.0
	12,112.4	14,103.5	17,024.9	19,713.0	18,115.5	21,230.0
	3,027.0	3,477.9	4,046.6	4,623.0	4,509.8	5,020.0
	335.9	386.9	421.8	553.2	706.5	760.0
	(51.5)	(36.7)	(25.8)	(30.9)	(45.5)	(50.0)
	8,801.0	10,275.4	12,582.3	14,567.7	12,944.7	15,500.0
	5.6	8.3	8.9	11.8	21.8	20.0
	$ 8,806.6	$10,283.7	$12,591.2	$14,579.5	$12,966.5	$15,520.0
	$ 710.2	$ 776.9	$ 890.2	$ 1,015.3	$ 935.5	$ 910.0
	1,472.5	1,794.8	1,670.3	2,058.1	2,626.5	2,650.0
	2,916.8	3,365.4	3,628.8	4,543.3	4,626.8	4,980.0
	241.1	294.2	147.9	(81.2)	180.8	210.0
	5,340.6	6,231.3	6,337.2	7,535.5	8,369.6	8,750.0
	3,466.0	4,052.4	6,254.0	7,044.0	4,596.9	6,770.0
	18.6	71.0	5.2	29.7	86.0	60.0
	3,447.4	3,981.4	6,248.8	7,014.3	4,510.9	6,710.0
	1,782.0	2,050.0	3,255.0	3,555.0	2,380.0	3,360.0
	$ 1,665.4	$ 1,931.4	$ 2,993.8	$ 3,459.3	$ 2,130.9	$ 3,350.0

Source: Corporate records.

clause. He felt certain that he could beat the inflation rate. The Ammco plant was the highest paying plant in the area. The result was a "good atmosphere and employees that don't want to leave."

Ammco plant workers were, for the most part, members of the United Steelworkers of America. Twenty-five people in the plant were not members, however, and did not pay dues. Wacker felt strongly that the open-shop concept was a fundamental worker right and vowed "I'll take a strike on it. Membership in the union should not be a condition of employment." His father had fought a case based on this principle all the way to the Supreme Court. It was Wacker's belief that labor and management need not have an adversary relationship. "Labor doesn't win unless management makes a profit. They rise and fall together."

Ammco's Executive Group

Wacker was always concerned with developing a good working executive group since the time he became the chief officer. Through the years he brought together his own operating staff. The group included:

J. Dragoni (55) joined Ammco in January 1956 as a New England district representative. After seven years, he was promoted to be the New England regional manager. During his tenure, he built up the New England sales force from four to 18 people. He was brought to the North

EXHIBIT 2
Balance Sheets for the Periods Ending December 31 ($000)

December 31,	1972	1973	1974	1975	1976	1977	1978	1979	1980
Cash	165.5	203.7	178.2	181.7	11.9	171.4	158.7	768.8	229.5
Securities	1050.0	325.0	325.0	1600.0	—	900.0	4874.7	3555.3	4947.2
Accounts receivable—net	1691.9	1365.3	1930.6	1819.1	2513.2	2672.3	3355.5	3745.4	4480.0
Due from Liquid Controls	5.6	76.6	116.1	14.7	11.9	35.1	39.6	20.3	
Inventories	1554.7	2209.9	2830.4	2648.5	3465.0	3782.9	3764.8	5834.9	5044.5
Inventory reserve—LIFO	—	—	(537.2)	(639.0)	(744.0)	(1221.0)	(1033.0)	(1246.0)	(1296.0)
Prepaid expenses	62.1	33.1	69.0	33.9	41.5	16.1	49.3	34.8	44.9
Total current assets	4529.8	4206.6	4912.1	5658.9	5299.5	6356.8	11209.6	12713.5	13450.1
Investment—LCC	800.0	850.0	850.0	1450.0	1130.0	1977.4	1658.6	1329.2	1078.9
Investment—rent-Ammco	—	—	—	1.0	800.0	438.6	438.6	—	—
Cash value of life insurance	174.9	236.9	297.2	351.6	409.0	528.9	686.0	827.9	399.1
Note receivable—Dayco	—	257.8	248.7	238.7	227.8	216.0	—	—	—
Other investments	36.4	36.4	36.4	36.4	482.4	1.6	1.6	1.6	1.7
Total investments	1011.3	1381.1	1432.3	2077.7	3049.2	3162.5	2784.8	2158.7	1479.7
Property, plant, and equipment	6072.7	7408.0	7855.0	8552.7	9833.0	11078.8	11878.3	14539.1	17151.2
Accumulated depreciation	(2429.1)	(2744.3)	(3359.0)	(3985.3)	(4646.0)	(5410.5)	(6178.8)	(7022.8)	(7788.0)
Net plant and equipment	3643.6	4663.7	4496.0	4567.4	5187.0	5668.2	5699.5	7516.3	9363.3
Patents and trademarks—net	11.2	13.1	13.0	13.1	12.9	12.8	12.4	1396.3	1286.0
Deferred federal income taxes	147.0	147.0	202.0	270.0	314.2	279.7	321.0	346.3	219.5
Total assets	9342.9	10411.5	11055.4	12587.1	13862.8	15480.2	20027.3	24130.9	25798.5
Notes payable to bank	—	—	—	—	—				
Accounts payable	366.2	448.8	459.9	410.4	717.8	416.6	519.9	963.3	790.0
Accrued expenses	774.6	610.9	692.2	730.6	730.5	854.0	1233.6	1621.8	2002.9
Federal and state inc. taxes	411.1	197.1	(126.3)	603.2	262.9	536.1	1976.1	1091.2	1211.4
Total current liabilities	1551.9	1256.8	1025.8	1744.2	1711.2	1806.8	3729.6	3676.3	4004.3
Long-term debt—Prud/other	850.0	941.3	900.7	324.3	392.1	322.1	292.6	1563.0	1034.9
Capital stock	1000.0	1000.0	1000.0	1000.0	1000.0	1000.0	1000.0	1000.0	1000.0
Earned surplus, Jan.	5519.5	5941.0	7214.4	8128.9	9518.6	10759.5	12350.9	14771.9	17891.6
Year to date profit	1661.1	1613.0	1254.1	1771.8	1665.4	1931.4	2993.7	3459.3	2130.9
Less: Dividends paid	(339.6)	(339.6)	(339.6)	(382.0)	(424.5)	(339.6)	(339.6)	(339.6)	(263.2)
Other	(900.0)								
Total equity	6941.0	8213.4	9128.9	10518.7	11759.5	13351.3	16005.0	18891.6	20759.3
Total Liabilities and Equity	9342.9	10411.5	11055.4	12587.2	13862.8	15480.2	20027.3	24130.9	25798.5
Current ratio	2.7	3.1	4.8	3.0	2.9	3.3	2.9	3.3	3.2
Book value per share	81.76	96.95	107.53	123.89	138.51	157.3	188.5	222.5	244.5

Source: Corporate records.

Chicago office in February 1979 as the Vice President of Sales to succeed L. Monteith. His mission was to increase export sales. Dragoni served as a B-29 navigator in the China–Burma–India theatre during World War II. He was married with two children.

L. Morrison (45) emigrated in 1950 from Israel where he worked for a racing-car company and auto shop. Before joining Ammco in 1972, he worked for Northwestern University building x-ray equipment. He joined the engineering department of Ammco, performing a wide variety of different functions at the entry level. He was gradually given increased responsibility until he was named a Vice President in 1977. Morrison succeeded Wally Mitchell, who retired in 1980 as head of research and development. He was married with no children.

A. D. Yankus (43) joined Ammco in 1959 shortly after obtaining a BS in accounting. His starting position was a junior accountant. He was promoted to Assistant Treasurer after eight years. He attended business school at night while he worked and was awarded an MBA in 1967. He was married and had two children.

Tom McPherson joined Ammco in 1961 as a Controller. He left the company at the age of 54. He had experience in a small printing company and the Toni Company, a division of Gillette, before joining Ammco. McPherson came to the company with a good background in data processing and aided in developing Ammco's computer-based information system. He assumed the added position of Treasurer in 1963 and during his tenure also served as Treasurer and Controller of Liquid Controls Corporation. In 1974 McPherson was promoted to General Manager, a position he held until leaving in 1977.

Wally Mitchell was another important member of the executive group until 1980. He had served as Vice President and Director of Manufacturing and Engineering. Although Mitchell had only a seventh-grade education, he had patented over 150 inventions, 20 of which were related to Ammco's business. Mitchell had worked in the 1930s under Fred Wacker, Sr. After leaving the company over some differences with Mr. Wacker, Sr., he returned under Fred Wacker, Jr. with whom he shared some common interests in the automotive field, including auto racing.

Mitchell was Fred Wacker, Jr.'s personal mechanic when Wacker was part of the French auto racing team. During his time with Ammco, he made many suggestions for streamlining Ammco's production system and designed some new items in the product line. Mitchell established a research group in Ammco to develop new products to solve problems encountered by large auto and brake companies which were customers of Ammco.

During Fred Wacker, Jr.'s tenure Mitchell was compensated as a consultant. He discontinued his activities with Ammco in 1980 at the age of 74.

Ammco's Development

Problems started to develop in the mid-1950s at Ammco. Many new products were introduced before being properly tested, and, as a consequence, the product line declined in quality. Ammco's plant and equipment were becoming obsolete. There were numerous bottlenecks and tie-ups in production. The situation worsened until 1967, when the cost of goods sold reached 56 percent of sales and profits dropped to 1.4 percent of sales. At one point, Wacker was not sure he would be able to meet the company's weekly payroll. Inventories became greater than unfilled orders, sales dropped, and Ammco's debt-to-equity ratio peaked at 70 percent.

In the summer of 1967, drastic measures were taken to turn the company around. These included: (1) reduction of the work force, (2) improvement of the existing products, and (3) use of only one production shift to aid in the reduction of inventories. By 1973 Ammco had $16 million in sales with 319 employees compared with $6 million in sales and 475 employees in 1967. The cost of goods sold was down to 44 percent of sales, and its after-tax profit was 10.6 percent of sales.

Throughout the 1970s, Ammco's sales (net shipments) increased at a fairly steady rate. Different elements converged to make the years 1971 to 1973 profitable years for Ammco. During that period, the company's profit rate was above the company's 10 percent profit goal.

Organizational Changes

Partly because of his firm's rapid expansion program, Wacker was concerned at the end of 1973. First, there was the problem of his succession and the future of the company. What would happen if he became disabled or he decided to retire? He knew that none of his other family shareholders was either able or willing to take the company over should such an event occur. Wacker's son was still very young and had not even decided which college he would like to attend.

In anticipation of a management succession problem, Wacker, early in 1974, modified his organization chart (Exhibit 3). At the same time, Tom McPherson was promoted from Treasurer and Controller to a newly created position of General Manager. Although he was not a family member, McPherson, in Wacker's mind, was being tested and trained to eventually take over the company should that become necessary. In his position McPherson had been responsible for the design, development, and introduction of new, computerized management information, inventory control, and production scheduling systems. McPherson was considered by many people in the company to be a likable person, respected in his job, and possessed important leadership abilities. As early as 1973, John Lauten, then Industrial Relations Manager, said: "I think Tom McPherson could do a good job of running the company and keeping the same atmosphere that Fred has established."

Ammco's rapid increase in sales and profits prompted a new investment program that was decided on in 1973. In 1976, these new capital investment programs were being implemented in order to keep pace with increased demand. There were two plants at that time:

1. Plant 1 in North Chicago, 108,330 square feet.
2. Plant 8, also in North Chicago, 60,000 square feet.

Plant 8 was enlarged by about 40,000 square feet at a cost of $19 a square foot. This increase in capacity was finished in 1977 and led to a major reorganization of Ammco's facilities. Machining was concentrated in Plant 1. The different parts were then transported the three miles to Plant 8 for assembly and shipping.

At Liquid Controls, a program of expansion was also undertaken: 23,400 square feet of space were added to the 49,000 square foot plant at a cost of $36 a square foot. The difference in cost was due to the fact that office space was added with a marble floor and expensive furniture.

EXHIBIT 3
Organization Chart, 1974

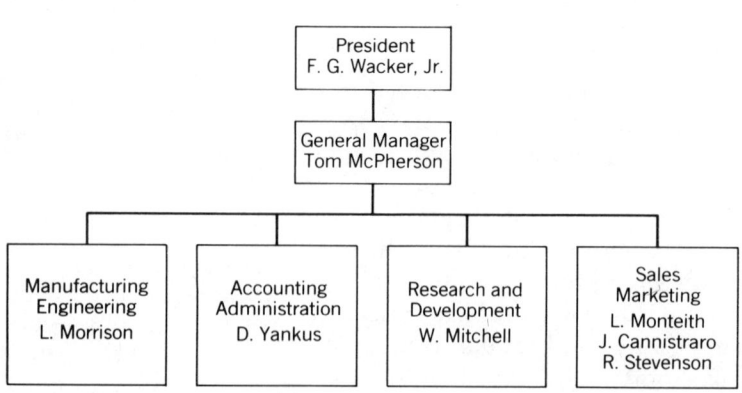

Source: Corporate records.

All this was done, as Wacker was proud to say, "without going to the banks, but financed out of retained earnings." In fact, in September 1976, the company did not have any long-term debt, and had been completely out of the banks and insurance company since the end of July 1975, when the balance of the Prudential loan was repaid.

This policy was also consistent with one of the company's basic objectives, which was "to finance growth through earnings rather than debt or public offerings." Wacker insisted on presenting this no-debt policy as one of the major elements of his business philosophy. (See Exhibit 4.) He said, "I do not want to be in anybody else's hands. In fact, I am not so much interested in growing fast as I am in growing solidly and securely."

According to him, internally generated cash would best allow a company to grow securely in the long run. A fair selling price should generate enough profits, which in turn should permit the company to expand. Although he recognized that his position was sometimes considered old-fashioned and too conservative, he was always eager to demonstrate that this policy was the only one that would enable a smaller size company like Ammco to survive in case of a recession or a drastic economic downturn.

Operating Changes

In August 1976, after long discussions and negotiations, all plant workers were taken off the incentive plan. The incentive system had been established in the late 1940s, and the rates had not substantially changed in the past 10 years. More than once, McPherson had recommended that shop workers on the floor be taken off this incentive plan. His argument against the plan was that some of the employees working on very big, slow-moving pieces had difficulty earning incentive.

For example, an average worker on one particular part was able to produce 7 pieces a day; another one, by pushing hard was eventually able to come up with 7.2 or 7.3 pieces during the same period, which did not allow him to substantially benefit from the incentive plan. For these reasons, nobody wanted to work on those jobs, which as a consequence always created back orders, delays, and scheduling problems. McPherson's idea was to give these workers a compensating pay raise and take them off the incentive plan.

Before the change, general supervisors met every morning in order to decide on the most important jobs, ones that had to be done during the day "to put out the fires." There was little scheduling in advance. Scheduling was complicated by the fact that there was often a shortage in certain critical small tools and accessories that were low-volume items.

McPherson had also remarked that workers were in fact metering their production and that there was significant group pressure not to go over the norms, so that the norms would not be revised: "What was supposed to be an incentive, was in fact a brake." Besides the problems created by the norms themselves, it

EXHIBIT 4
Basic Objective

Our basic objective is to operate a profitable, growth, manufacturing, and sales corporation selling quality products, competitively priced, to the automotive aftermarket.

Supporting objectives are to broaden the line of products, diversify into other lines not necessarily related to the automotive aftermarket, and to put profits back into the business, which, with the overall objective, indicates a conservative dividend policy.

Our further policy is to finance growth through earnings rather than debt or public offering.

With respect to employees, our policy is to pay well, operate both an annual bonus and a deferred profit-sharing plan, and in return expect maximum performance.

Further, we will have no planned obsolescence.

We will try to be a model of what is right about the free, competitive enterprise system.

Source: Corporate records.

was also difficult to find toolmakers. Although they were paid the highest hourly rate, they were not included in the incentive plan. Finally, Ammco was caught in a circular problem. It had the production capacity to turn out more units, but since the sales force was not selling enough, there was no pressure to produce more.

In 1976, after numerous lengthy discussions, McPherson finally convinced the plant manager and Wacker to shift to the new plan. Wacker agreed, but subject to the condition that the time–study person would go on doing his duties and "keep the old program going," just in case it proved necessary to revert to the old system. As soon as the paycheck ended up being bigger than before, the union accepted the change, scheduling improved, and problems started to disappear.

At the same time, however, production went down. The standard hours efficiency rate (the ratio of hours worked to units produced) was always in the 52 to 54 percent range before August 1976. After the change, it quickly went down and stabilized around 44 percent.

In terms of cost, the change did not cause any modification in the payroll for the workers who were included in the incentive plan previously. Their new rate was derived from their average weekly earnings divided into 40 hours. For the other workers, who were not directly included in the incentive plan before, there was a pay increase because they were in fact out of line with the other category.

Ammco's Position in the Automotive Industry

Ammco Tools, Inc., had six major product lines:

1. Heavy equipment: brake service—brake lathes and brake-shoe grinders.
2. Accessories: shop benches, facing sets, silencers, adaptors.
3. Small tools: cylinder and brake hones, ridge reamers, torque wrenches, declerometers.
4. Stones and cutters: tool bits, stone sets, and abrasive belts.
5. Wheel service: wheel alignment, gauges, instrumentation, and drive-on racks.
6. Parts: replacement parts for the heavy equipment.

Sales and profitability by product line are shown in Exhibit 5. The heavy number of models and products is indicated in Exhibit 6. Ammco's heavy equipment line dominated the business. The company had approximately 60 to 70 percent market share in this area with five major competitors. In the small-tool business, Ammco's share was more limited: between 10 and 15 percent of the market. Ammco faced many small competitors in various segments of the business. Snap-On Tools distributed various Ammco small tools through their direct-selling truck fleet.

Ammco was relatively new in the wheel service sector. Its major products were wheel alignment systems and drive-on racks. Although Ammco entered that line of business in 1963, sales remained rather flat and limited until 1974 (from $306,453 in 1966 to $369,487 in 1974). However, the sales of wheel service equipment started to increase rapidly after 1975. Ammco's share of this market was around three percent according to company estimates.

Marketing Philosophy

The products that Ammco designed were evaluated on the basis of whether they would appeal to the mechanics who would be using them. Wacker believed this was the way to beat his competitors. He did not believe in planned obsolescence. As a result the Ammco products continued to make a profit for their customers for a long time.

Ammco sold its products through warehouse distributors and automotive jobbers. Consequently, warehouse distribution amounted

EXHIBIT 5
Income Statements by Product Group Periods Ending December 31 (000s)

		1972	1973	1974	1975	1976	1977	1978	1979	1980 (budget)
	Sales by product group									
1	Heavy equipment	$ 8,275	$ 9,140	$10,645	$12,293	$12,808	$15,028	$17,150	$19,763	$21,400
2	Accessories	2,183	2,280	2,246	2,207	2,305	2,478	2,672	3,031	3,300
3	Small tools	1,904	1,932	2,018	2,508	2,303	2,554	2,772	4,132	4,600
4	Stones and cutters	1,698	1,839	1,867	2,358	2,729	3,086	3,543	2,725	2,900
5	Wheel service	304	272	369	770	2,083	2,280	2,770	2,962	3,600
6	Parts	398	505	456	587	684	757	967	1,093	1,200
9	Other	15	2	—	—	3	5	9	329	—
	Total	$14,777	$15,970	$17,601	$20,723	$22,915	$26,188	$29,883	$34,034	$37,000
	Gross profit by group									
1	Heavy equipment	$ 5,181	$ 5,233	$ 5,633	$ 6,084	$ 7,107	$ 8,425	$ 9,831	$11,580	$12,500
2	Accessories	1,366	1,361	1,234	1,217	1,315	1,428	1,557	1,766	1,920
3	Small tools	1,068	963	1,026	1,303	1,189	1,276	1,389	2,477	2,820
4	Stones and cutters	1,000	1,068	1,110	1,383	1,610	1,781	2,298	1,763	1,840
5	Wheel service	145	116	198	350	1,071	1,188	1,306	1,580	1,820
6	Parts	290	348	310	374	423	452	607	649	700
9	Other	2	2	—	—	1	3	5	161	—
	Total	$ 9,002	$ 9,091	$ 9,511	$11,431	$12,716	$14,533	$16,992	$19,904	$21,600

EXHIBIT 6
Product Line 1981

	Models	Replacement Parts/ Accessories
Alignment rack	5	
Air jacks	1	
Camber/caster gauges	1	1
Toe gauge—optical	1	4
Wheel clamps	2	—
Storage cabinets	4	—
Alignment tool sets	2	—
Scuff detector	1	—
Portable alignment testor	2	—
Brake shops/lathes	7	32
Brake drum grinder	2	4
Brake shoe grinder	4	10
Brake service tools	6	1
Cylinder hones	9	24
Brake bleeder/washers	2	7
Miscellaneous tools	28	

to 50 to 55 percent of total sales. Wacker considered going directly to the consumer like Snap-On Tools, Inc., and Sun Electric. He believed that he could reduce the price of a lathe substantially if he went directly to the consumer. He was afraid, however, that doing this might have a negative effect on the company's other lines.

Wacker believed that a business could compete on price, promotion, advertising, service, quality, or product differentiation, but that "you can't compete on all at the same time." He went on to say that "we compete on quality and service and try to be the highest-priced line, yet we give the best value per dollar spent. I care about profit, not volume." Wacker believed that salespeople focused too much on volume to the exclusion of relationship of a price charged and the service provided. It was his perception that he was not charging enough for the meters in LCC. "I have been trying to raise the price singlehandedly." He felt that while LCC devices cost more, the consumer got more value. "Salespeople always figure to sell on price." John Dragoni, the most recent Vice President of Sales has been asked to train the salespeople to look at sales from the company's point of view.

One of the problems that concerned Wacker was his belief that the new cars were more complicated than the old ones. Also, the older, heavier cars were more frequently in need of brake service than some of the newer, compact cars. The new brake repair machines had to be more complicated, yet perhaps would be used less frequently.

Marketing Wheel-Service Products

Sales of the wheel-service line, started in 1963, experienced uneven growth. Sales reached $306,453 in 1966, and fell to $177,983 in 1969 before recovering to $369,487 in 1974. A full line of products had been developed that included portable alignment testers, scuff detectors, wheel stand sets, four different types of drive-on rack sets, and a series of specific tools such as toe gauges, camber/caster gauges, and adjusting tools. The products were available, but the sales force ignored them and instead concentrated on selling the brake-service line. Thus, in November 1975, it was decided to introduce the Rent-Ammco program to gain a bigger share of the market in wheel alignment.

This program was a form of time payment that Ammco decided to finance internally as long as it was possible to do so. Ammco sold the wheel-alignment equipment to a dealer and at the same time lent money to a buyer who would buy it from a dealer. The buyer would then pay back in installments. The buyer who decided not to keep the equipment could easily terminate the contract on short notice.

McPherson and Wacker did not interpret this program in the same way. For the general manager this was a very useful marketing tool that was designed to attract more customers by easing the terms of the purchase plan. Moreover, he had always felt that this was a very flexible program that could easily be discontinued whenever necessary. Wacker, however, had always been reluctant to initiate this program, because of its possible drain on cash. He discovered somewhat later by examining the financial statements in March 1977 that the effect of the Rent-Ammco program on the company was even worse than he had expected. The program had gone above the projected $800,000 level and was already causing a cash drain of more than $1 million by the end of February.

Although it was using cash, the program was instrumental in overcoming customer resistance and, consequently, helped increase sales. The idea had originated from the salespeople themselves, who had always said that it would be very helpful to have a financing plan to aid in overcoming buyers' resistance.

At the time the Rent-Ammco program was in progress, a second program was implemented to increase the sales of wheel-alignment equipment. It was decided to put pressure on the sales force by increasing the number of salespersons and by redesigning and reducing sales territories. As a result the salesperson had to develop the sales of wheel-alignment units in order to be able to increase his or her compensation.

Finally, in 1976, L. Monteith, a new, aggressive sales manager launched the VAN program. He persuaded McPherson to decide on that program without Wacker's final approval. Formerly, each of the 100 salespersons had a van or station wagon that carried a demonstration unit. Monteith wished to introduce a new slogan: "Call the Ammco man in the blue van," and thought that each salesperson should have a van with two brake lathes in the back. These completely equipped vans would permit salesmen to make product demonstrations in the presence of any potential buyer. According to this plan, the company would buy the vans at fleet prices, install the demonstrator units inside, and carry the financing up to $7,000 a piece. Each salesperson had the choice to sign up for that program and acquire a new van (Dodge, Ford, or Chevrolet). The corresponding price would be deducted from salary and commissions over a two-year period. Wacker had been willing to consider this option, but only reluctantly. The program nevertheless was very popular, and about half the salespersons signed up for it. Since the company was cash-rich at that time, McPherson and Monteith had decided to finance the program directly.

Problems of the Expansion Program and Declining Sales

Over the summer of 1976, Wacker got somewhat worried about the extent of the expansion program itself. Early in September, he called McPherson into his office to express his doubts:

Wacker: What if anything goes wrong?

McPherson: Nothing will go wrong. The cash generated internally will be more than enough to finance our investment program.

Wacker: Well, I don't want to get caught off guard. Why don't you go and talk to the three major banks in Chicago and check with them about obtaining a line of credit?

A few weeks later, Wacker had not heard anything from McPherson about the line of credit. He asked him again. A few days later, Wacker talked to McPherson about the problem and discovered he had sent the Treasurer (Dennis Yankus) to check with the different banks on the possibility of obtaining that line of credit. By mid-October, McPherson had not presented any option for a line of credit; so Wacker decided to check himself with Northern Trust, which was co-executor of his father's estate. Northern Trust agreed to grant $1 million in revolving credit and a $0.5 million credit line.

In November, it was necessary to decide on the level of bonuses and dividends. The company had a fixed profit-sharing plan in which everybody participated. As usual, Wacker asked McPherson for his recommendations. The general manager proposed an increase in bonus by 51 percent over the previous year. He also recommended $42,450 in additional dividend payments. These recommended increases would mean the outlay of an additional $171,303 in cash for 1976 over the $634,596 paid in 1975 (bonus and dividends). Wacker was assured that this could be done without "getting into the bank." The following month, at the December meeting of the board of directors, Wacker proposed a resolution to increase the dividend and it was passed unanimously.

January 1977 proved to be a difficult period for the company. Although Ammco's sales were not significantly seasonal, January had traditionally been a weak month. Usually the two middle quarters accounted for about 53 percent of sales, whereas the winter and fall quarters only 47 percent. December, January, and February usually had lower sales. Sales in January 1977, however, were considerably below expectations. Net shipments amounted to only $1,003,038, a figure 5.5 percent lower than the corresponding figure a year before and 36.8 percent and 54.6 percent lower than net shipments for December 1976 and November 1976, respectively. Income statements and balance sheets for this period are shown in Exhibits 7 and 8.

Wacker tried to understand what went wrong. The explanation he received from his general manager was that external factors—not under company control—had caused very low sales and, consequently, very low shipments. Salespersons were just not bringing back any orders, and the few orders that were obtained could be processed at record speed.

Unshipped orders in December 1976 amounted to $858,514; at the end of January 1977, they were up to $886,149 but went back

EXHIBIT 7
Monthly Income Statements March 1976 to February 1977

	1976				
	Mar	Apr	May	June	July
Automotive					
Gross shipments	$1922.3	$2003.6	$2269.7	$2547.4	$1294.3
Less returns/allowances	32.6	23.0	41.8	23.0	30.8
Net shipments	1889.7	1980.6	2227.9	2524.1	1263.5
Cost of sales	920.4	926.5	983.2	1104.1	623.8
Gross Profit	969.3	1054.1	1244.7	1420.3	639.7
Other costs					
Commissions	251.8	254.3	297.2	343.4	164.5
Freight out	31.7	29.1	28.0	32.4	24.0
Other	(6.2)	(3.0)	(3.2)	(2.7)	(4.2)
Automotive Income	692.0	773.7	922.7	1047.2	455.4
Meter Income (LCC)	0.4	0.4	0.9	0.7	0.2
Total Income	$ 692.4	$ 774.1	$ 923.6	$1047.9	$ 455.6
Departmental Expense					
Engineering expense	58.3	53.1	54.1	54.2	60.1
Selling expense	127.7	149.0	113.4	109.6	116.7
Administrative expense	231.0	223.2	216.9	231.8	240.2
Other expense, net	10.4	19.0	17.3	23.7	24.6
Total departmental	427.4	444.3	401.7	419.3	441.6
Operating Income	265.0	329.8	521.9	628.6	14.0
Interest expense	—	—	—	—	—
Net Income	265.0	329.8	521.9	628.6	14.0
Tax provision	132.0	167.0	261.0	316.0	7.0
Net Profit	$ 133.0	$ 162.8	$ 260.9	$ 312.6	$ 7.0

down to $537,978 at the end of February. At Ammco an average backlog of orders of $1 million was considered normal. It amounted to about two weeks work of orders ($0.5 million was a minimum since it took about one week just to process an order).

In addition to weak demand, Yankus, the treasurer, felt that past increases in prices may have played a role. Prices might have been over the competitive level at that time. In fact, after the freeze in prices and wages, the trend was reversed in 1974. Inflation set in and with newly liberated prices and wages, costs went up. In order to maintain the profit margin, Ammco started to raise its prices twice a year to recover cost increases. In 1974, the biggest increase amounted to 19 percent; then prices increased every 6 months at an average yearly rate of 8 to 12 percent until they started to stabilize in 1977.

Wacker discovered that internal reasons also played a role in the low shipments. In a conversation with the plant manager, he found out that production had been stopped for a week in January in order to take a new inventory. The physical inventory figures did not match the computerized inventory figures. There were large discrepancies, apparently because of recordkeeping problems with a new inventory control system.

On February 2, McPherson came to see Wacker and asked that $500,000 be borrowed as interim working capital in order to alleviate the consequences of the poor January sales performance. Wacker agreed, after being assured that this sum would be adequate for the

	1976					1977	
	Aug	Sept	Oct	Nov	Dec	Jan	Feb
	$2057.4	$2038.5	$2214.2	$2241.0	$1633.2	$1039.2	$2094.5
	46.8	32.6	36.0	34.1	46.3	36.2	58.6
	2460.6	2005.9	2178.2	2206.9	1586.9	1003.0	2035.9
	1087.3	951.8	1031.1	1090.6	788.6	727.1	926.7
	1373.3	1054.1	1147.1	1116.3	798.3	275.9	1109.2
	322.0	265.4	289.4	293.1	212.9	141.4	274.6
	26.4	41.6	25.4	31.8	32.2	22.0	24.7
	(7.9)	(4.2)	(3.9)	(4.3)	(3.4)	(3.7)	(5.1)
	1032.8	751.3	836.2	795.7	556.6	116.2	815.0
	0.4	0.4	0.3	0.4	0.4	0.4	2.0
	$1033.2	$ 751.7	$ 836.5	$ 796.1	$ 557.0	$ 116.6	$ 817.0
	57.4	63.2	66.3	73.9	74.2	67.4	67.3
	87.1	172.2	118.9	143.9	146.8	119.6	139.9
	232.4	226.0	234.4	252.9	378.8	273.7	275.6
	3.8	23.5	23.1	8.4	77.6	14.6	11.8
	380.7	484.9	442.7	479.1	677.4	475.3	494.6
	652.5	266.8	393.8	317.0	(120.4)	(358.7)	322.4
	(1.2)	—	—	—	(7.4)	—	(2.9)
	651.3	266.8	393.8	317.0	(137.8)	(358.7)	319.5
	326.0	134.0	195.0	158.0	(12.0)	(180.0)	163.0
	$ 325.3	$ 132.8	$ 198.8	$ 159.0	$(125.8)	$(178.7)	$ 156.5

foreseeable future. Three weeks later, McPherson asked that an additional $300,000 be borrowed. Again Wacker sought and received assurances that this amount would be sufficient. On March 3, McPherson asked that $200,000 more be borrowed. The following exchange ensued:

Wacker: In September you said we would not need anything and did not even bother to go to the banks in order to ask for a line of credit. Then you said we had to borrow $500,000 and that this would be enough. Then $300,000 more, and now we are up to $1 million. Are you sure that this will be the last time.

McPherson: Yes. This will be enough.

McPherson again explained that the problem in January could not have been foreseen and that borrowing money was the only way to reduce the adverse effects on the company's financial statements. Sales for February of $2,035,858 were much higher than in January. A loss of $178,687 in January and profit of $156,410 in February still left the company in a net loss position. On March 7, McPherson was again in Wacker's office:

McPherson: Despite past projections, I think we're going to need to draw down another $500,000 from our line of credit.

Operating Problems—Turnaround Efforts

In March 1977, Wacker was concerned about the recent incorrect cash projections from his

EXHIBIT 8
1977 Balance Sheet—Through June 30, 1977

	December 31, 1974	December 31, 1975	December 31, 1976
Cash	$ 178,198	$ 181,720	$ 11,869
Securities	325,000	1,600,000	
Accounts receivable—net	1,930,580	1,819,056	2,513,216
Due from LCC	116,112	14,724	11,907
Inventories	2,830,364	2,648,480	3,464,989
Inventory reserve—LIFO	537,100	639,000	744,000
Prepaid expenses	68,985	33,907	41,510
Total current assets	4,912,139	5,658,887	5,299,491
Investment—LCC	850,000	1,450,000	1,130,000
Investment—rent-Ammco		1,000	800,000
Cash value of life insurance	297,161	351,629	408,976
Note receivable—Dayco	248,669	238,699	227,848
Note receivable—JWB	—	—	480,710
Other investments	36,420	36,420	1,650
Total investments	1,432,250	2,077,748	3,049,184
Property, plant, and equipment	7,855,047	8,552,697	9,832,970
Accumulated depreciation	3,359,073	3,985,257	4,645,989
Net plant and equipment	4,495,974	4,567,440	5,186,981
Patents and trademarks	13,015	13,078	12,911
Deferred federal income taxes	202,000	270,000	314,274
Total Assets	11,055,378	12,587,153	13,862,841
Notes payable to bank	—	—	—
Accounts payable	459,866	410,362	717,780
Accrued expenses	692,239	730,575	730,466
Federal and state income taxes	126,345	603,185	262,909
Total current liabilities	1,025,760	1,744,122	1,711,155
Long-term debt Prud	650,000	—	—
Long-term debt—bank	—	—	—
Long-term debt—other	250,699	324,395	392,151
Capital stock	1,000,000	1,000,000	1,000,000
Earned surplus, Jan. 1	7,214,412	8,128,919	9,518,637
Year to date profit	1,254,107	1,771,768	1,665,400
Less dividends paid	339,600	382,050	424,500
Other	—	—	—
Total equity	9,128,919	10,518,637	11,759,537
Total Liabilities and Equity	$11,055,378	$12,578,153	$13,862,841
Current ratio	4 .8	3.0	2.9
Book value per share	107 .53	123.80	138.51

	January 31, 1977	February 28, 1977	March 31, 1977	April 30, 1977	May 31, 1977	June 20, 1977
	$ 48,332	$ 152,000	$ 165,261	$ 41,004	$ 113,963	$ 214,758
	—	—	—	—	—	—
	1,894,005	2,492,754	2,890,416	3,440,843	3,586,485	3,260,186
	12,129	43,380	15,946	48,117	42,457	23,657
	3,877,347	4,074,120	4,273,603	4,061,599	3,735,342	3,533,871
	744,000	780,000	780,000	780,000	780,000	780,000
	26,022	64,133	519	172,517	158,744	170,460
	5,113,835	6,046,447	6,565,745	6,784,080	6,856,971	6,422,962
	1,120,000	1,110,000	1,060,000	1,060,000	1,060,000	1,060,000
	900,000	1,060,000	1,111,892	1,163,015	1,209,203	1,188,209
	408,976	408,976	408,976	408,976	408,976	408,976
	226,902	225,949	224,989	224,022	223,049	222,069
	559,621	618,525	677,422	851,312	850,195	954,071
	1,650	1,650	1,650	1,650	1,650	1,650
	3,217,149	3,425,100	3,484,929	3,708,975	3,753,073	3,834,979
	10,016,617	10,154,025	10,246,943	10,397,094	10,582,029	10,729,700
	4,720,909	4,795,989	4,870,989	4,945,989	5,020,989	5,095,959
	5,295,628	5,358,036	5,375,954	5,451,105	5,561,040	5,633,711
	12,811	12,711	12,611	12,511	12,411	12,311
	114,274	314,274	314,274	314,274	314,274	314,274
	13,953,697	15,156,568	15,753,513	16,270,945	16,497,769	16,278,253
	—	—	500,000	500,000	500,000	500,000
	1,234,893	1,083,443	740,683	949,892	440,854	456,872
	152,102	976,371	786,703	811,807	927,934	874,364
	14,298	148,702	381,702	402,952	710,109	333,359
	1,972,697	2,208,516	2,409,088	2,664,651	2,578,897	2,164,595
	—	—	—	—	—	—
	—	800,000	1,000,000	1,000,000	1,000,000	1,000,000
	400,151	408,151	411,816	419,816	427,816	411,461
	1,000,000	1,000,000	1,000,000	1,000,000	1,000,000	1,000,000
	10,759,537	10,759,537	10,759,537	10,759,537	10,759,537	10,759,537
	78,687	22,277	257,973	511,843	816,420	1,032,321
	—	—	84,900	84,900	84,900	169,800
	11,680,850	11,737,260	11,932,610	12,186,480	12,491,057	12,622,058
	$13,953,697	$15,156,568	$15,753,513	$16,270,945	$16,497,769	$16,218,233
	2.4	2.6	2.6	2.4	2.5	2.8
	136.41	138.25	140.55	143.54	147.13	148.67

general manager. He decided to write him a letter indicating the specific objectives to be accomplished by the end of the year. (See Exhibit 9.) A copy of the letter was sent to the other top executives of the company in order to "bring Ammco's situation out in the open and in order that all will share in the responsibility of turning the company around."

Among the items mentioned were the following:

- Incur no additional debt and liquidate all existing debt.
- Incur no more capital expenditures without Wacker's approval.
- Increase shipments to $26 million a year, reduce inventory to $3.1 million, and increase inventory turnover to 3.8.
- Earn 9.6 percent on sales after tax by year end.

On the same list were other programs that Wacker wanted reduced or refinanced in order to decrease the financial burdens on the company.

In addition, Wacker had grown dissatisfied with the company's organization structure. All important information had been filtered to him through the general manager. He decided to reorganize his top corporate management team, and, at the same time, take some responsibilities away from McPherson. Thus, the responsibility of the plant was given entirely to Lenny Morrison, who was placed in charge of manufacturing and engineering. McPherson was assigned to a newly created position, Vice President in charge of Administration. An executive committee was also formed, composed of Wacker, McPherson (administration), Yankus (treasurer), Morrison (manufacturing and engineering), and Wally Mitchell (research and development).

Inventory problems continued throughout July 1977. The difference between the physical inventory and computer inventory figure could not be reconciled. Wacker finally

EXHIBIT 9
Letter from Wacker to McPherson

AMMCO TOOLS, INC/2100 COMMONWEALTH AVENUE/NORTH CHICAGO, ILLINOIS 60064
March 16, 1977

Tom McPherson
General Manager

Dear Tom:

In order that Ammco Tools, Inc., may eliminate its indebtedness to the Northern Trust Company before the end of this year, please make it your business to achieve the following objectives as soon as possible:

1. *Van Program*
   No more vans to be ordered by Ammco after the 12 on order are delivered. Please attempt to refinance the 32 vans at the National Bank of North Chicago or elsewhere. The proposed van program desired by Mr. Cannistraro can be carried out and completed providing the financing is not done by Ammco. Please let me know as soon as this is completed.

2. *Rent—Ammco*
   Please see that the Rent-Ammco program is discontinued immediately, and by that I mean: no more new business is to be written.

3. *Inventory*
   Inventory to be reduced to $3,100,000, which should support shipments of $26,000,000 at 3.8 inventory turns per year at present prices.

4. No new obligations of any sort to be taken on without my approval.

5. I wish to sign all capital equipment or other requisitions for $500.00 or more. This does not include purchases for inventory, which will be controlled by item #3 above.

6. No additional employees to be hired other than sales representatives. Both attrition and terminations, as necessary, will serve to reduce work force in office and plant.

7. No salary increases are to be given, and I will approve none in any case, until our situation is turned around.

8. You have stated that you believe that our 9.6%

(*Continued*)

EXHIBIT 9 (Continued)

after tax profit on sales is too high to achieve. I believe it's too low as an objective. With proper management we should be able to achieve it and go beyond it.

Please let me know if you have any questions with respect to any of the above as there should be no misunderstandings.

Fred G. Wacker, Jr.

cc: Mr. W. F. Mitchell
Mr. Len Morrison
Mr. Dennis Yankus

Source: Corporate records.

---

retained a consulting firm, which after review presented him with some preliminary conclusions and a list of recommendations.

Essentially these were:

1. The company was running too many computers. One would be enough. In fact, there were three computers: One IBM 360-40 at Ammco and two IBM 360-30's—one at Liquid Controls and the other one reserved for programming tests. This was primarily because of the fact that during the 1960s, Wacker was upset about Liquid Control's dependency on Ammco. In fact, Liquid Controls was a second fiddle. Ammco's problems were always solved first. For this reason, the companies were completely separated in 1967, but were not in two separate buildings. Later on, the same decision was made for the computer. Liquid Controls would have its own computer so that it could get proper service and would not have to wait for Ammco's programs to be run first.

2. The company had too many people in both the office and the plant. A reduction of the size of the staff was needed. The consulting firm was proposing a $64,610 payroll reduction through the termination of four employees.

McPherson had been in close contact with the consultants since the beginning of the study and had been aware of their preliminary conclusions. Early in September, the head of the consulting firm, Sam Rose, called Wacker about McPherson's lack of cooperation:

Rose: Fred, we can't get anywhere. You paid for these studies. We proposed a few changes, but McPherson is still "stonewalling" my recommendations for change.

On Friday, September 9, 1977, Wacker terminated McPherson's employment with Ammco. The following morning McPherson called him at home and wanted to see him. Wacker set up a Monday meeting.

At the meeting McPherson handed Wacker a letter. In the letter McPherson regretted the fact that he had disappointed Wacker, reviewed his work history, and argued that he would be the best individual to implement the recommendations from the computer consultants, Sam Rose and Company. McPherson concluded the letter:

> You have many efforts going on to reach the objectives you have set for the company. When it comes to setting up and running internal controls systems in all of these areas, the best person you could have working to accomplish this is myself, simply because of my experience with both companies over the years. There is also the highly important fact that I am well liked and respected by most people in the company, which gives me the ability to work with them without representing an unknown or threatening force that any newcomer must necessarily overcome. While both of us do not subscribe to the indispensable person theory, it is nevertheless true that someone other than myself would have to go through a familiarization period, both in learning how all things I have mentioned are done and in working toward rapport with all the other people concerned.
>
> To get the job done right and as expeditiously as possible, I believe I am your best man.

On the basis of McPherson's letter and their conference together on Monday morning, Wacker told McPherson a few days later that he could return.

After his return, McPherson let it be known that he did not agree with some of the consultant's proposals. He was particularly adamant about not changing either the computers and/or computer personnel. Wacker and Rose talked on the phone once more about the decisions that would have to be made and about McPherson's lack of flexibility in carrying them out. Wacker again asked for McPherson's resignation. McPherson left the company on September 30, 1977.

Reflecting on this event, Wacker said:

> To this day I like Tom. I felt sorry about it, but there was no other way except to let him go. I told McPherson, "You got me in debt. I asked you to do some things and you didn't do them." He didn't follow through. He worked with me long enough. He knew what I wanted.

During the fall, they effectively started to do the work of two companies on a single computer (IBM 360-40). The elimination of the two IBM 350-30's was effective as of October 12 for Ammco and November 12 for Liquid Controls. Wacker still received the same reports as he did before.

In terms of material management, Ammco's inventory reduction program proceeded on schedule. At a meeting with the consultant and Ammco's top executives on October 12, it was announced that coding had been completed for all manufactured parts and that appropriate run quantities (economic order quantities) and appropriate reorder points would be calculated and available for review by October 17.

Following the consultant's recommendation three people were dismissed. At the same time, Wacker felt that Ammco was slightly overstaffed in terms of production personnel; therefore, no new people were added to the production floor in 1977, and consequently, the size of the work force decreased from 211 persons in January to 196 at the end of December as a result of attrition.

In an interview Wacker made the following points:

- In April and May, the company experienced record sales.
- In October, monthly shipments exceeded $3 million for the first time.
- In March, April, and May, the profit rate exceeded the 10 percent target.
- The last portion of the $1.5 million line of credit was paid back in October.

In reviewing the new organizational structure, Wacker felt that he had made a mistake earlier. He noted:

> When Tom was general manager, he had, in fact, the position of an executive vice-president. All the other executives reported to him instead of reporting directly to me. Therefore, I did not always get the whole story. I lost touch with what was going on. Now, in the new structure, everybody reports directly to me. There is no one in between. Communications are more direct, better, and more satisfying.

Ammco's Development After the 1977 Turnaround

The departure of McPherson was followed by the appointment of J. Dragoni as Sales Manager replacing L. Monteith, who had initiated the VAN program. Wally Mitchell retired at 74 as Director of Research and Development and was succeeded by Lenny Morrison.

Wacker ran the company through an informal executive group, consisting of Morrison, Yankus, and the Vice President of Sales and Marketing, Dragoni. Morrison had gradually assumed responsibility for research and development as Mitchell moved toward retirement at the age of 74.

Wacker also changed Ammco's Canadian distribution, replacing an outside organization

EXHIBIT 10
New Organization Chart

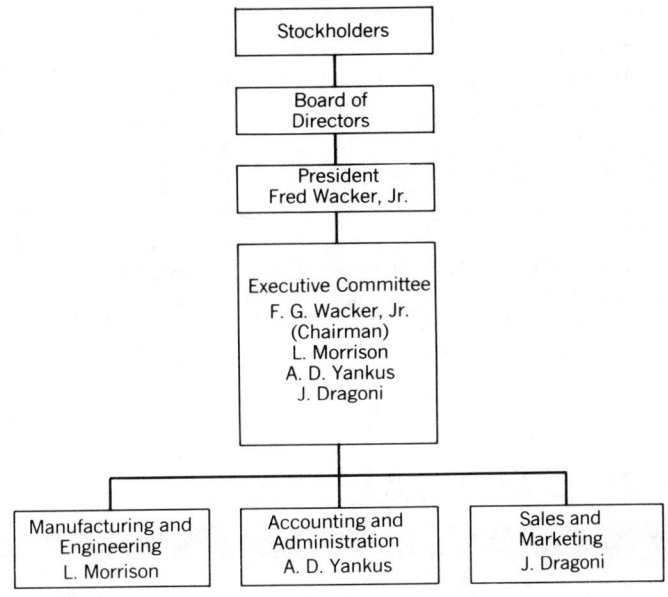

Source: Corporate Records.

with direct Ammco people, as in the United States. The responsibility of sales and product distribution in Canada was taken over by an employee of Ammco's sales department in the headquarters office. A new Ammco plant scheduled to open in 1980 was delayed until the spring of 1981 because of construction problems. Because of the delay, production at the old plant had to be modified several times in the first quarter of 1980. Sales declined in the first quarter of 1980 after a strong fourth quarter in 1979. Inventory reached a level of $6.86 million. Wacker initially responded by putting the hourly workers on a four-day work week. He then let 15 employees go. Inventory levels remained high despite the reduced production, however, and an additional 100 employees were laid off before the problem was ultimately resolved.

After a number of years of touring the trade shows looking for companies to purchase, Wacker initiated discussions with four firms about the possibility of acquisition. Discussion with one company was ended when the owner kept increasing the price each time an agreement appeared imminent. A second set of negotiations was successful. In 1979 an agreement to purchase Magnum Corporation was completed approximately one year after negotiations were initiated. The final sales price was $2.5 million. Magnum was a small, family-run corporation. The owner and senior manager was an older man who ran the company with the assistance of his son-in-law. The Ohio-based company was roughly 10 years old. Its sole product was a patented, automatic tire changer.

In reflecting on the company's performance, Wacker wondered how effectively he had dealt with McPherson and the cash-drain problem that occurred in 1977. He was also concerned with immediate and future changes needed to be implemented to achieve his long-term goal of "staying alive" in a highly competitive and rapidly changing industry. While satisfied with the past financial performance of the company, he found the most recent financial data disappointing. (See Exhibits 1 and 2.)

The rapid increase in small cars also presented a challenge and market opportunity for Ammco. Small engines would have to be rebuilt, particularly if people tended to keep cars longer. This would result in an increased demand for engine-rebuilding tools. Brakes on smaller cars also tended to wear out sooner and would demand increased service. This also held true for tires and wheel alignment.

Management succession was also a matter Fred Wacker had given consideration. He expressed great confidence in Lenny Morrison as an executive who was adept in manufacturing, engineering, and product development. He stated that his son looked like the only real possibility to succeed him at this time. Although his son had worked in the plant for three summers while in college, Fred Wacker was not sure if his son had made up his mind to commit himself to the business.

5 INTERNATIONAL

BORDADOS MATY, S. A.

Twenty years ago, Señora Carolina Garcia turned out a child's dress on her home Singer sewing machine and sold it. Today that machine is ensconced in her plush, feminine, pink-upholstered Vice President's Office.

Based in Aguascalientes, Bordados Maty is one of the largest apparel manufacturers in Mexico. "Maty Group" includes a number of product line divisions including unconsolidated subsidiaries for tax purposes. Approximately 85 percent of revenues come from the Apparel Division. The basic product line has always been dresses for little girls, in which the firm remains dominant. Other lines include women's dresses as well as clothing for little boys. These two lines are active, but have never been fully developed and promoted.

Sra. Garcia, as Founder and Vice President, spends much of her time walking through production facilities and communicating with her son and Executive Vice-President Carlos on matters that need to be corrected. She also heads a Design Department of 20 people. One of her subordinates in the Design Department is Carlos' wife. At least three times a year, the key design people travel to Europe and the United States seeking fashion information.

The Design Department is considered an expensive function that few firms in the industry can duplicate. The department nominally reports to the Sales Manager, but because of the family relationship of the key design people, it actually reports to the general management level.

The industry consists of hundreds of small producers of limited lines. These producers have no design departments; they openly copy others' successful designs. Frequently, they do not pay taxes and various fringe benefits that the Government requires. Only three or four

---

Source: This case was prepared by Lincoln W. Deihl. Permission to use granted by Lincoln W. Deihl.

producers in Mexico operate on the scale of Maty Group.

Maty is the name of Sra. Carolina's mother and daughter. The latter is a university student who is frequently seen in temporary jobs at the company. Senora Carolina's husband, Don Carlos, is President, but largely occupies himself in a small, woodworking shop built for him on the ground floor beneath the Executive Offices. The family home is near the center of the walled compound that encloses the main plant.

Carlos, the son of the founders, at age 33 is Executive Vice-President and General Manager. He left school at 13 to work in the factory his parents had recently founded. He worked at various jobs in the plant, such as cutting and folding. At age 22, Carlos directed production; at 32, he directed marketing. He took on these positions as the respective functions became dominant in the firm. There was little interest at this time in "administracion," the control function.

Gradually, Carlos became aware of the need for expanding the function of general management. Several years ago, he took the IPADE course, a high-quality Executive Program offered both in Mexico City and Guadalajara. As a result, he has become quite a sophisticated general manager. All of his top-level managers currently are taking the IPADE course, flying in a chartered airplane to Guadalajara Tuesday noons and returning Wednesday evenings. Middle-level managers are making plans to attend the course within the next year.

Meetings of Management

On the evening of June 9, 1980, two important meetings were held to implement the new organization structure designed by Carlos and Planning Director, Raúl González. The first meeting at 5:00 P.M was attended by the Executive Committee: the newly named Head of the Human Resources Division, Jose Antonio Torres (age 29); the Head of the Administrative Services Division, Humberto Salazar (age 30); the Head of the Apparel Division, Rolando Garcia (age 34); the Head of Comarco, the Domestic Products subsidiary, Francisco Avayo (age 33); the Head of the Bordamex subsidiary, Javier Medina (age 32); the Head of Production in the Apparel Division, Jose de la luz Lopez (age 27). The remaining member, the Head of the Industrial Division, had not yet been named. (See Exhibit 1.)

Later that evening, lower-level managers were brought into the meeting. Carlos announced that the new structure was designed by him and the Planning Director. Some questions were asked, particularly about the level of Bordamex. Carlos explained that the capital structure and growth prospects for Bordamex required that it be this level. The organization structure and the rationale were apparently well accepted.

Comarco (Domestic Division)

Francisco Avayo, the new Head of Comarco, S. A. (Domestic Division), has been with Maty Group for 10 months. With his marketing degree from Iberro–Americana University, he spent nine years in Mexico City in marketing and organization development positions with Nestlé. Originally from Aguascalientes, he accepted the opportunity to return, recognizing the element of risk in his career move.

Francisco has the task of establishing an autonomous profit center. Traditionally called the Domestic Division, it has been an integral part of the firm from the beginning. But with the economic growth of Mexico, there was a great demand for ready-made clothing; this is where the firm placed its priorities. Today the Apparel Division generates 85 percent of revenues, and the Domestic Division generates most of the rest.

Comarco, S. A. is now being established as a separate profit center to replace the Domestic Division. The biggest problem is finding production facilities. Arrangements have been made with the Governor of the State to

EXHIBIT 1
Bordados Maty, S. A.

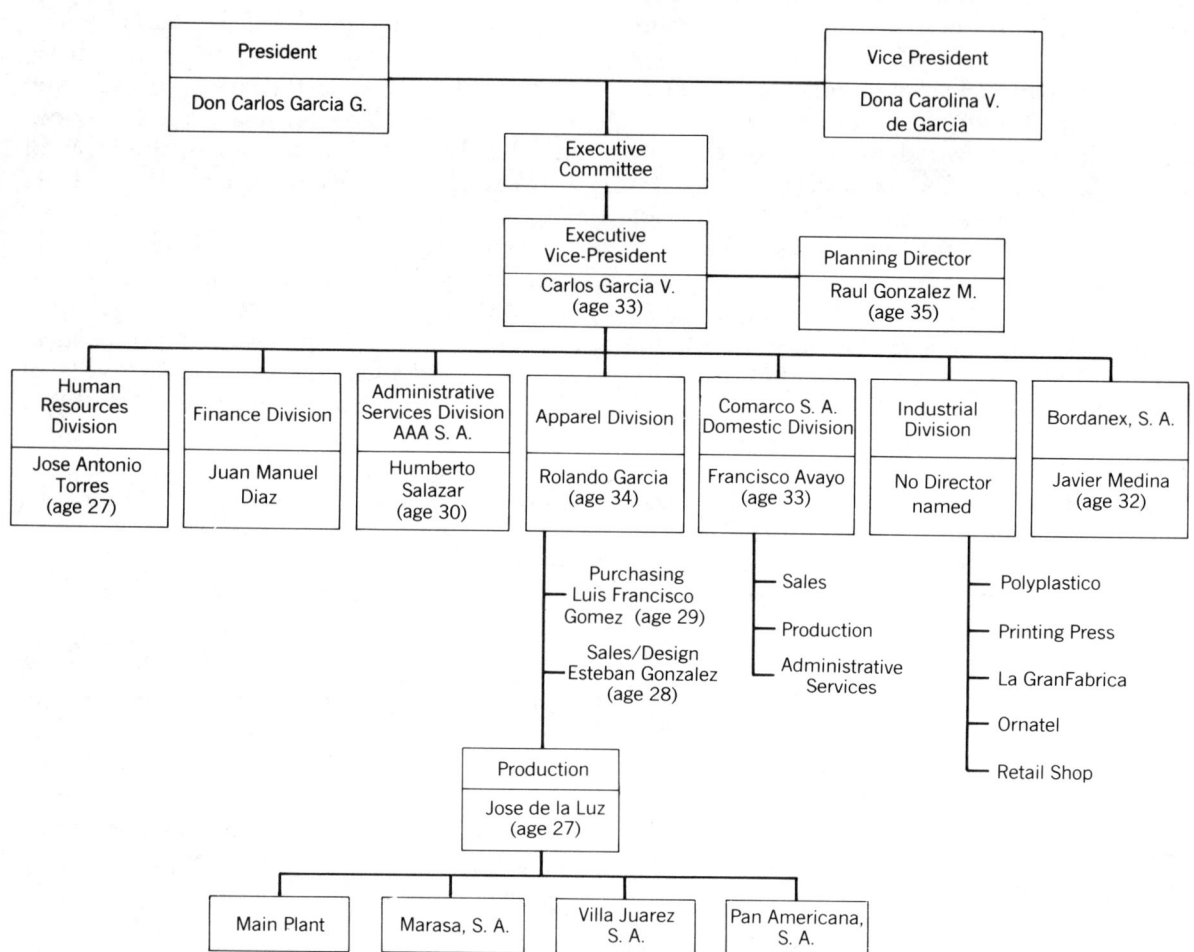

set up two new factories in an underdeveloped part of the state. Construction is already underway. Present output for the division is 49,000 items per month. Current demand is for 85,000 items. Product lines include textiles for the home: kitchen, bathroom, bedroom, living room, and dining room and for institutional needs: hotels, restaurants, hospitals, military, etc. Institutions normally are supplied on a long-term contract basis. Francisco believes there is a vast potential market, virtually untapped, particularly in institutions. He has recently hired a production manager and a manger of administration and finance. He will take care of marketing himself at present; he sees no major marketing problems at present.

Distribution is through the five sales offices of the Apparel Division. The same physical facilities are used in Monterrey, Guadalajara, Mexico City, and Mazatlan. Separate facilities are used in Vera Cruz. Comarco now has its own people in all these facilities.

Francisco sees no serious problem in obtaining supervisory and middle-management personnel. These people are available in Maty Group and can be transferred. They are frequently willing to come for promotion and added responsibility. It will probably not be possible to find many skilled workers locally because the new plants are somewhat remote. But the firm will provide transportation for workers from Aguascalientes.

Francisco has developed his own control system, relatively simple and economical. He will utilize the Administrative Services Division only for data collecting.

Human Resources

José Torres, newly named Head of the Division of Human Resources, has a Business Administration degree with a major in Industrial Relations from Iberro–Americana University in Mexico City where he was a scholarship holder. While studying, because of financial need, he held a full-time job in Industrial Relations with Alfa Group, a major Mexican holding company. He found the pace "killing" and went with Famosa, a firm in Monterrey. After two years, he accepted an industrial relations job with Maty Group. He was named Head of Division after one year.

José's biggest problem is getting the line managers to recognize that training and development is a line responsibility and that HR is only there to assist and provide resources. He sees a problem in filling new training positions with specialists because these people are scarce. He is uncertain whether his key subordinates can really adapt and change to the new reality of the significance of HR. He believes that top management is now convinced of the importance of developing human resources if the firm is to continue to grow. Marc Rouvroy (age 27) is Belgian and related to the family: his mother was a sister of Sra. Carolina. He came to work in the company two years ago as an alternative to military service. The Belgian government permits work in a Third-World country as a military alternative.

Marc has worked in Human Resources, Production, Administrative Services, and the Domestic Division. Usually, he has been in staff rather than line activities. He has prepared several studies of operations in various units. Currently, he is involved in distribution with some supervisory responsibility for personnel in sales offices. Also, he is concerned with coordination of Purchasing and Production activities.

The Company is sending Marc to IPADE in Mexico City for two years to earn his Master of Business Administration degree. He expects to remain in the company several more years, but is uncertain as to his future. He has learned Spanish while in Mexico and is well accepted by others. If the company expands its export activities, he would like to establish a sales office in the United States.

Marc sees possible problems in Industrial Relations. Traditionally, the company has had good relations as a paternalistic employer. The majority of employees are women at low levels. There is a single labor union—Government sponsored—which employees are required to join. Management is on good terms with union representatives. Carlos and the head of the local union are good friends.

Marc sees a number of instances of favoritism, unfairness, and discrimination; he feels these may cause problems. For example, night watchmen work 13-hour shifts at below-standard wages. He feels the company could face many industrial relations problems in the future as workers become more aware.

Labor Problems at Villa Juárez

Recently, there was a work stoppage for the first time at Villa Juárez, a rural plant. The cause was dissatisfaction over the profit-sharing arrangement. Work resumed after several hours only when Carlos, Sra. Carolina, and the labor union representative visited the plant.

The Government requires that 8 percent of profits be shared with workers. Each year the plant labor representative and the Company sign a document setting forth the agreement for the annual profit distribution. Then, 15 days later the distribution actually takes place. Profit-sharing is based on each plant as a profit center.

At the Villa Juárez plant, workers actually received only about 65 percent of the previous year's distribution. This was apparently because of some problems and inefficiencies at the plant during the past year. Operations and piece-rate earnings were very much affected by problems with flow and quality of raw materials.

Two agitators among the workers apparently spread the story that the company was manipulating figures and trying to cheat them. After all, the company is supposed to have been growing and expanding in the past year. So, workers all went out on an illegal work stoppage. The plant manager happened to be in Aguascalientes at the time. Headquarters was notified by radio because this is the only means of rapid communication.

A number of meetings were held at headquarters as the plant manager rushed to Villa Juárez. Carlos and the head of the labor union for the state eventually went to the plant as well. In the first meeting with the workers, the labor union head impressed upon them that the company had always been fair, that the work stoppage was illegal, and that they could be fired. As a result, most returned to work.

In a subsequent meeting with workers who stayed out, the labor union head apparently promised vaguely that the company would provide some additional compensation. Apparently, this had been discussed at Headquarters as an alternative; however, several managers had opposed such "capitulation" as setting a dangerous precedent.

At any rate, everyone eventually returned to work, including the two identified agitators who showed "remorse." The company now has the problem of determining whether and how much additional compensation should be granted.

The agitators have been identified as being affiliated with a socialist political party–labor union that has been increasingly active in various parts of the country. In particular, in the southern city of Oaxaca, agitation was accompanied by violence. This political party–labor union presently has approximately 3,000 families illegally occupying a camp in Aguascalientes. The Governor has taken a low-key approach to the problem and avoided violence.

The town of Villa Juárez has near the plant two Government-operated, but Communist-controlled teacher-training institutions. The company feared that instructors at the institutions would attempt to take advantage of the labor situation at the nearby plant, but this has not yet happened.

The Villa Juárez plant manager is the right-hand man of José de la Luz. He has been here for 10 months and expects to be replaced in two months. He will then become a coordinator of plant managers. As such, he will travel to the various plants to try to improve coordination with Purchasing and balance the work load among plants. A new plant manager cannot yet be developed internally. The new manager will probably be shifted from the nearby rural plant at Palo Alto.

Presently, the Villa Juárez manager sees no problems with the workforce. But he says that management is watching carefully for trouble, especially among the identified agitators. He expects no further labor problems. At the moment he speaks, the plant again is experiencing problems with the water supply for essential worker facilities.

There are problems at Villa Juárez with continuity of supplies. Production workers were laid off the previous week for this reason. They are now trying to contract work from the Pan Americana and the Mara (Palo Alto) rural plants to keep workers busy.

Administrative Services Division (AAA, S.A.)

The Administrative Services Division is organized as a subsidiary to sell data analysis services and systems to clients both within Maty

Group and outside as well. As yet, however, there are virtually no outside clients.

A supervisor in the Operations Research Section, Juan Bosco, returned a year ago from Pennsylvania State University with a Master's degree in Operations Research. He took a job for two months with a brewery in Monterrey and has been with Maty Group about 10 months. He admits to personal problems in adjusting on re-entry.

Juan sees various problems in transferring systems and management skills—but not technology. Systems require people to make them work; because of what he calls the "Mexican mentality," transfer requires considerable time and patience to make it work. Juan feels that the people in his group have limited skills, such as in statistics. He has not yet been able to get the support that he feels he needs from the top; probably, he will not stay with the company.

Financial Planning

At age 35, Raúl González is the oldest member of management. He is also the most American oriented member with his Master of Business Administration degree from Eastern Michigan University and Master of Industrial Engineering degree from the University of Michigan. As Planning Director, Raúl fills the traditional role. He is also a key communication link between middle-level and top management. As the Director of the Industrial Division has not been named, the heads of those five departments and subsidiaries report to him.

Raúl is trying to encourage the planning function within the various functions and divisions. He is trying to set up realistic five-year projections. In the past, such projections have been much too optimistic—based on what the various managers want rather than what is possible.

Raúl does not want a separate planning department, but tools and guidance must be provided so planning can be done within the divisions. Progress is being made. There is general acceptance of the need. Managers are now coming up with more realistic projections.

The net profit figures are 4.8 million pesos (22.7 pesos to the U. S. dollar) for 1979 and 2.9 million for 1978. (See Exhibit 3.) In actuality, according to Raúl, net profit is probably closer to 20 million because of "tax planning." The difference is in cost of goods sold. Transfer prices are kept deliberately high in order to lower profit for the parent company and raise profit for the subsidiaries. The parent company tax rate is 42 percent while that of the subsidiaries is 30 or 20 percent. This "tax planning" is considered acceptable and within the limits of the law. The Government accepts such "tax planning" in order to encourage industrialization.

There are only 20 or 30 copies of the audited financial statements. (See Exhibits 2, 3, and 4). Circulation is strictly controlled. The Mexican auditors are affiliated with Touche Ross & Co.; their acceptance of the reports is without reservations.

Raúl points out that selling and administrative expenses (Exhibit 2) include rent of installations—land and buildings. The owners own all facilities and rent them to the company.

The financial reports are only for Bordados Maty S. A.; it is not consolidated. This is not required. Probably by 1985, the firm will "go public" and then be required to publish consolidated statements. The process of going public is a gradual one. Now, partners are being invited in to certain subsidiaries—such as Bordamex, Ornatel, and Polyplastics. These partners are close, well-known to the owners, and they have a small financial interest. This process of bringing in partners will be widened over the coming years as the company prepares for the complex task of "going public." Inevitably, as the company continues to grow, there will be a need for outside capital.

Marketing

There is little need for demand creation. Production is to order and it rarely meets demand.

EXHIBIT 2
Balance Sheet

	December 31	
	1979	1978
Assets		
Current Assets		
Cash	5,877,860	1,665,073
Accounts Receivable (it is not considered necessary to estimate bad debts)		
Accounts Receivable from Customers	64,653,309	43,159,139
Accounts Receivable from Subsidiaries	5,438,613	—
Advance Payment to Supplier	1,464,343	—
Other Receivables	4,598,982	3,094,827
	76,155,247	46,253,966
Inventories		
Finished goods	11,664,357	4,112,174
In-process goods	19,572,208	18,981,358
Raw Materials	42,334,056	30,097,785
In-transit merchandise	3,213,399	127,820
	76,784,020	53,319,137
Advance Payments (i.e., insurance and rents)	123,049	622,587
Sum of Current Assets	158,940,176	101,860,763
Investments (Credit Union)	804,000	804,000
Plant and Equipment		
Machinery and equipment	14,685,163	7,531,981
Office furniture and equipment	8,762,111	3,308,999
Vehicles	1,830,404	1,237,570
Installations (electrical, plumbing)	1,839,887	1,047,887
	27,117,565	13,126,437
Less accumulated depreciation and amortization	18,596,077	6,141,883
	178,340,253	108,806,646
Liabilities and Equity		
Current Liabilities		
Notes Payable	26,877,493	4,965,854
Accounts Payable to Suppliers	71,619,237	52,801,002
Accumulated Expenses and Taxes, except income tax	6,169,032	7,810,559
Income Tax	—	1,116,979
Participation of Workers in Profits	835,039	641,922
Affiliated Companies—Accounts Payable	5,522,885	4,054,486
Current Portion of Long-Term Loan	2,431,244	2,773,193
Sum of Current Liabilities	113,454,930	74,163,995
Long-Term Loans—less amount to be paid in one year	24,110,458	11,451,468
Equity		
Capital—42,000 common shares to bearer in 1979 and 18,000 shares in 1978, with par value of 1,000 pesos each	42,000,000	18,000,000
Paid-in capital	(5,983,979)	—
	36,016,021	18,000,000

(Continued)

EXHIBIT 2 (Continued)

	December 31	
	1979	1978
Retained Earnings	4,758,844	5,191,183
	40,774,865	23,191,183
	178,340,253	108,806,646

Note: 22.7 peso to the U. S. dollar.

Salesmen take orders several times a year, and the factory normally produces 80–90 percent of what customers order. However, Esteban Gonzalez, the sales manager is convinced that some "publicidad" should be undertaken to stress the image of the firm as a quality producer. He feels this would be advantageous as the firm competes with many low-cost producers. Also, he feels it would facilitate adding new product lines in the future.

Distribution is through five regional sales offices: Guadalajara, Monterrey, Mexico City, Pacific, and Surreste. These offices have been operated by independent commission agents. No inventories are maintained.

Recently, the firm has apparently been moving toward staffing the offices with com-

EXHIBIT 3
Statement of Results of Operation and Accumulated Profits

	Year Ending December 31	
	1979	1978
Net Sales	290,209,382	214,463,420
Costs and Expenses		
Cost of Goods Sold	215,318,721	156,768,600
Selling Expenses	31,436,623	31,246,255
Administrative Expenses	23,823,352	12,621,241
Financial Expenses	9,680,724	7,258,570
	280,259,420	207,894,666
Profit Before Taxes and Worker's Participation in Profit	9,949,962	6,568,754
Income Tax	4,356,079	3,096,034
Worker's Participation in Profit	835,039	600,594
	5,191,118	3,696,628
Net Profit	4,758,844	2,872,126
Retained Earnings at the Beginning of the Year	5,191,183	2,319,057
Capitalization of Profits	5,191,183	—
Retained Earnings at the End of the Year	4,758,844	5,191,183
Net Profit per Share	132.13	159.56

EXHIBIT 4
Statement of Sources and Uses of Funds

	Year Ending December 31	
	1979	1978
Sources of Funds		
From the Operation		
Net profit	4,758,844	2,872,126
Depreciation and amortization	1,599,431	1,214,242
Total funds from the operation	6,358,275	4,086,368
Long-term financing	15,090,232	5,191,862
Sales of fixed assets	—	633,121
	21,448,507	9,911,351
Uses of Funds		
Acquisition of plant and equipment	1,228,785	3,360,810
Payment of the current portion of long-term loan	2,431,244	3,368,775
Increase in working capital	17,788,478	3,181,766
	21,448,507	9,911,351

pany managers. The company discovered that the agent in Guadalajara was not making visits to service large customers. After lengthy meetings between Carlos and the agent, the contract was cancelled and a company manager was placed in charge of the Office. As a direct result of the problems in Guadalajara, the agent in Monterrey communicated with Carlos seeking clarification of his relationship with the company. After several communications, that contract was also cancelled and a company manager placed in charge. Reportedly, the relationship with the agent in Mexico City currently is shaky.

It appears that the intention of the Company is to have employee-staffed sales offices exclusively. The policy in the past had been to have employees in charge of certain functions—such as collections—in the sales agencies. This policy is making the transition to company offices easier as someone is on hand prepared to take charge.

The commission on sales paid to agents was at one time on gross sales, but this has since been related to net sales which takes into account collections and returned merchandise at end of season. Commissions paid were originally 9.9 percent; then they were reduced to 5.9 percent. Now negotiations are underway to reduce commissions to 2 percent. In a typical case, with 420,000,000 pesos sales, the agent gains 21,000,000 pesos in commissions just for order taking. In negotiations, Carlos is attempting to show agents that with anticipated sales projections their commissions will not drastically change, even at 2 percent. Carlos feels that traditionally agents have been well-compensated for doing little.

Sales offices have relatively few customers, mainly large wholesalers and some major retailers such as Sears and Roebuck. Customers have considerable influence over prices and design. There are serious problems in returned merchandise. In the past, customers received perhaps 80 percent of what they ordered, and often substitute colors and designs were included. Consequently, they usually ordered more than they actually expected.

Now, the company supplies closer to 100 percent of what is ordered. Consequently, customers at the end of season are returning large amounts of unsold merchandise; this presents a problem. Labels are removed, and the merchandise has been sold in a retail shop on the premises of the main plant. Now, the company is considering establishing a network of company-operated retail shops in outlying areas of the state to retail this returned merchandise. Also, an attempt is being made to rationalize selling so that merchandise can be moved to other parts of the Republic when the season ends in a particular area.

The Planning Director recently made a study of pricing in the industry and concluded that Maty's prices were well below average. As a result, there are plans to increase prices significantly, as it is felt that the Company should recover its substantial design costs.

Normally, new designs have been produced each season, then discontinued. Then competitors have copied them. Now, Maty will attempt to extend the life of designs to a three to five-year period.

The current penetration of the total market by Maty's apparel lines is estimated by the Planning Director as follows:

Women	1.3%
Juveniles (age 15–20)	0.7
Girls (age 1–12)	3.5
Boys (age 5–14)	0.2
Babies (age 0–4)	1.6

It is hoped that by the end of 1980 a start may be made on entering the export market by selling to Costa Rica, a stable country that imports nearly all of its apparel. Such a move would force the company to improve its quality standards in general and would be in line with the Government's priorities of increasing exports.

Initially, Maty would simply set up a Commission agent in Costa Rica and receipts would be paid into a "post office box company" to be set up in a "tax haven" such as the Grand Cayman Islands. Such a "triangular relationship" is acceptable tax planning, according to the Planning Director. He and Carlos intend to make a trip to Costa Rica, probably in September. Raúl has had some experience in Costa Rica having made a number of trips there when he was employed by a Monterrey firm.

The export market is deemed essential as sales are clearly slowing this year. This is due to several factors: consumers have clearly slowed buying, unemployment is rising, wages and salaries have not kept pace with inflation, and a new 10 percent Value Added Tax (VAT) is in effect.

Sales volume was 214.5 M pesos in 1978 and 290.2 M in 1979 (Exhibit 3). The Sales Department estimates 464.0 M in sales for 1980, but Raúl considers this overly optimistic and thinks they will do well to reach 410.0 M, a 36 percent gain. Over the years, the sales managers have tended to overestimate sales.

All materials and supplies, including zippers and fasteners, must be purchased from domestic suppliers in Mexico City. No imports are permitted. Purchasing Manager Luis Gomez utilizes about 40 sources in order to assure continuity, quality, and prices. According to Luis, there are problems in continuity and quality, but these are being resolved. However, it is not uncommon for work stoppages to occur in the Cutting and Sewing Room because of lack of materials. Luis would like to have earlier and better information from Sales in order to facilitate purchasing, but he understands the problem in providing a longer lead time. Also, Luis would like a narrowing of types of materials needed, but the Sales Manager clearly wants to provide wide product lines.

Production

Patterns are drawn on large sheets of paper and juxtaposed to minimize waste. Cutting is a semiskilled activity. A power jigsaw is manipulated by hand as it cuts through a stack of cloth. Presently, the company is investigating the purchase of computer-guided cutters. There is a problem of matching bolts of cloth with varying shades of color. This is a quality problem with suppliers.

The main plant is to be moved in September 1980 to a building now under construction in the new Industrial Park. Only a few operations and offices will remain behind: ironing, cutting, packaging, and distribution. The new building has been under construction for two months; it is expected to be finished in September, and production should begin there in October.

The moving of production equipment is to be done in one day and night to minimize production disruption. The machines are not considered particularly difficult to transport. A possible problem is transportation of employees. Studies have been made and assurances given that transportation will be adequate; it is a municipal function but privately contracted. Public transportation is a chronic problem in Mexico, but the company does not anticipate that they will have to provide transportation.

Ornatel

One of the units in the Industrial Division reporting to the Planning Director is Ornatel, a woven garment label subsidiary in which he has a financial stake. A newly organized subsidiary, Ornatel appears to have ample back orders. Just now, however, the General Manager and Supervisor need to spend considerable time in Guadalajara visiting old customers of the plant from which machinery was bought assuring them that their needs will be met. This is a task that can only be accomplished in person—perhaps over lunch—not by telephone or mail.

Only in its second week of operation, the plant is operating more smoothly than in the previous week. The Designer is Acting Supervisor at the moment, and Raúl looks in a couple times a day.

A personal project that also requires that Raúl look in several times a day is a small tortilla producing plant. His partner is a relative who handles deliveries to small groceries in his car. Another relative and partner is the young supervisor who has been able to cope thus far with the numerous breakdowns of the second-hand equipment as well as supervising the unskilled young women in the labor-intensive operation.

Rural Plants

Bordamex makes sewn ornaments for apparel. Equipment includes two large automatic programmed machines for making fancy emblems. Each machine cost 8 million pesos. Two more machines are on order. The present prefab building will be extended to accommodate them.

Presently, 80 percent of Bordamex output is sold to Maty and the balance is sold outside. The goal is to reverse this within a year or two.

The Pan Americana plant receives textiles from Maty's centralized cutting room and sells its entire output to Maty. Management acknowledges some problems with continuity of supplies. The plant has some training problems because workers are accustomed to field work and must adapt to operating sewing machines. But they do fairly well, with the help of Human Resources people from Maty. The plant has had some experience in utilizing the Japanese concept of quality control circles in an effort to resolve quality problems.

Home for the Aged

Rising not far from the Villa Juárez rural plant is Señora Carolina's favorite social project, the Home for the Aged (Rouvroy Hogar Para Ancianos). It will have a total cost of 40,000,000 pesos. The foundation is in place as well as facilities for pigs and chickens. In one year, the first stage should be in place with accommodations for 20 persons.

A rural plant, La Fran Fabrica, should generate net revenues of 2,500,000 pesos a year which is to be used to cover operating expenses of the Home. The Senora and the Planning Director are now actively seeking 1,000,000 pesos from six local banks for fixed assets. Local suppliers have been persuaded to furnish building supplies at lower prices, free in some instances. The well digger and the pipeline supplier have donated services and supplies. The architect often asks local merchants to sell supplies and materials at lower prices. The state and federal governments are expected to provide some support. Plans have been made to solicit contributions from individuals and to raise funds through such activities as lotteries and movies.

Marc Rouvroy opposes the Home for the Aged, even though the project bears his family name. He feels that the need for such an institution in Mexico is limited because the extended family system takes care of its own. At one time, Marc says he raised some questions regarding the project's feasibility with Señora Carolina; she would not speak to him for weeks. He feels that sponsoring a primary school or training school for Maty workers or a literacy program would be better.

La Gran Fabrica, the rural plant that is to cover operating expenses for the Home, is managed by Lupita, Sra. Carolina's daughter. Lupita is an efficient, capable manager. A walk through the plant convinces one that she organizes well and is respected by workers.

Lupita's husband is manager of Polyplasticos, S. A., a company subsidiary that produces mostly plastic garment hangers. The two operated a dry cleaning business in Guadalajara until it went bankrupt.

Meeting with the Consultants

Rather unexpectedly, two consultants arrived from Kurt Salmon Associates, an international textile industry consulting firm based in Atlanta. Presumably, this was to be an exploratory visit. The purpose apparently was to find ways and means of increasing plant productivity. There was a general feeling that productivity is low and that this could have substantial impact on profitability. It was also felt that equipment is being underutilized.

First, the consultants toured production facilities with Production Head José de la Luz. OR Supervisor Juan Bosco was enlisted to translate. While this was taking place, several executives with the Planning Director were sitting together to determine where to focus the efforts of the consultants. Rolando was anxious to have the study focus on production within his division. There was some feeling that the study ought to focus on recurrent efforts at standardization and extension of models in the product lines. Unfortunately, Rolando had to leave the meeting to fly to Guadalajara for the weekly IPADE course.

The group then met with the consultants as efforts continued to determine the direction of the proposed study. The Planning Director understood the importance of the "readiness" of the organization for the consultants. He was aware that the client needed to focus the effort and that the consultants had a product line—a "package"—to sell.

Carlos, who had apparently instigated the exploratory visit by the consultants had gone off to Spain a week earlier on a business trip of several weeks. The next morning, a beaming Señora Carolina came through the offices to report that Carlos had just telephoned from Spain where he had arrived safely.

A second meeting with the consultants included the Human Resources Director, the Sales Manager, the Planning Director, and the Production Head. The Purchasing Manager was too busy elsewhere. The OR Supervisor was again included because of his language skills, since the Sales Manager and Production Manager spoke little English. Bob Langley, the senior consultant, spoke some Spanish while his colleague, Gary Ratliff, spoke none.

The consultants were told that growth is to be based on contracting out production to small shops in the area. It is recognized that this is more expensive than in-house capability, but it is essential as capital is needed for growth. Small shops exist in the area with unutilized capacity.

The group was convinced that strategic planning is necessary as well as ambitious objectives. What do we want and what do we need to get there? It is also necessary to have people who will make decisions to see that we reach the goals.

The group felt that in addition to use of contractors, productivity must be optimized in present plants. The Production Head stated that solving his "loading problem" would increase productivity five to seven percent.

The consultants felt that productivity could be increased 50 percent in Cutting and 25–40 percent in other areas. These were cited as "ballpark figures." With 180 sewing machines in Plant #1 and 2,300 square meters, 100 machines could be added. Each operator now has 13 square meters; she should have seven to eight.

Another problem cited was that of direct labor to supervisors, now 40–1. The consultants felt that a good look should be taken at the new arrangement, where Cutting, Ironing, Packaging, and Shipping are to be centralized in the new building at the Industrial Park. The consultants felt this is probably "a good fit."

Near the end of the meeting, the consultants proposed a detailed study of production operations as well as direct and indirect labor and the effect on gross margins with a view to improving return on capital. The managers present expressed doubt as to whether this direct–indirect labor ratio can be reduced.

Also, the consultants felt they should look at operational systems and subsystems including work scheduling and process controls as well as manufacturing in general. They assume that product design is adequate and that the company is meeting its sales objectives.

In the diagnostic stage, a project Manager would be assigned. He or she would be a person with experience and background and would be responsible for coordinating the project. It is estimated that four people in all would be needed. Probably they should be at the principal (manager) level rather than staff-consultants. One or two people should be in manufacturing as material utilization is highly technical. Estimated calendar time: three to four months.

Fees were not proposed yet. Billing is to be every two weeks; due in 30 days. The fee rate depends on the number of people. For implementing, staff-consultants are used—60–80 hours staff, 90–125 hours for principals. Added to fees would be travel, transportation, and report preparation costs as well as living expenses, apartment, and car. The report would provide a sequence of priorities that would include evaluating the sales organization and its method of operating.

The consultants left at 7:00 in the evening for the two-hour drive in a rented Dodge Dart to the airport in Leon. The complete proposal was promised for the following week's mail.

Most of the managers met early the following morning to evaluate the consultants' visit. It was tentatively decided that at this point they really do not need a full-scale study. The managers have only been in their jobs a few months on the average. Most of them feel they have a "pretty good handle" on the problems they face and have been developing plans to cope with them. They feel they already know their problems and can solve them. It is a little like the farmer who told the County Agricultural Extension Agent: "I only farm half as well as I know how now."

The managers calculated that a full-scale diagnostic study, including apartment and car, would cost 1,500,000 pesos; and resources seem particularly scarce this year. The general feeling of the group was that a limited study might be recommended on how to improve the loading factor and eliminate line-of-balance delays. This would involve improved coordination with suppliers, economic lot inventories, and ways and means to keep production lines functioning smoothly.

F. W. WOOLWORTH AND CO., LIMITED (WOOLWORTH, U. K.[1])

Woolworth's fiscal year 1981,[2] Geoffrey Rodgers' first year as Chairman and Chief Executive of the variety store multiple, completed a decade of evolutionary change within the company. Rodgers had continued the program of changes that had been made throughout the 1970s.

Despite these actions, 1981 had been a difficult year. See Exhibit 1 and 2 for Woolworth's financial performance, Exhibit 3 for Woolworth's share price performance, and Exhibit 4 for a comparison of Woolworth's performance with competitors. Industry observers, the "City,"[3] media, and customers continued to express confusion over which direction Woolworth was following, attributing its weakness

---

Source: This case was prepared by Professor X. Gilbert as a basis for class discussion rather than to illuminate either effective or ineffective handling of an administrative situation. Copyright © 1981 by IMEDE (International Management Development Institute), Lausanne, Switzerland. Reproduced by permission.

[1]F. W. Woolworth and Co., Limited (or, "Woolworth, U. K."), is a U. K. quoted Company, of which the American parent is a major shareholder, as opposed to wholly owned subsidiaries such as those in Canada, Mexico, and Germany. Throughout the case, Woolworth, U. K. will be referred to as Woolworth.

[2]Fiscal year 1981 referred to the period of February 1, 1980 through January 31, 1981.

[3]In England, "The City" refers to the major banks, brokerage houses, and other financial institutions of London.

EXHIBIT 1
1981 Financial Statements

Consolidated Balance Sheet at 31 January 1981	1981 £000	1981 £000	1980 £000	1980 £000
Fixed Assets				
Properties		484,185		483,518
Fixtures and equipment		41,581		35,056
		525,766		518,575
Assets Leased to Third Parties		3,988		4,004
Interest in Subsidiary Company		1,224		1,230
Advance Corporation Tax		5,784		5,784
Current Assets				
Stock	194,581		195,715	
Debtors	41,070		31,003	
Bank balances, deposits, and cash	17,462		5,729	
	253,113		232,447	
Current Liabilities				
Creditors	96,463		91,526	
Bank loans and overdrafts	73,489		57,744	
Current taxation	12,414		9,419	
Proposed final dividend	13,496		13,496	
	195,862		172,185	
Net Current Assets		57,251		60,262
		594,013		589,854
Issued Capital		94,537		94,537
Reserves		483,826		476,835
Stockholders' Funds		578,363		571,372
Term Loans		11,336		10,250
Minority Interests		787		
Deferred Taxation		877		3,082
Corporation Tax, payable 1 February 1982		2,650		5,150
		594,013		589,854

Consolidated Profit and Loss Account for the year ended 31 January 1981	1981 £000	1981 £000	1980 £000	1980 £000
Turnover (including value added tax)		1,067,846		977,995
Deduct: Value added tax		116,232		89,847
Turnover: (excluding value added tax)		951,614		888,148
Trading Profit		59,538		74,244
Deduct: Depreciation	12,182		10,295	
Interest	13,765		9,208	
		25,947		19,503
		33,591		54,741
Add: Rent Income	2,780		1,693	
Surplus on property disposals, excluding sale and leasebacks	2,845		819	
		5,625		2,512
Profit Before Taxation		39,216		57,253

(*Continued*)

EXHIBIT 1 (*Continued*)

Consolidated Balance Sheet at 31 January 1981	1981 £000	1981 £000	1980 £000	1980 £000
Taxation		8,909		15,708
Profit After Taxation		30,307		41,545
Add: Extraordinary items		8,649		
		38,956		41,545
Deduct: Foreign currency differences		492		754
Profit for Year		38,464		40,791
Dividends		18,127		18,590
Retained Profit added to reserves		20,337		22,201
Earnings per Ordinary Stock Unit of 25p		8.02p		10.99p

Consolidated Source and Application of Funds for the Year Ended 31 January 1981	1981 £000	1981 £000	1980 £000	1980 £000
Source of Funds				
Arising from trading:				
Profit before taxation	39,216		57,253	
Depreciation	12,182		10,295	
	51,398		67,548	
Minority interests	82			
Surplus on disposals of fixed assets	(2,111)		175	
Exchange differences on net current assets	(140)		(319)	
		49,229		67,404
From other sources:				
Disposals of fixed assets	29,701		4,750	
Issue of shares by overseas subsidiary	533			
		30,234		4,750
		79,463		72,154
Application of Funds				
Purchase of fixed assets		33,013		22,038
Purchase of subsidiary		16,790		
Payment of taxation		12,377		15,180
Payment of dividends		18,127		17,363
Increase in working capital:				
Stock—increase	(6,041)		29,268	
Debtors—increase	9,535		9,469	
Creditors—decrease	(1,469)		(13,383)	
		2,025		25,354
Purchase of assets leased to third parties		348		4,078
		82,680		84,018
Movement in Borrowings				
Loans and overdrafts less deposits and cash balances				
At beginning		62,265		50,406
New subsidiary at acquisition date		1,881		

(*Continued*)

EXHIBIT 1 (Continued)

Consolidated Balance Sheet at 31 January 1981	1981 £000	1981 £000	1980 £000	1980 £000
At end		67,363		62,265
Increase		3,217	increase	11,859

Consolidated Value Added Statement for the Year Ended 31 January 1981	1981 £000	1981 £000	1981 Percent	1980 £000	1980 £000	1980 Percent
Sales and Other Income		1,083,929	100		981,512	100
Cost of merchandise and services		737,494	68		670,080	68
Value Added		346,432	32		311,432	32
Applied						
Employees						
Pay and pension contributions		155,237	45		144,578	46
Government						
Corporate taxation	9,293			15,708		
Value added taxation	116,232			89,847		
		125,525	36		105,555	34
Replacement of Assets and Business Development						
Depreciation	12,182			10,295		
Retained profit	20,337			22,201		
		32,519	9		32,496	11
Providers of Capital						
Interest on borrowings	15,024			10,213		
Dividends to stockholders	18,127			18,590		
		33,151	10		28,803	9
		346,432	100		311,432	100

Note: The difference between this figure and the stock difference between 1980 and 1981 shown in the balance sheet is accounted for entirely by H × Q stock shown in 1981, but not 1980.

EXHIBIT 2
F. W. Woolworth and Co., Limited and Subsidiary Companies Financial Record: 1970–1981

£000's	1970	1971	1972	(1) 1973/74	1975	1976	1977	1978	1979	1980	1981
Turnover	322,332	334,247	378,368	452,575	489,727	607,658	700,879	767,940	875,185	977,995	1,067,846
Profit before taxation	34,563	37,266	40,626	43,310	30,649	36,252	40,609	46,780	53,104	57,253	39,216
Taxation (note 2)	14,056	14,947	12,450	20,414	16,591	19,246	21,133	22,135	12,584	15,708	8,909
Earnings (note 2)	20,507	22,319	28,176	22,896	14,058	17,006	19,476	24,645	40,520	41,545	30,307
Foreign currency difference							(2,312)	(933)	(357)	(754)	(492)
Extraordinary items					734	(1,714)	762	554	(781)		8,649
Ordinary dividends—gross	18,900	18,900	20,319								
—net				14,934	14,934	14,934	14,934	15,785	16,900	18,590	18,127

(Continued)

EXHIBIT 2 (Continued)

£000's	1970	1971	1972	(1) 1973/74	1975	1976	1977	1978	1979	1980	1981
Retained	1,607	3,419	7,857	7,962	(142)	358	2,992	8,481	22,482	22,201	20,337
Fixed assets and investments	158,829	204,967	210,580	219,439	224,444	233,768	243,444	244,484	513,658	523,808	530,978
Advance Corporation Tax				4,415	5,074	9,999	11,839	6,398	6,043	5,784	5,784
Stock	43,086	54,566	51,016	71,351	83,878	96,143	117,865	128,301	166,447	195,715	194,581
Debtors	4,437	4,014	5,190	6,574	7,886	9,604	12,731	17,036	21,534	31,003	41,070
Creditors	31,380	31,537	31,882	40,139	42,926	52,817	65,529	68,693	78,143	91,525	96,463
Working Capital	16,143	27,043	24,324	37,786	48,838	52,930	65,067	76,644	109,838	135,192	139,188
Bank and Cash	20,076	13,664	28,271	9,807							
Short-Term Borrowings					9,578	23,011	38,857	38,436	40,406	52,015	56,027
Current taxation	15,368	13,392	13,183	27,555	9,900	7,850	10,458	9,804	14,609	9,419	12,414
Dividend	13,702	13,702	20,319	10,303	10,303	10,303	10,303	11,154	12,269	13,496	13,496
Net current assets	7,149	13,613	19,093	9,735	19,057	11,766	5,449	17,250	42,554	60,262	57,251
Net Assets	165,978	218,580	229,673	233,589	248,575	255,533	260,732	268,132	562,255	589,854	594,013
Stockholders' funds	147,768	177,363	184,157	193,598	193,456	193,814	196,806	261,079	549,385	571,372	578,363
Deferred taxation	4,250	18,172	16,110	20,865	32,221	43,363	55,946			3,082	877
	152,018	195,535	200,267	214,463	225,677	237,177	252,752	261,079	549,385	574,454	579,240
Term loans		10,045	16,026	18,526	21,826	14,465	5,000		10,000	10,250	11,336
Minority interests											787
Corporation Tax (payable after 12 months)	13,960	13,000	13,380	600	1,072	3,891	2,980	7,053	2,870	5,150	2,650
Capital employed	165,978	218,580	229,673	233,589	248,575	255,533	260,732	268,132	562,255	589,854	594,013
Earnings per stock unit Note 2	5.19p	5.90p	6.50p	6.05p	3.72p (13 months)	4.50p	5.15p	6.52p	10.72p	10.99p	8.02p

Source: F. W. Woolworth and Co., Limited., Annual Report and accounts, 31 January, 1980/1981.

Note: Value Added Tax (VAT) was introduced in the U. K. in 1973, and subsequently changed several times until a 15 percent flat rate was fixed in June 1979.

Notes
1. For the 13 months ended 31 January 1974.
2. The earnings for 1973/1974 to 1980 are affected by the change to the imputation system of corporation tax, by which dividends are paid net of tax. The taxation change and earnings for 1978 and later years are not comparable with those for pre-1978 years because of the change in accounting policy for deferred taxation.
3. In 1972 and 1973/1974 sums of £1,099,000 and £1,933,000 (net), respectively, were charged direct to reserves principally to cover foreign exchange fluctuation and in 1973/74 on restatement £3,400,000 was transferred from deferred taxation to capital reserve.
4. Dividend stated gross and not comparable with 1973/1974 and later years.

EXHIBIT 3
Woolworth Share Price Performance

Share Prices	Price History	1976	1977	1978	1979	1980
	High	80	69	73	87	71½
	Low	40	48	61	56	50
	Stockholder funds per share	51	51	66[a]	145[b]	151

[a] Increase reflects transfer of deferred tax to reserves.
[b] Property revaluation.

EXHIBIT 3 (Continued)

EXHIBIT 4
Comparison of Performance with Competitors
Pre-tax Profit (Percent of Pre-tax Profit to Sales in Parentheses)

£ 000's	1970	1971	1972	1973	1974	1975	1976	1977	1978	1979	1980	1981
F. W. Woolworth	34,563 (10.7)	37,266 (11.1)	40,626 (10.7)	43,310 (9.6)		30,649 (6.3)	36,252 (6.0)	40,609 (5.8)	46,780 (6.1)	53,104 (6.1)	57,253 (5.9)	39,216 (3.7)
Marks & Spencer	43,705 (12.9)	50,115 (12.8)	53,766 (12.2)	70,036 (13.4)	79,208 (13.1)	81,906 (11.3)	83,774 (9.3)	102,445 (9.6)	117,915 (9.5)	161,554 (11.0)	173,650 (10.2)	181,200 (9.5)
British Home Stores					15,464 (12.8)	18,596 (11.5)	21,911 (10.4)	25,498 (10.4)	27,022 (9.9)	33,578 (10.3)	41,830 (10.4)	39,700 (9.5)
Littlewoods			10,609 (8.1)	22,778 (9.1)	28,200 (5.7)	36,630	36,400	48,800	50,900 (4.4)	37,000 (3.7)	3,500 (0.03)	
Boots	20,200 (9.0)	25,000 (9.7)	34,200 (11.3)	56,700 (15.4)	63,700 (15.4)	65,200 (9.9)	72,200 (11.8)	91,100 (12.4)	107,000 (12.1)	113,000 (10.7)	121,300 (10.1)	121,000 (8.8)
W. H. Smith	4,585 (3.8)	6,518 (5.0)	9,860 (6.4)	9,875 (5.9)	10,779 (6.4)	9,266 (4.3j)	11,251 (4.2)	15,627 (4.8)	20,172 (5.1)	20,190 (4.3)	18,617 (3.4)	16,100 (2.4)
Sainsbury	5,083 (3.8)	6,585 (3.8)	10,035 (3.8)	11,338 (3.8)	13,542 (3.7)	14,337 (3.2)	15,372 (2.8)	25,303 (3.8)	27,139 (3.3)	31,838 (3.2)	46,030 (3.8)	62,100 (3.9)
Tesco	15,278 (6.6)	17,248 (6.6)	20,857 (6.9)	25,516 (7.1)	24,558 (5.8)	23,248 (4.6)	25,052 (4.1)	30,187 (4.3)	28,562 (3.0)	37,641 (3.1)	36,500 (2.4)	35,600 (1.9)

Note: For Woolworth, the years 1970 to 1972 corresponded to the calendar year; 1973 corresponded to the period January 1, 1973 to January 31, 1974; the years 1975 onwards corresponded to the 12 months ending on January 31 of the year. Marks & Spencer figures include U. K. and overseas stores.

to being "caught halfway between its established role as a variety store and its desire to become a specialist store. This marketing schizophrenia has left the stores unprofitably suspended between the two."[4]

Rodgers, who had been with Woolworth for 40 years, characterized himself as an "in at the bottom, out at the top man, one of the traditional Woolworth's people who maybe have been criticized in the past."[5] As he began a new decade, he wanted to avoid the short-term focus for which he and his predecessors had often been criticized by maintaining two corporate objectives: variety was the core of the business and earnings per share had to be kept in line with inflation. His long-term thinking, however, centered on the variety concept itself. Variety had been Woolworth's very successful formula for over one-half a century. Rodgers considered whether the variety strategy, as he used to know it and in which he had always placed his faith, was still the foundation on which Woolworth would meet the challenges of the 1980s, or whether it was, as many contended, a mature concept in need of revision or even replacement.

Company Background

F. W. Woolworth and Company, Limited was a public limited company with 52.7 percent of the equity held by F. W. Woolworth Company, Incorporated of the U. S. The business of the company was to trade as retail merchants offering a wide variety of low-priced goods for sale. In 1981, the business was operated nation-wide through 957 variety stores[6] in the U. K. and 38 abroad, 12 department stores under the "Woolco" banner, 43 Shoppers' World catalogue discount stores, of which 14 units operated within Woolworth stores, 2 Furniture World furniture shops, one Burgermaster fast-food restaurant, 39 recently acquired B & Q do-it-yourself (DIY) stores. Compared with other U. K. multiples, Woolworth had the second greatest number of stores, the lowest sales per square foot, and was fourth in turnover. Appendix A provides biographical data on the executive members of the Board of Directors in mid-1981.

1909–1960: The Boom Years

Frank Winfield Woolworth, who founded the Woolworth organization in Lancaster, Pennsylvania in the United States in 1879, opened his first U. K. store in Liverpool in 1909, reputedly causing riots with his new concept. The sale counters were mobbed by women, shop attendants fainted, and customers helped themselves to the goods. His formula included offering a wide variety of low-value merchandise displayed openly under one roof to encourage browsing.

From one store in 1909, 26–30 stores were opened each year, so that there were 700 stores by 1939. During the 1950s, another 300 stores were built. Woolworth performance during the expansion years was highly successful.

1960–1969: Profit Plateau

During the 1960s, the steam ran out of the expansionist strategy. Whereas an average of one store had been opened per fortnight from 1909 until the mid-1960s, approximately 60 stores were added during the 1960s. At the peak of development, 1150 stores were in operation in the U. K. in virtually every high street of every town. A vast mixture of types and locations of stores had resulted from the rapid geographical spread.

In 1964–1965, Woolworth profits plateaued as Woolworth and the variety concept began to be challenged by both the environment and competition. Whereas the traditional downmarket Woolworth customer had comprised a majority of the population, the U. K. post-war economy had boomed and newly af-

---

[4]"British Woolworth Troubles," *The New York Times,* August 30, 1980.
[5]*Marketing Week,* Vol. 3, No. 17, June 27, 1980, pp. 30–32.
[6]The variety stores constituted the main business of Woolworth and, accordingly, represent the focus of this case.

fluent customers traded up, began to purchase different items, and demanded a wider choice, as well as more specialized service in each product area.

Industry observers noted that Woolworth's competitors, who had previously adhered to a similar retailing concept, had responded more quickly to customer demands and a changing retailing concept. Each altered its strategy to take advantage of customer changes by establishing a clearly recognizable specialty. For example, Marks and Spencer and British Home Stores, who had had difficulty competing with Woolworth, developed the clothing and food lines. Exhibit 5 provides a sales and profit comparison of Woolworth and Marks and Spencer for 1952–1980.

EXHIBIT 5
Comparative Growth Record Woolworth/M & S (1952–1980)

	Sales £M		Pre-Tax Profit £M		Net Profit to Sales		Number of Stores	
	W	M & S	W	M & S	W	M & S	W	M & S
1952/3	113.9	86.5	16.3	7.0	14.3%	8.1%	782	234
1955/5	147.7	118.0	22.5	10.0	15.2%	8.5%	914	234
1957/8	166.5	126.6	24.1	14.1	14.5%	11.1%[a]	992	235
1958/9	178.7	130.2	25.6	15.1	14.3%	11.6%	1,018	236
1959/60	193.8	143.3	28.3	17.8	14.6%	12.4%	1,035	236
1960/1	212.0	161.2	31.3	20.5	14.8%	12.7%	1,053	237
1961/2	223.9	166.2	32.8	21.3	14.7%	12.8%	1,068	238
1962/3	234.1	177.1	35.5	22.5	15.2%	12.7%	1,078	239
1963/4	248.3	193.0	37.6	25.1	15.1%	13.0%	1,094	239
1964/5	259.4	210.4	37.7	27.7	14.5%	13.2%	1,110	239
1965/6	270.6	227.9	39.2	29.8	14.5%	13.1%	1,119	239
1966/7	273.6	244.9	38.7	30.9	14.1%	12.6%	1,126	239
1967/8	272.0	269.2	36.7	34.1	13.5%	12.7%	1,134	241
1968/9	295.7	299.4	39.4	38.1	13.3%	12.7%	1,137	243
1969/70	311.6	337.7	37.1	43.7	11.9%	12.9%	1,140	244
1970/1	322.3	388.3	34.6	50.1	10.7%	12.9%	1,124	245
1971/2	334.3	432.2	37.3	53.8	11.2%	12.5%	1,113	248
1972/3	378.4	513.3	40.6	70.0	10.7%	13.6%	1,097	248
1973/4	452.6	591.5	43.3	76.8	9.6%	13.0%	1,072	251
1974/5	489.7	739.5	30.6	81.8	6.3%	11.1%	1,067	252
1975/6	607.7	884.1	36.3	85.8	6.0%	9.7%	1,056	252
1976/7	700.9	1.003.9	40.6	106.9	5.8%	10.6%	1,048	252
1977/8	767.9	1.193.3	46.8	120.6	6.1%	10.1%	1,035	253
1978/9	875.2	1.431.7	53.1	161.0	6.1%	11.2%	1,034	253
1979/80	978.0	1.677.1	57.3	170.5	5.9%	10.2%	1,039	251
1980/81	1.067.8	1.902.3	39.2	176.8	3.7%	9.3%	1,095	

[a] M & S Simplification Exercise 1956 onwards.
Note: M & S Sales and Profits for U. K. stores only, Sales VAT inclusive—net after Refunds.

Rodgers attributed the problem not to a lack of success on Woolworth's part, but to the tremendous success of its competitors first in copying the Woolworth concept and later in initiating strategic changes in response to customers' needs. He maintained that Woolworth's continued success pre-1970 had obviated the necessity for drastic change in its retailing concept.

1970–1980: Evolutionary Change

The need for change was first recognized during the mid-1960s when profits plateaued. This recognition coupled with the change in 1969 from an autocratic to a more realistic and humanistic Chief Executive Officer ushered in an era of self-assessment. In 1970, outside consultants strongly recommended that Woolworth place a high priority on marketing throughout the organization to help transform Woolworth from a buying to a customer-needs orientation. It was also strongly recommended that Woolworth undertake the highly complex task of measuring the relative profitability of various mixes of their 30,000 product lines. Woolworth's first outside executive was brought in to develop a marketing department and to better coordinate the buying, sales, and advertising functions.

The Stores

Classification and Performance

In 1981, 90 percent of all Woolworth's 10 million square feet of selling space was represented by the 957 variety stores (excluding Woolco, Shoppers World, etc.). The variety stores varied in size from 2,000 square feet to over 50,000 square feet. The average net selling area of Woolco was 65,000 feet; Shoppers World free-standing and in-store catalogue showrooms averaged less than 2,500 square feet. Exhibit 6 provides sales and gross profit performance by store type.

EXHIBIT 6
Sales and Gross Profit Performance by Store Type

	1977/78	1978/79	1979/80	1980/81
	(£ sale/gross profit per sq ft per year)			
Variety Stores (including Eire)	75/22	85/25	95/28	100/28
Catalogue Stores (Shoppers World)	172/38	199/40	236/49	277/53
Woolco Stores (excluding Hypermarket)	66/21	72/18	86/16	91/20
Woolco—Hypermarket	158/32	164/28	184/28	198/33

Variety Stores (including Eire)[a]
(£ sale/gross profit per sq ft per year by class: 1979/80 before attribution of shrinkage)[b]

Class		Class		Class	
1	107/32	6	105/31	11	77/24
2	116/34	7	108/32	12	72/24
3	111/33	8	96/29	13	70/33
4	105/30	9	86/27	14	71/23
5	102/30	10	82/26		

[a]Variety represented over 95 percent of turnover.
[b]Shrinkage referred to total loss including theft, damage, anticipated and unanticipated mark-down, etc.

EXHIBIT 7
Store Classification and Performance by Size 1980–1981 (Variety Chain Only; includes Eire)

Store Class	Number of Stores	Square Feet	Selling Area as a Percent of Total	Sales as a Percent of Total Variety Sales	Net Profit as a Percent of Total Net Profit
1	32	40,000+	14	14.2	3.8
2	12	35,000–39,999	4	4.7	2.7
3	23	30,000–34,999	6½	7.2	3.6
4	31	25,000–29,999	7	7.2	6.0
5	60	20,000–24,999	11	12.1	7.8
6	43	17,750–19,999	6½	7.3	7.9
7	45	15,000–17,499	6	6.8	6.8
8	77	12,500–14,999	8	8.6	11.2
9	99	10,000–12,499	8½	7.5	10.3
10	78	8,500–9,999	5½	5.3	9.2
11	141	7,000–8,499	8	7.1	11.2
12	159	5,500–6,999	7½	6.5	10.3
13	138	4,000–5,499	5½	4.5	7.4
14	38	2,000–3,999	1	1.0	1.8

Until 1974, Woolworth had classified its stores on a volume turnover basis only. In 1981, it classified its variety stores for the purposes of merchandising, promotional decisions, and fixturization on the basis of 14 size categories ranging from class 1 at 40,000 square feet or more down to class 14 at 2,000–3,990 square feet. All stores, whatever their size, were managed similarly and, with few exceptions, carried the same departments. There were approximately 180 stores in the range of 2,000–5,500 square feet, which represented under 7 percent of total selling space. More than 40 percent of total selling area was concentrated in the 158 stores above 20,000 square feet. Some of the most profitable stores per square foot tended to fall in the medium-sized category. Management hypothesized that this was either because the present merchandising formula was best suited to that store size or because those stores tended to be situated in towns where rent was low or had not increased and where competing multiples such as Marks and Spencer and British Home Stores were unrepresented.[7] Exhibit 7 provides store classification and performance by size.

The Corporate Planning department believed that a neighborhood type classification that represented a generalized socio–economic evaluation of a store's trading environment would, if adopted, provide the basis for more locality demand. See Appendix B for a description of this classification and for a performance breakdown prepared on its basis.

Image and Environment

According to management, the appearance and shopping environment of Woolworth's variety stores had become a major problem before the 1970s largely because of an excessive degree of independence, or "entrepreneurship," on the part of store managers. Because

---
[7] In calculating the profitability of a store, Woolworth deducted expenses including either actual rent paid or, in the case of freehold properties, a "market rent differential" that Woolworth assigned based on local trading conditions.

store managers' pre-1970 performance had been based solely upon store profits, sufficient expenditure had not been made on repairs, refixturization, or refurbishment in many years. As there had been little or no central control during the pre-1970 era, there had developed a lack of conformity with regard to layout, space allocation, display, and in-store promotion. Some members of management believed that this environment had resulted in the gradual erosion of the Woolworth store image to one of a confusing and old-fashioned store.

It was to remedy this erosion of image that Woolworth began a program of store refixturization and refurbishment in the early 1970s to complement its new focus on higher-ticket merchandise. Woolworth also followed the general move in retailing by closing its smaller, less profitable units. It expanded stores or opened larger stores to offer the customer a wider choice of merchandise. Since 1974, the store closure program had resulted in a net reduction of 71 stores. Exhibit 8 shows the number of stores built, extended, repaired, improved, and modernized during the 1970s.

The 10-year program of store improvement, planned to run at £25 million per year, was designed to modernize 100 stores per year, and add $1\frac{1}{2}$ percent of new sales area. Cash flow problems lowered the original goal to less than £16 million per year, largely taken up by commitments on new or existing stores, and many stores received only a temporary "facelift." Management described the problem as a "chicken and egg" situation: the ultimate profitability of the new, more upmarket merchandise policy was dependent upon upgrading the images of the stores and vice versa. It was estimated that each store required a facelift at least once every 10 years. At a minimal cost of £12 to £13 per square foot, Woolworth needed to invest more than £10 million each year to maintain the status quo. In 1980, industry observers, critical of the slowdown in store modernization, estimated that an immediate investment of at least £50 million was required to raise the store refurbishment program to a level necessary to successfully support the proposed merchandising changes.

In addition to the investment in store improvement begun during the 1970s, an attempt was made to introduce greater professionalism and uniformity within the stores. New displays and point-of-sales requirements were carefully documented and detailed store operating manuals were produced that contained precise instructions for in-store signage and merchandise display. Line drawings of specimen layouts were prepared for all major product groups and display specialists were appointed to all stores.

Studies had been conducted during the 1970s to determine projected sales, market potential, physical, and seasonal characteristics of the merchandise. The findings of the studies became the basis of detailed space allocation formulas that were applied to shelf space and department location of Woolworth's more than 60 merchandise departments in each of the fourteen class stores. Exhibit 9 provides a listing of merchandise departments; Exhibit 10 contains departmental space allocation guidelines, expressed in terms of footage requirement per department, for the mid-point size store in each store class.[8]

In 1980, as part of its program, Woolworth commissioned an outside agency to conduct market research regarding the Woolworth store image, especially as compared with the images of four of its competitors. Exhibit 11 provides the results of one part of the study.

In spite of its efforts to achieve uniformity, Woolworth management admitted that there were also special circumstances to be considered in building, modernizing, or managing a store. There was debate among management

---

[8] In January 1982, these space allocation guidelines were changed from footage requirement for the mid-point size store in each store class to the footage requirement for the low-point size store in each store class. This left more space in the various stores of a class to be allocated to the promotion of merchandise that the district and store managers felt had local potential.

EXHIBIT 8
Store Development 1970–1980[a]

Openings and Closures within Each Year	1970	1971	1972	1973/4[b]	1975	1976	1977	1978	1979	1980	1981
Woolworth stores: New, relocated, and rebuilt	8	11	14	6	6	7	4	3	2	4	
Extended and modernized	44	73	88	81	65	10	23	17	97	104	
Woolco Stores opened	1	1	1	1	2	2	3	—	1	—	
Shoppers World Stores opened	—	—	—	—	14	4	1	—	1	1	
Furnishing World Stores opened											2
Footlocker Stores opened											4
Burgermaster Stores opened											1
B & Q Stores acquired											39
Overseas Stores opened	—	—	6	2	1	—	1	—	—	—	
Closures	23	8	23	29	24	20	15	16	11	6	
Number of Stores at End of Year											
Woolworth U. K.	1081	1077	1055	1027	1005	988	975	966	958	956	957
" Republic of Ireland	23	22	21	21	21	21	21	19	19	19	19
" West Indies	7	7	11	13	13	13	14	14	13	13	14
" Zimbabwe Rhodesia	2	2	4	4	4	4	4	4	4	4	4
" Cyprus	—	—	—	—	1	1	1	1	1	1	1
Woolco	4	5	6	7	9	11	14	13	13	13	12
Shoppers World	—	—	—	—	14	18	19	17	18	19[c]	29[c]
Total	1117	1113	1097	1072	1067	1056	1048	1034	1026	1025	

[a]The first heading in the breakdown of this information shows new, relocated, and rebuilt stores. In Woolworth terminology, new means a new trading area, relocated implies a different site in an existing trading area, and a rebuild is merely reinstating a modern building on an existing site with no extension.
[b]For the 13 months ended 31 January 1974.
[c]In addition, 14 Shoppers World units are operated in Woolworth stores.

EXHIBIT 9
List of Merchandise Departments

List of Departments	Director	
General Manager, DIY Division 250, 251, 252, 260, 261, 270, 320, 331	Buying Controller 010, 015, 022, 023, 024, 025, 030, 031, 032, 033, 034, 035, 036, 200, 201, 241, 341	Buying Controller 091, 150, 151, 190, 200, 211, 220, 221, 222, 230, 231, 232, 290, 300, 301
Assistant to General Manager Dept. 250—Home decorating Dept. 251—Curtain fittings Dept. 252—Cabinet and builders hardware Dept. 260—Electrical hardware Dept. 261—Lighting Dept. 270—Auto and motorcycle accessories Dept. 320—Horticulture Dept. 331—Bathroom	Dept. 010—Confectionery Dept. 015—Seasonable confectionery Dept. 022—Ice cream Dept. 023—Provisions and delicatessen Dept. 024—Fresh meat and poultry Dept. 025—Fresh fish Dept. 030—Grocery Dept. 031—Frozen foods Dept. 032—Fresh fruit and vegetables Dept. 033—Biscuits Dept. 034—Bread and cakes Dept. 035—Wines and spirits Dept. 036—Pets and pet supplies	Dept. 040—Clocks, watches, and watch straps Dept. 041—Jewelry Dept. 070—Records and music Dept. 071—Audio, TV, radio, and musical instruments Dept. 091—Ladies handbags Dept. 110—Footwear Dept. 111—Footwear accessories Dept. 150—Hair goods Dept. 151—Haberdashery Dept. 190—Christmas seasonable stationery Dept. 200—Stationery
Responsibility for merchandise for R. J. Stores	General Manager, Restaurants Assistant General Manager	
	Dept. 020—Restaurants	Dept. 021—Take-away foods

regarding the criteria to be used for such decisions. The Milton Keynes mall "superstore,"[9]

---

[9]Woolworth referred to its 66 class 1–3 stores (35,000–40,000 square feet or more) as "superstores." Collectively, the superstores failed to produce an adequate return on the investment, even though the average purchase per sale was £1.50–1.75, or 25 percent above the Woolworth average. Some of the superstores, taken individually, showed a good profit.

for example, to which over 50 percent of the clientele traveled more than one hour to visit, represented the optimal layout and image. It was large, modern, well laid-out and clearly marked, cheerfully painted, and brightly lighted. Store personnel were pleasant and attentive. Although it was known that it would not produce an adequate return, management had approved the investment in order to occupy a

List of Departments		
Buying controller 040, 041, 070, 110, 111, 262, 271, 275, 330, 340, 342, 343, 350, 400		General Manager, Textiles 090, 130, 160, 170, 180, 181, 182, 183, 184
Dept. 201—Household stationery	Dept. 290—Christmas ornaments and decorations	Distribution Coordinator, Import Range Coordinator Buying Coordinator, 090, 130, 170, 181, 182(G & H), 184
Dept. 210—Greeting cards	Dept. 300—Toys	
Dept. 211—Childrens and adults books	Dept. 301—Hobbies	Dept. 090—Fashion accessories
Dept. 220—Toiletries	Dept. 330—Kitchenware	Dept. 130—Handkerchiefs
Dept. 221—Cosmetics	Dept. 340—Household utensils	Dept. 160—Domestic textiles
Dept. 222—Home brew	Dept. 341—Household goods	Dept. 170—Ladies hosiery
Dept. 230—Photo goods	Dept. 342—Furniture and floor coverings	Dept. 180—Ladies' wear
Dept. 231—Travel goods	Dept. 343—Carpets and rugs	Dept. 181—Mens' wear
Dept. 232—Gifts	Dept. 350—Tableware	Dept. 182—Children's wear
Dept. 241—Cigarettes and tobacco	Dept. 400—Weighing machines, photo machines	Dept. 183—Baby wear (up to 2 years)
Dept. 262—Appliances		Dept. 184—Boys' wear
Dept. 271—Cycles and accessories		
Dept. 275—Leisure and camping equipment		

strategic location that they thought would eventually pay out.

On the other hand, Woolworth stores located in central London or other large city centers, such as Birmingham or Glasgow, presented an unresolved investment dilemma. Management was undecided as to whether these stores should be modernized or closed. In recent years, two stores had been closed in central London and converted into profitable ventures. One was turned into office space and the other into a small shopping mall. Typical of this dilemma and located in one of London's busiest shopping streets was the Oxford Street store, which was visited by crowds of tourists, and was also highly visible to the opinion leaders of England (media, press, financial institutions). Although it had been one

EXHIBIT 10
Departmental Space Allocation Guidelines[a]

Store Class	1	2	3	4	5	6	7	8	9	10	11	12	13	14	
Dept	4000*	3500–3900 3750	3000–3499 3250	2500–2999 2750	2000–2499 2250	1750–1999 1876	1500–1799 1624	1250–1499 1376	1000–1249 1124	850–999 926	700–849 775	550–699 625	450–549 477	200–399 300	Dept
010			114		108		88	80	80	72	72	72	68	68	48	44	32	18	010
015				108		88										015
020				—			—	—	—	—	—	—	—	—	—	—	020
021			12	12	12	—	8	8	8	—	—	—	—	—	—	—	021
022			—	—	8											022
023			70	60	60	—	56	42	42	42	42	42	—	—	—	—	023
024			32	—	—	56										024
025			—				—									025
030			80	60	12	—	12	48	8	40	8	—	—	—	—	—	030
031			24	20	20	56	14	14	14	14	14	12	—	—	—	—	031
032			—	—	—	14										032
033			24	20	—	—	12	—	12	—						033
034			28	24	24	12	20	16	18	12	12	12	—	—	—	—	034
035			—	—	—	20										035
036			24	20	8	—	6	12	4	8	2	2	2	2	2	—	—	—	036
040			32	24	24	16	16	12	12	12	12	8	8	8	8	6	2	2	040
041			20	16	16	16	16	12	12	8	8	8	—	—	—	—	041
070			120	106	106	16	78	68	72	64	68	60	52	44	40	28	24	16	070
071			88	72	76	78	68	44	48	36	44	20	18	8	4	4	2	2	071
090			—	—	—	68										090
091			28	24	24	—	20	16	16	16	18	16	16	12	12	12	6	4	091
110			60	52	52	20	44	40	40	36	36	18	24	20	??	16	12	8	110
111			16	16	16	44	16	12	12	12	12	12	12	12	8	8	8	4	111
130			—	—	—	12										130
150			12	8	12	—	4	4	4	4	4	4	4	24	4	4	4	4	150
151			80	76	76	4	66	60	60	42	42	22	20	12	12	8	8	8	151
160			112	84	92	66	76	60	64	56	50	52	48	36	28	20	16	10	160
170			—	—	—	76										170
180			—	—	—											180
181			614	516	516	—	424	352	352	280	260	222	180	150	123	99	77	48	181
182			—	—	—	424										182
183			—													183
184			—	—												184
190			—													190
200			64	56	60	—	48	40	44	38	40	36	36	30	26	20	16	8	200
201			28	24	28	48	24	20	24	18	20	16	16	12	12	12	8	8	201
210			28	??	24	24	29	18	16	16	18	16	16	12	12	8	8	4	210
211			52	40	44	36	40	28	32	24	28	20	20	16	12	8	8	4	211
220			112	108	112	84	88	72	76	64	68	64	60	56	44	32	28	14	220
221			54	68	76	60	68	56	80	56	60	52	48	40	28	24	20	12	221
222			24	16	80	18	20	12	16	12	16	12	8	8	8	8	4	4	222
230			32	24	29	20	24	16	20	16	16	12	8	8	8	8	4	4	230
231			66	30	54	44	44	40	40	36	36	28	28	24	20	16	12	8	231
232			44	24	36	12	20	16	20	—	—	—	—	—	—	—	—	—	232
241			—					—	—	—	—	—	—	—	—	—	241
250			80	72	72	66	60	52	52	48	48	44	40	36	32	30	24	16	250
251			16	72	12	72	12	8	12	8	8	8	8	8	4	4	4	4	251
252			80	72	72	60	60	52	52	44	44	44	36	28	24	20	12	8	252
260			74	66	66	52	52	42	42	38	38	32	32	28	24	16	12	8	260
261			106	86	86	72	72	62	62	58	58	52	40	28	24	20	16	8	261
262			48	40	40	32	32	20	20	16	16	12	8	8	6	6	4	4	262
270			52	44	44	36	36	24	24	20	20	20	12	12	8	4	4	4	270
271			28	24	24	20	20	20	20	20	20	4	4	4	4	—	—	271
275			28	28	28	20	21	16	20	18	16	18	12	8	8	8	4	275
290			—												—	290
300			112	100	108	84	92	68	72	60	58	56	48	44	40	36	28	12	300

(Continued)

EXHIBIT 10 (Continued)

Store Class	1	2	3	4	5	6	7	8	9	10	11	12	13	14	
Dept	4000*	3500–3900 3750	3000–3499 3250	2500–2999 2750	2000–2499 2250	1750–1999 1876	1500–1799 1624	1250–1499 1376	1000–1249 1124	850–999 926	700–849 775	550–699 625	450–549 477	200–399 300	Dept
310			16	14	14	12	14	8	8	8	8	8	6	6	8	6	—	—	310
320			84	80	80	64	64	62	60	52	52	52	44	40	32	24	20	12	320
330			96	84	84	64	64	52	56	52	52	44	40	32	28	20	16	12	330
331			28	24	24	24	24	20	20	20	20	20	12	12	12	8	8	6	331
340			36	32	36	28	32	24	24	20	20	20	16	16	12	12	8	4	340
341			40	32	32	28	32	28	28	28	28	24	24	16	12	12	12	6	341
342			152	156	164	96	100	72	72	52	54	44	28	22	16		—	—	342
350			40	32	32	28	28	20	20	20	20	12	4	4	4	4	2	2	350
													926	775	625	477	300		
	4000*	3750	3250	2750	2250	1876	1624	1376	1124	926	775	625	477	300	

*a*Units given are expressed in lineal footage of counter space available. The ratio of square feet of floorspace to lineal footage used in the above table was 10:1, although in 1981 management believed it was in fact closer to 7:1.

of the first stores to be modernized in the early 1970s, it had benefitted from only partial improvements, because management did not think that a higher investment would show a sufficient return. By 1981, the early improvements had begun to age. However, modernization still would not be justified by a sufficient return. As a result, management had not decided whether the store should now be remodernized or closed down. This situation was compounded by a merchandise mix and display techniques that had been improvised to appeal to the crowd of tourists, low-market clientele, and idle strollers characteristic of certain areas of Oxford Street. Price-slashing signs that cluttered the merchandise displays and blacked the department markers, a wide mix of high-appeal, tourist-oriented, cheap merchandise that normally occupied the front of the store, and Woolworth's difficulty in attracting qualified sales personnel in Central London all concurred to the lack of coherence and low-market image that was so often attributed to Woolworth. Some members of management recognized that, although it had a high sales figure per square foot, the Oxford Street store failed to reflect the numerous changes that had been made in an attempt to upgrade Woolworth's image. This situation was in contrast with the neighboring stores of Woolworth's usual competitors and other Woolworth stores throughout the country where established merchandise, display, and service policies appeared to be maintained.[10]

Store Personnel

Store personnel had sometimes been criticized by shoppers for untidy appearance, laziness, and for not being very familiar or helpful with merchandise selection. A 1976 attitudinal survey indicated very low morale among employees, thought to be largely due to the previous autocratic management style and the resulting sense of alienation from the top.

The Personnel Director had, since 1976, implemented several action plans designed to improve the situation. First, the lines of communication were opened up by the formation of participative groups and committees for all levels of personnel designed to increase communication with the Board. A new publication, *Management Quarterly*, was established with the sole objective of acquainting all management with the background to executive decisions. The training function was revamped

---

[10]The Oxford Street store, together with 25 others, was eventually put on the market for disposal in March 1982.

EXHIBIT 11
Woolworth Store Image

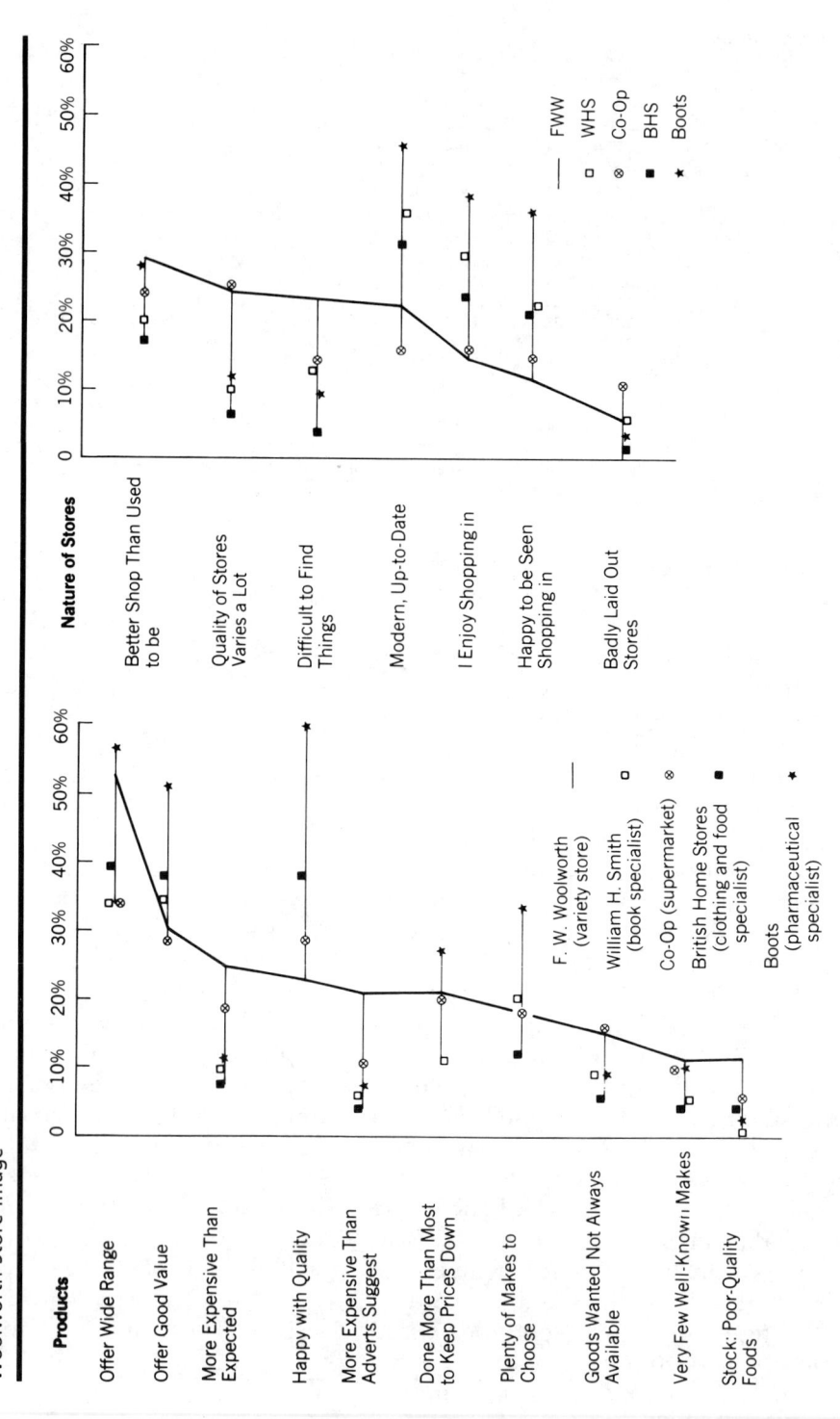

Source: Woolworth Records.
Base: All Shoppers

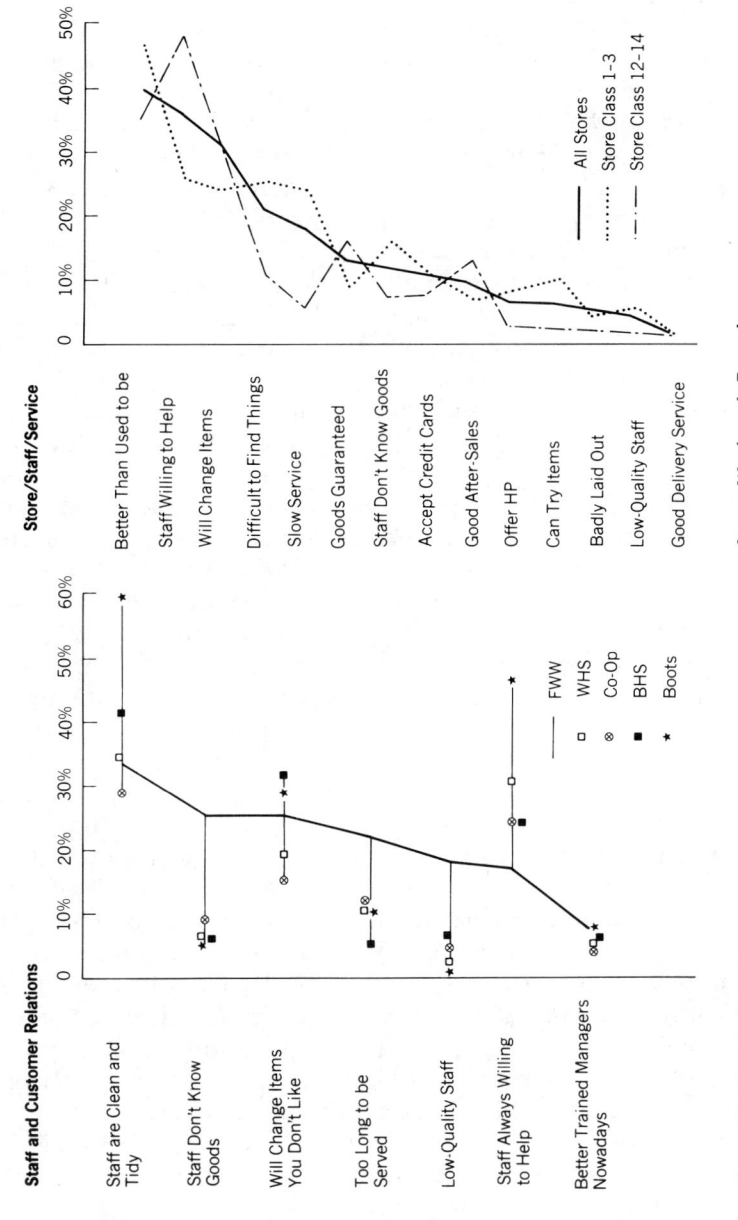

and decentralized to the four geographic regions. Strenuous training programs were developed for staff and managers that included management training, previously reserved for only top management. Salary structures and benefits were reviewed and Woolworth staff became more competitively rewarded.

In 1981, Woolworth had 37,815 equivalent full-time employees. Its sales per employee were less than half those of Marks and Spencer and profits per employee were less than a quarter, although improvements were being made. Retail industry turnover was normally high (60–70 percent) because of the number of part-time people, but given the economic climate, 1981 turnover was very low. Woolworth turnover figures followed the same industry pattern.

Buying and Merchandising

"The Company's essential trading base," Woolworth explained in its Management Plans—1980–84, "will remain the Woolworth variety store format." Buying and merchandising, as noted in the Plan, were therefore directed towards ensuring support to this basic concept.

Buying

Woolworth's buying function was carried out by approximately 60 buyers, each responsible for a number of merchandise groups (see Exhibit 9). The decision to buy a particular item rested essentially with the buyer responsible for the merchandise group to which this item belonged. Woolworth's buying philosophy was thus essentially one of "shopping around," whereby the buyers sourced the items that they estimated might sell well at a reasonable price in a Woolworth store. Woolworth maintained relationships with 5,500 to 6,000 suppliers, some of whom did virtually all their business with Woolworth. This number could be compared with Marks and Spencer's suppliers, which were less than 600. Woolworth made an attempt to guide its suppliers by providing them with explicit product specifications, such as choice of raw materials, production process, production planning, or quality standards. "Of course, a Woolworth buyer buys. In other words, he has to make decisions on the basis of what is available from the suppliers," commented the Chairman. In fact, according to one of the buying executives, much of the market information on which buying decisions were made was obtained from the suppliers themselves.

Merchandise Groups

In 1981, Woolworth carried approximately 60 merchandise groups representing 30,000 product lines,[11] the largest merchandise range of any U. K. multiple retailer. Woolworth officially recognized four product groups: Food; Textiles; DIY; Variety Base. These product groups did not all correspond to organizational entities. Two divisions had been established in 1980, corresponding to two of these product groups: the Textiles Division and the DIY Division. A third division, Catering, was part of the food product group. These divisions had been set up in an attempt to obtain some product-line coordination within broad, but coherent product groups. Within these divisions, the buyers reported to the Division Manager, instead of reporting to a Buying Controller.

Exhibit 12 shows the merchandise space, sales, and net profit of the four official product categories during the 1970 to 1981 period. The Planning Department had unofficially divided the Woolworth merchandise into 16 product groups for purposes of analysis and layout as well as to encourage product group thinking. Exhibit 13 provides performance results of the 16 product groups from 1975 to 1980.

In Woolworth's merchandise mix, the proportion of relatively slow-moving items was

---

[11]Only a few merchandise groups, such as audio and furniture, were not listed in every store. Woolco, which shared the same buying, carried the same departments but 3,000 to 4,000 lines more than Woolworth.

EXHIBIT 12
Merchandise Space, Sales, and Net Profit: 1970–1981
Variety Chain Only (Before Shrinkage)

	1970	1975	1980	1981
Percent of Total Space				
Variety Base	55.5	56.0	58.5	58.4
Food	15.0	12.0	4.5	4.3
Textiles	15.0	17.0	20.0	20.4
DIY	14.5	15.0	17.0	16.9
Percent of Total Sales (before mark-down)				
Variety Base	53.5	56.0	61.0	61.9
Food	25.0	21.5	9.5	8.7
Textiles	10.0	10.0	14.0	14.1
DIY	12.5	12.5	15.5	15.3
Percent of Net Profit				
Variety Base	77.0	78.0	73.0	66.8
Food	0	−4.0	−6.5	−6.1
Textiles	6.0	0	0.5	5.3
DIY	17.0	26.0	33.0	34.0

[a]Refers to clothing and domestic textiles (sheets, linens).

increasing as noted by the Management Services Executives: "In 1970, 52 percent of the items sold by Woolworth had sales of less than six units per store, per week. In 1975, 81 percent of the merchandise had sales of less than six units per store, per week. I estimate that in 1980, this would be the case for approximately 90 percent of Woolworth's merchandise."

Changes in the Merchandise Mix

During the 1970s, Woolworth had dramatically altered its merchandise mix, a change that could be summarized as "out of food and into clothing." The rapid growth of the large supermarket chains, such as ASDA (Associated Dairies Association) and TESCO, had put tremendous pressure on Woolworth's food departments, that in 1970 had represented 35 percent of turnover and that had been present in virtually all Woolworth stores. The June 1977 price war in the already low-margin food sector forced Woolworth's decision to phase out

EXHIBIT 13A
Performance by Variety Chain Merchandise Group[a] (1975–1980)

Sales (after mark-down)	Percent of Total Company Sales					
	1975	1976	1977	1978	1979	1980
1. Textiles	9.90	9.88	10.70	10.85	12.38	13.04
2. Leisure/Activity	14.36	15.40	15.36	17.03	17.70	18.69
3. Jewelry and Gifts	2.77	2.85	2.84	3.11	3.53	3.31
4. Household Consumables (i) and (ii)	12.52	11.77	11.53	11.07	10.62	10.33
5. DIY	12.60	12.82	13.20	13.39	14.57	15.62
6. Furniture and Electronics	3.02	3.17	3.34	3.27	3.21	3.23
7. Personal Grooming	3.87	3.66	3.47	3.31	3.35	3.38
8. Christmas Cards and Decorations	1.92	1.99	2.01	2.21	2.53	2.56
9. Catering	1.34	1.32	1.36	1.34	1.48	1.50
10. Confectionary	9.01	8.84	9.10	8.89	8.77	9.07
11. Concessions	3.44	3.37	3.73	4.18	5.50	6.01
12. Daily Foods (i)	9.53	10.52	9.84	8.74	6.96	5.39
13. Daily Foods (ii)	2.49	2.67	2.51	2.19	1.66	1.40
14. Weekly Food	9.04	7.76	7.08	6.53	3.57	2.04
15. Housewares	2.49	2.44	2.38	2.60	2.84	3.02
16. Footwear	1.54	1.53	1.58	1.36	1.36	1.41

[a]See Exhibit 13C for a definition of department groups. Excludes Woolco.

EXHIBIT 13B
Performance by Variety Chain Merchandise Group[a] (1975–1980)

	\multicolumn{6}{c}{Percent of Total Company Sales}
Net Profit (after mark-down)	1975	1976	1977	1978	1979	1980
1. Textiles	−18.01	−14.17	−8.74	−2.78	−2.64	−18.18
2. Leisure/Activity	19.64	21.68	19.71	28.66	27.71	28.15
3. Jewelry and Gifts	7.88	9.80	7.85	8.69	3.03	4.55
4. Household Consumables (i) and (ii)	14.32	12.32	11.95	11.32	11.21	11.14
5. DIY	38.31	36.49	31.81	35.38	36.29	43.81
6. Furniture and Electronics	−4.42	−3.00	−1.55	−2.18	−2.16	−3.48
7. Personal Grooming	7.03	5.77	5.36	5.00	4.99	5.94
8. Christmas Cards and Decorations	17.87	16.89	13.93	14.15	14.66	17.66
9. Catering	4.45	4.51	3.69	3.63	4.09	4.16
10. Confectionary	17.25	18.12	16.88	12.44	9.26	12.81
11. Concessions	1.41	1.33	1.25	0.38	0.20	0.34
12. Daily Foods (i)	−1.01	−0.02	−0.12	−1.89	−2.73	−1.02
13. Daily Foods (ii)	2.75	2.43	2.33	0.10	0.30	0.23
14. Weekly Food	−15.59	−12.67	−7.97	−13.29	−7.95	−5.73
15. Housewares	4.38	2.20	2.46	3.01	3.15	2.88
16. Footwear	3.39	2.73	3.33	1.26	0.94	1.14

[a] Excludes Woolco.

EXHIBIT 13C
Performance by Variety Chain Merchandise Group (Product Group Definitions)

Major Product Groups	Department Included (see Exhibit 9)
1. Textile Divison	090—130—160—170—180—181—182—183—184.
2. Leisure/Activity	070—071—151—211—230—231—271—275—300—301.
3. Jewelry/Gifts	040—041—091—210—232.
4. Household Consumables (i)	201—340—341
Household Consumables (ii)	111—200—220
5. DIY Division	250—251—242—260—261—320—270.
6. Furniture and Electronics	262—342.
7. Personal/Grooming	150—221.
8. Christmas Decorations and Cards	190—290.
9. Catering Division	020—021.
10. Confectionary	010—015.
11. Concessions/Kiosks	035—241.
12. Daily Food (i)	022—023—024—025—031—032.
13. Daily Food (ii)	034.
14. Weekly Food	030—033—036.
15. Housewares	330—350.
16. Footwear	110.
Grand Total	All Departments

Departments 222, 331, and 343 are included in 220, 330, and 342, respectively.

of food gradually. By 1981, food represented only 8.8 percent of turnover and a loss amounting to 6.3 percent of net profits, with more than 700 food departments having been closed since 1977, mostly in small and medium-sized stores. It was anticipated that by 1984, no stores of less than 12,000 sq. ft. would retain any food. At that point, 85 Woolworth and Woolco units would still be operating full grocery departments, while fresh daily foods and a supporting package of selected other grocery items would still be carried by approximately 200 stores. These food outlets were expected to generate a turnover of approximately £100 million at that time. However, management made it clear that if such a rationalization failed to yield the expected return, a complete withdrawal from grocery retailing would take place.

Variety Base

Competition resulting from merchandise diversification by the food multiples was felt by Woolworth in several nonfood areas of its traditional variety base. Consumables were seen by management as being most exposed to such competition. In household stationery, household goods, personal consumables, toiletries, cosmetics and confectionery, Woolworth was indeed loosing market share or expecting to do so in the near future. However, in household utensils a growth in market share was forecast "to be achieved through exploitation of high-gross own-brand items backed up by competitively priced and well promoted consumables."[12] In the cosmetic markets also, where own-brands had been particularly successful, Woolworth expected "to prevent a further decline by reducing margins on the consumable elements in the range whilst placing display emphasis on higher-gross 'exclusive' range elements such as fragrances."[13]

Within its variety base, Woolworth also expected several ranges to play an "anchor role" as secure areas for future trading. These were toys and games, cycles, electrical appliances, footwear accessories, hair goods, stationery, gift ranges and greeting cards. Finally certain variety areas were expected to achieve growth in market share: footwear, haberdashery, books, records and tapes, audio and TV, clocks and watches, jewelry, travel goods, and handbags. Growth was expected to result from a combination of numeric strength of its outlets, improved merchandising techniques, improved quality and design, merchandise upgrading, traditional Woolworth strength, and "cultivating a 'Department Store' image."[14] However, competition was also expected to increase in all of these areas.

Since 1970, in an attempt to increase the amount spent per purchase and to get growth, Woolworth had begun to focus on higher-margin, higher-priced products such as furniture, audio and clothing, in addition to its traditional, low-price variety base. Woolworth general merchandise quality had traditionally been judged inferior to average, but its low prices and variety had been its main attractions. However, its reputation for low prices was being challenged by customers who, in a 1980 research project, expressed concern that Woolworth prices were becoming very uncompetitive. Rodgers explained: "It wasn't that the prices of existing merchandise were increasing, but that the mix itself was changing, a fact perhaps not clearly recognized by Woolworth's public." The Director of Corporate Planning added: "We have probably made a mistake in trying to generate higher sales per square foot, higher average sales per customer or higher margins through higher-price goods such as audio or furniture. The intrusion of higher-price goods seems to have confused our clientele."

---

[12]Woolworth Management Plans—1980–84.
[13]*Ibid.*

[14]Woolworth Management Plans—1980–84.

DIY

DIY was one of the three merchandise groups, together with Textiles and Catering that had been designated for development. With 15.6 percent of sales, 15.8 percent of space, and 44 percent of net profits in 1981, the DIY group was expected to nearly double turnover and increase market share from 8 to 10.5 percent by 1984. Although the growth rate of the DIY industry had displayed significant variations (i.e., + 7.8 percent in 1979; + 2.3 percent in 1980), Woolworth management expected it to continue. In 1981, as a part of its development plans in the DIY sector, Woolworth acquired B & Q, a successful, young DIY firm that operated 39 outlets, mainly in converted out-of-town facilities. This acquisition complemented Woolworth's plans to expand its DIY business by dedicating an average of 20 percent of floorspace to DIY lines in the Woolworth and Woolco stores, through: (1) stockroom space conversions, of which 10 were made in 1980 with 18 more planned before 1982; (2) low-cost bungalow extensions, 25 of which were to be built from 1981 to 1984; (3) improved display techniques. The DIY plans represented an annual capital spending of £2 million to £2.5 million from 1980 to 1984. The number of B & Q stores was to be doubled over a two to three-year period. At the end of 1981, Woolworth acquired the 34 store DIY chain Dodge City, thus forming with B & Q the largest chain of DIY supercenters in the country with a total of $2\frac{1}{2}$ million square feet of retailing space.

Textile

The Textile group, which had been set up in February 1980 by grouping clothing and domestic textiles, represented in 1981 13 percent of company sales, 20.6 percent of space, and a loss amounting to 19 percent of company net profits. With market shares of 1.5 percent in clothing and 5 percent in domestic textiles, Woolworth intended to reach 2 percent and 6 percent, respectively, by 1984. The reason for selecting clothing was that, whereas food represented the area of greatest consumer expenditure, clothing was second. Clothing was admittedly an area of great competition in the high street, strongly dominated by Marks and Spencer and to a lesser extent British Home Stores. To this, a Woolworth executive responded by saying: "Then it must make them more vulnerable." In management's view, the move into clothing would be facilitated by the complementary decision to attempt to upgrade the Woolworth image. A new image would allow Woolworth to gain credibility with a more upmarket clientele for higher priced purchases. It was Woolworth's objective to increase clothing to 30–35 percent of turnover by 1985. The principal objective was "the creation of a good quality, price competitive, co-ordinated range covering the entire apparel spectrum."[15] This implied reducing an acknowledged bias towards children's wear, underwear, and hose, "so as to fall more closely in line with the average profile of the U. K. market."[16] In the domestic textiles area, the emphasis was to be placed "on color coordination and 'fashion-conscious' marketing."[17] Management considered that textile had adequate floor space in the larger stores. However, they recognized that a significant increase was needed to exploit fully the potential of the smaller suburban and country–town stores.

Catering

The Catering group was, in management's view, a move to indicate a "commitment to the continued enhancement of existing restaurant and take-away food operations and to an aggressive development program embracing both new in-store catering units and a new concept in free-standing, fast-food operation."[18] At the beginning of 1980, the company operated 63 restaurants in Woolco and Wool-

---
[15]*Woolworth Management Plans—1980–84.*
[16]*Ibid.*
[17]*Ibid.*
[18]*Ibid.*

worth town center stores. With 1.6 percent of company sales and 4.9 percent of net profits in 1981, catering had a 1.25 percent market share in the total U. K. restaurant market. It planned to achieve 1.75 percent by 1984, through a total of 103 in-store restaurants. At the same time, Woolworth intended to develop the "takeaway" sector through improved menus and better fixturization, promotion, and display. In 1981, 120 stores had a "sandwich-bar" takeaway food operation, producing a turnover of £1.9 million. In 1980, Woolworth also opened its first free-standing "fast-food" unit under the name of "Burgermaster." It anticipated that 22 such units would be in operation in free-standing locations by the end of 1984. A number would also be opened in Woolworth stores.

Diversification

In addition to the developments implemented in the existing areas of merchandise, Woolworth also set up new retail approaches in several sectors. Its catalogue retail operation, "Shoppers World," started in 1974, had 43 units in 1980, 14 of which were operated within Woolworth stores. A total of 64 units were planned to be opened by 1984. Woolworth's main competitor in the catalogue retail sectors was Argos, a subsidiary of British American Tobacco Industries, which operated 102 showrooms.

In the furniture sector, Woolworth opened in 1980 a large out-of-town furniture center under the name of "Furnishing World." Six more such units were planned with selling areas of more than 25,000 sq. ft. per store. The "Furnishing World" stores were to offer a wide range of furniture in a wide spectrum of prices. A number of joint DIY, "Furnishing World," and Garden Centers were planned.

In 1980, Woolworth also opened four specialty stores for sports footwear and clothing under the name of "Footlocker." The "Footlocker" concept had been imported from the parent operation in the U. S., where over 200 such stores had been found very successful.

Merchandising strategy was complicated by the diversity of Woolworth's traditional product strengths.

Product	Share of U. K. Market
Confectionary	5% (Number 1)
Angling equipment (minus bait)	12% (Number 1)
Low-priced lawn mowers	12% (Number 1)
Rosebushes	n/a (Number 1)
DIY market (not including B & Q)	8%
Luggage sales	24%
Records and cassettes	15% (by value)
Electric light bulbs	27%
Paint market	13%
Motor oil	(No. 1 retail outlet)
Greenhouse market	9%

Woolworth was hesitant to give up areas where it enjoyed such a preeminent position and hoped to maintain these strengths while shifting its emphasis to the higher margin merchandise.

Departmental profitability studies, undertaken each year, provided an estimate of departmental net profit contribution. Modifications in space allocation, range, etc. were considered on the basis of the studies. The 1970 study indicated an imbalance in profit production among various merchandise groups which still characterized the mix in 1980. The Food department, then representing 15 percent of selling space, was estimated to be operating at a break-even level in 1970 with all other departments (recognized at that time) producing some profit. Nearly one-third of 1970 sales floor space had been devoted to merchandise providing little or no net return. In 1981, management characterized the sucess of its efforts at increasing the return in these areas as very limited.

In spite of the various merchandise and new retailing developments, Woolworth's chances of success were still considered with some skepticism by numerous observers. Referring to the B & Q acquisition in particular, Rodgers explained: "We don't feel it's going to transform the Woolworth business overnight. But I hope that in 10 years' time someone will say, 'Well, at least they did something—they didn't wait until somebody else had succeeded.'" Referring to the diversification moves in general, one critic remarked that perhaps Woolworth was doing "too little, too late." In 1981, it was estimated that diversification represented approximately 2 percent of Woolworth's total turnover.

Pricing

Pricing decisions were made by the buying organization on the basis of a target gross margin for each product group. Buyers negotiated with their suppliers to obtain a purchase price that would be compatible with what they perceived the market conditions to be, after addition of the target gross margin.

Advertising and Branding

Advertising

Woolworth's advertising campaigns during the 1970s were aimed at both improving the image of Woolworth and improving the sales of featured products to the customers, especially to increase awareness of the new higher-margin, higher-price product ranges. Particularly on television, advertising spots had emphasized the variety concept with the message that you could find anything at Woolworth. Woolworth's themes as advertised on window stickers and in radio and television messages had also been "The Wonder of Woolworth" in 1975 but, more recently, was "Everybody Needs Woolworth Sometime" and in 1981, "You'll Love the Change."

Woolworth's total media expenditures from 1975–1980 represented the third largest in the retail industry. Table 1 provides Woolworth's media expenditures.

Although Woolworth's expenditure increased beyond that of media inflation, Woolworth's TV expenditure in real terms had decreased considerably between 1975–1979. Woolworth's media split from 1975–1980 had changed significantly. Table 2 provides a breakdown of television and press expenditures.

Woolworth also conducted special promotions, such as fashion shows, seasonal promotions, and, in selected stores, special storewide "10 percent off all merchandise" sales. These were decided upon by the Sales and Advertising Director with the collaboration of the Buying Director. Management considered that

TABLE 1
Woolworth Media Spend (Total)

Fiscal Year (Feb–Jan)	Total £ M	Of Which, Suppliers Contribution	Nominal Increase Percent	Media Inflation Percent
1976	3.25	.75	—	—
1977	4.40	1.2	35.4	22
1978	5.80	1.9	31.8	18
1979	7.20	3.0	24.1	15
1980	9.50	4.0	31.9	15
1981	10.90	5.0	14.7	24
1982 (forecast)	11.80	4.7	8.3	—

Source: Woolworth Records.

TABLE 2
Woolworth Media Split

	Percent TV	Percent Press
1975–1976	80	20
1976–1977	56	44
1977–1978	45	55
1978–1979	56	44
1979–1980	52	48
1980–1981	65	35

Source: Woolworth Records.

pressure on pricing and promotion strategies had both resulted in a gradual drop in margins over the years, especially in consumables' departments, in order to compete with the rapidly increasing number of discounters.

Branding

Until the early 1970s, Woolworth had allowed a large number of private brands to develop. "When I joined Woolworth as Marketing Manager," commented the Director of Corporate Planning, "there were some 30 different private brands, nearly one for any product group: paints, cosmetics, food, strationery, . . ." The decision was then made to reduce the number of private brands to just a few, the most important of which was "Winfield." In 1980, the decision was made to change "Winfield" to "Woolworth." In 1981, private brand merchandise represented 21 percent of all merchandise.

Finance and Real Estate

The relatively weak performance of Woolworth was frequently commented upon by financial analysts who tended to focus on early quarterly results. However, as in many retailing organizations, up to 60 percent of a year's profits were earned in the fourth quarter (November, December, and January), which made it more difficult to speculate on the year-end results.

Some observers attributed part of Woolworth's problem to what they called a short-sighted approach on the part of the American parent company. Woolworth, U. K. had long been more profitable than its parent company which, financial analysts believed, welcomed the yearly flow of dividends. This was seen by some as depriving Woolworth, U. K. of a much needed source of financing for its modernization program. U. K. management quickly refused this argument. In fact, according to management, the policy of the parent company was much less a problem than the lack of attractive investment opportunities. If such opportunities were shown to exist, funds could be made available through a decrease of dividends, divestments in the order of £30 million to £40 million, or an increase in debt.

Capital spending for 1981, previously forecast as £42.5 million, was £49.8 million, including the £16.8 million acquisition of B & Q. Yearly capital spending for the years 1981–1984 was forecast at approximately £40 million, inflation-adjusted. These figures included all capital requirements, that is, not only new stores and modernizations, but warehousing, distribution, fixtures, data-processing equipment, etc. Spending would be partly financed by the sales of property, which in 1981 represented £29.7 million, a £25 million increase over 1980.

Woolworth's situation with respect to stores and property ownership was somewhat unique in the U. K. retail industry. Uncharacteristic of this industry, nearly 80 percent of total Woolworth selling space was classified as either freehold (owned) or long leasehold (99 year leases).

The Woolworth Customer

According to surveys conducted in the fall of 1980, a large proportion of the British public (92 percent in 1980) had visited a Woolworth store at least once. This figure had remained relatively stable over the years. However, the frequency with which shoppers visited the

TABLE 3
Percent of General Public Having Shopped at Woolworth During Week Prior to Interview

Year	1973	1974	1975	1976	1977	1978	1979	1980
%	37	33	37	37	39	38	36	33

stores had declined slightly, as shown in Table 3.

Compared with competition, Woolworth had suffered from the greatest drop in frequency during the prior year. Exhibit 14 provides a comparison of customer shopping frequency among Woolworth and its competitors.

Woolworth believed that a breakdown of its customers reflected the class proportions of the U. K. population, thus making it a "classless store." Exhibit 15 compares the Woolworth once-a-week customer profile, as well as competitors', with the U. K. population. Studies had shown that, in spite of attempting to move upmarket, Woolworth had witnessed a recent downward shift in clientele, as shown in Table 4.

According to surveys, the public had a rather poor image of the Woolworth customer who often, in fact, did not wish to admit to shopping at Woolworth. The Woolworth customer was characterized as older, lower class, with poor taste, somewhat ignorant and different from the respondent. A comparison of this characterization with the actual figures of age and class of customers revealed that the characterization was a problem of perception, rather than actual customer profile. Commenting on the consumer impression, management stated, "It is far easier to create a reputation

EXHIBIT 14
Shopping Frequency Comparisions

once/week	once/2weeks	once/month	ever	Store
30	46	69	94	Boots
19	28	49	89	Marks and Spencer
14	21	39	75	W. H. Smith
28	34	44	73	Co-op
6 / 10	22		67	British Home Stores
23	35	57	91	F. W. Woolworth

Base: All in Great Britain.

EXHIBIT 15
Customer Profiles—Woolworth and Competitors Comparison with U. K. Population (1979)

	Once a Week Shoppers						
Total	General Public 100%	Woolworth 100%	Boots 100%	M & S 100%	W. H. Smith 100%	Co-Op 100%	B. H. S. 100%
Men	48	36	32	35	52	40	35
Women	52	64	68	65	48	60	65
Aged							
15–24	19	17	23	14	18	14	18
25–34	17	17	18	16	17	14	20
35–54	31	32	31	33	34	33	30
55+	32	34	28	36	31	39	32
Class[a]							
ABC1	38	32	40	42	45	31	33
C2	33	39	34	31	35	34	37
DE	29	29	26	27	20	35	31

Source: Woolworth Records.
Base: All in Great Britain.
[a] ABC1: Upper-Middle Class, Middle Class, and Lower-Middle Class; C2: Skilled Laborer; DE: Laborer and Subsistence Level.

than to change one." Many customers also had good experiences with Woolworth and often wrote to Woolworth to comment favorably upon or to congratulate Woolworth on the organization's unchanged concept of variety. Appendix C provides examples of letters received by management.

Interviews conducted in 1980 indicated mixed trends in customer purchasing behavior regarding intended vs. actual purchase and intended vs. actual expenditure. The interviews also indicated that a number of Woolworth clients were either frustrated buyers (those who intended to buy, but did not for some reason) or impulse buyers (those who had not intended to buy, but did). Product unavailability was generally the reason that an intended purchase was not made. The percentage of impulse and frustrated buyers varied among product groups (see Exhibits 16 and 17).

A study of willingness to buy products from Woolworth showed that the products respondents were willing to buy from Woolworth tended to be among those considered as traditional Woolworth stock, such as confectionery, lamps and lampshades, toiletries, haberdashery, paints, etc. (see Exhibit 18). A few of Woolworth's newer products, such as houseplants and records and cassettes, had been widely accepted by customers, but they had remained reluctant about purchasing other newer lines, such as men's and women's clothing, major items of furniture, cameras

TABLE 4
Woolworth Once-a-Week Clientele: 1979–1980

Class	1979	1980
ABC$_1$	32%	31%
C$_2$	39%	35%
DE	29%	34%

Source: Woolworth Records.
ABC$_1$: Upper, Middle, and Lower-Middle Class.
C$_2$: Skilled Laborer.
DE: Laborer and Subsistence Level.

EXHIBIT 16
Woolworth Customer/Purchasing Behavior

Intended vs. Actual Purchasing Behavior

	Purchase	
Year	Percent Intending to Buy	Percent Who Bought
1975	73%	82%
1977	70%	78%
1980	70%	72%

	Expenditure	
Year	£ Intended to Spend	£ Spent
1977	1.97	1.81
1980	2.33	2.03

Base: Woolworth Shoppers.

Frustrated and Impulse Buyers (1980)

	Bought	Did Not Buy
Intended to buy	81%	19%
Did not intend to buy	50%	50%

Reasons for Nonpurchase: Trends

Reason for Nonpurchase	1977 %	1980 %	% ±
Didn't have/couldn't find specific item	37	34	−3
Didn't have/couldn't find type of item	25	29	+4
Didn't have size	9	11	+2
Too expensive/cheaper elsewhere	14	8	−6
Changed mind	8	8	0

Base: All failing to buy intended purchase (35 percent).

EXHIBIT 17
Impulse and Frustrated Purchases

	Impulse Purchasers %	Frustrated Purchasers %
Toys and games	59	42
Greeting cards	58	21
Women's casual clothes	56	47
Cosmetics	54	26
Confectionary	51	13
Toiletries	47	24
Household cleaners	46	10
Gardening products	45	46
Stationery	45	20
Records and cassettes	39	40
Shoes	37	36
Children's clothing	33	44
Any food	33	13
Haberdashery	29	30
Electrical hardware	26	24
Cigarettes and tobacco	22	2
Paint and decorating materials	16	25

Source: Company records.
Impulse Purchasers: Percentage of buyers of each product type who did not intend to buy that product type (base = all buyers of that product type).
Frustrated Purchasers: Percentage of those intending to buy each product type who did not actually buy that product type (base = all intending to buy each product type).

and photographic goods, stereo units, and music centers.

Interviewees would also cite a sense of muddle, the difficulty of locating sections in the store, a sense of claustrophobia because of the narrow aisles, not being able to find what they wanted, the casual or unhelpful staff, and high prices for not very high-quality products as reasons for their reluctance to buy.

Overall, surveys indicated some degree of confusion as to what Woolworth was aiming at, perhaps resulting from the intrusion of larger, more expensive items among the small items customers were used to and for which they wanted to visit a Woolworth store. Customer comments included the following:

> "It sells a bit of everything, a wide range of things."
> "It is everyone's favorite . . . it has a wider appeal than most other stores."
> "Convenient and local, for 'bits and bobs,' general, everyday, useful goods rather than any one thing."

EXHIBIT 18
Customer Willingness to Buy Merchandise at Woolworth's

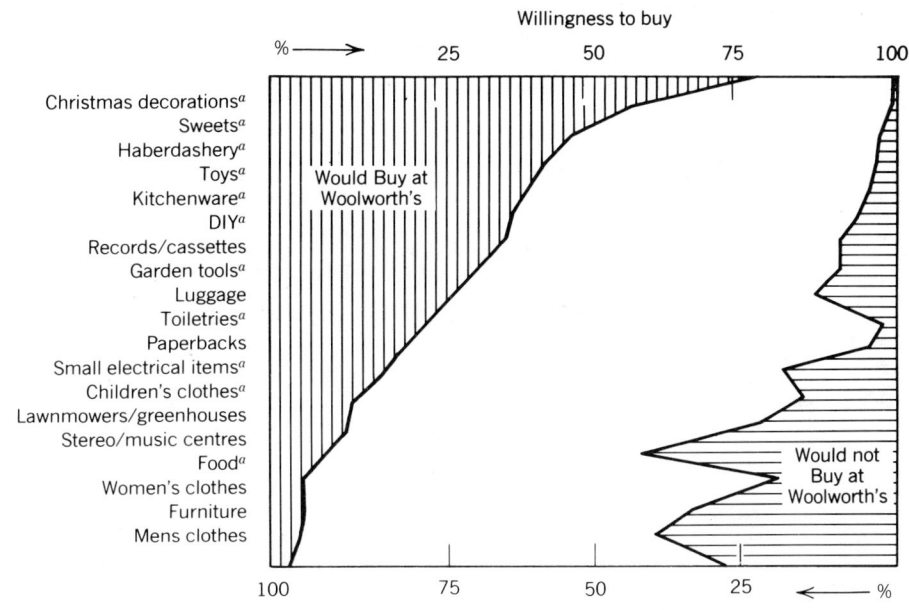

Source: RBL 1979.

*a*Traditional Strengths.

"The store to go when you are not sure what you want."
"For lower quality goods."

Issues for the 1980s

The question of the variety strategy itself was still much debated among Woolworth's top management at the end of 1981. Many observers of the retail sector had expressed strong doubts regarding the viability of the variety concept, but several members of Rodgers' management team had pointed out the irony of the numerous specialized retail chains that seemed to be moving increasingly in the direction of variety by adding new merchandise lines. On the other hand, one could not help but appreciate the success stories of the more specialized retail chains.

APPENDIX A
Biographical Sketch of Directors

G. RODGERS (CHAIRMAN AND CHIEF EXECUTIVE)

Joined Woolworth as a Management Trainee and subsequently managed a number of stores in the Liverpool Region. From 1961 has held the following executive positions:

District Manager

Assistant Regional Manager

Executive Responsible for Decimalization

Regional Manager

Director and Regional Manager

Joint Managing Director

Deputy Chairman and Chief Executive

Chairman and Chief Executive

H. R. JOHNSON (JOINT MANAGING DIRECTOR)

Joined Woolworth as a Management Trainee and progressed through Store Management in the Liverpool Region. Had extensive experience setting up overseas companies and managing stores in the West Indies.

Since 1962 has held the following Executive posts:

District Manager

Regional Departmental Manager

Supervisor Overseas Stores

Buyer—various departments

Executive responsible for formation of catalogue division

General Manager—Shoppers World

Seconded to NCR on management exchange program

Store Operations Executive

Director—responsible for developing departments

Joint Managing Director

R. E. JONES (JOINT MANAGING DIRECTOR)

Joined Woolworth as a Management Trainee, subsequently managing a number of stores in the Metropolitan Region. Has held the following executive positions since 1969:

District Manager

Seconded to work with P. A. Consultants on special project

Merchandise Coordinator

Buyer

Store Planning Executive

Assistant Regional Manager

Regional Manager

Director and Regional Manager

Joint Managing Director

J. H. BRADWELL (JOINT DIRECTOR OF BUYING)

Joined Woolwroth as a Management Trainee and progressed through Store Management in the Birmingham Region. Since 1959 has held the following executive posts:

District Manager

Regional Departmental Manager

Buyer—various departments

Buying Supervisor

Executive in charge of Buying

Director of Buying

J. BLAIR (DIRECTOR OF REAL ESTATE, CONSTRUCTION, AND FIXTURES)

Joined Woolworth as a Management Trainee and subsequently managed stores in the Birmingham Region. From 1961 has held the following positions:

District Manager

Executive in charge of Research

Buyer—Woolworth

Buyer—Woolco

Assistant Buying Supervisor—Woolco

Buying Supervisor—Woolco

Director—responsible for developing departments

Director—in charge of Real Estate, Construction, and Fixtures

K. J. WILLOUGHBY (DIRECTOR OF CORPORATE PLANNING)

Joined Woolworth in 1971. Previous experience with Nestlé and the Co-operative Wholesale Society. Joined Woolworth as Marketing Manager. Subsequently became:

Director of Store Operations

Director of Corporate Planning

M. P. DOWNS (DIRECTOR OF PERSONNEL)

Joined Woolworth in 1974. Previous experience had been in retailing in South Africa and Rhodesia. Became Personnel Manager for British Home Stores and later Personnel Manager for the Regional Hospital Boards. Joined Woolworth as Personnel Manager and subsequently appointed Personnel Director.

R. J. KIRKMAN (DIRECTOR OF CORPORATE FINANCING)

Background in accountancy in retail industry and immediately prior to joining Woolworth was Chairman and Managing Director of UDS Group Finance Ltd. Joined Woolworth in 1978 as Director of Finance, following two consecutive incumbents hired since 1971 from outside the Company had occupied the position and left.

D. COLLIER (DIRECTOR OF SALES AND ADVERTISING)

Joined Woolworth as a Management Trainee and progressed through Store Management in the Kensington Region. Since 1968 has held the following Executive positions:

District Manager

Regional Sales Manager

Sales Promotion Executive—major stores

Company Sales and Advertising Executive

Director of Sales and Advertising

J. G. DODDS (JOINT DIRECTOR OF BUYING)

Joined Woolworth as a Management Trainee and subsequently managed both Woolworth and Woolco stores. From 1973 has held the following executive posts:

Assistant General Manager—Woolco

Assistant Regional Manager—Woolworth

Regional Manager

Director and Regional Manager

Joint Buying Director

APPENDIX B
Classification of Stores by Neighborhood

Area Code	Description
1	*City Centers*—Twelve major centers of national importance and influence.
2	*Other Major Conurbations*—Major towns of regional importance including suburban retail nuclei in city center-based conurbations.
3	*Major Conurbations:* Secondary Sites
4	*Metropolitan Regions*—Urbanized regions with well-developed communication and employment infrastructure. Regional town centers exerted strong influence over these surrounding urbanized catchments.
5	*Metropolitan Region:* Secondary Center
6	*Rural Regions*—Areas with limited urban development, isolated from metropolitan centers, predominantly served by "self-contained" market centers of long standing.
7	*Rural Region:* Secondary Center

Table B1 indicates the number of stores, selling area, and performance by neighborhood classification. Table B2 provides a performance breakdown of the Woolworth stores according to this classification.

TABLE B1
Space and Performance by Neighborhood Classification

Area Code	Title	Number of Stores	Selling Area (Sq Ft)	Percent Total Space	Sales/Sq Ft
1	City Centers	23	519,000	6 %	130
2	Other Major Conurbations	60	1,409,950	16 %	107
3	Major Conurbations: Secondary Sites	175	1,161,325	13 %	82
4	Metropolitan Regions	197	2,266,350	25½%	102
5	Metropolitan Regions: Secondary Center	226	1,377,575	15½%	89
6	Rural Regions	89	1,010,000	11½%	102
7	Rural Regions: Secondary Center	207	1,084,400	12½%	97

Source: Company Records.

TABLE B2
Number of Stores and Average Sales/Sq. Ft. by Area Code 1979/80[a]

Area Code Store Class	Number of Stores Average Sales/Sq. Ft.						
	1	2	3	4	5	6	7
1—3	12	28	1	16	2	7	0
4	2—126	6— 90	3—101	12—110	1—136	3— 83	1— 82
5	3—117	8—114	5— 96	27—108	2— 70	11— 94	2— 96
6	1—100	4—147	6— 95	11—111	6—107	5—120	3—128
7	2—117	3—118	7— 87	17—119	8—110	7—129	4— 98
8	2—137	4—100	10— 84	19—105	18— 91	15—120	6—122
9	.	3—103	18— 83	21— 99	14— 84	11—101	22— 98
10	.	.	15— 82	18— 95	27— 88	5— 86	20—101
11	1—112	2— 81	26— 80	20— 89	38— 88	13— 88	28— 98
12	.	.	37— 75	20— 85	58— 78	2— 88	46— 95
13	.	2— 99	40— 75	14— 71	40— 82	9— 85	54— 86
14	.	.	7— 72	2— 67	14— 90	3— 98	21— 95
4—14	11	32	174	181	226	84	207
1—14 Total	23—130	60—107	175— 82	197—102	228— 89	91—102	207— 97

[a] 1980–1981 breakdown not available; no change in trading patterns anticipated.

APPENDIX C
Examples of Letters from Customers

G. Rodgers, Esquire,
Chairman and Chief Executive,
F. W. Woolworth & Co. Limited,
Woolworth House,
242–246 Marylebone Road,
LONDON NW1 6JL.

Dear Mr. Chairman,

My Wife and I thank you for the interesting and informative copies of your Company's Annual Report and Accounts for the year ended 31 January 1980 and compliment you, your Co-Directors, and Staff on the results achieved during a difficult trading year.

I assume from page 8 of the report that you have no Stores in Denmark, Norway, and Sweden. Is this assumption correct please or is the explanation that F. W. Woolworth & Co. Limited have separate companies registered in those countries?

While writing I would mention that I have found the plastic zips used on your travelling cases unsatisfactory as evidenced by one case I purchased at your Boscombe (Bournemouth) Stores, which case unfortunately burst open when being handled at the airport due to the plastic zip. Other travelling cases purchased at the same Stores with a metal zip have proved more satisfactory. Having moved from Bournemouth to Spalding I reported the defective zip to your Spalding Stores and desire to compliment Mrs. Cooper, your supervisor there, for the most courteous and efficient manner in which she dealt with this matter.

Being now retired, I can no longer afford to attend annual general meetings of Companies, but I have returned proxies in your favour duly signed direct to your Transfer Office.

With best wishes to you and everyone connected with F. W. Woolworth & Co. Limited, which makes a splendid contribution to our country and the community.

Yours sincerely,

Mr. G. Rogers   9 March 1981

Dear Sir,

Since your TV announcement that prices in Woolworth's Stores were being cut, I have been studying and comparing prices in our nearest town—Dereham, where Boots International Stores and Key Market are your biggest competitors. (Marks & Spencer is some 25 miles away and Sainsburys about 20 miles away.) First, I compared the prices of toiletries with Boots, and fresh foods, i.e., cheese, bacon, ham, etc. with the other stores. In all cases I was delighted to find that not only was I able to buy name proprietary brand of goods 3–4p cheaper, but quality fresh food at very reasonable prices.

Next I sought the Manager, Mr. Shorter (I asked his name because he was both courteous and helpful) to enquire if this was a temporary boost or a long-term policy. He explained the three-coloured system by which you hope to maintain prices in 1981.

If this is so, may I say I think it is a real shot in the arm, not only for your company, but also for us, your customers in these particularly difficult times. In Norfolk especially, people do not earn high wages, but they do shop in the market towns, which have several good local shops, an open market with cheap good green grocery *and* a Woolworth Store. We also have a thriving Women's Institute in nearly all the villages and towns, and it is through these that the word is spread. (I shall do my bit in Buston!)

However may I also add that prices alone do not influence the shopper. The customer looks for

1. Quality and cleanness in food.
2. A competent and helpful staff (very good in Norfolk, but sadly lacking in the south of England).
3. The British label.

I told Mr. Shorter I shall continue to observe, but in the meanwhile I am very satisfied with what I purchased last Saturday.

Yours faithfully,

NAUTICA S. A.

In the late afternoon of November 26, 1981, Mr. Harold Ehrenstrom, President of Bangor Punta Overseas S. A., a subsidiary of Bangor Punta Corporation in the United States, was piloting a Piper Seneca from Geneva, Switzerland to Nantes, France. This route was well known to him since Bangor Punta Corporation had acquired Nautica S. A. in Les Herbiers (60 kilometers from Nantes) in 1969. At that time, Nautica's sales had only been FF 20 million. Mr. Ehrenstrom had been actively involved in the company's constant growth since then, and the company had reached sales of FF 206 million in 1981[1] and had become the largest boat manufacturer in Europe.

That morning, Mr. Ehrenstrom together with Mr. Michael Marchand, Managing Director of Nautica S. A., had attended a presentation given by a group of participants in IMEDE's MBA Program. This group had been assigned by Mr. Ehrenstrom to conduct a study of the leisure boat industry and Nautica's performance, and to make recommendations of a strategic nature to Nautica. The presentation had confirmed Mr. Ehrenstrom's concerns with regard to Nautica's operations, the need to insure continued growth, and a specific plan for moving abroad had been proposed.

Nautica's sales growth had slowed down in 1980 after a rapid growth in 1975–1979, and the sales increase expected for 1981 had stemmed mainly from the successful diversification of Nautica into a new market with a new product, the Microcar. However, Nautica's profit margins had been steadily decreasing since 1976 and some product lines were clearly not profitable in 1981. Diversification into the windsurfing market had not met expectations and the sales of Nautica's windsurfer had been moving very slowly.

Furthermore, the majority of Nautica's sales had been in the French market and the growth of leisure boat sales in this market had decreased significantly. The next few years should be challenging ones. On the one hand, leisure activities were booming and so were some leisure-related industries. On the other hand, a new political majority had just come to power in France. Socialism could mean more leisure time availability.

Messrs. Ehrenstrom and Marchand were wondering how much of the decrease in the French market could be attributed to the general recession in Europe and in which markets efforts should be made in the years to come. Bénéteau, Nautica's major competitor, had been increasing its market share in France and

---

Source: This case was prepared by Professor Jacques Horovitz as a basis for class discussion rather than to illuminate either effective or ineffective handling of an administrative situation. Copyright © 1982 by IMEDE (International Management Development Institute), Lausanne, Switzerland. Reproduced by permission.

[1]Sales figures are for the financial year ending on August 31, 1981.

was threatening Nautica's position as the largest boat manufacturer in Europe. At the same time, many companies were going out of business announcing liquidation or their willingness to sell.

It was clear to Mr. Ehrenstrom that some major changes were taking place in the leisure boat industry and its competitive environment, and that adapting to these changes would have implications for Nautica's strategic choice with regard to product lines and markets. He was proud of Nautica's position in the leisure boat industry, wanted to strengthen this position, and ensure continued growth and profitability. He wanted to review the situation with Mr. Marchand and come up with a plan that would have long-range as well as short-range implications for Nautica as a competitor in the leisure-boat industry and a successful operating unit of Bangor Punta Corporation.

The Leisure Boat Industry in Europe[2]

A casual visitor to one of the various boat shows taking place each year in Hamburg, London, Paris, and many other cities around the world would be astonished by the versatility of the products, companies, and the countries from which those companies come. The industry that supplied the market generated by leisure-time water activities had become both international and interrelated with various other industries serving the manufacturers and buyers of leisure boats. The industry's turnover, including sales of boats, engines, boat equipment, accessories, servicing, and mooring facilities was estimated at FF 90 billion in 1980 with sales of new leisure boats amounting to only one-third of this amount.

Development of the Leisure Boat Market

Boats were not purchased to any significant extent by individuals for recreational purposes until the twentieth century, and the first of these were custom-built for the affluent. Thus, until after World War II, owners of leisure boats constituted an insignificant minority of the world's population. Partly as a result of post-war prosperity, the boating industry expanded rapidly after World War II, including powerboats, and sailboats for the lake as well as for the sea. The development, however, took place mostly in the United States with the European industry lagging a few years behind. The rapid growth in Europe did not occur until the end of the 1950s and soon the European manufacturers did reach a level of sophistication equal to that of their American counterparts. In 1980, total sales of European-manufacturers amounted to FF 7 billion. Exports within and out of Europe totalled FF 3 billion. Imports of European countries amounted to FF 2 billion (including imports from other European countries).

The total number of boats in 1980 in the United States and Europe combined was estimated to be 17 million boats (of all sizes, including inflatable boats), of which 12.5 million were in the United States only. The number of boat users was estimated to be at least twice the number of boats. Sweden had the highest number of boats in Europe, while concentration of boats per capita was the highest in Norway. Germany and France accounted for the largest share of sales in Europe in 1980, with sales in Germany amounting to FF 1.5 billion and in France to FF 1.1 billion. For selective data on sales and number of boats per capita in Europe in 1980, see Exhibit 1.

The European countries differed with regard to consumer requirements, both in terms of product type and product design. For example, the demand for powerboats was relatively higher in Germany and Italy compared to other European countries, and consumers in those countries demanded fancier boats—with teak decks and luxury interior design.

The leisure boat market had proven to be highly influenced by economic trends, stagnat-

---
[2]Many times French industry data has been selected as representative of the trends in Europe.

EXHIBIT 1
Sales, Number of Boats, and Boats per Capita in Europe in 1980

Country	Sales (FF Million)	Number of Boats (Thousands)	Boats per 1000 Inhabitants
France	1,100	488	9
Germany	1,500	438	7
Italy	950	414	7
U. K.	890	680	14
Holland	510	200	14
Sweden	960	800	100
Denmark	440	180	30
Finland	380	515	100
Norway	420	660	160
Spain	390	80	2

ing in times of recession and picking up again in times of economic growth. Thus, in the years until 1974 and from 1976 to 1979, the market in Europe had grown constantly at a rate of above 10 percent per year, while the recessions in 1975 and 1980 brought a decline. As an example that illustrates the pattern throughout Europe, Exhibit 2 shows sales between 1972 and 1980 in France. The growth rate in France, England, and the Scandinavian countries had traditionally been the highest in Europe. By 1980, the countries in which the market had suffered a higher decrease than others were England and Holland, compared to a levelling off of sales in Italy, Germany, and France. The German market was predicted to grow at a rate of above 5 percent in the 1980s, and Spain also was considered to have a promising growth potential.

The rapid expansion of the number of boats in Europe was limited by the availability of mooring facilities. In 1980, potential leisure boat buyers were facing congested marinas preventing them from acquiring a new boat. Furthermore, the cost of mooring space had climbed steeply and, in some marinas, this cost per year amounted to 10 percent of the price of a medium-sized boat.

The Product

Leisure boats were classified as either "power" or "sail" boats. Further subclassification of powerboats was into dinghies (or runabouts), inflatables, and cabin cruisers. Sailboats were

EXHIBIT 2
New Boat Sales and GNP Evolution in France 1972–1981

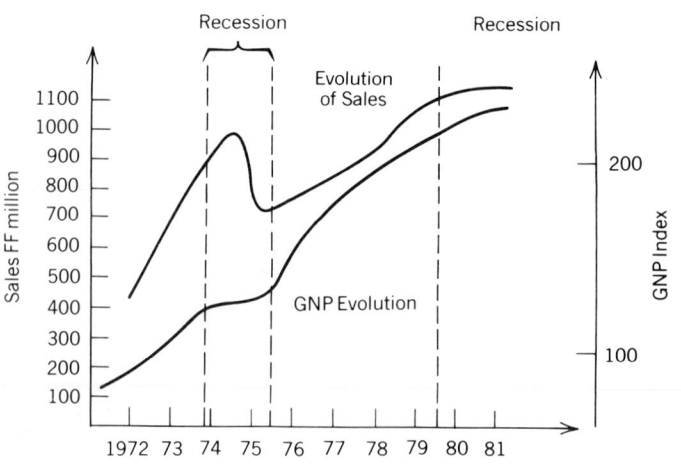

subclassified as sailing dinghies and yachts (equipped with auxiliary motor). Exhibit 3 provides an illustration of boats in the different categories. Exhibit 4 depicts the size and price range in each category, their percentage of units and sales in France in 1980. Although it may vary slightly from country to country, the proportion is the same throughout Europe.

The product in each category could be further classified by the hull material, displacement, beam, sail areas, and motor size. Another classification was related to the use/design of the boat: day cruisers, fishing, sailing, and powerboats, etc.

New models in each category were continuously introduced with the average marketing life of each new model being three years for the smaller size boats and five years for the larger ones. These new models also would initiate new life cycles of the different categories. For example, while the sales of sailing dinghies as a whole had declined, the windsurfer had emerged and represented the high growth product in the years 1977–1980.

The evolution of sales of the different product types was related very much to the economic trends and buying behavior. The steep climb of fuel costs following the oil crisis in 1973 depressed sales of powerboats, mainly small outboard dinghies and medium-sized (5 to 9 meters) power cruisers. Buyer preferences were changing to sailboats, not only because of fuel costs, but because of the trend for "back-to-nature" and ecology. In some lakes in

EXHIBIT 3
Product Categories (Different Scale—Downs)

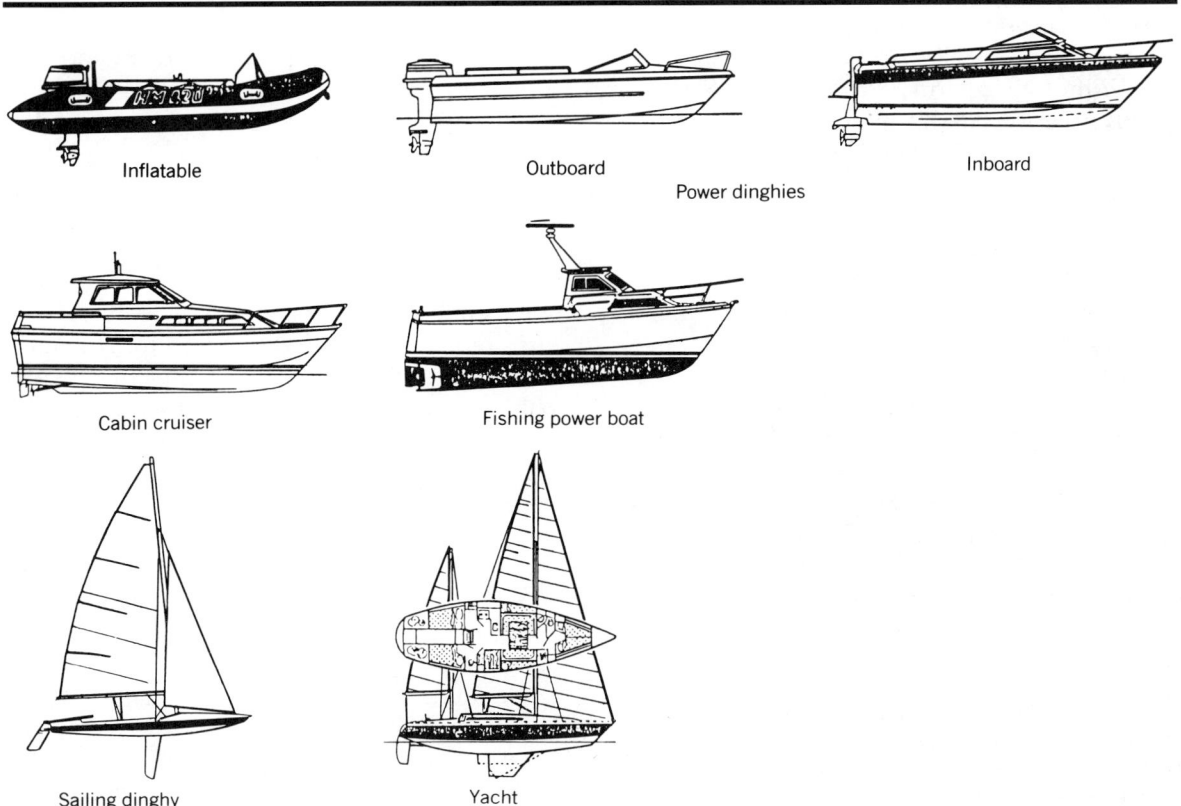

EXHIBIT 4
Breakdown of Sales by Product Category in France in 1980

Product Category	Size Range (meters)	Price Range (FF)	Percent of Unit Sales	Percent of FF Sales
Sailing dinghies	2.50–5.50	5,000–20,000	15%	10%
Yachts	<9.00	20,000–200,000	12%	23%
Yachts	>9.00	>200,000	6%	36%
Power dinghies and runabouts (inboard and outboard)	3.00–6.00	5,000–130,000	11%	11%
Cabin cruisers	>5.50	>50,000	5%	14%
Inflatables	2.50–8.00	2,000–50,000 (without engine)	<u>51%</u>	<u>6%</u>
			100%	100%

Switzerland and Germany, the use of powerboats was prohibited as a consequence of ecologist pressures. Fishing boats, which were traditionally built for the professional use of fishermen, were becoming more and more popular among buyers who thought of combining their hobby with the pleasure of cruising with their families.

In the sailing cruiser category, the manufacturers followed the buyers' trend to trade up and introduced boats of larger sizes. Thus, whereas most of the production in 1970 was of the 5 to 7 meter size, by 1980 more and more manufacturers were offering sailing cruisers of the size 9 to 14 meters.[3]

The prices of models within each category, even of the same size, varied considerably. In fact, the size of the boat could hardly be taken as a basis for price comparison and it was more so the larger the boat. For example, in France there were 12-meter sailing cruiser models selling for FF 200,000, but also models of the same size selling for FF 900,000 per boat.

The expensive models were custom-built with special interiors and exterior designs, containing a large variety of accessories that were not available in the low-price models. Furthermore, a buyer of a low-priced, standardized sailing cruiser model would have to add 20 to 40 percent of the purchase price in order to equip the boat according to his needs.

Technology

Whereas in the 1950s and 1960s the majority of boats were made of wood, the use of GRP (generic name for reinforced polyester) had become increasingly important. Special skills were required for producing the mold itself, but the manufacturing process from the mold was simple and required very little skill compared to building wood boats. The use of GRP molds enabled the production of boats in large series reducing the time required for the manufacture of each unit. However, the design of a boat and the construction of a mold for a nine-meter sailing cruiser required approximately six months, and the mold could be used for the production of 100 boats. Thus, manufacturing boats using the GRP molds process was advantageous in larger series manufacturing. Also, since the cost of the mold was about the price of a finished boat, the larger the series, the easier it was to change models from an economic point of view.

In the 1970s, aluminium was also introduced as construction material. However, the manufacturing process using aluminium was

---

[3] Motor and sailing yachts of larger sizes were considered a completely different market in which boats were mostly custom-built for the affluent by a small number of manufacturers who specialized exclusively in that segment.

EXHIBIT 5
Use of Materials for Boat Construction
Percent of Total Number of Boats Constructed[a]

Material Product Type	1965			1980		
	Wood	GRP	Aluminium	Wood	GRP	Aluminium
Sailboats <9 meter	54%	46%	—	0.5%	98%	1.5%
Sailboats >9 meter	55%	35%		3%	84%	7%
Power dinghies	60%	38%		2%	98%	—
Power cruisers	85%	7%		2%	98%	—

[a]Percentages do not add up to 100% because of the use of other materials.

very expensive compared to GRP and thus was used by only a few manufacturers, mainly in the production of larger size boats. Exhibit 5 compares the use of the different materials in 1965 and 1980.

With the improvement of materials technology, developments in manufacturing processes also were made. Besides the traditional job-shop operation building 5 to 10 custom-designed boats per year, medium and large-size manufacturers had started to grow by building a few standard models in large series. The term "large series," however, might be misleading because a medium-size, large-series manufacturer would have an output of 300 units per year and would in fact manufacture 30 to 40 units per model. For instance, the "large" manufacturers, such as Nautica and Bénéteau in France, with an output of above 3,000 units per year, would have a maximum output per model of 200 units. To use an analogy, the leisure boat industry was transforming itself as the light aircraft industry had done 30 years ago with 10 times the size. The light aircraft industry, in turn, had followed the same industrial transformation as the automobile industry with only 1/1000 of the size.

The Suppliers

The suppliers serving the leisure boat manufacturers represented a large variety of industries. They could be divided into three categories: manufacturers–suppliers of primary materials, such as the fiberglass resin, aluminum, and wood; manufacturers–suppliers of power systems; manufacturers–suppliers of components, such as masts, sails, and winches. The first group usually consisted of large established multinationals, such as *Saint-Gobain Pont-A-Mousson* (SGPM) in France and ICI in England, that were supplying their products to a variety of other industries. Sales to leisure boat manufacturers comprised a small percentage of their total sales. To reach significant volume purchases with these suppliers was rather difficult; only the large-boat manufacturers could enjoy certain volume discounts ranging from 5–10 percent. The same could be said about the power system suppliers, such as Volvo, Renault, and Yamnar, although the engines manufactured by them for the boat industry were special models designed for boats. On the other hand, the manufacturers–suppliers of components consisted of hundreds of small firms. For example, the turnover of Goiot, the largest deck fittings manufacturer in France, was under FF 100 million. Many of the components manufacturers were offering the same product at the same quality for use only in boats. Thus, competition among these suppliers was fierce, and even medium-size boat manufacturers could obtain discounts for volume orders. These discounts ranged between 20 percent for the

EXHIBIT 6
Primary Materials and Components in Different Product Types (GRP Boats)

	Powerboat (5.7 m)	Sailboat (7.6 m)	Sailboat (11.4 m)
Engine	58%	28%	17%
Fiberglass	13	18	18
Components			
Interior	11	16	17
Mast/Sail	—	17	23
Windows	9	3	2
Wood	6	8	8
Deck Fittings	3	5	11
Iron cast (ballast)	—	5	4
	100%	100%	100%

small to medium-size manufacturers up to 35 percent for the large-size manufacturers.

The relative weight of primary materials, engines, and components in the cost structure of the different product categories varied significantly, as shown in Exhibit 6. Purchases represented up to 70 percent of the ex-factory price for a medium-size powerboat and 50 percent for a medium-size yacht. On average, purchases represented 53 percent of French manufacturers sales in 1980.

Market Characteristics

With the increasing popularity of boat activities, the leisure boat industry served a market of buyers from all age groups and professions. In general, the majority of small sailboat and outboard dinghy users were young people around the age of 20, whereas large motor and sailing cruisers were purchased by people of 30 to 60 years old. As an illustration, Exhibit 7 depicts a breakdown of users of different categories by age and by profession in one country, France, in 1980.

Buyer groups could also be classified according to how they used a boat. One could identify the following groups:

EXHIBIT 7
Boat Ownership in France in 1980

	By Profession		
	Sailing Dinghies	Powerboats	Yachts
Professionals	6.2%	4.4%	8.6%
Upper Management	13.2%	11.4%	18.0%
Middle Management	16.0%	16.0%	17.4%
Office Employees	13.0%	17.7%	11.5%
Blue Collar	7.2%	15.0%	6.0%
Large-Business Owners	1.1%	2.6%	2.4%
Small-Business Owners	7.6%	14.3%	8.4%
Farmers	1.4%	1.0%	0.6%
Students	3.1%	0.8%	0.7%
Retired	6.7%	9.5%	8.4%
Companies	16.7%	3.8%	14.6%
Associations	6.1%	0.7%	0.4%
Others	2.5%	3.0%	2.8%
	100%	100%	100%

	By Age[a]	
Age	Sailing Dinghies	Yachts
<20 years	51%	17%
20–30 years	27%	22%
30–50 years	14%	30%
>50 years	8%	31%

[a]Data for powerboats not available.

The Enthusiast or Professional Sailor

This buyer would spend most of his free time on his boat, be a member of a sailing club, and participate in races. The performance of the boat (mainly speed) would be of major importance to him, reputation of the manufacturer being somewhat less important and price of very little importance. The enthusiast would be well informed of market offerings and very selective in his purchase, tending to change boats every two to three years. It was estimated that this group accounted for 20 percent of boat purchases in 1980.

Pleasure Buyers

This group purchased the boat for use in a limited time of the year—a few weekends and the summer vacation—amounting to four to five weeks per year. Price was of major importance to this group as well as service availability for the boat. The pleasure buyer also relied very much on the manufacturer's reputation. It was not unusual for this type of buyer to shop around visiting many dealers until he made his final decision as to which boat to buy and where. Once a boat had been bought by this buyer, he would use it for at least four to five years before changing to a new one. It was estimated that this group accounted for 65 percent of boat sales in 1980.

Charter Companies

Faced by the difficulties of financing the purchase and the maintenance of new boats and because of the fact that people were actually using their boats for a limited time in a year, new arrangements were created to sell a boat for a limited period of time. The most common arrangement was the chartering offered by a growing number of companies that purchased a fleet of boats and located them in the most popular cruising areas around the world. The number of chartering companies had increased at the rate of 20 percent per year between 1975 and 1980. In France only, their number had increased from less than 100 in 1975 to about 150 in 1980. Many of these companies owned only three or four boats and combined the chartering business with dealership operations.

The charter companies offered mainly large sailboats of the sizes above 9 meters. Their major buying criterion was price, but they also placed high importance on the durability and functional features of the boat, such as easy handling of the boat, number of berths, etc. Most of these companies owned their own service facilities and required direct assistance of the manufacturers only for major breakdowns. A charter company used the boats for a period of five years on average. It was estimated that this group accounted for 10 percent of total sales in 1980.

Institutions

This group consisted mainly of sailing schools, clubs, and hotels in the yacht areas. They purchased windsurfers and small sailing boats of the sizes up to 5 meters and small powerboats for water skiing. Their major buying criteria were price and durability of the boat. It was estimated that this group accounted for 5 percent of sales in 1980.

Buyers would usually choose as their first boat a small or medium-sized model that they would substitute for a larger size within a few years. The new model would not necessarily be purchased from the same manufacturer because the old brand loyalty was very much related to a product line offered by a manufacturer. Full-line manufacturers enjoyed brand loyalty to the extent of having 60–70 percent of their sales made to buyers who had already owned one of their boats.

With an increasing number of leisure boat users replacing their old boats with new ones, the second-hand market had been growing rapidly each year. Whereas in 1970 only about 15 percent of purchased boats were used ones, it was believed that in 1980 at least 60–70 percent of the purchases were of second-hand boats.

The long life of a boat had in fact commanded a relatively high second-hand price until recently. Until 1978, an owner could recover the nominal purchase value when selling, but since then it was not true any more. Prices of second-hand boats dropped sharply in 1979 and 1980. Still, a fully equipped three-year old sailboat would sell for 70 percent and a 10-year old for 40 percent of the purchase price of a new boat. Prices of powerboats tended to depreciate faster bringing the price of a three-year old second-hand boat to 50–60 percent of the price of a new one.

With the expansion of the number of leisure boat users, the increasing amount of information available to them, and the increasing number of second and third-time buyers, buyers in 1980 were becoming more choosy in their selection of a boat. It was not unusual for buyers to "shop around" in boat shows and question different dealers until they made their final choice. By-results of this phenomenon were the customized needs of the new buyers that the manufacturers had to satisfy and sometimes found very difficult to do, as well as an increased need for professionalism among dealers and the increased importance of boat shows.

In addition to chartering, an increasing number of leisure boat users chose other arrangements, such as time-sharing and multiple ownership, to overcome the high purchase price and maintenance costs of a boat. The time-sharing was very similar to chartering, but the organizing companies financed the purchase of boats by selling in advance limited cruising times for a specific period in a year. Multiple ownership was done mostly on a private basis with a few users buying a boat together and dividing among themselves the time for the use of the boat.

Distribution

In most cases, manufacturers sold their products in local markets through independent dealers. A distributor would only be used in export markets. He would generally be a big dealer who would appoint other dealers to cover the geographical areas in the market that he could not reach. It was generally agreed that a buyer relied heavily on the dealer when buying a boat and would often make his final decision at the dealer's shop.

A buyer would usually approach the dealer nearest to him, either where he lived or, as in most cases, where he planned to use the boat and required service for it. Thus, the dealers mostly were concentrated in the main recreational areas. In France, for example, there were about 500 dealers in 1981, most of them situated on the Mediterranean and the Atlantic.

The majority of the dealerships were operations that had been initiated by boat enthusiasts who had decided to combine pleasure with business. They had begun by trading in used boats, then selling accessories, and sometimes offering repair services as well as renting out boats to their customers in some cases. They typically sold a relatively full line of marine equipment, including boats, inboard and outboard engines, boat trailers, hardware, and accessories, and in addition provided maintenance facilities. In 1980, 50 percent of an average dealer's turnover came from the sale of new boats, 25 percent from the sale of second-hand boats, and 25 percent from the sale of accessories and maintenance services. On the latter, however, the dealer had the highest margins, sometimes up to 50 percent, while on new boats the margin was about 15 percent and hardly any profit was made on used boats. The average turnover of a dealer in France in 1980 was FF 1.2 million and he employed three to four people. He might carry two 7 to 9 meter boats in inventory. However, some dealers were more than 10 times bigger than the average, and it was estimated that in 1980, 10 percent of the dealers accounted for more than 50 percent of sales. Virtually all dealerships were independent operations. Some manufacturers—mainly the small ones—sold their products directly from the factory rather than, or in addition to, using dealers.

Dealers seldom carried more than one or two lines of directly competing products. In return, boat and engine manufacturers could try to protect their dealer by avoiding having another one in the same geographical area. Dealers typically carried several complementary boat lines in order to broaden the range of sizes and/or types of boats offered to customers. Thus, only manufacturers who had a full-product line, and these were not many, could have a dealer who would exclusively represent them.

In general, manufacturers were not offering dealers many incentives. The most common ways of pushing sales through the dealers were margins and credit terms. The margins ranged between 10–20 percent of the manufacturer's price list and credit terms were generally 60 days after delivery of the boat.

In 1980, the dealers were facing difficulties. A very competitive market and the increased "shopping around" of buyers forced them to increase discounts offered to buyers (discounts of 5–10 percent were most common, thus bringing a dealer's margin on a new boat to 5 percent). Additional pressure came from the need to offer trade-in arrangements forcing the dealers to take on an old boat when selling a new one. Having a few old boats in inventory would use up their capital for a long period of time, sometimes four or six months to a year. Since many of the dealers were financially weak to start, it meant that they could not purchase new boats for inventory and exhibition purposes. The financial difficulties also were caused by the seasonality of sales that occurred between February and June when the dealer had to begin purchasing and receiving the boats in late fall and complete most buying by April. In order to assist the dealers, the manufacturers had been forced to extend the terms of payment which were usually 60 days to up to 90 and even 120 days.

Leisure Boat Manufacturers

Historically, boat manufacturers had chosen to compete in narrow segments of the market defined by the design and/or function of their boat. Traditionally, they were small entrepreneurial companies that had specialized in building boats of a specific design in a limited range of sizes. Because of the myriad boat types, functions, designs, and sizes, the product lines of even the larger manufacturers seldom would be identical to one another.

In the 1960s and 1970s, however, the trend toward larger broad-line boat manufacturers was commenced by firms that had grown large by developing a market for their existing narrow product lines and sought further growth through both broadened product lines and mergers and acquisitions. Still in the 1970s, there were many companies entering the market in the good years and just as many exits in recession periods, such as in 1975 and 1980. The result was that the boat manufacturing industry in Europe in 1980, which was estimated at 2,200 boat builders, was fragmented and made up predominantly of small firms (one to ten employees) while the larger firms (50 or more employees) accounted for the majority of the sales. This can be seen in the following table referring to the sales volume of the 200 manufacturers operating in France in 1980. Five companies in France in 1980 accounted for 55 percent of total national sales. This trend of four to five companies acquiring more than 50 percent of the market was common in all European countries, but the degree of concentration would still vary, as shown in Exhibit 8.

The profitability of boat manufacturers was rather low, with the better performing companies (and these were very few) making around 5 percent net profit on sales after taxes. Many companies had incurred losses in 1980, and in 1981, profitability was even lower with sales dropping in most European countries. Exhibit 9 shows average 1978 operating results of a group of 20 manufacturing firms in France that accounted for more than 70 percent of the sales. Financial problems also beset boat manufacturers because of the seasonality of the boating business, except for large boats that were sold also out of season. To prepare for the selling period between February and June, most production took place in the preceding months. As a result, substantial interim financing was required. Most manufacturers in France, for instance, had an equity level of about 20 percent, long-term debt of 30 percent,

TABLE 1

Year	Turnover in FF Million:	0–1	1–5	5–10	10–20	+20	Total Sector
1978	Number of companies	71	47	15	8	11	160
1979		98	55	12	13	11	189
1980		114	48	14	8	15	199

and short-term liabilities of 50 percent of the total liabilities of the firm. Many manufacturers, who attempted to alleviate the problem of seasonal sales by concentrating production in the months immediately preceding the selling season, faced labor problems inherent in a seasonal business.

Production methods used by boat manufacturers varied from custom-building large yachts to meet customers' specifications to large batch production of smaller standardized boats. Although custom-building had been traditional in the industry, the increased sales volumes of the larger companies and the adaptability to "mass" production of new hull materials, like fiberglass, had led the larger manufacturers towards production line techniques. Fiberglass hulls, for example, were typically molded at one station, then finished (e.g., decks, interiors, and equipment were installed) at succeeding stations.

"Large-series" manufacturers were not only attempting to cut costs by standardizing the manufacturing process, but also trying to standardize the design of the models within a product line and across product lines. This was one of the ways to reduce raw materials and work-in-process inventory levels since a large-size boat contained about 5,000 different parts. Apart from cutting costs, standardization partly answered the problem of anticipating sales levels of the different models in the season. Orders were made by the dealers according to the demand of buyers and this demand could neither be directed nor anticipated. This was mostly true for new models

Large manufacturers were trying to increase the success prospects of a new model by

EXHIBIT 8
Concentration Levels in Different European Countries

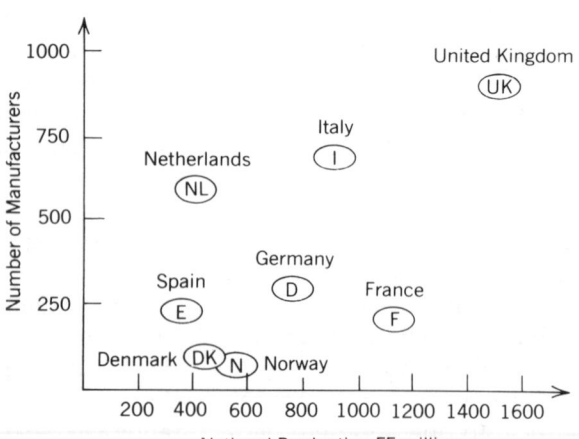

EXHIBIT 9
Industry Income Statement—1978
French Boat Manufacturers

	Ex-Factory Price	100%
	Cost of Materials	48.1%
	Other Purchases	13.8%
	Value Added	38.1%
	Personnel Costs[a]	29.3%
	Operating Income	8.8%
	Financing Costs	2.5%
	Depreciation	2.8%
	Provisions	1.7%
	Profit before Tax	1.8%

[a]Direct and Indirect Labor.

having it designed by a well-known boat architect who had a reputation for designing "winning models." Architects would usually charge 1.5 to 3 percent of sales as royalty fees. Some manufacturers were trying to overcome the problems of anticipating demand and the need to "customize" boats by selling a "kit"—just the molded parts of the boat—leaving it up to the buyer's desire and capability to "finish up" the boat.

Pricing was subject to some controversy in the boating industry. While the large-series manufacturers attempted to price their boats in the lower price range for each size category in order to attract buyers, the small manufacturers that could not compete on price had to offer higher margins to dealers or sell the boats directly to the end user. Industry practice varied with respect to advertising and promotion. French manufacturers spent an average of 2 percent of sales on advertising and promotion. Generally speaking, advertising budgets had increased in the last 10 years. Most promotional efforts were essentially restricted to factual advertising in specialized boating periodicals, exhibitions, and boat shows and providing sales aid to dealers. Boat shows were considered a particularly effective marketing tool, but participation in two to three boat shows in a national market in a year was quite expensive, costing around FF 100,000 per show. Here again, the larger manufacturers had the advantage of being able to set up an exhibition spread on a large floor area presenting a large variety of models with many salesmen around them (the salesmen were usually the company's dealers who, of course, had an interest in coming for the period of the boat show to realize sales there) that could attract the attention of the majority of the thousands of visitors to the show.

Trade magazines were not used only for advertising, but manufacturers attempted to have results of boat tests reported in these magazines as well as introduction reports on new models and general descriptive reports about the company's product line. The majority of boat users read at least one trade magazine per month and these reports were considered a highly influential tool. Similar to that was the coverage received on participation in boat races in which manufacturers participated with their current models or prototype. Winning a race would bring publicity to the company and was used afterwards as a promotional theme in the company's advertising. Participating in a race would mostly mean extending credit, if the boat was sold to the sponsor, or a repurchase agreement in the case of leasing.

Nautica S. A.

Some 30 years ago, Henri Cocteau, a keen powerboat racer, began to construct wooden boats to his own design, at first for himself and then for his friends. His designs were so successful that he gave up his hardware business and devoted himself to building boats. In the 1950s a leisure boat was inevitably made of wood. Henri Cocteau was one of the first manufacturers to look into the possibilities of plastics. By 1959, he was offering polyester hulls with wooden decks and by 1960 boats made entirely of polyester.

In 1964, the company changed its legal status to that of a corporation, thereafter trading under the name of Société Nautica Constructions S. A. In September 1969, Bangor Punta Corporation, an American diversified multibusiness company looking for business opportunities in Europe, acquired a 75 percent interest in Nautica S. A. At that time, Bangor Punta Corporation already owned three successful yacht and powerboat manufacturing companies in the United States (O'Day, Jensen-Marine, and Starcraft), with sales amounting to $60 million.

Mr. Cocteau remained as general manager of Nautica S. A. until he sold out the rest of his shares and left the company in 1972. Mr. Michel Marchand, who had been with the company since 1968, was appointed General Manager. By 1981, Nautica's sales reached over FF 200 million, representing 4.5 percent of Bangor Punta Corporation's consolidated sales.[4] Nautica had become the largest boat manufacturer in Europe with an annual output of above 6,000 units of its different models. Financial data for the company in the years 1975–1981 are shown in Exhibit 10.

Nautica's management, however, was quite concerned by a few factors that had accompanied this growth. First, profit margins had been constantly decreasing, from a profit before tax of 30 percent on sales in 1970 to 6 percent in 1981. Nautica, which traditionally had much higher profit margins than the industry average, was losing this edge. Second, Nautica's main competitor, Bénéteau, had significantly increased its market share in France in 1980 and 1981, while Nautica's market share remained constant at around 18 percent since 1979. Furthermore, the French market in which 75 percent of Nautica's boat sales were realized, was showing signs of decreasing growth rate in 1981. Finally, production problems had appeared as a result of difficulties to estimate market demand for Nautica's different models. With Nautica's wide product line, this meant high inventory levels of some of the models, while the output of others could not meet the demand.

Product Policy

Nautica had followed a consistent strategy of constantly adding new models to the different types of leisure boats. By 1981, it was the only manufacturer in France with a full line of powerboats and sailboats with more than 50 models covering three ranges:

Powerboats: dinghies, outboard, and cabin cruisers from 3.60 to 9.60 meters.

Fishing/leisure crafts and canoes from 3.10 to 8.30 meters.

Sailboats and sailing cruisers from 5.50 to 14.00 meters.

Exhibit 11 presents Nautica's product line in 1981 giving the introduction year of each model.

Nautica's approach was not to build beautiful and sophisticated boats, but simple and sturdy family cruising boats focusing not on racing, but on family and vacation use. Recently, however, the newer larger models (Sun Fizz, Espace, Trinidad) were as sophisticated and highly finished as its competitors'. Models were usually designed to enable competitive pricing while maintaining high gross margins compared to the industry average.

However, gross margins as well as the price competitiveness were not equal along the product lines. Gross margin on the sailboats in 1981 was the highest, about 23 percent, while powerboats generated 20.5 percent and fishing boats only 15 percent. Prices of the sailboats were very competitive, positioning Nautica's boats in the low-price range in any size. For example, the "Rush," a 9.20 meter sailboat, was priced at FF 160,000, compared to the competitors' sailboats of the same size priced

---

[4]Bangor Punta Corporation also owns Piper Aircraft, a light aircraft manufacturer aimed at the leisure and business market, and Smith and Wesson, a handgun manufacturer.

EXHIBIT 10
Financial Statements 1975–1981 (FF thousands)

Income Statement	1975	1976	1977	1978	1979	1980	1981
Sales (in constant 1981 francs)	103,647	140,664	168,234	176,752	215,200	193,137	206,116
Net Sales[a]	53,983	80,356	109,243	125,445	169,182	172,444	206,116
Cost of Sales							
Materials	24,174	36,625	45,035	54,512	74,355	78,859	92,660
Labor	9,742	11,475	22,649	29,458	36,181	39,146	56,567
Overhead (including depreciation)	2,192	7,923	6,280	6,255	9,171	8,686	15,704
Gross Profit	17,875	24,333	35,279	35,220	49,525	45,753	41,185
Sales and General Administration	5,225	6,778	8,710	9,114	9,715	16,562	22,113
Management Fee and Commission[b]	1,445	2,023	1,997	2,047	2,246	1,965	2,789
Employee Profit Shares	739	1,073	1,683	1,755	2,886	1,591	—
Total Operating Expenses	7,409	9,874	12,390	12,916	14,847	20,118	24,902
Operating Income	10,466	14,459	22,889	22,304	34,678	25,635	16,283
Other Income (Expenses)							
Interest Expense	(238)	(47)	(288)	(617)	(621)	(2,917)	(6,312)
Interest Income	782	389	484	345	515	746	557
Miscellaneous Income	406	739	615	551	1,084	549	(1,242)
Profit before Tax	11,416	15,540	23,700	22,483	35,656	24,002	11,770
Taxes	5,504	7,556	11,625	10,858	17,386	10,882	5,667
Net Profit	5,912	7,984	12,075	11,625	18,270	13,120	6,103

Balance Sheet	1975	1976	1977	1978	1979	1980	1981
Current Assets							
Cash and Equivalents	7,029	15,922	13,903	8,658	15,957	13	3,423
Receivables	12,518	17,188	19,269	23,282	32,633	25,080	47,961
Inventories (FIFO)	14,813	12,872	21,069	28,914	32,104	64,216	67,966
Other Current Assets	606	665	1,393	1,980	2,880	6,445	5,623
Total Current Assets	34,966	45,647	55,634	62,834	83,574	95,754	124,973
Plant, Property, and Equipment	14,955	16,190	23,070	28,083	39,113	48,321	56,018
Less Accumulated Depreciation	4,330	5,565	7,183	9,854	13,278	16,530	21,009
Net	10,625	10,625	15,887	18,229	25,835	31,791	35,059
Intangible Assets Net	347	234	122	20	20	128	165
Other Assets	6	108	14	1,666	1,319	269	1,506
Total Assets	45,943	56,614	71,657	82,749	110,748	127,942	161,703
Current Liabilities							
Short-Term Debt	—	—	—	—	—	—	17,090
Long-Term Debt Due	5	5	5	5	5	5	5
Accounts Payable	4,132	5,970	6,953	9,503	12,098	12,559	24,709
Accrued Liabilities	2,906	4,528	6,520	8,219	10,141	15,387	16,782
Accrued Income Tax	672	4,489	6,248	2,581	10,593	—	—
Employees' Profit Sharing	739	1,073	1,684	1,755	2,886	1,591	—
Other Current Liabilities	380	441	1,691	1,563	1,088	12,543	4,399
Total Current Liabilities	8,833	16,506	23,101	23,626	36,811	42,085	62,985
Deferred Income	—	—	998	3,214	2,738	2,484	2,178

(Continued)

EXHIBIT 10 (Continued)

Income Statement	1975	1976	1977	1978	1979	1980	1981
Deferred Income Taxes	444	573	1,064	1,575	1,610	3,680	4,556
Long-Term Debt	37	32	27	22	17	11	9,209
Stockholders Equity	36,628	39,502	46,467	54,312	69,572	79,682	82,775
Total Liabilities	45,943	56,614	71,657	82,749	110,748	127,942	161,703

[a] Current terms.
[b] To Bangor Punta Overseas S. A.

at FF 200,000 and more. Prices were not as competitive in the fishing boat and powerboat lines. For example, the "Esteou 630," a 6.3 meter fishing boat, was priced at FF 84,000 compared to the competitors' price of FF 53,000 for a similar boat.

Development of sales was different for different product lines. While unit sales of all product lines had constantly increased from 1972 until 1981, the major growth was in the sailboat line. 1,400 units of this line were sold in 1980 compared to 390 units in 1972. (See Exhibit 12 for unit sales development of the different product lines between 1972 and 1981.)

Within the product lines, certain changes were also apparent. In the powerboat line, small powerboats (under 6 meter) dominated unit sales—83 percent of powerboats sold in 1980, but within the sailboat product line large sailboats (above 9 meter) were becoming more important: from 17 percent of total sailboats sold in 1976 to 32 percent in 1980.

While sailboats represented only 18 percent of unit sales in 1980, they were the major cash generators, bringing in 65 percent of sales and 70 percent of gross profit because of the higher gross margins in this line. The weight of the different product lines in sales and gross profits for the years 1979–1981 is shown in Exhibit 13.

Within the product lines, three to four models would usually account for the majority of sales (about 60 percent). A review of Nautica's sales by model reveals that a successful model might account for up to 40 percent of the units sold in its product line and this would be reached two to three years after the model's introduction. For example, the "Flirt," which was introduced in 1976 reached 43 percent of sailboat unit sales in 1978 and dropped to 14 percent in 1980. The "Skanes 510," which was introduced in 1977, reached 30 percent of powerboat unit sales in 1978 and dropped to 21 percent in 1980.

Nautica's management believed that it was very difficult to predict the success of a new model before its introduction to the market and the evolution of its sales. However, dealers related the success of the "Rush," a 9.20 meter sailboat, to filling the gap that existed in the market in that size and the success of the "Sun Fizz," a 11.75 meter sailboat, which was also introduced in 1980, to the fit of the design and the price for the requirements of the charter market. Sales of the Sun-Fizz, which was priced at about FF 320,000 (net ex-factory price), reached 180 units in 1981 compared to forecasted sales of 80 units.

Marketing in France

Nautica's sales in France represented 79 percent of its total sales in 1981. Its share of the French market had increased from 12 percent in 1976 to 18 percent in 1979 and remained the same in 1980 and 1981.

Nautica sold directly to dealers. Its dealer network in France in 1981 comprised 130 dealers geographically spread to cover all of France. This was the largest dealer network in

EXHIBIT 11
Nautica's Product Line

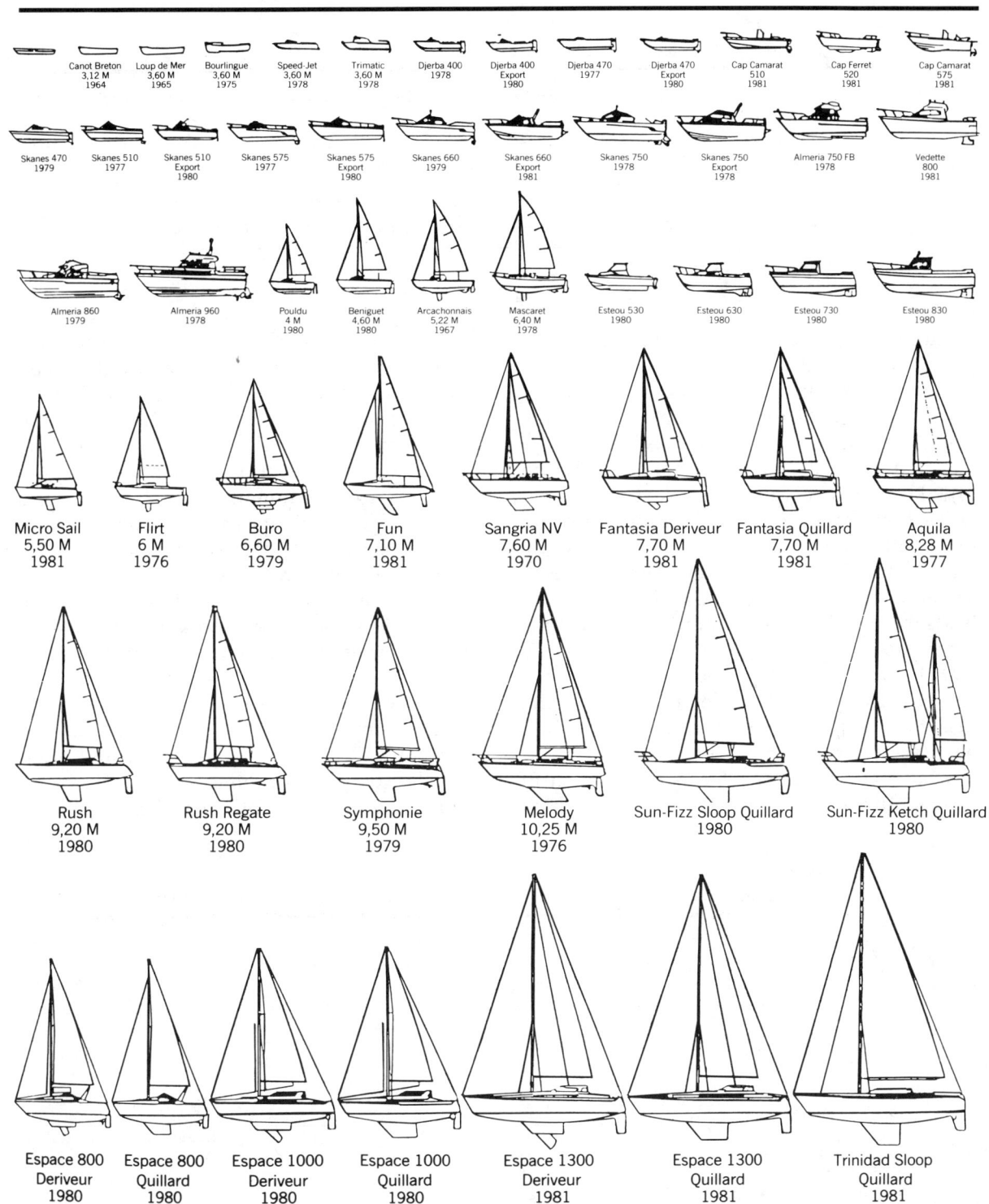

EXHIBIT 12
Evolution of Unit Sales by Product Line

	1972	1973	1974	1975	1976	1977	1978	1979	1980	1981
Sailboats	390	557	774	572	934	1280	1425	1642	1398	1059
Powerboats	790	1053	1165	1271	1482	1570	1656	2114	1578	1748
Fishing boats	425	387	475	510	595	671	674	678	982	810
Dinghies	732	381	639	1179	1252	1269	1040	1087	3775[a]	2691[a]
Total	2337	2378	3053	3532	4263	4790	4795	5521	7733	6308

[a]Including windsurfers.

the industry (Bénéteau, Nautica's main competitor, had 110 dealers).

Nautica's management tried to emphasize loyalty of dealers urging them to buy only from Nautica. Dealers who had originally represented both Nautica and Bénéteau had been urged by both companies to make a choice and at least 50 percent of them had chosen to remain with Nautica. The dealer was offered the whole range of Nautica's product line. Few separate dealerships for powerboats or sailboats existed. The wide product line was thus considered an advantage from both Nautica's and the dealer's point of view.

Nautica supplied the different boats to the dealers two to four weeks after an order had been placed. The terms of payment were usually 60 days, but longer terms were given in the months of September to February, which were considered off-season months. The pressures faced by dealers in 1980 and 1981 forced Nautica's management to increase the terms of payment to 90 days and even 120 days in the weak months. Most dealers had certain boats in inventory; however, Nautica did not supply boats on a consignment basis. A dealer was furnished with Nautica's promotional material, but Nautica did not participate in any local advertising initiated by dealers.

Nautica's relationship with its dealers was considered to be quite good and the turnover among dealers was very low. Nautica did not have any salesmen. Dealers were visited irregularly by Nautica's sales manager or other company executives—mostly upon the requirement of the dealer. Dealers would often visit the company's premises in Les Herbiers. In 1981, a program of "regional meetings"

EXHIBIT 13
Percentages of Total Sales and of Total Gross Contribution of Nautica's Product Lines

	1979		1980[a]		1981[a]	
Percentage of:	Sales	Total Gross Contribution	Sales	Total Gross Contribution	Sales	Total Gross Contribution
Sailing boats	60%	65%	65%	70%	67%	73%
Powerboats	25	21	16	15	15.5	15
Fishing boats	12	10	14	10	12	9
Others[b]	3	4	5	5	5.5	3
	100%	100%	100%	100%	100%	100%

[a]Not including Microcar sales.
[b]Small boats, windsurfers, and service parts.

with dealers had been initiated. Dealers from a certain region were invited for a one-day meeting in which Nautica's management reviewed new products and marketing programs and listened to dealers' problems or requests. The meetings were planned to take place at least once a year in each region.

Dealers in France received price lists quoting the final price to the buyer and were invoiced on the price lists minus 15 percent. While the maximum price was that recommended by Nautica in the price list, most dealers gave discounts to buyers ranging from 5–10 percent, as was normal in the industry. While promotion on a local basis was the responsibility of the local dealers, Nautica promoted its products nation-wide. The elements of the promotion were:

Advertising in most trade magazines.

Participation in all boat shows.

Participation in boat races with prototypes of existing models.

Special promotion projects such as cooperative promotion campaigns with a car manufacturer.

With an increasing competition, the promotion budget was augmented substantially over the years—from FF 750,000 in 1976 to FF 3.5 million in 1981. In terms of percentage of sales, this budget was not high compared to the industry average, but the amount enabled Nautica to maintain a higher promotion level than most of its competitors. In 1981 the budget was allocated as follows:

Advertising (including brochures)	50%
Boat shows	24%
General promotion (special projects and exhibits)	26%

Nautica's advertisement was divided into three categories: general company ads featuring such themes as the wide product line and dealer network; ads of special services, such as the financing program and the used boats data center; specific model ads. Generally, these advertisements were considered to reflect a conservative image that would appeal to the family leisure group. Nautica did not make special promotional efforts to generate sales to institutions and charter companies.

Nautica's management was not sure whether the low promotion levels in the years preceding 1981 had not affected adversely Nautica's market share growth in France or whether the budget allocation in 1981 for the different promotion tools had the optimum effectiveness.

Nautica offered through its dealers in France a number of special services for prospective buyers:

Financing arrangements. Nautica had reached an agreement with a French finance company to offer a financing package for the purchase of a new boat.

Insurance. Nautica offered a one-year "all risk" insurance coverage.

Guarantee. All boats had a one-year full guarantee for the hull and parts.

Second-hand trading data center. Information about used boats available at its dealers throughout France was processed by Nautica's computer and the lists were distributed to the dealers or advertised at Nautica's expense.

A second-hand boat market. This had been opened by Nautica on the Seine in Paris for the use of Nautica's dealers. New boats were also on permanent exhibition there and Nautica's dealers, who did not (and many of them could not) hold certain boats in inventory, would send prospective buyers to see the boats in this center.

Unlike some other competitors, Nautica did not operate a chartering company for its boats.

Marketing Abroad

While Nautica's management always maintained the importance of acquiring export markets, Nautica's exports were usually less than

EXHIBIT 14
Export Sales (FF Thousands)

Europe	1978/1979	1979/1980	1980/1981
United Kingdom	1,805	2,601	9,567
Switzerland	4,103	5,346	4,842
Italy	1,578	1,305	4,813
Greece	177	376	4,687
Germany	2,990	2,948	4,332
Belgium	1,899	2,833	2,737
Norway	98	—	1,682
Netherlands	5,358	2,455	1,630
Austria	804	343	1,051
Portugal	165	—	798
Spain	32	1,619	411
Denmark	590	750	352
Yugoslavia	99	—	—
Overseas Markets	4,154	2,207	2,549
Total	23,401	22,783	39,452

20 percent of its total annual sales. These exports were divided among more than 10 countries, but the majority of sales were realized in England, Italy, and Switzerland. Data with regard to exports by country in the years 1975 to 1981 are given in Exhibit 14. Most of the increase in exports in 1981, mainly to the U. K., Italy, Greece, and Germany was due to sales of the "Sun-Fizz."

Nautica did not sell directly to dealers in any of the export markets. Rather it contacted an importer/distributor in each country offering him the complete product line. Only in 1981 did Nautica appoint separate importers for powerboats and sailboats in Italy and additional importers of powerboats in Germany. The boats were not modified to suit local needs, unless it was required by the import authorities.

The importers were charged by Nautica on the basis of ex-factory price in French francs, identical to the selling price to French dealers. The decision and implementation of the marketing policy in each country, including appointment of dealers, promotion, and even pricing, was left up to the importer. Thus, Nautica's sales in any of the export markets were heavily dependent on the competence of the local importer. This can be seen in the following examples of Germany and Switzerland.

Germany

Mr. Lungern had been Nautica's importer to Germany since 1969. He was a keen sailor, who constantly participated in races with Nautica's boats, thus acquiring a reputation for him and the boats. He did not have a showroom or service facilities and his office was situated in his house near Hamburg. Mr. Lungern sold directly to local buyers, not using any dealers. Thus, his coverage of the market was small. He spent very little on advertising, but participated in all the three boat shows in Germany. Nautica's participation in his promotion expenses was limited to 2 percent of his total purchases.

Sales to Germany had been very volatile and in 1981 Nautica's sales of FF 4.8 million (including FF 700,000 realized by the powerboat importers) represented less than $\frac{1}{2}$ percent of the German boat market. The sales of another French manufacturer, Dufour, in Germany amounted to FF 28 million that year.

Switzerland

Mr. Hedinger had been Nautica's importer and distributor in Switzerland since 1972. His business combined the sales of other leisure products, such as camping vans with that of Nautica's complete product line. He had a large showroom and service facilities in Uttwil, near Lake Constance, and operated a dealer network of 16 dealers for the sale of Nautica's boats. The dealers were independent, but sold Nautica's boats as their major line and had regional exclusivity. Mr. Hedinger priced the boats relatively high adding a markup of up to 40 percent on the landed cost (Nautica's ex-factory price plus transportation). The dealers received 10 percent of this price. He regularly advertised in national and local trade magazines allocating 5 percent of his sales turnover for this purpose. His dealers were highly appreciative of his backing and were very loyal to him. For example, in a case of a sale realized to a buyer coming from a region where one of his dealers was operating, Mr. Hedinger would transfer to that dealer the margin due to him.

In 1981, having the agreement of Nautica's management, Mr. Hedinger had appointed two dealers on the German side of Lake Constance; thus he acquired a foothold in the southern part of Germany. Mr. Hedinger was also receiving 2 percent of his total purchases as Nautica's participation in his promotion expenses.

Nautica was outperforming its French competitors in the Swiss market. By 1981 its sales to Switzerland amounted to FF 5.1 million, representing 16 percent of total boat imports to Switzerland that year and 13 percent of the Swiss market.

It was not unusual for foreigners to buy Nautica boats through French dealers. Nautica's management did not have exact figures with regard to this indirect exporting, but it was estimated that it amounted to about 5 percent of Nautica's total sales. Some of the importers were complaining about the fact that French dealers could offer a better price than them as a result of having the same ex-factory price, but less overhead costs.

Production

In the years of fast expansion, Nautica's management policy had been that of continuous upgrading of production facilities pursuing efficient production and implementing a better inventory control.

Nautica's production facilities covered 62,000 m^2 of floor space in 1981 compared to 15,000 m^2 in 1970. They included three molding centers, five assembly and finishing halls, carpentry, upholstery, and stainless-steel workshops. The assembly and finishing facilities were divided by product line: powerboats, dinghies, small sailboats, large sailboats, and the Microcar assembly. There were 845 production workers of average skill, except in such areas as carpentry and tooling where higher skills were needed.

The production process began with the hull and upper deck molding, by applying several layers of fiberglass impregnated by resin inside the mold. The finished molded parts then would be transferred to the assembly hall where first the deck would be fitted onto the hull and the wooden enforcements placed in the hull. The boat would then be placed across in the same hall where all the other parts would be mounted on it. In each of the stages, there would be a team of three to six workers performing the tasks on each boat. Each model required a different number of labor hour input. For planning and pricing purposes, standard labor hours per model were taken as a basis.

Comparing Nautica's standard labor input to the industry average shows that less labor hours were used in the manufacture of sailboats and about the same in the manufacture of fishing and powerboats (see Exhibit 15 A). Furthermore, labor hours per unit constantly decreased each year (see Exhibit 15 B).

Although there was similarity in the assembly process and the tools used for the construction of all models, labor force flexibility within the plant was somewhat limited since an assembly team would become specialized in the final assembly of a specific model and only a few tasks were performed as general construction (i.e., wood structure fitting, electricity, etc.).

Each of Nautica's models was broken down into references representing the components to be used in its construction. In 1981, 8,000 different references existed for Nautica's 50 models with each boat representing between 50 to 1,500 references. Little similarity existed in references per model in the different product lines, but limited similarity existed *within* the product lines.

EXHIBIT 15
Labor Hours Per Boat

Type	Nautica	Industry
Sailboat (12 m)	1550	2000
Sailboat (7 m)	280	300
Powerboat (7 m)	480	280
Fishing boat (6 m)	350	240

Labor Hours Input Per Boat (average per unit)

Product Line	Year		
	1978	1979	1980
Sailboats	516	486	474
Powerboats	173	146	107
Fishing boats	262	258	151

According to the production schedule, a computerized order form would be issued to the main storage center. The storage center would then transfer all the parts needed for the assembly of a complete boat to the work-in-process storage room, which was usually situated in each assembly hall. From there the parts would be distributed to each of the assembly stations. The transfer of the parts to the work-in-process storage room was done every 10 days based on the production schedule for that period. There was no inventory control at the work-in-process stage.

While the facilities outlay and the manufacturing process were geared to enable flexibility in production, it was not unusual to have congestion problems and loss of labor hours because of a change in production schedule. Some people in production were of the view that there were frequent changes in production schedules and these were due to the lack of sales planning by the marketing department. The marketing people, however, maintained that long-range forecasting was impossible, but they were giving short-term forecasts that were sufficient to revise schedules in a controlled manner.

Purchasing

In general, Nautica's purchasing policy stressed spreading orders among a few suppliers of certain items and shopping around for the best price. Its size gave Nautica the advantage of getting higher discounts than most of its competitors. These discounts amounted to 5 to 10 percent for the commodity purchases, such as resin and motor supplies, and to 20–35 percent from component suppliers. This advantage was reflected in Nautica's purchasing costs as a percentage of sales, which in 1980 was 46 percent compared to the industry average of 53 percent. However, back in 1973 Nautica's purchasing costs as a percentage of Sales had been 45 percent compared to the industry average of 60.5 percent that year.

While the total number of suppliers used by Nautica was about 1,000, the majority of supplies came from a much smaller number of suppliers. In 1980, out of total purchases of FF 105 million, 32 percent came from 10 suppliers. FF 12 million of fiberglass purchases was supplied by three companies and FF 16 million of engine supplies was supplied by five companies.

The large suppliers, such as fiberglass and engine suppliers, were contracted on a yearly basis according to projected sales. The smallest suppliers were contracted on an ad hoc basis. In recent years, Nautica had moved into in-house manufacturing of some components. This was the case in most of the woodwork, the stainless-steel parts, and the upholstery. Nautica's management did not believe that with the supply capacity and the competitive situation among other components' suppliers it was worthwhile to manufacture other components such as masts and sails in-house.

Purchasing was usually done on the basis of forecasted sales according to inventory levels. By 1981, a computerized system was being introduced to assist in the coordination of purchases and inventory.

EXHIBIT 16
Nautica's Organization Chart

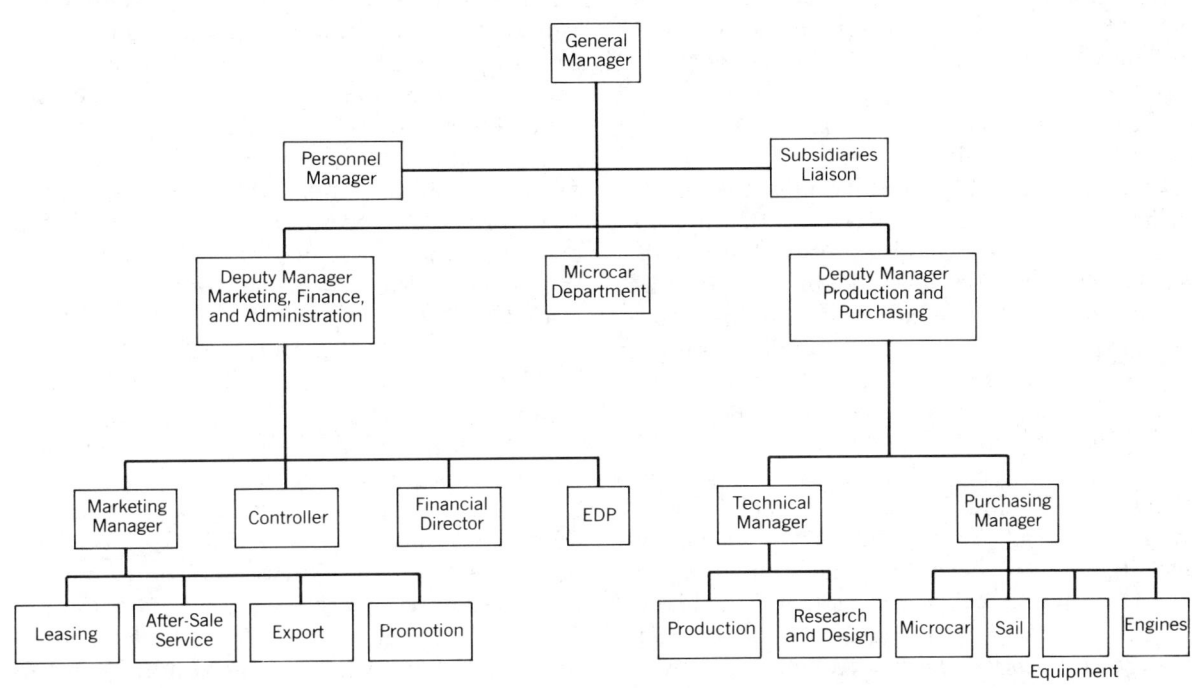

Organization

Nautica's organization had been developed along functional lines. Exhibit 16 depicts its organizational structure in 1981. Since the organization had grown rapidly in the years of expansion, problems of communication between functions had arisen. For instance, production managers wanted longer runs and less schedule changes. The marketing people, on the other hand, gave sales estimates that were likely to change because market requirements were difficult to predict. The purchasing department required minimization of inventories, but production pressed for higher inventories to enable the frequent changes in production schedules. The functioning of the Research and Design Department was frequently criticized. This department was in charge of studying and defining the bill of materials as well as the manufacturing process of each model.

Diversification Moves

In 1980, a decision was taken to begin the manufacture of the Microcar, a 49 cc, fiberglass body, two-seater vehicle. It sold mostly in rural areas because it did not require a driver's license and so could be sold to the older population as a means of local transportation for short trips, such as for shopping. The diversification fitted with the company's existing resources in two ways: (1) the production of the body was based on the same technology as building boats (i.e., fiberglass moldings), and (2) the employment of product labor force could be steadied through the year overcoming slack production periods because of the seasonality in boat purchases.

Sales of the Microcar started in early 1981. By September 1981, 1,340 units had been sold, generating 8 percent of sales that year and 3.6 percent of profits. Sales in 1982 were expected to climb to 7,000 units or 35 percent of Nautica's sales.

Upon requests of its dealers, Nautica's management had also decided in 1979 to market a windsurfer. The production of the windsurfer had been subcontracted, and its manufacturer used the fiberglass technology. This caused the price of the windsurfer to be uncompetitive as the fiberglass technology was more expensive than injection molding or thermo forming technology used by other manufacturers, mainly Dufour. Dufour had gained price leadership in this market with its FF 2,500 windsurfer compared to Nautica's price of FF 3,500. While Dufour had reached sales of more than 50,000 units in 1980, Nautica's sales were less than 3,000. Nautica's management had also chosen not to become engaged in heavy marketing efforts, and sold the windsurfer mostly through its regular dealers and only a few through specialized windsurfer outlets.

As sales of the windsurfer did not seem to meet expectations, Nautica's management had decided, at the beginning of 1981, to withdraw gradually from this market. The contract with the subcontractor was not renewed, but sales of the windsurfer from the remaining inventory were continued.

Nautica's Main Competitors in Europe

Bénéteau

Bénéteau represented a success story among French manufacturers. The firm, which had been started by Mr. Benjamin Bénéteau in 1884, had been busy for several years after World War II renewing the Bénéteau fishing fleet with its traditional 50-ton trawlers. The average life of a trawler was 15 to 20 years, so there were not many new boats to build. Moreover, wood was gradually giving way to steel which Bénéteau was not able to handle. Mrs. Annette Roux, Bénéteau's granddaughter, took over the business from her father in 1964 when it was a tiny, ailing boatyard with 17 employees. Mrs. Roux decided to enter the growing leisure boat market with a small polyester boat that her father had designed. By 1981 the company had become the second largest manufacturer in France with a turnover of FF 190 million and 700 employees, which produced 3,000 boats per year in five factories on the Vendée coast in France. To implement this growth, Mrs. Roux had followed a consistent policy of expanding the product line, improving manufacturing techniques, and building up a wide dealership network and heavy promotion.

The expansion of the product line had taken the form of adding new models of larger sizes to the first successful model. Thus, the "pêche-promenade" line was built up until 1975 when the "Evasion" line was introduced. This line included in 1981 six models of the sizes 6.70 to 11.30 meter. In 1977, the first model of the "First" line was introduced aiming at the classical high performance sector of the market. The first model of this line was a prize-winning, nine-meter racing yacht designed by a well-known French architect, and by 1981 the "First" line included eight models ranging from 7.50 to 13 meters. In 1979, the line of "Flyer" powerboats with five models of the sizes 5.20 to 7.50 meter was introduced, and to complete the expansion of the product line six power and sailing/fishing boats were introduced in 1980 together with one model of a windsurfer and a sporty sailing dinghy.

Mrs. Roux also realized the importance of a large and strong dealer network for the high-growth strategy. Thus, she followed a very systematic and aggressive policy of entering existing dealerships. One or two models were introduced to the dealer as a complementary item in their line, and then the dealer was "followed up" continuously with regular visits from Bénéteau people. By this policy, Bénéteau acquired many of its competitors' dealers, reaching a dealer network of 110 dealers by 1980, second only to Nautica which had 130 dealers in France.

The emphasis on dealers was accompanied by heavy promotion using all the tools available in the market and initiating new promotional programs. Mrs. Roux built up the image of a dynamic, successful, and high-growing company through constant exposure of her and the company to the media—she gave frequent interviews that had appeared in trade magazines, management periodicals, and daily and weekly newspapers. The introduction of each new model was made public by having news conferences reported thereafter in the different magazines. In addition to that, Bénéteau advertised heavily in all trade magazines in colorful advertisements spreading over six to ten pages of a magazine concentrating on the theme of an "experienced boat builder who builds reliable and excellent performing boats." It also offered the services of a computerized data center for used boats and initiated a program of chartering, whereby Bénéteau would rent out boats sold to its customers, which could save up to 50 percent of the purchasing price of a boat. Participants in the market who were questioned about this plan tended to believe that it was not very realistic and considered it to be another promotional gimmick among the many used by Bénéteau.

Bénéteau's pricing was very competitive in all product lines, and while the quality of the boat was standard, buyers considered it as good value for the money.

Bénéteau had a high debt, even by industry standards. Its short-term liabilities were 64 percent of total liabilities and long-term debts were 21 percent in 1979. Competitors were questioning its financial capabilities. However, its profitability was above the industry average. Financial statements for 1978–1981 are shown in Exhibit 17.

By 1980 Bénéteau had reached a 17 percent share of the French market. At the same time, Bénéteau's management was making efforts to penetrate other European markets concentrating mostly on Germany. Bénéteau's reputation in this country was rather low and

EXHIBIT 17
Bénéteau Financial Statement 1979–1981 (FF Thousands)

	1978	1979	1980[a]	1981
Income Statement				
Sales	74,389	123,211	220,254	198,284
Cost of Materials	33,448	54,298	96,773	93,149
Other Purchases	4,147	7,931	11,521	12,880
Labor Costs	17,358	28,621	58,143	50,406
Depreciation	2,141	4,168	9,529	11,163
Gross Margin	17,295	28,193	44,288	30,686
General and Administration	3,607	6,050	14,371	12,892
Employee Profit Shares	1,505	2,572	1,510	365
Financing Costs	2,126	3,359	10,443	13,056
Profit Before Tax	10,057	16,212	17,964	4,373
Income Taxes	5,378	8,895	7,321	2,351
Net Profit	4,679	7,317	10,643	2,022

(Continued)

EXHIBIT 17 (Continued)

	April 30, 1978	April 30, 1979	August 31, 1980	August 31, 1981
Balance Sheet				
Current Assets				
Cash and Equivalents	8,344	5,766	838	3,417
Receivables[b]	15,022	19,004	20,646	38,658
Inventories	16,530	28,859	54,982	55,597
Taxes Refund Due	1,700	1,554	2,796	2,104
Other Current Assets	621	2,110	5,352	4,284
Total Current Assets	42,217	57,293	84,614	104,060
Fixed Assets				
Plant, Property, and Equipment	17,339	26,986	54,814	61,477
Depreciation	6,075	10,088	19,617	25,316
Net	11,264	16,898	35,197	36,161
Intangible Assets	238	357	375	486
Total Assets	53,719	74,548	120,186	140,707
Current Liabilities				
Short-Term Debt	1,881	3,496	9,146	24,949
Accounts Payable	22,094	23,701	32,314	23,693
Accrued Liabilities	1,212	3,205	2,416	660
Accrued Income Tax	3,562	4,869	630	1,198
Employees' Profit Sharing	840	1,175	1,438	1,913
Other Current Liabilities	8,327	4,663	13,360	21,447
	32,916	41,109	59,304	73,860
Deferred Income Taxes				
Long-Term Debt	3,251	1,280	5,732	6,031
Shareholders' Equity	7,558	13,151	25,704	31,004
Reserves and Accrued Income	1,800	3,600	4,800	4,800
Total Liabilities	8,194	15,408	24,646	25,012
	53,719	74,548	120,186	140,707

[a]16-month period.
[b]Excluding amount of invoices that were cashed in at the bank, but still have not been paid by customers. The coverage in case of nonpayment rests on the company. These amounts were (in FF mil.): 1978: 17.7; 1979: 31.6; 1980: 24.2; 1981: 30.3.

the products were not conceived to be up to the requirements of the German buyer. Thus, Bénéteau had formed a service center in Hamburg in which special accessories for the German market had been added for the boats. It also attempted to build up a wide dealer network in cooperation with the German importer assisting the importer and dealers in the promotion efforts. For example, Bénéteau paid all the expenses for participation in the three large German boat shows.

Dufour

In 1974, Dufour was the largest boat manufacturer in France with sales of FF 64 million. However, its sales in 1976 had dropped to FF 42 million, had climbed again to FF 105 million in 1980, and had dropped to FF 91 million in

1981. More significantly, Dufour had not shown a profit since 1973, except for 1979 which was an exceptionally good year for all manufacturers. Its losses in 1981 amounted to FF 8 million.

Dufour's product line consisted only of sailboats with 14 models ranging between 6 and 14 meters. It was the first company to manufacture sailboats in large series using aluminum as the hull material. In 1978 it had also introduced a windsurfer that was manufactured in a process based on plastic foam injection and was sold at a bottom-of-the-line price. The windsurfer became Dufour's biggest success and the company became the largest windsurfer manufacturer and exporter in France with a total production of about 50,000 units per year. Its other product line, however, had suffered decreasing sales and low profitability. The aluminum hull model was believed to be priced under cost and had contributed to Dufour's constant losses. Baron Bich, who owned Dufour, had separated in 1981 Dufour's boat line from the windsurfer line and had made them two legal entities. Rumors indicated that he wanted to get rid of the money-losing boat activities.

Dufour had traditionally the highest export percentages among French manufacturers. By 1980 it was exporting more than 50 percent of its production. The company had built a very strong position in the German market, reaching about a 5 percent market share. This was mostly due to a very active importer who developed a wide distribution network and was giving margins of up to 20 percent to its dealers.

While successful in Germany, Dufour boats in France, despite their reliability and durability, were considered to have inferior design compared to Nautica's and Bénéteau's boats. It was also lagging behind in promotion efforts. Its advertising levels were low and usually featured specific models rather than building up the brand name. Much effort was put into participation in races.

Yachting France

Yachting France represented a consolidation of four different boat builders: Alcoa, Jouet, Jean Morin, and Lanaverre. Each of these groups was specialized in one product category. Thus, Yachting France represented in 1981 a full-line manufacturer with sailboats from 5.50 to 13 meters, five models of fishing boats from 4 to 8 meters, powerboats and cabin cruisers from 5 to 10 meters, one motor sailor, and a catamaran model. The company had increased its sales from FF 50 million in 1976, the first year of consolidation, up to FF 102 million in 1981, becoming third after Bénéteau and Nautica. Thirty-five percent of Yachting France's sales in 1981 were realized by sale of the fishing cruisers line "Artaban." Yachting France sold through about 60 dealers in France and exported mainly to European countries. The export figures were very low (around 10–15 percent of sales). The company's promotion was limited to local advertising and participation in boat shows. It did not participate in races. Yachting France's product line was priced at the low end of the range as were Nautica and Bénéteau.

Amel and Wauquiez

These two companies, belonging to the medium-size traditional French boat makers, had many things in common in their strategy. Wauquiez, with FF 43 million in sales in 1980 (up from FF 30 million in 1978 and FF 37 million in 1979) manufactured only four models of sailboats of the sizes 10.8 to 13 meters. Amel had sales of FF 26 million in 1980 (up from FF 22 million in 1978; FF 24.5 million in 1979) producing a line of sailboats with three models of the sizes 12 up to 15.8 meters. The owners/managers of both companies were enthusiastic sailors who built their promotion—mostly in advertising and boat shows—on their brand name, which stood for fine design, excellent quality, and good performance. Their boats were priced at the medium/high-price range. They sold around 50 boats each per year with Wauquiez selling 50 percent of its production in export markets and Amel reaching 75 percent in exports mostly to Italy and Germany.

Nautor

Nautor was Finland's largest boat builder with an estimated turnover of FF 115 million in 1981. Its parent company, Oy Schauman—a Finnish conglomerate—ensured a steady financial base since a cash crisis had taken place in 1971.

The "Swan" line of Nautor's motor sailors was regarded as the "Rolls Royce" of the industry. It included eight models ranging from 11.20 to 21 meters. The boats were of a very high-quality with a luxurious design and finish. They were also highly priced. For example, the Swan 37 (11.20 meters) was priced[5] at FF 700,000 compared to FF 430,000 for Nautica's "Sun-Fizz" (11.75 meters). The Swan 44 (13.55 meters) was priced at FF 1,400,000 compared to FF 790,000 for Nautica's "Trinidad" (14.00 meters).

Nautor exported most of its production and sold through agents who covered all of Europe. It also had five agents in the United States and was planning to appoint agents in Australia, Japan, and the Far East.

---

[5]Prices refer to retail selling price and include 17.6 percent value-added tax.

JOHN CURRIE AND INTERNAV LTD., SYDNEY, NOVA SCOTIA

My father was originally from Cape Breton and like most Capers, wanted to get back. My mother was from Massachusetts. I was born and brought up in New York. Apart from the duration of World War II, I spent all of my summers here in Cape Breton, first with my parents, then after marriage, with my wife and children. One summer we came here and never did go back. It is not very often that people on summer vacation leave their house and home and never go back. That's a rarity. My kids never did go back to their old home. By the time they went back to straighten everything out, our house was sold to somebody else. They never even saw their friends again. My dog is still an illegal immigrant in Canada. We've been coming here so many summers that moving was not really a problem. Cape Bretoner's are very friendly people. It's one of the easiest areas of the world to move into. I can't really say why I made that decision; it was, I think, partially personal. I did like the area, and I'm sure that that is part of it, but it definitely looked to me like an area that had to blossom for my kind of oceanographic fishing-type equipment.

With these words, John Currie, President of Internav Ltd., described how he came to set up his company on Cape Breton Island, Nova Scotia, close to where Alexander Graham Bell developed the telephone and the hydrofoil and Guglielmo Marconi built the first station for transmitting wireless telegraphy signals across the Atlantic to Europe.

Having grown up in New York City, John Currie studied physics at Queen's College in Buffalo, New York, and on graduation, took his first job with the Sperry Gyroscope Company on Long Island. He worked for Sperry for about 10 years, first on inertial guidance systems for the B-58 and the X-15 aircraft and then

---

Source: This case was prepared by Professor Michael Martin and Professor Philip Rosson, Dalhousie University. The authors gratefully acknowledge the financial support of the Federal Department of Industry, Trade, and Commerce, Technological Strategy Branch in the development of the case. Permission to use granted by Michael Martin.

helped develop the Loran C navigational system for the U. S. military. He was then invited to join the Laboratory For Electronics (LFB) company in Boston to develop a Loran C capability there. LFB had developed the navigational and bombing system for the F-105 fighter plane. He worked at LFB and a couple of other companies in the Boston area for several years and then decided that he really wanted to get out of the defense business and start his own company. He felt that the Loran C system had commercial potential outside of the aerospace business. By this time, he had acquired both management and engineering experience. Shortly before leaving Sperry, he had been promoted to senior engineer, which was the last position before entering management. At LFB he started out as a project engineer and later became program manager for various Loran C programs on aircraft and helicopters. He had tried to interest LFB in developing a commercial-type Loran C receiver, but had been completely unsuccessful; this was one of the reasons why he left that company.

He started his own company in Waltham, Massachusetts in October 1971, being its first president and owning (and still owning) about 48 percent of the stock. This company, International Navigation Ltd., is still operating in Massachussets. With this company he developed and produced the first low-cost Loran C receivers to be used on fishing boats and, for a long time, International Navigation was the only manufacturer in that market. He quickly discovered that there were a lot of other seafarers besides fishermen who wanted to navigate, and the company did a fair amount of work for hydrographics surveying teams. It helped develop a system called Pulse 8 that is used by Decca Surveying in the U. K. Decca bought a large number of receivers for work in the North Sea exploration program. When he formed the company, Mr. Currie anticipated that the Loran C navigational system would be adopted by the U. S. Coast Guard and, in effect, gambled on that outcome, since the Coast Guard had yet to get congressional approval for doing so. Eventually, the system was adopted by the U. S. Coast Guard. By 1976, he recognized that it would be a good move for Canada to join in an hemispherical Loran C system, rather than trying to go its own way, so that Loran C would also become the Canadian navigational system for at least a decade or so. He decided to set up Internav Ltd. in Sydney, Nova Scotia.

His choice was based upon several considerations. First, it provided him an opportunity to return to his father's "native heath" of Cape Breton. Second, the total Atlantic Canadian fishing areas and fleets of about 20,000 vessels are encompassed in a 500-mile radius about Sydney, which represented a lucrative market for his products. Third, he could reasonably expect a good amount of government support, because Sydney was located in a depressed area. He recalled that one of the reasons why Massachusetts had become so strongly entrenched in the electronics industry was because government money had been pumped into that state from the 1920s onward to compensate for the closing down of the wool mills there. He believed that a similar investment potential could develop in Cape Breton. Fourth, he knew the area pretty well from his numerous summer vacations and had relatives and friends living there. It also had a lot of favorable attributes from a "quality of life" standpoint. The Bras D'Or lakes offer some of the best boating in the whole world and the Cape Breton highlands constitute an area of outstanding natural beauty. Both are within a short drive of Sydney so, in the long run, he thought it would be a very good area into which he could entice professional-type people to move.

Internav began operations in February 1977 with three people from the plant in the States and 10 people hired locally. Two of the three Americans returned to Massachusetts, and the third stayed in Sydney as the general manager. In the summer of 1977, Mr. Currie and his family started their annual vacation in Cape Breton and, as was stated earlier, have stayed there ever since.

Internav's Markets

The principal of the Loran C navigational system is outlined in Exhibit 1 and is very simple. A Loran C receiver on a seagoing vessel receives the specially timed Loran signals from the master station and two or more secondary stations in a Loran C chain. The receiver then measures the difference in arrival time between the master signals and the secondary signals to devise two intersecting lines of position which it computes into the corresponding latitude and longitude coordinates of the vessel's current location. Other important navigational data are provided, depending on the sophistication of the receiver installed on the vessels. A Loran C receiver is a relatively inexpensive and accurate navigational instrument, but is clearly dependent upon the existence of a chain of Loran C transmitter stations. The major markets for the company's products are small fishing and pleasure boats operating in seas provided with Loran C coverage. The markets therefore developed in step with the development of Loran C coverage. The Cana-

EXHIBIT 1
The Loran C System

Loran is the acronym that stands for *LOng RAnge Navigation* and actually refers to a hyperbolic system of radio navigation.

The Loran A system began during World War II when it became necessary to have a means of determining position that was independent of the weather. By 1971, 83 Loran A stations were in service around the world, operated and maintained by the U. S. Coast Guard and foreign government agencies.

During the late 1950s and early 1960s, when the nature of radio wave propagation was better understood, an improved system was developed, Loran C. This system proved to be much more accurate and dependable than Loran A and the usable range of the system increased greatly. Loran C's very stable groundwave signals mean that position accuracy in good coverage areas can be extremely high—often as close as a few tens of meters. At longer ranges, beyond about 900 to 1,000 miles, the system's skywave signals can also be used, though extra care is required by the operator and accuracies are correspondingly lower.

Today, there are 20 Loran C chains in operation around the world providing efficient coverage for many of the world's navigable waterways. Still more are proposed.

Since the introduction of Loran C, surprising advances in electronics technology have brought this versatile navigation system within the economic reach of thousands of commercial and pleasure boat owners. The microprocessor has had incredible impact, making it possible to store vast amounts of information in very small spaces, efficiently and economically.

It is for these reasons—the superior performance, reliability, and dependability of Loran C—that in January 1981, the U. S. Loran A system was terminated and Loran C will be exclusively maintained.

Loran C is more than just a tool for the navigator. It can be used in a variety of ways. Extremely accurate clocks have been built that use the Loran C frequency of 100 kHz as a timing standard. It is also an important element in vessel traffic control systems, providing position information to dispatchers in distant locations.

How does the LC 360 make use of this remarkable system? Once operating, the LC 360 receives the specially timed Loran signals from the master station and two or more secondary stations in a Loran C chain. The LC 360 then measures the difference in the arrival time between the master signals and the secondary signals to derive two intersecting lines of position or LOP's. Then the LC 360 goes much further, converting the Loran C Time Differences into the corresponding latitude and longitude and providing a variety of important navigation data.

dian coverage has expanded steadily from 1977, beginning with British Columbia, the Great Lakes, and the Atlantic Seaboard. When a new transmitter opens up in Labrador in the spring of 1983, there will be complete coverage along the whole of the Atlantic Canadian coastline. The timetable for the installation of Loran C transmitters is known in advance, so the company can readily predict the size of its target markets as they grow with this expansion. Later the company should expand into some of the areas of the Arctic where localized low-cost systems also will apply. Ignoring this last possibility, the total Canadian market constitutes some 25,000 vessels.

The company manufacturers and markets a product range of Loran C receivers and peripheral equipment that retail at prices between $1,000 and $5,000 (see Exhibit 2). Most of these units are sold through a dealer network. The dealers provide any "after sales" services required and enjoy a relatively high price mark-up of 50 percent (that is a dealer will pay $2,000 for a unit that he retails at $3,000). Internav also sells about 5 percent of its products to the military for installation on RCN vessels. The military market contributes rather more than 5 percent of the total sales revenue, because military land and sea receivers require special product enhancements that significantly increase their prices. Total market size is strongly influenced by the rate of technological change in the microelectronics industry. Products are being continuously improved to exploit the latest performance improvements and cost reductions in microelectronic technology. Thus, a product becomes obsolescent before it wears out. Although a few of International Navigation's customers are still using receivers that they bought up to 10 years ago, many replace units every three to five years. After, say, four years they find that they can buy a new receiver that is about 10 times as effective as the old one at the same dollar price as they paid earlier. Given the present inflation rates, customers recognize that they are getting a much better buy for their money, so they scrap the old unit to replace it with a new one.

Offshore Markets

International Navigation at Woburn, Massachusetts (where it has relocated from Waltham) and Internav at Sydney exclusively manufacture and market products for the United States and Canada, respectively. Each holds the "world-wide" or "offshore" rights to market products developed in its own facility. That is, International Navigation has the world-wide rights for selling products developed at Woburn, and Internav the corresponding rights for products developed at Sydney. International Navigation presently holds the major portion of these offshore rights because it has been in operation longer, but Internav should enjoy a growing proportion of these rights as it develops its own products. Internav has sold about 15 percent of its products offshore during the first few years of its operation, but again, this proportion should increase in two or three years.

In both North America and world-wide, competition in the marketplace is quite tough. There are several American and two Japanese companies that provide strong competition. All these companies are small, but those in Japan have the advantage that their government subsidizes all their R & D for them.

Start-Up Financing

The company was founded with an initial capitalization of $200,000. $50,000 was provided by International Navigation, approximately $90,000 by a grant from the Department of Regional Economic Expansion (DREE), and approximately $60,000 by a loan from Industrial Estates Limited (IEL). Initial working capital was mostly provided through loans from the parent company. Later on, the Cape Breton Development Corporation also provided loans to support the initial R & D efforts. The Corporation also provided initial support in terms of

EXHIBIT 2
Description of Internav Ltd. Products[a]

LC-360 Navigation System
Combined receiver navigation computer displays TD's, Lat/Long, true speed and course made good, plus range, bearing, track error, and time to go to any of 40 waypoints. Includes Steer Command, Cycle Guard, nonvolatile memory, four internal notch filters, AC or DC power.

LC-204 Receiver
Dual seven-digit readouts, memory, two external notch filters. AC or DC power.

Option: serial or parallel data output

LC-123 Receiver
Dual six-digit readouts, memory, steering, time to go, SNR, blink, Cycle Guard, up to four internal notch filters (specify operation area with order), DC power only.

Options: Steering, time to go, SNR, blink, Cycle Guard, retrofit package, two external notch filters

LC-112 Receiver
Single seven-digit readout. Alternating TD display can be "split" to continuously show last three digits of two LOPs, five position memory recall, SNR, blink, Cycle Guard, two internal notch filters, 12 VDC power.
As above, with four internal notch filters for Canadian East Coast

Options: two external notch filters
24 VDC or 115 VAC power

CC-2 Navigation Computer
Displays present position in latitude and longitude. Shows true course made good and groundspeed, plus distance, time, true bearing, and cross track error to any of nine preselected waypoints, AC or DC power.

CC-2 is an add-on option to LC-204, 123, and 112.

TP-2 Track Plotter
Plots track made good on 10 × 15 in. X–Y chart. Wide-scale range, AC or DC power

TP-2 is an add-on option to LC-360, LC-204, 123 or 112.

IL Remote Display
Simultaneously repeats Loran LOPs (or lat long from CC-2 or LC-360) at remote location in chartroom or steering station, AC or DC power.

IL is an add-on option to LC-360, LC-204, 123, and 112

Accessories
Antenna Cable (75 feet supplied)
Operator handbook (one supplied)

[a]Descriptions extracted from company brochure.

site selection and the rental of physical plant at lower than market rates.

By early 1982, all of these loans were paid off and the company was entirely Canadian owned. In early 1982, Mr. Currie owned 80 percent of the equity of the company with the balance owned by the Federal Business Development Bank. Further financial information is shown in Exhibit 3.

Manufacturing Operations

Internav began manufacturing operations in 1977, initially making the range of Loran C receivers that had been developed in the Ameri-

EXHIBIT 3
Financial Information

Summary of Income and Expenses
Three Years Ended December 31, 1981

	1981 (Unaudited)	1980	1979
	$	$	$
Sales	2,159,105	1,806,270	1,707,280
Cost of Goods Sold			
Inventory, beginning	471,902	424,870	315,107
Materials	1,081,930	1,020,382	917,665
Freight In	29,462	26,251	15,058
Direct Labor	238,655	185,751	223,580
Overhead	269,696	223,452	225,083
	2,091,645	1,884,706	1,696,493
Inventory, ending	652,945	471,902	424,870
	1,438,700	1,412,804	1,271,623
Gross Profit	720,405	393,466	435,657
	33.4%	21.8%	25.5%
Expenses			
Selling	177,699	218,098	190,306
Administrative	265,243	179,214	152,165
Engineering	37,092	27,553	18,510
	480,034	424,870	360,981
Operating Income (loss)	240,371	(31,404)	74,676
Other Income (loss)	—	63,887	(39,527)
Income before taxes	240,371	32,483	35,149
Income Taxes			
Current		(2,433)	2,433
Deferred	32,000	12,648	
	32,000	10,215	2,433
Net Income	208,371	22,268	32,716
Sales	9.6%	1.2%	1.9%

Unaudited Balance Sheet
December 31, 1981

	$
Assets	
Current	
Cash	1,564
Receivables	632,764
Inventory	652,945
	1,287,273
Receivables	7,929
Equipment, at cost less depreciation	293,723
Deferred product development costs	276,823
	1,865,748

(Continued)

EXHIBIT 3 (Continued)

Unaudited Balance Sheet
December 31, 1981

	$	$
Liabilities		
Current		
Bank Indebtedness	373,164	
Payables and Accruals	377,713	
Long-Term Debt Payable within one year	45,000	
	795,877	
Payable to Director	75,911	
Loans Payable International Navigation	53,492	
Long Term	299,365	
Deferred government assistance	45,427	
	1,270,072	
Deferred income taxes	44,648	
	1,314,720	
Shareholders' Equity		
Capital Stock	600	
Contributed Capital	49,400	
Retained Earnings	501,028	
	551,028	
	1,865,748	

can company and selling them in the Canadian market. In its early years of operations, International Navigation was acutely aware of its lack of marketing expertise, so it granted the offshore world-wide marketing rights of its products to Simrad, a Norwegian company that had a well-established "top-notch" reputation for selling echo-sounders and communications gear to the fishing industry throughout the world. For some strange reason, Simrad's "world-wide" marketing rights applied everywhere except to Canada, so Internav was able to sell products in the Canadian market without violating the original agreement with the Norwegian company. A description of Internav's 1982 product range is shown in Exhibit 2.

The company began its operations in 1977 with a workforce of 10 people and, with continuous sales growth, the workforce grew steadily to a peak of 55 in the summer of 1981. Products are manufactured on a quite straightforward assembly line basis, but the "seasonality" of the marketplace is a continuing problem for the company. Winter (December) sales are much lower than summer (July) sales. Ideally, the company would like to follow a constant production-rate manufacturing strategy, but so far this has proved to be financially infeasible. Ideally, Mr. Currie would have liked the company to have been making pre-tax profits of $200,000 year by 1981, but it was actually making only $35,000–40,000 a year, because sales growth had not been as rapid as had been initially anticipated. Internav needs to generate $130,000 a month to break even and, historically, has been unable to generate sufficient cash flow during the peaks of its season to provide enough working capital to "make-to-stock" during the succeeding troughs. The seasonality in the company's sales is illustrated in Exhibit 4.

EXHIBIT 4
Seasonality of Business

Monthly Cash Receipts as a Percentage of Annual Totals

Month	Percentage of Annual Cash Receipts
January	5
February	5
March	7
April	7
May	10
June	13
July	13
August	13
September	10
October	7
November	5
December	5
	100%

R & D Activities

For the first years of its operations, Internav was essentially a manufacturing branch–plant of the U.S. company. Mr. Currie initiated an R & D endeavour in 1978. This R & D facility now (January 1982) has five graduate engineers, four "technologists" who are graduates of two-year programs of the College of Cape Breton, and a number of technicians. The latter are nondegreed individuals who have developed a capability for understanding electronics "on-the-job." While under training, these technicians have been partially subsidized by Canada Manpower support programs, which Mr. Currie has found to be very valuable in terms of subsidizing his in-house training program.

The company performs two categories of R & D:

1. Contract work to determine the propagation characteristics of Loran C transmitters in various geographical locations. Such detailed signal-strength field studies are vital preliminary investigations in the development of new Loran C navigational systems. The company has performed studies on the Great Shield in Ontario and much work with the Canadian Coast Guard off the East Coast. It has also performed some work for the French lighthouse service in the Mediterannean. Currently, it is performing a survey in the Beaufort Sea with Dome Petroleum. These projects have enabled the company to establish a good understanding of marine navigational problems and the role of the Loran C systems in helping solve these problems.

2. At the same time, the company has built up its skills in microprocessor development and programming as applied to shipboard Loran C systems. This has enabled them to add a succession of incremental technological improvements in established product lines and to develop new products. For example, they have developed a new receiver, the LC-720, that they are planning to market in Spring 1982, and are also developing an airborne receiver under contract with the Department of Supply and Services, Science Procurement Branch. The company views contract R & D for the development of new electronic systems as a profitable activity that it hopes to increase in the future.

In the present (early 1982) business climate, the company finds it very difficult to support an R & D group on the profits from its sales, so it finds contract R & D (particularly the propagation field strength studies) very important from the standpoint of maintaining stability in its R & D operations.

Future Plans

Turning to the future, Mr. Currie recognizes that by about 1987 the Loran C business will have begun to fall-off. Every vessel will be equipped with a Loran C unit, the market will be saturated, and only the replacement market will remain. Therefore, Internav has a good solid market for another two or three years, but after that must find new products. To do this the company plans to utilize its general navigational expertise in a number of different ways.

First, it intends to support high-precision positioning applications offshore for the oil industry, which should be a growing lucrative market as offshore hydrocarbon resources are increasingly extracted.

Second, Internav is developing an airborne Loran C receiver that will enable it to expand out of the seasonal marine navigational market.

Third, Mr. Currie wants to expand R & D contract services to the RCN. He recognizes that the navy's frigate program will require all kinds of radio navigational expertise in terms of computer programming, signal processing, etc. He wishes to expand his R & D capabilities and offer contracted services over and above those required as an adjunct to the development of new receivers. He is currently seeking military security clearance for his staff so that the company can expand into that market.

All navigational aids have a useful life and then they are replaced by something else. They are also initially developed by the military, and the military is now planning to develop a satellite (as against shore) based navigational system. Once such a system has been developed, it will subsequently be made available for civilian use and then a "new" offshore vessel market will be created. The 25,000 vessels currently being equipped with the land-based Loran C system will require replacement receivers to use the new satellite-based system.

In the shorter term, Internav anticipates an annual growth rate of 10–15 percent for a few years. This is based upon the continuing Loran C business, plus a growth in exports based upon the new products currently being developed and an increasing involvement in the offshore hydrocarbon industry. This should lead to a growth in employment from the present level of 40 to 100 people, with a corresponding increase in annual dollar sales turnover.

The biggest potential growth opportunity, however, is presented by expected developments in new technology and has necessitated setting up a new company Micronav Ltd.

Micronav Ltd.

When Mr. Currie worked for LFB in Boston, the Vice President of R & D was Dr. Morris Myer who was the founding father of a replacement for the instrument landing system (ILS) that is used in all the world's airports at present. This replacement is known as Microwave Landing System (MLS) and will be introduced into airports beginning in 1985 or 1986. Micronav has been established to exploit the market opportunities created by the introduction of this new system. The world-wide market is expected to reach $3–4 billion with the Canadian market amounting to about $200 million. Micronav seeks to capture a significant share of these markets.

The new company is beginning the substantial R & D effort ($5–6 million of R & D investment over the next three to four years) required to develop "hardware" to secure this market share. It will develop flight-testing facilities at Sydney Airport. Mr. Currie estimates that he will require $3 million to come up with the first prototype equipment. He has raised $300,000 of private capital and hopes to match that figure from the Province's venture capital sources. He would like the federal government to provide the balance of financial support required and is already receiving $429,000 from federal industry minister Herb Gray and the National Research Council (see Exhibit 5). If successful, Micronav should enjoy $20–30 million a year annual sales and employ 500 people by 1990.

EXHIBIT 5
Two News Stories

*Cape Breton Firms to
Receive Government Aid*

By CLAYTON CAMPBELL
Sydney Bureau

SYDNEY—Two Cape Breton companies will receive government assistance totalling $349,000 to aid in the expansion and development of operations and equipment.

Under the capital assistance project of the ocean industry development agreement signed recently between Nova Scotia and federal governments, Industrial Welding Limited of Cheticamp will receive a $210,200 development grant to assist in the expansion of hydraulic deck gear and other metal fabricated products.

The firm, owned by Roger and Raymond Deveau, will receive a similar amount under the regional development incentives program to help in expansion of the firm's operations.

Micronav Company Limited of nearby Point Edward will be awarded a $429,000 grant from the National Research Council to assist in the development of a microwave landing system for sale in Canada and abroad.

Industry Minister Herb Gray made the announcements at a news conference here Monday.

"My department is pleased to support these local firms," he said.

"The two development incentives awarded to Industrial Welding are examples of how the recently-signed ocean development agreement will be used to supplement and complement other federal government programs, and to support and encourage the development of ocean related activities throughout Nova Scotia," he said.

Mr. Gray pointed out that the microwave landing system (MLS) is the most advanced type of landing system under development, and is expected to be used in all airports.

The MLS is a new type of equipment designed to enable aircraft to land in adverse weather conditions. It will replace the instrument landing system (ILS) now in use throughout the world.

The minister told the conference the MLS market value is expected to be several hundred million dollars, and "it is hoped Micronav will be able to address this very large market in an effective and timely way."

Cape Breton-The Sydneys MP Russell MacLeilan said the announcements are "encouraging for the economy of Cape Breton, and will have a direct bearing on industrialization and economic opportunities."

He said Internav Company Limited, from which Micronav was founded, is one of the top companies in Canada manufacturing technical marine navigation equipment.

"MLS is the system of the future, and Micronav is the only company in Canada that is looking to supply the department of transport (and) to sell the system abroad as well," Mr. MacLeilan added.

He called the local development of the MLS an "exciting prospect that, if successful, will produce hundreds of jobs in this area."

He indicated that further government assistance may be forthcoming as the MLS project progresses.

Cape Breton-East Richmond MP Dave Dingwall told a news conference that Mr. Gray's announcements are "good news in tough economic times." He said the monies made available to the local firms "will go a long way to lessen unemployment in Cape Breton."

Micronav president John Currie said sale of the MLS in Canada would total about $200 million, with worldwide sales reaching $3 billion to $4 billion.

He said the company has started preliminary work on what will be "a gigantic program."

He said two technical people have been hired, with 11 more to be added to the staff within six months.

Another 17 will be hired in 1983 and 10 more in the third year of operation.

"This is a long-term program that will require by the early 1990s about 400 employees," he said, adding that it will take up to 30 years to equip all the airports in the world.

Mr. Currie said the company will have "all kinds of training programs for this highly-technical project. But we are not in any hurry. We have plenty of time to do it right."

EXHIBIT 5 (Continued)

DREE's New Sydney Office 'Will Provide Closer Liaison'

By CLAYTON CAMPBELL
Cape Breton Bureau

SYDNEY—The department of regional economic expansion Sydney office will strengthen the department's close involvement with all economic and related developments in Cape Breton. Industry, Trade and Commerce Minister Herb Gray said here Monday.

Speaking at the official opening of the downtown office, Mr. Gray said it will provide a closer liaison with the business community, local groups and other development agencies in Cape Breton.

Besides providing advice and assistance regarding government programs, the office will coordinate its activities with other federal departments and agencies, including the Cape Breton Development Corporation.

"The three-member office will encourage the establishment of export industries, which are technologically advanced and competitive in world markets," he said. "Concurrently, work will be undertaken to foster smaller indigenous manufacturing industries based on local resources, producing for local markets."

Emphasis will also be placed on steel, coal, coke, offshore resources and the resulting spinoff industries.

Mr. Gray went on to mention that the new office will work closely with the Sydney Steel Corporation (Sysco) and the provincial government to develop further steel-related opportunities such as foundry and metal fabrication.

"Of considerable importance is the potential that exists for offshore industries in the areas of research, management and utilization of the resources of the Atlantic Shelf and Eastern Arctic," he said.

Cape Breton-The Sydneys MP Russell MacLeillan says the office will make Cape Bretoners aware of the department's functions and programs.

He pointed out that the office will serve the entire island, and "it is up to all of us to utilize it."

Cape Breton East-Richmond MP Dave Dingwall says a local DREE office "is long overdue."

"I am glad to see that it is finally here, for it will provide benefits of economic and professional assistance to the people of Cape Breton," he added.

Senator Al Graham said the office is "a manifestation of the accepted role of the federal government to bring government closer to the people."

The office, he said, will mean that the people of Cape Breton can count on greater government efficiency in the future.

6 SOCIAL RESPONSIBILITY

WELGRO CHEMICAL COMPANY

What follows is an excerpt from an August 1976 report on the CBS Evening News.

Dan Rather: One of the familiar environmental themes a few years ago concerned phosphates, chemicals used in detergents and boycotted by environmentalists. In Florida's Polk County, another phosphate battle now is starting up at the source. Bruce Hall reports.

Bruce Hall: It's called Bone Valley; 5000 acres strip-mined every year. It's not the coal fields of West Virginia or Montana; it's the phosphate mines of Florida, the residue from prehistoric seas and creatures that left the area with one of the most bountiful supplies of phosphate in the world.

Florida produces 80 percent of the nation's phosphates, and more than one-third of the world's supply. Phosphates are essential in the production of fertilizer, and have been mined here since the turn of the century. And it has grown into a $3-billion business that employs 61,000 people.

Now, however, because of pressure from many city and county officials, the Environmental Protection Agency has, in effect, called for a moratorium on new phosphate mining and plant construction until an environmental study of the area is completed. The study may take up to 18 months, and industry spokesmen say it is unnecessary.

Homer Hooks (Executive Director, Florida Phosphate Council): We opposed the EPA study from the outset because we felt that there—we know there are presently 16 studies being conducted in and about the industry by all levels of government.

Source: Prepared by William G. Callarman, Denzil Strickland, and Victor J. LaPorte, Jr., University of Central Florida. Permission to publish granted by William G. Callarman.

Hall: The federal government ordered the environmental impact study after critics complained the industry's air pollution controls are inadequate; that too much land is being destroyed, left as huge barren gullies; that the industry's extremely heavy use of water is depleting the fresh water resources of the state; that the slime ponds filled with waste products have in the past collapsed, polluting nearby agricultural lands and streams.

The phosphate producers claim all federal standards for air and water pollution are being met, and further that they are now reclaiming much of the strip-mined land. But a preliminary study by the EPA now indicates that many homes built on that reclaimed land are trapping high levels of radioactive radon gas inside the structures. Radon is caused by the decay of uranium, which is often found with phosphates and can cause lung cancer. County, state, and federal agencies are trying to measure the amount of radon in more than 1000 homes, but it will be at least the end of the year before any conclusive results are known.

Richard Guimond (EPA): To tell you the truth, when we first came down here we really didn't expect to find as much radon, particularly in structures, as we did. From the standpoint of the average levels we've found in the structures so far, if someone was to live there on an annual basis, we would estimate that after approximately six to eight years, they could double their risk of lung cancer.

Hall: Industry spokesmen say the danger of radon has been blown out of proportion, and further, that homes are able to be built in a way to minimize the risk.

Hooks: We think that there are reasonably simple ways to handle this, such as, for instance, the construction of residences six or eight or ten inches above the ground to allow for ventiliation. Air-conditioners would be a solution—anything to keep the air moving. Normal home ventilation might be the answer.

Hall: The phosphate industry concedes it has been a dirty business in the past, but isn't any more; that stiffer regulations could cause a fertilizer shortage, and raise world food prices. Nevertheless, state and federal agencies are expected to insist on tighter industry controls before any new land is mined.

—Bruce Hall, CBS News, Polk County, Florida

History

The Product

Phosphate is mined in Florida primarily in an area about 50 miles long and 40 miles wide in Polk and Hillsborough Counties. Roughly, this mining area lies between Tampa and Orlando, Florida.

Processed phosphate is used principally in high-analysis fertilizers. In addition, phosphate is used in the production of food preservatives, cloth dyes, gasoline and oil additives, toothpaste, shaving cream, soap, and many other products.

World Market

Morocco accounts for about one-third of the world's exports and controls about two-thirds of the world's known phosphate reserves. Morocco's reserves appear to be much larger than those in the United States and are believed to be sufficient to last for hundreds of years. (According to University of Florida Professor David Anthony, statistics from the Bureau of Mines indicate that of the present mining rate the United States will be out of phosphates by the year 2000.)

According to a *Wall Street Journal* article in August 1976, Morocco seems to be headed toward a dominating position in the world phosphate market. In 1974, Morocco took a cue from OPEC and successfully pushed the price of phosphate up as high as $68 a ton compared to $14 a ton in 1973.

Prices soon returned to normal, however, as companies in the United States and elsewhere increased production. Also, consumption declined as farmers began to buy less phosphate because of the high prices. Other major exporters of phosphate, besides Morocco and the United States, are the Soviet Union, Tunisia, and Jordan.

Mining Process

The phosphate-mining operation itself is a gigantic operation beginning with prospecting and site surveys. The survey stage includes extensive planning for drainage and water supply requirements, waste disposal and electric power distribution systems, the mining layout itself, and railroad tracks and roads necessary for transportation.

The first step in mining is the removal of from 5 to 40 feet of sand lying above the phosphate deposits. This "overburden" is scooped up by mammoth, electrically operated draglines and is deposited into an adjacent mined out area. After the overburden is stripped away, the dragline digs up the phosphate ore. Phosphate mining would be a simple matter if this ore were pure phosphate, but the phosphate deposits are actually a matrix of phosphate, sand, and clay. The remainder of the mining process consists of separating the phosphate from the rest of the matrix.

The matrix is dumped into a shallow pit called a "sump," where high pressure water guns convert it into a fluid mixture known as "slurry." The slurry is propelled by centrifugal pumps from the mining site through a pipeline to the phosphate washer and recovery plant. This plant may be located as far as five miles from the mining site.

At the plant the slurry first goes through a washing operation. Basically, washing is a screening operation to clean and separate the larger phosphate pebbles from the slurry. These pebbles are conveyed to loading bins and the slurry is processed further. The finer particles of phosphate remaining in the slurry are removed by screening or chemical flotation processes.

Phosphate can be shipped in a wet rock or dry rock form. Wet rock is simply phosphate materials as they come out of the washing operation with no further processing. Dry rock is phosphate that has undergone drying in large rotary kilns to lower its moisture content, making it easier to use in chemical processes and to transport. In some cases dried rock is sent to grinding plants to be ground to a specified size for the individual needs of phosphate users. Modern methods of phosphate recovery have made it possible for companies to recover about two-thirds of the phosphate in the ore.

Environmental Problems

Although contemporary phosphate processing is certainly more efficient than ever before, it has been the target of criticism because of historical environmental problems that have worried environmentalists for decades. To begin with, the strip-mining operation is far from aesthetically pleasing. As Orval Jackson, a writer for UPI points out, from the air, parts of southwest Florida look like the moon, with giant craters and mountains of barren grey earth. This provides a startling contrast to the rest of the area's subtropical greenery.

As can be readily noted from the description of the phosphate-mining process, the industry uses great amounts of water in various stages of the mining and recovery operations. It has been estimated that it takes 10,000 gallons of water to mine one ton of marketable phosphate. Critics contend that the phosphate industry is thus depleting Florida's water resources. They point to the lower water table levels in the area as proof of this contention.

Not only is there the fear that the water level is dropping, but that existing water sources may be contaminated by the mining process. The major portion of the water used by the phosphate plant is pumped into clay settling ponds where contaminants are allowed to precipitate to the bottom over a period of time allowing the clean water at the top to be discharged and recycled for further use. Critics fear that spills from these ponds could contaminate fresh sources of water in the vicinity.

Although the mining of phosphate is not a major contribution to air pollution despite the vastness of the area that is mined, there has been some problem with the release of particulate matter into the air from the drying and grinding processes as well as gaseous emissions from the various chemical processes. Among the most harmful contaminants has been fluoride, which attacks the bone structure of animals. In addition, critics of the industry have claimed that it can be harmful to plant life, including citrus, a mainstay of Florida economic life.

Perhaps ironically, the latest criticism of the industry has come about through its efforts to improve an earlier criticism. Following mining operations, the land which was disturbed is now required by Florida law to be reclaimed by grading with bulldozers and other earth-moving equipment. It has been determined that associated with the phosphate deposits are low concentrations of uranium. Since the mining of phosphate disturbs the overburden, radioactivity contaminates the overburden used in land reclamation. The critical question is just how dangerous this radioactivity may be. Critics claim that any exposure to radioactivity is harmful because of its cumulative effects over the years.

In the face of many criticisms, the phosphate industry has attempted to make major adjustments. An important voice for the industry in Florida has been the Florida Phosphate Council. Homer Hooks, Executive Director of the Phosphate Council, sees these adjustments as not only a reaction to environmental law, but an adjustment in environmental attitude.

> The old myths of the big, dirty, nasty phosphate industry, poisoning the air and the water and ruining the landscape—that's no more.

Don't misunderstand—our hands were dirty for a long time, a very long time. But I think that's changed. Within the last 10 years, since we've organized the Phosphate Council and pulled these companies together to improve what we do, there has been a marked change, both in our performance, and in our attitude. We are now complying with the environmental regulations.

The Phosphate Council

The Florida Phosphate Council is a nonprofit trade association organized and operated for the welfare of 11 phosphate mining and processing companies, and Welgro Chemical Company is one of those 11. The purpose of this council is to act as a public relations body for the member firms with respect to the citizenry, the press, and government. It is in the latter role as lobbyist that the Council does much of its most vital work. Routine functions of the Council include publication and distribution of Environment Fact Sheets, Economic Fact Sheets, a weekly summary of newspaper articles concerning the phosphate industry, and numerous miscellaneous brochures introducing the phosphate industry or presenting the phosphate industry's viewpoint on given issues. Member companies depend on the Council to represent their best interests and serve as a point of contact in matters involving their mutual concern. In many respects, the Council has become the spokesman for the phosphate industry in Florida.

Gerald Sims, Manager of the Environmental Control Department at the Welgro Chemical Company, has this to say about the Council:

> (The Phosphate Council is) geared to the needs of local Florida operations. . . . I would say they are . . . a watchdog on legislative matters on a county and state basis. . . . They also sponsor tours; they are available for public speaking engagements. They are principally P.R.

An example of the work the Council has done in the past is their efforts in 1969 to lobby against a state imposed severance tax on the phosphate industry. A Phosphate Council publication at the time contended:

A severance tax is the most serious threat to the continued growth of Florida's mining industries.

Such a tax would not produce nearly as much money for the State as some persons predict. Any income realized from this source would be largely offset by losses in other tax-producing areas.

Phosphate, the largest segment of Florida's mining industry, is particularly vulnerable to such a tax.

If Florida's phosphate deposits were the only ones in the world, or the biggest, or the richest, or the most strategically located, perhaps the industry could absorb a modest severance tax.

But Florida has no monopoly on phosphate, and none of these advantages exists.

The severance tax came into effect in 1971.

The public relations efforts of the Council have not always stimulated the desired response in readers. In one case, a copy of the Economic Fact Sheets 1976 spurred an editorial in the *Daytona Beach Journal* that labeled the publication as "propaganda." Taking a hardline on the phosphate industry in general and the Phosphate Council in particular, the editorial concluded with:

> We hope that our legislators will take a hard look at who makes up the "Florida" phosphate council, look at the danger to this state its propaganda does not recognize, and decide that there is a need for further legislative action to control the situation.

Welgro Chemical Company and Environmental Control

One of the important member firms of the Florida Phosphate Council is the Welgro Chemical Company. Welgro is an old and respected name in the fertilizer business with a history going back before the turn of the century. After several changes of ownership, Welgro Chemical is now a subsidiary company of The Bradford Companies of Fort Worth, Texas, a diversified company with assets of over $1.5 billion. Other major Bradford companies include Bradford Steel Company, Bradford Energy Company, Bradford Exploration Company, Bradford Pipe Line Company, and Bradford Realty Corporation.

Welgro is a completely integrated company in that it is involved in the phosphate mining and processing operations from the time the phosphate rock is removed from the ground until it is sold to consumers as Welgro fertilizer. Besides its rock mines in Florida, Welgro operates seven fertilizer production plants in the United States along with many terminals and market outlets.

Corporate Attitude Toward Environment

A Welgro publication details a number of voluntary public-interest projects in which the company participates:

> Today Welgro has forest lands in Hillsborough and Polk counties that encompass some 45,000 acres under a scientific forestry program. . . . The harvesting of these forest products creates additional jobs, and generally adds to the local economy.
>
> The company is an active participant in the Nationwide "Tree Farm" Program. Since 1936 more than 11,000,000 pine seedlings have been planted. Welgro Chemical Co. works actively with the U. S. Forest Services, Colleges, and forest industries in establishing test plantings and conducting forest fertilization research.
>
> Over the years Welgro Chemical Co. has donated and leased lands to various local civic, conservation, and recreational groups. . . .
>
> Fields of grain, planting of citrus, forage for cattle, and beautiful forests stand in testimony of our interest in returning mined out land to useful production. The lakes which accompany reclaimed lands are a veritable fisherman's paradise and offer unlimited recreation for people in central Florida.

Gerald Sims, Manager of Environmental Control, commenting on regulation, says:

> We have a past history of cooperation with the (regulatory agencies).

He adds:

> We don't entirely agree with all the rules and regulations . . . and in some cases we have actually gone to court action to rectify and correct some of those regulations. . . . Welgro . . . wishes to comply with any reasonable law that is promulgated by the EPA or the state.

Richard Guimond of the EPA agrees that Welgro is cooperative. He explains:

> We began our study of the Florida phosphate industry in June 1974, with a meeting with the Florida Phosphate Council, the member companies, and the local government leaders. During the meeting we outlined the study plans and requested their cooperation.
>
> Shortly after this meeting, we began environmental investigations in and around the facilities of several companies including Welgro. Since that time we have conducted field studies at Welgro's mines, benefication plant, drying plant, and phosphoric acid plant. . . During each of these field trips, Welgro's management ensured that their staff answered all of our questions and provided us with access to any areas we required.
>
> Further, since some of our equipment required electricity in remote areas along with other special needs, they made provision for these requirements.
>
> In general, because of their excellent cooperation, we were able to gather much environmental data and information in a very short period of time. Because of their assistance, we were able to devote time to our scientific investigation which otherwise would have been needed for logistical support.

Environmental Control Department

In the late 1940s and 1950s pollution projects at Welgro were assigned to personnel as required. In 1958, the company established a one person Pollution Control Department, and in 1964 a technician was added.

Presently five persons are assigned to the Environmental Control Department. Also at each chemical plant there is a small staff responsible for pollution control, involving a total of 15 persons. In addition, one person is assigned to monitor water discharge at each mining location.

Budget for the corporate environmental control staff was about $150,000 in 1975. Welgro will budget from $3 million to $10 million per year for capital and maintenance of pollution control items in just their Florida operations.

Responsiveness of Industry to Regulation

Dr. David Anthony, a University of Florida biologist, has said that the phosphate industry had to be "dragged, kicking and screaming, into the twentieth century. It has been consistently resistant to even minimal regulation. It has a history of reacting nonresponsibly."

Replies Phosphate Council Director Homer Hooks:

> Dr. Anthony's statement does not hold up under examination of the facts of the past 10 years. The industry worked closely with the State Department of Pollution Control in development and promulgation of the very strict dam construction and maintenance regulation in 1972. Other control regulations . . . have likewise been accomplished with industry cooperation and participation. . . . I am afraid Dr. Anthony was merely repeating old perceptions about the industry which are no longer true.

Still, those perceptions persist. Waldo Proffit, Jr., a writer for the *Sarasota Herald Tribune*, wrote in June 1976, that phosphate companies were not taking advantage of existing technology to reduce fluoride emissions.

> It would seem that an industry sincerely concerned about the public would exert every reasonable effort to reduce fluoride emissions below the liberal legal maximums. Especially when the technology to do it has been available for 10 years and when those years have seen unparalleled prosperity in the industry.
>
> The lesson for the Florida citizenry is clear. When discussing rules and regulations for any aspect of the phosphate industry, pay no attention to what the industry tells you it CAN do. Insist on a specific definition of what it MUST do.

Dr. Herschel H. Nelson, Chairman of the Social Science Division at Polk Community College, Winter Haven, and a member of the Environmental Task Force of Winter Haven, agrees with the view of an industry resisting regulation. Commenting on the sincerity of the companies in the phosphate industry in attempting to correct environmental problems, he says:

> They will do as little as they can up to the point where they are concerned and forced to take corrective measures. The nature of their business is to reduce expenses and maximize profits, so it is only when profits . . . are threatened by unfavorable publicity, boycott, expensive after-the-fact corrective measures, or fines in the form of penalties will they respond effectively.

One *Sarasota Herald Tribune* writer wrote in early 1976 that the industry's attitude is "the public be damned." Not so, says James L. Cox of Lakeland, a phosphate management consultant for over 20 years:

> I think the industry has got environmental religion. Some of it was not voluntary, but whether they got religion or not, they are going to church regularly. What I'm saying is that the industry is very responsive to community and social needs. This was not true 15 years ago.

"As for environmental religion," counters University of Florida biologist Anthony, "just get up in an airplane, look at the mining area, and determine for yourself. Note, also, whether land reclamation is predominantly along major highways."

Contemporary Environmental Problems

Reclamation of Land

Effective July 1, 1975, Florida law made it mandatory that mined land be restored to "an acceptable condition" after mining operations end. This had been done in the past by phosphate companies on a voluntary basis. To help phosphate firms accomplish this restoration, the government paid between $8.5 and $9 million in 1975 in rebated severance taxes. But when it became known that this restored land was susceptible to radiation, the EPA stepped in to study the extent of the problem.

Wayne King of the *New York Times* described the land reclamation situation in this way:

> According to Mr. Hooks (of the Phosphate Council), Florida, in essence, requires only that mined land be returned to some useful purpose. Thus, on the vast majority of land, little or nothing is done after mining, and it is still considered reclaimed. It may simply be dubbed a wildlife preserve, pasture land, or something similar. Even where the land is used for development, it may be left as it was, rutted and hilled, with the great mesas of sifted earth, 10 stories high, still standing.
>
> Mr. Hooks says this is more aesthetic, lending more interest to the landscape. Florida is very flat, as you know.

It is this restored land upon which dwellings had been built which concerned the EPA most, since the radioactive radom gas was felt to be especially dangerous when trapped in dwelling structures.

Richard Guimond of the EPA states:

> Based upon our present knowledge, we estimate that continuous occupancy of the structure with the highest average radon daughter level we have measured over the past year (0.1 working level) would double the occupant's risk of lung cancer after about six to eight years of residence. Occupancy for longer periods would proportionately increase the risk. Ventilation is a very important factor in the radon daughter levels within a structure. Increasing ventilation by opening windows or otherwise diluting the indoor air with outdoor air can greatly reduce the indoor radon daughter concentrations in the air. Conversely, structures that are closed up will provide the opportunity for build up of the radiation levels in the structure. Concrete can provide a barrier to prevent radon from diffusing through the ground into a structure. However, the thickness and quality of the concrete are very important in determining the effectiveness of the barrier. If the concrete is very thin or has many cracks in it, the radon will be able to be transported through the floor into the structure.
>
> In general, the radiation problems in open areas are minimal because of the great diffusing power of the atmosphere. The primary concern in open areas is the potential uptake of radionuclides in food crops that may be grown on the land.

Welgro's Gerald Sims comments:

> They (the EPA) embarked on a one-year study. At the end of five weeks they had some results, and they issued a report from the EPA to the Governor of the State of Florida on five weeks of a 12-month survey. This was preliminary data and the Governor, in fact, handled the situation very admirably, in that he indicated the State would not be moved into some decision that may be wrong down the road. We need more data.

Despite industry claims that the EPA's results were only preliminary, Hillsborough County imposed a temporary moratorium on residential construction on land reclaimed from phosphate mining in the summer of 1975.

Dr. Charlton Prather, of the state health office, was quoted in the press as saying that there was no evidence of increased cancer caused by residing in phosphate-mining areas. Scientists studying the problem made the suggestion that miners save the 10 feet of top soil stripped from the land and replace it during the reclamation project. This would restore nature's protective blanket over any radioactive material.

Homer Hooks of the Phosphate Council pointed out that this was possible but that it would greatly increase reclamation costs. He added,

> First of all, we need to find out if it's necessary to do it. We're not convinced it is. If it's necessary, okay, this is one of the reclamation techniques we may have to adopt.... When we find out the scientific facts, we want to be prepared to take whatever remedial steps are indicated to assure safety to everybody.

Gerald Sims explained:

> I've read some reports from the EPA and from the state people where there's a possibility of air spacing from the foundation to the dwelling floors.... Shielding... these things have to be investigated. They indicate that (concrete) does act as somewhat of a shield, but not a complete shield. They are talking about metal, lead, something of this nature. It would increase construction costs, but, again, I haven't seen any real firm figures on this at all.

With respect to the possibility of bringing topsoil in from a different area entirely, Mr. Sims replied:

> To translocate topsoil from another area, to our previously mined areas... that would be an impossibility. The economics there would not be justified.... I want to emphasize that you are talking about a tremendous acreage, and a tremendous earth movement by sorting the piles in our present mining, but to take from other areas would be an impossibility.... How would you move Hardee County into Polk County?

Richard Guimond of the EPA said of the control measures:

> With respect to potential control methods for precluding the problem of contaminated lands in the future economic practicability of various control actions would be a valid consideration in determining the most suitable control means. However, at this time the Environmental Protection Agency has no authority to require specific types of mining or reclamation technology by industry in order to control this pollutant.... We can only make recommendations to the state of Florida and the local governments concerning acceptable radiation levels in structures and land contamination levels.

In July 1976, a symposium was held in Lakeland (Polk County), Florida to discuss the dangers of radiation on the populace of Central Florida. Few persons attended the symposium, however. Observed Dr. Hershel Nelson of Polk Community College and moderator of the panel:

> While radiation from reclaimed phosphate is measurable, it is not intense enough to arouse public alarm nor prompt public action to take measures to curtail it.... Unfortunately, not many people are trained in matters of radiation and need tangible, visible evidence to be convinced it poses a health problem. Even when long-range effects of radiation damage add up to a cancer condition, the cause is in dispute and may be attributed to a variety of things that are more convincing in the minds of the public.

When asked how he felt county politicians viewed the radiation problem, Dr. Nelson replied:

> Commissioners are members of the public also and are subject to the same limitations in considering radiation damage—especially if economic advantages of an immediate nature outweigh arguments for spending money to limit radiation from reclaimed phosphate land. If it ever comes to a decision requiring drastic expenditures on the part of phosphate companies to correct radiation dangers, and these expenditures are coupled with economic penalties (increased cost of products, layoffs, closing of sections of the industry, etc.), county commissioners will minimize (the dangers of) radiation.

By late 1976 the phosphate industry was awaiting the results of the first phases of the EPA's radiation study.

Air and Water Pollution

A recent brochure published by the Florida Phosphate Council makes the following points:

> The modern phosphate industry in Florida is a far cry from the operations of the early opportunists who saw, took, and left. Today's industry is devoting time, money, and total cooperation in making the term, "good business citizen," mean all that it should. . . .
>
> Air and water quality play an important part in phosphate operations. Dedicated and often voluntary efforts (at a cost of over $200 million in the past 10 years) have attacked the problems of pollution. . . .
>
> Waterborne emissions have been cut by over 90%. And the industry's techniques of air pollution control are so successful they're studied as models by industries throughout the world.
>
> Preservation of our environment is vital. So is the production of phosphate.
>
> The environment nurtures us. Phosphate feeds us.
>
> We need both.

With few exceptions the phosphate industry is now meeting state and federal standards on permissible air and water emissions. In 1967, the Florida State Legislature passed the Air and Water Pollution Control Act which established a 5500 pound per day level for fluoride emissions into the atmosphere. IMC Inc., a large phosphate producer, makes the following claim: ". . . by this time, the phosphate industry had voluntarily reduced its fluoride emissions to 3000 pounds per day at full-production capacity, even though phosphoric acid production was rapidly increasing. Today, emissions are barely above 2000 pounds."

In May 1972, the EPA approved an even more stringent Florida State Implementation Plan that required compliance by July 1, 1975. According to spokesmen for both the Atlanta regional office of the EPA and the Florida Department of Environmental Regulation (DER), the Florida phosphate industry is more than adequately meeting these standards.

The phosphate industry is far from out of the woods with regard to air pollution. Constant monitoring is conducted by the DER and from time to time cases of noncompliance are uncovered. In June 1976, the *Sarasota Herald Tribune* reported the following:

> . . . the State Department of Environmental Regulation (DER) has filed suit in Hillsborough County Circuit Court seeking to shut down operations of the Gardinier Phosphoric Inc. phosphate-processing plant at Gibsonton. . . .
>
> According to technicians of the Hillsborough County Environmental Protection Commission, the plant had registered 11 instances of excessive emissions since installation of the monitors in 1975. . . .

The water emission situation is very similar. In general, the industry is complying with state and federal standards. In 1972 the Florida Legislature enacted the Water Resources Act, which established five water-management districts within the state. The Southwest Florida Water Management District is responsible for the area where the bulk of the phosphate industry is located in Florida. In addition, corporate scientists constantly monitor water samples to assure compliance with published standards.

Most of the pollutants resulting from the phosphate-mining process are contained in the clay solids that are separated from phosphate pebble. Because it takes as long as 10 to 15 years for the clays to stabilize in the industry's settling ponds, public concern is always present regarding the threat of a dam failure. In an article appearing in the *Tampa Tribune*, UPI writer Orval Jackson made the following observations:

> . . . while in use, these ponds pose the threat of pollution through spillage. (Homer) Hooks says new dam construction techniques minimize this danger. But twice in the last 10 years, slime spills have turned the picturesque Peach

River and part of Charlotte Harbor chalky and white and killed millions of fish before the waters cleared.

Hal Scott of the Florida Audubon Society expresses the opinion:

> The phosphates present a real risk of water pollution. Considerable damage has been done to the Peach River over the years. With the expansion of the mining region, other areas will be threatened with the same thing.

Thomas Love, staff writer for the *Washington Star*, summarizes the position of critics:

> According to opponents of the industry, the mining operations pose a major pollution threat to Florida's beautiful and economically important rivers. They feed the estuaries which are dependent on the fresh water for their production of aquatic life.

Homer Hooks responds:

> We raise families, send our kids to school, breathe the air, drink the water and enjoy the scenic beauties of Florida with everybody else. I'm a lifelong resident, and I'm not about to countenance the ruination of the place where I live. I'm not going to dirty my nest and I don't think anybody else in this industry wants to either.

Water Usage

Perhaps more imperative than the long-standing debates over air and water quality is the recent controversy over water usage. Phosphate mining taps huge quantities of water from southwest Florida's supply. The Southwest Florida Water Management District says that phosphate companies draw 244 million gallons of water a day. This water comes from the huge underground freshwater reservoir that stretches the length and breadth of the state: the Floridan aquifer. Critics are quick to point out that the City of Tampa requires only 59 million gallons of water a day to supply its 320,000 residents.

The Florida Phosphate Council says that, through the industry's conservation practices, 85 percent of the water used by phosphate companies is recycled water, not water from the aquifer. In addition, the industry returns another 30 million gallons of water a day back into the Floridan aquifer by recharge wells. IMC, the industry's largest producer, is quick to point out the fact that:

> ... in the last 15 years, approximately 115 fewer inches of rain fell than normal. This translates into some 20 billion gallons of water per day less than normal.... While industry might be thought to be the greatest water consumer, figures show it is not; irrigation for agriculture holds that distinction.... In a study of Consumptive (Water) Use in Florida conducted by Black, Crow, and Eidsness, Inc., a firm of consulting hydrologists, irrigation accounted for 69 percent of the total water used, with municipal's share estimated at 13 percent, industry's 9 percent, and other usages 9 percent.... Presently, IMC... recycles 89 percent of the water used at its four processing plants and withdraws 11 percent from the aquifer. However, IMC believes it can do better. Its goal is zero "consumptive" use of water from the aquifer....

These future efforts are apparently unacceptable to critics who point out the present dangers of the situation. An editorial in the *Sarasota Herald Tribune* in June 1976 expressed the opinion:

> We were blessed, in the month of May, with rainfall—more than in any May in recent memory.
>
> Watering bans imposed earlier in the spring get lifted now, and the temptation is to think that the water crisis has passed.
>
> But the improvement in our water situation is largely superficial. The problem is a long-term, continuing one.... And we are faced, in these counties, with proposals for unprecedented drawdowns of multibillions of dollars of fresh water from the Floridan aquifer in the next few years by phosphate-mining and chemical processing companies.
>
> Data collected in May, district hydrologist Horace Sutcliffe, Jr. of the U. S. Geological Survey told the Manasota Basin Board this week,

made it "very obvious the zone of closed contours has expanded considerably."

A "zone of closed contours" is, in a manner of speaking, a subterranean sump—an area where the underground water supply has been so depleted that ground water from the surrounding areas in all directions tends to flow toward the sump.

And this particular sump, from which too much water has been sucked, is in turn robbing water from an area covering about half of Manatee County where a combination of overuse and rain-short years has caused the water table to drop to the average level of the Gulf of Mexico.

That, of course, means that sea water presses inland, rendering well water unfit for consumption and for crops. . . .

And as Sutcliffe warned the water board, the process is almost irreversible. It took all the millions of years since this peninsula emerged from the sea for our supply of ground water to accumulate.

We have been wastefully mining the essential resource.

And that must stop.

Gerald Parker, a recently retired hydrologist for the Southwest Florida Water Management District, also points out the dangers of saltwater intrusion. He claims that the aquifer in Manatee County has dropped to 10 feet below sea level 35 miles inland from the Gulf Coast. In Mr. Parker's words, "If the present conditions continue, both Manatee and Sarasota Counties will be in serious trouble."

Homer Hooks agrees that great quantities of water are essential to the phosphate industry. But he points to studies that show that alternate mining methods are unfeasible. Dry mining, Hooks says, would increase the cost of the raw product and create a new pollution problem: dust.

Expansion Into Other Areas

During the summer of 1976, Manatee County became the battleground for environmentalists and the phosphate interests. At issue: Would Beker Phosphate Corporation and Phillips Petroleum Company be allowed to mine phosphate in Manatee County?

In Manatee County, phosphate deposits were located about 50 feet below ground level. Before the recent increase in phosphate prices, the industry had not believed that mining in Manatee County would be particularly profitable.

"We've got everything going for us here," said vocal environmentalist, Sheila D. Leach, also the wife of the mayor of Bradenton. "It's a beautiful county. Don't we have a right to determine our destiny?"

One of the key points of contention in the controversy was the industry's use of water. Officials in adjoining Sarasota County pointed out that half of Sarasota's water supply came from reserves in Manatee County. Furthermore, officials argued that the problem would worsen in future years because projections indicated that population in the Sarasota area would double in the next decade.

Also at issue was the detrimental effect that industry critics claimed mining would have on tourism, the largest industry in Manatee and Sarasota counties.

Much of the opposition indeed came from neighboring Sarasota County. In particular, the *Sarasota Herald Tribune* took a strong antiphosphate stance. The Sarasota County Commission also entered the antiphosphate fight as an interested party when Manatee County Commissioners granted Beker Corporation the first permit to mine in Manatee County.

So active were both of these phosphate opponents in their efforts that in April Beker filed a $2 million lawsuit against the Sarasota County Commissioners, charging them with harrassment. A $10 million libel suit was filed against the Sarasota paper the same day. The suit against the paper was later dropped, but was then refiled in August.

In May, President Gerald Ford, in Florida during the 1976 campaign, was briefed by David Linsay, Jr., editor of the *Herald Tribune*.

Later, at the President's request, the President's Council on Environmental Quality ordered an intensive and sweeping study of the environmental impact of phosphate mining in Florida.

Opposition to mining in Manatee County also came from environmental groups in Manatee County. The primary effort of these groups was to petition for a referendum on phosphate mining. In addition, one of the newspapers conducted a mail survey to determine the attitudes of Manatee County citizens toward phosphate mining. Over 95 percent of the respondents opposed mining in Manatee County, the paper later reported.

In July, in the eastern part of the county, a homeowner's association obtained 2500 signatures on a petition protesting mining in the county.

Phosphate Council spokesmen also were active during the summer: "I don't believe we need any kind of governmental restriction on mining." Homer Hooks was quoted as saying in an August newspaper article.[1] "The demand for food supply around the world requires that those of us who are in the food chain do the best job we can to feed these people."

> Those who say "Cut your mining rate in half and it will last twice as long"—well, that sounds good in theory, but who are we going to tell they cannot have phosphate fertilizer to grow a food crop? We can't play God. You've got people starving in Bangladesh, Pakistan, the Congo, and other areas that desperately need food.

"If we are to keep feeding the world, expansion is necessary," Phosphate Council Director of Information Bobby Barnes told a Kiwanis Club.

Hooks was reported as saying in another interview:[2]

> World population is gaining at the rate of 200,000 persons every day. It will double early in the next century, and these people must be fed. Therefore, we have to mine the phosphate which the Lord put under the soil of Florida. It's simply a matter of the baby crop vs. the food crop.

To counter arguments by critics that phosphate mining in harmful to tourism, Hooks often pointed out that Cypress Gardens is only seven miles from an active phosphate mine and Disney World is 22 miles away from a mine.

As the expansion fight continued through the summer, many newspapers, government officials, and radio stations became active participants in the controversy. Below is an excerpt from an August editorial aired by a radio station in Sarasota:

> In this coming election, phosphate mining is becoming an issue. Most candidates are opposed to the mining of phosphate in Manatee County. They just simply do not want it anywhere around us. If you ask why they'll tell you it's ugly, how much water is used, the possibility of radiation, the possibility of the sludge contaminating our rivers. Everything is based on a possibility. Anyone being for phosphate mining now . . . is condemned.
>
> Well, the facts are these. According to the *St. Pete. Times*, without artificial fertilizers, food production in the United States would be cut 50 percent. The cost of food would more than double, millions of people here in America and overseas would go hungry and perhaps starve. . . . Suppose every area in the world took the same attitude on all mining and drilling. Where would we get coal, oil, iron ore, bauxite, uranium, copper, and so one?
>
> . . . Here we sit in Manatee and Sarasota using all the world's goods—oil, steel, paper, food. Yes and even fertilizer in our agriculture products—tomatoes, oranges, etc. But we will not produce; we take, but we don't give. It's not right. It's not fair. It's unjust.
>
> We know we'll be heavily criticized for our attitude. But before you do we want everyone of

---

[1] Orval Jackson, "Florida Phosphate Industry A Big Business," *Tampa Tribune*, August 17, 1976.
[2] Charles Patrick, "Phosphate Mining Involves Trade-offs," *St. Petersburg Times*, May 13, 1976.

you to stop using products that are grown from commercial fertilizer—tomatoes, bread, oranges, orange juice, all meat, all cereals, all vegetables, all fruit. Then when you do and give up these products forever we'll believe you are definitely against phosphate mining.

In late summer, the Manatee County Commission met to review the mining request of Phillips Petroleum Company.

Welgro: Expansion Strategy

A major expansion program completed in 1975 included a new 3½ million ton per year phosphate rock mine in Polk County; modernization of two other Polk County mines; construction of a deep-water terminal on Tampa Bay with loading facilities for phosphate rock; a new ammonia plant in Oklahoma; and finally, a new urea plant in Arkansas.

Demand for Phosphate

Welgro's President, Carl J. Martin, wrote in a letter to stockholders:

Looking to the future, the industry prospects are favorable. Fundamental strength still stems from the increasing need for food...

In the United States during 1975, 574 million acres were used for crops, representing essentially all of the arable acreage available. Increased requirements for agricultural products, for both domestic consumption and for export, can be met only by increasing yields per acre. This will require progressively larger amounts of fertilizer.

Participation with Foreign Countries

Welgro is currently participating in several foreign projects. Welgro is, through a 25 percent interest, participating in the Korean Seventh Fertilizer Complex. In addition, Welgro is a 25 percent equity holder in a proposed phosphate project in Jordan. Welgro has a 30 percent interest in a proposed nitrogen venture in Pakistan.

According to Mr. Martin, other projects are being evaluated in Southeast Asia, Europe, South America, and the Middle East.

EXHIBIT 1
Consolidated Statement of Income

(Thousands except per share amounts)	Years ended December 31,	
	1977	1976
Income		
Sales and services revenue	$1,239,588	$1,002,590
Investing income	9,675	15,916
Share of Peabody Holding net loss	(2,064)	—
Other income (deductions)—net	(5,963)	1,636
Total income	1,241,236	1,020,142
Costs and expenses		
Costs and operating expenses	940,426	756,677
Selling, general and administrative expenses	142,828	127,839
Interest accrued	61,024	56,551
Interest capitalized	(2,111)	(5,241)
Total costs and expenses	1,142,167	935,826
Income before income taxes	99,069	84,316
Provision for income taxes	33,758	23,120
Net income	$ 65,311	$ 61,196
Earnings per common and common equivalent share	$2.61	$2.44

Expansion in the United States

Other expansion projects either underway or planned are a second ammonia plant in Oklahoma and facilities in Louisiana to permit the receipt of phosphate rock from Florida and the loading of ships with the finished product.

Financial Condition

The selected financial information shown in Exhibits 1, 2, and 3 indicates the company's financial condition. Figures 1 to 4 show mining sites and various sections of reclaimed land.

EXHIBIT 2
Consolidated Balance Sheet

Assets (Thousands)	December 31, 1977	December 31, 1976
Current assets		
Cash	$ 10,893	$ 15,052
Short-term investments	64,181	47,693
Receivables	136,494	112,319
Inventories	242,673	196,154
Prepayments	4,756	5,337
Total current assets	458,997	376,555
Noncurrent investments	203,088	206,616
Property, plant and equipment, at cost	1,407,626	1,262,555
Less accumulated depreciation and depletion	254,216	203,701
Property, plant and equipment—net	1,153,410	1,058,854
Other assets and deferred charges:		
Cost in excess of fair value of tangible assets of businesses acquired	30,763	31,094
Other	36,549	35,666
Total other assets and deferred charges	67,312	66,760
Total assets	$1,882,807	$1,708,785

Liabilities and stockholders' equity (Thousands)	December 31, 1977	December 31, 1976
Current liabilities		
Notes payable	$ 23,000	$ 10,000
Accounts payable	113,016	99,093
Accrued liabilities	48,734	39,499
Income taxes	24,388	22,281
Long-term debt due within one year	32,617	19,388
Total current liabilities	241,755	190,261
Long-term debt	722,917	677,331
Deferred credits		
Income taxes	174,720	139,325
Other	26,764	25,214
Total deferred credits	201,484	164,539
Stockholders' equity		
Preferred stock	48	115

(*Continued*)

EXHIBIT 2 (Continued)

Liabilities and stockholders' equity (Thousands)	December 31, 1977	December 31, 1976
Common stock	24,887	25,452
Capital in excess of par value	200,995	205,207
Retained earnings	493,908	463,854
Net unrealized loss on marketable equity securities	(3,187)	(2,718)
Treasury stock, at cost	—	(15,256)
Total stockholders' equity	716,651	676,654
Total liabilities and stockholders' equity	$1,882,807	$1,708,785

EXHIBIT 3
Financial Information by Profit Center

		The Companies				
Millions except per share amounts		1977	1976	1975	1974	1973
Revenues	Chemical Company (Fertilizer)	$ 592.7	$ 481.0	$518.5	$461.8	$312.0
	Pipe Line Company (Energy)	100.7	87.4	78.4	68.6	64.1
	Energy Company (Energy)	209.9	185.4	144.6	128.6	78.9
	Exploration Company (Energy)	89.3	25.8	13.7	—	—
	Metals Company (Metals)	269.6	223.0	126.7	169.2	133.7
	Intercompany eliminations	(22.6)	—	—	—	—
	Total revenues	$1,239.6	$1,002.6	$881.9	$828.2	588.7
Operating profit	Chemical Company (Fertilizer)	$ 76.5	$ 57.9	$150.2	$146.0	$ 43.6
	Pipe Line Company (Energy)	49.8	40.7	37.2	32.1	30.1
	Energy Company (Energy)	8.8	13.1	12.4	10.7	9.6
	Exploration Company (Energy)	9.0	1.4	(.4)	—	—
	Metals Company (Metals)	14.8	15.2	8.1	23.5	13.8
	Total operating profit	$ 158.9	$ 128.3	$207.5	$212.3	$ 97.1
Other income (expense) items	Interest accrued	$ (61.0)	$ (56.5)	$(51.2)	$(41.7)	$(34.3)
	Interest capitalized	2.1	5.2	16.0	14.9	1.6
	Investing income	9.6	15.9	13.7	2.5	16.7
	Share of Peabody Holding net loss	(2.1)	—	—	—	—

(Continued)

EXHIBIT 3 (*Continued*)

		The Companies				
Millions except per share amounts		1977	1976	1975	1974	1973
	General corporate expenses	(9.2)	(8.7)	(8.4)	(7.6)	(4.3)
	Other income (deductions)—net	0.7	0.1	0.5	(6.8)	(3.3)
	Total other income (expense) items	$ (59.9)	$ (44.0)	$(29.4)	$(38.7)	$(23.6)
Income	Income before income taxes	$ 99.0	$ 84.3	$178.1	$173.6	$ 73.5
	Provision for income taxes					
	Excluding investment tax credits	(45.6)	(33.2)	(85.2)	(83.4)	(30.4)
	Investment tax credits	11.9	10.1	24.3	3.3	1.0
	Income from continuing operations	65.3	61.2	117.2	93.5	44.1
	Income from discontinued operations	—	—	6.6	2.1	4.3
	Net income	$ 65.3	$ 61.2	$123.8	$ 95.6	$ 48.4
Earnings per share	Primary					
	Income from continuing operations	$ 2.61	$ 2.44	$ 4.84	$ 3.98	$ 2.11
	Income from discontinued operations	—	—	0.27	.09	.21
	Net income	$ 2.61	$ 2.44	$ 5.11	$ 4.07	$ 2.32
	Fully diluted:					
	Income from continuing operations	$ 2.61	$ 2.44	$ 4.84	$ 3.95	$ 1.95
	Income from discontinued operations	—	—	0.27	0.09	0.18
	Net income	$ 2.61	$ 2.44	$ 5.11	$ 4.04	$ 2.13

Social Responsibility 719

Figure 1
Mining Site

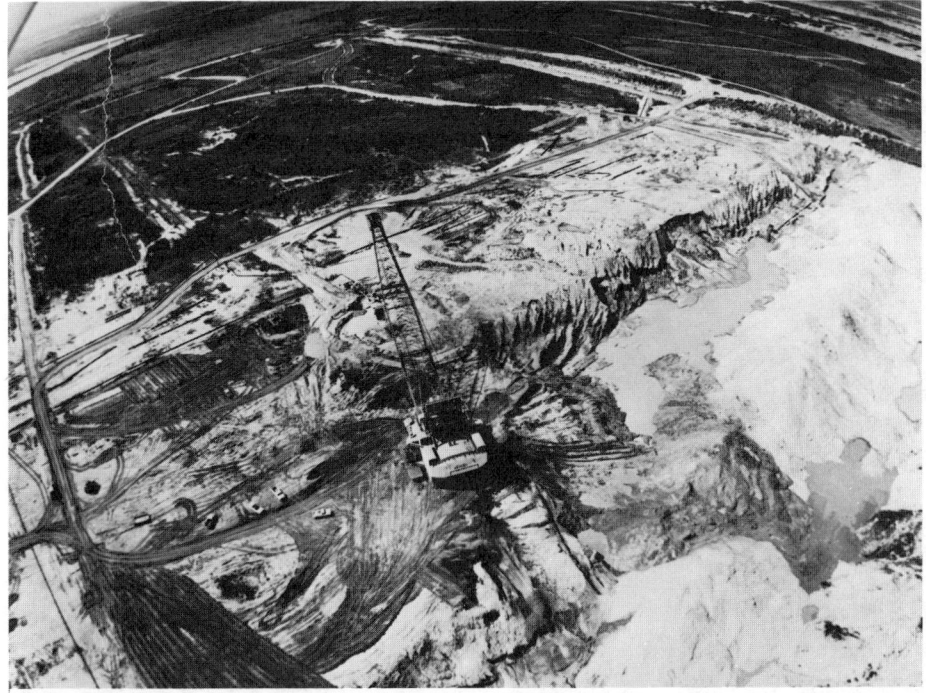

Figure 2
Mining Site (Dragline in Center)

Figure 4
Reclaimed Land

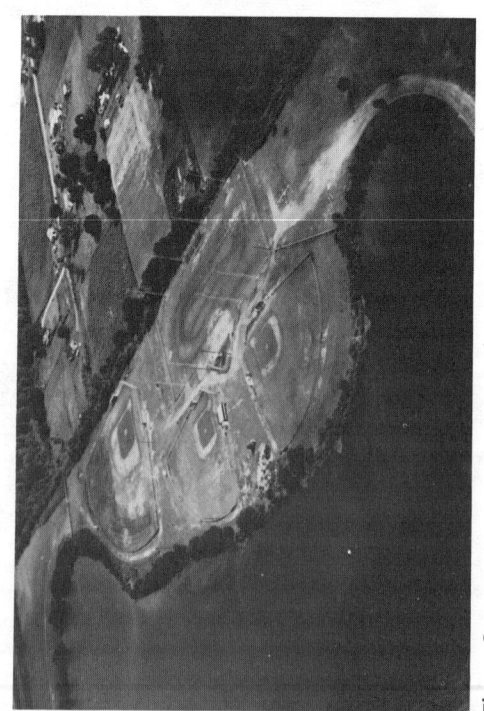

Figure 3
Reclaimed Land

THE ANACONDA SMELTER

Ralph Cox, Executive Vice-President of the Atlantic Richfield Company (ARCO) and President of the Anaconda Company, sat back wearily in his chair. The date was September 15, 1980, and he had just returned to his office in Denver, Colorado. Another in a recent series of rather lengthy meetings with most of the other senior executives of the Anaconda Company had just adjourned.

The major topic of discussion of this recent series of meetings was the status of the Anaconda Company's primary activities in the State of Montana. More specifically, the immediate question of interest was what to do with the firm's copper-smelting operation in Anaconda, Montana.

Among the options from which Anaconda might choose were the following:

1. Maintain the status quo, at least over the short-run, and operate the smelter under approved variances from both state and federal clean-air regulations.
2. Continue to operate the smelter and commit the company to a program that would redesign and reconstruct the smelter into compliance with the various environmental regulations.
3. Continue to operate the smelter for several years while a new smelter was being built.
4. Shut down the smelter immediately and ship the copper concentrate emanating from the company's open-pit mine in Butte, Montana to Japan for further processing (tolling).

Ralph Cox knew that the decision would affect the lives of literally thousands of residents of Montana. A plant closure would be devastating to the local economy—in both the short and the long-run. The decision would also affect the future strategic position of the overall Anaconda Company. Finally, the decision would most likely receive close scrutiny by a wide variety of interested parties.

Organization of the Case

Because of the importance of the decision for the small town of Anaconda, Montana, much of the case material will focus on the smelter located there. The smelter, however, was not operating in isolation. The operations in Anaconda were the middle part of a geographic (and product flow) triangle that had corners in Butte, Montana (an open-pit mine and concentrator) Anaconda, Montana (the smelter), and Great Falls, Montana (the copper refinery). In addition, a complex set of variables affected the productivity and economic viability of all three of these operations. Therefore, it will be necessary to discuss in some depth these variables and the relationship of these three cities with each other and the State of Montana.

The first major section of the case will review the copper industry as of 1976 (when ARCO bought Anaconda). The history and background of the Anaconda Company will be presented in the second major section. The period surrounding the merger between ARCO and Anaconda will then be discussed. The next major section will deal with the smelter and refinery evaluation process and some factors which affected the productivity of these operations. Finally, the decision at hand and the predicted effects of the possible alternatives will be presented.

The Copper Industry

Although commercial deposits of copper ore were known to exist on almost every continent, five general areas contained about 75 percent of the world's known reserves as of

---
Source: This case was prepared by Mary Pat Cormack and Professor M. Edgar Barrett. Materials for this case were taken totally from public sources. Permission to use granted by Professor M. Edgar Barrett.

1976. These areas, listed in order of total past production tonnage were: the Rocky Mountain and Great Basin area of the United States; the west slope of the Andes Mountains in Chile and Peru; the central plateau of Africa in Zaire and Zambia; the Precambrian shield area of central Canada and its extension into northern Michigan; and, the Soviet Union (see Table 1). The greatest known reserve of copper ore in one body was the deposit at Chuquicamata, Chile.

Three of the top six copper-producing countries in the world were third-world countries. They also figured prominently in total smelting capacity. They did not, however, have a substantial amount of refining capacity and consumed very little of the end product. Conversely, Japan accounted for a little over one percent of the copper production in the world. However, the country figured strongly in smelting and refining capacity and the consumption of fabricated copper.

A wave of nationalization hit the copper industry during the late 1960s and early 1970s when the governments of Chile, Peru, Zaire, and Zambia all took control of the copper mines located within their national borders. By 1976, 35 percent of all the free world's output of copper ore was controlled by four governments.

The same four countries organized the International Council of Exporting Countries in 1967. The primary goal of the organization was to achieve stability of the price of copper. However, since the countries took over, they had operated at full capacity despite slackening demand. The main problem was that most of the governments were deep in debt and in desperate need of foreign exchange. In addition, they wanted to avoid laying off workers. For these reasons, the organization had never been very successful as a price stabilization mechanism.

The Copper Industry in the United States

Approximately 80 percent of the copper output in the United States during 1977 was from open-pit mining. Copper ore usually yielded other metals as byproducts, including gold and silver.

The five leading copper companies in the United States in 1976 were: Kennecott, Phelps Dodge, Anaconda, Magma, and ASARCO. Domestic production from these companies declined on an annual compounded basis by almost 3 percent from 1972 to 1976 (see Table 2). Exhibit 1 shows performance measurements for the leading copper companies.

TABLE 1
Leading Copper Countries as of 1976 (Percentage of Total World Production)

Leading Countries	Mining	Smelting	Refining	Consumption of refined copper
Canada	9.1	6.1	5.8	a
Chile	12.6	10.7	a	a
Japan	a	10.8	9.7	12.3
United States	18.4	18.0	19.3	20.8
U. S. S. R.	15.1	15.0	16.2	14.6
West Germany	a	a	5.0	8.7
Zaire	5.6	5.1	a	a
Zambia	8.9	8.8	a	a

Source: "Metals—Nonferrous," *Standard and Poor's Industry Surveys,* October 1978, pp. M173–6.
[a]Less than 5 percent of total.

TABLE 2
Leading Copper Companies in the United States (Production in Short Tons)

	1976	1975	1974	1973	1972
Kennecott	346,427	288,104	402,213	471,721	460,576
Phelps Dodge	330,960	249,686	281,338	319,566	305,432
Anaconda	164,089	149,547	190,059	200,454	233,471
Magma	149,121	132,767	149,645	152,263	149,492
ASARCO	106,718	78,551	81,062	75,180	71,714

Source: "Metals—Nonferrous," *Standard and Poor's Industry Surveys*, October 1978, p. M174.

Generally, United States and Canadian products had established fixed prices for copper sold in North America. The established price was changed infrequently and in large steps. Foreign copper, on the other hand, had a commodity status. Selling prices were determined by the quotations on the London Metal Exchange (LME). In the past, trends in LME quotes had dictated copper prices throughout the world. Whenever a considerable disparity developed between LME and the U. S. prices, domestic producers usually adjusted their prices in an effort to maintain orderly markets. Since the end of 1974 the price of foreign copper had been lower than the price of domestic copper. The average price of copper in North America was $0.688/lb. in 1976, whereas, the average price of foreign copper was $0.639.

EXHIBIT 1
Performance Measurements of the Nonferrous Metal Industry—1976

	Return on Equity		Debt/ Equity Ratio	Return on Total Capital		Net Profit Margin
	Five-Year Average	1976		Five-Year Average	1976	
Copper						
Cyprus Mines	12.4%	3.5%	0.3	13.3%	4.6%	3.4%
General Cable	10.8	8.1	0.4	8.4	6.6	5.1
Phelps Dodge	10.2	5.8	0.6	8.6	4.7	5.6
Kennecott	6.7	1.7	0.3	6.1	2.3	2.7
Anaconda	4.0	0.4	0.4	3.6	1.0	0.4
Revere	deficit	deficit	1.5	deficit	deficit	deficit
Medians	8.5	2.6	0.4	7.3	3.5	3.1
Aluminum						
Medians	8.2	7.3	0.8	5.4	5.0	3.7
Diversified Metals						
Medians	18.2	11.6	0.4	12.1	7.5	6.2
Industry Medians	10.8	7.4	0.4	8.6	5.0	3.4
All-Industry Medians	12.7	12.9	0.4	9.1	9.8	4.6

Source: "29th Annual Report on American Industry; The Industry Reports: Metals," *Forbes*, January 1, 1977, p. 158.

EXHIBIT 2
Performance Measurements of the Copper Industry—1980

	Return on Equity		Debt/ Equity Ratio	Return on Total Capital		Net Profit Margin
	Five-Year Average	1980		Five-Year Average	1980	
Copper						
NVF	14.1%	7.9%	2.4	3.5%	11.5%	2.5%
Revere Copper	11.1	14.3	1.2	8.5	6.1	3.0
Phelps Dodge	6.1	9.8	0.6	6.7	4.9	7.0
Kennecott	3.4	5.7	0.4	5.8	3.7	4.0
Medians	8.6	8.9	0.9	6.3	5.5	3.5
Aluminum						
Medians	16.5	21.5	0.5	13.8	10.3	9.2
Diversified Metals						
Medians	14.3	23.6	0.3	18.3	10.0	7.8
All-Industry Medians	15.8	16.1	0.4	11.0	11.1	5.0

Source: "33rd Annual Report on American Industry," *Forbes*, January 5, 1981, pp. 84, 238, 240.

The profit margins of most domestic producers were squeezed to zero as the price fell toward $0.60/lb (see Exhibit 2).

The costs associated with producing copper, which varied by location and type of ore deposit, had maintained a strong upward trend in recent years. Costs for labor, fuel, materials, and transportation had all increased. In addition, many new programs to control air pollution at copper smelters and refineries were introduced. Estimates for pollution control costs ran to as much as $0.15/lb.

By the middle 1970s, the domestic producers were quite concerned about the availability of cheap foreign copper. These companies demanded government production measures. Some firms cut back production and rumors of plant closures became more frequent. The quoted share price of many of the firms fell to their lows for the decade.

In addition, domestic producers were concerned about their inability to make capital investments. "When the price was 70¢, H. Myles Jacob, chairman and chief executive officer, Inspiration Consolidated Copper Co., Miami, Arizona, said that the price was inadequate to justify copper industry development of new mines. 'With inflation, the cost of new construction has escalated wildly over the price tags of fixed assets now in use,' said Jacob. 'In addition, government-mandated pollution control equipment further balloons the price of new production capability.'"[1]

Shortly thereafter, the various copper companies began to be cited as obvious takeover targets. Copper was seen by some as an undervalued asset that was expected to appreciate in value. In addition, leading economic indicators pointed to a strong 1978. Copper was essential to the capital goods industry. Thus, the future of the industry appeared strong.

Labor Unions in the U. S. Copper Industry

The nonferrous (copper) mining industry encompassed multiple unions and locations and complex sets of work practices. As a result,

---
[1]*Purchasing*, September 7, 1976, p. 59.

labor negotiations in the copper industry were described as among the most complex in the United States. Following an industry-wide nine-month strike in 1969, the industry established the concept of common contract expiration dates and coordinated bargaining on behalf of all the relevant unions. The National Nonferrous Industry Conference (essentially controlled by the United Steelworkers of America) was responsible for setting bargaining goals for all of the unions in the industry and approving the settlement made by each company. The economic aspects of labor settlements in the copper industry were heavily influenced by settlements in the steel and aluminum industries, where the union contracts were negotiated earlier in the same year.

The Anaconda Company

Anaconda was a major industrial corporation engaged in the mining and processing of minerals and the manufacturing of metal products. See Exhibit 3 for financial data. The company operated mines and plants in 55 locations in the United States and Canada, employing over 22,000 employees during 1975 (see Exhibit 4). Approximately 75 percent of sales came from manufacturing during that year and the remainder from mining. This split of sales revenues initially resulted from some Chilean problems. Later it was shaped by a conscious diversification program that management believed was essential to maintain stability through bad years.

EXHIBIT 3
Financial Statements Five-Year Summary of Operations (Millions of Dollars, Except per Share Figures)

	1975	1974	1973	1972	1971
Sales and Other Operating Revenue	$1,087.8	1,672.7	1,343.1	1,011.6	946.5
Operating Costs and Expenses					
Cost of sales and expenses	1,065.2	1,448.4	1,200.6	911.3	882.3
Provision for depreciation and depletion	51.3	50.7	45.7	44.1	46.9
	1,116.5	1,499.1	1,246.3	955.4	929.2
Operating Income (loss)	(28.7)	173.6	96.8	56.2	17.3
Equity in net income of affiliated companies	5.8	16.7	15.3	10.0	4.2
Income from Chilean investments	9.4	5.4			
Interest and miscellaneous income	6.1	5.6	4.8	4.3	1.6
Interest expense	(32.0)	(29.7)	(23.2)	(21.7)	(25.2)
Gains (losses) on foreign exchange	0.8	(10.4)			
Income (loss) before Taxes and Extraordinary Income	(38.6)	161.2	93.7	48.8	(2.1)
Provision for income taxes	1.2	54.5	24.6	5.4	3.9
Income (loss) before Extraordinary Income (loss)	(39.8)	106.7	69.1	43.4	(6.0)
Extraordinary income (loss)		140.4	17.7	88.3	(347.9)
Net Income (loss)	$ (39.8)	247.1	86.8	131.7	(353.9)
Per share of common stock					
Income (loss) before extraordinary income (loss)	$ (1.80)	4.83	3.13	1.97	(.28)
Extraordinary income (loss)		6.36	0.80	4.00	(15.89)
Net income (loss)	$ (1.80)	11.19	3.93	5.97	(16.17)
Dividends paid					
Amount	$ 16.6	22.1	11.0	2.7	10.9
Per share of common stock	$ 0.75	1.00	0.50	0.125	0.50

EXHIBIT 3 (*Continued*)
Sales and Operating Income by Division (Millions of Dollars)

	1975	1974	1973	1972
Sales and other operating revenue				
Montana Mining and General Mining Divisions	$ 278.1	378.5	341.3	341.8
Uranium Division	24.0	28.6	29.5	18.2
Natural Resource Divisions	302.1	407.1	370.8	360.0
Aluminum Division	311.2	384.0	276.2	198.4
Brass Division	347.2	616.4	497.3	346.5
Wire and Cable Division	294.1	502.0	390.5	286.1
Walworth Division (Acquired October 1975)	11.6			
Forest Products Division (Sold June 1972)			9.7	24.6
Less sales between divisions	(178.4)	(236.8)	(201.4)	(204.0)
Net sales and other operating revenue	$1,087.8	1,672.7	1,343.1	1,011.6
Operating income (loss)				
Montana Mining and General Mining Divisions	$ (40.7)	41.1	49.9	27.2
Uranium Division	0.5	4.5	10.1	5.8
Natural Resource Divisions	(40.2)	45.6	60.0	33.0
Aluminum Division	17.4	48.9	(2.9)	3.9
Brass Division	(1.8)	30.1	24.9	10.3
Wire and Cable Division	9.2	61.3	23.9	13.8
Walworth Division (Acquired October 1975)	.8			
Forest Products Division (Sold June 1972)				3.6
Unallocated corporate expenses	(13.2)	(11.0)	(9.1)	(8.4)
Consolidating adjustments	(0.9)	(1.3)		
Operating income (loss)	$ (28.7)	173.6	96.8	56.2

Five-Year Sales by Class of Products (millions of dollars)

	1975	1974	1973	1972	1971
Copper and copper products	$ 625.1	1,163.1	960.9	701.3	662.5
Aluminum and aluminum products	335.8	403.8	299.7	220.2	177.0
Uranium oxide	24.0	28.6	29.5	18.2	20.4
Other metals, forest products, etc.	102.9	77.2	53.0	71.9	86.6
Total	$1,087.8	1,672.7	1,343.1	1,011.6	946.5

Primary Production

	1975	1974	1973	1972	1971
Copper (short tons)	149,622	197,543	208,110	242,955	227,415
Aluminum (short tons)	243,591	298,737	217,950	177,618	171,677
Uranium oxide (short tons)	1,736	2,025	2,069	2,022	1,763
Silver (thousands of ounces)	2,352	3,571	4,256	3,979	3,869

(*Continued*)

EXHIBIT 3 (*Continued*)
Consolidated Balance Sheet (Thousands of Dollars)

	December 31	
	1975	1974
Assets		
Current Assets		
Cash	$ 19,933	$ 8,472
Short-term securities, at cost (approximates market)	22,518	61,434
Receivables, less allowance for doubtful accounts of $3,711 (1974—$3,563)	151,928	149,720
Inventories	260,235	233,878
Supplies	28,609	25,825
Prepaid expenses	2,278	2,872
Total current assets	485,501	482,201
Chilean notes and OPIC insurance claims	172,436	192,723
Investments	88,011	89,622
Property, plant, and equipment	1,205,350	1,115,276
Other assets and deferred charges	56,155	51,450
	$2,007,453	$1,931,272
Liabilities		
Current Liabilities		
Notes payable	$ 16,000	
Long-term debt and capitalized lease obligations due within one year	60,697	$ 16,812
Accounts payable and accrued expenses	138,002	123,247
Accrued taxes	23,580	28,813
Total current liabilities	238,279	168,872
Long-term debt	335,872	273,755
Capitalized lease obligations	133,321	131,890
Other liabilities and deferred credits	62,276	58,039
Reserve for estimated expropriation costs	26,787	31,444
	796,535	664,000
Shareholders' Equity		
Common stock outstanding—22,090,826 shares	557,648	557,648
Retained earnings	653,270	709,624
Total shareholders' equity	1,210,918	1,267,272
	$2,007,453	$1,931,272

Statement of Changes in Consolidated Financial Position (Thousands of Dollars)

	1975	1974
Financial resources were provided by		
Income (loss) before extraordinary income	$(39,786)	$106,757
Charges (credits) to income not affecting working capital:	51,289	50,716
Depreciation and depletion	8,361	8,569
Amortization relating to mining joint ventures	(92)	(11,233)
Equity in undistributed income of affiliated companies	(2,939)	(5,450)

(*Continued*)

EXHIBIT 3 (Continued)
Statement of Changes in Consolidated Financial Position (Thousands of Dollars)

	1975	1974
Undistributed income from Chilean investments	3,816	15,723
Other, including gains and losses on foreign exchange	20,649	165,082
Extraordinary income		
Portion of settlement with Chilean government of 1971 expropriation loss received in cash		65,075
Utilization of income tax loss carryforwards, exclusive of amounts relating to Chilean settlement		46,766
		111,841
Other sources	120,499	40,211
Long-term debt borrowings	4,826	7,494
Increase in capitalized lease obligations	15,982	6,634
Sales of fixed assets and investments	24,439	
Reduction in Chilean investments, principally notes		310
Issuance of capital stock	165,746	54,649
Total resources provided	186,395	331,572
Financial resources were used for		
Payment of dividends	16,568	22,087
Additions to—plant and equipment	68,679	118,256
—mining joint ventures	59,973	75,644
Deferred mine development	20,803	7,283
Reduction of—long-term debt	58,014	27,925
—capitalized lease obligations	3,395	3,384
Acquisition, less working capital acquired of $25,974	14,053	
Other noncurrent assets and liabilities	11,017	25,028
Total resources used	252,502	279,607
Increase (decrease) in working capital	$ (66,107)	$ 51,965

Source: Anaconda 1975 Annual Report.

The Loss of Chilean Operations

Anaconda mines located in Chile supplied two-thirds of the company's primary copper output and generated approximately 75 percent of its earnings during the 1960s. However, during 1969, Anaconda sold a 51 percent interest in its two Chilean mines (Chuquicamata and El Salvador) to the Chilean government. The government agreed to purchase the remaining interest before 1982. Unexpectedly, in 1971, the country expropriated the mines. According to Chilean law, compensation for expropriated properties was to be based on their Chilean book values with deductions to be made for assets deemed not to have been received in good operating conditions and for "excessive profits" earned by the operating company.

In October 1971, Chile announced that it had determined that "excessive profits" and other deductions from Chuquicamata and El Salvador exceeded their book values by $78 million. However, the country agreed on a settlement of $7.5 million (on a book value of $14.8 million) for Exotica, a new property that Anaconda also lost.

Anaconda appealed to the Overseas Private Investment Corporation (OPIC), a United States government corporation that has the responsibility to insure domestic companies op-

EXHIBIT 4
Anaconda Company Operations

Some other subsidiaries and affiliates
In Australia:
　Anaconda Australia Inc., Sydney
In Brazil:
　Fios e Cabos Plasticos do Brasil S.A., Rio de Janeiro
　S. A. Marvin, Rio de Janeiro
In Canada:
　Anaconda Canada, Ltd., Toronto
　Anaconda CATV Limited, Vancouver
In Iran:
　Anaconda-Iran, Inc., New York, N.Y.

In Jamaica:
　Alumina Partners of Jamaica, Jamaica
　Anaconda Jamaica Inc., New York, N.Y.
In Mexico:
　Compañia Minera de Cananea, S.A., Mexico City
　Condumex, S. A., Mexico City
　Nacional de Cobre, S. A., Mexico City
　Swecomex, S. A., Guadalajara
In The Netherlands:
　Anaconda, B. V., Amsterdam
In The United Kingdom:
　F.T.L. Company, Limited, Morley, Leeds, U.K.

W—Wire and Cable Division　B—Brass Division　A—Aluminum Division
MM—Montana Mining Division　GM—General Mining Division
U—Uranium Division　M—Metallurgical Division

Source: Anaconda 1974 Annual Report.

erating overseas against nationalization losses. In September 1972, Anaconda received $11.9 million from OPIC for the loss of Exotica. However, OPIC formally rejected claims of $159 million against the Chilean government for Chuquicamata and El Salvador. Finally, in 1974, the company received $65 million in cash and $188 million in promissory notes from the government of Chile as a settlement.

In addition to the settlement, the company was left with approximately $160 million of consolidated tax-loss carryforwards available through 1981. However, by this time, all of the other parts of Anaconda had begun to feel the effects of the loss of the Chilean operations.

The State of Montana

Montana was the fourth largest state in terms of area and the 42nd in terms of population in 1976. In fact, only three states (Alaska, Wyoming, and Nevada) had lower population density figures. The state's populace was strongly oriented toward the out-of-doors, summer and winter sports, and hunting and fishing. The state's largest source of income was agriculture, with livestock accounting for about two-thirds of cash income and crops the remainder. However, Montana, with its far north-central location, found itself relatively far from the markets for their cattle, grain, lumber, metals, and petroleum, as well as from the nation's manufacturing and supply centers.

Montana had done little to attract industry to the state. According to an editorial that appeared in a Montana newspaper, "Cities, counties, and states which care about industrial development offer tax incentives, building assistance, and a host of services to prospective investors. Montana has never really joined this game. Not long ago, we're told, the owner of a fishing equipment company looked into the possibility of building a plant in Montana. . . . But the businessman finally turned to Idaho . . . because of incentives offered in that state as well as an open-arms attitude toward industrial growth."[2]

The roots of the Anaconda Company can be traced back to the Anaconda copper vein in Butte, Montana. The mining, smelting, and refining operations had a great effect on the state of Montana. Conversely, the state which was just described genuinely affected the company.

Relative to the frontier on which these three operations began, they were considered to be quite sophisticated. These operations required an infrastructure previously not known in that area. In addition, they utilized a wide variety of skilled craftsmen and tradesmen. As a result, the company built—at each location—its own support system consisting of foundries, blacksmith shops, electrical repair facilities, machine shops, railroads, water companies, lumber operations, coal companies, newspaper operations, and hotels.

The company did not have the same amount of influence in 1976 that it once possessed. Its vast timberlands in western Montana and many other assets had been sold. Still, the presence of the company was very heavily felt. Anaconda's economic clout simply made it the town's (Anaconda, Montana) unofficial leader. This fact produced a love–hate relationship on the part of many residents. It had been estimated that approximately 80 percent of the employment in Anaconda, Montana was a result, either directly or indirectly, of the firm's smelting complex and its affiliated work sites. Critics charged that Anaconda's influence went beyond the town. Some felt that the firm had an undue influence on the state legislature. One Anaconda manager in Butte, however, responded to a similar criticism by saying, "We don't want a company town. We're tired of it. If the weather is bad, it's blamed on the Anaconda Company."[3]

---

[2]*The Independent Record*, Helena, Montana, October 2, 1980, p. 4.
[3]"An Open-pit dilemma for Butte, Mt." *Business Week*, December 1, 1973, p. 94.

The Butte, Anaconda, and Great Falls Triangle

Since the turn of the century, copper ore had been mined in Butte, Montana and hauled 25 miles to Anaconda to be melted into concentrate (a process known as smelting). It was then shipped by rail to Great Falls for refining. These three cities were where Anaconda had its origin. For a very long time, they had represented the hub of Anaconda's domestic-mining operations.

Butte

The principal ore body located in Butte often has been dubbed "the richest hill on earth." The area produced billions of dollars of wealth from gold, silver, copper, and zinc deposits since the first prospectors rushed to the town in the 1860s. The area's overwhelming success, however, came from high-grade ore and easily extractable copper deposits. During World War I, Butte boomed. In 1916, more than 262 million pounds of copper were mined (a record that never has been surpassed).

For many years, copper was mined in underground mines. However, by the early 1950s, the costs associated with underground mining began to exceed the price received. This economic change was due to a combination of declining levels of the ore grade and rising underground mining costs. In 1955, Anaconda opened the Berkeley open pit and gradually phased out the underground mining operations. Copper produced from the open pit was lower grade and higher volume than that from the underground mine. By the 1970s, Berkeley ore averaged about 0.5 percent copper. Thus, it was necessary to mine one ton of ore to produce 10 pounds of copper.

As noted earlier, the loss of the Chilean mines had a great effect on the overall Anaconda Company. The most noticeable changes took place in Butte. The Berkeley pit became the company's largest source of copper, accounting for approximately 50 percent of its total production of 150,000 tons in 1975.

The Kelley underground mine was reopened and extensive drilling and testing operations began in the hope of locating higher grade ore deposits. At the same time, the loss of the Chilean mines forced the firm to become significantly more cost-conscious. As a result, the workforce in Butte was cut from 3,000 to 1,700 people in the middle 1970s, although production stayed the same.

Butte ore was trucked to the primary crusher, where it was crushed to pieces less than four inches in size. It was then transported by a network of conveyor belts to a secondary crushing system and then fed into the grinding section of the concentrator where a substance having the consistency of gritty talcum powder was produced. An additional step further reduced the amount of waste materials. At the completion of this series of steps, the ore had been upgraded to a copper slurry consisting of about 26 percent copper (see Exhibit 5).

Anaconda

The copper slurry was transported to the smelter in Anaconda where it, along with several off-site sources, supplied the smelter's feedstock. The smelter process involved many steps that started with copper slurry and ultimately produced anodes that weighed 460 pounds each and were 99 percent pure copper.

The Anaconda smelter was situated on top of a mesa overlooking a wide, flat area. Its enormous stack towered 585 feet in the air. Over 1,200 people were employed at the smelter.

Great Falls

Anodes from the Anaconda smelter were transported 160 miles to Great Falls for refining. The finished product was known as a cathode. It weighed about 180 pounds and was 99.9 percent pure copper. It was then shipped to Anaconda manufacturing divisions or sold to outside customers. For the most part, refined copper was fabricated into intermediate

EXHIBIT 5
Montana Production Flowchart

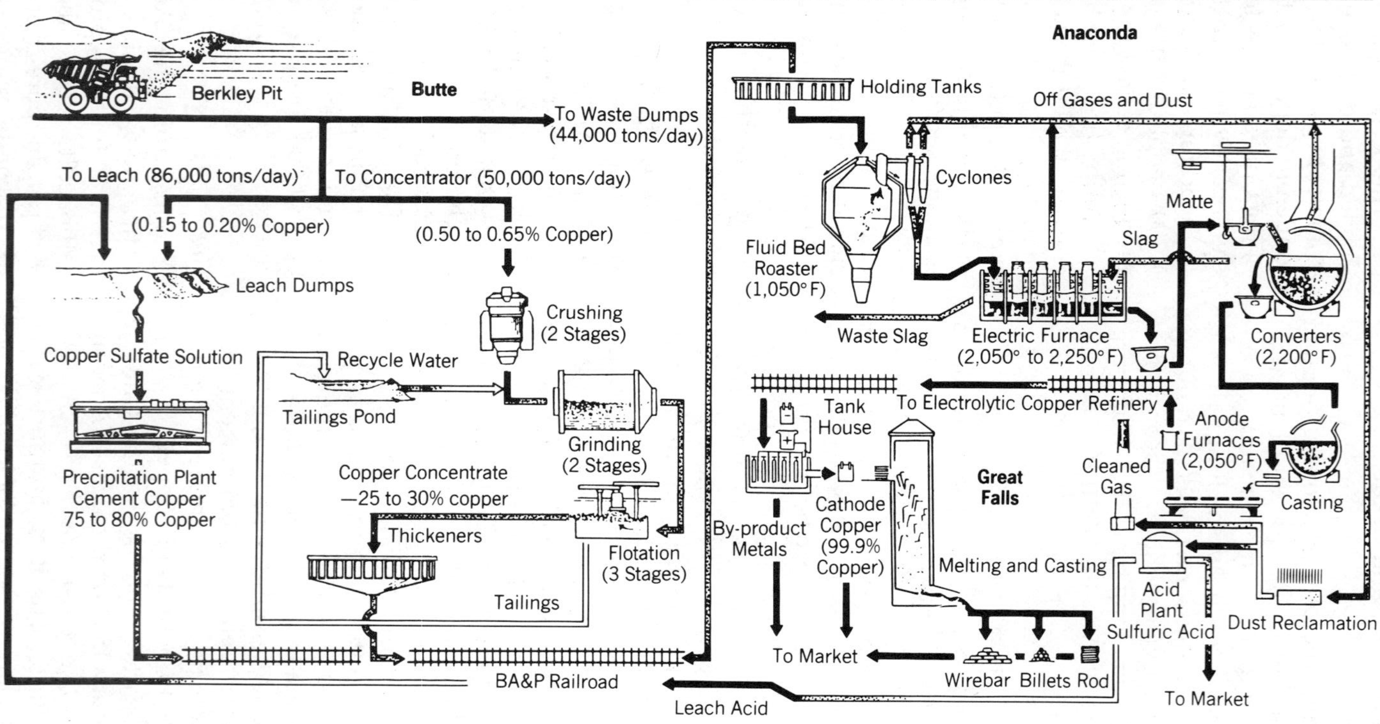

Source: Montana Copper, Anaconda Copper Company.

and finished articles by wire and brass mills. Over 500 people were employed at the refinery.

Problems that Faced the Anaconda Smelter

The Federal Clean Air Act of 1970 required each applicable state to submit to the Environmental Protection Agency (EPA) plans for reducing copper smelter air pollution. The State of Montana submitted a plan in 1972. During the next couple of years, the State, the EPA, and the Anaconda Company attempted to develop a reasonable compliance plan for the smelter.

By 1976, the company spent or committed to spend $60 million to improve the smelter. In 1974, a new "baghouse" was installed to capture particulate emissions. A baghouse was a filter that was attached to the top of the smelter's stack. It was designed to capture solid particles that had once been dispersed for miles into the air by the smelter's huge stack.

The next major improvement was the installation of a sulfuric acid plant. This plant was designed to remove sulfur dioxide from the smelter's gas stream and convert it into sulfuric acid. Again the Company attempted to capture emissions that had once been dispersed into the atmosphere. However, the conversion of sulfur dioxide to sulfuric acid resulted in a byproduct that had many applications.

Sulfuric acid was used in the copper industry for the leaching of metals from low-grade material and the reduction of uranium ore. It was also used in the production of commercial fertilizer. It was not unusual for sulfuric acid to be produced on almost a one-to-one (ton) basis with copper. Anaconda, most likely, did not make very much money from this large volume byproduct because of the cost of freight to get the product to established markets in the Midwest and Gulf Coast areas.

In addition to environmental improvements, the Company replaced the smelter's natural gas reverberatory furnaces with electric furnaces. This expenditure was designed to considerably reduce the amount of energy used, thereby lowering operating costs in an attempt to offset the higher costs incurred because of environmental-related improvements. Despite these efforts to improve the smelter, the level of compliance that Anaconda's management had anticipated was not attained.

The Atlantic Richfield—Anaconda Merger

By mid-1975, Anaconda's management most probably suspected that there was a very real possibility that they would be a takeover candidate. After posting a net income of almost $107 million for 1974, the first half of 1975 produced one of the company's worst sets of financial results. The company blamed an abnormally low demand for their products, particularly in the automotive, construction, and electrical markets, for the sharp decline in their sales. In addition, the company was in need of cash at this time. Anaconda had just started the development of the Carr Fork mine near Salt Lake City. This new copper mine had an initial estimated cost of $135 million. Also, the aluminum business would most likely need extra capital in order to help complete the process of raising the level of the firm's activities to a "critical mass."

In August 1975, the Crane Company announced an exchange offer for five million shares of Anaconda stock. By mid-February 1976, Crane had acquired 4.1 million shares, making Crane the company's largest shareholder, with over 18 percent of its stock. However, in early February 1976, Anaconda announced an agreement with Tenneco under the terms of which the latter was to pay $25.50 per share for all the remaining shares of the former. In March 1976, ARCO entered the picture. The corporation tendered $27 per share for a 27 percent interest and forced Tenneco to back away.

The Atlantic Richfield Company

ARCO was the eighth largest domestic oil company in 1976. Production of crude oil and natural gas were obtained principally in the United States, including the Gulf of Mexico and Alaska. Foreign production was primarily in Iran, Indonesia, and the United Kingdom.

In 1968, Robert O. Anderson, Chairman of the Board, made two major decisions that were to strongly impact ARCO, and ultimately, the Anaconda Company as well. Anderson was convinced that there was too much political risk in large-scale foreign investments. Thus, he decided to sink capital in Alaska where discoveries had been made but where the cost to produce and transport the crude oil and natural gas was extremely high. In addition, he rejected the idea of trying to acquire the Anaconda Company at that time because of the copper company was very dependent on its Chilean mines. Both of Anderson's decisions proved to be correct. Anaconda lost Chile in 1971 and, by 1976, ARCO could see the end of the their long struggle to get their Alaskan crude to market.

ARCO was again evaluating Anaconda as a prospective acquisition candidate in early 1976. It quickly moved to get its "foot in the door" by acquiring 27 percent of Anaconda's stock.

What they saw was a minerals company whose share price was well below book value ($55 per share) and had substantial reserves of copper, uranium, and bauxite. In addition, they saw a company that had $215 million in tax-loss carryforwards. However, even a casual analysis of the Montana mining operations would identify a very old smelter and working conditions at all three cities that were not in line with those normally found in the oil industry. The studies done at that time estimated that ARCO would have to spend $100 million to bring the smelter up to EPA standards.

On July 2, 1976, ARCO offered cash and stock worth $32 per share or over $500 million for the remaining 73 percent of Anaconda's shares. They also loaned Anaconda $100 million for near-term capital needs. The merger was finalized in January 1977.

The Adjustment Period

In the spring of 1978, headquarters for the Anaconda Company were moved from New York to Denver. For many different reasons, few Anaconda executives made the move. As a result, the influx of ARCO executives into the Anaconda Company was probably quicker than originally had been anticipated by both companies.

In 1979, Anaconda was reorganized into Anaconda Industries, Anaconda Copper Company, and Anaconda Coal Company, each an operating entity of the Atlantic Richfield Company. This move imposed an organizational structure typical of the major oil company on a copper company. See Exhibit 6 for financial data.

EXHIBIT 6
Financial Data: Atlantic Richfield Company (Millions of Dollars)

	1979	1977	1975
Sales			
Petroleum	$14,033	$9,488	$7,383
Chemicals	2,242	1,235	681
Metals	2,173	1,692	—
Coal	68	1	7
Other	(1,839)	(1,003)	(324)
Total	$16,677	$11,413	$7,747
Income before Taxes			
Petroleum	$2,379	$1,022	$721
Chemicals	117	77	87
Metals	179	136	—
Coal	(12)	(18)	(30)
Other	(519)	(248)	83
Total	$2,144	$969	$861
Total Assets			
Petroleum	$9,270	$7,969	$6,491
Chemicals	2,076	1,763	755
Metals	2,237	1,777	—
Coal	266	143	78
Other	(16)	40	(14)
Total	$13,833	$11,692	$7,310

Source: *Atlantic Richfield Company Annual Report*, 1979, p. 34.

The Smelter/Refinery Evaluation Process

As mentioned earlier, the Anaconda smelter had been running under variances for many years. ARCO knew at the time of the merger that additional capital would be needed to bring the smelter into compliance.

During 1978, additional controls on emissions were issued. The State of Montana promulgated regulations that limited sulfur-dioxide emissions from the smelter to 11,800 pounds per hour based on a 24-hour average. Meanwhile, the Occupational Safety and Health Administration (OSHA) issued arsenic regulations that required the company to install engineering controls to reduce the workers' exposure to inorganic arsenic. The new regulation required that the exposure be limited to less than 10 micrograms per cubic meter on an eight-hour weighted basis, which was said to be the smallest, measurable amount.

Industry Evaluation

The changes in existing regulations served to expedite the company's decision to fully evaluate the smelter and refinery decision, a process that ultimately cost ARCO $15 million. Starting in July 1978 and continuing for eight months, Anaconda conducted a study of the world's smelting industry. The company wanted to determine how the United States' smelting position compared to that of the rest of the world and, more important, how Anaconda compared to the rest of the industry. Table 3 shows how sulfur-dioxide standards in the United States compared to other countries.

Since Japan was considered the main area of competition for the United States and, since the possibility of tolling had been considered, the Japanese copper industry was evaluated in some depth. The study stated that Japanese smelters were generally located near major population centers, although three were located in national parks. All of them were required to meet stringent sulfur-dioxide regulations. For the most part, Japanese smelters used the technology of the 1950s and 1960s. However, relative to the United States technology—which dated from the 1940s, it was considered advanced, energy-efficient technology (see Table 4).

The Smelting Industry in the United States

There were 16 copper smelters operating in the United States during 1978. Historically, the

TABLE 3
Sulfur Dioxide Regulations—1980

	Sulfur Dioxide Concentration (parts per million)	Average Time (hours)
Current		
U. S. EPA	0.50	3
	0.14	24
Canada	0.34	1
(Federal) actual	0.10	24 not currently enforced
	(0.17)	1
proposed	(0.06)	24
West Germany	0.14	1
Japan (Federal)	0.10	1
Proposed		
Montana	0.50	1
	0.10	24

Source: Sept. 1980 Smelter/Refinery Decision, Anaconda Copper Company.

TABLE 4
Japanese Smelter Capacity/Utilization

Smelter/Owner	Capacity	Utilization (April 1980)	Type
Kosaka/Dowa	128	85	Flash
Miyako/Rasa	62	—	Blast
Onahama/Onahma	468	75	Reverb
Hitachi/Nippon	168	0	Flash
Ashio/Furukawa	84	63	Flash
Naoshima/Mitsubishi	336	77	Reverb
	104	95	M. I.
Hibi/Mitsui	136	75	Blast
Tamano/HBI-Kyodo	264	85	Flash
Toyo/Sumitomo	312	72	Flash
Saganoseki/Nippon	480	60	Flash
Total	2,542		

Source: Sept. 1980 Smelter/Refinery Decision, Anaconda Copper Company.

TABLE 5
United States Smelter Capacity

Smelter/Owner	Capacity	Type
Asarco		
El Paso, TX	200	Reverb
Hayden, AZ	360	Reverb
Tacoma, WA	200	Reverb
Kennecott		
McGill, NV	156	Reverb
Hurley, NM	260	Reverb
Hayden, AZ	260	Reverb
Salt Lake, UT	580	Noranda
Inspiration, AZ	300	Electric
Magma, AZ	400	Reverb
Phelps Dodge		
Douglas, AZ	220	Reverb
Morenci, AZ	490	Reverb
Ajo, AZ	180	Reverb
Hidalgo	360	Flash
Louisiana Land, MI	180	Reverb
Cities Service, TN	120	Electric
Anaconda	360	Electric
Total	4,626	

Source: Sept. 1980 Smelter/Refinery Decision, Anaconda Copper Company.

typical smelter was built near a source of ore. Although seven smelters were located in Arizona, the others were in nine different states (see Table 5). Thus, many different sets of regulations applied to the group of smelters.

Conclusions resulting from the Anaconda study of the U. S. smelting industry were: (1) most smelters used obsolete, energy-inefficient, "reverb" technology, (2) some of the smelters were operating at less than rated capacity because of environmental curtailments; (3) most smelting capacity in the United States was committed; (4) energy and labor costs to operate these facilities were high.

The Retrofit Evaluation Program

The first part of the retrofit evaluation program began in September 1978.[4] Anaconda signed separate contracts with Furakawa (a Japanese firm) and Lurgi (a German firm) to independently develop a retrofit program that would achieve compliance with the federal environmental regulations. Each company received identical input and produced their final reports in March 1979. The two reports called for designs that were quite similar. Anaconda's engineers combined the engineering results and philosophies of the two reports and developed their own composite retrofit program.

Retrofit Detailed Engineering

A decision was made in July 1979 to proceed with the detailed engineering of the composite retrofit program. Bids were received from five contractors and, finally, Lurgi was selected.

The detailed retrofit engineering program called for $480.6 million in capital expenditures (see Table 6). Anaconda engineers modified the Lurgi plans slightly. The modifications resulted in a decrease in the estimated operating reliability of the plant. They also resulted in a decrease in the estimated capital costs of over $80 million. Thus, the final Anaconda estimate for retrofit was determined to be approximately $400 million.

---
[4]Retrofit is a term used to describe the process of redesigning and reconstructing existing facilities.

TABLE 6
Capital Costs—Detailed Retrofit

Item	Millions of Dollars
Roaster	44.7
Electric Furnace	18.9
Copper Converter	65.2
Slag-Cleaning Furnace	28.7
Anode Furnace	6.6
Fugitive Gas System	59.9
Wet Gas-Cleaning System	53.9
Sulfuric Acid Plant	61.1
Wastewater Treatment Plant	14.0
Utilities	25.6
Total, Lurgi estimate	378.6
Less: Lurgi's contingency	21.0
Plus: Construction management	2.0
Owner's cost	5.0
Escalation	53.0
Contingency (15%)	63.0
Total	480.6

Source: Sept. 1980 Smelter/Refinery Decision, Anaconda Copper Company.

In addition to the capital costs, operating expenses were expected to increase because of the retrofit program. Also, the output of sulfuric acid was expected to increase greatly. It was at this point that the estimated operating costs, plus depreciation began to equal and exceed the cost of shipping concentrate to Japan. When this final figure was applied to the overall smelter decision economics in May 1980, it was decided that a full retrofit of the smelter was not economical. Thus, the retrofit detailed engineering program was stopped.

Modified and Minimum Retrofit Programs
As a result of the decision not to proceed with the full retrofit program, a task force was formed to review the technical concepts and try to identify the parameters for a modified retrofit design. The task force concluded that a number of changes could be made that would reduce capital costs to $310 million. However, they determined that operating reliability would be seriously affected and there was no guarantee that the modified retrofit design would ensure compliance with environmental standards as they existed at the time of the study.

The concept of a minimum retrofit program was also explored. It was concluded that the investment required by such a program would be at least $200 million. However, this type of program would have required the production rate to be reduced by as much as 50 percent of normal capacity. In addition, the study raised serious doubts as to whether the minimum retrofit program would ensure compliance with federal regulations. It was determined, however, that the minimum retrofit program would definitely not achieve compliance with the proposed Montana sulfur-dioxide standards.

The New Smelter/Refinery Option
Late in 1979, prior to the final data being assembled on the retrofit programs, management decided that other alternatives should also be explored. Thus, a decision was made to initiate a detailed study in respect to the possibility of building a completely new smelter and refinery.

Many different types and sizes of smelters and refineries were considered. In addition, various locations were explored. Thus, the combination of alternatives was very large. The resulting difference in cost estimates was also substantial. The results of the overall study were received in July 1980. Capital cost estimates ran up to close to one billion dollars for a large new smelter and refinery.

Alternatives
By June 1980, five alternatives were being considered. These were: (1) modify the smelter and refinery and, as a result of the reduced capacity, toll excess concentrate to other Anaconda smelters; (2) build a 50 million pound per month new smelter and refinery in Louisiana with a partner; (3) build a 30 million pound per month new smelter in Montana and

modify the refinery; (4) build a 15 million pound per month smelter, modify the refinery, and toll excess concentrate to other Anaconda smelters; (5) close the Anaconda smelter and Great Falls refinery and toll the concentrate.

Shortly after the list of alternatives was narrowed to five options, two environmental factors changed. The State of Montana Board of Health adopted an ambient sulfur dioxide standard that was more restrictive than the federal standards. The new Montana standard was 0.5 parts per million (ppm)/1 hour average compared to the federal standard of 0.5 ppm/3 hour average. None of the retrofit alternatives considered would have met the new Montana standards.

Concurrently, the EPA issued rules and requirements for obtaining a nonferrous smelter order (NSO). This legal variance allowed relief from compliance with federal standards, while research was conducted on possible compliance alternatives. The terms of an NSO required that final compliance be attainable by 1988. Because of the change in environmental factors, Anaconda added qualifying for an NSO to its list of alternatives and eliminated the medium-size Montana smelter. Most of the managers from the original Anaconda firm were, at the least, receptive to the possibility of qualifying for an NSO.

Labor Negotiations in Montana

Local negotiations began on May 6, 1980. This was the first set of negotiations that took place after the influx of ARCO personnel. Therefore, the company was undoubtedly concerned about the outcome of the negotiations and the precedent that would be set.

A major concern on the part of management was productivity improvement. Because of a complex set of union rules, many jobs only could be done by certain people. The company wanted the unions to ease the rules that kept workers confined to limited jobs. Understandably, this was not a popular issue with the unions. They knew the end result probably would be fewer workers.

Apparently, little real progress was made on either the local or national levels by June 30, 1980—the day the industry contracts expired—an industry-wide copper strike began at midnight July 1. All Montana operations were shut down.

Meanwhile, bargaining had begun on a national level at the end of August. Kennecott settled shortly thereafter. As expected, the union wanted to use the settlement as the industry pattern. They wanted all companies to make settlements equal to Kennecott's. This was probably not expected, as Kennecott led the industry in wages and benefits. Thus, this would mean substantial increases for many companies.

The Decision at Hand

Anaconda's management had developed five alternatives concerning the smelter that fell basically into four categories: build, retrofit, close and toll, and apply for the NSO (go on as is).

Earlier that year, management developed a set of key questions that could be used to aid in the evaluation process. All alternatives were to be studied in light of the likely answers to each of the following questions: (1) How would Montana be impacted by shutting down the smelter and refinery or relocating them? What would be the impact of the resulting reduction in employment? (2) Which alternative would enable wise industrial strategy in terms of future smelter capacity, capital input and competitive position? (3) Should mine, smelter, and refinery production be matched? (4) Would the chosen alternative meet Anaconda standards and produce a quality product from all Anaconda concentrates? (5) Would the chosen alternative be able to meet future, perhaps more stringent environmental regulations? (6) Would the chosen alternative be economically feasible in terms of return on capital investment, operating costs, and energy requirements?

Management knew that approximately 1,500 people would be directly affected by a closing of the smelter and refinery. Although some could be relocated at Butte and other Anaconda operations, this would not take care of the majority of the people. Regardless of relocation efforts, a choice to close the smelter would cause a strong rippling effect on the local community, unless new industry was convinced to move to Anaconda.

From the recent studies that had been conducted and from inquiries that had been made with the Japanese, Anaconda's management apparently believed that excess smelting capacity existed in Japan. In light of anticipated capital expenditures that would be made if the smelter was not closed, the Japanese tolling option was apparently determined to be an economically feasible alternative.

7 SHORT CASES INVOLVING STRATEGIC ISSUES

MOLDEX COMPANY

At the end of the Vietnam conflict, Bruce Train was in the plastics business but it failed and he lost his entire investment in the corporation. He felt that his failure was due to (1) lack of working capital, (2) too low a bid on a fixed-price military contract, and (3) becoming so engrossed in the technical and sales side of the business that his indirect, general, and administrative expenses expanded too rapidly, that is, many more indirect and office workers were hired than were actually needed. Mike Scott has been a long-time friend of Train and has had a moderately successful career. Although both Train and Scott dislike figures, "efficiency experts," and accounting data, they have resolved not to make the same mistakes in undertaking a new venture together. They also want to make sure that they keep control of the company, so that they do not build up a successful business only to find that some other person is able to squeeze them out and gain control. They have had considerable experience in the aviation and plastics industries, and have amassed between them approximately $75,000 that they would like to invest in some business with possibilities for profits and capital gains.

In the course of their business experience, they became acquainted with Robert House, now President and General Manager of the Atlantic Chemical Company. This company, engaged in the manufacture of industrial plastics, has a brilliant young chief engineer, Fred Bates, who invented and developed a special light and strong plastic board of high strength, low weight, and exceptional insulating qualities. Moreover, it is easily shaped to any desired form and is made largely of low-cost, noncritical wood pulp and waste-paper material. Although the product has some use in the

---

Source: This case is patterned from a case prepared by teaching assistants of H. Koontz in 1961–1963. Robert Schellenberger obtained the original through Professor A. P. Raia, University of California, Los Angeles. Permission to use granted by Robert E. Schellenberger.

manufacture of industrial plastics, Train and Scott have discovered that it is admirably suited for the manufacture of portable, easily constructed, and highly insulated military huts and radar nose domes for aircraft. Train, who has much experience in selling articles to the military, expects a strong demand for such products because of the increased concern in a strong national defense capability.

The plastic board product that Train and Scott are considering has been patented by the Atlantic Chemical Company under the name of Moldex. Investigation has disclosed that only one other product is competitive with Moldex, Soft-Ply, which is manufactured by a very large well-known company, the Standard Plywood Products Company. Although Soft-Ply has similar qualities to Moldex, its manufacturing cost is considerably higher and it does not form and shape as easily.

On January 1, 1984, Mr. House said that for personal reasons and because it would take his company out of its main line of business, he was not interested in producing Moldex and would be willing to give an exclusive license for its manufacture to Train and Scott on an exclusive royalty basis of $0.05 per square foot. The next day Mr. House informed Mr. Train that he had another manufacturer anxious to obtain the license and he must have Train's answer by the close of business on January 15.

In examining the possibility of starting the manufacture of Moldex for arctic huts and radar domes, Train and Scott developed the following facts and estimates:

1. *Production facilities.* These alternatives are open for obtaining production facilities:

   a. Mr. House indicated that Train and Scott can utilize unused space in the Atlantic Chemical Company factory in Allentown on a three-month renewable-lease basis. There is enough space at least to manufacture 100,000 square feet of Moldex per month. Further, Mr. House has promised to allow the use of certain high-priced plastic presses. The cost of this space would be $1,000 per month plus an estimated additional cost of $1,000 per month for the use of the presses. A further advantage of this arrangement is that chief engineer Bates could be easily available for technical consultation; Train and Scott feel that his technical advice is highly desirable for a period of time, no matter which facilities are used. With the use of the space and presses, it is estimated that Train and Scott would have to spend $25,000 for machinery to handle production to a capacity of 100,000 square feet per month. This equipment may be moved to another location—in which case, equipment purchase requirements at the new location would be reduced by $20,000.

   b. Train and Scott can lease a plant in Scranton for a minimum of a five-year period at an annual rental of $15,000. This plant has ample space for production at a rate of 1,000,000 square feet per month. However, certain large presses have to be acquired and the total cost of facilities for a capacity of 100,000 square feet per month would be $100,000 and for 1,000,000 square feet capacity, $150,000. Sixty thousand dollars of the $100,000 represents equipment for which loans may be obtained. Intermediate capacity presses are not available.

   c. Train and Scott can have a plant, suitable for 1,000,000 square feet of capacity per month, built in Allentown in three months at a cost of $125,000 for land and plant. Cost of machinery and other facilities for such a plant would be the same as in alternative (b).

2. *Production costs.* As soon as production begins, costs per square foot would be as shown in Table 1 (cost includes everything except interest and selling expense, that is,

TABLE 1
Total Costs per Square Foot of Moldex

Location	Plant Capacity	Total Costs per Square Foot
Atlantic Chemical Company	50,000	0.285
Atlantic Chemical Company	100,000	0.209
Scranton	100,000	0.205
Scranton	200,000	0.200
Scranton	300,000	0.183
Scranton	600,000	0.168
Scranton	1,000,000	0.154
Allentown	100,000	0.212
Allentown	200,000	0.203
Allentown	300,000	0.182
Allentown	600,000	0.168
Allentown	1,000,000	0.154

material, royalties, rent, depreciation, labor, etc.).

3. *Sales possibilities and policies.* Army and Air Force authorities have indicated that they are contracting for competitive Soft-Ply at 25¢ per square foot average for flat and rounded shapes. Quantities now under contract average 600,000 square feet per month, although much larger quantities are likely to be sought in the immediate future. Train now owns a business engaged in the buying and selling of aircraft materials and believes that, temporarily at least, his sales organization could be used for selling Moldex to the Defense Department. Both Train and Scott agree that no attempt should be made now to sell this product to the civilian market, although possibilities for future sales should be kept in mind.

4. *Financing.* In addition to the $75,000 in capital that Train and Scott have, informal inquiries have disclosed that the Atlantic Chemical Company would be willing to invest $100,000 in the Moldex venture: John Mann, a friend in the aviation industry, would be willing to invest up to $150,000 if the venture looks sound; additional funds could be obtained from a loan on inventory and accounts receivable, if a contract from either the Army or the Air Force is obtained. (Such loans would be a maximum of one-half of inventory plus accounts receivable). Train will assume responsibility for general management and sales. Consequently, his salary will come under general and administrative costs. Scott will assume responsibility for production and personnel. Consequently, his salary will be included in direct labor costs.

Source: This case was prepared by Robert E. Schellenberger, East Carolina University and Joseph Tomey, Sperry Univac. Permission to use granted by Robert E. Schellenberger.

KEYSTONE INSTRUMENTS, INC.

You are a management consultant called in by the management of Keystone Instruments, Inc. to attempt to assist them in solving a major production problem that they now face. It is January 3, 1980, and you are talking with the president of Keystone, Joe Marcell, who is relating the background of the problem.

Conversation with Joe Marcell

One of Keystone's main lines of business is the production of integrated circuits that are used as components in the production of a circuit board used by many organizations. Such circuit boards are the heart of many electronic devices including radios, TVs, etc. Keystone began production on a major contract with National Automobile Company on April 1, 1979. National produces approximately 1.5 million automobiles annually. Approximately two-thirds of these automobiles are equipped with a system used by automobile garages for diagnosing and evaluating the performance of the automobile. One system diagnoses the pressure within the engine to ascertain engine wear. One system can be used to ascertain the mixture of gasoline and oxygen, etc. Each of the circuit boards which are the heart of this system include five individual integrated circuits. Keystone is one of two suppliers providing integrated circuits to the National Automobile Company, thus this contract represents 2.5 million integrated circuits. The system used in the car has both passive and active elements. For example, the tests for engine wear can be made only in the confines of an automobile garage—passive system. The system that deals with the fuel oxygen mixture functions all of the time and indeed functions to adjust the carburetor so that the appropriate fuel mixture is present under varying operating conditions, that is, an active system. In either case, the failure of a system is significant inasmuch as the results of system failure are costly and potentially dangerous. The failure of fuel monitoring system to provide the correct fuel mix could indeed cause the car to cut off and not operate. Or, for example, the failure of the passive system for evaluating engine wear could either predict the presence of engine wear when none is there or fail to predict the presence of engine wear when there is engine wear present. Consequently, National Automobile demands a very high rate of product reliability.

The award of the contract from National Automobile Company was the culmination of two long, hard years and a substantial amount of effort. Indeed, 18 months ago we delivered 14,000 of these integrated circuits to National Automobile Company. Four thousand of these were used in National Automobile Company's very thorough product-testing process. The remaining 10,000 were installed in demonstrator automobiles at the beginning of the 1979 model year. These prototype integrated circuits have more than met the requirements for reliability established by National Automobile Company. Indeed, most of the circuits installed in National's 1979 models have been in use for close to 15 months. There have been no reported failures of those circuits.

Since November 15, 1979, through January 2, 1980, we have received a total of 147 reported cases of failure. The table shown below depicts the pattern of failures over time.

Week of	Total Circuit Failures in All Cars	Number of Our Circuits Failing
Oct. 1	0	0
Oct. 8	2	1
Oct. 15	1	0
Oct. 22	3	2
Oct. 29	2	1
Nov. 5	1	0
Nov. 12	8	6
Nov. 17	10	9
Nov. 24	14	11
Dec. 1	15	13
Dec. 8	18	16
Dec. 15	21	20
Dec. 22	24	21
Dec. 29	28	26
Total	147	126

We have been producing between 50,000 and 60,000 circuits per week beginning April 1, 1979. The production process involves the production of the integrated circuit less lead wires in our U. S. plant. These circuits are shipped to our overseas plant for the insertion of lead wires and the addition of a plastic encasement around the circuit. These circuits are then returned to the U. S. plant for inspection and then shipped to the National Automobile Company. It takes approximately six weeks from the time the first circuits are manufactured in the U. S. plant until they arrive at National Automobile Company. National Automobile then begins the assembly of their circuit board, which then is installed when the final product is assembled. Thus, the first set of circuit boards were available approximately June 15 at the final assembly plant. The final assembly of the automobile began in mid-August so that all automobile dealers were supplied with a representative sample of the automobiles for the October 1, 1980 model year.

Analysis of a representative sample of the circuits that have failed clearly indicates that moisture penetration on the circuit is the cause of the vast majority of the failures. What is most frustrating is the fact that the circuits provided by the other supplier are not experiencing an abnormal failure rate. National Automobile is very concerned about the problem. They are threatening not only cancellation of the contract but legal action to force Keystone to pay for any recall expenses and/or damage to the reputation of National Automobile Company. Needless to say the problem is acute.

Brief Description of Integrated Circuit Production

In this case, the important considerations in the production of integrated circuits are those that are related to the potential causes of moisture in the integrated circuit. There are a number of procedures that eliminate or inhibit the effects of moisture. The circuit is encased in either a plastic or metal package that is used for installing the circuit in the circuit board. In addition, the metal package is made so that it provides a completely airtight container. All prototype circuits are made in metal packages. However, all production circuits are made in plastic packages, otherwise, the company would lose money on the contract. Very few purchasers have found it desirable or advisable to purchase metal encasements. Although the plastic encasement can never be made airtight, the design of the encasement can have some effect on inhibiting the entrance of moisture. A better design will more severely restrict the entrance of moisture.

However, the primary mechanism to eliminate moisture from the circuit is to coat the circuit with silicon dioxide (essentially a covering of glass). These coatings, if properly done, will virtually eliminate the potential for entrance of moisture into the circuit.

It is essential that the glass (silicon dioxide) coating cover completely and not include minute cracks that allow the entrance of moisture. In order to prevent the presence of microcracks, phosphorus is mixed with the silicon dioxide. It is important that the proper amount of phosphorus be included. Excess phosphorus in the presence of moisture creates phosphoric acid which can erode the pads on which the wires are attached, thus causing failure in the circuits. An inadequate amount of phosphorus does not prevent the presence of microcracks.

A second course of action open to the organization is to include "guard rings." Guard rings operate to decrease the impact of moisture when present. In these circuits, the major danger of moisture is that the current is passed through the circuit when it should not be. Thus, guard rings are an internal barrier that inhibit the flow of current when it should not flow.

The following reports from engineering, production, research, and quality control indicate their findings regarding the problem and what they believe should be done in order to overcome the problem.

Memo from Engineering

We believe the problem is due to the overseas assembly of circuits. We have never experienced this problem during domestic manufacturing. We recommend domestic manufacturing until the manufacturing problem overseas can be cleared up.

We are well aware of manufacturing's belief that guard rings should be included in the design of our product. However, guard rings are only useful in inhibiting the effects of moisture. We believe the major concern should be with eliminating any moisture rather than accepting the presence of moisture and dealing with it. Likewise, we are aware that production believes we should redesign the plastic encasement. Again, our response is that the plastic encasement can only serve to reduce or delay the impact of moisture once present.

Another potential cause of the problem is the slipshod way that manufacturing in the United States trained the new personnel to operate the new silicon dioxide machines. These machines were purchased to handle the increase in production of integrated circuits when the national car contract began.

Report from Research Department

In the design phase for the circuits used by National Automobile, we completed both accelerated life tests, that is first testing the product at 125°C to simulate extended life for the product and second the 85–85 test (85°C and 85 percent humidity). All products showed more than acceptable tolerance limits in both of these tests. Further, in the design phase we did phosphorus content analysis on the prototypes. This analysis is designed to insure that the phosphorus content is within acceptable limits of tolerance. It showed acceptable tolerance limits for phosphorus.

Since the problem has existed we have ascertained that the failures have almost universally been due to the presence of moisture in the units that have failed. Both accelerated life tests, that is, 125°C and the 85–85 test, show: (1) an initial early life period with relatively few failures, (2) a second exponential failure pattern, and (3) finally a leveling of the failure rate. Because phosphoric acid is not present on the failed circuits, we have not conducted the test for phosphorus content since the failures began.

We are aware that engineering believes the problem may rest with overseas assembly which involves inserting lead wires and adding the plastic encasement. Installation of the wire may leave the pad underneath the wire exposed. However, the presence of moisture on this pad underneath the wire is harmless unless mixed with phosphorus. Since we have found no phosphoric acid, we are inclined to dismiss this concern. The other impact of improper wiring would be a failure of the wire to connect. Since the basic cause of failure is due to moisture, we may dismiss this concern about whether the wires are properly connected.

Report from Quality Control

Quality control engages in a constant testing program on the circuits as they are produced and after they are completed. The microchips that are the heart of the circuit are tested thoroughly so that only acceptable chips have been used. Once the encased circuit is completed, all of the internal circuitry is thoroughly checked and those circuits of improper circuitry are rejected. Upon return of the wired circuits from overseas, all of the circuitry is checked again and those with improper circuitry are rejected. While our rejection rates on this product are high, they have been within expected limits. Some of our testing has been done on a sampling basis rather than a 100 percent inspection basis. Further, the extended life tests and phosphorus content tests are not routinely conducted. We believe we should move to 100 percent inspection throughout the quality control process and routinely conduct extended life tests.

Memo from Production

We have thoroughly reviewed and checked the overseas assembly process and cannot find any weaknesses in the overseas assembly. We believe that the guard ring should be used in our product inasmuch as our competitor's product is not having failure difficulties and it used the guard ring design. Further, we believe a new plastic encasement design should be used, patterned after the plastic encasement design used by our competitor. We agree with the quality control department in endorsing the extended life testing program on all items produced.

ALABAMA CLOTHING, INC.

At 8:45 A.M. on Wednesday, October 8, 1981, two of the owners of Alabama Clothing sat in a meeting room faced with a crucial decision. Dave Edwards and Jim Andrews, the company's President and Executive Vice-President, respectively, had just heard a full confession of embezzlement from the store manager of the most profitable store in the company. By 10:00 A.M., when the store opened, Mr. Edwards and Mr. Andrews had to decide what they would do about this unprecedented problem.

Alabama Clothing

Alabama Clothing Inc., a retail apparel company, catered to people of all ages and incomes. It was located in Alabama, where it was regarded as the state's fashion leader. When it was founded in 1921 by Martin Edwards and Thomas Smith, it consisted of one store in downtown Birmingham. The company built its reputation by demonstrating its belief that the customer was "somebody special" and should, therefore, be treated accordingly. Salespeople strictly abided by the company policy that "the customer is always right" and "no customer should leave unhappy." In addition to the royal treatment from the salespeople, the customer also received free gift wrapping, free alterations, interest-free credit, and an unrestricted merchandise return policy.

Since its founding in 1921, Alabama Clothing has continued to be family-owned and operated. When Martin Edwards died in 1953, his son Charles became President. Eight years later, Mr. Smith retired and his son-in-law, Eric Jones, took his place as Vice President. There were no further management changes until January 1975 when Jim Andrews, an outside professional, was offered the position of Treasurer as well as an option to buy into the company. Jim accepted and began January 1, 1975. Later that same month, Dave Edwards, Charles' son, was promoted from a Division Merchandising Manager to General Merchandising Manager. Finally, in January 1976, Mr. Jones resigned and sold his stock to Mr. Andrews. At the same time, Charles Edwards became Chairman of the Board, Dave succeeded him as President, and Jim Andrews became Executive Vice President (see Exhibit 1).

Eight additional stores had been opened throughout Alabama since 1921. Although the vast majority of its business was clothing, four of the stores had expanded to include housewares and linens. The average store had 50,000 square feet and was run by management consisting of a Store Manager, two Assistant Store Managers, 14 department managers, and as many as 25 Assistant Department Managers (see Exhibit 2).

The number of salespeople per store varied from 64 in the smallest store to 110 in the largest. In 1978, the company instigated a sales development program which was unique in the industry.

The program based its promotions on individual customer sales. Entry-level sales positions (Sales Assistant) were paid an hourly wage plus one percent commission on net sales. When the Sales Assistant's sales reached a specified dollar amount (this specified amount varied with the different departments in the store), he or she was promoted to Sales Associate. At this level, the commission was $1\frac{1}{4}$ percent in addition to the hourly wage. If and when sales reached the next higher specified amount, the person was promoted to Senior Sales Associate (with a commission increase to

---

Source: This case was prepared by Andy Abroms, Curt Leathers, and John Greening under the direction of Associate Professor Jeffrey A. Barach, as a basis for class discussion. It is not intended to illustrate either the effective or the ineffective handling of an administrative situation. Copyright © by the School of Business, Tulane University. Reproduced with permission.

746 Cases

EXHIBIT 1
Organization Chart

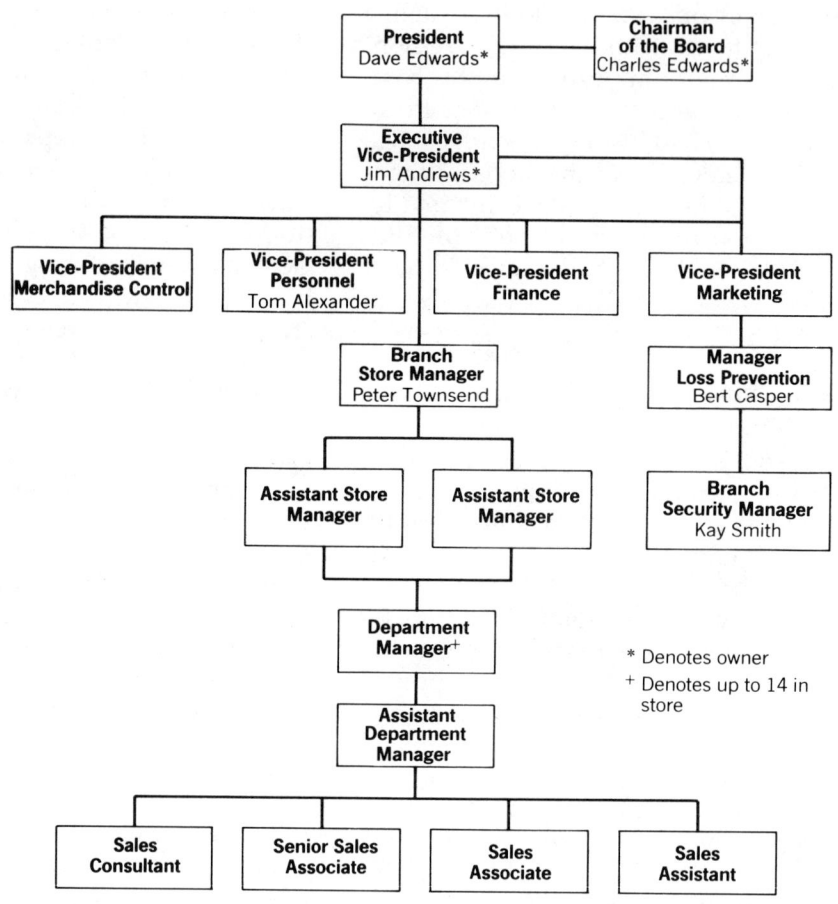

EXHIBIT 2
Dates of Store Openings

Location (Mall)	City	Date Opened
Downtown	Birmingham, AL	April 1921
Riverside	Birmingham, AL	July 1963
Oakwood	Decatur, AL	October 1963
Lakeway	Birmingham, AL	March 1965
Regency	Birmingham, AL	October 1969
Indian Springs	Huntsville, AL	February 1976
Sunshine Valley	Montgomery, AL	August 1979
Glendale	Florence, AL	August 1978
Century	Tuscaloosa, AL	July 1981

1½ percent). At the next sales plateau, the promotion was to Sales Consultant. In addition to 2 percent commission, Sales Consultants received an extra week paid vacation (in addition to the normal two weeks), four personal holidays, subscriptions to trade magazines of their choosing, and an achievement award display in their department. About 15 percent of the salesmen were Sales Consultants and the number-one salesman in the company had net sales in excess of $600,000 per year.

After working for one year, all 2,500 of the company's employees, regardless of status, were included in a profit sharing plan. Employees also were covered by an optional comprehensive health plan, paid 50 percent by the employee and 50 percent by the company.

Peter Townsend

Peter Townsend was born and raised in Birmingham, Alabama. Shortly after graduating from the University of Alabama, he opened his own retail clothing business. After three years of hard work and few results, he sold his business and took a job at Alabama Clothing. During his first three years at the company, he was the buyer of Ladies Coats. As his four children got older and the demands on him to travel to markets became increasingly great, Peter requested a transfer to a branch store. He was transferred to the Regency branch and installed as the store manager. At that time, the Regency branch was 30,000 square feet and did an annual volume of $10,000,000.

Mr. Townsend was liked by everyone in the store. Both the customers and employees knew if they had any problems he would find a solution. In fact, many of the customers would come into the store for the sole purpose of saying hello to him or to show him the most recent pictures of their grandchildren. Townsend was a firm believer that the "customer is always right" and he made absolutely sure that *no* customer left unhappy. Once, for instance, a customer was dissatisfied with a leather jacket he special ordered from the men's department. The customer had ordered this jacket specifically to match his brand new Lincoln Continental, but when the jacket came in, it was a different shade of brown. After learning from the manufacturer that it would be impossible to make a jacket the exact color that the customer wanted, Mr. Townsend had the customer's car painted to match the jacket.

Alabama Clothing Company's policies concerning employee theft and shoplifting were no less defined. Neither action was tolerated by the company and such instances were expected to be immediately disclosed to the District Attorney.

After 13 years at Regency, Peter had built a reputation that was more than respected. The owners regularly received praise from customers who told of how well they were treated at Regency and swore they would never take their business elsewhere. Employees also enjoyed working with Peter and regarded him as a friend, in addition to store manager. The store itself had grown to 75,000 square feet, the biggest of its kind in the city. In 1981, Regency's net sales totaled $23,000,000, the highest of any store in the chain. The employees were happy, the customers were happy, and Peter Townsend, who was earning $61,000 a year, was happy.

His reputation, however, was by no means limited to his managing expertise. Socially, he was regarded by his friends as being the father of one of the community's nicest families. A dedicated father, he always spent time with his family, often planning extravagant family junkets to Hilton Head. His wife and four children were each admired and respected by their peers.

His family was a member of the same country club as both the Edwards family and the Andrews family, where they often played tennis together. All things considered, Peter Townsend was a success in every sense of the word. Recently, however, Townsend had suffered several family traumas. His brother had died a month before and his father had been stricken with a heart attack only a week ago.

Catastrophe

On Tuesday, October 7, Tom Alexander, Vice President of Personnel, called Mr. Andrews to report a serious problem concerning Peter Townsend. An hour later, Mr. Andrews had been briefed by Bert Casper, Director of Loss Prevention, and Mr. Alexander concerning the events since Monday morning.

Early Monday morning, two sales associates approached Kay Smith, Security Manager of the Regency store, with a claim that Mr. Townsend was stealing money from the cash drawer of their department. The two associates were not sure how he was doing this, but they suspected it had something to do with the cash books. Ms. Smith, having assured the informants of their confidentiality, called Bert Casper and gave him a full report. That evening, Bert went to the Regency store and examined Townsend's office. He found two partially used cash books. Since the only person authorized to have possession of the cash books was the Service Desk Manager, Bert became highly suspicious. He noted the serial numbers of the books. He then told Kay Smith to check the departments constantly to see if those books ever turned up on the sales floor. The next morning (Tuesday), Kay found the books in two different departments on the sales floor. She immediately reported this to Mr. Casper who, in turn, reported it to Mr. Alexander.

Still in disbelief, Andrews listened as Bert detailed his suspicions. Bert explained how cash books were delivered from the Service Center in large boxes. Each book consisted of 50 two-part (one part green and one part white) cash tickets and a sheet of carbon. When a salesperson recorded a cash sale, the white copy was given to the customer while the green copy remained in the book.

Whenever a department needed a new cash book, an associate would go to the Service Desk and request one. The Service Desk Manager would take one out of the box and record its serial number on a computer sheet. This recording would put the cash book on "control." At the end of each day, a computer sheet was sent to the Service Center where it was fed into the computer. Also at the end of each day, each department "closed-out" its cash drawer. This was done by adding the total dollar sales reported on each green copy of each book and comparing that total with the total cash in the cash drawer. If all went well, the two totals balanced. If the totals did not balance, the associate in charge of closing-out the cash drawer (every day a different associate was assigned this task) would complete an "over/under" form. He or she would then put the cash, cash books, and "over/under" form into a deposit bag and deliver it to the Service Desk. The Service Desk personnel would reconcile the cash count and send all complete cash books to the Service Center. At the Service Center, a list of these completed books was fed into the computer which verified that every book that went on "control" was returned.

What Peter was doing, Bert reasoned, was taking cash books out of the box before they went on "control." He would place his own cash books in different departments and the salespeople would use them as if they were ordinary cash books. Before the end of the day, Peter would retrieve his cash books, total the amount of sales, and remove that amount of cash from the respective cash drawers. When the drawer was closed-out at night, it would balance and, since the cash books did not go on control, the computer would not record a discrepancy.

What tripped up Townsend, Bert explained further, was the salespeople losing their commission. Most of the salespeople who worked in the store were professionals; they had a pretty good idea of the amount of merchandise they sold in a given week. When the commission fell short of their expectation week after week, they became suspicious and a little more aware of what was going on around the cash drawer. This is how the two associates at Regency became suspicious.

After the three executives thoroughly discussed these suspicions and the consequences, they asked the company lawyer to advise them on how to proceed. The attorney, Mr. Andrews, Mr. Casper, and Mr. Alexander met at the Regency store after Townsend left. Their purpose was to make an in-depth examination of his office. Upon inspection of Townsend's desk, they found the same two cash books that Bert had discovered the night before (which were the sames ones that Kay Smith had found on the sales floor earlier that day), along with $3,000 in cash.

Jim was shattered. His worst suspicions seemed to be true. While the lawyer was making notes on the incident, Mr. Andrew called Dave Edwards (the president) and informed him of the entire story. They decided to sleep on it and make a decision on what to do the next morning. Jim made an appointment with the lawyer for 7:00 A.M. and went home.

After a night of tossing and turning, Mr. Andrews met Mr. Edwards and their lawyer at the lawyer's office. After meeting for an hour, the three men decided to confront Peter with the problem in hopes that he would offer a simple explanation.

When the three men appeared in his office, however, Peter became completely unnerved. Before they could even finish the story of what had happened, he broke down and offered a full confession. Andrews and Edwards were mortified. This long-time friend and fellow employee was looking them in the eye and telling them that he had been embezzling company funds for the last year and a half. His method was exactly what Bert had suspected. The only question the two owners could muster was "Why?" Peter went on to explain that all four of his children were either in college or about to enter, and he simply needed the money. He kept repeating, "I wanted a better life for my family." Finally, Mr. Edwards asked him how much he had stolen, and the reply was "somewhere between $10,000 and $12,000."

When all had been confessed, Mr. Edwards and Mr. Andrews excused themselves to a vacant meeting room. As they sat down, they laid out three possible alternatives for dealing with Townsend. Whichever one they chose, the decision had to be made by 10:00 A.M.

Alternatives

1. *Terminate and Prosecute Peter Townsend.* According to the company's policy regarding employee theft, this was the alternative that should have been chosen. Furthermore, although nothing of this magnitude had ever happened before, Edwards and Andrews felt this action would serve as a deterrent to others. This alternative, however, had four disadvantages. Townsend was so well-known and so well-liked that the social repercussions of such an action might be devastating. The vast numbers of customers and associates of Alabama Clothing that liked Townsend so much might view the company as being ruthless, and thus damage the outstanding reputation the company worked so hard to obtain. Another disadvantage was the timing of the incident. Since Townsend's brother had just died and his father was seriously ill, Edwards and Andrews felt that it might be too much for Townsend's family to have to cope with Peter being prosecuted for embezzling. A third disadvantage was justifying putting a man of Townsend's business and social capabilities in jail. Who would gain if Townsend served a prison sentence? Finally, if the company decided to prosecute, the informants' identities could not possibly be kept confidential. The two informants had been promised confidentiality, and Edwards and Andrews intended to ensure this promise was kept.

2. *Terminate Mr. Townsend.* Edwards and Andrews thought that terminating him might be punishment enough. After all, putting him in jail would not get their money back. It would only serve to hurt Townsend even more. There was one problem with this alternative; Edwards and Andrews did not

know exactly what to say concerning Townsend's departure. They could not announce that he was stealing because they would have to prosecute in conjunction with the company's employee theft policy. Therefore, they had to provide some reason for his dismissal so the employees would be convinced that the appropriate action was taken. The question was whether or not Edwards and Andrews would go out on a limb and announce they terminated him for some other reason, therefore not having to prosecute him.

3. *Ask for Money Back and Don't Terminate Him.* This was the most economical, efficient alternative. Having chosen this alternative, the company would get its money back, no one's life would be ruined, Alabama Clothing would retain a good store manager, and the store's image would not be in jeopardy. A problem, however, would arise if anyone found out that he confessed and no action was taken against him. At the time, the only people who knew were Edwards, Andrews, and their lawyer. Everyone else, including the two associates who brought it to Ms. Smith's attention, merely suspected him. But if anyone found out that Townsend stole thousands of dollars from the store and nothing was done to him, how could the company deal with the next associate who was caught stealing? This alternative would lead to a potential problem of double standards.

With the store opening at 10:00 A.M., a decision was required within an hour and a quarter.

GULF COAST SEAFOOD

Ben Thompson, President and owner of Gulf Coast Seafood, paused to think. It had been a typically long day. All morning had been spent on the phone trying to find several more customers along a proposed delivery truck route to Indiana. Now another problem faced him. While making a final evening walk through his plant, he accidentally discovered two cases of shrimp (worth $600) hidden in the company trash truck. Two long-suspected employees, Jerry Johnson and Jim Avery, probably had some connection with the hidden shrimp. It would be easy to watch the truck and catch the thieves red-handed. Yet Ben's policy until now had been to avoid confrontations with employees suspected of theft. Was this the perfect opportunity to alter that policy? Ben knew he had little time to decide.

Company Background

Gulf Coast Seafood (GCS) was located in a small rural community on the Gulf Coast. Mr. Thompson's father and grandfather started a small operation in 1890. In 1946, Ben joined the business with a desire to expand it. He was a hard worker whose tight-fisted policies and long hours at the plant paid off in significant company growth. By the mid-1960s GCS was recognized as an established seafood distributor. By 1980, GCS's market extended throughout the Southeast with gross sales of $20 million.

The company processed, packed, and distributed oysters, shrimp, and fish as well as other seafood upon request. It also provided a variety of services to local shrimp boat operators. These included sale of fuel, marine sup-

---

Source: This case was written by David Berry and another student who prefers to remain anonymous under the supervision of Associate Professor Jeffrey A. Barach as a basis for class discussion rather than to illustrate either or ineffective administrative practices. Copyright © by the Graduate School of Business Administration, Tulane University. Reproduced with permission.

plies and ice, provision of docks and workspace, and accounting and bookkeeping services.

Mr. Thompson was developing business contacts along the East Coast in hopes of further market expansion. One of his sons, Leon, was studying for an MBA and would soon rejoin the firm. Ben had encouraged Leon to attend graduate school. He thought the professional training would be useful to Leon, as well as the company. Another son, Fred, was currently working for GCS, and a third was just beginning college.

Employee Relations

GCS was a major employer in the area. Plant workers lived in the neighboring small towns and rural communities. The nonunion workforce numbered about 150, depending on the season. Approximately half worked only during the peak season and generally felt no strong loyalty to the company. Others had grown up with the firm, working summers while in high school and full-time upon graduation. Many of the workers had known one another since childhood. The small-town setting provided frequent opportunities for friendly interaction outside of the job.

Mr. Thompson felt he offered competitive wages and tried to "make work" for his full-time employees during slow times of the year. He was always available to pay bail or provide small loans to help workers out of tight spots. He also believed working conditions were very good since his new plant came on-line in 1977. This air-conditioned building was a fivefold expansion of the old facilities. Its modern equipment eliminated much of the strenuous manual labor traditionally associated with the seafood industry.

Although GCS was a major employer, there were a number of other job possibilities. An individual could also farm, work on the shrimp boats, or take a job with one of the numerous support businesses for farming or seafood. Because of the seasonality of the local industry, most of the workforce had some encounter with the GCS plant. For example, during the slow season, many farmers worked on the shrimp boats that used the services provided by GCS. Others, who worked in support industries (like net shops), would make deliveries to the shrimp boats at GCS docks. A person choosing to leave GCS for another job would still have some contact with GCS employees and management.

Management Opinions on the Theft Policy

Until now Mr. Thompson's philosophy had always been to "cover the rat holes." He sought to keep the peace by making sure that a theft could not happen again. For example, numerous locks and one-way seals[1] were used throughout the plant. He felt, in a sense, responsible for the employee pilfering since he controlled the environment that offered the potential for workers to steal. Ben was also anxious not to falsely accuse employees and was not convinced that the hassles of confronting employees were worth the benefits.

Once a local restaurant called to inform him that one of his truck drivers was offering a case of shrimp for sale at a bargain price. Apparently, the driver had slipped the crate on the truck without it being counted by the loader. Mr. Thompson thanked the caller for the information, but never said anything to the driver. He had received several such calls over the past five years. Mr. Thompson knew that if a large theft was discovered it would have to be investigated and the thieves confronted, but so far no such large theft had occurred and no one had ever been fired for stealing.

"Red" Smith,[2] the Manager of the garage was in agreement with Mr. Thompson. His feeling was that if stealing were a continual

---

[1]Seals permit detection of any unauthorized opening of locked areas. The locks had common keys and could be altered to take new keys when necessary (at least once per year).
[2]See Appendix A for a table of key personnel.

problem in large quantities, then it might be necessary to confront employees in order to stop it. "Employees are like children and candy—you have to take the temptation away because they can't resist by themselves. Besides, if you're hungry, five pounds of shrimp feed the family—they might not steal a wrench, but food is different." Mr. Smith believed company policy should be to prevent pilfering and only prosecute large-scale theft. "It's their nature to be dishonest. You have to take the temptation away by following up with paperwork, inventories, and checks and balances. The only time to put your foot down is when somebody is trying to clean out your cooler."

Fred Thompson, Manager of the physical site and refrigeration equipment, shared his father's opinion. "Petty theft can't be stopped. As long as it is kept to a minimum we're OK. The cost would be too high to do something about it. After all, they know when they've been found out, and so do most of the other employees." He believed that trust in the employees bred honesty and distrust bred dishonesty. Further, he thought the establishment and implementation of a formal policy would be a waste of time. "So far it hasn't been necessary to do anything. Daddy's the boss. He owns the company and he can do as he pleases."

Tom Rutherford did not agree with the informal policy of nonconfrontation. He was called the "straw boss" and was responsible for 75 percent of the workforce. His duties included assigning workers to various jobs, monitoring production, and making recommendations for raises, as well as the number of hours individuals should work.

> I don't condone stealing. It's hard to work around people you know are dishonest. I can't see keeping those people around since it makes it hard to delegate responsibility. I let some things slide because of Mr. Thompson's feelings on the matter, but it's getting to be a joke. They're just trying to see how much they can get away with. Besides, if other workers

APPENDIX A
Table of Key Personnel

Name	Age	Position	Previous Employment	Years with GCS	Education
Ben Thompson	58	Owner–manager	U. S. Navy—WWII, ensign's mate	35	High school
Fred Thompson	26	Plant maintenance engineer	Part-time and summers at GCS	10 part-time 4 full-time	4 years college B.A., Economics
Leon Thompson	24	Will take position in marketing	Part-time and summers at GCS	10 part-time	4 years college B.A., Economics MBA—General Administration
"Red" Smith	38	Manager of garage	Family farm and U. S. Army Reserves	12	4 years college B.A., Business Administration
Jack Burnsides	46	Controller and treasurer	U. S. Navy—Lt. Bell Telephone	20	4 years college B.A., Accounting
Tom Rutherford	38	Plant manager	Nichol's Stevedoring Company (six years)	9	3 years college
G. G. Green	28	Electrician	Family electrical business	2	High school
Jerry Johnson	40	Truck driver	U. S. Army	20	High school
Jim Avery	40	Low-level supervisor	U. S. Army	12	High school

see these people getting off scott-free they'll be tempted to steal too.

He also was concerned about GCS's responsibility to the community. "It's like we're harboring criminals. We have some of the dregs of the earth down here working on the boats. I wonder how the community feels about a business that attracts people like that?"

Tom did not believe GCS had a serious problem with theft, but was concerned that the same names were mentioned as suspects whenever anything was missing.

> Not being confronted gives them the idea that anything goes. These guys steal just to steal. They're always bragging about their illegal deer hunting activities. They make sport of dishonesty. In fact, I see a lot more potential dishonesty, but being around production all the time I have the chance to intercept it and straighten things out. I don't report all the suspicious incidents. After all, it's Mr. Thompson's business and he can handle it any way he pleases.

Jack Burnsides, the controller, understood Tom's feelings, but agreed with Mr. Thompson's policy.

> For a long time I thought something should be done. When you're young you may handle things a bit recklessly, but you mellow out with age. More than 10 years ago Ben's policy really upset me. Now I understand his side of it. It's tough to fire someone and then see them at the grocery store or church the next week.

> We had a lawyer advise us once. He said unless we have a very strong case we better be careful, since if we're wrong we're subject to prosecution. We have to weigh the cost of confrontation against the benefits.

> Here at GCS it would be hard to eliminate stealing altogether. To stop it we'd have to take drastic measures, like installing a closed circuit surveillance system. Even if we did catch and prosecute thieves, we wouldn't end the pilfering. All we would probably get is bad press in town.

While admitting he could not know for sure, Mr. Burnsides believed the magnitude of the problem was low.

> We're not losing much, but there is still a shrinkage problem—even with a computerized inventory system and numerous doublechecks. There's nothing to indicate large shortages, but a few years back one truck driver bragged at a coffee shop that he made $40,000 a year by stealing from GCS.[3]

> In the accounting department, we see such large numbers that one hundred pounds of shrimp or two gallons of oysters are relatively small figures. However, it is hard to get managers to watch costs if they see thefts occurring and nothing is done. But, in the last analysis, the Lord forgives, shouldn't we?

The Suspects

Mr. Thompson's prime suspect was Jerry Johnson, 40, who had been with the company over 20 years. He worked part-time while a high-school student. Upon graduation, he worked full-time until he was drafted and rejoined the firm afterwards. Jerry had been involved in a number of suspicious incidents. However, he was the company's best truck driver. Ben knew it was not too difficult to find drivers able to handle a tractor–trailer rig. But he wondered whether a new driver could be trusted any more than Jerry. At least Jerry could be depended upon to take good care of the $100,000 rig and deliver (in acceptable form) 99.9 percent of the $200,000 load of seafood. Yet, Jerry's name was the first mentioned whenever something was missing.

Jim Avery, 40, was a good friend of Jerry's and another prime suspect. He had grown up in the surrounding community and had been

---

[3] It was theoretically possible for the driver's boast to be true. He would need to sell 2–3 cases per week. Normally that amount would be noticed, but if he were collaborating with a loader, it could have happened. Each truck had capacity for 500–600 cases. Mr. Burnsides believed, in this case, it was nothing more than an idle boast.

on the company payroll for 12 years. He was a truck driver until his heart attack. Afterwards he was given a position as a low-level supervisor responsible for loading trucks. Mr. Thompson wondered whether Avery's heart condition might make confrontation and/or dismissal particularly risky to his health. Jim's brother worked full-time in general maintenance and also had a history of heart trouble. Avery's wife had been working for GCS for nine years and was considered a good employee.

The Alternatives

Ben Thompson had a number of options for dealing with the discovered shrimp. The most viable were:

1. Quietly replace the shrimp in the freezer and do nothing.
2. Replace the shrimp, lock the truck and inform the watchman and janitor to report any suspicious activity.
3. Leave the seafood and stake out the truck in hopes of catching and confronting the thieves.
4. Inform the sheriff and have him stake out the truck.

Subsequent Events

Mr. Thompson returned the shrimp to the freezer. Then he went and found one of the spare locks he kept for occasions such as these and padlocked the trash truck. As he left, he instructed the janitor and watchman to be on the lookout. The next morning the security guard related the following incident.

Soon after Ben left, the janitor saw Jerry Johnson talking to the watchman over by the garage. He wondered if Johnson was detaining the guard and hid to see what would happen. G. G. Green, another employee, approached the trash truck and tried to open the door. He noticed the lock, seemed confused, and left. A moment later, Jim Avery approached the truck and went through the same process. Later Johnson, Green, and Avery were seen leaving the grounds together.

Mr. Thompson was surprised that G. G. Green was involved. For years Green's father, an independent electrician, had serviced GCS's electrical repair needs. When Green's father retired two years ago, G. G. was hired by GCS to handle electrical as well as other general repairs. G. G. was an obvious choice since he had worked with his father for a number of years.

It seemed to Ben that Avery and Johnson were a bad influence on young Green. He wondered if his policy of nonconfrontation had actually encouraged Green's involvement (not to mention other employees). He also was concerned about the effect on other employees once news of the incident became widely circulated.

Although Ben expected the stories to cause a stir among company workers, he believed the event was insignificant and not worth any more of his time. In any event, Ben would make sure that, in the future, all bay doors would be locked after hours.

Ben aired the incident among trusted management as the discovery and closure of "another rat hole." Red Smith agreed that the trash truck should have been locked anyway, as a matter of policy since this was a well-known means for stealing goods from businesses. All were disturbed that G. G. Green was involved. They had not believed Green to be so gullible as to join Johnson and Avery.

Postcript

His father's policy on company theft had always bothered Leon Thompson. In speaking with Burnsides on the subject, Leon said:

> Ben missed his opportunity to confront the thieves. They don't have to be fired and prosecuted—jail doesn't do anybody any good. But the situation was perfect for Ben at least to tell the older employees in private, 'Don't put me on the spot like that. The company is changing and some day I'm going to have to put my foot

down!' He could also have scolded Green with a warning, 'Don't let it happen again, or else!'

Burnsides believed the company should voice opposition when the evidence was conclusive.

Leon was in general agreement. He believed the policy should be modified, but was unsure exactly how to proceed.

THE KHASHOGGI AFFAIR

Financial dealings between U. S. corporations and foreign government officials in 1975 and 1976 resulted in the toppling of two Western governments, the resignation of many officials, and numerous public apologies. These financial arrangements (see Exhibit 1) were revealed for the most part during U. S. Senate and SEC hearings examining the practices of multinational corporations. A result of these revelations was Senator Abraham Ribicoff's (D-Conn.) Resolution 265, advocating that business contracts between U. S. nationals and foreign companies or governments be illegal when finder's fees, kickbacks, bribes, or other questionable payments were involved.

Corporations in domestic U. S. operations had long accepted these rules as the norm and usually applied them beyond the levels set by law. Yet, even following the scandals that emerged from the congressional hearings, 48 percent of 531 top and middle managers, representing a broad spectrum of business interests, believed that such practices—including bribery—should be allowed when prevalent in a foreign country. This apparent paradox may be better understood by examining U. S. trade with Saudi Arabia, and the role of one of its most prominent businessmen, Adnan Mohamad Khashoggi.[1]

Saudi Arabia in 1975 was the largest source of surplus investment capital in the world. The earning surpluses amassed by Saudi Arabia and its United Emirate neighbors in 1974 dollars, would in 9.2 years have been sufficient to buy the entire New York Stock Exchange or in 3.2 years all the gold held by central government banks or in 79 days the Exxon Corporation. In 1975, Saudi Arabia's Council of Ministers approved a five-year plan calling for $140 billion in investment in addition to proposed military expenditures. Since 1973, U.S. exports had kept pace with Saudi growth and had accounted for over one-third of Saudi imports. U. S. companies, therefore, were in a good position to obtain a significant portion of this business. But during the period, Japan, Germany, France, and Britain had managed to increase their share of the Saudi market, and any legislation that could be perceived as anti-Arab by the Saudis would threaten the U. S. position in the market.

Adnan Khashoggi has been described as the Rockefeller of the 1970s. Over a 20-year period, he amassed a personal fortune of $100 million and assembled a $400 million financial empire. His Triad Corporation was the first Arab-owned multinational corporation. He controlled 80 percent of Triad's assets, with 10

Source: This case was prepared by Terry White under the supervision of Professor William H. Warren. Permission to use granted by William H. Warren.

[1] Adnan M. Khashoggi has been interviewed by students at the School of Business of The College of William and Mary on three occasions. The first, on February 17, 1975, was conducted on the college campus in Williamsburg, Va. The second was conducted by telephone to Riyadh, Saudi Arabia. The third interview, on October 21, 1975, also was conducted by telephone, in this case to London. At the time of the third interview, Mr. Khashoggi had departed the United States after being issued a subpoena to testify before the Securities and Exchange Commission. Unless noted otherwise, quotations by Mr. Khashoggi presented in this case were derived from one of these interviews.

EXHIBIT 1
Newspaper Article Reporting Political Contributions of U.S. Corporations

Millions Are Involved

(C) New York Times Service

NEW YORK—Following is a compilation of reported payments abroad by American corporations for political contributions, sales commissions, bribes and other purposes that have recently come into question. Many of these payments are legal in the countries where paid, and may or may not violate U.S. law:

ASHLAND OIL CO.: $190,000 to two government officials in Gabon: $40,000 to middlemen in the Dominican Republic; $3,000 to a Libyan official; $100,000 to a consultant in Libya; $30,000 to a Nigerian consultant; $77,500, not accounted for.

CASTLE & COOKE FOODS, INC.: $30,000 a year paid to functionaries in Latin-American governments for several years.

EXXON CORP.: $27 million authorized payments to Italian political parties; $19 million to $22 unauthorized payments to Italian political parties; $1,250,000 to Canadian political parties.

FORD MOTOR CO.: $20,000 a year to Canadian political parties.

GENERAL MOTORS CORP.: $250,000, 1972 political contribution in South Korea; $229,000, 1974 and 1975 contributions to Korean national defense fund; $100,000 to Canadian political parties.

GRUMMAN CORP: $6 million commission paid to consultant to Iran.

GULF OIL CORP.: $4.8 to Democratic Republic party of South Korea; $450,000 to late President Rene Barrientos of Bolivia; $50,000 to pro-Arab publicity campaign in Lebanon.

LOCKHEED AIRCRAFT CORP.: $7.9 million to various foreign officials and consultants; $7.1 million to Yeshio Kodama, Japanese rightist; $2.2 million to Marubeni Corp., Japanese trading firm; $2.2 million to various Japanese officials; $1.1 million to government official in the Netherlands; $112,000 to Mexican officials; $200,000 to senior air force officers in Colombia.

MCDONNELL DOUGLAS CORP.: $2.5 million to unidentified foreign government and air force officials.

MOBIL OIL CORP.: $2 million to Italian political parties.

NORTHROP CORP.: $30 million to foreign consultants; $1.8 million to agents in Switzerland; $450,000 to two Saudi Arabian generals.

PHILLIPS PETROLEUM CO.: $700,000 to foreign officials and consultants.

ROCKWELL INTERNATIONAL: $570,000 to government officials or employees in four foreign governments.

G.D. SEARLES & CO.: $1.3 million to employees of foreign governments.

TENNECO, INC.: $12 million from 1970 to 1975 to overseas lawyers, advisers, consultants, and agents in connection with operations in 24 countries.

UNITED BRANDS CO.: $1.25 million to Honduran government officials.

WHITTAKER CORP.: $75,000 a year paid for six years for foreign tax avoidance purposes.

Source: Richmond Times Dispatch.

percent controlled by each of his two brothers. During the early 1970s he appeared as a "jet-age Bedouin," managing over 70 companies in 35 nations. Khashoggi's wealth was not the result of personal petroleum assets or royal standing. Rather, it originated from his profound abilities as a middleman—an agent.

In Saudi Arabia, wealth is centralized in a very small percentage of the populace. Unlike the United States where wealth is obtained by the citizens and then funneled to the government through taxes, in Saudi Arabia wealth originates with the government through its oil assets and then is distributed to the populace. This centralization of capital with the government officials makes connections and influence with the royal family an essential element of doing business in that country. From birth, although not of royalty, Adnan Khashoggi had access to the royal family. His father, Dr. Mohamed Khashoggi, was Saudi Arabia's first native physician, serving as personal physician to the late King Ibn Saud. Although Adnan chose not to follow in his father's footsteps in medicine, the childhood friendships he established with the royal family became an immense asset in his business endeavors.

By the time Mr. Khashoggi was 28-years-old, he had established himself with the Saudi government as being able to deliver Western products of high quality. At the same time, he was perceived as a most valuable liason and agent by Western companies seeking to do business with the government. In 1964, he signed his first contract with Lockheed Corporation—a $2000 monthly fee to research the market for the F-104 Starfire. Although Mr. Khashoggi failed to make the sale, his direct contacts with the late King Faisal convinced him that a strong market existed in Saudi Arabia for major defense systems. His big breakthrough came in 1965 when he negotiated for Raytheon the $122 million sale of the Hawk surface-to-air missile to the Saudi Defense Ministry. He had by 1977 bought out the Raytheon regional sales company and obtained a $240 million renewal of the Hawk order as well as the accompanying contracts for automatic replacement and spare parts. By 1970 Raytheon's contracts through Khashoggi had exceeded $1.5 billion. Soon Khashoggi found himself providing agent services for the sale of Lockheed's C-130 and L-1011's, Northrop's F-5 fighters, McDonald Douglas, British Aircraft Company, France's national arms-export agency, Belgian ordnance, and Italian military vehicles. His fees for these contracts were as impressive as the list of corporations he served: he received $106 million in commissions from Lockheed, $45 million for the sale of French tanks, and $40 million from Northrop.

It would be incorrect, however, to consider Adnan Khashoggi's business interests as solely devoted to military sales. In fact, over two-thirds of his income was from nonrelated areas. He was the sales agent for Chrysler trucks and cars: for these services he received over $50 million in commissions (15 percent of sales) over the past 20 years. He owned a government granted 50-year monopoly on the development of gypsum deposits in Saudi Arabia. Furthermore, he invested heavily in real estate in the American Southwest, with a majority interest in two banks in California (now divested), and contemplated constructing a $1 billion trade center in Egypt—complete with the erection of a new pyramid and a Disneyland-equivalent amusement park nearby.

But what did Mr. Khashoggi have to do with Senator Ribicoff's Senate Resolution? In March 1975, as Mr. Khashoggi landed in his private jet at Las Vegas, the SEC presented him with a subpoena to testify before them. Khashoggi refused to accept it, left for the Caribbean, and has not returned to the United States since. Earlier Senate and SEC hearings had disclosed that many large American companies—among them Northrop and Lockheed—had been paying large sums to bribe and influence government officials of foreign nations. The Northrop Corporation charged that Mr. Khashoggi had demanded $450,000 to bribe two Saudi generals to influence defense contracts on purchase of the F-5 aircraft. Another document released by Northrop reported that

> A Saudi Prince approached a representative of Northrop at the time of a major contract signing and indicated he deserved a commission on the sale and not in the case of government-to-government sales such as the one under discussion. Representatives of the Saudi govern-

ment also approached the Northrop representative and indicated that there was a disagreement with the Prince and they considered this to be most unfortunate, and hoped that things would be worked out to his satisfaction.

Lockheed's Chairman of the Board, Daniel J. Haughton, did not specify any specific cases of bribery, but noted that Mr. Khashoggi had received $106 million in agent's fees between 1970 and 1975. He testified that Mr. Khashoggi had told him that bribes were necessary and that some of the fees paid to him were used for that purpose. Furthermore, he revealed that other Lockheed officials had been told directly by Saudi government officials that payment of bribes would be necessary and that, in addition to those funneled through Mr. Khashoggi, payments had been made directly to Saudi officials through bank accounts in Switzerland and Lichtenstein.

Moreover, both companies testified that they believed it impossible to do business in Saudi Arabia without the utilization of Mr. Khashoggi or some other prominent agents. In fact, Khashoggi had maintained a virtual monopoly over Saudi Defense Ministry contracts. According to one source, he had gathered 80 percent of the contracts from that office. There was no doubt that he enjoyed an extremely close rapport with the Saudi Minister of Defense, Prince Sultan.

In light of Senator Ribicoff's resolution, the case writers in an interview with Mr. Khashoggi attempted to discriminate between finder's fees, kickbacks, and bribes—and whether Saudi cultural recognizes any distinction for indeed in many cases one may result in providing the medium for the other. Addressing this issue, Mr. Khashoggi said,

> I regret that Senator Ribicoff has not differentiated between kickbacks, bribes, and finder's fees because he has destroyed the free enterprise system by even suggesting to mix the three together. And if this is the goal, he will succeed because finder's fees are part of your system. Banks get finder's fees, real estate agents get finder's fees, manufacturer's representatives get fees, marketing organizations get their fees.

Many countries in the Middle East actually require by law that agents be utilized on government contracts involving foreign corporations. In exploring this issue with Mr. Khashoggi, the casewriters learned that an underlying issue was a distrust of foreigners, which can be reduced by dealing with a middleman of a common culture. In some cases, religion provided this basis. Mr. Khashoggi emphasised that Muslims "have to go to prayer five times a day. It is not just a Sunday prayer." He emphasized that the religious process was a continual "checking of your own morals, and that is why we feel morals are very high, and you can make a deal by shaking hands—and that is it. A man sticks to it." The need for Westerners to have 10 or so lawyers always available for advice has partially led to this distrust of foreigners, according to Mr. Khashoggi. Consequently, except for military hardware, the Saudi government requires that an agent be involved, and the agent must be Muslim.

There is also the matter of the Arabic language's complexity. The degree of complexity involved may best be indicated by citing the periods required by the U. S. Defense Language Institute to study various languages; for the Romance languages 24 weeks of intensive study are involved, 32 weeks for German, 62 weeks for Mandarin Chinese, and 85 weeks for Arabic. Unfortunately, there have been business contracts concluded wherein Western manufacturers were unaware, because of language misinterpretations, of the total job requirements. The ill will resulting from such misunderstandings, both on the part of the purchaser and the seller, has encouraged Arab nations to insist on the use of Arab agents.

Another major reason for Arab insistence on the use of agents was because of the sophistication of the modern equipment being sought. In many cases the Saudi government did not have the expertise to screen out all the offers it receives. In one such case involving a decision as to which of two jet aircraft to purchase, the King of one Arab nation sent his son to the United States to test fly each of the aircraft and make the decision. The Prince, who had less than 500 hours flight time, concluded that both were good aircraft and therefore each should be purchased. The two aircraft were designed for the same tactical mission, and therefore the purchase of both provided no strategic advantage, only the coupled costs and difficulties of providing a redundant logistics base for each. Such examples led the Arab nations to rely more heavily on the expertise of agents in evaluating and screening systems.

Even when not required by law, agents may be a necessity when dealing with Arab nations. There is a classical example of a new vice president of a U. S. firm who, after reviewing company agent's fees, decided that the agent's contract could be cancelled. All that the company had in the country at that time was a continuous, but lucrative servicing contract that had been negotiated years before. Within 48 hours after the agent had been cancelled, all local work permits of the company's employees were withdrawn. Needless to say, the agent was reinstated.

It would be inaccurate for one to assume that agents serve only the purchaser. While in earlier times in Saudi Arabia agent's fees were paid by the purchaser, today they are paid by the seller. Even if the above situation could be reversed, it is doubtful that U. S. companies could operate in Saudi Arabia successfully without an agent and without agent's services. Over and above the language problems, most U. S. businessmen simply did not have the patience and cultural understanding to tolerate the procedures required to obtain permits in Saudi Arabia.

According to Mr. Khashoggi, the personal gifts and individual attention he gave to the royal family were not a "bribe," but the expected social interactions. He related that at one time he was told by the royal family of a Bedouin school in one locality that needed textbooks. Mr. Khashoggi provided them—without reimbursement. He was told that a Bedouin chief near the boarder with Yemen needed 12 trucks to transport his goats back and forth from one oasis to another. He provided them—without compensation. Although these practices may seem questionable in western culture, Mr. Khashoggi reported that it was considered as loyalty to the royal family. He further ridiculed reports that he used such favors to influence Prince Sultan and other members of the royal family. He reminded the case writers that the royal family initially owned all the wealth represented by the oil reserves and that what they chose to distribute to the country was their prerogative.

The financial costs associated with establishing one's base may also far exceed expectations of American businesses. Saudi regulations require that companies with as few as 40 employees provide their own housing and arrange for local transportation, because of the degree to which these facilities have been overtaxed. Furthermore, although a company may be able to develop a successful negotiating team, this would probably be inadequate. Because of the harsh environment, limited social opportunities, and strict Muslim standards for women, companies have found that half of the managers they send are unwilling to remain in the country for over one year.

The case writers asked Mr. Khashoggi what an agent did to earn his commission.

> Some people seem to have the idea that maybe I met somebody in a bar recently and said 'I have friends and I can get your contract approved if you make it worthwhile for me.' Well the real story is quite the opposite. We have worked for 20 years to establish the offices and staff and know-how in both Saudi Arabia and with American business to do this work.
>
> As you know, if you do not have someone to show you around and tell you what to do or who to meet, it is very difficult for you, as a

stranger, to be able to market your product there. So, the local agent plays this important role. But if he is not also efficiently organized to follow-up later, then the whole effort of the visit can fall apart.

Additionally, Mr. Khashoggi had elsewhere noted that the agent in reality was the risk taker.

> They take the risk of introducing the product into the market, and receive what's due to them only if they succeed in selling the product. If they don't they lose out. Because of that, the most important function of an agent is to evaluate the kind of products that can be sold in the area. If we select a good product, we stand a good chance of selling it.

He also pointed out to the case writers that although his fees may have seemed high, his investment was quite large. For example, although his commission from Lockheed was approximately $106 million, he had invested over $3 million in selling Lockheed's products before he was able to break into the market. If he had not been successful, that loss would have been his. The cost, including spare parts, of a single L-1011 was a little over $17.5 million. Furthermore, the $106 million received was earned over a period of 15 years, so that the annual fees were approximately $7 million. In the case of Northrop where he received $40 million, he noted, "my estimate is that we invested $6 million to $9.5 million in managerial overhead and services in helping Northrop on the pending contract."

One of the best summaries of what was expected of an agent has been reported in *The Saudi Arabia Market, a Guide for U. S. Businessmen*, published by the U. S. Department of Commerce. According to that publication, agents routinely provided for such necessities as visas and arranging for meetings of company officials with government personnel, and for a higher level, a good local representative maintains close contacts with the various ministries in order to obtain timely information on upcoming contracts. If he is aggressive, he convinces officials that his principal's product or service is unique. A comparison of this statement with Northrop's contract with Mr. Khashoggi's Triad Corporation provided no apparent inconsistencies.

Why then was the Church Subcommittee on Multinational Corporations so concerned with the role of agents if agents' fees in themselves in most cases were not illegal? The problem seemed to be with the role of the agent. The Chairman of Lockheed's testimony revealed that Mr. Khashoggi told him that part of his fees were used as bribes. The role thus permitted bribery without the direct contact of the corporation. Also, if the agent was able to influence government officials (this is suggested to be his primary purpose), is it not conceivable that he would sell that nation the product for which he is offered the highest commission? Considering that the product may or not be that which is best suited for national interests, this became especially critical in sales involving military equipment.

According to congressional testimony, the influence of a local agent on procurement, as one example, resulted in the purchase of an aircraft that had been plagued with maintenance problems. Because of these maintenance difficulties, the country had been unable to maintain a readiness posture of more than three aircraft in an operationally ready status at any one time. The same agent was also influential in selling a European-built vehicle that was totally incompatible with the harsh desert operating conditions. The result was a 100 percent failure of the vehicles during the hot summer months. Such events were not only potentially catastrophic during military operations, but could be politically embarassing for the nation of the seller as well.

In many cases, the reliability of a company's military products was viewed, whether fairly or not, as an indication of the technological expertise and integrity of the selling nation because it allowed the sale of those products to its allies. There was also the obvious factor that the United States had a vital interest in ensuring that its allies possessed tactically and technically proficient weapons systems. It could not afford for the level of an agent's commission to be the deciding factor. Mr. Khashoggi acknowledged that at one time this could have happened. "If the British paid higher commissions, then I could get a higher commission, and they got the business," he said.

Because of the national defense implications involved, Iran, Kuwait, Israel, and Saudi Arabia have forbidden agent's fees in the sale of weapons themselves. However, these restrictions did not apply to system components, update modifications, or supply parts. Consequently, manufacturers continued to maintain agents in these countries. Furthermore, since they stood to gain profits in the field of systems components, it is likely that the agents did attempt to influence original purchases. On this point, Mr. Khashoggi said "I think business has to be build around the package—(1) the product, (2) the market, and (3) the incentive for both sides."

The Senate hearings however, produced accusations of direct bribery. Northrop presented documents indicating that they had paid $450,000 to Mr. Khashoggi, earmarked for two Saudi generals. The money was intended to influence their support for the procurement of Northrop's F-5 fighter. According to Northrop officials, Khashoggi requested this sum of money in addition to his commission fees in order to assure the generals' cooperation. Northrop personnel knew that one of the generals involved had previously presented problems to Northrop and feared that he might do the same again.

In an overseas telephone interview with the case writers, Mr. Khashoggi countered the Northrop accusations by saying that payment of the generals was entirely Northrop's idea and that he refused to complete the transaction. He claimed that Northrop was "concerned about General Hashim at that time and wanted to reach him because they were afraid that maybe he had already been approached by Lockheed." Mr. Khashoggi related,

> The final report of Northrop, which is public knowledge by now, showed that their earlier report ignored the fact that they issued a check for $200,000 in the name of the general, and that when I was confronted with the fact that this check was to be delivered to the general, I stopped them from ruining their reputation and our reputation, the government's, and everybody's. At that time you know I had my own differences with them on certain fees and compensations, as you see it is in the minutes of the Ernst and Ernst report. So it was a good opportunity for me to—what can we call it—penalize them or take advantage of the situation or whatever it was, to collect our fees which were due to us. On this issue of the generals which we stopped them from making a mistake, I must stress at this point that you do not have to bribe to do business in the area if you are organized properly and you are doing a professional job. Their actions (Northrop's) were typical of the naivety of a salesman.

Although the Senate hearings concluded that there was no way to ascertain with certainty whether Mr. Khashoggi or Northrop suggested the payment to the generals, some facts were uncontested. First, Northrop wrote the checks with the intent of influencing the F-5 decision. Second, no proof was ever provided showing that Mr. Khashoggi had requested payment to the generals. Third, Mr. Khashoggi acknowledged receipt of the checks and the fact that he kept them. Fourth, and perhaps as important as any fact, there has been a great misunderstanding in the Western world of the term *baksheesh*, the traditional payment in the Arab world for favors received. To mistake what the Saudis regarded as a form of good manners for low-level graft was an error that had proven costly to many Western businessmen.

After the Senate Hearings

Mr. Khashoggi, American business, and the Arab government officials were to different degrees affected by the Church Committee hearings and continued repercussions internationally were expelled. Mr. Khashoggi was denied payment of his fees from Northrop. Mr. Khashoggi believed, however, that he would eventually receive all of his compensation. But why did he refuse to appear before the SEC hearings if, as he claimed, he did nothing illegal? Mr. Khashoggi told the case writers that he could produce letters wherein he offered to provide the SEC any documentation that it required, and agreed to allow them to question him outside the United States if it would aid in their investigation. He strongly contended however, that he should not be involved in proceedings that would influence U.S. policy. He told the case writers:

> I think what happened in the U. S. is an international affair, but it is something which you are involved with in your own companies and your own morals. God bless you. Whatever you think is best for your country, do it. But, according to the words of His Majesty the late King Faisal, 'we are not going to be involved in the business of influencing the American people in one way or the other. And, Americans between themselves should settle their own issues, and we should not be part of them . . . only those that are American should be talking to Americans.' (Khashoggi had, in fact, presented this argument on several occasions before the hearings had been suggested.)

The second party of interest, American business, found itself internationally in much the same position it had been in on pollution control before the federal government mandated national policies on pollution abatement and control. A company attempting to maintain higher pollution standards than the norm was at a competitive disadvantage. The more consciencious firms that made unrequired pollution expenditures would have found themselves being squeezed out of the market. In the same sense that state laws could not resolve the problems and it was left to the federal government do so, U. S. legislation on ethical standards may be insufficient in an international environment. During the Senate hearings, however, Senator Church said, "I find it hard to believe that governments could resist an agreement of that kind (to prevent bribes and payoffs) if it was universal and applied to all arms manufacturing companies."

Mr. Baughton (CEO of Lockheed), however, was less than optimistic about the ratification of such an agreement. He presented for the record an article written by a French correspondent entitled "Bribes Boost French Arms." According to the article, the French Defense Ministry, nicknamed by many the "Ministry of Bribes," not only condoned such practices, but strongly encouraged them as a means of boosting French exports and enhancing France's international position. Mr. Haughton concluded,

> I am not arguing that it is a good practice and I am not arguing that it is a necessary practice. I am saying unless everybody plays by the same set of rules, if you are going to win, it is necessary. It is a competitive choice you have when you decide whether to get out of the competition and lose it or compete and lose it, or whether you want to play by the same set of rules as your competitors.

Although it cannot be concluded that Mr. Khashoggi's affairs were a cornerstone of U.S.–Arab relations, there was little doubt that how Arab business interests are welcomed does play a major role. At the time of the Senate hearings, the Saudi Ambassor, Ali A. Alireza, complained officially to the State Department about the "harassment" of Mr. Khashoggi. Prince Sultan agreed that bribery would be punished if discovered, but stressed "the right to make a profit and the agent's right to compensation." He denounced the "fake concern being shown for methods of concluding commercial deals," and said that the aim is "to undermine the standing and harm the reputation of Arabs."

There was also a question on the part of the Arabs as to whether Arab money has not been "painted a different color." They noted that Senator Church, Chairman of the Senate Subcommittee, long had been a strong supporter of Israel. Following 20 years of American foreign policy in the Middle East, the American outrage over the oil embargo of 1973, and rising fears of Arab economic dominance, Saudi claims may have been at least in part, valid. Mr. Khashoggi explained to the William and Mary student case writers in February 1974, "we are trapped in a political atmosphere and also in the oil problem. People are mixing this with individual investments, and so we are in a hostile attitude (in America)."

This hostile attitude was in part confirmed by the newspapers' accounts of the October 1975 interview with Mr. Khashoggi. Students who participated in the interview were astonished at the derogatory tone of the accounts. This generally expressed attitude was best summed up by one of the students:

> I think the newspapers wrote their respective articles as they did because they were trying to feed the public information which it wanted to hear. . . . These papers, which must rely on the public for support, must dress Arabs in the color of black to generate public interest.

A COMMUNITY COALITION PLANS A CONFERENCE ON EMPLOYEE ASSISTANCE PROGRAMS

In 1984, a coalition of community organizations in a Midwest city planned a national conference dealing with the issues of employee assistance programs in business and industry. As a board member of one organization, this case writer fortuitously had access to documents and observation of formal and informal activities characterizing the conflict that emerged between the coalition and a local labor union over the choice of a nonunion hotel for the conference site. The coalition consisted of the Occupational Programming Division of a local medical center, the local chapter of the National Council on Alcoholism, and a local community college department representative for alcohol studies. The Association of Labor/Management Administrators and Consultants on Alcoholism, Inc. was listed as a sponsor, but was not involved in the planning of the conference.

Ensuing events and activities of the conference coalition and the local labor union officials to resolve the conflict illustrate a matrix of independent and dependent relations challenged in the process as vested interests are disturbed and new issues emerge. The critical issue of the case focuses on the local chapter of the National Council on Alcoholism withdrawing as one of the conference sponsors. The purpose of this case is to examine current decision models and to apply decision analysis skills to a decision dilemma in one empirical setting.

Background

Policy makers in labor, business, and industry, who are continually concerned about improving productivity and performance, have given serious attention in recent years to various forms of employee assistance programming. Among these forms of assistance are recovery programs for employees who are having drinking problems. During the 1970s, au-

---

Source: This case was prepared by Joseph P. Caliguri. Permission to use granted by Joseph P. Caliguri.

thorities in the field of alcoholism assisted business and industry organizations that wished to assist alcoholic employees in lieu of dismissal as the only alternative. Some of the major issues emerging from development of employee assistance programming relate to cost-effectiveness, legal aspects of confidentiality, employee and company rights, financial costs of insurance and health care because of illness and premature death of employees, different referral procedures, and the search for advanced intervention techniques. The conference referred to in this case was to be an annual event on employee assistance programming. Its intent was to present some of the most knowledgeable authorities to address the issues mentioned previously for the participants who had policy administration responsibilities in their organizations.

Definition of Terms

Synoptic–Rational Model—Selecting the best course of action when a decision-maker has a clear goal, identifies various alternatives to achieve the goal, and considers probabilities related to possible outcomes for each alternative. Evaluation of a decision is summative–judgement about the selected alternative having the expected result.

Incremental Model—Alternative solutions that differ only slightly from existing policy are considered, and that, if chosen, would cause only incremental change from the status quo. Decisions are pragmatic and subject to negotiation among many actors to accommodate various values through consensus.

Politics—The art of appropriate decision-making when there is disagreement concerning goals in deference to consensus decision-making by reasonable actors.

Coercive Power—is based on fear. A leader scoring high in coercive power is seen as inducing compliance because failure to comply will lead to punishments such as undesirable work assignments, reprimands, or dismissals.

Connection Power—is based on the leader's "connections" with influential or important persons inside or outside the organization. A leader scoring high in connection power induces compliance because others aim at gaining the favor or avoiding the disfavor of the powerful connection.

Legitimate Power—is based on the position held by the leader. The higher the position, the higher the legitimate power tends to be. A leader scoring high in legitimate power induces compliance from or influences others because they feel that this person has the right by virtue of position in the organization to expect that suggestions be followed.

Reward Power—is based on the leader's ability to provide rewards for other people. They believe that their compliance will lead to gaining positive incentives such as pay, promotion, or recognition.

Dispute Over Hotel Site
Mars Management Conference

In October 1984 plans were made by a coalition of organizations to hold an Employee Assistance Programming Industrial Workshop during a week in October 1985 in a Midwest city. The purposes of the workshop were to attract labor and major business representatives who would pay $250 to $350 to participate and to raise funds to finance future programs.

But, an intense disagreement sparked by a local union labor leader about a nonunion hotel site selected for the conference two months before the conference date resulted in almost two-thirds of the scheduled speakers (who had ties to organized labor) cancelling their appearance.

Charges and countercharges began to escalate on the issue. In a newspaper account, the coordinator of the event, a director of a local community college Alcohol Studies department exclaimed, "local labor leaders are incensed because they were not invited as main speakers, especially John Jones of the United Labor Member Assistance Program."

Mr. Jones retorted, "being bypassed as a speaker was neither here nor there, it's a non-union hotel and I am not going to participate."

Another employee of the United Labor Member Assistance Program called the charges against Jones very untrue. He said that the local hotel–motel workers union here were angered by national advertisements of the conference as a joint labor–business event. He added, "they are on the pity pot for not doing their homework."

The coordinator explained that the hotel was chosen after an extensive search found that the only available unionized hotels were already booked or were inappropriate. Subsequent to these charges, Blue Cross–Blue Shield as a support organization dropped out to avoid the risk of offending the local labor council. The local chapter of the National Council on Alcoholism in an August 26, 1984 meeting of its executive committee and other representatives of the coalition sponsoring the conference concluded that:

> The two conditions for continued participation of the local chapter on alcoholism had not been met. These conditions were: (1) move the conference to a union hotel, and (2) encourage Mr. Jones of the local labor council to accept a main speaker invitiation for the conference. After extensive discussion, the executive committee thanked the conference coalition representatives and a motion to withdraw as a co-sponsor was carried without opposition.

The Director of the alcohol agency stated:

> We are largely financed by United Way and do not want to jeopardize its contributions to our agency. Labor has strong influence on the United Way Board. We have withdrawn because of pressures applied from a variety of sources having to do mainly with unions. It's a no-win situation. If we alienate unions, we cut ourselves off from that segment of the population. The sad part is that our intent was to help people learn to deal with alcoholism on the job. We were prepared to allocate $7000 from an industrial grant fund we have to support the conference.

The Medical Center that had donated $10,000 to promote the conference remained as the sponsor along with the community college. The Medical Center also offers business and industry organizations a consultant fee service to assist them in developing their own employee assistance programs. It was interested in conducting a conference every year to raise funds for the coalition as well as to develop contacts among national leaders in the field.

On September 23, 1984, the Executive Director of the Alcohol Chapter made the following comments in an informal interview with the case writer:

> In retrospect, our agency yielded to political pressures to withdraw in order to sustain our funding level with United Way in the future. I feel that we have lost some independence as an agency in requesting funds from United Way on the basis of merit—our worth to the community, so to speak.
>
> On the other hand, we have never participated in a coalition sponsorship of a program, had no policy or guideline procedures, but for sure we learned that protocol is very important to labor unions. You have to check with union leaders on such things as hotel sites and leadership participation in any activity that affects their union people.
>
> Also, let's face it, they have their own alcoholism assistance programs and we are competing with them for funds and prestige in the field of alcoholism.
>
> I've realized that we need to get a strong labor representative from their central labor council on our board to facilitate better communication and cooperation with labor. On a last point, I have met with members of the Central Labor Council here. They are displeased with Mr. Jones' tough tactics and actions and there is agreement that for future conferences a protocol link will be established with them.
>
> Despite the setbacks and ensuing attempts to resolve the conflict, the coordinator of the conference acquired replacements with less national prestige for the lectures.

THE CLASSIC CAR CLUB OF AMERICA

The Collector Car Hobby

The collector car hobby in the United States is a broad and wide-reaching activity involving a large number of Americans. Basically, a "collector car" is any automobile owned for purposes other than normal transportation. The most widely read collector car magazine, *Hemmings Motor News*, had a circulation of over 210,000 in March 1984, and its circulation has been steadily growing for many years. Thus, a figure of 250,000–300,000 would probably be a conservative estimate of the number of Americans engaged in this hobby.

Collector car is a loose term, ranging from turn-of-the-century "horseless carriages" to currently built, but limited-production cars, such as Italian super-sports cars and American convertibles. Naturally, owners of collector cars enjoy the company of other persons with similar interests, and thus, a wide variety of car clubs exist to suit almost any particular segment of this vast hobby. The largest of these clubs, the Antique Automobile Club of America, caters to owners of virtually all cars 25 years old or older, and in 1984, was close to achieving a membership level of 50,000.

History and Background

The Classic Car Club of America, Inc. (CCCA) was formed in 1952 by a small group of enthusiasts interested in the luxury cars of the late 1920s and 1930s. Certain high-priced, high-quality, and limited production cars were designated as "Classic Cars," and the peiord of 1925–1942 was chosen as the limits of the "Classic Era." It was felt that cars built prior to 1925 had not yet reached technical maturity, and that after World War II, the quality of most so-called luxury cars had succumbed to the economic pressures of mass production.

Over the years, the list of CCCA-recognized Classics was modified and expanded, and the time period was extended to 1948 to include certain pre-WWII models that continued in production for a few years after the war. Although all cars included on the list were of considerably higher price and quality than the mass-production cars of the era, there was also a wide variance in original price and quality of these recognized Classics. For example, in 1930 a new Ford Model A (not a Classic) cost about $450. Two of the many CCCA-recognized Classics of 1930 are the Auburn Eight, priced as low as $1195, and the Duesenberg Model J, which sold in the $12,000–$14,000 range. The Auburn, although a car of middle price and quality, is considered a Classic because its styling was exceptional at the time, while the Duesenberg was the highest priced and most exotic American car of its era, carrying custom-built bodies and bought by an exclusive clientele of movie stars, playboys, and other super-rich personalities. Most classics fell somewhere between these two extremes, with original prices in the $2000–$5000 range. Table 1 lists those cars recognized as CCCA in 1984.

CCCA Activities and Organization

When the CCCA's fiscal year ended on October 31, 1983, the club had 4560 members as indicated here:

Active (regular membership—1983 dues $25/yr)   3796
Associate (for spouses, no publications—$3/yr)   578
Life (one-time charge of $350 after 10 years) 142
Life Associate (spouse of Life—$35)   37
Honorary (famous car designers, etc)   7
    4560

CCCA members receive a variety of benefits from their membership. A magazine, *The Classic Car*, is published four times a year.

Source: This case was prepared by Matthew C. Sonfield. Permission to use granted by Matthew C. Sonfield.

TABLE 1
CCCA-Recognized Classic Cars

A. C.	Farman*	Moon*
Adler*	Fiat*	Nash*
Alfa Romeo	Franklin*	Packard*
Alvis*	Frazer–Nash*	Peerless*
Amilcar*	Graham–Paige*	Peugeot*
Armstrong–Siddeley*	Hispano–Suiza*	Pierce–Arrow
Aston Martin*	Horch	Railton*
Austro–Daimler	Hotchkiss*	Raymond Mays*
Auburn*	Hudson*	Renault*
Ballot*	Humber*	Reo*
Bentley	Invicta	Revere
Benz*	Isotta-Fraschini	Riley*
Blackhawk	Itala	Roamer*
B. M. W.*	Jaguar*	Rohr
Brewster*	Jensen*	Rolls–Royce
Brougham Superior*	Jordan*	Ruxton
Bucciali	Julian*	Squire
Buick 90	Kissell*	S. S. Jaguar
Bugatti	Lanchester*	Stearns–Knight
Cadillac*	Lancia*	Stevens–Duryea
Chrysler*	Lagonda*	Steyr*
Cord	La Salle*	Studebaker*
Cunningham	Lincoln*	Stutz
Dagmar*	Lincoln Continental	Sunbeam*
Daimler*	Locomobile*	Talbot*
Darracq*	Marmon*	Talbot-Lago
Delage*	Maserati*	Tatra*
Delaunay Belleville*	Maybach	Triumph*
Delahaye*	McFarlan	Vauxhall*
Doble	Mercedes	Voisin
Dorris	Mercedes–Benz*	Wills Ste Claire*
Duesenberg	Mercer	Willys–Knight
du Pont	M. G.*	
Excelsior*	Minerva*	

*Indicates that only certain models of this make are considered classic and/or post-WW II models require individual approval from the club for classic status.

High in quality, it features full-color photos of classics on the front and back covers, 48 pages of articles and black-and-white photos of classics, and a list of CCCA activities. A CCCA *Bulletin* is also published eight times per year, and contains club and hobby news, technical columns, and members' and commercial ads for classic cars, parts, and related items. A further publication is the club's *Handbook and Directory*, published annually. It contains the CCCA bylaws, judging rules, etc., as well as a listing of current members and the Classic Cars they own.

The CCCA also sponsors three national events each year. The Annual Meeting in January includes business meetings and a car-judging meet, and is held in a different location in the United States each year. In July, a series of "Grand Classic" judging meets are held simultaneously in a number of locations around the country. In 1983, 365 classics were judged or exhibited at six different Grand Classics from coast to coast. At CCCA judging meets, cars are rated by a point system that takes into account the authenticity of restoration and the general condition of the car, both cosmetically and mechanically.

Each summer the club sponsors one or more "Classic CARavans" in various parts of the United States and Canada. The CARavan is a tour in which more than 100 classics join together in a week-long planned itinerary.

The CCCA also has available technical advisors to assist members, and makes available for sale to members certain club-related products, such as hats and ties with a classic car design.

The club is managed by a 15-person Board of Directors, with President, Vice Presidents, Treasurer, Secretary, etc. All are club member volunteers (from all over the United States), who have shown a willingness and ability to help run the CCCA, and have been elected by the total membership to three-year terms of office. They are not reimbursed for their expenses, which include attending monthly board meetings, most of which are held at headquarters offices that are rented in Madison, New Jersey. The only paid employees of the club are a part-time secretary and the publications editor. An organization chart of the CCCA is shown in Table 2.

In addition to belonging to the National CCCA, the majority of members also pay dues and belong to a local CCCA Region. In 1984 there were 24 regions throughout the United States. (See Table 3.) Each region sponsors a variety of local activities for members and their Classics, and publishes its own magazine or newsletter. Many of the regions also derive revenues from the sale of Classic Car replacement parts or service items, offered to all members of the national club.

Current Problems that Face CCCA

Although the officers and directors of the CCCA believe the club to be strong, both financially and in its value to its members, a variety of concerns about the future exist. As indicated in the financial statements provided in Table 4, the CCCA experienced a small negative cash flow for the 1983 fiscal year.

Of primary concern is the effect of inflation on the club's ability to maintain its current level of service and benefits to the membership. In particular, the cost of publications, headquarters office administration, and rent have risen considerably in recent years. The Board of Directors has responded by both watching costs carefully and raising dues several times, but it recognizes that certain cost increases are unavoidable, and that raising dues too high will result in a loss of members.

One way to overcome this problem is to increase the number of members and, thus, create greater revenues for the club. The directors know that many Classic owners do not belong to the CCCA. Although CCCA members owned about 6500–7000 Classics in 1983, no one really knows how many Classics and owners are not in the club. Club efforts in recent years to increase membership have been targeted at these Classic-owning non-CCCA members. Letters have been sent to past members who failed to renew their CCCA membership (about 5–10 percent each year), region officers have contacted local non-CCCA members known to own Classics, and a few articles about CCCA activities, as well as paid CCCA membership advertisements have been placed in old-car hobby magazines.

Furthermore, although some CCCA members do not own classics, most do, for much of the pleasure of belonging to the club derives from participating in the various activities with a Classic Car. Thus, although Classic enthusiasts who do not own a Classic might also be an appropriate target for CCCA new membership efforts, the primary focus has been on persons currently owning a Classic.

Unless the listing of recognized Classics is expanded, the number of Classics in existence is fixed, and with it, by and large, the number of Classic owners. There are varying opinions

TABLE 2
Organization Chart

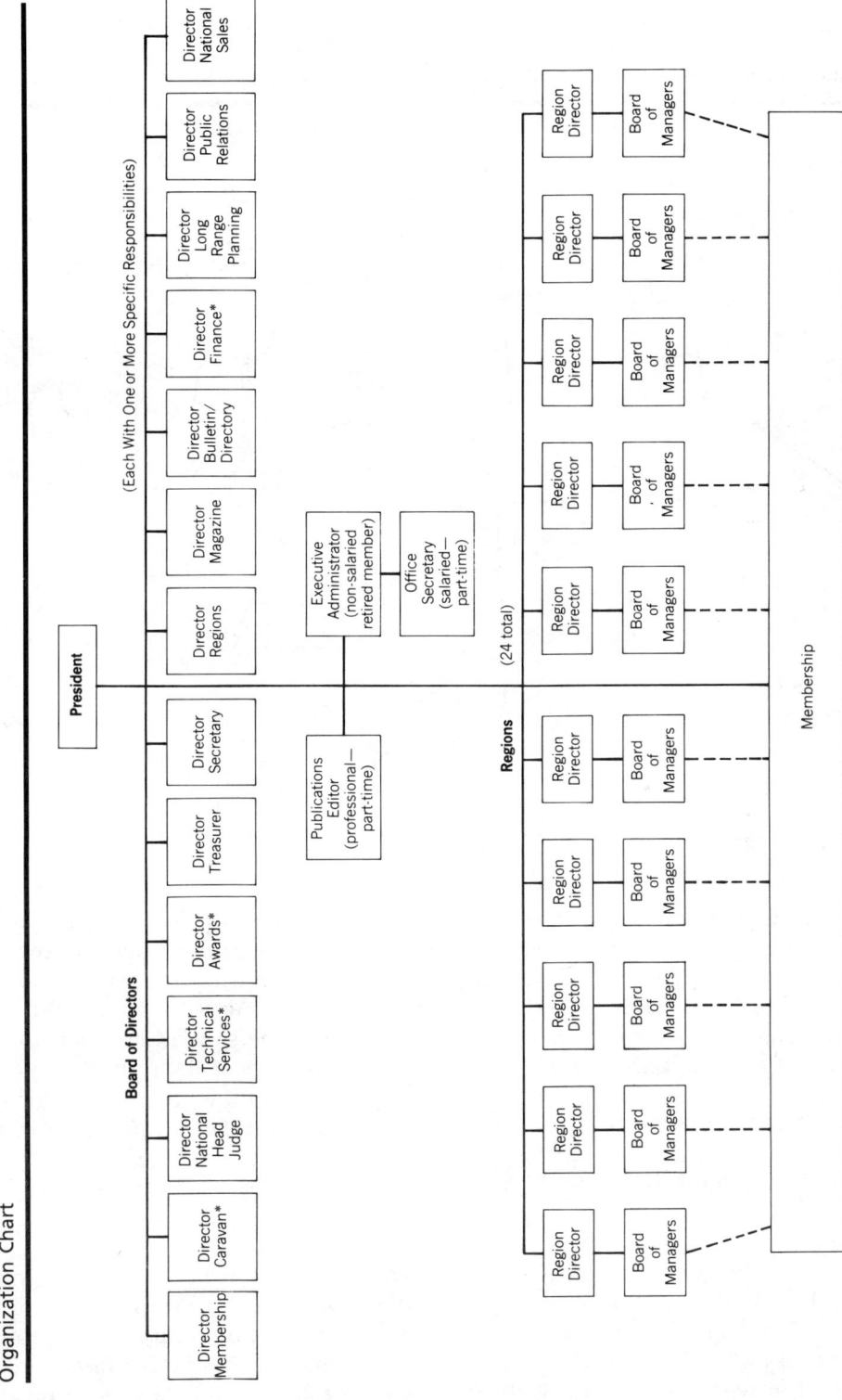

*This director chairs a committee for this functional responsibility comprised of other directors and members.

TABLE 3
Map Showing Boundaries of Regions of Classic Car Club of America

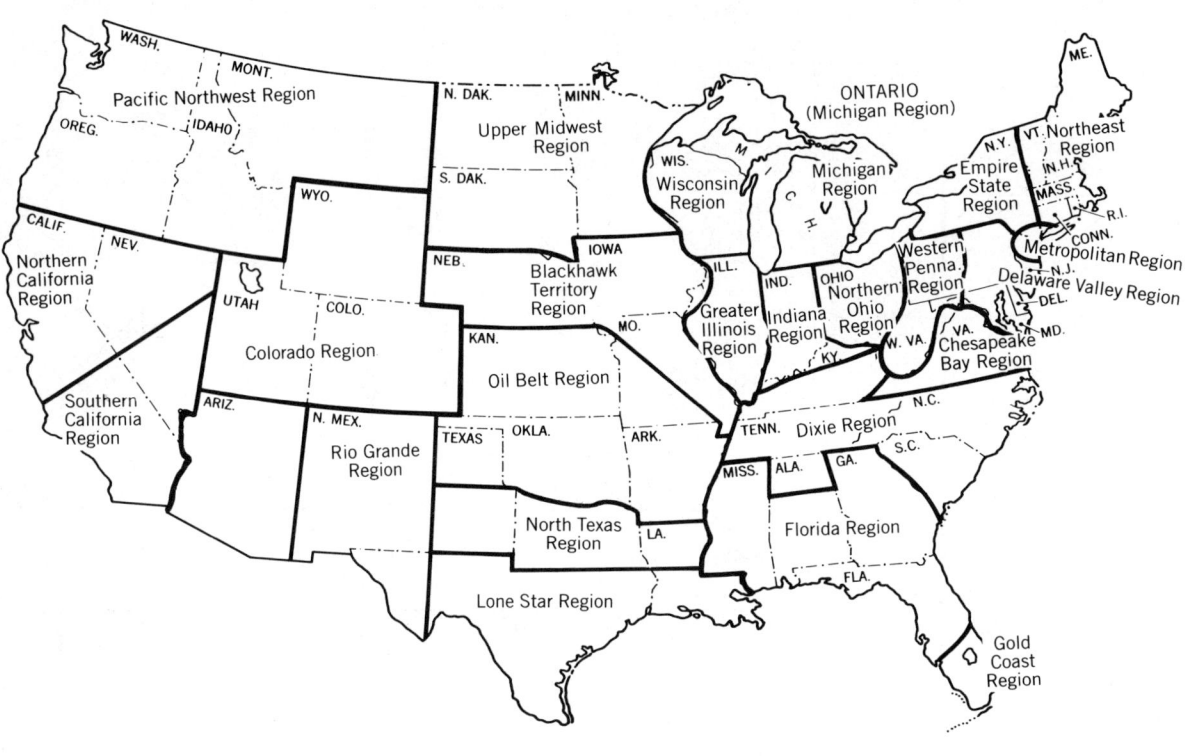

within the CCCA with regard to expanding the current listing of Classics. Although there is some debate over adding further makes and models within the current 1925–1948 year limits, the main controversy concerns whether or not to add cars built after 1948.

The minority of members who favor this post-1948 expansion make several arguments. They say that some high-quality cars were built after 1948 and these should also be considered "Classic." Furthermore, they argue that the club is currently not attracting young members (only 20 percent of CCCA members are under 45); this is because younger people are less able to afford the cost of a Classic and are unable to "identify" with a 1925–1948 car as they can with a car of the 1950s or 1960s.

Although prices of Classics vary greatly, depending on the make of car, its condition, and type of body, all prices rose significantly in the 1970s. Also it is true that many current CCCA members own Classics because of nostalgia for the cars of their youth.

On the other hand, most members of the Board of Directors, along with a clear majority of the membership, argue against expansion of the list of Classics past 1948. The primary argument is that a Classic Car is more than just a high-quality luxury car. Rather, it is the product of a "Classic Era," when the truly wealthy lived a separate lifestyle from the rest of the population, and an elite group of auto makers and custom-body craftsmen were willing and able to produce cars to meet this upper-class

TABLE 4
CCCA Financial Statements

	FY 1983	FY 1982	FY 1981
Receipts			
Active Dues (dues received for current fiscal year)	$47950	$43900	$41199
Prepaid Active Dues (received for next fiscal year)	54975	47370	33440
Associate Dues ($3.00/yr 1983, 1982, 1981)	972	978	801
Prepaid Associate Dues (for next fiscal year)	1227	762	648
Life Membership (1983: $350; 1982 and 1981: $250)	7310	5375	6775
Publications (back issue, individual copy sales)	3429	3472	4202
Bulletin Advertising	3663	3396	1459
Magazine Advertising	3567	1658	2752
Awards (payments from members for judging meets and meetings)	5240	5091	5230
CARavan (current years)	5300	5646	5900
CARavan (prepaid for next fiscal year)	6360	1500	1550
National Sales Items (badges, jewelry, clothing)	5235	4045	609
Interest Earned	10416	8750	9957
Regional Insurance (reimbursements from regions)	1100	1550	1300
Miscellaneous and Foreign Exchange	887	2330	322
Total Receipts	$157631	$135823	$116144
Assets			
Bank Balance	$5356	$1891	$5485
Investments (at cost; notes, CD's, money market funds)	96566	88997	85236
(includes life membership fund)	(37245)	(29800)	(24255)
Liabilities			
None			
Disbursements			
Bulletin	$18961	$17036	$13739
Magazine	57123	42099	33756
Directory	16181	9277	9237
Awards (judging, meetings, trophies, etc.)	8888	9648	10025
General Administration	8786	7573	10843
Office (salaries, rent, utilities, etc.)	28573	21824	16934
CARavan	5069	5564	4252
National Sales Items	1710	4123	126
Membership (recruitment)	5670	3401	1619
Regional Insurance	1600	1177	1279
Regional Relations	454	462	431
Computer Services	3678	3611	8011
Miscellaneous and Foreign Exchange	2562	1972	1142
Total Disbursements	$159225	$127767	$111394
Surplus	$(−1624)	$ +8056	$ +4750

Note 1. Cash basis reporting.
Note 2. Security transactions not included.
Note 3. Other assets not included (furniture, fixtures, sales items, trophies, deposits, etc.)

lifestyle. By the end of World War II, it is argued, social upheavals ended this lifestyle and economic pressures closed down the custom-body builders and most of the independent luxury car makers, with the remaining luxury cars generally becoming simply bigger, heavier, and better-appointed versions of other cars made by multiline manufacturers. Furthermore, it is argued, although a few truly special car models were made after 1948, the quantities produced were small and the addition of these cars to the list would bring in few new members to the CCCA.

Beyond the board's concerns about the future financial strength of the club, there is a concern about the use of members' Classics and the nature of CCCA activities. As previously mentioned, the value of classics has risen significantly over the years. In 1952 when the club was founded, most people viewed Classics simply as "old cars" that could generally be bought for a few hundred to a few thousand dollars. Today, Classics are viewed as a major investment item, with professional dealers and auctions a significant factor in the marketplace. Although some less exotic and unrestored Classic models can be found for under $10,000, most sell for $10,000–$75,000 and the most desirable classics (convertible models with custom bodies, 12 and 16-cylinder engines, etc.) can sell for $100,000 and more. Furthermore, judging meets have become very serious events, with high scores adding significantly to a classic's sales value. Thus, many top-scoring Classics are now hardly driven at all, and are trailered to and from judging meets. Although most classic owners still enjoy driving their cars, the emphasis in the club is definitely moving from the driving to the judging, and this upsets many CCCA members.

Still another concern of some members involves possible future gasoline shortages in the United States. If such a shortage arose, how would the public view Classic Cars and the old-car hobby in general? Would the ownership and driving of cars for non-transportation purposes be considered unpatriotic or antisocial?

Membership Survey

In response to these various concerns, the CCCA board established a Long-Range Planning Committee to study issues about the future of the club and to make recommendations to the board. In late 1983, a membership questionnaire was developed and sent to all members along with their 1984 membership renewal material. The response rate was excellent—about 75 percent of the club's members returned a completed questionnaire with their 1984 dues. Table 5 presents this questionaire and a tabulation of quantifiable responses.

It is more difficult to summarize the responses to the open-ended questions. Although no one sentiment represented a majority or even a large minority of the membership, some themes were frequently repeated:

A concern about trailered cars and professionally restored cars competing with other classics in judging.

Too much emphasis in the CCCA on judging, and not enough on driving. A focus on cosmetics rather than mechanics.

To attract younger members, the club must expand the listing of classics beyond 1948.

"The ———— (which I happen to own) should be recognized as a classic. It is as fine a car as the ————, which is recognized by the CCCA as a classic."

The CCCA should not dilute the meaning of "Classic." Hold fast to the 1925–1948 limits.

Future Direction of CCCA

In 1984 the CCCA Board of Directors was studying these issues. The board members knew that they could not ignore the problem of rising costs, and that the response must go beyond raising dues. Although the survey

TABLE 5
Membership Questionnaire

CLASSIC CAR CLUB OF AMERICA

MEMBERSHIP QUESTIONNAIRE

Please help your National Board of Directors guide the CCCA in the path that you desire by completing this questionnaire and returning it with your membership renewal.

1. I have been a member of the CCCA
   ☐ less than 2 years   ☐ 2 - 5 years   ☐ 5 - 10 years   ☐ more than 10 years
         11%   20%   18%   51%
2. I live in the _____ region (or state if there is no region)
3. My age is ☐ under 25   ☐ 25 - 34   ☐ 35 - 44   ☐ 45 - 54   ☐ 55 - 64   ☐ 65 and over
               1%   3%   17%   30%   28%   22%
4. I am a member of a CCCA Region   ☐ yes 69% ☐ no 31%
   If not, why not? _____
5. I have attended
   64% ☐ One or more Grand Classics
   19% ☐ One or more National CCCA CARavans
   24% ☐ One or more Annual Meetings
   52% ☐ One or more Regional Events
6. I belong to _____ (how many) other car clubs.
      9% 19% 23% 17% 12% 7% 5% 2% 2% 1% 3%
      0   1   2   3   4   5   6   7   8   9 10&+
   I am more active in some of these clubs than I am in the CCCA.   ☐ yes 44% ☐ no 56%
   If "yes," why? _____
7. Compared to other car clubs, the CCCA is
   ☐ the best 31%   ☐ better than most 47%   ☐ average 21%   ☐ poor 1%
8. Compared to other car clubs, the value I receive for my CCCA dues is
   ☐ the best 27%   ☐ better than most 40%   ☐ average 31%   ☐ poor 3%
9. Overall, I rate *"THE CLASSIC CAR"* magazine   ☐ excellent 74% ☐ good 24% ☐ fair 1% ☐ poor 0%
10. Overall, I rate the *"CCCA BULLETIN"*   ☐ excellent 35% ☐ good 51% ☐ fair 13% ☐ poor 1%
11. In *"THE CLASSIC CAR"*, the types of articles I enjoy most are:
    Rate each: 3 = enjoy a great amount   2 = enjoy a fair amount   1 = enjoy a little   0 = do not enjoy

2.3	Grand Classic articles	2.4	Articles on classic car designers
1.5	Annual Meeting articles	2.7	Car photos from the Classic Era
2.1	CARavan articles	2.3	Reprints from classic era publications
2.7	Stories and photos of members' cars	1.5	Book reviews
2.8	Historic articles on classic cars or coachbuilders	1.6	Articles on regional events
2.4	Technical articles	1.3	Articles on non-CCCA car events
2.5	Restoration articles	1.7	Classic car humor
2.4	Articles on car collections or car museums	1.8	Letters to the editor
___	Other: _____		

12. I would prefer
    28% ☐ to continue to have the *HANDBOOK-DIRECTORY* published every year
    72% ☐ to have it published every other year if a significant savings to the club would result
13. Currently the club's By-Laws require that 7 candidates run each year for election to 5 open National Board positions. While this gives the membership a choice in their voting, it also means that the two least-known candidates generally lose and will not seek election to the Board again.
    I think it is important to continue the system of 7 candidates for 5 positions.   ☐ yes 64% ☐ no 36%

(Please continue on other side)

TABLE 5 (*Continued*)

14. With regard to the CCCA's listing of recognized Classic Cars,
    - **69%** ☐ I basically think the current listing is good
    - **28%** ☐ I think the listing should be expanded
    - **3%** ☐ I think the listing should be reduced

    Comments: _____
    _____
    _____

15. With regard to the CCCA 100-point judging system,
    - **86%** ☐ I basically think the current system is good
    - **14%** ☐ I think the system could be improved

    If so, how? _____
    _____
    _____

16. Overall, I would rate the Grand Classics as
    ☐ excellent **50%** ☐ good **30%** ☐ fair **2%** ☐ poor **1%** ☐ don't know **17%**

17. Overall, I would rate the Annual Meetings as
    ☐ excellent **15%** ☐ good **22%** ☐ fair **5%** ☐ poor **0%** ☐ don't know **59%**

18. Overall, I would rate the CARavans as
    ☐ excellent **28%** ☐ good **16%** ☐ fair **2%** ☐ poor **0%** ☐ don't know **54%**

19. I think the CCCA should have additional National Judging Meets. ☐ yes **23%** ☐ no **77%**

    If "yes," what type? _____

20. I think the CCCA could be improved by:
    _____
    _____
    _____
    _____
    _____
    _____
    _____
    _____

Other comments: _____
_____
_____
_____
_____
_____
_____
_____
_____

Thank you for your assistance.

clarified some of the opinions of the membership, the board did not view this survey as a ballot, with the board obligated to follow the majority preference in every question area.

As they met for their monthly Board of Directors meeting, the 15 officers and directors of the CCCA asked themselves the following questions:

1. How do we deal with rising costs to the club?
2. What should be our policy with regard to future dues increases?
3. Should we consider the reduction of CCCA services to our membership in the future?
4. Is expansion of the listing of recognized Classic Cars desirable?
5. What are the alternative ways to increase membership in the club?
6. How can younger people be attracted to the CCCA?
7. Are there other sources of revenue for the club?
8. Were important questions not included in the 1983 membership survey that should be included in a future survey?
9. Are there other long-range issues or concerns that the club has not yet addressed?

THE CHARGER COMPANY (A)

The phone rang, and highly indignant words blared: "Fasters, what do you mean by submitting a report to all the executives without first talking it over with the division manager!"

Fasters replied, "My men made every effort to see him. They never got past his secretary. He instructed her to have them talk to the works manager."

"I don't believe a word of it. Lining is up in arms. He says the report is vindictive. What are you trying to do—embarrass the division manager? I don't believe your men ever tried to see Lining and I question the veracity of their statements!" The phone on the other end was hung up with a bang.

Fasters said to himself, "Bunn must be hot under the collar or he wouldn't have called me when I was away from my own office, visiting another plant."

The next day, Fasters' office received Bunn's letter confirming this telephone conversation and demanding an explanation. A week later, Fasters received a letter from Bunn's superior, Mr. Cordan, stating, "I have read the aforementioned report and discussed it with Mr. Bunn. He has advised me that the report is essentially untrue, inaccurate, and overstated. I am not satisfied to have such wide differences of opinion and have scheduled a meeting to be held in my office on ——— ———. I would appreciate it if you would be present."

In light of the phone call and the two letters, Mr. Fasters decided to reassess all events leading to this climax.

The cast of characters is as shown in Exhibit 1. The Charger Company had an elaborate organizational structure because of its scale of operation. At the headquarters office of the corporation, the president had a group of staff vice-presidents in charge of functions. Mr. Fasters was a staff department head reporting to the vice president, manufacturing. The headquarters staff departments assisted in policy formulation and made staff studies for the operating organization when requested. Members of such departments were encouraged to offer ideas for the good of the com-

Source: This case was prepared by William Brant, The American College. Permission to use granted by William Brant.

EXHIBIT 1
Organization Chart

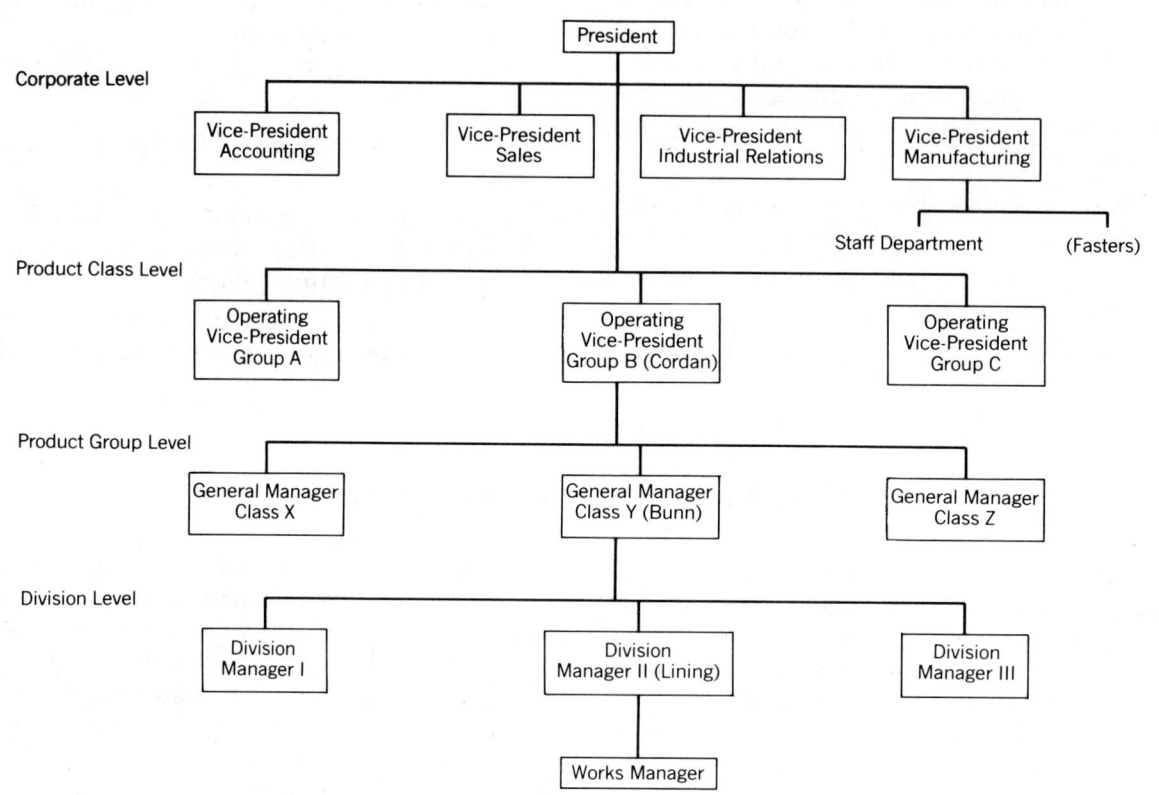

pany. Their proposals were considered by a management committee consisting of the vice presidents at the headquarters level and the operating vice-presidents in charge of product groups. Mr. Cordan of this case was the operating vice-president, Product Group "B."

Under the Vice Presidents of the product groups, there were general managers of product classes. They supervised the division managers, who were in charge of the sales and manufacturing operations of one or more plants. Mr. Bunn was general manager of Product Class "Y." One of the four division managers under him was Mr. Lining of Division II.

Two years before this incident occurred, Mr. Fasters' staff department proposed to the management committee, with the approval of the vice president, manufacturing, that representatives of Mr. Fasters' office join with representatives of the vice president, accounting, to make studies in each plant of the procedures for and actual practices regarding expense control. The suggestion was approved, and enthusiastically endorsed by the general managers. They sent a letter through channels to each division manager advising that periodically a team of two men would visit each plant to make a comprehensive analysis of expense-control practices and systems.

After a visit these field representatives of headquarters were to prepare a report giving findings and recommendations. They were to discuss it with the appropriate division manager and his staff. Thus, they would be able to incorporate any specific plans of action set in motion by division managers. Next, a report was to be submitted to Mr. Fasters. Both his department and the accounting office were to make comments. The final document was then to be submitted to the vice president, accounting; the vice president, manufacturing; the operating vice-president, product group; the general manager, product class; and the division manager concerned.

This general procedure had worked smoothly within the company until general manager Bunn of Product Class "Y" exploded. In the first plant studied, the two team members spent approximately four weeks examining documents, interviewing line management, interrogating industrial engineers, observing operations, etc. The employees of this plant were very cooperative. Some of the facts revealed by them could have been embarrassing to the division manager. The team was enabled to make specific recommendations for improvement to the division manager. His reception of the report was good. According to him, the study had given him an opportunity to review his situation and get his house in order. He intended to implement the recommendations unless they were changed in the review process at a higher level. Sixteen other plants were visited with reasonably good acceptance of the work of the team.

In his review of the Division II situation, Mr. Fasters found that the team had observed all the required organization routines. Mr. Sawyer, representing Mr. Fasters, had a master's degree in industrial engineering and 12 years with the company. Mr. Peters, from the accounting office, had served that department for 30 years. Both men had shown ability to gain confidences and use them discreetly. They were considered straightforward, conscientious, and unobtrusive in their work. In Division II the team obtained from plant personnel considerable information that pointed up a number of practices and procedures requiring improvement. In the opinion of the team members, the operating organization at the lower levels sincerely wanted to make these changes. The team thought that there was some resistance at some level within the division to these suggestions, and, in fact, to any from headquarters.

While the study was in process, Mr. Sawyer advised Mr. Fasters about the possible impact of the information that was being collected. Mr. Fasters emphasized the necessity of reporting it to the division manager, and Mr. Sawyer promised that he and Mr. Peters would do so.

The team made several efforts to see the division manager, but his secretary informed them that he was busy. They questioned the secretary closely to learn if the manager had knowledge of the procedural requirement that he and his staff go over the report with the team. She replied that he knew the requirements, but was too busy to discuss a headquarters program. He would ask his assistant, the works manager, and several staff members to go over it, and what they approved would be all right with him. Eventually, this meeting was held.

The members of the local management staff took a very reasonable attitude; they admitted the bad situation portrayed in the analysis and offered their assurances that immediate steps would be taken towards improvement. The team members thought that the local management staff was glad to have their problem brought out in the open, and were delighted to have the suggestions of the headquarters representatives.

When Mr. Fasters reviewed the report, both team members expressed their complete dissatisfaction with the brush-off they got from the division manager. Fasters took this as a cue to question them extensively concerning their findings and recommendations. In view of the sensitive character of the situation and the possible controversy that it might create, he was reluctant to distribute the report. It was the consensus of the remainder of the staff and the representatives of the accounting office that the usual transmittal letter should be prepared and distribution made. Mr. Fasters signed this letter and took no other action until the telephone call came from Mr. Bunn.

THE CHARGER COMPANY (B)

Mr. Cordan, operating vice-president, Product Group "B" of the Charger Company, called a meeting to review the report submitted by Mr. Fasters' staff department and the accounting office. Mr. Cordan, Mr. Bunn, Mr. Fasters, the vice president, accounting, and the vice president, manufacturing attended. In a very constructive, two-hour meeting, the report was evaluated and many conclusions were confirmed.

Division manager Lining was not present. Mr. Cordan had not invited him because he wanted to keep "heat" out of the meeting. Mr. Cordan regarded Mr. Lining as an "individual operator," who on more than one occasion had shown definite disrespect for headquarters' functions and programs.

There was some heat in the meeting, nevertheless. Mr. Bunn stated that Mr. Fasters should have discussed the report with him. Thus, he might have had an opportunity to take executive action at his level. When a division manager failed to consider a report, the superior should have a chance, even though the formal procedure did not provide for it. Mr. Bunn said that Mr. Fasters should have known that. Mr. Bunn also read a letter that had been prepared by Mr. Lining. It generally and categorically denied most of the statements in the report that were unsatisfactory to him. The vice president, accounting and Mr. Fasters, however, had certain information and supplementary reports that seemed to discount the effectiveness of the letter of rebuttal.

Before too much time elapsed, Mr. Cordan turned the discussion into ways of bringing about improvement in the future. "Where there was so much smoke," he observed, "there might be some fire." He suggested that men of higher rank review the work of the two team members; this would serve either to confirm or modify their findings. This step seemed advisable in order to assuage the feelings of the local division manager.

The meeting ended on a very harmonious note. Mr. Cordan asked Mr. Bunn to see Mr. Lining. "He needs to understand and appreciate that he has a responsibility to find time to review and comment on the type of reports being made by team members."

Mr. Fasters was pleased by the results of the meeting and the follow-up actions. Mr. Bunn must have talked with Mr. Lining. Whatever was said may have contributed to better working relationships. Plant cooperation immediately improved. The division manager cleared any obstacles interfering with the success of the program. His influence was particularly noticeable in its effect on the behavior of the line-supervisory organization. According to Mr. Fasters, cooperation rather than resistance was now encouraged. The home-office team became the advisory team it was intended to be.

In reviewing this experience Mr. Fasters said, "There was bound to be some form of blow-up because Lining had the reputation of thinking he did not have to conform to company-wide programs unless it was to his advantage. Further, he was more rugged in nature than Bunn. On many occasions Bunn was inclined to support Lining. There has been a very definite change in this respect during the latter part of this year."

Source: This case was prepared by William Brant, The American College. Permission to use granted by William Brant.

APPENDIX A

ADDITIONAL SOURCES OF INFORMATION

Frequently, the analyst may wish to obtain more information on the firm or the industry than is provided in the case. Information on the environment in which an organization operates is extremely important. This appendix provides a conceptual framework whereby the analyst may search for additional information, as well as providing a limited number of specific references deemed most useful. Analysts are encouraged to obtain a comprehensive reference such as David M. Brownstone and Gordon Carruth, *Where to Find Business Information: A Worldwide Guide for Everyone Who Needs the Answers to Business Questions*, 2e (New York: John Wiley and Sons, 1982) or Paul C. Wasserman, C. C. Georgi, and J. Woy, *Encyclopedia of Business Information Sources*, 4e (Detroit: Gale Research Company, 1980). Milutinovich[1] has developed an excellent framework that the analyst should find very useful in searching for additional information.

Figure 1 is the general business reference sources which includes all the sources that are generally available in the university library. Because there are so many government publications and these publications are so useful to the analyst, Milutinovich has developed a separate framework for them. This framework is provided in Figure 2. The sections that follow will break the government and general business reference sources framework into selected component parts that are most useful to the analyst.

Figure 3 presents a model that one may find useful in searching for relevant information. The model includes the basic steps that the analyst should go through in searching for information, beginning with a requirement for information and concluding with organized information useful in decision making.

GOVERNMENT PUBLICATIONS

- Andriot, John L., ed. *Guide to U. S. Government Publications* (U. S. Government, McLean, VA: Documents Index), Annual, 1973 to date. Annotated guide to publications of the various U. S. Government Agencies. Volume 1 contains a list of publications in existence as of January 1973; Volume 2 covers publications of

---

[1]Jugoslav S. Milutinovich, "Business Facts for Decision Makers: Where to Find Them," *Business Horizons*, April, 1985.

Appendix A

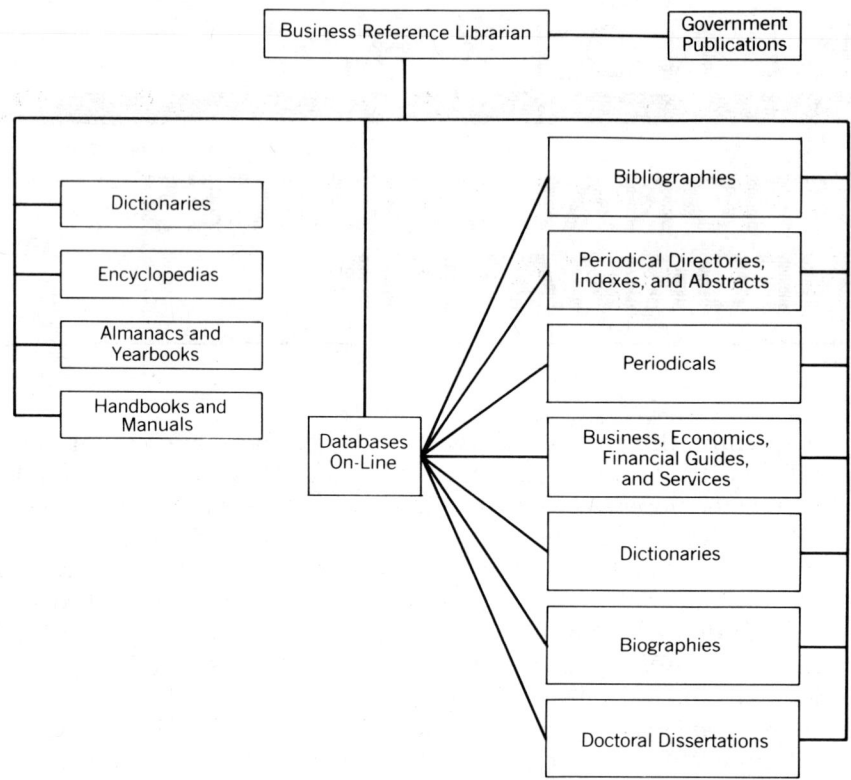

Figure 1
General Business Reference Sources

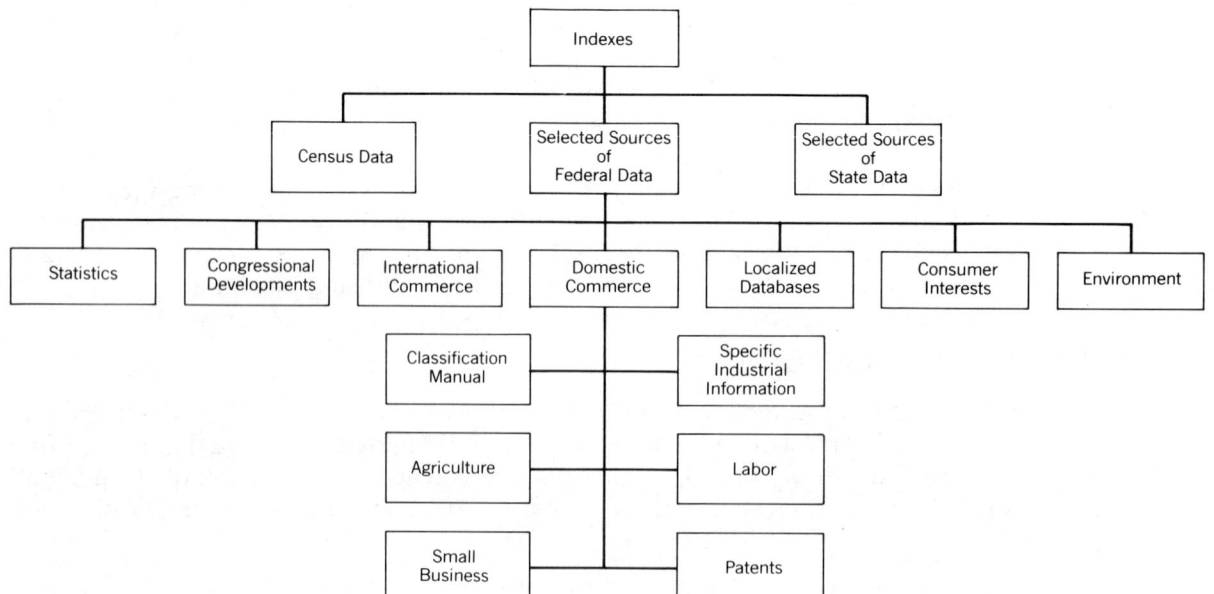

Figure 2
Government Publications

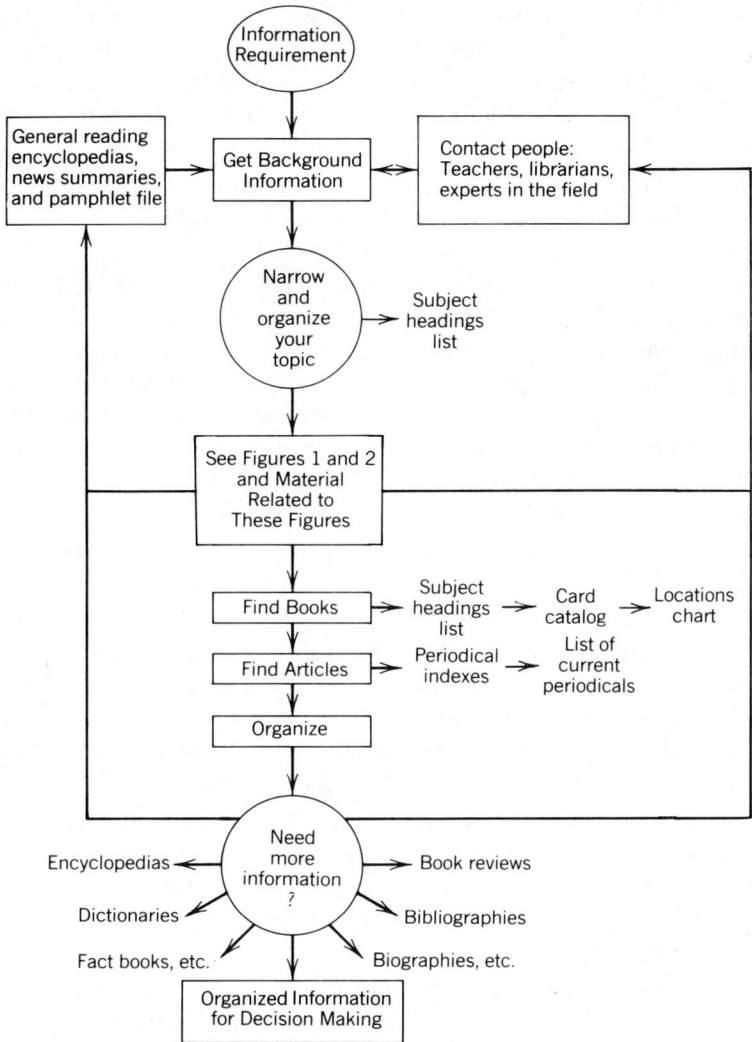

Figure 3
Strategy for Library Information Research

abolished agencies and discontinued publications; Volume 3 explains and outlines the Superintendent of Documents classification scheme.

- *The Federal Register* (Washington, D. C.: Division of the Federal Register, The National Archives). Published daily. The Register contains all regulatory matter issued by all national agencies and governmental bodies. These listings are both complete and official, and are indexed.
- *Bureau of the Census Catalog of Publications* (Washington, D. C.: U. S. Department of Commerce, Bureau of the Census). Issued quarterly with monthly supplements and accumulated annually. An all-encompassing index of Census Bureau data, publications, and unpublished materials.

- *Census of Population* (Series PC). (Washington, D. C.: GPO, Bureau of the Census). Issued every 10 years. Detailed characteristics of the population for states, counties, cities, and towns in a series of reports that give data on number of inhabitants, general population characteristics, general social and economic characteristics.
- *Census of Business* (Washington, D. C.: Bureau of the Census). Issued every five years. Multivolume. Contains statistical data on retail and wholesale trade of selected service industries in the United States.
- *Census of Manufacturers* (Washington, D. C.: U. S. Department of Commerce, Bureau of the Census). Issued every five years. Supplies data on U. S. manufacturing firms categorized under the headings of Final Area Reports and Final Industry Reports. *Final Area Reports* presents statistics on value added by manufacturing, employment, payrolls, new capital expenditure, and number of establishments. *Final Industry Reports* includes a series of separate reports on value of shipments, capital expenditures, value added by manufacturing, cost materials, and employment for approximately 450 manufacturing industries.
- *Business Conditions Digest* (Washington, D. C.: Department of Commerce, Bureau of Economic Analysis). Published monthly. Provides a look at many of the economic time series found most useful by business analysts and forecasters.
- *Economic Report of the President (together with the Annual Report of the Council of Economic Advisors* (Washington, D. C.: President). Annual. The annual report of the CEA comprises the major portion of this publication. It discusses economic policy and outlook, economic trends of the year, and includes statistical tables relating to income, employment, and publication.
- *Statistical Abstract of the United States* (Washington, D. C.: U. S. Department of Commerce, Bureau of the Census, GPO). Published annually. A reliable source for statistical summaries on the economy, business, population, and politics. Emphasis is on information of national scope, plus tables for regions, states, and some local areas.
- *U. S. Government Manual* (Washington, D. C.: U. S. Government Printing Office). Published annually. An indispensible official handbook of the federal government describing personnel, purposes, and programs of most government agencies.
- *Overseas Business Reports* (Washington, D. C.: Bureau of International Commerce). Annual. Each report deals with a group of countries' basic economic structure, trade regulations, practices and policies, market potential, and investment laws. Designed to aid business in gaining access to, and increasing its share of, foreign markets.
- *Standard Industrial Classification Manual* (Washington, D. C.: U. S. Government Printing Office, 1973). Developed for use in the classification of establishments by type of activity in which engaged; for purposes of facilitating the collection, tabulation, presentation, and analysis of data relating to establishments; for promoting uniformity and comparability in the presentation of statistical data col-

lected by various agencies of the U. S. government, state agencies, trade associations, and private research organizations. It covers an entire range of economic activities.

- *Minerals Yearbook* (Washington, D. C.: Bureau of the Mines). Annual. Three volumes. Statistics on metals, minerals, and mineral products, along with economic and technical developments and trends in the U. S. and foreign countries.
- *Mineral Industry Surveys* (Washington, D. C.: Bureau of Mines). Irregular issue. Contains statistical data on metals, nonmetals, and fuels, regarding production, consumption, and shipments.
- *Area Trends in Employment and Unemployment* (Washington, D. C.: Manpower Administration). Monthly. Describes area labor market developments and outlook for 150 major employment centers, with separate brief summaries for selected areas, including those with concentrated presistent unemployment and underemployment.
- *Area Wage Surveys* (Washington, D. C.: Bureau of Labor Statistics). Annual. Provides occupational earnings data for nearly 100 SMSAs, published separately for each SMSA. Useful information for wage and salary administration, collective bargaining, and determining plant location.
- *Small Business Bibliographies* (Washington, D. C.: Small Business Administration). Irregular issue. Briefly describes particular business activities and has a substantial bibliography, which includes federal, state, and nongovernmental publications. The preface of each issue may be helpful to those seeking career information.
- *Monitor, Environmental Impact Statements* (Washington, D. C.: Council on Environmental Quality). Monthly. Provides abstracts of environmental impact statements of federal agencies concerning proposed projects, as well as legislation relating to environmental impact statements.

GENERAL REFERENCE SOURCES OF BUSINESS INFORMATION AND IDEAS

Business Reference Librarian

The business reference librarian should be consulted as a time-saving first step in gathering business facts. This specialist has the best sources at her/his fingertips and can give expert guidance. He or she compiles booklists concerning specific areas, identifies special library collections, and is aware of books scheduled for publication. By use of networking, this specialist is aware of the holdings in all business reference libraries in the general area, and in university, public, and corporate libraries open to the public.

The business reference librarian can also tap into the interlibrary loan system—a free, cooperative exchange system of books and periodicals from member libraries across the country.

On-Line Databases

- *Directory of Computer-Based Services* (Washington, D. C.: Telenet Communications Corp.) Published annually. It lists data banks, commercial service bureaus, educational institutions, and companies that offer interactive computer-based services to the public through the nation-wide Telenet network.
- *Directory of Online Information Resources* (Rockville, MD: CSG Press, 1980). Easy-to-use guide to selected, publicly accessible bibliographic and nonbibliographic on-line databases. 225 databases available, file descriptions, coverage, and size.
- *ABI/INFORM* August 1971 through the present. 134,636 records. All phases of business management and administration. Stresses general decision sciences information that is widely applicable. Specific product and industry information included. 400 primary publications in business and related fields are scanned.
- *Management Contents* (Skokie, IL: Management Contents, Inc.) 1974 to present. Monthly updates. Current information on a variety of business and management-related topics for use in decision making and forecasting. Articles from 200 U. S. and foreign journals, proceedings, and transactions are fully indexed and abstracted to provide up-to-date information in areas of accounting, marketing, operations research, organizational behavior, and public administration.
- *Predicasts Terminal System* (Cleveland: Predicasts, Inc.). Bibliographical and statistical database providing instant access to many business journals and other special reports for searches of current articles, statistics, and geographic location of companies. Abstracts wide range of periodical abstracts and indexes.
- *Disclosure II* (Washington, D. C.: Disclosure, Inc.) 1977 to present. Updated weekly. Extracts of reports filed with the U. S. Security and Exchange Commission by publicly owned companies. 11,000 company reports provide reliable and detailed sources of public financial and administrative data. Source of information for marketing intelligence, corporate planning and development, portfolio analysis, legal and accounting research.

Bibliographies

- Brownstown, David M. and Gordon, Carruth. *Where to Find Business Information: A World-Wide Guide for Everyone Who Needs the Answers to Business Questions*. 2e. (New York: John Wiley and Sons, 1982). Source list of 5,000 current foreign and domestic, private and public business information.
- *Management Information Guides* (Detroit, Gale Research Co.) A group of bibliographical references to information sources for various business sources in many fields. Each volume includes general reference works, film strips, government, and institutional reports.

Periodical Directories, Periodicals, Indexes, and Abstracts

- *Business Periodicals Index.* (New York: Wilson Company). 1958 to present. Published monthly with monthly and annual cumulations. Cumulative subject index covering 270 business periodicals in the English language.
- *Predicasts' F & S Index United States.* (Cleveland: Predicasts, Inc.) 1960 to present. Published weekly, with monthly, quarterly, and annual cumulations. Index covering company, industry, and product information from business-oriented periodicals and brokerage house reports in the United States.
- *Management Contents.* (Skokie, IL: G. D. Searle and Co.) Published biweekly. Reproduction of the tables of contents of a selection of 150 of the best business/management journals.
- *New York Times Index.* (New York: The New York Times Co.) 1913 to present. Published every two weeks. Annual cumulation. Detailed index summarizing and classifying news alphabetically via subject, persons, and organizations. Cross references. Also on-line database from January 1969.
- *Wall Street Journal Index.* (New York: Dow Jones Company, Inc.) 1958 to present. Published monthly. Annual cumulation. A complete report on current business. Subject index of all articles that have appeared in the Journal, grouped in two sections—Corporate News and General News.

Business, Economic, and Financial Guides and Services

- *Business and Investment Service.* (New York: International Statistical Bureau, Inc.) Published weekly. Relates to analyses of production in basic industries. Some political analyses of interest are included, along with a section entitled "Selected Securities Guide." Herein is presented stock market trends and indexes, as well as earnings and prices of stocks in selected industries.
- Grant, Mary M. and Norma Cote, eds. *Directory of Business and Financial Services.* 7e. (New York: Special Libraries Association, 1976). Guide to existing national and international business, economic, and financial services describing 1051 publications issued by 421 publishers.
- *Moody's Bond Record.* (New York: Moody's Investor's Service). Published weekly. Provides statistics, prices, and other information for bonds of all types, including municipals.
- *Moody's Dividend Record.* (New York: Moody's Investor's Service). Published weekly. Gives current information on dividend declarations, payment dates, ex-dividend dates, dividend dates, income bond-interest payments, payments on bond and default, stock split-ups, stock subscription rights, and preferred stocks called.
- *Moody's Handbook of Common Stocks.* (New York: Moody's Investor's Service). Published quarterly. Covers 1000 plus selected common stocks listed alpha-

betically. Each company page has a 10-year statistical history, a 15-year price chart, company's background, recent developments, and investment quality.

Directories

- Benjamin, William A., ed. *Directory of Industry Data Sources.* 2e. (Detroit, MI: Gale Research Company, 1982). Includes over 15,000 annotated entries describing a wide range of information sources on 60 industries.
- *Thomas Register of American Manufacturers.* (New York: Thomas Publishing Co.) Published annually. Comprehensive U. S. directory restricted to manufacturing firms. Volumes 1–7 are indexes to manufacturers by product. Volume 7 includes a list of trade names. Volume 8 lists manufacturer by company name, including information similar to Standard and Poors Register. Volumes 9–12 are compilations of manufacturer's catalogues.

Statistical Sources Index

- Predicasts, Inc. *Predicasts Forecasts.* (Cleveland, OH: University Circle Research Center). Published quarterly, cumulated annually. Abstracts business and financial forecasts for specific U. S. industrial products and general economy. Presents composite data for economic, construction, energy, and other indicators.

APPENDIX B

FINANCIAL AND RATIO ANALYSIS

Many students have not worked with financial analysis for an extended time. Those students probably need a bit more guidance than others who recently have taken a course in corporate or managerial finance. This appendix provides a review of some basic financial analysis, including financial ratios, a cost-percentage analysis, and a sources and uses of funds statement. For discussion and illustration, Exhibits 1 and 2 are provided

EXHIBIT 1
XYZ Manufacturing Company
Comparative Operating Statements (1980–1983)
Fiscal Years End December 31 (in $1,000s)

	1980	1981	1982	1983
Net sales	2,728	3,830	4,415	3,723
Cost of goods sold				
Material	1,624	2,566	3,048	2,102
Direct labor	166	254	269	181
Manufacturing expense	454	667	779	745
Total manufacturing cost	2,244	3,487	4,096	3,028
Inventory variation increase (decrease)	11	(34)	(237)	(9)
Total cost of goods sold	2,255	3,453	3,859	3,019
Gross margin	473	377	556	704
Selling and administrative expense	161	186	222	309
Operating profit (loss)	312	191	334	395
Other income (expense)	(2)	(12)	(9)	(19)
Federal taxes	132	87	197	239
Net profit (loss)	178	92	128	137
Retained earnings	85	243	298	384
	263	335	426	521
Dividends				
Preferred	20	10	8	5
Common	—	27	34	32
Retained earnings	243	298	384	484

EXHIBIT 2
XYZ Manufacturing Company
Comparative Balance Statements (1980–1983)
Fiscal Years End December 31 (in $1,000s)

	1980	1981	1982	1983
Current assets				
Cash	141	43	75	106
Receivables (net)	146	191	53	42
Inventory	320	426	682	672
Investments: life insurance	3	3	3	4
Prepaid expenses	8	12	12	15
Total	618	675	825	839
Current liabilities				
Notes payable—bank	—	100	—	—
Accounts payable	86	167	238	40
Accrued expenses	41	34	55	88
Provision for income taxes	132	81	197	239
Total	259	382	490	367
Working capital	359	293	335	472
Fixed assets				
Land	7	8	14	23
Buildings	127	176	181	190
Machinery and equipment	183	238	295	316
Less depreciation	93	110	154	205
Net after depreciation	90	128	141	111
Total	224	312	336	324
Net Assets	583	605	671	796
Capital stock				
Preferred stock	172	133	109	74
Common stock	166	170	173	222
Capital in excess of par value[a]	2	4	5	16
Retained earnings	243	298	384	484
Total Equity	583	605	671	796

[a]Net gains from stock sales and retirements.

RATIO ANALYSIS

The basic information on the financial health of a company comes from ratios calculated from the financial data. The authors suggest the use of four major categories: (1) liquidity ratios, (2) leverage ratios, (3) activity ratios, and (4) profitability ratios.

For the ratio analysis to be meaningful, there must be some base against which the calculated ratios may be compared. Two types of comparisons are suggested: trend analysis and norms for the company over time. Also the calculated ratios should be compared with the norms of the industry. Frequently, norms for the specific industry may not be available, and the analyst must revert to norms for American Industries in general. Appendix A provides references to assist the analyst in finding the norms for various industries. *Dun and Bradstreet's Key Business Ratios* is an excellent reference the analyst may wish to consult. In analyzing companies that manufacture or market more than a single product, the analyst should be careful to separate the financial ratio analysis by product when possible. For example, one product may supply 56 percent of total sales while the remaining three products supply 44 percent of total sales. However, the analyst may find that it is not always possible to do this because the financial data presented in the case is often combined into consolidating financial statements. In such cases, the judgment of the analyst becomes very important in interpreting the ratios.

The set of ratios discussed under each category is a compromise between an exhaustive set designed to cover all situations and a limited list designed for a particular case. The financial data of the XYZ Manufacturing Company will be used to illustrate the calculation and interpretation of each ratio.

Categories of Financial Ratios

Liquidity Ratios. The first category is *liquidity ratios*. Liquidity ratios are designed to measure a firm's ability to meet its maturing obligations. Two of the most frequently used liquidity ratios are the current ratio and the quick ratio.

The *current ratio* is current assets divided by current liabilities. Current assets normally include cash, marketable securities, accounts receivable, and inventories. Current liabilities are composed of accounts payable, short-term notes payable, taxes payable, and accrued expenses, such as wages that are owed but not paid. The current ratio is generally accepted as a measure of short-term solvency. It indicates the extent to which the claims of short-term creditors are covered by assets convertible to cash in a time period corresponding to the maturity of the claims. The generally accepted standard for American industry is a ratio of 2.5 to 1.

From the standpoint of creditors, a high current ratio is desirable. A high current ratio by itself, however, does not guarantee that the company will be able to generate a sufficient volume of cash to meet its commitments. For example, a high current ratio could mean that the organization has abnormally high inventories. The current ratio from the company's standpoint is the cushion used for adversity. Thus, companies that operate in a very stable environment where the demands for both assets and liabilities are steady do not need as high a ratio as a company operating in an industry with widely fluctuating demands for these resources. For example, the demand for assets and liabilities for a utility company are fairly steady. The utility company also operates in a stable environment. On the other hand, an electronics company operates in a dynamic environment with erratic demands for assets and liabilities. Clearly, the current ratio for the utility company need not be as high as that for the electronics company.

The *quick ratio* is calculated by deducting inventories from current assets and dividing the remainder by current liabilities. It provides a measure of the extent to which the company could pay off its short-term obligations without relying on the sale of inventories, since inventories are the least liquid and more likely to result in a higher loss on sales relative to other current assets. The norm for all American industries is 1 to 1. Again, the higher the firm's calculated ratio, the more positively it is viewed by short-term creditors. Like the current ratio, a requirement of 1 to 1 depends on the stability of the organization.

Leverage Ratios. The second category is leverage ratios. These ratios measure the contributions of owners compared with the financing provided by the firm's creditors. Leverage ratios are important for a number of reasons. First, creditors look to the equity provided by the owners to provide a margin of safety. If the owners are providing only a small portion of the total financing, the risks are borne by the creditors. Second, by selling debt the owners are able to maintain control of the firm with a limited investment. Third, if the firm earns more on the debt than it pays in interest on the debt, the additional earnings belong to the owners of the firm.

The first leverage ratio is *times interest earned*. To calculate this ratio, the analyst divides earnings before interest and taxes by the interest charges. The ability to pay interest is not affected by income taxes because income taxes are computed after deducting interest expense, hence the before-tax figure is used in the numerator. This ratio measures how much earnings may decline before the firm finds itself unable to meet its annual interest costs. The American industry norm for the times interest earned ratio is 8 to 1. Obviously, the higher the ratio, the greater the margin of safety for the creditors. Further, when the ratio drops below the industry norm it provides the financial manager with an indication that additional debt may be difficult to secure.

Frequently, in case analysis, the financial information necessary to compute the times interest earned ratio is not available. When this is the case, an alternate ratio may be used. The suggested alternate ratio is a *debt ratio*. This ratio measures the firm's percentage of total funds provided by creditors. Creditors prefer moderate debt ratios because the lower the ratio, the greater the cushion against creditors' losses in the event of liquidation. Owners may prefer a high ratio to magnify earnings or because raising equity means giving up some control. An American industry norm for the debt ratio is 40 percent.

Activity Ratios. Activity ratios, the third category of financial ratios, are used to measure how effectively the firm is employing the resources at its command. Like other categories of financial ratios, a number of ratios fall within the activity category, but only two will be discussed.

The first activity ratio, *inventory turnover*, is measured by dividing cost of goods sold by average inventory. A manager must compromise between being out of stock and over-investing funds in inventory. A declining or low turnover may provide clues that the company is overstocked, whereas a high ratio may indicate a danger that the firm may run out of stock. Industry norms for inventory turnover are relatively meaningless because inventory turnover varies so widely from industry to industry. However, the overall norm for American industry is 9 to 1. It should be remembered, however, that inventories of relatively small, inexpensive items are apt to turnover much faster than inventories of large, expensive items. Consequently, if there is no information on industry turnover available, the analyst can look at the characteristics of the industry and the value of the industry's product and ascertain whether he or she expects the turnover level to be higher or lower than the norm for American industry in general. Also, the analyst can examine the changes in inventory turnover over time to see whether the company is doing better or worse than it has in the past.

The second activity ratio is the *average collection period*—a measure of the accounts receivable turnover. This is best calculated in a two-step method. First, annual sales are divided by the number of days in the year. The authors suggest using the number 360. This gives sales per day. Second, sales per day are divided into average accounts receivable. This determines the number of days of sales tied up in receivables, which is the average collection period. Again, norms for American industry are relatively meaningless because the standards on trade credit vary so widely from industry to industry. The norm for American industry is 36 days. The analyst can look at the characteristics of the specific industry in order to ascertain whether he or she would expect this industry to be above or below the norm. Since this figure is so dependent on the terms normally provided in the industry for trade credit, little can be gained from a general discussion. In part, the analyst may have to look at the changes in the average collection period over time to see whether the company is doing better or worse than it has in the past. Again, industry information is the best basis for ascertaining the effectiveness of the collection policies of the company.

Profitability Ratios. Profitability is the result of the firm's policies and decisions. There are many measures of a firm's profitability, and caution must be used in deciding which profitability ratio to use. Industry peculiarities can greatly influence these ratios. Two of the better known ratios are discussed here.

The first profitability ratio is *sales margin or return on sales*. Net profit after taxes divided by net sales indicates the extent to which costs per dollar of sales can increase or unit selling prices can decline before the firm suffers an overall loss. Again, the industry norm varies from industry to industry. The norm for American industry is 5 percent. Again, the expected sales margin from industry to industry varies markedly, and the analyst must use available industry reference data.

The second profitability ratio is *return on investment* or *return on net worth*. The ratio of net profit after taxes to net worth or investment measures the productivity of the resources that the owners of the firm have committed to the operation of the business. The return on net worth or investment is probably the best single measure of overall performance for the firm. The average for American industries varies from year to year, depending on economic conditions. The range for American manufacturing industries is 15 to 18 percent. Although the norms for industries may vary, in evaluating overall performance there is little justification for accepting a rate of return on net worth or investment significantly lower than this figure, unless it is a temporary condition.

Analysis for the XYZ Manufacturing Company

Table 1 shows the calculation of financial ratios for the XYZ Manufacturing Company for 1980 through 1983. The table also shows the ratios for the norms for American industry. It should be noted that the American industry norms are for 1983.

The first two ratios are concerned with the ability of the company to face short-term adversity. We see that the XYZ Manufacturing Company has both a low current ratio and quick ratio. This means that it has limited resources to cover its current liabilities (i.e., its obligations to creditors). The debt ratio is high relative to industry norms, and it would be desirable for this company to decrease its debt ratio. The inventory turnover figure for 1983 is low relative to the norms for American industry. This suggests that inventory may be high. Also, it can be seen that the inventory turnover continues to decrease between the years 1980 through 1983. Combining the findings of the quick and inventory turnover ratios leads one to conclude that the inventories are rapidly increasing. These ratios indicate that the

TABLE 1
Financial Ratios for XYZ Manufacturing Company

	1980	1981	1982	1983	1983 American Industry Norm[a]
Current ratio $\frac{\text{Current assets}}{\text{Current liabilities}}$	$\frac{618}{259} = 2.386$	1.767	1.683	2.286	2.5
Quick ratio $\frac{\text{Current assets—inventory}}{\text{Current liabilities}}$	$\frac{298}{259} = 1.151$	0.652	0.292	0.455	1.0
Debt ratio $\frac{\text{Total debt}}{\text{Total assets}}$	$\frac{259}{583} = 0.444$	0.631	0.730	0.461	40%
Inventory turnover $\frac{\text{Cost of goods sold}}{\text{Inventory}}$	$\frac{2255}{320} = 7.06$	8.11	5.66	4.49	9.0
Average collection period $\frac{\text{Receivables}}{\text{Sales per day}}$	$\frac{146}{2728/360} = 19.267$ days	17.95 days	4.32 days	4.06 days	36 days
Return on sales $\frac{\text{Net profit after taxes}}{\text{Net sales}}$	$\frac{178}{2728} = 6.52\%$	2.4%	2.8%	3.6%	5.0%
Return on net worth $\frac{\text{Net profit after taxes}}{\text{Total net worth}}$	$\frac{178}{583} = 30.53\%$	15.2%	19.1%	17.2%	15–18%

[a] For American Industry average norms, see Eugene F. Brigham, *Fundamentals of Financial Management*, 3 (New York: The Dryden Press, 1983).

company should further investigate its inventory management to see if improvements can be made.

Looking at the average collection period, one can see that receivables are down to 4.06 days, an almost unbelievably low and very desirable figure. There is no way one can expect improvement on this figure. Indeed while it is desirable for XYZ to maintain this rapid collection, it is reasonable to expect that this figure will increase in future periods.

The return on sales figure is below the norm for American industry. It is the highest it has been in the last three years, showing significant improvement, but lower than it was in 1980. The return on net worth averages for the last three years are very close to the American industry norm. Consequently, we must conclude that the company is performing reasonably well.

In summary, the quick ratio indicates some question regarding the ability to weather short-term adversity, and this condition would be materially helped by a reduction in the size of the inventory. Accounts receivable management is very effective. But inventory management is questionable. Debt capital management appears to be something that XYZ should reexamine, and it would be desirable for XYZ to lower its level of debt.

COST-PERCENTAGE ANALYSIS

A second technique useful in appraising the financial health of an organization is cost-percentage analysis. This technique looks at all costs on the income statement as a percentage of net sales. Table 2 shows the cost percentages for the years 1980 through 1983.

This analysis shows that all 1981 costs were higher than 1980 costs except for

TABLE 2
XYZ Manufacturing Company

	Cost Percentages			
	1980	1981	1982	1983
Net sales	100%	100%	100%	100%
Materials	59.5	67.0	69.0	56.5
Direct labor	6.1	6.6	6.1	4.9
Manufacturing expense	16.6	17.4	17.6	20.0
Total manufacturing cost	82.2	91.0	92.7	81.3
Inventory variation	0.4	(0.9)	(5.4)	(0.2)
Cost of goods	82.6	90.2	87.4	81.1
Gross margin	17.3	9.8	12.6	18.9
Selling and administrative expenses	5.9	4.9	5.0	8.3
Operating profit (loss)	11.4	5.0	7.6	10.6
Other income	—	(0.3)	(0.2)	(0.5)
Taxes	4.8	2.3	4.5	6.4
Net after-tax income	6.5	2.4	2.9	3.7

selling and administrative costs. 1982 shows a continued increase in costs with only direct labor costs declining slightly. The movement in 1983 is desirable on almost all fronts, except increasing manufacturing expenses. It is suggested that direct labor and manufacturing expenses be combined because one increases or decreases at the expense of the other.

SOURCES AND USES OF FUNDS

A third technique useful in appraising the financial condition of a company is a source and use of funds statement. The source and use of funds statement tells the analysts how the organization acquired and used funds. It is especially useful to conduct the analysis over a large number of years. This enables the analyst to see the patterns of behavior that the organization displays in acquiring and using its capital resources. The sources and uses of funds analysis begins with a simple calculation in all categories of the balance sheet of the differences from year to year. By subtracting the first year from the second year, we calculate the differences. Some of the items will be negative and some positive. Those asset items that are negative represent sources of funds. It should be remembered that depreciation is a source of funds. Conversely, when liabilities increase, they become a source of funds. An increase, for example, in accounts payable represents a source of funds because we are using trade credit as a source of funds. An increase in long or short-term notes is an obvious source of funds. If we are paying off more accounts

TABLE 3
Sources and Uses of Funds for XYZ Manufacturing Company

	1980	1981	(1981–1980) Difference	Source or Use	1982	(1982–1981) Difference	Source or Use	1983	(1983–1982) Difference	Source or Use
Assets										
Cash	141	43	−98	Source	75	32	Use	106	31	Use
Receivables	146	191	45	Use	53	−138	Source	42	−11	Source
Inventories	320	426	106	Use	682	256	Use	672	−10	Source
Other	11	15	4	Use	15	0	Source	19	4	Use
Land	7	8	1	Use	14	6	Use	23	9	Use
Buildings	127	176	49	Use	181	5	Use	190	9	Use
Machinery and equipment	183	238	55	Use	295	57	Use	316	21	Use
Depreciation	93	110	−17	Source	154	−44	Source	205	−51	Source
Liabilities										
Notes	0	100	100	Source	0	−100	Use	0	−198	
Accounts payable	86	167	81	Source	238	71	Source	40	33	Use
Accrued expense	41	34	−7	Use	55	21	Source	88	42	Source
Taxes	132	81	−51	Use	197	116	Source	239		Source
Equity										
Preferred stock	172	133	−39	Use	109	−24	Use	74	−35	Use
Common stock	166	170	4	Source	173	3	Source	222	49	Source
Capital in excess of par	2	4	2	Source	5	1	Source	16	11	Source
Retained earnings	243	298	55	Source	384	86	Source	484	100	Source

Data given in thousands of dollars.

payable, we must use funds to do so. Finally, an increase in net worth represents a source of funds and a decrease represents a use of funds. If retained earnings increase, it is because we have committed our funds to the business. If they decrease, it means we have removed them from the business. Table 3 shows the calculation of the sources and uses of funds for the XYZ Manufacturing Company.

For 1981 the major sources of funds were the use of cash, notes, accounts payable, and retained earnings. The major uses of those funds were to build inventories and receivables, as well as invest in buildings, machinery, and equipment. It should also be noted that XYZ decreased its tax liability as well as retired some preferred stock. When the sources and uses of funds statements for 1981 and 1982 are compared, some interesting differences emerge. In 1982, XYZ's major sources of funds were the reduction of receivables, increases in the accounts payable, and increases in retained earnings. The major uses of the funds were to continue building inventories and pay off the short-term notes. In 1983, the major sources of funds were from depreciation, increases in retained earnings, and the sale of common stock. The major uses of funds were to reduce accounts payable, retire some preferred stock, and build the cash position. The sources and uses of funds statement not only indicates how funds were acquired and used, but says something about the stability of a company's financial policies, especially if each account is examined across a large number of years.

ADDITIONAL INFORMATION ON FINANCIAL PERFORMANCE

Most students conducting a financial review of an organization find certain information useful in most cases. That information includes data on (1) consumer price index (CPI) and population growth; (2) compound growth. Tables 4 and 5 provide this information.

TABLE 4
Information on Consumer Price Index (CPI) and Population

Year	CPI (Base Year 1967)	U. S. Population (in Millions)
1983	297.1	234.2
1982	289.1	232.1
1981	272.4	229.8
1980	246.8	227.7
1979	217.4	225.1
1978	195.4	222.6
1977	181.5	220.2
1976	170.5	218.0
1975	161.2	216.0
1974	147.7	213.9

Statistical Abstract of the United States: 1984, U. S. Department of Commerce, Bureau of Census, 104th ed.

TABLE 5
Compound Growth Table

	Years									
Percentage	1	2	3	4	5	6	7	8	9	10
1	1.010	1.020	1.030	1.041	1.051	1.062	1.072	1.083	1.094	1.105
2	1.020	1.040	1.061	1.082	1.104	1.126	1.149	1.172	1.195	1.105
3	1.030	1.061	1.093	1.126	1.160	1.194	1.223	1.267	1.305	1.343
4	1.040	1.082	1.125	1.170	1.217	1.265	1.316	1.369	1.423	1.480
5	1.050	1.103	1.158	1.215	1.276	1.340	1.407	1.477	1.551	1.629
6	1.060	1.124	1.191	1.262	1.338	1.418	1.504	1.594	1.689	1.791
7	1.070	1.145	1.225	1.311	1.403	1.501	1.602	1.718	1.838	1.967
8	1.080	1.166	1.260	1.360	1.469	1.587	1.714	1.851	1.999	2.159
9	1.090	1.188	1.295	1.412	1.539	1.677	1.828	1.993	2.172	2.367
10	1.100	1.210	1.331	1.464	1.611	1.772	1.949	2.144	2.358	2.594
11	1.110	1.232	1.368	1.518	1.685	1.870	2.076	2.305	2.558	2.839
12	1.120	1.254	1.405	1.574	1.762	1.974	2.211	2.476	2.773	3.106
13	1.130	1.277	1.443	1.630	1.842	2.082	2.353	2.658	3.000	3.395
14	1.140	1.300	1.482	1.689	1.925	2.195	2.502	2.853	3.252	3.707
15	1.150	1.323	1.521	1.749	2.011	2.313	2.660	3.059	3.518	4.046
16	1.160	1.346	1.561	1.811	2.100	2.436	2.826	3.278	3.803	4.411
17	1.170	1.369	1.602	1.874	2.192	2.565	3.001	3.511	4.108	4.807
18	1.180	1.392	1.643	1.939	2.288	2.700	3.185	3.759	4.435	5.234
19	1.190	1.416	1.685	2.005	2.386	2.840	3.380	4.021	2.785	5.695
20	1.200	1.440	1.728	2.074	2.488	2.990	3.583	4.300	5.160	6.191
21	1.210	1.464	1.772	2.144	2.594	3.138	3.798	4.595	4.450	6.728
22	1.220	1.488	1.816	2.215	2.703	3.297	4.023	4.908	5.987	7.305
23	1.230	1.513	1.861	2.289	2.815	3.463	4.260	5.239	6.444	7.926
24	1.240	1.538	1.907	2.364	2.932	3.635	4.508	5.590	6.931	8.594
25	1.250	1.563	1.953	2.441	3.052	3.815	4.769	5.960	7.451	9.313

APPENDIX C

STUDENT CASE ANALYSIS
Overseas National Airways (ONA)

BACKGROUND

Overseas National Airways is a charter airline company that was organized in 1950 and experienced rapid growth until 1958. The realized growth was from military contracts for flying cargo and personnel. ONA won a large contract by underbidding, resulting in termination of operations because of financial difficulties.

The company was refinanced and back into operation in 1960. Again it grew rapidly because the CAB awarded it authority for transatlantic flights at a time when U. S. tourist travel to Eastern Europe was experiencing a great surge. During the late 1960s and early 1970s ONA had its authority extended to fly to other foreign locations, while at the same time continuing to receive military contracts as well as expanding their share of the tourist market. During this boom period, ONA built its fleet and diversified into other businesses, including steamboats and real estate. During this time period two attempts by other companies to acquire ONA were unsuccessful.

In 1975, ONA again went into a financial tailspin resulting from aircraft accidents, poor financial management, increased competition, and deregulation of fares for the scheduled airlines. The situation at ONA at the end of 1977 is summarized below:

- Three serious crashes between 1975 and 1977 destroyed two DC-10 jets and one DC-8.

- Sold fleet of DC-8 jets and spare parts. This improved the cash flow position by paying debt commitments and providing cash for future requirements. Four DC-8's and one DC-9 jet was subleased to other operators. ONA was left with two DC-10 jets, down from 21 in 1975.

- A third DC-10 aircraft was ordered from McDonnel Douglas for delivery in June 1978 to be used for the summer tourist peak season. With the third aircraft, ONA was operating near break-even operation for 1978 (loss of more than $12 million in 1977).

- The primary market was flights between the United States and Europe. Other markets included the Islamic pilgrims from African countries to Saudi Arabia for the Holy season. The nontransatlantic markets included Hong Kong, Tahiti, Rio, Lima, and South Africa (off-season destinations).
- Charter business was sold through about 20 established wholesale tour agencies that contracted for ONA's flight services. ONA continued to receive about 20 percent of its revenue from contracts with the U. S. military for transport of military personnel. At times, foreign airlines sought ONA's aircraft for charter flights over their routes during peak seasons.
- ONA exits the charter cargo business.
- Operating revenues dropped from a peak of $89.6 million in 1975 to nearly $80 million in 1977.
- ONA reorganized and a new chairman assumed leadership. All diversified and auxiliary businesses were divested.

Significant information concerning the current status of ONA is:

- Forty-nine percent of ONA is controlled by two individual investors and 51 percent is publicly owned.
- ONA's only business is passenger charters, and it is completely booked for 1978, including bookings on the third and yet to be delivered DC-10.
- ONA is taking measures to improve its safety record. These measures include equipment standardizations, improved safety procedures, strict inspection and maintenance programs, and employment of highly qualified personnel.
- Employee morale is high in spite of the reorganization and drastic reduction in work force.

DEFINING THE BUSINESS

The mission of ONA is to provide low-fare charter flights to tourists from the United States to world-wide destinations.

EXTERNAL ENVIRONMENTAL CHANGES

- Two DC-10 aircraft lost in serious accidents during 1976.
- Deregulation of the airline industry by CAB in 1977.
- Liberalization of U. S. charter regulations.
    Reduction/elimination of advanced ticket purchase requirements.
    Reduction in minimum size of charter groups from 40 to 20.
    Elimination of minimum stay requirements.
    Elimination/reduction of constraints (volume, frequency, regularity) on off-route charter flights by scheduled carriers.

Under consideration by CAB: part charter services on scheduled flights at charter rates; permit scheduled carriers substantial price reductions—up to 35 percent less than standard industry fare level.
- Strike at McDonnel Douglas delaying delivery on ordered DC-10.
- Declining value of U. S. dollar.

CHARTER INDUSTRY CHARACTERISTICS

- Cyclical
- Seasonal
- Pleasure travellers, not business travellers
- Oligopoly
- Intense competition—price based (more than 40 common carriers authorized to operate transatlantic charter services)
- Barriers to entry is high
- Barriers to exit—costly
- Power of substitutes is high
- Buyer power is high and seller power is low
- Very low net profit margins
- High fixed costs

OPPORTUNITIES AND THREATS

Opportunities

- Some deregulations are beneficial—minimum stay requirements, advanced ticket sales requirement, and minimum charter size.
- A number of scheduled airlines sold narrow-bodied aircraft reducing charter capacities.
- The number of tourists from the U. S. is increasing.

Threats

- Nondelivery of DC-10 until October 1978—ONA will miss the summer peak season when two thirds of annual profits are earned.
  Result: substantial loss in 1978 (see Addendum A & B)
- Rights of scheduled carriers to operate off regular routes expanded.
- Increased competition because of deregulation.
- Scheduled carriers offer high commissions to travel agents.

KEY SUCCESS FACTORS

- Be able to match competitors' fares.
- Frequent flights to bring up volume of passenger revenue.
- Good image.
- Attractive tour packages.
- Efficient operations to hold down operating expenses.
- Match unusually high commissions given by scheduled carriers to travel agents on individual ticket sales.
- Be able to operate on 100 percent load factor.
- Quality equipment and highly qualified technical personnel.

ASSESSING STRENGTHS AND WEAKNESSES OF ONA VIS-À-VIS ITS COMPETITORS

Strengths

- High morale and spirit of employees
- Highly trained technical staff
- High-quality maintenance operations

Weaknesses

- Weak financial position (see addendum 1 and 2 for details)
- ONA currently losing money (see addendum 1)
- Competitors are profitable and strong financially (see addendum 1)
  World Airways loaded with cash; TIA has backing of $1.2 billion parent.
- Weak image because of accidents

REASSESSING ONA'S MISSION

The analysis of the case does not require that the mission be changed. Therefore, the mission of ONA remains as originally stated. The mission of ONA is to provide low-fare charter flights to tourists from the United States to world-wide destinations.

STRATEGIC OBJECTIVES

- In the short run, to increase profitability to break-even.
- Remain in the charter flights market, but increase share of market to generate additional revenues.
- Complete the implementation of the reorganization.
- Secure services of newly ordered DC-10 or an alternative.

ASSESSING ORGANIZATIONAL STRATEGY

Current strategy—retrenchment.
Recommended alternative strategies.

- Lease its DC-10 fleet to other airlines.
- Lease a DC-10 from someone else for the summer 1978.
- Sell the company.
- Sell the aircraft and liquidate the company.

Recommending the new organizational strategy.
ONA should remain in the retrenchment strategy on the corporate level for now. It may be premature to sell the company, sell the aircraft, and liquidate, or lease its aircraft out to others. ONA should continue to cut back on operations until it has a lean, efficient staff. To get through the summer months and carry out its commitments, it should lease an aircraft until the new DC-10 is available. It may seek damages from McDonnel Douglas for its delay. At the conclusion of 1978, ONA needs to reevaluate its strategy because the retrenchment strategy will have had time to be fully implemented. Indeed, if at that time losses are still occurring it may be wise for ONA to consider liquidation. On the other hand, if losses are reduced ONA should consider continuing operations with a turn-around corporate strategy and consider differentiation (quality of service and equipment to build image) and focus (only charter flights) business strategies.

ADDENDUM 1
Financial Analysis of ONA and Competitors

	Selected Financial Ratios								
Ratios	1977 ONA	1976 ONA	1977 Capital	1976 Capital	1977 TIA	1976 TIA	1977 World	1976 World	Industry Average
Current	1.03	0.39	0.62	0.45	0.32	0.33	2.8	3.0	2.5
Quick	0.87	0.52	0.41	0.24			2.6	2.8	1.0
Debt (%)	86	59	63	62	53	65	39	40	33
Average Collection Period (days)	27	26	7	11	16	23	38	29	20
Return on Sales (%)	−15.4	−4.65	1.24	5.6	4.8	2.4	2.5	3.1	5
Return on Investment (%)	−12.8	−6.02	2.9	9.1	5.9	1.6	1.2	1.9	—

ADDENDUM 2
ONA's Cost-Percentage Analysis

Cost %'s	1977	1976	1975	1974
Net Sales	100%	100%	100%	100%
Flight Operations	91%	103.85%	90.5%	87.6%
Marketing and General Administration	8.41%	8.47%	7.04%	7.24%
Interest and Debt Expenses	5.3%	2.47%	0.76%	0.97%
Gain (Loss) on Disposal of Assets	(3.87)%	13.16%	2.8%	2.44%
(TOT) Other Income (Loss)	(8.89)%	13.12%	3.44%	2.88%
Net Income (Loss)	(15.5)%	(4.65)%	1.7%	2.82%

ADDENDUM 3
Major Competitor's Cost-Percentage Analysis

Cost %'s	1977	1976	1975	1974	1973
Sales	100%	100%	100%	100%	100%
Operating	78.4%	79%	70.7%	77.6%	82.1%
Selling and General Administration	8.8%	11.4%	9.4%	11.9%	12.4%
Aircraft Rentals	8.3%	11.7%	10.0%	11.7%	7.5%
Interest	1.6%	1.9%	2.3%	2.6%	3.0%
Income Tax Expenses	2.5%	3.3%	1.7%	−1.3%	−2.2%
Net Income	3.1%	2.5%	6.8%	21.7%	1.1%

CASE INDEX

Alabama Clothing, Inc.
  Andy Abroms, Curt Leathers, John Greening, and Jeffrey A. Barach, 745–750
Albertson's, Inc.
  Melvin J. Stanford and Dan R. Willis, 390–416
Allied Chemical Company
  Sexton Adams, 506–518
American Express Company, The
  James R. Lang, 333–350
Ammco Tools, Inc.
  Serge Oreal, Robert D. Hamilton, III, and Thomas J. McNichols, 601–620
Anaconda Smelter, The
  Mary Pat Cormack and M. Edgar Barrett, 721–739
Apartment Store, The
  Richard Levin and Bettye Painter, 147–160
Apple Computer, Inc.
  Marlene Carle, Robert Carle, Richard Edwards, Paula Walters, and Sexton Adams, 519–333
ASDIC Limited
  Philip Rosson and Michael Martin, 533–543

Bordados Maty, S. A.
  Lincoln W., Deihl, 620–632

Casual Male, The: Off-Price Men's Apparel Retailing
  Richard S. Tedlow, 267–287
Charger Company (A) and (B), The
  William Brant, 775–778
Classic Car Club of America, The
  Matthew C. Sonfield, 766–775
CML Group, Inc.: Twelve Years Old
  Laura L. Nash, 460–477

Community Coalition Plans a Conference on Employee Assistance Programs, A
  Joseph P. Caliguri, 763–765
Crested Butte Athletic Club
  M. Agee, J. Buckeye, and A. K. Wickesberg, 160–172

Diamond Valley Savings and Loan Association
  Julius S. Brown, 325–332
Dickenson Mines Limited
  Peter Nerby and David C. Shaw, 544–559

Electronic Data Systems Corporation
  Deborah Weaver, Monique Hensel, Jeff Bell, Sexton Adams, and Adelaide Griffin, 307–324

F. W. Woolworth and Co., Limited (Woolworth, U. K.)
  X. Gilbert, 632–666

Gulf Coast Seafood
  David Berry and Jeffrey A. Barach, 750–755

Holiday Inns, Inc.
  Timothy Mescon and Richard Robinson, 439–459

John Currie and Internav Ltd., Sydney, Nova Scotia
  Michael Martin and Philip Rosson, 692–702

Kerr-McGee Corporation
  Mark W. Bushell and Roger M. Atherton, 478–497

Keystone Instruments, Inc.
   Robert E. Schellenberger and Joseph Tomey, 741–744

Khashoggi Affair, The
   Terry White and William H. Warren, 755–763

McLean Trucking Company, The
   Bernie Berger, Jim Buchanan, Teresa Dawn, Dave Thompson, Sexton Adams, and Adelaide Griffin, 287–306

Marion Laboratories, Inc.
   Marilyn L. Taylor and Kenneth Beck, 559–576

Mary Kay Cosmetics, Inc.
   Mark Kever, George Macias, John Sanders, Ken Schoenherr, and Sexton Adams, 350–366

Masco Corporation
   Janet Lorenzen and Joe G. Thomas, 497–505

Midland County Hospital
   Alan Sheldon, 201–233

Mobil Corporation
   Bill Clark and M. Edgar Barrett, 576–600

Moldex Company
   Robert E. Schellenberger, 739–741

Nautica, S. A.
   Jacques Horovitz, 666–692

Oshman's Sporting Goods, Inc.
   Robert E. Schellenberger, 367–390

Overnite Transportation Company
   William H. Warren, 246–266

Parker Drilling Company (1984)
   Robert E. Schellenberger, 417–438

Slumbering Valley, Inc.
   G. Michael, E. L. Parke and R. Lorenz, 173–195

Theatrical Society, The
   Robert Broadbent, Leonard A. Fuchs, III, James J. Wiley, and Glenn Boseman, 196–201

Wal-Mart Stores, Inc.
   Monya Giggar, Gregg Gunchick, David Miller, and Sexton Adams, 234–246

Welgro Chemical Company
   William G. Callarman, Denzil Strickland, and Victor J. LaPorte, Jr., 703–720

AUTHOR INDEX

Anderson, M. J., Jr., 85
Ansoff, H. I., 67

Bates, Donald L., 61, 62
Boseman, Glenn, 139
Bower, Marvin, 4

Drucker, Peter, 58

Eldridge, David L., 61, 62

Gerstein, Marc, 102, 103, 105
Gluck, Frederick W., 16, 17
Glueck, William F., 60, 66, 122

Hall, William K., 88
Hamermesh, R.G., 85, 88
Harris, J. E., 85
Herskovits, Melville J., 96
Higgins, James M., 95
Hofer, Charles W., 11, 73, 74, 77, 83

Jauch, Lawrence R., 122

Kapor, Mitchell, 49, 51
Kaufman, Stephen P., 17
Kotler, Philip, 84, 86

Levitt, Theodore, 7
Linden, Eugene, 101
Lorange, Peter, 102

McAfee, Jerry, 49, 50
Maisonrouge, Jacques G., 51
Milutinovich, Jugoslav S., 779
Murphy, Declanc, 102

Patel, Peter, 88, 89
Pierce, John A., II, 95
Porter, Michael E., 83, 85

Reisman, Heather, 102, 103, 105
Robinson, Richard B., Jr., 95

Salter, Malcolm S., 111, 112
Schellenberger, Robert E., 139
Schendel, Dan E., 11, 73, 74, 77, 83
Silk, S.B., 88
Steiner, George A., 10, 16, 95

Uytergoeven, Hugo E.R., 62

Walleck, A. Steven, 17

Younger, Michael, 88, 89

SUBJECT INDEX

Activity ratios, 790–791
  average collection period, 791
  inventory turnover, 790–791
Average collection period ratio, 791

Boston consulting group growth-share matrix, 78–81
Business strategies:
  generic, 83–84
  situational, 84–89
Business strategy, 10, 74
  analysis, 83–89

Case analysis:
  appraisal framework, 127–142
  major steps, 123–127
  written and oral, 123
Case method, 122
Control of organizational strategy, 115–118
Corporate culture and strategy implementation, 96–99
Corporate strategy, 10, 73–74
  analysis, 76–83
  generic alternatives, 58–68, 69
  identifying current, 75–76
Cost percentage analysis, 793-794
Current ratio, 789

Debt ratio, 790
Differentiation, 84, 85

Environmental analysis, 24–27
Evolution of formal strategic management, 16–18

Financial ratios, 789–793
  activity, 790–791
  leverage, 790
  liquidity, 789–790
  profitability, 791

Functional strategy, 10, 74–75
  analysis, 90

General Electric business portfolio matrix, 81–83
Generic business strategies, 83–84
  differentiation, 84
  focus, 84
  overall cost leadership, 83

Human resources and strategy implementation, 102–108

Inventory turnover ratio, 790–791

Key success factors, 27–28
  identification of, 28–36

Leverage ratios, 790
  debt ratio, 790
  times interest earned, 790
Liquidity ratios, 789–791
  current, 789
  quick, 789–791

Mission, organizational, 7, 45–49

Objectives, strategic, 9, 53–58
  characteristics of effective, 56–58
  formulation of, 54–56
Opportunities and threats, identification of, 22–23
Organizational levels and strategic management, 14–16
Organizational mission, 7, 45–49
Organizational philosophy, 7–9, 49–52
Organizational policies, 9, 52–53
Organizational rewards and strategy implementation, 109–115
Organizational strategy, 9–11
  choosing an, 90–91

Subject Index

Organizational strategy, (*Continued*)
  control of, 11, 115–118
  implementation of, 10–11, 94–115
Organizational structure and strategy implementation, 99–101

Philosophy, organizational, 7–9, 49–52
Planning, strategic, 5–6
Policies, organizational, 9, 52–53
Portfolio analysis, 77–83
  Boston Consulting Group growth share matrix, 78–81
  General Electric business portfolio matrix, 81–83
Profitability ratios, 791
  return on investment, 791
  sales margin, 791

Quick ratio, 789–791

Ratio analysis, 788–793
Return on investment, 791
Return on net worth, 791
Return on sales, 791

Sales margin, 791
Situational business strategies, 84–89
Societal strategy, 9–10, 72–73
Sources and uses of funds, 794–795
Strategic decisions, 12–14
Strategic management:
  defined, 4
  evolution of formal, 16–18
  and organizational levels, 14–16
  steps, 6–11
Strategic objectives, 9, 53–58
  characteristics of effective, 56–58
  formulation of, 54–56
Strategic planning, defined, 5–6
Strategy, organizational, 9–10, 72–92
Strategy implementation, 6, 10–11, 94–119
  and corporate culture, 96–99
  and human resources, 102–108
  and organizational rewards, 109–115
  and organization structure, 99–101
Strengths and weakness, evaluation, 36–41
SWOT analysis, 6–7
  conceptual framework, 21–22
  evaluation of strengths and weaknesses, 36–41
  key success factors, 27–28
  opportunities and threats, 22–23

Times interest earned ratio, 791